Lecture Notes in Computer Science 14108

Founding Editors

Gerhard Goos
Juris Hartmanis

Editorial Board Members

The series Lecture Notes in Computer Science (LNCS), including its subseries Lecture Notes in Artificial Intelligence (LNAI) and Lecture Notes in Bioinformatics (LNBI), has established itself as a medium for the publication of new developments in computer science and information technology research, teaching, and education.

LNCS enjoys close cooperation with the computer science R & D community, the series counts many renowned academics among its volume editors and paper authors, and collaborates with prestigious societies. Its mission is to serve this international community by providing an invaluable service, mainly focused on the publication of conference and workshop proceedings and postproceedings. LNCS commenced publication in 1973.

Osvaldo Gervasi · Beniamino Murgante ·
Ana Maria A. C. Rocha · Chiara Garau ·
Francesco Scorza · Yeliz Karaca ·
Carmelo M. Torre
Editors

Computational Science and Its Applications – ICCSA 2023 Workshops

Athens, Greece, July 3–6, 2023
Proceedings, Part V

Springer

Editors
Osvaldo Gervasi ⓘ
University of Perugia
Perugia, Italy

Ana Maria A. C. Rocha ⓘ
University of Minho
Braga, Portugal

Francesco Scorza ⓘ
University of Basilicata
Potenza, Italy

Carmelo M. Torre ⓘ
Polytechnic University of Bari
Bari, Italy

Beniamino Murgante ⓘ
University of Basilicata
Potenza, Italy

Chiara Garau ⓘ
University of Cagliari
Cagliari, Italy

Yeliz Karaca ⓘ
University of Massachusetts Medical School
Worcester, MA, USA

ISSN 0302-9743 ISSN 1611-3349 (electronic)
Lecture Notes in Computer Science
ISBN 978-3-031-37116-5 ISBN 978-3-031-37117-2 (eBook)
https://doi.org/10.1007/978-3-031-37117-2

This Springer imprint is published by the registered company Springer Nature Switzerland AG
The registered company address is: Gewerbestrasse 11, 6330 Cham, Switzerland

Preface

These 9 volumes (LNCS volumes 14104–14112) consist of the peer-reviewed papers from the 2023 International Conference on Computational Science and Its Applications (ICCSA 2023) which took place during July 3–6, 2023. The peer-reviewed papers of the main conference tracks were published in a separate set consisting of two volumes (LNCS 13956–13957).

The conference was finally held in person after the difficult period of the Covid-19 pandemic in the wonderful city of Athens, in the cosy facilities of the National Technical University. Our experience during the pandemic period allowed us to enable virtual participation also this year for those who were unable to attend the event, due to logistical, political and economic problems, by adopting a technological infrastructure based on open source software (jitsi + riot), and a commercial cloud infrastructure.

ICCSA 2023 was another successful event in the International Conference on Computational Science and Its Applications (ICCSA) series, previously held as a hybrid event (with one third of registered authors attending in person) in Malaga, Spain (2022), Cagliari, Italy (hybrid with few participants in person in 2021 and completely online in 2020), whilst earlier editions took place in Saint Petersburg, Russia (2019), Melbourne, Australia (2018), Trieste, Italy (2017), Beijing, China (2016), Banff, Canada (2015), Guimaraes, Portugal (2014), Ho Chi Minh City, Vietnam (2013), Salvador, Brazil (2012), Santander, Spain (2011), Fukuoka, Japan (2010), Suwon, South Korea (2009), Perugia, Italy (2008), Kuala Lumpur, Malaysia (2007), Glasgow, UK (2006), Singapore (2005), Assisi, Italy (2004), Montreal, Canada (2003), and (as ICCS) Amsterdam, The Netherlands (2002) and San Francisco, USA (2001).

Computational Science is the main pillar of most of the present research, industrial and commercial applications, and plays a unique role in exploiting ICT innovative technologies, and the ICCSA series have been providing a venue to researchers and industry practitioners to discuss new ideas, to share complex problems and their solutions, and to shape new trends in Computational Science. As the conference mirrors society from a scientific point of view, this year's undoubtedly dominant theme was the machine learning and artificial intelligence and their applications in the most diverse economic and industrial fields.

The ICCSA 2023 conference is structured in 6 general tracks covering the fields of computational science and its applications: Computational Methods, Algorithms and Scientific Applications – High Performance Computing and Networks – Geometric Modeling, Graphics and Visualization – Advanced and Emerging Applications – Information Systems and Technologies – Urban and Regional Planning. In addition, the conference consisted of 61 workshops, focusing on very topical issues of importance to science, technology and society: from new mathematical approaches for solving complex computational systems, to information and knowledge in the Internet of Things, new statistical and optimization methods, several Artificial Intelligence approaches, sustainability issues, smart cities and related technologies.

In the workshop proceedings we accepted 350 full papers, 29 short papers and 2 PHD Showcase papers. In the main conference proceedings we accepted 67 full papers, 13 short papers and 6 PHD Showcase papers from 283 submissions to the General Tracks of the conference (acceptance rate 30%). We would like to express our appreciation to the workshops chairs and co-chairs for their hard work and dedication.

The success of the ICCSA conference series in general, and of ICCSA 2023 in particular, vitally depends on the support of many people: authors, presenters, participants, keynote speakers, workshop chairs, session chairs, organizing committee members, student volunteers, Program Committee members, Advisory Committee members, International Liaison chairs, reviewers and others in various roles. We take this opportunity to wholehartedly thank them all.

We also wish to thank our publisher, Springer, for their acceptance to publish the proceedings, for sponsoring part of the best papers awards and for their kind assistance and cooperation during the editing process.

We cordially invite you to visit the ICCSA website https://iccsa.org where you can find all the relevant information about this interesting and exciting event.

July 2023

Osvaldo Gervasi
Beniamino Murgante
Chiara Garau

Welcome Message from Organizers

After the 2021 ICCSA in Cagliari, Italy and the 2022 ICCSA in Malaga, Spain, ICCSA continued its successful scientific endeavours in 2023, hosted again in the Mediterranean neighbourhood. This time, ICCSA 2023 moved a bit more to the east of the Mediterranean Region and was held in the metropolitan city of Athens, the capital of Greece and a vibrant urban environment endowed with a prominent cultural heritage that dates back to the ancient years. As a matter of fact, Athens is one of the oldest cities in the world, and the cradle of democracy. The city has a history of over 3,000 years and, according to the myth, it took its name from Athena, the Goddess of Wisdom and daughter of Zeus.

ICCSA 2023 took place in a secure environment, relieved from the immense stress of the COVID-19 pandemic. This gave us the chance to have a safe and vivid, in-person participation which, combined with the very active engagement of the ICCSA 2023 scientific community, set the ground for highly motivating discussions and interactions as to the latest developments of computer science and its applications in the real world for improving quality of life.

The National Technical University of Athens (NTUA), one of the most prestigious Greek academic institutions, had the honour of hosting ICCSA 2023. The Local Organizing Committee really feels the burden and responsibility of such a demanding task; and puts in all the necessary energy in order to meet participants' expectations and establish a friendly, creative and inspiring, scientific and social/cultural environment that allows for new ideas and perspectives to flourish.

Since all ICCSA participants, either informatics-oriented or application-driven, realize the tremendous steps and evolution of computer science during the last few decades and the huge potential these offer to cope with the enormous challenges of humanity in a globalized, 'wired' and highly competitive world, the expectations from ICCSA 2023 were set high in order for a successful matching between computer science progress and communities' aspirations to be attained, i.e., a progress that serves real, place- and people-based needs and can pave the way towards a visionary, smart, sustainable, resilient and inclusive future for both the current and the next generation.

On behalf of the Local Organizing Committee, I would like to sincerely thank all of you who have contributed to ICCSA 2023 and I cordially welcome you to my 'home', NTUA.

On behalf of the Local Organizing Committee.

Anastasia Stratigea

Organization

ICCSA 2023 was organized by the National Technical University of Athens (Greece), the University of the Aegean (Greece), the University of Perugia (Italy), the University of Basilicata (Italy), Monash University (Australia), Kyushu Sangyo University (Japan), the University of Minho (Portugal). The conference was supported by two NTUA Schools, namely the School of Rural, Surveying and Geoinformatics Engineering and the School of Electrical and Computer Engineering.

Honorary General Chairs

Norio Shiratori	Chuo University, Japan
Kenneth C. J. Tan	Sardina Systems, UK

General Chairs

Osvaldo Gervasi	University of Perugia, Italy
Anastasia Stratigea	National Technical University of Athens, Greece
Bernady O. Apduhan	Kyushu Sangyo University, Japan

Program Committee Chairs

Beniamino Murgante	University of Basilicata, Italy
Dimitris Kavroudakis	University of the Aegean, Greece
Ana Maria A. C. Rocha	University of Minho, Portugal
David Taniar	Monash University, Australia

International Advisory Committee

Jemal Abawajy	Deakin University, Australia
Dharma P. Agarwal	University of Cincinnati, USA
Rajkumar Buyya	Melbourne University, Australia
Claudia Bauzer Medeiros	University of Campinas, Brazil
Manfred M. Fisher	Vienna University of Economics and Business, Austria
Marina L. Gavrilova	University of Calgary, Canada

Sumi Helal	University of Florida, USA and University of Lancaster, UK
Yee Leung	Chinese University of Hong Kong, China

International Liaison Chairs

Ivan Blečić	University of Cagliari, Italy
Giuseppe Borruso	University of Trieste, Italy
Elise De Donker	Western Michigan University, USA
Maria Irene Falcão	University of Minho, Portugal
Inmaculada Garcia Fernandez	University of Malaga, Spain
Eligius Hendrix	University of Malaga, Spain
Robert C. H. Hsu	Chung Hua University, Taiwan
Tai-Hoon Kim	Beijing Jaotong University, China
Vladimir Korkhov	Saint Petersburg University, Russia
Takashi Naka	Kyushu Sangyo University, Japan
Rafael D. C. Santos	National Institute for Space Research, Brazil
Maribel Yasmina Santos	University of Minho, Portugal
Elena Stankova	Saint Petersburg University, Russia

Workshop and Session Organizing Chairs

Beniamino Murgante	University of Basilicata, Italy
Chiara Garau	University of Cagliari, Italy

Award Chair

Wenny Rahayu	La Trobe University, Australia

Publicity Committee Chairs

Elmer Dadios	De La Salle University, Philippines
Nataliia Kulabukhova	Saint Petersburg University, Russia
Daisuke Takahashi	Tsukuba University, Japan
Shangwang Wang	Beijing University of Posts and Telecommunications, China

Local Organizing Committee Chairs

Anastasia Stratigea	National Technical University of Athens, Greece
Dimitris Kavroudakis	University of the Aegean, Greece
Charalambos Ioannidis	National Technical University of Athens, Greece
Nectarios Koziris	National Technical University of Athens, Greece
Efthymios Bakogiannis	National Technical University of Athens, Greece
Yiota Theodora	National Technical University of Athens, Greece
Dimitris Fotakis	National Technical University of Athens, Greece
Apostolos Lagarias	National Technical University of Athens, Greece
Akrivi Leka	National Technical University of Athens, Greece
Dionisia Koutsi	National Technical University of Athens, Greece
Alkistis Dalkavouki	National Technical University of Athens, Greece
Maria Panagiotopoulou	National Technical University of Athens, Greece
Angeliki Papazoglou	National Technical University of Athens, Greece
Natalia Tsigarda	National Technical University of Athens, Greece
Konstantinos Athanasopoulos	National Technical University of Athens, Greece
Ioannis Xatziioannou	National Technical University of Athens, Greece
Vasiliki Krommyda	National Technical University of Athens, Greece
Panayiotis Patsilinakos	National Technical University of Athens, Greece
Sofia Kassiou	National Technical University of Athens, Greece

Technology Chair

Damiano Perri	University of Florence, Italy

Program Committee

Vera Afreixo	University of Aveiro, Portugal
Filipe Alvelos	University of Minho, Portugal
Hartmut Asche	University of Potsdam, Germany
Ginevra Balletto	University of Cagliari, Italy
Michela Bertolotto	University College Dublin, Ireland
Sandro Bimonte	CEMAGREF, TSCF, France
Rod Blais	University of Calgary, Canada
Ivan Blečić	University of Sassari, Italy
Giuseppe Borruso	University of Trieste, Italy
Ana Cristina Braga	University of Minho, Portugal
Massimo Cafaro	University of Salento, Italy
Yves Caniou	Lyon University, France

Ermanno Cardelli	University of Perugia, Italy
José A. Cardoso e Cunha	Universidade Nova de Lisboa, Portugal
Rui Cardoso	University of Beira Interior, Portugal
Leocadio G. Casado	University of Almeria, Spain
Carlo Cattani	University of Salerno, Italy
Mete Celik	Erciyes University, Turkey
Maria Cerreta	University of Naples "Federico II", Italy
Hyunseung Choo	Sungkyunkwan University, Korea
Rachel Chieng-Sing Lee	Sunway University, Malaysia
Min Young Chung	Sungkyunkwan University, Korea
Florbela Maria da Cruz Domingues Correia	Polytechnic Institute of Viana do Castelo, Portugal
Gilberto Corso Pereira	Federal University of Bahia, Brazil
Alessandro Costantini	INFN, Italy
Carla Dal Sasso Freitas	Universidade Federal do Rio Grande do Sul, Brazil
Pradesh Debba	The Council for Scientific and Industrial Research (CSIR), South Africa
Hendrik Decker	Instituto Tecnológico de Informática, Spain
Robertas Damaševičius	Kausan University of Technology, Lithuania
Frank Devai	London South Bank University, UK
Rodolphe Devillers	Memorial University of Newfoundland, Canada
Joana Matos Dias	University of Coimbra, Portugal
Paolino Di Felice	University of L'Aquila, Italy
Prabu Dorairaj	NetApp, India/USA
Noelia Faginas Lago	University of Perugia, Italy
M. Irene Falcao	University of Minho, Portugal
Cherry Liu Fang	U.S. DOE Ames Laboratory, USA
Florbela P. Fernandes	Polytechnic Institute of Bragança, Portugal
Jose-Jesus Fernandez	National Centre for Biotechnology, CSIS, Spain
Paula Odete Fernandes	Polytechnic Institute of Bragança, Portugal
Adelaide de Fátima Baptista Valente Freitas	University of Aveiro, Portugal
Manuel Carlos Figueiredo	University of Minho, Portugal
Maria Celia Furtado Rocha	PRODEB–PósCultura/UFBA, Brazil
Chiara Garau	University of Cagliari, Italy
Paulino Jose Garcia Nieto	University of Oviedo, Spain
Raffaele Garrisi	Polizia di Stato, Italy
Jerome Gensel	LSR-IMAG, France
Maria Giaoutzi	National Technical University, Athens, Greece
Arminda Manuela Andrade Pereira Gonçalves	University of Minho, Portugal

Louiza de Macedo Mourelle	State University of Rio de Janeiro, Brazil
Nadia Nedjah	State University of Rio de Janeiro, Brazil
Laszlo Neumann	University of Girona, Spain
Kok-Leong Ong	Deakin University, Australia
Belen Palop	Universidad de Valladolid, Spain
Marcin Paprzycki	Polish Academy of Sciences, Poland
Eric Pardede	La Trobe University, Australia
Kwangjin Park	Wonkwang University, Korea
Ana Isabel Pereira	Polytechnic Institute of Bragança, Portugal
Massimiliano Petri	University of Pisa, Italy
Telmo Pinto	University of Coimbra, Portugal
Maurizio Pollino	Italian National Agency for New Technologies, Energy and Sustainable Economic Development, Italy
Alenka Poplin	University of Hamburg, Germany
Vidyasagar Potdar	Curtin University of Technology, Australia
David C. Prosperi	Florida Atlantic University, USA
Wenny Rahayu	La Trobe University, Australia
Jerzy Respondek	Silesian University of Technology Poland
Humberto Rocha	INESC-Coimbra, Portugal
Jon Rokne	University of Calgary, Canada
Octavio Roncero	CSIC, Spain
Maytham Safar	Kuwait University, Kuwait
Chiara Saracino	A.O. Ospedale Niguarda Ca' Granda - Milano, Italy
Marco Paulo Seabra dos Reis	University of Coimbra, Portugal
Jie Shen	University of Michigan, USA
Qi Shi	Liverpool John Moores University, UK
Dale Shires	U.S. Army Research Laboratory, USA
Inês Soares	University of Coimbra, Portugal
Elena Stankova	St. Petersburg University, Russia
Takuo Suganuma	Tohoku University, Japan
Eufemia Tarantino	Polytechnic of Bari, Italy
Sergio Tasso	University of Perugia, Italy
Ana Paula Teixeira	University of Trás-os-Montes and Alto Douro, Portugal
M. Filomena Teodoro	Portuguese Naval Academy and University of Lisbon, Portugal
Parimala Thulasiraman	University of Manitoba, Canada
Carmelo Torre	Polytechnic of Bari, Italy
Javier Martinez Torres	Centro Universitario de la Defensa Zaragoza, Spain

Giuseppe A. Trunfio	University of Sassari, Italy
Pablo Vanegas	University of Cuenca, Equador
Marco Vizzari	University of Perugia, Italy
Varun Vohra	Merck Inc., USA
Koichi Wada	University of Tsukuba, Japan
Krzysztof Walkowiak	Wroclaw University of Technology, Poland
Zequn Wang	Intelligent Automation Inc, USA
Robert Weibel	University of Zurich, Switzerland
Frank Westad	Norwegian University of Science and Technology, Norway
Roland Wismüller	Universität Siegen, Germany
Mudasser Wyne	SOET National University, USA
Chung-Huang Yang	National Kaohsiung Normal University, Taiwan
Xin-She Yang	National Physical Laboratory, UK
Salim Zabir	France Telecom Japan Co., Japan
Haifeng Zhao	University of California, Davis, USA
Fabiana Zollo	University of Venice "Cà Foscari", Italy
Albert Y. Zomaya	University of Sydney, Australia

Workshop Organizers

Advanced Data Science Techniques with Applications in Industry and Environmental Sustainability (ATELIERS 2023)

Dario Torregrossa	Goodyear, Luxemburg
Antonino Marvuglia	Luxembourg Institute of Science and Technology, Luxemburg
Valeria Borodin	École des Mines de Saint-Étienne, Luxemburg
Mohamed Laib	Luxembourg Institute of Science and Technology, Luxemburg

Advances in Artificial Intelligence Learning Technologies: Blended Learning, STEM, Computational Thinking and Coding (AAILT 2023)

Alfredo Milani	University of Perugia, Italy
Valentina Franzoni	University of Perugia, Italy
Sergio Tasso	University of Perugia, Italy

Advanced Processes of Mathematics and Computing Models in Complex Computational Systems (ACMC 2023)

Yeliz Karaca	University of Massachusetts Chan Medical School and Massachusetts Institute of Technology, USA
Dumitru Baleanu	Cankaya University, Turkey
Osvaldo Gervasi	University of Perugia, Italy
Yudong Zhang	University of Leicester, UK
Majaz Moonis	University of Massachusetts Medical School, USA

Artificial Intelligence Supported Medical Data Examination (AIM 2023)

David Taniar	Monash University, Australia
Seifedine Kadry	Noroff University College, Norway
Venkatesan Rajinikanth	Saveetha School of Engineering, India

Advanced and Innovative Web Apps (AIWA 2023)

Damiano Perri	University of Perugia, Italy
Osvaldo Gervasi	University of Perugia, Italy

Assessing Urban Sustainability (ASUS 2023)

Elena Todella	Polytechnic of Turin, Italy
Marika Gaballo	Polytechnic of Turin, Italy
Beatrice Mecca	Polytechnic of Turin, Italy

Advances in Web Based Learning (AWBL 2023)

Birol Ciloglugil	Ege University, Turkey
Mustafa Inceoglu	Ege University, Turkey

Blockchain and Distributed Ledgers: Technologies and Applications (BDLTA 2023)

Vladimir Korkhov   Saint Petersburg State University, Russia
Elena Stankova   Saint Petersburg State University, Russia
Nataliia Kulabukhova   Saint Petersburg State University, Russia

Bio and Neuro Inspired Computing and Applications (BIONCA 2023)

Nadia Nedjah   State University of Rio De Janeiro, Brazil
Luiza De Macedo Mourelle   State University of Rio De Janeiro, Brazil

Choices and Actions for Human Scale Cities: Decision Support Systems (CAHSC–DSS 2023)

Giovanna Acampa   University of Florence and University of Enna
                                  Kore, Italy
Fabrizio Finucci   Roma Tre University, Italy
Luca S. Dacci   Polytechnic of Turin, Italy

Computational and Applied Mathematics (CAM 2023)

Maria Irene Falcao   University of Minho, Portugal
Fernando Miranda   University of Minho, Portugal

Computational and Applied Statistics (CAS 2023)

Ana Cristina Braga   University of Minho, Portugal

Cyber Intelligence and Applications (CIA 2023)

Gianni Dangelo   University of Salerno, Italy
Francesco Palmieri   University of Salerno, Italy
Massimo Ficco   University of Salerno, Italy

Conversations South-North on Climate Change Adaptation Towards Smarter and More Sustainable Cities (CLAPS 2023)

Chiara Garau	University of Cagliari, Italy
Cristina Trois	University of kwaZulu-Natal, South Africa
Claudia Loggia	University of kwaZulu-Natal, South Africa
John Östh	Faculty of Technology, Art and Design, Norway
Mauro Coni	University of Cagliari, Italy
Alessio Satta	MedSea Foundation, Italy

Computational Mathematics, Statistics and Information Management (CMSIM 2023)

Maria Filomena Teodoro	University of Lisbon and Portuguese Naval Academy, Portugal
Marina A. P. Andrade	University Institute of Lisbon, Portugal

Computational Optimization and Applications (COA 2023)

Ana Maria A. C. Rocha	University of Minho, Portugal
Humberto Rocha	University of Coimbra, Portugal

Computational Astrochemistry (CompAstro 2023)

Marzio Rosi	University of Perugia, Italy
Nadia Balucani	University of Perugia, Italy
Cecilia Ceccarelli	University of Grenoble Alpes and Institute for Planetary Sciences and Astrophysics, France
Stefano Falcinelli	University of Perugia, Italy

Computational Methods for Porous Geomaterials (CompPor 2023)

Vadim Lisitsa	Russian Academy of Science, Russia
Evgeniy Romenski	Russian Academy of Science, Russia

Workshop on Computational Science and HPC (CSHPC 2023)

Elise De Doncker	Western Michigan University, USA
Fukuko Yuasa	High Energy Accelerator Research Organization, Japan
Hideo Matsufuru	High Energy Accelerator Research Organization, Japan

Cities, Technologies and Planning (CTP 2023)

Giuseppe Borruso	University of Trieste, Italy
Beniamino Murgante	University of Basilicata, Italy
Malgorzata Hanzl	Lodz University of Technology, Poland
Anastasia Stratigea	National Technical University of Athens, Greece
Ljiljana Zivkovic	Republic Geodetic Authority, Serbia
Ginevra Balletto	University of Cagliari, Italy

Gender Equity/Equality in Transport and Mobility (DELIA 2023)

Tiziana Campisi	University of Enna Kore, Italy
Ines Charradi	Sousse University, Tunisia
Alexandros Nikitas	University of Huddersfield, UK
Kh Md Nahiduzzaman	University of British Columbia, Canada
Andreas Nikiforiadis	Aristotle University of Thessaloniki, Greece
Socrates Basbas	Aristotle University of Thessaloniki, Greece

International Workshop on Defense Technology and Security (DTS 2023)

Yeonseung Ryu	Myongji University, South Korea

Integrated Methods for the Ecosystem-Services Accounting in Urban Decision Process (Ecourbn 2023)

Maria Rosaria Guarini	Sapienza University of Rome, Italy
Francesco Sica	Sapienza University of Rome, Italy
Francesco Tajani	Sapienza University of Rome, Italy

Carmelo Maria Torre   Polytechnic University of Bari, Italy
Pierluigi Morano   Polytechnic University of Bari, Italy
Rossana Ranieri   Sapienza Università di Roma, Italy

Evaluating Inner Areas Potentials (EIAP 2023)

Diana Rolando   Politechnic of Turin, Italy
Manuela Rebaudengo   Politechnic of Turin, Italy
Alice Barreca   Politechnic of Turin, Italy
Giorgia Malavasi   Politechnic of Turin, Italy
Umberto Mecca   Politechnic of Turin, Italy

Sustainable Mobility Last Mile Logistic (ELLIOT 2023)

Tiziana Campisi   University of Enna Kore, Italy
Socrates Basbas   Aristotle University of Thessaloniki, Greece
Grigorios Fountas   Aristotle University of Thessaloniki, Greece
Paraskevas Nikolaou   University of Cyprus, Cyprus
Drazenko Glavic   University of Belgrade, Serbia
Antonio Russo   University of Enna Kore, Italy

Econometrics and Multidimensional Evaluation of Urban Environment (EMEUE 2023)

Maria Cerreta   University of Naples Federico II, Italy
Carmelo Maria Torre   Politechnic of Bari, Italy
Pierluigi Morano   Polytechnic of Bari, Italy
Debora Anelli   Polytechnic of Bari, Italy
Francesco Tajani   Sapienza University of Rome, Italy
Simona Panaro   University of Sussex, UK

Ecosystem Services in Spatial Planning for Resilient Urban and Rural Areas (ESSP 2023)

Sabrina Lai   University of Cagliari, Italy
Francesco Scorza   University of Basilicata, Italy
Corrado Zoppi   University of Cagliari, Italy

Gerardo Carpentieri	University of Naples Federico II, Italy
Floriana Zucaro	University of Naples Federico II, Italy
Ana Clara Mourão Moura	Federal University of Minas Gerais, Brazil

Ethical AI Applications for a Human-Centered Cyber Society (EthicAI 2023)

Valentina Franzoni	University of Perugia, Italy
Alfredo Milani	University of Perugia, Italy
Jordi Vallverdu	University Autonoma Barcelona, Spain
Roberto Capobianco	Sapienza University of Rome, Italy

13th International Workshop on Future Computing System Technologies and Applications (FiSTA 2023)

| Bernady Apduhan | Kyushu Sangyo University, Japan |
| Rafael Santos | National Institute for Space Research, Brazil |

Collaborative Planning and Designing for the Future with Geospatial Applications (GeoCollab 2023)

Alenka Poplin	Iowa State University, USA
Rosanna Rivero	University of Georgia, USA
Michele Campagna	University of Cagliari, Italy
Ana Clara Mourão Moura	Federal University of Minas Gerais, Brazil

Geomatics in Agriculture and Forestry: New Advances and Perspectives (GeoForAgr 2023)

Maurizio Pollino	Italian National Agency for New Technologies, Energy and Sustainable Economic Development, Italy
Giuseppe Modica	University of Reggio Calabria, Italy
Marco Vizzari	University of Perugia, Italy
Salvatore Praticò	University of Reggio Calabria, Italy

Geographical Analysis, Urban Modeling, Spatial Statistics (Geog-An-Mod 2023)

Giuseppe Borruso	University of Trieste, Italy
Beniamino Murgante	University of Basilicata, Italy
Harmut Asche	Hasso-Plattner-Institut für Digital Engineering Ggmbh, Germany

Geomatics for Resource Monitoring and Management (GRMM 2023)

Alessandra Capolupo	Polytechnic of Bari, Italy
Eufemia Tarantino	Polytechnic of Bari, Italy
Enrico Borgogno Mondino	University of Turin, Italy

International Workshop on Information and Knowledge in the Internet of Things (IKIT 2023)

Teresa Guarda	Peninsula State University of Santa Elena, Ecuador
Modestos Stavrakis	University of the Aegean, Greece

International Workshop on Collective, Massive and Evolutionary Systems (IWCES 2023)

Alfredo Milani	University of Perugia, Italy
Rajdeep Niyogi	Indian Institute of Technology, India
Valentina Franzoni	University of Perugia, Italy

Multidimensional Evolutionary Evaluations for Transformative Approaches (MEETA 2023)

Maria Cerreta	University of Naples Federico II, Italy
Giuliano Poli	University of Naples Federico II, Italy
Ludovica Larocca	University of Naples Federico II, Italy
Chiara Mazzarella	University of Naples Federico II, Italy

Stefania Regalbuto   University of Naples Federico II, Italy
Maria Somma   University of Naples Federico II, Italy

Building Multi-dimensional Models for Assessing Complex Environmental Systems (MES 2023)

Marta Dell'Ovo   Politechnic of Milan, Italy
Vanessa Assumma   University of Bologna, Italy
Caterina Caprioli   Politechnic of Turin, Italy
Giulia Datola   Politechnic of Turin, Italy
Federico Dellanna   Politechnic of Turin, Italy
Marco Rossitti   Politechnic of Milan, Italy

Metropolitan City Lab (Metro_City_Lab 2023)

Ginevra Balletto   University of Cagliari, Italy
Luigi Mundula   University for Foreigners of Perugia, Italy
Giuseppe Borruso   University of Trieste, Italy
Jacopo Torriti   University of Reading, UK
Isabella Ligia   Metropolitan City of Cagliari, Italy

Mathematical Methods for Image Processing and Understanding (MMIPU 2023)

Ivan Gerace   University of Perugia, Italy
Gianluca Vinti   University of Perugia, Italy
Arianna Travaglini   University of Florence, Italy

Models and Indicators for Assessing and Measuring the Urban Settlement Development in the View of ZERO Net Land Take by 2050 (MOVEto0 2023)

Lucia Saganeiti   University of L'Aquila, Italy
Lorena Fiorini   University of L'Aquila, Italy
Angela Pilogallo   University of L'Aquila, Italy
Alessandro Marucci   University of L'Aquila, Italy
Francesco Zullo   University of L'Aquila, Italy

Modelling Post-Covid Cities (MPCC 2023)

Giuseppe Borruso	University of Trieste, Italy
Beniamino Murgante	University of Basilicata, Italy
Ginevra Balletto	University of Cagliari, Italy
Lucia Saganeiti	University of L'Aquila, Italy
Marco Dettori	University of Sassari, Italy

3rd Workshop on Privacy in the Cloud/Edge/IoT World (PCEIoT 2023)

Michele Mastroianni	University of Salerno, Italy
Lelio Campanile	University of Campania Luigi Vanvitelli, Italy
Mauro Iacono	University of Campania Luigi Vanvitelli, Italy

Port City Interface: Land Use, Logistic and Rear Port Area Planning (PORTUNO 2023)

Tiziana Campisi	University of Enna Kore, Italy
Socrates Basbas	Aristotle University of Thessaloniki, Greece
Efstathios Bouhouras	Aristotle University of Thessaloniki, Greece
Giovanni Tesoriere	University of Enna Kore, Italy
Elena Cocuzza	University of Catania, Italy
Gianfranco Fancello	University of Cagliari, Italy

Scientific Computing Infrastructure (SCI 2023)

Elena Stankova	St. Petersburg State University, Russia
Vladimir Korkhov	St. Petersburg University, Russia

Supply Chains, IoT, and Smart Technologies (SCIS 2023)

Ha Jin Hwang	Sunway University, South Korea
Hangkon Kim	Daegu Catholic University, South Korea
Jan Seruga	Australian Catholic University, Australia

Spatial Cognition in Urban and Regional Planning Under Risk (SCOPUR23)

Domenico Camarda	Polytechnic of Bari, Italy
Giulia Mastrodonato	Polytechnic of Bari, Italy
Stefania Santoro	Polytechnic of Bari, Italy
Maria Rosaria Stufano Melone	Polytechnic of Bari, Italy
Mauro Patano	Polytechnic of Bari, Italy

Socio-Economic and Environmental Models for Land Use Management (SEMLUM 2023)

Debora Anelli	Polytechnic of Bari, Italy
Pierluigi Morano	Polytechnic of Bari, Italy
Benedetto Manganelli	University of Basilicata, Italy
Francesco Tajani	Sapienza University of Rome, Italy
Marco Locurcio	Polytechnic of Bari, Italy
Felicia Di Liddo	Polytechnic of Bari, Italy

Ports of the Future - Smartness and Sustainability (SmartPorts 2023)

Ginevra Balletto	University of Cagliari, Italy
Gianfranco Fancello	University of Cagliari, Italy
Patrizia Serra	University of Cagliari, Italy
Agostino Bruzzone	University of Genoa, Italy
Alberto Camarero	Politechnic of Madrid, Spain
Thierry Vanelslander	University of Antwerp, Belgium

Smart Transport and Logistics - Smart Supply Chains (SmarTransLog 2023)

Giuseppe Borruso	University of Trieste, Italy
Marco Mazzarino	University of Venice, Italy
Marcello Tadini	University of Eastern Piedmont, Italy
Luigi Mundula	University for Foreigners of Perugia, Italy
Mara Ladu	University of Cagliari, Italy
Maria del Mar Munoz Leonisio	University of Cadiz, Spain

Smart Tourism (SmartTourism 2023)

Giuseppe Borruso	University of Trieste, Italy
Silvia Battino	University of Sassari, Italy
Ainhoa Amaro Garcia	University of Alcala and University of Las Palmas, Spain
Francesca Krasna	University of Trieste, Italy
Ginevra Balletto	University of Cagliari, Italy
Maria del Mar Munoz Leonisio	University of Cadiz, Spain

Sustainability Performance Assessment: Models, Approaches, and Applications Toward Interdisciplinary and Integrated Solutions (SPA 2023)

Sabrina Lai	University of Cagliari, Italy
Francesco Scorza	University of Basilicata, Italy
Jolanta Dvarioniene	Kaunas University of Technology, Lithuania
Valentin Grecu	Lucian Blaga University of Sibiu, Romania
Georgia Pozoukidou	Aristotle University of Thessaloniki, Greece

Spatial Energy Planning, City and Urban Heritage (Spatial_Energy_City 2023)

Ginevra Balletto	University of Cagliari, Italy
Mara Ladu	University of Cagliari, Italy
Emilio Ghiani	University of Cagliari, Italy
Roberto De Lotto	University of Pavia, Italy
Roberto Gerundo	University of Salerno, Italy

Specifics of Smart Cities Development in Europe (SPEED 2023)

Chiara Garau	University of Cagliari, Italy
Katarína Vitálišová	Matej Bel University, Slovakia
Paolo Nesi	University of Florence, Italy
Anna Vaňová	Matej Bel University, Slovakia
Kamila Borsekova	Matej Bel University, Slovakia
Paola Zamperlin	University of Pisa, Italy

Smart, Safe and Health Cities (SSHC 2023)

Chiara Garau	University of Cagliari, Italy
Gerardo Carpentieri	University of Naples Federico II, Italy
Floriana Zucaro	University of Naples Federico II, Italy
Aynaz Lotfata	Chicago State University, USA
Alfonso Annunziata	University of Basilicata, Italy
Diego Altafini	University of Pisa, Italy

Smart and Sustainable Island Communities (SSIC_2023)

Chiara Garau	University of Cagliari, Italy
Anastasia Stratigea	National Technical University of Athens, Greece
Yiota Theodora	National Technical University of Athens, Greece
Giulia Desogus	University of Cagliari, Italy

Theoretical and Computational Chemistry and Its Applications (TCCMA 2023)

Noelia Faginas-Lago	University of Perugia, Italy
Andrea Lombardi	University of Perugia, Italy

Transport Infrastructures for Smart Cities (TISC 2023)

Francesca Maltinti	University of Cagliari, Italy
Mauro Coni	University of Cagliari, Italy
Francesco Pinna	University of Cagliari, Italy
Chiara Garau	University of Cagliari, Italy
Nicoletta Rassu	University of Cagliari, Italy
James Rombi	University of Cagliari, Italy

Urban Regeneration: Innovative Tools and Evaluation Model (URITEM 2023)

Fabrizio Battisti	University of Florence, Italy
Giovanna Acampa	University of Florence and University of Enna Kore, Italy
Orazio Campo	La Sapienza University of Rome, Italy

Urban Space Accessibility and Mobilities (USAM 2023)

Chiara Garau	University of Cagliari, Italy
Matteo Ignaccolo	University of Catania, Italy
Michela Tiboni	University of Brescia, Italy
Francesco Pinna	University of Cagliari, Italy
Silvia Rossetti	University of Parma, Italy
Vincenza Torrisi	University of Catania, Italy
Ilaria Delponte	University of Genoa, Italy

Virtual Reality and Augmented Reality and Applications (VRA 2023)

Osvaldo Gervasi	University of Perugia, Italy
Damiano Perri	University of Florence, Italy
Marco Simonetti	University of Florence, Italy
Sergio Tasso	University of Perugia, Italy

Workshop on Advanced and Computational Methods for Earth Science Applications (WACM4ES 2023)

Luca Piroddi	University of Malta, Malta
Sebastiano Damico	University of Malta, Malta
Marilena Cozzolino	Università del Molise, Italy
Adam Gauci	University of Malta, Italy
Giuseppina Vacca	University of Cagliari, Italy
Chiara Garau	University of Cagliari, Italy

Sponsoring Organizations

ICCSA 2023 would not have been possible without the tremendous support of many organizations and institutions, for which all organizers and participants of ICCSA 2023 express their sincere gratitude:

 Springer Nature Switzerland AG, Switzerland
(https://www.springer.com)

 Computers Open Access Journal
(https://www.mdpi.com/journal/computers)

 National Technical University of Athens, Greece
(https://www.ntua.gr/)

 University of the Aegean, Greece
(https://www.aegean.edu/)

 University of Perugia, Italy
(https://www.unipg.it)

 University of Basilicata, Italy
(http://www.unibas.it)

 Monash University, Australia
(https://www.monash.edu/)

 Kyushu Sangyo University, Japan
(https://www.kyusan-u.ac.jp/)

 University of Minho, Portugal
(https://www.uminho.pt/)

Universidade do Minho
Escola de Engenharia

Referees

Francesca Abastante	Turin Polytechnic, Italy
Giovanna Acampa	University of Enna Kore, Italy
Adewole Adewumi	Algonquin College, Canada
Vera Afreixo	University of Aveiro, Portugal
Riad Aggoune	Luxembourg Institute of Science and Technology, Luxembourg
Akshat Agrawal	Amity University Haryana, India
Waseem Ahmad	National Institute of Technology Karnataka, India
Oylum Alatlı	Ege University, Turkey
Abraham Alfa	Federal University of Technology Minna, Nigeria
Diego Altafini	University of Pisa, Italy
Filipe Alvelos	University of Minho, Portugal
Marina Alexandra Pedro Andrade	University Institute of Lisbon, Portugal
Debora Anelli	Polytechnic University of Bari, Italy
Mariarosaria Angrisano	Pegaso University, Italy
Alfonso Annunziata	University of Cagliari, Italy
Magarò Antonio	Sapienza University of Rome, Italy
Bernady Apduhan	Kyushu Sangyo University, Japan
Jonathan Apeh	Covenant University, Nigeria
Daniela Ascenzi	University of Trento, Italy
Vanessa Assumma	University of Bologna, Italy
Maria Fernanda Augusto	Bitrum Research Center, Spain
Marco Baioletti	University of Perugia, Italy

Ginevra Balletto	University of Cagliari, Italy
Carlos Balsa	Polytechnic Institute of Bragança, Portugal
Benedetto Barabino	University of Brescia, Italy
Simona Barbaro	University of Palermo, Italy
Sebastiano Barbieri	Turin Polytechnic, Italy
Kousik Barik	University of Alcala, Spain
Alice Barreca	Turin Polytechnic, Italy
Socrates Basbas	Aristotle University of Thessaloniki, Greece
Rosaria Battarra	National Research Council, Italy
Silvia Battino	University of Sassari, Italy
Fabrizio Battisti	University of Florence, Italy
Yaroslav Bazaikin	Jan Evangelista Purkyne University, Czech Republic
Ranjan Kumar Behera	Indian Institute of Information Technology, India
Simone Belli	Complutense University of Madrid, Spain
Oscar Bellini	Polytechnic University of Milan, Italy
Giulio Biondi	University of Perugia, Italy
Adriano Bisello	Eurac Research, Italy
Semen Bochkov	Ulyanovsk State Technical University, Russia
Alexander Bogdanov	St. Petersburg State University, Russia
Letizia Bollini	Free University of Bozen, Italy
Giuseppe Borruso	University of Trieste, Italy
Marilisa Botte	University of Naples Federico II, Italy
Ana Cristina Braga	University of Minho, Portugal
Frederico Branco	University of Trás-os-Montes and Alto Douro, Portugal
Jorge Buele	Indoamérica Technological University, Ecuador
Datzania Lizeth Burgos	Peninsula State University of Santa Elena, Ecuador
Isabel Cacao	University of Aveiro, Portugal
Francesco Calabrò	Mediterranea University of Reggio Calabria, Italy
Rogerio Calazan	Institute of Sea Studies Almirante Paulo Moreira, Brazil
Lelio Campanile	University of Campania Luigi Vanvitelli, Italy
Tiziana Campisi	University of Enna Kore, Italy
Orazio Campo	University of Rome La Sapienza, Italy
Caterina Caprioli	Turin Polytechnic, Italy
Gerardo Carpentieri	University of Naples Federico II, Italy
Martina Carra	University of Brescia, Italy
Barbara Caselli	University of Parma, Italy
Danny Casprini	Politechnic of Milan, Italy

Piero Di Bonito	University of Campania Luigi Vanvitelli, Italy
Chiara Di Dato	University of L'Aquila, Italy
Michele Di Giovanni	University of Campania Luigi Vanvitelli, Italy
Felicia Di Liddo	Polytechnic University of Bari, Italy
Joana Dias	University of Coimbra, Portugal
Luigi Dolores	University of Salerno, Italy
Marco Donatelli	Università of Insubria, Italy
Aziz Dursun	Virginia Tech University, USA
Jaroslav Dvořak	Klaipeda University, Lithuania
Wolfgang Erb	University of Padova, Italy
Maurizio Francesco Errigo	University of Enna Kore, Italy
Noelia Faginas-Lago	University of Perugia, Italy
Maria Irene Falcao	University of Minho, Portugal
Stefano Falcinelli	University of Perugia, Italy
Grazia Fattoruso	Italian National Agency for New Technologies, Energy and Sustainable Economic Development, Italy
Sara Favargiotti	University of Trento, Italy
Marcin Feltynowski	University of Lodz, Poland
António Fernandes	Polytechnic Institute of Bragança, Portugal
Florbela P. Fernandes	Polytechnic Institute of Bragança, Portugal
Paula Odete Fernandes	Polytechnic Institute of Bragança, Portugal
Luis Fernandez-Sanz	University of Alcala, Spain
Maria Eugenia Ferrao	University of Beira Interior and University of Lisbon, Portugal
Luís Ferrás	University of Minho, Portugal
Angela Ferreira	Polytechnic Institute of Bragança, Portugal
Maddalena Ferretti	Politechnic of Marche, Italy
Manuel Carlos Figueiredo	University of Minho, Portugal
Fabrizio Finucci	Roma Tre University, Italy
Ugo Fiore	University Pathenope of Naples, Italy
Lorena Fiorini	University of L'Aquila, Italy
Valentina Franzoni	Perugia University, Italy
Adelaide Freitas	University of Aveiro, Portugal
Kirill Gadylshin	Russian Academy of Sciences, Russia
Andrea Gallo	University of Trieste, Italy
Luciano Galone	University of Malta, Malta
Chiara Garau	University of Cagliari, Italy
Ernesto Garcia Para	Universidad del País Vasco, Spain
Rachele Vanessa Gatto	Università della Basilicata, Italy
Marina Gavrilova	University of Calgary, Canada
Georgios Georgiadis	Aristotle University of Thessaloniki, Greece

Ivan Gerace	University of Perugia, Italy
Osvaldo Gervasi	University of Perugia, Italy
Alfonso Giancotti	Sapienza University of Rome, Italy
Andrea Gioia	Politechnic of Bari, Italy
Giacomo Giorgi	University of Perugia, Italy
Salvatore Giuffrida	Università di Catania, Italy
A. Manuela Gonçalves	University of Minho, Portugal
Angela Gorgoglione	University of the Republic, Uruguay
Yusuke Gotoh	Okayama University, Japan
Mariolina Grasso	University of Enna Kore, Italy
Silvana Grillo	University of Cagliari, Italy
Teresa Guarda	Universidad Estatal Peninsula de Santa Elena, Ecuador
Eduardo Guerra	Free University of Bozen-Bolzano, Italy
Carmen Guida	University of Napoli Federico II, Italy
Kemal Güven Gülen	Namık Kemal University, Turkey
Malgorzata Hanzl	Technical University of Lodz, Poland
Peter Hegedus	University of Szeged, Hungary
Syeda Sumbul Hossain	Daffodil International University, Bangladesh
Mustafa Inceoglu	Ege University, Turkey
Federica Isola	University of Cagliari, Italy
Seifedine Kadry	Noroff University College, Norway
Yeliz Karaca	University of Massachusetts Chan Medical School and Massachusetts Institute of Technology, USA
Harun Karsli	Bolu Abant Izzet Baysal University, Turkey
Tayana Khachkova	Russian Academy of Sciences, Russia
Manju Khari	Jawaharlal Nehru University, India
Vladimir Korkhov	Saint Petersburg State University, Russia
Dionisia Koutsi	National Technical University of Athens, Greece
Tomonori Kouya	Shizuoka Institute of Science and Technology, Japan
Nataliia Kulabukhova	Saint Petersburg State University, Russia
Anisha Kumari	National Institute of Technology, India
Ludovica La Rocca	University of Napoli Federico II, Italy
Mara Ladu	University of Cagliari, Italy
Sabrina Lai	University of Cagliari, Italy
Mohamed Laib	Luxembourg Institute of Science and Technology, Luxembourg
Giuseppe Francesco Cesare Lama	University of Napoli Federico II, Italy
Isabella Maria Lami	Turin Polytechnic, Italy
Chien Sing Lee	Sunway University, Malaysia

Marcelo Leon	Ecotec University, Ecuador
Federica Leone	University of Cagliari, Italy
Barbara Lino	University of Palermo, Italy
Vadim Lisitsa	Russian Academy of Sciences, Russia
Carla Lobo	Portucalense University, Portugal
Marco Locurcio	Polytechnic University of Bari, Italy
Claudia Loggia	University of KwaZulu-Natal, South Africa
Andrea Lombardi	University of Perugia, Italy
Isabel Lopes	Polytechnic Institut of Bragança, Portugal
Immacolata Lorè	Mediterranean University of Reggio Calabria, Italy
Vanda Lourenco	Nova University of Lisbon, Portugal
Giorgia Malavasi	Turin Polytechnic, Italy
Francesca Maltinti	University of Cagliari, Italy
Luca Mancini	University of Perugia, Italy
Marcos Mandado	University of Vigo, Spain
Benedetto Manganelli	University of Basilicata, Italy
Krassimir Markov	Institute of Electric Engineering and Informatics, Bulgaria
Enzo Martinelli	University of Salerno, Italy
Fiammetta Marulli	University of Campania Luigi Vanvitelli, Italy
Antonino Marvuglia	Luxembourg Institute of Science and Technology, Luxembourg
Rytis Maskeliunas	Kaunas University of Technology, Lithuania
Michele Mastroianni	University of Salerno, Italy
Hideo Matsufuru	High Energy Accelerator Research Organization, Japan
D'Apuzzo Mauro	University of Cassino and Southern Lazio, Italy
Luis Mazon	Bitrum Research Group, Spain
Chiara Mazzarella	University Federico II, Naples, Italy
Beatrice Mecca	Turin Polytechnic, Italy
Umberto Mecca	Turin Polytechnic, Italy
Paolo Mengoni	Hong Kong Baptist University, China
Gaetano Messina	Mediterranean University of Reggio Calabria, Italy
Alfredo Milani	University of Perugia, Italy
Alessandra Milesi	University of Cagliari, Italy
Richard Millham	Durban University of Technology, South Africa
Fernando Miranda	Universidade do Minho, Portugal
Biswajeeban Mishra	University of Szeged, Hungary
Giuseppe Modica	University of Reggio Calabria, Italy
Pierluigi Morano	Polytechnic University of Bari, Italy

Filipe Mota Pinto	Polytechnic Institute of Leiria, Portugal
Maria Mourao	Polytechnic Institute of Viana do Castelo, Portugal
Eugenio Muccio	University of Naples Federico II, Italy
Beniamino Murgante	University of Basilicata, Italy
Rocco Murro	Sapienza University of Rome, Italy
Giuseppe Musolino	Mediterranean University of Reggio Calabria, Italy
Nadia Nedjah	State University of Rio de Janeiro, Brazil
Juraj Nemec	Masaryk University, Czech Republic
Andreas Nikiforiadis	Aristotle University of Thessaloniki, Greece
Silvio Nocera	IUAV University of Venice, Italy
Roseline Ogundokun	Kaunas University of Technology, Lithuania
Emma Okewu	University of Alcala, Spain
Serena Olcuire	Sapienza University of Rome, Italy
Irene Oliveira	University Trás-os-Montes and Alto Douro, Portugal
Samson Oruma	Ostfold University College, Norway
Antonio Pala	University of Cagliari, Italy
Maria Panagiotopoulou	National Technical University of Athens, Greece
Simona Panaro	University of Sussex Business School, UK
Jay Pancham	Durban University of Technology, South Africa
Eric Pardede	La Trobe University, Australia
Hyun Kyoo Park	Ministry of National Defense, South Korea
Damiano Perri	University of Florence, Italy
Quoc Trung Pham	Ho Chi Minh City University of Technology, Vietnam
Claudio Piferi	University of Florence, Italy
Angela Pilogallo	University of L'Aquila, Italy
Francesco Pinna	University of Cagliari, Italy
Telmo Pinto	University of Coimbra, Portugal
Luca Piroddi	University of Malta, Malta
Francesco Pittau	Politechnic of Milan, Italy
Giuliano Poli	Università Federico II di Napoli, Italy
Maurizio Pollino	Italian National Agency for New Technologies, Energy and Sustainable Economic Development, Italy
Vijay Prakash	University of Malta, Malta
Salvatore Praticò	Mediterranean University of Reggio Calabria, Italy
Carlotta Quagliolo	Turin Polytechnic, Italy
Garrisi Raffaele	Operations Center for Cyber Security, Italy
Mariapia Raimondo	Università della Campania Luigi Vanvitelli, Italy

Bruna Ramos	Universidade Lusíada Norte, Portugal
Nicoletta Rassu	University of Cagliari, Italy
Roberta Ravanelli	University of Roma La Sapienza, Italy
Pier Francesco Recchi	University of Naples Federico II, Italy
Stefania Regalbuto	University of Naples Federico II, Italy
Rommel Regis	Saint Joseph's University, USA
Marco Reis	University of Coimbra, Portugal
Jerzy Respondek	Silesian University of Technology, Poland
Isabel Ribeiro	Polytechnic Institut of Bragança, Portugal
Albert Rimola	Autonomous University of Barcelona, Spain
Corrado Rindone	Mediterranean University of Reggio Calabria, Italy
Maria Rocco	Roma Tre University, Italy
Ana Maria A. C. Rocha	University of Minho, Portugal
Fabio Rocha	Universidade Federal de Sergipe, Brazil
Humberto Rocha	University of Coimbra, Portugal
Maria Clara Rocha	Politechnic Institut of Coimbra, Portual
Carlos Rodrigues	Polytechnic Institut of Bragança, Portugal
Diana Rolando	Turin Polytechnic, Italy
James Rombi	University of Cagliari, Italy
Evgeniy Romenskiy	Russian Academy of Sciences, Russia
Marzio Rosi	University of Perugia, Italy
Silvia Rossetti	University of Parma, Italy
Marco Rossitti	Politechnic of Milan, Italy
Antonio Russo	University of Enna, Italy
Insoo Ryu	MoaSoftware, South Korea
Yeonseung Ryu	Myongji University, South Korea
Lucia Saganeiti	University of L'Aquila, Italy
Valentina Santarsiero	University of Basilicata, Italy
Luigi Santopietro	University of Basilicata, Italy
Rafael Santos	National Institute for Space Research, Brazil
Valentino Santucci	University for Foreigners of Perugia, Italy
Alessandra Saponieri	University of Salento, Italy
Mattia Scalas	Turin Polytechnic, Italy
Francesco Scorza	University of Basilicata, Italy
Ester Scotto Di Perta	University of Napoli Federico II, Italy
Nicoletta Setola	University of Florence, Italy
Ricardo Severino	University of Minho, Portugal
Angela Silva	Polytechnic Institut of Viana do Castelo, Portugal
Carina Silva	Polytechnic of Lisbon, Portugal
Marco Simonetti	University of Florence, Italy
Sergey Solovyev	Russian Academy of Sciences, Russia

Maria Somma	University of Naples Federico II, Italy
Changgeun Son	Ministry of National Defense, South Korea
Alberico Sonnessa	Polytechnic of Bari, Italy
Inês Sousa	University of Minho, Portugal
Lisete Sousa	University of Lisbon, Portugal
Elena Stankova	Saint-Petersburg State University, Russia
Modestos Stavrakis	University of the Aegean, Greece
Flavio Stochino	University of Cagliari, Italy
Anastasia Stratigea	National Technical University of Athens, Greece
Yue Sun	European XFEL GmbH, Germany
Anthony Suppa	Turin Polytechnic, Italy
David Taniar	Monash University, Australia
Rodrigo Tapia McClung	Centre for Research in Geospatial Information Sciences, Mexico
Tarek Teba	University of Portsmouth, UK
Ana Paula Teixeira	University of Trás-os-Montes and Alto Douro, Portugal
Tengku Adil Tengku Izhar	Technological University MARA, Malaysia
Maria Filomena Teodoro	University of Lisbon and Portuguese Naval Academy, Portugal
Yiota Theodora	National Technical University of Athens, Greece
Elena Todella	Turin Polytechnic, Italy
Graça Tomaz	Polytechnic Institut of Guarda, Portugal
Anna Tonazzini	National Research Council, Italy
Dario Torregrossa	Goodyear, Luxembourg
Francesca Torrieri	University of Naples Federico II, Italy
Vincenza Torrisi	University of Catania, Italy
Nikola Tosic	Polytechnic University of Catalonia, Spain
Vincenzo Totaro	Polytechnic University of Bari, Italy
Arianna Travaglini	University of Florence, Italy
António Trigo	Polytechnic of Coimbra, Portugal
Giuseppe A. Trunfio	University of Sassari, Italy
Toshihiro Uchibayashi	Kyushu University, Japan
Piero Ugliengo	University of Torino, Italy
Jordi Vallverdu	University Autonoma Barcelona, Spain
Gianmarco Vanuzzo	University of Perugia, Italy
Dmitry Vasyunin	T-Systems, Russia
Laura Verde	University of Campania Luigi Vanvitelli, Italy
Giulio Vignoli	University of Cagliari, Italy
Gianluca Vinti	University of Perugia, Italy
Katarína Vitálišová	Matej Bel University, Slovak Republic
Daniel Mark Vitiello	University of Cagliari

Plenary Lectures

A Multiscale Planning Concept for Sustainable Metropolitan Development

Pierre Frankhauser

Théma, Université de Franche-Comté, 32, rue Mégevand, 20030 Besançon, France
`pierre.frankhauser@univ-fcomte.fr`

Keywords: Sustainable metropolitan development · Multiscale approach · Urban modelling

Urban sprawl has often been pointed out as having an important negative impact on environment and climate. Residential zones have grown up in what were initially rural areas, located far from employment areas and often lacking shopping opportunities, public services and public transportation. Hence urban sprawl increased car-traffic flows, generating pollution and increasing energy consumption. New road axes consume considerable space and weaken biodiversity by reducing and cutting natural areas. A return to "compact cities" or "dense cities" has often been contemplated as the most efficient way to limit urban sprawl. However, the real impact of density on car use is less clear-cut (Daneshpour and Shakibamanesh 2011). Let us emphasize that moreover climate change will increase the risk of heat islands on an intra-urban scale. This prompts a more nuanced reflection on how urban fabrics should be structured.

Moreover, urban planning cannot ignore social demand. Lower land prices in rural areas, often put forward by economists, is not the only reason of urban sprawl. The quality of the residential environment comes into play, too, through features like noise, pollution, landscape quality, density etc. Schwanen et al. (2004) observe for the Netherlands that households preferring a quiet residential environment and individual housing with a garden will not accept densification, which might even lead them to move to lower-density rural areas even farther away from jobs and shopping amenities. Many scholars emphasize the importance of green amenities for residential environments and report the importance of easy access to leisure areas (Guo and Bhat 2002). Vegetation in the residential environment has an important impact on health and well-being (Lafortezza et al. 2009).

We present here the Fractalopolis concept which we developed in the frame of several research projects and which aims reconciling environmental and social issues (Bonin et al., 2020; Frankhauser 2021; Frankhauser et al. 2018). This concept introduces a multiscale approach based on multifractal geometry for conceiving spatial development for metropolitan areas. For taking into account social demand we refer to the fundamental work of Max-Neef et al. (1991) based on Maslow's work about basic human needs. He introduces the concept of satisfiers assigned to meet the basic needs of "Subsistence, Protection, Affection, Understanding, Participation, Idleness, Creation, Identity and Freedom". Satisfiers thus become the link between the needs of everyone and society and may depend on the cultural context. We consider their importance, their location and their accessibility and we rank the needs according to their importance for individuals or households. In order to enjoy a good quality of life and to shorten trips and to reduce automobile use, it seems important for satisfiers of daily needs to be easily accessible. Hence, we consider the purchase rate when reflecting on the implementation of shops which is reminiscent of central place theory.

The second important feature is taking care of environment and biodiversity by avoiding fragmentation of green space (Ekren and Arslan 2022) which must benefit, moreover, of a good accessibility, as pointed out. These areas must, too, ply the role of cooling areas ensuring ventilation of urbanized areas (Kuttler et al. 1998).

For integrating these different objectives, we propose a concept for developing spatial configurations of metropolitan areas designed which is based on multifractal geometry. It allows combining different issues across a large range of scales in a coherent way. These issues include:

- providing easy access to a large array of amenities to meet social demand;
- promoting the use of public transportation and soft modes instead of automobile use;
- preserving biodiversity and improving the local climate.

The concept distinguishes development zones localized in the vicinity of a nested and hierarchized system of public transport axes. The highest ranked center offers all types of amenities, whereas lower ranked centers lack the highest ranked amenities. The lowest ranked centers just offer the amenities for daily needs. A coding system allows distinguishing the centers according to their rank.

Each subset of central places is in some sense autonomous, since they are not linked by transportation axes to subcenters of the same order. This allows to preserve a linked system of green corridors penetrating the development zones across scales avoiding the fragmentation of green areas and ensuring a good accessibility to recreational areas.

The spatial model is completed by a population distribution model which globally follows the same hierarchical logic. However, we weakened the strong fractal order what allows to conceive a more or less polycentric spatial system.

We can adapt the theoretical concept easily to real world situation without changing the underlying multiscale logic. A decision support system has been developed allowing to simulate development scenarios and to evaluate them. The evaluation procedure is based on fuzzy evaluation of distance acceptance for accessing to the different types of amenities according to the ranking of needs. We used for evaluation data issued from a great set of French planning documents like Master plans. We show an example how the software package can be used concretely.

References

Bonin, O., et al.: Projet SOFT sobriété énergétique par les formes urbaines et le transport (Research Report No. 1717C0003; p. 214). ADEME (2020)

Daneshpour, A., Shakibamanesh, A.: Compact city; dose it create an obligatory context for urban sustainability? Int. J. Archit. Eng. Urban Plann. 21(2), 110–118 (2011)

Ekren, E., Arslan, M.: Functions of greenways as an ecologically-based planning strategy. In: Çakır, M., Tuğluer, M., Fırat Örs, P.: Architectural Sciences and Ecology, pp. 134–156. Iksad Publications (2022)

Frankhauser, P.: Fractalopolis—a fractal concept for the sustainable development of metropolitan areas. In: Sajous, P., Bertelle, C. (eds.) Complex Systems, Smart Territories and Mobility, pp. 15–50. Springer, Cham (2021). https://doi.org/10.1007/978-3-030-59302-5_2

Frankhauser, P., Tannier, C., Vuidel, G., Houot, H.: An integrated multifractal modelling to urban and regional planning. Comput. Environ. Urban Syst. **67**(1), 132–146 (2018). https://doi.org/10.1016/j.compenvurbsys.2017.09.011

Guo, J., Bhat, C.: Residential location modeling: accommodating sociodemographic, school quality and accessibility effects. University of Texas, Austin (2002)

Kuttler, W., Dütemeyer, D., Barlag, A.-B.: Influence of regional and local winds on urban ventilation in Cologne, Germany. Meteorologische Zeitschrift, 77–87 (1998) https://doi.org/10.1127/metz/7/1998/77

Lafortezza, R., Carrus, G., Sanesi, G., Davies, C.: Benefits and well-being perceived by people visiting green spaces in periods of heat stress. Urban For. Urban Green. **8**(2), 97–108 (2009)

Max-Neef, M. A., Elizalde, A., Hopenhayn, M.: Human scale development: conception, application and further reflections. The Apex Press (1991)

Schwanen, T., Dijst, M., Dieleman, F. M.: Policies for urban form and their impact on travel: The Netherlands experience. Urban Stud. **41**(3), 579–603 (2004)

Graph Drawing and Network Visualization – An Overview – (Keynote Speech)

Giuseppe Liotta

Dipartimento di Ingegneria, Università degli Studi di Perugia, Italy
giuseppe.liotta@unipg.it

Abstract. Graph Drawing and Network visualization supports the exploration, analysis, and communication of relational data arising in a variety of application domains: from bioinformatics to software engineering, from social media to cyber-security, from data bases to powergrid systems. Aim of this keynote speech is to introduce this thriving research area, highlighting some of its basic approaches and pointing to some promising research directions.

1 Introduction

Graph Drawing and Network Visualization is at the intersection of different disciplines and it combines topics that traditionally belong to theoretical computer science with methods and approaches that characterize more applied disciplines. Namely, it can be related to Graph Algorithms, Geometric Graph Theory and Geometric computing, Combinatorial Optimization, Experimental Analysis, User Studies, System Design and Development, and Human Computer Interaction. This combination of theory and practice is well reflected in the flagship conference of the area, the *International Symposium on Graph Drawing and Network Visualization*, that has two tracks, one focusing on combinatorial and algorithmic aspects and the other on the design of network visualization systems and interfaces. The conference is now at its 31st edition; a full list of the symposia and their proceedings, published by Springer in the LNCS series can be found at the URL: http://www.graphdrawing.org/.

Aim of this short paper is to outline the content of my Keynote Speech at ICCSA 2023, which will be referred to as the "Talk" in the rest of the paper. The talk will introduce the field of Graph Drawing and Network Visualization to a broad audience, with the goal to not only present some key methodological and technological aspects, but also point to some unexplored or partially explored research directions. The rest of this short paper briefly outlines the content of the talk and provides some references that can be a starting point for researchers interested in working on Graph Drawing and Network Visualization.

2 Why Visualize Networks?

Back in 1973 the famous statistician Francis Anscombe, gave a convincing example of why visualization is fundamental component of data analysis. The example is known as the *Anscombe's quartet* [3] and it consists of four sets of 11 points each that are almost identical in terms of the basic statistic properties of their x– and y– coordinates. Namely the mean values and the variance of x and y are exactly the same in the four sets, while the correlation of x and y and the linear regression are the same up to the second decimal. In spite of this statistical similarity, the data look very different when displayed in the Euclidean plane which leads to the conclusion that they correspond to significantly different phenomena. Figure 1 reports the four sets of Anscombe's quartet. After fifty years, with the arrival of AI-based technologies and the need of explaining and interpreting machine-driven suggestions before making strategic decision, the lesson of Anscombe's quartet has not just kept but even increased its relevance.

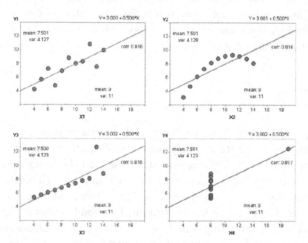

Fig. 1. The four point sets in Anscombe's quartet [3]; the figure also reports statistical values of the x and y variables.

As a matter of fact, nowadays the need of visualization systems goes beyond the verification of the accuracy of some statistical analysis on a set of scattered data. Recent technological advances have generated torrents of data that area relational in nature and typically modeled as networks: the nodes of the networks store the features of the data and the edges of the networks describe the semantic relationships between the data features. Such networked data sets (whose algebraic underlying structure is a called graph in discrete mathematics) arise in a variety of application domains including, for example, Systems Biology, Social Network Analysis, Software Engineering, Networking, Data Bases, Homeland Security, and Business Intelligence. In these (and many other) contexts, systems that support the visual analysis of networks and graphs play a central role in critical decision making processes. These are human-in-the-loop processes where the continuous interaction between humans (decision makers) and data mining or optimization algorithms (AI/ML components) supports the data exploration, the development of verifiable theories about the data, and the extraction of new knowledge that is used to make strategic choices. A seminal book by Keim et al. [33] schematically represents the human-in-the-loop approach to making sense of networked data sets as in Fig. 2. See also [46–49].

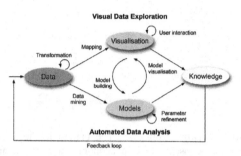

Fig. 2. Sense-making/knowledge generation loop. This conceptual interaction model between human analysts and network visualization system is at the basis of network visual analytics system design [33].

To make a concrete application example of the analysis of a network by interacting with its visualization, consider the problem of contrasting financial crimes such as money laundering or tax evasion. These crimes are based on relevant volumes of financial transactions to conceal the identity, the source, or the destination of illegally gained money. Also, the adopted patterns to pursue the illegal goals continuously change to conceal the crimes. Therefore, contrasting them requires special investigation units which must analyze very large and highly dynamic data sets and discover relationships between different subjects to untangle complex fraudulent plots. The investigative cycle begins with data collection and filtering; it is then followed by modeling the data as a social network (also called *financial activity network* in this context) to which different data mining and data analytic methods are applied, including graph pattern matching, social network analysis, machine learning, and information diffusion. By the network visualization system detectives can interactively explore the data, gain insight and make new hypotheses about possible criminal activities, verify the hypotheses by asking the system to provide more details about specific portions of the network, refine previous outputs, and eventually gain new knowledge. Figure 3 illustrates a small financial activity network where, by means of the interaction between an officer of the Italian Revenue Agency and the MALDIVE system described in [10] a fraudulent pattern has been identified. Precisely, the tax officer has encoded a risky relational scheme among taxpayers into a suspicious graph pattern; in response, the system has made a search in the taxpayer network and it has returned one such pattern. See, e.g., [9, 11, 14, 18, 38] for more papers and references about visual analytic applications to contrasting financial crimes.

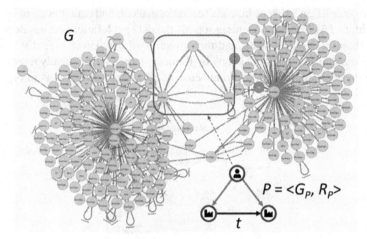

Fig. 3. A financial activity network from [10]. The pattern in the figure represents a SuppliesFromAssociated scheme, consisting of an economic transaction and two shareholding relationships.

3   Facets of Graph Drawing and Network Visualization

The Talk overviews some of the fundamental facets that characterize the research in Graph Drawing and Network Visualization. Namely:

- Graph drawing metaphors: Depending on the application context, different metaphors can be used to represent a relational data set modeled as a graph. The talk will briefly recall the matrix representation, the space filling representation, the contact representation, and the node-link representation which is, by far, the most commonly used (see, e.g., [43]).
- Interaction paradigms: Different interaction paradigms have different impacts on the sense-making process of the user about the visualized network. The Talk will go through the full-view, top-down, bottom-up, incremental, and narrative paradigms. Pros and cons will be highlighted for each approach, also by means of examples and applications. The discussion of the top-down interaction paradigm will also consider the hybrid visualization models (see, e.g., [2, 24, 26, 28, 39]) while the discussion about the incremental paradigm will focus on research about graph storyplans (see, e.g., [4, 6, 7]).
- Graph drawing algorithms: Three main algorithmic approaches will be reviewed, namely the force-directed, the layered), and the planarization-based approach; see, e.g., [5]. We shall also make some remarks about FPT algorithms for graph drawing (see, e.g., [8, 19, 20, 25, 27, 40, 53]) and about how the optimization challenges vary when it is assumed that the input has or does not have a fixed combinatorial embedding (see, e.g., [12, 13, 16, 17, 23]).
- Experimental analysis and user-studies: The Talk will mostly compare two models to define and experimentally validate those optimization goals that define a "readable"

network visualization, i.e. a visualization that in a given application context can easily convey the structure of a relational data set so to guarantee efficiency both in its visual exploration and in the elaboration of new knowledge. Special focus will be given to a set emerging optimization goals related to edge crossings that are currently investigated in the graph drawing and network visualization community unedr the name of "graph drawing beyond planarity" (see, e.g., [1, 15, 29, 35]).

The talk shall also point to some promising research directions, including: (i) Extend the body of papers devoted to user-studies that compare the impact of different graph drawing metaphors on the user perception. (ii) Extend the study of interaction paradigms to extended reality environments (see, e.g., [21, 30, 36, 37]); (iii) Engineer the FPT algorithms for graph drawing and experimentally compare their performances with exact or approximate solutions; and (iv) Develop new algorithmic fameworks in the context of graph drawing beyond planarity.

We conclude this short paper with pointers to publication venues and key references that can be browsed by researchers interested in the fascinating field of Graph Drawing and Network Visualization.

4   Pointers to Publication venues and Key References

A limited list of conferences where Graph Drawing and Network Visualization papers are regularly part of the program includes *IEEE VIS, EuroVis, SoCG, ISAAC, ACM-SIAM SODA, WADS,* and *WG.* Among the many journals where several Graph Drawing and Network Visualization papers have appeared during the last three decades we recall *IEEE Transactions on Visualization and Computer Graphs, SIAM Journal of Computing, Computer Graphics Forum, Journal of Computer and System Sciences, Algorithmica, Journal of Graph Algorithms and Applications, Theoretical Computer Science, Information Sciences, Discrete and Computational Geometry, Computational Geometry: Theory and Applications, ACM Computing Surveys,* and *Computer Science Review.* A limited list of books, surveys, or papers that contain interesting algorithmic challenges on Graph Drawing and Network Visualization include [5, 15, 22, 29, 31–35, 41–45, 50–52].

References

1. Angelini, P., et al.: Simple k-planar graphs are simple (k+1)-quasiplanar. J. Comb. Theory, Ser. B, **142**, 1–35 (2020)
2. Angori, L., Didimo, W., Montecchiani, F., Pagliuca, D., Tappini, A.: Hybrid graph visualizations with chordlink: Algorithms, experiments, and applications. IEEE Trans. Vis. Comput. Graph. **28**(2), 1288–1300 (2022)
3. Anscombe, F.J.: Graphs in statistical analysis. Am. Stat. **27**(1), 17–21 (1973)
4. Di Battista, G., et al.: Small point-sets supporting graph stories. In: Angelini, P., von Hanxleden, R. (eds.) Graph Drawing and Network Visualization. GD 2022, LNCS, vol. 13764, pp. 289–303. Springer, Cham (2022). https://doi.org/10.1007/978-3-031-22203-0_21

5. Battista, G.D., Eades, P., Tamassia, R., Tollis, I.G.: Graph Drawing: Algorithms for the Visualization of Graphs. Prentice-Hall, Hoboken (1999)
6. Binucci, C., et al.: On the complexity of the storyplan problem. In: Angelini, P., von Hanxleden, R. (eds.) Graph Drawing and Network Visualization. GD 2022. LNCS, vol. 13764, pp. 304–318. Springer, Cham (2023). https://doi.org/10.1007/978-3-031-22203-0_22
7. Borrazzo, M., Lozzo, G.D., Battista, G.D., Frati, F., Patrignani, M.: Graph stories in small area. J. Graph Algorithms Appl. **24**(3), 269–292 (2020)
8. Chaplick, S., Giacomo, E.D., Frati, F., Ganian, R., Raftopoulou, C.N., Simonov, K.: Parameterized algorithms for upward planarity. In: Goaoc, X., Kerber, M. (eds.) 38th International Symposium on Computational Geometry, SoCG 2022, June 7–10, 2022, Berlin, Germany, LIPIcs, vol. 224, pp. 26:1–26:16. Schloss Dagstuhl - Leibniz-Zentrum für Informatik (2022)
9. Didimo, W., Giamminonni, L., Liotta, G., Montecchiani, F., Pagliuca, D.: A visual analytics system to support tax evasion discovery. Decis. Support Syst. **110**, 71–83 (2018)
10. Didimo, W., Grilli, L., Liotta, G., Menconi, L., Montecchiani, F., Pagliuca, D.: Combining network visualization and data mining for tax risk assessment. IEEE Access **8**, 16073–16086 (2020)
11. Didimo, W., Grilli, L., Liotta, G., Montecchiani, F., Pagliuca, D.: Visual querying and analysis of temporal fiscal networks. Inf. Sci. **505**, 406–421 (2019)
12. W. Didimo, M. Kaufmann, G. Liotta, and G. Ortali. Didimo, W., Kaufmann, M., Liotta, G., Ortali, G.: Rectilinear planarity testing of plane series-parallel graphs in linear time. In: Auber, D., Valtr, P. (eds.) Graph Drawing and Network Visualization. GD 2020. LNCS, vol. 12590, pp. 436–449. Springer, Cham (2020). https://doi.org/10.1007/978-3-030-68766-3_34
13. Didimo, W., Kaufmann, M., Liotta, G., Ortali, G.: Rectilinear planarity of partial 2-trees. In: Angelini, P., von Hanxleden, R. (eds.) Graph Drawing and Network Visualization. GD 2022. LNCS, vol. 13764, pp. 157–172. Springer, Cham (2023). https://doi.org/10.1007/978-3-031-22203-0_12
14. Didimo, W., Liotta, G., Montecchiani, F.: Network visualization for financial crime detection. J. Vis. Lang. Comput. **25**(4), 433–451 (2014)
15. Didimo, W., Liotta, G., Montecchiani, F.: A survey on graph drawing beyond planarity. ACM Comput. Surv. **52**(1), 4:1–4:37 (2019)
16. Didimo, W., Liotta, G., Ortali, G., Patrignani, M.: Optimal orthogonal drawings of planar 3-graphs in linear time. In: Chawla, S. (ed.) Proceedings of the 2020 ACM-SIAM Symposium on Discrete Algorithms, SODA 2020, Salt Lake City, UT, USA, January 5–8, 2020, pp. 806–825. SIAM (2020)
17. Didimo, W., Liotta, G., Patrignani, M.: HV-planarity: algorithms and complexity. J. Comput. Syst. Sci. **99**, 72–90 (2019)
18. Dilla, W.N., Raschke, R.L.: Data visualization for fraud detection: practice implications and a call for future research. Int. J. Acc. Inf. Syst. **16**, 1–22 (2015)
19. Dujmovic, V., et al.: A fixed-parameter approach to 2-layer planarization. Algorithmica **45**(2), 159–182 (2006)
20. Dujmovic, V., et al.: On the parameterized complexity of layered graph drawing. Algorithmica **52**(2), 267–292 (2008)

21. Dwyer, T., et al.: Immersive analytics: an introduction. In: Marriott, K., et al. (eds.) Immersive Analytics, LNCS, vol. 11190, pp. 1–23. Springer, Cham (2018)
22. Filipov, V., Arleo, A., Miksch, S.: Are we there yet? a roadmap of network visualization from surveys to task taxonomies. Computer Graphics Forum (2023, on print)
23. Garg, A., Tamassia, R.: On the computational complexity of upward and rectilinear planarity testing. SIAM J. Comput. 31(2), 601–625 (2001)
24. Di Giacomo, E., Didimo, W., Montecchiani, F., Tappini, A.: A user study on hybrid graph visualizations. In: Purchase, H.C., Rutter, I. (eds.) Graph Drawing and Network Visualization. GD 2021. LNCS, vol. 12868, pp. 21–38. Springer, Cham (2021). https://doi.org/10.1007/978-3-030-92931-2_2
25. Giacomo, E.D., Giordano, F., Liotta, G.: Upward topological book embeddings of dags. SIAM J. Discret. Math. 25(2), 479–489 (2011)
26. Giacomo, E.D., Lenhart, W.J., Liotta, G., Randolph, T.W., Tappini, A.: (k, p)-planarity: a relaxation of hybrid planarity. Theor. Comput. Sci. 896, 19–30 (2021)
27. Giacomo, E.D., Liotta, G., Montecchiani, F.: Orthogonal planarity testing of bounded treewidth graphs. J. Comput. Syst. Sci. 125, 129–148 (2022)
28. Giacomo, E.D., Liotta, G., Patrignani, M., Rutter, I., Tappini, A.: Nodetrix planarity testing with small clusters. Algorithmica 81(9), 3464–3493 (2019)
29. Hong, S., Tokuyama, T. (eds.) Beyond Planar Graphs. Springer, Singapore (2020). https://doi.org/10.1007/978-981-15-6533-5
30. Joos, L., Jaeger-Honz, S., Schreiber, F., Keim, D.A., Klein, K.: Visual comparison of networks in VR. IEEE Trans. Vis. Comput. Graph. 28(11), 3651–3661 (2022)
31. Jünger, M., Mutzel, P. (eds.) Graph Drawing Software. Springer, Berlin (2004). https://doi.org/10.1007/978-3-642-18638-7
32. Kaufmann, M., Wagner, D. (eds.): Drawing Graphs, Methods and Models (the book grow out of a Dagstuhl Seminar, April 1999), LNCS, vol. 2025. Springer, Berlin (2001). https://doi.org/10.1007/3-540-44969-8
33. Keim, D.A., Kohlhammer, J., Ellis, G.P., Mansmann, F.: Mastering the Information Age - Solving Problems with Visual Analytics. Eurographics Association, Saarbrücken (2010)
34. Keim, D.A., Mansmann, F., Stoffel, A., Ziegler, H.: Visual analytics. In: Liu, L., Özsu, M.T. (eds.) Encyclopedia of Database Systems, 2nd edn. Springer, Berlin (2018)
35. Kobourov, S.G., Liotta, G., Montecchiani, F.: An annotated bibliography on 1-planarity. Comput. Sci. Rev. 25, 49–67 (2017)
36. Kraus, M., et al.: Immersive analytics with abstract 3D visualizations: a survey. Comput. Graph. Forum 41(1), 201–229 (2022)
37. Kwon, O., Muelder, C., Lee, K., Ma, K.: A study of layout, rendering, and interaction methods for immersive graph visualization. IEEE Trans. Vis. Comput. Graph. 22(7), 1802–1815 (2016)
38. Leite, R.A., Gschwandtner, T., Miksch, S., Gstrein, E., Kuntner, J.: NEVA: visual analytics to identify fraudulent networks. Comput. Graph. Forum 39(6), 344–359 (2020)

39. Liotta, G., Rutter, I., Tappini, A.: Simultaneous FPQ-ordering and hybrid planarity testing. Theor. Comput. Sci. **874**, 59–79 (2021)
40. Liotta, G., Rutter, I., Tappini, A.: Parameterized complexity of graph planarity with restricted cyclic orders. J. Comput. Syst. Sci. **135**, 125–144 (2023)
41. Ma, K.: Pushing visualization research frontiers: essential topics not addressed by machine learning. IEEE Comput. Graphics Appl. **43**(1), 97–102 (2023)
42. McGee, F., et al.: Visual Analysis of Multilayer Networks. Synthesis Lectures on Visualization. Morgan & Claypool Publishers, San Rafael (2021)
43. Munzner, T.: Visualization Analysis and Design. A.K. Peters visualization series. A K Peters (2014)
44. Nishizeki, T., Rahman, M.S.: Planar Graph Drawing, vol. 12. World Scientific, Singapore (2004)
45. Nobre, C., Meyer, M.D., Streit, M., Lex, A.: The state of the art in visualizing multivariate networks. Comput. Graph. Forum **38**(3), 807–832 (2019)
46. Sacha, D.: Knowledge generation in visual analytics: Integrating human and machine intelligence for exploration of big data. In: Apel, S., et al. (eds.) Ausgezeichnete Informatikdissertationen 2018, LNI, vol. D-19, pp. 211–220. GI (2018)
47. Sacha, D., et al.: What you see is what you can change: human-centered machine learning by interactive visualization. Neurocomputing **268**, 164–175 (2017)
48. Sacha, D., Senaratne, H., Kwon, B.C., Ellis, G.P., Keim, D.A.: The role of uncertainty, awareness, and trust in visual analytics. IEEE Trans. Vis. Comput. Graph. **22**(1), 240–249 (2016)
49. Sacha, D., Stoffel, A., Stoffel, F., Kwon, B.C., Ellis, G.P., Keim, D.A.: Knowledge generation model for visual analytics. IEEE Trans. Vis. Comput. Graph. **20**(12), 1604–1613 (2014)
50. Tamassia, R.: Graph drawing. In: Sack, J., Urrutia, J. (eds.) Handbook of Computational Geometry, pp. 937–971. North Holland/Elsevier, Amsterdam (2000)
51. Tamassia, R. (ed.) Handbook on Graph Drawing and Visualization. Chapman and Hall/CRC, Boca Raton (2013)
52. Tamassia, R., Liotta, G.: Graph drawing. In: Goodman, J.E., O'Rourke, J. (eds.) Handbook of Discrete and Computational Geometry, 2nd edn., pp. 1163–1185. Chapman and Hall/CRC, Boca Raton (2004)
53. Zehavi, M.: Parameterized analysis and crossing minimization problems. Comput. Sci. Rev. **45**, 100490 (2022)

Understanding Non-Covalent Interactions in Biological Processes through QM/MM-EDA Dynamic Simulations

Marcos Mandado

Department of Physical Chemistry, University of Vigo, Lagoas-Marcosende s/n, 36310 Vigo, Spain
mandado@uvigo.es

Molecular dynamic simulations in biological environments such as proteins, DNA or lipids involves a large number of atoms, so classical models based on widely parametrized force fields are employed instead of more accurate quantum methods, whose high computational requirements preclude their application. The parametrization of appropriate force fields for classical molecular dynamics relies on the precise knowledge of the non-covalent inter and intramolecular interactions responsible for very important aspects, such as macromolecular arrangements, cell membrane permeation, ion solvation, etc. This implies, among other things, knowledge of the nature of the interaction, which may be governed by electrostatic, repulsion or dispersion forces. In order to know the balance between different forces, quantum calculations are frequently performed on simplified molecular models and the data obtained from these calculations are used to parametrize the force fields employed in classical simulations. These parameters are, among others, atomic charges, permanent electric dipole moments and atomic polarizabilities. However, it sometimes happens that the molecular models used for the quantum calculations are too simple and the results obtained can differ greatly from those of the extended system. As an alternative to classical and quantum methods, hybrid quantum/classical schemes (QM/MM) can be introduced, where the extended system is neither truncated nor simplified, but only the most important region is treated quantum mechanically.

In this presentation, molecular dynamic simulations and calculations with hybrid schemes are first introduced in a simple way for a broad and multidisciplinary audience. Then, a method developed in our group to investigate intermolecular interactions using hybrid quantum/classical schemes (QM/MM-EDA) is presented and some applications to the study of dynamic processes of ion solvation and membrane permeation are discussed [1–3]. Special attention is paid to the implementation details of the method in the EDA-NCI software [4].

References

1. Cárdenas, G., Pérez-Barcia, A., Mandado, M., Nogueira, J.J.: Phys. Chem. Chem. Phys. **23**, 20533 (2021)
2. Pérez-Barcia, A., Cárdenas, G., Nogueira, J.J., Mandado, M.: J. Chem. Inf. Model. **63**, 882 (2023)

3. Alvarado, R., Cárdenas, G., Nogueira, J.J., Ramos-Berdullas, N., Mandado, M.: Membranes **13**, 28 (2023)
4. Mandado, M., Van Alsenoy, C.: EDA-NCI: A program to perform energy decomposition analysis of non-covalent interactions. https://github.com/marcos-mandado/EDA-NCI

Contents – Part V

International Workshop on Information and Knowledge in the Internet of Things (IKIT 2023)

Opportunities and Challenges of Digital Transformation in the Public
Sector: The Case of Ecuador 3
    Datzania Villao, Gonzalo Vera, Vilma Duque, and Luis Mazón

Real-Time Anomaly Detection Business Process for Industrial Equipment
Using Internet of Things and Unsupervised Machine Learning Algorithms 16
    Emrullah Gultekin and Mehmet S. Aktas

Recycling Bin Based on the Internet of Things for Santa Elena Province 32
    Maria Campuzano, Marcia Bayas, and Ronald Rovira

Arduino and the Construction of a Height and Heart Rate Meter 44
    Andrade Vera, José Catuto González, and Carlos Mendoza González

Effects of the Olympics on Citizens' Interest in Foreign Cultures: Evidence
from the Tokyo 2020 Games 58
    Takumi Kato

How 5G Will Transform Smart Cities: A Literature Review 70
    Isabel Lopes, T. Guarda, A. J. G. Fernandes, and Maria Isabel Ribeiro

FPGA-Based Hardware/Software Codesign for Video Encoder on IoT
Edge Platforms 82
    Cuong Pham-Quoc

Impact of ICT on the Agricultural Sector's Sustainability: Evidence Based
on Practices 97
    Maria I. B. Ribeiro, Teresa Guarda, Isabel M. Lopes,
    and António J. G. Fernandes

Identification of Bus Stations on the Urban Transport Network Based
on GPS Tracking Data 110
    Washington Daniel Torres Guin, Luis Enrique Chuquimarca Jiménez,
    Samuel Baldomero Bustos Gaibor, José Miguel Sánchez Aquino,
    and Marjorie Alexandra Coronel Suárez

Augmented Computing and Smart Cities Sustainability   123
Teresa Guarda, Isabel Lopes, Samuel Bustos, Isabel Ribeiro,
and António Fernandes

IOHIVE: Architecture and Infrastructure of an IOT System for Beehive
Monitoring and an Interactive Journaling Wearable Device for Beekeepers   133
Charalambos Alifieris, Theodora Chamaidi, Katerina Malisova,
Dimitrios Mamalis, Evangelos Nomikos, Chrysostomos Rigakis,
Evangelos Vlachogiannis, and Modestos Stavrakis

Emerging Data Driven Smart City and Its Solutions for Sustainability: The
Case of Cuenca-Ecuador   150
Datzania Villao, Maritza Pérez, Soraya Linzan, and Mónica Tumbaco

Adoption of the Rules of the General Data Protection Regulation
on the Websites of Municipalities   166
Pascoal Padrão, A. J. G. Fernandes, and Isabel Lopes

International Workshop on Collective, Massive and Evolutionary Systems (IWCES 2023)

Preliminary Results of Group Detection Technique Based on User
to Vector Encoding   179
Giulio Biondi, Valentina Franzoni, and Alfredo Milani

Sentiment Processing of Socio-political Discourse and Public Speeches   191
Gulmira Bekmanova, Banu Yergesh, Aru Ukenova, Assel Omarbekova,
Assel Mukanova, and Yerkyn Ongarbayev

Multidimensional Evolutionary Evaluations for Transformative Approaches (MEETA 2023)

Community Archive as Place-Based Decision-Making Process: A Proposal
for the "Archivio Atena"   209
Ludovica La Rocca, Chiara Mazzarella, Stefania Regalbuto,
Maria Somma, and Alessandro Imbriaco

Culture and the City: Towards a Context-Aware Assessment Framework   226
Irene Bianchi and Ilaria Tosoni

Smart Circular Cities and Stakeholders Engagement: A Literature Review
to Explore the Role of Artificial Intelligence   239
Sabrina Sacco, Ferdinando Di Martino, and Maria Cerreta

Evaluating Energy Communities: A New Social and Economic Model
for Implementing the Ecological Transition 259
    Martina Bosone, Barbara Pirelli, and Domenico Vito

Participatory Art and Co-creation Methodology in the "Viale delle
Metamorfosi" Project 277
    Sveva Ventre and Maria Cerreta

Tailored Urban Regeneration Process: A Multi-method Evaluation
for Waterfront Brownfield 295
    Maria Lucia Raiola, Gaia Daldanise, and Maria Cerreta

Exploring Transformative Potentials of Urban Cemeteries Through
an Evolutionary Evaluation Approach: The Case Study of "Poggioreale"
in Naples (Italy) 311
    Giuliano Poli, Piero Zizzania, Giovangiuseppe Vannelli,
    and Angela D'Agostino

Landscape-Based Fire Resilience: Identifying Interaction Between
Landscape Dynamics and Fire Regimes in the Mediterranean Region 328
    Jinlai Song, Daniele Cannatella, and Nikos Katsikis

GIS-Based Hierarchical Fuzzy MCDA Framework for Detecting Critical
Urban Areas in Climate Scenarios 345
    Barbara Cardone, Ferdinando Di Martino, and Vittorio Miraglia

Urban Regeneration Strategies for Implementing the Circular City Model:
The Key Role of the Community Engagement 359
    Mariarosaria Angrisano and Francesca Nocca

Building Multi-dimensional Models for Assessing Complex Environmental Systems (MES 2023)

Civic Uses as Complex Socio-Ecological System: A Proposal
for an Analytical Framework 379
    Danny Casprini, Alessandra Oppio, and Francesca Torrieri

Evaluation of NBS Solutions for Climate Resilience and Adaptation
in the Sub-saharan Africa: The Case of Ghana's Ashanti Region 398
    Martina Corti, Vanessa Assumma, and Francesco Pittau

Supporting the Resources Allocation for Inner Areas by the Use
of the FITradeoff Method 415
    Marta Dell'Ovo, Alessandra Oppio, Eduarda Asfora Frej,
    and Adiel Teixeira de Almeida

Renewable Energy Sources and Ecosystem Services: Measuring
the Impacts of Ground-Mounted Photovoltaic Panels 429
  Caterina Caprioli, Federico Dell'Anna, and Francesco Fiermonte

NBS Design and Implementation in Urban Systems: Dimensions,
Challenges and Issues to Construct a Comprehensive Evaluation
Framework 444
  Giulia Datola and Alessandra Oppio

How to Address Marginalization in Small Towns: An MCDA Approach
to Evaluating Different Strategies in Campania Region 455
  Marco Rossitti, Fabiana Forte, and Francesca Torrieri

Learning Urban Sustainability by Playing 468
  *Isabella M. Lami, Francesca Abastante, Marika Gaballo,
  Beatrice Mecca, and Elena Todella*

The Canvas Model to Support the Circular Urban Regeneration Projects 483
  Mariarosaria Angrisano

Supporting the Management Plan of a World Heritage Site Nomination
Through a Multi-step Evaluation Approach 498
  *Sebastiano Barbieri, Marta Bottero, Caterina Caprioli,
  and Giulio Mondini*

Evaluating Nature-Based Solutions Impacts: A Preliminary Framing
of Assessment Methods 512
  *Vanessa Assumma, Giulia Datola, Carlotta Quagliolo,
  and Alessandra Oppio*

An Evaluation Model to Support Strategic Urban Planning in Italy: The
Application of Community Impact Evaluation 528
  Giulio Cavana and Federico Dell'Anna

**Mathematical Methods for Image Processing and Understanding
(MMIPU 2023)**

Mathematical Models and Neural Networks for the Description
and the Correction of Typical Distortions of Historical Manuscripts 545
  Pasquale Savino and Anna Tonazzini

A Mathematical Model for the Analysis of Eye Fundus Images in Healthy
and Diabetic Patients 558
  Arianna Travaglini and Gianluca Vinti

Mapped Variably Scaled Kernels: Applications to Solar Imaging   577
   Francesco Marchetti, Emma Perracchione, Anna Volpara,
   Anna Maria Massone, Stefano De Marchi, and Michele Piana

Fruit Fly Detection and Classification in IoT Setup   593
   Syed M. Fasih, Asad Ali, Talha Mabood, Atif Ullah, Muhammad Hanif,
   and Waqar Ahmad

A Finite Differences-Based Metric for Magnetic Resonance Image
Inpainting   608
   Marco Seracini, Claudia Testa, and Stephen R. Brown

Improving Color Image Binary Segmentation Using Nonnegative
Matrix Factorization   623
   Ciro Castiello, Nicoletta Del Buono, and Flavia Esposito

Truncated Minimal-Norm Gauss–Newton Method Applied to the Inversion
of FDEM Data   641
   Federica Pes

Blind Source Separation of Color Noisy Blurred Images   659
   Giulio Biondi, Antonio Boccuto, and Ivan Gerace

Quadratically Transformed Luminance Chrominance Spaces   676
   Giulio Biondi, Antonio Boccuto, and Ivan Gerace

Author Index   695

International Workshop on Information and Knowledge in the Internet of Things (IKIT 2023)

Opportunities and Challenges of Digital Transformation in the Public Sector: The Case of Ecuador

Datzania Villao[1](✉) ⓘ, Gonzalo Vera[1] ⓘ, Vilma Duque[1] ⓘ, and Luis Mazón[2] ⓘ

[1] Universidad Estatal Península de Santa Elena, La Libertad, Ecuador
datzaniavillao@gmail.com
[2] BITrum Research Group, Leon, Spain

Abstract. Electronic government has several benefits, especially in improving the provision of public services, transparency and accountability, citizen participation, efficiency and cost savings and economic development. However, there is still no extensive literature on the characteristics of e-government in developing countries. That is why the purpose of the paper is to identify the opportunities and challenges of digital transformation in the public sector of Ecuador. For this, a multidimensional theoretical framework of e-government was used that in composed for socioeconomic and political factors to identify the opportunities and challenges of a country. Bibliographic research was conducted for which secondary information was used, especially from public documents of the country and international reports. As a result, since 2000 Ecuador has started its digital Transformation until now with the implementation of a new model for the digital transformation of the country that includes the supply of digital infrastructure, as well as the digitalization of public services, promoting the access of these by creating regulatory norms that allow the development of e-government. However, despite the advances that the country has had in the public sector, there are still challenges such as improving interoperability between the different public institutions, improving the security and protection of government data, and training specialized human talent. In the same way, it is established that to have a positive impact, it is important to take into account that the successful implementation of e-government requires adequate planning, investment in technological infrastructure and the training of government personnel, as well as consideration of security issues, privacy and access to technology.

Keywords: e-government · Digital infrastructure · Digital Transformation · Public services

1 Introduction

E-government is a powerful tool to modernize and transform public administration. Electronic government, also known as e-government or digital government, refers to the use of information and communication technologies (ICTs) to improve the administration and delivery of government services to citizens, businesses, and other entities [1, 2].

O. Gervasi et al. (Eds.): ICCSA 2023 Workshops, LNCS 14108, pp. 3–15, 2023.
https://doi.org/10.1007/978-3-031-37117-2_1

This model of government has had a boom in recent years. That is why, according to data from the International Data Corporation (IDC), by 2023, 45% of States will deploy state-of-the-art technology to process data obtained through the Internet of Things (IoT), networks or other devices [3]. The importance of e-government lies in several key aspects. First, it improves the efficiency and effectiveness of government through the automation of government processes, which leads to greater efficiency in the delivery of services and in the internal management of government [4–6]. Second, it expands government services by facilitating access to government services through digital channels, allowing citizens and businesses to access information, carry out procedures, and participate in democratic processes more conveniently and quickly [6, 7]. Third, greater transparency and accountability, since electronic government can promote government transparency and accountability by facilitating access to public information and allowing citizen participation in the supervision and evaluation of government activities, which contributes to strengthening the confidence of citizens in the government and its institutions [8]. Fourth, promotion of innovation and technological development since electronic government promotes the adoption of new technologies in the public sector, which promotes innovation and technological development in the government and in society in general, which in turn can have a positive impact on the economy, competitiveness and job creation in the ICT sector [9]. Fifth, the promotion of citizen inclusion and participation, since it promotes citizen inclusion and participation by facilitating access to government services for different segments of the population, including people with disabilities, low-income people, and residents of rural areas [10]. In addition, e-government encourage citizen participation in government decision-making through online participation tools, such as surveys, consultations, and social networks.

The Electronic Government in Ecuador has been an important initiative to modernize and improve the public administration of the country. The Ecuadorian Government during its evolution towards a digital transformation has focused on various areas, including the automation of government processes, the improvement in the provision of public services, transparency and accountability, as well as the promotion of citizen participation [11]. The main e-government initiatives implemented in Ecuador include the Electronic Government Portal, which is the main access point for online government services in Ecuador [12]. It has also implemented the Electronic Signature, which is a tool used to validate the authenticity and integrity of electronic documents. It has developed the Electronic Public Procurement Platform that allows government entities and suppliers to carry out procurement processes for goods and services electronically, which improves transparency, efficiency, and competitiveness in the public procurement process [13]. Moreover, online citizen participation has improved through various online tools such as online consultations and surveys, citizen participation platforms and social networks [14]. However, despite all this progress, several weaknesses have been identified in some sectors.

The current literature presents a large amount of research in which the benefits of using everything related to electronic government can be highlighted, especially in developed countries, there is still little research on the characteristics of electronic government in developing countries, since each country has a different context. That is why the purpose of the research is to identify the opportunities and challenges of digital transformation in the public sector of Ecuador. The importance of this research lies in the fact that Ecuador has gone through several transitions and governments with different policies, which has created a series of interactions in everything related to the implementation of an electronic government. In the same way, a multidimensional theoretical framework of e-government composed by socioeconomic and political factors was used to identify opportunities and challenges in developing countries.

The research is organized as follows: The following section presents the characteristics of the multidimensional theoretical framework developed by Gulnoza Kuldosheva 2021 to explain opportunities and challenges in e-government for developing countries [15]. The third section identifies the opportunities and challenges of Ecuador using the multidimensional theoretical framework. The last sections discuss the case and concludes the paper.

2 Multidimensional Framework of E-government for Developing Countries

In 2021, Gulnoza Kuldosheva developed a multifunctional theoretical framework to explain how e-government works for developing countries, which is presented at Fig. 1 [15].

2.1 Socio-economic Component

This component has a first phase that is an analysis of the stages that a government has had to go through on its way to digital transformation, which lays the foundations for projects related to electronic government that a government can implement. The second phase for this component are the current status of projects on electronic government. To analyze the projects, it is necessary to explore the institutionality of a government, the technological infrastructure component and the quality of the services offered by an electronic government.

Institutionality
Institutionality has to do with the governance that is exercised through public and private organizations, and society in general, in charge of carrying out activities of design, formulation, implementation, regulation, and control in an impartial, transparent, objective, and Non-partisan of government policies, no transient political influences. Accompanied by a regulation that complies with and enforces national policy and that only makes decisions that fall within its scope of legal competence, independent and capable of applying the general policies of the government. It is very important to promote the transversally of this process of change, which can be achieved by generating regulations that create the necessary governance conditions [16].

Infrastructure
Understood as the physical and non-physical medium through which one has access to information and communication, which is considered the variable that determines and

sizes the digital divide in a country. In this sense, access to ICTs and information must consider, among others, three dimensions such as geographic access, economic access and socio-cultural access. This section includes the internet coverage that a country has, the number of platforms that it has to provide different public services, the number of people with internet access and with access to a mobile phone and internet technology infrastructure [17].

Services
This dimension is defined by the products, services, applications and digital content that the government can offer and demand. Government products and services are tied to the type of technology used to deliver services, applications, and digital content. In this dimension, it is important to identify all the public services that a government can offer through different platforms. They are usually interactive portals where information is collected from a user and then distributed to different government departments to make decisions about a specific area. The quality of these public services that a government offers may depend on factors such as the lack of qualified personnel in the government or the lack of promotion of the services to the community [18].

2.2 Political Factors

Transparency and Citizen Participation
One of the theories of electronic government is that it seeks to promote citizen participation in decision-making and in the provision of government services. This theory holds that technology can facilitate meaningful citizen participation in public policymaking, accountability, and government oversight. Electronic government seeks to empower citizens and promote transparency and collaboration in public management. That is why in democratic countries one of the duties of the State is to inform citizens of its management and work on Digital Transformation initiatives [19]. For this reason, information on the progress and execution of each of the actions that are articulated need to be available to citizens through official government channels. The published information serves so that each actor knows about the management of public institutions.

Electronic government can facilitate citizen participation and collaboration in the development of public policies through digital platforms that allow consultation, dialogue, and feedback from citizens [5, 6]. This can contribute to greater inclusion and representativeness in government decision-making and strengthen participatory democracy.

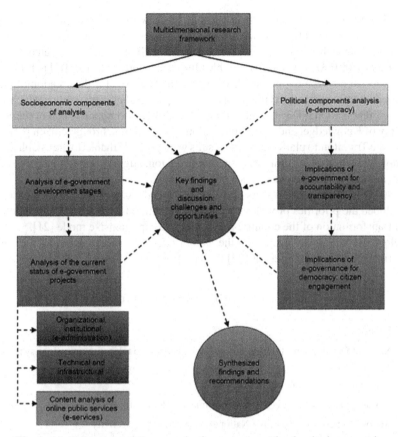

Fig. 1. Multidimensional Framework of e-government for developing countries

3 Opportunities and Challenges for E-government in Ecuador

3.1 Socio-economic Analysis

Analysis of E-government Development Stages in Ecuador
The development of the Electronic Government of Ecuador began in year 2000, when the first National Plan for the Development of Telecommunications was published, whose main purpose was the dissemination of the internet at the national level. From there, the Ecuadorian Government has undertaken with initiatives, plans and strategies, to include information and communication technologies at the State level. Precisely in this year, in accordance with Resolution No. 380-17-CONATEL-2000, universal access to telecommunications services was declared as State policy [20]. Since then, the country has been implementing different public policies towards the transformation of a digital government. A good evidence to demonstrate the progress of electronic government in the country was the United Nations Electronic Government Development Index (EGDI), which measures topics such as online services, telecommunications infrastructure and human capital. In 2018 Ecuador was ranked 84 out of 193 countries with an index

of 0.613, evidencing constant growth and placing it with this result above the world and regional average [11]. Ecuador has also shown progress year after year, that can be observed through the 2018 E-GOVERNMENT SURVEY where it rated Ecuador with an index of 0.37, a value that doubles the result obtained in 2010 [11]. For this, the Ecuadorian government has worked on several initiatives for the creation of public policy and improvement of services with the participation of citizens, among which stand out the current National Development Plan 2017–2021, the Organic Code of the Social Economy of Knowledge; and the simplification of procedures through citizen proposals through the Tramiton.to platform. These results were possible thanks to the establishment and implementation of instruments with a single vision, aligned with national objectives and articulation with different actors.

In 2021, Ecuador presented its first Digital Agenda as a public policy instrument that included the priorities of various sectors and identified joint actions to promote the digital transformation of the country, focused on a comprehensive mode [21].

Below are the main events in the country in its process towards the digital transformation of the Government [22] (Table 1).

Table 1. Phases of E-government in Ecuador

Year	Event
2000	National Development Plan declares universal access to telecommunications systems as a public policy
2001	The Connectivity Commission is created
2003	National Program for Electronic Government and the Information Society
2005	Action Plan 2005–2010 of the National Agenda for Connectivity
2008	The use of free Software is used as a public policy
2011	Creation of the Information Technology Secretary
2012	Implementation of the software platform called "Government Services Bus (BSG)"
2013	Creation of the Secretary of Electronic Government
2014	Creation of the first National Electronic Government Plan 2014–2017
2018	Regulatory improvement and administrative simplification are declared as State policy
2021	First Digital Agenda of Ecuador 2021–2022 was created and implemented

Institutionality

Among the institutions that lead the digital transformation of the country is the Presidency of the Republic, which dictates the guidelines and policies at the national level, the Ministry of Telecommunications and the Information Society, and the different Ministries that are the ones that make up the Central Public Administration and the Other State powers and provincial, local and parish GAD who collaborate and coordinate with the different Ministries [23]. Figure 2 presents the structure of the main actors in the Digital Transformation of the Ecuadorian Government.

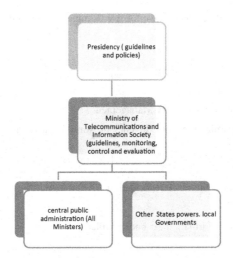

Fig. 2. Multidimensional Framework of e-government for developing countries

The Ministry of Telecommunications and the Information Society has the competence to exercise the rectory, issue and implement policies, guidelines and regulations aimed at the Digital Transformation of the country [24]. These policies, guidelines, and regulations should focus on the use and appropriation of ICTs in the health, education, productivity, labor, tourism, and agriculture sectors, in coordination with the governing bodies of these sectors. To establish the Governance of the Digital Transformation Agenda, the competent entities permanently analyze the need to create or modify the different legal, juridical and strategic instruments for a correct execution of the Agenda within their sectors and institutions. In this sense, the mentioned actors work based on the following regulations that are presented in Table 2, which in turn are aligned with Ecuador's Plan for the Creation of Opportunities 2021–2025, and the United Nations 2030 agenda and the 17 Sustainable Development Goals SDGs.

Technology and Infrastructure
By 2020, 53.2% of households in Ecuador had Internet access, rural coverage was 34.7% of households and the proportion of people who used Smartphones was 81.8% [25]. Another data that stands out is the percentage of households in Ecuador that have access to fixed Internet, which is 45.50%. Regarding the Internet Access Service - IAS, as of June 2022 the national density per household represented 54.64%, with more than 2.59 million accounts. Of the national total, 68.32% corresponds to fiber optic connections. In the same way, until July 2022, 15,639 WIFI points were reported, distributed in 126 cities of the country, that is, 57% of cities have WIFI points installed [25].

However, the fact that progress has been made in the implementation of technological infrastructure in the country, Ecuador is still vulnerable to cyber threats. For example, according to the Global Cybersecurity Index (GCI), issued by the ITU, published in

Table 2. Normative for E-government in Ecuador.

Laws and Programs
Constitution of the Republic of Ecuador
Telecommunications Organic Law
Organic Law on Data and Civil Identity Management
Organic Law for the Optimization and Efficiency of Administrative Procedures
Executive Decrees
Digital Transformation Policy
Information Society Plan - Digital Transformation
Electronic Government Plan
Telecommunications and Information Technology Plan

2020, the country is ranked 119 out of 182, being one of the countries with the highest vulnerabilities worldwide [25].

Services

In 2018 The Ecuadorian Government promoted the implementation of online services in its different Ministries. For example, in this year, 130 public institutions that belongs to central government had a web portal and official social networks and the 80% of these Institutions have a web portal with accessibility features. This institutions, 9% have mobile applications that allow citizen procedures to be carried out. In addition, there were 12.5 thousand officials who used electronic signatures to issue official communications through the "Quipux Document Management System", signing around 4.2 million documents, generating savings of 1.9 million dollars per Costs associated with printing documents [25]. In the same way, by the year 2020, 75% of Ecuadorians had access to electronic financial products and services, and 90% of this group had carried out electronic transactions in international portals. On the other hand, in Jan 2022 the e-Government index was 0.70 [26].

However, despite all this progress, the use of the digital channels of the Central Government Institutions is not distributed equally since there is a direct relationship with the socioeconomic and educational level. This means that not everyone can access the benefits provided by the State, aggravating social inequalities. Likewise, despite the potential that online procedures have in terms of reducing time, costs and limiting corruption, only 21.4% of central government procedures can be started online and 11% can be completed online [25]. This added to the fact that many public services that have been implemented online have lacked a prior analysis to simplify it. This lack of understanding and improvement of the process behind the implemented system often makes the automated public service even more cumbersome than the original manual version. For example, there are the procedures of the Ecuadorian Institute of Intellectual Property -IEPI- and the form of assets of the Comptroller's Office.

Another problem has arisen in the interoperability of State Institutions. For example, 65 local governments use information that resides in databases of other Central Government institutions to provide services to citizens, however, there are still a large number of local governments that still do not have these services for which continues to request copies of documents from citizens such as identity cards for the different procedures.

Digital Talent

This pillar refers to people as the fundamental factor of digital transformation, which seeks to strengthen basic skills in digital technologies in the entire population and encourage the development of new skills, as well as technical and professional skills in these technologies. Currently, it is no longer enough to equip the new generations with a fixed set of skills or knowledge, it will be necessary for them to develop a wide variety of skills and abilities to adapt to change. Leaving in evidence, the need to have a vision at the country level, to promote digital talent permanently, in which people acquire new and more relevant skills throughout their lives.

However, currently it has been detected that there is insufficient specialized human resources in the development of systems, databases, process automation tools and project management in relation to the scale of operations of the institution [27].

3.2 Political Analysis

Transparency

Regarding transparency in relation to the publication of information for citizens, according to a report issued by the Ombudsman's Office in January 2020, more than 97% of the institutions that belongs to the Central Government, publish their activities through institutional web portals, in compliance with article 7 of the Organic Law on Transparency and Access to Public Information, LOTAIP14. For this, the National Government has promoted the implementation of online services. On the other hand, there is the Open Data Inventory (ODI), an organization that evaluates the coverage and openness of official statistics through open data. In the 2016 index, Ecuador ranked 31 out of 173 countries, being the leader in South America with a score of 56 [25].

Citizen Participation

Ecuador has important advances in citizen participation and government transparency by electronic means. For example, in 2022, the United Nations Organization issued the results of the Electronic Participation Index in the ease of access to information provided by the government to citizens, Ecuador got a score of 70%. Related to the involvement of citizens in the contribution and deliberation on public policy and services, Ecuador got a score of 78.3% in this criterion and finally in citizen co-participation in the joint design of policies and services, with a score of 54.6%. For this, the Ecuadorian government has worked on various initiatives to create public policy and improve services with the participation of citizens, among which the current National Development Plan stands out; the Organic Code of the Social Knowledge Economy; and the simplification of procedures through citizen proposals through the Tramiton.to platform. Digital media have also been implemented that allow citizen interaction with the State.

However, one of the challenges to improve citizen participation in electronic government is to improve knowledge about the usefulness of the information that is generated and presented on the different pages of Government Institutions. This is because of there is still a lack of knowledge regarding the economic benefit and social and political impact that its exploitation can generate. In addition, there are 20% of State institutional portals that do not have web accessibility features, which represents an access barrier for people with disabilities [28].

Another of the great challenges in increasing participatory democracy in the country. Although the results of the United Nations and the systems implemented by the government show progress on this issue, it is still an uncommon practice for government institutions to take advantage of these digital tools for the generation of public policy or improvement of services.

4   Discussion

Ecuador has made very significant progress in the implementation of an electronic government, especially at the level of regulations and application of technological infrastructure. However, there are still very big challenges such as improving the interoperability of the different public institutions and improving the knowledge of the population in the use of public services, the training of human talent specialized in the technical part for the design and implementation of electronic government and the vulnerability of public systems since the country is still vulnerable to cyber threats [6, 29].

Regarding the multidimensional framework used to identify the opportunities and challenges for developing countries, it can be pointed out that although there are many similarities with the dimensions of this framework, there are also differences such as in the dimension of socio-economic factors, especially in the projects of electronic government for Ecuador. For example, the multidimensional framework points out that there are three sub-dimensions such as the institutional part, the technical and infrastructure part, and the quality of the electronic services. However, in Ecuador according to the model of the Ecuador's Digital Transformation Agenda 2022–2025, a new dimension is established, which is "digital talent and training", which is one of the main measures to promote adaptation to the effects of digital transformation on employment, since it makes it easier for servers to public whose roles are affected by this process take on new tasks. Table 3 presents the main opportunities and challenge of each dimensions analyzed, both in socioeconomic and political factors.

Table 3. Opportunities and Challenges for E-government in Ecuador

Dimensions	Opportunities	Challenges
Socioeconomic factors		
Institutional Dimension	Regulations that establish the development of electronic government	Improve interoperability between public institutions
Technological Dimension	Mass use of ICT access by mobile phones	Vulnerability for cyber threats
Public service quality dimension	Increased access to automated public services	Lack of knowledge of the population about the existence of digital platforms for public procedures
Digital talent	Rapid development of technological innovation	Deficit of qualified human talent
Political factors		
Transparency	Online service mechanisms to meet citizen needs	Limited Organizational integration
Citizen Participation	Growing interest of citizens for new spaces for participation	Lack of Knowledge of the population about the existence of web pages of public institutions

5 Conclusion

Electronic government is important because it improves government efficiency, broadens access to government services, promotes transparency and accountability, fosters technological innovation, and promotes citizen inclusion and participation. It is a powerful tool to modernize and transform public administration, improve the quality of government services and strengthen the relationship between government and citizens [29]. Electronic Government in Ecuador has had a significant impact in improving government efficiency, infrastructure, transparency and citizen participation in decision-making. However, it also faces challenges in terms of expansion of technological infrastructure, training of specialized personnel, coordination of interoperability of different ministries and raising awareness of the population about the use of online services. In its process of continuing to advance its digital agenda, the country needs to continue working directly together with existing elements that include national and international laws, plans, guidelines and regulations that seek to align the government with the different efforts and existing regulatory reality. The fundamental basis for creating a model that helps the organization of Electronic Government in Ecuador must understand how key regulations such as the Constitution of Ecuador, the National Development Plan, strategies and indicators of the United Nations Organization are related. The Government of Ecuador must continue to work in an organized way, investing in technological infrastructure and the training of government personnel, as well as considering issues of security, privacy and access to technology in order to modernize and improve public administration in the country.

References

1. ADB Institute (April de 2021). ADB Institute. https://www.adb.org/sites/default/files/public ation/696281/adbi-wp1248.pdf
2. Almarabeh, T., AbuAli, A.: A general framework for e-government: definition maturity challenges, opportunities, and success. Eur. J. Sci. Res. **39**(1), 29–42 (2010). https://d1wqtxts1xzle7.cloudfront.net/65828927/A_General_Framework_for_E-Government_D ef20210228-6753-54bzs7.pdf?1614572197=&response-content-disposition=inline%3B+fil ename%3DA_General_Framework_for_E_Government_Def.pdf&Expires=1681514109& Signature=Gx3i-Ps
3. Bayona, S., Morales, V.: E-government development models for municipalities. J. Comput. Meth. Sci. Eng. **17**(1), 547–559 (2017). https://doi.org/10.3233/JCM-160679
4. Ekos (30 de April de 2021). Ekos. (Ekos). https://ekosnegocios.com/articulo/3-retos-tecnol ogicos-para-el-nuevo-gobierno-en-ecuador
5. Gobierno Electrónico (2000). Gobierno Electrónico. (Gobierno Electrónico). https://www. gobiernoelectronico.gob.ec/ano2000/
6. Gobierno Electrónico (2018). Gobierno Electrónico. https://www.gobiernoelectronico.gob. ec/wp-content/uploads/2018/09/PNGE_2018_2021sv2.pdf
7. Gobierno Electrónico. (August de 2018). Gobierno Electrónico. (Gobierno Electrónico). https://www.gobiernoelectronico.gob.ec/wp-content/uploads/2018/10/Desarrollo-de-Gob ierno-Electr%C3%B3nico-en-la-Administraci%C3%B3n-P%C3%BAblica-de-Ecuador-1. pdf
8. Gobierno Eléctrónico. (s.f.). Gobierno Eléctrónico. (Gobierno Eléctrónico). https://www.gob iernoelectronico.gob.ec/
9. Gobierno Electrónico. (2018 de Septiembre). Gobierno Electrónico. (Gobierno Electrónico). https://www.gobiernoabierto.ec/wp-content/uploads/2018/11/Libro-Blanco-y-el-Plan-Nac ional-de-Gobierno-Electr%C3%B3nico.pdf
10. Guarda, T.I., Oliveira, P., Ribeiro, M.I., Fernandes, A.J.: How to measure the performance of a smart city. In: Workshops at the 3rd International Conference on Applied Informatics 2020, vol. 2714, pp. 77–86. CEUR Workshop Proceedings, Ota (2020). https://ceur-ws.org/ Vol-2714/icaiw_aiesd_5.pdf
11. Guarda, T., Anwar, S., Leon, M., Mota Pinto, F.J. (eds.): Information and Knowledge in Internet of Things. EICC, Springer, Cham (2022). https://doi.org/10.1007/978-3-030-75123-4
12. Guarda, T., Augusto, M.F., Haz, L., Díaz-Nafría, J.M.: Blockchain and government transfor-mation. In: Rocha, Á., Ferrás, C., López-López, P.C., Guarda, T. (eds.) ICITS 2021. AISC, vol. 1330, pp. 88–95. Springer, Cham (2021). https://doi.org/10.1007/978-3-030-68285-9_9
13. Guarda, T., Fernandes, C., Augusto, M. F.: Technology, Business, Innovation, and Entrepreneurship in Industry 4.0. Springer, Cham (2023). https://doi.org/10.1007/978-3-031-17960-0
14. Gupta, M. P., Jana, D.: E-government evaluation: a framework and case study. Gov. Inf. Q. **20**(4), 365–387 (2003). http://103.27.10.17/bitstream/handle/12345678/1111/guptagov2002. pdf?sequence=1&isAllowed=y
15. Halachmi, A., Greiling, D.: Transparency, e-government, and accountability: some issues and considerations. Publ. Perform. Manage. Rev. **36**(4), 562–584 (2013). https://www.tandfo nline.com/doi/abs/10.2753/PMR1530-9576360404

16. ITahora. (May de 2022). ITahora. (ITahora). https://itahora.com/2022/05/16/escasez-de-tal ento-humano-en-ciberseguridad/
17. Lopes, I.M., Guarda, T.: The relationship between smart cities and the internet of things in low density regions. In: Antipova, T., Rocha, A. (eds.) DSIC18 2018. AISC, vol. 850, pp. 369–378. Springer, Cham (2019). https://doi.org/10.1007/978-3-030-02351-5_42
18. Medjahed, B., Rezgui, A., Bouguettaya, A., Ouzzani, M.: Infrastructure for e-government web services. IEEE Internet Comput. **7**(1), 58–65 (2003). https://doi.org/10.1109/MIC.2003. 1167340
19. Muñoz-Cañavate, A., Hípola, P.: Electronic administration in Spain: from its beginnings to the present. Gov. Inf. Q. **28**(1), 74–90 (2011). https://doi.org/10.1016/j.giq.2010.05.008
20. Mustafa, D., Farida, U., Yusriadi, Y.: The effectiveness of public services through E-government in Makassar City. Int. J. Sci. Technol. Res. **9**(1), 1176–1178. https://www.res earchgate.net/profile/Yusriadi-Yusriadi/publication/338594999_The_Effectiveness_Of_P ublic_Services_Through_E-Government_In_Makassar_City/links/5e1ebe3f299bf136303ad 34f/The-Effectiveness-Of-Public-Services-Through-E-Government-In-Makassar-Ci
21. Nkwe, N.: E-government: challenges and opportunities in Botswana. Int. J. Humanit. Soc. Sci. **2**(17), 39–48 (2012). https://citeseerx.ist.psu.edu/document?repid=rep1&type=pdf&doi=e86 332923fc092fdca4067ec941b1434f4774e76
22. Plataforma de Contratación Pública del Ecuador. (s.f.). Plataforma de Contratación Pública del Ecuador. (Plataforma de Contratación Pública del Ecuador). https://portal.compraspubli cas.gob.ec/sercop/
23. Rowley, J.: E-Government stakeholder who are they and what do they want? Int. J. Inf. Manage. **31**(1), 53–62 (2011). https://doi.org/10.1016/j.ijinfomgt.2010.05.005
24. *Telecommunications Ministry. (Septiembre de 2018). Telecommunications Ministry.* https:// publicadministration.un.org/egovkb/en-us/Data/Country-Information/id/52-Ecuador
25. Telecommunication Ministry. (2021). Telecommunication Ministry. (Telecommunication Ministry). https://www.telecomunicaciones.gob.ec/wp-content/uploads/2021/05/Age nda-Digital-del-Ecuador-2021-2022-222-comprimido.pdf
26. Telecommunications Ministry. (2022). Telecommunications Ministry. https://www.teleco municaciones.gob.ec/wp-content/uploads/2022/12/Anexo-31

Real-Time Anomaly Detection Business Process for Industrial Equipment Using Internet of Things and Unsupervised Machine Learning Algorithms

Emrullah Gultekin[✉][iD] and Mehmet S. Aktas[iD]

Computer Engineering Department, Yildiz Technical University, Istanbul, Türkiye
emrullah.gultekin@std.yildiz.edu.tr, aktas@yildiz.edu.tr

Abstract. Today, it is evident that the Internet of Things, real-time data processing, and artificial intelligence technologies are essential in industrial settings to enable early warning autonomous anomaly detection systems. Such systems can detect anomaly situations that could cause failures shortly after they occur, allowing necessary maintenance to be performed promptly. In this research, a software platform has been designed and developed to collect data from sensors placed on industrial equipment to monitor their condition using the required IoT infrastructure. The real-time data collected from this platform is analyzed using real-time data processing techniques. Here, a business process is introduced for instant anomaly detection using real-time clustering analysis methods. To validate the proposed business process architecture, a prototype software has been developed, and its ability to detect anomaly situations has been evaluated. The results show that the proposed business process architecture is effective in real-time anomaly detection and can successfully detect anomalies that can lead to industrial equipment failures.

Keywords: internet of things · anomaly detection · artificial intelligence · clustering · real-time unsupervised machine learning · real-time streaming-data prediction

1 Introduction

The way we connect with the world around us has changed as a result of the Internet of Things (IoT). IoT devices provide enormous amounts of data in real-time, which may be leveraged to get insightful knowledge and improve decision-making. Anomalies or outliers in this data may, however, also be a sign of issues or security breaches. Real-time detection of these anomalies is essential to avoiding infrastructure damage, income loss, and other undesirable effects.

In today's highly competitive industrial landscape, businesses are under increasing pressure to maintain their operational efficiency and profitability.

O. Gervasi et al. (Eds.): ICCSA 2023 Workshops, LNCS 14108, pp. 16–31, 2023.
https://doi.org/10.1007/978-3-031-37117-2_2

Industrial equipment such as machines, pumps, and turbines play a critical role in the smooth functioning of manufacturing processes, and any downtime or malfunction can have a significant impact on productivity and profitability. Real-time anomaly detection is an essential tool for businesses to proactively detect and address issues before they result in equipment failure or downtime.

The advent of the IoT and Artificial Intelligence (AI) technologies has transformed the industrial equipment landscape, allowing businesses to monitor and analyze equipment data in real-time. By leveraging IoT sensors, businesses can collect vast amounts of data on equipment performance, which can then be analyzed using AI algorithms to detect anomalies and predict potential issues.

Unsupervised learning techniques have become a promising answer to these problems. Unsupervised learning techniques may adapt to changes in the data distribution without needing labeled data, which is crucial in dynamic contexts where the data's features can vary over time.

There are various difficulties with real-time anomaly detection on streaming IoT data. First, it is challenging to analyze IoT data using conventional statistical techniques since it is frequently noisy, high-dimensional, and missing values. Second, algorithms that can process massive amounts of data rapidly and effectively are needed since streaming data must be analyzed in real-time. Finally, as anomalies are uncommon occurrences, it may be challenging to train a supervised learning model to recognize them because the training data may not adequately represent them.

This paper presents a real-time anomaly detection business process for industrial equipment using IoT and unsupervised machine learning algorithms. The proposed business process involves collecting data from IoT sensors on equipment performance, preprocessing the data to extract relevant features, and using clustering algorithms to detect anomalies in real-time. The detected anomalies are then sent to a notification system for further analysis and action.

The subsequent sections of this paper are organized as follows: We initiated our investigation by identifying pertinent research issues. In Sect. 3, we conducted a thorough review of the relevant literature. The proposed methodology was introduced in Sect. 4. In Sect. 5 we present the prototype application and evaluation. Finally, in Sect. 6, we provide a succinct summary of the research findings.

2   Research Problem

The task of real-time anomaly detection on streaming IoT data is critical and requires advanced techniques that can handle the vast and rapidly changing data. Real-time unsupervised machine learning methods have shown promise in this area and can be used to improve decision-making and prevent negative outcomes in IoT applications. However, further research is needed to develop more sophisticated real-time unsupervised learning techniques that can handle the complexity and diversity of IoT data, as well as to evaluate their effectiveness in practical settings.

Four key research questions that need to be addressed in this context are:

(1) What is a good software architecture design of a unsupervised machine learning based business process for detecting anomalies, which can lead to failures of industrial machines, on the streaming data coming from IoT devices?
(2) Can clustering algorithms be used effectively for real-time anomaly detection in streaming IoT data?
(3) How can we perform real-time anomaly detection on streaming unlabeled data in an IoT system?
(4) Which real-time unsupervised machine learning algorithms are best suited for detecting anomalies in streaming IoT data?

Answering these questions will enable researchers to develop more effective and efficient anomaly detection systems for IoT applications.

3   Related Work

Real-time anomaly detection on streaming IoT data has grown in significance due to the proliferation of IoT devices and the increasing amount of data they generate. The identification of anomalies in streaming IoT data has been successfully accomplished through the use of supervised and unsupervised learning techniques. This paper focuses on the significance of real-time anomaly detection in IoT, the challenges it poses, and potential solutions based on unsupervised learning.

Real-time anomaly detection in unsupervised machine learning, particularly in the context of clustering, has been an active research area in recent years. Several methods and algorithms have been proposed to address the challenges of real-time anomaly detection in clustering. In this section, we review some of the relevant literature on real-time anomaly detection methods for unsupervised machine learning, specifically in the context of clustering.

The utilization of streaming data in numerous real-world applications, such as e-commerce, banking, sensor data, and telecommunications logs, has led to an increasing interest in the field of data stream mining [4]. In contrast to batch classification, the classification of data streams differs in terms of how learning and predictions occur. The classifier in data stream classification uses the existing model to predict at any time with continuously streaming data [5].

In our previous work, we proposed a workflow architecture utilizing stream-based machine learning algorithms to provide predictive maintenance in IoT systems [1]. The proposed workflow employs various supervised machine learning algorithms, including Adaptive Random Forest, Hoeffding Tree, Leveraging Bagging, SPegasos, and Single Drift Classifier classification algorithms. A prototype application is provided to demonstrate the utility of the proposed workflow, and a prototype experiment is presented to investigate the efficacy of the prediction. In this study, real-time anomaly detection was performed in IoT streaming data using unsupervised machine learning techniques.

Mollaoglu et al. [2] suggested an approach for identifying fraud situations using tagged customer data in telecommunications, utilizing machine learning algorithms and big data analytics platforms. In contrast, we provide a full solution that leverages machine learning for anomaly detection in the IoT space, with distinct dataset, algorithm, and success criteria.

Kayacik et al. [3] presented a methodology for anticipating anomalous behavior in real-time streaming customer data, utilizing supervised machine learning techniques in the communications field. In comparison, we present a comprehensive business process that applies unsupervised machine learning to IoT real-time anomaly detection, with distinct dataset, techniques, and success criteria.

Liang et al. [12] suggested a bearing health indicator using a recurrent neural network to estimate the residual life values of bearings. Our research has a similar objective but with a distinct methodology and structure, focusing on preventive maintenance using IoT systems and employing unsupervised machine learning techniques to detect anomalies in real-time unlabeled data.

Akbar et al. [6] proposed a proactive IoT architecture for predicting complex events using real-time data through Complex Event Processing (CEP) and machine learning. In contrast, our work focuses on a methodology for predictive maintenance of IoT systems using unsupervised machine learning algorithms to ensure the system's reliability.

Certain studies concentrate on the analysis of provenance data, which encompasses the interactions between user agents, data, and processes. Such data is employed to extract valuable insights from these interactions in diverse domains, including social computing [11], social networking [13,14], numerical weather prediction [10], and others. However, our investigation diverges from these studies as we analyze streaming IoT data for the purpose of anomaly detection using unsupervised machine learning algorithms.

Online clustering algorithms update the cluster model continuously as new data points arrive, while also allowing for the removal of outdated data points to adapt to changing data patterns. CluStream is a popular online clustering algorithm that uses micro-clusters to represent the approximate distribution of data points and identifies anomalies based on the deviation of data points from the micro-cluster centroids. Aggarwal et al. proposed a framework for clustering evolving data streams, which includes online clustering algorithms, for real-time anomaly detection in data streams [14].

In the context of this research, a system design has been proposed that enables protective maintenance to be implemented utilizing Internet of Things technology for large physical machinery (such as motors). The proposed system uses real-time clustering analysis methods on data from IoT sensors to identify abnormal operating conditions that could result in the motors failing. We observe metadata management solutions for web service-based systems in the literature [16,17]. However, in this study, real-time system data analysis is used to find abnormal operating conditions. Additionally, we also observe studies that focus on distributed systems built on web services developed for a number of study fields [10,18–22,24,30,31,33]. In contrast to these studies, a restful web service-based system is being developed in this research to detect unexpected conditions in the operation of motors. Different data labeling methods have been developed for usage data obtained during the use of systems in the literature [25, 28, 29]. In this research, the focus is on real-time analysis and interpretation of data obtained from sensors, and data labeling methods are not included. Among the studies in the literature, there are also those that focus on software quality for developed software [26, 27]. However, software quality examination has not been performed in this study. When the literature is examined, it is also observed that studies have been conducted on real-time data analysis and detecting compliance with rules [15, 32]. In this research, real-time data analysis is performed on data from IoT sensors to detect unexpected operational behaviors.

4   Proposed Methodology

In our study, we aim to detect and intervene in the errors of large industrial machines without causing any damage to the machines by using real-time unsupervised machine learning methods on unlabeled data. The goal is to detect and intervene in errors in real-time through the proposed process as shown in Fig. 1. Here, sensor environment data and sensor device data are first obtained from IoT devices equipped with a mobile operating system (such as Contiki NG). Then, the streaming data undergoes various operations and is clustered using clustering algorithms within a streaming machine learning library (such as the MOA framework). Data that does not belong to any cluster is considered anomalous after the clustering process.

In the current study, we aimed to complement our prior work by investigating a methodology for real-time anomaly detection using unsupervised machine learning methods. Specifically, the effectiveness of unsupervised machine learning algorithms was evaluated to detect anomalies in IoT systems. This stands in contrast to the previous work, which utilized supervised machine learning methods.

The proposed process consists of various modules, which are detailed below.

4.1   Feature Extraction Module

Real-time anomaly detection in IoT systems requires the extraction of relevant features from a variety of sensor data streams. These features are used to train a machine learning model to detect anomalies in the data and trigger alerts or responses in real-time.

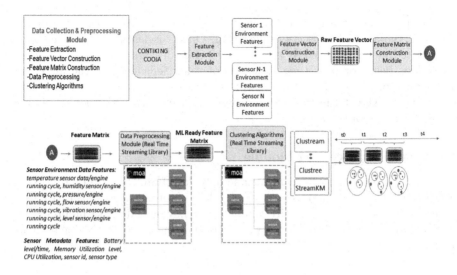

Fig. 1. Proposed Business Process

Domain-specific features such as temperature gradients, pressure differentials, humidity sensor values, flow sensor values, level sensor values and vibration patterns can be used to extract information specific to the IoT system being monitored. These features can be used to identify anomalies that are unique to the system or the environment it is operating in. In addition to these, metadata information related to the specific features of IoT devices can be added. Information such as battery level, memory status, CPU status, sensor ID, and sensor type can also be extracted.

4.2   Feature Vector Construction Module

In IoT systems, real-time anomaly detection requires the construction of a feature vector that captures the relevant features of the data. The feature vector is used as input to a machine learning algorithm to detect anomalous behavior in real-time.

The construction of a feature vector involves selecting and extracting the most relevant features from the data and combining them into a single vector. The feature vector should be constructed in a way that maximizes the accuracy and efficiency of the anomaly detection algorithm.

At this stage, the relevant features are identified, normalized, and combined. Additionally, dimensionality reduction and updating the feature vector are performed in this step.

4.3   Feature Matrix Construction Module

The construction of a feature matrix involves selecting and extracting the most relevant features from the data and organizing them into a matrix. The feature matrix should be constructed in a way that maximizes the accuracy and efficiency of the anomaly detection algorithm. Once the feature matrix has been constructed, it can be used as input to a machine learning algorithm to detect anomalous behavior over time. The accuracy and efficiency of the algorithm will depend on the quality of the feature matrix, so it is important to carefully select and construct the features and organize them in a way that maximizes the performance of the algorithm.

4.4 Data Preprocessing Module

To achieve high accuracy in real-time anomaly detection, the data preprocessing step is crucial. Such systems require careful data preprocessing to ensure that the algorithm can accurately identify anomalous behavior. The data preprocessing step involves cleaning, transforming, and normalizing the data to prepare it for analysis.

4.5 Clustering Algorithms Module

For clustering we propose the MOA (Massive Online Analysis) framework which is a popular open-source platform for real-time machine learning and data stream mining. MOA provides a range of clustering algorithms that can be used for anomaly detection in IoT systems.

Here are some real-time clustering algorithms that can be used for anomaly detection using streaming based machine learning library (i.e. the MOA library):

CluStream Clustering: CluStream is a clustering algorithm specifically designed to handle data streams that exhibit concept drift. It operates on two levels of clustering, macro-clusters, and micro-clusters, where macro-clusters represent the overall data distribution, and micro-clusters represent local regions in the data distribution. By maintaining micro-clusters, CluStream can detect changes in the data distribution and update macro-clusters accordingly, making it suitable for handling concept drift.

ClusTree Clustering: ClusTree is a hierarchical clustering algorithm that performs online, incremental hierarchical clustering of evolving data streams. It handles noisy, high-dimensional data by using a projection-based clustering approach that maps data into a lower-dimensional subspace. ClusTree maintains a tree structure of clusters, where each node represents a cluster of data points. The tree is incrementally updated by merging nodes as new data arrives, and the height of the tree can be adjusted to control the granularity of the clustering.

StreamKM Clustering: StreamKM is an assignment-based streaming clustering algorithm and a streaming variant of the k-means clustering algorithm. It updates the cluster centers incrementally and maintains a set of potential outliers, which can detect concept drift or outliers in the stream. StreamKM is efficient in the data stream setting, where data arrives continuously and can only be processed once.

These clustering algorithms can be used in combination with the streaming based machine learning libraries (such as the MOA library). In turn, this will lead to incremental learning capabilities to detect anomalous behavior in real-time. The choice of clustering algorithm will depend on the nature of the data and the requirements of the anomaly detection task. It is important to carefully evaluate the performance of different clustering algorithms and tune their parameters to achieve the best results.

In the proposed software architecture, we indicate that any streaming based machine learning library that can support aforementioned streaming based clustering algorithms can be utilized. In the prototype implementation of the proposed architecture, we use the MOA framework for the streaming ML library to be able to cluster real-time data and detect anomalies in the running observation data of the industrial equipment. We use the Clustream, Clustree and StreamKM clustering algorithms available in the MOA library to cluster the data and identify outliers that do not belong to any cluster as anomalies. This approach will enable us to detect anomalies in real-time and take appropriate actions to prevent any potential damage. The proposed business process described in this section, addresses research problem-1 presented in Sect. 2.

5   Prototype Application and Evaluation

We developed a prototype version of the proposed methodology to assess its effectiveness. We performed performance testing on the prototype and evaluated the suggested methodology using an actual dataset. Specifically, we utilized the NASA dataset [7], which leveraged C-MAPSS to simulate engine degradation under different operating conditions and failure modes. The dataset comprises four subsets, each of which represents a unique combination of operating conditions and failure modes. The dataset does not have any labeled data.

To construct a model in a big data platform environment, we first labeled the data using clustering algorithms. By passing through this model, incoming data in the streaming data is determined whether it belongs to any existing clusters. If the data does not belong to any cluster, it is considered an anomaly.

We employed the MOA framework (version 21.07), which is a big data processing framework, to train and test real-time streaming IoT data. We implemented unsupervised machine learning algorithms such as Clustream, Clustree, and StreamKM. This procedure was performed on a machine with 4 Core CPUs, 16GB RAM and 2.9 GHz.

In this study, we focus on detecting anomalies in streaming IoT data using unsupervised machine learning techniques, which do not require labeled data and are well-suited for real-time detection. These techniques are particularly useful in dynamic contexts where the features of the data can change over time and require adaptation to changes in data distribution.

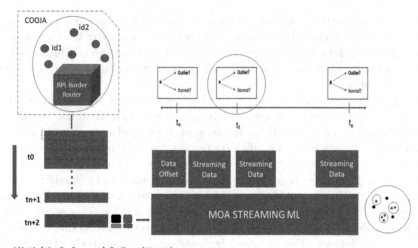

id1: t1, {x1, x2, x3, ... xn}, Outliner / Normal

Fig. 2. Proposed Data Processing and Analysis Process

In alignment with our previous work, the data used in this study originates from IoT devices that run on the Contiki NG operating system. To simulate the system, we used Cooja, a network simulator. Contiki NG is specifically designed for wireless sensor networks. For hosting the Contiki NG operating system, we employed Docker containers. NodeJS and REST architecture services were utilized to present data to the external environment. We saved the NASA Turbofan Jet Engine data as if it originated from this system in a PostgreSQL database. The application retrieves this data from the database and sends it to the model as streaming data.

5.1 Dataset

For testing our proposed process, we utilized the Nasa Turbofan Jet Engine dataset, which contains a larger number of records and presents a challenging problem for anomaly detection. The dataset is part of NASA's C-MAPSS simulation tool for turbofan engines and includes fourteen input parameters that allow simulation of a variety of operating behaviors [8]. The dataset comprises 61249 running observation data of industrial equipment (i.e. NASA turbo fan engine). Each running observation data consists of attributes, IoT sensor environment data, describing the running performance of the motor. The data includes anomalies (varying levels of deterioration over time) until the system failure [9].

The data are provided in a compressed text file containing 26 columns of separated integers, with each row representing a sampling of data collected during a single operational cycle and each column representing a unique variable.

5.2   Test Design

In order to test the prototype system on the aforementioned dataset, we first conducted data preprocessing (i.e. filtering) on the data. By filtering unnecessary columns and using clustering algorithms, we aim to identify anomalous patterns and improve the accuracy of predictive models.

The NASA Turbofan Jet Engine data is originally stored in text files, which are presented as four separate train and test data. In order to easily access and process the data, we transferred it to a relational database, specifically PostgreSQL. Some columns in the dataset do not experience significant changes and, thus, do not have much effect on the result. By filtering these columns, only the necessary fields were transferred to the model for improved efficiency.

We started the realtime clustering process with an offset dataset. First we feed the system with 35% offset data as shown in Fig. 2. As time progressed, the system was fed with subsequent data with 15% offset, and unsupervised machine learning algorithms were used to analyze the data. These algorithms separated the data into clusters, and any data not included in a cluster was considered an outlier. The number of outliers that occurred over time was calculated to evaluate the effectiveness of the algorithms.

To determine outliers for each clustering type, we applied the following methodology. For each data point, we tested whether it belongs to the current clusters by performing cluster membership testing for all clusters. We did this by measuring the distance between the data point and the centroid of the relevant cluster. If the distance value was above a certain threshold value, we considered the data point as not a member of the tested cluster. A data point that did not belong to any cluster using this membership test was classified as an outlier. Different threshold values were used for the distance-based membership test for different clustering algorithms. For CluStream, ClusTree, and StreamKM, these threshold values were chosen to be 35, 35, and 350, respectively. For outlier detection, the euclidean distance formula was used to determine the distances of the data to the clusters and compared with a threshold value. The v-measure values of these clusters were calculated to measure the quality of the clustering process.

With this experimental study test design, we aim to answer research problem 3, which we presented in Sect. 2.

5.3   Evaluation Result and Discussion

In this study, we evaluated the real-time anomaly detection process we proposed for industrial equipment using IoT and AI technologies. We worked with data from the NASA dataset, specifically the data numbered 4. In this dataset, the engines operate until they experience a fault. The main idea of our study is that by analyzing data from industrial machines, possible faults can be detected in advance and addressed through predictive maintenance. We aimed to detect anomalies before faults occur by analyzing unlabeled data using unsupervised machine learning techniques. Machines can exhibit many anomaly indicators before experiencing a fault, and we expect these anomaly situations to exhibit an increasing trend close to the occurrence of a fault. In our study, we first train our model using the Clustream, Clustree, and StreamKM clustering algorithms in the MOA framework on the initial 35% offset section of 61,249 data points. Then, we input data in 15% sections into the system to detect anomalies. As the data comes in, we observe that anomalous situations not initially present in the system increase towards the end.

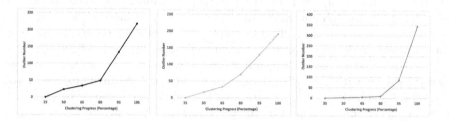

Fig. 3. The figure on the left indicates the clustream clustering algorithm results. The figure in the middle represents the clustree clustering algorithm result. The figure on the right shows the streamkm clustering algorithm results

Table 1 shows the anomaly detection data for the evaluated Clustream algorithm. As seen in the figure, while there are no outliers in the initial 35% offset data, 23, 34, 49, 134, and 218 outliers were detected in the 50%, 65%, 80%, 95%, and 100% data, respectively.

Table 2 contains the data for the Clustree algorithm. Similarly, in the results of this algorithm, although there were no outliers initially, 17, 33, 70, 130, and 192 outliers were detected in sequence. An increase in the number of outliers close to the occurrence of a fault was also observed here.

Table 3 contains the data for the Stream KM algorithm. Unlike other algorithms, it is necessary to determine the cluster count. For the detection of K cluster count, the Silhouette method was used, and the cluster number was determined as 3 for this data. As seen in the table, although there were no outliers initially, 3, 5, 9, 85, and 343 outliers were detected over time. An increase in the number of outliers towards the fault time is also noteworthy here. The results for the clustering algorithms presented in Fig. 3.

We used the V-Measure method to measure the quality of clustering results. It can be seen that the clustering performed with all three algorithms is of high quality according to the V-Measure values.

This results indicates that algorithms using IoT and AI technologies may be more suitable for real-time anomaly detection in industrial equipment. This section addresses research problems 2 and 4 presented in Sect. 2.

Overall, the proposed business process demonstrated good performance in detecting anomalies in real-time. The combination of IoT sensors, data preprocessing techniques, and unsupervised machine learning algorithms enabled the system to detect anomalies with a high degree of accuracy, minimizing the risk of equipment failure and downtime.

Table 1. Realtime Analysis Results of Clustream Clustering on IoT Sensor Data

Observation Number	Progress (Percentage)	Cluster Count	Outlier Number	V-Measure
21311	35	100	0	0.99460
30557	50	100	23	0.99557
39697	65	100	34	0.99704
48903	80	100	49	0.99630
58059	95	100	134	0.99703
61249	100	100	218	0.99737

Table 2. Realtime Analysis Results of Clustree Clustering on IoT Sensor Data

Observation Number	Progress (Percentage)	Cluster Count	Outlier Number	V-Measure
21311	35	352	0	0.98702
30557	50	314	17	0.99037
39697	65	330	33	0.99016
48903	80	316	70	0.99211
58059	95	331	130	0.99373
61249	100	280	192	0.99575

Table 3. Realtime Analysis Results of StreamKM Clustering on IoT Sensor Data

Observation Number	Progress (Percentage)	Cluster Count	Outlier Number	V-Measure
21311	35	3	0	0.96640
30557	50	3	3	0.99336
39697	65	3	5	0.96265
48903	80	3	9	0.99894
58059	95	3	85	0.99970
61249	100	3	343	0.99153

However, there were some limitations to our study. First, we used the NASA dataset, and the performance of the system may vary with different datasets. Second, we only evaluated a limited number of clustering algorithms, and there may be other algorithms that could perform better in detecting anomalies.

We also observe that as the number of outliers in the running observation data increases, the industrial equipment is more likely to fail. Hence, such real-time anomaly detection systems can prevent the system from failures by keeping track of the increasing anomaly behaviours.

The system can be customized for specific equipment types and integrated into existing equipment monitoring systems to improve operational efficiency and minimize downtime. Further research is needed to evaluate the system's performance with larger datasets and to explore the use of other clustering algorithms for anomaly detection.

6   Conclusion and Future Work

In this study, we proposed a real-time anomaly detection business process for predictive maintenance of industrial equipment. The proposed process utilizes IoT sensors and real-time unsupervised machine learning techniques, which do not require labeled data and are well-suited for real-time detection. The system uses IoT sensors to collect data from equipment in real-time and applies data preprocessing techniques and streaming-based clustering algorithms to detect anomalies. To facilitate testing of the proposed business process, we implemented a prototype application. The protoype application was evaluated using the NASA Turbofan Engine Degradation Simulation dataset, which contains sensor readings from aircraft engines that can be used to predict when an engine is likely to fail, in a streaming data fashion. The experimental study results are promising in detecting anomalies in real-time. The results also indicate that as the number of outliers in the running observation data of the industrial equipment increases, they are likely to fail. Hence, we claim that such real-time anomaly detection systems can prevent the industrial equipment from failures by keeping track of the increasing anomaly behaviours. We calculate the number of outliers over time using Clustream, Clustree, and StreamKM streaming clustering algorithms. The results show that the increase in the number of outliers over time is correlated with the trend of approaching an error condition. These anomaly situations can be detected before an error occurs, allowing for early intervention. These results demonstrate the potential of unsupervised machine learning techniques for real-time anomaly detection in IoT applications, and highlight the need for further research to develop more sophisticated techniques that can handle the complexity and variety of IoT data.

There are several areas for future work to improve the proposed real-time anomaly detection business process. First, the system could be evaluated with different datasets. Second, additional clustering algorithms could be evaluated to determine if they perform better than the algorithms used in this study. Third, the proposed system could be integrated with other AI technologies, such as deep learning or reinforcement learning, to further improve the accuracy of anomaly detection. Deep learning algorithms could be used to learn complex patterns in the data, while reinforcement learning could be used to optimize the clustering algorithms in real-time.

References

1. Gultekin, E., Aktas, M.S.: A business workflow architecture for predictive maintenance using real-time anomaly prediction on streaming IoT data. In: 2022 IEEE International Conference on Big Data (Big Data), Osaka, Japan (2022). https://doi.org/10.1109/bigdata55660.2022.10020384
2. Mollaoğlu, A., Baltaoğlu, G., Çakir, E., Aktaş, M.S.: Fraud detection on streaming customer behavior data with unsupervised learning methods. In: 2021 International Conference on Electrical, Communication, and Computer Engineering (ICECCE), Kuala Lumpur, Malaysia, pp. 1–6 (2021). https://doi.org/10.1109/ICECCE52056.2021.9514152

3. Kayacik, A.F., Özcan, B., Baltaoğlu, G., Çakir, E., Aktaş, M.S.: Real-time fraud prediction on streaming customer-behaviour data. In: 2021 International Conference on Electrical, Communication, and Computer Engineering (ICECCE), Kuala Lumpur, Malaysia, pp. 1–6 (2021). https://doi.org/10.1109/ICECCE52056.2021.9514169

4. Homayoun, S., Ahmadzadeh, M.: A review on data stream classification approaches. J. Adv. Comput. Sci. Technol. **5**, 8 (2016). https://doi.org/10.14419/jacst.v5i1.5225

5. Gomes, H.M., Bifet, A., Read, J., et al.: Adaptive random forests for evolving data stream classification. Mach. Learn. **106**, 1469–1495 (2017). https://doi.org/10.1007/s10994-017-5642-8

6. Akbar, A., Khan, A., Carrez, F., Moessner, K.: Predictive analytics for complex IoT data streams. IEEE Internet Things J. **4**(5), 1571–1582 (2017). https://doi.org/10.1109/JIOT.2017.2712672

7. Saxena, A., Goebel, K., Simon, D., Eklund, N.: Damage propagation 893 modeling for aircraft engine run-to-failure simulation. In: Proceedings of the International Conference 894 Prognostics Health Management, pp. 1–9 (2008)

8. Asif, O., Haider, S.A., Naqvi, S.R., Zaki, J.F.W., Kwak, K.-S., Islam, S.M.R.: A deep learning model for remaining useful life prediction of aircraft turbofan engine on C-MAPSS dataset. IEEE Access **10**, 95425–95440 (2022). https://doi.org/10.1109/ACCESS.2022.3203406

9. Muneer, A., Taib, S.M., Fati, S.M., Alhussian, H.: Deep-learning based prognosis approach for remaining useful life prediction of turbofan engine. Symmetry **13**, 1861 (2021). https://doi.org/10.3390/sym13101861

10. Tufek, A., Gurbuz, A., Ekuklu, O.F., Aktas, M.S.: Provenance collection platform for the weather research and forecasting model. In: 2018 14th International Conference on Semantics, Knowledge and Grids (SKG), Guangzhou, China, pp. 17–24 (2018). https://doi.org/10.1109/SKG.2018.00009

11. Riveni, M., Baeth, M.J., Aktas, M.S., Dustdar, S.: Provenance in social computing: A case study. In: 2017 13th International Conference on Semantics, Knowledge and Grids (SKG), Beijing, China, pp. 77–84 (2017). https://doi.org/10.1109/SKG.2017.00021

12. Guo, L., Li, N., Jia, F., Lei, Y., Lin, J.: A recurrent neural network based health indicator for remaining useful life prediction of bearings. Neurocomputing **240C**(2017), 98–109 (2017). https://doi.org/10.1016/j.neucom.2017.02.045

13. Tas, Y., Baeth, M.J., Aktas, M.S.: An approach to standalone provenance systems for big social provenance data. In: 2016 12th International Conference on Semantics, Knowledge and Grids (SKG), Beijing, China, pp. 9–16 (2016). https://doi.org/10.1109/SKG.2016.010

14. Aggarwal, C.C., Han, J., Wang, J., Yu, P.S.: A framework for clustering evolving data streams. In: Proceedings of the 29th International Conference on Very Large Data Bases - Volume 29 (VLDB '03), vol. 29. VLDB Endowment, pp. 81–92 (2003)

15. Baeth, M.J., Aktas, M.S.: An approach to custom privacy policy violation detection problems using big social provenance data. Concurr. Computat. Pract. Exp. **30**, e4690 (2018). https://doi.org/10.1002/cpe.4690

16. Aktas, M.S., Fox, G.C., Pierce, M., Oh, S.: XML metadata services. Concurr. Computat. Pract. Exp. **20**, 801–823 (2008). https://doi.org/10.1002/cpe.1276

17. Aktas, M.S., Pierce, M.: High-performance hybrid information service architecture. Concurr. Computat. Pract. Exp. **22**, 2095–2123 (2010). https://doi.org/10.1002/cpe.1557

18. Fox, G.C., et al.: Real time streaming data grid applications. Distributed Cooperative Laboratories: Networking, Instrumentation, and Measurements, pp. 253–267. Springer, Boston (2006). https://doi.org/10.1007/0-387-30394-4_17

19. Aktas, M.S., Fox, G.C., Pierce, M.: Fault tolerant high performance information services for dynamic collections of grid and web services. Future Gen. Comput. Syst. **23**(3), 317–337 (2007). https://doi.org/10.1016/j.future.2006.05.009

20. Aydin, G., Sayar, A., Gadgil, H., Aktas, M.S., Fox, G.C., Ko, S., Bulut, H., Pierce, M.E.: Building and applying geographical information system grids. Concurr. Computat. Pract. Exp. **20**, 1653–1695 (2008). https://doi.org/10.1002/cpe.1312

21. Fox, G.C., Aktas, M.S., Aydin, G., et al.: Algorithms and the grid. Comput. Visual Sci. **12**, 115–124 (2009). https://doi.org/10.1007/s00791-007-0083-8

22. Aktas, M., Aydin, G., Donnellan, A., et al.: iSERVO: Implementing the international solid earth research virtual observatory by integrating computational grid and geographical information web services. Pure Appl. Geophys. **163**, 2281–2296 (2006). https://doi.org/10.1007/s00024-006-0137-8

23. Aydin, G., Aktas, M.S., Fox, G.C., Gadgil, H., Pierce, M., Saya, A.: SERVOGrid complexity computational environments (CCE) integrated performance analysis. In: The 6th IEEE/ACM International Workshop on Grid Computing, 2005, Seattle, p. 6 (2005). https://doi.org/10.1109/GRID.2005.1542750

24. Pierce, M.E., et al.: The QuakeSim Project: Web services for managing geophysical data and applications. In: Tiampo, K.F., Weatherley, D.K., Weinstein, S.A. (eds) Earthquakes: Simulations, Sources and Tsunamis. Pageoph Topical Volumes. Birkhäuser Basel (2008). https://doi.org/10.1007/978-3-7643-8757-0_11

25. Uygun, Y., Oguz, R.F., Olmezogullari, E., Aktas, M.S.: On the large-scale graph data processing for user interface testing in big data science projects. In: 2020 IEEE International Conference on Big Data (Big Data), Atlanta, pp. 2049–2056 (2020). https://doi.org/10.1109/BigData50022.2020.9378153

26. Sahinoglu, M., Incki, K., Aktas, M.S.: Mobile application verification: A systematic mapping study. In: Computational Science and Its Applications - ICCSA 2015. ICCSA 2015. Lecture Notes in Computer Science, vol. 9159. Springer, Cham (2015). https://doi.org/10.1007/978-3-319-21413-9_11

27. Kapdan, M., Aktas, M., Yigit, M.: On the structural code clone detection problem: A survey and software metric based approach. In: Computational Science and Its Applications - ICCSA 2014. ICCSA 2014. Lecture Notes in Computer Science, vol. 8583. Springer, Cham (2014). https://doi.org/10.1007/978-3-319-09156-3_35

28. Olmezogullari, E., Aktas, M.S.: Pattern2Vec: Representation of clickstream data sequences for learning user navigational behavior. Concurr. Computat. Pract. Exp. **34**(9), e6546 (2022). https://doi.org/10.1002/cpe.6546

29. Olmezogullari, E., Aktas, M.S.: Representation of click-stream datasequences for learning user navigational behavior by using embeddings. In: 2020 IEEE International Conference on Big Data (Big Data), Atlanta, pp. 3173–3179 (2020). https://doi.org/10.1109/BigData50022.2020.9378437

30. Nacar, M.A., et al.: VLab: collaborative grid services and portals to support computational material science. Concurr. Computat.: Pract. Exper. **19**, 1717–1728 (2007). https://doi.org/10.1002/cpe.1199

31. Dundar, B., Astekin, M., Aktas, M.S.: A big data processing framework for self-healing Internet of Things applications. In: 2016 12th International Conference on Semantics, Knowledge and Grids (SKG), Beijing, China, pp. 62–68 (2016). https://doi.org/10.1109/SKG.2016.017

32. Baeth, M.J., Aktas, M.S.: Detecting misinformation in social networks using provenance data. In: 2017 13th International Conference on Semantics, Knowledge and Grids (SKG), Beijing, China, pp. 85–89 (2017). https://doi.org/10.1109/SKG.2017.00022

33. Aktas, M., et al.: Implementing geographical information system grid services to support computational geophysics in a service-oriented environment. In: NASA Earth-Sun System Technology Conference, University of Maryland, Adelphi, Maryland (2005)

Recycling Bin Based on the Internet of Things for Santa Elena Province

Maria Campuzano(✉) ⓘ, Marcia Bayas ⓘ, and Ronald Rovira ⓘ

TECED Research Group, Universidad Estatal Peninsula de Sana Elena, La Libertad, Ecuador
{mcampuzano,mbayas,rrovira}@upse.edu.ec

Abstract. As municipal solid waste keeps growing, waste management becomes a more complex issue for developing and developed nations. Latin America has fast population growth and low recovery rates. In Ecuador, Santa Elena is one of the few provinces which have not initiated segregated waste collection. Internet of Things has great potential to improve waste management systems at various points. The research objective was to analyze the current municipal solid waste management system and to propose a solution that incorporates Internet of Things technology to achieve segregated waste collection in an efficient way tailored for the municipalities of Santa Elena province. First, the current waste management system of the three municipalities of Santa Elena province was identified using literature review and interviews to municipal workers and recyclers. Analyzing similar waste management applications and considering local conditions, an improved waste management system was designed incorporating Internet of Things. The proposed solution includes solar-powered recycling bins which incorporate filling-level sensors and smoke sensors. Data is sent using a Wi-Fi module to a web server so real-time monitoring can be performed and updated efficient collection routes generated.

Keywords: waste management · Internet of Things · recycling bin · waste collection · Santa Elena province

1 Introduction

As cities continue to grow and industrialize, municipal solid waste (MSW) management has become a more complex issue worldwide [1]. Urban waste management represents a great challenge for modern societies, and it is an important pillar for sustainable development [2]. This matter requires urgent attention as the waste managed improperly affects people and the environment mainly in developing economies where this topic may be overlooked [3]. Municipal waste management can be expensive, as it represents around 4 to 20% of local budgets [4]. Traditional practices need to be improved with smart technologies to increase waste management systems' efficiency and to migrate to a circular economy towards sustainability [5].

Around 80% of Latin America's population dwells in urban areas [6]. Despite significant breakthroughs, municipal solid waste management in Latin America has not developed as fast as population growth. This region still has low recovery rates and open

O. Gervasi et al. (Eds.): ICCSA 2023 Workshops, LNCS 14108, pp. 32–43, 2023.
https://doi.org/10.1007/978-3-031-37117-2_3

dumps which affect sanitation and may be a threat to human health and the environment [7]. Waste usually has a high percentage of organic materials, which is common in developing countries [8]. Sorting and recycling have not yet been widely implemented around this region in comparison to similar economies in different parts of the world [6].

Despite that Ecuador is one of the first countries to create a national program on integrated solid waste management and to incorporate into its constitution nature's rights, current waste management systems need to be improved [9, 10]. Only 52% of municipalities operate landfills as the final disposal stage. The Ministry of Environment intended to close open dumps and temporary cells before 2018, however, it has not been done yet [11]. Household waste represents a great amount of urban solid waste [12]. Municipalities are responsible for collecting, treating, and disposing waste under a figure called decentralized autonomous governments [13]. Ministry of Environment Agreement 161 establishes extended producer responsibility principles for different products like mobile phones, batteries, pesticide containers, and used tires [11].

Not every Ecuadorian municipality has implemented mechanized waste collection in the cities. It is not uncommon to see piles of garbage bags on street corners. There are municipalities like Ambato, which installed waste bins more than 15 years ago. On the other hand, in municipalities like Salinas, you can see waste collectors loading by hand waste bags into waste collection trucks. Cities like Ambato, Cuenca, Riobamba, Quito, Guayaquil, among others have a mechanized residential solid waste collection. On average, 13,653 tons of waste are collected per day in Ecuador. Although differentiated collection is in place, only 34% of municipalities have implemented formal segregation; therefore, only 15% of waste is collected separately [14, 15].

Smart cities use information and communication technology (ICT) to improve cities' operations toward sustainability [16]. Frequent areas managed smartly include energy, transportation, green building, water supply, waste management, and land management [17]. Internet of Things (IoT) technology has brought attention to a wide range of applications in the science and engineering world where wired and wireless networks can be used [18]. IoT connects citizens, activities, data, and things converting information into actions that have generated exceptional possibilities to reshape assets and services [19]. IoT combines various technologies to create an interconnected network of small and large devices with sensors and actuators. Devices can communicate and exchange information through the internet so autonomous decisions can be made [20]. Developed and developing countries use Internet of Things applications to grow sustainably. As developing nations face financial and technical restrictions towards implementing smart city concepts, it is important to create an adequate environment to launch IoT initiatives [21].

Waste management supported by Internet of Things technology has become an important subject for research [22]. IoT has great potential to improve waste management systems at various points so circular economy and sustainability can be achieved. IoT devices can be installed in landfills [23, 24], energy conversion facilities [25], recycling centers [26], waste collection vehicles [20], dustbins [27], among others. Bins and containers integrated with filling sensors may be able to reduce overfilled or unnecessary collected bins through platforms that update waste collection routes in real-time [28].

Sathish Kumar et al. and Joshi et al. are some of the first researchers to be published on using IoT for smart waste management with wireless sensor networks together with cloud computing to optimize dustbin picking [29, 30]. Sathish Kumar et al. paired ultrasonic sensors with Arduino UNO to monitor filling levels to alert when bins require to be emptied. RFDI tags were included, and a system was created to monitor in real-time bins. An Android application was programmed and related to a web server for sending alerts and remote monitoring [30]. Waste management using Internet of Things for India was proposed using a solar-powered compacting dustbin with a wireless connection to transmit filling-level data to a cloud server to generate optimized collection routes. Operational waste collection costs were calculated to be reduced by 80% [31]. Monitoring systems applied to smart bins integrated with wireless filling sensors to update collection routes have also been studied in South Korea [27]. Shyam et al. proposed an algorithm to update and optimize daily routes for picking smart dustbins. The innovation relies on that not only daily data sent by sensors is analyzed but historical data which aids to predict future conditions relating to factors such as traffic and cost-efficiency [20].

IoT has been studied under different scopes and applications to improve waste management, not only to optimize collection routes but to aid waste segregation towards circular economy. Deep-learning convolution neural networks were created to classify waste in the initial collection stage into six categories. IoT devices allowed information exchange between dustbins and waste management centers to improve routes and maintenance [32]. Rahman et al. also used deep learning together with IoT for waste classification. IoT was used for controlling in real-time from anywhere and Bluetooth allowed data monitoring in the short-range trough a mobile application [33]. Internet of Things technology was used to improve accountability in household waste segregation in China [34].

In the Ecuadorian context, a smart waste monitoring system was developed for Riobamba city. An existing waste container was retrofitted with a solar panel and a device to send data collected by level, temperature, humidity, and pH sensors. The scope included database, web page, and server implementation [35]. For Cuenca city, a smart recycling container was designed and built. Through capacitive sensors, it identifies if it is a plastic bottle or a can so it can be sent by a rotary tray to the right part of the container. An ultrasonic filling sensor was also used to monitor the filling level of the bin to optimize collection routes [36]. Even though IoT has been studied before in Ecuador, it was only analyzed for Riobamba and Cuenca cities where mechanized collection is in place and have implemented waste classification. The research objective was to analyze the current municipal solid waste management system and to propose a solution that incorporates IoT technology to achieve segregated waste collection in an efficient way for the municipalities of Santa Elena province.

2   Materials and Methods

2.1   Study Area

Santa Elena province is in the southwestern part of the coastal region of Ecuador (Fig. 1). This province has an area of 3691 km^2 and an altitude from 0 to 800 m.a.s.l. Almost 45% of the land is rural. It is dived into three cantons: Santa Elena, La Libertad, and Salinas [37].

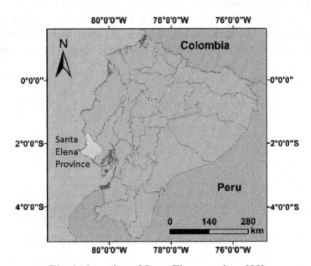

Fig. 1. Location of Santa Elena province [38]

Ecuador's average waste composition for 2021 was: 55% organic, 11% plastic, 6.5% non-hazardous sanitary, 5.1% cardboard, and 4.6% paper. No current information is available for Santa Elena province. In Ecuador, only 34% of municipalities have initiated or operated waste segregation process. Santa Elana is one of the few provinces which have non-existing waste classification programs executed by municipalities. Average waste generation for Santa Elena province is around 0.8 kg per day [14]. Waste pickers, which may be part of an association or not, perform urban mining. There are few private recycling initiatives and recyclers associations.

2.2   Methodology

This research was divided into two phases (Fig. 2). The purpose of phase one was to identify the current waste management system of the three municipalities of Santa Elena province. First, literature review was performed to analyze current waste management practices in the municipalities. Scarce research was available; therefore, it was necessary to obtain more information through field visits and interviews in the three municipalities. Municipal workers in charge of waste management were interviewed using semi-structured questionnaires to establish the current urban waste management system and the willingness to accept IoT implementation. Formal and informal recyclers were interviewed too to establish where they perform their activities and what kind of materials they work with. Their willingness to perform formal recycling aided with IoT was assessed too. The purpose of phase two was to propose an improvement for the current system incorporating IoT using the information gathered in phase one towards implementing differentiated waste collection. For the second phase, exploratory research was performed using scientific articles on similar IoT solutions to choose the best options for Santa Elena province reality. The main stages of the province waste management system were evaluated and improved incorporation IoT smart recycling bins and considering recycling streams. The recycling bin was designed using Autocad 3D and the circuit to be implemented inside the waste bins was designed using Proteus Professional 8. Route planning mechanisms were not included in the scope of the research.

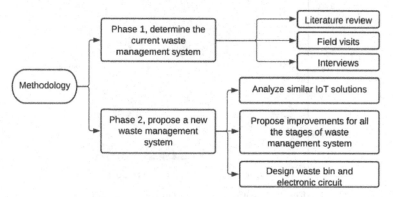

Fig. 2. Methodology used for the research.

3 Results and Discussion

The three municipalities of Santa Elena province were visited to assess the current municipal solid waste management system. Salinas and La Libertad municipalities have a municipal solid waste department while Santa Elena municipality has created a public company for managing waste called EMASA-EP. It is considered a better practice to create public companies for urban waste. None of the municipalities have implemented landfills and final disposal is performed at open dumpsites (Fig. 3). During field visits, it was noticed that in general MSW is placed into plastic bags at street corners, and in a few cases, it is placed into closed bins or containers. Recyclers open the bags to get valuable materials like plastic, paper, cardboard, metal, or electronic waste. During interviews with recyclers, it was mentioned that some of them are part of associations and others are informal recyclers. Municipalities have not implemented a segregated collection of MSW. Waste trucks transport the load to the open dumpsite of each municipality. At the dumpsites, there are also recyclers who collect materials. Formal and informal recyclers sell and transport the materials to Guayaquil city, which is located in another province.

When interviewed, stakeholders showed interest in participating in projects to increase the efficiency of waste management where recyclable materials are recovered in a formal way.

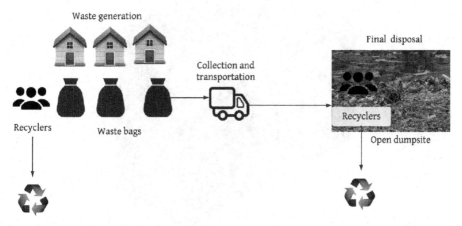

Fig. 3. Current municipal solid waste management system of municipalities of Santa Elena province

Since citizens are not used to separate waste, it would be useful to start a differentiated collection with smart recycling bins, first in Santa Elena municipality since they have a more advanced waste management system. It also should be considered that recycling bins should be gradually introduced so people may be more familiar with separating waste. The proposed improved system includes a bin for recyclable materials and another for common solid waste (Fig. 4). The recycling container will be for plastic, paper, and cardboard which are the main recycling materials. Since there is no electricity supply at the streets where waste is collected, solar panels and rechargeable batteries were considered for the bins. Containers have a capacity of 120 L, each one. Low-cost technologies have been selected to implement IoT inside the waste bins. Filling levels and smoke alarms are sent wirelessly to the cloud through internet. Collection routes are updated based on filling levels to avoid static routs and static schedules which may result in picking empty bins. Waste truck workers have access to mobile devices so they can perform collection as planned and inform of any inconvenience they may find during their work. IoT will improve efficiency and save money and time. Because the current system does not have a recycling center, it is proposed to merge a transfer station and the IoT monitoring center. It is considered that is better for recyclers to pick recyclable materials from general waste at the transfer station to avoid health hazards at the final disposal stage. It is advisable for the municipalities' authorities to consider landfills instead of open dumpsites to reduce environmental and health hazards (Fig. 5). Later, organic waste should be converted into compost or to produce energy using biogas or landfill gas.

IoT components and photovoltaic power system are shown in Fig. 6 and Fig. 7. The type of solar panels chosen for this research was polycrystalline (p-Si) since they are less expensive than monocrystalline ones; however, they have 5% less efficiency. If a waste

Fig. 4. Proposed solar-powered smart bins

Fig. 5. Proposed waste management system

collector detects dust on the solar panel glass, he can clean it to increase the energy the system receives. The rechargeable module and battery will allow stored energy to be supplied when there is not enough solar radiation. The microcontroller board Arduino UNO was selected because it has a small size that fits into the bin, has an average price, and fulfills the needs to process data from the two sensors. Further research should consider using an ultra-low-power and highly-integrated microcontroller that may have better performance concerning battery life [39]. The HC-SR04 ultrasonic distance sensor measures the filling level by sending an ultrasound that bounces back when it finds an obstacle. The distance is calculated using speed and time. An ultrasonic sensor was chosen because it measures levels for liquid and solid materials and does not need to be in contact with the measured material. This type of sensor was selected because IR sensors have shorter ranges and sunlight, hardness and colors may affect their accuracy [40]. However, further research might be necessary to increase accuracy as creating tailored caps to reduce detection angles that may avoid lateral surfaces detection [41] or installing two ultrasonic sensors in the waste bin [42] or using different type of sensors to triangulate data. HC-SR04 sensor is not expensive and has a measurement range from 2 cm to 400 cm with a resolution of 0.3 cm, which is adequate considering that the height of the bin is no more than 150 cm. The MQ2 gas sensor is used to detect gas and smoke, it is used to alert if there is smoke produced by a fire inside the bin. The NRF 905 module connects the sensor node and the gateway sensor. This device has a communication range of up to 1000 m. The Wi-Fi module ESP8266 is a system on chip (SoC) that includes a TCP/IP protocol stack that gives Arduino UNO access to the Wi-Fi network and it is widely used for IoT applications. Communication through Wi-Fi was selected for this work under the scenario that the government program of Santa Elena of becoming a digital province is fulfilled. However, other communication technologies such as Narrowband IoT and LoRa should be also considered to transfer data [43]. The generated data is stored and processed for real-time monitoring and waste collection improvement. Based on the amount of waste stored inside the bin, collection routes will be generated.

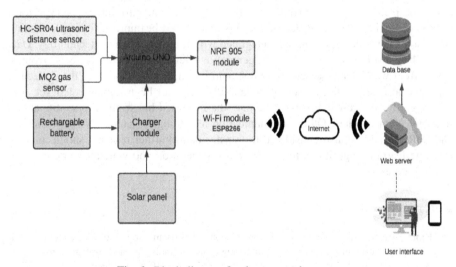

Fig. 6. Block diagram for the proposed system

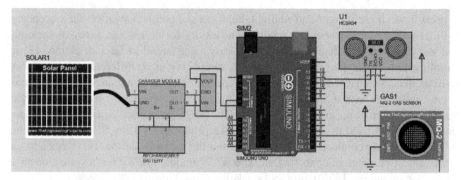

Fig. 7. Solar-powered circuit to be integrated into the waste bins

4 Conclusions

The current municipal solid waste management system of the three municipalities of Santa Elena province does not include waste bins; therefore, waste is placed in plastic bags that sometimes can be broken prior to collection. Waste classification has not been formally implemented by the municipalities. However, it does not mean that all recyclable materials go to open dumpsites because formal and informal recyclers perform the task of picking recyclable materials. This situation may be improved by implementing smart solar-powered recycling bins integrated with Internet of Things technology. Data from filling-level sensors will allow the generation of efficient dynamic collection routes. The current waste management system should be improved not only at the collection stage but also at the final disposal as landfills have not been implemented yet. The next stage for the research should validate the proposed bin from an operational and financial point of view. Other communication technologies such as Narrowband IoT and LoRa should be also considered to transfer data. Further research should include machine learning algorithms to predict waste generation and generate more efficient picking routes.

References

1. Kundariya, N., et al.: A review on integrated approaches for municipal solid waste for environmental and economical relevance: monitoring tools, technologies, and strategic innovations. Bioresour Technol. **342**, 125982 (2021). https://doi.org/10.1016/j.biortech.2021.125982
2. Rossit, D.G., Nesmachnow, S.: Waste bins location problem: a review of recent advances in the storage stage of the municipal solid waste reverse logistic chain. J. Clean Prod. **342**, 130793 (2022). https://doi.org/10.1016/J.JCLEPRO.2022.130793
3. Vyas, S., Prajapati, P., Shah, A.v., Varjani, S.: Municipal solid waste management: dynamics, risk assessment, ecological influence, advancements, constraints and perspectives. Sci. Total Environ. **814**, 152802 (2022). https://doi.org/10.1016/J.SCITOTENV.2021.152802
4. Kaza, S., Yao, L., Bhada-Tata, P., van Woerden, F.: What a waste 2.0: a global snapshot of solid waste management to 2050. World Bank Publications, Washington, DC (2018)
5. Lin, K., et al.: Toward smarter management and recovery of municipal solid waste: a critical review on deep learning approaches. J. Clean. Prod. **346**, 130943 (2022). https://doi.org/10.1016/J.JCLEPRO.2022.130943

6. Hettiarachchi, H., Ryu, S., Caucci, S., Silva, R.: Municipal solid waste management in Latin America and the Caribbean: issues and potential solutions from the governance perspective. Recycling **3**, 19 (2018). https://doi.org/10.3390/recycling3020019

7. Margallo, M., et al.: Enhancing waste management strategies in Latin America under a holistic environmental assessment perspective: a review for policy support. Sci. Tot. Environ. **689**, 1255–1275 (2019). https://doi.org/10.1016/j.scitotenv.2019.06.393

8. Bottausci, S., Midence, R., Serrano-Bernardo, F., Bonoli, A.: Organic waste management and circular bioeconomy: a literature review comparison between Latin America and the European Union. Sustainability **14**(3), 1661 (2022). https://doi.org/10.3390/su14031661

9. Villalba Ferreira, M., Dijkstra, G., Scholten, P., Sucozhañay, D.: The effectiveness of inter-municipal cooperation for integrated sustainable waste management: a case study in Ecuador. Waste Manage. **150**, 208–217 (2022). https://doi.org/10.1016/J.WASMAN.2022.07.008

10. Campuzano, M.G., Crisanto, T.: E-waste management: a case study of municipalities of Santa Elena province - Ecuador. Commun. Comput. Inf. Sci. **1307**, 587–598 (2020). https://doi.org/10.1007/978-3-030-62833-8_43/COVER

11. Holland Circular Hotspot: Study Waste Management in the LATAM region (2021)

12. Negash, Y.T., Sarmiento, L.S.C., Tseng, M.L., Lim, M.K., Ali, M.H.: Engagement factors for household waste sorting in Ecuador: improving perceived convenience and environmental attitudes enhances waste sorting capacity. Resour. Conserv. Recycl. **175**, 105893 (2021). https://doi.org/10.1016/J.RESCONREC.2021.105893

13. Burneo, D., Cansino, J.M., Yñiguez, R.: Environmental and socioeconomic impacts of urban waste recycling as part of circular economy. The case of Cuenca (Ecuador). Sustainability **12**, 3406 (2020). https://doi.org/10.3390/su12083406

14. Instituto Nacional de Estadísticas y Censos: Estadística de Información Ambiental Económica en Gobiernos Autónomos Descentralizados Municipales: Gestión de Residuos Sólidos 2021. INEC, Quito, Ecuador (2022)

15. Ortiz, C., et al.: Evaluation of municipal solid waste management system of Quito - Ecuador through life cycle assessment approach. LALCA: Revista Latino-Americana em Avaliação o Ciclo de Vida **4**, e45206–e45206 (2020). Instituto Brasileiro de Informação em Ciência e Tecnologia. https://doi.org/10.18225/LALCA.V4I0.5206

16. Camero, A., Alba, E.: Smart city and information technology: a review. Cities **93**, 84–94 (2019). https://doi.org/10.1016/J.CITIES.2019.04.014

17. Mingaleva, Z., Vukovic, N., Volkova, I., Salimova, T.: Waste management in green and smart cities: a case study of Russia. Sustainability **12**(1), 94 (2019). https://doi.org/10.3390/SU12010094

18. Peña, M., Llivisaca, J., Siguenza-Guzman, L.: Blockchain and its potential applications in food supply chain management in Ecuador. Adv. Intell. Syst. Comput. **1066**, 101–112 (2020). https://doi.org/10.1007/978-3-030-32022-5_10/COVER

19. Guarda, T., et al.: Internet of Things challenges. In: Iberian Conference on Information Systems and Technologies, CISTI (2017). https://doi.org/10.23919/CISTI.2017.7975936

20. Shyam, G.K., Manvi, S.S., Bharti, P.: Smart waste management using Internet-of-Things (IoT). In: Proceedings of the 2017 2nd International Conference on Computing and Communications Technologies, ICCCT 2017, pp. 199–203 (2017). https://doi.org/10.1109/ICCCT2.2017.7972276

21. Sharma, M., Joshi, S., Kannan, D., Govindan, K., Singh, R., Purohit, H.C.: Internet of Things (IoT) adoption barriers of smart cities' waste management: an Indian context. J Clean Prod. **270**, 122047 (2020). https://doi.org/10.1016/J.JCLEPRO.2020.122047

22. Hong, I., Park, S., Lee, B., Lee, J., Jeong, D., Park, S.: IoT-based smart garbage system for efficient food waste management. Sci. World J. **2014**, 1–13 (2014). https://doi.org/10.1155/2014/646953

23. Gopikumar, S., Raja, S., Robinson, Y.H., Shanmuganathan, V., Chang, H., Rho, S.: A method of landfill leachate management using internet of things for sustainable smart city development. Sustain. Cities Soc. **66**, 102521 (2021). https://doi.org/10.1016/J.SCS.2020. 102521

24. Mabrouki, J., Azrour, M., Fattah, G., Dhiba, D., Hajjaji, S. El: Intelligent monitoring system for biogas detection based on the Internet of Things: Mohammedia, Morocco city landfill case. Big Data Min. Anal. **4**, 10–17 (2021). https://doi.org/10.26599/BDMA.2020.9020017

25. Anagnostopoulos, T., et al.: Challenges and opportunities of waste management in IoT-enabled smart cities: a survey. IEEE Trans. Sustain. Comput. **2**, 275–289 (2017). https://doi.org/10. 1109/TSUSC.2017.2691049

26. Ramly, R., Sajak, A.A.B., Rashid, M.: IoT recycle management system to support green city initiatives. Indonesian J. Electr. Eng. Comput. Sci. **15**, 1037–1045 (2019)

27. Roy, A., Manna, A., Kim, J., Moon, I.: IoT-based smart bin allocation and vehicle routing in solid waste management: a case study in South Korea. Comput. Ind. Eng. **171**, 108457 (2022). https://doi.org/10.1016/J.CIE.2022.108457

28. Kumaravel, G., Ilankumaran, V.: IoT based smart battery power and wastage level tracking system for solar powered waste bin by GSM technology. IOP Conf. Ser. Earth Environ. Sci. **1055**, 012014 (2022). https://doi.org/10.1088/1755-1315/1055/1/012014

29. Joshi, J., et al.: Cloud computing based smart garbage monitoring system. In: 2016 3rd International Conference on Electronic Design, ICED 2016, pp. 70–75 (2017). https://doi. org/10.1109/ICED.2016.7804609

30. Sathish Kumar, N., Vuayalakshmi, B., Prarthana, R.J., Shankar, A.: IOT based smart garbage alert system using Arduino UNO. In: IEEE Region 10 Annual International Conference, Proceedings/TENCON., vol. 1028–1034 (2016). https://doi.org/10.1109/TENCON.2016.784 8162

31. Saha, H.N., et al.: Waste management using Internet of Things (IoT). In: 2017 8th Industrial Automation and Electromechanical Engineering Conference, IEMECON 2017, pp. 359–363 (2017). https://doi.org/10.1109/IEMECON.2017.8079623

32. Wang, C., Qin, J., Qu, C., Ran, X., Liu, C., Chen, B.: A smart municipal waste management system based on deep-learning and Internet of Things. Waste Manage. **135**, 20–29 (2021). https://doi.org/10.1016/J.WASMAN.2021.08.028

33. Rahman, M.W., Islam, R., Hasan, A., Bithi, N.I., Hasan, M.M., Rahman, M.M.: Intelligent waste management system using deep learning with IoT. J. King Saud. Univ. Comput. Inf. Sci. **34**, 2072–2087 (2022). https://doi.org/10.1016/J.JKSUCI.2020.08.016

34. Wang, B., Farooque, M., Zhong, R.Y., Zhang, A., Liu, Y.: Internet of Things (IoT)-Enabled accountability in source separation of household waste for a circular economy in China. J. Clean. Prod. **300**, 126773 (2021). https://doi.org/10.1016/J.JCLEPRO.2021.126773

35. Veloz-Cherrez, D., Lozada-Yanez, R., Rodríguez, J., Mayorga, P., Panchi, J.: Smart waste monitoring system as an initiative to develop a digital territory in Riobamba City. Information **11**, 231 (2020). https://doi.org/10.3390/INFO11040231

36. Mejía, C., Llivisaca, C., Astudillo, F., Vázquez-Rodas, A.: Recolección y clasificación automática de desechos reciclables. Maskana **8**, 331–340 (2017)

37. Herrera-Franco, G., et al.: Geosites and georesources to foster geotourism in communities: case study of the Santa Elena Peninsula Geopark project in Ecuador. Sustainability **12**, 4484 (2020). https://doi.org/10.3390/SU12114484

38. Morante-Carballo, F., Gurumendi-Noriega, M., Cumbe-Vásquez, J., Bravo-Montero, L., Carrión-Mero, P.: Georesources as an alternative for sustainable development in COVID-19 times—a study case in Ecuador. Sustainability (Switz.) **14**, 7856 (2022). https://doi.org/ 10.3390/SU14137856/S1

39. Anggrawan, A., Hadi, S., Satria, C.: IoT-based garbage container system using NodeMCU ESP32 microcontroller. J. Adv. Inf. Technol. **13**, 569–577 (2022)

40. Misra, D., Das, G., Chakrabortty, T., Das, D.: An IoT-based waste management system monitored by cloud. J. Mater Cycles Waste. Manag. **20**, 1574–1582 (2018). https://doi.org/10.1007/S10163-018-0720-Y/METRICS

41. Addabbo, T., et al.: A LoRa-based IoT Sensor node for waste management based on a customized ultrasonic transceiver. In: 2019 IEEE Sensors Applications Symposium, Conference Proceedings, SAS 2019 (2019). https://doi.org/10.1109/SAS.2019.8705980

42. Nirde, K., Mulay, P.S., Chaskar, U.M.: IoT based solid waste management system for smart city. In: Proceedings of the 2017 International Conference on Intelligent Computing and Control Systems, ICICCS 2017, January 2018, pp. 666–669 (2017). https://doi.org/10.1109/ICCONS.2017.8250546

43. Zhu, Y., Jia, G., Han, G., Zhou, Z., Guizani, M.: An NB-IoT-based smart trash can system for improved health in smart cities. In: 2019 15th International Wireless Communications and Mobile Computing Conference, IWCMC 2019, pp. 763–768 (2019). https://doi.org/10.1109/IWCMC.2019.8766748

Arduino and the Construction of a Height and Heart Rate Meter

Andrade Vera⊙, José Catuto González$^{(\boxtimes)}$ ⊙, and Carlos Mendoza González$^{(\boxtimes)}$ ⊙

Universidad Estatal Península de Santa Elena, La Libertad, Santa Elena, Ecuador
{aandrade,jose.catutogonzalez,cmendoza}@upse.edu.ec

Abstract. Due to the health emergency caused by the disease called COVID-19, the health authorities of each country implemented preventive measures, including maintaining a social distance of at least 2 m. Clinical laboratories perform a wide variety of tests, which is why they have a large influx of patients every day, in the same way, the first process they perform is the taking of vital signs, being this, the taking of height and cardiac pulse, which has been affected by the pandemic, as it involves direct contact with people, increasing the likelihood of contagion. Due to the above mentioned, the objective of this article is the development of a height and heart rate meter in order to avoid physical contact in the taking of vital signs in the clinical laboratory "Inmunolab", which will work in conjunction with a web and mobile application, which can be used by the following users: doctor in charge and worker. The height and cardiac pulse meter are based on several electrical components for its correct functioning, being these: Arduino NANO, ultrasonic sensor HC SR04, led display, potentiometer, heart rate sensor, 9v battery and bluetooth module HC-0.

Keywords: Arduino · Web application · Mobile application

1 Introduction

Evolution has been something that everyone has had to experience and more in these times where absolutely everything is being optimized by computer processes, in all areas of daily life there are changes, from being able to monitor a house to be able to buy everything online with the comfort and simplicity through the use of a mobile device, regardless of the economic level of people, human beings have become very dependent on technologies, because of this, all individuals have a technological device with which they can interact with all the services offered by the vast network of internet [1].

Coronavirus is an infectious disease caused by the SARS - CoV-2 virus, causing a pandemic that has drastically changed daily life and the way people relate to each other [2].

Covid-19 is easily spread through physical contact from person to person, for this reason and to avoid contagion [3], the World Health Organization (WHO) recommends keeping a social distance in enclosed and open-air places, being cautious about physically interacting with other individuals, since the virus can spread even if the infected person has no symptoms [2].

O. Gervasi et al. (Eds.): ICCSA 2023 Workshops, LNCS 14108, pp. 44–57, 2023.
https://doi.org/10.1007/978-3-031-37117-2_4

The COVID-19 pandemic has generated that some processes that used to work correctly now turn out to be inefficient. In that sense, the detection of these problems in the processes most affected by the current situation is a matter of survival for different organizations, not only in the field of business, companies, or enterprises, but also in health, which has been very important and at the same time has been the most affected in the pandemic that is going through the whole world [4].

The coronavirus pandemic accelerated the adoption of technological trends and in the following years we will witness how organizations will integrate the use of these, to manage the crisis and prepare for an eventual recovery; it will be an important year where digital technologies will play a fundamental role to overcome some challenges that the world is currently facing, for example, remote work through the new forms of interaction in public spaces [5].

A new trend that has revolutionized and thrived in this era is the Internet of Medical Things (IoMT), which refers to a system of machines and objects equipped with technologies capable of collecting data and communicating with each other. It has different applications and its use ranges from tele-medicine to the development of wearables, which are versatile technologies, such as smart watches [6].

In view of what has happened in the world with the COVID 19 pandemic, people have opted to optimize many processes that omit physical contact to avoid contagion [7].

The clinical laboratory "INMUBOLAB", is an establishment that performs different types of tests, so it has a large influx of patients. Before any examination it is necessary for each patient to have his vital signs taken, because it is a standard that must be followed with obligatory nature, the physical contact was inevitable, since, in the process of taking the height, the patient must stand next to a measuring tape that is usually located on the wall, therefore, a healthy distance was not maintained, making the risk of contagion remain throughout the process. For the taking of the cardiac pulse, it is true that there are devices that allow this work to be done, but there is still physical contact.

It is important for a clinical laboratory to have a device that allows non-contact pulse and height measurements because this reduces the risk of infectious disease transmission. Non-contact devices, such as pulse sensors and laser-based height gauges, allow laboratory personnel to take accurate measurements without having to touch the patient [8].

In addition, non-contact devices may also be more comfortable for patients, especially those who may be uncomfortable with physical contact. This may be especially important for patients with infectious diseases or immunocompromised patients, for whom physical contact may pose a greater risk [9].

Finally, non-contact devices can be more accurate and consistent in taking measurements, which may be important for monitoring and follow-up of patients with chronic diseases or recovering from injury or surgery. In summary, the adoption of non-contact devices in a clinical laboratory can improve the safety, convenience and accuracy of patient measurement taking [10].

The device that covers the present proposal, being able to take height and cardiac pulse, contains two of the main data in a sign taking, which avoids all contact between the medical team and patient. Technologies are created to evolve and optimize processes, which is what this project seeks to improve.

This article shows the development of a height and heart rate meter to avoid physical contact in taking vital signs in the clinical laboratory "INMUNOLAB" in times of covid19, to improve the process of taking signs and maintain a prudent distance, all the information obtained will be stored in a database to be managed in the best way and then be displayed by the laboratory for their results. The project will be divided in two parts, the first one will be focused in all that is Hardware, for this reason the IoT architecture model will be used, which is composed of four levels [8], in the second part we work on the development of the web and mobile application.

2   Theoretical Foundations

This section presents the theoretical and technological bases on which the development of the height and heart rate meter is based. First, the Arduino concept and its application on the Internet of Medical Things is described. Secondly, the development and application of the device is presented.

2.1   Arduino

Arduino is an open-source platform, used for the creation of electronics, which is based on free hardware and software, is flexible and easy to use by developers and creators [11].

This platform allows you to create different types of microcomputers from a single board and can be used for different purposes [11]. Among the benefits of using Arduino, it can be highlighted that: it simplifies the process of working with microcontrollers, it is low cost, being more accessible compared to other platforms, the software works on the Windows, Mac OS, and Linux operating systems, the programming environment is simple and straightforward, it is expandable, as it is open-source, and it is hardware extensive, providing users with the opportunity to build the development board version, understanding how it works and saving money [11]. Taking this into account, technological advances nowadays have allowed us to visualize from another perspective a world interconnected completely by all commercial, industrial, and domestic sector [12].

In recent years, information and communication technologies have evolved significantly in the creation of interconnected electronic devices and virtual machines, giving rise to the Internet of Things (IoT), allowing for intelligent automation of processes from anywhere, exchanging information and interacting with each other [12].

The technology applied to healthcare clearly represents devices capable of communicating via the internet to transfer data about patients. This is called Medical Internet of Things (IoMT), which is the application of technology in the healthcare sector, covering one of the areas where the benefits are most significant [13]. To implement IoMT, it is necessary to integrate technological methods to provide network-based services [13]. One of the devices that stands out in the Medical Internet of Things is Arduino, allowing the creation of devices such as telemedicine, wearables, drones, augmented reality, sensors, among others [14]. This generates great benefits, such as providing real-time information on the patient's health status, allowing personalized patient tracking, efficient management of available medical resources, reducing errors in diagnosis and treatment, reducing treatment time, and improving the patient's experience in the healthcare center [12].

2.2 Arduino and Its Application in Medical Internet of Things

In recent years, Arduino has become a popular tool for prototyping and solutions in the field of Internet of Things (IoT), including its application in the field of medicine.

In medicine, IoT devices based on Arduino are used for a wide variety of applications, from real-time patient monitoring to the automation of medical devices. One of the key benefits of Arduino is its flexibility and adaptability to different needs and environments [15].

For example, sensors connected to Arduino devices can be used to measure and monitor a variety of physiological variables, such as heart rate, blood pressure, temperature, and blood oxygen concentration. The data collected by the sensors can be transmitted over the Internet to a cloud platform, where it can be analyzed and visualized [15].

In addition, Arduino devices can also be used to control medical devices, such as infusion pumps, vital sign monitors, and diagnostic equipment, by automating their functions and integrating with other systems [16].

Arduino has become a popular tool for creating IoT devices in the field of medicine, and its adaptability and flexibility make it suitable for a wide variety [16].

2.3 Importance of Computer Systems in Clinical Laboratories

Computer systems are essential in clinical laboratories due to their ability to automate processes and improve efficiency in data management and analysis. Some of the main reasons why they are important are as follows [17]:

1. Improved efficiency: Computer systems allow for the automation of routine processes, such as data entry, which reduces time and human errors in these tasks. This improves the overall efficiency of the laboratory, resulting in faster and more accurate patient care [17].
2. Data management: Computer systems allow for the efficient management of substantial amounts of patient data, which can include test results, clinical history information, and billing details. The ability to quickly organize and access this data improves the quality of patient care and enables better clinical decision-making [17].
3. Accuracy of test results: Computer systems allow for automated analysis and interpretation of test results, which reduces the possibility of human errors and improves the accuracy of the results [17] systems can incorporate robust security measures to protect the privacy and security of patient data [17].

Computer systems are fundamental to improving efficiency and accuracy in clinical laboratories, as well as protecting the privacy and security of patient data. These systems allow for more effective management of patient data and better clinical decision-making, resulting in better care and outcomes for patients.

2.4 Technological Advances in the Healthcare Sector for Social Distancing

During the COVID-19 pandemic, social distancing has become an important measure to prevent the spread of the virus. Technology has played a key role in enabling people to maintain social distance while receiving medical care. The following are some technological advances in healthcare for social distancing [18]:

1. Telemedicine: Telemedicine has allowed patients to receive medical care from the comfort of their homes, reducing the risk of exposure to the virus. Patients can schedule virtual appointments with their doctors, get diagnoses and prescriptions, and receive health follow-up through online platforms and applications [19].
2. Medical robots: Medical robots have been used in hospitals to reduce the exposure of healthcare workers to the virus. These robots can perform tasks such as cleaning and disinfecting rooms, transporting supplies, and delivering food and medication to patients [20].
3. Wearables: Wearables are portable devices that allow remote health monitoring. Patients can use devices such as smartwatches and bracelets to monitor their heart rate, physical activity, and sleep and share data with their doctors [21].
4. Artificial intelligence: Artificial intelligence has been used to develop early detection systems for COVID-19 and to analyze large amounts of data related to the pandemic. It has also been used to develop algorithms that can help doctors make decisions about patient treatment [22].
5. Virtual reality: Virtual reality has been used to create telepresence experiences that allow patients to interact with doctors and other patients in virtual environments. This can be particularly useful for patients who cannot leave their homes due to the pandemic [23].

These technological advances have been crucial in enabling people to maintain social distance while receiving medical care during the COVID-19 pandemic. Additionally, many of these advances have the potential to improve healthcare in the future and improve accessibility to medical care for people living in remote areas or having difficulty accessing traditional medical care.

2.5 Web Application

A web application is a version of a webpage that adapts to any mobile device, regardless of the operating system it uses, meaning they are multi-platform apps. They are based on HTML, CSS, or JavaScript [24].

Web applications require a browser to function, and therefore, do not need to be downloaded from a store such as Play Store, App Store, among others. They do not take up memory on mobile devices and do not require updates, so users will always be able to view the latest version of the application [24].

Such apps are distinguished into three levels, the upper level that interacts with the user, the lower level that provides information, and the intermediate level that processes data [24].

A web application is software designed to run in a web browser. Unlike desktop applications that are installed on a computer, web applications run on a remote server and are accessed via the internet. Users can interact with the application through a web interface, which usually consists of web pages designed specifically for the application [24].

Web applications are commonly used in a wide variety of situations, from email and social networking applications to business management and e-commerce systems. Because there is no need to install software on the user's computer, web applications are easy to use and accessible from anywhere with an internet connection. Additionally, web applications can be updated and improved without requiring users to download and install updates on their computers, making them more convenient for developers and users [24].

2.6 Mobile Application

A mobile application is one that is developed specifically for a particular operating system, known as a Software Development Kit or SDK. Each platform, such as Android, IOS, or Windows Phone, has a distinct system and requires downloading and installation, and needs to be updated by the user [25].

Technology plays a very important and significant role in the healthcare sector, often being decisive in the processes of sample collection or diagnosis development. Therefore, an essential part of clinical laboratory management is the incorporation of technologies that are suitable for procedures and serve as support in the development of medical services [26].

A mobile application (also known as an "app") is software designed to run on mobile devices such as smartphones, tablets, and smartwatches. Mobile applications are designed to perform various functions and offer different services, from social networks and games to productivity and finance applications. These applications can be downloaded and installed from application stores such as Apple's App Store or Android's Google Play Store. Mobile applications can also be native, designed specifically for a mobile operating system, or they can be web-based, cloud-based, and accessible through a web browser on a mobile device.

3 Construction of the Height and Heart Rate Meter

The system structure is modeled based on the Client-Server Architecture as shown in Fig. 1. The process starts from the client, where Arduino detects the height and heart rate, and establishes a connection with the server. If communication is successful, Arduino sends a request via URL using the HTTP protocol with the obtained data, establishing a connection with the database, to subsequently save patient information in the mobile application. Similarly, users can interact on the web and mobile application through various graphical interfaces, making queries on the web service, linked to the database hosted on the server.

The electronic components used in the hardware architecture are arduino nano or uno, HC SR04 ultrasonic sensor, LED display, buzzer, heart rate sensor, 9V battery + connectors, and HC-06 Bluetooth module. Figure 2 shows the electronic components used to make the microcontroller connection.

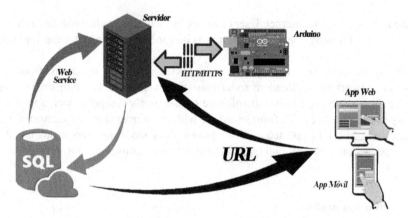

Fig. 1. System architecture [27].

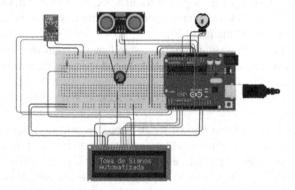

Fig. 2. Connection of the microcontroller with all the devices [27].

The following is the configuration of the microcontroller.
Heart Rate Sensor Library.

```
#include <PulseSensorPlayground.h>
```

Led Display Library.

```
#include <LiquidCrystal.h>
LiquidCrystal lcd(12, 11, 5, 4, 3, 2);
int led=13;
char buffer[10];
```

Heart rate sensor variables.

```
int PulseSensor = A0; // Conecte el cable rojo del sensor
en pin analógico cero
int Signal = 0;
float sensorvalor;
```

Distance sensor variables.

```
#define pEcho 10  //Conecta pin echo
#define pTrig 9  //Conecta el trigger
int duracion;  //Captura el pulso que emite el echo
int duracion1;
int ultrasonico=0; //Captura la distancia
void setup()
{
```

Speed configuration.

```
lcd.begin(16,2);
Serial.begin(9600);         //Inicia la velocidad en 9600
baudios
pinMode(pEcho, INPUT);
pinMode(pTrig, OUTPUT);
```

Pin declaration.

```
pinMode(led,OUTPUT);
digitalWrite(led,LOW);
lcd.setCursor(0,0);// col fila
lcd.print("Toma de Signos");
 lcd.setCursor(0,1);// col fila
lcd.print("Automatizada");
delay(3000);
lcd.clear();
}
float lectura_ultrasonico()
{
```

Sending low pulse to trigger.

```
digitalWrite(pTrig, LOW);
```

2 µs delay,

```
delayMicroseconds(2);
```

Generates trigger pulse.

```
digitalWrite(pTrig, HIGH);
```

10 µs delay

```
            delayMicroseconds(10);
            digitalWrite(pTrig, LOW);
            duracion=pulseIn(pEcho, HIGH);
            duracion1 =(duracion*0.034) /2;
            ultrasonico= 180 - duracion1;
            return ultrasonico;
 }
 float lectura_sensor()
 {
```

Reading data from heart rate sensor

```
    Signal = analogRead(PulseSensor);
    if(Signal <= 360){
     sensorvalor = sensorvalor-sensorvalor;
     }else{
       sensorvalor = (Signal/10) +25;
       delay(500);
       }
     delay(100);
          return sensorvalor;

   }
   void loop()
   {
```

Storing data sent from functions

```
int dist = lectura_ultrasonico();
int puls = lectura_sensor();
sprintf(buffer, "%d,%d",puls,dist);
Serial.println(buffer);
lcd.setCursor(0,0);
lcd.print("Pulso = ");
lcd.print(puls);
lcd.print("  LPM");
lcd.setCursor(0,1);//col fila
lcd.print("Altura = ");
lcd.print(dist);
lcd.print("  CM");
delay(1000);
lcd.clear();
}
```

Figure 3 shows the connection of the HC-06 Bluetooth module with Arduino. The selection of this module is due to its signal coverage being suitable for the construction of the meter.

Fig. 3. Connection of the HC-06 Bluetooth module with Arduino [27].

The graphical interfaces of the mobile application were created in App Inventor. Meanwhile, the web application is developed using Bootstrap, PHP, MySQL, and Ajax.

4 Results

Figure 4 shows the processing and storage of information collected by the devices. The information is recorded in the database after laboratory workers carry out the customer care process based on the data captured by the height and heart rate meter.

The mobile application allows authorized healthcare personnel to register vital signs and search for patients to record vital signs.

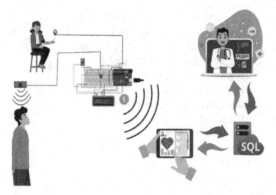

Fig. 4. Project Infrastructure [27].

The administrator must search for the patient by entering their ID number and then record pulse and height measurements as shown in Fig. 5. For this, the patient is placed under the height sensor as shown in Fig. 6. Once the data has been taken, a one-minute wait is required before capturing and storing the data in the application.

Fig. 5. Patient search and sensor registration interface [27].

In the web application, the administrator role can register, update, and delete user data, as well as view reports.

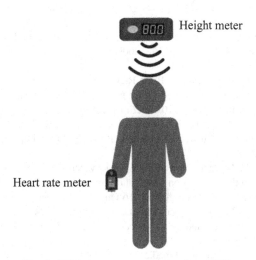

Height meter

Heart rate meter

Fig. 6. Vital signs measurement scheme [27].

5   Conclusions

By complementing the clinical laboratory with an automated height and heart rate meter, a better control and organization of patient measures and exams was achieved, maintaining an adequate distance to prevent contagion.

The height and heart rate meter were designed using the Arduino Uno microcontroller, which sends information by connecting via Bluetooth to a mobile application, storing the patient's vital signs.

The administrative process of the clinical laboratory was improved. To determine this, the time it takes for users to register the patient, height, and heart rate was calculated, concluding that waiting times are reduced by 40%, contributing to the management of said procedure.

If new functionalities are desired for the systems, it is recommended to review the tools used in this project since if other programs are used, there may be compatibility issues.

Migration of the applications to a permanent web server is recommended to always have access to information and places since it is currently on a free server.

Creating a pulse meter using Arduino can be an interesting and useful project to learn about programming and electronics. By using a pulse sensor and an Arduino microcontroller, it is possible to measure a person's heart rate and display it on an LCD screen or mobile application.

Additionally, this project can be customized and improved to fit different needs and requirements. For example, alarms can be added to indicate when the heart rate is too high or too low, or a data logging function can be added to track changes in heart rate over time.

Creating a pulse meter using Arduino can also be an excellent way to foster creativity and innovation and can serve as a foundation for more advanced projects in the future.

References

1. Jeong, D.-Y., et al.: Digital twin: technology evolution stages and implementation layers with technology elements. IEEE Access **10**, 52609–52620 (2022). https://doi.org/10.1109/ACCESS.2022.3174220

2. Huang, C., Yang, L., Pan, J., Xu, X., Peng, R.: Correlation between vaccine coverage and the COVID-19 pandemic throughout the world: based on real-world data. J. Med. Virol. **94**(5), 2181–2187 (2022). https://doi.org/10.1002/jmv.27609

3. Ciotti, M., Ciccozzi, M., Terrinoni, A., Jiang, W.-C., Wang, C.-B., Bernardini, S.: The COVID-19 pandemic. Crit. Rev. Clin. Lab. Sci. **57**(6), 365–388 (2020). https://doi.org/10.1080/10408363.2020.1783198

4. Antonini, M., et al.: An analysis of the COVID-19 vaccination campaigns in France, Israel, Italy and Spain and their impact on health and economic outcomes. Health Policy Technol. **11**(2), 100594 (2022). https://doi.org/10.1016/j.hlpt.2021.100594

5. Lustosa Rosario, A.C., et al.: "Open configuration options Higher Education Digital Transformation in Latin America and the Caribbean," Washington, D.C., December 2021. https://doi.org/10.18235/0003829

6. Razdan, S., Sharma, S.: Internet of medical things (IoMT): overview, emerging technologies, and case studies. IETE Tech. Rev. **39**(4), 775–788 (2022). https://doi.org/10.1080/02564602.2021.1927863

7. Brem, A., Viardot, E., Nylund, P.A.: Implications of the coronavirus (COVID-19) outbreak for innovation: which technologies will improve our lives? Technol. Forecast. Soc. Change **163**, 120451 (2021). https://doi.org/10.1016/j.techfore.2020.120451

8. Davila, M.I., Lewis, G.F., Porges, S.W.: The PhysioCam: a novel non-contact sensor to measure heart rate variability in clinical and field applications. Front. Publ. Health **5** (2017). https://doi.org/10.3389/fpubh.2017.00300

9. Abuella, H., Ekin, S.: Non-contact vital signs monitoring through visible light sensing. IEEE Sens. J. **20**, 3859–3870 (2019). https://doi.org/10.1109/JSEN.2019.2960194

10. An, J.Y., Shin, H.J., Yang, M., Park, D.-Y., Yang, J., Kim, H.J.: Non-contact diagnosis of sleep breathing disorders using infrared optical gas imaging: a prospective observational study. Sci. Rep. **12**(1), 21052 (2022). https://doi.org/10.1038/s41598-022-25637-w

11. Monk, S.: Programming Arduino: Getting Started with Sketches, 1st edn. McGraw-Hill Education, New York (2012). https://www.accessengineeringlibrary.com/content/book/9780071784221

12. Singh, R.: Internet of Things with Raspberry Pi and Arduino (2020)

13. Mohd Aman, A.H., Hassan, W.H., Sameen, S., Attarbashi, Z.S., Alizadeh, M., Latiff, L.A.: IoMT amid COVID-19 pandemic: application, architecture, technology, and security. J. Netw. Comput. Appl. **174**, 102886 (2021). https://doi.org/10.1016/j.jnca.2020.102886

14. Kondaveeti, H., Mathe, S.: A systematic literature review on prototyping with Arduino: applications, challenges, advantages, and limitations. Comput. Sci. Rev. **40** (2021). https://doi.org/10.1016/j.cosrev.2021.100364

15. Mihat, A., Mohd Saad, N., Shair, E.F., Aslam, A.B.N., Abdul Rahim, R.: Smart health monitoring system utilizing internet of things (IoT) and Arduino. Asian J. Med. Technol. **2**(1), 35–48 (2022). https://doi.org/10.32896/ajmedtech.v2n1.35-48

16. Aldujaili, A.A., Dauwed, M., Meri, A., Abduljabbar, S.S.: Smart internet of things kindergarten garbage observation system using Arduino uno. Int. J. Electr. Comput. Eng. (IJECE) **12**(6), 6820 (2022). https://doi.org/10.11591/ijece.v12i6.pp6820-6828

17. Kaplan, B.: Initial impact of a clinical laboratory computer system. J. Med. Syst. **11**(2–3), 137–147 (1987). https://doi.org/10.1007/BF00992348

18. Sivasankar, G., Anand, A.P., Susela Sruthi, K.: Internet of Things based wearable smart gadget for COVID-19 patients monitoring. In: 2022 International Conference on Wireless Communications Signal Processing and Networking (WiSPNET), pp. 130–134. IEEE, March 2022. https://doi.org/10.1109/WiSPNET54241.2022.9767173

19. Omboni, S., et al.: The worldwide impact of telemedicine during COVID-19: current evidence and recommendations for the future. Connect. Health 1, 7-35 (2022). https://doi.org/10.20517/ch.2021.03

20. Heng, W., Solomon, S., Gao, W.: Flexible electronics and devices as human-machine interfaces for medical robotics. Adv. Mater. 34(16), 2107902 (2022). https://doi.org/10.1002/adma.202107902

21. Vavrinsky, E., et al.: The current state of optical sensors in medical wearables. Biosensors (Basel) 12(4), 217 (2022). https://doi.org/10.3390/bios12040217

22. van de Sande, D., et al.: Developing, implementing and governing artificial intelligence in medicine: a step-by-step approach to prevent an artificial intelligence winter. BMJ Health Care Inform. 29(1), e100495 (2022). https://doi.org/10.1136/bmjhci-2021-100495

23. Kolecki, R., et al.: Assessment of the utility of Mixed Reality in medical education. Transl. Res. Anat. 28, 100214 (2022). https://doi.org/10.1016/j.tria.2022.100214

24. Pelet, J.-É., (ed.): Advanced Web Applications and Progressing E-Learning 2.0 Technologies in Higher Education. IGI Global (2019). https://doi.org/10.4018/978-1-5225-7435-4

25. Li, X., Zhao, X., (Ato) Xu, W., Pu, W.: Measuring ease of use of mobile applications in e-commerce retailing from the perspective of consumer online shopping behaviour patterns. J. Retail. Consum. Serv. 55, 102093 (2020). https://doi.org/10.1016/j.jretconser.2020.102093

26. Drew, D.A., et al.: Rapid implementation of mobile technology for real-time epidemiology of COVID-19. Science 368(6497), 1362–1367 (2020). https://doi.org/10.1126/science.abc0473

27. Gonzáñez, J.C.: Elaboración de un medidor de altura y pulso cardiaco para evitar el contacto físico en la toma de signos vitales en el laboratorio clínico Inmunolab en tiempos de COVID19. Universidad Estatal Península de Santa Elena, La Libertad (2022)

Effects of the Olympics on Citizens' Interest in Foreign Cultures: Evidence from the Tokyo 2020 Games

Takumi Kato[✉] [iD]

Meiji University, Tokyo, Japan
takumi_kato@meiji.ac.jp

Abstract. Governments worldwide are competing to internationalize their cities. During the 2020 Tokyo Olympics and Paralympics, Japan promoted not only the construction of stadiums but also multilingual support of city facilities. However, to truly internationalize a city, considering the above facilities and systems alone is insufficient. The perspective of citizen consciousness is lacking. Existing literature on Olympic effects is largely limited to three aspects: development of urban facilities, economic effects, and strengthening of a city's brand. Academically, little has been discussed about the impact of the Olympics on the international consciousness of citizens. Thus, this study clarified the impact of hosting the Olympics on citizen's interest in foreign cultures. Online surveys conducted in 2019–2022 in Japan showed that, despite the COVID-19 pandemic and the Olympics, citizens' interest in foreign cultures and their overall happiness did not change. However, by applying a multiple regression analysis, a positive interaction was detected between holding the Olympics and citizens' happiness. Therefore, citizen's interest in foreign cultures brought by the Olympics is conditional on citizens' sense of happiness. Hence, public sentiment should be improved before the Olympics is held. Practitioners should not depend on the Olympics to instantly improve public sentiment across the board. Practitioners should consider facilities and public sentiment as two key components of urban design. Even if governments invest in equipment, if they do not obtain the cooperation of its citizens, trouble will occur, and sustainable growth will be difficult.

Keywords: Urban Planning · Internationalization · Olympic Effects

1 Introduction

Gaining competitive advantage through city internationalization has received considerable attention from academics and practitioners [1]. Many cities including Washington, D.C. [2], Frankfurt [3], Marseille [4], Barcelona [5], and Helsinki [6] have promoted urban planning aimed at internationalization. Governments and companies worldwide have started to explore city rating indexes, including Global Liveability Index by CNN [7], Global Cities Index by A.T. Kearney [8], and Global Power City Index [9].

© The Author(s), under exclusive license to Springer Nature Switzerland AG 2023
O. Gervasi et al. (Eds.): ICCSA 2023 Workshops, LNCS 14108, pp. 58–69, 2023.
https://doi.org/10.1007/978-3-031-37117-2_5

In Japan, the Tokyo Metropolitan Government has clearly expressed its intention to internationalize. Aiming to grow its tourism [10] and finance industries [11], the city is continuing to internationalize. One of its activities was the Tokyo Olympics and Paralympics 2020 (hereafter, Tokyo Olympics). By holding this mega event, the Tokyo Metropolitan Government aimed to realize multilingual support by constructing stadiums and other facilities, digital signages, and smartphone applications [12, 13].

However, to truly achieve city internationalization, considering only the above facilities and systems is insufficient owing to the lack of public awareness. For example, in the tourism context, frustrated locals have constantly voiced their complaints about the hordes of foreign tourists [14]. Residents have negative impressions of tourists for many reasons, such as rising land prices and some tourists' rude behavior. Some local governments have passed ordinances against using apartments for Airbnb at the behest of residents [15]. This state of over tourism is called "tourism pollution" [16]. However splendid the facilities are, internationalization remains difficult when such negative sentiments remain among citizens.

Therefore, this study clarified the impact of hosting the Olympics on citizen's interest in foreign cultures. Existing literature on Olympic effects is largely limited to three aspects: development of urban facilities, economic effects, and strengthening of a city's brand. This study complements Olympic effects with a new aspect of citizens' interest in foreign cultures.

2   Existing Literature and Hypotheses

This section derives hypotheses based on existing literature on Olympic effects.

2.1   Representative Olympic Effects

Despite the huge costs, countries have offered to host the Olympics to benefit from the Olympic effects. The following three are mainly known as Olympic effects.

Development of Urban Facilities. As the Olympics provides a great opportunity to improve cities, Olympic functions are key urban development strategies. Hence, the International Olympic Committee requires cities to bid for the Olympics to develop legacy strategies to create sustainable assets after the Olympics [18]. Particularly, the necessity for the Green Olympics, which emphasizes the development of environmentally friendly transportation and buildings, has been appealed [19]. Hence, to prepare for the 2008 Summer Olympics, Beijing made significant environmental cleanup efforts. This reduced deaths and outpatient visits in the city due to lower air pollution [20].

Economic Effect. Hosting the Olympics attracts tourists from around the world and contributes to related businesses [21]. The effect is not limited to the Olympic period. From 8 years before to 16 years after the Olympics, the arrival of tourists from abroad significantly increased [22, 23]. Moreover, hosting the Olympics stimulates the export industry. This is attributable to not the actual act of hosting a mega event but the contribution of the country's information to the world [24].

Strengthening of a City's Brand. The host country aims to promote the country's brand image (e.g., advanced industries and cultural history) [25]. By hosting the Winter Olympics in 2006, Turin transformed into an internationally recognized "cultural city" [26]. The 2008 Beijing Olympics also provided China with a marketing opportunity to globally enhance its brand [27].

2.2 Citizen's Interest in Foreign Cultures

On the public attitude aspect of Olympic effects, close exposure to sports can increase citizens' health awareness and frequency of sports participation [28]. Generally, the number of medals won at the Olympics reflects a country's economic scale. However, hosting a country leads to more medals than the economic scale [29, 30]. Hence, hosting events in one's own country tends to increase awareness of sports among citizens. Another aspect of civic attitudes is the culture of other countries. Athletes from many countries interact with citizens [31], and the media also introduces foreign cultures and cuisine [32]. Accordingly, following hypothesis was formulated in this study:

H1: Hosting the Olympics positively impacts citizen's interest in foreign cultures.

However, egoism is prevalent in modern society, and people focus on their own interests above all else [33]. People with low self-esteem are particularly concerned about themselves, which makes them more likely to be jealous of others [34]. Conversely, people with high self-esteem are more likely to be interested in others [35]. Hence, the magnitude of the effect on citizen's interest in foreign cultures changes depending on people's sense of well-being in life. Accordingly, the following hypothesis was proposed in this study:

H2: Hosting the Olympics positively impacts citizen's interest in foreign cultures among happy citizens.

3   Method

This section describes the survey and verification methodology.

3.1 Survey

This study used online surveys targeting Japan's capital (around Tokyo Prefecture) and Kansai (around Osaka Prefecture) areas. Surveys were conducted once yearly, four times in total from 2019 to 2022 (April 19–25, 2019; April 17–23, 2020; April 16–22, 2021; April 15–21, 2022) by the Yoshida Hideo Memorial Foundation. Table 1 shows that the total sample size is 13,131. Ages range from teens to 60s.

Table 2 shows the 12 questions used in this study: basic attributes (Nos. 1–5), happiness (No. 6), life values (Nos. 7–11), and interest in foreign cultures (No. 12). Questions about values include items related to money and shopping that affect life satisfaction.

3.2 Verification

Multiple regression analyses including interaction was adopted as the verification method. Table 3 shows that in addition to each survey item, after the COVID-19 dummy (1 for the 2020–2022 survey, and 0 for others) and after the Olympic dummy (1 for the 2021–2022 survey, and 0 for the others) were added. To verify H1, the objective variable included degree of interest in foreign cultures (No. 12), the explanatory variable was the Olympic dummy, and other variables were control variables (Model 1). For H2 verification, I applied interaction between and after Olympic dummy and happiness (Model 2). For the analysis, the statistical analysis software R was used.

Table 1. Respondent attributes.

Item	Content	Number of Respondents	Ratio
Year	2019	3,197	24.3%
	2020	3,379	25.7%
	2021	3,244	24.7%
	2022	3,311	25.2%
Age	10s (15–19)	587	4.5%
	20s	1,944	14.8%
	30s	2,721	20.7%
	40s	3,639	27.7%
	50s	2,913	22.2%
	60s	1,327	10.1%
Gender	Male	6,736	51.3%
	Female	6,395	48.7%
Marital Status	Married	8,365	63.7%
	Unmarried	4,766	36.3%
Residence	Capital Area (Around Tokyo)	8,559	65.2%
	Kansai Area (Around Osaka)	4,572	34.8%

Table 2. List of questions.

No	Question	Type	Option
1	Please choose your age	single answer	10s, 20s, 30s, 40s, 50s, 60s
2	Please choose your gender	single answer	Male, Female, Prefer not to say
3	Please choose your marital status	single answer	Married, Unmarried
4	Please choose your annual household income	single answer	1: Ten - twenty thousand USD, 2: Twenty - thirty thousand USD, 3: Thirty - forty thousand USD, 4: Forty - fifty thousand USD, 5: Fifty - sixty thousand USD, 6: Sixty - seventy thousand USD, 7: Seventy - eighty thousand USD, 8: Eighty - ninety thousand USD, 9: More than ninety thousand USD
5	Please choose your residence area	single answer	Capital Area (Around Tokyo), Kansai Area (Around Osaka)
6	I am satisfied with my life	five-point Likert scale	1: Definitely not agree, 5: Definitely agree
7	Compared to the beginning of the year, the family budget situation has improved	five-point Likert scale	1: Definitely not agree, 5: Definitely agree
8	I feel that the economy will improve in five years	five-point Likert scale	1: Definitely not agree, 5: Definitely agree
9	I generally strive to buy products at the lowest price	five-point Likert scale	1: Definitely not agree, 5: Definitely agree
10	I always strive for the best quality	five-point Likert scale	1: Definitely not agree, 5: Definitely agree
11	I enjoy exchanging ideas with people from other cultures and countries	five-point Likert scale	1: Definitely not agree, 5: Definitely agree
12	I am interested in learning more about people who live in other countries	five-point Likert scale	1: Definitely not agree, 5: Definitely agree

Table 3. Variable list.

No	Variable	Description	Data Type	Mean	SD
1	Age	Age	1:10s, …, 6: 60s	3.787	1.335
2	Female	Female dummy	0/1	0.487	0.500
3	Married	Married dummy	0/1	0.637	0.481
4	Household_Income	Annual household income	1: Ten - twenty thousand USD, …, 9: More than ninety thousand USD	5.878	2.191
5	Capital	Dummy of living in capital area	0/1	0.652	0.476
6	Happiness	Degree of happiness	5-point Likert scale	2.874	1.086
7	Family_Budget	Family budget situation	5-point Likert scale	3.352	0.918
8	Economy	Economic outlook	5-point Likert scale	3.434	0.991
9	Low_Price	Degree of low price orientation	5-point Likert scale	2.869	1.016
10	High_Quality	Degree of high quality orientation	5-point Likert scale	3.282	0.981
11	Communication	Degree of interest in communicating with foreigners	5-point Likert scale	2.972	1.033
12	Foreign_Culture	Degree of interest in foreign cultures	5-point Likert scale	2.882	1.059
13	Covid19	After Covid19 dummy	0/1	0.757	0.429
14	Olympic	After Olympic dummy	0/1	0.499	0.500

4   Results and Implications

4.1   Results

The mean values of happiness and interest in foreign cultures by year were confirmed. Figure 1 shows that happiness in the years 2019 (2.837), 2020 (2.871), 2021 (2.877), and 2022 (2.911) show little fluctuation. Figure 2 shows that interest in foreign cultures also roughly has the same score as 2019 (2.866), 2020 (2.872), 2021 (2.888), and 2022 (2.901).

Table 4 shows that the results of Model 1's multiple regression analysis show no significant effect of the Olympics on interest in foreign cultures. Adjusted R-squared was 0.660, confirming the validity of this model. The maximum variance inflation factor of this model is 1.491, and there is little concern about multicollinearity. Hence, H1

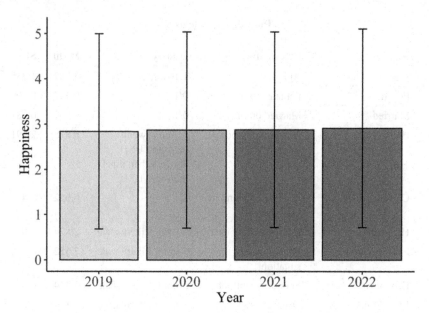

Fig. 1. Mean happiness by year.

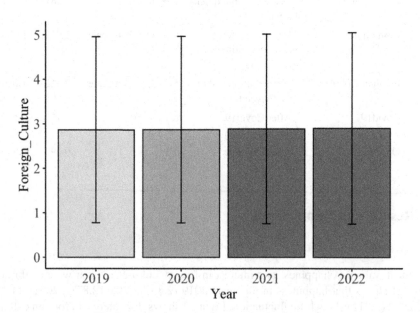

Fig. 2. Mean interest in foreign cultures by year.

Table 4. Results of regression analysis.

Variable	Model 1				Model 2			
	Estimate	SE	p-value		Estimate	SE	p-value	
Intercept	0.304	0.041	0.000	***	0.402	0.041	0.000	***
Olympic	0.016	0.013	0.237		0.015	0.013	0.242	
Happiness	0.031	0.006	0.000	***	0.031	0.006	0.000	***
Age	−0.002	0.005	0.710		−0.002	0.005	0.697	
Female	−0.040	0.011	0.000	***	−0.040	0.011	0.000	***
Married	0.023	0.013	0.085		0.023	0.013	0.079	
Household_Income	−0.005	0.003	0.091		−0.005	0.003	0.082	
Capital	−0.010	0.011	0.402		−0.009	0.011	0.423	
Family_Budget	0.023	0.007	0.001	**	0.023	0.007	0.001	**
Economy	0.002	0.006	0.804		0.001	0.006	0.853	
Low_Price	−0.007	0.005	0.216		−0.007	0.005	0.223	
High_Quality	0.015	0.006	0.012	*	0.015	0.006	0.013	*
Communication	0.815	0.006	0.000	***	0.815	0.006	0.000	***
Covid19	−0.008	0.015	0.624		−0.007	0.015	0.639	
Olympic * Happiness					0.022	0.010	0.029	*
Adjusted R-squared	0.660				0.661			

was unsupported. Model 2 shows that a significantly positive interaction was detected between the Olympics and happiness. Figure 3 shows that people with low (high) happiness exhibit a negative (positive) effect of interest in foreign cultures. Therefore, H2 was supported.

4.2 Implications

Existing literature on Olympic effects has been largely confined to three aspects: development of urban facilities, economic effects, and strengthening of a city's brand. This study focused on the citizen's opinions necessary for internationalizing cities and theoretically expanded the aspect of this effect.

The four main practical implications of this study are as follows. First, to internationalize a city, consideration should be given not only to physical facilities but also to citizens' feelings. Even if governments invest in equipment, if they do not obtain the cooperation of its citizens, trouble will occur, and sustainable growth will be difficult [14–16]. Hence, facilities and public sentiment should be considered as two key components of urban design.

Second, citizen's interest in foreign cultures brought by the Olympics is conditional on citizens' sense of happiness. Hence, public sentiment should be improved before the

Olympics is held. Practitioners should not depend on the Olympics to instantly improve public sentiment across the board.

Third, public well-being has not been significantly damaged by COVID-19. Despite the negative tone of the media on the impact of the pandemic, no change in consumer well-being responses was found. Making decisions based on objective data is essential, without being misled by the excessive discourse in the world.

Fourth, knowledge should be managed thoroughly by clarifying the basis of decision-making for mega-events such as the Olympics. In the case of large events, the wide variety of people involved makes the rationale for strategies ambiguous, and the fact that knowledge is not passed on is a major problem. Practitioners should take advantage of the data and analysis that technology brings and actively apply it to practical issues.

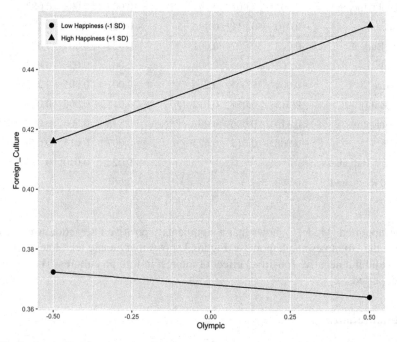

Fig. 3. Interaction between the Olympics and happiness on interest in foreign cultures.

4.3 Limitations and Future Work

This study has the following limitations. First, the results' generalization is limited because the study only targets the Japanese market. Second, this study is limited in that the evaluation results were obtained during the COVID-19 period. Many negative opinions were expressed about holding the Olympics during the pandemic [36]. The effect on citizens' interest in foreign cultures may be different from the regular Olympics. Therefore, conducting similar verification under normal circumstances may be an ideal topic for future research.

5 Conclusion

Academically, little has been discussed about the im-pact of the Olympics on the international consciousness of citizens. Thus, this study clarified the impact of hosting the Olympics on citizen's interest in foreign cultures. The result of applying multiple regression analysis to the multiple survey in Japan from 2019 to 2022 showed that citizen's interest in foreign cultures brought by the Olympics is conditional on citizens' sense of happiness. Hence, public sentiment should be improved before the Olympics is held.

Acknowledgement. This study uses data provided by the Yoshida Hideo Memorial Foundation.

References

1. Christofi, M., Iaia, L., Marchesani, F., Masciarelli, F.: Marketing innovation and internationalization in smart city development: a systematic review, framework and research agenda. Int. Mark. Rev. **38**(5), 948–984 (2021). https://doi.org/10.1108/IMR-01-2021-0027
2. Abbott, C.: The internationalization of Washington, DC. Urban Affairs Rev. **31**(5), 571–594 (1996). https://doi.org/10.1177/107808749603100501
3. Keil, R., Ronneberger, K.: Going up the country: internationalization and urbanization on Frankfurt's northern fringe. Environ. Plan. D: Soc. Space **12**(2), 137–166 (1994). https://doi.org/10.1068/d120137
4. Giovinazzi, O.: The internationalization of the Marseille waterfront: An integrated approach. Waterfronts Revisited, pp. 207–221. Routledge (2016)
5. Roig, A., Sun-Wang, J.L., Manfredi-Sánchez, J.L.: Barcelona's science diplomacy: towards an ecosystem-driven internationalization strategy. Human. Soc. Sci. Commun. **7**(1), 1–9 (2020). https://doi.org/10.1057/s41599-020-00602-y
6. Vanolo, A.: Internationalization in the Helsinki metropolitan area: Images, discourses and metaphors. Eur. Plan. Stud. **16**(2), 229–252 (2008). https://doi.org/10.1080/09654310701814538
7. Marcus, L.: The world's most liveable cities for 2022. CNN, June 23 (2022). https://edition.cnn.com/travel/article/economist-world-most-liveable-cities-2022/index.html. Accessed 10 Jan 2023
8. Kearney, A.T.: Readiness for the storm: The 2022 global cities report. A.T. Kearney (2022). https://www.kearney.com/global-cities/2022. Accessed 10 Jan 2023
9. Mori Memorial Foundation. Global power city index. Mori Memorial Foundation (2022). https://www.kearney.com/global-cities/2022. Accessed 10 Jan 2023
10. Reidy, G.: With Japan still shut to travelers, it is out of sight and out of mind. April 6) (2022). https://www.japantimes.co.jp/opinion/2022/04/06/commentary/japan-commentary/japan-tourist-trade/. Accessed 10 Jan 2023
11. CNN.: The Global Financial City of the Future. CNN) (2023). https://sponsorcontent.cnn.com/int/tokyo-sustainable-recovery/global-financial-city/. Accessed 10 Jan 2023
12. Tokyo Metropolitan Government. Policy for promotion of the global city strategy. Tokyo Metropolitan Government (2022). https://www.seisakukikaku.metro.tokyo.lg.jp/en/news/diplomacy/policy-for-promotion-of-the-global-city-strategy.html. Accessed 10 Jan 2023
13. Japan External Trade Organization. Tourism government initiatives. Japan External Trade Organization (2023). https://www.jetro.go.jp/en/invest/attractive_sectors/tourism/government_initiatives.html. Accessed 10 Jan 2023

14. Sugiyama, S.: Kyoto's love-hate relationship with tourists endures as yen weakens. Japan Times, July 4 (2022). https://www.japantimes.co.jp/news/2022/07/04/business/kyodo-tourism-uncertainty/. Accessed 10 Jan 2023

15. Reidy, G.: With Japan still shut to travelers, it is out of sight and out of mind. Japan Times, April 6 (2022). https://www.japantimes.co.jp/opinion/2022/04/06/commentary/japan-commentary/japan-tourist-trade/. Accessed 10 Jan 2023

16. Duignan, M.B., Everett, S., McCabe, S.: Events as catalysts for communal resistance to overtourism. Ann. Tour. Res. **96**, 103438 (2022). https://doi.org/10.1016/j.annals.2022.103438

17. Brasor, P.: Japan is struggling to deal with the foreign tourism boom. Japan Times, May 5 (2018). https://www.japantimes.co.jp/news/2018/05/05/national/media-national/japan-struggling-deal-foreign-tourism-boom/. Accessed 10 Jan 2023

18. Agha, N., Fairley, S., Gibson, H.: Considering legacy as a multi-dimensional construct: The legacy of the Olympic Games. Sport Manag. Rev. **15**(1), 125–139 (2012). https://doi.org/10.1016/j.smr.2011.08.004

19. Long, X., Chen, B., Park, B.: Effect of 2008's Beijing Olympic Games on environmental efficiency of 268 China's cities. J. Clean. Prod. **172**, 1423–1432 (2018). https://doi.org/10.1016/j.jclepro.2017.10.209

20. Schleicher, N., et al.: The effect of mitigation measures on size distributed mass concentrations of atmospheric particles and black carbon concentrations during the Olympic Summer Games 2008 in Beijing. Sci. Total Environ. **412**, 185–193 (2011). https://doi.org/10.1016/j.scitotenv.2011.09.084

21. Ferreira, R.R.: The location effect: How some Atlanta clubs won the "Olympic Ring." Cornell Hotel Restaurant Admin. Quart. **39**(5), 50–58 (1998). https://doi.org/10.1177/001088049803900510

22. Chong, T.T., Hui, P.H.: The olympic games and the improvement of economic well being. Appl. Res. Qual. Life **8**(1), 1–14 (2013). https://doi.org/10.1007/s11482-012-9176-8

23. Vierhaus, C.: The international tourism effect of hosting the Olympic Games and the FIFA World Cup. Tour. Econ. **25**(7), 1009–1028 (2019). https://doi.org/10.1177/1354816618814329

24. Rose, A.K., Spiegel, M.M.: The Olympic effect. Econ. J. **121**(553), 652–677 (2011). https://doi.org/10.1111/j.1468-0297.2010.02407.x

25. Kassens-Noor, E., Fukushige, T.: Olympic technologies: Tokyo 2020 and beyond: the urban technology metropolis. J. Urban Technol. **25**(3), 83–104 (2018). https://doi.org/10.1080/10630732.2016.1157949

26. Bondonio, P., Guala, C.: Gran Torino? The 2006 Olympic Winter Games and the tourism revival of an ancient city. J. Sport Tourism **16**(4), 303–321 (2011). https://doi.org/10.1080/14775085.2011.635015

27. Berkowitz, P., Gjermano, G., Gomez, L., Schafer, G.: Brand China: using the 2008 Olympic Games to enhance China's image. Place Brand. Publ. Dipl. **3**(2), 164–178 (2007). https://doi.org/10.1057/palgrave.pb.6000059

28. Contreras, J.L., Corvalan, A.: Olympic Games: No legacy for sports. Econ. Lett. **122**(2), 268–271 (2014). https://doi.org/10.1016/j.econlet.2013.12.006

29. Weed, M., et al.: The Olympic Games and raising sport participation: a systematic review of evidence and an interrogation of policy for a demonstration effect. Eur. Sport Manag. Q. **15**(2), 195–226 (2015). https://doi.org/10.1080/16184742.2014.998695

30. Choi, H., Woo, H., Kim, J.H., Yang, J.S.: Gravity model for dyadic Olympic competition. Physica A **513**, 447–455 (2019). https://doi.org/10.1016/j.physa.2018.09.045

31. Rice, C.: Culture, exchange and equality: How Tokyo 2020 is crafting its legacy. University of Southern California Center on Public Diplomacy (2021). https://uscpublicdiplomacy.org/blog/culture-exchange-and-equality-how-tokyo-2020-crafting-its-legacy. Accessed 10 Jan 2023

32. International Olympic Committee. The press at Tokyo 2020. International Olympic Committee (2021). https://olympics.com/ioc/news/the-press-at-tokyo-2020. Accessed 10 Jan 2023

33. Clohesy, W.W.: Altruism and the endurance of the good. Voluntas: Int. J. Volunt. Nonprofit Organiz. **11**(3), 237–253 (2000). https://doi.org/10.1023/A:1008923809507

34. Parker, J.G., Low, C.M., Walker, A.R., Gamm, B.K.: Friendship jealousy in young adolescents: individual differences and links to sex, self-esteem, aggression, and social adjustment. Dev. Psychol. **41**(1), 235–250 (2005). https://doi.org/10.1037/0012-1649.41.1.235

35. Mendiburo-Seguel, A., Páez, D., Martínez-Sánchez, F.: Humor styles and personality: A meta-analysis of the relation between humor styles and the Big Five personality traits. Scand. J. Psychol. **56**(3), 335–340 (2015). https://doi.org/10.1111/sjop.12209

36. Kato, T.: Opposition in Japan to the Olympics during the COVID-19 pandemic. Human. Soc. Sci. Commun. **8**(1), 1–9 (2021). https://doi.org/10.1057/s41599-021-01011-5

How 5G Will Transform Smart Cities:
A Literature Review

Isabel Lopes[1,2,3]([ORCID]), T. Guarda[3,4]([ORCID]), A. J. G. Fernandes[1,5]([ORCID]),
and Maria Isabel Ribeiro[1,5]([ORCID])

[1] Instituto Politécnico de Bragança, Campus de Santa Apolónia,
5300-253 Bragança, Portugal
{isalopes,toze,xilote}@ipb.pt
[2] UNIAG, Instituto Politécnico de Bragança, Campus de Santa Apolónia, 5300-253 Bragança,
Portugal
[3] Algoritmi, Universidade do Minho, Largo do Paço, 4704-553 Braga, Portugal
[4] Universidad Estatal Península de Santa Elena, La Libertad, Ecuador
[5] Centro de Investigação de Montanha (CIMO), Laboratório Associado Para a Sustentabilidade
e Tecnologia em Regiões de Montanha (SusTEC), Instituto Politécnico de Bragança, Campus de
Santa Apolónia, 5300-253 Bragança, Portugal

Abstract. The expectation created around 5G is great. Major changes are foreseen, in very different areas, which will have a great impact on people's daily lives.
It is expected that smart cities will be more efficient, more sustainable and safer,
with significant impacts on the people who inhabit them and also on the people
who visit them. 5G technology is not being implemented in the world in a comprehensive and similar way, there are countries that already have a large coverage
of this network and others that are still barely talking about this fifth-generation
technology of mobile communications. Given that there is still a great unknown
and uncertainty in relation to 5G, the question that this research work intends to
address is to what extent this technology can initiate an intelligent era, which, in
turn, provides a better quality of life for people, which each they are in greater
numbers, living in cities. Thus, this work intends to cross these growing trends,
with the new paradigm that is the implementation of 5G. For this, the Scopus
database was used, where a search was carried out in the most recent scientific
literature on these topics, since they are very current trends. The results are discussed in the light of the literature and future work is identified with a view to
contributing to the enrichment of those who are dedicated to these recent themes
but which are in great exponential growth.

Keywords: 5G Network · Smart Cities · Technology

1 Introduction

If we focus on the evolution of cities, we are clearly faced with a phenomenon that
is no longer new. The displacement of citizens to large urban centers is increasingly
evident and notorious, a phenomenon that makes the rural environment increasingly
depopulated.

© The Author(s), under exclusive license to Springer Nature Switzerland AG 2023
O. Gervasi et al. (Eds.): ICCSA 2023 Workshops, LNCS 14108, pp. 70–81, 2023.
https://doi.org/10.1007/978-3-031-37117-2_6

It is estimated that more than 50% of the world's population now lives in large urban areas, compared to just 34% in 1960. This population relocation poses new challenges to governments and local authorities, as demands in areas as disparate as Health, Environment and housing are major challenges that cities have to face.

Challenges that raise some important questions, which are linked to the incitement to guarantee quality of life for the populations that live there and also how to make urban spaces more innovative, participatory, connected and sustainable places.

The answer to these questions can be given if cities become more and more intelligent, more inclusive, more sustainable and more technological. One thing is for sure, "the intention underlying any of these situations is to make the city a community which can be friendly to people and for the people" [1].

The concept of "smart cities" has come to dominate both the academic literature and the public policies agenda. Several worldwide projects are being conceived and implemented, with different characteristics, motivations, maturity levels, government models and funding sources. However, the motto is always the use of information and communication technologies to make urban life easier [2].

Undoubtedly, the way people live in smart cities "has changed significantly due to various technological advances. There are many skyscrapers in smart cities, replacing old buildings. They are much smarter, not just because of the innovation of building materials science, but also because of the rapid development of sensor technology and the convergence of new data streams" [3].

These technologies are now applied on a large scale, and a large number of cities around the world are already considered "smart cities". This is the current reality! What is expected with the application of 5G technology is to accelerate the transformation of cities into even more promising scenarios.

Thus, this research work, in addition to contextualizing what is meant by smart cities and what is the fifth generation of mobile communications, aims to answer the following questions:

What is the relationship between technology and smart cities?

How should 5g accelerate the transformation of smart cities?

What are the main changes expected in cities with 5G?

The structure of this research work begins with this brief introduction, followed by the contextualization of the fifth generation of mobile networks and smart cities (Sects. 2 and 3). Next, we will address the methodology used to carry out this research work. Then, in Sect. 5, we present possible changes that can be expected in cities with 5G. The last section presents the main conclusions of the present study, as well as the identification of future works that can be carried out in these themes, since the desirable and expected knowledge in such current areas is a great umbrella where so many other points deserve attention from researchers.

2 Fifth Generation of Mobile Communications

The fifth generation of mobile communications is being rolled out albeit at different rates around the world. There are countries where 5G has already reached the homes of many citizens, regardless of whether they live inside or outside large urban centers, and others where little or nothing has yet been done to implement this new generation of mobile communications, as in some countries it has not yet been implemented. They have so little 3 and 4G. But as the standards underlying this new technology become more mature, industry observers predict that societal developments will lead to changes in the way communication systems are used and that these developments will, in turn, lead to a significant increase in mobile and wireless traffic volume; such traffic volume is expected to increase a thousand-fold over the next decade. Observations such as this one are common in the literature positioning the technology: "Unlike previous generations of mobile networks, the fifth generation (5G) technology is expected to fundamentally transform the role that telecommunications technology plays in the society" [4].

5G is expected to satisfy various requirements regarding latency, data rates, bandwidth, coverage, connectivity, and energy consumption [5, 6]. The fifth mobile generation will make it possible to connect, on an almost infinite scale, smart devices that communicate with each other at high speed [7, 8].

This new generation of communications began in the 1970s with 1G and continues to the present day, where 5G technology is now beginning to see the light of day. The evolution of different mobile communication generations from 1G to 5G with time are in Fig. 1.

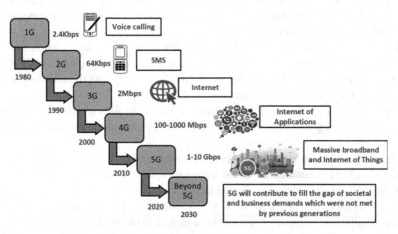

Fig. 1. Timeline of Mobile communication generations [9]

5G is a revolution and a potential discontinuity in the country's socio-economic progress over the next decade:

- **Companies** – is the fundamental basis for the competitiveness of companies in the next decade in the Industry 4.0 *framework*;
- **Cities and territories** – it is a fundamental basis for the intelligence of cities, for territorial cohesion and for environmental development;
- **Education/Training** – is the fundamental basis for new forms of teaching/learning, more immersive and centered on the student/trainee and/or on the context;
- **State** – is the fundamental basis for a new generation of more efficient and inclusive public services;

- **Health** – it is the fundamental basis for a more efficient and more effective health through all the added intelligence throughout the chain;
- **People** – and the fundamental basis for improving the quality of life of families benefiting from the economic and social progress of these new companies, cities and public services.

5G is an opportunity for start-ups and highly innovative companies to have access to more and better data, namely taking advantage of Artificial Intelligence, and to create new businesses taking advantage of the innovative features of 5G through real-time services and a integration of millions of devices never seen before [7, 10] (Fig. 2).

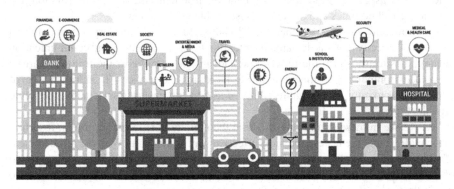

Fig. 2. Uses of 5G technology [11].

It is expected that the fifth generation of mobile communications will structurally change the role that telecommunications technologies play in society, a result that was not as noticeable in previous generations of mobile communications. 5G is also expected to enable further economic growth and pervasive digitization of a hyperconnected society, where not only are all people are connected to the network whenever needed, but also many other devices/things virtually creating the society with everything connected (i.e. Internet of Everything) [12, 13].

With 5G, cities will undergo transversal transformations, which depend on excellent mobile communications, impacting various sectors and industries, such as health, environment, transport, education and public safety. "We talk, for example, about improving air quality and energy consumption, reducing pollution and waste or implementing mobility systems that reduce traffic; to facilitate access to healthcare systems, powered by telecare, wearables for measuring vital signs and remote diagnostics; and the reinforcement of public safety by monitoring and reacting instantly in case of emergencies, using drones or connected ambulances" [14].

3 Smart City

The smart city concept "smart city" has come to dominate both the academic literature and the public policy agenda. Several projects are being conceived and implemented worldwide, with different characteristics, motivations, levels of maturity, governance models and funding sources, despite the motto always being the use of information and communication technologies to facilitate the urban life [15].

Defining what smart cities are "smart cities" and measuring levels of sustainability, quality of life and well-being are topics that still lack consensus.

However, the first step in this direction seems to have been taken: the publication of the ISO 37120:2014 standard is the first ISO reference (the International Organization for Standardization) with indicators for cities, measuring the ability to provide services and quality of life [16].

Although a universally accepted concept of "smart city" is not clear. There is a set of aspects that are referred to with greater or lesser incidence in the definition of smart cities. These aspects are the concern for the environment, the use of information and knowledge technologies and urban and sustainable development.

But how can you define a "smart city"? The International Data Corporation defines a smart city "as a city that has declared its intention to use information and communication technologies to transform the modus operandi in one or more of the following areas: energy, environment, government, mobility, buildings and services. The ultimate goal of a smart city is to improve the quality of life of its citizens, ensuring sustainable economic growth" [17].

As we see in these definitions, the term technology is repeatedly present, resorting to technology and the fastest and most effective way to innovate. With the advancement of technology, today there are more and more innovations that contribute to the growth of the concept of Smart Cities and that can be applied in the daily lives of citizens who live in these cities.

According to the IESE Cities in Motion index, for a city to be considered smart, it is important that it uses a large number of these solutions [18]:

– Use of information and communication technologies (ICT)
– Building automation and control
– Efficient urban planning
– Urban mobility and sustainable public transport
– Smart management of solid waste
– Improved environmental sustainability
– Concern for the social environment
– Technologies applied to education
– Technologies applied to health
– E-commerce system
– Transparency between governments and citizens
– Shared data in Open Data

This number of solutions are of the utmost importance for cities to be smart, however many of them applied in isolation would not have the desired effect by themselves. The sum of many of these complementary solutions is necessary (see Fig. 3). For example, it is not enough for the city to have only a strong economy, if wealth is not well distributed or if the means of production harm the environment.

Fig. 3. Complementary solutions to each other.

4 Methodology

The methodology adopted for this research work was done through a brief systematic review of the literature, where several scientific articles present in the Scopus databases were selected, according to the themes under study [19].

The systematic review of the literature intends to provide a small theoretical contribution, since it brings together the most recent knowledge in the area of 5G and smart cities, also serving to expand knowledge through empirical research carried out.

The process began by searching the Scopus databases under "article title, abstract, keywords" with the following keywords related to the theme of this work: "smart cities"; "5G smart cities applications"; "using 5G in smart cities". This research had the first filter by restricting the time horizon to the last decade (2013–2023). This choice was due to the fact that both 5G technology and smart cities are very current topics.

The first search resulted in 36 documents, of which only 17 were left for a second phase of analysis. This second filter was due to the fact that the excluded articles did not respond in any way to the main question of this research work, which is to know how far to what extent 5G technology can initiate a smart era in our cities, which in turn provides a better quality of life for its inhabitants.

The 17 articles resulting from the search and initial filters considered eligible and included in the study. The exclusion of the remaining documents results from the reading of the respective articles and the verification that they would not be relevant because they are not related to the question for this study (see Fig. 4).

But the inclusion and exclusion criteria (see Table 1) went beyond the question posed in the previous paragraph.

It was the application of these three inclusion criteria and four exclusion criteria that delimited the horizon of the articles that will serve as a basis for the literature review of this research work [19] (Table 2).

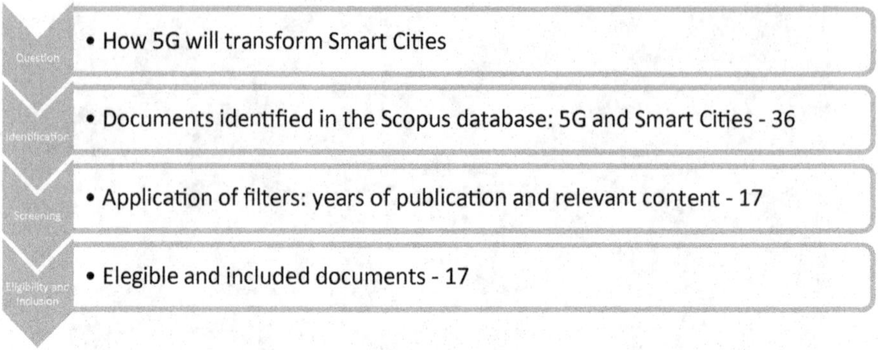
Question
• How 5G will transform Smart Cities
Identification
• Documents identified in the Scopus database: 5G and Smart Cities - 36
Screening
• Application of filters: years of publication and relevant content - 17
Eligibility and Inclusion
• Elegible and included documents - 17

Fig. 4. Document search and evaluation steps. Adapted from [19, 20].

Table 1. Inclusion and Exclusion Criteria [19]

Inclusion Criteria	Exclusion Criteria
– Articles in English; – Magazine articles, lectures, congresses, technical reports and conferences; – Articles that meet the question that this work wants to answer	– Articles prior to 2013; – Articles such as company web pages; – Short articles of less than 4 pages; – Articles not available

Table 2. Title and publication year of the selected paper

Paper title	Year
How the 5G network will boost the concept of Smart Tourism in Portugal	2023
Using 5G in smart cities: A systematic mapping study	2022
Securing Cyberspace of Future Smart Cities with 5G Technologies	2022
5G Smart IoT Poles	2022
Research on Application of 5G to Smart City	2021
Urban Mobility Services based on User Virtualization and Social IoT	2020
5G Promoting the development of smart cities	2020
5G Boosting Smart Cities Development	2020
Application Analysis of 5G in Environmental Protection Informatization	2019
Smart cities and 5G networks: An emerging technological area?	2019
5G smart city vertical slice	2019
Standardization: The Road to 5G	2018
Impact of 5G Technologies on Smart City Implementation	2018
Analysis of smart city transportation using IoT	2018
Integrating smart city applications in 5G networks	2018
Analysis of vehicular mobility in a dynamic free-flow high way	2017
Deploying 5G-Technologies in Smart City and Smart Home Wireless Sensor Networks with Interferences	2015

These 17 articles were fundamental to answer the main research question of this work, with their analysis described in the section that follows.

5   Changes Predicted in Cities with 5G

To realize the potential of Internet of Things (IoT) for smart cities, with 5G and AI, we present a framework for IoT systems (see Fig. 3). The framework is organized into 4 dimensions: data collection; the data centers; data processing; and applications.

Large amounts of cities data can be collected from various IoT devices and then sent to data centers via 5G. This data will be processed through AI techniques and models, and then distributed through 5G to the various IoT devices (see Fig. 5).

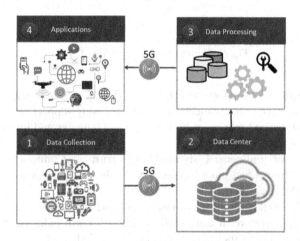

Fig. 5. Framework of 5G and AI-empowered IoT systems for smart cities.

All generations of mobile communications have influenced the development of the smart cities. With 5G it is expected, given its characteristics of high speed, large bandwidth, high confidentiality and low latency, a significant advance over 4G.

These essential 5G advances lead us to think about the challenges associated with taking advantage of these resources in cities. The Fig. 6 describes these possible uses:

Resilience - It is important to have ways of efficient recovery in order to automatically recognize and handle erroneous operations in 5G communication networks [21].

Standardization - Enormous efforts are needed to develop 5G communication network standards to be compatible with existing technologies and future technologies, many of which will be paramount for the evolution of smart cities [21, 22].

Energy efficiency - For the fifth generation of mobile communications, it is of paramount importance to achieve high energy efficiency for wireless communications in cities.

Scalability – This is yet another challenge in the design and implementation of 5G-enabled smart city solutions, where mass communications will stand out.

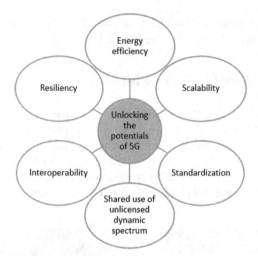

Fig. 6. Harnessing 5G capabilities [21].

Interoperability - To support a wide range of IoT "application scenarios, 5G communication networks need efficient mechanisms to effectively support heterogeneous data handling capabilities and manage different radio technologies and integrated mobility management schemes" [21].

Shared use of unlicensed dynamic spectrum - Communication network researchers need to conduct more research on the development of effective spectrum management techniques [21].

You can't talk about 5G without talking about the IoT because the connection between them is intrinsic. Therefore, it can be said that the 5G will enhance the "Internet of Things" and allow Smart Cities to develop [19, 23, 27, 28].

The IoT is emerging as an essential use case for this new 5G technology. It is common knowledge of the impact that IoT can have on the transformation of any city and this combination with 5G will build a scenario in cities that was unthinkable a decade or two ago. The IoT discussion is extending "beyond applications such as connected cars and smart metering to encompass the full range of business activities in industry verticals such as manufacturing, utilities and raw material production" [23].

It is expected that the following 5G-related technologies will contribute in the future in urban management [24, 25]:

- Artificial Intelligent
- Wireless Network Technology
- Cloud Computing and Big Data
- Precise Positioning Technique
- Terminal and Chip Technology

5G technology will bring both quantitative and qualitative changes, allowing for new features and a significant increase in the number and speed of connections.

Although 5G succeeds previous generations, its characteristics indicate that it will not only bring incremental improvements. For example, video surveillance can take advantage of 5G high-bandwidth technology, remotely controlled drones can be operated through low latency services, and sensors such as water quality monitoring can be operated through large-connection services. In short, many successful cases have emerged in the innovative application of "5G + smart city" [26].

Next, we will analyses the advantages of 5G applied to smart cities from five scenarios [29]:

Smart Security - The characteristics of 5G such as large bandwidth can meet the needs of video transmission, in addition, applying 5G technology in surveillance solutions, the near elimination of latency will provide a boost to the camera's responsiveness and real-time tracking.

Smart governance - The characteristics of 5G, such as high bandwidth, will allow many online applications, applications that began to transmit online various aspects of our daily lives that will streamline the lives of citizens living in large urban centers.

Intelligent protection of the environment – The characteristics of 5G will bring environmental gains, which result from the use of applications that allow better real-time monitoring of the conditions of agricultural land, energy, waste management and traffic in cities or weather conditions, through different devices, many of them connected to IoT technology [30].

Smart medical – The characteristics of 5G will allow through advanced IoT technology to perform interaction between patients and medical resources. Telemedicine is based on low-latency, high-definition image transmission technology, allowing doctors to remotely diagnose and even treat patients. In addition, during outdoor emergency care, the 5G network can ensure the quality of communication between the ambulance and hospital medical staff.

Intelligent transport – The characteristics of 5G will create favorable conditions for the realization of new scenarios for the application of intelligent transport [23]. Car remote control is one of the application scenarios of intelligent transport, which requires the car image data can be transmitted to the control room in time, so it has higher requirements on the uplink bandwidth. On the other hand, "the vehicle mobility model under the assumption of time-varying vehicle speed is quite challenging" [31].

6 Conclusion

Smart cities are characterized by smart heterogeneous devices that can interact and cooperate with each other by exchanging regularly low amounts of data in the context of IoT [32, 33].

On the other hand, 5G technology "offers a number of features that will positively affect digital experiences and smart cities. In addition to greater speed for uploading and downloading data, it guarantees very short latency times and the ability to connect multiple devices simultaneously. The combination of high density and low latency will profoundly transform our cities" [34].

5G and the emerging 6G must be further investigated to address the security needs of fast-growing smart cities and improve the quality of life [21].

In this research work, we discuss the positive effects and how 5G can accelerate the transformation of smart cities. However, smart cities are a complex ecosystem that involves all aspects of our society [35, 36]. Thus, we propose as future work the approach of the challenges that smart cities will face with the fifth generation of mobile communications.

Acknowledgements. The authors are grateful to the Foundation for Science and Technology (FCT, Portugal) for financial support through national funds FCT/MCTES (PIDDAC) to CIMO (UIDB/00690/2020 and UIDP/00690/2020) and SusTEC (LA/P/0007/2020).

The authors are grateful to the UNIAG, R&D unit funded by the FCT— Portuguese Foundation for the Development of Science and Technology, Ministry of Science, Technology and Higher Education. "Project Code Reference: UIDB/04752/2020 e UIDP/04752/2020".

References

1. Lopes, I.M., Oliveira, P.: Can a small city be considered a smart city? Procedia Comput. Sci. **121**, 617–624 (2017). CENTERIS - International Conference on ENTERprise Information Systems, Barcelona (Spain)
2. Silva, C., Selada, C., Guerreiro, D., Afonso, P., Melo, R.: Índice de Cidades Inteligentes – Portugal. INTELI – Inteligência em Inovação, Centro de Inovação (2012)
3. Yang, C., et al.: Using 5G in smart cities: A systematic mapping study. Intell. Syst. Appl. **14** (2022)
4. GSMA. Road to 5G: Introduction and migration (2018). https://www.gsma.com/futurenet works/wp-content/uploads/2018/04/Road-to-5G-Introduction-and-Migration_FINAL.pdf
5. Agiwal, R., Saxena, M., Agiwal, A., Roy, N.: Saxena Next generation 5G wireless networks: A comprehensive survey. IEEE Commun. Surv. Tutor. **18**(3), 1617–1655 (2016)
6. Gupta, A., Jha, R.K.: Survey of 5G network: Architecture and emerging technologies. IEEE Access **3**, 1206–1232 (2015)
7. Santos, P.M., Gomes, P.Z.: 5G: E depois do "Big Band"? Exame (2021)
8. Minoli, D., Occhiogrosso, B.: Practical aspects for the integration of 5G networks and IoT applications in smart cities environments. Wirel. Commun. Mobile Comput. **2019** (2019)
9. Meraj, M., Kumar, S.: Evolution of mobile wireless technology from 0g to 5g. Int. J. Comput. Sci. Inf. Technol. **6**(3), 2545–2551 (2015)
10. Vignaroli, L., et al.: The touristic sector in the 5G technology era: The 5G-TOURS project approach. In: 2020 IEEE Globecom Workshops (GC Workshops), pp. 1–6 (2020)
11. Domazon. https://www.domazon.in/. Accessed 31 July 2022
12. Heejung, Y., Howon, L., Hong-Beom, J.: What is 5G? Emerging 5G mobile services and network requirements. Sustainability **9**(10), 1–22 (2017)
13. GSMA. Understanding 5G – A guide for local communities. https://www.gsma.com/gsmaeu rope/resources/understanding-5g-a-guide-for-local-communities/
14. Antunes, M.E., Santiago, A., Vaz, P.: 5G: A revolução também passa pelas nossas cidades, Revista Smart Cities - Cidades Sustentáveis, fev (2020)
15. Silva, C., Selada, C., Guerreiro, D., Afonso, P., Melo, R.: Índice de Cidades Inteligentes – Portugal, INTELI – Inteligência em Inovação, Centro de Inovação (2012)
16. Cardoso, F.: Primeira norma ISO para as cidades, Revista Smart Cities, Agosto (2014)
17. Coimbra, G.: Smart Cities Benchamark 2015. International Data Corporation (IDC) (2015)
18. IESE. Cities in Motion Index (CIMI). https://blog.iese.edu/cities-challenges-and-manage ment/2020/10/27/iese-cities-in-motion-index-2020/
19. Lopes, I., Guarda, T., Fernandes, A., Ribeiro, M.I.: How the 5G network will boost the concept of smart tourism in Portugal: A literature review (2023)

20. Xiao, Y., Watson, M.: Guidance on conducting a systematic literature review. J. Plan. Educ. Res. **39**(1), 93–112 (2019)
21. Akhunzada, A., Islam, S.U., Zeadally, S.: Securing cyberspace of future smart cities with 5G technologies. IEEE Netw. **34**, 336–342 (2020)
22. Al-Dulaimi, A., Wang, X., Lin, I.C.: Standardization: The road to 5G. In: 5G Networks: Fundamental Requirements, Enabling Technologies, and Operations Management, pp. 691–708. Wiley, IEEE Press, Hoboken (2018)
23. Rao, S.K., Prasad, R.: Impact of 5G technologies on smart city implementation. Wireless Pers. Commun. **100**(1), 161–176 (2018)
24. Kochetkov, D., Vuković, D., Sadekov, N., Levkiv, H.: Smart cities and 5G networks: An emerging technological area? J. Geograph. Inst. "Jovan Cvijić" SASA. **69**(3), 289–295 (2019)
25. Xu, H.: 5G Promoting the development of smart cities. Zhang Jiang Technol. Rev. **1**, 34–37 (2020)
26. Chen, H., Yuan, L., Jing, G.: 5G boosting smart cities development. In: 2020 2nd International Conference on Artificial Intelligence and Advanced Manufacture (AIAM), pp. 154–157. IEEE (2020)
27. Lynggaard, P., Skouby, K.E.: Deploying 5G-technologies in smart city and smart home wireless sensor networks with interferences. Wireless Pers. Commun. **81**, 1399–1413 (2015)
28. Satyakrishna, J., Sagar, R.K.: Analysis of smart city transportation using IoT. In: 2018 2nd International Conference on Inventive Systems and Control (ICISC), pp. 268–273. IEEE (2018)
29. Xu, Y., Jia, S.: Research on application of 5G to smart city. IOP Conf. Ser. Earth Environ. Sci. **760** (2021)
30. Pei-Jun, L.I., Ji-Xiang, S., Amp, S.P.: Application analysis of 5G in environmental protection informatization. Comput. Knowl. Technol. (2019)
31. Zarei, M., Rahmani, A.M.: Analysis of vehicular mobility in a dynamic free-flow high way. Vehicul. Commun. **7**, 51–57 (2017)
32. Anedda, M., Giusto, D.D.: Urban mobility services based on user virtualization and social IoT. In: 2020 IEEE International Symposium on Broadband Multimedia Systems and Broadcasting (BMSB), Paris, France, pp. 1–4 (2020)
33. Tung, Y.-C., Zhan, Z.-Q., Chuang, M.-H., Peng, S.-H., Ho, C.-H., Chen, C.-C.: 5G Smart IoT Poles. In: 2022 International Conference on Wireless Communications Signal Processing and Networking (WiSPNET), Chennai, India, pp. 153–157 (2022)
34. 5G e Cidades Inteligentes: soluções para um futuro hiperconectado. https://www.reply.com/pt/telco-and-media/5g-smart-cities
35. Usman, Y., Asghar, M.M.R., Granelli, F., Qaraqe, K.: Integrating smart city applications in 5G networks. In: Proceedings of the 2nd International Conference on Future Networks and Distributed Systems, pp. 1–5 (2018)
36. Stefanescu, R.B., et al.: 5G Smart city vertical slice. In: 2019 IFIP/IEEE Symposium on Integrated Network and Service Management (IM), Arlington, pp. 13–19 (2019)

FPGA-Based Hardware/Software Codesign for Video Encoder on IoT Edge Platforms

Cuong Pham-Quoc[1,2]([envelope]) [ORCID]

[1] Ho Chi Minh City University of Technology (HCMUT), 268 Ly Thuong Kiet street, District 10, Ho Chi Minh City, Vietnam
[2] Vietnam National University - Ho Chi Minh City (VNU-HCM), Thu Duc, Ho Chi Minh City, Vietnam
cuongpham@hcmut.edu.vn

Abstract. Recently, image/video-based applications have been widely used for many domains, such as traffic, medical, or robotics. In this context, IoT-based systems with video processing implemented on edge devices have been applied extensively, for example, surveillance, object detection and monitoring, or intelligent home/building systems. Although algorithms for images/videos encoder with various standards produce good results, they usually require high computing power that is limited with edge platforms. Therefore, we propose an efficient hardware/software codesign approach to accelerate the video encoder process with FPGA-based IoT edge computing platforms in this work. The design flow exploits the effectiveness of the high-level synthesis process to quickly and efficiently generate FPGA-based hardware accelerator cores to improve system performance. We use the H.264 encoder as our case study to verify the proposed design flow and evaluate the accelerator ability compared to general-purpose processors. An FPGA Ultra96-v2 edge computing board is used for conducting experiments with a certified dataset. Experimental results show that we obtain speed-ups by up to 14.9× compared to a 4-core ARM processor. Our experimental system also saves up to 6.24× energy consumption compared to the ARM processor.

Keywords: FPGA · Hardware accelerator · H.264 encoder · Edge Computing · IoTs

1 Introduction

With the rapid development of technology and the internet, videos are used in various areas of the internet ranging from entertainment to supervising and monitoring. However, one of the most critical issues of network streaming video applications is the communication network bandwidth and the cost of transferring recorded videos from cameras to cloud storage or data centers. One promising approach to tackle this issue is to use edge computing platforms to process or pre-process videos and transfer only critical frames of objects detected

O. Gervasi et al. (Eds.): ICCSA 2023 Workshops, LNCS 14108, pp. 82–96, 2023.
https://doi.org/10.1007/978-3-031-37117-2_7

from videos to servers or cloud services. Edge computing platforms offer several advantages over traditional cloud computing solutions [3]. Edge computing reduces latency by processing data closer to where it's generated, reducing the time it takes for data to travel to and from the cloud. This ability is particularly beneficial for applications that require real-time processing, such as industrial automation, self-driving cars, and object detection.

Although this promising approach can be a solution for high-traffic and cost-ineffective video data transferring, low computing performance and limited energy capacity and storage of edge computing platforms are obstacles that should be considered carefully [15]. Therefore, in this work, we propose an approach for acceleration video encoders on FPGA-based edge computing platforms to overcome the obstacles of edge computing performance with energy efficiency. Our proposed approach first profiles the encoders for extracting the computationally-intensive functions that are good candidates for accelerating by FPGA fabrics. We then use high-level synthesis (HLS) tools to exploit different optimizations, such as loop unroll or pipeline, to generate the most optimized accelerator core. Finally, the system is built based on the hardware accelerator architecture [12] to exploit the advantages of both general-purpose processors and FPGA-based accelerator cores.

Due to its optimization, the H.264 video compression standard, also known as MPEG-4 Part 10, is one of the most well-known and widely used video coding standards for video streaming or video-based object monitoring. H.264 offers several advantages compared to other standards, such as high-quality video compression, enabling efficient video content storage and transmission without compromising image quality. Hence, we use the H.264 video encoder as our case study to validate the proposed approach. We develop our experimental system with the Ultra96-v2 FPGA edge computing platform to evaluate the acceleration ability compared to an embedded ARM processor. Experimental results with HD videos in Derf test media collection [23] show that our system achieves speed-ups by up to 14.9× compared to a 4-core ARM processor at 1.2 GHz.

The main contributions of our paper can be summarized in three folds.

1. We propose an efficient hardware/software codesign approach to accelerate the streaming video encoder for edge computing platforms on FPGA devices. A high-level synthesis process is used to generate hardware descriptions for the accelerator cores.
2. We present a case study with a well-known video coding format H.264 and the Ultra96-v2 FPGA board.
3. We show our experimental results with HD videos to reference other future studies.

The rest of the paper is organized as follows. Section 2 presents the background and related work. We introduce our proposed design approach in Sect. 3. Section 4 shows the implementation of the H.264 encoder as our case study. Experiments with HD videos on the Ultra96-v2 FPGA board are discussed in Sect. 5. Finally, Sect. 6 concludes our paper.

2 Background and Related Work

This section presents the background for video codec in general and H.264 in details. We then discussed related work in the literature focusing on acceleration video codec on FPGA.

2.1 Video Codec & H.264 Encoder

A video compression process requires two main components *encoder* and *decoder*. While the encoder encapsulates original video streams to compressed bitstreams with reduced data size for transferring and storing, the decoder converts the encapsulated bitstreams back to the original videos. The encoder usually includes three main functions for compressing: prediction model, spatial model, and entropy encoder. The decoder converts the compressed videos to original ones by using coefficients and prediction parameters of the encoder to calculate the entropy decode function, inverse transform, and reconstruction. Figure 1 summarizes the CODEC process based on the H.264 format [14].

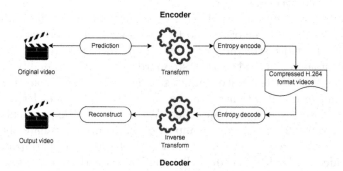

Fig. 1. The generic process of video encoder and decoder based on the H.264 format

As mentioned above, this work uses the H.264 encoder as a case study to demonstrate our proposed approach for FPGA edge computing platforms. The H.264 video compression standard uses hybrid video coding to encode and decode video data efficiently. The encoding process involves several steps, starting with video pre-processing, including resizing, color space conversion, and noise reduction. Figure 2 presents the syntax of the H.264 video compression standard. First, a sequence of an original video's frames is encoded to Network Adaption Layer Units (NALUs) packages. Each package stores parameters and a list of slices representing video frames. A slice consists of a header with encoding information followed by a list of macroblocks that encode a 16×16 pixels block of a video frame. Next, the encoding process applies compression techniques, such as intra-prediction, inter-prediction, and transform coding, to reduce redundancies in the video data and improve compression efficiency.

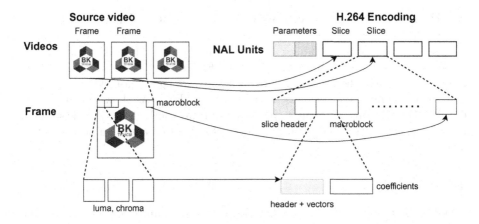

Fig. 2. The H.264 encoding process

2.2 Related Work

In recent years, many studies have focused on acceleration video encoders by hardware implementation. An entropy-based encoder for 8K video implemented on FPGA is introduced in [17]. In this work, the binarizer is customized, and pipeline techniques are exploited for massive parallelism to improve performance. However, this approach targets ultra-HD videos and is used in high-performance computing only. Researchers in [20] present their OpenCL-based and FPGA-powered H.266 acceleration. This approach implements the transformation and quantization steps on FPGA to improve performance. The experimental system is built with high-end FPGA devices instead of edge computing platforms like our work. Authors of [9] accelerate hexagon-diamond search (HEXDS) block matching algorithm on FPGA to improve performance of High-Efficiency Video Coding (HVEC) standard. This research only accelerates part of the encoding process and targets another compression standard. A heterogeneous CPU-FPGA computing architecture is used for HEVC video encoder [13]. The proposed system targets the OpenPOWER high-performance computing platform. A high-level synthesis approach, like our work, is used for acceleration of interpolation filter in HEVC video standard [16]. The proposed system targets high-end FPGA with a Virtex 6 device. Researchers in [10] design and build an ASIC accelerator core with the 90-nm TSMC technology for improving the performance of the HEVC video encoder. Due to the ASIC approach, the work achieves much improvement in performance. Versatile video coding (VVC) with 64×64 2D discrete sine/cosine transforms is proposed in [4]. This work focuses on the transformation step instead of the entire encoding process.

3   Proposed Hardware/Software Codesign Flow

This section proposes our design approach based on high-level synthesis (HLS) to accelerate video streaming encoder with FPGA edge computing platforms. Figure 3 illustrates the proposed hardware/software codesign flow for accelerating video streaming encoder based on FPGA and HLS. As shown in the figure, the flow consists of four main steps, starting from the high-level programming languages source code and ending with an FPGA-based edge computing implementation.

3.1   Profiling

The flow is started with the certified source code for an encoder method. The main purpose of this step is to get profiling data to make the most optimized hardware/software partition to improve system performance with hardware computation. The source code (usually in C/C++) is executed and profiled with a general-purpose processor to identify computationally intensive functions and data communication. Data communication is considered because transferring data across the computing cores also contributes much to the execution time of the entire system.

3.2   Hardware/Software Partition

Based on profiling data of the previous steps, the time-consuming functions are selected to build with dedicated hardware computing cores on the FPGA fabrics to take advantage of the reconfigurable technology (high parallelism, a massive amount of resources, and quickly adapting the design change). However, hardware fabrics cannot host all software functions due to the capability of resources and suitability of the functions. Therefore, this step needs to partition the source code into the software and hardware parts. The software part will continue processing with a general-purpose processor, while dedicated hardware cores will perform the hardware part. Due to dedications and hardware processing, the performance of these cores is higher than that of software-based processing.

This step also defines the interface for data communication between software functions and hardware cores. The target platforms should be taken into account for introducing the most optimized hardware/software interconnect. This interface can be a bus, crossbar, share memory, or network-on-chip based on the type of general-purpose processors that execute the software part. This software-hardware interconnect plays an important role in the system because communication overhead may require up to 50% execution times [11].

3.3   High-Level Synthesis

After determining functions accelerated by hardware-dedicated cores previously, this step generates HDL-based (hardware description language) processing cores.

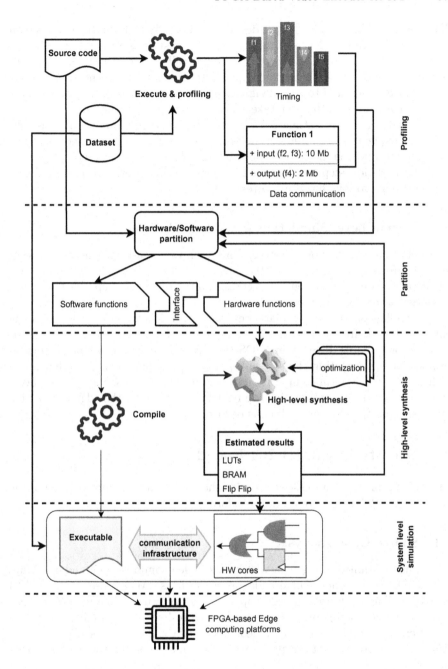

Fig. 3. The proposed design flow for video streaming encoder with HLS and targeting FPGA edge computing platforms

Although HDL-based cores can be developed manually by hardware designers, in this work, we use high-level synthesis (HLS) tools such as Vitis [22] from Xilinx or Stratus HLS [2] from Cadence for automatically creating the cores in HDL. HLS can offer many advantages compared to manual implementation, such as efficiently building and testing designs or exploiting various optimizations [8].

As shown in Fig. 3, this step takes optimization rules into account to generate HDL-based cores with estimated results in terms of the number of resources, working frequency, and latency. The HLS process can be performed in several iterations to find the most optimized solution. However, we sometimes need to redo the partition step since the IoT edge platforms' hardware resources may not be enough for the hardware cores.

3.4   System Level Simulation & Implementation

As the last step of the flow, after verifying with the high-level synthesis process, all parts are integrated and simulated during this step. Although the HLS process simulates and verifies the generated cores, simulation in this step is at the system level instead of the core level.

Depending on the target platforms, the general purpose processors can be embedded hardwired processors (for example, ARM or PowerPC) or softcore processors (for example, RISC-V or NIOS-II). These general-purpose processors are responsible for executing the software part of the application, while hardware-dedicated cores perform computationally intensive functions. This process needs to be supported by a system development kit provided by the edge target platforms such as Vivado from Xilinx as our experiments.

4   Case Study with H.264 Encoder

This section presents our case study with the H.264 encoder implemented on the Ultra96-v2 FPGA edge computing platform.

4.1   Source Code Analysis

H.264, as mentioned above, is a well-known video compression standard. Many certified H.264 encoder source codes exist, such as JM software [7] or ITU-T H.264 [6]. This work uses the x264 open-source software from VideoLAN Organization [19] as the reference source code. Figure 4 shows the main parts of the H.264 encoder implemented by VideoLAN software. The four processes, Filter, Analysis, Encode, and Entropy, are the four main computationally intensive functions.

The source code is then profiled with the perf tools [18] for extracting the timing values of functions. Although many profiling tools can be used for this purpose, we use perf because it is already integrated into most Linux kernels. Table 1 presents the perf results for the top computationally intensive source code functions.

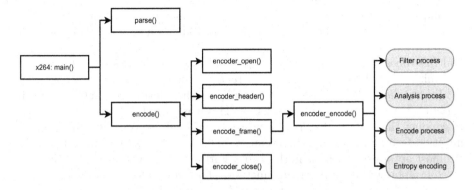

Fig. 4. Overview of H264 encoder main functions

Table 1. Timing profiling results with the perf tool for H.264 encoder

Function name	Overhead
x264_pixel_satd_8x4	26.12%
x264_pixel_avg_16x16	24.81%
x264_pixel_sad_16x16	14.67%
get_ref	14.24%
quant_4x4x4	10.43%
others	9,73%

The table shows that the `get_ref` function is also time-consuming along with the four functions x264_pixel_satd_8x4, x264_pixel_avg_16x16, x264_pixel _sad_16x16, and quant_4x4x4. However, this function collects data from external memory that an FPGA-based accelerator core cannot accelerate. Therefore, only the four functions, x264_pixel_satd_8x4, x264_pixel_avg_16x16, x264_pixel _sad_16x16, and quant_4x4x4, are suitable for accelerating by FPGA fabrics. Consequently, in this work, we optimize the five functions with HLS to generate accelerator cores for these functions. The following section presents the optimization techniques applied to the HLS processes.

4.2 High-Level Synthesis Optimization

High-level synthesis (HLS) [5] generates hardware circuits from high-level programming languages such as C or MATLAB. HLS has several advantages over traditional hardware design methods such as RTL (register transfer level). Compared to the traditional approach, HSL offers many advantages, such as higher productivity, faster design iterations, improved design quality, better portability, and reduced time to market. In this work, we exploit the faster design iterations of HLS by considering different optimization approaches for the four functions mentioned above. Those are *pipeline*, *unroll*, and *arry partition*. The *pipeline* technique helps reduce the initiation interval of a loop or a function by applying concurrent operations. The *unroll* approach produces a copy of RTL logic for computing multiple operations concurrently instead of a single block executed multiple times. Finally, the *array partition* optimization creates HDL description for multiple small blocks of memory or registers instead of a large memory [22].

Table 2 shows the HLS estimation results for the above four functions regarding latency and hardware resource usage. This work uses the Xilinx Vitis tool [1] to conduct the high-level synthesis process. Although we consider various optimization techniques for each function, we only show the estimation results with the most optimized methods in this table. Furthermore, the table shows that the *pipeline* approach is used for all functions. Therefore, all four cores use many flip flops (FFs) as pipeline registers and Look-up tables (LUTs) for computing functions.

Table 2. HLS estimation results

Function	Optimized techniques	Resource estimates	Latency
x264_pixel_satd_8x4	pipeline	DSP: 1	$11.370\mu s$
	array partition	FF: 2165	
		LUT: 2340	
x264_pixel_avg_16x16	unroll	DSP: 96	$75.360\mu s$
	pipeline	FF: 3672	
		LUT: 6178	
x264_pixel_sad_16x16	array partition	DSP: 0	$11.050\mu s$
	pipeline	FF: 2075	
		LUT: 2364	
quant_4x4x4	array partition	DSP: 2	$1.900\mu s$
	pipeline	FF: 4088	
		LUT: 3791	

4.3 System Implementation

After optimizing and generating HDL-based hardware descriptions for the four accelerator cores, we build our testing system based on the hardware accelerator computing paradigm [12]. Our case study uses the Xilinx MPSoC Ultra96v2 edge computing board [21] as our evaluation platform. Our testing system features a 4-core ARM Cortex functioning as a host processor and FPGA fabrics, which can be utilized to construct different components such as local memory (buffer), exchange registers for handling IP cores, and accelerator IP cores for computing the time-consuming functions mentioned above. Figure 5 illustrates the platform's overall setup. All components inside the MPSoC FPGA device are connected through a standard AXI bus. Due to space constraints, only the system's primary features are displayed in the image.

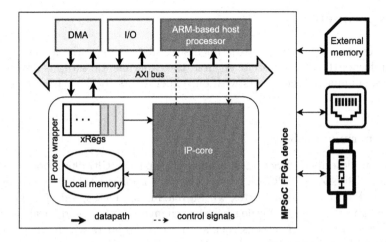

Fig. 5. Overview the FPGA-based edge computing system for H.264 encoder

4.4 Further Improvement with the Pipeline Technique

Due to the multi-processing cores implemented (hardware IP cores and a general-purpose processor), we can further improve the system's performance with the pipeline technique to achieve better performance. In general, while hardware accelerator cores calculate the accelerated functions, the general processor fetches new data to the local memory of the IP cores and processes the output of these cores. Figure 6 illustrates our scheduling for pipeline processing over seven cycles. Stages with the same color represent the processing of one piece of data. Our pipeline processing is divided into four stages. The general purpose processor executes one stage with the **get_ref** function at first and other functions when the hardware cores are finished following. The four hardware accelerator cores designed in the previous steps perform the rest three stages. Due to the pipeline approach, we need a more significant local memory for storing the current being processed data and the next piece of data.

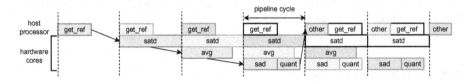

Fig. 6. Pipeline scheduling for the system

5   Experiments

In this section, we present our experiments to validate and estimate the acceleration ability of the above system. At first, the experimental setup is introduced. Then, we summarize the results with our experiments to illustrate the goals of our work.

5.1   Experimental Setup

The system described in Sect. 4 is evaluated using the Ultra96v2 board, which contains a Xilinx Zynq FPGA featuring over 70K Look-up Tables, 950 KB Block RAMs, and a 4-core ARM Cortex with a maximum clock speed of 1.5GHz. IP cores generated by HLS, Verilog-based exchange registers and local memory descriptions are utilized to construct all IP core wrappers within the FPGA's programmable logic part of the MPSoC device. An AXI bus connects the computational cores to the ARM Cortex as the host processor.

To assess the effectiveness of the proposed computing system, we compare our system with the processing capabilities of only the ARM processor. The following platforms are examined in detail:

1. *Our system* is a hardware accelerator architecture consisting of both the ARM processor and hardware cores for the four computationally-intensive of H.264 encoder, including x264_pixel_satd_8x4, x264_pixel_avg_16x16, x264_pixel_sad_16x16, and quant_4x4x4. The hardware cores perform the four functions when they are invoked, while the ARM processor handles the other parts of the encoder. In this setup, the ARM processor operates at its maximum frequency (1.5 GHz), while the hardware cores run at 230 MHz.
2. *The ARM system* uses all cores of the 4-core ARM processor for processing the entire H.264 encoder in parallel with the support of the x264 source code. Like our system, the ARM processor functions at the maximum frequency of 1.5 GHz for a fair comparison. However, the FPGA fabrics (hardware cores) are disable since only the ARM processor is utilized.

To test and compare our system with the ARM system, uncompressed videos from the Derf media collection are used [23]. In addition, we randomly chose three HD videos from the dataset to evaluate the proposed system's performance and energy efficiency. The following section presents our experimental results.

5.2   Experimental Results

At first, our system is synthesized with Xilinx tools to configure the Ultra96v2 board. The synthesis report shows that our system can function at 230 MHz and requires 4.208 W of power consumption. Figure 7 depicts the percentage of hardware resources our system used compared to the total amount of resources offered by the FPGA device. The figure shows that we use a lot of BRAM compared to the other types of resources due to our pipeline approach. More precisely, many block RAMs are used for building local memory. However, according to the figure, more room exists for increasing the hardware cores or replicating existing accelerators to improve system performance.

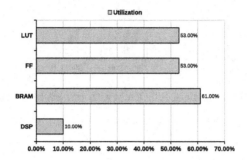

Fig. 7. Hardware resources usage for the whole system

Three HD videos from the dataset are collected to test the proposed system. Table 3 presents our performance in terms of execution evaluation of the system. According to the table, we achieve speed-ups by up to 14.9× compared to the ARM system. For the HD video *in_to_tree_420_720p50* (1280 × 720 resolution), we can process up to 47 frames per second.

Table 3. Performance comparison in terms of execution time (second)

Video input	#frames	Our system	ARM system	Output size
riverbed_1080p25	250	117.53	1057.78	11 MB
in_to_tree_420_720p50	500	10.53	156.88	648 KB
ducks_take_off_420_720p50	500	22.30	266.93	2.6 MB

Figure 8 compares the speed-ups of the proposed system with the ARM processor. As shown in the figure, we achieve speed-ups from 9× to 14.9×. The figure also depicts the energy consumption comparison between the two systems (energy = power × time). Compared to the ARM processor, our system is up to 6.24× energy efficiency.

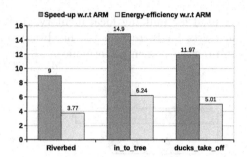

Fig. 8. Speed-ups and energy-efficiency with respect to the ARM system

6   Conclusion

The use of image and video-based applications has become widespread across various domains, including traffic management, medical fields, and robotics. With the rise of IoT-based systems, video processing has been implemented on edge devices for surveillance, object detection and monitoring, and intelligent home or building systems. However, while image and video encoder algorithms have produced satisfactory results, they typically require high computing power, which is constrained in edge platforms. To address this, we propose an efficient hardware/software co-design approach to accelerate the video encoder process using FPGA-based IoT edge computing platforms. Our design flow utilizes high-level synthesis to rapidly and efficiently generate FPGA-based hardware accelerator cores to enhance system performance. We use the H.264 encoder as a case study to verify our design flow and evaluate its accelerator capabilities compared to general-purpose processors. Our experiments with a certified dataset on an FPGA Ultra96-v2 edge computing board demonstrate that our system achieves up to 14.9× speed-up compared to a 4-core ARM processor, while also reducing energy consumption by up to 6.24× compared to the ARM processor.

Acknowledgement. We acknowledge Ho Chi Minh City University of Technology (HCMUT), VNU- HCM for supporting this study.

References

1. AMD Xilinx. Vitis^{TM} unified software platform overview (2023). https://www.xilinx.com/products/design-tools/vitis/vitis-platform.html. Accessed 01 Apr 2023
2. Cadence. Stratus high-level synthesis fastest path from specification to silicon (2023). https://www.cadence.com/content/dam/cadence-www/global/en_US/documents/tools/digital-design-signoff/stratus-high-level-synthesis-ds.pdf. Accessed 01 Apr 2023

3. Caprolu, M., Di Pietro, R., Lombardi, F., Raponi, S.: Edge computing perspectives: Architectures, technologies, and open security issues. In: 2019 IEEE International Conference on Edge Computing (EDGE), pp. 116–123 (2019). https://doi.org/10.1109/EDGE.2019.00035
4. Garrido, M.J., Pescador, F., Chavarrías, M., Lobo, P.J., Sanz, C., Paz, P.: An FPGA-based architecture for the versatile video coding multiple transform selection core. IEEE Access **8**, 81887–81903 (2020). https://doi.org/10.1109/ACCESS.2020.2991299
5. Gupta, R., Brewer, F.: High-Level Synthesis: A Retrospective, pp. 13–28. Springer, Netherlands (2008). https://doi.org/10.1007/978-1-4020-8588-8_2
6. International Telecommunication Union. H.264.2: Reference software for itu-t h.264 advanced video coding (2016). https://www.itu.int/rec/T-REC-H.264.2. Accessed 01 Apr 2023
7. Joint Video Team. H.264/14496-10 AVC reference software manual (2009). https://iphome.hhi.de/. Accessed 01 Apr 2023
8. Martin, G., Smith, G.: High-level synthesis: Past, present, and future. IEEE Design Test Comput. **26**(4), 18–25 (2009). https://doi.org/10.1109/MDT.2009.83
9. Mukherjee, A.: VLSI architecture design of motion estimation block with hexagon-diamond search pattern for real-time video processing. In: 2021 IEEE 18th India Council International Conference (INDICON), pp. 1–6 (2021). https://doi.org/10.1109/INDICON52576.2021.9691531
10. Pastuszak, G.: Multisymbol architecture of the entropy coder for h.265/hevc video encoders. In: IEEE Transactions on Very Large Scale Integration (VLSI) Systems vol. 28, no. 12, pp. 2573–2583 (2020). https://doi.org/10.1109/TVLSI.2020.3016386
11. Pham-Quoc, C., Al-Ars, Z., Bertels, K.: A heuristic-based communication-aware hardware optimization approach in heterogeneous multicore systems. In: 2012 International Conference on Reconfigurable Computing and FPGAs, ReConFig 2012 (2012). https://doi.org/10.1109/ReConFig.2012.6416720
12. Pham-Quoc, C., Heisswolf, J., Werner, S., Al-Ars, Z., Becker, J., Bertels, K.: Hybrid interconnect design for heterogeneous hardware accelerators. In: 2013 Design, Automation & Test in Europe Conference & Exhibition (DATE), pp. 843–846 (2013). https://doi.org/10.7873/DATE.2013.178
13. Qiu, Y., et al.: A heterogeneous HEVC video encoder system based on two-level CPU-FPGA computing architecture. In: 2021 IEEE 14th International Conference on ASIC (ASICON), pp. 1–4 (2021). https://doi.org/10.1109/ASICON52560.2021.9620382
14. Richardson, I.E.: The H.264 Advanced Video Compression Standard, 2nd edn. Wiley Publishing (2010)
15. Roman, R., Lopez, J., Mambo, M.: Mobile edge computing, fog et al.: A survey and analysis of security threats and challenges. Future Gen. Comput. Syst. **78**, 680–698 (2018). https://doi.org/10.1016/j.future.2016.11.009
16. Sjövall, P., Rasinen, M., Lemmetti, A., Vanne, J.: High-level synthesis implementation of an accurate hevc interpolation filter on an FPGA. In: 2021 IEEE Nordic Circuits and Systems Conference (NorCAS), pp. 1–7 (2021). https://doi.org/10.1109/NorCAS53631.2021.9599653
17. Tao, L., Gao, W.: A hardware implementation of entropy encoder for 8k video coding. In: 2022 IEEE International Conference on Multimedia and Expo (ICME), pp. 1–6 (2022). https://doi.org/10.1109/ICME52920.2022.9859988
18. The Linux Kernel Archives: perf: Linux profiling with performance counters (2023). https://perf.wiki.kernel.org/. Accessed 01 Apr 2023

19. VideoLAN Organization: x264, the best h.264/avc encoder (2013). http://www.videolan.org/developers/x264.html. Accessed 01 Apr 2023

20. Waidyasooriya, H.M., et al.: Opencl-based design of an FPGA accelerator for h.266/vvc transform and quantization. In: 2022 IEEE 65th International Midwest Symposium on Circuits and Systems (MWSCAS), pp. 1–4 (2022). https://doi.org/10.1109/MWSCAS54063.2022.9859281

21. Xilinx. Zynq ultrascale+ mpsoc (2021). https://www.xilinx.com/products/silicon-devices/soc/zynq-ultrascale-mpsoc.html. Accessed 01 Apr 2023

22. Xilinx, A.: Vitis high-level synthesis user guide (ug1399) (2022). https://docs.xilinx.com/r/en-US/ug1399-vitis-hls. Accessed 01 Apr 2023

23. Xiph.org. Video test media [derf's collection] (2016). https://media.xiph.org/video/derf/. Accessed 01 Apr 2023

Impact of ICT on the Agricultural Sector's Sustainability: Evidence Based on Practices

Maria I. B. Ribeiro[1](✉) ⓘ, Teresa Guarda[2,3] ⓘ, Isabel M. Lopes[3,4] ⓘ,
and António J. G. Fernandes[1] ⓘ

[1] Centro de Investigação de Montanha (CIMO) e Laboratório associado para a Sustentabilidade e Tecnologia em Regiões de Montanha (SusTEC), Instituto Politécnico de Bragança, Campus Santa Apolónia, 5300-253 Bragança, Portugal
`{xilote,toze}@ipb.pt`
[2] Universidad Estatal Península de Santa Elena, La Libertad, Ecuador
[3] Algoritmi Centre, Minho University, Guimarães, Portugal
`isalopes@ipb.pt`
[4] Unidade de Pesquisa Aplicada em Gestão – Instituto Politécnico de Bragança, Bragança, Portugal

Abstract. Despite being an emerging phenomenon, the literature on how ICT impact the adoption of sustainable agriculture has aroused growing interest on the part of farmers, scientific and business communities and policy makers. Therefore, the main objective of this study was to investigate the state-of-the-art of ICT use in agriculture with an impact on the sustainability of the sector. In order to achieve this objective, a computer-assisted bibliographic search was performed in February, 2023. This search included all publications available in the Scopus database and was based on the words "Impact" OR "Contributions" AND "information" AND "Communication" AND "Technologies" AND "Sustainability" AND "Agriculture". Subsequently, publications were selected taking into account the following criterion: empirical studies that demonstrate evidence of the impact or contribution of ICT to sustainable agriculture. For each publication, it was collected information about authorship and publication date, place where the study was developed, type of study, methods, objectives and findings. All studies show positive contributions as a result of the use of ICT and artificial intelligence for the adoption of a sustainable agriculture with lower resources' consumption, namely, improvement of soil quality, greater efficiency in the use of water and energy with the use of solar energy, greater efficiency in the application of nitrogen, minimization of the use of inorganic fertilizers, reduction of food waste and improvement of food security, greater involvement of farmers with sustainability concerns and promotion of more sustainable consumption.

Keywords: Agriculture · Sustainability · ICT

1 Introduction

The agricultural sector is crucial to increase the economic growth and development of the countries and to reduce poverty, especially in developing countries whose economies depend heavily on this sector [1]. In addition, the role of agriculture in rural development

O. Gervasi et al. (Eds.): ICCSA 2023 Workshops, LNCS 14108, pp. 97–109, 2023.
https://doi.org/10.1007/978-3-031-37117-2_8

is highly expressive, with regard to maintaining rural populations, protecting cultural heritage and agricultural trade, activities that shape the cultural heritage and identity of rural regions [2].

Worldwide, the use of ICT has been impactful in reducing poverty and in the economic empowerment of poor women and men in rural areas [3]. Furthermore, agriculture supports other industries by providing raw materials, leveraging demand for many products, allowing industrial expansion and wealth generation [4].

A potential mechanism to increase farmer's income is the use of improved agricultural technologies such as fertilizers, seeds and cultivation techniques. In this sense, digital technologies are most often considered as an opportunity to enable a sustainable future in agriculture and rural areas [5]. In the age of information technology, the numerous electronic devices and existing software applications can offer very important contributions to the challenges that agriculture, especially the food sector, faces such as sustainability, economy and food security [6]. However, to ensure that technological innovations increase productivity and guarantee the sustainability of the sector, Governments must promote locally sustainable ICT, such as mobile phones, Internet-based digital tools and services [4]. For example, precision agriculture is considered an instrument for more sustainable agriculture [7] that analyzes the spatial and temporal variability of agricultural fields using ICT with the aim of optimizing profit, sustainability and the protection of agro ecological services [8]. However, many farmers despite having the necessary technology to operate specifically on site, for whatever reason do not use it in practice and therefore the available ICT systems are not used to their fullest potential [7]. Thus, it is fundamental that several competences and scientific disciplines act together to help strengthen the sustainable development of agriculture through a transdisciplinary approach that can impact society in various domains. For example, the implementation of educational programs on ICT is important to ensure greater involvement of farmers and communities around sustainability issues [9].

Given the importance and recognition of the role of technologies, most countries have already adopted a national strategy for their use in the agricultural sector [10, 11]. In Europe, the European Commission has established as one of its objectives to fully connect farmers and the countryside to the digital economy in order to achieve a smarter, more modern and sustainable future for the food and agricultural sectors [12]. Despite its importance, the use of ICT to increase and ensure the sustainability of the agricultural sector is still an emerging area of research [13]. In addition, the impacts or contributions to the sustainability of agriculture are often only visible in the medium and long term. Such reasons may justify the existence of few articles in this line of research.

In this context, the main objective of this study was to investigate the state-of-the-art of ICT use in agriculture with an impact on the sustainability of the sector, based on the Preferred Reporting Items for Systematic Reviews and Meta-Analyses (PRISMA) statement.

This article is organized into four sections. In the first section, the importance of the theme that is the object of the study is justified, the objective is presented, the methodology used is briefly described and the structure of the article is presented. In the second section, the literature review is organized. The third section describes with more detail the methodology used. The fourth section presents the results including detailed content analysis. Finally, the fifth and last section presents the main conclusions and suggests guidelines for future research.

2 Background

From the 21st century, the digital paradigm brought with it a new way of thinking about innovation in the various sectors of activity through the introduction of the Internet of Things (IoT) and ICT [14]. The agricultural sector is currently facing the great challenge of increasing agricultural production to feed a growing and prosperous population in a scenario of reduced availability of natural resources and related problems. In fact, the water scarcity, the decline of soil fertility, the effects of climate change, and the rapid decrease of fertile agricultural land due to urbanization are some of the problems faced by current societies. Faced with such constraints, ICT in agriculture can provide or enhance the increase in efficiency, productivity and sustainability of the sector, providing information and promoting knowledge sharing [15]. The use of technologies, in particular emerging ones, provide multiple benefits to the agricultural sector, not only economically, but also with regard to sustainability of the use of natural resources [16].

Sustainability or sustainable development has been a topic of global interest in recent decades triggered by environmental disasters caused by human action that endanger life on the Planet. In this way, making the Planet more sustainable means harmonizing conflicts between the economic, environmental and social spheres through the rescue of ancient knowledge of traditional communities combined with the development of clean and innovative technologies capable of mitigating the impacts of human actions while, at the same time, generates financial returns and social well-being. Sustainability can be understood as meeting present human needs without compromising the needs of future generations [17]. The term "sustainable" covers other spheres in addition to the environmental issue, namely, economic, cultural and social issues [18]. The concept of agricultural sustainability encompasses valuing the internal resources of productive agricultural systems, their maintenance and, consequently, its productivity over time [19]. For agriculture to be sustainable, it will have to adopt a production model that minimally affects the environment, preserves the characteristics of agroecosystems for long periods, combines conventional and innovative practices in food cultivation, and worry about the social situation of farmers [20].

Promoting sustainability is part of the agenda of policy makers in all economies. In this sense, the impact of ICT, which have significantly increased the sharing of information, can be significant in reducing waste, increasing productivity and food security [21]. ICT are imperative to achieve long-term sustainable development [22]. Increasing agricultural production and optimizing the use of inorganic fertilizers are some of the most important objectives for agricultural and environmental sustainability [23]. Technology is an instrument of excellence to build relationships, mitigate environmental and climate impacts [24], as well as to increase environmental sustainability in regions, since it has the capacity to provide innovations and sustainability to the agricultural sector and increasing productivity as an alternative and complement to agricultural extension [10].

3 Methods

From a methodological point of view, a systematic review of the literature was carried out, which enabled data collection and subsequent analysis. For this, some criteria were defined that allow the collection of data in a reliable and replicable way [25] making the literature review process scientific and transparent [26]. The present systematic literature review was based on the PRISMA statement [27], as shown in Fig. 1.

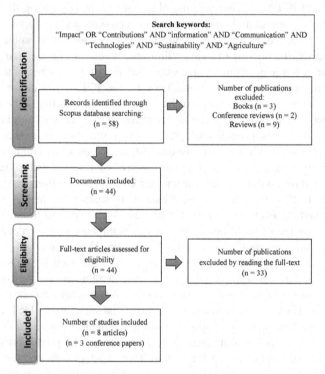

Fig. 1. PRISMA flow diagram of data collection process and analysis.

In the context of the PRISMA Statement, the Scopus database was screened. The search was performed in February 25, 2023, using the keywords "Impact" OR "Contributions" AND "Information" AND "Communication" AND "Technologies" AND "Sustainability" AND "Agriculture". A total of fifty-eight publications were found (Fig. 1). Of these, fourteen documents were removed, namely, Books (n = 3), Conference reviews (n = 2) and Reviews (n = 9), as shown in Fig. 1.

Publications were selected taking into account the following criterion: empirical studies that demonstrate evidence of the impact or contribution of ICT to sustainable agriculture. After full reading the publications, 11 publications were considered (Fig. 1). Then, for each document, information was collected about authorship and publication date, place (country and continent) where the research took place, type of study, methodology used, study objectives and findings.

4   Results and Discussion

Table 1 presents all the included publications by ascending order of publication data. As mentioned before, this table also contains information about authorship, type of study, region/country/continent where the research was developed, sample size, objectives and contributions.

The selected studies were developed in Europe (5), Asia (3), America (2) and Africa (1). Most of the studies carried out on the European Continent [8, 28–31] were case studies [8, 28, 30, 31].

An experimental study developed in Andalucia, Spain involved the development of an easy-to-use application that allowed farmers to manage reusable water and fertilizers used in the olive grove more efficiently [28], as shown in Table 1.

Other researchers [8] tested it in Italy through the use of an unmanned aerial vehicle and satellite platforms, whether the images obtained were useful and reliable to assess the conditions of cultivated areas (Table 1).

Table 1. General data, objectives and findings of the articles selected for the systematic literature review.

Author (date) [Reference]	Place Type of study Methods	Objective of the study Findings
1. Aldakhil et al. (2019) [22]	- South Asia (Asia) - Secondary study - Quantitative study - Data: data times series from 1975 to 2016 - Robust Least Square (RLS) Regression	To examine the role of ICT (e.g. telephone, mobile phone and internet), advanced technological factors (e.g. farm machinery and high-tech exports, specific growth factors (e.g. research and development spending by *per capita* income, investment flows direct foreign exchange, trade openness and industrial added value)) and the resultant carbon impact of fossil fuel emissions The results show that landlines, mobile phones and internet servers significantly influenced fossil fuel carbon emissions. Furthermore, agricultural machinery, e.g. tractors, substantially increase fossil fuel carbon emissions in a region
2. Jimenez & Castro (2019) [16]	- Colombia (America) - Experimental study - Quantitative study - Case study	To propose a prototype identification system, designed and validated to provide an information system for monitoring African oil palm crops to implement precision agriculture The results were promising and provide a good basis for the implementation of Precision Agriculture

(*continued*)

Table 1. (*continued*)

Author (date) [Reference]	Place Type of study Methods	Objective of the study Findings
3. Alcaide Zaragoza et al. (2020) [28]	- Andalucia, Southern Spain (Europe) - Quantitative study - Experimental study	To develop a mobile application for Android devices, the REUTIVAR-App, which provides farmers and technicians with an easy-to-use tool that facilitates the management of fertirrigation using reused water to irrigate olive groves The mobile application adapted the scheduling of fertirrigation to real weather conditions and adjusted the allocation of water throughout the irrigation season, avoiding additional costs to the farm. The REUTIVAR-App also showed that, thanks to the nutrient applied via water, no additional application of fertilizer was necessary, saving 100% of the fertilizers used by the farmer. In summary, the use of the application improved the efficiency of water and fertilizer use and increased farmers' involvement with sustainability concerns
4. Broad (2020) [32]	- Brooklyn, New York, United Sates (America) - Qualitative study - Case study	To examine the work of Square Roots, a Brooklyn-based vertical farming company co-founded by the entrepreneur Kimbal Musk and tech CEO Tobias Peggs Proponents of indoor vertical farming presented the enterprise as the key to the future of food, an opportunity to use technological innovation to increase local food production, bolster urban sustainability and create a world where there is "real food" for everyone. At the same time, critics have raised concerns about the costs, energy use, social impacts and overall agricultural viability of these efforts
5. Espelt (2020) [29]	- Barcelona, Spain (Europe) - Primary study - Qualitative study: qualitative interviews with the main stakeholders (CSA and suppliers) Data: Agro-ecological network generated by the 56 CSA in Barcelona, and their 177 providers	To identify Community Supported Agriculture (CSA) models with greater potential for the consumer, highlighting the role of ICT in meeting this challenge The results show that, when communities are professionalized, with optimized adoption of ICT and constituted as agro ecological platform cooperatives, they have a greater impact and greater potential to promote a model of food consumption based on agro ecology

(*continued*)

Table 1. (*continued*)

Author (date) [Reference]	Place Type of study Methods	Objective of the study Findings
6. Messina et al. (2020) [8]	- Italy (Europe) - Experimental study - Case study	To evaluate the reliability of multispectral images (MS) collected at different spatial resolutions by an unmanned aerial vehicle (UAV) and PlanetScope and Sentinel-2 satellite platforms in monitoring onion crops ("Cipolla Rossa di Tropea" Protected Geographical Indication) on three different dates. Two types of soil cover, namely, bare soil and onions were spatially identified using object-based geographic classification, and their spectral contribution was analyzed by comparing the Soil-Adjusted Vegetation Index (SAVI) calculated considering only the crop pixels (i.e. SAVI onions) and which was calculated considering only uncovered soil pixels (i.e. SAVI soil) with the SAVI of the three platforms The results showed that the satellite images, coherent and correlated with the UAV images, can be useful to evaluate the general conditions of the field while the UAV allows to discriminate localized circumscribed areas that the lower resolution of the satellites lost, where there are conditions of heterogeneity in the field, determined by abiotic or biotic stresses
7. Mylona et al. (2020) [30]	- Egeia Island of Andros (Greece) - Experimental study - Case study	To present a case study of the re-cultivation of abandoned terraces on the Aegean Island of Andros, using a climate-smart agriculture system, which involves the establishment of an extensive meteorological network to monitor the local climate and hydrometeorological forecast. Along with terrace site mapping and soil profile, the performance of cereal and legume crops was evaluated in a low-intake farming system The results revealed that terrace soil quality could be improved through cultivation to support food security and prevent land degradation. In line with global studies, this study suggests that marginal terrace cultivation is opportune through a climate-smart agriculture system as a holistic approach to improving land quality and serving as a means of combating the impacts of climate change

(*continued*)

Table 1. (*continued*)

Author (date) [Reference]	Place Type of study Methods	Objective of the study Findings
8. Fatumo et al. (2021) [21]	- Eastern Cape province, South Africa (Africa) - Primary study - Quantitative study - Case study - Data: 104 farmers out of 120 - Descriptive statistics; binary regression model; Spearman Rho correlation	To analyze the level of knowledge and the impact of ICT in the practice of family farming The results show that few farmers use some ICT tools in agriculture improving food security in their own way. Farmers share information about the availability of their individual products, resulting in waste, jeopardizing food security. However, the result of using ICT was considered beneficial
9. Khan et al. (2021) [23]	- Afghanistan (Asia) - Observational study - Primary study - Quantitative study - Data: National dataset from 7987 rural households - Regression analysis	To evaluate the potential of the mobile phone, mobile phone promotion policy, and whether the mediation role of human capital in reducing the application of inorganic fertilizers, ensuring environmental and agricultural sustainability goals The results showed that the use of the mobile phone significantly reduced the use of inorganic fertilizers by improving the human capital of farmers. In addition, evidence from the technique showed that mobile phone promotion policies decreased the application of inorganic fertilizers
10. Li et al. (2022) [33]	- Zhejiang, China (Asia) - Observational study - Primary study - Quantitative study - Data: 400 agricultures	To investigate the association between a digital extension service ("Zhe' yang' shi" WeChat app) and the adoption of soil testing and fertilization, a precision fertilization technology The empirical results show that the use of the "Zhe' yang' shi" WeChat application significantly increases the adoption of soil testing and formula fertilization. The findings enrich the literature on the influence of ICT on the behavior of farmers in adopting sustainable agricultural technology. It provides a valuable example for developing countries to promote sustainable agriculture through the use of digital technology

(*continued*)

Table 1. (*continued*)

Author (date) [Reference]	Place Type of study Methods	Objective of the study Findings
11. Medel-Jiménez et al. (2022) [31]	- Vienna, Austria (Europe) - Experimental study - Case Study	To present a comparative life cycle assessment of a conventional winter wheat production system with and without the use of a crop sensor for variable rate nitrogen application The results demonstrate that using optical crop sensors for variable rate nitrogen application could have a limited but positive environmental impact and highlights the importance of applying site-specific soil models to estimate field emissions (ICT components contributed less than 1% to all impacts assessed, namely, environmental impacts of the fertilization process only; and comparison of soil emissions simulated by DeNitrification-DeComposition with soil emissions from a production process of reference wheat), and highlights the importance of applying site-specific soil models to estimate field emissions

Another study [30] presents the case of the re-cultivation of abandoned terraces on the Aegean Island of Andros, Greece using a smart farming system to monitor and review the local climate. The results proved that the re-cultivation of marginal terraces was feasible with the use of a smart agriculture system and, this way, it was possible to improve soil quality and combat the impacts of climate change (Table 1).

Finally, another study [31] proved that the use of a crop sensor for nitrogen application has very positive environmental impacts. On the European Continent, other study [29] of observational and qualitative nature aimed, using ICT, to identify Community Supported Agriculture models with the potential to promote a more sustainable food consumption model (Table 1).

The three studies developed on the Asian continent are of observational nature [22, 23, 33], two are primary studies [23, 33] and one is a secondary study [22]. While a study [23] evaluated the potential of the mobile phone in the application of inorganic fertilizers in Afghanistan, other study [33] tested the use of a precision technology for soil and fertilization testing. The study which was based on data from a time series from 1975 to 2016 in South Asian countries [22], proved the need to develop green technologies in order to promote more sustainable agriculture. The authors support their study by stating that the technological footprint was considered the main factor that negatively affected the environment, sabotaging the United Nations Sustainable Development Goals [22]. Given the above, the authors argued that more efficient green technologies are needed to conserve the natural environment. In this context, the authors examined the role of ICT, advanced technological factors and specific growth factors and the resulting impact of fossil fuel carbon emissions in South Asia. Results proved that only specific growth factors, i.e. research and development spending, were negatively correlated with carbon emissions, reinforcing the premise that greener technologies and equipment are needed to adopt more sustainable agriculture.

In the American continent, two experimental studies were developed, one quantitative [15] and the other qualitative [32]. The quantitative study, carried out in Colombia, consisted of testing a prototype designed to monitor African oil palm crops, providing data that would support the implementation of precision agriculture in this agricultural sector [15]. The qualitative study was based on examining the work of a company located in Brooklyn that is committed to Vertical Agriculture. While advocates of this type of agriculture consider it an innovative opportunity that makes use of technology to increase local production of healthier and more sustainable food, the most skeptical question its viability due to the high energy and social costs. This situation will be overcome if this type of agriculture resorts to the use of solar energy [32].

Finally, it is worth mentioning the primary and quantitative study carried out on the African continent [21], which aimed to assess the level of knowledge and the impact of ICT on family farming based on the application of a questionnaire to 104 farm owners or respondents of a total of 120. The results showed that small farmers from a small rural community in South Africa are highly information deprived, which significantly affects their ICT awareness. And, although there are very few who use ICT, the results are beneficial. In this context, it is necessary to raise awareness among farmers about the role of ICT to improve agricultural productivity and the level of sustainability in agriculture [21].

5 Conclusion

This study intends to be another contribution to the growing academic research on the impact or contribution of ICT in the adoption of sustainable agriculture, allowing a better understanding of the phenomenon. For this, a systematic literature review was performed according the PRISMA statement. In this context, a computer-assisted bibliographical search was carried out in the Scopus database on February, 2023. The search involved the use of keywords such as: impact, contributions, information, communication, technologies, sustainability and agriculture. After applying the PRISMA statement, of the initial 58 publications, only 11 were included in this study, namely, 8 articles and 3 conference papers.

The results allowed to conclude that all publications show positive contributions, at an environmental, economic and social level, as a result of the use of ICT, namely, mobile phone, internet, APPS, sensors, servers, unmanned aerial vehicles and prototypes. Also, the publications show the contribution of AI for the adoption of a more sustainable agriculture that use less resources. Examples of this are: the improvement of soil quality and its homogeneity; greater efficiency in the use of water; the use of reusable water; greater efficiency in the use of energy; greater use of solar energy; greater efficiency in the application of nitrogen; minimization of the use of inorganic fertilizers; reduction of food waste; improvement of food security; increase of farmer engagement with sustainability concerns; and promote a more sustainable consumption.

This research is supported only by publications from the Scopus database. Despite this limitation, the quality of the systematic literature review is not affected because this is considered the most comprehensive bibliometric database in terms of peer-reviewed publications. However, other international databases, such as Web od Science should be included in future research that will support an empirical research whose study object should be the Portuguese farmers. In fact, it is intended to survey young Portuguese farmers affiliated in the association of young farmers of Portugal (AJAP). The main objective of the study should be: to verify if young farmers are concerned about the sustainability of the agriculture they practice and, to what extent, do they use ICT in their daily lives in order to achieve the agriculture sustainability.

Acknowledgments. The authors are grateful to the Foundation for Science and Technology (FCT, Portugal) for financial support through national funds FCT/MCTES (PIDDAC) to CIMO (UIDB/00690/2020 and UIDP/00690/2020) and SusTEC (LA/P/0007/2020).

References

1. Slafer, G., Savin, R.: Comparative performance of barley and wheat across a wide range of yielding conditions. Does barley outyield wheat consistently in low-yielding conditions?. Eur. J. Agron. **143**, 1–8 (2023)
2. Ragkos, A., Theodoridis, A., Batzios, A., Batzios, C., Vazakidis, A.: Multifunctional agriculture and ICT: incompatibility or a recipe for territorial development? CEUR Workshop Proc. **2030**, 371–376 (2017)
3. Golmohammadi, T.: Rural tele-centers in sustainable agriculture and rural development in Iran: situations and problems (case study: South Khorasan province - east of Iran). CEUR Workshop Proc. **1152**, 707–725 (2011)
4. Chandio, A., Gokmenoglu, K., Sethi, N., Ozdemir, D., Jiang, Y.: Examining the impacts of technological advancement on cereal production in ASEAN countries: does information and communication technology matter? Eur. J. Agron. **144**, 126747 (2023)
5. Rijswijk, K., Klerkx, L., Bacco, M., Scotti, I., Brunori, G.: Digital transformation of agriculture and rural areas: a socio-cyber-physical system framework to support responsibilisation. J. Rural Stud. **85**, 79–90 (2021)
6. Durresi, M.: (Bio)Sensor integration with ICT tools for supplying chain management and traceability in agriculture. Compr. Anal. Chem. **74**, 389–413 (2016)
7. Lindblom, J., Lundström, C., Ljung, M., Jonsson, A.: Promoting sustainable intensification in precision agriculture: review of decision support systems development and strategies. Precis. Agric. **18**(3), 309–331 (2016). https://doi.org/10.1007/s11119-016-9491-4
8. Messina, G., Peña, J.M., Vizzari, M., Modica, G.: A comparison of UAV and satellites multispectral imagery in monitoring onion crop. An application in the 'Cipolla Rossa di Tropea' (Italy). Remote Sens. **12**(20), 1–27 (2020)
9. Klimova, A., Rondeau, E., Andersson, K., Rybin, A., Zaslavsky, A.: An international Master's program in green ICT as a contribution to sustainable development. J. Cleaner Prod. **135**, 223–239 (2016)
10. Haggag, W.M.: Agricultural digitalization and rural development in COVID-19 response plans: a review article. Int. J. Agric. Technol. **17**(1), 67–74 (2021)
11. Trendov, N.M., Varas, S., Zeng, M.: Digital Technologies in Agriculture and Rural Areas - Status Report. Food and Agriculture Organization of the United Nations, Rome (2019)

12. Commission, E.: The Future of Food and Farming. European Commission, Brussels (2017)
13. Ratten, V.: Social entrepreneurship through digital communication in farming. World J. Entrepreneurship Manag. Sustain. Dev. **14**(1), 99–110 (2018)
14. Bucci, G., Bentivoglio, D., Finco, A., Belletti, M.: Exploring the impact of innovation adoption in agriculture: how and where precision agriculture technologies can be suitable for the Italian farm system? IOP Conf. Ser. Earth Environ. Sci. **275**(1), 012004 (2019)
15. Awuor, F., Kimeli, K., Rabah, K., Rambim, D.: ICT solution architecture for agriculture. In: 2013 IST-Africa Conference & Exhibition, pp. 1–7 (2013)
16. Jimenez, J.C., Castro, K.A.C.: Design of an identification system for crop monitoring as first step to implementing precision agriculture technology: the case of African palm. Commun. Comput. Inf. Sci. **1027**, 353–363 (2019)
17. United Nations: Report of the World Commission on Environment and Development. United Nations, Rio de Janeiro, Brazil (1988)
18. Lírio, E., Arnholz, E., Martins, L., Scalzer, J.: Agricultura sustentável: uma ferramenta para educação ambiental no campo. Revista Educação Ambiental em Ação **46**, 1–19 (2013)
19. Gomes, E., Mello, J., Mangabeira, J.: Estudo da sustentabilidade agrícola em um município amazônico com análise envoltória de dados. Pesquisa Operacional **29**(1), 23–42 (2009)
20. Ehlers, E., Veiga, J.: O que se entende por Agricultura Sustentável? Dissertação de Mestrado em Ciência Ambiental, Universidade de São Paulo, Brasil (1994)
21. Fatumo, D.E., Ngwenya, S., Shibeshi, Z., Aduradola, O.J., Azeez, A.N.: Impact of information and communication technology in enhancing food security in a rural area: Alice community as a case study. In: 2021 IST-Africa Conference (IST-Africa), pp. 1–8 (2021)
22. Aldakhil, A.M., Adyia Zaheer, A., Younas, S., Nassani, A.A., Abro, M.M.Q., Zaman, A.M.: Efficiently managing green information and communication technologies, high-technology exports, and research and development expenditures: a case study. J. Cleaner Prod. **240**, 118164 (2019)
23. Khan, N., Ray, R.L., Kassem, H.S., Ansah, S., Zhang, S.: Toward cleaner production: can mobile phone technology help reduce inorganic fertilizer application? Evidence using a national level dataset. Land **10**(10), 1023 (2021)
24. Chen, M., Zhang, L., Teng, F., Wang, Z., Li, Y.: Climate technology transfer in BRI era: needs, priorities, and barriers from receivers' perspective. Ecosyst. Health Sustain. **6**(1), 1–12 (2020)
25. Xiao, Y., Watson, M.: Guidance on conducting a systematic literature review. J. Plan. Educ. Res. **39**, 93–112 (2019)
26. Tranfield, D., Denyer, D., Smart, P.: Towards a methodology for developing evidence informed management knowledge by means of systematic review. Braz. J. Manag. **14**(3), 207–222 (2003)
27. Moher, D., Liberati, A., Tetzlaff, J., Altman, D.G.: The PRISMA group: preferred reporting items for systematic reviews and meta-analyses: the PRISMA statement. PLoS Med. **6**(7), e1000097 (2009)
28. Alcaide Zaragoza, C., González Perea, R., Fernández García, I., Camacho Poyato, E., Rodríguez Díaz, J.A.: Open source application for optimum irrigation and fertilization using reclaimed water in olive orchards. Comput. Electron. Agric. **173**, 105407 (2020)
29. Espelt, R.: Agroecology prosumption: the role of CSA networks. J. Rural. Stud. **79**, 269–275 (2020)
30. Mylona, P., Sakellariou, M., Giannakopoulos, C., Psiloglou, B., Kitsara, G.: Terrace landscapes as green infrastructures for a climate-smart agriculture to mitigate climate change impacts. CEUR Workshop Proc. **2761**, 236–243 (2020)
31. Medel-Jiménez, F., Piringer, G., Gronauer, A., Krexner, T., Kral, I.: Modelling soil emissions and precision agriculture in fertilization life cycle assessment - a case study of wheat production in Austria. J. Cleaner Prod. **380**, 134841 (2022)

32. Broad, G.M.: Know your indoor farmer: square roots, techno-local food, and transparency as publicity. Am. Behav. Sci. **64**(11), 1588–1606 (2020)
33. Li, B., Zhuo, N., Ji, C., Zhu, Q.: Influence of smartphone-based digital extension service on farmers' sustainable agricultural technology adoption in China. Int. J. Environ. Res. Public Health **19**(15), 9639 (2022)

Identification of Bus Stations on the Urban Transport Network Based on GPS Tracking Data

Washington Daniel Torres Guin⬤, Luis Enrique Chuquimarca Jiménez[(✉)] ⬤,
Samuel Baldomero Bustos Gaibor⬤, José Miguel Sánchez Aquino⬤,
and Marjorie Alexandra Coronel Suárez⬤

Facultad de Sistemas y Telecomunicaciones, Universidad Estatal Península de Santa Elena,
Santa Elena, Ecuador
lchuquimarca@upse.edu.ec

Abstract. In contemporary urban settings, inhabitants use public transportation to engage in events and commercial transactions; therefore, transportation holds significant relevance. This study introduces an approach for identifying critical public transportation stations based on integrating information from sensors on the pedestrian walkway of the sector and GPS locations. Urban transportation systems can incorporate technologies that generate large amounts of information, which can be analyzed to obtain valuable insights related to mobility. In the first place, the topology of the road network is considered as the dynamic characteristics of the flow of traffic, to develop a mechanism that identifies the autobus stations considering the spatiotemporal ones from the GPS traces obtained from the spatial detection of the affluence of people. Later, an algorithm is presented that uses the structure of the road network and the influence of traffic between nearby roads to identify critical roads based on traffic volume. Finally, the bus-GPS track sector data compiled in Santa Elena, Ecuador is analyzed. We conducted a thorough analysis to observe the spatiotemporal changes in bus services, the most relevant routes, and intersections. Furthermore, the correlation coefficient has been used to evaluate the algorithm's performance in identifying multiple critical points. The findings indicate that this method is more effective and practical than the conventional congestion index analysis. The research carried out should be useful in the management of urban transport and the creation of alternative stations.

Keywords: Urban Transport · Big Data · GPS Trajectories · Autobus Stations

1 Introduction

The process of urbanization in cities has generated a growing need for citizen mobility, making it a critical issue. The geographical structure of urban environments implies that people must move around to carry out social and economic activities. In this sense, public transportation systems are the cornerstone of urban mobility, representing the population's most efficient, sustainable, and economical transportation mode [1]. Understanding the relationship between citizen flow to critical points within the urban area and public transportation is essential to improving city mobility. To meet the changing demands of urban areas, such as housing, offices, and markets, drivers make additional unplanned stations based on passengers' needs rather than the municipality's planned stations. Some of these stations are maintained and become designated long-term stations. Therefore, most unplanned autobus stations are possible candidates for new autobus stations due to increased public demand from rapid urbanization. Designing a platform to extract location and real-time data from users at these unplanned autobus stations provides an accurate estimate of the new autobus stations required by public authorities. On the other hand, the collected information can help travelers know all autobus stations and their schedules through application interfaces, making travel more scheduled and efficient. Therefore, the study of the infrastructure of the urban public transport network in the cities has received considerable attention in research and practice [2, 3]. Modern smart cities are using technology to improve urban services [4]. One of the research fields related to smart cities is Intelligent Transportation Systems (ITS), which use technological systems to track the location of buses and improve mobility regarding road service for buses, cars, and pedestrians. Additionally, large amounts of urban data can be collected to understand citizen mobility better [5].

The urban public transportation system is a complex network comprising a physical road network and a traffic demand network. In turn, it is made up of intersections and street segments. The flow of traffic on the traffic demand network reflects the movement of vehicles off the roadway. However, the street sections of the urban transit network do not have the same importance, because some paths or stations are less traveled. Therefore, it is crucial to acknowledge the significance of proper road usage and optimal station placement within road networks. Furthermore, identifying critical routes and stations is essential to alleviate urban traffic congestion, develop emergency response plans, and implementing effective urban transportation planning and management.

One of the main objectives of the analysis of the urban transport network is to determine the most important routes and stations that directly imply the information on the routes of the urban public transport lines, the duration of the journey and distances between the stations, which would be useful to design a more efficient urban transport network. Various methods have been studied in the literature to identify metrics in quantifiable graphs, such as the distance between stations and the number of elementary travel lines [6]. Therefore, it is possible to use it to quantify the relative importance of stations in an urban road network. However, it needs to consider detailed traffic flow. In the same way, we proposed a measure of centrality called DelayFlow, which considers the time of delay of the trip and the volume of the flow of passengers, to decide the critical stations in an urban transport network [7]. In addition, a method that can determine the critical stations of the urban transport network according to the measure of the local system [8, 9]. On the other hand, a fundamental objective of urban transportation road network analysis is to identify critical routes. Various measures have been proposed to evaluate the criticality of routes, some of which can be found in studies [10, 11].

Since 2012, Big Data has become an access point for research in all areas of life, such as academia, industry, education, medical services, and government agencies, among others. Big Data analysis is of great importance in multiple areas of life. Large traffic data in the city can be used effectively to improve transport management and urban road planning. The Global Positioning System (GPS) sensor in mobile vehicles has been used to automate data extraction related to traffic and urban roads. As an essential part of the public transportation system, buses are one of the most popular means of transportation that serve citizens in urban and suburban areas. GPS trajectory data from buses contain a wealth of spatiotemporal information, which enables the potential for gaining knowledge in understanding urban commerce, human mobility behavior, and road network dynamics. Understanding the dynamics of mobility is crucial to improving transport systems. For example, to improve the quality of the urban bus services, a method for detecting abnormal tray sectors online is proposed to analyze the points in which the buses are stopped with the longest time to collect or leave users. This proposed method was evaluated based on GPS trajectories of the buses in real time, the travel patrons of the passengers on the entire route were modeled based on GPS trajectories of the urban buses for the identification of stations [13, 14]. According to this model, specific parameters were established to evaluate the performance of urban road transportation. The effectiveness of the proposed algorithm was validated using GPS data from buses collected in Santa Elena, Ecuador. The results revealed that the method could provide high-quality inspection and detailed information about urban traffic to construct stations in the urban road network. However, there are several challenges in identifying autobus stations, especially unplanned ones. Unplanned autobus stations may also include ad-hoc locations due to traffic congestion or other similar factors and may not necessarily be actual boarding points for passengers.

The urban transport network is a dynamic multimodal network that includes road networks with static structural characteristics on the roads and traffic flow with dynamic characteristics. Methodologies for identifying critical stations and segments of the urban transport network associated with the static structure have been extensively researched in the last decade. However, only some studies have considered the dynamic traffic charac-teristics in the urban transport network. In this article, we will develop a complex network algorithm to capture the urban transport network's static and dynamic characteristics. The main contributions are summarized below:

– An urban transport network is proposed through the combination of the static structure of the road network and the dynamic traffic flow. The static structure represents the roads that connect the city, while GPS data provides detailed information about dynamic changes in urban traffic flow. Therefore, the proposed model allows for capturing both the temporal and spatial characteristics of the urban transport network.
– As a case study, a comprehensive analysis was conducted using data collected from the GPS-equipped buses in Santa Elena, Ecuador, to visualize the spatiotemporal changes in bus services, critical routes, and critical stations. Furthermore, the corre-lation coefficient was used to quantify the algorithm's performance in identifying mul-tiple critical points. The results demonstrate that the proposed algorithm effectively identifies critical lanes and stations in the urban transport network.

The rest of this document is organized as follows. In Sect. 2, a weighted complex network is proposed for an urban transport network. Next, Sect. 3 provides a mixed Implementation of intelligent solutions in the urban transport system. Section 4 presents the results of the benefits of urban public transport by incorporating state-of-the-art technologies. Finally, the conclusions and our future work are presented in Sect. 5.

2 Proposed System

Complex networks have been applied in various fields, such as biology, engineering, medical science, social sciences, telecommunications, transportation, and more. Of course, the application of the complex networks focused on the study of the transport network has greater relevance. For the urban transport network, there is a dual alternative representation of the road network, where its stations become nodes. This approach allows for analyzing and studying the relevant topological characteristics of the urban transportation network [15].

Depending on the direction of the roads, there is unidirectional and bidirectional traffic on the urban transport network. The circulation of descending traffic is directly influenced by ascending traffic. Similarly, the flow of ascending traffic is also affected by the flow of descending traffic in case of blockages. The importance of the stations in the urban transport network on the ground is affected by its ascending and descending station, but also by the topology of the urban road network. Therefore, the importance of nodes in the urban transportation network is examined from two perspectives: the spatial position of the station in the static road network and the dynamics of traffic flow in the urban transportation network.

2.1 Description and Pre-processing of Data

The GPS trajectory data are compiled in the city of Santa Elena, Ecuador. Santa Elena is the capital of the province of Santa Elena in zone 5 of Ecuador. There are 39,681 inhabitants in the urban sector of the province of Santa Elena [16]. The urban area of Santa Elena is 632.4 square kilometers (see Fig. 1). There are 8 urban transport cooperatives with 240 units in the province of Santa Elena in the cities of La Libertad, Salinas, and Santa Elena [17]. The data from the GPS tray sector of the buses has been compiled from September to December 2020. The GPS log is periodically sent to the data center via a GPS-enabled device on board the bus. Each record provides the identification, length, latitude, time stamp, movement speed, direction and operating status of the vehicle. The sampling interval of the trajectories point is 30 s.

Raw GPS tracking data often contains abnormal signals due to random and systematic errors. However, to address missing points in time intervals of less than 30 s, the linear interpolation method adds a missing point between adjacent positions in the urban road network. In this article, the characteristics of the urban transport network are analyzed for a period of one hour.

Data analysis involves collecting and processing raw data to extract relevant information that provides supporting evidence for decision-making (see Fig. 2). Therefore, a space-time algorithm of the urban transport network was built based on GPS track sector data. The suitable main network model includes approximately 235 bus service stations.

The data analysis process begins and ends in real time. In urban environments, this involves collecting raw data from a city, such as in the case of Santa Elena. For him, the data analysis process on the GPS trajectories of the public urban transport buses is made up of several phases. Initially, the raw data needs to be processed, which involves organizing them into tables, reviewing datasets, and refining them to detect corrupt or inaccurate records. After that, the analysis of the data is carried out using algorithms

Fig. 1. Map of Expansion Urbana-Ciudad Santa Elena (GAD)

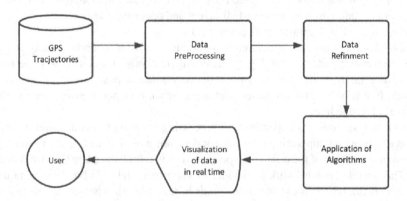

Fig. 2. Data analysis workflow applied in this work.

that have the objective of describing the behavior of urban transport. Urban data often come from diverse and dynamic sources, such as sensors and mobile devices, making it necessary to detect inaccuracies for urban data analysis. Finally, the results are typically communicated to the user using visualization techniques.

The objective of the visualization of data is to efficiently show the quantities measured through graphs. However, urban data analysis involves the combination of quantitative and qualitative data, which requires more advanced means of visualizing results effectively. Since urban data often have a vital geographic component, urban data visualization combines classical statistical charts with geographic information systems (GIS).

2.2 Analysis of the Conditions of Urban Traffic

A system of evaluation of the congestion of the traffic according to the conditions of the road traffic of the province has been established. Urban public transport is one of the many components that the National Traffic Agency (NTA) tries to manage and control, according to the established statutes and regulations [18]. However, NTA mentions that urban transport buses commonly have a problem due to infractions received regarding speed limits. NTA seeks an alternative to reduce accidents and violations caused by public transport, it presents information systems for road routes in public transport to improve traffic management.

The buses are allowed to move at 50 km/h inside the urban center following the NTA [19]. The congestion level in a city varies over time and space, depending on the daily travel demand of urban residents. The variation in rural traffic occurs due to congestion on the road due to business hours. The moons increase gradually, and the maximum peaks are at 7:00 am and 6:00 pm. The main reason is the entrance to the institutions and exit from the same. On weekends, vehicle congestion is less than on weekdays. However, this is because the activities of urban residents tend to be more regular on weekdays than on weekends.

2.3 Data Collection System

The bus stations are the places where an autobus stations for a finite duration. Therefore, it is possible to extract two locations from the urban roads using the GPS device, observing the points where the speed of the bus is zero. In order to analyze the spatio-temporal characteristics of the locations of the stations, a field study was carried out to extract several GPS points from the stations on the urban roads considering designated stations and unscheduled stations.

The special coverage average between stations is between 100 m, however, for some urban bus stations they can go further than 100 m. Therefore, it is essential to consider that both the spatial and temporal distribution of bus stations exhibit high variability, making it challenging to use a threshold-based approach to detect autobus stations automatically. The average waiting time for buses at non-designated stations also varies considerably.

2.4 Passenger Information System

A passenger information system is based on a digital monitor designed to track the location of each bus using GPS technology. In addition, all the information is stored and processed on a web server that provides bus locations in real time, together with web applications for use by each passenger (see Fig. 3).

The design of the passenger information system uses a data base and a server connected to the satellite. The GPS is installed in each bus and the information screens are installed in each bus station. In addition, the passenger information will be available at the stations as well as on their mobile devices. Finally, the passenger information system would be monitored from the central Urban Public Transport office in the city of Santa Elena.

2.5   Mobile GPS Monitoring Device

There is a GPS tracking module on the bus, together with a GSM modem and a micro-controller that serves to transmit information in the form of bus position coordinates. The latitude and longitude information are stored on the server, which data are in real time. In addition, the bus routes, departure and arrival time, number of passengers and bus speed can be stored.

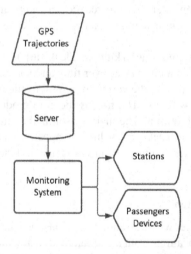

Fig. 3. Scheme of the passenger information system

The electronic devices obtain the data from the GPS and periodically transmit and verify the information on the server. The GPS device sends the information to the server using the SIM card to later download the information to the passenger application. To obtain the signal from the satellite, the GPS device is activated, which is able to obtain the current location of the bus (latitude and length) in each time interval.

With a mobile application for the passenger, you can facilitate the arrival at destinations with the suitable number of buses, which will be found in an interactive way with a pleasant user interface. The users with the application of the passenger information system will tend to access the current position of the bus until the time of arrival at the station. In addition, the system also refreshes or updates the coordinates of the time of arrival of the bus to the passengers.

When the passenger enters the bus, the information about the unit is updated in a database, which is available to the rest of users, which can decide whether there are places available on the bus. In addition, users have the ability to see the bus route or other information contained in the application. On the other hand, when selecting the bus, the application shows its position on the user's screen and informs the time of arrival and departure.

A modern passenger information service is a control and monitoring system that is used to provide a reliable and real-time transport base that helps plan the transport system of the city of Santa Elena. In addition, it is an intelligent transport system for urban areas in Ecuador, especially in the city of Santa Elena.

3   Intelligent Urban Transport System

An intelligent urban transport system for the needs of the city of Santa Elena implies implementing intelligent solutions in the existing urban transport system. In the big cities there are street networks for urban transport using buses, which is a dominant form of public transport. Therefore, a paradigm shift is needed in the modern urban transportation system.

Smart solutions for urban transport should include intelligent issuance of tickets and automated collection of fares; fast transit bus systems: buses; and autobus stations based on smart GPS.

3.1   Issuance and Automated Collection of Tickets

The use of urban public transport helps to reduce road congestion, managing to increase the mobility of people, which in turn indirectly contributes to the productivity of the city of Santa Elena. The automated issuance of tickets is one of the technologies that reduce the operating cost and facilitate passages to the passengers of urban public transport. Automatic ticket issuing is a system that utilizes a microchip, embedded in a smart card, to store the information of a travel ticket electronically. The automated issuance of tickets is a useful tool for the sectors of urban public transport and the bodies in charge due to which they can track the number of passengers on the routes, the time taken by the passengers, and the accounting of earnings is carried like a box common This system will help for future planning in the development of urban public transport routes. Additionally, tickets are more secure against fraudulent activities. The electronic card can be deactivated once the theft is reported, and the remaining balance can be refunded or transferred to a new electronic card. Automated ticket issuing also strengthens the case for mobile ticketing. Figure 4 shows a schematic of the electronic card process for issuing tickets to passengers.

3.2   Fast Transit Bus Route

The traffic congestion on the main routes of Santa Elena, La Libertad, and Salinas poses a challenge to the mobility of urban public transportation, including buses. The limitations for buses mobility are:

−   Size and number of buses in the fleet.

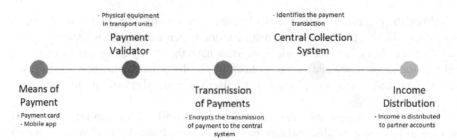

Fig. 4. Scheme of the passenger information system

– Congestion of vehicles on the main urban roads at peak hours.
– Technology implemented on the buses.

A possible solution to the limitations mentioned in urban public transportation mobility is implementing a system known as Bus Rapid Transit (BRT), which offers a high-quality urban service that is fast, comfortable, and affordable urban service for all passengers. BRT utilizes exclusive bus lanes, the priority right of way for buses, level boarding platforms, and other quality services like information technology. Therefore, this allows for combining the flexibility of buses with the high-performance standards and design of metro transportation systems, resulting in a surface-level transportation style like a metro. The proposal is to construct an exclusive bus lane like a metro line.

The exclusive rails for the buses guarantee a fast and reliable service, which is why it is essential to have exclusive rails on the sides of the road on the main avenues that possess only one-way, to be effective and free of obstacles. The central rails must be separated from the other vehicle and motor rails with a continuous physical divider.

In the city center, BRT systems have a shared central station instead of two separate autobus stations, one for each direction. These stations are in the middle of the roadway, between both directions of traffic, and provide access to buses traveling in both directions.

The central stations are more compact and take up less space than two edge stations, making them more cost-effective in construction and operation than bus stations on both sides of the bus lanes.

The central stations managed to optimize the use of space on the street.

3.3 Bus System and Bus Stations Based on GPS

The current issue in the bus transportation system of the city of Santa Elena is the need for real-time information for passengers regarding the location of buses and arrival/departure schedules. Due to the lack of information in real time, passengers arrive late at work and, at times, are forced to take private transport such as taxis. The passenger information system facilitates access to information about buses, timetables and estimated arrival times. It is possible to obtain the location of the buses by enabling them with GPS technology (see Fig. 5).

The studies in the city of Santa Elena show that some of the passengers arrive late at their destination because they decide to wait for a bus without knowing if the bus is arriving punctually. On the other hand, the location of the buses in the cities would be beneficial for the passenger to plan the exit to the bus station.

The information system for passengers is based on a GPS track stored in the cloud that incorporates a prediction algorithm to provide real-time information about the bus service. The passenger information system provides at any time given the location of the buses and can predict the time of arrival of the bus to the station. This technology allows travelers to obtain information on the number of passengers in real time, in addition, through interfaces on websites, applications for smart phones and screens of stations at autobus stations.

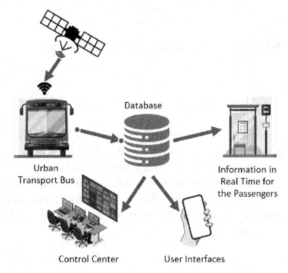

Fig. 5. GPS-based bus and bus station transport system diagram

4 Results

The architecture of the proposed system consists of several modules through which passengers can draw the maximum benefit from urban public transport through the incorporation of latest generation technologies. The architecture can be divided into three modules:

- Bus Transmitter Module;
- Bus Control Module;
- Passenger Service Module.

4.1 Bus Transmitter Module

The bus location is obtained through a GPS module connected to a high-performance single-board computer called Raspberry Pi (Rpi) and a GSM module (see Fig. 6). The

GPS module provides the bus location, which the Rpi processes. Additionally, data from a passenger count sensor on the bus is collected and processed by the Rpi, and updates are transmitted via WiFi. The sensor for counting the number of passengers can be an infrared sensor. The WiFi/GSM module transmits the information to the bus terminal control module.

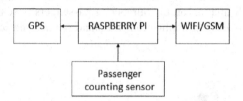

Fig. 6. Block Diagram of the Bus Transmitter Module.

4.2 Bus Control Module

The module consists of a WiFi-enabled RPI that receives the bus coordinates, arrival times, and passenger information on board. Subsequently, the RPI processes this information and sends it in real time to a central server. It can be accessed through a user interface like a smartphone application and displayed in real time at the bus station (see Fig. 7). Passengers can check live updates of the location and arrival times of their desired bus at the station from the comfort of their homes through the smartphone application that allows wireless internet access.

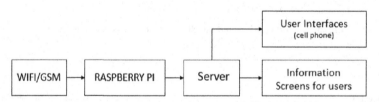

Fig. 7. Block diagram of the bus control module.

4.3 Passenger Service Module

The passenger service module consists of a smartphone with an application to locate the bus and estimate its arrival time at the station. As such, it is beneficial for passengers to plan their departure from home to the bus station, having advance information about the bus arrival time. The passenger service module may also include screens at the bus stations to display the coordinates and arrival schedules of the buses. Additionally, information about the number of passengers on board the bus is also reflected in the information channels. Passengers can access the schedule information through the wireless Internet connection available on smartphones. By using the passenger information system in real time, we can also respond quickly to complicated situations such as robots through the implementation of panic buttons.

5 Conclusion

The urban public transport buses in the cities of Santa Elena, La Libertad and Salinas in Ecuador, were inspired to plan viable technological solutions in an efficient way for the sustainable growth of the cities and their inhabitants. The objective of having a management and monitoring system in these cities is a challenging aspect, but it can be achieved with the active participation of citizens. In this work, a proposal was presented in one of the sectors of an intelligent city, which is transport in modernized urban buses. Different solutions related to urban public transport were compared, such as the BRT system, electronic cards for tickets, buses with GPS technology and bus stations with information screens interconnected to a central cloud system. In the proposed model, passengers will not have to wait for buses without prior planning. Models have been implemented that allow passengers to accurately access information about the location of buses and arrival/departure schedules by incorporating cutting-edge technological solutions into the existing bus transportation system. Passengers can now obtain information about urban transportation through smartphone applications. The limitation of the project lies in the lack of detailed information regarding the implementation process and specific challenges encountered. While the study presents an approach to identify critical public transportation stations through the integration of sensor information and GPS locations.

In future work, it is important to continue exploring the potential of integrating advanced technologies into urban transportation systems. The approach proposed in this study, which combines sensor information from pedestrian walkways and GPS locations, shows promise in identifying critical public transportation stations. Future research can focus on refining and expanding this approach to larger urban areas, evaluating its effectiveness in diverse urban contexts, and integrating it with other smart city initiatives.

References

1. Grava, S.: Urban transportation systems. Choices for communities (2003)
2. Feng, S., Hu, B., Nie, C., Shen, X.: Empirical study on a directed and weighted bus transport network in China. Physica A **441**, 85–92 (2016)
3. Xing, Y., Lu, J., Chen, S.: Weighted complex network analysis of shanghai rail transit system. Discrete Dyn. Nat. Soc. (2016)
4. Deakin, M.: From intelligent to smart cities. In: Smart Cities. Routledge, pp. 27–44 (2013)
5. Putra, A.S., Warnars, H.L.H.S., Gaol, F.L., Soewito. B., Abdurachman, E.: A proposed surveillance model in an intelligent transportation system (ITS). In: 2018 Indonesian Association for Pattern Recognition International Conference (INAPR), pp. 156–160. IEEE (2018)
6. Hawick, K., James, H.: Node importance ranking and scaling properties of some complex road networks (2007)
7. Cheng, Y.Y., Lee, R.K.-W., Lim, E.P., Zhu, F.: DelayFlow centrality for identifying critical nodes in transportation networks. In: Proceedings of the 2013 IEEE/ACM International Conference on Advances in Social Networks Analysis and Mining, pp. 1462–1463 (2013)

8. Shao-Hai, L., Jin-Zhao, W., Na, A.: An identification method for the hub node of urban transport network based on the local modularity. J. Theor. Appl. Inf. Technol. **48** (2013)
9. Zhang, X., Li, W., Deng, J., Wang, T.: Research on hub node identification of the public transport network of Guilin based on complex network theory. In: CICTP 2014: Safe, Smart, and Sustainable Multimodal Transportation Systems, pp. 1302–1309 (2014)
10. Scott, D.M., Novak, D.C., Aultman-Hall, L., Guo, F.: Network robustness index: a new method for identifying critical links and evaluating the performance of transportation networks. J. Transp. Geogr. **14**, 215–227 (2006)
11. Taylor, M.A., Sekhar, S.V., D'Este, G.M.: Application of accessibility-based methods for vulnerability analysis of strategic road networks. Netw. Spat. Econ. **6**, 267–291 (2006)
12. Zhang, H., Dai, L.: Mobility prediction: a survey on state-of-the-art schemes and future applications. IEEE Access **7**, 802–822 (2018)
13. Harb, R., Yan, X., Radwan, E., Su, X.: Exploring precrash maneuvers using classification trees and random forests. Accid. Anal. Prev. **41**, 98–107 (2009)
14. Bermingham, L., Lee, I.: A probabilistic stop and move classifier for noisy GPS trajectories. Data Min. Knowl. Disc. **32**(6), 1634–1662 (2018). https://doi.org/10.1007/s10618-018-0568-8
15. De Vos, J.: The influence of land use and mobility policy on travel behavior: a comparative case study of Flanders and the Netherlands. J. Transp. Land Use **8**, 171–190 (2015)
16. Acosta, R.Á., Guale, L.N., Pineda, F.C., Tarabó, A.E.M.: Production and commercialization of fish skin tanning products, Santa Elena-Ecuador. J. Soc. Sci. **26**, 353–367 (2020)
17. Arce Bastidas, R.F., Suárez Domínguez, E., Solís Argandoña, E.V., Argudo Guevara, N.: Analysis of tourist products: the case of Península de Santa Elena, Ecuador, Podium, pp. 139–158 (2020)
18. Tinoco, W.W., Montalvan, E.A., Tinoco, W.W., et al.: Análisis Del Expenditure Tributario En La Exoneración De Impuestos A La Piedad Vehicular: Caso De Estudio De Santa Elena, 2021. Revista Universidad de Guayaquil **135**, 45–54 (2022)
19. Pico, Á.A.R., Jumbo, K.J.S., Torres, L.J.A.: Traffic ordering models in the City of Loja. Science **21**, 31–43 (2019)

Augmented Computing and Smart Cities Sustainability

Teresa Guarda[1,2(✉)] ⓘ, Isabel Lopes[2,3] ⓘ, Samuel Bustos[1] ⓘ, Isabel Ribeiro[4,5] ⓘ,
and António Fernandes[4,5] ⓘ

[1] Universidad Estatal Peninsula de Santa Elena, La Libertad, Ecuador
tguarda@gmail.com
[2] Algoritmi Centre, Minho University, Guimarães, Portugal
[3] Applied Management Research Unit (UNIAG) - Instituto Politécnico de Bragança (IPB),
5300-253 Bragança, Portugal
[4] Centro de Investigação de Montanha (CIMO) - Instituto Politécnico de Bragança, Bragança,
Portugal
[5] Laboratório Associado para a Sustentabilidade e Tecnologia em Regiões de Montanha
(SusTEC) - Instituto Politécnico de Bragança, Bragança, Portugal

Abstract. Smart Cities promote a great improvement in urban environments in terms of sustainability, leveraged by the use of technologies that allow the optimization and monitoring of different systems, from waste management systems to public safety. There are several technologies that can play a key role in this process, highlighting augmented computing, augmented reality, virtual reality, artificial intelligence, and machine learning. In this context, smart cities collects and analyses, optimizing the various systems processes. There are many challenges that arise in order to have sustainable smart cities, challenges in terms of privacy and data security, but also in promoting inclusion and equity. It is important to adopt an inclusive and holistic approach that involves all stakeholders and takes into account the specific needs and objectives of a city. With this in mind, the adoption of augmented computing technologies facilitates the creation of more livable and also more sustainable urban environments. The main objective of this work is to explore the area of augmented computing in the context of smart cities sustainability.

Keywords: Augmented Computing · Smart City · Virtual and Augmented
Reality · Machine Learning · Artificial Intelligence

1 Introduction

Sustainability is becoming a priority in all facets of society and urban environments around the world are recognizing its role in creating a sustainable future. With buildings consuming a significant proportion of global energy and therefore directly contributing to a city's overall environmental impact there is great momentum to improve this situation through the use of interconnected technologies (Aurigi & Odendaal, 2021).

O. Gervasi et al. (Eds.): ICCSA 2023 Workshops, LNCS 14108, pp. 123–132, 2023.
https://doi.org/10.1007/978-3-031-37117-2_10

The perspective of sustainability applied to the urban environment, in order to achieve the necessary success to implement the related fundamental rights, gives rise to the concept of a sustainable city (Al Sharif & Pokharel, 2022), from an environmental point of view, corresponding to the optimization of the relationship between people and the environment, with a view to guaranteeing natural resources for future generations.

In a smart city, the environment, economy and society are necessarily intertwined and coexist in a single ecosystem. The connectivity infrastructure is fundamental in providing the services and processes offered (Allam, Sharifi, Bibri, Jones, & Krogstie, 2022).

Smart cities use technologies, programs, data and digital solutions with the aim of improving the quality of life of their inhabitants (Casini, 2017). In this context, augmented computing has a transformative potential in terms of the functioning of smart cities, making them more efficient, sustainable and also livable (Bibri & Krogstie, 2017).

Smart cities make use of various technologies, such as sensors, IoT devices, and monitoring solutions (Saleem, Zeebaree, Zeebaree, & Abdulazeez, 2020), which allow optimizing the various city systems, such as energy, waste, and transport, with the aim of improve the efficiency and sustainability of urban areas (Strielkowski, Veinbender, Tvaronavičienė, & Lace, 2020). As example we can have smart traffic lights can use real-time data to optimize traffic flow, thus reducing congestion and fuel consumption, and also smart buildings can use sensors to monitor energy consumption and thus optimize building systems, reducing the energy consumption. For example, smart waste management systems can use sensors to optimize waste collection, reducing the energy and fuel needed by garbage trucks. With intelligent transport systems is possible optimize the traffic flow and encourage citizens to use alternative transports (public transports, bicycle's, electrics, and others), and that can also help reducing carbon emissions (Meneguette, De Grande, & Loureiro, 2018).

The main objective of this work is to explore the area of cognitive computing in the context of smart cities sustainability, with the aim to have a perception of the challenges and impact of augmented computing (AC).

This work is organized in five sections. The second section provides an overview of augmented computing and the technologies used. The third is about the smart city and its sustainability, focusing on sustainable development. The fourth section explores the challenges of new technologies, specifically AC and its impact on the sustainability of smart cities. The last section presents the conclusions.

2 Augmented Computing

The first computational systems, and the first approaches to artificial intelligence, were registered at the beginning of the 20th century (Gershman, Horvitz, & Tenenbaum, 2015), being the beginning of the era of augmented computing, which evolved throughout the century, highlighting the appearance of the first systems of virtual reality, of intelligence artificial and machine learning (Xiong, Hsiang, He, Zhan, & Wu, 2021), which was fundamental for the development and evolution of augmented computing technologies.

Augmented computing uses different technologies, being highlighted: artificial intelligence (AI); machine learning (ML); virtual reality (VR); and augmented reality (AR).

With these technologies is possible improved the efficiency and productivity of the urban areas (Alzahrani & Alfouzan, 2022) (Fig. 1). The combined use of these technologies allows creating powerful augmented computation systems, allowing human-computer relationships to be smarter and more immersive.

Currently, AC has widespread use, in education to health among others, improving human work capabilities in terms of effectiveness and efficiency.

One of the main areas of development in augmented computing is virtual reality and augmented reality. VR and AR are two technologies that have different characteristics and objectives, while VR takes us to a new environment created by computer; AR includes projections of content and complementary information in the real world (Kohli, Tripathi, Chamola, Rout, & Kanhere, 2022).

Both technologies need an intermediary to be accessed, which can be an application or an accessory, offering completely different experiences for users.

VR allows users to experience immersive digital environments, while AR overlays digital information and graphics onto the real world.

AR is about the real world. It's when you look at an existing environment and see overlapping elements, with information and graphics specific to a location, for example.

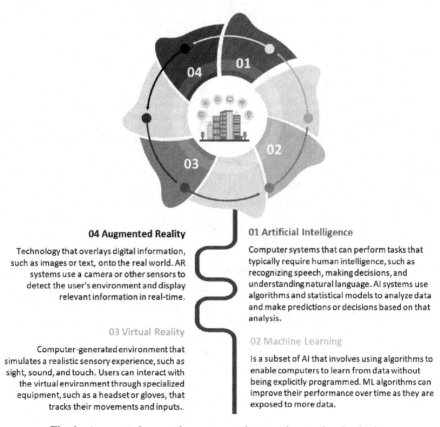

04 Augmented Reality

Technology that overlays digital information, such as images or text, onto the real world. AR systems use a camera or other sensors to detect the user's environment and display relevant information in real-time.

03 Virtual Reality

Computer-generated environment that simulates a realistic sensory experience, such as sight, sound, and touch. Users can interact with the virtual environment through specialized equipment, such as a headset or gloves, that tracks their movements and inputs..

01 Artificial Intelligence

Computer systems that can perform tasks that typically require human intelligence, such as recognizing speech, making decisions, and understanding natural language. AI systems use algorithms and statistical models to analyze data and make predictions or decisions based on that analysis.

02 Machine Learning

Is a subset of AI that involves using algorithms to enable computers to learn from data without being explicitly programmed. ML algorithms can improve their performance over time as they are exposed to more data.

Fig. 1. Augmented computing augmented computing used technologies.

AR can be defined as a system that: combines virtual elements with a real environment; it is interactive and has real-time processing; it is conceived and displayed in three dimensions.

Augmented computing enabled a more efficient and productive use of resources, providing an important role in the sustainability of smart cities. AI and ML can be used in the optimization of the use of resources, predicting and preventing equipment failures, optimizing energy use in buildings, and others.

AC can have a significant impact on the sustainability of cities, analyze the possible negative impacts, to be possible maximize the benefits of AC on the sustainability of cities.

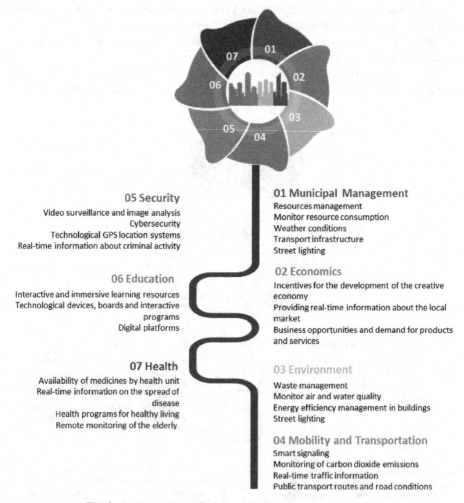

Fig. 2. Augmented computing application areas in smart cities.

05 Security
Video surveillance and image analysis
Cybersecurity
Technological GPS location systems
Real-time information about criminal activity

06 Education
Interactive and immersive learning resources
Technological devices, boards and interactive programs
Digital platforms

07 Health
Availability of medicines by health unit
Real-time information on the spread of disease
Health programs for healthy living
Remote monitoring of the elderly.

01 Municipal Management
Resources management
Monitor resource consumption
Weather conditions
Transport infrastructure
Street lighting

02 Economics
Incentives for the development of the creative economy
Providing real-time information about the local market
Business opportunities and demand for products and services

03 Environment
Waste management
Monitor air and water quality
Energy efficiency management in buildings
Street lighting

04 Mobility and Transportation
Smart signaling
Monitoring of carbon dioxide emissions
Real-time traffic information
Public transport routes and road conditions

There are several areas of application for augmented computing in smart cities, such municipal management, economics, environment, mobility and transportation, security, education, and health (Fig. 2).

3   Smart Cities and Sustainability

The bases of the concept of smart cities are the economic development, the citizen's life quality, and the sustainability. The overall objective of smart and sustainable cities is to improve sustainability with the help of technologies (Albino, V., Berardi, U., & Dangelico, R. M. (2015). Smart cities: Definitions, dimensions, performance, and initiatives, 2015).

The concept of Smart Cities is closely related to the digital transformation paradigm that can be explained as changes in the way of connecting, collecting and analyzing data caused by the adoption of new information and communication technologies (Caragliu, Del Bo, & Nijkamp, 2011). The simplest definition of a smart city is a city that through the use of technology improves the life quality of the citizens (Abadía, Walther, Osman, & Smarsly, 2022).

A smart city aims to create a more efficient, sustainable and livable environment, through the use of technologies that allow monitoring and optimizing the various systems. Sensors, Internet of Things (IoT) devices, and digital solutions leverage optimization and monitoring processes, facilitating data collection and subsequent analysis, thus making it possible to automate and optimize different processes and systems (Whaiduzzaman, y otros, 2022). By using technology to optimize and monitor various systems, cities can reduce resource consumption and waste production, leading to a more sustainable and livable environment.

The sustainable city is the most durable type of human settlement, providing an acceptable standard of living for all without serious damage to the ecosystem or the biogeochemical cycles on which it depends, as opposed to the current urbanization model, which considers natural resources inexhaustible and free (Newman & Jennings, 2012).

Sustainability is very important in some areas, particularly: sustainable development; the environment; the energy; the foods; the transport; consumption and production (Fig. 3) (United Nations, 2015).

Sustainable development expresses the relationship between economic growth, environmental conservation and social concern (Moreno, Allam, Chabaud, Gall, & Pratlong, 2021; Jiang, Gao, Jin, & Liu, 2021). Based on society's awareness of the irrational use of natural resources and the environmental impacts generated by human action, the concept of sustainable growth emerges as an alternative, which promotes the interdependence between economy, environment and society (Sachs, 2015).

Sustainable development is anchored in the economic development of humanity based on the conservation of natural resources. Thus, development in a sustainable manner means that natural resources are used rationally, that is, without their depletion, with a view to conserving these resources for future generations. Therefore, society's economic progress is sought based on the importance of environmental resources for productive activities and also on their conservation, in a clear concern for the future of humanity (United Nations, 2015).

Despite the problem of urbanization and the design of smart cities, a global concern has already turned to the issue of sustainability, as it enables us to provide a future for the next generations in our cities. The vision of sustainability helps us to seek innovative solutions, for example, for the excessive volume of solid supplements produced daily in cities and to combat the fuel produced by proteins and the volume of vehicles on the streets, but without reducing employability levels (Marjanović-Halburd, Halburd, & Manfredi, 2017).

However, the United Nations itself has expanded this concept of sustainability in recent years, maintaining the guarantee of opportunity for all, that is, social inclusion is part of this more current concept, since urbanization has brought a world where poverty and inequalities are endemic, which results in greater ecological problems (Caragliu, Del Bo, & Nijkamp, 2011).

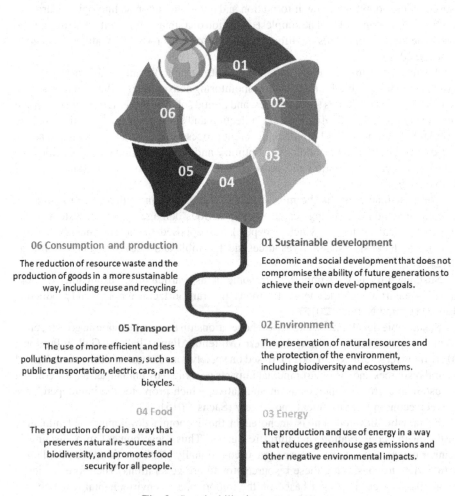

06 Consumption and production

The reduction of resource waste and the production of goods in a more sustainable way, including reuse and recycling.

05 Transport

The use of more efficient and less polluting transportation means, such as public transportation, electric cars, and bicycles.

04 Food

The production of food in a way that preserves natural re-sources and biodiversity, and promotes food security for all people.

01 Sustainable development

Economic and social development that does not compromise the ability of future generations to achieve their own devel-opment goals.

02 Environment

The preservation of natural resources and the protection of the environment, including biodiversity and ecosystems.

03 Energy

The production and use of energy in a way that reduces greenhouse gas emissions and other negative environmental impacts.

Fig. 3. Sustainability important areas.

Therefore, the design of smart cities needs to encompass sustainability actions aimed at recovering and maintaining our consumed natural resources, promoting the use of renewable energy conversion, treatment and cleaning of rivers that supply cities, treatment of the volume exponential growth of solid waste, the use of innovative construction solutions, among others. Smart city will be in how sustainable development will concern future nations and promote resilience, avoiding shortages of natural resources, new epidemics or other natural disasters (Ramirez Lopez & Grijalba Castro, 2020).

4   Challenges and Impact of AC on Smart Cities Sustainability

With the increase of urban population, the cities grow and face more challenges in terms of sustainability (Biadacz & Biadacz, 2021).

With the transformations imposed by the effects of globalization around the world, society and cities have been undergoing profound transformations in their most diverse aspects (Kara, 2019). In this context, it is urgent to look for innovative solutions that help solve these problems, and to carefully analyze the challenges and impact of technologies, namely AC, which must be used responsibly and sustainably in smart cities.

In the main challenges of AC in the smart cities sustainability it is worth mentioning its integration with other smart cities technologies (IoT, AI, ML, Bid Data, among others), and it depends of the development of the sustainable technologies, that must ensuring the privacy and security of the users data.

In the process of developing sustainable technologies for smart cities, the environmental sustainability cannot be neglected. It should be taken into account that privacy and security of user data must be guaranteed.

For a better use of AC in smart cities, training is essential. This is the only way to take advantages of the benefits offered by AC, and at the same time minimize the possible negative impacts (Javed, y otros, 2022). For that regulation is vital to ensure the responsible and sustainable use of AC in smart cities.

AC technologies can be used in smart cities to improve the efficiency and sustainability of urban areas. We can highlight: training in virtual reality: maintenance of augmented reality; intelligent transport; predictive maintenance; smart buildings; intelligent energy management; and waste management (Fig. 4).

Augmented computing can have a significant impact on the sustainability of cities on several levels: improving energy efficiency, environmental monitoring; developing innovative solutions; and improving life quality (Ismagilova & Raman, 2019).

AC can also have a negative impact on the sustainability of smart cities, such as the digital exclusion, lack of security and privacy in data collection, and lack of regulation, among others.

With the introduction of new technologies in smart cities, which present different scenarios and new challenges, the concern with regulation in terms of privacy and security of personal data prevails The regulation must accompany the new technologies adoption.

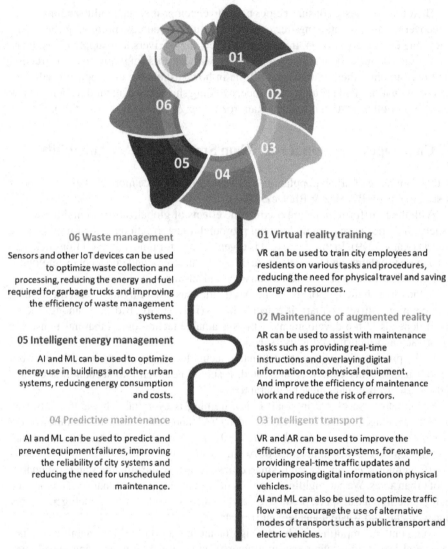

06 Waste management

Sensors and other IoT devices can be used to optimize waste collection and processing, reducing the energy and fuel required for garbage trucks and improving the efficiency of waste management systems.

05 Intelligent energy management

AI and ML can be used to optimize energy use in buildings and other urban systems, reducing energy consumption and costs.

04 Predictive maintenance

AI and ML can be used to predict and prevent equipment failures, improving the reliability of city systems and reducing the need for unscheduled maintenance.

01 Virtual reality training

VR can be used to train city employees and residents on various tasks and procedures, reducing the need for physical travel and saving energy and resources.

02 Maintenance of augmented reality

AR can be used to assist with maintenance tasks such as providing real-time instructions and overlaying digital information onto physical equipment. And improve the efficiency of maintenance work and reduce the risk of errors.

03 Intelligent transport

VR and AR can be used to improve the efficiency of transport systems, for example, providing real-time traffic updates and superimposing digital information on physical vehicles.
AI and ML can also be used to optimize traffic flow and encourage the use of alternative modes of transport such as public transport and electric vehicles.

Fig. 4. Areas of smart cities that can be improved by technologies in terms of efficiency and sustainability of urban areas.

5 Conclusions

Smart cities and augmented computing have the potential to significantly improve the sustainability of urban areas. By using technology to optimize and supervise various systems, cities can reduce their resource consumption and waste production, improve the energy efficiency and environmental monitoring, developing innovative solutions, leading to a more sustainable and livable environment. Augmented computing can also contribute to the sustainability of smart cities by enabling more efficient and productive use of resources. As these technologies continue to advance, it is important to consider their potential impact on sustainability and to develop strategies to maximize their benefits for the environment.

However, the use of AC in smart cities also presents challenges and ethical issues such as privacy, security and equal access to technology. Furthermore, the production and disposal of electronic devices for accessing AC can have negative impacts on smart cities sustainability such as the digital exclusion, lack of security and privacy in data collection.

Therefore, it is important that the impacts and challenges of augmented computing on the sustainability of smart cities are carefully considered, to ensure the responsible and sustainable use of this technology for the benefit of society.

Acknowledgement. The authors are grateful to the Foundation for Science and Technology (FCT, Portugal) for financial support through national funds FCT/MCTES (PIDDAC) to CIMO (UIDB/00690/2020 and UIDP/00690/2020) and SusTEC (LA/P/0007/2020).

References

Abadía, J.J., Walther, C., Osman, A., Smarsly, K.: A systematic survey of Internet of things frameworks for smart city applications. Sustain. Cities Soc. **83**, 1–19 (2022). https://doi.org/10.1016/j.scs.2022.103949

Al Sharif, R., Pokharel, S.: Smart city dimensions and associated risks: Review of literature. Sustain. Cities Soc. **77**, 1–14 (2022). https://doi.org/10.1016/j.scs.2021.103542

Albino, V., Berardi, U., Dangelico, R.M.: Smart cities: Definitions, dimensions, performance, and initiatives. J. Urban Technol. **22**(1), 3–21 (2015). https://doi.org/10.1080/10630732.2014.942092

Allam, Z., Sharifi, A., Bibri, S.E., Jones, D.S., Krogstie, J.: The metaverse as a virtual form of smart cities: Opportunities and challenges for environmental, economic, and social sustainability in urban futures. Smart Cities **5**(3), 771–801 (2022). https://doi.org/10.3390/smartcities5030040

Alzahrani, N.M., Alfouzan, F.A.:. Augmented reality (AR) and cyber-security for smart cities—A systematic literature review. Sensors **22**(7), 2792 (2022). https://www.mdpi.com/journal/sensors

Aurigi, A., Odendaal, N.: From "smart in the box" to "smart in the city": Rethinking the socially sustainable smart city in context. J. Urban Technol. **28**(1–2), 55–70 (2021). https://doi.org/10.1080/10630732.2019.1704203

Biadacz, R., Biadacz, M.: Implementation of "Smart" solutions and an attempt to measure them: A case study of Czestochowa, Poland. (MDPI, Ed.) Energies **14**(18), 5668 (2021). https://doi.org/10.3390/en14185668

Bibri, S.E., Krogstie, J.: On the social shaping dimensions of smart sustainable cities: A study in science, technology, and society. Sustain. Cities Soc. **29**, 219–246 (2017). https://doi.org/10.1016/j.scs.2016.11.004

Caragliu, A., Del Bo, C., Nijkamp, P.: Smart cities in Europe. J. Urban Technol. **18**(2), 65–82 (2011). https://doi.org/10.1080/10630732.2011.601117

Casini, M.: Green technology for smart cities. IOP Conf. Ser. Earth Environ. Sci. **83**(1), 1–8 (2017). IOP Publishing. https://doi.org/10.1088/1755-1315/83/1/012014

Gershman, S.J., Horvitz, E.J., Tenenbaum, J.B.: Computational rationality: A converging paradigm for intelligence in brains, minds, and machines. Science **349**(6245), 273–278 (2015). https://doi.org/10.1126/science.aac6076

Ismagilova, E.H., Raman, K.R.: Smart cities: Advances in research—An information systems perspective. Int. J. Inf. Manage. **47**, 88–100 (2019). https://doi.org/10.1016/j.ijinfomgt.2019.01.004

Javed, A.R., et al.: Future smart cities requirements, emerging technologies, applications, challenges, and future aspects. Cities **129**, 103794 (2022). https://doi.org/10.1016/j.cities.2019.102397

Jiang, M., Gao, Y., Jin, M., Liu, S.: Sustainable development of the business environment in smart cities: A hierarchical framework. Kybernetes **50**(5), 1426–1448 (2021). https://doi.org/10.1108/K-03-2020-0148

Kara, B.: The impact of globalization on cities. J. Contemp. Urban Affairs **3**(2), 108–113 (2019). https://doi.org/10.25034/ijcua.2018.4707

Kohli, V., Tripathi, U., Chamola, V., Rout, B.K., Kanhere, S.S.: A review on virtual reality and augmented reality use-cases of brain computer interface based applications for smart cities. Microprocess. Microsyst. **88**, 104392 (2022). https://doi.org/10.1016/j.micpro.2021.104392

Marjanović-Halburd, L., Halburd, M., Manfredi, S.: Can smart cities be sustainable cities? Sustainability **9**(10), 1794 (2017). https://doi.org/10.3390/su9101794

Meneguette, R.I., De Grande, R., Loureiro, A.A.: Intelligent transport system in smart cities. Springer, Cham (2018). https://doi.org/10.1007/978-3-319-93332-0

Moreno, C., Allam, Z., Chabaud, D., Gall, C., Pratlong, F.: Introducing the "15-Minute City": Sustainability, resilience and place identity in future post-pandemic cities. Smart Cities **4**(1), 93–111 (2021). https://doi.org/10.3390/smartcities4010006

Newman, P.W., Jennings, I.: Cities as sustainable ecosystems: Principles and practices. Island Press (2012)

Ramirez Lopez, L.J., Grijalba Castro, A.I.: Sustainability and resilience in smart city planning: A review. Sustainability **13**(1), 1–25 (2020). https://doi.org/10.3390/su13010181

Sachs, J.D.: The age of sustainable development. In: The Age of Sustainable Development. Columbia University Press (2015)

Saleem, S.I., Zeebaree, S., Zeebaree, D.Q., Abdulazeez, A.M.: Building smart cities applications based on IoT technologies: A review. Technol. Rep. Kansai Univ. **62**(3), 1083–1092 (2020). Obtenido de https://www.academia.edu/download/63243187/30-4-2020_Saleem_Subhi_Diyar_Adnan20200508-53466-10f8emd.pdf

Strielkowski, W., Veinbender, T., Tvaronavičienė, M., Lace, N.: Economic efficiency and energy security of smart cities. Econ. Res. Ekon. istraživanja **33**(1), 788–803 (2020). https://doi.org/10.1080/1331677X.2020.1734854

United Nations. Transforming our world: The 2030 Agenda for Sustainable Development (2015). Obtenido de https://sustainabledevelopment.un.org/content/documents/21252030%20Agenda%20for%20Sustainable%20Development%20web.pdf

Whaiduzzaman, M., et al.: A review of emerging technologies for IoT-based smart cities. Sensors **22**(23), 9271 (2022). https://doi.org/10.3390/s22239271

Xiong, J., Hsiang, E.L., He, Z., Zhan, T., Wu, S.T.: Augmented reality and virtual reality displays: Emerging technologies and future perspectives. Light: Sci. Appl. **10**(1), 2016 (2021). https://doi.org/10.1038/s41377-021-00658-8

IOHIVE: Architecture and Infrastructure of an IOT System for Beehive Monitoring and an Interactive Journaling Wearable Device for Beekeepers

Charalambos Alifieris[1], Theodora Chamaidi[1] , Katerina Malisova[1] ,
Dimitrios Mamalis[2], Evangelos Nomikos[1] , Chrysostomos Rigakis[1],
Evangelos Vlachogiannis[1], and Modestos Stavrakis[1(✉)]

[1] Department of Product and Systems Design Engineering, University of the Aegean,
84100 Syros, Greece
{babis,theodora.chamaidi,katemalisova,v.nomikos,chr.rigakis,
evlach,modestos}@aegean.gr
[2] Kudzu P.C., 84100 Syros, Greece
dimitris.mamalis@kudzu.gr

Abstract. IOHIVE is a project that focuses on the development of a smart apiculture system that incorporates sensors to monitor the weight, temperature, humidity, pressure, and sound of beehives. Additionally, the project involves the development of a wearable device that beekeepers use to interactively keep notes (journaling) of their empirical observations during beehive inspections at the apiary. This paper presents the architecture of the IOHIVE system/service, which consists of hardware infrastructures, including sensors, microcontrollers, network infrastructure (LoRA, Wifi, GSM/4G), as well as the wearable and its hardware and software. The software infrastructure includes the IOHIVE Service API, database, and the IOHIVE web application and its frontend and backend. The paper also describes the IOHIVE approach to smart beehive monitoring and journaling including the scenarios of the beehive inspection workflow, which includes the minimal and standard inspection scenarios. The IOHIVE system provides bee stakeholders, beekeepers and/or researchers (both mentioned from now on as beekeepers) with real-time monitoring of the beehives, enabling them to make informed decisions in time, resulting in improved bee health and productivity. The wearable device, coupled with the IOHIVE web application, provides a digital beekeepers' journal that assists people in recording their observations in real-time on the field, enabling them to maintain accurate records of their beehives and bee colonies, and potentially identify trends over time.

Keywords: Beehive · Monitoring · Journaling · Smart Apiculture · IoT · Wearable

O. Gervasi et al. (Eds.): ICCSA 2023 Workshops, LNCS 14108, pp. 133–149, 2023.
https://doi.org/10.1007/978-3-031-37117-2_11

1 Introduction

The design of technologies for sustainable apiculture can help people, in many ways, including monitoring and management of bee colonies, pest and disease detection and control, as well as improving the efficiency of honey production. In the past few years, the use of smart technologies in apiculture has been steadily increasing, while the introduction of the Internet of Things further boosted the development of various systems and applications in the field. Today, there are numerous examples of successful implementations that combine such technologies for remote beehive monitoring with automation and data analytics. Moreover, several systems and applications have also been developed to assist users during the beehive inspections and more specifically with beehive journaling. These can be categorized as mobile applications, web-based platforms and IoT hybrid monitoring systems. The IOHIVE project deals with the development of an integrated platform that combines a similar functionality with the aforementioned implementations in terms of monitoring, but also adds an additional layer of interaction regarding beehive journaling in real-time when performing inspections in the field/apiary.

In summary, the general objectives of the IOHIVE project are to design and develop technological infrastructures and services for: a) remote hive monitoring of beekeeping data, b) the growth of bee collonies in accordance with local climatic conditions, honey yield, and other hive-derived products, c) the support of beekeeping practices and management techniques targeting the proliferation and development of bee populations, d) the endorsement and exploitation of all products stemming from the practices of beekeeping. The project intends to collect, process, and display both quantitative and qualitative data to enhance operational efficiency and elevate the standard of the products [6]. This manuscript predominantly concentrates on the evaluation of the general structure and infrastructure fabricated to meet the project's requirements. Accordingly, the paper is structured in the following sections. The introduction describes an overview of the current status in smart beekeeping, precision apiculture and IoT, it discusses the benefits and challenges of using these related technologies. In the second section, beehive monitoring and journaling are discussed, outlining the key factors that should be monitored and recorded for optimal beehive management. In the third section, we describe the IOHIVE approach to smart beehive monitoring and journaling, including the hardware and software components, data collection and analysis methods, and user interface and interactions. Finally, the fourth section presents a short critical analysis of the advantages and limitations of the IOHIVE approach and outlines future directions for research and development.

1.1 The Value of Technology Assisted Apiculture

Smart beekeeping, precision apiculture, and the Internet of Things (IoT) along with other technologies and beekeeping systems have revolutionised the way bee stakeholders, including beekeepers, bee product producers and bee researchers, manage their hives. In recent years, advancements in sensor technology, data analytics, and wireless communication have enabled the aforementioned bee stakeholders to monitor their hives in near real-time, collect and analyze data, and make informed decisions based on the insights gained. On the one hand, smart beekeeping can help beekeepers increase hive productivity, reduce hive losses, and optimize resource use.

In a broader sense, smart beekeeping involves utilizing a range of technologies to achieve its objectives in supporting the beekeeping process. By leveraging sensors, cameras, robotics, drones, wearables, mobiles and other advanced technologies, smart beekeeping aims to monitor the health of the beehive and gather data on important factors ranging from environmental conditions such as temperature, humidity to bee or beekeeper activity and physiology. This data can then be further utilised to inform critical decisions about the relationship of people with the bee colonies, develop strategies for beekeeping and thus influence the actual practices of beehive observation, inspection and management. In a similar fashion, Precision Apiculture aims to help bee stakeholders identify and address specific issues related to bee management based on precise and data-driven strategies [1–3]. It involves collecting and analyzing data at a more granular level with numerous techniques and goals. It incorporates a number of different technologies ranging from geographical information systems (GIS), satellite imagery analysis and sensors to robotics and other advanced digital tools, to afford different applications for sustainable beekeeping [2, 4, 5]. These include: a) **site selection** to ensure that bees have access to sufficient pollen and nectar resources while minimizing competition with other colonies, b) **hive management** to create hive-specific management plans (e.g. for feeding, pest control, queen replacement etc.), c) **pollination services** to optimize the pollination for specific crops, d) disease and pest management by monitoring the health of individual colonies and detect signs of disease or pest infestations early on and thus provide guidelines for efficient prevention strategies, e) **breeding programs** to improve bee breeding by identifying and selecting desirable traits, such as disease resistance or high productivity, based on the analysis of colony data and genetic information, f) **resource management** to optimise resource usage, such as feed, treatments, and equipment, based on the specific needs of each colony or location, and g) **environmental monitoring** to develop conservation strategies, such as habitat restoration or the creation of pollinator-friendly landscapes. Precision apiculture aims to maximize productivity, minimize resource use, and promote sustainable beekeeping practices by using technology and data to optimize hive management decisions at the micro-level. In summary, smart beekeeping can be considered a subset of precision apiculture. While both concepts involve using technology and data-driven techniques to improve beekeeping, precision apiculture takes a more comprehensive approach, emphasizing precise, customised management strategies for individual colonies and locations [6].

Moreover, advancements in computing and the Internet of Things (IoT) are playing an increasingly important role in supporting technology-assisted beekeeping [7–9]. IoT technologies mainly focus on interconnecting physical devices that are embedded with sensors, software and networking capabilities. The goal is to enable these devices to collect and exchange data with each other and the central systems they are connected to. In the context of beekeeping, IoT technology can be used to remotely monitor apiaries and beehives, automate tasks such as hive monitoring, data collection, and reporting, and reduce the need for frequent on-site visits by beekeepers. By using IoT-based monitoring systems, beekeepers can collect real-time data on factors such as temperature, humidity, and sound levels in their hives, and remotely assess the health of their colonies. This helps to minimize the amount of stress placed on the bees and can reduce the number of interventions required to manage the hives, improving colony health and productivity [10, 11].

On the other hand, there are challenges associated with using these technologies, such as the high cost of implementation, the need for technical expertise, and the potential for data overload [9]. Furthermore, concerns have been raised about the privacy and security of data collected through IoT devices, as well as the potential for these devices to interfere with bee behavior [7, 12]. Despite these challenges, the benefits of using smart technologies and IoT in beekeeping are clear, and these technologies have the potential to revolutionize the industry in the coming years. As such, it is important for beekeepers and researchers to continue exploring and developing these technologies, while also addressing the challenges and concerns associated with their use.

2   Beehive Monitoring and Journaling

Beekeeping is an agriculture-related practice that requires significant labor and attention in order to maintain the health and productivity of bee colonies. [13]. In their everyday practice, beekeepers routinely inspect the frames of each beehive almost daily, varying frequency based on the season and objectives. Through diligent journaling of observations and practices during field visits, beekeepers can draw insightful conclusions regarding the status of the beehive and forecast its future health. In addition, such journaling practices are also an effective means to validate the efficacy of beekeeping protocols, by tracking the progress and outcomes of the monitored practices. [13, 14]. Beekeeping inspections are often complex and journaling at the same time can become a challenging task as the beekeeper must deal with various tools and processes. Beekeepers often rely on empirical methods and tools, such as paper journals, to record notes on their observations during or after the inspection. These notes may include the use of symbols, numbers, or other shorthand to record their observations. However, the process of journaling during beehive inspections can be distracting and disrupt the beekeeper's focus.

The subsequent two paragraphs will be focused on presenting technologies and research that are associated with the practice of journaling and monitoring beehives.

2.1   Technologies Used for Beehive Journaling and Monitoring

A broad array of systems, services, and applications have been developed for note-taking or journaling during beehive inspections, along with monitoring conducted via sensors [2]. This includes both systems and services rooted in academic research and those available commercially, along with mobile applications accessible in most mobile marketplaces. Noteworthy open-source systems explicitly addressing the need for journaling encompass the Beep App, an online web service, accompanied by the Beep Scale [15], and OSBeehives application, supported by the BuzzBox beehive monitoring system [16]. Both services provide diary functionality to beekeepers and researchers, enabling them to take notes on the current status, treatments, and any changes made during inspections, among other factors, for each hive. Additionally, monitoring conducted via sensors is stored in databases and presented to users via various visualisation techniques, such as graphs, charts, and widgets. Both systems classify information according to the inspection checklists prevalently utilised within the beekeeping community [17]. As both systems are currently under substantial development, their graphical user interfaces and core functionalities are undergoing continuous updates, enabling users to seamlessly navigate via both their mobile and desktop devices.

Manual journaling by beekeepers is often complemented by automated systems that monitor a variety of data pertinent to an apiary, including beehive status and the micro-climate of the surrounding area. The monitored data is captured and scrutinised by an array of systems and techniques, such as audio/acoustic or sound analysis [18, 19], motion/track analysis [20, 21], population estimation and variability [22, 23], behaviour analysis [24], vibration [25], image analysis, and computer vision for detecting diseases and parasites [26], energy consumption [27], and environmental data [28]. Several systems have also been developed to monitor combinations of the aforementioned data based on multi-sensor arrays, which fall under the domain of Internet of Things (IoT). Such systems typically monitor temperature, humidity, weight, audio, video, vibrations, among other factors. Some recent examples include BeePi [29], Beemon [10], an IoT concept for precision beekeeping [7], and an IoT project of a low-power beekeeping safety and conditions monitoring system [30].

2.2 Inspection and Journaling Workflow

Following the user research phase, the design team developed two standard inspection scenarios that run parallel to the monitoring of sensor data from beehive sensors and local weather stations. These scenarios are referred to as the 'Minimal Inspection Scenario' and the 'Standard Inspection Scenario'. Detailed information about these scenarios is presented in another paper that has been submitted to another journal and is currently under review. Therefore, we will provide a brief summary of these scenarios here.

The Minimal Inspection Scenario

The "Minimal Inspection Scenario" primarily centres on the steps that a beekeeper follows to assess the current status of a beehive by solely observing it without any interventions or beehive management. This scenario assumes that the beekeeper only observes the beehive status in the following pattern, consisting of two inspections named "Inspection 1" and "Inspection 2", (e.g., two weeks). It is important to note that the actual time duration may differ from the specified interval and has been presented for scenario representation purposes only (Fig. 1).

During "Inspection 1," which takes place on Day 1, the beekeeper performs the following tasks and observations in two hive states: "Hive State 1," which describes the beehive's condition before the beekeeper opens it, and "Hive State 1'," which describes the beehive's status after the beekeeper's inspection. In this scenario, the beekeeper only observes the condition of the beehive without any interventions, and therefore, "Hive State 1" and "Hive State 1'" are not heavily influenced by any beekeeping protocols. However, the state of the beehive is considered different primarily because even this mild intervention alters the status of the colony, as observed by the monitored data, such

Minimal Inspection Scenario

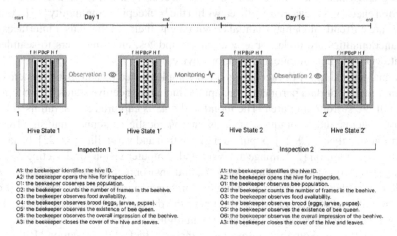

Fig. 1. Diagram representing the 'Minimal Inspection Scenario'

as changes in temperature and sound frequency. During "Inspection 1," the beekeeper performs the following observations and actions:

A1: the beekeeper identifies the beehive ID.

A2: the beekeeper opens the beehive for inspection.

O1: the beekeeper observes bee populations.

O2: the beekeeper counts the number of frames in the beehive.

O3: the beekeeper observes food availability.

O4: the beekeeper observes brood (eggs, larvae, pupae).

O5: the beekeeper observes the existence of bee queen.

O6: the beekeeper observes the overall impression of the beehive.

A3: the beekeeper closes the cover of the beehive and leaves.

During "Inspection 2," which takes place on the following apiary visit (Day 16 on this example), the beekeeper follows a similar approach, but the actual status of the beehive is altered due to the following reasons: a) the actual evolution that takes place because of the actions performed by the colony, b) environmental conditions, and c) human interventions (even by observing).

The Standard Inspection Scenario that includes both user observations and interventions is more complicated as it involves significant alterations to the beehive's status by the human following a specific beekeeping protocol. This scenario is beyond the scope of this paper and is analysed in a separate publication.

3 The IOHIVE Approach to Smart Beehive Monitoring and Journaling

In this project we have developed the IOHIVE approach which utilizes a combination of digital technologies and human-beehive interactions to provide a comprehensive under-standing of the current conditions within an apiary, including the state of individual beehives. Specifically, in-beehive sensors, weather stations, and wearable devices are employed to monitor the health, activity, and productivity of the hives. The following figure provides a high-level overview of the IOHIVE architecture (Fig. 2).

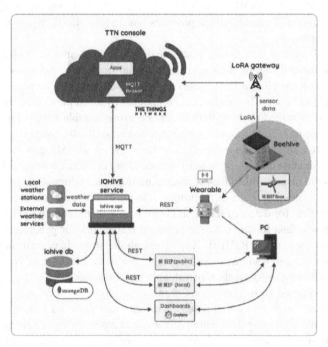

Fig. 2. IOHIVE System and Service Architecture

In this section, we will describe the different components used in the IOHIVE architecture and the related infrastructures that have been developed to fulfill the system/service's purposes. These components include the IOHIVE Architecture, LoRa/LoRaWAN implementation, LoRa Nodes and Gateways, Sensors, Weather Stations, and Wearables.

3.1 The IOHIVE Architecture

The IOHIVE architecture is centered around the IOHIVE Service, which is responsible for orchestrating the various data flows as described in the following sections. The IOHive Service acts as a bridge between the different devices involved, managing the different protocols and data streams coming from the users. These devices include monitoring devices, such as sensors, gateways, and weather stations, as well as wearable devices used in the field to perform inspections, and desktop clients where end-users can store and analyze data.

From a technical standpoint, the IOHIVE Service is a scalable application developed using NodeJS/NestJS, which subscribes to a TTN MQTT broker [31] for receiving data from the connected devices. Additionally, the service offers REST endpoints for receiving and serving data to users. The IOHIVE Service seamlessly integrates with both the public BEEP application [15] and a fork installation of the actual IOHIVE application [32], which extends BEEP's functionality to meet the project's requirements. The main service stores all data from the related services offered by the various projects' components in a MongoDB cluster, which provides timeseries collections and the powerful aggregation framework.

In practical applications taking place in the field (e.g. apiary), LoRa nodes are employed for the purpose of data aggregation from beehives. These nodes establish a connection with the closest LoRa gateway, which subsequently forwards the data to the public TTN network. The payload, accompanied by a unique device ID and timestamp, is then transmitted to the IOHIVE Service using suitable payload decoders and webhooks. Moreover, certain devices are equipped with 3G/4G connectivity and have the capability to communicate using SMS technology via an SMS gateway, a solution designed to surmount challenges posed by areas lacking in LoRa coverage. The IOHIVE Service bears the responsibility for preprocessing the data, encompassing tasks such as validation and formatting, before committing it to the database. In addition, the service furnishes endpoints for data extraction and aggregation that are intended for use by the IOHIVE App. Grafana functions as the principal framework for generating charts and integrating them within the IOHIVE App. Through the strategic utilisation of both the MongoDB aggregation framework and Grafana, a framework for data visualization is portrayed, facilitating the derivation of valuable insights (Fig. 3).

The data gathered from continuous monitoring of the beehive and its surrounding environment can be cross-referenced with the data gathered during inspections. By extracting and analyzing data windows for each inspection cycle, the user can gain insights into the issues encountered during the previous inspection period and plan appropriate corrective actions. The attainment of this can be facilitated through the deployment of suitable visualisation techniques.

However, the availability of communication channels such as LoRa, 3G, or SMS, poses several restrictions related to data rate, payload size, and cost. For instance, LoRaWAN has a raw maximum data rate of 27 kbps, which has been studied extensively to understand its limitations [33]. The Things Network website [31] provides a useful summary of these limitations and best practices. Therefore, it is essential to take these limitations into account when designing both the architecture and the interaction techniques used in the IOHIVE system.

The current state of the IOHIVE architecture integrates both the BEEP app (application/platform) and the BEEP base (hardware scale). The IOHIVE Service facilitates

Fig. 3. The IOHIVE early v2 prototype interface includes visualisations and charts that display various information related to beehive monitoring and local weather data.

the transmission of data from various sensors to the BEEP app. Additionally, wearable devices transmit inspection data directly to the IOHIVE API service, which then forwards the data to the BEEP app.

To address the outcomes of the user research that took place in a previous stage and presented in this publication [11], a series of inspection checklists were developed. A data transformation layer, integrated into the IOHIVE Service, is responsible for converting data from multiple sources into formats that are optimally compatible with different interfaces. This capability enables the development of dynamic and configurable checklists that that meet the specific requirements of end-users.

Despite the BEEP framework's provision of configurable checklists, our inspection requirements necessitated an extension of this capability. As a result, we have extended IOHIVE app to accommodate our specific needs for inspection, which can be encapsulated in the following abstract, BEEP-agnostic Data Transfer Model (DTO) (Fig. 4).

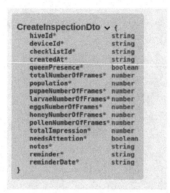

Fig. 4. IOHIVE's inspection data model.

We have created a mapping of this model to the aforementioned checklist to integrate it with BEEP and leverage BEEP's functionality and accumulated experience in the field.

Hive Monitoring and Workflow

The architecture outlined above and its integration with BEEP and IOHIVE apps enables efficient management of apiaries and hives, connected monitoring devices, and alert mechanisms, such as low battery notifications, right out of the box.

The following sequence diagram illustrates the monitoring process. Sensor data, such as that from weather stations, scales, and temperature sensors, is predominantly transmitted via Lora. Lora Gateways then transmit the data to TTN, and our service receives the messages, stores, transforms, and forwards them to BEEP installations, in combination with interactive Grafana charts (Fig. 5).

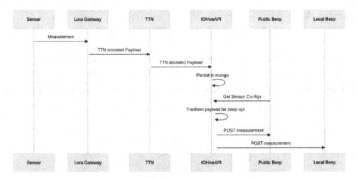

Fig. 5. IOHIVE Sequence diagram

Inspection Workflow

The sequence diagram below presents the inspection flow. A user wearing such a device initially scans the QR on every hive in order to identify the inspection target. The device fetches either from local storage or from IOHIVE Service at the last inspection. The user adjusts the values (see model above) based on her observations and data is being either persisted locally or directly transmitted through IP/REST to our service. The service persists, transforms and publish inspections to beep installations (Fig. 6).

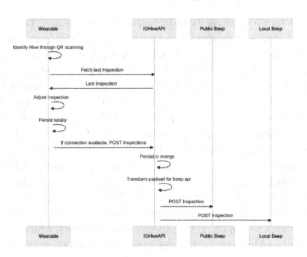

Fig. 6. Inspection Workflow Diagram

IOHIVE Service API

The IOHIVE Service provides three distinct APIs (Fig. 7):

- IOHIVE Sensor (Data) API - responsible for the integration of sensor data
- IOHIVE Weather (Data) API - responsible for the integration of weather data
- IOHIVE Inspection (Data) API - responsible for the integration of inspection data

Fig. 7. IOHIVE Service API

3.2 LoRa/LoRaWAN Implementation

Drawing on the design requirements and research gathered during the initial stages of implementation, the focus of this project is to utilise IoT technologies that provide long-range wireless communication at a low bitrate between connected objects, including sensors that operate on a battery. The IOHIVE project employs LoRa, a long-range, low-power wireless technology, to remotely monitor beehives. By operating in the unlicensed radio spectrum and offering low data rates, it enables the deployment of cost-effective, energy-efficient IoT devices for beekeeping. LoRaWAN, a wide area network protocol, standardizes the communication and system architecture for the network, including end nodes, concentrators, network servers, and application servers. Given its far-reaching transmission capabilities, LoRa is an optimal solution for connecting beehive sensors and actuators across varied landscapes, thereby supporting the development of the IOHIVE project. LoRaWAN networks, employed in the IOHIVE project, use a bidirectional ALOHA-based protocol to facilitate uplink and downlink communication. In uplink, end devices send messages without targeting specific concentrators, which forward them to the Network Server, and ultimately, the Application Server processes the data. Downlink follows the reverse order, with the Application Server sending encoded messages back to end nodes. LoRaWAN's combination of modulation technology, system architecture, and unlicensed ISM band operation makes it an ideal choice for large-scale IoT applications like IOHIVE. With open and freely available LoRaWAN implementations, minimal technical expertise is required to establish such infrastructure, thereby supporting the growth of the project.

Why and how LoRa-Based Infrastructure can be used for Beehive Monitoring and Journaling

Apiculture is often practiced in remote areas and over large spatial distances. Typically, intensive apiculture areas are located in non-urban regions where conventional radio technologies, such as cellular or WiFi, are not accessible. Satellite radio technologies, which are available globally, are relatively expensive and require high transmission power, making them unsuitable for low-power IoT systems. Therefore, the use of LoRa and LoRaWAN technologies is being advocated as a solution. The high link budget of LoRa signals allows them to travel long distances and penetrate obstacles commonly found in the apiculture domain, such as high vegetation and landscape geography. The low power requirements for transmitting and receiving messages make it possible to extend the battery life of LoRa-compatible IoT devices or even use energy harvesting techniques. Additionally, setting up a private local LoRaWAN network infrastructure has become effortless. Concentrators are available as standalone devices and can be connected to open-source LNSs deployed on-premises or utilize publicly available open-source and free-to-use LNSs. Furthermore, the availability of public networks deployed worldwide can enable the use of the technology without the need to build a private infrastructure. In other words, LoRa and LoRaWAN infrastructure can be effortlessly used as-is, expanded by collaborating with existing infrastructure or deployed privately on-premises without requiring licensing or pay-per-use schemes.

Hardware Used for Wearable, LoRa Sensor Nodes and Gateways
A common issue of deployed IoT technologies is interoperability of systems and architecture. In order to accommodate this issue, a different approach was required. Journaling and monitoring of apiculture procedure requires both the use of stationary low power IoT devices which can operate autonomously in a harsh environment for long periods of time and the use of high-power wearable devices. Both these different types of systems require different data acquisition, processing and transmission techniques and technologies. Thus, the complexity of developing such a unified system is regarded as high. Sprout IoT platform [34], implemented for the purposed of the IOHIVE project, abstracts the common procedures which differentiate high power wearable devices from stationary low power ones. Two of the main procedures which normally require different design schemes are power management and data transmission. The developed abstraction embedded in the Sprout IoT platform hardware, brings the power consumption and usage schemes and the use of different radio communication technologies to the configuration level allowing for designers and developers to focus on the rest of the application procedure. The end result is a unified platform which can be used in either way without the need to design specific power management and transmission techniques.

IOHIVE Wearable
The IOHIVE Wearable is a device designed for beekeepers to efficiently journal their beekeeping practices during hive inspections. The device is designed on the basis of the following user requirements and design specifications: a) Sprout-based: The wearable is built upon the versatile Kudzu Sprout platform, ensuring compatibility and seamless integration with other Sprout-based devices, such as scales, b) Rechargeable Battery: The device operates on a rechargeable battery, promoting eco-friendliness and cost-effectiveness with many hours of operation in the field, c) Wi-Fi Connectivity: The

wearable supports Wi-Fi uplink and downlink for real-time data transmission, allowing beekeepers to sync their journal entries quickly and easily with the IOHIVE app, d) LoRa and LoRaWAN Compatibility: The wearable is designed to work with LoRa and LoRaWAN technology, enabling long-range, low-power communication for remote connectivity, e) NFC Scanner: Equipped with an NFC scanner, the wearable can quickly read information from NFC tags, streamlining data collection from the beehives, f) User Interface: The intuitive UI includes buttons, LEDs, a rotary encoder, and a screen, facilitating smooth navigation and interaction for beekeepers, g) User-Friendly Design: With a focus on usability and wearability, the IOHIVE Wearable ensures comfort and functionality, making it an indispensable tool for beekeepers, h) Dedicated Software: The device's software is tailored for beekeeping inspections, providing a comprehensive and efficient solution for monitoring and managing hives. Throughout the development process, the IOHIVE Wearable has undergone various prototyping stages. In the following figures we provide CAD models and images of the 3D-printed prototypes that showcase the evolution of the design, including the electronics and circuits, to offer a detailed insight into the wearable's creation. The CAD models of the IOHIVE Wearable's design are readily available on our online IOHIVE Digital Repository [32], which we update frequently to showcase the latest advancements and improvements in the open design process (Fig. 8).

Fig. 8 IOHIVE Wearable Prototype.

LoRa Sensor Nodes and Gateways

Devices (nodes and gateways) used in this project utilize LoRa low-power wide-area network modulation. Some node devices, supporting 3G/4G, communicate via SMS technology, ensuring coverage in areas with limited LoRa access. The aim is to install low power LoRa nodes in apiaries, connecting to the nearest LoRa gateway [35, 36]. The gateways relay data to The Things Network [31]. Utilising suitable payload decoders and webhooks, the payload is supplemented with a unique device ID and timestamp, and subsequently conveyed to the IOHIVE Service.

3.3   Sensors and Weather Stations

The IOHIVE platform boasts an open and extensible architecture, deliberately crafted to facilitate the integration of diverse end devices. It is hardware-agnostic, meaning that it allows for the integration of end devices, regardless of their manufacturer, model, or specifications. IOHIVE's core role is to facilitate remote beehive monitoring, collection of weather and environmental data, and inspection data. Metrics such as a) hive weight, b) internal/external hive temperature, c) humidity and d) internal hive sound offer critical insights into bee colony status. Broad area climatic and apiary-specific microclimatic data serve as valuable environmental indicators. Furthermore, beehive inspection data, supplied by beekeepers, presents an invaluable additional information layer. This empirically derived data, rooted in observation and experience, offers a subjective measure of phenomena as experienced firsthand by the beekeepers. The significance of this data is undeniable, and it can be further employed in correlating with sensor-derived data. An overview of the end devices already integrated into the platform is provided in the subsequent figures (Fig. 9):

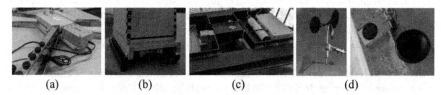

(a)   (b)   (c)   (d)

Fig. 9. IOHIVE end devices. a) BEEP base, b) SaveBees SMS scale, c) Kudzu scale based on Sprout, and d) MeteoHelix IoT Pro weather station MeteoWind IoT Pro wind sensor.

4   Advantages and Future Directions

IOHIVE presents a novel approach aimed at enhancing apiculture-related activities by promoting sustainable beekeeping practices through the use of digital technologies for monitoring and journaling. These practices aid in conserving bees as essential pollinators while also fostering the economic viability of the beekeeping community. The IOHIVE approach provides scalability, security, interoperability, and decentralisation for large-scale IoT deployments for smart and precision apiculture. Future directions for research and development will focus on evaluating the wearable/tangible device, improve the design and UX of the GUIs of the web appplication, expanding network coverage through optimized network planning and deployment, integrating AI and data analytics, developing standards and protocols for beekeeping, and optimizing costs through cloud-based solutions and automation.

Acknowledgements and Funding. This research was co-financed by the European Union and Greek national funds under the Operational Program 'Research Innovation Strategies for Smart Specialisation in South Aegean ΟΠΣ 3437', call South Aegean Operational Plan 2014–2020 (project code: ΝΑΙΓ 1–0043435). The study involved collaboration with project partners including the Institute of Mediterranean Forest Ecosystems and Forest Products Technology (Dr. Sofia Gounari) and Kudzu P.C. [34].

References

1. Howard, S.R., Ratnayake, M.N., Dyer, A.G., Garcia, J.E., Dorin, A.: Towards precision apiculture: traditional and technological insect monitoring methods in strawberry and raspberry crop polytunnels tell different pollination stories. PLoS ONE **16**, e0251572 (2021)
2. Hadjur, H., Ammar, D., Lefèvre, L.: Toward an intelligent and efficient beehive: a survey of precision beekeeping systems and services. Comput. Electron. Agric. **192**, 106604 (2022)
3. Zacepins, A., Brusbardis, V., Meitalovs, J., Stalidzans, E.: Challenges in the development of Precision Beekeeping. Biosys. Eng. **130**, 60–71 (2015)
4. Bourouis, A., Benahmed, T., Mokeddem, K.A.M., Benahmed, K., Lairedj, A.S.: IoT for smart apiculture: issues and solutions. In: 2022 3rd International Conference on Embedded & Distributed Systems (EDiS), pp. 61–66 (2022)
5. González Pacheco, M.A., Barragán Ocaña, A.: Sustainability and innovation in the beekeeping sector: a first approach. In: Estrada, S. (ed.) Digital and Sustainable Transformations in a Post-COVID World: Economic, Social, and Environmental Challenges, pp. 161–189. Springer International Publishing, Cham (2023)
6. Abu, E.S.: The use of smart apiculture management system: review paper. Asian J. Adv. Res. **3**, 6–16 (2020)
7. Zacepins, A., Kviesis, A., Pecka, A., Osadcuks, V.: Development of internet of things concept for precision beekeeping. In: 2017 18th International Carpathian Control Conference (ICCC), pp. 23–27 (2017)
8. Dasig, D.D., Mendez, J.M.: An IoT and wireless sensor network-based technology for a low-cost precision apiculture. In: Pattnaik, P.K., Kumar, R., Pal, S. (eds.) Internet of Things and Analytics for Agriculture, Volume 2. SBD, vol. 67, pp. 67–92. Springer, Singapore (2020). https://doi.org/10.1007/978-981-15-0663-5_4
9. Ochoa, I.Z., Gutierrez, S., Rodríguez, F.: Internet of things: low cost monitoring beehive system using wireless sensor network. In: 2019 IEEE International Conference on Engineering Veracruz (ICEV), pp. 1–7. IEEE (2019)
10. Tashakkori, R., Hamza, A.S., Crawford, M.B.: Beemon: An IoT-based beehive monitoring system. Comput. Electron. Agric. **190**, 106427 (2021)
11. Chamaidi, T., et al.: IOHIVE: design requirements for a system that supports interactive journaling for beekeepers during apiary inspections. In: Soares, M.M., Rosenzweig, E., Marcus, A. (eds.) Design, User Experience, and Usability: UX Research, Design, and Assessment, pp. 157–172. Springer International Publishing, Cham (2022)
12. Zabasta, A., Kunicina, N., Kondratjevs, K., Ribickis, L.: IoT Approach application for development of autonomous beekeeping system. In: 2019 International Conference in Engineering Applications (ICEA), pp. 1–6 (2019)
13. Sperandio, G., et al.: Beekeeping and honey bee colony health: a review and conceptualization of beekeeping management practices implemented in Europe. Sci. Total Environ. **696**, 133795 (2019)
14. Durant, J.L., Ponisio, L.C.: A regional, honey bee-centered approach is needed to incentivize grower adoption of bee-friendly practices in the almond industry. Front. Sustain. Food Syst. **5**, 261 (2021)
15. BEEP: digital tools for beekeepers. https://beep.nl/index.php/home-english. Accessed 11 Feb 2022

16. OSBeehives - BuzzBox Hive Health Monitor & Beekeeping App. https://www.osbeehives. com. Accessed 11 Feb 2022
17. beeXML.org – Collaboration platform for the standardization of the exchange of data about bees and beekeepers – BeeXML. https://beexml.org/beexml/. Accessed 30 Jan 2022
18. Hodzic, A., Hoang, D.: Detection of deviations in beehives based on sound analysis and machine learning (2021)
19. Terenzi, A., Cecchi, S., Spinsante, S.: On the importance of the sound emitted by honey bee hives. Vet. Sci. **7**, 168 (2020)
20. Kulyukin, V., Mukherjee, S.: On video analysis of omnidirectional bee traffic: counting bee motions with motion detection and image classification. Appl. Sci. **9**, 3743 (2019)
21. Spiesman, B.J., et al.: Assessing the potential for deep learning and computer vision to identify bumble bee species from images. Sci Rep. **11**, 7580 (2021)
22. Campbell, J., Mummert, L., Sukthankar, R.: Video monitoring of honey bee colonies at the hive entrance, vol. 4 (2008)
23. Chen, C., Yang, E.-C., Jiang, J.-A., Lin, T.-T.: An imaging system for monitoring the in-and-out activity of honey bees. Comput. Electron. Agric. **89**, 100–109 (2012)
24. Tu, G.J., Hansen, M.K., Kryger, P., Ahrendt, P.: Automatic behaviour analysis system for honeybees using computer vision. Comput. Electron. Agric. **122**, 10–18 (2016)
25. Aumann, H.M., Aumann, M.K., Emanetoglu, N.W.: Janus: a combined radar and vibration sensor for beehive monitoring. IEEE Sensors Lett. **5**, 1–4 (2021)
26. Schurischuster, S., Remeseiro, B., Radeva, P., Kampel, M.: A preliminary study of image analysis for parasite detection on honey bees. In: Campilho, A., Karray, F., ter Haar Romeny, B. (eds.) ICIAR 2018. LNCS, vol. 10882, pp. 465–473. Springer, Cham (2018). https://doi. org/10.1007/978-3-319-93000-8_52
27. Hadjur, H., Ammar, D., Lefèvre, L.: Analysis of energy consumption in a precision beekeeping system. In: Proceedings of the 10th International Conference on the Internet of Things, pp. 1–8. Association for Computing Machinery, New York (2020)
28. Rahman, A.B.M.S., Lee, M., Lim, J., Cho, Y., Shin*, C.: Systematic analysis of environmental issues on ecological smart bee farm by linear regression model. IJHIT **14**, 61–68 (2021)
29. Kulyukin, V.: Audio, image, video, and weather datasets for continuous electronic beehive monitoring. Appl. Sci. **11**, 4632 (2021)
30. Kontogiannis, S.: An internet of things-based low-power integrated beekeeping safety and conditions monitoring system. Inventions. **4**, 52 (2019)
31. The Things Network. https://www.thethingsnetwork.org/. Accessed 11 Apr 2023
32. IOHIVE Project Website and Services. https://iohive.aegean.gr. Accessed 11 Apr 2023
33. Adelantado, F., Vilajosana, X., Tuset-Peiro, P., Martinez, B., Melia-Segui, J., Watteyne, T.: Understanding the limits of LoRaWAN. IEEE Commun. Mag. **55**, 34–40 (2017)
34. Kudzu P.C.: https://kudzu.gr/. Accessed 11 Feb 2022
35. Sinha, R.S., Wei, Y., Hwang, S.-H.: A survey on LPWA technology: LoRa and NB-IoT. ICT Express. **3**, 14–21 (2017)
36. Bor, M., Vidler, J.E., Roedig, U.: LoRa for the Internet of Things. In: Presented at the EWSN '16 Proceedings of the 2016 International Conference on Embedded Wireless Systems and Networks, AUT February, vol. 15 (2016)

Emerging Data Driven Smart City and Its Solutions for Sustainability: The Case of Cuenca-Ecuador

Datzania Villao$^{(\boxtimes)}$ ⓘ, Maritza Pérez, Soraya Linzan ⓘ, and Mónica Tumbaco ⓘ

Universidad Estatal Península de Santa Elena, La Libertad, Ecuador
datzaniavillao@gmail.com

Abstract. The rapid urban growth of cities has produced several economic, social and environmental problems. This has brought the need to seek alternatives to develop more sustainable, resilient and equitable cities. One of the models that present one of the solutions for these sustainability problems are data driven sustainable smart cities, which are smart cities that use big data to generate a large amount of information that once it has been collected, stored, processed, and analyzed by different institutions with technical and specific competencies, implement actions to achieve their sustainability. Although there is no extensive literature on the characteristics of these cities, there is a theoretical framework that explains the characteristics of this type of cities. The objective of this paper is to identify the potential of the city of Cuenca in Ecuador to become a data driven sustainable smart city using this theoretical framework. The research is descriptive using the city of Cuenca as a case study, for which different sources of secondary information such as public documents about the city were used. As a result, it was identified that the city of Cuenca uses sensors to monitor traffic, air quality and noise, the implementation of smart lighting systems and the creation of a digital platform to improve the management of public services such as water, electricity and garbage collection, which makes it fit in certain characteristics to the model of a data driven sustainable smart city. However, one the main factors to fit the data driven sustainable city is the national and local context of a city.

Keywords: Data Driven · Smart City · Sustainability · Big Data

1 Introduction

Currently, more than half of the world's population lives in cities, and it is estimated that by 2050 almost seven out of ten people will live in urban areas. This rapid urbanization process has brought new problems, such as social inequality, traffic congestion, environmental pollution and health problems [1]. These problems create the need to seek mechanisms to achieve more sustainable cities. Sustainability is understood as "what makes it possible to satisfy the needs of the present without compromising the ability of future generations to satisfy their own needs" [2]. That is why the United Nations has established the Sustainable Development Goals (SDG), among which is SDG 11, which seeks to achieve more sustainable and inclusive cities through the development of more innovative models for cities [3].

O. Gervasi et al. (Eds.): ICCSA 2023 Workshops, LNCS 14108, pp. 150–165, 2023.
https://doi.org/10.1007/978-3-031-37117-2_12

The use of ICTs has become in one of the tools to achieve more sustainable cities. First, because thanks to the development of smart cities, which main component are stable, secure, reliable and interoperable technologies that are integrated into a significant volume of applications allow different services to be provided in an efficient and sustainable manner [4, 5]. Thanks to recent advances in the field of Internet of Things (IoT), artificial intelligence (AI), digital twins, robotics, and smart electricity networks and meters are driving and supporting the development of smart cities at world scale. Second, thanks to ICTs through the IoT [6], which is a rapidly expanding network of devices with embedded sensors and software that connect with each other and share data, it allows billions of devices and objects equipped with smart sensors connect with each other and collect information in real time and send this data, wirelessly, to centralized control systems for subsequent decision making [7, 8]. Third, thanks to ICTs, everyday millions of digital data are generated worldwide that different institutions, whether public or private, can store for later use. This accumulation, processing, study and use of data on a large scale is called Big Data [9]. The data obtained thanks to Big Data is undoubtedly a valuable source of information for the private sector, which until now has been the one that has benefited the most from its use, but Big Data is also called to play a key role in sustainable development from the public and institutional sphere. Big Data for sustainable development seeks to gather, cross-reference and relate data from physical components with data on social components [10]. These data, in turn, are extracted mainly from satellite photos and public databases, requiring public-private collaboration. As a result, when crossing all these data, it can help to avoid geopolitical conflicts, understand human behavior in the face of natural disasters or humanitarian crises and understand vulnerability and resilience in different situations [11].

Smart cities are taking advantage of the power of big data, for example, to manage the mobility and behavior of citizens in a much more intelligent way [6]. This is how the term "data driven smart city" has emerged, which is a city that uses the data generated by different technologies in order to improve and optimize its operations, services, strategies and policies in a specific area [12]. For example, the data generated by big data can improve security, since it can be used to know which are the most conflictive areas of a city and make decisions about it [13]. This data can also encourage sustainable growth through proper city planning, as maps can be created based on the needs of different parts of a population. The data also allow optimize operations and make better decisions in traffic management planning. For example, cities like Madrid, Barcelona and Valencia are already taking advantage of electric mobility in their urban buses [14]. Thanks to big data and the interconnection between teams, cities can access information they have never had available before and offers the possibility of making better decisions in real time. These data can also improve the environment due to air quality sensors, efficient buildings, among others. All these benefits that the information generates through ICTs brings the term "data driven sustainable smart cities", which is an innovative city that uses ICTs together with the interconnection of urban systems that allow controlling its resources in a sustainable way in order to improve their citizens' quality of life [15].

However, currently a large body of literature present exclusively the benefits of big data and the Internet of Things in a smart city. Few research focuses on the solutions that big data can bring to sustainability in smart city context. One of these few investigations on how big data can generate solutions for the sustainability of a smart city is the work of Bibri and Krogstie 2020 and Bribi 2021 in which the integration of sustainable urbanism and smart urbanism was analyzed and identified a conceptual framework for data-driven sustainable smart cities [16]. This paper aims to explore the potential of the city of Cuenca to be considered a data driven sustainable smart city. The importance of this research is that each city has a particular context for which it is necessary to analyze its specificities in terms of big data generation and how it can be used to help achieve its sustainability.

This paper is structured as follows. Section 2 provides the details of the data-driven sustainable smart cities. Section 3 presents the methodology adopted for this research. Section 4 presents the findings of elements of each dimension of the conceptual framework applied to Cuenca. Finally, this paper concludes.

2 A Conceptual Framework for Data-Driven Sustainable Smart Cities

2.1 Data Driven City

Collecting large amounts of data, processing it and sharing it in real time in the form of relevant information generates added value for a city. The data, converted into information for decision-making also facilitates synergies and interoperability, within the city itself and with other supra-municipal services and systems, such as transport, energy or health and drives innovation in areas such as mobility, safety, efficiency and energy [17].

Mobility

In this line of action, data driven city is put at the service of an integrated logistics and transport system for a city, efficient and with low environmental impact. It includes traffic management, the urban distribution of goods and the management of sustainable, safe and interconnected transport systems, which integrate buses, trams, trains, subways, bicycles, scooters and pedestrians, allowing to easily change modes of transport and prioritizing clean and non-motorized options, in addition to providing users with useful information in real time [18]. The managers of these systems use enabling technologies to provide a better service and receive feedback from citizens, who can provide information to the system in real time, which in turn allows for better service planning.

Security

Smart cities must create safe spaces, protect sensitive infrastructures and areas from threats and be able to react effectively and quickly in the event of emergencies. There are video surveillance systems and security systems based on and supported by the use of cameras, cybersecurity against attacks on essential public services, transportation security, command and control centers for emergency management, public alerts, technological location systems and video surveillance solutions applied to the protection of heritage and infrastructures [19].

Energy Efficiency
In this line of action of a smart city, everything related to the environment of cities, are the greatest generators of impacts, both due to the consumption of water, energy and raw materials, as well as the generation of waste and pollution. However, for this type of problem, there are solutions for the promotion of renewable energies, intelligent measurement systems for energy and water consumption, pollution monitoring and control, the renovation of buildings and urban equipment, as well as the efficiency, reused and recycling of resources [20]. In this sense, there are solutions for the integration of all urban services in integrated systems, which not only put technology at the service of providing services, but also for their operation and management. On the other hand, urban public lighting deserves special attention. For this, it is important to have the connectivity infrastructure for other services, given its regular distribution throughout the entire city, its permanent connection to the electricity grid and its elevation above sources of distortion and communications interference [21].

2.2   Data Driven Sustainable Smart City

One of the research about data driven smart sustainable city is the one of Bibri (2020) who points out that a data driven smart sustainable city is a city that has several components of ICT and use all these technology and solutions in order to generate, store, process, analyze and take advantages of urban data to make better decisions in different areas with the purpose to improve quality of life of its citizens [12]. The results of the research was the design of a framework for data driven sustainable smart cities that is composed of several dimensions interrelated such us technology, competences, processes and practices as it is presented in figure [16].

This theoretical framework based on the information generated from two Spanish cities presents dimensions such as technology, the competences of different actors and the processes and practices that can be implemented. All this interaction between the existing technologies of a smart city allows the generation of different operations and services which are managed by different institutions or actors with specific skills and abilities that seek to apply sustainable and equitable practices to improve the standard of living of their citizens. The data driven sustainable smart city model is based on all this interaction and integration of dimensions, which will be explained in detail below.

Technology
Within a successful smart city system that generates data, the technological infrastructure has been identified as a fundamental pillar in the model, which allows the collection, storage, processing and analysis of data. In this sense, the exchange of data between different actors and the creation of solutions based on the information analyzed is important. At this level there are platforms applied by the administration and control of a city [4]. As part of the infrastructure is everything related to accessibility such as the density of the Wi-Fi network, internet access, level of fiber optic penetration, number of wireless

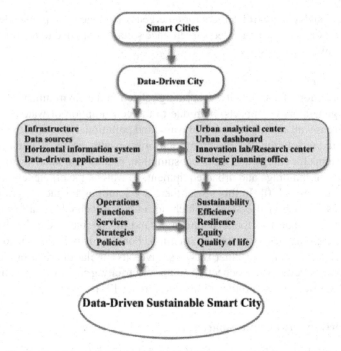

Fig. 1. A conceptual framework for data driven sustainable smart cities.

internet points in public places, broadband speed, capacity networks among others [22]. An important aspect is the sources of information, such as the presence of open and online data, electronic and mobile payment systems, use of social networks, Internet use as a percentage of the population, proportion of computer owners, proportion of residents with smartphones and number of visits from municipal services on the web portal. Another tool is surveillance sensors and cameras, in highway traffic, public transit, parking lots, public lighting, cleaning and garbage collection, and control of polluting gas emissions [4, 23].

Technology is a very important dimension of the conceptual framework because it evolved all related to a cyber-physical system that offers comprehensive management of all the elements that it encompasses through different technological tools that help collect and analyze data to meet the objectives of efficiency, sustainability, productivity and safety [24]. Intelligent infrastructures are based not only on their physical structure, cabling, sensors, among others, but also on principles such as data, applications, analytics, feedback, and adaptability [4, 6]. It is an infrastructure that collects data, processes information, takes appropriate actions in a completely autonomous and dynamic way. This classification usually includes smart grids, smart transportation, smart buildings, smart civil infrastructures, especially to provide basic services, security, and citizen participation.

Intelligent Networks

An intelligent network is one that can efficiently incorporate the behavior and actions of all the users that are connected to it, in such a way there are few losses and a high quality and security of supply. An example would be the Horizontal Information System, which is software for managing the information of one or several administrative procedures that affect the scope of several departments, even when the competence in the management and definition of the affected procedures falls on a single department [25].

These systems generally use sensors that store information at different points in a city. Some examples of these systems are Sentilo and city OS. In this area is the transport network that, thanks to its intelligent network, enjoys greater automation, integration and management of all the devices connected to it, thus achieving an efficient and sustainable distribution. Mobility technologies in cities such as Barcelona and London stand out as they use data driven technology for transport. Hybrid buses are also used to decrease emissions and a bicycle sharing system that can be available for citizens to go for short trips in the city [26]. There is also a Biking app that check the availability of bicycles. Another example of these technologies would be the case of the city of Bogotá, which uses the Intelligent Transport System (SIT)20, which is made up of a set of technological tools that serve to collect, store, provide traffic information and monitored in real time [27]. The Traffic Management Center is the place that Bogotá mobility system is managed for decision-making and dissemination regarding accidents, congestion, the environment and citizen perception based on the integration of information, knowledge, technologies and processes. The generation of these intelligent transport systems allows acquiring much more friendly transport with the environment such as electric buses. One of the greatest examples is Spain, which in many of its cities has emigrated from traditional buses to fully electric buses, cities like Madrid, Barcelona, Sevilla and Zaragoza follow this trend [14]. The growing number of people living in cities, makes necessary to [4, 6]. The use of intelligent traffic lights, it is possible to distribute the volume of vehicles, improving traffic and promoting more sustainable mobility. For example, countries like China are already beginning to carry out this type of initiative, implementing intelligent traffic lights, which are capable of decongesting large urban areas [28]. These traffic lights collect information such as the number of vehicles that have approached the traffic light, waiting times, or the state of traffic. The information is processed and allows the traffic light to decide the optimal moment to stop or move traffic, thus avoiding traffic jams [6].

Smart Energy

Thanks to energy technology, it is possible to automate, control, monitor and optimize the energy of cities. To achieve this, it is necessary for cities to have an efficient infrastructure made up of sensors, advanced technology meters, renewable energy sources or control and analysis systems. These types of methods multiply the savings and efficiency of energy in cities, one of the most valuable resources and the one that generates the most waste. One of the cities using this technology is Oslo in Norway, which has 650,000 LED bulbs that are connected to processing stations [29]. These bulbs can intelligently adjust the power of the light according to the need of the moment. Another case of cities that apply this technology is Singapore, that through hundreds of thousands of sensors installed in various regions of the country permanently monitor energy consumption, waste generation and the use of drinking and residual water, over time [30]. All these devices provide public service providers, residents, the government, industries and civil organizations with exact information on the use of resources and services, thus it is possible to identify sources of waste, reduce costs, make more efficient delivery, better distribution of resources, and above all, creating awareness among the population.

Citizen Security

Another of the most controversial global issues in recent years is the application of Artificial Intelligence in relation to citizen security. The increase in surveillance devices on streets around the world generates acceptance and rejection in equal parts. However, today's smart cities take advantage of technology in a more realistic and effective way. For example, through security and surveillance cameras, models can be applied that alert about certain suspicious movements or actions by citizens. Clear cases can be violent acts or robberies, thus resulting in great allies in reducing crime. Other elements such as facial identification have applications from simple capacity control to the identification of individuals in response to criminal cases [31].

Citizen Participation

Citizen participation is a collaboration tool between citizens and governments. To facilitate citizen participation, it is not only about incorporating the use of new technologies and promoting digital governments, but also about facilitating physical and virtual spaces for citizens to participate in the entire process of proposal, execution, and evaluation through the use of new technologies. For example, Medellín Ciudad Inteligente, encourages citizen participation through free access to the Internet in public spaces and facilities. The open data platform Mi-Medellín also allows the collection and use of data for the co-creation of the city. Moreover, the city has an Intelligent Mobility System, A Early Warning System, A Noise Monitoring Network, An Air Quality Network, and the Integrated Metropolitan Emergency and Security System, citizen-oriented initiatives that, through ICT, they respond efficiently to security, mobility and environmental problems [32].

Competencies

Data oriented competencies can be technical and institutional, which are characteristics and abilities can allow the right functioning, management and planning of different activities that can be interrelated. The institutions that develop different competencies can be training centers, study institutes for the generation of urban information, universities, strategic planning offices, analytical centers and urban dashboards [16]. These institutions or departments have the mission of processing the information and then analyzing it to make decisions to solve some sustainability problems. For example, the Analytical Centers operate through a smart city board, whose objective is to create innovative platforms for the use and application of big data. In the case of Urban dashboards, they are very useful for collaborating in the analysis of data that can be interpreted by experts or not. Other key institutions in the development of competencies are strategic planning offices, which are generally public and play a fundamental role in the development of sustainable projects. Likewise, the academy is key to managing big data information, since many universities create training programs for the creation or management of big data information and sustainable projects. Universities usually have Innovative Labs and Research Centers, that seek to develop and improve solutions for sustainability. For example, in Brasil, Sau Paulo, there is the Secretary of Innovation and Technology that has the MobiLab laboratory, which is an organization recognized nationally and internationally for innovation in the urban mobility segment, whose open data allowed the launch of a series of applications and tools focused on transportation and traffic [27]. In 2019 it became Mobilab+, focusing since then on the search for solutions related to education, health, housing, well-being, the environment and mobility, among others [33]. In this sense, these institutions can provide real-time information to users about transportation schedules, bicycle availability, weather, air pollution, and traffic level. All this information can help in the planning of a city, if there is a clear planning of the management model of a city and the role played by each of the actors involved.

Processes and Practices
The processes and practices are totally related to the technology and competences that a smart city may have. For example, depending on technology and infrastructure that a city has, different services can be provided and various operations can be carried out or specific strategies can be created and even different policies can be applied. These operations are generally related to transportation, traffic congestion, urban infrastructure management, citizen security, gas emissions, equal access to education, health, other social services, citizen participation, and urban planning. In the same way, the practices that can be applied in a smart city to make it more sustainable, efficient, equitable and resilient depend on the different skills and abilities developed by the different institutions involved.

3 Methodology

This is a descriptive investigation, since a specific case study of the city of Cuenca is used, which has been chosen because in 2022 it was evaluated and recognized as the best smart and sustainable city in Ecuador [34]. This is based on the International Model of Sustainable Smart Cities of the International Telecommunications Union of the United Nations and evaluated by the Ministry of Telecommunications in 2022 among 60 cities in the country. This indicates that this city is applying technologies for the development of different sustainable projects in the social, political and environmental areas. In this sense, development plans, programs, projects, public documents and other secondary data of the city were reviewed. In the same way, the research is of a deductive type since it goes from the general to choosing a theoretical framework on data driven sustainable smart city and adjusting it to a specific case study such as the city of Cuenca.

4 Results of the Case Study of Cuenca

The conceptual framework for data driven sustainable smart cities, as presented in Fig. 1, generates data in different areas. The generation, collection, management and control of this data depend on two large dimensions such as Technology, which implies the physical and non-physical part of ICTs, which are in charge of the different operations, functions and services in the city. The other important dimension is the competences that are generated from the different actors that can be planning departments, universities, urban analysis centers and research centers which are in charge of managing the information generated by a smart city in order to use the information in sustainability projects. That is why, based on this framework applied to Cuenca (Fig. 2).

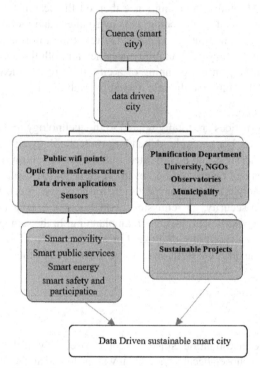

Fig. 2. Cuenca a data driven sustainable smart city

Technology

Internet coverage in Cuenca is relatively good. Most of the urban areas of the city have access to high-speed internet through technologies such as ADSL, cable, fiber optics and Wi-Fi. The most popular internet provider companies in the city are Claro, Movistar, CNT and TV Cable. For example, there is an infrastructure of 85% of fiber optics in the city and according to the 2019 Multipurpose Survey, 79.02% of households in the urban area of the city have internet [34]. In addition, the city has more than 600 public Internet points in parks, markets, squares and train areas [35]. This internet coverage allows the city to offer services with a mass focus, applying emerging technologies such as IoT and Big Data.

Transport, Traffic, and Mobility

Cuenca is a city where points of interest are within short distances. It has accessible and safe routes and attractive routes that allow people to enjoy the urban landscape, more direct routes that help optimize travel time and correctly resolve conflicting points.

Its mobility infrastructure allows it to articulate with other modes of transport. In the downtown area of the city, there are sensors to monitor vehicular traffic, as well as smart lighting systems to save energy [36]. The city also has 100 km of cycle paths, and non-polluting transport such as the Tram that allows reducing the carbon footprint as well as the collection of waste and recycling [34]. For example, there is the Cuenca Electro-mobility Plan born from the Transformative Urban Mobility Initiative (TUMI) which, through the German Cooperation for Sustainable Development (GIZ), seeks to accelerate the adoption of sustainable mobility in the world supporting developing countries [37]. In addition, the city has the "BiciCuenca" public bicycle program that adds to the initiative to build safer spaces and streets for cyclists by redesigning street intersections with an accessible design [38]. Moreover, with the purpose of providing support in the traffic operations of the city, the Mayor's Office of Cuenca and its Mobility, Transit and Transportation Company, EMOV EP, through the use of drones, detect mobility difficulties on the roads with the highest circulation [39]. During overflights, the images and videos captured by the drones are sent to a Command Center where it is coordinated with group leaders and supervisors so that contingency plans are immediately activated that allow a better vehicular flow.

Environment

It was pointed out in the Cuenca Air Quality Report 2018, the Cuenca Air Quality Monitoring Network has generated reliable information through internationally recognized methods and procedures. Since June 2012, the Basin Monitoring Network operates an automatic station installed in the Historic Center. This infrastructure records the levels of air pollution and the values of the main meteorological parameters in real time. Since June 2016, they have also been operating with automatic sensors for fine particulate matter, which record the concentrations of this pollutant in the area of influence of the Cuenca Industrial Park [40].

On the other hand, within the urban area there are levels of auditory emissions higher than the norm, with few exceptions, especially at night time for measurement. It is worth mentioning that as part of a noise control project, the platform http://gis.uazuay.edu. ec/proyectos/ruido-continuo/ was created, which works in real time, reporting the noise level in 7 stations located in different points of the urban area of the city [41]. In addition, there are sustainable energy projects in which solar energy systems have already been implemented in various public and private buildings.

Citizen Security

It is the function of the Municipal local Government to create and coordinate municipal citizen security councils, with the participation of the National Police, the community and other organizations related to security matters, which formulate and execute local policies, plans and evaluation of results on prevention, protection, security and citizen coexistence. The Cuenca Citizen Security Council (CSC) was created in December 2002. This institution attached to the Municipality has the primary function of planning and coordinating in an articulated manner with the entities in charge of citizen security and developing public policies for the benefit of the Cuenca people. This drives the neighborhood organization to achieve a concept of mutual aid. The CSC works jointly with the Government of Azuay, the Ministry of Public Health, the Fire Department, among others. The SIS ECU 911system has high technology and has a video-surveillance system and monitoring of events in the city in real time. Specifically, an intelligent video surveillance system was implemented in the historic center of the city, where there are more than 600 security cameras connected to SIS ECU 911 to monitor vehicular and pedestrian traffic, as well as to prevent crime and guarantee the safety of citizens and tourists. This modern equipment has video analytics such as face detection, loitering patterns, license plate detection and a loudspeaker system for immediate alert [42].

Citizen Participation

Cuenca has various forms of citizen participation that seek to involve the population in decision-making of the city planning. One of the main forms of citizen participation is through the Citizen Participation Boards, which are neighborhood organizations created to encourage citizen participation in local management. Another form of citizen participation in Cuenca is through the Consultative Councils, which are forums for dialogue between the municipality and different sectors of society, such as business, academics, and the community. These councils aim to encourage collaboration between society and local authorities to improve city management. For this, there are digital platforms for citizen participation, such as the virtual platform for citizen complaints, which allows citizens to report problems in their area. Another platform is "Cuenca Participa", which aims to promote citizen participation in decision-making [43]. In the same way, a digital platform has been developed to improve the management of public services such as water and garbage collection. Through this platform, citizens can make requests and report problems more efficiently, which has improved efficiency and transparency in service management.

Competencies

The planning model of Cuenca has different actors that play fundamental roles in the collection, management, administration and analysis of data in the city, which are presented in Fig. 3.

Each of these actors play important and fundamental roles that are clearly specified in the Annual Development Plan of the of Cuenca city. In this sense Cuenca Municipality is the actor that coordinates and plans the different operations in the city. Below is a summary of the powers and functions of each Institution (Table 1).

Discussion

Urban planning in Cuenca is an important and relevant issue for the development of the city. The city has a Develop Plan that focuses on improving the quality of life of the inhabitants and promoting the sustainable development of the city. The plan establishes a series of objectives and long-term goals. It also defines the strategies and actions necessary to achieve them. Among the main objectives of the plan are: Promote the protection of the cultural and natural heritage of the city, improving accessibility and urban mobility, by promoting public transport and promoting the use of bicycles and the tram.

Within its planning, the creation of an integrated public transport system has been established, which allows the mobility of citizens in an efficient and sustainable manner, promoting the development of tourist and cultural projects. That is, urban planning in

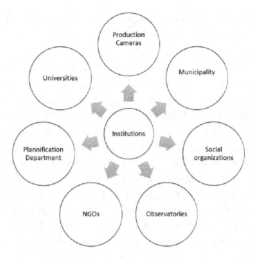

Fig. 3. Institutions of the data driven sustainable smart city in Cuenca

Table 1. Competences and Functions of Institutions

Competences	Functions
Planning Department	Participating in the process of formulating Cuenca Development Plan Making use of data to guide urban planning Using data, identifying patters and solving problems
Universities	Designing sustainable projects for the city and then presenting them to the Municipality. Ex. Design and implement the Monitoring, Follow-up and Evaluation System (SME) of Development programs and projects Offering educational programs of big data
Production Cameras	Finance development and sustainability projects
Observatories	Preparing periodic special reports on the progress in the objectives and goals of the Development plan. Ex. The Territorial Development Observatory (ODET) aims to observe and monitor the quality of life of the population Facilitating the evaluation of the actions undertaken within the city
NGOs	Providing technical, methodological and operational tools and regulations for the identification, prioritization, execution and coordinated evaluation of plans, programs and projects. Ex. Institute for Transportation & Development Policy Integrating resources and expertise through collective intelligence
Social organizations	Participating in decision-making, seeking the concretion of spaces for permanent dialogue between institutional actors and citizens in order to strengthen cantonal participatory democracy. Ex. Cuenca participa

the city focuses on the sustainable development of the city, the protection of cultural and natural heritage, the improvement of the quality of life of the inhabitants and the promotion of economic development. Planning and management is carried out jointly between the local, private camera, universities, observatories and social organizations. Decision-making and definition of strategies is articulated in a participatory manner, with horizontal relationships, despite the existence of a hierarchical position between society and local government and that the public administration bodies have the power to execute the resolutions. However, the framework of data driven sustainable smart city that was inspired in cities such us Barcelona and London, has different characteristics of Cuenca city, for example Cuenca has centralized its development plan in its Municipality through its public enterprises that play critical roles specially in the mobility, delivery of public services and sustainability projects. Moreover, the Planning Department is the one that coordinate the activities with the rest of the institutions. In the case of sustainable projects, universities and NGOS are the one that design sustainable projects and specific programs about new technologies. On the other hand, social organization, and observatories participate in the decision-making process in the city.

5 Conclusion

The rapid urban growth of cities generates the need to seek more sustainable and habitable cities and technology leads the way to build them. Thanks to digitization, the elements that make up these urban centers can be connected to each other and improve the well-being of millions of people. That is why a Smart City is one of the best options since it is characterized by taking advantage of the full potential of Information and Communication Technologies to create healthier, safer, more efficient and inclusive spaces. In these urban spaces, the connectivity of the devices is of great importance since it allows communication between them and the emission and reception of data. This information is ordered, classified and analyzed thanks to Big Data, which is capable of studying large volumes of data in real time to obtain trends and anticipate solutions, so that those responsible for the services can make the right decisions. This is where the term data driven smart city appears, which together with the need to make cities more sustainable become and data driven sustainable smart cities, which are cities that use ICTs to collect information through big data to then make decisions to achieve a more sustainable city. Although there is still no extensive literature on the data sustainable smart cities, a theoretical framework has been established for this type of cities that includes technology that include infrastructure, applications and data sources which depending on the progress of this, produces different operations and strategies to be developed in a city. Another dimension is the competencies that are abilities that various institutions have within a smart city to process, classify and analyze the information which projects and actions are created to achieve sustainability, equity and resilience in a city. As established in the objective of the research, it was sought to identify the potential of the city of Cuenca that fit into this framework since it is considered as a smart city that uses technological infrastructure with the skills of the different actors involved to apply sustainable projects. Among the initiatives that the city has applied are the use of sensors to monitor traffic, air quality and noise, the implementation of smart lighting systems and the creation of a digital platform to improve the management of public services such as water and garbage collection. However, despite the fact that much progress has been made with the implementation of ICTs, this city has a very different context from cities like Barcelona and London, which were the cities that inspired the theoretical framework used. It is important to mention that to achieve the sustainability of a city, it depends to a great extent on the national and local contexts, especially with its public policies, the level of technological infrastructure installed, and the skills developed by the institutions involved. However, there are still many gaps in this topic of data driven sustainable smart cities, such as identifying whether other cities in the country can adapt to the theoretical framework used, as well as identifying opportunities and challenges to develop data driven smart sustainable cities, the public policies necessary to promote this type of cities among other topics that could be explored in future researches.

References

1. Battista, G., Evangelisti, L., Guattari, C., Basilicata, C., Lieto Vollaro, R.: Buildings energy efficiency: interventions analysis under a smart cities approach. Sustainability **6**(8), 4694–4705 (2014). https://doi.org/10.3390/su6084694
2. Batty, M.: Smart cities, big data. Environ. Plann. B. Plann. Des. **39**(2), 191–193 (2012). https://doi.org/10.1068/b3902ed
3. Batty, M.: Big data, smart cities and city planning. Dial. Hum. Geogr. **3**(3), 274–279 (2013). https://doi.org/10.1177/2043820613513390
4. Bibri, S.E.: Data-driven smart sustainable cities of the future: an evidence synthesis approach to a comprehensive state-of-the-art literature review. Sustain. Fut. **3**(100047), 1–23 (2021). https://doi.org/10.1016/j.sftr.2021.100047
5. Bibri, S.E., Krogstie, J.: The emerging data–driven Smart City and its innovative applied solutions for sustainability: the cases of London and Barcelona. Energy Inf. **3**(1), 1–42 (2020). https://doi.org/10.1186/s42162-020-00108-6
6. Bici Publica Cuenca. (Bici Publica Cuenca) Recuperado el 1 de April de 2023 (2022). https://www.bicicuenca.com/
7. CAF. (CAF) Recuperado el 1 de April de 2023. https://www.caf.com/es/conocimiento/visiones/2020/06/brasil-lider-govtech-de-america-latina/
8. Calzada, I., Cowie, P.: Beyond smart and data-driven city-regions? Rethinking stakeholder-helixes strategies. Reg. Maga. **308**(4), 25–28 (2017). https://doi.org/10.1080/13673882.2017.11958675
9. Center by International Government Innovation. (Center by International Government Innovation) Recuperado el 1 de April de 2023 (2018). https://www.cigionline.org/articles/smart-cities-need-local-democracy/?utm_source=google_ads&utm_medium=grant&gclid=CjwKCAjwitShBhA6EiwAq3RqA291LySBNhtgsWJXnBvmbgy_FxMuv_Nx39EEbkK55y9poIL4Iu0qMRoCPIoQAvD_BwE
10. CEPAL. (CEPAL) Recuperado el 1 de April de 2023 (2022). https://repositorio.cepal.org/bitstream/handle/11362/48000/1/S2200488_es.pdf
11. Copaja, M., Esponda, C.: Tecnología e innovación hacia la ciudad inteligente. Avances, perspectivas y desafíos. Bitacora Urbano Territorial **29**(2) (2019). https://doi.org/10.15446/bitacora.v29n2.68333
12. Cuenca Municipality. (Cuenca Municipality) Recuperado el 1 de April de 2023 (2022). https://www.cuenca.gob.ec/content/cuenca-la-mejor-puntuada-en-el-pais-como-ciudad-inteligente-y-sostenible

13. Cuenca Municipality. (Cuenca Municipality) Recuperado el 1 de April de 2023 (2022). https://www.cuenca.gob.ec/content/inicia-plan-piloto-de-electromovilidad-en-cuenca
14. Cuenca Municipality. (Cuenca Municipality) Recuperado el 1 de April de 2023 (2022). https://www.cuenca.gob.ec/content/drones-monitorean-la-circulaci%C3%B3n-vehicular-en-cuenca
15. Cuenca Municipality. (Cuenca Municipality) Recuperado el 1 de April de 2023 (2022). https://www.cuenca.gob.ec/sites/default/files/planificacion/dic2022/2_1_Diagnostico.pdf
16. Cuenca Municipality. (Cuenca Municipality) Recuperado el 1 de April de 2023 (2022). https://www.cuenca.gob.ec/content/alcald%C3%ADa-de-cuenca-present%C3%B3-mapa-de-ruido-y-gu%C3%ADas-did%C3%A1cticas
17. Cuenca Municipality. (Cuenca Municipality) Recuperado el 1 de April de 2023 (2022). https://cuencaparticipa.cuenca.gob.ec/?locale=es
18. de la Harpe, A., Thurner, T.W.: The critical role of information system integration in a horizontal merger. J. Cases Inf. Technol. (JCIT) **21**(4), 1–13 (2019)
19. El Comercio. (El Comercio) Recuperado el 1 de April de 2023 (2023). https://elmercurio.com.ec/2023/01/20/cuenca-ciudad-inteligente-sostenible-2022/
20. Future Space. (Future Space) Recuperado el 1 de April de 2023. https://www.futurespace.es/uso-ia-smart-cities-para-eficiencia-energetica-y-sostenibilidad/
21. Guarda, T.I., Oliveira, P., Ribeiro, M.I., Fernandes, A.J.: How to measure the performance of a smart city. In: CAIW 2020: Workshops at the Third International Conference on Applied Informatics 2020, vol. 2714, pp. 77–86. CEUR Workshop Proceedings, Ota (2020). https://ceur-ws.org/Vol-2714/icaiw_aiesd_5.pdf
22. Guarda, T., Fernandes, C., Augusto, M.F.: Technology, Business, Innovation, and Entrepreneurship in Industry 4.0. Springer, Cham (2023). https://doi.org/10.1007/978-3-031-17960-0
23. Guarda, T., et al.: Internet of Things challenges. In: IEE (ed.) 12th Iberian Conference on Information Systems and Technologies (CISTI), pp. 1–4. IEEE (2017). https://ieeexplore.ieee.org/stamp/stamp.jsp?arnumber=7975936&casa_token=X1wQ9Y2C_pgAAAAA:dMCNRggeTj9DJ9IZoY1Wzy1w40NuKutNtVpNzyk4igHfKH5wnwcSa1-6fzWNeSigXBkki8Nhggw&tag=1
24. Happle, G., Wilhelm, E., Fonseca, J.A., Schlueter, A.: Determining air-conditioning usage patterns in Singapore from distributed, portable sensors. Energy Procedia **122**, 313–318 (2017). https://doi.org/10.1016/j.egypro.2017.07.328
25. Hashem, I.A., et al.: The role of big data in smart city. Int. J. Inf. Manag. **36**(5), 748–758 (2016). https://eprints.soton.ac.uk/394830/1/IJIM_Big_Data_in_Smart_City_Final.pdf
26. Ismagilova, E., Hughes, L., Rana, N.P., Dwivedi, Y.K.: Security, privacy and risks within smart cities: literature review and development of a smart city interaction framework. Inf. Syst. Front. **24**, 1–22 (2020). https://doi.org/10.1007/s10796-020-10044-1
27. ITU WRC. (ITU) Recuperado el 1 de abril de 2023 (2021). https://www.itu.int/es/mediacentre/backgrounders/Pages/smart-sustainable-cities.aspx
28. Lacinák, M., Ristvej, J.: Smart city, safety and security. Procedia Eng. **192**, 522–527 (2017). https://doi.org/10.1016/j.proeng.2017.06.090
29. Laufs, J., Borrion, H., Bradford, B.: Security and the smart city: a systematic review. Sustain. Cities Soc. **55**, 102023 (2020). https://doi.org/10.1016/j.scs.2020.102023
30. Lopes, I.M., Guarda, T.: The relationship between smart cities and the internet of things in low density regions. In: Antipova, T., Rocha, A. (eds.) DSIC18 2018. AISC, vol. 850, pp. 369–378. Springer, Cham (2019). https://doi.org/10.1007/978-3-030-02351-5_42
31. Martins, F., Patrão, C., Moura, P., Almeida, A.T.: A review of energy modeling tools for energy efficiency in smart cities. Smart Cities **4**(4), 1420–1436 (2021). https://doi.org/10.3390/smartcities4040075

32. United Nations. Recuperado el 1 de April de 2023. https://www.un.org/es/impacto-acad%
    C3%A9mico/page/sostenibilidad#:~:text=En%201987%2C%20la%20Comisi%C3%B3n%
    20Brundtland,de%20satisfacer%20sus%20necesidades%20propias
33. Pal, D., Triyason, T., Padungweang, P.: Big data in smart-cities: current research and chal-
    lenges. Indon. J. Electr. Eng. Inf. (IJEEI) **6**(4), 351–360 (2018). https://doi.org/10.11591/ijeei.
    v6i1.543
34. Pedrotti, A.: Portal Movilidad España. (Portal Movilidad España) Recuperado el 1 de April
    de 2023 (2022). https://portalmovilidad.com/si-a-los-buses-electricos-en-espana-los-operad
    ores-y-ciudades-con-los-planes-mas-ambiciosos/
35. Portal Diverso. Portal Diverso. (Portal Diverso) Recuperado el 1 de April de 2023
    (2022). https://portaldiverso.com/los-controles-de-seguridad-en-cuenca-y-la-provincia-dan-
    buenos-resultados/
36. Radu, L.D.: Disruptive technologies in smart cities: a survey on current trends and challenges.
    Smart Cities **3**(3), 1022–1038 (2020). https://doi.org/10.3390/smartcities3030051
37. Ruggieri, R., Ruggeri, M., Vinci, G., Poponi, S.: Electric mobility in a smart city: European
    overview. Energies **14**(2), 315 (2021). https://doi.org/10.3390/en14020315
38. SER. (SER) Recuperado el 1 de April de 2023 (2020). https://cadenaser.com/emisora/2020/
    08/06/ser_cuenca/1596714103_942271.html
39. Telefónica, F.: Smart Cities: un primer paso hacia la internet de las cosas. Fundación Telefónica
    (2011)
40. The Copenhagen Centre on Energy Efficiency. (The Copenhagen Centre on Energy Efficiency)
    Recuperado el 1 de April de 2023. https://c2e2.unepccc.org/kms_object/oslo-norways-street-
    lighting-retrofit/
41. Toli, A.M., Murtagh, N.: The concept of sustainability in smart city definitions. Front. Built
    Environ. **6**(77) (2020). https://doi.org/10.3389/fbuil.2020.00077
42. United Nations. (United Nations) Recuperado el 1 de April de 2023/ https://www.un.org/sus
    tainabledevelopment/es/cities/
43. Zanella, A., Bui, N., Castellani, A., Vangelista, L., Zorzi, M.: Internet of things for smart cities.
    IEEE Internet Things J. **1**(1), 22–32 (2014). https://doi.org/10.1109/JIOT.2014.2306328

Adoption of the Rules of the General Data Protection Regulation on the Websites of Municipalities

Pascoal Padrão[1], A. J. G. Fernandes[1,2] ⓘ, and Isabel Lopes[1,3,4(✉)] ⓘ

[1] Instituto Politécnico de Bragança, Campus de Santa Apolónia, 5300-253 Bragança, Portugal
{toze,isalopes}@ipb.pt

[2] Centro de Investigação de Montanha (CIMO), Laboratório Associado para a Sustentabilidade e Tecnologia em Regiões de Montanha (SusTEC), Instituto Politécnico de Bragança, Campus de Santa Apolónia, 5300-253 Bragança, Portugal

[3] UNIAG, Instituto Politécnico de Bragança, Campus de Santa Apolónia, 5300-253 Bragança, Portugal

[4] Algoritmi, Universidade do Minho, Largo do Paço, 4704-553 Braga, Portugal

Abstract. With the advent of technologies, the amount of information processed by these means has increased dramatically. In this sense, the protection of personal data has become urgent to guarantee people's freedom of thought and to avoid possible abuses in terms of invasion of privacy and preservation of personal information. Thus, the European Union created a Regulation, in 2016, with the aim of standardizing legislation and practices with regard to data protection, in order to protect its citizens and increase transparency in the processing of their data, the same is called the "General Regulation on Data Protection" (GDPR). After 7 years since its creation and five since its entry into force and since the GDPR also affects websites, we intend with this study to verify if the websites of some Portuguese municipalities (belonging to CIM-TTM, CIM-AT and CIM Douro) include the necessary dynamics to comply with the rules dictated by the regulation.

Keywords: General Regulation on Data Protection · Municipalities · Data Protection Officer · Information systems · Safety

1 Introduction

The technological evolution of the beginning of the century and globalization promoted a transverse revolution in our society and led us to new challenges in terms of personal data protection, imposing a solid and more coherent protection framework in the European Union (EU).

The need for the EU to create a more solid framework in terms of data protection was undoubtedly due to the great technological evolution that led to more and more information being stored digitally, but also to standardize the various existing regulations

O. Gervasi et al. (Eds.): ICCSA 2023 Workshops, LNCS 14108, pp. 166–176, 2023.
https://doi.org/10.1007/978-3-031-37117-2_13

and standards in a more robust and unique framework that all EU Member States must abide by through its implementation.

As a result of these findings, the EU created Regulation (EU) 2016/679, with the aim of updating legislation on data protection, aligning it with the new digital age, in addition, it also intended to harmonize legislation in all States EU Members, reinforce the rights of citizens, protecting them from risks and threats in the use of their personal data.

This EU legal imperative in terms of time should have been implemented 5 years ago. Thus, it is imperative to know in this research work, not the state of its implementation in general, but rather, to verify if the Websites include the necessary dynamics mentioned in the regulation.

This regulation applies to all organizations based in the EU. Companies and public entities are required to prove compliance with all requirements arising from the application of this Regulation. Thus, in this study and since Municipalities deal daily with a lot of information from their residents, we find it pertinent to know if the content of their Websites is adjusted to the directives that the GDPR imposes.

The municipalities under study are Portuguese and as the intention is to analyze the Websites of the 308 existing municipalities, the focus of this work will focus on a part of the Portuguese territory located in the north interior, covered by the Municipalities belonging to three Intermunicipal Communities (CIM). In other works, other territories will be covered until the total analysis of the 308 existing Municipalities.

The Intermunicipal Communities are an association of Municipalities, within the Portuguese legal framework, through the creation of a superior local entity, to which the associated Municipalities delegate part of the functions or powers conferred upon them by law, with the aim of providing services to all its members. According to Law No. 75/2013 of September 12, there are currently 23 intermunicipal entities. This study focuses on three:

- Intermunicipal Community of Terras de Trás-os-Montes (CIM-TTM)
- Intermunicipal Community of Alto Tâmega and Barroso (CIM-AT)
- Douro Intermunicipal Community (CIM-Douro)

The structure of this research work begins with this introduction, followed by a brief review of the literature on the general data protection regulation. The methodology used for this research work follows, a methodology that takes us to the point of the results of this study. Finally, the conclusions are briefly presented, as well as the verified limitations and future works are identified.

2   General Regulation on Data Protection

Regulation (EU) 2016/679 (2016), published on April 27, 2016, more commonly known as the General Data Protection Regulation, which puts into effect the new regulations relating to the protection of natural persons, with regard to the processing of personal data and the free movement of such data, thus revoking the previous Directive 95/46/EC, which had as its fundamental objectives to ensure compliance with legislation in all Member States, as well as to allow citizens and business structures to benefit from the digital economy and e-commerce, reforming the way organizations work with personal data, and above all, protecting the personal data of European citizens, since the GDPR creates new duties for the business and public sector.

The GDPR is a legal framework that provides guidelines for collecting and processing personal information from individuals [1]. GDPR seeks to clarify data protection issues for personal data collected and processed in the EU [2]. Personal data is any information that relates to an individual who can be directly or indirectly identified. Names, email addresses, location information, ethnicity, gender, biometric data, religious beliefs, web cookies, and political opinions can also be personal data [3].

In this way, having unified and up-to-date legislation with regard to data protection is essential to safeguard the fundamental right to data protection, as well as to enable the growth of a consolidated digital economy and strengthen the fight against crime and terrorism. The GDPR is generally regarded as the most strict privacy policy released and enforced to date [4, 5].

The GDPR was ratified in 2016 by the European Union and entered into force only in May 2018, directly applicable in all Member States [6, 7].

The same applies to all entities that work with personal data, of natural persons, and the same entities that process personal data must analyse, without exception, the rules provided for therein.

However, it should be noted that the GDPR, despite being a European diploma, is not governed by the correction and penalty of companies that process data worldwide, since the GDPR takes as a paradigm the technology available today for processing personal data and, therefore, aims to reconcile the use of technological solutions in their current and future state of development, and the risks they entail, with the defense of the rights and freedoms of persons whose data are processed [8].

The strictest rules presented by it translate into:

1. there is greater control, by people, over their personal data;
2. there is equal competition from which companies benefit.

The main innovations of the General Data Protection Regulation are [9]:

1. "New rights for citizens.
2. The creation of the post of Data Protection Officer (DPO).
3. Obligation to carry out Risk Analyses and Impact Assessments to determine compliance with the regulation.
4. Obligation of the Data Controller and Data Processor to document the processing operations.
5. New notifications to the Supervisory Authority: security breaches and prior authorisation for certain kinds of processing.
6. New obligations to inform the data subject by means of a system of icons that are harmonised across all the countries of the EU.
7. An increase in the size of sanctions.
8. Application of the concept 'One-stop-shop' so that data subjects can carry out procedures even though this affects authorities in other member states.
9. Establishment of obligations for new special categories of data.

10. New principles in the obligations over data: transparency and minimisation of data".

Key steps organizations need to take to get their Websites GDPR compliant [10].

1. Improve Your Privacy Policy
2. Create a Cookie Collection Notice
3. Display Notices on All Website Forms
4. Make Sure All Plugins Are GDPR Compliant
5. Use the Double Opt-in
6. Add Unsubscribe Links
7. Delete Personal Data on Request
8. Don't Buy Mailing Lists

The General Data Protection Regulation is thus the most recent and one of the strictest data protection regulations approved by the EU. Fundamentally, it aims to protect the Rights and Freedoms of all individuals included in its terms; ultimately the privacy and security of all our personal data [11].

The introduction of the GDPR enables users to control how their data is accessed and processed, requiring consent from users before any data manipulation is carried out on their (personal) data by smart devices or cloud-hosted services [12].

In addition to the changes already mentioned, the GDPR also affects websites, as these are increasingly a source of data collection.

The GDPR "has changed the way websites collect and process customer data. Its effective implementation in May 2018 brought changes in the construction of procedures for requesting, storing and processing data, as well as in the interaction with consumers regarding information on how, why and where data is stored. Websites must include some dynamics in order to comply with the rules dictated by the GDPR" [13]. These dynamics go through:

- Inform consumers of the basics of data collection;
- Ensuring that consumer rights are being fulfilled;
- Provide updated Privacy and Cookie Policies;
- Allow contact to exercise the Rights of Holders.

In addition, some ways to make a website GDPR compliant are [14]:

- Update Privacy Policy;
- Cookie Consent Policy;
- Secure Data Storage;
- Comply with Data Requests;
- Penetration Testing.

There is no one-size-fits-all approach or solution for websites to be GDPR compliant, because every organization is different, the most important thing is that the GDPR protects the privacy of users and ensures that their information is properly protected.

3 Research Methodology

Document analysis was the method used in this study through the articulation between the literature review on the subject under study with the records collected on the websites of each municipality.

Document analysis becomes revealing throughout the investigation process, as it enables the interpretation of its content and enables the understanding of practices in context [15].

As already mentioned in the summary, and although the analysis of the websites of the 308 Portuguese municipalities would be optimal, this study initiated this study, restricting it to all the municipalities that make up the CIM of Terras de Trás-os-Montes, Alto Tâmega and Barroso and Douro (see Fig. 1).

As observed in Fig. 1 the CIMs under study were three of the CIMs that are part of NUTS III. The CIM of Terras de Trás-os-Montes is made up of 9 Municipalities, the CIM of Alto Tâmega and Barroso is made up of 6 Municipalities and the CIM Douro which is made up of 19 Municipalities. Thus, in this study, 34 websites belonging to the Municipalities that integrate these three CIM's were analyzed.

The analysis of the websites of these 34 municipalities was carried out between August 1, 2022 and September 30, 2022.

In order to respond to the objectives of this study, the analysis of the municipalities' websites began with a search for the terms "General Data Protection Regulation" and "GDPR".

However, the collection of search records on the websites of each municipality by the terms "GDPR" and "General Data Protection Regulation", did not have a great effect,

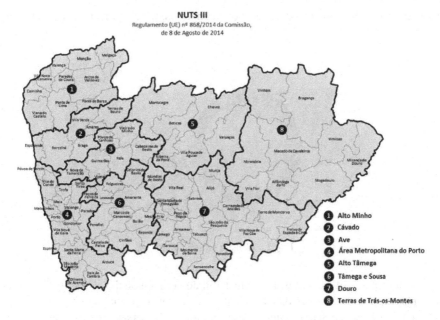

Fig. 1. CIM's study participants (5, 7 and 8)

as we found that, in a large part of them, did not return any results. Since we knew a priori that one of the municipalities had already implemented the GDPR norms and on its website, the aforementioned search did not return any value, a more exhaustive investigation was carried out, whereby we denoted that the term used would be "Privacy and Data Protection Policy".

That said, we reformulated the survey carried out so far and included the two terms in the research, "General Data Protection Regulation" and "Privacy and Data Protection Policy", no longer using the terminology "GDPR" in the research.

4 Results

The first step towards carrying out this investigation was to carry out a survey on each website of the respective municipalities in order to assess whether they contemplated some form of protection of personal data in them.

As such, the following search terms were entered in the search engine of each of the websites: "General Data Protection Regulation" and "Privacy and Data Protection Policy", as previously mentioned, in the item "Adjustments to the Planned Study" in the previous chapter, in a first phase the research focused only on the term "General Data Protection Regulation"; However, we found that most websites use the term "Privacy and Data Protection Policy".

Thus, in a universe of 34 websites researched, carrying out 68 searches in total, that is, carrying out the search for the two terms listed in the methodology, per website, 20 of them presented positive results, which corresponds to 59%, and 14 of them did not return any given that it included any of the search terms, which corresponds to 41% (see Fig. 2).

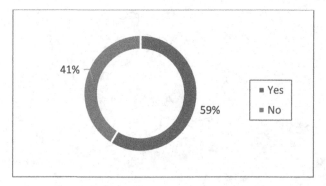

Fig. 2. Website search results

The percentage of 41% of websites that still do not include the necessary dynamics for compliance with the rules dictated by the regulation seems to us to be a somewhat still high figure, given that, after more than five years of the mandatory implementation of the norms contained in the GDPR we are faced with municipalities that still do not comply with these norms.

Since in the methodology we selected three CIM as a sample for this study, it is pertinent at this point to present individually the response of each of the municipalities, as well as the CIM they are part of. As such, in Table 1, we present the result of the search on the website of each municipality, corresponding to the " ✗" to a negative result and the " ✓" to a positive result, in the return of the search carried out by the two terms carried out.

In Table 1 we have all the Municipalities belonging to the three CIM's, then each of the CIM's is presented graphically. Figure 3, shows the percentage of websites that comply with the rules dictated by the GDPR belonging to the CIM-TTM. A can be seen, most CIM-TTM Municipalities comply with these rules, only 33% do not make any reference to the GDPR.

When we talk about CIM-TTM we are talking about 9 Municipalities that integrate it and as we can in Table 1 the Municipalities that translate on their Website what the data protection regulation dictates are: Alfandega da Fé, Bragança, Macedo de Cavaleiros, Miranda Douro, Mogadouro and Vimioso. On the other hand, those that do not make any reference on their Websites when we carry out searches with the defined keywords are: Mirandela, Vila Flor and Vinhais.

The question that must be asked is whether the Municipalities that do not include the dynamics present in the GDPR on their Websites have implemented the GDPR or not. Because there is a departure, the GDPR will hardly be present on websites if the regulation is not yet a reality in that Municipality.

Regarding the CIM-Douro, the largest of the three CIMs under analysis in this research work, we found that only 53% of the Municipalities comply with the standards on their websites (see Fig. 4). The figure of 47%, corresponding to 9 Municipalities

Table 1. Results by CIM

CIM-TTM	CIM-AT	CIM-Douro
✓ Alfandega da Fé	✗ Boticas	✓ Alijó
✓ Bragança	✓ Chaves	✓ Armamar
✓ Macedo de Cavaleiros	✓ Montalegre	✗ Carrazeda de Ansiães
✓ Miranda do Douro	✗ Ribeira de Pena	✗ Freixo de Espada à Cinta
✗ Mirandela	✓ Valpaços	✗ Lamego
✓ Mogadouro	✓ Vila Pouca de Aguiar	✓ Mesão Frio
✗ Vila Flor		✗ Moimenta da Beira
✓ Vimioso		✓ Murça
✗ Vinhais		✗ Penedono
		✓ Peso da Régua
		✓ Sabrosa
		✓ Santa Marta de Penaguião
		✗ São João da Pesqueira
		✗ Sernancelhe
		✗ Tabuaço
		✗ Tarouca
		✓ Torre de Moncorvo
		✓ Vila Nova de Foz Côa
		✓ Vila Real

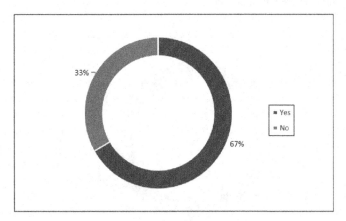

Fig. 3. CIM TTM result

among the 19 that make up the CIM-Douro, is relatively high, considering the time period since the entry into force of the GDPR and this study. Municipalities that do not have their websites in compliance are: Carrazeda de Ansiães, Freixo de Espada à Cinta, Lamego, Moimenta da Beira, Penedono, São João da Pesqueira, Sernancelhe, Tabuaço and Tarouca.

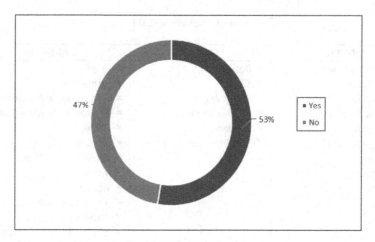

Fig. 4. CIM Douro result

Finally, CIM Alto Tâmega e Barroso, which is the CIM with the fewest Municipalities in this study, has only 6 Municipalities in its composition, 4 of which already comply with the stipulations of the GDPR on their Websites.

As shown in Fig. 5, most municipalities comply with GDPR rules on their websites, only 33% of municipalities make no reference to data protection. Only two Municipalities disagree: Boticas and Ribeira de Pena.

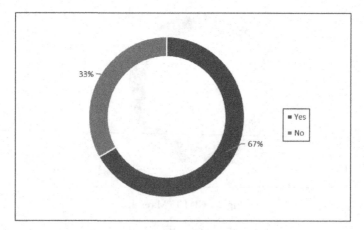

Fig. 5. CIM AT result

As already mentioned, the new General Regulation on Data Protection came into force in 2018. This document represented one of the biggest changes in the way of processing personal data ever made, with an enormous impact on all natural persons and private organizations or public entities that operate with them.

Public organizations, by virtue of their functions, have a high impact. These public organizations include the Municipalities, which due to their proximity to citizens, care in the processing of personal data must be redoubled.

Municipalities have a dual function, in addition to having to implement the GDPR, as they incur heavy fines, as they have websites with a very high consultation by citizens and which can be accessible to anyone, the compliance of these digital platforms with what dictates the GDPR is of no lesser importance.

5   Conclusions

With the development of the Information Society, organizations are getting more and more intertwined data, and the struggle to balance between protecting information resources and the need for sharing information is a daily concern. It implies potential security risks and, on the other hand, the expected benefits from the information sharing process; this balancing is not easy to achieve [16]. The need to share and the need to protect information are at first sight two opposing phenomena.

Ensuring total information security is the aim of many organizations, but the word "totality" when talking about security is very ambitious. But the GDPR will certainly contribute a lot to organizations to better protect the personal data they process.

In this research work regarding the compliance of the Websites of the 34 Municipalities with the GDPR, we realized that most of the websites of the municipalities already respect this dynamic, as 59% of the municipalities have references to the GDPR on their websites.

Although there are still 41% of the Municipalities, that is 14 of the 34 that constitute the universe of this study. This percentage can be considered high if we consider that the regulation entered into force five years ago.

When presenting these results regarding the presence of the GDPR on the websites, there is a question that arises, is whether the Municipalities that do not include the dynamics present in the GDPR on their websites, have or have not implemented the GDPR. Although this survey was not within the scope of the present work, it can be pointed out as a limitation of this study.

As future work, we propose opening this study to more CIM's so that we can better assess whether the Websites of the Municipalities include the necessary dynamics to comply with the rules dictated by the regulations.

Acknowledgements. The authors are grateful to the Foundation for Science and Technology (FCT, Portugal) for financial support through national funds FCT/MCTES (PIDDAC) to CIMO (UIDB/00690/2020 and UIDP/00690/2020) and SusTEC (LA/P/0007/2020).

The authors are grateful to the UNIAG, R&D unit funded by the FCT—Portuguese Foundation for the Development of Science and Technology, Ministry of Science, Technology and Higher Education. "Project Code Reference: UIDB/04752/2020 e UIDP/04752/2020".

References

1. Alshamsan, A.R., Chaudhry, S.A.: A GDPR compliant approach to assign risk levels to privacy policies. Comput. Mater. Continua **74**(3), 4631–4647 (2023)

2. GDPR, Retrieved 25 October 2022. https://gdpr-info.eu/. Accessed 3 Feb 2023
3. Aslan, U., Şen, B.: GDPR compliant audit log management system with blockchain. In: 15th Turkish National Software Engineering Symposium (UYMS), Izmir, Turkey (2021)
4. What is GDPR the EU's new data protection law? (2019). https://gdpr.eu/what-is-gdpr/. Accessed 1 Feb 2023
5. Asif, M., Javed, Y., Hussain, M.: Automated analysis of pakistani websites' compliance with GDPR and Pakistan data protection act. In: International Conference on Frontiers of Information Technology (FIT), Islamabad, Pakistan, pp. 234–239 (2021)
6. EUR-Lex - 31995L0046 - PT. https://eur-lex.europa.eu/legal-content/PT/TXT/HTML/?uri=CELEX:31995L0046&from=EL. Accessed 6 Feb 2023
7. Vojkovic, G.: Will the GDPR slow down development of smart cities? In: 41st International Convention on Information and Communication Technology, Electronics and Microelectronics (MIPRO), Opatija, Croatia, pp. 1295–1297 (2018)
8. Parecer N.o 20/2018, CNPD (2018). https://www.uc.pt/site/assets/files/475840/20180502_parecer_20_cnpd.pdf. Accessed 8 Feb 2023
9. Primavera. Regulamento Geral de Proteção de Dados, Saiba como adaptar a sua empresa! (2022). https://pt.primaverabss.com/pt/tudo-que-precisa-saber-sobre-o-rgpd/. Accessed 14 Nov 2022
10. Bochis, N.: 8 Steps To Be GDPR Compliant With Your Website. https://www.online-tech-tips.com/web-site-tips/8-steps-to-be-gdpr-compliant-with-your-website/. Accessed 26 Nov 2023
11. Gobeo, A., Fowler, C., Buchanan, W.J.: GDPR and Cyber Security for Business Information Systems, in GDPR and Cyber Security for Business Information Systems, River Publishers (2020)
12. Barati, M., Rana, O., Petri, I., Theodorakopoulos, G.: GDPR compliance verification in Internet of Things. IEEE Access **8**, 119697–119709 (2020)
13. Metakia. https://metakia.com/blog/como-integrar-o-rgpd-no-seu-website/. Accessed 23 Dec 2023
14. Cobalt. https://www.cobalt.io/blog/is-my-website-gdpr-compliant. Accessed 23 Dec 2023
15. Patton, M.Q.: Qualitative Research & Evaluation Methods, 3rd edn. Sage (2002)
16. Anderson, C., Baskerville, R.I., Kaul, M.: Information security control theory: achieving a sustainable reconciliation between sharing and protecting the privacy of information. J. Manag. Inf. Syst. **34**(4), 1082–1112 (2017)

International Workshop on Collective, Massive and Evolutionary Systems (IWCES 2023)

Preliminary Results of Group Detection Technique Based on User to Vector Encoding

Giulio Biondi[1] , Valentina Franzoni[1,2](✉) , and Alfredo Milani[1]

[1] Department of Mathematics and Computer Science, University of Perugia, Perugia, Italy
{giulio.biondi,valentina.franzoni,alfredo.milani}@unipg.it
[2] Department of Computer Science, Hong Kong Baptist University, Hong Kong, China

Abstract. This paper presents a novel approach for detecting groups of users based on observations of co-occurrences of user behavior. A Deep Neural Network is trained to encode users into a vector representation using an innovative adaptation of the word embedding architecture used in Natural Language Processing, which has been recently applied and modified for various domains, including graph data, recommender systems, and DNA gene sequence embedding. Preliminary experiments show promising results for the proposed adaptation to group detection based on the user-to-vector encoding derived from behavior observations in a variety of scenarios.

Keywords: user behaviour detection · user to vector encoding · machine learning

1 Introduction

Word2Vec [20] denotes a group of algorithms designed to learn high-order word embeddings from large textual datasets. Originally tested on word similarity tasks, the development of efficient word embedding techniques have enabled their application to a range of Natural Language Processing tasks, [13,14] including recommender systems, [1] sentiment analysis, [3,11,17] and question classification. [16,27] The underlying concept of Word2Vec has been successfully applied to various domains. For instance, in graph data analysis, the skip-gram technique has been utilized to generate higher-order graph node representations. [4,5,12,18] In this context, node ids are treated as words, and sentences are constructed from sequences of ids collected through random walks on the graph. Node embeddings have been employed to address several network tasks such as graph classification [26] and link prediction. [7] Other notable applications include recommender systems, [24] where items are embedded by leveraging their attributes and user interactions, and gene sequence embedding for understanding DNA replication mechanisms [25]. The versatility of Word2Vec and its

O. Gervasi et al. (Eds.): ICCSA 2023 Workshops, LNCS 14108, pp. 179–190, 2023.
https://doi.org/10.1007/978-3-031-37117-2_14

ability to learn meaningful representations of data has made it a popular tool in various fields. Its success in generating high-order word embeddings has inspired researchers to adapt the technique to other types of data, leading to the development of new methods and applications. As research in this area continues, we will likely see more innovative uses of Word2Vec and related techniques in the future.

In this work, we present preliminary results for a novel approach for detecting groups of users, based on observations of co-occurrences of user behavior. Observations are used to train a Deep Neural Network (DNN) to learn and encode users into a vector representation by an innovative adaptation of the popular word embedding technique used in Natural Language Processing. The paper is organized into four sections. Section 2 introduces a new method for encoding users into vectors for group detection, introducing a reference scenario for user observations, scheme and algorithmic details of the proposed group detection method, and the metrics used to assess performances. Section 3 presents the experimental phase including a description of the dataset, experimental settings, and a discussion of the results. Finally, Sect. 4 concludes the paper and summarizes the main findings.

2   User to Vector Encoding for Groups Detection

2.1   User Observation Scenario

We introduce for clarification purposes a scenario for user observation where group detection will be held. Let us assume, for example, that users belonging to known groups (e.g., classes of students in a given school) are observed during random social behavior. For instance, student detectors are available at school gates and record the entry/exit flow of students at the beginning/end of the school day.

An observation is a set of students observed while passing at the gates in a given time interval. It is easy to note, as shown in Fig. 1, that each observation is a set of individuals characterized by subgroups of students belonging to the same group/class, this is because people in the same class tend to exit school at the same moment, and tend to stay grouped at least in pairs or larger sets. At the same time, people in a subgroup tend to vary randomly, and subgroups in a single observation likely belong to different classes/groups [2]. On the other hand, observations with no subgroups (i.e. made only of single individuals all belonging to different classes/groups) are very unusual in a real social scenario, where people tend to interact and cluster. The goal is to collect multiple observations along days and devise a method to infer the groups to which the individual belongs, exploiting pattern regularities in subgroups observed over time. Despite Fig. 1 showing group labels by different graphical textures, in real observations data individuals would not be labeled with their group, but we assume every single person can be recognized through multiple passages.

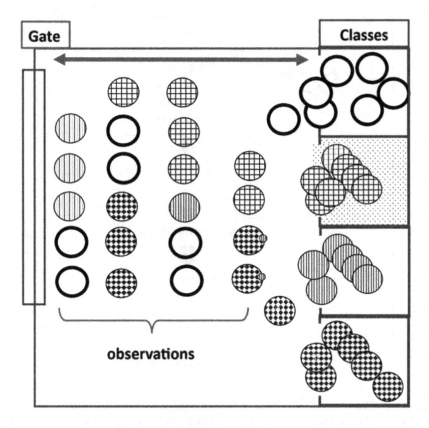

Fig. 1. Group Detection Scenario: classes of students

2.2 Proposed Method

The word encoding architecture, originally proposed in [20], was introduced to learn word embeddings (e.g., meaningful projections of words in a higher-dimensional vector space) from large corpora of texts. [6,8] In the vector space, words that frequently appear in the same context in a reference corpus are considered semantically close, then projected to close vector points according to a distance metric (e.g., euclidean distance) in the multidimensional space of embedding.

The core idea of our adaptation of word2Vect architecture is to assume observed users as single words and to consider observations of users as sentences composed of words. Therefore, conducting user-to-vector encoding on the user sequences represented by the observations would project in the vectorial multi-dimensional space users which co-occur more often in observations, representing them by closer points. Therefore, after computing user embedding, the set of a group of students can be easily detected by applying a geometric clustering technique to the encoded points, i.e. the generated vectorial representation.

The general workflow of the proposed method is shown in Fig. 2.

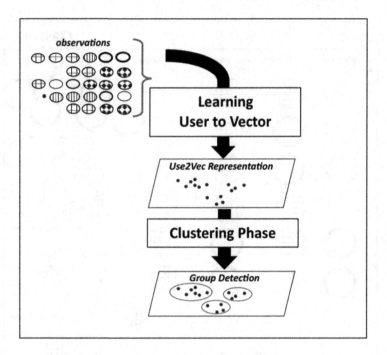

Fig. 2. Group Detection Workflow

Learning User Embedding. Embeddings are learned either through a Continuous-Bag-of-Words (CBOW) approach, predicting a word based on the surrounding context, or employing the skip-gram technique and predicting the context, given a word; in this work, we use the skip-gram technique. Word2Vec skip-gram-based methods require setting the values for the following hyper-parameters:

- *minimum count* parameter defines the minimum number of occurrences for a word to be considered significant and thus included in the vocabulary for subsequent embedding. [22] Unfrequent words are removed from the tokenized sentences in the preprocessing phase, before the embedding computation; a value of 1 means that all the words in the corpus are retained for embedding.
- *context size* c, or window size, defines the left and right context for a given word w: words in a sentence at a distance $<= c$ from w are considered semantically close to w, with weight proportional to their distance. Common window sizes for applications in large corpora are 2, 5, or 10.
- *embedding size*, specifies the number of components of the embedding vectors, in [21]; an intuitive criterion is that projecting the elements to be embedded in a higher-dimension space allows better discrimination, but too large values can be detrimental for performance.

In our implementation of user embedding, different parameters setting has been explored and tested on an experimental basis.

Clustering Vector Representations of User. A suitable candidate algorithm for clustering users (i.e., points in the multidimensional space obtained by the embedding phase) is K-Means [15,19]. K-means is an iterative clustering algorithm that partitions elements in a domain by randomly computing a list of points, called led *centroids*, in the multidimensional space of the domain, and assigning each element to the closest centroid. The centroids are re-computed by averaging all the elements in the group, which are then re-assigned to the new closest centroid; the aim is to minimize the intra-cluster sum of square differences between each point and the centroid. The desired number of clusters is a parameter of the algorithm, along with the number of iterations and the specification of the k-means procedure, e.g., *lloyd*, and *elkan* procedures.

2.3   Metrics

The following metrics are typically used in the literature for assessing clustering quality compared to the ground truth (i.e., the real groups to which the users belong); all the metrics have a lower bound of 0, indicating total independency between the clustering results and the ground truth labels, and an upper bound of 1 for perfect labeling.

- *Homogeneity score* [9,23] describes to which extent the points in the computed clusters belong to the same ground-truth group, ranging from 0 (i.e., each cluster contains two elements from the same group) to 1 (i.e., completely homogeneous clusters).
- *Completeness score* [23] measures the rate of aggregation of elements from the same group in the computed clusters: a value of 0 means that all the elements from the same group fall into different clusters, while 1 means that the fall into the same cluster.
- *V_measure score* [23] is the harmonic mean of homogeneity and completeness.
- *Fowlkes-Mallows score* (FMI) [10] is the geometric mean of the pairwise precision and recall measures:

$$FMI = \frac{TP}{\sqrt{(TP + FP)(TP + FN)}}$$

where TP counts the pairs in the same group clusterized together, FP the pairs in the same group but not in the same cluster, and FN in the same cluster but not in the same group.

3 Experiments

3.1 Observations Dataset

Two different scenarios derived from the reference user observation scenario (see Sect. 2.1) were analyzed, with 10 groups/classes of 10 elements/students each, and 10 groups/classes of 25 elements/students each. (*Scenario 1*)(*Scenario 2*). For each grouping, 4 datasets of observations have been randomly produced, containing respectively 1000, 2500, 5000, and 10000 observations with random elements; each observation contains subgroups of size from 2 to 5 elements from 3 different groups, thus having a minimum length of 6 and a maximum length of 15. We applied randomization using a Gaussian normal distribution to every decision step of the generation of a single observation. Decisions about which groups to include, the size of each subgroup, and the extraction of each individual from its group are also randomized in the same way.

3.2 Experiment Settings

The following settings are applied to the *user to vector learning* phase: the window size is set to 5, and the minimum count to 1 since no individual user had to be discarded when building the embedding. For each scenario, various embedding sizes are considered (i.e., 2, 5, 10, 25, 50, 100, and 200). The k-means algorithm is used to cluster the individuals according to the embeddings created from the user observations; the number of desired clusters is set to 10 for all the experiments (i.e., equal to the number of groups/classes in the ground truth), k-means++ is the chosen initialization technique.

3.3 Experimental Results

In Table 1 the results for experiments with 10 groups, of 10 individuals each, are reported. In Table 2 the results for experiments with 10 groups, of 25 individuals each, are reported. In Table 2 the results for experiments with 10 groups, of 25 individuals each, are reported. It is apparent that, regardless of the scenario and the vector size, 1000 observations are not sufficient to learn any meaningful embedding. Scaling with the number of observations, Scenario 1 Word2Vec produces embeddings that allow perfect clustering with 2500 observations, albeit for high embedding sizes only (i.e., 100, and 200). The same number of observations proves not sufficient for Scenario 2, under any setting (Table 3).

Table 1. Test 1 results: scenario 1 (10 groups, 10 individuals per group)

# Observations	Embedding size	Homogeneity	Completeness	V_Measure	Fowlkes-Mallows
1000	2	0.2363	0.2439	0.2401	0.1146
1000	3	0.2445	0.2476	0.2461	0.1119
1000	5	0.2194	0.2251	0.2222	0.0998
1000	10	0.2570	0.2631	0.2600	0.1238
1000	25	0.2366	0.2429	0.2397	0.1171
1000	50	0.2383	0.2541	0.2459	0.1185
1000	100	0.1702	0.1877	0.1785	0.0974
1000	200	0.1561	0.1682	0.1620	0.0866
2500	2	0.2756	0.2911	0.2832	0.1473
2500	3	0.3643	0.3829	0.3734	0.1917
2500	5	0.5530	0.5645	0.5587	0.3870
2500	10	0.5810	0.6086	0.5944	0.4106
2500	25	0.9062	0.9284	0.9172	0.8332
2500	50	0.9177	0.9427	0.9300	0.8496
2500	100	1.0000	1.0000	1.0000	1.0000
2500	200	1.0000	1.0000	1.0000	1.0000
5000	2	0.5916	0.6079	0.5997	0.3777
5000	3	0.8378	0.8801	0.8585	0.7231
5000	5	1.0000	1.0000	1.0000	1.0000
5000	10	1.0000	1.0000	1.0000	1.0000
5000	25	0.9398	0.9698	0.9546	0.8756
5000	50	1.0000	1.0000	1.0000	1.0000
5000	100	1.0000	1.0000	1.0000	1.0000
5000	200	1.0000	1.0000	1.0000	1.0000
10000	2	0.7784	0.7934	0.7859	0.6639
10000	3	0.9854	0.9859	0.9857	0.9789
10000	5	1.0000	1.0000	1.0000	1.0000
10000	10	1.0000	1.0000	1.0000	1.0000
10000	25	1.0000	1.0000	1.0000	1.0000
10000	50	1.0000	1.0000	1.0000	1.0000
10000	100	1.0000	1.0000	1.0000	1.0000
10000	200	1.0000	1.0000	1.0000	1.0000

Table 2. Test 2 results: Scenario 2(10 groups, 25 individuals per group)

# Observations	Embedding size	Homogeneity	Completeness	V_Measure	Fowlkes-Mallows
1000	2	0.0721	0.0728	0.0724	0.0948
1000	3	0.0715	0.0720	0.0718	0.0944
1000	5	0.1000	0.1017	0.1009	0.1087
1000	10	0.0652	0.0657	0.0654	0.0946
1000	25	0.0864	0.0907	0.0885	0.1102
1000	50	0.0798	0.0836	0.0817	0.1104
1000	100	0.0900	0.0926	0.0913	0.1060
1000	200	0.0855	0.0938	0.0895	0.1124
2500	2	0.1587	0.1663	0.1624	0.1345
2500	3	0.1795	0.1822	0.1808	0.1468
2500	5	0.1919	0.1930	0.1924	0.1535
2500	10	0.2972	0.2987	0.2979	0.2243
2500	25	0.4061	0.4123	0.4091	0.3130
2500	50	0.5160	0.5205	0.5182	0.3906
2500	100	0.5847	0.5987	0.5916	0.4561
2500	200	0.4759	0.4827	0.4793	0.3325
5000	2	0.4631	0.4767	0.4698	0.3068
5000	3	0.5782	0.5874	0.5827	0.4529
5000	5	0.9231	0.9236	0.9233	0.8961
5000	10	0.9398	0.9690	0.9542	0.8816
5000	25	1.0000	1.0000	1.0000	1.0000
5000	50	1.0000	1.0000	1.0000	1.0000
5000	100	1.0000	1.0000	1.0000	1.0000
5000	200	1.0000	1.0000	1.0000	1.0000
10000	2	0.6764	0.7023	0.6891	0.5324
10000	3	0.9780	0.9781	0.9780	0.9757
10000	5	1.0000	1.0000	1.0000	1.0000
10000	10	1.0000	1.0000	1.0000	1.0000
10000	25	1.0000	1.0000	1.0000	1.0000
10000	50	1.0000	1.0000	1.0000	1.0000
10000	100	1.0000	1.0000	1.0000	1.0000
10000	200	1.0000	1.0000	1.0000	1.0000

Table 3. Test 3 results: Scenario 2 (10 groups, 25 individuals per group), 20 clusters

# Observations	Embedding size	Homogeneity	Completeness	V_Measure	Fowlkes-Mallows
1000	2	0.1870	0.1496	0.1662	0.0814
1000	3	0.1809	0.1402	0.1580	0.0675
1000	5	0.1494	0.1168	0.1311	0.0622
1000	10	0.1751	0.1391	0.1551	0.0752
1000	25	0.1803	0.1421	0.1589	0.0716
1000	50	0.1652	0.1345	0.1483	0.0772
1000	100	0.1761	0.1405	0.1563	0.0728
1000	200	0.1824	0.1442	0.1611	0.0716
2500	2	0.2452	0.1950	0.2172	0.1006
2500	3	0.2794	0.2197	0.2460	0.1208
2500	5	0.2863	0.2239	0.2513	0.1206
2500	10	0.3703	0.2889	0.3246	0.1623
2500	25	0.4926	0.3844	0.4318	0.2488
2500	50	0.5932	0.4654	0.5216	0.3256
2500	100	0.8078	0.6312	0.7087	0.5529
2500	200	0.7153	0.5637	0.6305	0.4395
5000	2	0.5005	0.3961	0.4422	0.2144
5000	3	0.6501	0.5104	0.5719	0.3514
5000	5	0.8976	0.7124	0.7944	0.6572
5000	10	0.9945	0.8038	0.8891	0.7876
5000	25	1.0000	0.8146	0.8978	0.7971
5000	50	1.0000	0.8231	0.9030	0.8260
5000	100	1.0000	0.8087	0.8942	0.7887
5000	200	1.0000	0.8133	0.8970	0.7979
10000	2	0.7321	0.5814	0.6481	0.4005
10000	3	0.9662	0.7641	0.8533	0.7185
10000	5	1.0000	0.8159	0.8986	0.8149
10000	10	1.0000	0.7928	0.8844	0.7559
10000	25	1.0000	0.7940	0.8852	0.7625
10000	50	1.0000	0.7945	0.8855	0.7646
10000	100	1.0000	0.8030	0.8907	0.7755
10000	200	1.0000	0.8023	0.8903	0.7802

4 Conclusions

In this work, we have introduced a novel technique of user group detection based on user-to-vector encoding learned from user behavior observations of a random group of unknown users. The approach leverages the co-occurrence of users in observations, which is used to induce group information. The preliminary experimental results are quite promising, yet a deeper and more systematic investigation is needed to evaluate the robustness of the approach in the presence of noisy observations and to use data from real domains. Moreover, results suggest that it is worth exploring the potential applications of techniques of learning vectorial representation embedding user behavior in a wide variety of domains, which will be the target of future works.

Acknowledgments. This work is partially supported by the Italian Ministry of Research under PRIN Project "PHRAME" Grant n.20178XXKFY. Supported also by KIT-Lab, Knowledge, and Information Technology Laboratory, University of Perugia, Italy.

References

1. Baek, J.W., Chung, K.Y.: Multimedia recommendation using word2vec-based social relationship mining. Multim. Tools Appl. **80**, 34499–34515 (2021). https://doi.org/10.1007/s11042-019-08607-9
2. Carpi, A., D'Alessandro, F.: On the commutative equivalence of bounded semi-linear codes. In: Mercaş, R., Reidenbach, D. (eds.) WORDS 2019. LNCS, vol. 11682, pp. 119–132. Springer, Cham (2019). https://doi.org/10.1007/978-3-030-28796-2_9
3. Chen, Q., Sokolova, M.: Specialists, scientists, and sentiments: Word2Vec and Doc2Vec in analysis of scientific and medical texts. SN Comput. Sci. **2**(5), 1–11 (2021). https://doi.org/10.1007/s42979-021-00807-1
4. Chiancone, A., Franzoni, V., Li, Y., Markov, K., Milani, A.: Leveraging zero tail in neighbourhood for link prediction. In: 2015 IEEE/WIC/ACM International Conference on Web Intelligence and Intelligent Agent Technology (WI-IAT), vol. 3, pp. 135–139. IEEE (2015)
5. Chiancone, A., Milani, A., Poggioni, V., Pallottelli, S., Madotto, A., Franzoni, V.: A multistrain bacterial model for link prediction andrea chiancone. In: 2015 11th International Conference on Natural Computation (ICNC), pp. 1075–1079. IEEE (2015)
6. D'Alessandro, F., Carpi, A.: On incomplete and synchronizing finite sets. Theoret. Comput. Sci. **664**, 67–77 (2017). https://doi.org/10.1016/j.tcs.2015.08.042
7. Du, X., Yan, J., Zhang, R., Zha, H.: Cross-network skip-gram embedding for joint network alignment and link prediction. IEEE Trans. Knowl. Data Eng. **34**(3), 1080–1095 (2022). https://doi.org/10.1109/TKDE.2020.2997861
8. Carpi, A., D'Alessandro, F.: On the commutative equivalence of context-free languages. In: Hoshi, M., Seki, S. (eds.) DLT 2018. LNCS, vol. 11088, pp. 169–181. Springer, Cham (2018). https://doi.org/10.1007/978-3-319-98654-8_14

9. Carpi, A., D'Alessandro, F.: On the hybrid černý-road coloring problem and Hamiltonian paths. In: Gao, Y., Lu, H., Seki, S., Yu, S. (eds.) DLT 2010. LNCS, vol. 6224, pp. 124–135. Springer, Heidelberg (2010). https://doi.org/10.1007/978-3-642-14455-4_13

10. Fowlkes, E.B., Mallows, C.L.: A method for comparing two hierarchical clusterings. J. Am. Statist. Assoc. **78**(383), 553–569 (1983). https://doi.org/10.1080/01621459.1983.10478008

11. Franzoni, V., Biondi, G., Milani, A.: A Web-Based System for Emotion Vector Extraction. In: Gervasi, O., et al. (eds.) ICCSA 2017. LNCS, vol. 10406, pp. 653–668. Springer, Cham (2017). https://doi.org/10.1007/978-3-319-62398-6_46

12. Franzoni, V., Chiancone, A., Milani, A.: A multistrain bacterial diffusion model for link prediction. Int. J. Pattern Recognit. Artif. Intell. **31**(11), 1759024 (2017)

13. Franzoni, V., Li, Y., Mengoni, P., Milani, A.: Clustering Facebook for biased context extraction. In: Gervasi, O., et al. (eds.) ICCSA 2017. LNCS, vol. 10404, pp. 717–729. Springer, Cham (2017). https://doi.org/10.1007/978-3-319-62392-4_52

14. Franzoni, V., Milani, A.: A pheromone-like model for semantic context extraction from collaborative networks. In: 2015 IEEE/WIC/ACM International Conference on Web Intelligence and Intelligent Agent Technology (WI-IAT), vol. 1, pp. 540–547. IEEE (2015)

15. Franzoni, V., Milani, A.: A semantic comparison of clustering algorithms for the evaluation of web-based similarity measures. In: Gervasi, O., et al. (eds.) ICCSA 2016. LNCS, vol. 9790, pp. 438–452. Springer, Cham (2016). https://doi.org/10.1007/978-3-319-42092-9_34

16. Franzoni, V., Milani, A., Mengoni, P., Piccinato, F.: Artificial intelligence visual metaphors in e-learning interfaces for learning analytics. Appl. Sci. **10**(20), 7195 (2020)

17. Franzoni, V., Poggioni, V., Zollo, F.: Automated classification of book blurbs according to the emotional tags of the social network Zazie. ESSEM@ AI* IA **1096**, 83–94 (2013)

18. Grover, A., Leskovec, J.: node2vec: Scalable feature learning for networks (2016)

19. Lloyd, S.: Least squares quantization in PCM. IEEE Trans. Inf. Theory **28**(2), 129–137 (1982). https://doi.org/10.1109/TIT.1982.1056489

20. Mikolov, T., Sutskever, I., Chen, K., Corrado, G.S., Dean, J.: Distributed representations of words and phrases and their compositionality. In: Burges, C., Bottou, L., Welling, M., Ghahramani, Z., Weinberger, K. (eds.) Advances in Neural Information Processing Systems, vol. 26. Curran Associates, Inc. (2013)

21. Patel, K., Bhattacharyya, P.: Towards lower bounds on number of dimensions for word embeddings. In: Proceedings of the Eighth International Joint Conference on Natural Language Processing (Volume 2: Short Papers), pp. 31–36. Asian Federation of Natural Language Processing, Taipei (2017)

22. Poggioni, V., Bartoccini, U., Carpi, A., Santucci, V.: Memes evolution in a memetic variant of particle swarm optimization. Mathematics **7**(5) (2019). https://doi.org/10.3390/math7050423

23. Rosenberg, A., Hirschberg, J.: V-measure: A conditional entropy-based external cluster evaluation measure. In: Proceedings of the 2007 Joint Conference on Empirical Methods in Natural Language Processing and Computational Natural Language Learning (EMNLP-CoNLL), pp. 410–420. Association for Computational Linguistics, Prague (2007)

24. Vasile, F., Smirnova, E., Conneau, A.: Meta-prod2vec: Product embeddings using side-information for recommendation. In: RecSys '16, pp. 225–232. Association

for Computing Machinery, New York (2016). https://doi.org/10.1145/2959100.2959160

25. Wu, F., Yang, R., Zhang, C., Zhang, L.: A deep learning framework combined with word embedding to identify DNA replication origins. Sci. Rep. **11**, 844 (2021). https://doi.org/10.1038/s41598-020-80670-x

26. Xie, Y., Liang, Y., Gong, M., Qin, A.K., Ong, Y.S., He, T.: Semisupervised graph neural networks for graph classification. In: IEEE Transactions on Cybernetics, pp. 1–14 (2022). https://doi.org/10.1109/TCYB.2022.3164696

27. Yilmaz, S., Toklu, S.: A deep learning analysis on question classification task using Word2vec representations. Neural Comput. Appl. **32**(7), 2909–2928 (2020). https://doi.org/10.1007/s00521-020-04725-w

Sentiment Processing of Socio-political Discourse and Public Speeches

Gulmira Bekmanova[1,2(✉)] ⓘD, Banu Yergesh[1,2] ⓘD, Aru Ukenova[1] ⓘD,
Assel Omarbekova[1,2] ⓘD, Assel Mukanova[3] ⓘD, and Yerkyn Ongarbayev[2] ⓘD

[1] Faculty of Information Technologies, L.N. Gumilyov Eurasian National University, 010000 Astana, Kazakhstan
gulmira-r@yandex.kz
[2] L.N. Gumilyov Eurasian National University, 010000 Astana, Kazakhstan
[3] Higher School of Information Technology and Engineering, Astana International University, 010000 Astana, Kazakhstan

Abstract. The article deals with the development of an ontological model of words in public political discourse and texts of public speeches in the Kazakh language. The article presents an ontological model of the subject area of elections, a referendum, examples of processing queries from the knowledge base are given. A sentimental analysis of political discourse in social networks in the Kazakh language was carried out in order to determine the mood of the discussion in these sources.

Keywords: Intelligent Synonymizer · Political discourse · Database · Kazakh language · Ontology

1 Introduction

The concept of sentiment analysis has many different names, interpretations, tasks, such as, for example, sentiment analysis, intellectual analysis of opinions, search for opinions, search for subjectivity, sentiment analysis, etc. Therefore, in this work, the concept of sentiment analysis was adopted and, in connection with it, the following concepts were clarified.

Sentiment - the emotional attitude of the author, who expressed an opinion on certain objects (product, organization, personality, etc.), events (elections, uprising, war, etc.), phenomena (eclipse, flood, etc.), process (education, service, etc.) or its properties described in the text.

Opinion is a concept about something, belief, judgment, conclusion, conclusion, point of view or statement on a topic in which it is impossible to achieve complete objectivity, based on the interpretation of facts and an emotional attitude towards them.

Sentiment analysis of text is a class of content analysis methods in computational linguistics designed for automated detection of emotionally colored vocabulary in texts and emotional evaluation of authors (opinions) in relation to objects, phenomena, events, processes or their properties.

O. Gervasi et al. (Eds.): ICCSA 2023 Workshops, LNCS 14108, pp. 191–205, 2023.
https://doi.org/10.1007/978-3-031-37117-2_15

Sentiment of an opinion is a sign off, which indicates that the opinion will be positive, neutral or negative. It is also called opinion polarity, sentiment direction, or semantic direction.

Many researchers are engaged in sentiment analysis, so there are many different methods and algorithms that are used in research. On the one hand, in the applied research of sentiment analysis, machine learning methods, lexicon-based methods or linguistic methods can be applied.

On the other hand, the classification of sentiment analysis methods may depend on the level of their classification, such as document, sentence, or aspect level. Sentiment analysis at the document level classifies the entire document as positive or negative. In this case, it is considered that the document describes one object. Sentence-level sentiment analysis categorizes each sentence in a document as subjective or objective, and categorizes subjective opinions as positive or negative. And at the level of the object and aspect, the relation of the object to a particular aspect is determined, because the user can leave different opinions on several aspects of one object in one review.

Sentiment analysis methods can be used on various types of data such as news, reviews, blogs, or social media posts.

Each type of data has its own characteristics that must be taken into account when collecting, preparing, pre-processing data and describing objects.

The topic of political discourse on the Internet, automatic detection of hotbeds of political discourse in social networks is an urgent task of modern researchers. The next important task is to determine the sentiment of discussions in the centers of political discourse. The prerequisites for this study are several works by the authors related to the identification of terrorist threats in social networks [1], the work on the sentiment analysis of texts [2–6], as well as the creation of a morphological analyzer [7, 8].

An important element of the political discourse processing system is the development and further use of an intelligent synonymizer, which significantly increases the efficiency of the system that solves the problem of socio-political discourse processing sentiment. The development of an intelligent synonymizer application for socio-political discourse and texts of public speeches is an important task in the field of natural language processing. The socio-political discourse and texts of public speeches are often characterized by the use of specialized terminology and jargon, as well as by the repetition of certain words or phrases [9–13]. This can lead to a lack of clarity and precision in communication, as well as a loss of audience attention and engagement.

An intelligent synonymizer application can help resolve these issues by providing users with a variety of alternative words and phrases that convey the same meaning as the original word or phrase. The application can recommend synonyms based on the context and meaning of the original word or phrase by combining rule-based and machine learning approaches [14–19]. Data gathering, preprocessing, feature extraction, model training, and evaluation are all steps in the development of such an application. The data collection step entails gathering a large corpus of socio-political discourse and public speech texts that can be used to train and evaluate the synonymizer model [20–23]. In the preprocessing stage, the data is cleaned and tokenized, and stop words and other noise are removed [24]. The feature extraction stage involves identifying relevant features of the text, such as word frequency, co-occurrence patterns, and syntactic structures. The model training stage involves selecting and implementing a machine learning algorithm, such as a neural network or a decision tree, and using the extracted features to train the model on the corpus of text. The evaluation stage involves testing the performance of the model on a separate test set of text, using metrics such as accuracy, precision, and recall [25–27].

Overall, the development of an intelligent synonymizer application for socio-political discourse and texts of public speeches has the potential to improve the quality of communication in these important domains, and to enhance audience engagement and understanding.

2 Related Works

Sentiment processing of socio-political discourse and public speeches is a subfield of natural language processing (NLP) that involves the identification and analysis of emotions, attitudes, and opinions expressed in text data related to socio-political issues and public speeches.

The work [28] explores the nature of sentiment analysis in political texts, outlines the challenges faced by analysts of political texts, and discusses how these challenges influence the reliability of findings. It demonstrates ongoing research that is creating an algorithm that analyzes stylistic devices (such as sarcasm, irony, and hyperbole) and offers choices for figuring out the sentiment of texts in sentences that contain these stylistic devices.

Social media opinions and comments that incite racial tensions have been seen as posing a significant danger to social, political, and cultural stability as well as the peace in various nations. As a result, social media should be watched closely, and offensive comments should be quickly identified and blocked. The research [29–31] uses sentiment analysis to identify tweets that contain racist text. Adopting the sentiment analysis model [32] also showed that the emotions associated with all of the identified themes are primarily negative sentiments expressed toward socio-political problems. Moreover, this study [33] examines the sentiment analysis of social media data for the purpose of detecting anxiety or despair using a variety of artificial intelligence methods. A multimodal hate speech detection algorithm tailored for Greek social media is presented by the authors in [34]. The research focuses on Greek-language tweets that criticize immigrants and refugees, particularly those that use racist and xenophobic language. Similar to this, [35] suggests an advanced machine learning-based method for the automatic detection of hate speech in Arabic social media networks. In order to analyze the data, a distinct set of features are used and various emotional states are recorded. The research employs four distinct machine learning techniques, including Naive Bayes (NB), DT, SVM, and RF, along with features from the TF-IDF, profile, and mood.

Another paper [36] offers PolSentiLex, a sentiment lexicon for the Russian language that is openly available and created to identify sentiment in user-generated content about social and political problems. The next method proposed in [37] for evaluating news using blockchain technology, smart contracts, and NLP has a lot of potential. Its system assesses news without prejudice or interference from sociopolitical factors using a combination of human and machine opinion. In order to gauge public sentiment regarding the spread of the COVID-19 virus and its potential societal repercussions, a sentiment analysis methodology was created in [38]. This was accomplished by extracting features using the TF-IDF and Lexical techniques, and classifying the data using Naive Bayes.

It was discovered that sentiment affects the way content is shared on social media, with emotionally charged Tweets getting more retweets and news content with high sentiment being more well-liked and getting more notice [39, 40]. Additionally, it has been demonstrated that including sentiment in recommendation systems raises the quality of recommendations by making them more specifically tailored to the participant's preferences [41]. However, the predominance of negative emotion in a collection of news stories may reduce the likelihood of meeting opposing views and getting a balanced media diet [42], as high levels of negative emotion indicate a bias in the news story [43].

Depending on the frequency and length of social unrest, there may be long-term consequences that raise risks in the financial, economic, and political spheres. The work [44] has annotated a dataset based on Nigeria's #EndSARS campaign to forecast the occurrence of societal unrest. A support vector classifier has also been used to model how the general public feels about the demonstration.

One of the potential challenges in developing an intelligent synonymizer in Kazakh language is the complexity and variability of the language used in socio-political discourse and public speeches. The use of specialized terminology, jargon, and metaphors can make it difficult to identify appropriate synonyms that convey the same meaning and nuance as the original text. In order to analyze texts in the Kazakh language that contain terrorist threats, this study [1] described a rule-based approach that used a dictionary. Additionally, the authors have published a number of works on sentiment analysis of texts [2–6] as well as morphological analysis [7, 8] for Kazakh language.

3 Development of a Database of Synonyms and an Ontological Model of Words in Public Political Discourse and Texts of Public Speeches

3.1 Review and Coordination of Sources of Political Discourse

While the term "discourse" comes from the Latin word discursus, meaning "conscious thought (reasonable thinking)", over time, this concept came to mean "scientific dispute", in some works discourse comes from the Latin "discurro – to wander", "discurrere" – to discuss, negotiate. Discourse is an attribute of the communicative-social field, it occurs where the statement has social consequences. Discourse is a concept that analyzes the social background of a thought, presented through an ambiguous conversation.

Currently, in connection with the events taking place in the world and the country, the study of political institutions, political processes, and political technologies is an urgent problem. Therefore, it is necessary to study the socio-political vocabulary, political texts written in the Kazakh language, to study them on their basis. Changes in the society that form the political cognitive consciousness of the society and the linguistic image of politics form the concept of political discourse in the relationship of humanity. For this reason, it is important to study political discourse to the fullest.

Political discourse is presented in many communication tools such as treaties, reports, election campaigns, editorials, newspaper comments, interviews and conferences. Politicians usually use regular language mixed with direct and colloquial language. They can also use proverbs and idioms. Through them, politicians make their language more informal, making it more understandable to the audience for many listeners who listen to them. Thus politicians often use two styles: for example, colloquial, and rhetorical style, which may also include political language, due to special terminology and speech structure.

Today, in addition to oral communication and dialogue, written texts in social networks and correspondence are also a form of social and political activity. The implementation of political action through text and conversation is the trend of the new time. They have political functions and consequences, so they are a source of political discourse.

The vast majority of political discourse studies are devoted to the texts and speeches of professional politicians or political institutions such as presidents and prime ministers, as well as governments, parliaments or political parties at the local, national and international levels. Therefore, political discourse is a tool that contributes to mass consciousness.

The object of our study will be political discourse on electoral topics, since here everyone is a participant in political discourse: the president, deputies, members of the government, political parties and social movements, as well as citizens who have the right to vote. As a source of political discourse, one can take texts and articles on the topic of elections and referendums, speeches and appeals of leaders of political and public associations, as well as candidates for deputies. And all this will be covered through the media.

3.2 Selection and Development of Text Data

It is necessary to prepare corrective textual data based on socio-political discourse. The subject area of elections and referendums was chosen for the analysis. A study was made of 1200 sources applicable to this area.

It was revealed that according to the tone of messages in the articles, negative - 2.58%, neutral - 95.5%, positive - 1.92%. Of all the data, the sources of information in social networks accounted for 33.33%, the media of information - 66.7% (Fig. 1).

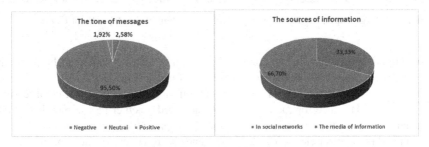

Fig. 1. Percentage of Sources

After analyzing the texts from these sources, more than 800 pages of textual data that met the requirements were collected and a text database was developed.

3.3   Ontological Model of the Subject Area of Elections, Referendum

To build an ontology there were collected, first of all, accumulated knowledge of the subject area and the basic concepts of selections from the collected texts. Their definitions, explanations, relationships to each other, subclasses, properties and axiomatic rules, their personalities were determined. The creation of the ontology was carried out in the Protégé environment.

A fragment of ontology classes "Electoral System of the Republic of Kazakhstan" is shown in Fig. 2.

To build an ontology, knowledge of the subject area and the basic concepts of samples from the collected texts were collected. Their definitions, explanations, relationships to each other, subclasses, properties and axiomatic rules, their personalities were determined. The creation of the ontology was carried out in the Protégé environment.

A fragment of ontology classes "Electoral System of the Republic of Kazakhstan" is shown in Fig. 2. Link to ontology https://clck.ru/33tTch.

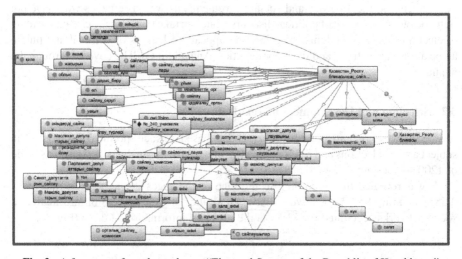

Fig. 2. A fragment of ontology classes "Electoral System of the Republic of Kazakhstan"

The figure shows the election commissions for the electoral system of the Republic of Kazakhstan, their types, definitions and terms of office (Fig. 3).

The figure reflects the central electoral commission, definition, term of office and members (Fig. 4). Since for each person it is indicated whether he is a member or the chairman of the central election commission, Reasoner automatically determines the chairman of the central election commission and the members of the central election commission.

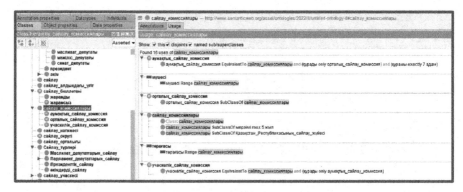

Fig. 3. Subclasses in the ontological model

The figure shows what qualities a candidate for the presidency should have. To do this, the following conditions must be met

$$
\begin{aligned}
\textit{office of president} &\equiv \exists\, \textit{state language proficiency} \,\sqcap\, \forall\, \textit{citizenship} \\
(\textit{The Republic of Kazakhstan}) &\sqcap\, \exists\, \textit{has Age} \geq 40 \,\sqcap\, \exists\, \textit{has higher education}
\end{aligned}
\tag{1}
$$

here: office of president, state language, the Republic of Kazakhstan, higher education – classes of ontology, proficiency, age, has – denote relationships between classes.

Only a candidate who meets this axiom (rule) can run as a presidential candidate (Fig. 5).

The following figure shows that the precinct election commission is formed exclusively by the territorial election commission, as well as how many people are included in it (Fig. 6). The commission's term of office is 5 years.

As a rule, the composition of the precinct election commission can be of two types:

With the number of voters $<=$ more than 2,000 people, the composition of the precinct election commission is 5–7 people.

With the number of voters $=>$ more than 2,000 people, the composition of the precinct election commission is 7–11 people.

In the created ontology, in accordance with the "Law of the Republic of Kazakhstan On Elections", a lot of provisions are created, as indicated above, and a definition of each concept is given.

With the help of ontology, we can get answers to various questions. To do this, we can create DL Query queries.

Fig. 4. Relationships and personalities in the ontological model

For example:

Question: "If there are 2 candidates marked on the ballot, is it valid or what ballot is it?" (Fig. 7).

Answer: Invalid

The question: "Who are the participants in the elections?" (Fig. 8).

Answer: election commission, voters, political parties, candidates (12).

Thus, the created ontology in the subject area "Electoral system of the Republic of Kazakhstan" includes rules, definitions, basic concepts and relationships that relate to the electoral system. Based on the rules, you can get new knowledge on demand from existing ones.

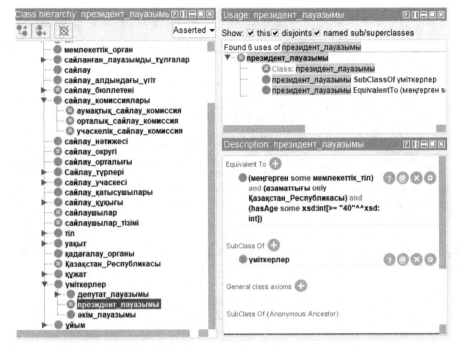

Fig. 5. Representation of axiomatic rules in the ontological model

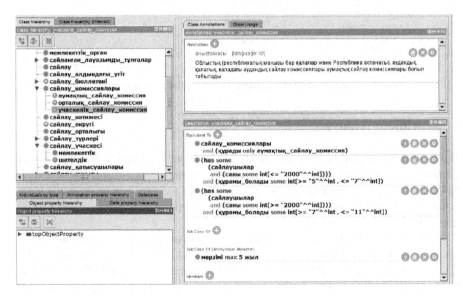

Fig. 6. Representation of axiomatic rules in the ontological model

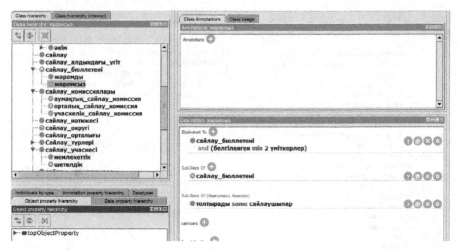

Fig. 7. Representation regarding the question "Is a ballot valid if 2 candidates are marked on the ballot or which ballot is it?"

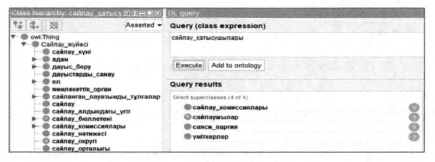

Fig. 8. Representation regarding the question "Who are the participants in the elections?"

4 Sentiment Analysis

The tasks of sentiment analysis are mainly implemented for English, Italian, Russian, Chinese and other languages, and research related to the sentiment analysis of texts in the Kazakh language has recently begun. Thus, there are very few ready-made tools, mathematical models, linguistic resources for the sentimental analysis of the Kazakh language.

To solve the problem of sentiment analysis, it is necessary to perform syntactic analysis after morphological analysis. For this, the syntactic rules of simple sentences of the Kazakh language were formalized and their constituent trees were built. The formalization of the syntactic rules of sentences was carried out using Chomsky's context-free (CS) grammar. During syntactic analysis, the components of the sentence are determined. More details about the sentiment analysis method can be found in the article [4].

Below is a model based on formalized production rules for determining the tonality of phrases in the text in the Kazakh language:

1) If the phrase consists of a noun with a positive coloring and a verb of a positive form with a neutral assessment following it, then the tone of this phrase is positive.

Displayed equations are centered and set on a separate line.

$$\frac{\omega \in L,\ \omega = \zeta \cdot \alpha \cdot \beta \cdot \xi,\ \alpha \in N,\ sent(\alpha) = 1,\ \beta = V\_Post,\ sent(\beta) = 0}{sent(\omega) = 1} \quad (2)$$

here and below ζ, ξ – any chains of words, including empty ones. For example, " инаугурация болды" ('the inauguration was"), "сыйыақы алды" ("received reward").

2) If a phrase consists of a noun with a negative connotation followed by a positive verb with a neutral evaluation, then the tone of this phrase is negative.

$$\frac{\omega \in L,\ \omega = \zeta \cdot \alpha \cdot \beta \cdot \xi,\ \alpha \in N,\ sent(\alpha) = -1,\ \beta = V\_Post,\ sent(\beta) = 0}{sent(\omega) = -1} \quad (3)$$

For instance, " бұрмалау тіркелді" ("tampering has been reported").

3) If the phrase consists a noun with a positive color and a verb of the positive form with a neutral color following it, and if after the verb there are words of negation (not/no), then the tonality of the phrase is negative.

$$\frac{\omega \in L,\ \omega = \zeta \cdot \alpha \cdot \beta \cdot \xi,\ \alpha \in N,\ sent(\alpha) = 1,\ \beta = V_{Post},\ sent(\beta) = 0,\ \gamma = @}{sent(\omega) = -1}$$

$$(4)$$

As an example, " бостандық берген жок" ("did not give freedom").

4) If a phrase consists a very positive adjective followed by a neutral noun, the tone of the phrase is very positive.

$$\frac{\omega \in L,\ \omega = \zeta \cdot \alpha \cdot \beta \cdot \xi,\ \alpha \in Adj,\ sent(\alpha) = 2,\ \beta = N,\ sent(\beta) = 0}{sent(\omega) = 2} \quad (5)$$

In this instance, " құрметті депутат" ("honorable deputy"), " көрнекті саясаткер" ("prominent politician").

5) If a phrase consists an adjective with a very negative connotation followed by a noun with a neutral connotation, then the tone of this phrase is very negative.

$$\frac{\omega \in L,\ \omega = \zeta \cdot \alpha \cdot \beta \cdot \xi,\ \alpha \in A,\ sent(\alpha) = -2,\ \beta = N,\ sent(\beta) = 0}{sent(\omega) = -2} \quad (6)$$

For example, " жемқор әкім" ("corrupt mayor").

6) If a phrase consists an adjective with a very positive coloring, a negative particle (emes) and a noun with a positive coloring following it, then the phrase has a negative coloring.

$$\frac{\omega \in L,\ \omega = \zeta \cdot \alpha \cdot \beta \cdot \gamma \cdot \xi,\ \alpha \in Adj,\ sent(\alpha) = 2,\ \beta = @,\ \gamma \in N,\ sent(\gamma) = 1}{sent(\omega) = -1}$$

$$(7)$$

For instance, " биік емес мәртебе" ("not a high status").

7) If a phrase consists a positive adjective followed by a neutral positive verb, then the tone of the phrase is positive.

$$\frac{\omega \in L,\ \omega = \zeta \cdot \alpha \cdot \beta \cdot \xi,\ \alpha \in Adj,\ sent(\alpha) = 1,\ \beta \in V\_Post,\ sent(\beta) = 0}{sent(\omega) = 1} \quad (8)$$

As an example, " дұрыс таңдайды" ("chooses correctly").

8) If a phrase consists an intensifying adverb (" өте" ("very"), " ең" ("the most")), followed by a positive adjective and then a noun with a neutral color, then this phrase has a very positive color.

$$\frac{\omega \in L,\ \omega = \zeta \cdot \alpha \cdot \beta \cdot \gamma \cdot \xi,\ \alpha \in AdvIntens,\ \beta = Adj,\ sent(\beta) = 1,\ \gamma = N,\ sent(\gamma) = 0}{sent(\omega) = 2}$$

$$(9)$$

In this instance, " өте перспективті саясаткер" ("the most perspective politician").

The tonality of the entire text is defined as the arithmetic mean of the measurements of the tonality of lexical units (sentences) and the rules for their combinations.

$$sent(L) = \frac{\sum_{i=1}^{n} sent(\omega)}{n} \quad (10)$$

This emotional speech recognition method is used to determine the mood of the conversation in these sources by analyzing the tone of texts obtained from official and unofficial political information sources posted on social media in the Kazakh language.

5 Conclusion

In order to address the practical issue of identifying the sources of political discourse, the tone of discussion in these sources, identifying hotspots of inciting hatred, negativity, enmity, or vice versa, and highlighting the political events, phenomena, and discussions that are most highly regarded by society. The resolution of this problem will aid in the implementation of the Hearing State Concept, and the sophisticated artificial intelligence methods used to complete the tasks will enhance the Republic of Kazakhstan's degree of technological and scientific advancement.

References

1. Bekmanova, G., Yelibayeva, G., Aubakirova, S., Dyussupova, N., Sharipbay, A., Nyazova, R.: Methods for analyzing polarity of the Kazakh texts related to the terrorist threats. In: Misra, S., et al. (eds.) ICCSA 2019. LNCS, vol. 11619, pp. 717–730. Springer, Cham (2019). https://doi.org/10.1007/978-3-030-24289-3_53
2. Yergesh, B., Bekmanova, G., Sharipbay, A.: Sentiment analysis of Kazakh text and their polarity. Web Intell. **17**(1), 9–15 (2019). https://doi.org/10.3233/WEB-190396
3. Bekmanova, G., Yergesh, B., Sharipbay, A.: Sentiment analysis model based on the word structural representation. In: Mahmud, M., Kaiser, M.S., Vassanelli, S., Dai, Q., Zhong, N. (eds.) BI 2021. LNCS (LNAI), vol. 12960, pp. 170–178. Springer, Cham (2021). https://doi.org/10.1007/978-3-030-86993-9_16

4. Bekmanova, G., Yergesh, B., Sharipbay, A., Mukanova, A.: Emotional speech recognition method based on word transcription. Sensors **22**(5) (2022). https://doi.org/10.3390/s22 051937

5. Yergesh, B., Bekmanova, G., Sharipbay, A.: Sentiment analysis on the hotel reviews in the Kazakh language. In: Paper Presented at the 2nd International Conference on Computer Science and Engineering, UBMK 2017, pp. 790–794 (2017). https://doi.org/10.1109/UBMK. 2017.8093531

6. Yergesh, B., Bekmanova, G., Sharipbay, A., Yergesh, M.: Ontology-based sentiment analysis of Kazakh sentences. In: Gervasi, O., et al. (eds.) ICCSA 2017. LNCS, vol. 10406, pp. 669–677. Springer, Cham (2017). https://doi.org/10.1007/978-3-319-62398-6_47

7. Zhetkenbay, L., Sharipbay, A., Bekmanova, G., Kamanur, U.: Ontological modeling of morphological rules for the adjectives in Kazakh and Turkish languages. J. Theor. Appl. Inf. Technol. **91**(2), 257–263 (2016)

8. Bekmanova, G., et al.: A uniform morphological analyzer for the Kazakh and Turkish languages. In: Paper Presented at the CEUR Workshop Proceedings, pp. 20–30 (2017)

9. Raxmatovna, B.N.: Specific features of political speech. Central Asian J. Lit. Philos. Cult. **3**(12), 80–87 (2022)

10. Tameryan, T.Yu., et al.: Political media communication: bilingual strategies in the pre-election campaign speeches. Online J. Commun. Media Technol. **9**(4), e201921 (2019)

11. Al Maani, B., et al.: The positive-self and negative-other representation in Bashar Al-Assad's first political speech after the Syrian uprising. Theory Pract. Lang. Stud. **12**(10), 2201–2210 (2022)

12. Sotvoldiyevna, U.D.: Political Euphemisms in English and Uzbek languages (A comparative analysis). Eurasian J. Learn. Acad. Teach. **9**, 92–96 (2022)

13. Dave, P.: Analysis of the political power speeches of Jr. Martin Luther King and Barrack Obama: in the light of critical discourse analysis as a literary research method. Vidhyayana-Int. Multi. Peer-Rev. E-Journal-ISSN **7**(5), 2454–8596 (2022)

14. Abdurashetona, A.M., Ismailovich, I.O.: Methods of tagging part of speech of Uzbek language. In: 2021 6th International Conference on Computer Science and Engineering (UBMK). IEEE (2021)

15. Fiorelli, M., et al.: Metadata-driven semantic coordination. In: Garoufallou, E., Fallucchi, F., William De Luca, E. (eds.) MTSR 2019. CCIS, vol. 1057, pp. 16–27. Springer, Cham (2019). https://doi.org/10.1007/978-3-030-36599-8_2

16. Langer, A.M.: Analysis and Design of Next-Generation Software Architectures. Springer, New York (2020). https://doi.org/10.1007/978-3-030-36899-9

17. Lai, C.: Fast retrieval algorithm of English sentences based on artificial intelligence machine translation. In: Atiquzzaman, M., Yen, N., Xu, Z. (eds.) 2021 International Conference on Big Data Analytics for Cyber-Physical System in Smart City, vol. 102. Springer, Singapore (2022). https://doi.org/10.1007/978-981-16-7466-2_117

18. Abdurashetona, A.M., Mokhiyakon, U.: Software features and linguistic features of Uzbek Synonymizer. In: 2022 7th International Conference on Computer Science and Engineering (UBMK). IEEE (2022)

19. Bekmanova, G., et al.: Linguistic foundations of low-resource languages for speech synthesis on the example of the Kazakh language. In: Gervasi, O., Murgante, B., Misra, S., Rocha, A.M.A.C., Garau, C. (eds.) Computational Science and Its Applications–ICCSA 2022 Workshops: Malaga, Spain, 4–7 July 2022, Proceedings, Part III. Springer, Cham (2022). https://doi.org/10.1007/978-3-031-10545-6_1

20. Ibrahim, M.: A corpus-based comparative analysis of assertive strategies in Pakistani democratic and dictatorial speeches. J. Appl. Linguist. TESOL **5**(4), 6–19 (2022)

21. Mohammed, T.A.S., Banda, F., Patel, M.: The Topoi of Mandela's death in the Arabic speaking media: a corpus-based political discourse analysis (2022)

22. Liu, M.: Stancetaking in Hong Kong political discourse: a corpus-assisted discourse study. Chin. Lang. Discourse **13**(1), 79–98 (2022)
23. Afzaal, M.: "Review of Literature." A Corpus-Based Analysis of Discourses on the Belt and Road Initiative: Corpora and the Belt and Road Initiative, pp. 17–37. Springer, Singapore (2023)
24. Anand, S., Keefer, R.: From description to code: a method to predict maintenance codes from maintainer descriptions. Maintenance Reliab. Condition Monit. **2**(2), 35–44 (2022)
25. Ma, Y., et al.: An end-to-end dialogue state tracking system with machine reading comprehension and wide & deep classification. arXiv preprint arXiv:1912.09297 (2019)
26. Saravanan, S., Sudha, K.: GPT-3 powered system for content generation and transformation. In: 2022 Fifth International Conference on Computational Intelligence and Communication Technologies (CCICT). IEEE (2022)
27. Dmytriv, A., et al.: Comparative analysis of using different parts of speech in the Ukrainian texts based on stylistic approach. In: CEUR Workshop Proceedings, vol. 3171 (2022)
28. Tretyakov, E., et al.: Sentiment analysis of social networks messages. In: Klimov, V.V., Kelley, D.J. (eds.) Biologically Inspired Cognitive Architectures 2021: Proceedings of the 12th Annual Meeting of the BICA Society. Springer, Cham (2022). https://doi.org/10.1007/978-3-030-96993-6_61
29. Goswami, S., Hudnurkar, M., Ambekar, S.: Fake news and hate speech detection with machine learning and NLP. PalArch's J. Archaeol. Egypt/Egyptol. **17**(6), 4309–4322 (2020)
30. Lee, E., et al.: Racism detection by analyzing differential opinions through sentiment analysis of tweets using stacked ensemble GCR-NN model. IEEE Access **10**, 9717–9728 (2022)
31. Alshalan, R., Al-Khalifa, H.: A deep learning approach for automatic hate speech detection in the Saudi Twittersphere. Appl. Sci. **10**(23), 8614 (2020)
32. Chu, K.E., Keikhosrokiani, P., Asl, M.P.: A topic modeling and sentiment analysis model for detection and visualization of themes in literary texts. Pertanika J. Sci. Technol. **30**(4), 2535–2561 (2022)
33. Babu, N.V., Kanaga, E.G.M.: Sentiment analysis in social media data for depression detection using artificial intelligence: a review. SN Comput. Sci. **3**, 1–20 (2022)
34. Perifanos, K., Goutsos, D.: Multimodal hate speech detection in Greek social media. Multimodal Technol. Interact. **5**(7), 34 (2021)
35. Aljarah, I., et al.: Intelligent detection of hate speech in Arabic social network: a machine learning approach. J. Inf. Sci. **47**(4), 483–501 (2021)
36. Koltsova, O., et al.: PolSentiLex: sentiment detection in socio-political discussions on Russian social media. In: Filchenkov, A., Kauttonen, J., Pivovarova, L. (eds.) Artificial Intelligence and Natural Language: 9th Conference, AINL 2020, Helsinki, Finland, 7–9 October 2020, Proceedings. Springer, Cham (2020). https://doi.org/10.1007/978-3-030-59082-6_1
37. Mahmud, Md.A.I., et al.: Toward news authenticity: synthesizing natural language processing and human expert opinion to evaluate news. IEEE Access **11**, 11405–11421 (2023)
38. Widodo, D.A., Iksan, N., Sunarko, B.: Sentiment analysis of Twitter media for public reaction identification on COVID-19 monitoring system using hybrid feature extraction method. Int. J. Intell. Syst. Appl. Eng. **11**(1), 92–99 (2023)
39. Holt, K., Ustad Figenschou, T., Frischlich, L.: Key dimensions of alternative news media. Digital Journalism **7**(7), 860–869 (2019). High-Choice Information Environments, vol. 25
40. Chang, W.-L., Tseng, H.-C.: The impact of sentiment on content post popularity through emoji and text on social platforms. In: Cyber Influence and Cognitive Threats, pp. 159–184. Academic Press (2020)
41. Dang, C.N., Moreno-García, M.N., De la Prieta, F.: An approach to integrating sentiment analysis into recommender systems. Sensors **21**(16), 5666 (2021)

42. Wu, C., et al.: SentiRec: sentiment diversity-aware neural news recommendation. In: Proceedings of the 1st Conference of the Asia-Pacific Chapter of the Association for Computational Linguistics and the 10th International Joint Conference on Natural Language Processing (2020)
43. Rozado, D., Al-Gharbi, M., Halberstadt, J.: Prevalence of prejudice-denoting words in news media discourse: a chronological analysis. Soc. Sci. Comput. Rev. 08944393211031452 (2021)
44. Oladele, T.M., Ayetiran, E.F.: Social unrest prediction through sentiment analysis on Twitter using support vector machine: experimental study on Nigeria's# EndSARS. Open Inf. Sci. 7(1), 20220141 (2023)

Multidimensional Evolutionary Evaluations for Transformative Approaches (MEETA 2023)

Community Archive as Place-Based Decision-Making Process: A Proposal for the "Archivio Atena"

Ludovica La Rocca[1], Chiara Mazzarella[1], Stefania Regalbuto[2], Maria Somma[1(✉)], and Alessandro Imbriaco[3]

[1] Department of Architecture, University of Naples Federico II, via Toledo 402, 80134 Naples, Italy
{cerreta,ludovica.larocca,chiara.mazzarella, maria.somma}@unina.it

[2] Department of Management, Ca' Foscari University of Venice, San Giobbe, Cannaregio 873, 30121 Venice, Italy
stefania.regalbuto@unive.it

[3] Studio Bellosguardo Aps, Via Montoggio 57, 00168 Rome, Italy

Abstract. The construction of a community archive can be a tool for analysis, public engagement and support for activating social innovation and urban regeneration processes. The study presents the methodological proposal developed in an educational laboratory in cooperation between public entities, universities, and the third sector, for a local cultural and social regeneration project in the historic centre of Atena Lucana in the South of Italy. The proposed community archive aims to archive in a digital system the architectural and urban heritage of Atena Lucana's historic centre to trigger processes of adaptive reuse and urban regeneration leveraging on a socio-spatial relationship. The paper proposed a methodology framework to co-design a multidimensional archive, which includes georeferenced hard and soft data deduced based on interviews, focus groups and collaborative mapping. A place-based community archive constitutes a spatial decision support system for urban regeneration. Based on specific objectives and methods, the community archive aims to develop sustainable and inclusive regeneration strategies.

Keywords: Community archive · digital archive · public space · spatial decision-support system · urban regeneration

1 Introduction

In the most recent scholarly literature, there is growing attention to community archives, initiatives often with relatively long histories but whose importance has only recently been widely recognised by cultural policymakers and professional organisations (https://www.ucl.ac.uk/information-studies/community-archives-and-identities-documenting-and-sustaining-community-heritage). The 2004 Task Force Archives

O. Gervasi et al. (Eds.): ICCSA 2023 Workshops, LNCS 14108, pp. 209–225, 2023.
https://doi.org/10.1007/978-3-031-37117-2_16

report, titled "Listening to the Past, Speaking to the Future" [1], stated that the community archives are a new and resourceful source, significant for society as institutional archives in public collections. At the same time, establishing community archives as structured and recognisable organisational identities poses the need to interpret what an archive and a community are. While Flinn, Stevens and Shepherd define community as "any kind of people who come together and present themselves as such" [2], on the other hand, Scotini [3] argues that the archive is not simply a collection of data, documents or information, but a fundamental practice with the power to restore visibility and voice to what has not been archived: a repressed, exiled identity, a memory. A community archive is configured as an "unresolved" operation since it arises in the paradox of something that, while aspiring to be archived, eludes archiving. More specifically, the community archive can be interpreted as the product of community attempts to document the history of their commonality, resulting in "collections of material collected primarily by members of a given community and over whose use community members exercise some level of control" [2].

Since both activist archiving techniques and data activism strongly emphasise involving communities of interested stakeholders in creating representations that assert their points of view, the Environmental Data and Governance Initiatives (EDGI) instance shows that there are striking parallels between both [4]. Caswell, Cifor and Ramirez assert that community archives can be an alternative to traditional archives "through which communities can make collective decisions about what is of lasting value to them, shape the collective memory of their past, and control how stories about their past are constructed" [5]. There where the two ways of understanding archives, namely the traditional and the community archives, are developed in a logic of opposition, the more recent literature introduces a "participatory turn" according to which the latter presents itself as an opportunity to re-configure the former mode, thus presenting a challenge to traditional archives. Also, in the light of the Faro Convention [6], according to which the involvement of communities in the identification, knowledge, protection and enhancement of tangible and intangible heritage is an indispensable practice to foster the preservation, Patricia Garcia pays particular attention to how communities practice the management and administration of archives, glimpsing in their participation in cataloguing a tool to enrich the ordinary archival structure [7].

In contrast to traditional archives, community members can be involved in every stage of archival creation, from defining the scope to describing materials to providing resistance to further advance movement building and solidarity. Huvila et al. [8] point how community archives suggest a shift of responsibility between archivist and user, harnessing community knowledge to reposition archives as sites of empowerment and solidarity, reflecting community needs [9]. In this sense, community archives are institutions in which community members "exercise some level of control" and community archivists as mediators between "professional heritage services" and communities [10]. Born mainly out of a long tradition of documentation of local history and social movements by volunteers and activists, community archives can be venues of representation of social minorities and told of custody, collection development and appraisal, processing, arrangement and description, organisation, representation and naming, collaboration, resource generation and allocation, activism and social justice, preservation, reuse, and sustainability [11]. Over time, community archives have emerged as part of the broader participatory movement to enhance cultural heritage [12–14].

In the renewed participatory turn of community archives, digital technology has played a relevant role by enabling community members to collect and digitise materials and share them [14, 15]. Community archives take the form primarily of digital storage that contains, preserves, and makes accessible the cultural, historical, and social heritage of a specific community or group of people and can include a variety of materials such as documents, photographs, audio and video recordings, oral histories, art, and personal objects. Digital platforms thus become particularly significant both for building interactive and long-lasting databases and for facilitating interaction among users [16], defining themselves as much in open-source digital resource management systems such as Omeka and Islandora [12, 17] as in geographic information systems (GIS) to support archiving.

The main objectives of community archives include: preserving the collective memory and history of one or more communities, helping to build a sense of identity and belonging; providing an educational resource for future generations, helping to understand the community's past and traditions; enhancing cultural diversity and promote intercultural dialogue by encouraging understanding and respect among different communities; support historical and socio-cultural research by providing a base of reliable data and sources; and facilitate community participation and civic engagement by involving people in collecting, preserving and sharing their heritage.

In an attempt to achieve these goals, multiple experiences have developed, especially in more recent times, around the world. The Community Archives and Heritage Group (CAHG) is a community archive project active since 2006 in the UK and Ireland. After three years, it was developed informally. Starting from the work on memory and identity and memory, the project has grown up to today and was established with a vision statement based on principles of inclusion, collaboration for creating value for more people and respect for the environment. The information is mapped and opened via a web platform, and all activities are advertised. The project developed with a creative perspective that went beyond mere archiving. In fact, the collection of work and team efforts over time have produced community-led projects (https://www.communityarchives.org.uk/index.php).

The project, Community Archives and Identities: Documenting and Sustaining Community Heritage, examined how community archives contributed to the construction of collective identities in historically marginalised "communities", focusing on how much such archives might advance broader social policy goals [10]. According to the study, there are five primary areas of practice where mainstream, publicly financed cultural organisations-especially archives-engage with community archives. These include administration, gathering, curation and dissemination, consulting, and advising. The categories' descriptions are meant to illustrate possibilities rather than exhaustive. A prominent worldwide photographic art gallery, Belfast Exposed celebrated its 30th anniversary in 2013 after beginning as a grassroots, community-based photography enterprise. To make the analogue collection more accessible to a wider audience, more than 3000 photographs from it had been digitally archived by 2005. By 2007, the gallery had created two digital libraries, one offline and one online, using archival and psychoanalytic social theory. Additionally, several works of art based on the collection that Belfast Exposed commissioned in the previous ten years have been examined as illustrations of new approaches to interacting with the archive [18].

Among the Italian experiences, the community archive of Manerba del Garda was born in 2021 based on participatory research and teaching activities begun in the 1970s, the result of collaboration with ASAR and some universities, with the aim of cataloguing information on the history and cultural heritage of the municipality. In continuous evolution, the archive consists of a School of Participatory Research aimed at its construction and expansion through conferences, guided tours, research activities for filing landscapes, sites and architecture, and dissemination. On the occasion of Matera 2019 Capital of Culture, the ARCO - ARchivio digitale di COmunità project was developed. The goal is not to lose the testimony of these moments of aggregation rooted in Lucanian agricultural culture, using photographs, videos, oral histories and newspaper articles collected by the community as tools of territorial investigation to be returned then within a web platform. On the other hand, the most recent Apulian experience sees the creation in 2022 in San Cesario di Lecce of the Community Sound Archive (ASC) "The City that Speaks." ASC is the result of a participatory process that involves citizens exercising self-representation and recognising the specificities of their place. The goal of ASC is to reconnect residents in a joint reflection on the places they live and to trigger proposals that can bring out community priorities (https://partecipazione.regione.puglia.it/proces ses/la-citta-che-parla/f/208/).

It is possible to access the archive through a travelling map app. It will be set up in physical form inside Distilleria De Giorgi, one of southern Italy's most exciting and impressive industrial archaeology sites, now converted into a cultural container. It emerges how in the landscape of community archives and the different declinations of the genre, the document represents the device whose interpretation changes the structure and approach with which to relate to archiving. Indeed, over time, the idea of "document" has expanded from written text to artefacts, monuments, products, and even entire neighbourhoods and cities [19].

In this perspective, documentation shifts from more sterile document preservation to a more dynamic collective design. At the same time, the archive, rather than a memory, is an aspiration, an anticipation of collective memory through value elicitation as a meta-intervention. As McKemmish [20] argues, archives are "always in flux", and their narratives depend on decisions about which objects are significant, which should be preserved and which should not. Precisely for this reason, the community archive becomes a tool of imagination and social design, inquiry and communication, of debate and desire at the same time.

The research is part of the planning of "Archivio Atena" - Community Archive of Atena Lucana" to design a place-based decision-making process by which to identify and catalogue, through collaborative approaches, the dimensions recognised as particularly representative of the material and immaterial heritage of the historic centre of Atena Lucana. In this perspective, the community archive is intended to investigate the multiple dimensions of the local identity of the area through visible and non-visible elements and bring out, more fully and complexly, its values through collaborative decision-making processes. The experimentation, which intends to structure a methodological-typical approach functional to activating a community archive, is configured simultaneously, as a tool for investigation and intervention, in Italy's inland areas and, specifically, in abandoned centres. In this way, the construction of the community archive represents a co-design challenge of an urban regeneration process that opens up some research questions:

- How to identify the characterising/representative elements for a place-based community archive?
- How to structure a scientific decision-making process as a participatory tool, simultaneously of self-representation and knowledge of communities?
- Can a community archive provide data to inform a decision support system for developing urban regeneration projects?

In an attempt to answer these questions, the article is structured into a first part devoted to the introduction and contextualisation of the research question within a panorama of international literature, a second part relating to the spatial and project context in which the study was developed, the third part in which the research methodology is expressed followed by the fourth part in which the decision-making process framework is described as a result of this initial positioning. Finally, in the fifth part, discussions and conclusions are gathered.

2 Archivio Atena: An Urban Regeneration Strategy

"Archivio Atena" is a winning project of the public notice, "Attractivity of the villages", part of the National Recovery and Resilience Plan (PNRR M1C3) financed by the Next Generation EU. The project's objective is to build the community archive of the Municipality of Atena Lucana, a small town in the province of Salerno, in the Campania Region, in southern Italy. The project is structured to create innovative tools for narrating the territory from part of the community through digitising the cultural heritage and establishing a permanent laboratory for the meeting of artists, scholars, cultural operators, institutions and individuals (Fig. 1). The Municipality of Atena developed this project with a significant partnership consisting of the Central Institute for Cataloging and Documentation (ICCD), ISIA Urbino, MAXXI L'Aquila, Legacoop, MIDA, Studio Bellosguardo Association, Amici San Ciro Association, Leel association, Le Case di Igea association, Artem association, Comunità Montana, National Cilento Park Vallo di Diano e Alburni, SC Hotel, Cartolibreria Etoile. The involvement of many institutional subjects but also local actors and different people, realities and visions in its events and activities (i.e. inhabitants, male and female students, male and female artists, entrepreneurial activities, territorial associations and census implementers) has the aim of making a collective work.

The Archivio Atena project aims to collect the local cultural heritage in a community archive. Through the digitalisation of private photographs, the creation of photographic campaigns, and the production of audio-visual material in the area, Archivio Atena intends to preserve and enhance the common identity of the inhabitants of Atena Lucana, safeguarding a historical-cultural wealth that risks being dispersed. Also, Archivio Atena is a project that invests in training and considers the teaching of traditional techniques

ARCHIVIO ATENA IS...

...A COLLECTIVE WORK   ...AN IDEA   ...REMEMBER
                         OF COUNTRY   TOGETHER

Fig. 1. Archivio Atena

and arts as a social glue and a precious resource to be disseminated. Increasing the village's attractiveness also means supporting the development of new job opportunities by redeveloping shared spaces, creating cultural aggregation initiatives and supplying technological tools and digital equipment for the country. Then, with several annual appointments, events, festivals, educational activities and artistic residencies, Archivio Atena is bringing young people, male and female students, to the area to encourage encounters and contamination and use the town as a party thanks to the participation and involvement of all citizens.

The project's leitmotif is the archive, i.e. the practice of collecting and digitising private photographs and material and immaterial, natural and environmental heritage, which defines the historical and cultural identity of Atena Lucana. In this context, the teaching and research laboratory is part of the RIVA research, teaching and third mission network of the Federico II Department of Architecture in Naples, to structure a place-based census technique able to integrate a critical census of architecture, and public space, considering tangible and intangible identity elements.

3 Material and Methods

As part of a worldwide push for increased decentralisation, accountability, and popular democracy [21–24], the notion of encouraging involvement in decision-making emerged in the late 1970s and 1980s. The idea is that people taking part in government is a step forward in the fight for democracy and equality. The essential basic characteristics of 'good governance' include responsibility and legitimacy and, under those ideas, transparency, inclusivity, respect, and efficacy [25–28].

In particular, Seale [29, 30] divides archives into two categories: primary sources, which are the original documents that have survived from the past, and secondary sources, which are "accounts created by people writing at some distance in space or time from the events described." Archives include unique data that is not accessible anywhere else. This information is also available in a wide variety of formats, such as text (which Seale further subdivides into oral sources, which are spoken sources that are subsequently transcribed, and documentary sources, which are written sources that are generated either during or after an event), images, family trees, and more [30].

The construction of community archives can constitute significant advantages in terms of active involvement in urban regeneration processes.

With this in mind, deliberative evaluation methods and tools are considered to be particularly relevant, becoming significant, especially in the collaborative exploration phases in which different stakeholders are involved in the recognition and elicitation of shared, plural and cultural values [31–34] that can contribute to constituting the characterising elements for the definition of a community archive.

Deliberation of shared values considers the collective and intersubjective meanings that, through social interactions, convey conceptions of the common good among people [34–37]. They are particularly relevant and significant in confronting practice, especially in collaborative exploration phases where different stakeholders recognise and elicithared, plural and cultural values [31–34]. The deliberative approach also arises to consider evaluative processes of equity and justice [37–39]. Irvine et al. [40] discuss the potential of deliberative evaluations as new democratic spaces, and Kenter [34] adds that such assessments can function as boundary objects between researchers, stakeholders and decision-makers [32].

From this perspective, the goal of integrating deliberation into evaluation is not only a more robust elicitation of values. However, it can provide more effective opportunities for recognising different voices in decision-making and building bridges between potentially conflicting perspectives and interests in decision-making [34].

Deliberative evaluation is an interactive evaluation method that leads different actors (politicians, citizens, etc.) to form value judgements by facilitating open dialogue between the parties, thus, taking into account ethical beliefs, moral commitments and social norms beyond individual and collective utility. Therefore, deliberative methods also can promote learning and reflection, encouraging people to go beyond self-interest to construct collective judgements that reflect a more comprehensive and socially just evaluation of public goods.

Kenter et al. [34] describe that a deliberative process can be structured around the following stages:

1. the search for, acquisition and social exchange of information, the addition of knowledge (from the report identified) and the expression and exchange of transcendental values and beliefs to form reasoned opinions;
2. the expression of reasoned opinions as part of the dialogical and civilised engagement between participants, respecting the different points of view held by participants, being able to openly express disagreement, providing equal opportunities for all participants to engage in deliberation and providing opportunities for participants to evaluate and re-evaluate their positions
3. identification and critical evaluation of options or 'solutions' that could address a problem, reflecting on the potential consequences and trade-offs associated with different options
4. integrating insights from the deliberative process to establish contextual values around different options and, finally, determine a preferred, informed and reasoned choice.

The scientific literature divides these techniques into deliberative, analytic -deliberative, potentially-interpretive deliberative, interpretive, psychometric-deliberative and psychometric [41, 42].

These techniques can be included in the broader categorisation of revealed preference-based and stated preference-related methods [43].

Revealed preference-based methods largely coincide with the techniques defined by Kenter as interpretive [41] and include:

- direct observation, as human action and behaviour reflect social value;
- documentation, as the consultation of textual, photographic, and historical material, returns information about human preferences concerning the topics discussed;
- media/social media analysis, as analysis of shared material on the topic or place of interest, yields significant data to reference values.

Declared preference methods, on the other hand, rely directly on the statements made by stakeholders questioned to express a value. These include the following potential-interpretive deliberative techniques:

- Interviews: gaining an in-depth understanding of the stakeholder's expression of opinion regarding a specific issue or place;
- Questionnaires: structured questions to gather information on the values expressed by the interviewees, generically traced back to a given set of values/actions and a Likert scale to assess relevance;
- Storytelling: analysis of participants' experiences, relationships, and stories to obtain information on the values expressed by them directly or indirectly [34];
- Participatory mapping: combines the tools of modern cartography with participatory methods to map the values and benefits found in a specific context by making a physical or digital map to indicate the value (and problematic) features and sometimes rank them by importance [44–47];
- Participatory GIS (PGIS): combines the method of participatory mapping with GIS techniques of spatial analysis [48, 49];
- Public Participation GIS (PPGIS): emphasises the local level of stakeholder involvement to promote knowledge production by local non-governmental groups;
- Focus groups: activates group discussions, enabling information to be obtained based on the interactions that arise during the thematic debate;
- Expert-based: uses experts' professional knowledge to assess the relevance of values, making explicit the benefits and critical issues at stake. An example of this is the Delphi method [50].

In particular, following the stated knowledge-based methods, the last decades have seen a proliferation of integrated theoretical and methodological approaches to GIS [51–56] setting the research effort for the interaction, not only between the technical/computational aspects with the participatory/collaborative ones but also, and above all, with intangible socio-cultural aspects that make the interaction with GIS an innovative tool that can lead to a much more profound knowledge of all the elements that contribute to the construction of a decision-making process and in this case of a community archive. As a result, the concept has evolved in research, development and practice domains consisting of different approaches and frameworks. In particular, spatial aspects (such as the domains of geo-computation and geo-visualisation) and spatial decision support systems have been integrated with new technologies increasingly related to the concepts of co-participation and collaboration, also known as: intelligent SDSS [57], planning support systems - PSS [58], collaborative GIS - CGIS [59], group SDSS [60], participatory GIS - PGIS [61–64], public participation GIS - PPGIS [62, 65, 66], spatial knowledge-based systems [67], spatial multi-agent systems [68]. All these tools constitute, on the one hand, the advancement of the concept of SDSS, which Malczewski [69] defines as "an interactive computer-based system designed to support a user or group of users in achieving more effective decision-making while solving a semi-structured spatial decision-making problem", and on the other hand the advancement to the critical issues raised over the years regarding the inability to have adequate tools for active public participation [66, 70] and thus of tools designed to support community knowledge and involvement in the production and use of geographic information [71–73]. The action of mapping this information, and making it accessible to all through GIS platforms, is a way to make it operational, making it available both for pure knowledge and also to stimulate planning considering local identity and memory. In this way, a community archive with specific and geolocated information becomes a Spatial Decision Support System (SDSS) [74, 75].

Participatory Maps and Participatory Mapping are 'maps' (representations of geographic information) created by a community or groups of individuals via participatory methods [48, 49, 76, 77]. They are based on local interests, needs, and (spatial) knowledge, and they use various mapping and elicitation techniques - they are an 'approach' rather than a single method [61, 66, 71, 76, 78, 79]. Moreover, as local spatial knowledge is complex, multi-source and multidimensional, collaborative mapping methods can help define future regeneration processes, some useful in bringing a place alive, rethinking, and reactivating it. The primary goal of collaborative mapping processes for community archives is to successfully capture the invaluable (yet often invisible) spatial knowledge of local natives and put it to better use for practical purposes in public policy [74, 76] or to revive a cultural identity that has been eroding over time. Local spatial knowledge is fundamental that describes living spaces and places, paying particular attention to understanding the directness of the elements and values that have defined a taxonomic identity for those settings. Public space and landscapes' symbolic, emotional, and mystical experience is crucial to local spatial knowledge. According to McCall M. [76] the 'laid of the land' defines cultural and activity areas and responsibility spaces. The understanding of the ontology of specific belief systems complicates what seems to be a simple binary separation between facts and values. In other words, what constitutes "facts" may differ depending on the meta-value system. (Spatial) ontologies organically integrate people's values of and about space with spatial facts regarding spatial analysis; these things are concatenated. Societies and cultures engage in lengthy, profound meta-value system construction and appropriation processes. The frame of identification and transmission of values is necessary for the designation and understanding of spatial facts. People's values may modify the interpretation of realised spatial facts, which feeds back into the ontological system that validates and re-frames the facts [80]. Translating facts and values, often ignored from the outside, inherent in and constituting a community archive into collaborative maps requires adequate representation and valid representativeness.

Facts matter more than values in representation, but values matter more than facts in representativity. Participatory mapping not only displays points but also seeks, finds, and maps valuable areas. Furthermore, the need to seek out representative voices applies equally to factual knowledge and its mapping to ethical principles. For these reasons, some of the deliberative approaches described above are fundamental, including interviews, questionnaires, focus groups and storytelling, which define a reasoned construction of a community archive aiming at co-design.

4 Methodology

In an attempt to produce an advance towards the construction of a place-based community archive, research activities developed as part of educational laboratories have been structured in four distinct phases according to the methodological process specifically designed and below (Fig. 2). The first two phases are preliminary to building the archive, effectively developing in the third and fourth phases. The archive structuring process involves using different approaches, methods, and tools, inferring soft and hard data and including other points of view.

Phase 1. Context and Community Knowledge. It is aimed at the definition and description of the analysis context (i), the identification of involved stakeholders (ii) and to defining of the objective underlying the construction of the community archive (iii), respectively addressed in the three steps in which phase 1 is divided: context analysis (1.1), stakeholder analysis (1.2), specific objective definition (1.3).

Phase 2. Archive Type Identification. This phase has been specifically structured to choose the most suitable supports to grasp the most significant features. To this end, the second phase is divided into two distinct steps, the first focusing on the tool selection (2.1) and the second aimed at identifying specific descriptive categories deduced from theoretical and operational frameworks (2.2).

Phase 3. Archive Elements Identification. Divided into four distinct steps and aimed at collecting information material, the structuring of the process is based on the integration of top-down and bottom-up approaches. In addition to specific phases of the stakeholders' consultation, the laboratory activities take place in the context of a research group, including experts and local community members. To define the most suitable categories, the ones that have been selected in the second phase have been then discussed in the context of the research team, involving experts and community, through a proper consultation phase (3.1), which has been deemed valuable to point the discussion. This step includes introducing the basic theoretical concepts, a critical interpretation of the same, and the basic knowledge for mapping information material. Then, starting from the critical considerations that have emerged, it has proceeded to identify and classify the most significant elements (tangible and intangible) of the archive's objective. Finally, the step provides for georeferenced mapping of the elements identified. Step 3.2 has been specially structured to classify the elements selected, providing an interpretative key of the main characteristics through brainstorming and literature study. Finally, step 3.3 is dedicated to collecting data valid for database structuring. Then, the database resulting from the research group is submitted to the local community as part of a consultation phase (3.4) which aims to test the built model in the actual context (through on-site visits, focus groups, and interviews) and detect the data helpful in making the archive (data collection is carried out through interviews, direct observation, and documentary analysis).

Phase 4. Archiving and Digitisation. In this phase, through four steps, the database produced as a result of step 3.3 is reworked based on the observations received from the local community. Therefore, mapping (4.1) and database (4.2) are revised. Subsequently, the data in the archive is digitised (4.3). Finally, to validate the archived material, a further phase of interaction involving the local community and the main stakeholders has been provided (4.4).

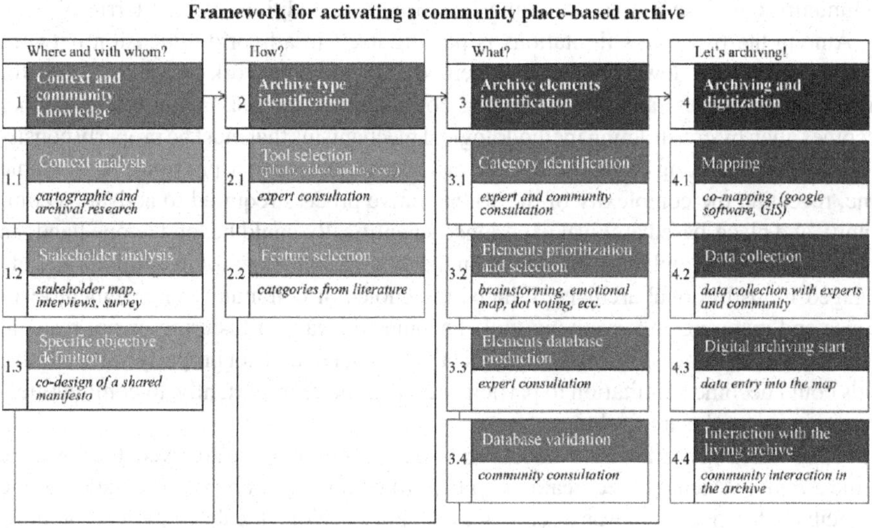

Framework for activating a community place-based archive

Where and with whom?		How?		What?		Let's archiving!	
1	Context and community knowledge	2	Archive type identification	3	Archive elements identification	4	Archiving and digitization
1.1	Context analysis — *cartographic and archival research*	2.1	Tool selection *(photo, video, audio, ecc.)* — *expert consultation*	3.1	Category identification — *expert and community consultation*	4.1	Mapping — *co-mapping (google software, GIS)*
1.2	Stakeholder analysis — *stakeholder map, interviews, survey*	2.2	Feature selection — *categories from literature*	3.2	Elements prioritization and selection — *brainstorming, emotional map, dot voting, ecc.*	4.2	Data collection — *data collection with experts and community*
1.3	Specific objective definition — *co-design of a shared manifesto*			3.3	Elements database production — *expert consultation*	4.3	Digital archiving start — *data entry into the map*
				3.4	Database validation — *community consultation*	4.4	Interaction with the living archive — *community interaction in the archive*

Fig. 2. The methodological workflow

5 Discussion and Conclusion

An analysis of the literature has shown that interest in community archives has grown significantly recently. Research has paid particular attention to the meaning of community, the values and urgencies expressed by the sponsoring communities, and the opportunities, in terms of professional skills and empowerment, that these experiences can offer. In particular, commonly, these experiences share a bottom-up view, an approach to the theme of the community archive that emerged and matured over time by citizens driven by shared cultural and social motives. However, less space has been given to the techniques and approaches proper for activating and curating a community archive.

The current research proposed a methodological framework for activating place-based community archives, starting from this gap and from the need to experiment with the community archive as an operational tool for urban regeneration in a central dimension between top-down institutional and bottom-up community-based. The aim was to systematise the various experiences and investigations activated to represent a collaborative process, replicable in other contexts as well, capable of orienting not the object of the archive but how it can be defined with the community of reference. In this endeavour, a method was structured to support independent groups, associations or public bodies that intend to trigger community and place-based urban regeneration processes in their territory. The proposal was born in the framework of the Archivio Atena project, which involves the territory of Atena Lucana and, in particular, the historic centre of Atena Lucana. In this sense, the methodological proposal fits, even more in detail, in the construction of valuable tools and methods of investigation and, above all, of a project to operate in "inland areas" and in abandoned areas starting from the values expressed by communities in close connection with uses, forms and traditions of their territory.

Among the proposal's limitations is placing itself in a hybrid dimension between bottom-up and top-down. Where the methodological framework becomes a tool for triggering the process and thus activating communities, the risk is that the researcher becomes alien by constructing methodological mechanisms that must be properly consistent with the inhabiting communities' characteristics, skills and aspirations. At the same time, revealing the complexity of the collaborative process required to activate a community and place-based archival experience scientifically could be, on the one hand, an obstacle to project implementation and, on the other, a challenge for institutions already engaged in institutional archives. Finally, the choice of community engagement techniques and mapping and archiving tools becomes relevant in fostering or not resident participation. In this case, the use of technically structured and not properly collaborative tools could become a limitation to participation and, more importantly, to communities' appropriation of the archival tool.

In constructing the database model for collecting the data to be archived, the presence of the Archivio Atena project team, with the project manager and representative of the municipal administration, was as crucial as the presence of a local community member. Because site-specific issues can change the elements that do or do not deserve to be surveyed, arguably, without any local community member, the model would have been repeated several times due to the discussion with the community or during the workshop. At the same time, a team of academics was an essential resource in the framework's design and, in particular, in building the structure of an archival database that would then have to be validated by the resident communities.

Future directions of the research include the application of the methodology in the context of the historic centre of Atena Lucana, in which the inhabitants will test and validate the database. Furthermore, particular attention will be given to testing collaborative approaches for selecting, prioritising and co-assessing the objects of which the archive is composed. In this sense, it will be necessary to build ad-hoc streamlined and operational techniques and tools through which communities can fully self-represent themselves at all times.

References

1. Netwon, C.: Listening to the past, speaking to the future. Rec. Manag. J. **14**, 133–134 (2004). https://doi.org/10.1108/09565690410566800
2. Flinn, A., Stevens, M., Shepherd, E.: Whose memories, whose archives? Independent community archives, autonomy and the mainstream. Arch. Sci. **9**, 71–86 (2009). https://doi.org/10.1007/s10502-009-9105-2
3. Scotini, M.: Archiviare l'inarchiviabile: Forme Del Tempo e Regimi Di Storicità. Archiviare l'inarchiviabile : forme del tempo e regimi di storicità, pp. 33–40 (2022). https://doi.org/10.1400/288446
4. Currie, M.E., Paris, B.S.: Back-ups for the future: archival practices for data activism. Arch. Manuscripts **46**, 124–142 (2018). https://doi.org/10.1080/01576895.2018.1468273
5. Caswell, M., Cifor, M., Ramirez, M.H.: To suddenly discover yourself existing': uncovering the impact of community archives. Am. Archivist **79** (2016)
6. Council of Europe, Council of Europe Framework Convention on the Value of Cultural Heritage for Society (2005)
7. Vukliš, V., Gilliland, A.: Archival activism: emerging forms, local applications. In: Filej, B. (ed.) Archives in the Service of People – People in the Service of Archives; Alma Mater Europea: Maribon, pp. 14–25 (2016)
8. Huvila, I.: Participatory archive: towards decentralised curation, radical user orientation, and broader contextualisation of records management. Arch. Sci. **8**, 15–36 (2008). https://doi.org/10.1007/s10502-008-9071-0
9. Zavala, J., Migoni, A.A., Caswell, M., Geraci, N., Cifor, M.: A process where we're all at the table': community archives challenging dominant modes of archival practice. New Pub.: Aust. Soc. Archivists **45**, 202–215 (2017). https://doi.org/10.1080/01576895.2017.1377088
10. Stevens, M., Flinn, A., Shepherd, E.: New frameworks for community engagement in the archive sector: from handing over to handing on. Int. J. Herit. Stud. **16**, 59–76 (2010). https://doi.org/10.1080/13527250903441770
11. Poole, A.H.: The information work of community archives: a systematic literature review. J. Documentation **76**, 657–687 (2020)
12. Sabharwal, A.: Functional frameworks for socialized digital curation: curatorial interventions and curation spaces in archives and libraries. Libr. Trends **69**, 672–695 (2021). https://doi.org/10.1353/LIB.2021.0009
13. Benoit, E., Eveleigh, A.: Participatory Archives: Theory and Practice, p. 263 (2019)
14. Liew, C.L., Goulding, A., Nichol, M.: From shoeboxes to shared spaces: participatory cultural heritage via digital platforms. Inf. Commun. Soc. **25**, 1293–1310 (2022). https://doi.org/10.1080/1369118X.2020.1851391
15. Gilliland, A., Flinn, A.: CIRN Prato Community Informatics Conference 2013: Keynote 1 Community Archives: What Are We Really Talking About? (2013)
16. Matusiak, K.K.: Evaluating a digital community archive from the user perspective: the case of formative multifaceted evaluation. Libr. Inf. Sci. Res. **44**, 101159 (2022). https://doi.org/10.1016/J.LISR.2022.101159
17. Cocciolo, A.: Community archives in the digital era: a case from the LGBT community. Preserv. Digital Technol. Cult. **45**, 157–165 (2017). https://doi.org/10.1515/PDTC-2016-0018/MACHINEREADABLECITATION/RIS
18. Blanco, P.P., Schuppert, M., Lange, J.: The digital progression of community archives, from amateur production to artistic practice: a case study of belfast exposed. Convergence **21**, 58–77 (2015). https://doi.org/10.1177/1354856514560299
19. Burgum, S.: This city is an archive: squatting history and urban authority. J. Urban Hist. **48**, 504–522 (2022). https://doi.org/10.1177/00961442209555165/ASSET/IMAGES/LARGE/10.1177_0096144220955165-FIG7.JPEG

20. McKemmish, S.: Are Records Ever Actual? (2016). https://doi.org/10.4225/03/57D77D8E7 2B71
21. Cooke, B., Kothari, U.: Participation The New Tyranny? 1st edn. Zed Books (2001)
22. Haklay, M.M.: Neogeography and the delusion of democratization **45**, 55–69 (2013). https://doi.org/10.1068/A45184
23. Hickey, S., Mohan, G.: Participation: From Tyranny to Transformation? Zed Books Ltd., 7 Cynthia Sreet, Londra N1 9JF, Regno Unito (2004)
24. Cavalier, D., Kennedy, E.B.:The Rightful Place of Science: Citizen Science. Arizona State University, Tempe, AZ (2016)
25. Grindle, M.S.: Good enough governance revisited. Dev. Policy Rev. **25**, 533–574 (2007). https://doi.org/10.1111/J.1467-7679.2007.00385.X
26. McCall, M.K.: Seeking good governance in participatory-GIS: a review of processes and governance dimensions in applying GIS to participatory spatial planning. Habitat Int. **27**, 549–573 (2003). https://doi.org/10.1016/S0197-3975(03)00005-5
27. Mccall, M.K., Dunn, C.E.: Geo-information tools for participatory spatial planning: fulfilling the criteria for 'Good' governance? Geoforum **43**, 81–94 (2012). https://doi.org/10.1016/J.GEOFORUM.2011.07.007
28. Towards Participatory Local Governance: Assessing the Transformative Possibilities. In: Hickey, S., Mohan, G. (eds.) Participation: From Tyranny to Transformation? pp. 25–41. ZedBook (2004)
29. Gilliland, A., McKemmish, S.: Building an infrastructure for archival research. Arch. Sci. **4**, 149–197 (2004). https://doi.org/10.1007/S10502-006-6742-6/METRICS
30. Seale, C.: Researching Society and Culture, pp. 1–664 (2017)
31. Cooper, N., Brady, E., Steen, H., Bryce, R.: Aesthetic and spiritual values of ecosystems: recognising the ontological and axiological plurality of cultural ecosystem 'Services.' Ecosyst. Serv. **21**, 218–229 (2016). https://doi.org/10.1016/J.ECOSER.2016.07.014
32. Ranger, S., et al.: Forming shared values in conservation management: an interpretive-deliberative-democratic approach to including community voices. Ecosyst. Serv. **21**, 344–357 (2016). https://doi.org/10.1016/J.ECOSER.2016.09.016
33. Everard, M., Reed, M.S., Kenter, J.O.: The ripple effect: institutionalising pro-environmental values to shift societal norms and behaviours. Ecosyst. Serv. **21**, 230–240 (2016). https://doi.org/10.1016/J.ECOSER.2016.08.001
34. Kenter, J.O.: Editorial: shared, plural and cultural values. Ecosyst. Serv. **21**, 175–183 (2016). https://doi.org/10.1016/J.ECOSER.2016.10.010
35. Farber, S.C., Costanza, R., Wilson, M.A.: Economic and ecological concepts for valuing ecosystem services. Ecol. Econ. **41**, 375–392 (2002). https://doi.org/10.1016/S0921-8009(02)00088-5
36. Fish, R., et al.: Participatory and Deliberative Techniques for Embeddingan Ecosystems Approach into Decision Making. Project Report. Defra, London, UK (2011)
37. O'Neill, J.: Markets, Deliberation and Environment, 1st edn. Routledge, London (2013). ISBN 9780203607169
38. Spash, C.L.: Deliberative monetary valuation and the evidence for a new value theory. Land Econ. **84**, 469–488 (2008). https://doi.org/10.3368/LE.84.3.469
39. Howarth, R.B., Wilson, M.A.: A theoretical approach to deliberative valuation: aggregation by mutual consent. Land Econ. **82**, 1–16 (2006). https://doi.org/10.3368/LE.82.1.1
40. Zografos, C., Howarth, R.B.: Deliberative ecological economics for sustainability governance. Sustainability **2**, 3399–3417 (2010). https://doi.org/10.3390/SU2113399
41. Kenter, J.O., et al.: What are shared and social values of ecosystems? Ecol. Econ. **111**, 86–99 (2015)

42. Cerreta, M.: Cultural, Creative, Community Hub: Dai Valori Condivisi Ai Valori Sociali Condivisi per La Rigenerazione Della Città Storica. In: Abitare il futuro; CLEAN, Napoli, pp. 134–146 (2016)
43. Cheng, X., Van Damme, S., Li, L., Uyttenhove, P.: Evaluation of cultural ecosystem services: a review of methods. Ecosyst. Serv. **37**, 100925 (2019)
44. Brown, G., Raymond, C.: The relationship between place attachment and landscape values: toward mapping place attachment. Appl. Geogr. **27**, 89–111 (2007)
45. Dramstad, W.E., Tveit, M.S., Fjellstad, W.J., Fry, G.L.A.: Relationships between visual landscape preferences and map-based indicators of landscape structure. Landsc. Urban Plan. **78**, 465–474 (2006)
46. Kenter, J.O.: Integrating deliberative monetary valuation, systems modelling and participatory mapping to assess shared values of ecosystem services. Ecosyst. Serv. **21**, 291–307 (2016). https://doi.org/10.1016/J.ECOSER.2016.06.010
47. Fish, R., et al.: Making space for cultural ecosystem services: insights from a study of the UK nature improvement initiative. Ecosyst. Serv. **21**, 329–343 (2016). https://doi.org/10.1016/j.ecoser.2016.09.017
48. Attardi, R., Cerreta, M., Poli, G.: A collaborative multi-criteria spatial decision support system for multifunctional landscape evaluation. In: Gervasi, O., et al. (eds.) ICCSA 2015. LNCS, vol. 9157, pp. 782–797. Springer, Cham (2015). https://doi.org/10.1007/978-3-319-21470-2_57
49. Cerreta, M., Panaro, S., Poli, G.: A spatial decision support system for multifunctional landscape assessment: a transformative resilience perspective for vulnerable inland areas. Sustainability **13**, 1–22 (2021). https://doi.org/10.3390/SU13052748
50. Nahuelhual, L., Carmona, A., Lozada, P., Jaramillo, A., Aguayo, M.: Mapping recreation and ecotourism as a cultural ecosystem service: an application at the local level in Southern Chile. Appl. Geogr. **40**, 71–82 (2013)
51. Chakhar, S., Mousseau, V.: GIS-based multicriteria spatial modeling generic framework **22**, 1159–1196 (2010). https://doi.org/10.1080/13658810801949827
52. Eastman, J.R., Kyem, P.A., Toledano, J.: GIS and Decisión Making. Explorations in Geographic Information Systems Technology; Ginebra (1993)
53. Laaribi, A., Chevallier, J.J., Martel, J.M.: A Spatial decision aid: a multicriterion evaluation approach. Comput. Environ. Urban Syst. **20**, 351–366 (1996). https://doi.org/10.1016/S0198-9715(97)00002-1
54. Malczewski, J.: GIS-based multicriteria decision analysis: a survey of the literature **20**, 703–726 (2007). https://doi.org/10.1080/13658810600661508
55. Nyerges, T.L., Jankowski, P.: Regional and Urban Gis: A Decision Support Approach. Guilford, New York (2010). ISBN 9781606233368
56. Sugumaran, R., DeGroote, J.: Spatial Decision Support Systems: Principles and Practices. CRC Press (2010). ISBN 9781420062120
57. Leung, Y.: Intelligent Spatial Decision Support Systems, p. 470. Springer, Cham (1997). https://doi.org/10.1007/978-3-642-60714-1
58. Geertman, S., Stillwell, J.: Planning support systems: an introduction. In: Planning Support Systems in Practice, pp. 3–22. Springer, Cham (2003). https://doi.org/10.1007/978-3-540-24795-1_1
59. Balram, S., Dragićević, S.: Collaborative Geographic Information Systems: Origins, Boundaries, and Structures (2006). https://services.igi-global.com/resolvedoi/resolve.aspx?doi=10.4018/978-1-59140-845-1.ch001, https://doi.org/10.4018/978-1-59140-845-1.CH001
60. Jankowski, P.: Integrating geographical information systems and multiple criteria decision-making methods **9**, 251–273 (2007). https://doi.org/10.1080/02693799508902036
61. Abbot, J.: Participatory GIS: opportunity or oxymoron? PLA Notes **33**, 27–34 (1998)

62. Craig, J.W., Harris, T.M., Weiner, D.: Community participation and geographic information systems. In: Community Participation and Geographical Information Systems, pp. 29–42. Taylor and Francis, New York (2002). ISBN 9780429203961

63. Harris, T., Weiner, D.: Empowerment, marginalization, and "Community-Integrated" GIS. Cartogr. Geogr. Inf. Sci. **25**, 67–76 (1998). https://doi.org/10.1559/152304098782594580

64. Peluso, N.L.: Whose woods are these? Counter-mapping forest territories in Kalimantan. Antipode **27**, 383–406 (1995). https://doi.org/10.1111/J.1467-8330.1995.TB00286.X

65. Obermeyer, N.J.: The evolution of public participation GIS **25**, 65–66 (2013). https://doi.org/10.1559/152304098782594599

66. Sieber, R.: Public participation geographic information systems: a literature review and framework. Ann. Assoc. Am. Geogr. **96**, 491–507 (2006). https://doi.org/10.1111/J.1467-8306.2006.00702.X

67. Zhu, X., Healey, R.G., Aspinall, R.J.: A knowledge-based systems approach to design of spatial decision support systems for environmental management. Environ. Manage. **22**, 35–48 (1998)

68. Parker, D.C., Manson, S.M., Janssen, M.A., Hoffmann, M.J., Deadman, P.: Multi-agent systems for the simulation of land-use and land-cover change: a review **93**, 314–337 (2008). https://doi.org/10.1111/1467-8306.9302004

69. Malczewski, J.: GIS and Multicriteria Decision Analysis. Wiley, New York (1999)

70. Pickles, J.: Ground truth: the social implications of geographic information systems. Ground Truth Soc. Implications Geogr. Inf. Syst. (1995). https://doi.org/10.1016/0268-4012(96)82860-x

71. Dunn, C.E.: Participatory GIS—A People's GIS? **31**, 616–637 (2016). https://doi.org/10.1177/0309132507081493

72. Cerreta, M., Mele, R., Poli, G.: Urban Ecosystem Services (UES) assessment within a 3D virtual environment: a methodological approach for the Larger Urban Zones (LUZ) of Naples, Italy. Appl. Sci. **10**, 6205 (2020). https://doi.org/10.3390/APP10186205

73. Bosone, M., Nocca, F., Fusco Girard, L.: The circular city implementation: cultural heritage and digital technology. In: Rauterberg, M. (ed.) HCII 2021. LNCS, vol. 12794, pp. 40–62. Springer, Cham (2021). https://doi.org/10.1007/978-3-030-77411-0_4

74. Poli, G., Muccio, E., Cerreta, M.: Circular, cultural and creative city index: a comparison of indicators-based methods with a machine-learning approach. Aestimum **81** (2023). https://doi.org/10.36253/AESTIM-13880

75. Cerreta, M., Mura, F.D., Muccio, E.: Digital platforms, imaginaries and values creation: opportunities for new urban dynamics. In: Calabrò, F., Della Spina, L., Piñeira Mantiñán, M.J. (eds.) New Metropolitan Perspectives, NMP 2022. LNNS, vol. 482, pp. 1505–1515. Springer, Cham (2022). https://doi.org/10.1007/978-3-031-06825-6_145/FIGURES/5

76. McCall, M.K.: Participatory mapping and PGIS: secerning facts and values, representation and representativity. Int. J. E-Planning Res. **10**, 105–123 (2021). https://doi.org/10.4018/IJEPR.20210701.OA7

77. Cerreta, M., Cannatella, D., Poli, G., Sposito, S.: Climate change and transformability scenario evaluation for Venice (Italy) Port-City through ANP method. In: Gervasi, O., et al. (eds.) ICCSA 2015. LNCS, vol. 9158, pp. 50–63. Springer, Cham (2015). https://doi.org/10.1007/978-3-319-21410-8_4

78. Brown, G., Brabyn, L.: An analysis of the relationships between multiple values and physical landscapes at a regional scale using public participation GIS and landscape character classification. Landsc. Urban Plan. **107**, 317–331 (2012). https://doi.org/10.1016/J.LANDURBPLAN.2012.06.007

79. Rambaldi, G., Weiner, D.: 3rd International Conference on Public Participation GIS, University of Wisconsin-Madison, 18–20 July 2004, Madison, Wisconsin, USA, vol. 3 (2004)
80. Nocca, F., De Toro, P., Voysekhovska, V.: Circular economy and cultural heritage conservation: a proposal for integrating level(s) evaluation tool. Aestimum **78**, 105–143 (2021). https://doi.org/10.36253/AESTIM-10119

Culture and the City: Towards a Context-Aware Assessment Framework

Irene Bianchi[(✉)] [iD] and Ilaria Tosoni [iD]

Department of Architecture and Urban Studies, Politecnico di Milano, Via Bonardi 3, 20133 Milan, Italy
{irene.bianchi,ilaria.tosoni}@polimi.it

Abstract. How to assess the capacity of cultural initiatives to generate social value in urban contexts? Which lenses allow capturing dynamics that affect their transformative potential? Assuming that the social value of cultural actions goes far beyond their direct impacts and depends on their capacity to intercept broader trajectories of change, the contribution identifies observation lenses capable of rendering a complex picture of relations between actors, actions, and context-specific variables. Through a process-oriented approach, the authors put contexts back at the centre and look not so much at impacts *per sè* as at impact generation mechanisms. Moving beyond economic impact evaluation, they look at culture-driven social value generated in three impact domains: health and well-being, urban regeneration, and social cohesion. Without proposing a comprehensive evaluation scheme, the contribution identifies obstacles and enabling factors influencing the transformative capacity of cultural actions on an urban scale. In line with the conceptual and methodological setting of the research - carried out within the H2020 MESOC (MEasuring the SOcial impacts of Culture) Project - the authors reflect on these evaluative objects and question whether (and to what extent) they support a reflection on specific cultural actions but also on the capacity of urban contexts with different characteristics to welcome and promote transformation dynamics towards social impact generation.

Keywords: social impact assessment · cultural-led transformation · place-sensitive evaluation

1 Introduction and Theoretical Background

From long before the emergence of the "creative city" label (Florida, 2003; Landry, 2009; Evans, 2017), urban studies and cultural research have explored the relationship between culture and urban transformation, often invoking cultural actions as an essential driver of change in cities. In this debate, a large body of literature focuses on the role of large-scale cultural policies and strategies, looking at their medium and long-term socio-spatial effects and identifying cities as the stage where these effects materialise. A different perspective lends more to the capacity of cultural actions to generate social impacts in specific settings and the role played by context-specific dynamics. This latter point of view often identifies cities as the preferred loci of cultural production and

O. Gervasi et al. (Eds.): ICCSA 2023 Workshops, LNCS 14108, pp. 226–238, 2023.
https://doi.org/10.1007/978-3-031-37117-2_17

artistic activation (Parkinson & Bianchini, 1993) or as fields of experimentation where social innovation processes can emerge and consolidate (Concilio & Tosoni, 2019). In this regard, particular attention is paid to local cultural actions - from urban cultural policies to grassroots initiatives - and their capacity to produce impacts beyond the usual economic terms. When reflecting on the social impact of cultural actions in cities, literature often refers to local development (Sacco et al., 2014; Sacco et al., 2013) and urban regeneration (García, 2004; Miles & Paddison, 2005), emphasising aspects related to community activation (Kay, 2000), social integration, and quality of life. In line with this perspective, more recent research and policy frameworks focus on cultural action's contribution to long-term and high-level "missions" (Mazzucato, 2017; Mazzucato & Dibb, 2019), exploring their capacity to trigger or accelerate, e.g. democratisation processes (Négrier, 2023) or sustainability transition (Loorbach, 2022). In this case, the transformative capacity of (local) cultural initiatives is defined by the extent to which they can align or interact with broader trajectories of change (Concilio et al., 2023).

In this last perspective, a key challenge is represented by assessing the effective contribution of cultural actions in terms of social value generation within specific urban contexts (Cerreta & La Rocca, 2021; Cerreta & Panaro, 2017; Cicerchia, 2022) Obstacles of various kinds contribute to this evaluation challenge, grounding on heterogeneous and - at times - conflicting conceptualisation of what "social value" is and how it is generated in complex social and spatial settings. Cultural policies and initiatives are frequently evaluated regarding the (inherently positive) economic outcomes they provide. Less consideration is given to their social repercussions and long-term effects, as they are often related to intangible elements that are difficult to capture (Cerreta & La Rocca, 2021). Also, because of conceptual ambiguities and a lack of operational definitions (Vanclay, 2002), attempts to assess social impact tend to focus on measurable impacts, rarely moving beyond the mere identification of project or policy outcomes. This focus is problematic, as it does not allow for capturing unexpected results, not trade-offs or spill-over effects that might be generated in different sectors or arenas. The issue pertains to the theoretical presumptions underlying these evaluation methods as well. Determining cultural actions' contribution to social value requires overcoming cause-effect linearity assumptions that often underlie evaluative models. Problematising the cause-effect nexus within complex open systems such as cities implies recognising that multiple factors can contribute to social impact generation. Reductionist approaches to social impact assessment do not allow assessing transformation dynamics through which social value can emerge in specific settings, nor capturing their contribution to high-level challenges to broader transformation dynamics.

Starting from the need to investigate culture-driven social impacts in the framework of broader transformative dynamics, the article proposes to move beyond economic impact evaluation, to which social impact assessment is often relegated, and to recognise the centrality (i) of intangible elements of social impacts; (ii) of the processes through which social value emerges; and (iii) of place-specific dynamics. Without proposing a complete assessment scheme, this contribution identifies analytical categories to capture culture-driven social impacts and to read them within broader urban transformation trajectories. Relying on the theoretical and empirical research carried out under the umbrella of the Horizon 2020 Project - MESOC (Measuring the Social Impacts of Culture), the authors reflect on evaluative objects and categories that might support the identification of obstacles and enabling factors affecting culture-led urban transformative dynamics. In particular, the contribution looks at culture-driven social value generated in three impact domains identified as crucial by the New European Agenda for Culture (European Commission, 2018): health and well-being, urban regeneration (in terms of better access to and use of urban spaces), and social cohesion.

After retracing the methodological steps that led to the identification of the observation dimensions and the corresponding evaluative objects, the authors reflect on the potential of the proposed approach, questioning whether (and to what extent) it can support the identification of obstacles and enabling factors affecting the transformative capacity of cultural actions at the city scale.

2 Materials and Methods

The authors are in the preliminary stages of building an evaluation model to assess the social impacts of (local cultural) actions in urban settings. In this process, they look for social value in three impact domains identified as crucial by the New European Agenda for Culture: health and well-being, urban regeneration and social cohesion. The investigation is carried out through an inductive approach inspired by the Theory of Change, as it investigates how and why an initiative works (Weiss, 1995). In doing so, it follows an open-ended and process-focused enquiry (Langley et al., 2013), which allows inferring a recursiveness of dynamics linking cultural actions to a set of designed or detectable social change impacts. The article relies on a triangulation of qualitative research methods, including desk research, surveys, semi-structured interviews and focus groups, grounding on empirical materials collected during the Horizon 2020 MESOC Project[1]. The methodology consists of two main steps (Fig. 1). First, the authors identified a sample of cultural actions targeting social value generation. By looking at their implementation, they identified relevant impacts and a first set of information about factors hindering or facilitating social impact generation. This analysis allowed drafting preliminary categories of enabling factors based on their recurrence across different settings (step 1, see chapter 2,1). In the second phase, impact generation dynamics were investigated through mediated interactions with policymakers and cultural operators from the city pilots. The conversations focused on contextual dynamics related to the uniqueness of urban areas and specific impact domains rather than single cultural actions. Based on a process of abstraction and synthesis, this step allowed for testing previous categories and for identifying broader observation dimensions and hypotheses about descriptors able to support social impact assessment processes (step 2, see chapter 2,2).

2.1 Analysis of Cultural Actions

The first step included the analysis of 35 cultural practices from 7 of the European cities directly involved in the MESOC Project. These actions included cultural policies

[1] The authors thank the MESOC partners involved in the collection of empirical material on the case studies, and in particular: Cluj-Culture Center, Centro Studi PIM, University of Barcelona, University of Valencia, the Municipality of Issy-Les-Moulineaux, DAEM.

Step 1	Focus: *Cultural actions*	Focus: *Social impact generation dynamics*	Step 2	Focus: *Social impact generation dynamics*	Focus: *cultural and urban context*
	Identification of 35 cultural actions targeting social value generation in the 3 impact domains (health and well-being, urban regeneration and social cohesion) Selection and analysis of 18 cultural actions from 6 European cities	Identification of factors enabling social impact generation and of corresponding categories *(clusters based on recurrence)*		Dialogues with 46 key actors from 9 European Cities Validation of the factors enabling social impact generation and of corresponding categories	Identification of context-sensitive observation dimension *(clusters based on recurrence and relevance)*

Fig. 1. Methodological steps

and strategies, but also emergent cultural practices explicitly seeking to generate social value in specific impact domains, namely: citizens' health and well-being in Valencia (ES) and Cluj-Napoca (RO); urban regeneration in Issy-Les-Moulineaux (FR), Rjieka (HR) and Milan (IT), and engagement and participation in Athens (HL) and Barcelona (ES). (For more insights: Bianchi et al., 2022; Bonet et al., 2023; Moro & Legale, 2023; Cacovean et al., 2022). Priority was given to well-documented activities already subjected to evaluation procedures. The initial sample was reduced to 18 cultural actions from 6 cities based on a selection based on the availability and quality of data and on the responsiveness of the initiative to the research objectives (see Table 1).

Data collection was guided by a survey completed by project partners in the pilot cities. More than a detailed description of the initiatives, the survey aimed to identify relevant dynamics for generating social impacts. Data was retrieved mainly through desk work. When necessary, stakeholders were contacted for clarification purposes. Within data availability limits, impacts were identified by observing how cultural policies and practices were defined, planned and implemented. Both social impacts and the enabling factors were identified through a set of exploratory questions investigating (i) changes recorded in the impact domains (beyond direct impacts); (ii) causal relations between these changes and specific cultural actions; and (iii) factors enabling or hindering the capacity of cultural actions to develop and generate impacts.

Data analysis was carried out through a textual analysis of the reports, which allowed identifying a first list of specific social impacts and recurrent conditions and dynamics affecting impact generation. This initial step lasted from September 2020 to February 2021. Numerous meetings with the Project's partners were held during this time to monitor the selection of examples and gather feedback. The first set of social impacts and enabling factors resulting from the analysis of cultural practices were grouped into thematic clusters according to recurrent features and characteristics.

Table 1. Cultural actions

Name of the Cultural Action (City)	social impact domain
Unspeakable: A music composition workshop for teenagers (Cluj-Napoca)	Health and well-being
Tablo: Training staff in the use of arts for the benefit of people with log-term conditions (Cluj-Napoca)	Health and well-being
Inner Space (Cluj-Napoca)	Health and well-being
Caixa dels Records: Memòria de una vida (Valencia)	Health and well-being
Museus per la Saluts: Records de Festa al Museu Faller de València (Valencia)	Health and well-being
Ocio inclusivo (Valencia)	Health and well-being
Istituto Comprensivo Sandro Pertini (Milan)	Urban Regeneration
Cascina Martesana (Milan)	Urban Regeneration
Caravanseray Selinunte San Siro (Milan)	Urban Regeneration
Le Temps des Cerises (Issy-Les-Moulineaux)	Urban Regeneration
Le CLAVIM - L'Espace Andrée Chedid (Issy-Les-Moulineaux)	Urban Regeneration
Musée Français de la Carte à Jouer (Issy-Les-Moulineaux)	Urban Regeneration
Culture in the Nieghbourhoods (Athens)	Social cohesion
Athens Garden Festival (Athens)	Social cohesion
Athens Escape Routes (Athens)	Social cohesion
Apropa Cultura|Una porta a la inclusió (Barcelona)	Social cohesion
Xamfrà, Centre de Música i Escena del Raval (Barcelona)	Social cohesion
En Palabras [relatos migrantes] (Barcelona)	Social cohesion

2.2 Dialogues with Key Actors

The second step consisted of a series of semi-structured dialogues with 46 critical actors from 9 cities between January and June 2022. The city sample was enlarged including Turku (FI) and Jerez de la Frontera (ES), to test the robustness of the initial set of enabling factors. Interlocutors included cultural operators, public officials, top/middle managers in charge of culture at the city level and stakeholders from the three impact domains. They were selected based on their role and degree of involvement in cultural actions targeting social value generation and their knowledge of contextual dynamics related to culture-led transformation. Interactions with stakeholders took the form of semi-structured interviews or focus groups. As for step 1, the dialogues were centred on identifying factors enabling culture-driven social impacts. In this second phase, guiding questions focused not so much on cultural actions' development and implementation but on contextual dynamics affecting them. A semantic analysis of interview transcripts based on codes derived from the initial enabling factors was also performed. A database associating text excerpts with codes and anonymised respondent profiles were built. On the one hand, the systematisation of text excerpts allowed identifying recurring factors affecting social impact generation and validating and integrating the categories mentioned above. On the other hand, this method made it possible to select those considered particularly relevant by the interviewees and to formulate hypotheses about general observation dimensions, potentially supporting the analysis of context-specific dynamics affecting social value generation.

3 Results

Mirroring what is described in the methodological section, this chapter reports the main results of the research.

3.1 Cultural Actions and Their Social Impacts

As mentioned in the methodology chapter, the final sample consists of 18 ongoing cultural actions from 6 cities aimed at generating social value in at least one of the three Projects' impact domains (see Table 1) and involving multiple cultural sectors, with a prominent role of performing arts, visual arts and audiovisual and multimedia. They were launched between 1997 and 2020, allowing for evaluating both established experiences and new initiatives. Most of the actions were initiated directly by public organisations (primarily municipal administrations or public cultural institutions). Public institutions also played an essential role in the community and private initiatives, mainly through well-established collaborative schemes. About half of the actions examined are permanent, while the rest are either one-time, fixed-term events or recurring activities (for example, Festivals). Most of the initiatives take place in a particular cultural or urban space, while a few take place simultaneously in different urban locations.

Analysing selected initiatives first allowed identifying impacts generated in the three social domains. If a comprehensive report of impacts is outside the scope of this research, some examples are provided for clarification purposes. Impacts recorded in the health and well-being domain include improvements in the quality and accessibility of healthcare services and healthcare personnel's skills, the spread of innovative therapeutic protocols and the use of well-being-focused space design in healthcare facilities. Still, others refer to higher awareness about health-related needs and gaps among decision-makers and increased cross-silos interactions across healthcare practitioners, cultural sector operators and local policy-makers. For what concerns urban regeneration, detected impacts include the valorisation of city history and heritage, the reactivation of underused urban spaces, the restoration and functional reuse of urban green areas and improved access to (green) public spaces in peripheral neighbourhoods. Some of the cultural actions analysed also synergised with educational activities and raised awareness among citizens and stakeholders on societal challenges related to urban sustainability futures. Finally, most initiatives targeting social cohesion and citizen engagement objectives succeeded (at least in part) in strengthening existing local networks, including citizens' alliances and collaborative schemes involving local decision-makers, private stakeholders and professionals. While some initiatives increased residents' participation in culture, others enhanced the social inclusion of marginalised groups (e.g. elderly, chronically ill patients, people suffering from mental diseases, and migrants).

Interestingly, initiatives developed in a single area (e.g. public health or urban regeneration) have impacted different domains. Recorded impacts could be traced back to different changes in the contexts. Some of them directly relate to the three impact domains and provide insights into the effectiveness of cultural actions in pursuing their intended scopes. These include (i) improvement of individual or group physical and phycological conditions (impact domain: health and well-being); (ii) betterment of physical facilities (impact domain: urban regeneration); (iii) empowerment of communities, reinforced identity and sense of belonging and (iv) higher participation in cultural activities (impact domain: social cohesion). Other impacts emerge transversely across social domains, impacting individuals and collective actors. They refer to the enhancement of artistic abilities, e.g. in terms of capacity for individual expression and interaction; better access to public and private resources; changes in governance and partnerships arrangements, with specific reference to the strengthening of social capital; design and provision of new policies and innovative services; and awareness raising and knowledge production.

3.2 Factors Enabling Social Impact Generation

The analysis of cultural actions allowed identifying an initial set of elements enabling social impact generation in the analysed domains. The set includes factors that recurrently emerged in the description of social impact generation dynamics. Table 2 illustrates the five categories and mentioned descriptors collected through case study analysis. These categories have been validated through interactions with key actors (including cultural operators and policymakers) from 9 cities. These dialogues allowed testing of the categories drafted in the previous phase. Their analysis, based on excerpts from interviews and focus groups, allowed for gathering further evidence and confirmed the validity of the preliminary set of enabling factors, supporting a more extensive description of the single categories.

The category "Networks and Partnerships" refers to linking, bonding and bridging social capital (Granovetter, 1973; Putnam, 2001) in designing and developing cultural actions towards social value generation. As the majority of the cultural actions analysed were promoted or supported by local public bodies, a key role in social impact generation was given to political recognition and support from institutional actors at different levels and to their direct involvement in collaborative schemes involving cultural operators, as well as third sector parties. In this context, the crucial role of cross-sectoral alliances -e.g. among cultural institutions and actors in the health or care sector was emphasised. The capacity of specific actions to generate impacts was also enhanced by well-established collaboration with other local and non-local cultural initiatives and involving target groups (e.g. patients or specific social groups) in the design and implementation of the action itself. A second category refers to "Resources and Infrastructures". Enabling factors grouped under this label refers to the capacity of cultural actions to mobilise or access different types of resources, including financial, infrastructural and human resources. While the former was needed for cultural action to take place, several interviewees stated that the availability of spaces and infrastructures and of dedicated working groups - including professionals, volunteers, or cultural operators - affected the effectiveness of the actions and their capacity to resonate in local contexts. Also, interviews revealed the relevance of the processes through which funds and resources

Table 2. Factors enabling social impact generation and corresponding descriptors. (Adapted from Concilio et al., 2023)

Enabling Factor	Descriptors (from the analysis of cases)
Networks and Partnerships	• Political recognition and support • Existence/Emergence of cross-sectoral collaborative schemes • Inclusion of consultants and professionals from different domains • Existence of well-established synergies with other cultural initiatives
Resources and Infrastructures	• Availability of financial resources • Capacity to mobilise new financial resources • Availability and accessibility of spaces and infrastructures • Availability of human resources
Norms and Regulations	• Existence of favourable normative frameworks in the cultural domain • Existence of favourable normative frameworks in the impact domain • Openness and flexibility of normative settings
Narratives and Discourses	• Development of a strong identity • Alignment with discourses from the cultural sector • Alignment with discourses from the impact domain
Knowledge and Abilities	• Enhancement of the skills and expertise of the actors involved • Capacity to build on the skills and expertise of the actors involved • Learning from other experiences

were mobilised, referring, e.g., to participation in calls for funding, activation of private-public partnerships and activation of broad and diversified support networks. A third recurrent factor, grouped under the label "Norms and Regulation", refers to favourable normative frameworks.

On the one hand, they include policy and regulatory frameworks that support the emergence of transformative cultural actions. On the other, they refer to organisational settings and procedures affecting the implementation process and its long-term effects. A third set of recurrent factors refers to the role of "Narrative and Discourses". The extent to which cultural actions were able to align with policy discourse from the cultural sector or from the impact domains deeply affected their transformative potential towards social impact generation. The use of words, images and symbols recognised as relevant in the contexts in which the action develops has made it possible to increase its perceived value in the eyes of the various subjects active in the urban ecosystem. Examples from the analysed cultural actions include the adaptation of high-level principles to context-specific dynamics and target groups; the promotion of emerging discourses from the social impact domains (e.g., promotion of well-being-focused design, prioritisation of mental health, embedment of local identity in the design of cultural initiatives' scopes and action areas). Finally, a key - intangible-element was recognised as "Knowledge and Abilities". This dimension refers to the ability to capitalise on existing knowledge and experience and trigger learning processes in the target groups. Concerning the former, attention was paid to the involvement of experts and practitioners from different domains (e.g., researchers, healthcare professionals, social scientists, and urban policy experts) and their interaction with cultural agents in the design and implementation phases. Regarding the latter, promoters of cultural actions stressed the relation between social impact generation and the enhancement of skills and expertise of different groups to which the cultural actions were addressed, including vulnerable social groups, early-career artists, and inhabitants of specific neighbourhoods. The analysis of cultural actions aimed at generating social value in specific domains has made it possible to identify transversal categories that affected their ability to generate impacts and trigger transformations on a local scale despite differences in urban settings and areas of action. The results of this first analysis were validated through a dialogue with a heterogeneous group of policymakers and cultural operators, different in origin, interests and points of view.

3.3 Lenses of Observation for a Context-Sensitive Assessment Framework

Dialogues with key actors have also made it possible to shift the perspective from cultural activities to the context in which they develop and to formulate some hypotheses on the observation lenses that can allow evaluating the capacity of urban and organisational systems to welcome, promote and proactively support the generation of culture-driven social value (Rausell-Köster et al., 2022; Bonet & Calvano, 2023; Rausell-Köster et al., forthcoming). These dimensions partially overlap with the ones described in the previous chapter. However, they are partially reframed to provide insights into the degree of readiness of specific contexts towards social impact generation.

1. Network changes. First, the observation of transformations taking place in local networks and social capital structures can provide insights into the degree of proactiveness of the social context and its capacity to trigger transformative processes towards social value generation. Beyond cultural actions' design and implementation, the existence and characterisation of interactions across policy levels and units, as well as among cultural actors, public agents, private stakeholders and local communities, constitute a relevant object of observation.
2. Market reactiveness. In line with the factors identified in the "Resources and Infrastructures" cluster, this lens of observation focuses on local market reactiveness in terms of capacity to detect unsatisfied needs and demands, propose new products and services and involve different categories of actors, including professionals from the cultural and creative industries and the impact domains. In addition, market dynamics might amplify the effects of single initiatives in the contexts of reference, supporting their capacity to "scale up, down and deep" (Moore et al., 2015) and to intercept broader trajectories of change.
3. Public policy sensitivity. The attention shown by public policies both to the objectives pursued in the single impact domains and to the role of cultural actions plays a fundamental role. Public policy sensitivity is manifested through favourable policy provisions and many other factors affecting social impact generation, including political recognition, the orientation of resources, the availability of public spaces and the definition of agreements and partnerships. At the same time, this lens can be explored through the observation of intangible dynamics, e.g. through the activation of symbolic resources and the emergence of new policy discourses.

4. Symbolic reactiveness. This observation lens examines dynamics related to "Narratives and Discourses" by abstracting them from their role in single actions. The degree of reactivity to the emergence of new discourses and new values, new models of sociality in the use of space and the interaction between groups contributes to determining the level of predisposition to change and might allow social impacts to resonate in contexts.

5. Learning awareness. Acknowledgement and access to critical information and expertise can be vital in initiating transformative processes towards social impact creation. Agents open to learning are generally more capable of recognising and mobilising valuable knowledge and embedding it in their activities. Therefore, an assessment of the degree to which the linkages between cultural experiences and social impact are acknowledged by media, educational bodies, and local associations can allow evaluation of the extent to which positive social impacts can emerge and diffuse in specific settings.

6. Spatial intelligence. Finally, understanding the relationship between cultural experiences and social impacts requires understanding its spatial determinants and the way spaces are used to facilitate social impact generation of awareness of socio-spatial needs and dynamics emerging alongside urban transformation processes. This dimension is critical to re-connect changes in the urban environment with positive social impact generation and to support context-sensitive cultural interventions. At the same time, spatial intelligence is required to avoid or minimise risks connected to negative socio-spatial impacts often triggered by cultural projects and practices.

4   Discussion and Concluding Remarks

The contribution assumes that the evaluation of the social impacts of cultural policies requires us to rethink how we look at social impact generation dynamics and to adopt a process-focused approach, more attentive to local context dynamics and the cross-cutting social and cultural consequences of public or private actions (Cicerchia, 2021, 2022). In line with the evaluation challenges described in the first section, the authors tried to identify evaluation approaches and objects capable of going beyond an economic-centred evaluation and rendering a complex picture of relations between actors, actions, and context-specific variables. Without presenting a comprehensive assessment scheme, the authors remark on evaluation objects that can help in the identification of impediments and enablers influencing the transformational capacity of cultural actions at the city scale. Rooting on the qualitative investigation carried out under the umbrella of the Horizon 2020 MESOC Project, the contribution first identifies dynamics affecting social impact generation and reflects on their recurrence across different urban settings. In particular, it identifies categories of factors affecting, driving, reinforcing, and multiplying impact generation and proposes to use them as sensors to identify changes in the interaction between cultural niches and broader urban change dynamics. In a second step, the article investigates to what extent the observation of impact generation dynamics triggered by single cultural initiatives can contribute to capturing the predisposition to change of specific contexts and evaluate their ability to trigger and consolidate transformative processes relevant.

While recognising the multiplicity of dimensions related to the culture-city nexus, the evaluative approach tries to reconcile the evaluation of specific cultural actions, the observation of contexts and their effect on the dynamics of generating social impact. In doing so, the contribution contributes to (i) a reflection on the role of cultural actions in urban transformation processes and (ii) to the debate on the assessment of cultural initiatives, which is still mainly focused on economic impact evaluation. Concerning this last point, this article acknowledges the complex character of impact generation mechanisms, thus freeing the observer from the theoretical conundrum that in any ecosystem, internal processes are unlikely to be linear (i.e. action x will not lead straight to result in y), which makes any impact assessment exercise virtually impossible to handle.

The article outlines evaluative objects and observation lenses, indicating a possible direction to follow in the definition of evaluation models capable of considering the effects of contextual dynamics on the mechanisms of generation of social impacts. Further research is needed to refine and test them, and to develop a comprehensive assessment scheme. The results presented in this work are affected by the way actors involved define "social impacts" and interpret social impact generation mechanisms. Future research should aim to include a broader range of participants and perspectives, to include a wider range of cities, and to further validate observation categories against existing assessment frameworks.

Authors' Contribution. Conceptualization, IB; methodology, IB and IT; case studies collection and analysis, IB and IT; writing the article, IB; final revision: IT. All authors have read and approved the final manuscript.

Funding. This article is developed and funded under the umbrella of the MESOC Project. MESOC (Measuring the Societal Value of Culture) Project has received funding from the European Union's Horizon 2020 Research and Innovation Programme under Grant Agreement No. 870935 (More info at: https://mesoc-project.eu/). The opinions expressed herein are solely by the authors and do not reflect the official point of any EU institutions nor of any other member of the MESOC Consortium.

References

Bianchi, I., Tosoni, I., Ghirardi, S.: Cultural interventions as drivers of well-being in cities. Insights from Valencia. In: From Wealthy to Healthy Cities Urbanism and Planning for the Well-Being of Citizens in Search of a New Planning Agenda for Urban Health, Socio-Spatial Justice and Climate Resilience: Proceedings of the 58th ISOCARP World Planning Congress, pp. 58–70 (2022)

Bonet, L., Calvano, G. (eds.): Measuring the Social Dimension of Culture: Handbook. Trànsit Projectes (2023). ISBN: 978-84-09-51172-3

Bonet, L., Calvano, G., Fernández Compañ, P.: Exogenous and endogenous factors affecting the social impact of cultural projects: the case of Barcelona ecosystem. City Territ. Archit. **10**(1), 9 (2023)

Cacovean, C.M., Dascal, M.D., Zbranca, M.R.: Developing a framework for culture-based interventions for well-being in Cluj-Napoca, Romania. City Territ. Archit. **9**, 37 (2022). https://doi.org/10.1186/s40410-022-00182-1

Cerreta, M., La Rocca, L.: Urban regeneration processes and social impact: a literature review to explore the role of evaluation. In: Gervasi, O., et al. (eds.) ICCSA 2021. LNCS, vol. 12954, pp. 167–182. Springer, Cham (2021). https://doi.org/10.1007/978-3-030-86979-3_13

Cerreta, M., Panaro, S.: From perceived values to shared values: a multi-stakeholder spatial decision analysis (M-SSDA) for resilient landscapes. Sustainability 9(7), 1113 (2017)

Cicerchia, A.: Che cosa muove la cultura: Impatti, misure e racconti tra economia e immaginario. Editrice Bibliografica (2021)

Cicerchia, A.: Indicators for local policies of cultural welfare: content, dimensions, and quality criteria. City Territ. Archit. 9(1), 32 (2022)

Concilio, G., Bianchi, I., Tosoni, I.: Signals of sustainability transition: sensing enabling factors through cultural initiatives. City Territ. Archit. 10(1), 5 (2023)

Concilio, G., Tosoni, I. (eds.): Innovation Capacity and the City: The Enabling Role of Design. Springer, Cham (2019). https://doi.org/10.1007/978-3-030-00123-0

European Commission. A New European Agenda for Culture—no. COM/2018/267 final (2018). https://eur-lex.europa.eu/legal-content/EN/TXT/PDF/?uri=CELEX:52018DC0267&from=EN

Evans, G.: Creative Cities–An International Perspective. In: Hannigan, J.A., Greg, R. (eds.) The SAGE Handbook of New Urban Studies, pp. 311–329. SAGE Publications Ltd. (2017)

Florida, R.L.: The Rise of the Creative Class: and How It's Transforming Work, Leisure, Community and Everyday Life. Pluto Press (2003)

García, B.: Cultural policy and urban regeneration in Western European Cities: lessons from experience, prospects for the future. Local Econ. J. Local Econ. Policy Unit 19(4), 312–326 (2004)

Granovetter, M.S.: The strength of weak ties. Am. J. Sociol. 78(6), 1360–1380 (1973)

Kay, A.: Art and community development: the role the arts have in regenerating communities. Commun. Dev. J. 35(4), 414–424 (2000)

Landry, C.: The Creative City: A Toolkit for Urban Innovation, 2nd edn., reprinted. Sterling (2009)

Langley, A., Smallman, C., Tsoukas, H., Van De Ven, A.H.: Process studies of change in organization and management: unveiling temporality, activity, and flow. Acad. Manag. J. 56(1), 1–13 (2013)

Loorbach, D.A.: Designing radical transitions: a plea for a new governance culture to empower deep transformative change. City Territ. Archit. 9(1), 30 (2022)

Mazzucato, M.: Mission-Oriented Innovation Policy: Challenges and Opportunities. UCL Institute for Innovation and Public Purpose Working Paper, vol. 43 (2017)

Mazzucato, P.M., Dibb, G.: Missions: A Beginner's Guide. UCL Institute for Innovation and Public Purpose, Policy Brief Series, vol. 11 (2019)

Miles, S., Paddison, R.: Introduction: the rise and rise of culture-led urban regeneration. Urban Stud. 42(5–6), 833–839 (2005)

Moore, M.-L., Riddell, D., Vocisano, D.: Scaling out, scaling up, scaling deep: strategies of non-profits in advancing systemic social innovation. J. Corp. Citizsh. 2015(58), 67–84 (2015)

Moro, A., Legale, E.: Stretching the boundaries of cultural policies for inclusive and sustainable urban contexts: the case of Issy-les-Moulineaux in France. City Territ. Archit. 10(1), 4 (2023)

Négrier, E.: Cultural policies and urban transitions green politics, democracy in the time of the pandemic. City Territ. Archit. 10(1), 8 (2023)

Parkinson, M., Bianchini, F. (eds.): Cultural Policy and Urban Regeneration: The West European Experience. Manchester Univ. Press (1993)

Putnam, R.D.: Bowling Alone: The Collapse and Revival of American Community (1. Touchstone ed.). Simon & Schuster [u.a.] (2001)

Rausell-Köster, P., et al.: Working Paper: a convergent model to explore the social impact of cultural and creative sectors. MESOC Project (forthcoming)

Rausell-Köster, P., Ghirardi, S., Sanjuán, J., et al.: Cultural experiences in the framework of "cultural cities": measuring the socioeconomic impact of culture in urban performance. City Territ. Archit. **9**, 40 (2022). https://doi.org/10.1186/s40410-022-00189-8

Sacco, P., Ferilli, G., Blessi, G.T.: Understanding culture-led local development: a critique of alternative theoretical explanations. Urban Stud. **51**(13), 2806–2821 (2014)

Sacco, P.L., Ferilli, G., Blessi, G.T., Nuccio, M.: Culture as an engine of local development processes: system-wide cultural districts I: theory: system-wide cultural districts: theory. Growth Chang. **44**(4), 555–570 (2013)

Vanclay, F.: Conceptualising social impacts. Environ. Impact Assess. Rev. **22**(3), 183–211 (2002)

Weiss, C.H.: Nothing as practical as good theory: exploring theory-based evaluation for comprehensive community initiatives for children and families. New Approach. Eval. Community Initiatives Concepts Methods Contexts **1**, 65–92 (1995)

Smart Circular Cities and Stakeholders Engagement: A Literature Review to Explore the Role of Artificial Intelligence

Sabrina Sacco, Ferdinando Di Martino, and Maria Cerreta(✉)

University of Naples Federico II, Naples, Italy
{sabrina.sacco,fdimarti,maria.cerreta}@unina.it

Abstract. The smart city concept describes the use of information and communication technologies (ICT) in a sustainable urban context to improve its services' efficiency and meet its inhabitants' requirements. This transition towards sustainability includes creating circular cities with a focus on the well-being of the entire ecosystem. By employing Artificial Intelligence (AI) systems and strategies for sustainable circular purposes, the aim of building a smart circular city is to raise the standard of living, optimize the utilization of resources, strengthen the relationships between various stakeholders and tackle climate, ecological, social and economic challenges. To be better fitted to the requirements of citizens and accelerate progress towards the SDGs, the AI models must include communities in the construction, implementation, and ongoing modification of AI systems, making a huge contribution to improving decision-making.

This study aims to investigate the direct and indirect relationships between AI, stakeholders' engagement, and the smart circular city, integrating the literature review with bibliometric maps elaborated through the VOSviewer tools. The findings of this study will contribute to defining the research gap about the role of AI technologies in encouraging and promoting stakeholders' participation in the collaborative decision-making process.

Keywords: Artificial Intelligence · Smart City · Stakeholders Engagement

1 Introduction

First introduced in the early 1990s, the concept of "Smart City" refers to an "urban labelling" phenomenon [1] generally related to the use of advanced technology and data analytics to improve the efficiency and sustainability of urban services and infrastructure [2–5]. Harrison et al. [6] defined a Smart City as an instrumented, interconnected, and intelligent city. However, the new urban challenges related to economic, environmental, ecological and social issues cannot be addressed only by increasing efficiency.

These challenges require new and innovative approaches to urban governance involving the "human factor" [7]. Creativity is a key driver to a Smart City, considering human and social infrastructure as crucial axes for city development [8]. Debates around Smart

© The Author(s), under exclusive license to Springer Nature Switzerland AG 2023
O. Gervasi et al. (Eds.): ICCSA 2023 Workshops, LNCS 14108, pp. 239–258, 2023.
https://doi.org/10.1007/978-3-031-37117-2_18

Cities have been advanced by the introduction of the concept of Cognitive City, an intelligent urban environment that constantly learns through interaction with citizens. This relatively new concept allows the development of an interdisciplinary approach to deal with complex urban issues [9]. "The citizen becomes an active element of urban governance, not only through civic participation but also through serving as a sensor for the operational state of the urban infrastructure" [10].

In a Cognitive City, citizens predominantly not only get information on urban infrastructure, but also provide information to others regarding their behaviours in the urban environment [11]. "Citizens as human sensor networks" [10] involve citizens as active players and active co-producers of services through a great degree of information, awareness, and engagement.

Providing services that fulfil the city's objectives and foster social innovation issues, requires the recognition of the centrality of collective action and capacitation, yielding social benefits rather than individual ones and bringing new values to society [12].

In this perspective, a central role is given to initiatives promoting social inclusion and equal participation [13], developing an integrated approach to linking governments, businesses, schools, non-profits, and citizens. This integration would involve three key elements: the satisfaction of the interests of actors; changes in socio-political arrangements; and empowerment of the participating actors [14].

Creating an environment where citizens are empowered to make decisions that are socially and environmentally responsible allows for encouraging of a balance between the environment, economy and the social aspects of a community in a circular and sustainable perspective, promoting social inclusion, economic development and resilience.

Promoting a sustainable and circular future development [15–18], the United Nations has identified 17 Sustainable Development Goals (SDGs) [19], which require complementary actions by governments, civil society, science, and businesses. Stakeholder engagement is an important part of sustainable development, as it ensures that the interests of all stakeholders - citizens, civil society organizations, governments, businesses, and other entities - are taken into consideration when making decisions about social issues.

This engagement process helps to better understand the potential impacts of decisions and allows for a more informed decision-making process. Artificial Intelligence (AI) systems could help define strategies for sustainable circular purposes that tackle climate, ecological, social, and economic challenges [20–23].

The participatory AI model [24] refers to the practice of involving humans in the development, deployment, and ongoing refinement of artificial intelligence systems. These models could fit the requirements of citizens and accelerate progress towards the SDGs, including communities in the construction, implementation, and ongoing modification of AI systems, making a huge contribution to improving decision-making. In particular, the integration of AI and the SDGs can be an effective tool for improving community engagement. Through AI-driven technologies, collaborative decision-making processes could be informed. Participatory AI involves engaging diverse stakeholders, such as end-users, domain experts, and community representatives, throughout the AI development process to ensure that the technology aligns with their needs, values, and priorities. AI can help to collect, analyse and interpret large amounts of data, targeting and addressing underrepresented stakeholders, identifying areas of need and potential areas of improvement and understanding the impacts of various initiatives.

AI can also be used to identify and prioritize potential development projects and programs. Integrating AI and stakeholder engagement requires understanding the various stakeholders involved and their respective roles in the process. Additionally, it's important to ensure that stakeholders are conscious of the purpose and scope of AI implementation. This approach can help to increase transparency, accountability, and trust in AI systems and can also help to identify and address potential biases and ethical concerns. The research intends to examine the scientific landscape of direct and indirect relationships that exist between AI, stakeholder engagement and smart circular city.

A bibliographic exploration done through the Scopus online database will be used to identify related articles, and the VOSviewer tool will be employed to build and illustrate the bibliometric networks.

The paper has been divided into three parts: Sect. 2 explains the methodology and the functional tools for bibliometric analysis; Sect. 3 presents the results of the study, including a literature review combined with the bibliometric maps of the scientific landscape; finally, Sect. 4 provides a discussion of the results and the conclusions.

2 Material and Methods

A literature survey has been implemented and visualised through the bibliometric approach of the scientific landscapes provided by van Eck and Waltman [25] (Fig. 1).

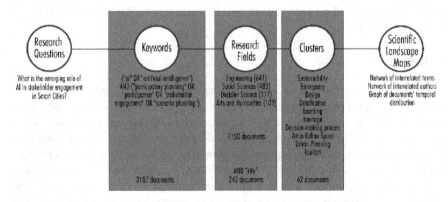

Fig. 1. The methodological steps for the scientific landscape maps.

The data collection process was carried out in the Scopus collection, a database for scientific publications, using the keywords ("ai" or "artificial intelligence") and ("participatory planning" or "participation" or "stakeholder engagement" or "scenario planning") to investigate the role of stakeholder engagement in processes using AI.

This generic research has allowed obtaining an interesting number of publications, for a total of 3187 documents. The database was filtered to refine the result obtained just, including the papers related to Social and Urban Science, for a total of 1150 papers. Then, the result obtained was filtered again, also considering the keyword "city", obtaining a total of 242 papers.

All 242 papers were exported in CSV format from Scopus with their specific data, including the number of times that the article, author, source, country, and references were cited, in addition to the title, abstract and all keywords. This information was necessary to produce and analyse bibliometric maps. These maps were generated with VOSviewer version 1.6.19 [26]: software able to create maps based on network data to be visualised and explored. Moreover, the software manual [27] explains how the maps are constructed from elements and links: network elements are the objects of interest to characterise through the maps, for example, publications, researchers, or terms present within the papers; the relations are the links between two elements, such as co-authorship, co-occurrence, citation, bibliographic coupling or co-citation links, depicted by a line of variable thickness that corresponds with the strength of the connection. The elements can then be grouped into clusters, which are identifiable by different colours.

Additionally, the software provides different ways of visualising the generated maps: network visualisation, where the elements' proximity or lack displays the connection between them and the size indicates their weight; overlay visualisation, where the variation of default colours indicates the range of elements from the oldest to the latest; density visualisation, which can be queried to obtain a density map of both elements and clusters. For the current research, maps of the scientific landscape were generated from network data extracted from the Scopus database to build a network of co-occurrence links between terms. Then a literature review was conducted. From these 242 papers thus filtered, we proceeded with the selection, one by one, of the most pertinent articles for the topic of study, eliminating all those with inconsistent titles and abstracts. This resulted in a sample of 62 analysed articles: the oldest dated 2010 and the most recent published in 2023.

3   Results

The search for scientific literature in Scopus using the keywords related to "artificial intelligence" and "stakeholder engagement" gave results of 1150 papers published between 2008 and 2023. A network data analysis, generated in VOSviewer, was done to understand and visualise the distribution and relationship between the terms frequently found in these articles. Through this map was possible to identify four main clusters related to "data", "education" and "learning", "industry", "management" and "decision" (Fig. 2).

The results were further refined, focusing on the term "city". A total of 242 papers was obtained. A co-authorship, filtered by country, network data analysis generated by VOSViewer shows that most of the publications come from the United States and China (Fig. 3).

A new network data analysis was done based on the 242 studied articles. The "Overlay" visualisation of this analysis (Fig. 4) allows us to discover the most recurrent terms and their related themes and when they were first introduced in the discussion.

By selecting the terms most pertinent to the main topics, VOSviewer uses chromatic gradation to depict the transition from 2018 (blue) to 2021 (yellow), indicating how relevant these issues have become recently.

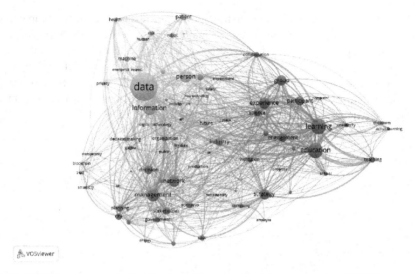

Fig. 2. VOSviewer network visualisation of the network data map based on 1150 documents.

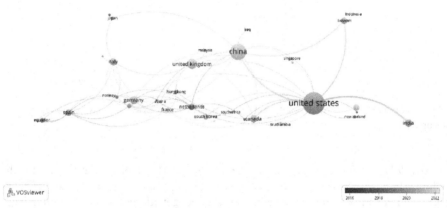

Fig. 3. VOSviewer network visualisation of the co-authorship filtered by country based on the bibliographic data of the 242 documents.

In 2018, terms such as "decision support system", "stakeholders", and "public participation" were widely used. During this time, AI was utilised in various ways to aid decision-making in various applications.

From 2019 to 2020, the debate investigated the possible connections of these terms to "city" and "urban planning". This was the first time the urban setting was explored as a field of study in terms of AI and stakeholder engagement. The yellow marks all the more widely shared terms between 2020 and 2021. The presence of "cultural heritage", "intangible cultural heritage", "big data", and "Smart City" in this cluster suggests that recent arguments point towards AI being pivotal in defining digital, sustainable, and circular growth processes in cities.

A selection, one by one, allows us to further filter the results. A total of 62 papers were analysed, as more relevant and related to the main topics of the research. A graph (Fig. 5) has been generated to facilitate the literature review. It is characterised by the years of publication (on the ordinates) and by the number of publications (on the abscissas) to understand the trend of publications on the topic of interest during the years. This graph shows the increasing interest in the research topics, especially from 2017 to 2022. Finally, the selected articles were classified into ten main clusters (Table 1).

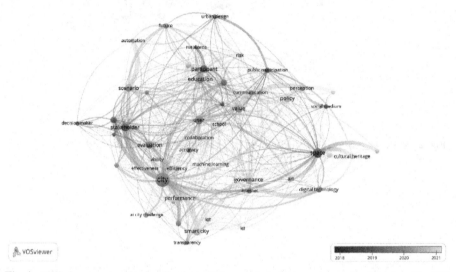

Fig. 4. VOSviewer network visualisation of the network data map's overlay based on the 242 documents.

Sustainability, in Terms of Sustainable City Growth. The implementation of AI technologies has the potential to revolutionize the current situation, promoting equal citizen participation and favouring sustainable growth. Deng et al. discuss how AI effectively investigates resource optimization strategies and model projections for resource-oriented cities. The authors emphasize that the success of these cities necessitates the involvement of governments, entrepreneurs, scientific research institutes, intermediary institutions and the general public. Gao et al. delve into the potential of AI to generate value from Open Government Data (OGD), which refers to information in the public sector that is available in open, reusable formats and free of charge. The goal of OGD is to ensure transparent administration and encourage citizen involvement. Sidani et al. provide a model based on a qualitative analysis of people's perceptions of how Smart Cities can promote sustainable social inclusion. Myeong et al. investigate how to incorporate data-driven approaches and citizen participation into efficient public sector pollution management in Smart Cities, encouraging integrated sensors and Big Data via the Internet of Things (IoT).

Emergency, in Terms of Strategies to Deal with Extreme Events. Recent advances in Deep Learning (DL) offer outstanding opportunities for modelling complex and dynamic

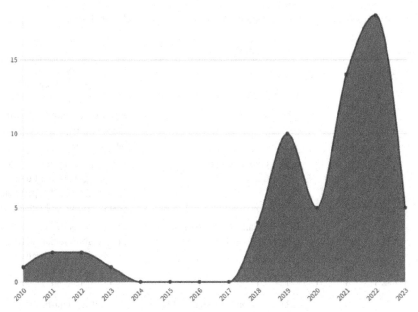

Fig. 5. Graph of the 62 articles published from 2010 to 2023 on the research topics.

systems, such as ecological, climate, and cyber systems. Hao et al. connect resilience theories with big urban data, utilising advanced urban sensing technologies and DL, to show how walkability, green spaces, and civic involvement can contribute to resilience. The findings demonstrate the mediating roles of communities' social and physical properties in diminishing the effects of extreme events, with data-driven proof. Li et al. devise a game to simulate the process when a city is struck by an earthquake that comprises one main shock and one aftershock. During the emergency response, citizens and the city, collaborate to finish the task of taking shelter and collecting data for regional damage evaluation. Smartphone-based monitoring techniques are identified to allow crowdsensing after extreme events, such as earthquakes.

Design, Including the Architectural and the Urban Scale Design. Dortheimer et al. suggest utilising novel information technologies to automate design interactions through crowdsourcing and AI technologies and promote citizen participation in the design process on an architectural scale. Quan creates the "Urban-GAN" system, a plural urban design computation system, to offer technical support for design empowerment and to enable the public to create their own designs. The system is composed of an urban form database and five process models, allowing users with little design knowledge to select urban form cases, generate designs and make design decisions. Burry compiles a catalogue of AI tools to direct urban development toward meaningful public participation in the urban design processes, with the goal of achieving more sustainable and resilient urban environments. Jutraž et al. analyse the pros and cons of various digital tools regarding their effectiveness in promoting public participation and education in urban

Table 1. Classification in ten clusters of the articles analysed.

Cluster	Year	Authors	Title
Sustainability	2023	Deng Y., Jiang W., Wang Z.	Economic resilience assessment and policy interaction of coal resource-oriented cities for the low carbon economy based on AI
	2023	Gao Y., Janssen M., Zhang C.	Understanding the evolution of open government data research: towards open data sustainability and smartness
	2022	Sidani D., Veglianti E., Maroufkhani P.	Smart Cities for a Sustainable Social Inclusion Strategy-A Comparative Study between Italy and Malaysia
	2021	Myeong S., Shahzad K.	Integrating data-based strategies and advanced technologies with efficient air pollution management in Smart Cities
Emergency	2023	Hao H., Wang Y.	Modeling Dynamics of Community Resilience to Extreme Events with Explainable Deep Learning
	2022	Li H., Chen X., Chen H., Wang B., Li W., Liu S., Li P., Qi Z., He Z., Zhao X.	Simulation of Smartphone-Based Public Participation in Earthquake Structural Response Emergency Monitoring Using a Virtual Experiment and AI
Design	2023	Dortheimer J., Yang S., Yang Q., Sprecher A.	Conceptual Architectural Design at Scale: A Case Study of Community Participation Using Crowdsourcing
	2022	Quan S.J.	Urban-GAN: An artificial intelligence-aided computation system for plural urban design

(continued)

Table 1. (*continued*)

Cluster	Year	Authors	Title
	2022	Burry M.	A new agenda for AI-based urban design and planning
	2010	Jutraž A., Zupančič T.	Evaluation of visual digital tools for public participation in urban design
Datafication	2022	Ziosi M., Hewitt B., Juneja P., Taddeo M., Floridi L.	Smart Cities: reviewing the debate about their ethical implications
	2022	Dyakonova M.A., Botasheva A.K., Kardanova M.L.	Socio-Economic and Political Transformation of "Smart Nations" as a Digital Society
	2022	Broomfield H., Reutter L.	In search of the citizen in the datafication of public administration
	2022	Roberts T., Zheng Y.	Datafication, Dehumanisation and Participatory Development
	2022	Marzá D.G., Calvo P.	Algorithmic democracy: a new structural change in public opinion?
	2021	Feher K.	Expectation of smart mentality and citizen participation in technology-driven cities
	2021	Singh U., Determe J.-F., Horlin F., De Doncker P.	Crowd Monitoring: State-of-the-Art and Future Directions
	2020	Alison Paprica P., Sutherland E., Smith A., Brudno M., Cartagena R.G., Crichlow M., Courtney B.K., Loken C., McGrail K.M., Ryan A., Schull M.J., Thorogood A., Virtanen C., Yang K.	Essential requirements for establishing and operating data trusts: Practical guidance co-developed by representatives from fifteen Canadian organizations and initiatives
Learning	2020	Jiang J.C., Kantarci B., Oktug S., Soyata T.	Federated learning in Smart City sensing: Challenges and opportunities

(*continued*)

Table 1. (*continued*)

Cluster	Year	Authors	Title
	2018	Pournaras E., Pilgerstorfer P., Asikis T.	Decentralized collective learning for self-managed sharing economies
	2018	Gugerell K., Platzer M., Jauschneg M., Ampatzidou C., Berger M.	Game over or jumping to the next level? How playing the serious game 'Mobility Safari' instigates social learning for a smart mobility transition in Vienna
Heritage	2022	Laužikas R., Žižiūnas T., Fomin V.	Novel Technologies as Potential Catalyst for Democratizing Urban Heritage Preservation Practices: The Case of 3D Scanning and AI
	2022	Li Q.	Intelligent Intangible Cultural Heritage Innovation Platform Under the Background of Big Data and Virtual Systems
	2022	Wang X., Liang M., Hou X., Song N.	Intelligent Computing of Cultural Heritage: A Case Study of European Time Machine Project
	2021	Kimura F., Ito Y., Matsui T., Shishido H., Kitahara I., Kawamura Y., Morishima A	Tourist Participation in the Preservation of World Heritage – A Study at Bayon Temple in Cambodia –
	2021	Flores-Ruiz D., Miedes-Ugarte B., Wanner P.	Relational Intelligence, Artificial Intelligence and Citizen Participation. The Case of the Cooperative Digital Platform Les Oiseaux de Passage
	2021	Yu X., Shan W., DIng H., Li B.	Research on Intangible Cultural Heritage Amusement Space Design from the Perspective of Artificial Intelligence

(*continued*)

Table 1. (*continued*)

Cluster	Year	Authors	Title
	2020	Mager T., Hein C.	Digital excavation of mediatized urban heritage: Automated recognition of buildings in image sources
	2019	Jeppson P.L., Muschio G., Levin J.	Computational Science, Convergence Culture, and the Creation of Archaeological Knowledge and Understanding
Decision-making process	2023	Zhou Y., Lei H., Zhang X., Wang S., Xu Y., Li C., Zhang J.	Using the Dual Concept of Evolutionary Game and Reinforcement Learning in Support of Decision-Making Process of Community Regeneration—Case Study in Shanghai
	2022	Purba F.N., Arman A.A.	A Systematic Literature Review of Smart Governance
	2022	Zhou Y., Chen J., Zhang X., Liu X., Lei H.	How to Support the Decision-Making Process of Community Regeneration proposed by Evolutionary Game and Reinforcement Learning? A case study in Shanghai
	2022	Rindzevičiūtė E.	AI, a wicked problem for cultural policy? Pre-empting controversy and the crisis of cultural participation
	2022	Mallah Boustani N., Merhej Sayegh M., Boustany Z.	Strengthening Public Institutions and Social Inclusion of Vulnerable Groups in A Developing Country - Innovation in Organizations and Artificial Intelligence Implications
	2022	Wilson C.	Public engagement and AI: A values analysis of national strategies

(*continued*)

Table 1. (*continued*)

Cluster	Year	Authors	Title
	2021	Weng M.-H., Wu S., Dyer M.	Ai augmented approach to identify shared ideas from large format public consultation
	2021	Haqbeen J., Sahab S., Ito T., Rizzi P.	Using decision support system to enable crowd to identify neighborhood issues and its solutions for policymakers: An online experiment at Kabul municipal level
	2021	Raineri P., Molinari F.	Innovation in Data Visualisation for Public Policy Making
	2021	Anastasiadou M., Santos V., Montargil F.	Which technology to which challenge in democratic governance? An approach using design science research
	2021	Hua Z.	Discussion Features of Public Participation in Space Governance in Network Media – Taking Yangzhou Wetland Park as an Example
	2019	Ramesh M.V.	Integration of participatory approaches, systems, and solutions using IoT and AI for designing smart community: Case studies from India
	2019	Shrestha R., Flacke J.	Leveraging citizen science to advance interactive spatial decision support technology: A swot analysis
	2019	Dixon B., Johns R.	Vision for a holistic Smart City-HSC: Integrating resiliency framework via Crowdsourced Community Resiliency Information System (CRIS)

(*continued*)

Table 1. (*continued*)

Cluster	Year	Authors	Title
	2019	Lee M.K., Kusbit D., Kahng A., Kim J.T., Yuan X., Chan A., See D., Noothigattu R., Lee S., Psomas A., Procaccia A.D.	Webuildai: Participatory framework for algorithmic governance
	2019	Duberry J.	Global environmental governance in the information age: Civil society organizations and digital media
	2019	Predescu A., Mocanu M.	Increasing Collaboration and Participation Through Serious Gaming for Improving the Quality of Service in Urban Water Infrastructure
	2019	Schütz L., Bade K.	Assessment user interface: Supporting the decision-making process in participatory processes
	2018	Boukchina E., Mellouli S., Menif E.	From citizens to decision-makers: A natural language processing approach in citizens' participation
	2018	Golini R., Guerlain C., Lagorio A., Pinto R.	An assessment framework to support collective decision-making on urban freight transport
	2012	Simm W., Whittle J., Nieman A., Portman A., Sibbald J.	OurCity: Understanding how visualization and aggregation of user-generated content can engage citizens in community participation
	2012	Skoric M.M., Pan J., Poor N.D.	Social media and citizen engagement in a city-state: A study of Singapore

(*continued*)

Table 1. (*continued*)

Cluster	Year	Authors	Title
	2011	Jensen M., Lowry P., Jenkins J.	Effects of automated and participative decision support in computer-aided credibility assessment
	2011	Mahmoud H., Arima T.	A web-based public participation system that supports decision making
Art in Urban Space	2022	Jiang X., Wang F., Jiang Z.	Study on the Path of Continuous Participation of Digital Art in Public Space in 6G IoT Communication
Urban Planning	2021	Kaklauskas A., Bardauskiene D., Cerkauskiene R., Ubarte I., Raslanas S., Radvile E., Kaklauskaite U., Kaklauskiene L.	Emotions analysis in public spaces for urban planning
	2021	Lieven C., Lüders B., Kulus D., Thoneick R.	Enabling digital co-creation in urban planning and development
	2020	Seifert N., Mühlhaus M., Petzold F.	Urban strategy playground: Rethinking the urban planner's toolbox
	2020	Kim H.-W., Kim G.-C.	Evaluating the quality of comprehensive plans for urban resilience: The case of seven metropolitan cities in South Korea
	2019	Aguilar-Castro J.L., Díaz-Villarreal F.J., Altamiranda-Pérez J.A., Cordero J., Chavez D., Gutiérrez-De Mesa J.A.	Metropolis: An emerging serious game for the Smart City
	2019	Costa R., Machado R., Gonçalves S.	Guimarães: innovative and engaged city
	2013	Taha D.S.	The influence of social networks in visiting, planning and living in cities. Alexplore: A pilot project in Alexandria

(*continued*)

Table 1. (*continued*)

Cluster	Year	Authors	Title
Tourism	2021	Pohjola T., Gronman J., Viljanen J.	Multi-Stakeholder Engagement in Agile Service Platform Co-Creation

design. The article was crafted to examine the possibilities of improving communication between actors in the urban design process.

Datafication, in Ethical and Citizen Emancipatory Terms. Ziosi et al. propose four dimensions for Smart Cities: network infrastructure, post-political governance, social inclusion and sustainability, with data playing a crucial role. Feher examines many trend reports, white papers and research summaries to analyse the expectations of smart mentality and citizen participation. The most expected human factors are open data, communities, collective participation, socio-technical engagement, and empowerment. Marzá et al. question if the algorithmic colonisation necessitates a new structural change of public opinion or, rather, the withdrawal of this concept. Alison Paprica et al. argue that data trusts need stakeholder engagement to be established. Broomfield et al. point out that smart government needs citizen participation and interactive processes for public policies and decisions. Roberts et al. stress the importance of including practical and emancipatory knowledge interests and monitoring and evaluation tools in the project cycle. Dyakonova et al. posit that digital technologies are essential for building Smart Nations. Singh et al. suggest the usage of DL algorithms, multi-agent systems, knowledge representation and explainable AI in crowd monitoring to enable privacy-preserving and public participation.

Learning, as Algorithmic and Collective Process. Jiang et al. investigate federated learning as an approach to Smart City Sensing, a concept which may be used to address the security and privacy issues that often accompany data collection. In addition, Pournaras et al. evaluate the potential of collective learning for the development of ethical and socially responsible participatory sharing economies via the Internet of Things (IoT). Moreover, Gugerell et al. use serious gaming to improve learning processes related to stakeholder involvement and citizen engagement in urban planning and governance.

Heritage, in Terms of Cultural Heritage Protection and Enhancement. The conflict between heritage protection and urban infrastructure development rationales has created a context for inclusion, participation and dialogue among different heritage-related communities. Laužikas et al. suggest that novel technological developments with the intent to increase community involvement and democratize administrative practices, will have direct effects through technology-based participatory practices, such as 3D representation of heritage. Li proposes a development model that focuses on intangible heritage protection and encourages the participation of the entire population. Wang et al. summarise a methodology that involves creating smart data for cultural heritage, breaking through the key technologies of intelligent computing of cultural heritage, developing digital standards and platforms for cultural heritage, visualising the virtual re-appearance of historical time and space and promoting multi-party cooperation and public partic-ipation. Jeppson et al. aim to encourage community participation and collaboration to advance the development of novel computer vision and pattern recognition technologies, allowing machine-based reconstructions of 3D objects. Flores-Ruiz et al. propose the cooperative digital platform "Les Oiseaux de Passage", which supports various Euro-pean heritage communities in enhancing their cultural heritage through activities related to the tourism sector. Yu et al. apply AI to define a design process, with different levels of interaction and participation of different age groups, about intangible cultural heritage amusement spaces. Kimura et al. investigate the possibility of tourists collaborating in a new heritage preservation system based on information and communication technol-ogy, 3D restoration technology via photographic data collection and AI. Mager et al. show how the combination of crowdsourcing, historical big data and deep learning can simultaneously raise questions and provide solutions in the field of architectural and urban planning history. Crowdsourcing can offer an important opportunity for partici-pation, incorporating their perspectives and arousing their interest in urban history and development questions.

Decision-Making Process, Including Gaming, Citizen Science and Active Participation Practices. Technology brings with it a range of advantages, yet several challenges must be dealt with, such as the processing of ever-more complex and growing data and the ethical and legal implications of AI. Governance is required to address these issues. Rindzevičiūtė furthers the participation in cultural policy, which involves engaging var-ious stakeholders at different stages of policy-making. Purba et al. urge for increased public involvement in smart governance through collaboration, partnership, and trans-parency. Mallah Boustani et al. explore ways in which AI tools can improve engage-ment in social and political life, particularly among young people. Wilson examines 16 national strategies for AI to assess how public engagement and participation may impact the development of AI governance regimes and decision-making by public administra-tors. Jensen et al. use decision-making theory to explain and forecast a higher acceptance of assessment aid recommendations when perceptual cues are provided by users. The authors design and test a hybrid decision aid which performs automated linguistic anal-ysis and elicits and analyses perceptual cues from an observer. Weng et al. use Natural Language Processing (NLP) toolkits to present a novel approach for identifying and visualising shared ideas from large-scale public consultation. Boukchina et al. employ NLP to extract valuable information from citizens' comments, applying Latent Seman-tic Analysis (LSA) on a corpus of comments to automatically identify the subjects addressed by citizens. Skoric et al. study how citizens' views of government control influence social media use and how this is linked to offline participation. The research suggests that social media alters the power dynamics between the government, media organisations and citizens, creating new spaces for online political discourse, which may encourage real-world political participation. Hua investigates the characteristics and differences of Internet users in urban public space governance issues. Online social media allows for free expression on urban social problems, allowing users to express their views, emotions, attitudes or opinions. Dixon et al. suggest the implementation of CRIS, a multi-modular crowdsourced Community Resiliency Information System (CRIS), as a means of creating a Holistic Smart City (HSC) which allows for scalable, customised solutions and ensures participation from a range of communities in Smart City technology. Golini et al. propose a framework to facilitate the aggregation and classification of information related to Urban Freight Transport (UFT) in cities, called the Smart City Logistics platform. This data was used to identify intervention priorities and evaluate alternative solutions in collaboration with stakeholders. Haqbeen et al. introduce a joint research program, namely, crowd-based communicative and deliberative e-planning (CCDP), which combined an AI-driven technology, a decision-support system and experimental participatory planning. Mahmoud et al. developed a system wherein stakeholders could visualise alternative proposals through virtual reality and share collected information and results. Zhou et al. explore the potential of incorporating scenario simulations of social attributes and social interaction dimensions into the research and development of digital twin cities.

Zhou et al. propose systematic decision support for community renewal with the use of deep reinforcement learning and evolutionary game modelling to build a conceptual framework for simulation and to provide optimal solutions for AI decision support. Predescu et al. construct a serious gaming platform combining crowdsensing and Augmented Reality (AR) to boost citizen participation in smart government. Raineri et al. discuss the use of citizen science, design thinking and accountability to promote civic engagement and data-driven policy making. Shrestha et al. discuss the SWOT of integrating citizen science and spatial decision support system analysing the literature. Ramesh considers IoT and AI key elements for a smart decision-making procedure, such as smart governance, smart energy, smart building, mobility, infrastructure, technology, healthcare, and citizens. Schütz et al. present a creative intelligent user interface to appraise participatory planning and decision process submissions. This technique of citizens' participation is a form of democracy where citizens are involved in the decision-making process regarding the growth of their society. Technologies permit citizens to take part in these processes by submitting inputs via digital media such as social media platforms or dedicated websites.

Simm et al. craft "OurCity", a site-specific digital artwork intended to accumulate, sum up and represent citizens' views on the cities in which they live, diminishing the gap between citizens and policymakers. Anastasiadou et al. enrich the discussion on which technology could be suitable to which major challenge of democratic governance, amplifying the influence of information and communication technologies-enabled public governance tools for government openness, public service efficiency and user-friendliness, citizen political participation and societal mobilization. Lee et al. introduce "WeBuildAI", a collective participatory framework that allows people to construct algorithmic policy for their communities. The main notion of the framework is to enable stakeholders to create a computational model that expresses their views and to have those models vote on their behalf to form algorithmic policy. By investigating some of the most-utilized current digital technologies and displaying some of the most remarkable emerging ones, Duberry shows how active civil society organizations operate and how ICTs sustain some of their roles and, thus their participation in global environmental governance.

Art, in Terms of Vibrancy of Urban Spaces. User participation is a key indicator of the vibrancy of public spaces in cities, and examining the elements that determine a user's willingness to stay involved can help guide the design and utilization of digital art in the ever-expanding IoT. Jiang et al. discuss how the 6G network can establish an "all-encompassing and intelligent" world based on abundant data, enabling AI implementation in diverse areas. Specifically, the authors analyse how emotional experience and media literacy can shape the likelihood of users.

Urban Planning, in Terms of Innovative Solutions able to Activate Co-creation Planning Processes. Since the mid-1900s, scientists have been exploring how to incorporate emotion into the urban planning process with qualitative methods. Kaklauskas et al. developed the "Affective System for Researching Emotions in Public Spaces for Urban Planning" (ASP System). This system combines maps data, such as observations of passers-by, climate information and air pollution levels, to help initiate citizen-centric planning solutions. Lieven et al. create an open source co-creating platform known as "DIPAS" (Digital Participation System) to get feedback from civil society. Seifert et al. propose the "Urban Strategy Playground" software framework, which uses AR to help planners develop strategies, evaluate them, and make them accessible for public participation. Kim et al. advocate for the integration of business, city planning and design and the community to achieve smart urban development. Aguilar-Castro et al. developed the city simulator game "Metropolis", which can be used by Smart Cities to make collective decisions, promote e-participation and serve as an e-decision-making tool. Costa et al. highlight how artificial intelligence, cognitive computing, and the IoT can define solutions that involve citizen engagement and participation. Finally, Taha et al. emphasize the potential of mobile social networking and geo-coding to inform decision-support systems for city planning.

Tourism, in Terms of Competitiveness and Sustainability. A systemic service platform approach and agile prototyping with smart emerging technologies such as AI, IoT, AR, 5G and Robotics, together with multi-stakeholder co-creation, as proposed by Pohjola et al., could give rise to a Smart Tourism Destination (STD), which seeks to offer strategic advantages, as well as to provide a data-driven management system to improve competitive and inclusive changes in a tourism ecosystem.

4   Discussion and Conclusions

As technology continues to become more pervasive and integrated into our everyday lives, the need to increase our participation in Artificial Intelligence (AI) is becoming more pressing. Participatory AI is a concept that emphasizes human input in the decision-making process. By leveraging the expertise of the people involved in the decision-making process, Participatory AI enables a collaborative approach to decision-making, where decisions are based on the collective insight and experience of the stakeholders. Involving stakeholders in the decision-making process means not only providing their participation but also increasing their understanding of the entire process, pros and cons related to the use of AI.

This degree of awareness allows them to be more likely to feel connected to the process and more likely to use the outcome. This can lead to satisfaction and loyalty, which can positively impact the outcomes of an urban decision-making process. This paper contributes to clarifying the opportunities given by the interaction between AI and stakeholders, giving a general literature review of methods adopted to encourage citizen participation.

Augmented Reality, Data Visualization, Interfaces, Digital Twins, and Evolutionary Games are such tools explored in this contribution, useful to engage general citizens in scientific research, thereby empowering them to participate in the decisions of the issues affecting them. The reconstruction of the scientific landscape around the fundamental concepts of "AI" and "stakeholder engagement", integrating the literature review with analysis of bibliometric maps, aimed to define a general framework to explore the role of citizen participation in urban decision-making processes using ai tools to deal with the future challenges. From this framework, the research intends to investigate the opportunities given using different types of AI in Smart Cities to encourage citizen participation as a key element of smart development, defining a new form of social engagement in a smart context.

Author Contributions. Conceptualization, M.C., F.D.M., S.S.; methodology, M.C., F.D.M., S.S.; validation, M.C. and F.D.M.; formal analysis, S.S.; investigation, S.S.; writing-original draft preparation, S.S.; writing-review and editing, M.C., F.D.M., S.S.; visualization, S.S.; supervision, M.C. and F.D.M. All authors have read and agreed to the published version of the manuscript.

References

1. Hollands, R.G.: Will the real smart city please stand up? City **12**(3), 303–320 (2008)
2. Washburn, D., Sindhu, U., Balaouras, S., Dines, R.A., Hayes, N.M., Nelson, L.E.: Helping CIOs Understand "Smart City" Initiatives: Defining the Smart City, its Drivers, and the Role of the CIO. Forrester Research Inc, Cambridge (2010)
3. Su, K., Li, J., Fu, H.: Smart city and the applications. In: Proceedings of IEEE International Conference on Electronics, Communications and Control (ICECC), pp. 1028–1031. Institute of Electrical and Electronics Engineers (IEEE), Ningbo (2011)
4. Mitton, N., Papavassiliou, S., Puliafito, A., Trivedi, K.: Combining Cloud and sensors in a smart city environment. EURASIP J. Wirel. Commun. Networking, 1–10 (2012)
5. Yin, C., Xiong, Z., Chen, H., Wang, J., Cooper, D., David, B.: A literature survey on smart cities. Sci. China Inf. Sci. **58**(10), 1–18 (2015). https://doi.org/10.1007/s11432-015-5397-4
6. Harrison, C., Eckman, B., Hamilton, R., Hartswick, P.: Foundations for smarter cities. IBM J. Res. Dev. **54**, 1–16 (2010)
7. Nam, T., Pardo, T.A.: Conceptualizing Smart City with dimensions of technology, people, and institutions. In: Proceedings of the 12th Annual International Digital Government Research, pp. 282–291. Association for Computing Machinery, College Park (2011)
8. Creating "the smart city". Rios, Patrice. https://archive.udmercy.edu/handle/10429/393. Accessed 14 May 2023
9. Cavoukian, A., Chibba, M.: Cognitive cities, big data and citizen participation: the essentials of privacy and security. In: Portmann, E., Finger, M. (eds.) Towards Cognitive Cities. SSDC, vol. 63, pp. 61–82. Springer, Cham (2016). https://doi.org/10.1007/978-3-319-33798-2_4
10. Mostashari, A., Arnold, F., Mansouri, M., Finger, M.: Cognitive cities and intelligent urban governance. Netw. Ind. Q. **13**(3) (2011)
11. Moyser, R., Uffer, S.: Cognitive Cities, From smart to cognitive: a roadmap for the adoption of technology in cities. In: Portmann, E., Finger, M. (eds.) Towards Cognitive Cities: Advances in Cognitive Computing and Its Application to the Governance of Large Urban Systems, pp. 61–82. Springer, Heidelberg (2016). https://doi.org/10.1007/978-3-319-33798-2_2

12. Kim, H.M., Sabri, S., Kent, A.: Smart Cities for Technological and Social Innovation, 1st edn. Academic Press (2020)
13. Partridge, H.: Developing a human perspective to the digital divide in the smart city. In: Proceedings of the Biennial Conference of Australian Library and information Association, Australia (2004)
14. Castro-Arce, K., Parra, C., Vanclay, F.: Social innovation, sustainability and the governance of protected areas: revealing theory as it plays out in practice in Costa Rica. J. Environ. Plan. Manag. **62**, 2255–2272 (2019)
15. Ellen MacArthur Foundation, Cities in the circular economy: an initial exploration. Available at https://www.ellenmacarthurfoundation.org/. Accessed 14 May 2023
16. Poli, G., Muccio, E., Cerreta, M.: Circular, cultural and creative city index: a comparison of indicators-based methods with a machine-learning approach. Aestimum **81** (2022)
17. Bosone, M., De Toro, P., Fusco Girard, L., Gravagnuolo, A., Iodice, S.: Indicators for ex-post evaluation of cultural heritage adaptive reuse impacts in the perspective of the circular economy. Sustainability **13**(9), 4759 (2021)
18. Sacco, S., Cerreta, M.: A decision-making process for circular development of city-port ecosystem: the East Naples case study. In: Gervasi, O., Murgante, B., Misra, S., Rocha, A.M.A.C., Garau, C. (eds.) Computational Science and Its Applications – ICCSA 2022 Workshops. ICCSA 2022. LNCS, vol. 13378. Springer, Cham (2022). https://doi.org/10.1007/978-3-031-10562-3_40
19. United Nations: Resolution adopted by the General Assembly on 6 July 2017, A/RES/71/313. https://unstats.un.org/sdgs/. Accessed 14 May 2023
20. Cardone, B., Di Martino, F.: A GIS-based fuzzy multiclassification framework applied for spatiotemporal analysis of phenomena in urban contexts. Information, Special Issue on Knowledge (2022)
21. Cardone, B., Di Martino, F., Senatore, S.: A fuzzy partition-based method to classify social messages assessing their emotional relevance. Inf. Sci. **594**, 60–75 (2022)
22. Cardone, B., Di Martino, F.: Fuzzy-based spatiotemporal hot spot intensity and propagation - an application in crime analysis. Electronics **11**(3), 370 (2022)
23. Cardone, B., Di Martino, F.: GIS-based hierarchical fuzzy multicriteria decision-making method for urban planning. J. Ambient. Intell. Humaniz. Comput. **12**(1), 601–615 (2020). https://doi.org/10.1007/s12652-020-02043-6
24. Birhane, A., et al.: Power to the people? Opportunities and challenges for participatory AI. In: Equity and Access in Algorithms, Mechanisms, and Optimization. EAAMO 2022, Article 6, pp. 1–8. Association for Computing Machinery, New York (2022)
25. Van Eck, N.J., Waltman, L.: Accuracy of citation data in Web of Science and Scopus. arXiv preprint arXiv:1906.07011 (2019)
26. Van Eck, N.J., Waltman, L.: Software survey: VOSviewer, a computer program for bibliometric mapping. Scientometrics **84**(2), 523–538 (2010). https://doi.org/10.1007/s11192-009-0146-3
27. Van Eck, N.J., Waltman, L.: VOSviewer Manual, vol. 1, no. 1, pp. 1–53. Univeristeit Leiden, Leiden (2013)

Evaluating Energy Communities: A New Social and Economic Model for Implementing the Ecological Transition

Martina Bosone[1]([⊠]) [iD], Barbara Pirelli[2], and Domenico Vito[3] [iD]

[1] Institute for Research on Innovation and Services for Development (IRISS) – National Research Council (CNR), Guglielmo Sanfelice Street, 8, 80134 Naples, Italy
m.bosone@iriss.cnr.it
[2] Studio Legale Avv. Barbara Pirelli, Roma Street, 12, 74123 Taranto, Italy
[3] Paris Observatory – HubZine Italia, Paris, France
domenico.vito@polimi.it

Abstract. The European Directive on the promotion of the use of energy from renewable sources, establishes the possibility of creating 'Renewable Energy Communities (REC)' for the production and consumption of energy from renewable sources, stimulating the transition from a centralized to a decentralized energy system.

By putting citizens at the center of the energy transition, REC represent a virtuous socio-economic community model in which citizens, businesses and administrations become 'prosumers', actively integrated in a participatory and democratic process to support the energy transition.

Considering both the complexity and the variety of factors that influence the evolution of this phenomenon and also the multidimensional implication of this new socio-economic model, this study aims to provide the Key Performance Indicators (KPIs) that influence citizens' energy communities and to establish a methodology to quantify or qualify these impacts.

In this study, 26 KPIs were identified and divided into three dimensions: environmental, economic and social.

The proposed KPIs were applied on two Italian case studies, selected as 'pioneers' examples of REC, allowing their comparison at multidimensional level.

The findings confirm that REC represent a model able to generate multiple benefits and, for this reason, their evaluation become a necessary step in monitoring progress (in itinere) and results (ex post).

This aspect makes KPIs particularly useful not only as an ex post evaluation tool but also as a method to support decision-making. Future research could test more case studies and verify the variation of the results obtained in relation to the different contexts considered.

Keywords: Energy Communities · Ecological Transition · Sustainable Development · Multidimensional Assessment · Key Performance Indicators

© The Author(s), under exclusive license to Springer Nature Switzerland AG 2023
O. Gervasi et al. (Eds.): ICCSA 2023 Workshops, LNCS 14108, pp. 259–276, 2023.
https://doi.org/10.1007/978-3-031-37117-2_19

1 Introduction

The European Commission's Clean Energy for All Europeans Package [1] affirms the prominent role that communities will play in the future energy system.

The package will contribute to decarbonizing the EU energy system in line with the objectives of the European Green Deal. Based on Commission proposals published in 2016, the package consists of 8 new laws. One of these laws is the Renewable Energy - Recast to 2030 (RED II) Directive (EU) [2], which aims to promote the use of energy from renewable sources: in Article 3 it sets an overall binding target for the Union by 2030, i.e. that Member States collectively ensure that the share of energy from renewable sources in the Union's gross final energy consumption in 2030 is at least 32%. The Commission will assess this target with a view to presenting, by 2023, a legislative proposal to increase it in case of further substantial reductions in the costs of renewable energy production, if this is necessary to meet the Union's international commitments to decarbonization or if such an increase is justified by a significant decrease in energy consumption in the Union.

Article 22 of the same Directive introduces the concept of a Renewable Energy Community, better known as the Energy Community. The Directive not only stipulates that by 2030 at European level, renewable energies should account for at least 32% of gross final energy consumption, but also sets the target that by 2050, 16% of electricity should come from community initiatives such as Energy Communities [3, 4].

In Italy, the term 'energy communities' only entered the official language in December 2020, when Parliament approved an amendment to the so-called 'Decreto Milleproroghe 162/2019' [5] that establishes the possibility of creating communities between several entities for the production and consumption of energy from renewable sources.

The reception of the European RED II Directive, therefore represented a fundamental step with which the Italian government in a timely manner aligned itself with several virtuous countries such as Denmark and Germany where the reality of energy communities has been present for years [6].

The excellent work of the 'GSE - Gestore dei Servizi Energetici' (Energy Services Manager) [7] during the consultations has provided the technical basis for standardization and for the effective and widespread implementation of these important innovations in Italy.

In fact, our country was quick from a regulatory point of view to transpose the European legislation, first by experimentally introducing small energy communities with plants up to 200 kW, and then definitively at the end of 2021 with the law transposing the European Directive, extending the possibility to plants up to 1 MW.

On the basis of the European Climate Law goals [8], investments and reforms contained in the Italian Green Transition Recovery and Resilience Plans (PNRRS) have been developed [9]. The PNRR foresees numerous investments in the renewable energy sector with the aim of ensuring clean and efficient energy use and sustainable public transport. Energy Communities are included in the social and territorial cohesion theme in order to support small territories at risk of depopulation. It is also important to take into consideration the Italian PTE (Plan for Ecological Transition) [10] in which the reduction of climate-changing emissions by 2030 is foreseen; this Plan - based on the objectives indicated in the PNRR - provides a framework for environmental and energy policies. It goes without saying that the progressive and capillary diffusion of Energy Communities is in line with the decarbonization objectives, but in order to evangelize them, it will be necessary to carry out targeted interventions on transmission, distribution and storage networks..

2 Energy Communities as a New Socio-economic Model

An energy community can be formed when individual citizens, local authorities or small companies and cooperatives join together to become co-owners of 'neighborhood' renewable energy plants, thus exchanging energy for self-consumption, but also with the possibility of feeding energy into the grid and receiving an incentive from the GSE. The latter can be shared (as in the case of a photovoltaic or wind power plant at the disposal of the community) or individual (as in the case of a photovoltaic plant installed on the roof of a house, a company, a public administration building or an apartment block).

In this way, a participatory form of renewable energy production is realized because passive consumers, consumers, are transformed into active consumers and producers, prosumers [11], as they have their own system to generate electricity for self-consumption, selling excess energy to other actors managed by a smart grid [12]. The smart grid paradigm suggests tackling energy management by increasing the flexibility of the electricity grid, using data and IT to remotely coordinate distributed generation and storage technologies so that they can actively respond to changing grid conditions. The infrastructure consists of a network that connects all actors in the energy community, monitored and controlled by state-of-the-art digital technologies to optimize every stage of energy production, consumption and exchange through innovative hardware and software solutions [13].

On this basis, new ways of governing energy communities are also being explored, for instance by coupling classical grid control methodologies with block chain technology [14].

According to the definition of Article 2(14) of the European Directive, a 'self-consumer of renewable energy' is a final consumer who, operating on its own site within defined boundaries or, if permitted by a Member State, on other sites, produces renewable electricity for its own consumption and may store or sell self-produced renewable electricity, provided that, for a self-consumer of renewable energy, other than a household (e.g. a business), these activities do not constitute its principal commercial or professional activity. In the next point, the Directive also specifies that 'self-consumers of renewable energy acting collectively' are constituted by a group of at least two self-consumers of renewable energy acting collectively and located in the same building or apartment block.

Point c of Article 2(16) of the European Directive explicitly states that the main objective of renewable energy communities is to provide community-wide environmental, economic or social benefits to their shareholders or members or to the local areas in which they operate, rather than financial profits.

RECs can represent a regenerative model not only for individual communities, at the local scale, but also at the territorial scale, emphasizing the role of communities as drivers of inclusive and sustainable development processes.

RECs can enable the development of local production chains, providing networking and employment opportunities for local communities and reducing energy dependency on other countries or regions. Moreover, RECs also contribute to the fight against energy poverty by reducing energy consumption, lowering supply tariffs and making the use of renewable energy sources more equitable and affordable [15].

The shift to decentralized energy production has many advantages, including the use of local energy sources, greater security of energy supply at the local level, shorter transport distances and less energy dispersion. This shift also promotes community development and cohesion through the availability of income sources and the creation of local jobs.

3 Case Studies Comparison: The Energy Communities of East Naples (NA, Italy) and Turano Lodigiano (LO, Italy)

According to the Symbola Report [16], there are currently around 7,000 active energy communities in Europe, involving 2 million inhabitants. This is a growing phenomenon, so much so that some estimates hazard a growth potential that could reach 264 million European citizens, generating 45% of the expected electricity demand by 2050 [17].

Enel relieved that the EU country with the largest number of Energy Communities, according to a study by the EU 2020 Joint Research Centre, is Germany, with 1,750 Communities, followed by Denmark (700) and the Netherlands (500) [6].

In Legambiente's 'Comunità Rinnovabili 2022' report [18], a census is made of 100 mapped practices. However, it argued that these numbers still appear to be totally insufficient to reach the target of 70 GW envisaged by 2030, pushing the time horizon of its realization further and further away.

Despite this, it is undeniable not to note how this phenomenon is growing rapidly and how the awareness of institutions and citizens is increasingly materializing in favor of virtuous initiatives and experiences of dialogue and collaboration.

In order to apply our evaluation methodology, we have therefore considered two case studies, the first being the energy community of San Giovanni a Teduccio, in the eastern suburbs of Naples, which was one of the first experiments of Renewable Energy Communities (RECs) in Southern Italy, and the other being that of Turano Lodigiano, where the first renewable energy community in Lombardy was born.

3.1 The Energy Community of San Giovanni a Teduccio (NA, Italy)

In the case of San Giovanni a Teduccio the proposal was initiated by Legambiente and was supported by the Fondazione con il Sud, which finances social development projects, with an initial contribution of 100,000 euros [19]. The cost of the installation is partially borne (42%) by tax deductions under the renovation bonus [20].

The first step in establishing the energy community was to start involving local people, breaking the initial sense of mistrust and illustrating the advantages of this model. In this phase, the intermediation of people already active in the area and recognized by the population for their civic commitment through environmental education projects, recovery of abandoned public areas, workshops with children and cultural initiatives was important. In fact, the president both of Legambiente Campania and the Fondazione Famiglia di Maria (a socio-educational center in the neighborhood) were personally involved in a local awareness campaign, emphasizing the great opportunity for redemption offered to this area. The project aroused enthusiasm in the community, which was willing to set up as an Energetic Community with an initial founding nucleus, formalized before a notary, and made up of three families of users, together with Mariateresa Imparato and Anna Riccardi (as representatives of Legambiente and the Foundation)[21]. Subsequently, the association expanded with the entry of twenty families from the neighbourhood. Thanks to the transposition of the European 'Red II' Directive in Italy, it was able to rely on a primary cabin, which would allow up to 40 families.

All the stakeholders involved started from the real needs of the local community, beginning with an analysis of the household's waste and energy expenditure management, and ending with the prediction of energy and economic savings as a solution to the energy poverty experienced by Ponticelli households.

From the outset, the proposed intervention targeted 40 families in distressed conditions, living in flats adjacent to the foundation, which would be easily connected to the same electricity box. These families were in absolute or near-absolute poverty, and very often live in conditions of 'energy illegality', so their joining the energy community had a social purpose even more than an environmental one, investing in their awareness as an active engine of change in the neighborhood's culture.

The next step was to install the photovoltaic system on the roof of the building of the Family of Mary Foundation, a 19th century building. The Foundation was active in the 19th century as an orphanage run by nuns. Today it is a secular educational institution, well known in the neighborhood, which cooperates with the social services of the municipality for the right to education.

The system consists of 166 panels with a total output of 53 kilowatts and is guaranteed for 25 years. It will be able to produce around 65,000 kilowatt hours in a year, 18% of which will be self-consumed by the Foundation, with the remainder being shared with the 40 local households. A storage system allows the energy to be stored and the extra energy to be fed into the grid and sold to the national grid. The proceeds will be distributed to the members at the end of the year for a return of between two hundred and three hundred euros per year per household, equivalent to the savings of two utility bills. In addition to this, households also benefit from the 20% discount that is applied on the utilities of those who have joined the energy community [7].

Over 25 years, the total incentives received, net of running costs, would amount to over 200,000 euros [19]. It is also estimated that real savings, in terms of reduced electricity consumption by all ERC members, would amount to around 300,000 euros [19].

This case study also emphasized the fundamental role of institutions as facilitators of the ecological transition, through an important assistance activity to the project's target households (a training course on renewable energy supply methods and the monitoring of electricity consumption and building quality in terms of heat dispersion) and an intensive information campaign on the benefits and potential of energy communities, in order to identify additional members.

3.2   The Energy Community of Turano Lodigiano (LO, Italy)

The second case study under analysis is that of Turano Lodigiano, a small municipality of just over 1,500 inhabitants. Here the first renewable energy community in Lombardy was born.

The ERC of Turano Lodigiano consists of 23 families, 1 parish and 9 municipal utilities, united in the free association called 'Solisca'. Established one year after the first project presentation on 2 October 2020, Solisca applied to the GSE for authorization to operate as an Energy Community in mid-January 2022. The shared energy is produced by two photovoltaic systems located on the roof of the locker rooms of the gymnasium and the municipal sports field, of 34 kW and 13 kW each respectively, totalling 46.5 kWp. The energy not self-consumed by the two PODs below the plants is shared by 23 residential consumers, the parish and 7 other municipal consumers.

In a first phase, only 10 of the 23 residential users shared energy: the next 13 were activated with the entry into force of the implementing regulations of Law 199 of 8/11/2021, which extended the scope of RECs to the primary cabin.

The initial investment in the plants covered the costs of the Energy Community's establishment and authorization process with 70,000 arriving to the municipality of Turano as ecological compensation for the construction of the turbogas power plant located in the municipality.

Supporting the Solisca community is a digital platform, which records real-time data - certified by block chain technology - of production and consumption, power flows, energy exchanges - produced, withdrawn, shared - and bill savings.

Members of the community are provided with an energy profile that can be accessed via an app, to receive advice on how to use the energy produced and exchanged and achieve even greater savings and efficiency.

Through the energy profile, users are also invited to adopt more conscious and sustainable consumption behavior through gamification initiatives.

Among the opportunities offered by the digital platform, there is also an estimated climate mitigation contribution generated by REC The system, in fact, calculates some environmental sustainability indicators such as CO_2 emissions not produced and the number of equivalent trees planted.

4   Assessing Energy Communities: KPIs for a Multi-criteria Assessment

As abovementioned, the energy communities are a promising model able to generate benefits at multidimensional level. However, to assess the effectiveness of an energy community, Key Performance Indicators (KPIs) need to be defined and monitored.

This study aims to provide the main indicators that influence citizens' energy communities and to establish a methodology to quantify or qualify these impacts.

To date, several studies have addressed the topic of evaluating energy communities. In many of them, the definition of Key Performance Indicators (KPIs) is adopted as an established method to provide an objective assessment of complex issues, such as energy communities and smart grids. A Key Performance Indicator (KPI) is a value that can be measured, evaluated and demonstrated in order to assess performance towards a specific goal [22].

KPIs can be expressed either as absolute values (e.g. energy production from renewable sources, carbon dioxide emissions, etc.) or as percentage values calculated with respect to a reference scenario (e.g. carbon dioxide reduction, increase in the share of renewables in the energy mix, etc.). They can be used to define high-level targets (linked to national and international energy visions) and local targets in the case of micro grids and energy communities [23]. Many authors suggest the use of KPIs in the design phase of a micro grid, as in Chan, where energy consumption savings and emission reductions are highlighted.

Community self-sufficiency and the self-consumption ratio are indicators most commonly identified [24–27] alongside other indicators more properly focused on environmental impact in terms of tons per year of avoided CO_2, NO_x and SO_2 [28, 29]. Other studies have also focused on the issue of identifying stakeholders as a determining factor in resolving the complexity of issues and needs related to each of them and to identify a multi-level energy performance analysis system, based on three different hierarchical levels - strategic, tactical and operational - and distributing KPIs among the different stakeholders in the system while maintaining their interdependence [30]. Cuesta et al. [31] conduct an extensive literature review to emphasize the need of considering social indicators in addition to the usual considerations of economic, technical, and environmental criteria, in order to refine the design of Hybrid Renewable Energy Systems (HRES).

In some studies, environmental and economic KPIs are considered in decision-making as a support system for strategic investment decisions in the field of micro grids [32–34], while in other studies, the focus is on how these decisions are conditioned by very heterogeneous factors [35].

Other authors have pointed out the interconnection between energy communities and other sectors positively influenced by them, such as mobility, economy, quality of space and innovation [24, 36].

In this regard, [37] et al. also emphasize the importance of taking a systemic approach in measuring the energy efficiency of communities, considering the entire life cycle of all components involved in the activation of an energy community (i.e. buildings, infrastructure and transport) [38, 39]. The authors propose indicators for each of these three categories.

Furthermore, both the Efkarpidis et al. study [27] and the Lightness project [40] introduce interesting indicators concerning the efficiency of energy consumption monitoring and detection tools, thus also including a dimension related to the possible distortion of results caused by technical error.

The potential KPIs that can be included in a multi-criteria evaluation framework are many and varied. For this reason, a filtering procedure was adopted in this study based on a number of basic criteria identified in the literature [41] concerning relevance, completeness, availability, measurability, reliability, familiarity, complementarity, non-redundancy and benchmarking capacity. Above all, they are interpreted as a tool within the reach of the consumer, and thus as a potential tool for self-assessment by the communities themselves, assisted by appropriate experts. For this reason, very significant indicators found in the literature (such as those concerning the calculation of emissions or technical aspects relating to energy production and consumption) were excluded and those of more immediate compilation and greater availability of information were considered, especially in view of the two case studies analyzed.

Furthermore, it is important to highlight that the definition of KPIs is fundamental to identify the main areas of impact of the Energy Community phenomenon, which is so dynamic and so variable with respect to so many different factors (types of users, environment, location, political framework, economy, etc.) [35, 40], constituting a valid support not only as an ex post evaluation tool but also as a method to support decision-making. In this sense, they express the performance expected from a given project and can then be used as part of a multi-criteria evaluation for decision-making, aimed at determining the best choice between different project scenarios.

In this study, 26 KPIs were identified, deduced from scientific studies, reports and projects and revised by the authors. They were divided into three dimensions: environmental, economic and social.

Environmental KPIs include issues related to both the energy performance of the community, in terms of the amount of renewable energy integrated and self-consumed, and the reduction of emissions. The latter is of particular relevance because it is a central issue in the energy transition [42, 43].

The economic KPIs focus on the financial viability and sustainability of the proposed solution for stakeholders and investors, but also on the convenience for users in terms of savings on electricity bills and tax deductions, as well as redistributive mechanisms whereby economic surpluses are reinvested in further community initiatives with consequent benefits.

Social KPIs highlight the importance of Energy Communities as a new model of active involvement and awareness-raising of citizens on sustainability issues, renewing the sense of cohesion and belonging even in the most degraded and marginalized places. This model also has an impact on the democratization of knowledge, widening access to specific content, stimulating the exchange of information and enabling citizens in the use of technologies. Therefore, it is important to consider feedback from users and community members, who are the first interlocutors to be addressed in order to detect the actual effectiveness of the implemented model. Lastly, the social aspects also include indicators, which in the literature are included in the category of 'legal' indicators, and which concern the transparency of the institutions on the data collected and shared by the other stakeholders and the consistency of the legislative framework adopted at the local level by the energy community with the national and European directives, since, in our opinion, they influence the social aspect of the overall satisfaction with the project and the relationship established between institutions and users.

The evaluation is based on both qualitative and quantitative indicators. Qualitative indicators were expressed using the Likert scale (5 = very high performance; 4 = high performance; 3 = medium performance; 2 = low performance; 1 = very low performance), while quantitative indicators were expressed through diverse units of measure.

Table 1 shows the 26 KPIs proposed in this study for the evaluation of Energy Communities and applied for the evaluation of the two selected Italian case studies.

Table 1. Proposed KPI framework for the evaluation of Energy Communities and their application on the two selected Italian case studies

Dimension	Indicatot	Description	Unit of Measure	Case study 1	Case study 2
Environmental	EN.1 Plant catchment area	Number of households using locally produced renewable energy	n	40	23
Environmental	EN.2 Size of the photovoltaic system	Number of photovoltaic panels	n	166	2
Environmental	EN.3 Total output of the photovoltaic system	The peak power, or nominal power of a photovoltaic system, is the maximum electrical power that the PV system is capable of producing under standard conditions of a temperature of 25 °C and incident solar radiation of 1000 W/m2. It is the sum of all the individual peak powers of each photovoltaic panel installed in the system	kWp (kilowatt peak)	53	46.5
Environmental	EN.4 Total energy produced	Amount of renewable energy produced locally by the energy community in a year	kWh/year	63,600	54,000

(*continued*)

Table 1. (*continued*)

Dimension	Indicatot	Description	Unit of Measure	Case study 1	Case study 2
Environmental	EN.5 Self-consumed energy	Total amount of renewable energy consumed locally (compared to all energy consumed) and not fed back into the grid	kWh/year	49,200	12,000
Environmental	EN.6 Exported energy	Amount of energy exported from the community to the grid compared to all energy generated locally	kWh/year	10,800	42,000
Environmental	EN.7 Energy payback time	Number of years required for the photovoltaic to produce the energy that was needed for its realisation	n	n.a.	n.a.
Environmental	EN.8 Reduction of GHG emissions	Amount of GHG emissions reduced in one year after installation of the photovoltaic system	tCO2eq/year	33.7[a]	29.6[b]
Economic	E.1 Economic Incentive	Annual incentive received by households from the GSE for energy produced and consumed collectively	€/year	200–300	1,428
Economic	E.2 Cost Savings	Euro per year saved overall by all member households of the energy community	€/year	12,000	15,000

(*continued*)

Table 1. (*continued*)

Dimension	Indicatot	Description	Unit of Measure	Case study 1	Case study 2
Economic	E.3 Payback period	Number of years needed to recover funds spent on an investment or to reach the break-even point	n	10	n.a.
Economic	E.4 Initial Economic Investment	Incentives received as initial investment for the installation and activation of the energy system	€	100,000	70,000
Economic	E.5 Tax Deductions	Percentage of tax deductions on total investment cost	%	42	n.a.
Economic	E.6 Level of local co-investment activated	Level of involvement of different stakeholders as investors in the activation of the energy community	Likert scale (1–5)	3	1
Economic	E.7 Redistribution of wealth	Percentage of economic surpluses reinvested in public benefit funds and other activities	%	n.a.	n.a.

(*continued*)

Table 1. (*continued*)

Dimension	Indicatot	Description	Unit of Measure	Case study 1	Case study 2
Social	S.1 Level of local community involvement	Awareness and involvement of tenants regarding the impact of its actions on energy consumption and consequent virtuous behaviour aimed at maximising collective self-consumption (surveyed through interviews)	Likert scale (1–5)	5	4
Social	S.2 Diversity of stakeholder categories involved	Number of different categories of stakeholders involved as co-producers of services	n	4	3
Social	S.3 Number of members of the energy community	Number of households in the energy community	n	20	33
Social	S.4 Social Cohesion	Improved sense of social cohesion and belonging among community members as a result of the activation of the energy community	Likert scale (1–5)	5	4
Social	S.5 Level of awareness	Activation of training, dissemination and awareness-raising activities following the activation of the energy community	Likert scale (1–5)	5	5

(*continued*)

Table 1. (*continued*)

Dimension	Indicatot	Description	Unit of Measure	Case study 1	Case study 2
Social	S.6 Level of acceptance	Level of acceptance of the use of new technologies (apps, sensors, etc.) by users in the energy community (surveyed through interviews)	Likert scale (1–5)	4	5
Social	S.7 Level of assistance to stakeholder	Support actions by promoters in accompanying members of the ERCs in the various fulfilment and authorisation processes required	Likert scale (1–5)	2	4
Social	S.8 Number of new jobs	Number of jobs directly generated as a result of the activation of the energy community	n	n.a.	n.a.
Social	S.9 Level of satisfaction with quality of life and well-being	Level of satisfaction of members of the energy community with respect to the improvement of their quality of life and perception of their level of well-being (surveyed through interviews)	Likert scale (1–5)	5	n.a.
Social	S.10 Level of data transparency	Level of user awareness regarding transparency on data collected and shared by other stakeholders (surveyed through interviews)	Likert scale (1–5)	n.a.	5

(*continued*)

Table 1. (*continued*)

Dimension	Indicatot	Description	Unit of Measure	Case study 1	Case study 2
Social	S.11 Level of consistency of the legislative framework	Level of coherence of the legislative framework adopted at local level by the energy community with national and European directives	Likert scale (1–5)	5	5

[a]In the case of the East Naples Energy Community plant:

1) Considering that 1,200 kWh per kWp [48] and that the plant in Naples is 53 kWp, this will result in a production of 63,600 kWh per year (1,200 kWh × 53 kWp).

2) If 1 Tonnes Oil Equivalent (TOE) is equivalent to 11,628 kWh [49]. The fuel saving will therefore be about 5.4 toe per year (63,600 kWh: 11,628 kWh).

3) The carbon dioxide emission 'avoided' each year can be calculated by multiplying the value of electricity produced by the photovoltaic system by the Italian electricity mix factor: 0.53 kg of CO2 avoided for every kWh produced by photovoltaics [48]. Thus, the Co2 saved through the use of the photovoltaic system will be equal to: 63,600 kWh × 0.53 = 33,708 kg of CO2 = 33.7t.

[b]In the case of the Turano Lodigiano Energy Community plant:

1) Considering that 1,200 kWh per kWp [48] and the fact that the Turano Lodigiano plant is 46.5 kwp, this results in a production of 55,800 kWh per year (1,200 kWh × 53 kWp).

2) If 1 Tonnes Oil Equivalent (TOE) is equivalent to 11,628 kWh [49]. The fuel saving will therefore be about 4.8 toe per year (55,800 kWh: 11,628 kWh).

3) The carbon dioxide emission 'avoided' each year can be calculated by multiplying the value of electricity produced by the photovoltaic system by the Italian electricity mix factor: 0.53 kg of CO2 avoided for every kWh produced by photovoltaics [48]. Thus, the Co2 saved through the use of the photovoltaic system will be equal to: 55,800 kWh × 0.53 = 29,574 kg of CO2 = 29.6t.

4) The annual economic incentive was calculated considering that of the 54 Mwh of energy produced, 30% is shared energy and receives an annual incentive of 119 €/Mhw given the current regulations.

5) The cost savings came from https://www.thegoodintown.it/solisca-la-comunita-energetica-di-turano-lodigiano/

The application of the proposed set of REC evaluation indicators on the two case studies showed that through this framework it is possible to compare different REC experiences through not only the energy or economic dimension, but also through a social and community involvement dimension.

Both case studies demonstrated the multiple benefits of REC.

The case of San Giovani a Teduccio has become a model to be copied and replicated in other cases, above all because it has shown that bottom-up approaches work as social activator, stimulating the creation of new communities based on a more raise awareness of the social, economic and environmental value of using renewable energy.

In the case of Turano Lodigiano emerged the role of technologies not only as a tool able to quantify the environmental benefits, but also as educational enabler of sustainable behaviour, opening to people the opportunity to better know and manage the impact of their own actions and thus, representing a real way to change the mindset towards a more ecological approach.

The involvement of citizens and local authorities in renewable energy projects through Renewable Energy Communities has brought significant added value in terms of local acceptance of renewable energy and access to additional private capital, resulting in local investment, greater consumer choice and increased citizen participation in the energy transition. This local involvement is even more important in a context of increasing renewable energy capacity. Measures to enable renewable energy communities to compete on an equal footing with other producers also aim to increase the participation of local citizens in renewable energy projects and thus increase the acceptance of renewable energy [44, 45].

5   Conclusions

The transition towards a more sustainable energy system requires a profound reform of economic and social models. Energy communities represent a new socio-economic model that can contribute to this transition process.

Energy communities offer several benefits, such as creating local jobs, lowering energy costs, increasing the security of energy supply and reducing greenhouse gas emissions. RECs are considered as activators of 'community resilience' [44, 46], because they stimulate participation in community life, strengthening the sense of individual and community responsibility and projecting actions towards the achievement of the common good [45].

However, there are also some challenges to be addressed in the creation and management of energy communities, such as the need to develop a clear and uniform legal framework at national and European level, the promotion of active participation of community members and the need to ensure fair access to energy for all community members.

The development of energy self-production and energy efficiency policies represent the best welfare policies for households, helping to reduce costs in energy bills and improve the social life of their members, especially in a context of energy and health crisis.

For this reason, RECs can be considered as a regenerative model that paves the way for processes of 'democratisation' and inclusion of citizens in the energy transition.

The motivations behind the activation of energy communities are varied, from the reliability of energy supply to self-sufficiency and the fight against energy poverty through the involvement of energy companies. But monetary benefits are not the only ones: environmental concerns and the desire for energy independence are equally strong motivations. For the first time, in fact, citizens can feel themselves to be real contributors to the energy transition process [4], implementing sustainable behavioral models in their lives and opening themselves up to welcome a change of mindset that offers real opportunities for integration and social development through the creation of new jobs. Bringing topics of global scope closer to the needs of specific local communities is the real strength of this model that reorganizes traditional market rules and relations between stakeholders that for a long time have had non-communicating objectives and fields of action.

To assess the effectiveness of an energy community, Key Performance Indicators (KPIs) need to be defined and monitored.

This study provides the main indicators that influence citizens' energy communities and to establish a methodology to quantify or qualify these impacts.

The application of the proposed set of REC evaluation indicators on the two case studies showed that through this framework it is possible to compare different REC experiences through not only the energy or economic dimension, but also through a social and community involvement dimension.

In addition, the KPIs identified can be a model for self-assessment as they allow organizations to assess their performance objectively and systematically against pre-established targets in order to identify areas for improvement and define future development objectives. In addition, KPI-based self-assessment facilitates the identification of the organization's strengths and weaknesses and allows it to focus on critical aspects for success [47].

The framework presented in this study is susceptible to future modifications and additions, especially considering that it was tested on only two case studies. Future research could test more case studies and verify the variation of the results obtained in relation to the different contexts considered.

Finally, it would be interesting to address the issue of self-assessment by trying to submit such a framework to a few sample communities and getting feedback on the real perceived usefulness of users as well as its ease of compilation.

References

1. European Commission: Clean energy for all Europeans Package. Clean energy all Eur. Packag. 14 (2017)
2. European Commission: Renewable Energy – Recast to 2030 (RED II). Eur. Comm. Off. Website. 2030 (2019)
3. Wilson, A.: Revision of the Renewable EnergyDirective: Fit for 55 package (2021)
4. European Commission: Energy communities. https://energy.ec.europa.eu. Accessed 12 May 2023
5. Ministero della Giustizia: Disposizioni urgenti in materia di proroga di termini legislativi, di organizzazione delle pubbliche amministrazioni, nonche' di innovazione tecnologica. Gazzetta Ufficiale - Serie generale - n. 305 del 31 dicembre 2019, Italy (2019)
6. Enel: Comunità energetiche in Italia e in Europa. https://www.enelgreenpower.com/it/paesi/europa/italia/comunita-energetiche-rinnovabili/comunita-energetiche-italia-europa
7. Gestore dei Servizi Energetici: Regole tecniche per l'accesso al servizio di valorizzazione e incentivazione dell'energia elettrica condivisa, Rome, Italy (2022)
8. European Commission: European Climate Law. Off. J. Eur. Union. 2021 (2021)
9. Ministero delle Imprese e del Made in Italy: PNRR - Piano Nazionale di Ripresa e Resilienza (2022)
10. Ministero Dell'Ambiente e della Sicurezza Energetica: Piano per la Transizione Ecologica (2022)
11. RSE & Fondazione Utilitatis: Orange book. Le comunità energetiche in Italia (2022)

12. van Summeren, L.F.M., Wieczorek, A.J., Bombaerts, G.J.T., Verbong, G.P.J.: Community energy meets smart grids: reviewing goals, structure, and roles in virtual power plants in Ireland, Belgium and the Netherlands. Energy Res. Soc. Sci. **63** (2020). https://doi.org/10.1016/j.erss.2019.101415

13. Frieden, D., Roberts, J., Gubina, A.F.: Collective self-consumption and energy communities: overview of emerging regulatory approaches in Europe. Compil. Proj. (2019)

14. Kotilainen, K., Valta, J., Systa, K., Makinen, S.J., Jarventausta, P., Bjorkqvist, T.: Exploring the potential of blockchain as an enabler for three types of energy communities. In: International Conference on the European Energy Market, EEM (2019). https://doi.org/10.1109/EEM.2019.8916261

15. United Nations: United Nations Transforming Our World: the 2030 Agenda for Sustainable Development. A/RES/70/1 (2015)

16. Ambrosini, C., Gallotti, L., Pagnoncelli, F., Renzi, F., Sturabotti, D.: CER - Le comunità energetiche contro la crisi (2022)

17. ENEA & AESS: La comunità energetica. Vademecum 2021 (2021)

18. Legambiente: Comunità rinnovabili (2022)

19. Fondazione con il Sud: Comunità Energetica e Solidale di Napoli Est. https://www.fondazioneconilsud.it/progetto-sostenuto/comunita-energetica-e-solidale-di-napoli-est/. Accessed 12 May 2023

20. Magliacane, C., Ruggieri, B., Coleandro, G.: La CER di Napoli est (2023). https://www.pilastrobologna.it/2023/03/14/la-cer-di-napoli-est/

21. Forte, M.: La comunità che si produce l'energia da sola a Napoli (2021). https://www.internazionale.it/notizie

22. Warren, J.: Key performance indicators (kpi) – definition and action. INTERNET Online Intell. Solut. (2011)

23. Lien, S.K., Sørnes, K., Walnum, H.T., Hauge, Å.L., Lindberg, K.B.: Selection of key performance indicators (KPIs) in the transition towards low-carbon urban communities. In: Eceee Summer Study Proceedings (2019)

24. Okwuibe, G.C., et al.: Evaluation of hierarchical, multi-agent, community-based, local energy markets based on key performance indicators. Energies. **15** (2022). https://doi.org/10.3390/en15103575

25. Cielo, A., Margiaria, P., Lazzeroni, P., Mariuzzo, I., Repetto, M.: Renewable energy communities business models under the 2020 Italian regulation. J. Clean. Prod. **316** (2021). https://doi.org/10.1016/j.jclepro.2021.128217

26. Mutani, G., Santantonio, S., Beltramino, S.: Indicators and representation tools to measure the technical-economic feasibility of a renewable energy community: the case study of villar pellice (Italy). Int. J. Sustain. Dev. Plan. **16** (2021). https://doi.org/10.18280/ijsdp.160101

27. Efkarpidis, N., et al.: A generic framework for the definition of key performance indicators for smart energy systems at different scales. Energies. **15** (2022). https://doi.org/10.3390/en15041289

28. Bianco, G., Bonvini, B., Bracco, S., Delfino, F., Laiolo, P., Piazza, G.: Key performance indicators for an energy community based on sustainable technologies. Sustain. 13 (2021). https://doi.org/10.3390/su13168789

29. Ceglia, F., Marrasso, E., Roselli, C., Sasso, M.: Small renewable energy community: the role of energy and environmental indicators for power grid. Sustainability **13** (2021). https://doi.org/10.3390/su13042137

30. Li, Y., O'Donnell, J., García-Castro, R., Vega-Sánchez, S.: Identifying stakeholders and key performance indicators for district and building energy performance analysis. Energy Build. **155** (2017). https://doi.org/10.1016/j.enbuild.2017.09.003

31. Cuesta, M.A., Castillo-Calzadilla, T., Borges, C.E.: A critical analysis on hybrid renewable energy modeling tools: an emerging opportunity to include social indicators to optimise systems in small communities. Renew. Sustain. Energy Rev. **122** (2020). https://doi.org/10.1016/j.rser.2019.109691

32. Pramangioulis, D., Atsonios, K., Nikolopoulos, N., Rakopoulos, D., Grammelis, P., Kakaras, E.: A methodology for determination and definition of key performance indicators for smart grids development in island energy systems. Energies **12** (2019). https://doi.org/10.3390/en12020242

33. Moretti, M., et al.: A systematic review of environmental and economic impacts of smart grids (2017). https://doi.org/10.1016/j.rser.2016.03.039

34. Tur, M.R., Bayindir, R.: Project surveys for determining and defining key performance indicators in the development of smart grids in energy systems. Int. J. Smart Grid **3**, 103–107 (2019). https://doi.org/10.20508/ijsmartgrid.v3i2.59.g54

35. Thomann, B.: Impact of Heterogenous Parameters on the Key Performance Indicators of Energy Communities (2023). https://repositum.tuwien.at/bitstream/20.500.12708/158337/1/ThomannBenjamin-2023-ImpactofHeterogenousParametersontheKey.pdf. https://doi.org/10.34726/hss.2023.103120

36. Sintef & NTNU: Zero Emission Neighborhoods in Smart Cities (ZEN) (2022)

37. Forsström, J., et al.: Measuring energy efficiency: Indicators and potentials in buildings, communities and energy systems. VTT Tied. - Valt. Tek. Tutkimusk (2011)

38. Angrisano, M., Fabbrocino, F., Iodice, P., Girard, L.F.: The evaluation of historic building energy retrofit projects through the life cycle assessment. Appl. Sci. **11**, 7145 (2021). https://doi.org/10.3390/app11157145

39. Gravagnuolo, A., Angrisano, M., Nativo, M.: Evaluation of environmental impacts of historic buildings conservation through life cycle assessment in a circular economy perspective. Aestimum, 241–272 (2020). https://doi.org/10.13128/aestim-10004

40. Barrios, B.: Lightness project - Deliverable 3.2: Report on the definition of the KPIs Assessment frameworks (2021)

41. Yang, Y., Jurasz, J., Li, H., Syrri, A.L.A., Yan, J.: Key performance indicators on flexibility of a multi-energy system. In: Applied Energy Symposium: Low Carbon Cities and Urban Energy Systems (CUE), Xiamen, China, pp. 1–7 (2019)

42. European Comission: New European Bauhaus. Europa.Eu (2021)

43. European Commission: The European Green Deal. Eur. Comm. (2019). https://doi.org/10.1017/CBO9781107415324.004

44. Caramizaru, A., Uihlein, A.: Energy communities: an overview of energy and social innovation (2019). https://doi.org/10.2760/180576

45. Eroe, K.: Le comunità energetiche rinnovabili (e solidali). Impresa Soc. **1** (2023). https://doi.org/10.7425/IS.2023.01.10

46. Cafer, A., Green, J., Goreham, G.: A community resilience framework for community development practitioners building equity and adaptive capacity. Community Dev. **50** (2019). https://doi.org/10.1080/15575330.2019.1575442

47. Attardi, R., Cerreta, M., Poli, G.: A collaborative multi-criteria spatial decision support system for multifunctional landscape evaluation. In: Gervasi, O., et al. (eds.) ICCSA 2015. LNCS, vol. 9157, pp. 782–797. Springer, Cham (2015). https://doi.org/10.1007/978-3-319-21470-2_57

48. Sigeim energia: Il manifesto dei Benefit e dei crediti ambientali. http://www.sigeim.it/i_vantaggi_ambientali.html. Accessed 12 May 2023

49. Energie Rinnovabili: Calcolo delle tonnellate equivalenti di petrolio (tep). http://nuove-energie-rinnovabili.blogspot.com. Accessed 12 May 2023

Participatory Art and Co-creation Methodology in the "Viale delle Metamorfosi" Project

Sveva Ventre[1][✉] and Maria Cerreta[2]

[1] Contemporary Art Curation and Social Innovation, Collettivo Zero APS, 80121 Naples, Italy
sv.ventre@gmail.com
[2] Department of Architecture (DiARC), Federico II University of Naples, 80134 Naples, Italy
maria.cerreta@unina.it

Abstract. The complex nature of social inequalities determined by top-down urban planning choices leads the new urban regeneration to new cultural strategies. Various artistic and social projects have seen the light in Italy and Europe, bringing a new democratic way of producing culture. Artists and cultural planners work collectively as 'territory entrepreneurs' whose sole purpose is to connect people and create community processes. Art disciplines play a social and public role, activating collaborative decision-making processes and experimenting with new power systems. Starting with the concept of community art from the previous century, this paper aims to investigate how art is increasingly becoming part of local regeneration processes. The case of the project *Viale delle Metamorfosi - Art makes its way*, in the eastern suburbs of Naples (Italy), is presented here as an example of innovation through the application of a co-creation methodological process, integrating participatory art and informal education. The most evident results, evaluated in a step-by-step approach in relation to the activities conducted, highlight the importance of multi-dimensional assessment in this type of process, able to mobilize realities and artists to explore new spatial participation opportunities and make it a practice of socio-cultural innovation.

Keywords: Community art · Culture-driven innovation · Community-centered design · Co-evaluation methodology · SOCRATES method

1 Introduction

1.1 Culture and Regeneration in Post-industrial Cities

The city is the result of a complex interaction between different planes: from the infrastructural to the cultural, from the economic to the political. Every city is a field of conflicts, alliances, and clashes, of power and imagination. Everything about it and its transformation is inevitably linked to these variabilities involving its inhabitants and those who pass through it [1]. The great urban and social transformations of the last century were related to industry development until all that was derived from it - factories, working-class districts, and places of aggregation - became the great ghost of post-modern times. Due to the decline of the Fordist city, the urban voids generated by the decommissioning of the factories became, thanks to the cultural engine, the home of the tertiary sector and knowledge-based activities [2]. The model of the post-industrial city is affirmed, where the cultural and tertiary sector progressively replaces the urban voids once occupied by factories. A.J. Scott underlines, "*[…] place and culture are persistently intertwined with one another, […]culture is a phenomenon that tends to have intensely local characteristics, thereby helping to differentiate places one another*" [3].

From the post-war period to the present day, regeneration strategies have radically altered our cities, using big tools and actions that should, instead, have known a more minute and careful sphere. It is no coincidence that when we speak of interventions in the regeneration of spaces, we speak of 'remembering', 'urban acupuncture', 'listening', 'sustainability' and 'identity', which remind us of the human and local dimension of action [4]. Many of the most recent experiences, in fact, challenge the limits of processes imposed from above (*top-down*) through traditional urban planning tools and seek to establish a horizontal relationship between those who execute and those who use, enhancing the components activated by participation as a creative drive from below (*bottom-up*). In this way, the process between public and private, large and small, is inverted so that the real resource to be valorised is the knowledge heritage of communities. This resource goes beyond the conventional idea of material goods, such as works of art, architectural heritage, museums, and cultural centres, to try to include elements such as the memories and identities of citizens, shared values, lifestyles, democracy and civic engagement. It goes without saying that a new narrative of the city revolves around the union of these 'commons', which inherently possess the potential for cross-sectoral and multi-sectoral action. In this sense, we go beyond the concept of urban regeneration to the point where culture is no longer a weapon to stop the decay of a city, but rather the process that draws from the identity matrix of the place and innovatively interprets its complex dimension [5]. For about a decade now, a new way of developing collaborative cultural projects, which exploits cooperative ways of designing, producing and distributing works, goods and services, has been spreading also in Italy [6]. Culture is no longer understood as elitist but as a collaborative practice. Suburban festivals, public art routes, and collaborative glossaries are emerging: territorial cultural projects that conduct innovative research on creating new horizons of possibility. The notion that tries to synthesize the phenomena is that of *cultural planning*, which restores centrality to 'cultural resources' [7] as a means of regeneration. Among these, a privileged role is reserved for art, which has long since experimented with opening to new audiences, becoming *community art* outside the canonical context of the museum or gallery.

Starting from the historical background of *community art* in the public and social spheres of the city, this article explores the use of participation as a tool for social involvement and awareness, both in artistic production and in interdisciplinary cultural projects. The following sections analyse the methodology (Sect. 2) and the context (Sect. 3) in which the project *Viale delle Metamorfosi* took place in South Italy (Naples) and the co-creation workshops activated together with the selected artists.

Social cohesion, which is one of the most important outcomes of culture-led regeneration, can only be achieved through the involvement of local communities in all its social components. Therefore, this article aims to show how the use of ex-ante evaluation tools can suggest proper models of governance in which regenerative processes ensure the representation of a coherent interpretation of the identity of places starting from their culture [8]. For this reason, at the end of the article, some considerations concerning the need for local authorities to consider results obtained with cultural actions have been included [9]. In conclusion, we can say that the potential of co-creation as a tool for communities, moreover when disadvantaged, to develop their role in society governance, express their knowledge and identity and contribute to action and change needs to be applied [10].

1.2 Community Art: The Spread of the Participatory Practice

According to the Report of the *Arts Council's Experimental Projects Committee* (UK) (June 1974) [11] "Community artists" are distinguishable not by the techniques they use but by their attitude towards the place of their activities in the society. One of the most relevant concerns is their effect on a specific community and the relationship they establish with it. *Community artists* aim to broaden and deepen the awareness of the community in which they operate by adopting different instruments of change (psychological, social, and political) and involving the community in the activities they promote. The above definition of *community artist* is very close to the meaning we recognize for *socially engaged art* today. These were, above all, at that time, unconventional art forms through which artists, who preferred to act in contexts of high cultural and economic deprivation, laid the foundations for political and social change from a co-authoring perspective. In the 1980s, socially engaged art was reinterpreted as a purely educational programme, which was considered one of the possible side effects of this practice, not its primary objective [12]. Unlike then, from 1990 to the present day, the rise of art activism and politically engaged art has marked the social turn of the contemporary arts, causing a sudden change of direction or even a fusion of art and activism. Compared to the 1970s, what made the difference was the recognition of participatory art as a genre on its own. The turning point of participation lies in trying to subvert the traditional roles of artist, work, and visitors: the artist goes from being an individualist producer of an object to a collaborator and promoter of situations/experiences; visitors, previously considered mere observers or spectators, are now repositioned in the role of co-producers and/or participants [13] (Fig. 1).

Nowadays, ensuring equal opportunities and a wider enjoyment of culture through the involvement of underrepresented groups is still a central point in the definition of access to culture in terms of increasing people participation and the removal of barriers. Participation took on the meaning of accessibility, becoming a central strategy of the democratic production of culture [14]. Furthermore, the 2022 OECD report "The Culture Fix: Creative people, places and industries" suggested and recognized that the Cultural and Creative Sectors (CCSs) can be drivers for the recovery of the cities, moreover where important regeneration processes can be stimulated [13]. The strong interconnection between cultural stakeholders and others from different economic sectors can be crucial to promote sustainable growth and innovation in peripheral areas.

This trend, which crosses art and several disciplines, represents an acknowledgement of how there are no longer postulates to follow in contemporary society, but rather a transformation of places, people and institutions is required [15]. The recent birth of the N.E.B. – New European Bauhaus – initiative, which takes its origins from the historical

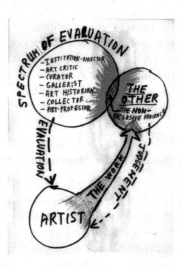

Fig. 1. Spectrum of evaluation (Source: T. Hirschhorn, 2010)

Bauhaus movement, promotes an interconnection between technology, arts and culture through the experimentation of innovative processes through sustainability, aesthetics (meant as the quality of life) and social inclusion [16].

It is no coincidence that in recent years, especially in Italy, we have witnessed a necessary redefinition of the patrimonial system in many ways still ongoing. The position once assumed by the *artivists* [17], a hybrid between an artist, an educator, and an activist, now takes on the value of a mixture of disciplines and languages. The recent experience of Documenta 15 (Kassel, Germany, 2022), curated by *ruangrupa*, a collective founded in 2000 and based in Jakarta, Indonesia, is clear evidence of this inclination. By curating the past edition of Documenta, they wanted to create a *globally oriented, collaborative and interdisciplinary art and culture platform* [18]. The artistic actions and performances were conceived as a place of comparison, learning, and sharing, making visible how the artistic process is rooted in the local ecosystem [19]. Art migrates towards life in this challenging present time, and the results are no longer classifiable as traditionally conceived art. However, it is closer to understanding by the community: the artist's action is valued for the change it brings and the commitment that artistic practices promulgate for the generation of new imaginaries. Only in this way is it possible to redefine the system of research, production, distribution, and promotion of culture.

2   Materials and Methods

The participatory arts model has contributed to the diffusion of a new approach, using experiential and situated methodologies that go beyond the conventional knowledge-generating practices of the various disciplines. The aim of such practices is to embrace more emotional perspectives that bring out a more affective and inclusive comprehension of places [20].

The Italian experience of *Artway of thinking* (Venice, 1993) represents one of the first integrated methodology-artwork approaches (Fig. 2), where the process constitutes the result. The artistic practice seeks the involvement of society and creates new relationships to listen to and perceive its community, with the aim of discerning the potential for development. The need to work with the complexity of the social texture has led to the use of a systemic approach to co-creation practices to trigger a sustainable mechanism of interrelation between the various disciplines and subjectivities. [21].

Fig. 2. *Artway of thinking*, Co-creation diagram, source: https://www.artway.info/cocreation-met hodology

The concept of 'co-creation' originated in the business world in the 1990s in connection with the involvement of customers in product development [22]. The concept extended to academia and was combined with the process of knowledge generation, drawing on different research practices developed through 'participatory action research' (PAR) [23] and arts-based research. Changing the hierarchy between artist and non-artist, as well as academic and non-academic, this approach seeks to balance the power dynamics involved in sharing knowledge.

Co-creation, in fact, necessarily implies participation, i.e. the construction of pathways through which certain individuals or social groups can make choices (and thus wield power) that can influence even minimally the outcomes of the process. This reinforces the need to define co-creation as a collective creative process involving communities and cultural professionals whose outcomes (not outputs) can be tangible or intangible in the form of artworks or experiences [24]. Co-creation is also an eminently political practice of *place-making*. It can therefore be said that the goal of co-creation is to public spaces of relation in which "*conflicting points of view confront each other without any possibility of final reconciliation*" [25]. When executed successfully, the co-creation methodology recognizes the tensions and power relations that are likely to exist between participants and can lead to establishing an environment of mutual trust. Therefore, place-making supported by co-creation is an innovative way of addressing territorial stigma by involving residents and local stakeholders in creative activities that highlight alternative representations of places and communities subjected to stigmatisation [26].

The methodology used in the case of the *Viale delle Metamorfosi* project in East Naples, which becomes an indispensable tool for the general understanding of the work of Collettivo Zero APS, envisages the articulation of the process in phases (Fig. 3). To facilitate intercultural and interdisciplinary group work, as a contemporary response to the reading of complexity and the production of innovation, this methodology alternates moments of connection between creative thinking and group dynamics, building a co-creation process shared by the individual and the group, at the same time sustainable for the environment. The main phases of the process follow:

1. *investigation*: phase of study and analysis of the social, cultural, and urban context. In this phase, links with local stakeholders and actors are determined; tools like data collection, data processing and data aggregation have been used;
2. *co-creation*: phase of proactive involvement and constant information of the beneficiary through multi-dimensional activities: workshops, educational laboratories and meetings between artists in residence and the community;
3. *restitution*: the final phase of the inauguration of the installations and/or artistic actions by means of a path through the neighbourhood, accompanied by a series of cultural and entertainment events;

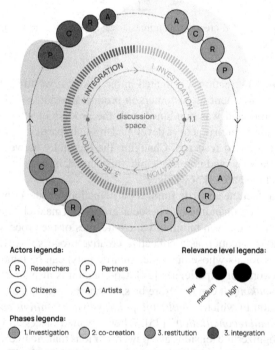

Fig. 3. *Viale delle Metamorfosi* Methodology diagram.

4. *integration*: inserting time into the process to metabolise the innovation: this phase consists of the integration of the process within the life of the place.

The here shown investigation process must be read as a practice which brings together different data and analysis. A co-creation methodology has been chosen to understand how a collaborative knowledge production between different actors, with respect to social and urban inequalities, can be established through arts-based methods. The co-creation process can be used as an interpretation of places and urban space, leading to a deeper understanding of communities living on the edges of the city [27]. By promoting the imagination of the participants and establishing new connections, relationships and encounters, co-creation is a matter of giving power, both in a project and in each cultural practice. This responds to a wider demand for connection and collaboration from cultural institutions. Co-create means to be part of the making of meaning, which can affect change both at personal and community levels [28].

3   Case Study

3.1   East Naples: A Post-disaster and Post-industrial Landscape

The urbanistic vicissitudes of East Naples, particularly of the Ponticelli district, where the Viale delle Metamorfosi project originates, tell of a still ongoing attempt to define the urban space on the eastern borders of the metropolitan city of Naples. Born as an autonomous settlement nucleus with a strong rural identity, Ponticelli was one of the *casali* that arose on the border of the main urban centre, then annexed to the city during the Fascist era. From the 1940s onwards, the district experienced growth with substantial residential expansion, accentuated by building speculation. As part of the drafting of the General Regulatory Plan (*Piano Regolatore Generale*) of 1972 and in accordance with Law 167/72, Ponticelli was identified as a place of the 'public city', i.e. an area only minimally built up, within which the project of public urbanization with popular settlements and neighbourhood facilities could be realized, in compliance with the Area Plan (*Piano di Area*) 167 [29]. In 1974 the administration introduced the theme of urban standards, launching the Framework Plan of Equipment (*Piano Quadro delle Attrezzature*), which accentuated the awareness of the minimum endowment of services and their distribution over the territory. In 1980, the Periphery Plan (*Piano delle Periferie*) was approved, the implementation of which would probably have been postponed if there had not been the great earthquake (November 1980), which led to the early approval of a national law aimed at resolving the housing emergency. Following the Irpinian earthquake, the Extraordinary Housing Plan (*Piano Straordinario di Edilizia Residenziale - P.S.E.R.*) was drawn up as a national law in favour of the earthquake-stricken population.

The city of Naples decided to develop a public housing project that would allow it to intervene in the suburbs and transform them to accommodate thousands of displaced people. The project included the construction of new buildings, the redevelopment of unbuilt areas and, finally, the consolidation and recovery of some existing structures. The plan was, however, part of a series of projects drawn up before the earthquake emergency and united by the same intervention strategy for the areas surrounding the city of Naples. In this way, the construction and development of production facilities and residential complexes for the working class were favoured, thus definitively affecting the survival of local agricultural activities. The eastern periphery of Naples was chosen above all because of all suburban areas, it showed the greatest architectural decay and a high rate of overcrowding. With the funds from the extraordinary plan (P.S.E.R.), it was preferred to invest in newly built structures rather than consolidate and retrofit historical housing estates already in use. In 1981, new housing estates were built in the former autonomous municipalities of San Giovanni a Teduccio, Barra and Ponticelli, which today constitute the Sixth Municipality of the metropolitan city of Naples. This area, which underwent significant development during the Bourbon era, acquired the name 'assembled landscape' in the literature over time, a definition that reflects the history of numerous and fragmented urban interventions [30]. In this area, industrial areas, residential districts, and road and railway infrastructures overlap, many of which are now disused.

Ponticelli, more than any other suburban district, reflects the fragmentation of these interventions, which show themselves in incomplete projects and spatial planning and, unlike the two other districts (San Giovanni a Teduccio and Barra), suffers even more from an awkward geopolitical position, which manifests itself through the absence of services. Due to its nature as a doubly isolated neighbourhood, it was defined as a 'satellite zone' for the city, a sort of residential outpost linking the city centre to the municipalities around Vesuvius (Fig. 4).

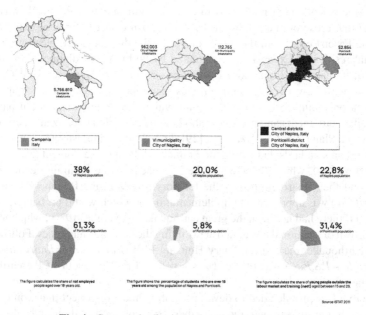

Fig. 4. Case-study district and statistical information

Following the settlement principles of functional autonomy from the urban centre (as in the English *New Towns* model), an attempt was made to build a community, planning oversized services and facilities with a view to constructing a satellite and self-sufficient neighbourhood. Only a small part of these services has been realized, thereby causing the phenomenon of the progressive abandonment of the facilities, not only because of their oversizing but also because of the inability to manage them. Large public containers have become ruins. The population - including pre-settled inhabitants (still tied to agriculture), 'white-collar workers' and the 'new poor' (displaced from the devastated historic centre of Naples in the 'temporary' camps of the 'Bipiani' and the 'Campo Evangelico', temporary asbestos houses which later became permanent residences), enclosed in ghetto districts built of prefabricated concrete and controlled by mafia, did not manage to turn into a community. At present, the legacy of unfinished plans and projects returns a heritage of elements and traces that is complex to stitch together, and in the unfinished spaces and systems of relations that have not been activated yet lies the malleability of a periphery, which is still in the process of finding its identity and its adaptability to the transformations [31].

ISTAT data provided by the Suburban Commission show that Ponticelli is the Italian district with the highest presence of young N.E.E.T. - Not in Education, Employment or Training - i.e. young people between 15 and 25 years of age who do not study and do not work, with strong disillusionment and low expectations for the future. Compared to a national average of 20 per cent, in Ponticelli there are 31 per cent of neet. The absence of employment, the continuous social isolation caused by the lack of services and cultural activities and widespread school dropout have made Ponticelli the neighbourhood with the youngest people who approach organized crime [32]. Indeed, in recent years, wars between clans (not very influential, but numerous) have taken place among the very young, with a youth mortality rate that exceeds other peripheral areas with the same mechanisms of Camorra control of the territory. Among the victims of the Camorra is the young man Ciro Colonna, after whom the Polyfunctional Centre, opened in 2019 in the former primary school in via Curzio Malaparte, is named. This public common was saved from abandonment by various associations, including *Maestri di Strada*, founded over 20 years ago and based its activities on the experimentation of new educational practices to tackle school dropout. The Centre, as well as the close building (see Atelier ReMida), is a site for workshops and activities organized by associations with similar goals: fighting educational poverty and organized crime through art, theatre, cinema and music, but also through research, active citizenship and reuse.

Ponticelli, together with the two districts of San Giovanni a Teduccio and Barra, represents a satellite area that seems far removed from the city centre of Naples, especially from a socio-economic and cultural point of view. But Ponticelli, unlike the other two, suffers even more from this isolation: it has no access to the sea and no sufficient public transport, all embedded in an extremely uneven urban texture. In this context, initiatives that focus on redeveloping public spaces and creating a community stand out. Among them the "Urban Social Garden" (*Orto sociale urbano*) in the Fratelli De Filippo park, which now boasts several European records. Associationism and artivism are a possibility of redemption and hope for the younger generations.

3.2 The Project Viale Delle Metamorfosi – Art Makes Its Way

In the year 2022, from March to October, the *co-creation* method was applied during two workshops organized in Ponticelli, an eastern suburb of the City of Naples (Italy). A long process of art production and performances involved the residents during the project *Viale delle Metamorfosi - Art makes its way*, an urban festival of contemporary arts curated by Collettivo Zero APS. *Viale delle Metamorfosi - Art makes its way* has been realized thanks to the open call *"I Quartieri dell'Innovazione"* promoted by the City of Naples and financed by the European funds PON Metro 2014–20 *"Spaces of Social Innovation – Paths of active inclusion"*. The project investigates the theme of *metamorphosis* through the languages of contemporary art and architecture to create a material and immaterial permanent heritage in the public spaces of the Ponticelli. Through the practice of *co-creation*, three artists were involved in two separate residencies. Each of them conducted research in the area, which led to the production of a new artistic heritage at the Ciro Colonna Polyfunctional Centre. Three artists participated in the project, two middle-career artists involved by invitation, Davide D'Elia and Anna Raimondo, and Edoardo Aruta, selected by open call. D'Elia and Aruta created two new works, both of which were donated to the community of the Ciro Colonna Centre. Anna Raimondo, instead, started a research project on gender issues.

Viale delle Metamorfosi adopts a methodology of participatory planning, in which art and culture stimulate a process of social change to enhance differences and fight stereotypes to build dialogue, networks and alliances with associations and institutions in the area. The aim is to promote and strengthen cooperation and the generation of a common heritage. By relating in particular to the public space of the district, which is often experienced as a limit and not as a "door" to the public city, the interventions, framed in a participatory dimension, do not represent a simple overlay to be inserted in the city, nor exclusively an element of tourist attraction, but rather become an action rooted in society, capable of supporting local identities and building new elements of distinctiveness for Ponticelli. The project aims to: raise awareness on the theme of diversity and listening, invite people to experience public space as a collective value to be regenerated and protected to foster new socio-cultural dynamics and trigger regeneration processes to improve the quality of life and local economies; experiment and disseminate inclusive and aggregative methodologies for communities, capable of developing a sense of identity and belonging to places. Each edition of the festival will develop one of the multiple declinations of the theme of *metamorphosis*, aiming to describe and analyze the dynamics related to the creation of personal identity in relation to social space.

The project is based on the theory of *change management*, a management model with which a transformation is approached through several phases of intervention: investigation, co-evaluation, co-creation, restitution and integration (Fig. 3) (Fig. 5).

The investigation phase engaged Collective Zero in studying the urban and social context and creating a network of associations and various entities. Community contexts are often ideal units of analysis to study the interaction between individual well-being and social sustainability [33], which is still terribly undermined today, especially in the present case, by social exclusion. From the *investigation* phase to the restitution phase, it was possible to use different tools.

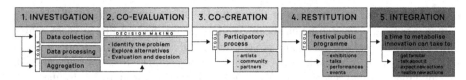

Fig. 5. Five phases applied methodology in the *Viale delle Metamorfosi* project

This phase, which took place in the exploration of the territory and the data collection, gave rise to a dense network of issues and actors that found their place in the process. In the territory analysis phase, we undertook a mapping of stakeholders, institutional and associative, and administered several interviews to residents. Among these stakeholders, many creative realities were present, especially related to street art, music, theatre, dance, art-education and circus arts. The objective was to map local competencies, to understand how services and spaces in the neighbourhood were perceived, what kind of life the people interviewed lived and what their expectations were. Community problems had to be identified, giving residents the opportunity to confirm or overturn project hypotheses. At the end of the stakeholder mapping process, which lasted one year and was conducted live and online, the co-creation phase was activated through three artist residencies, with accompanying workshops and laboratories.

The fundamental phase of *co-creation*, in which the guests of the artist residency program involve the local community in the realisation of their works (*"La Penna, La Spada"*, Edoardo Aruta, 2022 – *"Bravo Alfredo"*, Davide D'Elia, 2022), is part of the above-mentioned methodology. Through a long mediation process in which Collettivo Zero is the activator, the associations operating in the area and within the Ciro Colonna Centre were key stakeholders in the execution of the process. The inclusive logic of co-creation animated the artistic residency, encouraging participants to build relationships of trust with artists and vice versa, to achieve mutual and to face issues related to traditional hierarchies. The aim of Edoardo Aruta's *La penna, la spada* project is to mark the daily life of the Ponticelli district with poems from the Neapolitan tradition: the goal is to punctuate the life of the quarter with the sentiments expressed in the poems of authors from the 16th century to the present day and to form a network of subliminal messages hidden on everyday objects (cutlery, utensils, aprons, bags, dishcloths).

The project aims to 'reach the distracted gaze', to be an invitation to discover alternative memories, to establish associations with the traditional culture to relocate in the neighbourhood the traces of Neapolitan literature, which struggles to reach the suburbs. A wide range of participants attended the co-creation workshop set up by E. Aruta: around twenty residents, including adolescents and adults - including educators and actors from the theatre permanent laboratory, young rappers, and a few interested outsiders - took part in the *'poetic activism exercises'*, experimenting with poetic writing and rap music. This activity aimed to create a relationship between the stories of Ponticelli inhabitants and the contemporary musical trends spread in the city's eastern suburbs. The meeting was aimed at composing musical texts from extracts of traditional Neapolitan poetry. The works created were then donated to the women's enterprise that set up the social canteen project *'Cucinapoli Est'* in the former refectory of the Ciro Colonna Centre.

In June, during his residency at Ponticelli, D. D'Elia introduced into the festival activities personal research he has been carrying out for the past fifteen years, which allowed him to develop a publishing project entitled '*Tiepido Cool*'. The poetic criterion of the work of art is introduced by the title: two perceptions, those of hot and cold, which symbolize two places dear to the artist (London and Rome), felt by the artist as antithetical, highlighting the hot-cold duality on which his work is based. D'Elia - during his stay in Naples - initiated an investigation that allowed him to delve into the generative themes of the work, with a view to participation and co-authorship, activating collaboration processes with project partners. Through them, it was possible to organize a two-day workshop entitled, which involved the young people of the Ciro Colonna Polyfunctional Centre, hosted by its associations. In the workshop, the artist decided to start by introducing the *"Tiepido Cool"* test and then submitting it to the participants. Davide D'Elia's test is made up of 20 boards, each presenting two images, dichotomies formed by abstract images of objects or subjects linked together, such as a pen flanked by a pencil or a cat together with a dog. The 35 participants had to associate each image with the concept of hot or cold, according to their own experience and personal vision; the test, in fact, does not provide correct or incorrect answers but is based exclusively on the spontaneous and instinctive reactions of each person. The different answers allowed the artist to create a dialogue with the participants and create a map of perceptions. The artist then collected the results of the test, which formed the basis for the second part of the workshop, held the following day in the forecourt of the Ciro Colonna Centre. For this activity, wooden boards of different shapes were prepared: rectangular or semicircular, to be combined according to instinct, and vinyl stickers. Once the dichotomies to be used had been chosen, compositions were made with the chosen images, always bearing in mind the Tiepid/Cool diagram and the tension between the perception of cold and heat. The adhesive images proposed by the artist in the form of stencils were applied to the boards, and then the anti-fouling paint, another recurring element in D'Elia's work, was applied. In this work of transforming wood with elements related to metamorphosis, the works, each with its own originality, took shape. The participatory work tried to give young people a sense of doing together, in a logic of co-creation of common heritage, but also a *win-to-win* logic, in which actors and users mutually benefit in the development of cultural actions.

The restitution phase was characterized by a three-day festival (7, 8 and 9 October 2022) in which the artistic interventions resulting from the process, now belonging to the community, were shared with the city. The events presented an opportunity to disseminate the work carried out in the preceding months and discuss the project's key themes with various guests. The festival public program was divided into three sections: exhibitions, talks with experts from different fields (art, architecture, urban planning, education, sociology, etc.) and extra events realized in collaboration with other associations. During the entire festival, each activity was free, except for the social lunches promoted by the association in the canteen of *Cucinapoli-est*. These include two guided tours through late 20th-century architecture and *street art* interventions in the neighborhood, theatre and dance performances and live music. This heterogeneous set of events tells of Collettivo Zero's desire to activate a stable network in East Naples for the construction of new projects. In addition, it declares the intention to activate an awareness-raising process, which in the long term will direct the dissemination of contemporary culture and cultural debate in places of physical and social marginality that are most affected by the distance from the centre of the city, such as the Ponticelli district.

4 Results and Discussion

4.1 Local Cultural Projects: Conflicts and Successes

The project presented in the previous paragraph gathers within it different creative practices linked to the sphere of community engagement through participation (crowdfunding, workshops, laboratories, exhibitions, talks, events, etc.), which are often conducted by civil participants, partners from the third sector and stakeholders to implement the regeneration process. Creative capital, in fact, can optimize local cultural resources to rebuild community relations, values and public spaces in a productive way [34], thus enhancing urban regeneration processes driven by culture and rooted in the territory. In peripheral neighbourhoods such as Ponticelli, which are in a state of substantial social exclusion, creative practices often rise from very small-scale interventions whose goal is to nurture the sense of local identity and cohesion. This is also true for community places that are temporally foreign, as in the case of the Centro Ciro Colonna in Ponticelli. This approach involves combining site-specific 'adaptive recycling' with the reinforcement of social and cultural values rooted at the local level [35].

In the case of *Viale delle Metamorfosi* project, the ability to generate social and affective values, as well as cultural values, around the artistic action and to build an extended network around the Centro Ciro Colonna was very effective. The first served to integrate the various dimensions of the generated value, making it a concrete result of culture-led regeneration. The second served to produce complex network value around a specific local context through 'chain reactions' between culture, economy and processes [36] (Fig. 6).

The preceding paragraphs have shown how the *Viale delle Metamorfosi* project bases its success on solid relations created in the East Naples area. Assessing the complexity of the social and community dimension of the Ponticelli district, it was necessary to apply a multi-criteria ex-ante evaluation using impact matrices. Each element of the matrix represents the performance of each option according to each evaluation criterion. In fact, there is no single 'ideal' solution, but rather compromise solutions, integrating a plurality of technical aspects and social viewpoints in its ex-ante impact assessment. For this reason, the Social Multi-Criteria Evaluation (SMCE) approach can provide a methodological framework in which the phase of comparing the options of a typical ex-ante evaluation, with dimensions, objectives, and evaluation criteria, leads to the coherent aggregation of different information. In the case of *Viale delle Metamorfosi*, the starting point was the power interest matrix generated by stakeholder mapping [37]. Their positioning within the quadrants confirmed the role they could play within the project (Fig. 7).

On this basis, the SOCRATES (SOcial multi-CRiteria AssessmenT of European policieS) method has been applied, which implements the SMCE and uses three fundamental analyses: multi-criteria, equity, and sensitivity analyses. Multi-Criteria analysis requires the definition of alternatives, which in the case of this project, concerns the

Project	Objectives	Benefits from the project impact
Viale delle Metamorfosi Ponticelli district, Naples (Italy) Collettivo Zero APS	- to develop a new sense of identity and belonging to spaces through creative participatory processes; - to experiment and disseminate inclusive and aggregative methodologies for communities; - to activate paths of inclusion through contemporary art and culture; - to minimize exclusion from the socio-cultural and political life of the formal city.	- creation of a new artistic and cultural heritage, both tangible and intangible; - custody/care of the co-created artistic interventions as a legacy of the participatory actions; - implementation of cultural art projects (events, art residencies, exhibitions and culture-led regeneration processes) on the territory; - increased recognition of the value of cultural work produced in the periphery by the central cultural sector; - increased interest of other stakeholders in the area of intervention; - activation of a dense network of collaboration and support in the area of intervention;

Fig. 6. Framework of the *Viale delle Metamorfosi* project with its resulting benefits

Fig. 7. Power Interest matrix in the *Viale delle Metamorfosi* project

choice of the specific process/action to be activated for the involvement of artists in the Ponticelli area. Considering the neighbourhood's complex cultural and social value, it was decided to opt only for qualitative data that emerged from the data collection of the first phase of the investigation. Secondly, relevant dimensions must be defined, which in this case have been selected between the economic, social and cultural dimension.

Dimensions are connected to objectives and criteria: cost of the intervention (to minimize), time of execution (to minimize), involvement of multiple interests (to maximize), visibility of the action (to maximize) and regeneration of places (to maximize). The use of weights as importance coefficients clarifies the role of criteria in the hierarchical structure. The here shown impact matrix includes only qualitative (good/bad) measurements of the performance of each alternative with respect to selected evaluation criteria. After defining this, SOCRATES constructs an outranking matrix. This provides an illustrative visualisation of the comparison between one alternative and another, taking all criteria into account. The final ranking of the impact matrix shows that the preferable alternative is *"More artists: Emerging artist(s) and international artist(s)"*. This alternative was also correctly reflected through the social impact and related dendrogram, within which the stakeholders identified in the previous power-interest matrix were included (Fig. 8).

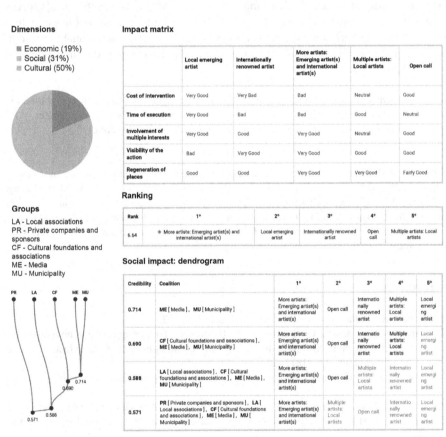

Fig. 8. SOCRATES method applied to the *Viale delle Metamorfosi* project

5 Conclusions

The proposed contribution presents a study started with Collectivo Zero for the realization of the project in question, which, due to the complex territory in which it is inserted, had to continuously adapt to uncertainties. What is common to the good practices already implemented locally are the methodologies and tools of investigation and action integrated and crossed by different disciplines to advance complex projects that enhance a very changing territory. The action taken by the association through art is neither the first nor the only one to have brought contemporary artists to act on the territory, where the decision-making process among the different stakeholders is oriented to the research and identification of shared cultural values. [38] But what this contribution wants to emphasize is the peculiarity of the proposal of *Viale delle Metamorfosi,* which, due to the quality of its methodology and its curatorial nature, extends the social process to contemporary culture. The use of SOCRATES as a multi-criteria tool in evaluation praxis is aimed at carrying out a sensitivity analysis which validates actual practice in the social and cultural field, confirming the outputs that have emerged from the ranking of the models inserted.

Acknowledgements. The obtained results of this research synthesise data collected within the ex-post evaluation process of the *"Viale delle Metamorfosi"* project, made by Collettivo Zero APS (https://www.collettivozero.org/ and https://www.vialedellemetamorfosi.com/).

Author Contributions. The authors jointly conceived and developed the approach and decided on the overall objective and structure of the paper: Conceptualization, M.C. and S.V.; Methodology, M.C. and S.V.; Software, S.V.; Validation, S.V.; Formal Analysis, S.V.; Investigation, S.V.; Data Curation, S.V.; Writing-Original Draft Preparation, S.V.; Writing-Review and Editing, M.C. and S.V.; Visualization, S.V.; Supervision, M.C. All authors have read and agreed to the published version of the manuscript.

References

1. Niessen, B.: Abitare il vortice, 1st edn. UTET, Milan (2023)
2. Cerreta, M., Daldanise, G., La Rocca, L., Panaro, S.: Triggering active communities for cultural creative cities: the "hack the city" Play Rech mission in the Salerno historic centre (Italy). Sustainability **13**, 11877 (2021)
3. Scott, A.J.: The Cultural Economy of Cities. Joint Editors and Blackwell Publishers Ltd. (1997)
4. Anele, R.: Rigenerazione urbana e Progetto sociale, 1 edn. Map Design project (2016)
5. Bodo, C.: World culture report 2000. Cultural diversity, conflict and pluralism. UNESCO (2000)
6. Franceschinelli, R.: Spazi del possibile – I nuovi luoghi della cultura e le opportunità della rigenerazione, 1 edn. Franco Angeli (2022)
7. Bianchini, F., Parkinson, M.: Cultural Policy and Urban Regeneration: The West European Experience, 1edn. Manchester University Press, Manchester (1993)
8. Sacco P., Blessi T.: The Social Viability of Culture-led Urban Transformation Processes: Evidence from the Bicocca District, Milan (2009)

9. Evans, G., Shaw, P.: The contribution of culture to regeneration in the UK: a review of evidence: a report to the Department for Culture Media and Sport (2004)
10. Cerreta, M., Panaro, S.: From perceived values to shared values: a multi-stakeholder spatial decision analysis (M-SSDA) for resilient landscapes. Sustainability **9**, 1113 (2017)
11. Community Arts: The Report of the Community Arts Working Party, Arts Council of Great Britain (1974)
12. Bishop, C.: Artificial Hells: Participatory Arts and the Politics of Spectatorship, 1st edn. Verso, London (2012)
13. Pioselli A.: Arte nello spazio urbano – l'esperienza italiana dal 1968 a oggi, 1 edn. Johan & Levi (2015)
14. European agenda for culture Open Method of Coordination (OMC) working fgorup of EU member States' experts on better access to and wider participation in culture work plan for culture (2011–2014)
15. Cerreta, M., Poli, G., Regalbuto, S., Mazzarella, C.: A multi-dimensional decision-making process for regenerative landscapes: a new harbour for Naples (Italy). In: Misra, S., et al. (eds.) ICCSA 2019. LNCS, vol. 11622, pp. 156–170. Springer, Cham (2019). https://doi.org/10.1007/978-3-030-24305-0_13
16. The Culture Fix: Creative People, Places and Industries, Local Economic and Employment Development (LEED), OECD Publishing, Paris (2022)
17. New European Bauhaus. https://new-european-bauhaus.europa.eu/about/about-initiative_en. Accessed 10 Apr 2023
18. Trione, V., Artivismo: arte, politica, impegno, 1st edn. Einaudi (2022)
19. Documenta 15, press release. https://documenta-fifteen.de/en/press-material/. Accessed 10 Apr 2023
20. Ruangrupa, collective's website. https://ruangrupa.id/en/documenta-fifteen/. Accessed 10 Apr 2023
21. Horvath, C., Carpenter, J.: Co-Creation in Theory and Praxis 2020 – Exploring Creativity in the Global North and Sputh, 1st edn. Bristol University Press, Bristol (2020)
22. Artway of thinking Association, Co-creation methodology. https://www.artway.info/cocreation-methodology. Accessed 10 Apr 2023
23. Vargo, S.L., Lusch, R.F.: Evolving to a new dominant logic for marketing. J. Mark. **68**, 1–17 (2004)
24. Whyte, W.F.: Participatory Action Research. Sage Publications, Thousand Oaks (1991)
25. Mouffe, C.: Art and Democracy: Art as an Agonistic Intervention in Public Space (2007). https://www.onlineopen.org/art-and-democracy
26. Carpenter, J., Horvath, C., Spencer, B.: Co-creation as an agonistic practice in the favela of Santa Marta, Rio de Janeiro. Urban Stud. J. **58**, 1906–1923 (2021)
27. Wacquant, L.: Territorial stigmatization in the age of advanced marginality. Thesis Eleven **91**(1), 66–77 (2007)
28. Heart of Glass & Battersea Art Centre: Considering Co-Creation, report (2021)
29. Castigliano, M.: Progettare città in periferia – La pianificazione di Ponticelli, Volume "Laboratorio trasformare il territorio 2019/20", 1 edn, p. 13. Department of Architecture, University of Naples Federico II (2020)
30. Lucci, R., Russo, M.: Napoli verso oriente, 1 edn. Clean Edizioni (2012)
31. Sunley, Peter, Martin, Ron, Tyler, Peter: Cities in transition: problems, processes and policies. Cambridge J. Reg. Econ. Soc. **10**(3), 383–390 (2017). https://doi.org/10.1093/cjres/rsx018
32. Rapporto della Comm. Parlamentare di inchiesta sulle condizioni di sicurezza e sullo stato di degrado delle città e delle periferie (2016)
33. Cerreta, M., Rocca, L.: Urban regeneration processes and social impact: a literature review to explore the role of evaluation. In: Gervasi, O., et al. (eds.) ICCSA 2021. LNCS, vol. 12954, pp. 167–182. Springer, Cham (2021). https://doi.org/10.1007/978-3-030-86979-3_13

34. Bertacchini, E.: Capital culturel, district culturel et biens communs, In Situ. Au regard des sciences sociales **2** (2021)
35. Gasparrini, C., Terracciano, A.: DROSSCITY. Metabolismo urbano, resilienza e progetto di riciclo dei drosscape, Trento-Barcellona (2016)
36. Cerreta, M., Daldanise, G., Sposito, S.: Public spaces culture-led regeneration: monitoring complex values networks in action. Urbani Izziv (2018)
37. Cerreta, M., La Rocca, L., Micelli, E.: Impact assessment for culture-based regeneration projects: a methodological proposal of ex-post co-evaluation. In: Calabrò, F., Spina, L.D., Mantiñán, M.J.P. (eds.) New Metropolitan Perspectives: Post COVID Dynamics: Green and Digital Transition, between Metropolitan and Return to Villages Perspectives, pp. 501–511. Springer International Publishing, Cham (2022). https://doi.org/10.1007/978-3-031-06825-6_47
38. Cerreta, M., Panaro, S.: Deliberative spatial multi-criteria evaluation (DSM-CE): forming shared cultural values. In: Gervasi, O., et al. (eds.) Computational Science and Its Applications – ICCSA 2017, pp. 747–763. Springer International Publishing, Cham (2017). https://doi.org/10.1007/978-3-319-62398-6_53

Tailored Urban Regeneration Process: A Multi-method Evaluation for Waterfront Brownfield

Maria Lucia Raiola[1]([⊠]) [iD], Gaia Daldanise[2] [iD], and Maria Cerreta[1] [iD]

[1] Department of Architecture (DiARC), University of Naples Federico II, Naples, Italy
{marialucia.raiola,maria.cerreta}@unina.it
[2] Institute of Research on Innovation and Services for Development (IRISS), National Research Council of Italy (CNR), Naples, Italy
g.daldanise@iriss.cnr.it

Abstract. The research aims to outline a tailor-made urban regeneration project for the urban brownfield area of Castellammare di Stabia waterfront, in southern Italy, structuring a multi-methodological and adaptive evaluation approach according to the Social Multi-Criteria Evaluation (SMCE) perspective.

The methodological process is elaborated in three main steps that integrate vertical and horizontal assessments to frame the multiplicity of aspects that characterise an urban regeneration decision-making process for a brownfield area. Starting from identifying environmental, economic and social issues, the proposed approach aims at defining a sustainable development strategy. The expected results consist of the selection of the preferred scenario among the outlined alternatives, spatialised in a multi-scale meta-project for the brownfield area of Castellammare di Stabia waterfront. Integrating quantitative and qualitative dimensions aims to build a decision-making process oriented towards developing an innovative model of well-being for the local community. In addition, the implementation of SMCE, combining the C.I.E. method and the NAIADE method, is an effective tool to support public policies in line with the impact assessment objectives set by the European Commission.

Keywords: Community Impact Evaluation · NAIADE · Urban regeneration · Waterfront · Scenario analysis

1 Introduction

The global crisis has highlighted the limits and criticality of a development model based solely on trade and pure economic return. The crisis is, however, an opportunity to launch a new model of urban development in which the economy is based on the exchange of knowledge and relationships between different actors. Furthermore, the waterfront could be read as part of a coastal zone system, considering the specific functional dimension that affects it, since in medium-sized cities in particular, the role of the waterfront directly influences the functions and image of the city [1]. In the context of small and medium-sized port cities, as in the case study presented below, a key element within the decision support system is the analysis of stakeholders and their needs to identify coalitions between stakeholder groups based on their perceptions [2] and synergies between local authorities belonging to the same coastal zone [3]. In this perspective, waterfront regeneration becomes a re-connection, in a circular perspective of integrated symbiosis that simultaneously involves all levels of relationships and capital, rebuilding and multiplying ties and making the system more resilient, making possible future development in this direction for port cities [4].

The use of integrated approaches can engage cooperation between academia and public authorities and promote integrated, spatially explicit, and strategic urban planning [5]. Through the creation of assessment maps, it is possible to trigger holistic regenerative and cyclical planning processes [6], solving the complexity of problems involving both spatial and environmental issues and social, cultural and economic ones. A significant aspect of the urban regeneration process is played by culture as an integrated and driving component, capable of renewing the synergic and symbiotic between business and territory, empowering citizens and guaranteeing efficiency, effectiveness, and equity [7]. This approach is able to enhance aware forms of a culture focused on people promoting the use of innovation and technology according to local conditions and citizens' needs, defining a complex space of social cohesion, creativity and quality of life, and synergies among natural, rural anche urban areas in which the landscape becomes an innovative action research field [8]. Issues related to environmental, social, and cultural values are assuming an increasing role in the evaluation of reuse projects related to urban regeneration from the perspective of the circular economy, where assessment tools are essential to understand the effectiveness and efficiency of this new model and to evaluate the multidimensional impacts it produces [9]. Investigating, mapping, and assessing the waterfront landscape is part of an approach that, through multidimensional geospatial data, allows us to address contemporary environmental issues and support decision-making related to sustainable management and planning [10], as an expression of a multidimensional interface about the meaning and the role of the different evaluation criteria, that contribute together to the definition of the scenarios, and the combined use of methods and techniques is crucial into tackling the complex decision process, making the evaluation process crucial both in planning and in identifying alternative solution in the spatial decision-making process [11].

Thanks to these processes, land assessment/action is an essential tool to identify possible development scenarios and becomes a method of integrated heritage enhancement for public administrations, according to the perspective of Social Multi-Criteria Evaluation (SMCE) [12]. The social multi-criteria evaluation method used is NAIADE (Novel Approach to Imprecise Assessment and Decision Environments) [13], explicitly designed for public policy, capable of providing appropriate responses to the objectives of efficiency, effectiveness, and consistency set by the European Commission on Impact Assessment [14]. Based on these assumptions, the research aims to identify a tailor-made urban regeneration process through the data spatialization in mapping scenario analysis and structuring an SMCE approach for the waterfront of Castellammare di Stabia, a city on the south coast of the province of Naples (Italy).

The paper is structured as follows: Sect. 2 presents the research methodological approach. Section 3 explores the cognitive framework of the territorial system. Section 4 is dedicated to building a tailor-made evaluation model. Finally, Sect. 5 relates to results, while Conclusions are presented in Sect. 6.

2 Materials and Methods

The methodological framework (Fig. 1) is fleshed out by analyzing hard and soft data, identifying and comparing social and economic transformations and issues with Sustainable Development Goals [15].

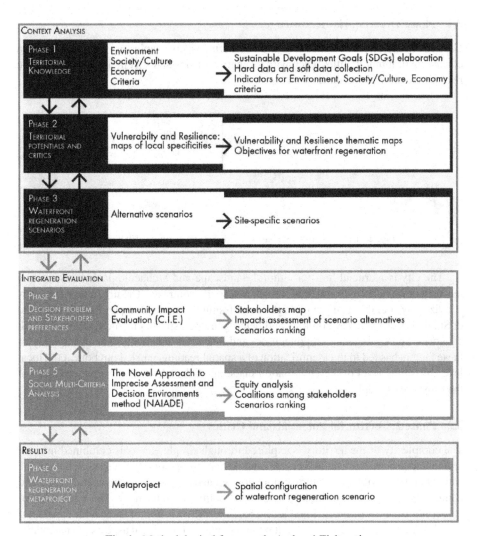

Fig. 1. Methodological framework, Authors' Elaboration

The interpretation of transformative processes and opportunities is made by analyzing the information collected and processed using specific indicators tailor made for the local context to identify the area's potentialities and criticalities concerning environmental, economic, and social criteria.

The primary purpose is to build specific territorial vulnerability and resilience maps, essential for identifying possible regeneration scenarios and elaborating a multi-criteria and site-specific assessment. According to a multi-methodological approach [16], the research addresses a complex decision-making problem.

3   Context Analysis

3.1   Phase 1: Territorial Knowledge

Castellammare di Stabia belongs to the Southern coast of Naples province, a wide area consisting of municipalities, each with its characteristics and specificities, which can be read as a territorial cluster (Fig. 2).

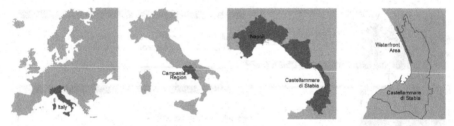

Fig. 2. Location of Castellammare di Stabia, Authors' Elaboration

The city is a crucial hub for cultural, landscape and archaeological tourism and a territory of intense environmental, urban, and social contrasts. The urban fabric is characterized by social housing with high social fragility. The landscape of Castellammare di Stabia is rich in highly complex and heterogeneous aspects in which social, cultural, economic and ecological components act and interact dynamically. The multiplicity of these factors has led to the identification of a spatial reading, carried out both at the local level and at the level of the conurbation made up of the towns of the southern coast of the province of Naples.

3.2   Phase 2: Territorial Potentials and Critics

The complexity of the territory is explored through simple elements combined in more articulated processes to build a careful and respectful reading of the specificities of the context and its population, return a more homogeneous and cohesive general vision and being able to represent the multidimensional quality of the territory. The assessment of vulnerability in multidimensional terms requires the selection of indicators capable of describing the complexity of the context in line with three critical aspects of sustainable development: environment, economy, and society.

Due to the specificity of spatial and territorial dynamics indicators is possible to illustrate and represent the territorial diversity of the natural environment and to assess the related impacts of the urbanization process [17].

The approach is appropriately structured to effectively reflect a synthetic framework for measuring sustainable transformation of the territory, which aims to improve the level of well-being of the entire community. To profile the territory quantitatively and qualitatively in the process of mapping environmental, economic and social vulnerability and resilience, we made use of census data from the Italian National Institute of Statistics (ISTAT) [18] and ISTAT's 8milaCensus [19] indicators built to meet the SDGs, interpolating different quantitative data to give qualitative and more realistic answers about the dynamics of the territory's development.

Two levels of data analysis were carried out for each indicator: first, for the Municipality of Castellammare di Stabia at the census years 1991, 2001, 2011, to understand local development trends; and second on national, regional, and conurbation scale consisting of the Cities and Towns of Naples, Portici, Ercolano, Torre del Greco, Torre Annunziata, and Castellammare di Stabia. In addition, several aspects were investigated in the mapping process: population and household structure, integration of foreigners, land use for housing purposes, housing stock, education level, population activity, unemployment and employment, mobility, and material and social difficulties, which produced thematic maps of spatial dynamics.

Specifically, the ranking of potential material and social difficulties considered the Social and Material Vulnerability Index developed by 8milacensus, which holds together seven different indicators and determines the position of the municipality of Castellammare di Stabia within the ranking of municipalities, allowing the local situation to be compared with other Italian municipalities. The high part of the ranking, where municipalities with a low-rank value are placed, corresponds to a high social and material vulnerability index.

INDICATORS	ITALIA	CAMPANIA	CASTELLAMMARE DIS TABIA	NAPOLI	ERCOLANO	PORTICI	TORRE DEL G RECO	TORRE ANNUNZIATA	VULNERABILIT/RESILIENCI	CRITICAL	POTENTIALS
Social and material vulnerability index	99,30	102,41	103,50	104,90	107,00	102,30	103,80	104,90	●	●	
Position in the municipalities vulnerability ranking	-	1,00	90,00	37,00	5,00	224,00	75,00	38,0	●		●
Improper housing incidence	0,22	0,35	0,20	0,70	0,30	0,20	0,30	0,50		●	●
Large families incidence	1,42	2,83	4,10	3,40	4,80	2,50	3,10	3,70		●	●
Families with potential economic hardship incidence	2,65	7,58	8,00	9,50	11,10	6,10	8,40	9,60	●	●	
Population in ov ercrowed conditions incidence	1,48	3,53	5,60	7,10	10,80	4,40	6,80	8,00	●		●
Young people out of the labor and training market incidence	12,30	20,36	20,70	22,80	27,20	15,90	23,20	24,80	●	●	
Families in need of assistance incidence	3,00	2,24	2,60	2,20	2,10	3,00	2,20	2,41	●	●	

Fig. 3. Potential material and social difficulties: comparisons on a national, regional and coastal scale (Source: 8milaCensus, http://ottomilacensus.istat.it/, Authors' Elaboration)

For Castellammare di Stabia, the social and material vulnerability index has remained relatively constant over the observed years, ranging from 105.0 in 1991 to 103.5 in 2011, remaining within a score range corresponding to 15 per cent of the national corresponding. However, the position within the vulnerability ranking changed considerably during the same observation period: position 651 for 1991, 200 for 2001, and 90 for 2011. This increase in vulnerability can be attributed to a movement of other Italian municipalities, which have activated practices aimed at improving their condition over the years. In the comparison with the other municipalities of the coastal strip analysed, Castellammare di Stabia is, in fact, the one with the lowest level of vulnerability after Portici and quite close to Torre del Greco, distancing itself from the others, which appears to be considerably higher, and therefore more vulnerable. Each indicator was then classified as an element of criticality/potentiality (Fig. 3.) and vulnerability/resilience, which structured the database to elaborate the territorial thematic mapping (Fig. 4).

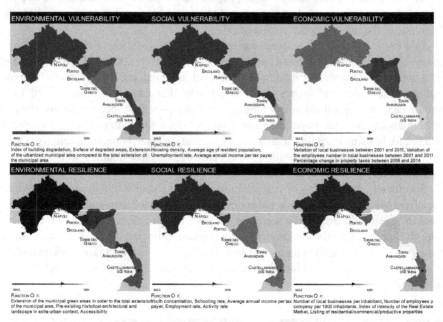

Fig. 4. Thematic maps, vulnerability and resilience (Source: 8milaCensus, http://ottomilacensus. istat.it/, Authors' Elaboration)

3.3 Phase 3: Waterfront Regeneration Scenarios

The exploration of the spatial context that flowed into the development of vulnerability and resilience maps led to the identification of a set of strategic urban regeneration goals for the Castellammare di Stabia's waterfront to 1) Promote a sustainable and innovative production process; 2) Realize a tourism system capable of enhancing environmental and archaeological potential; 3) Improve the quality of housing supply; 4) Implement a functional mix capable of responding to the heterogeneous needs of the social system. The four strategic goals become possible scenarios of sustainable development and regeneration of the waterfront and territorial poles with a specific vocation on which the scenario analysis and multi-criteria analysis focus on identifying the preferable alternative for the specific local context (Fig. 5).

Goal 1, promoting sustainable and innovative production processes, is embodied in the Productive Hub|S1 scenario, in which the implemented activities are commercial, corporate, and of the culture-education sphere, the majority private, with a small percentage public and social linked mainly to the involvement of universities.

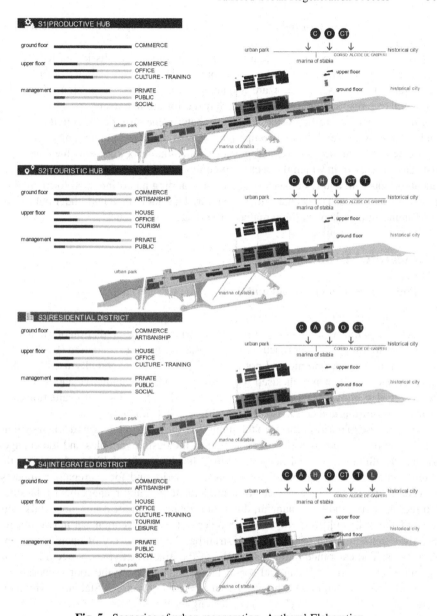

Fig. 5. Scenarios of urban regeneration, Authors' Elaboration

Goal 2, which is related to the tourist reception system, due to the proximity of the new marina, and protected archaeological and natural sites that are part of the World Heritage Sites (Archaeological Excavations of Pompeii and Herculaneum, Sorrento Peninsula, Islands of Capri and Ischia), is related to the Touristic Hub|S2 scenario, which sees an increase in commercial, craft and tertiary activities, increases the residential share, and allocates about one-third of the total activities to tourist reception and hospitality. It is an almost exclusively privately managed scenario.

Goal 3, improvement in the quality of housing supply, results in the Residential District|S3 scenario, where the increase in commercial and craft activities, offices, and the culture and education sector are accompanied by a large proportion of area for residential use, responding to the growing demand for urban housing.

Finally, Goal 4 corresponds to the need for heterogeneous types of activities, which can hold together several distinct components related to different community needs and requirements. Implementing a heterogeneous functional mix generates the Integrated District|S4 scenario, in which the sectors of commerce, handicrafts, offices, culture and education, tourism, and residences are increased, adding a part intended for recreation and leisure activities. The scenario thus configured has more than half under public and social management, leaving the remainder to private management.

4   Integrated Evaluation

4.1   Phase 4: Decision Problem and Stakeholders Preferences

A heterogeneous and complex territorial context requires an assessment model that considers the plurality of elements involved and prioritises the prediction of impacts on the local community. The approach of the Community Impact Evaluation (C.I.E.) [20], which can integrate economic and not economic analysis, was initially used to assess the impacts of the four hypothesised scenarios, combining quantitative and qualitative aspects. It also allows for conducting financial, cultural, and social evaluations and managing coalitions and conflicts between different stakeholder groups.

After a phase of the description of the status quo, the entire regional and urban system, comparison of options, as well as explication of the design variables and the changes associated with them, the analysis phase brings the observed variables and data into the system, producing different matrices for each scenario, and for aggregating impacts. For each scenario, the impacts related to implementation and management (classified as direct financial, indirect financial, direct non-financial, indirect non-financial) were assessed about the objectives of the urban regeneration intervention, set in two macro-objectives: rehabilitation of disused industrial buildings; recovery of open spaces and green areas. The examined variables consist of the mix of activities, space allocation, and interventions on the urban and social fabric characterising the four scenarios for the sustainable regeneration of the waterfront of Castellammare di Stabia, of which the aggregation of these impacts (Fig. 6.) concerning the set objectives follows.

Next, the sector preference assessment was conducted, corresponding to the convenience and interest of each category being part of the producer-operator, and user groups for the four scenarios, resulting in a matrix of results aggregated by sectors (Fig. 7).

Systematizing the results of the aggregate impact matrix with that of sectoral preferences required an additional level of interpretation of the values obtained. Finally, the complexity of the environmental system, the heterogeneity of the needs, and the multiplicity of types of subjects constituting the community led to the elaboration of the information into a structure organized by macro-criteria (economic/financial, environmental, socio-cultural) related to the common goal of the regeneration of the Castellammare di Stabia waterfront (Fig. 8).

AGGREGATE IMPACTS

Objectives	Variables	Scenarios				Realization DF	Realization IF	Realization DNF	Realization INF	Management DF	Management IF	Management DNF	Management INF
RECOVERY OF DISUSED INDUSTRIAL BUILDINGS:	artisanship	1	2	3	4	X				X		X	
	healt care		2	3	4	X		X		X	X	X	X
	bed and breakfast		2		4	X				X		X	X
	libraries	1	2	3	4			X				X	X
	house of the music				4	X		X		X		X	X
	educational didactic center			3	4			X	X			X	X
	commerce	1	2	3	4	X				X		X	
	co-working	1	2	3	4	X		X		X		X	
	hotel		2			X				X			X
	infopoint		2					X				X	X
	environmental research institute			3	4		X	X			X	X	X
	laboratories	1	2	3	4	X				X		X	
	toy library		2	3	4			X				X	X
	sea museum				4	X		X		X	X	X	X
	hostels		2		4	X				X		X	X
	houses		2	3	4	X	X			X	X	X	X
	food activities	1	2	3	4	X	X			X	X	X	X
	work training school	1		3	4		X	X			X	X	X
	social housing		2	3	4	X	X	X	X	X	X	X	X
	offices	1	2	3	4	X				X	X		X
RECOVERY OF PUBLIC SPACES AND GREEN AREAS:	event areas	1	2	3	4	X		X		X		X	X
	play areas	1	2	3	4			X				X	X
	rest areas	1	2	3	4			X				X	X
	bike sharing	1	2	3	4			X				X	X
	thematic gardens	1	2	3	4			X	X			X	X
	green mobility	1	2	3	4			X	X			X	X
	urban gardens	1	2	3	4			X	X			X	X
	parks	1	2	3	4			X	X			X	X

LEGEND:
DF → Direct Financial DNF → Direct Non-Financial
IF → Indirect Financial INF → Indirect Non-Financial

Fig. 6. Community Impact Evaluation (C.I.E.): Aggregate Impacts, Authors' Elaboration

AGGREGATE RESULTS BY SECTORS

Sectors of the community	Comparison between the Scenarios: S1| Productive Hub	S2| Touristic Hub	S3| Residential District	S4| Integrated District
Producers and Operators				
1 municipal administration	more or less good	good	more or less good	very good
2 organisation non-governmental	more or less good	good	good	very good
3 region, metropolitan city	more or less good	good	more or less good	very good
4 private subjects (companies, individuals)	very good	very good	good	good
5 university, research institutes	good	more or less good	more or less good	good
Users				
6 researchers	good	more or less good	more or less good	good
7 traders	good	very good	good	very good
8 self-employmed (company employees, professionals)	very good	more or less good	good	good
9 non-preschool and school-age residents	very good	more or less good	very good	very good
10 residents of the city of Castellammare di Stabia	good	good	very good	very good
11 tourists	more or less good	very good	good	good
12 users of collective equipment	good	very good	good	very good

Fig. 7. Community Impact Evaluation (C.I.E.): Aggregate Results by Sectors, Authors' Elaboration

CRITERIAS	INDICATORS	DIRECTION (max, min)	IMPACT TYPE D/I - F/E/C/S	MEASUREMENT UNIT	CURRENT CONDITION | S0	PRODUCTIVE HUB | S1	TOURISTIC HUB | S2	RESIDENTIAL DISTRICT | S3	INTEGRATED DISTRICT | S4
ECONOMIC - FINANCIAL macro criteria									
PROMOTION OF TOURISTIC CULTURAL ENVIRONMENTAL NETWORKS	Promotion of tourist flows	max	DF, IS, IC	qualitative judgment	-	-	+++	-	+
	Organization of major events and manifestations, exhibitions, shows	max	DF, DS, DC	yes / no	no	yes	yes	yes	yes
	Expansion of accommodation activities	max	DF, IS	qualitative judgment	-	-	+++	-	+
	Strengthening of tourist mobility services	max	DF, IF, IS, IC	yes / no	no	no	yes	no	yes
ENHANCEMENT OF PUBLIC MOBILITY	Improving local accessibility	max	IF, DS	yes / no	no	yes	yes	yes	yes
	Increasing collective public mobility	max	DF, IS	yes / no	no	yes	yes	yes	yes
PROMOTION OF PUBLIC-PRIVATE-SOCIAL PARTNERSHIP	Establishment of new collaborative relationships and partnerships	max	DF, IF	qualitative judgment	--	++	++	+++	+++
	Involvement of non-governmental associations	max	DF, IF, DS, IS	yes / no	-	yes	yes	yes	yes
PROMOTION OF JOB SECTOR	Reduction in the unemployment rate	min	DF, IF, DS, IS	qualitative judgment	+++	---	--	-	--
	Increased activities for the tourism sector	max	DF, IF, IS	m^2	-	0,00	21362 ,20	0,00	4272 ,44
	Increased activities for the culture - education - training sector	max	DF, IF, DS, DC, DE	m^2	--	8408 ,66	2500 ,00	10681 ,10	25634 ,64
	Increase in activities for the craft sector	max	DF, IF, IS	m^2	--	20137 ,43	8054 ,97	8054 ,97	12082 ,46
	Increased activities for the trade sector	max	DF, IF, IS	m^2	--	20137 ,43	32219 ,89	32219 ,89	28192 ,41
	Increase in activities for the tertiary and production sector	max	DF, IF, IS, IE	m^2	--	34316 ,47	10318 ,05	10681 ,10	6409 ,39
PROMOTION OF HOUSING AND SERVICES SECTOR	Increase in residential activity	max	DF, IF, DS, IS	m^2	--	0,00	8544 ,88	21362 ,93	6408 ,66
DEVELOPMENT OF THE REAL ESTATE MARKET DYNAMICS	Increase in market value for premises for productive use	max	DF, IF, IS	yes / no	no	yes	yes	yes	yes
	Increase in market value for residential premises	max	DF, IF, IS	yes / no	no	no	yes	yes	yes
	Increase in market value for office and tertiary premises	max	DF, IF, IS	yes / no	no	yes	yes	yes	yes
ENVIRONMENTAL macro criteria									
ENVIRONMENTAL SUSTAINABILITY EDUCATION	Formation of environmental awareness at pre-school age	max	DS, IS, DE, IE, IC	qualitative judgment	--	+	+	++	+++
	Training and education for the environment and sustainability	max	DS, IS, DE, IE, IC	qualitative judgment	--	+	+	++	+++
PROMOTION OF RESEARCH AND PROTECTION PROGRAMS	Activation of research and environmental protection programs	max	DS, IS, DE, IE, IC	yes / no	no	no	no	yes	yes
REDUCTION OF ENERGY CONSUMPTION	Containment of energy consumption in work activities	min	IF, DE, IE	qualitative judgment	nd	+++	+++	+++	+++
	Use of alternative and renewable energy sources	max	IF, DE, IE	yes / no	no	yes	yes	yes	yes
	Low energy buildings	max	IF, DE, IE	yes / no	no	yes	yes	yes	yes
	"Passive" residences	max	IF, DE, IE	yes / no	no	no	yes	yes	yes
CREATION OF A GREEN URBAN SYSTEM	Re-naturalisation of abandoned green areas	max	IS, DE, IE	m^2	0	116133 ,33	116133 ,33	116133 ,33	116133 ,33
	Creation of play areas	max	DS, IS, DE, IE	yes / no	no	yes	yes	yes	yes
	Construction of parking areas	max	DS, IS, DE, IE	yes / no	no	yes	yes	yes	yes
	Realization of thematic gardens and urban gardens	max	DS, IS, DE, IE, IC	yes / no	no	yes	yes	yes	yes
	Establishment of a public bike sharing service	max	IF, IS, DE, IE	yes / no	no	yes	yes	yes	yes
SOCIO - CULTURAL macro criteria									
PROMOTION OF CULTURAL EDUCATION ACTIVITIES	Activation of educational-educational projects for the school age	max	IF, DS, DE, IE, DC	qualitative judgment	--	+	+	++	+++
	Activation of educational projects for the resident population	max	DS, DE, IE, DC	qualitative judgment	--	+	+	++	+++
SOCIAL REGENERATION OF THE URBAN CONTEXT	Creation of a museum of the sea and industrial tradition	max	DF, IF, IS, DC, IC	yes / no	no	no	no	no	yes
	Creation of spaces of aggregation and relationship	max	DS, IS, IE, IC	yes / no	no	yes	yes	yes	yes
	Creation of common workspaces	max	DF, IF, IS, IE, IC	yes / no	no	yes	yes	yes	yes
	Creation of common craft workshops	max	DF, IF, IS, IE, IC	yes / no	no	yes	yes	yes	yes
	Activation of a public library and book sharing service	max	DS, IS, IE, DC, IC	yes / no	no	yes	yes	yes	yes
	Activation of a public play room service	max	DS, IS, IE, DC, IC	yes / no	no	yes	yes	yes	yes
	Realization of social housing and cohousing	max	DF, IF, DS, IS	yes / no	no	no	yes	yes	yes

Fig. 8. Community Impact Evaluation (C.I.E.): Information Matrix, Authors' Elaboration

The comparison shows that the preferred alternative is Scenario 4 (Fig. 9), which generates positive community impacts in the short and long term in a holistic and sustainable development vision for the coastal zone.

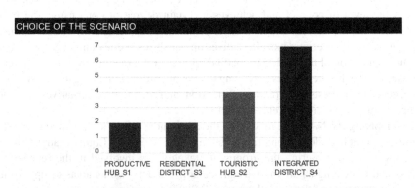

Fig. 9. Community Impact Evaluation (C.I.E.): Chosen Scenario, Authors' Elaboration

4.2 Phase 5: Social Multi-criteria Analysis

NAIADE [13], an acronym for Novel Approach to Imprecise Assessment and Decision Environments, is a multi-criteria assessment method in the fuzzy domain that enables an integrated approach by constructing outperformance relationships between alternatives concerning an assessment criterion with different types of measures, using conflict analysis procedures to be integrated with multi-criteria results. A significant aspect consists in predicting coalitions and conflicts thanks to the different positions of the various groups of actors involved [21].

NAIADE makes it possible to arrive at a defensible and equitable decision, which reduces the level of conflict and achieves a certain degree of consensus. The procedure performs pairwise comparisons of alternatives under each criterion, resulting in aggregation of all criteria; ranks alternatives and analyses social conflicts.

The application of the NAIADE method allows for the ranking of solutions to compromise, sorting the alternatives according to a set of criteria, indicating the possibility of convergence of interests and coalition formation, and sorting the alternatives according to impacts on groups or preferences of actors.

For applying the NAIADE method to the case study, Scenario 0, related to Existing Conditions, was included among the possible alternatives. The Equity matrix (Fig. 10) was constructed by entering the groups of stakeholders involved in the regeneration process and indicating as alternatives all scenarios understood as areas of opportunity for the enhancement of the Castellammare di Stabia waterfront.

GROUPS	ALTERNATIVE Existing Conditions|S0	Productive Hub|S1	Touristic Hub|S2	Residential District|S3	Integrated District|S4
PRODUCERS | OPERATORS					
Local Municipality	PERFECT	VERY GOOD	GOOD	VERY GOOD	PERFECT
Regione Campania	MORE OR LESS GOOD	GOOD	VERY GOOD	MORE OR LESS GOOD	VERY GOOD
Metropolitan City of Napoli	MORE OR LESS GOOD	GOOD	VERY GOOD	MORE OR LESS GOOD	VERY GOOD
Real estate operators	PERFECT	VERY GOOD	VERY GOOD	GOOD	PERFECT
Touristic operators	MORE OR LESS GOOD	MODERATE	PERFECT	MODERATE	VERY GOOD
Nautical operators	GOOD	PERFECT	VERY GOOD	MORE OR LESS GOOD	VERY GOOD
ICT operators	MORE OR LESS GOOD	PERFECT	MORE OR LESS GOOD	MORE OR LESS GOOD	PERFECT
University and Research Institutions	MODERATE	PERFECT	GOOD	GOOD	VERY GOOD
USERS					
Cultural associations	MODERATE	MODERATE	VERY GOOD	VERY GOOD	PERFECT
Social associations	MODERATE	MODERATE	VERY GOOD	VERY GOOD	VERY GOOD
Traders	GOOD	GOOD	PERFECT	VERY GOOD	VERY GOOD
Professionals - corporate employees	GOOD	PERFECT	VERY GOOD	VERY GOOD	VERY GOOD
Resident citizens	GOOD	VERY GOOD	GOOD	VERY GOOD	PERFECT
Non resident citizens	GOOD	MODERATE	GOOD	MORE OR LESS GOOD	VERY GOOD
Young people	GOOD	VERY GOOD	GOOD	VERY GOOD	PERFECT
Tourists	MORE OR LESS GOOD	MODERATE	PERFECT	MORE OR LESS GOOD	VERY GOOD
Users of collective equipments	MORE OR LESS GOOD	GOOD	VERY GOOD	VERY GOOD	PERFECT

Fig. 10. NAIADE: Matrix of Equity, Authors' Elaboration

Each alternative/group intersection corresponds to qualitative output as an expression of judgments of interest to analyse the conflicts between the groups through a linguistic evaluation of the alternatives according to the following scale: perfect/very good/good/more or less good/moderate/more or less bad/bad/very bad/extremely bad.

Each scenario identified contributes to structuring a possible positive-sum regeneration strategy in which the triggered process activates social and economic growth. Consequently, within the NAIADE matrices, the alternatives/scenarios did not receive negative ratings.

The NAIADE software returns the Coalition Dendrogram (Fig. 11) through a fuzzy clustering algorithm, which makes the coalitions and the level of conflict between the groups visualizable, with the relative index for each partnership alternative. Through the dendrogram, it is possible to check the level of agreement of the preferred alternative and, consequently, improve the participation process in collective choices to make the Integrated District scenario for sustainable waterfront development.

The ranking of alternative Scenarios (Fig. 11) presents the Integrated District|S4 as the preferred scenario, which meets the demand for increased activities, services and housing and improved community welfare with a heterogeneous functional mix.

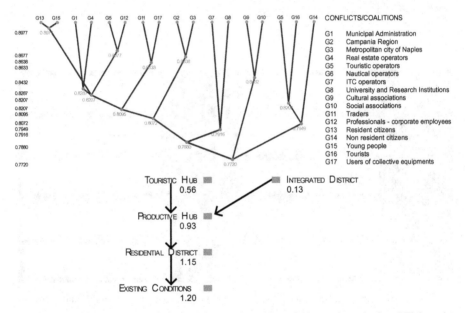

Fig. 11. NAIADE: Dendrogram of Coalitions and Ranking of Alternatives, Authors' Elaboration

5   Results

5.1   Phase 6: Waterfront Regeneration Metaproject

The outcome of the evaluation process for the tailor-made regeneration of the waterfront of Castellammare di Stabia provides an elaboration of Scenario 4, Integrated District concretized in a metaproject vision (Fig. 12), that includes new public and cultural areas obtained from the reconversion of disused industrial buildings; activities able to revitalise the supply of employment and livability thanks to open spaces and new housing;

renewed mobility system, configuring a green infrastructure for the local community. The buildings that accommodate the functional mix of the scenario create a new urban fabric, similar in layout to the already operational and functioning Marina di Stabia Tourist Port hub and draw a novel urban pattern: the built-up areas are punctuated by paved public spaces, connected to the road axis by a green infrastructure that changes continuously.

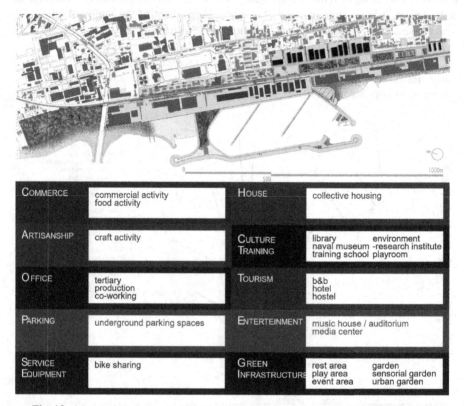

Fig. 12. Metaproject: Integrated District|S4 and Functional mix, Authors' Elaboration

6 Conclusions

The research aimed to structure, through the study of the territory, the mapping operation of vulnerability and resilience, scenario analysis and a multi-criteria social assessment, a site-specific regeneration process for Castellammare di Stabia waterfront, attentive to the needs and requirements of the community and respectful of the local context. Applying the C.I.E. and NAIADE methods in such a complex and heterogeneous context made understanding the conflicts and coalitions that characterize the construction of the decision-making problem more accessible and proved to be an effective decision-making process in achieving consensus by the actors involved. Therefore, the research dimension did not involve more detailed planning and design activities, left to later phases of investigation and work, focusing instead on structuring specific responses to the possibility of activating a process of urban regeneration in an integrated approach that created new connections, relationships and values between the community and the landscape.

Acknowledgement. The paper was developed from the master's thesis work of Maria Lucia Raiola, entitled: "Processi situati di rigenerazione urbana per aree dismesse. Valutazione di scenari per Castellammare di Stabia", Department of Architecture, University of Naples Federico II, tutor: prof. Maria Cerreta.

Author Contributions. Conceptualization, M.C., M.L.R., G.D.; methodology, M.C. and M.L.R.; validation, M.C., M.L.R., G.D.; formal analysis, M.L.R.; investigation, M.L.R.; writing— original draft preparation, M.L.R.; writing-review and editing, M.L.R. and G.D.; visualization, M.L.R.; supervision, M.C. and G.D. All authors have read and agreed to the published version of the manuscript.

References

1. Coccossis, H., Papatheochari, T.: Development of a waterfront regeneration tool to support local decision-making in the context of integrated coastal zone management. Ocean Coast. Manag. **169**, 284–295 (2019). https://doi.org/10.1016/j.ocecoaman.2018.12.013
2. Niavis, S., Papatheochari, T., Coccossis, H.: Supporting stakeholder analysis within ICZM process in small and medium-sized Mediterranean coastal cities with the use of q-method. Theor. Empir. Res. Urban Manag. **14**(1), 53–74 (2019). https://www.jstor.org/stable/265 90929
3. Rempis, N., Alexandrakis, G., Tsilimigkas, G., Kampanis, N.: Coastal use synergies and conflicts evaluation in the framework of spatial, development and sectoral policies. Ocean Coast. Manag. **166**, 40–51 (2018). https://doi.org/10.1016/j.ocecoaman.2018.03.009
4. Attardi, R., Bonifazi, A., Torre, C.M.: Evaluating sustainability and democracy in the development of industrial port cities: some Italian cases. Sustainability **4**(11), 3042–3065 (2012)
5. Somma, M., Campagna, M., Canfield, T., Cerreta, M., Poli, G., Steinitz, C.: Collaborative and sustainable strategies through geodesign: the case study of Bacoli. In: Gervasi, O., Murgante, B., Misra, S., Rocha, A.M.A.C., Garau, C. (eds.) Computational Science and Its Applications – ICCSA 2022 Workshops. ICCSA 2022. Lecture Notes in Computer Science, vol. 13379, pp. 210–224. Springer, Cham (2022). https://doi.org/10.1007/978-3-031-10545-6_15
6. Cerreta, M., Mazzarella, C., Somma, M.: Opportunities and challenges of a geodesign based platform for waste management in the circular economy perspective. In: Gervasi, O., et al. (eds.) ICCSA 2020. LNCS, vol. 12252, pp. 317–331. Springer, Cham (2020). https://doi.org/ 10.1007/978-3-030-58811-3_23
7. Cerreta, M., Daldanise, G., La Rocca, L., Panaro, S.: Triggering active communities for cultural creative cities: the "hack the city" play rech mission in the Salerno historic centre (Italy). Sustainability **13**(21), 11877 (2021)
8. Cerreta, M., Panaro, S.: From perceived values to shared values: a multi-stakeholder spatial decision analysis (M-SSDA) for resilient landscapes. Sustainability (Switzerland) **9**(7), 1113 (2017)

9. Nocca, F., De Toro, P., Voytsekhovska, V.: Circular economy and cultural heritage conservation: a proposal for integrating Level(s) evaluation tool. Aestimum **78**, 105–143 (2021)

10. Mele, R., Poli, G.: The evaluation of landscape services: a new paradigm for sustainable development and city planning. In: Gervasi, O., et al. (eds.) ICCSA 2015. LNCS, vol. 9158, pp. 64–76. Springer, Cham (2015). https://doi.org/10.1007/978-3-319-21410-8_5

11. Cerreta, M., Panaro, S., Cannatella, D.: Multidimensional spatial decision-making process: Local shared values in action. In: Murgante, B., Gervasi, O., Misra, S., Nedjah, N., Ana, M.A., Rocha, C., Taniar, D., Apduhan, B.O. (eds.) Computational Science and Its Applications – ICCSA 2012, pp. 54–70. Springer Berlin Heidelberg, Berlin, Heidelberg (2012). https://doi.org/10.1007/978-3-642-31075-1_5

12. Munda G.: Economic evaluation: the contemporary debate. In: Cerreta M., Concilio G., Monno V. (eds.), Making Strategies in Spatial Planning. Knowledge and Values, 329–338. Serie Urban and Landscape Perspectives. Springer, New York (2010). ISBN 978-90-481-3105-1, e-ISBN 978-90-481-3106-8

13. Munda, G.: A NAIADE based approach for sustainability benchmarking. Int. J. Environ. Technol. Manage. **6**(1–2), 65–78 (2006). https://doi.org/10.1504/IJETM.2006.008253

14. Munda, G.: Qualitative reasoning or quantitative aggregation rules for impact assessment of policy options? a multiple criteria framework. Qual. Quant. , 1–19 (2021). https://doi.org/10.1007/s11135-021-01267-8

15. UN Sustainable Development Goals. https://sustainabledevelopment.un.org. Accessed 10 May 2023

16. Cerreta, M., De Toro, P.: Integrated spatial assessment (ISA): a multi-methodological approach for planning choices. In: Burian, J. (eds.), Advances in Spatial Planning, pp. 77–108 InTech, Rijeka (2012). ISBN 978-953-51-0377-6

17. Cerreta, M., De Toro, P.: Urbanization suitability maps: a dynamic spatial decision sup-port system for sustainable land use. Earth Syst. Dyn. **3**(2), 157–171 (2012)

18. ISTAT Istituto Nazionale di Statistica. https://www.istat.it/. Accessed 10 May 2023

19. 8milaCensus. http://ottomilacensus.istat.it/. Accessed 10 May 2023

20. Lichfield, N.: Community Impact Evaluation: Principles and Practice, 1 edn. Routledge, Abingdon (1996). https://doi.org/10.4324/9780203991282

21. Munda, G.: Multicriteria evaluation in a fuzzy environment: the naiade method. In: Multicriteria Evaluation in a Fuzzy Environment, pp. 131–148. Physica-Verlag, Heidelberg (1995). ISBN 978-3-7908-0892-6, electronic ISBN 978-3-642-49997-5

Exploring Transformative Potentials of Urban Cemeteries Through an Evolutionary Evaluation Approach: The Case Study of "Poggioreale" in Naples (Italy)

Giuliano Poli, Piero Zizzania[✉], Giovangiuseppe Vannelli, and Angela D'Agostino

Department of Architecture, University of Naples Federico II, Naples, Italy
{giuliano.poli,piero.zizzania,giovangiuseppe.vannelli,
angdagos}@unina.it

Abstract. The article analyses theoretical framework and methodological pathways to investigate the potential impacts of transforming cemeteries into multifunctional landscapes that benefit citizens living in urban areas, fostering a paradigm shift in their conceptualisation from "Heterotopia" to "Hypertopia". With recognising of several levels of environmental, health and wellbeing, and cultural services, cemeteries are becoming relevant examples of places which provide citizens with multiple landscape and ecosystem services. This contribution is part of a University of Naples "Federico II" funding project, referred to as "Rethinking lastscapes Perspective", and it aims to investigate people's viewpoints concerning the current state and transformative potentials of Italian cemeteries, with a particular focus on the case study of the "Poggioreale" cemetery system in Naples (Ita-ly). A literature survey has allowed the scientific landscape to be explored relating to urban studies focused on cemeteries. Stated Preference Methods (SPM) and Volunteered Geographic Information (VGI) have been selected as the best-fit methods to be implemented in a preliminary research stage. These qualitative methods were beneficial during earlier phases of evaluations to gather fast feedback, exploration, and pilot testing, from an Evolutionary Evaluation (EE) perspective. Therefore, participants were asked to express their opinions concerning three main topics, considered more consistent with the research purposes: most recurring emotions, potential landscape services, and people's concerns attached to these places. Furthermore, the survey respondents were asked to map the preferred paths during the park visit. The findings are expected to have relevant implications for citizens and policymakers who experience the cemetery as a place supplying multiple potential landscape services.

Keywords: Cemeteries · Multifunctional Landscapes · Evolutionary Evaluation

1 Introduction

Evidence from around the world shows that cemeteries serve purposes beyond their traditional role of burying the dead and commemorating their lives [1]. They also provide cultural and recreational spaces similar to parks [2] and contribute to the vitality and

O. Gervasi et al. (Eds.): ICCSA 2023 Workshops, LNCS 14108, pp. 311–327, 2023.
https://doi.org/10.1007/978-3-031-37117-2_22

health of natural ecosystems for future generations [3], making them similar to green infrastructure, which is a network of natural and semi-natural areas that are strategically planned, designed, and managed to provide a range of environmental, social, and economic benefits to people and wildlife [4, 5].

This contribution is part of a University of Naples "Federico II" funding project referred to as "*Rethinking lastscapes Perspective (R.l.P.)*", and it aims to investigate people's viewpoints concerning the current state and transformative potentials of Italian cemeteries in providing citizens with Landscape Services (LS).

Landscape Services (LS) are the benefits people receive from the land that has been transformed by human activities, i.e.: agriculture, built environment or urbanisation processes [6]. Ecosystem Services (ES) are the benefits that humans receive from ecosystems and have been conceptualised at the foundations of Ecological Economics [7, 8] by expressing the value of natural ecosystems in monetary terms to make Decision-Makers aware of global consequences related to their depletion or lost [9]. The concepts are not interchangeable but should be used according to the contexts and purposes of the studies. LS, indeed, refer to a range of services provided by particular landscape's elements, such as the historical greenery or urban built-up areas with architectural and symbolic value [10–12] which cemeteries offer as places of memory, history, architecture, religion, and collective identity. ES are the benefits that humans receive from nature, such as clean air and water, food production, and climate regulation. On the contrary, LS are often related to the services provided by the landscape, but they extend beyond it to encompass especially the immaterial benefits provided by ecosystems.

Cemeteries can be, thus, conceived as multifunctional landscapes [13] since they integrate nature, culture, history, and social values into spaces which are unique and different from other green urban areas [14].

Inadequate management of cemetery areas can lead not only to problems of maintenance and deterioration of the built heritage but also to the loss of significant ecosystem and landscape services. For this reason, the identification of these services constitutes a fundamental strategy of conservation and valorisation from the perspective of evaluating preferable actions linked to the use of these spaces.

Several frameworks to classify, assess, and map ES and LS have been provided by international expert working groups. Among these, MAES is a framework developed by the European Environment Agency (EEA) to assess the current state of ecosystems and the services they provide for humans [15]. This framework allows for the identification of pressures on ecosystems, their resilience, and the services that ecosystems can provide. Moreover, MAES can help identify the most effective policy measures to ensure the sustainability of interventions by including the mapping and assessment of ecosystems, the classification of their services, and the impact evaluation of programs and planning on their functioning and provisioning. This work helps provide scientific and policy support for the sustainable use and management of landscapes.

The Economics of Ecosystems and Biodiversity (TEEB) represents a further international initiative to draw attention to the global economic benefits of biodiversity, led by Pavan Sukhdev, Special Adviser and Head of UNEP's Green Economy Initiative and Study Leader of TEEB [16]. It evaluates the economic value of biodiversity and ecosystems and how their destruction can hurt the global economy. It also examines how to best integrate the value of nature into decision-making processes at all levels, from local to global.

However, the initiative most consistent with the proposed research is the Common International Classification of Ecosystem Services (CICES), a standardised framework for categorising and describing the various types of ecosystem services that are provided by nature [17]. It was developed by the European Environment Agency (EEA) in collaboration with other international organisations. CICES provides a common language and set of categories for describing ecosystem services, which can help researchers, policymakers, and stakeholders better understand the value of natural systems and make more informed decisions about how to manage and protect them. The classification system is based on a hierarchical structure that includes three levels of detail: divisions, groups, and classes.

At the highest level, CICES includes three main divisions that encompass all ecosystem services: (i) Provisioning services, those that provide products such as food, water, and timber; (ii) Regulation and Maintenance services, those that help to regulate environmental conditions and support the maintenance of ecosystem integrity such as climate, air and water quality, and disease; (iii) Cultural services, those that provide non-material benefits such as recreational opportunities, cultural heritage, and aesthetic values. Each division is further divided into groups and classes, providing a detailed breakdown of the different types of ecosystem services within each category.

The LS classification proposed by Valles-Planells et al. (2014) follows the CICES framework by integrating new groups of services related to daily activities, regulation of the spatial structure, health, enjoyment, self-fulfilment, and social fulfilment.

In this perspective, the LS concept is esteemed to be consistent with the purposes of this research since it promotes interdisciplinary knowledge, assessment of spatial landscape pattern-functioning relationships at a local scale, collaborative tools for practitioners and policymakers [18].

The presented research aims to examine the transformative potentials of cemeteries using participant documentation, survey, and unstructured observations, and it is framed in the Evolutionary Evaluation (EE) first phase referred to as: "Process and Response". The transformative potential was conceptualised in terms of the capacity of cemeteries to provide multiple LS for citizens beyond their standard use. The investigation was addressed to explore people's perceptions related to current conditions, values attached to places, and their possible transformations. The "Poggioreale" cemetery park in Naples (Italy) was selected as a testing area to lay the foundations for the evolution of programs which shape these spaces from "heterotopia" to "hypertopia"[19].

The research questions which motivate this study follow:

- How can Evolutionary Evaluation inform a design process of cemetery spaces to make a paradigmatic change from heterotopia to hypertopia?
- Does the Evolutionary Evaluation provide practitioners and researchers with a best-fit framework to evaluating and planning of transformative scenarios?
- Is it possible to combine Evolutionary Evaluation to Landscape Services, conceived as a boundary object for different disciplines, to explore transformative potentials of urban cemeteries?
- Is there a potential demand of Landscape Services that citizens attach to cemeteries?

– To what extent Landscape Services framework can support Policy-Makers to make a step forward in the management of cemeteries?

The article shows a preliminary investigation of the proposed research questions from the *R.I.P.* project.

The remainder of the paper proceeds as follows: Sect. 2 presents the scientific landscape which links the research issues to the framework of Evolutionary Evaluation (EE); Sect. 3 shows material and methods implemented for the case study of the "Poggioreale" cemeterial system in Naples (Italy); Sect. 4 shows the preliminary results and expands on their implications in the future steps of the research; Sect. 5 concludes the article with limitations and potentials of the proposed approach.

2   The Scientific Landscape

An exploration of the scientific literature relating the studies on Evolutionary Evaluation, Landscape and Ecosystem Services, and cemeteries was performed by means of the software provided by van Eck and Waltman (Eck & Waltman, 2019) and referred to as *vosViewer*, which made it possible to analyse and display an emerging scientific landscape consisting of more than 500 articles.

The search has been led on *Scopus* indexing database, selecting open-access publications in the range 1993–2023. The keywords entered and related logical operators were: ("cemetery" OR "cemeteries" OR "burial sites" OR "memorial park" OR "funerary grounds" OR "graveyard") AND ("landscape services" OR "ecosystem services" OR "integrated assessment" OR "assessment" OR "evaluation" OR "evolutionary evaluation" OR "sustainable design" OR "sustainable planning"). The fields relevant to the research issues have been selected within the categories related to Social Sciences, Arts and Humanities, Environmental Science, Agricultural and Biological Sciences, Engineering, and Energy.

The overall number was reduced to 108 articles, combined from the titles, keywords and abstracts. The most recurring terms are listed in the ranking head: 1. Area (375); 2. Age (229); 3. Burial (226); 4. Population (223); 5. Risk (149); 6. City (147); 7. Burial site (145); 8. Value (127); 9. Soil (120).

The network visualisation in Fig. 1 shows the three clusters of topics which have been detected from database search (Fig. 1): Cluster 1 (blue colour) – Cemeteries have been analysed from a socio-cultural perspective, through surveys on the historical and artistic heritage and investigations on the remains found in the tombs; Cluster 2 (cyan colour) – Cemeteries have been studied from the perspective of risk, especially health risk associated with soils and burial sites; Cluster 3 (green colour) – Cemeteries have been analysed from a regional and urban perspective, highlighting their contribution to the natural ecosystem.

The proximity of two items in the visualisation approximates their relatedness in terms of co-citation links. By selecting the most frequently cited keywords and concepts, it has been feasible to collect and examine literature that is oriented towards specific goals in recent years. The weight of clusters denotes the number of occurrences of the term in the scientific literature. In the period analysed, the articles reporting themes from cluster 1 have been mostly stressed in the United States and Germany. Starting from 2010, the

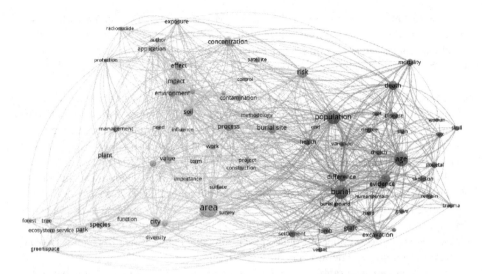

Fig. 1. Graph of the most recurring terms in scientific publications from *Scopus* database in the range 1995–2023.

themes of cluster 2 have been increased and deepened, while research relating to cluster 3 has only increased in the last 5 years, including Italy, Poland, Russia, Canada, and France.

The literature study focus has been shifting towards urban studies in which the spatial dimension has highlighted new research trends underlining the importance of cemeteries as places which provide citizens with ecosystem services, combining "city studies", "plant and biodiversity", "forest and green areas" within the Cluster 3. The development of cities in terms of urbanisation has determined the progressive approach of inhabited centre's boundaries to cemetery areas, that were historically peripheral, and, thus, the need to investigate environmental risks (Cluster 2) and the new role of these areas has emerged in a holistic dimension and multidimensionality of the contemporary city. The scientific landscape has been clearly showing that cemetery areas must be investigated from an interdisciplinary perspective integrating different assessment methodologies to inform programs, projects, and the management of these complex sites. These studies include the socio-cultural and anthropological dimension [20], environmental justice [21, 22], risk assessment [23], and ecosystems and cultural biodiversity [24–26].

Regarding the most common survey-based methods for assessing LS/ES - and, in general, various urban dynamics - the authors have detected the following four categories from the analysis of the scientific landscape: Stated Preference Method (SPM); Contingent Valuation Method (CVM); Choice Experiment Method (CEM); and Citizens Science approaches.

Stated Preference Methods are a type of survey-based research technique that seeks to understand how people value goods, services, or other attributes. These methods involve asking individuals to express their preferences for hypothetical scenarios or choices.

Contingent Valuation Method (CVM): CVM is a survey-based approach that asks people how much they would be willing to pay for a good or service or how much they would accept as compensation for a negative outcome, such as environmental damage. CVM can be used to estimate the monetary value that people place on non-market goods, such as clean air or scenic views.

Choice Experiment Method (CE): CE is a survey-based approach that presents individuals with a series of hypothetical choices between alternatives with different combinations of attributes. By analysing the choices made by participants, researchers can estimate the relative importance of each attribute and the trade-offs people are willing to make between them [27].

Both CVM and CE are widely used in environmental economics and health economics to estimate the economic value of public goods and services.

Citizen Science involves volunteers in scientific research by collecting data and contributing observations [28]. In the context of geographic mapping, citizen science projects can involve volunteers collecting data on environmental features, wildlife habitats, social concerns, feelings, or other aspects of the landscape.

Crowdsourced geographical mapping methods are techniques that involve using volunteers or the general public to collect and contribute geographic data to digital maps. These methods rely on a distributed network of individuals who use mobile devices, GPS units, or other tools to collect, validate, and edit geographic information. Some of the common crowdsourced geographical mapping methods and tools are:

OpenStreetMap (OSM): OSM is a collaborative project that aims to create a free, editable map of the world. Volunteers can contribute data by mapping roads, buildings, points of interest, and other features using OSM's web-based editing tools or mobile applications.

Participatory GIS (PGIS): PGIS is a collaborative approach that involves stakeholders in the process of mapping and analysing geographic data. This approach can be used to support community-based planning and decision-making by giving residents a voice in how geographic data is collected and used [29–31].

Crowdsourced geographical mapping methods have become increasingly popular in recent years due to the widespread availability of mobile devices and the growth of online communities. These methods can be used to create detailed, up-to-date maps of areas that are not well-served by traditional mapping methods, such as remote or underdeveloped regions. However, these methods also present challenges, such as ensuring data quality, addressing privacy concerns, and managing conflicts among contributors.

2.1 The Evolutionary Evaluation (EE) Approach to Assessing LS Cemetery Parks

The Evolutionary Evaluation (EE) concept is a framework for evaluating and assessing the effectiveness of social interventions or programs over time. It is based on the idea that social interventions and programs are complex adaptive systems that are constantly evolving and changing in response to their environment and that the evaluation of these interventions needs to be dynamic and flexible to capture these changes [32]. This concept is concerned with understanding the long-term impact of transformative interventions and programs, as well as how they adapt and evolve over time. It recognizes that planning is often subject to external factors such as changes in policy, funding, and community attitudes, which can impact their effectiveness [33].

The key principles of EE fit with the purpose of this research which is to investigate cemetery visitors' perceptions and needs to provide new design strategies which spark the landscape and ecosystem potential linked to these places.

The EE approach, indeed, gets an emphasis on adaptation and learning processes since evaluators must be open to adapting their evaluation approach in response to changes in the program or intervention being evaluated. Furthermore, the EE promotes collaboration and partnership between evaluators and program stakeholders to ensure that the evaluation is relevant and useful. In addition, the evaluation should consider the multiple variables that influence program success or failure, including social, economic, and environmental factors. In this perspective, the operational frameworks of LS and ES could inform planning and evaluation processes by implementing indicator-based methods to identify, categorise, and assess cemetery potentials to provide multiple benefits for citizens.

The use of the above-mentioned mixed and iterative assessment methods aids in capturing the complexity of the afforded issues and in gathering regular feedback and learning cycles which constantly inform program adaptation and improvement. The commonly used evaluation methods to assess ES and LS can be implemented to categorise and rank the cemeteries according to their capacity in providing services for citizens in an urban context. In the surveyed scientific literature, the most recurring methods to assess ES and LS can be grouped and listed as follows:

1. Economic valuation methods. They involve placing a monetary value on the ecosystem services, usually through methods such as cost-benefit analysis, contingent valuation, revealed preference, travel cost [34], hedonic price models [35], and real estate market changes [36].
2. Qualitative methods. They are used to assess the value of ecosystem services that cannot be quantified in monetary terms, through interviews and surveys, focus groups, and other qualitative approaches [37]
3. Biophysical methods. These methods measure the physical quantities of ecosystem services. Examples include remote sensing and field-based measurements of primary production, wildlife population surveys, water quality monitoring, and urban wetlands [38].
4. Modelling approaches. These methods involve the use of computer models to simulate the flow of ecosystem services over time, based on data from multiple sources. Examples include ecosystem services models, landscape models, and ecological surveys [39] which use Geographic Information Systems (GIS) for spatial analysis and data visualisation.

The authors have implemented qualitative methods as a starting point for their research on the transformative potentials of cemeteries in the urban context of Naples (Italy). Overall, the EE concept provides a framework for evaluating new design strategies for cemeteries that acknowledge their complexity and the need for a flexible, dynamic approach to evaluation. Figure 2 show the main steps of EE - as proposed by Urban et al. (2014) - which relate programs to evaluation, as follows:

- "Process and Response" relates to "Initiation"
- "Change" relates to "Development phase"
- "Comparison and control" relates to "Stability"
- "Generalizability" relates to "Dissemination"

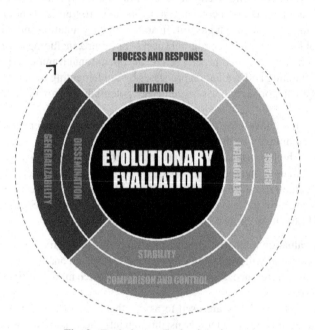

Fig. 2. Evolutionary Evaluation phases.

This contribution aims to show the first step of EE referred to as "Process and Response" by which the preliminary findings of people's feelings and perceptions about cemetery spaces have been investigated.

3 Materials and Methods

The proposed methodology aims to provide Decision-Makers with a framework to make a step forward in the valorisation and management of cemeteries by recognising the LS that these places can supply to citizens. As part of the above-mentioned *R.l.P.* interdisciplinary research, the contribution aims to show the results obtained from two qualitative methods, namely the Stated Preference (SP) method and Volunteered Geographic Information (VGI), implemented through a georeferenced survey for cemetery visitors. In particular, the methodological workflow in Fig. 3 shows the preliminary phase of the research which has been related to the first step of the EE framework (Fig. 3).

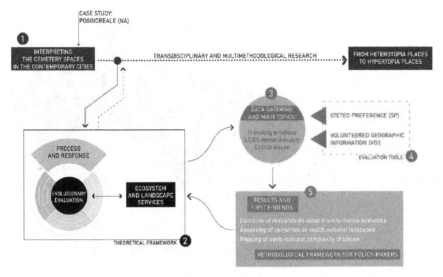

Fig. 3. Methodological workflow.

The methodological steps are as follows:

- Step 1. Problem definition and research purpose. Starting from the main goal of R.l.P. project, which aims to trigger cemeteries transformation from Heterotopia to Hypertopia, the problem statement related to this contribution has been defined in terms of suggesting management models which include LS and ES. In this step, the case study of Naples cemeterial system of "Poggioreale" (Italy) has been selected as a testing area;
- Step 2. Theoretical framework. Three theoretical frameworks and evaluation approaches have been selected for this research: the Evolutionary Evaluation, Landscape Services, and Ecosystem Services.
- Step 3. Data gatering and main topics. The primary topics to be explored have been established as: prevailing emotions linked to cemeteries, demand and supply of landscape and ecosystem services, and critical issues and visitor's concerns.
- Step 4. Evaluation tools. Two qualitative methods were esteemed to be useful to obtain results: Steted Preference (SP) method and Volunteered Geographic Information (VGI).
- Step 5. Results and first findings. The preliminary results from SP and VGI were provided to expand the goal and address the future research steps.

Next Sections show the case study and results from the methodology Step 4.

3.1 The Case Study

The burial sites laying on the "Poggioreale" hill in Naples (Fig. 4) structure a complex urban system. Starting from the ancient city centre toward north-east, coherently with a process of expulsion of burial sites from the city of the living since 1763, 11 cemeteries have transformed the hill.

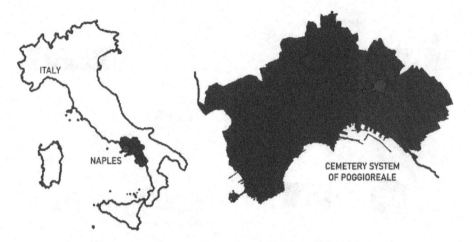

Fig. 4. Location of the "Poggioreale" cemetery in Naples (Italy).

Following the extraordinary "Cimitero delle 366 fosse" by Ferdinando Fuga, the east-side of Naples has been enriched of many different burial sites conceived for different religions, for diverse economic status, and as a response for health crises. Beyond this, the 11 enclosed citadels dedicated to the dead establish different relationships with the surrounding neighbourhood and with both the landscape of the hill and the landscape that from the hill can be perceived: the Neapolitan Bay. Moreover, the "Poggioreale" cemeteries system bear witness to different historical phases through many design approaches that have originated the 11 enclosed cities of the dead. Nowadays, the whole complex system of cemeteries is framed by the urban expansions traceable back to the last century. This urban area is made of walls enclosing mono-functional architectures generating a deep marginalisation in terms of public space, green areas, and, more generally, cultural infrastructures. This urban sector of the city could benefit from the cemeteries system if this would be reconsidered. In this direction, a first step could be the insertion of the foreseeable "Poggioreale" park within the protected area referred to as "Parco delle Colline Metropolitane" in Naples [40]. Such an envisaged political shift could be an operative way to experiment the theoretical shift from Heterotopia to Hypertopia.

4 Results

Within the R.l.P. project, the SPM was operationalised through on-field multiple-choice survey for the "Poggioreale" cemetery visitors and users. Interviewers were asked to express their opinions concerning three main topics, considered more consistent with the research purposes: most recurring emotions, potential landscape services, and problematics concerned with shaping cemeteries into multifunctional parks. Furthermore, the survey respondents were asked to map the preferred paths during the visit.

Next Sects. 4.1 and 4.2 show the preliminary results from SPM and VGI.

4.1 Stated Preference Method: Most Recurring Emotions, Potential Landscape Services, and Respondents 'Opinions

As show in Fig. 5, the sample of responding users is mostly over 55 years old, while less than 20% of respondents are under 25 years old. The respondents are 86% Neapolitan.

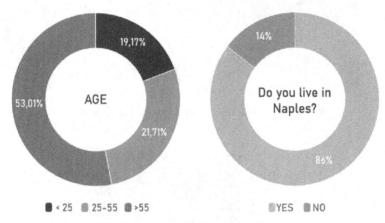

Fig. 5. Age and residency of respondents.

Subsequently, the mode of travel was investigated, highlighting how the majority of citizens find it easier and more convenient to reach the cemetery with their own private vehicle (Fig. 6).

Regarding the uses of the cemetery area, a particularly significant data is reported in Fig. 7, which shows that more than 60% of users visits cemetery solely to visit the graves of their relatives, highlighting the traditional prevailing use. Furthermore, only 20% of the sample identified green areas as relevant services, while the most recurring response was related to the need for basic utilities, e.g., benches and seats and internal mobility services.

In relation to the development scenario of a multifunctional park, respondents were asked if they believed it was possible to imagine a more open cemetery and to motivate their response. As show in Fig. 8, the collected answers were divided into three groups corresponding to three possible scenarios deduced from the collective imagination. Indeed, 59.76% believe that the cemetery should remain closed, only improving the services connected to the cemetery function. The 40.24% of the sample show a greater inclination towards negotiating the cemetery space, and it is distributed as follows: 17.07% propose to implement spaces for relaxation and existing services, also in the logic of an urban park; while 23.17% foster a more open vision of the cemetery, also implementing existing functions (such as play areas for children, refreshment areas, etc.), always emphasizing the need to think in terms of compatible uses. Indeed, over 80% of respondents are concerned that a more open and multifunctional cemetery scenario may desecrate the place and disturb funeral rituals, increasing the risk of profanation of graves.

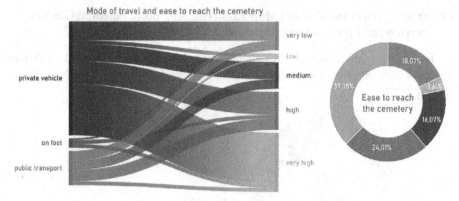

Fig. 6. Mode of travel and ease to reach the cemetery.

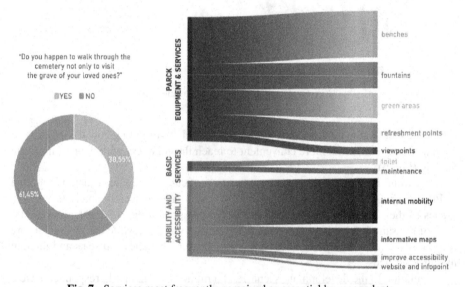

Fig. 7. Services most frequently perceived as essential by respondents.

An overview of gathered responses showed that the prevailing emotions linked to the place remain melancholy and sadness. Many people highlight feelings of peace and serenity associated with cemetery spaces. Often, the anger emotion is mentioned, which is linked to the lack of services or poor maintenance of some areas of the cemetery (Fig. 9).

The preliminary results highlighted the need to investigate the cultural issues underlying the cemetery collective consciousness to build a methodological tool to assess new design perspectives generating outcomes exportable in different contexts.

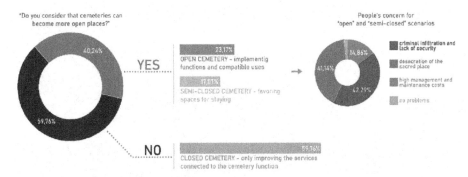

Fig. 8. Three scenarios for urban cemetery and people's concerns.

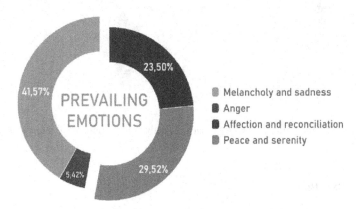

Fig. 9. Prevailing emotions attached to the cemetery by respondents.

4.2 Volunteered Geographic Information

On-field interviews have been conducted using a mobile digital support, and respondents were asked to mark on the cemetery map some particularly significant points and the main paths taken. The collected data was processed with the software Q-GIS into an heatmap of the most frequent markers (Fig. 10).

This allowed the visualization of areas with a higher number of signals due to the presence of famous persons tombs, viewpoints, or monuments. The most frequented paths correspond to the main internal roads of the cemetery, confirming that it is mainly used to reach the graves.

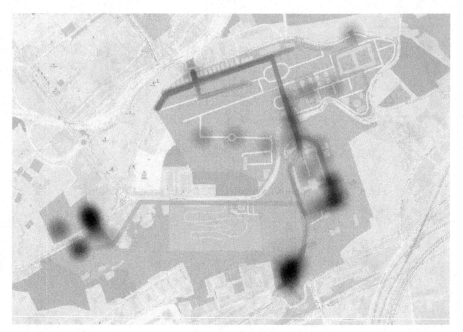

Fig. 10. Crowdsourced map of most recurring paths and points of interests sketched by respondents.

5 Conclusions

The results achieved in this preliminary phase of the wider *R.I.P.* project, implementing the EE approach, provide a general theoretical framework capable of organising guidelines from experts of different disciplines and the demands from citizens to support policymakers in the development of the design process for cemetery spaces from Heterotopia to Hypertopia. This approach, combined with the concepts of LS and ES, has allowed the construction of a methodological proposal capable of investigating the current conditions and guiding the construction of transformative scenarios for cemeteries.

The implemented methodology has indeed demonstrated that there is a real demand for landscape services from citizens. The collected data were useful in understanding the main social and cultural issues related to cemetery spaces and how cemeteries are used in Naples today. Furthermore, they clearly highlight how the different transformative hypotheses and proposed scenarios need to be informed by a wider multidimensional and transdisciplinary process of evaluation and investigation of the transformative potential of urban cemeteries. In conclusion, LS identification and mapping can be suitable approaches to manage recreational landscape that offers cemetery visitors a place to reflect, learn, and appreciate nature.

The findings of this study are expected to have relevant implications for citizens and policymakers who experience cemeteries as potential areas of multiple landscape services provision. Limitations include the small sample size and the use of self-reported measures. Nonetheless, qualitative methods implemented in this research were particularly useful during earlier phases of evaluations to gather fast feedback, exploration, and pilot testing, in an Evolutionary Evaluation perspective.

References

1. Kowarik, I., Buchholz, S., von der Lippe, M., Seitz, B.: Biodiversity functions of urban cemeteries: evidence from one of the largest Jewish cemeteries in Europe. Urban For. Urban Green. **19**, 68–78 (2016). https://doi.org/10.1016/J.UFUG.2016.06.023
2. Lovell, S.T., Taylor, J.R.: Supplying urban ecosystem services through multifunctional green infrastructure in the United States. Landsc. Ecol. **28**, 1447–1463 (2013). https://doi.org/10.1007/S10980-013-9912-Y/TABLES/2
3. Nocca, F., De Toro, P., Voysekhovska, V.: Circular economy and cultural heritage conservation: a proposal for integrating Level(s) evaluation tool. Aestimum **78**, 105–143 (2021). https://doi.org/10.36253/AESTIM-10119
4. McClymont, K., Sinnett, D.: Planning cemeteries: their potential contribution to green infrastructure and ecosystem services. Front. Sustain. Cities. **3**, 136 (2021). https://doi.org/10.3389/FRSC.2021.789925/BIBTEX
5. Sallay, Á., Mikházi, Z., Tar, I.G., Takács, K.: Cemeteries as a part of green infrastructure and tourism. Sustainability **14**, 2918 (2022). https://doi.org/10.3390/SU14052918
6. Vallés-Planells, M., Galiana, F., Van Eetvelde, V.: A classification of landscape services to support local landscape planning. Ecol. Soc. **19** (2014). https://doi.org/10.5751/ES-06251-190144
7. Costanza, R., et al.: The value of the world's ecosystem services and natural capital. Nature **387**, 253–260 (1997). https://doi.org/10.1038/387253a0
8. Costanza, R., et al.: Changes in the global value of ecosystem services. Glob. Environ. Chang. **26**, 152–158 (2014). https://doi.org/10.1016/J.GLOENVCHA.2014.04.002
9. Daily, G.C., Matson, P.A.: Ecosystem services: from theory to implementation. Proc. Natl. Acad. Sci. **105**, 9455–9456 (2008). https://doi.org/10.1073/PNAS.0804960105
10. Girard, L.F., Nocca, F.: Climate change and health impacts in urban areas: towards hybrid evaluation tools for new governance. Atmosphere (Basel) **11**, 1344 (2020). https://doi.org/10.3390/ATMOS11121344
11. Zaccone, M.C., Santhià, C., Bosone, M.: How Hybrid organizations adopt circular economy models to foster sustainable development. Sustainability **14**, 2679 (2022). https://doi.org/10.3390/SU14052679
12. Iodice, S., Toro, P. De, Bosone, M.: Circular Economy and adaptive reuse of historical buildings: an analysis of the dynamics between real estate and accommodation facilities in the city of Naples (Italy). Aestimum **2020**, 103–124 (2020). https://doi.org/10.13128/AESTIM-8476
13. Cerreta, M., Inglese, P., Malangone, V., Panaro, S.: Complex values-based approach for multidimensional evaluation of landscape. In: Murgante, B., et al. (eds.) ICCSA 2014. LNCS, vol. 8581, pp. 382–397. Springer, Cham (2014). https://doi.org/10.1007/978-3-319-09150-1_28
14. Rae, R.A.: Cemeteries as public urban green space: management, funding and form. Urban For. Urban Green. **61**, 127078 (2021). https://doi.org/10.1016/J.UFUG.2021.127078
15. Mapping Europe's ecosystems (MAES) — European Environment Agency. https://www.eea.europa.eu/themes/biodiversity/mapping-europes-ecosystems/mapping-europes-ecosystems-maes. Accessed 11 May 2023
16. The Economics of Ecosystems and Biodiversity (TEEB)—Italiano. https://www.isprambiente.gov.it/it/attivita/biodiversita/documenti/the-economics-of-ecosystems-and-biodiversity-teeb. Accessed 11 May 2023

17. Haines-Young, R., Potschin, M.: Common International Classification of Ecosystem Services (CICES) V5.1 and Guidance on the Application of the Revised Structure. https://cices.eu/. Accessed 04 May 2023
18. Termorshuizen, J.W., Opdam, P.: Landscape services as a bridge between landscape ecology and sustainable development. Landsc. Ecol. **24**, 1037–1052 (2009)
19. Vannelli, G., D'Agostino, A., Occhiuto, R.: Ripensare i lastscapes. Da spazi altri a spazi pubblici: ipertopie al di là dei recinti. Ri-Vista. Res. Landsc. Archit. **19**, 102–119 (2021)
20. Długozima, A., Nejman, R.: Attractiveness of cemeteries versus socioeconomic and spatial development of non-metropolitan cities in Poland. Acta Sci. Pol. Adm. Locorum. **21**, 83–104 (2022). https://doi.org/10.31648/ASPAL.6824
21. Bennett, G., Davies, P.J.: Urban cemetery planning and the conflicting role of local and regional interests. Land Use Policy **42**, 450–459 (2015). https://doi.org/10.1016/J.LANDUS EPOL.2014.08.011
22. Blanks, J., Abuabara, A., Roberts, A., Semien, J.: Preservation at the intersections: patterns of disproportionate multihazard risk and vulnerability in louisiana's historic African American cemeteries. Environ. Justice. **14**, 1–13 (2021). https://doi.org/10.1089/ENV.2020.0044
23. Gonçalves, V., Albuquerque, A., Carvalho, P., Almeida, P., Cavaleiro, V.: Groundwater vulnerability assessment to cemeteries pollution through GIS-based DRASTIC index. Water **15**, 812 (2023). https://doi.org/10.3390/W15040812
24. Larcher, F., Battisti, L., Gullino, P., Pagotto, U., Devecchi, M.: Cemeteries as important urban green spaces: ecosystem services provided by trees in "Cimitero Parco" (Turin, Italy). Acta Hortic. **1331**, 159–164 (2021). https://doi.org/10.17660/ACTAHORTIC.2021.1331.22
25. Długoński, A., Dushkova, D., Haase, D.: Urban cemeteries—places of multiple diversity and challenges. a case study from Łódź (Poland) and Leipzig (Germany). Land **11**(5), 677 (2022). https://doi.org/10.3390/land11050677
26. Quinton, J.M., Duinker, P.N.: Beyond burial: researching and managing cemeteries as urban green spaces, with examples from Canada. Environ. Rev. **27**, 252–262 (2019). https://doi.org/10.1139/ER-2018-0060
27. Cerreta, M., Daldanise, G., Di Girasole, E.G., Torre, C.M.: A cultural heritage low entropy enhancement approach: an ex post evaluation of creative practices. Sustain. **13**, 1–22 (2021). https://doi.org/10.3390/SU13052765
28. Cardone, B., Di Martino, F., Senatore, S.: Improving the emotion-based classification by exploiting the fuzzy entropy in FCM clustering. Int. J. Intell. Syst. **36**, 6944–6967 (2021). https://doi.org/10.1002/INT.22575
29. Cerreta, M., Mazzarella, C., Somma, M.: Opportunities and challenges of a geodesign based platform for waste management in the circular economy perspective. In: Gervasi, O., et al. (eds.) ICCSA 2020. LNCS, vol. 12252, pp. 317–331. Springer, Cham (2020). https://doi.org/10.1007/978-3-030-58811-3_23
30. Somma, M.: New tools to analyse the wastescapes of the cities: the case study of the metropolitan city of Naples. Lect. Notes Civ. Eng. **146**, 171–179 (2021). https://doi.org/10.1007/978-3-030-68824-0_18/FIGURES/4
31. Somma, M.: towards regenerative wasted landscapes: index of attractiveness to evaluate the wasted landscapes of road infrastructure. Geoj. Libr. **128**, 297–310 (2022). https://doi.org/10.1007/978-3-030-78536-9_19/TABLES/3
32. Urban, J.B., Hargraves, M., Trochim, W.M.: Evolutionary evaluation: implications for evaluators, researchers, practitioners, funders and the evidence-based program mandate. Eval. Program Plann. **45**, 127–139 (2014). https://doi.org/10.1016/J.EVALPROGPLAN.2014.03.011
33. Urban, J.B., Linver, M.R., Thompson, J., Davidson, R., Lorimer, D.: Evaluating youth character development programs using evolutionary evaluation and the systems evaluation protocol. Appl. Dev. Sci. **22**, 245–257 (2018). https://doi.org/10.1080/10888691.2017.1285236

34. Alberini, A., Kahn, J.R.: Handbook on Contingent Valuation. Elgar Pub, Cheltenham (2006)
35. Park, J.H., Lee, D.K., Park, C., Kim, H.G., Jung, T.Y., Kim, S.: Park accessibility impacts housing prices in Seoul. Sustainability **9**, 1825 (2017). https://doi.org/10.3390/SU9020185
36. De Toro, P., Nocca, F., Renna, A., Sepe, L.: Real estate market dynamics in the city of naples: an integration of a multi-criteria decision analysis and geographical information system. Sustainability **12**, 1211 (2020). https://doi.org/10.3390/SU12031211
37. Poli, G., Daldanise, G.: Creative ecosystem services: valuing benefits of innovative cultural networks. In: Gervasi, O., et al. (eds.) ICCSA 2021. LNCS, vol. 12954, pp. 193–209. Springer, Cham (2021). https://doi.org/10.1007/978-3-030-86979-3_15
38. Pan, M., Hu, T., Zhan, J., Hao, Y., Li, X., Zhang, L.: Unveiling spatiotemporal dynamics and factors influencing the provision of urban wetland ecosystem services using high-resolution images. Ecol. Indic. **151**, 110353 (2023). https://doi.org/10.1016/J.ECOLIND.2023.110305
39. Villaseñor, N.R., Escobar, M.A.H.: Cemeteries and biodiversity conservation in cities: how do landscape and patch-level attributes influence bird diversity in urban park cemeteries? Urban Ecosyst. **22**, 1037–1046 (2019). https://doi.org/10.1007/S11252-019-00877-3/TABLES/4
40. D'Agostino, A., Vannelli, G.: Soils' tales, recycling beyond death: the Parco Cimiteriale di Poggioreale towards possible extensions. Upl. - J. Urban Plann. Landsc. Environ. Des. **4**, 113–134 (2019). https://doi.org/10.6092/2531-9906/6615

Landscape-Based Fire Resilience: Identifying Interaction Between Landscape Dynamics and Fire Regimes in the Mediterranean Region

Jinlai Song, Daniele Cannatella[✉], and Nikos Katsikis

Delft University of Technology, 2628 CD Delft, The Netherlands
J.SONG-6@student.tudelft.nl, {D.Cannatella, N.Katsikis}@tudelft.nl

Abstract. Wildfires are widely viewed as key evolving inputs of Mediterranean ecosystem. But anthropogenic climate changes and other socioecological recessions have transformed normal wildfire into megafire. The paradigm shift is needed since the suppression capacity has been increasingly overcome from the fire department. This research is aiming to integrate diverse landscape dynamics and fire regimes, to interpret the interactions between them and identify a series of heterogeneous fire typologies in the Mediterranean region in order to support the application of landscape-based approaches. By classifying the land system dynamics into meteorologic, physiographic, biological and anthropogenic indicators (in relation with wildfire ignition and propagation), geographic information system based approaches and statistic analysis are applied to create diagnostic mappings. The results establish 10 types of landscape-based fire typologies which can be used as the decision support tool to prioritize risk mechanism and then lead to mitigate wildfire risk by changing contextual territorial elements in landscape system in order to create an integral long time territorial design.

Keywords: Mediterranean land system · wildfire regimes · landscape dynamics · land cover · fire management

1 Introduction

The Mediterranean ecosystem is a unique and diverse environment that has been formed by natural and anthropic processes. Wildfires are an important input to this ecosystem, as they play a critical role in maintaining biodiversity and reshaping the landscape (Pausas et al. 2008). In recent years, normal fires have become increasingly destructive since the growing climate activism and social movements, leading to severe natural and socioeconomic damages. Although such catastrophic events have been apparent and partly-solved for some time, contemporary wildfire management policies in Mediterranean climate regions have continued to focus almost entirely on short-sighted fire suppression-led reaction (Curt and Frejaville 2018). They are seeking to minimize burned area in the short-term during the crisis-happening phase and react to public opinion with ever-expanding investment in firefighting capacity, while failing to adequately and proactively address the underlying causes of the problem. This can result in extensive damage with loss of life, property damage, and environmental degradation. The paradigm shift and pragmatist approach are urgently needed (Moreira et al. 2020) when confronted with the demand to coexist with wildfire in Mediterranean Basin. It is also the privileged area for a broad scale with geo-information and geo-modelling based study.

The high urbanization rate of most bordering countries in Mediterranean Basin (Aggestam and Pülzl 2018), coupled with a widely known sensitivity to natural hazard, the persistence of old agricultural practices, and the diversity of ecosystems form a high and local complex heterogeneity landmark ensemble (Egidi et al. 2020). Events such as political instability also have significant impacts on the region's human-environment balances. Large-scale spatial implications can result from changes in land use patterns, displacement of people, and disruption of traditional practices. In this context, the landscape-based fire typologies are defined as the unique but homogeneous combination of natural or artificial factors interacts with wildfire regimes that makes landscape distinctive. Then the ignition and propagation of wildfires change within these diverse amalgamations on spatial and temporal scales.

Recent work has begun to investigate the comprehension of historical wildfire and spread patterns change in non-linear processions (Sequeira et al. 2020). New prevention landscape approaches aiming for predicting fire behaviours and providing basic information for management are called landscape-based fire scenarios which refer to multiscale land-type planning units for a fire generation model with different applications at national (Montiel Molina and Galiana-Martín 2016), regional (Molina et al. 2019) and local (Sequeira et al. 2020) scale in Spain. The Mediterranean Basin as a fire-prone area is all the more fantasized, as it is almost never studied as a whole (Darques 2015).

In this paper we work on a broader Mediterranean scale among complex landscape and atmospheric heterology, and create an integrated method of accumulating all the landscape reality in a vertical direction spatially (from subsoil to climatic factors). By exploring the relationship between landscape dynamics and fire regimes through meteorological, physiographic, biological and anthropogenic perspectives, we can identify landscape typologies in relation with fire behaviors, determine their spatial distributions and even represent the Mediterranean land system with the context of wildfire risk. The result of typology definition creates manageable units that can be used for policy making and decision support tool, monitor changes in dynamic values in order to develop the potential approaches in reducing territorial vulnerability and facilitating adaptation and resilience of wildfire in a holistic and proactive way.Subsequent paragraphs, however, are indented.

2 Theoretical Basis

The theoretical underpinning expounded in this paper serves to contextualize the classification of indicators for fire-landscape interaction and to establish the foundation for the methodology. The terminology of pyrogeography as an emerging discipline provides the intellectual framework of this research to understand and classify the complexity of fire and landscape index on in a global context. It enables currently isolated scholars studying varied aspects of fire to add value to each other's work. (Krawchuk et al. 2009; Roos et al. 2014). Such a synergy of perspectives is crucial given the increasing evidence that current fire management paradigms are unable to cope with the manifold challenges associated with wildland-urban interface, and the rural exodus leaving behind abandoned and increasingly flammable land-use systems, increasingly severe fire weather under the global climate change, and finally the increasing tension between biodiversity conservation and fire management objectives (Kruger 2014; O'Connor et al. 2011). What's more, the field of landscape character assessment establish certain assumptions and evaluate the landscape accordingly (Meeus 1995). While risk management cycle including preparedness, mitigation, prevention, response and recovery provide continuous perspective for evaluating landscape typologies and the direction to build upon the upcoming strategies. Finally, socio-economic-spatial structure reinterprets the movement and state policy differentiation on wildfire management, which becomes a crucial anthropic variable characterizing landscape features.

3   Material and Methods

3.1   Study Area

The study area is defined within a spatial extent in the European part of Mediterranean Climate Regions by focusing on areas surrounding the Mediterranean Sea in north side that share similar atmospheric and biophysical characteristics (see Fig. 1), as it describes the approximate extent of representative Mediterranean natural and political communities (Olson et al. 2001). Peninsulas of Iberian, Apennine, Balkan and Anatolia are included in this extent. The average density of the Mediterranean countries exceeds

Fig. 1. Study area (partially France, Portugal, Italy, Spain, Croatia, Bosnia & Herzegovina, Montenegro, Albania, Turkey; completely Monaco, Greece, Malta, Cyprus)

100 inhabitants/km^2, making it among the regions with highest human influence. The ecoregion is characterized by the Mediterranean specific regional features: a climate of hot dry summers and humid, cool winters. The surprising hilly landscape contains high mountains and rocky shores, thick scrub and semi-arid steppes, coastal wetlands and sandy beaches as well as a myriad of islands dotted across the sea.

3.2 Landscape Classification

The landscape dynamic in relation with fire regimes are classified into four main groups incorporating in 14 sub-variables. The first group of meteorological perspectives includes air temperature, humidity and wind speed. Then the physiographic indicators changes in slope, south aspect and elevation. The biological group covers fuel cover intensity, soil moisture and river density. The last group of anthropogeny are comprised by WUI(wildland and urban interface), population vulnerability (population exposed in WUI), road density, land use change and forest management intensity.

The spatial vehicle of variables are operated on a 10*10 km grid within the extent of study area in order to meet the average resolution of raster data. Thus, the goal of identifying fire patterns on a resolution able to capture the spatial variability of fire-environment interactions in heterogeneous landscape mosaics.

3.3 Spatial Analysis of Territorial Dynamics

Meteorological Change. Mediterranean climate is characterized by high temperatures and low relative humidity during the summer months which can create conditions conducive to the ignition and rapid spread of wildfires (Syphard et al. 2009). The presence of dry fuels, such as dead vegetation, can further increase the risk of fire. The timing and distribution of precipitation occurs during the winter season, leading to a build-up of vegetation and fuel for fires during the dry summer months. This creates a situation in which wildfires can quickly spread and become difficult to control. Wind speed and direction can also have a significant impact on wildfire behavior. High-pressure systems can create dry and windy conditions while during the winter months, low-pressure systems can bring wet and windy conditions that can make fire suppression efforts more difficult.

Physiographic Conditions. Specific mountain areas in the Mediterranean region of the European part where topography influences wildfire behaviors include the Pyrenees, the Alps, and the Apennines (Pérez-Sanz et al. 2013; Tinner et al. 2000). These mountain ranges have a range of elevations, slopes, and aspects. For example, steep slopes and south-facing aspects in the Pyrenees and Alps can create conditions conducive to wildfire ignition and spread, while higher elevations in the Apennines can provide cooler and moister conditions that reduce the risk of fire. In addition to these larger mountain ranges, there are also smaller, isolated mountainous areas in the Mediterranean region, such as the mountains of Corsica and Sardinia. These steep canyons or ridgelines that can create chimney-like conditions that accelerate fire spread (Clarke et al., 1994).

Biological Diversity. The study area is characterized by a high degree of biological diversity, with a range of plant and animal species that have adapted to the unique climatic conditions of the region (Pausas and Vallejo 1999). Wildfires shapes these ecosystems with many species having evolved to thrive in fire-prone environments. Mediterranean pine trees and eucalyptus have developed thick bark and serotinous cones that allow them to survive and regenerate after fire. High-intensity wildfires can lead to significant tree mortality, reducing tree cover density and altering the structure and composition of forest ecosystems. In addition, fires can cause changes in hydrological conditions, increasing the risk of soil erosion and altering water quality (Bodí et al. 2014). Specific river valleys and soil types can be particularly vulnerable to the impacts of wildfire, with erosion and sedimentation leading to decreased biological diversity and degraded ecosystem services.

Anthropogenic Uncertainties. HumSans and fuel are important parts of the system and that reciprocal effects exist between many components of the system (Riley et al. 2019). Firstly, the wildland-urban interface (WUI) in Mediterranean countries is characterized by a mix of land uses, challenging topography, and limited infrastructure and resources, which pose significant challenges for managing wildfire risk (Mitsopoulos et al. 2015). In southern Spain, the WUI is characterized by the extensive development of tourist resorts and urban areas along the coast, which are located in close proximity to natural areas. Additionally, the abandonment of agricultural production has led to a proliferation of wildland areas that are more susceptible to wildfire. Since the beginning of the 20th century, economic development has lead to a massive abandonment of agricultural land in Mediterranean regions (Nainggolan et al. 2012). In Spain and Portugal this evolution has been quite dramatic resulting in the abandonment of many marginal lands due to both heavy stocking reduction and crop abandonment. The selective abandonment of marginal agriculture land in more mountainous areas and the concentration of crop fields in valley bottoms near urban centres can lead to an increased homogeneity of (semi-)natural land use/cover types, such as shrublands and forests.

3.4 Data Description

More data and data with higher thematic and spatial resolution were available for the European part of the region (Table 1). The following criteria were used when choosing the data: 1). Highest spatial resolution; 2). Data were as recent as possible and kept almost in the same temporal scale; 3). Data underwent validation. This way we could ensure independence of the data and later analyze how the occurrence of land systems relates to population distributions. All input maps were resampled to 10*10 km grid in an Lambert equal area projection.

Table 1. Data used in indicators categories.

Categories	Factors	Units	Format	Resolution	Source
Meteorological	wind speed	m s-1	raster	3 km	New European Wind Atlas
	humidity	kg kg-1	raster	0.5° × 0.5°	Copernicus Climate Change Service
	annual temperature	K	raster	0.5° × 0.5°	Copernicus Climate Change Service
Physiographic	slope	degree	raster	30 km	Copernicus
	aspect	N-NE-E-SE-S-SW-W-NW, Flat	raster	30 km	Copernicus
	elevation	m	raster	30 km	Copernicus
Biological	fuel density	% proportion of total forest from land area	raster	1 km	European Forest Institute
	soil moisture	Soil Moisture Index (SMI) 0–1	raster	5 km	EEA geospatial data catalogue
	river density	m	polyline	/	HydroSHEDS
Anthropogenic	WUI proportion	Percentage of cell area (%)	raster	1 km	EFFIS
	population vulnerability	Percentile (%)	raster	1 km	EFFIS
	road density	m	polyline	/	European Environment Agency
	land-use change	/	polygon	/	CORINE Land Cover
	forest management intensity	/	raster	1 km	BBN session

3.5 Methods and Techniques

Considering fire typologies as landscape units which are defined through the analysis and interpretation of quite diverse territorial factors, geographic information system based methods perform a spatial analysis of the area attributes of homogeneity (Galiana-Martín and Montiel-Molina 2011). The landscape indicator groups in the extent of Mediterranean are resampled in the spatial vehicle of 10 km*10 km grid, which allows the normalization of fire-prone data intervals. Clustering analysis are used for the aggregation of feature similarity which is based on the set of attributes in order to find the spatially correlated landscape patterns (Wu 2004) (see Fig. 2).

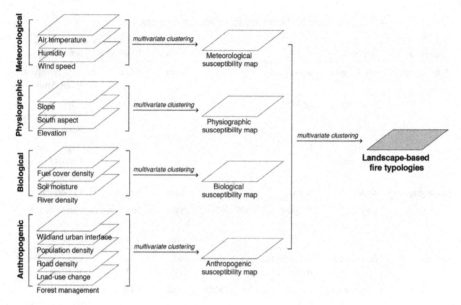

Fig. 2. GIS-base methodology

4   Results and Discussion

4.1   Landscape-Based Fire Typologies

The diagnostic map of landscape-based fire typologies in terms of both composition and configuration is one of the main outputs of this research that is shown in Fig. 3 and 4. Figure 5 illustrates the proportion of each typology in the extent of whole study area and their dominant features, which is also the basis for naming and grouping. Wildfires are produced and interact with identified ground realities among each of the landscape typologies, corresponding to part of Mediterranean land system features simultaneously (Blondel 2006).

Settlement Distribution. The typology of urban interface mixed with unmanaged wildland is characterized by the peri-urban areas have expanded into previously successive uninhabited wildland. Socio-economic trends in Europe towards more urban land use in rural regions and shrub encroachment are resulting to spatial change of interface (Modugno et al. 2016). The human properties are placed at high risk of woodlands and shrubs as the source of fuel for wildfires. Most of this type of landscape is often found at the foothills of south Alps and Apennine and middle Portugal. The second typology in this group is characterized by a combination of densely populated coastal areas and vegetation that is highly flammable under several transitional climate types and sub-types. The vegetation has a high concentration of oils and resins, making them highly combustible. For instance, Holm oak (Quercus ilex L.) is a climazonal species along the western Mediterranean, mostly in Croatian coast. Aleppo pine (Pinus halepensis Mill.) is a typical Mediterranean species that accounts for about 10% of all forests in the Mediterranean (Rosavec et al. 2022). The fragmented villages with multiple rainfed agricultural

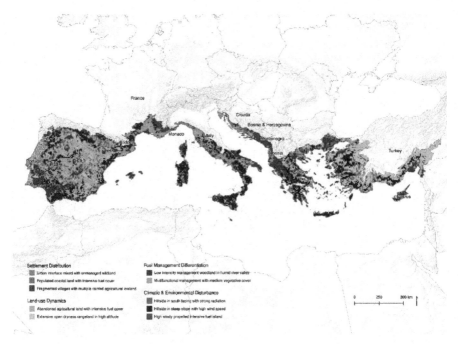

Fig. 3. Mediterranean landscape-based fire typologies

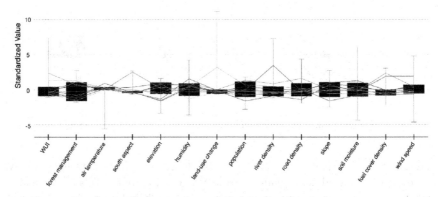

Fig. 4. Plot-box statistic of each variables

lowland type is basically distributed in the river basin of Guadiana and southern Tagus. The clustered villages among intensively used croplands, rangelands and seminatural lands parallel with altered fire regimes tend towards ecosystem process.

Land Use Dynamics. The typical Mediterranean region often shows human pressure affects the landscape characteristics through littoralisation, intensive agricultural practices, land abandonment, urban sprawl, and tourism concentration which leads soil deterioration and Land Use/Land Cover Changes (LULCCs) (Bajocco et al. 2012). This

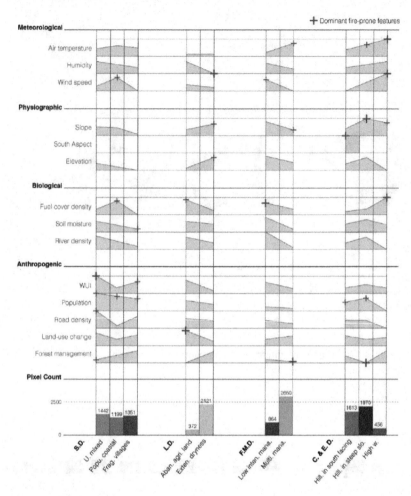

Fig. 5. Dominant features of each landscape-based fire typologies

trend can be reflected in the fire typology of abandoned agricultural land with intensive fuel cover in the inland depopulation area in Spain and Portugal. This land abandonment results in unmanaged vegetation prone to fire and then, leading the soil erosion, deforestation and habitat fragmentation. In the Anatolia peninsula and Balkan regions, the next fire typology is identified as the extensive open rangelands with dry, arid conditions in remote areas with a lower population density. These areas are typically used for grazing livestock and are often located at high altitudes, where temperatures are cooler with lower potential evapotranspiration and vegetation is sparse. Wildfires in these areas tend to spread quickly due to the lack of vegetation and can be difficult to control.

Fuel Management Differentiation. Sustainability and multifunctionality have been the guiding European forest policy models (Aggestam and Pülzl 2018) within which

forest management with local conditions has been embedded in fire typologies definition. In this case, the river valleys of Durance in France, the Pindus Mountain ridge
in Greece, and the Montenegro mountains areas are characterized as the next fire type.
This close-to-nature management covers across large, interconnected areas may lead
some natural wildfire ignitions. But at the same time, they are often located in a high
river density context, where humid basin can help to prevent fires from spreading. The
type of multifunctional management with medium vegetative cover is mainly distributed
in the inland of Spain and northern Greece. The vegetation there exhibits fragmented
patterns mixed with multifunctional and intensively managed forests which are aiming
to more than one objective occurring e.g. timber, water production, erosion protection,
biodiversity, climate mitigation and adaptation and recreation (Nabuurs et al. 2019).

Climatic and Environment Distribution. The last group of fire typologies characterization shows their specialities in hillside and archipelagos. One of the hillside types
with particularly obvious landscape feature that is under the south facing hillside with
strong radiation which promotes fire ignition and propagation. The pattern in dark blue
represents the fire type of hillside in steep slope and canyons with high wind speed
which illustrates some similarities with Mediterranean mountain system and often consistent with dense fuel configuration e.g. the Sistema Central in Spain and Portugal, the
Apennines, and the Pindus Mountain in Greece. The devastating fires are associated
with short episodes of severe fire weather generated by hot and dry winds (Moritz et al.
2010). Noteworthy, hillside should not be considered as the isolated landscape feature
in fire typologies. The smallest proportion typology of high windy propelled intensive
fuel island shows its speciality in the Aegean archipelago and Malta. Of the various
types of vegetation that make up the forests and woodlands on the islands, fire statistics
indicate that most of the blazes occur in the Turkish pine (Pinus brutia) forests and, to
a somewhat lesser extent, in shrub lands (Ne'eman and Trabaud 2000). Prevention of
fires on the islands, including the use of prescribed burning, is relatively inadequate, and
public participation in fire prevention remains limited.

4.2 Representation of Land System

Contemporary landscapes are contingent outcomes of past and present patterns, processes and decisions (Rounsevell et al. 2012). Thus, the land system is central to understand the relationship between human and environment. Some researches have previously
combined territorial indicators to classify land use systems, touching less with natural
crisis. The biomass in Anthropocene on global scale has been mapped by Erle C. Ellis
(Ellis 2011), which framed a systematic classification of the hybrid socio-ecological
fabric associated with the long and continuous human use of the earth's surface. The
result from Tomáš Václavík (Václavík et al. 2013) reveals diversity across the global land
system archetypes. European scale characterizations are mapped by Christian Levers etc.
(Levers et al. 2018) and reflected as the land-system archetypes and archetypical change
trajectories mainly within cropland, grassland or mosaic systems. Our approach moves
forward the existing classification systems by accounting for the land system conditions
with their specific landscape disturbance for the Mediterranean region. The 10 typologies

in the groups of settlement distribution, land-use dynamics, fuel management differentiation, climatic & environmental disturbance reinterpret the Mediterranean landscape at the first time under a novel semantic system of wildfire risk, revealing another way of understanding territorial realities (Fig. 6). Considering the possible degradation of landscape value and the loss of the cultural pattern in the Mediterranean region (Čurović et al. 2019), this identification of fire-landscape system could also put the existing characteristics in a dynamic process of climate change, ecosystem evolution and settlement emigration.

4.3　The Population Susceptibility

In the European Mediterranean regions, there exists a complex interrelationship between fire and population density. Although the effectiveness of higher population densities in keeping fire incidence low decreased in the last decades (Moreira et al. 2023). The phenomenon of high population and housing density has been still found to increase the likelihood of anthropogenic ignition due to the accumulation of fuel resulting from agricultural abandonment or even deliberate field cleaning in some areas (Chergui et al. 2018). Consequently, such regions are more prone to frequent fires that pose significant threats to human lives and infrastructure. Conversely, post-fire changes in the landscape may trigger settlement emigration (Henriques and Khachani 2006).

　　The population's vulnerability to certain factors is visually represented in Fig. 7 through the juxtaposition of population density data from 2020 with the previous diagnostic map (see Fig. 3), aiming to investigate the distribution of human settlements across various fire-landscape types. The fragmented rural settlements are mostly located in the typology 4, which is abandoned agricultural land with intensive fuel cover, particularly in central Portugal and peri-urban of Madrid in Spain (see Fig. 7,a,b). The changes of productive land ("baldio" and "dehesa") in the Iberian peninsula have been bringing highly mixed of village, cropland and forest which altered the fire regimes (Maranon 1988). The littoralization process of Mediterranean countries shows obviously in Spain and southern France (see Fig. 7, b). Urban clusters in these areas are overlayed with the typology 1,2 and 9 corresponding to the specific contexts. The typology 1 that presents wildland-urban interface appears more in the peripheral metropolis of central Italy (see Fig. 7,c) where changes in the socio-economic context have widely influenced the expansion of high- and medium-density settlements shaping a complex fringe landscape(Salvati et al. 2014). The interface type can also be seen in peri-urban of Athens (see Fig. 7,e), Lisbon and Coimbra (see Fig. 7, a). The densified urban areas along the Dinaric Alps mountain range are reflected in the typology with steer slope where the huge topographic differentiation propels fire into the human settlements (see Fig. 7, d). The inhabitants of the islands located in the Aegean Sea and western Anatolia are susceptible to the hazard under conditions of high wind-propulsion, as classified as typology 10 (see Fig. 7, e).

4.4　Application of Results for Wildfire Risk Management

The results of this research on the interplay between fire regimes and landscape dynamics in Mediterranean Climate Regions of the European part have produced a diagnostic map and typologies catalogue with significant implications for wildfire risk management.

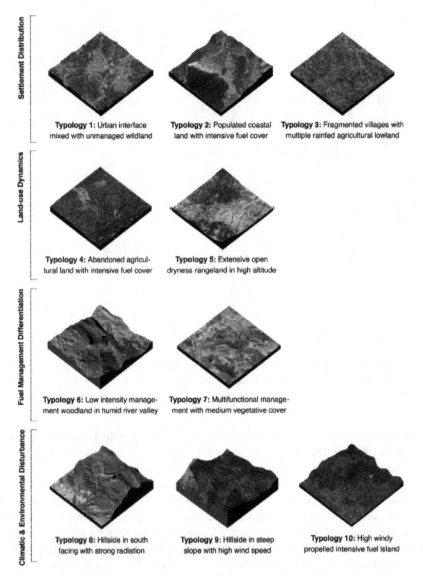

Fig. 6. Representing landscape system in relation with fire in Mediterranean Climate Regions (EU part)

This aggregation of territorial realities offers a novel methodology for characterizing fire hazard and landscape interaction that accurately identify the most risk-prone areas and can inform proactive and effective strategies. The fire-landscape types delineated in the map can be employed as a framework for implementing multiple landscape-based approaches to mitigate fire risk, including fuel reduction treatments (Collins et al. 2010), prescribed burning (Fernandes and Botelho 2003), vegetation management, and other measures tailored to the specific landscape typology. In addition, the visualized and

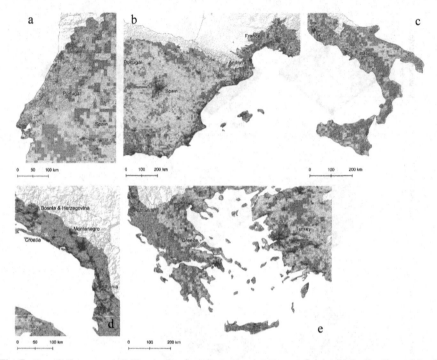

Fig. 7. Population susceptibility in key locations (central Portugal, central Spain, littoral Spain and French, central and southern Italy, the Dinaric Alps, part of Greece and western Anatolia peninsula)

represented typology study and spatial patterns can serve as a decision and negotiation support tool with stakeholders in wildfire risk management, enabling stakeholders to better understand potential risks and prioritize management actions.

Furthermore, the defined typologies are provided with a discrete class assigned to each pixel and thus ignore within-pixel heterogeneity. So that downscaling works are necessary pursuing sub-nations, regional and local investigation in diverse contexts that follows the same method. By developing relatively high-resolution models, for example 1 km*1 km grid, it is able to quantify substantial spatial variation in the key driver of some of the most costly wildfire in some specific locations. Macro-scale fire fisk variables exhibit a wide spectrum of complexity (Williams and Abatzoglou 2016) in global earth system, which also need to embed with necessitate quantitative modelling to better understand future fire responses. Furthermore, to enhance our comprehension of the territorial susceptibility that contribute to the occurrence and disturbance, e.g. flooding, erosion, over-exploitation etc., these models facilitate the identification and assessment of areas at greatest natural hazards to examine scenarios of land-use trajectories and inform targeted management plans.

4.5 Data Uncertainties

The presence of semantic inconsistencies arising from the combination of various remote sensing and modelling products can result in inaccuracies in datasets (Fritz and See 2008). In the present study, the spatial resolution differences across the datasets have been mitigated to a certain extent via resampling and reassignment. However, the primary source of uncertainty in the data is attributed to temporal scale variations. On one hand, it may limit its use in applications where shorter-term biodiversity or ecosystem changes prevail. For instance, fuel cover density data comes from EU forest map, version 2011. But its highly related fuel management intensity data is generated during 2019 (Nabuurs et al. 2019). On others, of the climatic variables under consideration, the precipitation index and annual average temperature are derived from the mean value spanning from 1979 to 2019 but the wind speed index for the same time period is absent.

The outputs of diagnostic map and statistic result provide a new methodology of territorial data assimilation to typify the spatial composition and configuration of fire-landscape in the extent of Mediterranean Climate Regions in European part. The characteristics of each typology cannot be only observed and measured by single sensors since the complexity and heterology of territorial systems. The iterations of data are required in the attributes of upcoming fire-landscape typology research under the same proposed method in order to ensure the accuracy of the clustered result.

5 Conclusion

Wildfires in the Mediterranean bioregion are widely reviewed as the crucial part of its ecosystem for centuries. In fact, the landscape system and the fire regimes have been evolving interactively which needs to be investigated in a comprehensive process. By understanding of Mediterranean pyrogeography, the dataset is developed by the perspective of meteorology, physiography, biology and anthropogeny based on a fire-prone data interval in order to reinterpret the fire-landscape interaction as a system. The output of this reidentification map reveals 10 fire-landscape typologies and their spatial distribution in the Mediterranean, which improves the understanding of land system with natural crisis and is a basis for assessment of future changes under the regional climate, land use and land cover change and changes in management intensity. It also provides a evaluation and decision support tool in some specific locations for fire management, biodiversity protection and conservation of landscape values. Thus, the downscale works of analysis are still needed for bridging the disconnection between Mediterranean research and landscape design practice. The prospective use cases must additionally account for the geopolitical and socio-cultural context of the region in question, as a means of establishing an integrated framework for fire management.

References

Aggestam, F., Pülzl, H.: Coordinating the uncoordinated: the EU forest strategy. Forests **9**(3), 125 (2018)

Bajocco, S., De Angelis, A., Perini, L., Ferrara, A., Salvati, L.: The impact of land use/land cover changes on land degradation dynamics: a Mediterranean case study. Environ. Manag. **49**, 980–989 (2012)

Blondel, J.: The 'design' of Mediterranean landscapes: a millennial story of humans and ecological systems during the historic period. Hum. Ecol. **34**, 713–729 (2006)

Bodí, M.B., et al.: Wildland fire ash: production, composition and eco-hydro-geomorphic effects. Earth Sci. Rev. **130**, 103–127 (2014)

Chergui, B., Fahd, S., Santos, X., Pausas, J.G.: Socioeconomic factors drive fire-regime variability in the Mediterranean Basin. Ecosystems **21**, 619–628 (2018)

Clarke, K.C., Brass, J.A., Riggan, P.J.: A cellular automation model of wildfire propagation and extinction. Photogramm. Eng. Remote. Sens. **60**(11), 1355–1367 (1994)

Collins, B.M., Stephens, S.L., Moghaddas, J.J., Battles, J.: Challenges and approaches in planning fuel treatments across fire-excluded forested landscapes. J. Forest. **108**(1), 24–31 (2010)

Čurović, Ž, Čurović, M., Spalević, V., Janic, M., Sestras, P., Popović, S.G.: Identification and evaluation of landscape as a precondition for planning revitalization and development of mediterranean rural settlements—Case study: Mrkovi Village, Bay of Kotor, Montenegro. Sustainability **11**(7), 2039 (2019)

Curt, T., Frejaville, T.: Wildfire policy in Mediterranean France: how far is it efficient and sustainable? Risk Anal. **38**(3), 472–488 (2018)

Darques, R.: Mediterranean cities under fire. a critical approach to the wildland–urban interface. Appl. Geogr. **59**, 10–21 (2015)

Egidi, G., Cividino, S., Vinci, S., Sateriano, A., Salvia, R.: Towards local forms of sprawl: a brief reflection on mediterranean urbanization. Sustainability **12**(2), 582 (2020)

Ellis, E.C.: Anthropogenic transformation of the terrestrial biosphere. Phil. Trans. Roy. Soc. A: Math. Phys. Eng. Sci. **369**(1938), 1010–1035 (2011)

Fernandes, P.M., Botelho, H.S.: A review of prescribed burning effectiveness in fire hazard reduction. Int. J. Wildland Fire **12**(2), 117–128 (2003)

Fritz, S., See, L.: Identifying and quantifying uncertainty and spatial disagreement in the comparison of Global Land Cover for different applications. Glob. Change Biol. **14**(5), 1057–1075 (2008)

Galiana-Martín, L., Montiel-Molina, C.: Landscape changes and wildfire behaviour: new fire scenarios in Spain. Landscape **9**, 13 (2011)

Henriques, M.C., Khachani, M. : Security and Migrations in the Mediterranean: Playing with Fire, vol. 50. IOS Press (2006)

Krawchuk, M.A., Moritz, M.A., Parisien, M.-A., Van Dorn, J., Hayhoe, K.: Global pyrogeography: the current and future distribution of wildfire. PLoS ONE **4**(4), e5102 (2009)

Kruger, F.: Fire in Mediterranean ecosystems: ecology, evolution and management. Int. For. Rev. **16**(1), 113–116 (2014)

Levers, C., et al.: Archetypical patterns and trajectories of land systems in Europe. Reg. Environ. Change **18**(3), 715–732 (2018). https://doi.org/10.1007/s10113-015-0907-x

Maranon, T.: Agro-sylvo-pastoral systems in the Iberian peninsula: dehesas and montados. Rangelands Arch. **10**(6), 255–258 (1988)

Meeus, J.: Pan-European landscapes. Landsc. Urban Plan. **31**(1–3), 57–79 (1995)

Mitsopoulos, I., Mallinis, G., Arianoutsou, M.: Wildfire risk assessment in a typical Mediterranean wildland–urban interface of Greece. Environ. Manag. **55**, 900–915 (2015)

Modugno, S., Balzter, H., Cole, B., Borrelli, P.: Mapping regional patterns of large forest fires in Wildland-Urban Interface areas in Europe. J. Environ. Manag. **172**, 112–126 (2016)

Molina, C.M., Martín, O.K., Martín, L.G.: Regional fire scenarios in Spain: linking landscape dynamics and fire regime for wildfire risk management. J. Environ. Manag. **233**, 427–439 (2019)

Montiel Molina, C., Galiana-Martín, L.: Fire scenarios in Spain: a territorial approach to proactive fire management in the context of global change. Forests **7**(11), 273 (2016)

Moreira, F., et al.: Wildfire management in Mediterranean-type regions: paradigm change needed. Environ. Res. Lett. **15**(1), 011001 (2020)

Moreira, F., et al.: Recent trends in fire regimes and associated territorial features in a fire-prone mediterranean region. Fire **6**(2), 60 (2023)

Moritz, M.A., Moody, T.J., Krawchuk, M.A., Hughes, M., Hall, A.: Spatial variation in extreme winds predicts large wildfire locations in chaparral ecosystems. Geophys. Res. Lett. **37**(4), 1–5 (2010)

Nabuurs, G.-J., Verweij, P., Van Eupen, M., Pérez-Soba, M., Pülzl, H., Hendriks, K.: Next-generation information to support a sustainable course for European forests. Nature Sustainabil. **2**(9), 815–818 (2019)

Nainggolan, D., de Vente, J., Boix-Fayos, C., Termansen, M., Hubacek, K., Reed, M.S.: Afforestation, agricultural abandonment and intensification: competing trajectories in semi-arid Mediterranean agro-ecosystems. Agr. Ecosyst. Environ. **159**, 90–104 (2012)

Ne'eman, G., Trabaud, L.: Ecology, biogeography and management of Pinus halepensis and P. brutia forest ecosystems in the Mediterranean Basin. Backhuys Publishers (2000)

O'Connor, C.D., Garfin, G.M., Falk, D.A., Swetnam, T.W.: Human pyrogeography: a new synergy of fire, climate and people is reshaping ecosystems across the globe. Geogr. Compass **5**(6), 329–350 (2011)

Olson, D.M., et al.: Terrestrial ecoregions of the world: a new map of life on eartha new global map of terrestrial ecoregions provides an innovative tool for conserving biodiversity. Bioscience **51**(11), 933–938 (2001)

Pausas, J.G., Llovet, J., Rodrigo, A., Vallejo, R.: Are wildfires a disaster in the Mediterranean basin?–a review. Int. J. Wildland Fire **17**(6), 713–723 (2008)

Pausas, J.G., Vallejo, V.R.: The role of fire in European Mediterranean ecosystems. In: Remote Sensing of Large Wildfires: in the European Mediterranean Basin, pp. 3–16 (1999)

Pérez-Sanz, A., et al.: Holocene climate variability, vegetation dynamics and fire regime in the central Pyrenees: the Basa de la Mora sequence (NE Spain). Quatern. Sci. Rev. **73**, 149–169 (2013)

Riley, K.L., Williams, A.P., Urbanski, S.P., Calkin, D.E., Short, K.C., O'Connor, C.D.: Will landscape fire increase in the future? a systems approach to climate, fire, fuel, and human drivers. Curr. Pollut. Rep. **5**, 9–24 (2019)

Roos, C.I., et al.: Pyrogeography, historical ecology, and the human dimensions of fire regimes. J. Biogeogr. **41**(4), 833–836 (2014)

Rosavec, R., Barčić, D., Španjol, Ž, Oršanić, M., Dubravac, T., Antonović, A.: Flammability and combustibility of two mediterranean species in relation to forest fires in Croatia. Forests **13**(8), 1266 (2022)

Rounsevell, M.D., et al.: Challenges for land system science. Land Use Policy **29**(4), 899–910 (2012)

Salvati, L., Ranalli, F., Gitas, I.: Landscape fragmentation and the agro-forest ecosystem along a rural-to-urban gradient: an exploratory study. Int. J. Sust. Dev. World **21**(2), 160–167 (2014)

Sequeira, C.R., Montiel-Molina, C., Rego, F.C.: Landscape-based fire scenarios and fire types in the Ayllón massif (Central Mountain Range, Spain), 19th and 20th centuries. Cuadernos de Investigación Geográfica **46**(1), 103–126 (2020). https://doi.org/10.18172/cig.3796

Syphard, A.D., Radeloff, V.C., Hawbaker, T.J., Stewart, S.I.: Conservation threats due to human-caused increases in fire frequency in Mediterranean-climate ecosystems. Conserv. Biol. 23(3), 758–769 (2009)

Tinner, W., Conedera, M., Gobet, E., Hubschmid, P., Wehrli, M., Ammann, B.: A palaeoecological attempt to classify fire sensitivity of trees in the southern Alps. The Holocene 10(5), 565–574 (2000)

Václavík, T., Lautenbach, S., Kuemmerle, T., Seppelt, R.: Mapping global land system archetypes. Glob. Environ. Chang. 23(6), 1637–1647 (2013)

Williams, A.P., Abatzoglou, J.T.: Recent advances and remaining uncertainties in resolving past and future climate effects on global fire activity. Curr. Clim. Change Rep. 2, 1–14 (2016)

Wu, J.: Effects of changing scale on landscape pattern analysis: scaling relations. Landscape Ecol. 19, 125–138 (2004)

GIS-Based Hierarchical Fuzzy MCDA Framework for Detecting Critical Urban Areas in Climate Scenarios

Barbara Cardone[1], Ferdinando Di Martino[1,2(✉)], and Vittorio Miraglia[1]

[1] Università degli Studi di Napoli Federico II, via Toledo 402, 80134 Naples, Italy
{b.cardone,fdimarti,vittorio.miraglia}@unina.it
[2] Centro di Ricerca Interdipartimentale "Alberto Calza Bini", Università degli Studi di Napoli Federico II, via Toledo 402, 80134 Naples, Italy

Abstract. In this research we propose a GIS-based multicriteria framework that implements a hierarchical MCDA fuzzy model aimed at the detection of urban risk areas in climate hazard scenarios. The fuzzy-based multi-criteria approach adopted has the advantage of adapting to the hierarchical modeling of urban systems and of implementing the approximate reasoning adopted by decision makers. The criteria are defined in a hierarchical structure where the leaf nodes consist of fuzzy numbers; each node is assigned a weight, called coefficient of relative significance, which represents its relevance in the generation of the parent node in the upper level. The fuzzy set in the parent node is implemented through a fuzzy operator of intersection of the fuzzy sets of the child nodes.

The framework was tested on a study area including densely populated neighborhoods in the municipality of Naples (Italy), with the aim of determining which subzones of the study area were most at risk in scenarios of heat waves in the summer months. The results obtained are consistent with the results of the evaluations carried out by experts in the field.

Keywords: Fuzzy Hierarchical model · GIS-based MCDA · Climate risk scenarios

1 Introduction

Recently various Multi-criteria Decision Analysis (MCDA) techniques were combined in GIS-based platforms in urban planning [1, 2, 8, 9, 13], landscape assessment [5–7] and land use analysis [10–12]. In many urban planning and land use models criteria need to modelled following the approximate reasoning used by the expert; in that case, it is necessary to resort to the use of fuzzy sets to implement the multicriteria model. In [3] a fuzzy GIS-based MCDA model for land use analysis is proposed; the area of study is partitioned in land parcels and fuzzy sets are used to manage criteria. The major benefits of this model compared to a traditional MCDA GIS-based model are its usability and its adaptation to various problems. Its main criticality is the impossibility of implementing complex criteria, which require partitioning by levels up to the composition of subcriteria that refer to atomic characteristics of the urban area analyzed. To overcome this restriction, in [4].

An extension of the model [3] is proposed in which a hierarchical structure of the criteria is constructed in which the leaf nodes represent the subcriteria referred to atomic urban characteristics. Each node in the hierarchy of criteria consists of a fuzzy set related to a criterion where the membership degree of an alternative to it represents how much how much the alternative meets the criterion. The user creates the fuzzy sets assigned to the leaf nodes; the fuzzy sets in the higher-level nodes are obtained starting from those in the child nodes.

In this research we test a GIS-based framework in which the fuzzy hierarchical model proposed in [4] is implemented in order to detect which sub-zones of the study urban area are more critical with respect to the population risk generated by heat wave scenarios. Following [4], each subzone of the study urban area constitutes an alternative. Four main criteria are taken into consideration, related to the density of residents, the presence of buildings in poor condition or old construction, the scarcity of urban green areas and the presence of waterproof open spaces. We have tested our framework on a study area consisting of the municipality of Naples, Italy; the subzones are made up of the individual districts into which the municipality is divided.

In the next section the hierarchical model [4] is briefly illustrated; the proposed framework is discussed in Sect. 2. Section 3 shows the results of the experimentation on the study urban area; final evaluation and future perspectives are described in Sect. 4.

2 Proposed Methodology

Figure 1 shows the flow chart which summarizes the structure of the proposed model.

Initially the area of study is partitioned in subzones taking into account the hierarchical model of criteria; then, the *Data extraction by subzone* component creates the *Subzones spatial dataset* extracting the characteristics of each subzone. The m subzones constitute the m alternatives for the hierarchical model.

In the next step the *Hierarchical Fuzzy subzone suitability assessment* (HFSSA) algorithm proposed in [4] is executed in order to assess the suitability of each subzone to the set of criteria.

Finally, the *Suitability thematic map* are created, where the spatial distribution of the suitability of the subzones to compliance with the criteria is shown. In addition, the Suitability thematic maps of the subzones to compliance each main criterion are performed.

In next subsection is detailed the HFSSA algorithm.

2.1 The Hierarchical Fuzzy Subzone Suitability Assessment Algorithm

Let the study area segmented in m subzones, representing the set $A = \{a_1, a_2,...,a_m\}$ of alternatives. Aim of the HFSSA algorithm is to find the alternatives more suited to compliance with a set of n criteria $r_1, r_2,...,r_n$, where the kth criterion r_k is expressed as a linguistic label of the fuzzy set:

$$R_k = \{\mu_{R_k}(a_1)/a_1, ..., \mu_{R_k}(a_i)/a_i, ..., \mu_{R_k}(a_m)/a_m\} \quad k = 1, 2, \ldots, n \quad (1)$$

with $\mu_{Rk}: A \rightarrow [0,1]$ membership function.

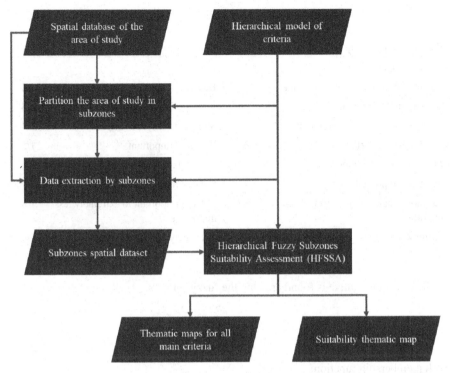

Fig. 1. Flow chart of the methodology

In [3] to the kth criterion is assigned a weight α_k called *Coefficient of Relative Significance* (for short, CRS), providing the relevance of the criterion in choosing the best alternative.

The coefficients of relative significance are assigned to each criterion by the decision maker, considering the constraint:

$$\frac{1}{n}\sum_{k=1}^{n}\alpha_k = 1 \qquad (2)$$

The CRSs are obtained by using the Saaty's AHP pairwise comparison method in which is constructed the pairwise comparison nxn matrix B whose elements b_{kj}, $k,j = 1,....,n$, represent the relevance of the criterion r_k with respect to the criterion r_j. The diagonal elements b_{kk} are set to 1 and $b_{jk} = 1/b_{kj}$.

In Table 1 are shown the pairwise comparison matrix values.

The coefficients of relative significance α_1, α_2,... α_n are obtained resolving the characteristic equation: $\det(\mathbf{B}-\lambda\mathbf{I}) = 0$ where $\mathbf{I}$ is the identity matrix.

If w_k is the k-th component of the eigenvector $\mathbf{w}$, the kth coefficient of relative significance is given by:

$$\alpha_k = n \cdot w_k \qquad (3)$$

Table 1. Values of the Saaty's pairwise comparison matrix.

Relevance of r_k on r_j	b_{kj}	Relevance of r_k on r_j	b_{kj}
Equally important	1		
Equally or slightly more important	2	Equally or slightly less important	1/2
Slightly more important	3	Slightly less important	1/3
Slightly to much more important	4	Slightly to way less important	1/4
Much more important	5	Way less important	1/5
Much to far more important	6	Way to far less important	1/6
Far more important	7	Far less important	1/7
Far more important to extremely more important	8	Far less important to extremely less important	1/8
Extremely more important	9	Extremely less important	1/9

The best alternative is found creating the fuzzy set:

$$R = \bigcap_{k=1}^{n} R_k^{\alpha_k} \qquad (4)$$

with membership function:

$$\mu_R(a_i) = \min_{k=1,..,n} \left(\mu_{R_k}^{\alpha_k}(a_i) \right) \qquad (5)$$

The most suitable subzone is given by the alternative a^* that best meets all the criteria, i.e. such that is, that the membership degree $\mu_R(a^*)$ is maximum.

Moreover, a suitability thematic map of the subzones is constructed, by classifying them based on the membership values $\mu_R(a_i)$ $i = 1,...,m$.

In order to handle the criteria complexity, in [4] is proposed an extension of this method in which each criterion is decomposed in subcriteria, following a hierarchical structure.

Let $r_1^{(1)} r_2^{(1)}, \ldots, r_n^{(1)}$ be the n criteria, where the subscript in round brackets (1) denotes the level in the hierarchy.

The kth criterion $r_k^{(1)}$ is decomposed in n_k subcriteria $r_{k1}^{(2)} r_{k2}^{(2)}, \ldots, r_{knk}^{(2)}$.

The fuzzy set $R_k^{(1)}$ is constructed starting from the subsets assigned to the subcriteria $r_{k1}^{(2)} r_{k2}^{(2)}, \ldots, r_{knk}^{(2)}$. It is given by the formula:

$$R_k^{(1)} = \bigcap_{h=1}^{n_k} \left(R_{kh}^{(2)} \right)^{\alpha_h^{(2)}} \tag{6}$$

Applying the min t-norm operator, the membership degree of the ith alternative to R_k is given by

$$\mu_{R_k}(a_i) = \min_{h=1,..,n_k} \left\{ \mu_{R_h^{(2)}}^{\alpha_h^{(2)}}(a_i) \right\} \tag{7}$$

This process can be iterated partitioning the subcriteria in a set of subcriteria in next level.

If a node in the hierarchical structure is a leaf node, the fuzzy set of the corresponding subcriterion is assigned by the decision maker using triangular or trapezoidal fuzzy numbers. The fuzzy set is constructed on the domain of a specific numerical characteristic given by an index calculated from the spatial dataset of the area of study.

For example, let the area of study be a municipality partitioned in district and a subcriterion in a leaf node is given by the fuzzy set *High percent of elderly population*. This fuzzy set is constructed on a numerical domain given by the interval [0, 100] and the characteristics is obtained summing the data of the number of residents and the number of elderly people in the district and calculating the ratio between the number of elderly people and the number of residents, converting this results in percent.

The decision maker assigns the CRSs of the subcriteria in a level $l + 1$ in which is partitioned a criterion in the level l creating the corresponding Saaty's pairwise comparison matrix.

Starting from the subcriteria in the leaf nodes, it builds the fuzzy sets of the criteria in the upper level; after constructing the fuzzy sets of the criteria in level 1, the suitability of the ith subzone is given by

$$s(a_i) = \min_{h=1,\ldots,n} \left\{ \mu_{R_h^{(1)}}^{\alpha_h^{(1)}}(a_i) \right\} \tag{8}$$

The most suitable subzone is given by the alternative a^* for which the suitability value is maximum.

In Algorithm 1 is schematized in pseudocode the HFSSA algorithm.

Algorithm 1. Hierarchical Fuzzy subzone suitability assessment (HFSSA)

Input:	Spatial dataset of the subzones Hierarchical model of criteria AHP comparison matrices among criteria
Output:	Spatial dataset updated with the suitability of each subzone to all main criteria and to the set of criteria

Set the m alternatives given by the m subzones

Set the n criteria r_1, r_2, ..., r_x, ..., r_n at the 0-level in the hierarchy

Import the L-levels hierarchical model of the criteria

For l = L-1 to 1

    For each node $R^{(l)}_k$ at the lth level

    If $R^{(l)}_k$ is a leaf node **then**

        Create as a fuzzy number the fuzzy set $R^{(l)}_k$ in the domain of the corresponding characteristics

    Else

        Create the AHP pairwise comparison matrix of the fuzzy sets in the child nodes of $R^{(l)}_k$

        Compute the coefficients of relative significance of the child nodes of $R^{(l)}_k$

        Construct the fuzzy set $R^{(l)}_k$

    End if

    Next node

Next l

Construct the fuzzy set R given by (4) with membership degree (5)

For i = 2 **to** m

    Compute the membership degree of the ith alternative to each main criterion $\mu_{R_k}(a_i)$ by (7)

    Compute the suitability s(a_i) by (8)

Next i

Return the updated spatial dataset

2.2 The Hierarchical Framework

We apply our model to evaluate which subzones of the study urban area are the most critical in the presence of heatwave scenarios.

The hierarchical structure of the criteria, composed by two levels, is shown in Fig. 2. In Fig. 2 are also shown the data need to calculate the characteristics of each subcriterion.

The hierarchical model is given by two levels; the expert creates the fuzzy sets related to the subcriteria in the second level. Each fuzzy set is constructed as a fuzzy number on

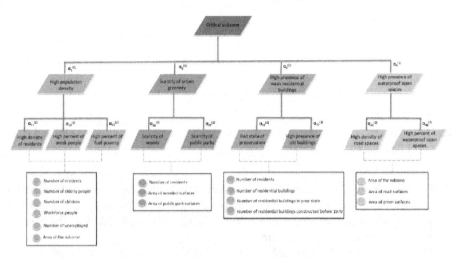

Fig. 2. Hierarchical structure of the criteria.

the domain of a characteristic. In the next paragraphs are detailed the four main criteria and their subcriteria; for each subcriterion is shown the corresponding fuzzy set.

High Population Density Criterion

The *High population density* criterion is partitioned in three subcriteria: *High density of residents*, *High percent of weak people* and *High percent of fuel poverty*.

The *High density of residents* subcriterion evaluates the impact of the density of residents. The correspondent fuzzy set is constructed on the domain of a characteristic given by the density of inhabitants per square kilometer. The *High density of residents* fuzzy set is given by the L-function fuzzy number in Fig. 3a.

The *High percent of weak people* subcriterion evaluates the presence of high concentrations of weak people, where by weak people we mean the elderly and children, whose health is particularly exposed to risk. The correspondent fuzzy set is constructed on the domain [0, 100] of an index measuring the percent of weak residents with respect to the total number of residents. The number of weak residents is given by the number of elderly people over the age of 74 and children under the age of 5. The *High percent of weak people* fuzzy set is given by the L-function fuzzy number in Fig. 3b.

The *High percent of fuel poverty* subcriterion evaluates the presence of high concentrations of fuel poverty people, understood as a population with difficulty in accessing essential energy services due to their high costs. The correspondent fuzzy set is constructed on the domain [0, 100] of an index measuring the percentage of unemployed compared to workforce people, where the workforce people is given by the number of residents aged 15 and over in the total workforce. The *High percent of fuel poverty* fuzzy set is given by the L-function fuzzy number in Fig. 3c.

Scarcity of Urban Greenery Criterion

The *Scarcity of urban greenery* criterion is partitioned in two subcriteria: *Scarcity of woods* and *Scarcity of public parks*.

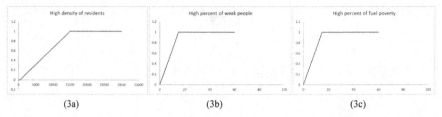

Fig. 3. Fuzzy sets High density of residents (3a) High percent of weak people (3b) and High percent of fuel poverty (3c).

The *Scarcity of woods* subcriterion evaluates the scarcity of woods and cultivated green areas. The correspondent fuzzy set is constructed on the domain of a characteristic given by square meters of woods and cultivated areas per inhabitant. This fuzzy set is given by the R-function shown in Fig. 4a.

The *Scarcity of public parks* subcriterion evaluates the scarcity of urban green areas as parks, as public parks and gardens, flowerbeds, etc. The correspondent fuzzy set is constructed on the domain of a characteristic given by square meters of urban green areas per inhabitant. This fuzzy set is given by the R-function shown in Fig. 4b.

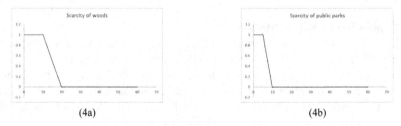

Fig. 4. Fuzzy sets *Scarcity of woods* (4a) and *Scarcity of public parks* (4b).

High Presence of Residential Buildings
The *High presence of residential buildings* criterion is partitioned in two subcriteria: *Bad state of preservation* and *High presence of old buildings*.

The *Bad state of preservation* sub-criterion evaluates the presence of buildings in bad state of conservation, without making any difference based on the construction period. The correspondent fuzzy set is constructed on the domain of a characteristic given by the percent of inhabitants living in bad state residential buildings. This fuzzy set is given by the R-function shown in Fig. 5a.

The *High presence of old buildings* sub-criterion evaluates the presence of buildings with ancient construction periods, regardless of their state of conservation. The correspondent fuzzy set is constructed on the domain of a characteristic given by the percent of inhabitants living in old residential buildings. This fuzzy set is given by the L-function shown in Fig. 5b.

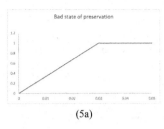 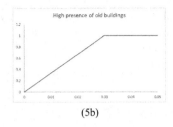

(5a)   (5b)

Fig. 5. Fuzzy sets Bad state of preservation (5a) and High presence of old buildings (5b).

High Presence of Waterproof Open Spaces

The *High presence of waterproof open spaces* criterion is partitioned in two subcriteria: *High density of road spaces* and *High percent of waterproof open spaces* (Fig. 6).

The *High density of road spaces* subcriterion evaluates the presence of road spaces in the subzone. The correspondent fuzzy set is constructed on the domain of a characteristic given by the percent of road areas with respect to the total area of the subzone. This fuzzy set is given by the L-function shown in Fig. 6a.

The *High percent of waterproof open spaces* subcriterion evaluates the percentage of waterproof open space surfaces with respect to the total open space surface in the subzone. The correspondent fuzzy set is constructed on the domain of a characteristic given by the percent of the ratio between the area covered by waterproof open spaces and the area covered by open spaces in the subzone. This fuzzy set is given by the L-function shown in Fig. 6b.

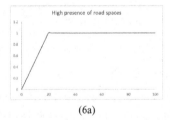 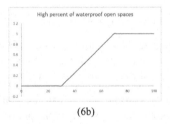

(6a)   (6b)

Fig. 6. Fuzzy sets High density of road spaces (6a) and High percent of waterproof open spaces (6b).

We've implemented our model in a GIS platform, using the ESRI ArcGIS Desktop 10.8 Tool GIS suite. The algorithm was implemented by using Python libraries.

3 Test Results

We test our framework an area of study given by the districts of the municipality of Naples, Italy. The municipality of Naples is a densely populated city divided into 30 districts with different urban characteristics. The districts of the historic centre are characterized by the prevalence of historic and old buildings and by a scarcity of green areas. Outlying districts have undergone more recent urban development; moreover, in the peripheral districts to the west of the city there is a greater presence of green wooded areas than in the districts of the eastern area.

The framework of the study urban area with the division into its districts is shown in the map in Fig. 7.

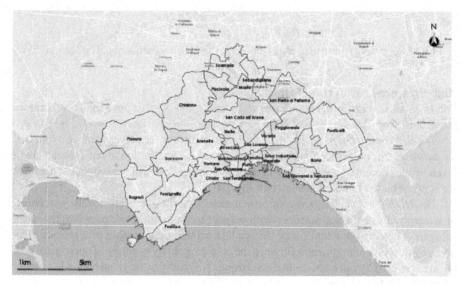

Fig. 7. The area of study: the municipality of Naples, Italy.

To test our framework, we have used the following data sources:

– Geo-Topographic data – scale 1: 5.000
– Census socio-demographic data – scale1: 10,000
– Partition of the municipality in districts – scale 1:2000.

All data were normalized in the planimetric coordinate system ETRS 1989 UTM Zone 33 Nord. Then, a set of spatial geoprocessing operator and spatial analysis functions are used in the GIS platform to summarize the data for district and to calculate the characteristics.

An expert urban planner was asked to assign values from Saaty's AHP pairwise comparison matrix for the criteria and corresponding subcriteria. In Table 2 are shown the four criteria and their subcriteria.

Table 3 shows the pairwise comparison matrix of the four criteria designed by the expert. It assigns a greater importance to the high population density than the scarce presence of green areas and the high presence of weak residential buildings and water-proof open spaces. The scarce presence of green areas is considered to be of greater importance than the high presence of weak residential buildings and waterproof open spaces. The high presence of weak residential buildings is considered to have a greater impact than the high presence of waterproof open spaces.

Table 4 shows the pairwise comparison matrices of subcriteria for the four criteria constructed by the expert.

Table 2. Criteria and their subcriteria in the hierarchical structure.

Criterion	Subcriterion
A High population density	
	A_1 High density of residents
	A_2 High percent of weak people
	A_3 High percent of fuel poverty
B Scarcity of urban greenery	
	B_1 Scarcity of woods
	B_2 Scarcity of public parks
C High presence of weak residential buildings	
	C_1 Bad state of preservation
	C_2 High presence of old buildings
D High presence of waterproof open spaces	
	D_1 High density of road spaces
	D_2 High percent of waterproof open spaces

Table 3. Pairwise comparison matrix of four criteria.

	A	B	C	D
A	1	3	4	5
B	1/3	1	2	3
C	1/4	1/2	1	2
D	1/5	1/3	1/2	1

Table 4. Pairwise comparison matrices of the subcriteria.

	A_1	A_2	A_3		B_1	B_2		C_1	C_2		D_1	D_2
A_1	1	1/5	1/4	B_1	1	3	C_1	1	4	D_1	1	1/2
A_2	5	1	2	B_2	1/3	1	C_2	1/4	1	D_2	2	1
A_3	4	1/2	1									

After constructed all pairwise comparison matrices, the hierarchical model is executed for each district. In Fig. 8 we show the thematic map obtained for the four criteria; to create each thematic map in those districts that belong to the fuzzy set connected to the criterion with a membership degree lower than or equal to 0.3 are labeled as "Low"; Medium Low those districts that belong to it with a membership degree between 0.3 and 0.6 and High those districts that belong to it with a membership degree greater than 0.6.

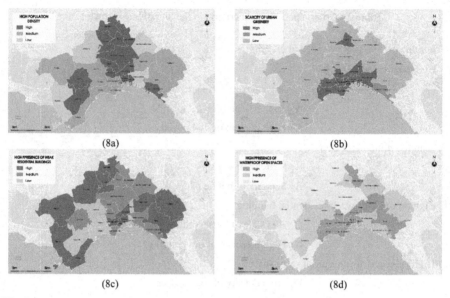

Fig. 8. Thematic maps of the four main criteria: High population density (8a), Scarcity of urban greenery (8b), High presence of weak residential buildings (8c), High presence of waterproof open spaces (8d).

Finally, we construct the suitability thematic map showing the critical subzone; the assessed suitability is partitioning into the three classes applied for the construction of the thematic maps of the main criteria. This map is shown in Fig. 9.

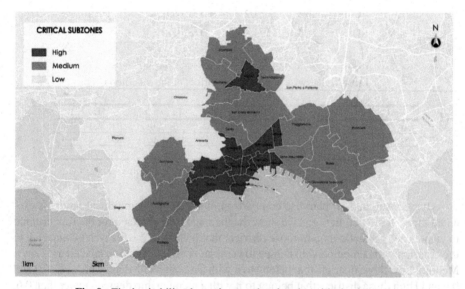

Fig. 9. Final suitability thematic map showing the critical subzones.

The suitability thematic map shows that the districts most at risk are, predominantly, the districts of the city center; they are the most populated, devoid of vegetation, with a high quantity of old or poorly-constructed residential buildings and mainly covered by waterproof open spaces. These results agree with the deductions made by the expert.

4 Conclusions

In this research we tested a GIS-based framework that implements the hierarchical MCDA fuzzy model [4] to detect which districts of the municipality of Naples are more critical with respect to the presence of heatwave scenarios.

The usefulness and adaptability of this approach to different issues are its key benefits over a traditional MCDA GIS-based model. It is feasible to get beyond the limitation of implementing complicated criteria, typical of other classic MCDA models, by building a hierarchical structure of criteria in which the sub-criteria correspond to atomic urban features. In this manner, the degree to which an alternative belongs to a fuzzy set relative to a criterion allows one to quantify the measure to which the alternative satisfies the requirement.

The critical subzone resulting thematic map highlights that the most critical subzones are those that cover the city center; this result is in line with the deductions of the expert.

The benefit introduced by the research consists of providing a MCDA tool with high usability and adaptability to model different urban problems involving complex criteria. IN fact, the criteria can be partitioned in a hierarchical fashion and the suitability of a subzone to meets the criteria is assessed starting using a fuzzy-based approach near to the approximate reasoning of the decision maker.

The limitation of the approach consists of not being able to obtain a more detailed analysis on a smaller scale since the data used are processed on a subzone scale. To carry out an analysis at a detailed scale, the input data summarized by subzone need to be substituted with data processed at a local scale.

In the future we intend to test our framework on different urban planning issues, increasing the complexity of the criteria and the number of levels of the hierarchical structure.

References

1. Akbulut, A., Özçevik, O., Carton, L.: Evaluating suitability of a GIS-AHP combined method for sustainable Urban and environmental planning in Beykoz District, Istanbul. Int. J. Sustain. Dev. Plann. **13**(8), 1103–1115 (2018). https://doi.org/10.2495/SDP-V13-N8-1103-1115
2. Alpagut, B., Lopez Romo, A., Hernández, P., Tabanoğlu, O., Hermoso Martinez, N.: A GIS-based multicriteria assessment for identification of positive energy districts boundary in cities. Energies **14**, 7517 (2021). https://doi.org/10.3390/en14227517
3. Arefiev, N., Terleev, V., Badenko, V.: GIS-based fuzzy method for urban planning. Procedia Eng. **117**, 39–44 (2015). https://doi.org/10.1016/j.proeng.2015.08.121
4. Cardone, B., Di Martino, F.: GIS-based hierarchical fuzzy multicriteria decision-making method for urban planning. J. Ambient. Intell. Humaniz. Comput. **12**(1), 601–615 (2020). https://doi.org/10.1007/s12652-020-02043-6

5. Cerreta, M., Panaro, S., Poli, G.: A spatial decision support system for multifunctional landscape assessment: a transformative resilience perspective for vulnerable inland areas. Sustainability **13**(5), 1–23, 2748 (2021). https://doi.org/10.3390/su13052748

6. Cerreta, M., Inglese, P., Malangone, V., Panaro, S.: Complex values-based approach for multidimensional evaluation of landscape. In: Murgante, B., et al. (eds.) ICCSA 2014. LNCS, vol. 8581, pp. 382–397. Springer, Cham (2014). https://doi.org/10.1007/978-3-319-09150-1_28

7. Cerreta, M., Mele, R., Poli, G.: Urban vulnerability assessment: towards a cross-scale spatial multi-criteria approach. In: Gervasi, O., et al. (eds.) ICCSA 2018. LNCS, vol. 10962, pp. 502–517. Springer, Cham (2018). https://doi.org/10.1007/978-3-319-95168-3_34

8. Chae, J.S., Choi, C.H., Oh, J.H., Chae, Y.T., Jeong, J.-W., Lee, D.: Urban public service analysis by GIS-MCDA for sustainable redevelopment: a case study of a megacity in Korea. Sustainability **13**, 1472 (2021). https://doi.org/10.3390/su13031472

9. Coutinho-Rodrigues, J., Simão, A., Henggeler Antunes, C.: A GIS-based multicriteria spatial decision support system for planning urban infrastructures. Decis. Support Syst. **5**(3), 720–726 (2011). https://doi.org/10.1016/j.dss.2011.02.010

10. Jelokhani-Niaraki, M., Malczewski, J.: A group multicriteria spatial decision support system for parking site selection problem: a case study. Land Use Policy **402**, 92–508 (2015). https://doi.org/10.1016/j.landusepol.2014.09.003

11. Memarbashi, E., Azadi, H., Baradi, A.A., Mohajeri, F., Van Passel, S., Witlox, F.: Land-use suitability in Northeast Iran: application of AHP-GIS hybrid model. ISPRS Int. J. Geo Inf. **6**(12), 396 (2017). https://doi.org/10.3390/ijgi6120396

12. Montgomery, B., Dragićević, S.: Comparison of GIS-based logic scoring of preference and multicriteria evaluation methods: urban land use suitability. Geogr. Anal. **48**, 427–447 (2016). https://doi.org/10.1111/gean.12103

13. Parizi, S.M., Taleai, M., Sharifi, A.: A GIS-based multi-criteria analysis framework to evaluate urban physical resilience against earthquakes. Sustainability **14**, 5034 (2022). https://doi.org/10.3390/su14095034

Urban Regeneration Strategies for Implementing the Circular City Model: The Key Role of the Community Engagement

Mariarosaria Angrisano[1]([✉]) and Francesca Nocca[2]

[1] Pegaso Telematic University, Naples, Italy
mariarosaria.angrisano@unipegaso.it
[2] University of Naples Federico II, Naples, Italy

Abstract. In an increasingly urbanized world such as the one we are living in today, the future of humanity is closely linked to cities, as also highlighted by the United Nations. The challenges of sustainable development are concentrated in the cities and thus the way they are planned and managed impacts the quality of life of the citizens who live in them. In this framework, the circular city model can contribute to operationalize the principles of sustainable development. By leveraging urban planning in urban regeneration as a tool for change, cities can transform their processes from linear to circular ones. This study presents the results of the URBES (Urban Regeneration and Best Energy Saving for our Cities) Erasmus+ project, coordinated by Pegaso Telematic University (Italy). In particular, the aim of the paper is to identify project alternatives for the regeneration of four case studies in the circular city model perspective, highlighting the key role of the community engagement. To this end, a questionnaire has been developed for the community to support the decision-making process. In particular, this process has put schools at its heart, with the awareness of the key role of the community engagement and that the circular economy model can be successful if it is supported from the bottom up and, thus, if it is supported by a strong cultural base.

Keywords: Urban regeneration · Circular city · Participatory processes

1 Introduction

As also highlighted by the United Nations, in an increasingly urbanized world such as the one we live in today, the future of humanity is closely linked to the cities [1]. Indeed, the main challenges of sustainable development, namely social inequalities, environmental degradation and economic crisis are concentrated in cities. Along with the growth of social inequalities, climate change is the most significant challenge facing the world in the 21st century.

A large number of resources are consumed in cities (which cover 3% of the earth's surface) with negative effects in terms of pollutants and climate alteration: cities are home to more than half of the world's population [2], consume 78% of the world's energy, produce more than 60% of greenhouse gas emissions and 50% of global waste [3]. Nevertheless, at the same time, cities are the places where wealth is produced and economic, social, environmental and cultural systems are interrelated, making the city a complex system [4]. Climate change is a natural phenomenon that has physical and meteorological effects and will impact not only the present but also future generations' health and wellbeing. It also poses a threat to the health of Mother Earth on which everything depends [5].

The rate at which climate change is proceeding exceeds humans' ability to react, which is often slow and ineffective. Bridging the gap between this status quo and a more desirable future is our primary challenge. The UN Agenda 2030 outlines a vision of a desirable future by setting 17 Strategic Goals (SDGs) to address the challenges of the 21st century [6], highlighting the necessity to shift towards a new paradigm: humanistic and ecological paradigm.

The SDGs goals are achievable in cities that, thus, play a key role in reaching sustainable development. The New Urban Agenda [7] represents the "spatial translation" of the above goals into physical space within cities. It promotes a shared vision about the urban development, rethinking the way of planning and managing cities for integrating and combining the dimensions of sustainable development, that is the economic, social, cultural and environmental dimensions.

The way cities are planned and managed impacts the quality of life of the citizens who live in them.

The document by which Europe has incorporated the United Nations' principles for achieving sustainable development is the Amsterdam Pact, a document that highlights the key role of adopting nature-based solutions and the circular economy in urban development [8].

Indeed, the linear economy model has been shown to be inefficient: it consumes natural resources and produces waste and degradation. In other words, it is unsustainable. So, a new economy model is required. In this perspective, the circular economy model is addressed in this study.

This research work is part of the URBES project, an European Erasmus+ project started in 2019 and ended in 2022, coordinated by Pegaso Telematic University, the 2nd Geniko Lykeio of Arta (Greece), the Kocasinan Anadolu Lisesi High School (Turkey), the Colegiul Vasile Lovinescu High School (Romania), the Sabatini Menna Artistic High School (Italy) and the BIMED Italia Association. The aim of the project has been to promote and connect the different cultural identities (of the four partner countries) to encourage cultural exchange.

Within this framework, the objective of the paper is to identify project alternatives for the implementation of the circular city model considering the key role that the community plays in the decision-making process. In particular, this work puts schools at its heart, with the awareness that the circular model can be successful if it is supported from the bottom up and thus if it is supported by a strong cultural base. Schools, in fact, are the places of condensation of citizenship, places of training in citizenship, that is, in collaboration and cooperation.

The paper is organized as follows: after the introduction in Sect. 1, the urban regeneration issue is addressed in Sect. 2, also identifying some good practices with a particular focus on the participatory processes. Section 3 shows the methodology. Then, in Sect. 4, four case studies of urban regeneration (identified with the involved schools) are presented. In Sect. 4, the participatory process is explained, describing also the survey conducted with the community. In Sect. 5 the results of the survey are discussed and the preferable project alternatives for the four urban regeneration case studies are defined. Finally, in Sect. 6 discussions are presented.

2 Urban Regeneration and the Circular Economy Model

The circular economy model, also endorsed by the United Nations both in Agenda 2030 and more explicitly in the New Urban Agenda, aims to implement sustainable development principles by following the concept that nothing in nature is wasted and everything can be used as a resource [9]. The goal of the circular economy is to maximize the value of products and materials by focusing on their entire life cycle, with the aim of "closing the loops" by reusing all waste as a resource for new production cycles.

The spatialization of the circular economy model is represented by the circular city model [10]. Several cities are embracing the circular economy as a development model and defining themselves as "circular cities" [11–15]. Cities such as London, Amsterdam, Rotterdam, Brussels, and Paris are some leading examples of this model in Europe [16].

These cities recognize the importance of mimicking natural systems and are taking strategic actions to transform their processes from linear to circular. These actions span across different sectors, including construction, agri-food, textiles, and more. However, the transition to a circular city model requires a systemic change that goes beyond technical solutions issues (as emerges from most of the good practices of circular cities). Urban planning can play a key role in promoting spatial proximity between resource flows, flexibility of buildings and spaces, and the incorporation of green spaces, among other initiatives that are fundamental to operationalize this urban development model [17].

By leveraging urban planning in city regeneration as a tool for change, cities can transform their organization, economy, community, and governance from linear into circular. The first studies on the concept of urban regeneration were initiated in the 19th century during the Victorian era in the United Kingdom as an attempt to improve the poor living conditions in cities caused by industrialization. The economic shift towards the peripheries of cities in the 1970 s resulted in many urban centers experiencing unemployment, inadequate quality of services and housing, street degradation, and public space neglect, which impeded the potential development of urban centers.

Today, urban regeneration is understood as a new strategy for urban development that can effectively improve the physical environment of cities, stimulate economic growth and preserve cultural heritage [18].

In terms of territorial dimension, empty, abandoned, or degraded spaces may not be visible or attractive, but they hold potential resources for the regeneration and self-sustainability of cities and regions. By creatively redesigning these spaces for new purposes, their actual and potential values can be brought to light and revitalized [19]. This is in line with the principles of the circular economy.

Urban regeneration projects can encompass interventions at the micro, meso, and macro scales, involving the revitalization of entire neighbourhoods, unused ancient buildings, abandoned industrial areas, and more. Urban regeneration aims to restore underutilized areas and redistribute opportunities, ultimately enhancing urban prosperity and improving the quality of life.

Scholars and researchers have examined urban regeneration from different perspectives. The literature on urban regeneration is diverse and multifaceted, reflecting the complex nature of the concept. It encompasses economic, social, environmental, and governance perspectives, emphasizing the need for integrated and sustainable approaches to revitalizing urban areas.

One important strand of literature focuses on the economic aspects of urban regeneration. It explores how regeneration projects can stimulate economic growth, attract investments, and create job opportunities in urban areas. Studies often analyze the role of public-private partnerships, financial instruments, and the impact of urban regeneration on local economies [20, 21].

Another significant line of the literature is on the social dimensions of urban regeneration. This includes topics such as community engagement, social cohesion, and the impacts of regeneration on vulnerable groups. Researchers investigate the effectiveness of participatory approaches, community empowerment, and inclusive development strategies in achieving social sustainability and improving the quality of life for residents [22, 23].

Furthermore, the environmental dimension of urban regeneration has gained attention in recent years. This literature focuses on sustainable development, green infrastructure, and the promotion of environmentally friendly practices in urban regeneration projects. It explores concepts such as eco-districts, brownfield redevelopment, and the integration of renewable energy sources to create more sustainable and resilient urban environments [24, 25].

Urban governance and policy play a crucial role in shaping urban regeneration processes. A significant strand of literature examines the role of planning policies, regulatory frameworks, and institutional arrangements in encouraging effective urban regeneration. It also considers issues of power dynamics, stakeholder collaboration, and the role of local government in driving successful regeneration initiatives [26, 27]. Case studies and comparative analyses have been conducted to examine urban regeneration projects in different contexts worldwide. These studies provide insights into the success factors, challenges, and lessons learned from specific regeneration initiatives, ranging from large-scale urban redevelopment projects to small-scale community-led interventions [28, 29].

Over time, several guidelines and laws have been established to facilitate the processes of urban regeneration in cities. One example is the "Toledo Declaration" (2010), which emphasizes the strategic significance of "integrated urban regeneration", i.e. a collaborative alliance among all stakeholders that are involved in the city-building process [30].

UN-Habitat develops various manuals and reports to guide urban regeneration projects, aiming to ensure that new city development initiatives can enhance economic accessibility, service provision, and engage local residents to promote local economic development [31].

The World Bank identifies different steps to carry out a successful urban regeneration project. The first step involves a scoping exercise, which entails engaging various stakeholders in specific meetings to determine the strategies to be implemented. The second step focuses on designing a web of actions and institutions, which involves establishing long-term development actions with the involved institutions. The third step revolves around fundraising, which can involve both private and public sources of funding. The final phase is the actual development of the project idea [32].

2.1 The Role of Participation in Urban Regeneration Processes

Citizen participation is a key component in urban regeneration projects, as it allows for the involvement of local communities in the decision-making processes and helps ensure that the project contribute to meet their needs and desires and, at the same time, reduce the conflicts among different point of views and interests. In addition, participation can promote social cohesion, build trust between different stakeholders, and increase the overall success and sustainability of the project. Healey in 1997 argued that participation can take many different forms, ranging from public consultations and workshops to more formalized forms of co-governance and co-production. Regardless of the specific form it takes, participation serves a number of important functions in urban regeneration projects [33–35]. By engaging with citizens and taking their views and concerns into account, urban regeneration projects can build greater legitimacy and support among local residents [36]. Furthermore, participation can help ensure that urban regeneration projects are more grounded in the local context and better aligned with local needs [37]. Moreover, participation can bring diverse perspectives and ideas to the table, which can help generate new and innovative solutions to complex urban challenges. By engaging with citizens and other stakeholders in collaborative and creative processes, urban regeneration projects can benefit from a wider range of insights and expertise [38].

Additionally, participation can help empower local communities by giving them a greater voice in decision-making processes and enabling them to play a more active role in shaping their own urban environments. This can help build greater resilience and capacity among local communities, as they are better equipped to respond to future challenges and changes [39, 40].

The project of urban regeneration influences the future of our cities and need clear and transparent tools to manage the conflict between public and private interests [41]. For this reason, in a lot of cities all over the world are activated participation processes to support the urban regeneration project during all the design phases. The actors involved in urban regeneration processes are citizens, associations in the area, governance, entrepreneurs, schools, etc.

The adoption of a participatory approach should guarantee the achievement of objectives that are coherent and responsive to the different territorial realities [42–44]. In the idea of participation referred to, the involvement of all social actors is essential, through a process that is fully inclusive and not limited to social categories or economic groups and/or organised groups and associations. This process should not be limited to the aspects of information and consultation but should have a character of continuity.

The participatory processes activate a process that aims to understand, listen, reason together, and discuss choices from the very beginning of the processes.

In Europe, there are various cities that have invested in urban regeneration projects, which can serve as good practices. Most often, these cities are port cities that are undertaking projects to redevelop small industrial districts along waterfronts [45]. There are many good practices of circular urban regeneration in which the participatory process has played a fundamental role, such as the Buiksloterham and De Ceuvel neighborhoods in Amsterdam [46], the reuse projects of HAKA-building boasts, Van Nelle Fabriek, and Venlo building in Rotterdam [47], the "Port House" project designed by Zaha Hadid in the Eilandje quarter in Antwerp [48], the reuse project of the Elbphilharmonie building in Hamburg port area [49], the industrial symbiosis processes activated in the port area of the city of Marseille [50] and the regeneration of Baxia Chado historic neighborhood in Lisbon [51].

3 Methodology

This research work, as anticipated in paragraph 1, is part of the URBES project. This project has been organized in five steps (see Fig. 1).

The first step has focused on analyzing the literature review and case studies on urban regeneration, also identifying good practices.

The second step has concentrated on selecting the case studies on which to carry out the decision-making process for urban regeneration, starting from the involvement of schools. In particular, within the four partner cities of the URBES project, workshops have been organized to discuss and identify case studies together. At the end of this step, the following case studies have been selected: Church of the Former Interdiocesan Seminary of Salerno (Italy), Castle of Arta (Greece); Autogării neighborhood (Romania), Seyyid Burhanettin Mosque (Turkey).

The third step has been related to analyzing the aforementioned case studies. This analysis aimed to develop the knowledge framework of pilot studies in order to identify criticalities and potential for supporting and orienting project choices.

In the fourth step, a participatory process has been activated in order to involve different stakeholders in the decision-making process to identify new project functions according to their needs, requirements, and desires. To this end, a survey has been developed with the community, through the submission of a questionnaire. It will be analyzed in the following paragraphs.

The last step, starting from the analysis of the results of the questionnaires (one for each case study) and the criticality and potential emerged from the third step, has aimed to determine the functions to be assigned to the four case studies and to define the preferable alternative projects.

The project was characterized by a strong dissemination process. In fact, students produced specific short films to share the results of the project and the various issues that emerged. They also developed an illustrative app to showcase the four projects. Furthermore, two international conferences were organized (the first one in Greece in November 2021 and the second one in Italy in November 2022) to share and discuss the project results. Finally, the entire project was also shared on some European platforms

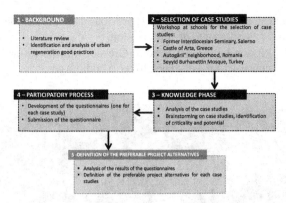

Fig. 1. The methodological framework

associated with the Erasmus+ Program. In addition to virtual collaboration, the project facilitated the mobility of professors, researchers and students. Four mobility events were organized in each partner country to discuss issues related to urban and environmental transformation.

4 The Selected Case Studies: An Overview

As described in the previous section, four case studies of urban regeneration have been identified by students and teachers from the four schools involved, with the support of university researchers.

The artistic high school Sabatini Menna in Salerno (Italy) identified the Church of the Former Interdiocesan Seminary of Salerno as a case study (see Fig. 2).

Fig. 2. Church of the Former Interdiocesan Seminary of Salerno, Italy

The Seminary, which served as the regional seminary headquarters, was constructed in 1929 by the bishops to the north of the city. Due to its grandeur, it represented the largest building project ever undertaken in Salerno.

In 1976, the Municipality of Salerno purchased the Seminary, and since then, the complex has been used for various purposes. Initially, a portion of the structure was used as the University headquarters, and currently, it houses the Art School Sabbatini Menna, the Arts theater, and an urban park. Despite its previous uses, the seminary buildings are now abandoned and in a poor state of conservation.

The case study chosen by the Art School (Greece) was the castle of Arta, Greece (see Fig. 3), whose construction dates back to the Middle Ages.

Fig. 3. The Castle of Arta, Greece

In the past, it served as the administrative and military center of the town, housing the rulers' palace and various religious buildings representing different ethnicities that had control over it.

During ancient times, there was no castle, but instead, an impressive fortification wall was constructed with neatly stacked stones. Subsequently, a castle was built within these walls, providing protection for the citizens during medieval invasions. Later, as part of a tourist development program for the area, a hotel was constructed within the walls. The surrounding area was enhanced with paths, gardens, stone stairs, terraces, and two tennis courts. Numerous trees were also planted, completely transforming the interior of the castle. The hotel played a significant role in the town's social life until 1992 when it ceased operations. Until then, it had attracted a large number of tourists and served as a center for leisure and entertainment for locals. Currently, the hotel is in a state of degradation and abandonment, and citizens no longer have access to its areas.

The case study selected by Fatilcenti school was the Autogării neighborhood in Romania (see Fig. 4).

Fig. 4. Autogării neighborhood, Romania

This neighborhood is located relatively centrally in Falticeni. This area serves as a transitional zone characterized by some commercial activity, a few bus stops, and several abandoned buildings. Within this area, a power plant was constructed, which ceased operations after the Second World War, having been in operation for over five decades. Adjacent to the power plant, housing units were built, which are currently abandoned.

In the year 2000, the Municipality initiated a regeneration project for this area, building apartments intended for student accommodation and a commercial zone. Over time, improvements have been made to the conditions of access and parking. However, despite these interventions, the area is still regarded as marginalized and unsafe.

Lastly, the Turkish school identified the redevelopment of the Seyyid Burhanettin Mosque as its case study (see Fig. 5).

Fig. 5. Seyyid Burhanettin Mosque

The mosque, constructed in 1797 near the historical center of Seyyid Burhaneddin city, is situated on a campus that encompasses a cemetery, a tomb, and another larger and older mosque known as Kalemkırdı. Spanning an area of 200 square meters, it continues to be utilized for public worship. However, the maintenance of the building is not optimal. Presently, the Municipality oversees its management, and it serves as a tourist attraction in the area.

As can be seen, they case studies are referred to three buildings and one neighborhood, highlighting the capacity to the circular economy to be operationalized at different scale.

5 The Participatory Process

The participatory process has been initiated for each school separately. Each school organized an initial meeting with various stakeholders, including other students, teachers, some municipal representatives, and sector associations. These meetings have served as moments of dialogue and discussion on the selected project area to identify the issues to be addressed through the survey.

A questionnaire has been then developed (one for each case study) aimed at identifying possible functions for the regeneration of the studied areas/buildings. The objective of the questionnaire was to gather needs and requirements of different stakeholders linked to the urban regeneration process and to understand their awareness about sustainability issue.

The questionnaire developed by each school has been administered over a period of approximately 2 months (from October to December 2020) to around 200 users each. It has been distributed in both paper and online form, through Google Forms. The paper format, distributed within the schools and through personal meetings with the community, has been the most successful in terms of collecting the highest number of responses.

The questionnaire has been divided into four sections, totalling 45 multiple-choice and open-ended questions, some of which including a space for respondents to explain their chosen option or provide suggestions and opinions.

The first section included questions to identify the interviewees' demographic information: age, profession, and level of education.

The second section consisted of questions aimed at understanding the interviewees' knowledge and awareness about environmental issues. For example, the questionnaire explored the interviewees' personal actions taken to protect the environment, identified major sources of pollution, assessed their perception of pollution in their city, and identified potential actions to raise awareness about sustainability and the environment.

In the third section, specific questions have been asked to identify the areas that, according to the interviewees, were the most degraded, with the objective of confirming the study area chosen in the first phase. Subsequently, they were asked if they had participated in decision-making processes related to other urban regeneration projects. Furthermore, some questions have investigated subjective aspects to assess the residents' perception of certain areas in their city.

The fourth section involves an investigation into how the interviewees assess the neighborhood or building to be regenerated in terms of accessibility, maintenance status, and offered services. They were asked if the selected areas hold any particular value for them, how involved they feel in the neighborhood's life, and what new functions they consider necessary for the building/neighborhood regeneration project.

6 Results: Analysis of the Questionnaires and Definition of the Project Alternatives

After the analysis and participatory phases, the co-design process to define the project alternatives has started. These alternatives have been identified by the students of the four school partners of the project with the support of researchers from Pegaso Telematic University.

At the end of the questionnaire submission process, Pegaso Telematic University and BIMED Association have analyzed the results and shared them with the students.

A number of important issues came up during this analysis about the four areas, their surroundings, and how the community perceives them. These findings provide useful information to orient design choices.

6.1 Former Interdiocesan Seminary in Salerno: Results

Regarding the Salerno case study, starting from the results of the questionnaire, the students have identified new functions for the reuse of the former Seminary's ecclesiastical building. The emerged preferable functions have been: info-point, health services, conference room, exhibition room, reading room, neighborhood library, an area for workshops, indoor play area, service center, and small bar. These functions are in line with the criticality emerged from the analysis phase in which they resulted lacking in the neighborhood.

In relation to the interviewee's awareness about sustainability issue, it was deemed satisfactory. In fact, in the open-ended answers, the respondents have suggested the use of technologies for improving the environmental sustainability of the building. The proposed technologies have been the following: innovative and green materials and technologies, green energy, water recovery systems, and home automation system. These design choices are closely linked to the new European Bauhaus principles, which recognizes that cultural heritage and historical monuments can contribute to achieve sustainable development goals by making them part of the green transition.

Starting from the above, the students have developed (with the support of the university researchers) the reuse project including the community point of view, that is integrating expert and community knowledge.

The objective of the project has been to bring back to life the Seminary building, providing functions for promoting inclusiveness and reducing the environmental impact (through the use renewable and clean energy).

The project has been careful to preserve the specific features of the building while changing its use value. It provides to maintain the spatial configuration of the Church, preserve the altar, and plan for the restoration of the wall paintings. By changing the function of the building (its use value), it is kept alive, which otherwise, in a state of abandonment, would have become "waste" (this is in line with the principle of circular economy to prolong the useful life of resources and reduce waste) [52, 53].

The building provides a range of different functions, including educational spaces such as labs, a neighborhood library, elderly care centers, indoor play areas, and spaces for temporary exhibitions, which will be used by both the inhabitants of the neighborhood and the city and the students from the art school. The reuse of buildings with a combination of functions (mixité) and flexible spaces is a characteristic of the circular economy model that is dynamic and allows for adaptation over time.

Subsequently, consistent with SDG 12, with regards to the energy upgrading of the building, the project has proposed the use of windows with thermal insulating glass, the construction of a new thermal insulating roof with the integration of photovoltaic tiles, and the use of plasters made of lime and hemp, which are rich in natural and thermoacoustic insulating properties.

To ensure inclusive access to the building spaces, the project has planned to connect the main entrance to the Church with the Seminary Park through stairways equipped with stairlifts. Additionally, the new multi-storey parking lot of the former Church will be equipped with a lift. In order to guarantee a sustainable mobility to reach the building, a bike sharing point near the Church has been planned (according to the 3, 7, 9 ,11, 13 SDGs).

This is also consistent with the principles of the "New European Bauhaus" launched-to by the European Commission in 2020, and the "New Green Deal" [54]. In particular, the public garden has been equipped with "smog eating" plant species in order to better the air quality. Furthermore, flowers of Mediterranean vegetation have been planted, that is plans linked to the local vegetation.

6.2 The Castle of Arta, Grecia: Results

Regarding the Greece case study, starting from the questionnaire, some functions have emerged to reuse the abandoned hotel and to improve the area surrounding the castle ruins (40 hectares) in order to return these now abandoned spaces to the community and make the place a tourist attraction. In particular, these functions have resulted from the survey: an equipped urban park, leisure facilities, a shopping centre, new housing, a children's playground areas (interactive educational), an outdoor cinema. Alongside these functions, some suggestions to improve the area have been proposed: pedestrian upgrade, maintenance of neoclassicals ruins, the construction of pedestrian paths for visiting the archaeological site, the restoration of the existing outdoor theater, the installation of new benches and new lights.

Moreover, respondents stated the need to reconvert the ex-hotel with more attractive functions, such as a cultural center, areas for permanent exhibitions, conference halls, info points for tourists, small stores selling local products, bar and restaurants repurposing byzantine and ottoman recipes. These last two functions highlight the respondents' desire to keep the local culture and history of the place alive while changing the original function of the building.

The interviewees demonstrated a satisfactory level of awareness regarding sustainability issues. They provided interesting suggestions related to the use of innovative and green materials, green energy, water recovery systems.

All these suggestions have been included in the project developed by the students and university researchers. The overall aim of the project has been, as said before, to return this large area to the community and, at the same time, to preserve the historical value and cultural identity of the place and the existing building. Therefore, the project has proposed the redevelopment of the entire park and the recovering of the castle archaeological ruins.

A cycle path connecting the castle park, runs along the castle's outer walls and reaches the historic centre have been proposed to improve the accessibility to the site and the connection with the city. Furthermore, the project includes the installation of telescopes on the castle walls to provide a top-down view of the city. Also a playground for children, an outdoor gym, and an open-air cinema contribute to the redevelopment of the park. Its usability and aesthetic attractiveness have been also improved by new benches and fountains, new lighting system and information panels sharing information on the history of the castle. The installation of these panels contributes to preserve and disseminate the history and identity of the place, both to current and future generations.

With regard to the redevelopment of the hotel, the priority intervention has been the consolidation of the building's structures. Furthermore, in line with the results of the questionnaire, a cultural centre has been provided. The latter included also the following functions: bar and restaurant serving dishes of local tradition (Byzantine and Ottoman tradition), a small shop for the sale of local products, an info point for visitors, a conference room, and an exhibition hall.

6.3 Autogării Neighborhood Romania: Results

By thoroughly analyzing the questionnaire results, the new functions for the regeneration of Autogării neighborhood, characterized by small residential buildings, disused industrial constructions, two dismissed shopping centers, the rehabilitation of an open-air market, and a closed school were determined to improve the area. These spaces therefore represent "waste" to be reintroduced into the loops, that is, to be brought back to life (circular economy principles) [55, 56].

The new functions for these spaces emerged from the questionnaire have included green spaces (planting new trees), equipped urban park, areas for sports and leisure, new streets to divert heavy traffic outside the district, new modern bus station, a system for better management of selective waste collection, new connections between the neighborhood and the center. Furthermore, other significant inputs have emerged from the survey. In particular, the modernization of existing buildings, the allocation of new functions for unused buildings, the restoration of a few old buildings in the area, and the improvement of the lighting of streets and green areas have been suggested from the respondents.

Regarding the interviewees' awareness about sustainability issues, it results to be satisfactory. Several sustainable technologies have been suggested to be implemented in the project. They included the use of innovative and eco-friendly materials and technologies, the adoption of green energy sources. Moreover, the necessity of achieving building energy autonomy, implementing water recovery systems, and promoting the recycling of urban waste have been highlighted (this allows the achievement, in particular, of the 12 SDG).

All these suggestions have been included in the project developed by the students (with the support of the university researcher as for the other case studies). The priority actions emerged from the questionnaire have been: the facade restoration of the small buildings that are still active, the attribution of new functions to the abandoned houses and disused industrial buildings (in line with the circular economy principles). To improve the connection of this area with the historic city center, the project has proposed the establishment of two bus stations and the cycle path (9, 12 SDG).

In the disused industrial buildings, new factions, in line with the results of the questionnaire, have been allocated by the project: two commercial centers, a cinema, a theater, a spa, green areas, co-working areas, and areas for exhibitions and events. Furthermore, the design project has included also various functions aimed at enhancing the urban environment, in line with many goals of the SDGs. These elements encompassed an urban park, new electric vehicle charging stations, an open-air market, new pedestrian pathways, new facilities for tertiary activities, new urban waste collection system, children's playground, and green interventions for existing buildings.

As in the previous case study, but at different scale (from building to city neighborhood), the project actions, identified through a synergic cooperation among common and expert knowledge, contribute to the achievement of the principles of the circular economy model. In particular, the reuse of "waste" areas/building, the provision of functions encouraging social inclusion and the adoption of green solutions and sustainable energy systems and technologies are in line with the principle of this new urban development model.

6.4 Seyyid Burhanettin Mosque, Turkey: Results

From the analysis of the questionnaires submitted by the Turkish school for the regeneration of Seyyid Burhanettin Mosque, various new functions to valorize the building and to improve its usability have emerged.

The existing function (the religious one) has been conserved, but it has been integrated with the provision of services to support the enjoyment of the mosque. In particular, the respondents have suggested restoring all the indoor spaces through the realization of new toilets and washrooms, waste collection boxes, a rest for coffins, an additional entrance for women. Furthermore, some suggestions for the restoration of the mosque emerged, as to install an underfloor heating system, to use of insulating paint, to enlarge and illuminate the women's area, to cover the floor with a more comfortable material, to use more energy-efficient light. About the requalification of the outdoor spaces, the respondents highlight the necessity to extend green areas, to plant further trees, to add recycling box and areas for feeding, watering and sheltering the animals.

The interviewees demonstrated a satisfactory level of awareness about sustainability issues. They provided valuable suggestions for incorporating various sustainable technologies into the project, as covering the building with insulated and natural materials, installing heating insulation, adding solar panels for heating the water, installing rainwater collector system to water the plants in the garden. This is in line with the principles of the New European Bauhaus that recognize the possible contribution of cultural heritage to green transition. This is also a characteristic of the circular city model [54]. Starting from the above suggestions and the issues emerged from the analysis phase, supported by the university researchers, the students developed the project. It has been coherent with the inputs from the questionnaire. The project has, for example, provided a specific room as a resting place during funeral prayers, as well as toilets (which were not present before) that are essential during prayer times. The entire building and roof have been insulated to improve heating and prevent energy and moisture loss. A rainwater recovery system has also been planned. Furthermore, the project has included the construction of an external area for prayer (covered with a removable canopy). On the roof of the mosque, 82 solar panels to generate electricity and hot water have been planned. Some interventions on the façade have been proposed to improve the visibility of the mosque to the citizens. For example, it was planned to replace the existing windows with wider ones, and to build a dome with colored glass so that light reaches the holy places. This contributes to strengthening the identity of the mosque, which is an important reference for the community.

7 Discussions and Conclusions

The findings of this study highlight the key role of the participatory processes in urban regeneration projects in order to bring the views, needs, and requirements of all stakeholders into the decision-making processes. Through the questionnaire administered to the community, it has been evident that involving local residents and other stakeholders can lead to more successful and shared outcomes that are better aligned with the needs and preferences of the community. Furthermore, participation allows to reduce the conflicts among different point of views and interests at stake [57, 58].

The results of this study also highlight the importance of effective communication and transparency throughout the urban regeneration process, through the integration of expert and common knowledge in a circular perspective, that is reciprocally ex-changing knowledge. By providing clear and accessible information to the community, and involving them in discussions and decision-making, it is possible to build trust and create a sense of ownership among different stakeholders. Overall, this study demonstrates that participation should be considered as an integral part of any urban regeneration project, rather than an optional add-on. By engaging with the community in a meaningful and inclusive way, urban planners and policymakers can ensure that regeneration projects are not only successful, but also sustainable and socially responsible.

It is important to recognize that community participation is not a one-time event, but a continuous process that requires ongoing communication and engagement with stakeholders throughout the project lifecycle.

While community participation can increase the social acceptance and sustainability of urban regeneration projects, it is important to balance the needs and perspectives of different stakeholders, including residents, business owners, and local authorities.

The use of a questionnaire as a tool for community participation can be effective in gathering quantitative data on community preferences and priorities, but it is important to complement this with qualitative data that can be deduced by different methodology, such as focus groups or interviews to capture more in-depth insights and perspectives. Community participation can help to build trust and transparency between project promoters and the local community, which can be particularly important in the context in which interests are conflictual.

Acknowledgments. The work presented in this paper is part of URBES project, European Erasmus+ project started in 2019 and ended in 2022, coordinated by Pegaso Telematic University and with the following partners: The 2nd Geniko Lykeio of Arta (Greece), the Kocasinan Anadolu Lisesi High School (Turkey), the Colegiul Vasile Lovinescu High School (Romania), the Sabatini Menna Artistic High School (Italy) and the BIMED Italia Association.

Author contributions. Conceptualization, M.A., F.N.; methodology, M.A., F.N.; survey analysis, M.A.; writing-original draft preparation, M.A., F.N.; writing-review and editing, M.A., F.N. All authors have read and agreed to the published version of the manuscript.

References

1. Bosone, M., Nocca, F.: Human circular tourism as the tourism of tomorrow: the role of travellers in achieving a more sustainable and circular tourism. Sustainability (Switzerland) **14**(19), 12218 (2022)
2. METABOLIC Homepage. www.metabolic.nl, (Accessed 22 Jan 2023)
3. UN-HABITAT Homepage. www.unhabitat.org, (Accessed 22 Jan 2023)
4. Pérez, M.G.R., Laprise, M., Rey, E.: Fostering sustainable urban renewal at the neighborhood scale with a spatial decision support system. Sustain. Cities Soc. **38**, 440–451 (2018)
5. Cerreta, M., Cannatella, D., Poli, G., Sposito, S.: Climate change and transformability scenario evaluation for venice (italy) port-city through ANP Method. In: Gervasi, O., et al. (eds.) ICCSA 2015. LNCS, vol. 9158, pp. 50–63. Springer, Cham (2015). https://doi.org/10.1007/978-3-319-21410-8_4

6. United Nations. Transforming Our World: The 2030 Agenda for Sustainable Development (2015)
7. United Nations. United Nations New Urban Agenda. In Proceedings of the United Nations Conference on Housing and Sustainable Urban Development (Habitat III), Quito, Ecuador, 17–20 October (2016)
8. Cerreta, M., Mazzarella, C., Somma, M.: Opportunities and challenges of a geodesign based platform for waste management in the circular economy perspective. In: Gervasi, O., et al. (eds.) ICCSA 2020. LNCS, vol. 12252, pp. 317–331. Springer, Cham (2020). https://doi.org/10.1007/978-3-030-58811-3_23
9. Ellen MacArthur Foundation. Growth within: A Circular Economy Vision for a Competitive Europe; Ellen MacArthur Foundation: London, UK (2015)
10. Nocca, F.: The role of cultural heritage in sustainable development: multidimensional indicators as decision-making tool. Sustainability **9**, 1882 (2017)
11. Agenda Stad. The Perspective of the Circular City; Agenda Stad: Amsterdam, The Netherlands (2015)
12. Circle Economy. Circular Prague; Circle Economy: Amsterdam, The Netherlands (2019)
13. Gemeente Rotterdam. Roadmap Circular Economy Rotterdam; Gemeente Rotterdam: Rotterdam, The Netherlands (2016)
14. LWARB. London's Circular Economy Route Map—Circular London; LWARB: London, UK (2017)
15. Mairie de Paris. White Paper on the Circular Economy of Greater Paris; Mairie de Paris: Paris, France (2017)
16. Nocca, F., Fusco, G.L.: Moving towards the circular economy/city model: which tools for operationalizing this model? Sustainability **11**(22), 6253 (2019). https://doi.org/10.3390/su11226253
17. Fusco Girard L., Nocca F.: Climate Change and Health Impacts in Urban Areas: Towards Hybrid Evaluation Tools for New Governance. Atmosphere **11**, 1344 (2020)
18. Cerreta, M., Mele, R., Poli, G.: Urban ecosystem services (UES) assessment within a 3d virtual environment: a methodological approach for the larger urban zones (LUZ) of Naples. Italy. Appli. Sci. **10**(18), 6205 (2020)
19. Gravagnuolo A., Angrisano M., Fusco Girard L.: Circular Economy Strategies in Eight Historic Port Cities: Criteria and Indicators Towards a Circular City Assessment Framework (2019)
20. Hall, P., Tewdwr-Jones, M. (eds.). Urban regeneration in the UK. Routledge (2010)
21. Begg, I., Sutherland, H.: Urban regeneration and economic development: The local state as entrepreneur. Urban Studies **42**(11), 2027–2048 (2005)
22. Evans, G.: Hard-branding the cultural city—From Prado to Prada. Int. J. Urban Reg. Res. **27**(2), 417–440 (2003)
23. Chaskin, R.J.: Improving community development through community organizing: Perspectives from residents and organizers. Urban Affairs Rev. **44**(6), 779–806 (2008)
24. Roberts, P., Sykes, H.: Urban regeneration: A handbook. SAGE (2000)
25. Newman, P., Jennings, I.: Cities as sustainable ecosystems: Principles and practices. Island Press (2008)
26. Healey, P.: Urban complexity and spatial strategies: Towards a relational planning for our times. Routledge (2007)
27. Blanco, H., Low, S. (eds.): The future of urban form: The impact of new technology. Routledge (2011)
28. Zukin, S.: Naked city: The death and life of authentic urban places. Oxford University Press (2010)
29. Harvey, D.: Rebel cities: From the right to the city to the urban revolution. Verso Books (2012)

30. Bianchi, A.: La rigenerazione urbana: un modo nuovo di pensare la città Economia della cultura n. **3**, 313–322 (2019)
31. UN-HABITA. www.unhabitat.org/topic/urban-regeneration, (Accessed on March 2023)
32. Rana Amirtahmasebi, Mariana Orloff, Sameh Wahba. Tools for urban regeneration. World Bank (2016)
33. Healey, P.: Collaborative planning in perspective. Plan. Theory Pract. **8**(2), 173–183 (1997)
34. Attardi, R., Cerreta, M., Poli, G.: A collaborative multi-criteria spatial decision support system for multifunctional landscape evaluation. In: Gervasi, O., et al. (eds.) ICCSA 2015. LNCS, vol. 9157, pp. 782–797. Springer, Cham (2015). https://doi.org/10.1007/978-3-319-21470-2_57
35. Somma, M.: Towards regenerative wasted landscapes: index of attractiveness to evaluate the wasted landscapes of road infrastructure. In: Amenta, L., Russo, M., van Timmeren, A. (eds) Regenerative Territories. GeoJournal Library, vol 128. Springer, Cham, (2022). https://doi.org/10.1007/978-3-030-78536-9_19
36. Imrie, R., Raco, M.: Urban renaissance and the regeneration of public participation. Local Gov. Stud. **29**(2), 1–17 (2003)
37. Blanco, I., Martins, J.: Citizen participation in urban regeneration: Tools and methods for collaborative planning. Habitat International 44, 304–311 (2014)
38. Cerreta, M., Poli, G., Somma, M.: assessing infrastructures alternatives: the implementation of a fuzzy analytic hierarchy process (F-AHP). In: Gervasi, O., et al. (eds.) ICCSA 2021. LNCS, vol. 12955, pp. 504–516. Springer, Cham (2021). https://doi.org/10.1007/978-3-030-87007-2_36
39. Balducci, A., Fedeli, V.: Citizen participation in urban regeneration: A tale of two Italian cities. Eur. Plan. Stud. **24**(6), 1076–1097 (2016)
40. Colding, J., Barthel, S.: Urban green commons: Insights on urban common property systems. Glob. Environ. Chang. **47**, 1–10 (2017)
41. Pruzan, P., Bogetoft, P.: Planning with Multiple Criteria. North Holland, Amsterdam, The Netherlands (1991)
42. Cerreta, M., Muccio, E., Poli, G., Regalbuto, S., Romano, F.: City-port circular model: towards a methodological framework for indicators selection. In: Gervasi, O., et al. (eds.) ICCSA 2020. LNCS, vol. 12251, pp. 855–868. Springer, Cham (2020). https://doi.org/10.1007/978-3-030-58808-3_61
43. Cerreta, M., Muccio, E., Poli, G., Regalbuto, S., Romano, F.: A multidimensional evaluation for regenerative strategies: towards a circular city-port model implementation. In: New Metropolitan Perspectives: Knowledge Dynamics and Innovation-driven Policies Towards Urban and Regional Transition, vol. 2, pp. 1067–1077. Springer International Publishing (2021). https://doi.org/10.1007/978-3-030-48279-4_100
44. Somma, M.: New tools to analyse the wastescapes of the cities: the case study of the metropolitan city of Naples. In: La Rosa, D., Privitera, R. (eds.) INPUT 2021. LNCE, vol. 146, pp. 171–179. Springer, Cham (2021). https://doi.org/10.1007/978-3-030-68824-0_18
45. Somma, M., Campagna, M., Canfield, T., Cerreta, M., Poli, G., Steinitz, C.: collaborative and sustainable strategies through geodesign: the case study of Bacoli. In: Gervasi, O., Murgante, B., Misra, S., Rocha, A.M.A.C., Garau, C. (eds) Computational Science and Its Applications – ICCSA 2022 Workshops. ICCSA (2022). Lecture Notes in Computer Science, vol. 13379. Springer, Cham, (2022)
46. Circle Economy. Circular Amsterdam. A Vision and Action Agenda for the City and Metropolitan Area. TNO: Amsterdam, The Netherlands (2016)
47. City of Rotterdam (Gemeente Rotterdam). Roadmap Circular Economy Rotterdam. City of Rotterdam: Rotterdam, The Netherlands (2016)
48. Invader. "Our Contribution to Sustainable Urban Development" Invader: Antwerp, Belgium (2016)

49. Homepage Port of Hamburg. www.hafen-hamburg.de, (Accessed 23 Feb 2023)
50. Homepage Marseille Fos. www.marseille-port.fr, (Accessed 23 April 2023)
51. Serdoura, F., Crespo, J., De Almeida, H.F.: Rehabilitation of baixa pombalina in lisbon. a strategy for environmental and economic sustainability. In: Sustainable Architecture and Urban Development (SAUD 2009 Conference) (2009)
52. Bosone, M., Nocca, F., Fusco Girard, L.: The circular city implementation: cultural heritage and digital technology. In: Rauterberg, M. (ed.) HCII 2021. LNCS, vol. 12794, pp. 40–62. Springer, Cham (2021). https://doi.org/10.1007/978-3-030-77411-0_4
53. Bosone, M., De Toro, P., Fusco Girard, L., Gravagnuolo, A., Iodice, S.: Indicators for ex-post evaluation of cultural heritage adaptive reuse impacts in the perspective of the circular economy. Sustainability **13**(9), 4759 (2021)
54. European Commission (EU). New European Bauhaus. European Commission (EU): Brussels, Belgium (2020)
55. Sacco, S., & Cerreta, M. Patrimonio plástico: a decision-making process for the re-use of an industrial architecture in montevideo vol. 11, pp. 92–102 - July 2020, 11, (2020)
56. Nocca, F., De Toro, P.: Voytsekhovska V: Circular economy and cultural heritage conservation: a proposal for integrating Level(s) evaluation tool. Aestimum **78**, 105–143 (2021)
57. Sacco, S., Cerreta, M.A: Decision-making process for circular development of city-port ecosystem: the east naples case study. In: Gervasi, O., Murgante, B., Misra, S., Rocha, A.M.A.C., Garau, C. (eds) Computational Science and Its Applications – ICCSA 2022 Workshops. ICCSA 2022. Lecture Notes in Computer Science, vol 13378. Springer, Cham (2022). https://doi.org/10.1007/978-3-031-10562-3_40
58. Bosone, M., Nocca, F.: Human circular tourism as the tourism of tomorrow: the role of travellers in achieving a more sustainable and circular tourism. Sustainability **14**(19), 12218 (2022)

Building Multi-dimensional Models for Assessing Complex Environmental Systems (MES 2023)

Civic Uses as Complex Socio-Ecological System: A Proposal for an Analytical Framework

Danny Casprini[1]([✉]), Alessandra Oppio[1], and Francesca Torrieri[2]

[1] Department of Architecture and Urban Studies,
Politecnico di Milano, via Bonardi 3, Milano (MI) 20133, Italy
danny.casprini@polimi.it
[2] Department of Industrial Engineering, Università degli Studi di Napoli Federico II,
via Claudio 21, Napoli (NA) 80125, Italy

Abstract. Civic use rights are a particular category of real rights over collective-owned or public lands that allows local communities to enjoy agri-pastoral-sylvan properties and use them for individual or commercial purposes. Properties encumbered by civic use rights have had a crucial importance in Italy to guarantee access to natural resources to local communities and contributed to shape the present cultural landscapes, especially in mountain and inner areas. In this sense, properties encumbered by civic uses represent strategic assets to preserve common natural resources and the landscape. Based on this, the Italian legislator recently guaranteed public bodies the faculty to transfer civic use rights from properties that lost their original agri-pastoral-sylvan purpose to another public property land of equal environmental value. This raised an evaluation question related to the assessment of the value of the land encumbered by civic use rights.

To answer this question, the current paper presents an analytical framework that supports in the definition of criteria to be addressed by decision-makers in cases of transferral of civic use rights. The framework combines different methodologies in a multidimensional model built on the basis of Ostrom's Design Principles (DPs) for the commons; the Socio-Ecological System Framework; and social impact assessment.

Keywords: Commons · Civic use properties · Socio-Ecological System · Ecosystem value · multidimensional evaluation model

1 Introduction

In western and central Europe, common ownership of properties and collective agriculture land-use systems have been widely maintained as traces from a past where common properties were seen as a mean to access economic and productive assets [1, 2]. As such different forms of collective ownership have been maintained in extensive or unproductive land-use settings, especially in inner areas [2, 3]. Additionally, in mountain areas, such as the Alps, the Pyrenees and the Carpathians, still nowadays it is possible to find common use of forests and grassland systems, such as pastures, that present different governance arrangements [2–6].

© The Author(s), under exclusive license to Springer Nature Switzerland AG 2023
O. Gervasi et al. (Eds.): ICCSA 2023 Workshops, LNCS 14108, pp. 379–397, 2023.
https://doi.org/10.1007/978-3-031-37117-2_26

The phenomenon of collective ownership of agri-pastoral-sylvan lands is extensively diffused also all over Italy, especially in mountain areas, where pastures and forests are shared among the different members of the local community [7]. A particular form of real rights over collective-owned lands or public properties is represented by civic use rights ("*usi civici*") that allow local communities to enjoy agri-pastoral-sylvan properties, and use them for sustenance or exploitative purposes, as recalled by Article 11 and 12, Law 1766/1927 and Article 3, Law 168/2017 [8]. Civic uses are particularly relevant as they cover almost 10% of the Italian territory with over 600,000 hectares of agricultural land and over 3 million hectares of national forests and graze encumbered by civic use rights [9–11]. In fact, this peculiar legal regime is typical of rural areas, where, historically, common ownership of the land was pursued and encouraged resulting in the creation of a common agri-pastoral-sylvan heritage. Additionally, civic uses also present a historical value recalling the history and development of the landscape and the territory at large [10, 12].

Collective use properties such as those encumbered by civic use rights represent a peculiar form of social arrangements that allow use and enjoyment of sylvan and agricultural lands through a self-organised management system, while preserving natural landscapes and the underpinned resources. In this sense, civic use properties became a fundamental mean for the protection and preservation of natural resources and rural landscapes in connection with Article 9 of the Italian Constitution, while promoting the generation of economic and social benefits for the local community [13]. Descending from this, one important challenge that civic use properties shares with common-pool resources is related to the detrimental effects to the ecological and social spheres deriving from both over-exploitation and under-use [2, 14–16]. However, this dynamic received little attention in literature even though in some cases civic uses have been characterised as socio-ecological systems [2, 4, 16, 17].

Based on the considerations made, this paper addresses civic use rights through the lens of socio-ecological systems (SES) developed by Ostrom to better understand the self-management model prescribed by the Law 168/2017 and assess how users' interactions with natural resources can support in the preservation of the ecological value of civic uses while generating social value for the local community. The use of Ostrom's socio-ecological system framework promotes the view of civic use rights as a complex system where natural and anthropic components interact with each other to generate social and ecological effects capable of influencing each other [1, 2, 14, 16]. Adopting the lens of SES supports in defining civic use properties according to the basic characteristics of the commons: non-exclusivity, scarcity and shared stewardship [18]. Thus, supporting to understand how crucial civic use rights are for the protection of environmental resources and agri-pastoral-sylvan landscapes. Additionally, using Ostrom's SES to analyse civic use properties allows to take into consideration also the social outcomes related to the collective use of agri-sylvan-pastoral properties, thus highlighting the social value of these lands in addition to their economic and ecological value that has been addressed in many previous studies [8, 9, 17, 19–21]. Lastly, Ostrom's SES framework allows to provide new contextual and conceptual insights also on the governance of civic use properties.

In this light, throughout the paper we aim to achieve two objectives. Firstly, we investigate applications of the Ostrom's socio-ecological system framework (SESF) to properties encumbered by civic use rights in a way to define the subsystems to be investigated and, secondly, we explore the connections between anthropic actions and the common resources. Descending from this, we aim to propose an analytical framework that allows to understand the social value connected to civic use properties and how it can enhance their potentiality to preserve natural ecosystems and cultural landscapes. According to this a set of multi-dimensional criteria will be defined to address a particular evaluation issue connected to the transferral of civic use rights as provided by the Italian legislation. The use of multi-dimensional criteria analysis has proven in many cases to enhance transparency and legitimacy in decision-making supporting public and private decision-makers in the process [22–24].

The paper is structured as follows: paragraph 2 presents the characteristics of civic use rights in the Italian legislative context, while paragraph 3 constructs the case to understand civic use properties as complex socio-ecological system and paragraph 4 addresses how to evaluate the social value of civic use properties. Building on the considerations made, paragraph 5 presents a proposal for a multi-dimensional analytical framework to analyse civic uses and to assess the case of transferral of civic use rights from a public property to another one. Discussion about the use of the analytical framework will be carried out in the conclusive paragraph.

2 Characteristics of Civic Use Rights in the Italian Context

In the Italian jurisdiction, civic uses are regarded as perpetual real rights over a public or private property attributed to a given community that can be exercised by all members part of it [8, 9]. Nowadays, civic uses can be found mainly over publicly-owned properties encumbered by collective use rights attributed to the community residing in the municipality or hamlet where the property is located [8]. Given their peculiarities, civic use rights are inalienable, nor subjected to acquisitive prescription; thus, inextinguishable rights (Article 3, Law 168/2017 and Article 12, Law 1766/1927).

Properties encumbered by civic uses are generally divided into two main categories: forest and grassland, on one side, and cultivated lands, on the other. The latter are commonly found in flat lands and former latifundio properties, as such, the modern rights descend from a concession from the landlord to use the land for sustenance purposes [25]. The non-cultivated properties, such as forests and graze, are typical of mountain areas where the local communities were historically used to share the resources to sustain themselves and the community at large [8–10, 25]. Over the centuries these rights evolved and together with the sustenance goal, the beneficiary communities started to use properties encumbered by civic use rights for exploitative purposes, especially with the development of the economy towards a capitalistic system [10, 25]. A process of de-privatisation of civic use properties started with the Law 1766/1927 and ownership of lands encumbered by civic use rights was transferred to municipalities and other local administrative bodies [13]. In this sense, the legislator ended the feudal practice of collective use rights and started to regard civic use rights as tools to protect natural resources and the cultural landscape as recalled by the Law 168/2017, given the fact that in vast majority act upon properties covered of woods and permanent graze.

Following the adoption of the Law Galasso, the relevance of civic use rights became crucial with regard to the preservation of natural heritage and landscape, thus revitalising the discussion about this peculiar form of collective use rights. The Constitutional Court in its jurisprudence recognised the primary role of civic uses to protect natural resources and landscapes, thus limiting administrative actions by the regions over properties encumbered by civic use rights. In the judgement given with sentence 345/1997 the Court addressing the Abruzzo Regional Law 23/1996, that provided a simplified procedure to change the destination of use of properties encumbered by civic uses when they lost their original purpose due to public interest, highlighted that for their very nature civic use rights are subjected to private law and thus excluded from the regional legislative power. The same is confirmed in Sentence 71/2020 where the Court analysing the Calabria Regional Law 24/2010 restated the private law nature of civic use rights and the primacy of national law over regional law with regard to civic use rights, thus excluding civic use properties from administrative actions and activities. Furthermore, the Court in the same judgment stated that the changes of destination of use can only be conducted according to the economic benefit for the beneficiary community, as prescribed by the Law 168/2017.

The Law 168/2017 also prescribes that even in cases of dissolution of civic uses rights, the land will retain its importance in conserving the natural and cultural landscape, thus preventing possible modifications that go against this interest. Moreover, with the latest reform to the Law 168/2017 new provisions regarding civic uses were added to Article 3 (paragraphs 8-bis, 8-ter and 8-quater). The new paragraphs provide that administrative bodies can allow municipalities to transfer civic use rights over superficial lands to their disposable assets, proven that there has been an irreversible and lawful transformation of the property itself. This means that civic use rights can be transferred from lands that no longer pursue the original destination of use (e.g. former graze hosting telecommunication infrastructures) towards lands with an equal ecological value as the original land encumbered by civic uses.

3   Understanding Civic Uses as Complex Socio-Ecological Systems

Civic uses, providing a right of collective enjoyment of agri-pastoral-sylvan properties, entail a way to manage common resources, that are non-exclusive and subtractable, thus capable of suffering from scarcity [18]. In fact, while none of the members of the community can prevent others to enjoy the property, the fact that one of them use a portion of land and the resources included therein it, limit others to benefit from the same pool of resources, subtracting a number of resources to the entire community [18]. This presents one of the typical problems of the commons: how to manage the available resources in a way that all members of the community can enjoy the resources available without over-exploit them [18].

In a way to better understand the issue and analyse the connection and interactions between anthropic activities and the set of natural resources underpinned a property encumbered by civic uses reference to the Socio-Ecological Systems developed by Ostrom will be made. Using this lens allows to investigate how the mentioned interactions can generate outcomes at the system levels and, thus, generating shared social value for the community of beneficiaries of civic uses. In conducting this assessment two different tools will be used: the Socio-Ecological System Framework (SESF) and the Design Principles (DPs) that supports to identify the variables to be taken into consideration when conducting an evaluation about the social value of a property encumbered by civic use rights.

3.1 Socio-Ecological System Framework

Socio-ecological systems are systems where human and natural aspects interact constantly in a way that natural resources promote the well-being of local communities and, at the same time, communities have an impact on natural resources determining their conservation or exhaustion [2, 14, 16]. In systems as such, different stakeholders collaborate with each other to protect the valuable resources and allow fair and just access to the resources for all members of the community [14]. In a complex SES, subsystems can be identified according to the framework provided by Ostrom: resource system; resource units; users; and governance system as shown in Fig. 1. In a system as such the life of the local community is highly interlinked with the preservation of natural resources, thus it is foreseeable that the local community will be able to define a management model that ensures everyone's enjoyment of the natural resources even in regime of scarcity, while preventing their overexploitation by users [14].

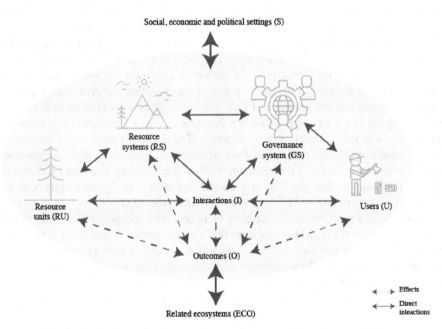

Fig. 1. Socio-Ecological System Framework adapted from Ostrom (2009)

As seen in the figure above, the different sub-systems have direct interaction with each other, in particular: the resource units (RU), for example the trees in a forest, are part of a broader resource system (RS), in this case the forest encumbered by civic uses [14, 26]. RU are generally used by the users (U), the community of beneficiary of civic use rights that might enjoy the resources for different purposes (e.g. harvesting, auto-consumption, exploitative or commercial purposes, touristic or cultural activities), thus enhancing the opportunities for different interactions (I) among the different subsystems and with the external actors and related ecosystems (ECO) [14, 26]. In a way to maximise enjoyment by different users and protect the resources, the community generally adopt a governance system (GS) that comprises a set of rules that all users decide to obey to [14, 26]. GS generally ranges from model of public management (top-down) to self-management models (community-based) and might enhance or hinder interactions between the other subsystems.

In a SES the interaction between the subsystems generates social and ecological outcomes (O) for the entire community and for the territory. In particular, the main interactions are related to the harvest of resources and the maintenance of the resource system according to natural re-generation patterns [14, 26]. This results in outcomes that are experimented by each subsystem in different ways and that contribute to the mitigation of scarcity of resources and to the overall benefit and well-being of community. The outcomes generated are also capable of influencing the GS adopted and change its conformation to adapt to the changes occurred at the SES level. Socio-ecological systems are influenced by the social, economic and political settings (S) and, at the same time, they have a series of impact on related ecosystems especially in terms of climate adaptation, pollution and social justice. For this reason, a set of variables has been defined by Ostrom to be taken into account and measured when dealing with SES (Table 1).

In cases of properties encumbered by civic uses, whether cultivated or sylvan-pastoral lands, the subsystems refer to natural resources (trees, grass, crops, soil, etc.) understood as the resource units; the forest, graze or cultivated land as the resource subsystem; the local community residing in the municipality or hamlet where the civic use property is located as users; and the presence of *Ente esponenziale* as a governance system. This body is typical of the Italian legal system that defines it as a legal entity that promotes and protect a general interest of the community. The law although does not prescribe a certain legal form for the creation of *Enti esponenziali*, leaving the decision about the governance arrangements to the community. Therefore, leading to a multi-stakeholder system that requires the adoption of a cooperative behaviour by all members of the community to overcome overexploitation of the resources [18].

Looking at a property encumbered by civic uses as a complex SES allows to take into consideration the typical interactions that are represented by anthropic activities in terms of harvesting and exploitation of natural resources as well as utilisation of the resource unit and the underpinned landscape for cultural or touristic purposes. Those interactions have effects on how the resources regenerate in the given property and how the collective use of the land can generate a distributive effect for the local community.

Table 1. Second-tier variables under first-level subsystems (S, RS, RU, U, I, O and ECO) in a SES framework. Ostrom (2009)

Social, economic and political settings (S)		
S1 Economic development	S2 Demographic trends	S3 Political stability
S4 Government resource policies	S5 Market incentives	S6 Media organisation

Resource systems (RS)	Governance systems (GS)
RS1 Sector (e.g. water, forests, pasture, fish)	GS1 Government organisations
RS2 Clarity of system boundaries	GS2 Nongovernment organisations
RS3 Size of resource system	GS3 Network structure
RS4 Human-constructed facilities	GS4 property-rights system
RS5 Productivity of system	GS5 Operational rules
RS6 Equilibrium properties	GS6 Collective
RS7 Predictability of system dynamics	GS7 constitutional rules
RS8 Storage characteristics	GS8 Monitoring and sanctioning process
RS9 Location	

Resource Units (RU)	Users (U)
RU1 Resource unit mobility	U1 Number of users
RU2 Growth or replacement rate	U2 Socioeconomic attributes of users
RU3 Interaction among resource units	U3 history of use
RU4 Economic value	U4 Location
RU5 Number of units	U5 Leadership/entrepreneurship
RU6 Distinctive markings	U6 Norms/social capital
RU7 Spatial and temporal distribution	U7 Knowledge of SES/mental models
	U8 Importance of resource
	U9 Technology used

Interactions (I) → Outcomes (O)	
I1 Harvesting levels of diverse users	O1 Social performance measures
I2 Information sharing among users	(e.g. efficiency, equity, accountability,
I3 Deliberation process	sustainability)
I4 Conflicts among users	O2 Ecological performance measures
I5 Investment activities	(e.g. overharvested, resilience, bio-diver-
I6 Lobbying activities	sity, sustainability)
I7 Self-organising activities	O3 Externalities to other SES
I8 Networking activities	

Related ecosystems (ECO)		
ECO1 Climate patterns	ECO 2 Pollution patterns	ECO3 Flows into and out of focal SES

3.2 Design Principles and SES Framework

In Ostrom's seminal work on commons' management eight Design Principles are proposed as rules of engagement to develop governance arrangements that promote the sustainable management of common resources [18]. Ostrom's DPs are detailed in Table 2 below. Using the DPs have proven to be relevant in in several other studies [2, 27].

If confronted with the SESF, DPs provides a set of normative prescriptions that can be found in the governance system within the SESF [2] supporting in the definition of the management arrangements that better suit the specific context. The adoption of the DPs as a starting point supports in the analysis of the context and it will have an influence on the different variables part of the SESF presented in Table 1 above, with particular reference to users and GS.

Table 2. Design principles (DPs) applicable to commons adapted from Ostom (1990)

Design Principles (Ostrom, 1990)
DP 1 Clearly defined boundaries
DP 2 Congruence between appropriation and provision rules and local conditions
DP 3 Collective-choice arrangements
DP 4 Monitoring
DP 5 Graduated sanctions
DP 6 Conflict-resolution mechanisms
DP 7 Minimal recognition of rights to organise
DP 8 Nested Enterprise

This analysis supports in understanding the factors that can be controlled by the local community in a way to enhance environmental and ecosystem conservation efforts and maximise the capacity of civic use rights to protect cultural landscapes. Therefore, what is necessary, in these cases, is to define a management system aiming to the long-term survival of the common resources that interact with the existing national and regional laws to promote shared ownership of the resources themselves while guaranteeing fair and just outcomes to the local communities that benefit from the property encumbered by civic use rights.

Performing an analysis according to the DPs and SESF can enhance the value of public properties subjected to civic use rights to pursue the general interest to preserve natural resources as recalled by the Law 168/2017 while empowering local communities to take actions in the natural resources' preservation in connection with administrative bodies and promote social and ecological benefits for the entire SES.

4   The Evaluation of the Social Value of Civic Uses

As presented above the SESF takes into account the outcomes created by the different kind of interactions between the subsystems: social outcomes can be generated by users' interaction with the resources and can be enhanced or hindered by the governance system, designed according to the DPs and put in place in the specific context, here understood as the resource system. The outcomes generated and experimented by the community shall be taken into consideration when addressing the social value of a land encumbered by civic use rights.

When dealing with the cases of civic use rights over a public property, social outcomes deal mainly with social justice, equitable access to resources and well-being of members of the local community [14, 28]. Thanks to the configurations of the governance model and management arrangements at the community level, additional outcomes can be generated in terms of innovative bottom-up solutions for the safeguards of the resources and the enhanced interaction between the SES and the external contexts [29]. Innovation also plays a role in promoting the protection of rural and cultural landscapes developing bottom-up solutions that involve the entire community in the effort and promotes further economic opportunities for all members [20, 30, 31].

When addressing the measurement of social outcomes, it is fundamental to take into account the issue of attribution of the effects to a certain activity in a way to establish a direct relationship between the stakeholders' actions and the effects that the community experiment [32–34]. Depending on the type of interactions inside the SES social outcomes may vary. For this reason, as a starting point, it is fundamental to address the analysis of the specific context where the property encumbered by civic use is located and the stakeholders' configurations within the community and their needs, capabilities and expectations [24]. In conducting this kind of assessment, the DPs defined by Ostrom and presented above can be applied as a guideline to better understand the case study and to rate the actual governance model in place. As a second step, the use of the lens provided by SESF becomes crucial to take into account two fundamental dimensions: social justice, in particular distributive equity and social inclusion, that may lead to the enhancement of capabilities of the users [28, 35].

Considering the social justice dimensions, it becomes necessary to evaluate the issue from two different perspectives: the results and the process. With reference to the former civic use rights represents a way to distribute resources among community members and the effects that this directly have for the users. In particular due consideration should be given to: the income effect, addressing how the use of the common property affects the economic return for the members of the community [2, 14]; the entrepreneurship effect, taking into consideration how access to a common land promotes different forms of entrepreneurship, either individual or collective, and the creation of jobs at the community level [2, 36]. On the other hand, when addressing the process of managing the properties encumbered by civic uses, a specific attention should be reserved to the inclusion of marginalised groups and to the democracy of the governance model designed to ensure higher results in terms of cohesion and sense of belonging to the community and how the presence of the civic use property is capable of affect community networks and relationships between different stakeholders [2, 14, 36].

The outcomes described and their combinations with other contextual factors might bring to the creation of additional benefits for the community. For this reason, an approach based on the Theory of Change (ToC) is useful to understand both the mechanisms behind the creation of shared value for the community and the processes that lead to the creation of specific effects and changes [34, 37]. An approach based on ToC allows to create a visual narrative model of the interactions (I) studied and to reflect on the causality nexuses that lead to the generation of the experimented outcomes (O), analysing whether those links are logical and realistic [38] In this sense, it becomes more important to assess the role that interactions between stakeholder and the available resources as well as to isolate some context specific variables that play a role in the generation of outcomes [38].

Lastly, given the fact that civic uses do not only protect the natural environment but also cultural landscapes, in addition to the assessment of social outcomes at community scale it becomes necessary to address the issue of social value at the territorial scale. In doing so, building on the ToC approach we can better understand the value that the civic use rights have at the territorial level and how the outcomes observed and studied are capable to shape the rural landscape over time [1, 31, 39]. In this sense the evaluation of the cultural value of the landscape shall be addressed in a dynamic way, taking into account different transformation of the territory over time and the effects that the social outcomes observed had on it as well as the role that the landscape played in the life of the community, [1], thus affecting mentioned outcomes.

5   A Proposal for an Analytical Framework

Against the background presented in the previous paragraphs, a framework to analyse the social value of properties encumbered by civic use rights is developed starting from Ostrom's SESF presented above. In particular, the analytical framework developed, on one side, add Ostrom's Design Principles to the SESF in a way to better understand the character of civic use properties in their context, especially with reference to the self-management of the civic use property. Whereas, on the other side, analysing the social value of a land encumbered by civic use rights will reinforce the measurement effort with reference to the outcomes in the SESF. Therefore, providing a way to analyse both the internal efficiency as suggested by Ostrom as well as external efficiency of the system that can be evaluated according to the social value of the property encumbered by civic uses. Furthermore, evaluating the social impact supports in understanding the relevance of the DPs and the SESF variables to understand the intrinsic and extrinsic characteristics that lead to the generation of positive societal impacts. This allows to combine the DPs and the SESF and to transform them in a rating model that provides recommendations on how to enhance the SES performances. The analytical framework is presented in Fig. 2 and discussed below.

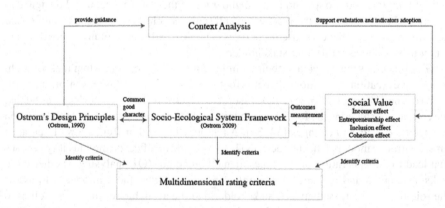

Fig. 2. General framework highlighting links between Ostrom's DPs, SESF, ES and Social Impact Assessment

The developed framework supports in conducting an analysis of the context according to Ostrom's DPs and allows to identify a set of multidimensional criteria to be addressed when managing common goods and collective use properties, as it is the case with civic use properties. The framework can be applied to different cases of collective rights over public or private property so that criteria can be adapted to the different contextual circumstances. In the cases of civic use rights transferral as provided by the Italian law, the present framework will provide a combination of criteria that public bodies shall consider in order to select a property not only of equal ecological value as the original one, but capable of generating positive outcomes for the community. Recurring to multidimensional framework will support public decision-makers in conceptualising the problem, analysing it according to a set of criteria and understanding how the decision taken might have effects in terms of environmental management, social justice and social cohesion at the community and territorial level [22, 40]. This will further enhance transparency and accountability in the decision-making process [22, 24].

5.1   The Issue of Transferral of Civic Use Rights (Article 3, Paragraph 8bis and 8ter, Law 168/2017)

As we have seen above, a recent change to the Law 168/2017 introduced specific provisions to allow municipalities to transfer civic use rights over superficial lands to their disposable assets, proven that there has been an irreversible and lawful transformation of the property itself. According to the law, the transferral is possible towards lands with an equal ecological value as the original land encumbered by civic uses. Methodological issues to be taken into consideration when evaluating the environmental value of a property encumbered by civic use rights have been discussed in literature, recurring to approaches such as the Total Economic Value [17, 21].

Moving the civic uses to another land entails some changes in terms of resource units (e.g. shifting from a chestnut grove to a pinewood), having effects also in terms of productivity of the property and the way in which the community make use of the resources. In this sense, applying the methodology described above can lead to define a set of criteria that guides decision-makers to enhance the sustainability of the civic use property seen as a SES, identifying *ex ante* possible social and cultural outcomes at the community and individual levels.

Proper understanding about the context (i.e. the territory) where the civic use property is located and the immaterial context formed by configurations of stakeholders and their interactions is needed. In doing, Ostrom's DPs and SESF provide a general framework that allow to understand better the local conditions and the specificities of the community that benefit from the civic use rights. Through the analysis of the DPs the evaluator can understand the collective choice arrangements and behaviours of the stakeholder, especially in cases of conflicts, as well as understand the legal boundaries and limitations that exists and whether the community agreed on monitoring and sanctions systems. At the same time, the evaluation allows to understand whether some sort of entrepreneurship and leadership have been nested in the context and what is their value at the community level by recurring to the combined analysis according to the DPs and SESF.

Conducting a dynamic assessment will give a guidance on how to shape the subsystem configurations to maximise the capacity to generate social outcomes, thus analysis also the efficiency and equity dimensions included in the SESF. In this light, an evaluation regarding social outcomes shall take into considerations:

- How the new resource system (land) will increase or decrease the income of the members of the community that use the common good;

- How the new configuration of interaction between the subsystems generates entrepreneurial opportunities or innovation patterns at the community level;
- How the new configuration includes actors or members of the community that were previously excluded;
- How the transfer of civic use rights enhances the sense of belonging to the community through the new configuration of interactions.

Based on these considerations, in the next paragraph we aim to identify a set of criteria that can be used when taking a decision related to transferral of civic use rights between from a land that lost its original destination of use to another public property. The set of criteria can be applied in different circumstances when decisions about the transferral of civic use rights is needed.

5.2 Defining a Set of Criteria for the Transferral of Civic Use Right

Given the general reconstruction of the decision problem, a set of criteria have been developed according to the analytical framework present above in a way to highlight direct and indirect effects of the interactions between the different subsystems. The criteria defined leads to a rating system based on efficiency (internal and external) and equity that can be applied to different cases of transferral of civic uses rights from a land that lost its original destination of use to another public property of equal environmental value. In this sense, the social value of civic uses should lead to select those lands that can guarantee inclusion, social cohesion and distributive justice through the civic use rights and, thus, acting upon a number of the second-tier variables included in the SESF that shall then be considered as criteria when addressing the issue of transferring civic use rights from a public property to another one.

The different criteria are presented in Table 3 and will be commented below. The criteria have been selected to be applicable to all cases in which a decision about transferral of civic use rights needs to be taken. Thus, a selection of the most appropriate DPs and SESF variables have been conducted based on a general decision-making problem that public bodies might face when recurring to the provisions for the transferral of civic use rights included in Article 3, par. 8-bis and 8-ter of the Law 168/2017. When selecting the criteria, a recognition of previous cases that used DPs and SESF to evaluate common use properties have been conducted [2, 4–6, 16]. The criteria shall be taken in consideration in an integrated way to rank different alternatives and to compare them to find the one that can better satisfy all criteria, or the higher number possible, according to specific context certain variables.

The framework so defined allows to understand the connection between the DPs and SESF when conducting the assessment of alternative lands to be encumbered by civic use rights. In doing so, each criterion and sub-criterion will be evaluated according to an interval scale ranging from 0 to 10, where "0" represent the worst level of performance and "10" represents the maximum level of performance in the given dimensions [41, 42]. Using an interval scale enhance consistency within each criterion and increase comparability of results from each proposed alternative [41, 42]. A scale constructed in this way allows to take into account different nuances that increase variability and differentiation. The scores assigned on the described scale will be attributed according

Table 3. Criteria and sub-criteria to be considered when deciding about the transferral of civic use rights from a public property to a new one.

DPs	SESF subsystem	Criteria	Sub-criteria
DP 1 Clearly defined boundaries	Resource systems (RS)	Clarity of system boundaries (RS2)	Proper definition of the boundaries of the civic use property and resources
		Size of the resource system (RS3)	Equal or comparable to the size of the original property
DP 2 Congruence between appropriation and provision rules and local conditions	Resource systems (RS)	Productivity of the system (RS5)	Comparability with original land
		Equilibrium properties (RS6)	Maximum harvest capacity of the system
		Predictability of system dynamics (RS7)	Predictability of the privileges coming from the new land
DP 3 Collective-choice arrangements	Governance system (GS)	Network structure (GS3)	Density of the social network
		Collective-choice rules (GS6)	Presence of multi-stakeholder governance arrangement
	Interactions (I)	Information sharing among users (I2)	Degree of information sharing among stakeholders
DP 4 Monitoring	Users (U)	Number of users (U1)	Capacity to change the number of users
		Socioeconomic attributes of the users (U2)	Capacity to promote diversity and inclusion among users
		History of use (U3)	Capacity to protect historical/cultural value of the civic uses and the landscape
	Resource Units (RU)	Spatial and temporal distribution (RU7)	Level of spatial distribution

(continued)

Table 3. (*continued*)

DPs	SESF subsystem	Criteria	Sub-criteria
			Level of temporal distribution
	Resource Unit (RU)	Economic Value (RU4)	Capacity to produce marketable amount of resources
DP 5 Graduated sanctions	Governance system (GS)	Monitoring and sanctioning (GS8)	Presence of a sanctioning mechanism
DP 6 Conflict-resolution mechanisms	Users (U)	Norms/social capital (U6)	Capacity to promote trust and shared ethical values at community level
	Interactions (I)	Conflicts among users (I4)	Capacity to resolve conflict among users
DP 7 Minimal recognition of rights to organise	Interactions (I)	Self-organising activities (I7)	Level of self-organisation within the community
DP 8 Nested Enterprise	Users (U)	Leadership/Entrepreneurship (U5)	Capacity to promote innovation through civic uses
		Technology used (U9)	Level of development of the technology employed
Outcome (o)			
Development opportunities for the community	Development opportunities for the community	Development opportunities for the community	Development opportunities for the community

to qualitative analysis of the characteristics of the alternative lands to be encumbered by civic uses and on how these characteristics can influence the generation of social outcomes. A comparison with the characteristics the original land will also be conducted. Based on the ranking obtained a difference between the initial situation and the proposed changes will be calculated and assessed how the new setting will affect the 4 social outcome dimensions taken into consideration.

Using a framework as such will support in the design of management arrangements that are capable of enhancing access to resources by a given community, promoting a model of self-organisation and have positive societal impacts on the members of the community. Below we will analyse some of the main criteria and how they should be addressed in the analysis.

The size of the resource system influences the capacity to create a self-management model and thus should be taken into consideration as a context variable when moving civic uses from one property to another one [14]. The choice of the new land, or portion of land, should privilege small and medium scale properties with an equal environmental value compared to the original one.

Transferring the civic use rights from one property to another one might change the resource available in the system and for this reason the productivity of the system (i.e. its capacity to generate goods/resources) and the predictability of the system dynamics (i.e. reaction of the resource system to harvesting by users) shall be taken into consideration when deciding about the transferral [2, 14]. In this sense the choice about the new property to be encumbered by civic use rights shall go in the direction of systems with a similar production pattern as the original one so that it can be predictable both in terms of quality and quantity of the resources available over the year. Connected with this, the decision-makers shall also take into consideration what are the effects that the transferral will have with regard to the economic value of resources to be calculated in terms of production that exceed the sustenance need of the community and that can be sold in the market [2, 14].

As mentioned above, the transferral of civic uses from one property to another one might have effects in terms of the number of users that benefit from collective resources which might result in changes to the network structure and the collective choice rules (i.e. the ability to take management decision at the SES level) [2, 14]. In this sense, once established the value of the land, its size and production pattern, public bodies shall privilege those alternatives that aim at inclusion of traditionally excluded groups and promote multi-stakeholder governance arrangement that extend the network structure and enable participatory decision making. To conduct this analysis the decision-maker shall also take into account the socioeconomic attributes of the members as they can represent important variables to contribute to social inclusion and social cohesion.

Furthermore, in a way to promote social innovation through civic uses, the leadership/entrepreneurship and the social capital variables shall be taken into consideration. The first one refers to the presence of entrepreneurial patterns inside the SES that can facilitate the self-organisation models at the community level and promote the generation of income and development effects as described above [14]. Additionally, the level of social capital and trust between the members of the community is crucial to achieve the mentioned social outcomes. In this sense, the transferral of civic use rights shall be regarded as an opportunity to foster the creation of social capital at the community level and promote forms of shared leadership.

Lastly, dealing with civic uses requires a knowledge of the history of its creation and the historical use of the property encumbered by civic uses [1]. In this sense, the public bodies, when transferring civic use rights, shall promote the preservation of historical use of the collective resource and look at properties that can guarantee continuity with the past and the traditions of the territory. This can have a positive effect in safeguarding the intangible heritage of the territory and protect the cultural landscape through the civic uses. In fact, knowing the history of use will privilege those properties that have a higher value for the preservation of the landscape that was shaped over the century by the presence of those real rights over the collective property and maintain the specificities of the context.

6 Conclusions

Civic use rights are conceptualized in the Italian legal system as perpetual use rights belonging to the members of a given community over a public or private property. Those rights evolved over time from a mean to guarantee access to agri-pastoral-sylvan properties to peasants subjected to a given landlord to a way to enhance access to natural resources and protect them. At present days, civic use rights are still present all over Italy in mountain and other inner areas where forest and grazelands are largely encumbered by different forms of collective use rights. As such, civic use rights became crucial to protect and preserve rural cultural landscapes (Law 431/1995 and Law 168/2017). In connection with this, a recent legal reform introduced paragraph 8-bis in Article 3 of the Law 168/2017 that allow municipality to transfer civic use rights from a property that lost its original purpose to give access to agri-pastoral-sylvan resources to another public-owned land proven that the latter has an equal environmental vale of the former one.

In the paper we presented a view of civic use properties can be understood as complex socio-ecological systems where the users agree on a model to manage the available resources in the system to prevent overexploitation and promote a shared stewardship for their conservation. Furthermore, throughout the interaction between the users and with the resources, a SES will generate positive environmental and social outcomes for the entire community and for connected ecosystem. Thus, understanding civic use properties as SES will facilitate their analysis as collective goods and resources allowing to valorise their management models in connection with their role in the preservation of natural and cultural landscapes.

Seen through this lens, the analysis of civic use properties requires the use of a multi-dimensional framework to understand the complexity of the issue. The framework provides a combination of Ostrom's DPs with SESF in order to define criteria and sub-criteria to be taken into consideration and the effects that the variation of those criteria might have over 4 social justice dimensions - income effect, entrepreneurship effect, inclusion effect and social cohesion effect - understood as the results of the external efficiency of the system. In this light, the innovation of the framework proposed lays not only in the combination of SESF and DPs, but also on the assessment of the social value of civic uses that will enhance understanding about the value of common use property.

The framework has been proposed for the assessment of the transferral of civic use rights from one property to another public-owned land in line with the requirements of the Italian law. Along this line, a general set of criteria to be taken into consideration by decision-makers have been defined according to social and socio-economic dimensions in addition to the equal environmental value criterion provided by the Law 168/2017. Using the proposed analytical framework will enhance the decision-making process by understanding the role of the community of users in the system and highlighting entrepreneurship, and possibly innovation, patterns that can further promote positive societal outcomes at the SES level.

Applications of the proposed analytical framework are still needed in order to understand its value and how it can be applied to different cases dealing with common-use property and transferral of civic use rights. Future research is needed to assess whether the developed framework can be useful in connection with economic evaluation methodologies that are generally used in cases of civic use properties.

References

1. Bruley, E., et al.: Historical reconfigurations of a social-ecological system adapting to economic, policy and climate changes in the French Alps. Reg. Environ. Change. **21**, 33–47 (2021). https://doi.org/10.1007/s10113-021-01760-8/Published
2. Brossette, F., Bieling, C., Penker, M.: Adapting common resource management to under-use contexts: the case of common pasture organizations in the black forest biosphere reserve. Int. J. Commons. **16**, 29–46 (2022). https://doi.org/10.5334/ijc.1138
3. Warde, P.: La gestion des terres en usage collectif dans l'Europe du Nord-Ouest. In: Les propriétés collectives face aux attaques libérales (1750–1914), pp. 61–77. Presses universitaires de Rennes (2003). https://doi.org/10.4000/books.pur.23653
4. Bassi, I., Carestiato, N.: Common property organisations as actors in rural development: a case study of a mountain area in Italy. Int. J. Commons **10**, 363–386 (2016). https://doi.org/10.18352/ijc.608
5. Eychenne, C., Lazaro, L.: Summer pastures: between "commons" and "public goods." Rev. Geogr. Alp. (2014). https://doi.org/10.4000/rga.2303
6. Sutcliffe, L., Öllerer, K., Roelling, M.: Wood-pasture management in southern Transylvania (Romania): From communal to where? In: Hartel, T., Plieninger, T. (eds.) European Wood-pastures in Transition, pp. 219–229. Routledge (2014). https://doi.org/10.4324/9780203797082
7. Marinelli, F.: Usi civici e beni comuni. Rassegna di diritto civile. **2**, 406–423 (2013)
8. Di Genio, G.E.B., Conte, E.: Beni Comuni e Usi Civici. Libreria Universitaria Edizioni, Limena (2016)
9. Marinelli, F.: Gli usi civici. Giuffré Editore, Milano (2013)
10. Deliperi, S.: Gli usi civici e gli altri diritti d'uso collettivi in Sardegna. Rivista Giurisica dell'ambiente. **3**, 387–417 (2011)
11. ISTAT: 6° Censimento Generale dell'Agricoltura Risultati definitivi. (2011)
12. Saleppichi, G.: La tutela costituzionale degli usi civici tra regime civilistico speciale e valenza paesistico-ambientale (a partire dalla sentenza della Corte Costituzionale n. 71 del 2020). Rivista Associazione Italiana dei costituzionalisti. **6**, 75–94 (2020)
13. Cervale, M.C.: Proprietà collettiva, usi civici e ordinamento civile in Italia. Collective ownership, civic uses and civil system in Italy (2021)
14. Ostrom, E.: A general framework for analyzing sustainability of social-ecological systems. Science 1979(325), 419–422 (2009). https://doi.org/10.1126/science.1170749
15. Ostrom, E.: Analyzing Long-enduring, Self-organized, and Self-governed CPRs. In: Governing the Commons. pp. 58–102. Cambridge University Press (1990). https://doi.org/10.1017/cbo9781316423936.004
16. Francucci, M.E.: Domini collettivi, forme di autogoverno per la gestione degli ecosistemi e lo sviluppo locale (2020). https://doi.org/10.13128/sdt-11863

17. Casprini, D., Oppio, A., Torrieri, F.: Usi civici: open evaluation issues in the Italian legal framework on civic use properties. Land (Basel) **12**, 871 (2023). https://doi.org/10.3390/land12040871

18. Ostrom, E.: Governing the Commons. Cambridge University Press (1990). https://doi.org/10.1017/CBO9780511807763

19. Piscopo, C., Buonanno, D.: Architettura E Beni Comuni. La Prospettiva Degli Usi Civici. Techne. **14**, 40–45 (2017). https://doi.org/10.13128/Techne-22140

20. Benedetti, R.: Gli Usi civici come pratica di rivalutazione e cura del territorio (2020)

21. Battisti, F., Pisano, C.: Common property in Italy. unresolved issues and an appraisal approach: towards a definition of environmental-economic civic value. Land (Basel). **11** (2022). https://doi.org/10.3390/land11111927

22. Oppio, A., Dell'Ovo, M.: Strategic environmental assessment (sea) and multi-criteria analysis: an integrated approach. In: Campeol, G. (ed.) Strategic Environmental Assessment and Urban Planning. GET, pp. 47–63. Springer, Cham (2020). https://doi.org/10.1007/978-3-030-46180-5_4

23. Oppio, A., Dell'Ovo, M., Torrieri, F., Miebs, G., Kadziński, M.: Understanding the drivers of urban development agreements with the rough set approach and robust decision rules. Land Use Policy **96**, 104678 (2020)

24. Dell'Anna, F., Dell'Ovo, M.: A stakeholder-based approach managing conflictual values in urban design processes. The case of an open prison in Barcelona. Land use Policy **114** (2022). https://doi.org/10.1016/j.landusepol.2021.105934

25. Cristoferi, D.: DA Usi Civici A Beni Comuni: Gli Studi Sulla Proprietà Collettiva Nella Medievistica E Modernistica Italiana E Le Principali Tendenze Storiografiche Internazionali (2016)

26. Farahbakhsh, I., Bauch, C.T., Anand, M.: Modelling coupled human-environment complexity for the future of the biosphere: strengths, gaps and promising directions. Philos. Trans. Royal Soc. B: Biolog. Sci. **377** (2022). https://doi.org/10.1098/rstb.2021.0382

27. Romagnoli, F., Masiero, M., Secco, L.: Windstorm impacts on forest-related socio-ecological systems: an analysis from a socio-economic and institutional. Perspective (2022). https://doi.org/10.3390/f13060939

28. Romolini, M., Conway, T.M., Saxena, P., De Guzman, E.B.: A socio-ecological approach to align tree stewardship programs with public health benefits in marginalized neighborhoods in Los Angeles, USA. Front, Sustainable Cities. **4**, 944182 (2022)

29. Silvetti, A., Bonaiti, C., Andrulli, F.: New life for mondonico: from "ghost village" to agro-forest university campus. ArchHistoR **7**, 1931–1948 (2020)

30. Shirvani Dastgerdi, A., Kheyroddin, R.: Policy Recommendations for Inte-grating Resilience into the Management of Cultural Landscapes. Sustainability (Switzerland) **14** (2022). https://doi.org/10.3390/su14148500

31. Cerreta, M., Elefante, A., La Rocca, L.: A creative living lab for the adaptive reuse of the morticelli church: The ssmoll project. Sustainability (Switzerland) **12**, 1–20 (2020). https://doi.org/10.3390/su122410561

32. Gates, E., Dyson, L.: Implications of the changing conversation about causality for evaluators. Am. J. Eval. **38**, 29–46 (2017)

33. Donaldson, S.I., Christie, C.A., Mark, M.M.: What Counts as Credible Evidence in Applied Research and Evaluation Practice? SAGE (2009)

34. Rawhouser, H., Cummings, M., Newbert, S.L.: Social impact measurement: Current approaches and future directions for social entrepreneurship re-search. Entrep. Theory Pract. **43**, 82–115 (2019)

35. Ebrahim, A., Rangan, V.K.: What impact? A framework for measuring the scale and scope of social performance. Calif. Manage. Rev. **56**, 118–141 (2014)

36. Piabuo, S.M.: Community forest enterprises in Cameroon: Tensions, para-doxes and governance challenges. Environ Dev. **44** (2022). https://doi.org/10.1016/j.envdev.2022.100762
37. Taplin, D.H., Clark, H.: Theory of Change basics. ActKnowledge, New York (2013)
38. Rolfe, S.: Combining theories of change and realist evaluation in practice: lessons from a research on evaluation study. Evaluation **25**, 294–316 (2019). https://doi.org/10.1177/135638 9019835229
39. Gravagnuolo, A., Micheletti, S., Bosone, M.: A participatory approach for "circular" adaptive reuse of cultural heritage. Building a heritage community in Salerno, Italy. Sustainability (Switzerland) **13** (2021). https://doi.org/10.3390/su13094812
40. Oppio, A., Forestiero, L., Sciacchitano, L., Dell'ovo, M.: How to assess urban quality: A spatial multicriteria decision analysis approach. Valori e Valutazioni **2021** 21–30 (2021)
41. Department of Communities and Local Government: Multi-criteria analysis: a manual (2009)
42. Abbas, A.E., Hupman, A.C.: Scale dependence in weight and rate multicrite-ria decision methods. Eur. J. Oper. Res. (2023). https://doi.org/10.1016/j.ejor.2022.12.038

Evaluation of NBS Solutions for Climate Resilience and Adaptation in the Sub-saharan Africa: The Case of Ghana's Ashanti Region

Martina Corti[1]([✉]) [iD], Vanessa Assumma[2,3] [iD], and Francesco Pittau[4] [iD]

[1] School of Architecture Urban Planning and Construction Engineering (AUIC), Politecnico di Milano, 20133 Milano, Italy
martina.corti@mail.polimi.it
[2] Department of Architecture and Urban Studies, Politecnico di Milano, 20133 Milano, Italy
vanessa.assumma@unibo.it
[3] Department of Architecture (DAStU), Università di Bologna, 40136 Bologna, Italy
[4] Department of Architecture, Built Environmental and Construction Engineering (DABC), Politecnico di Milano, 20133 Milano, Italy
francesco.pittau@mail.polimi.it

Abstract. The new challenge of the century is the development of sustainable projects. It is crucial to consider integrated solutions to evaluate project consequences at the social, geographical, physical, ecological, and technological levels in a future where climate hazards will increase owing to anthropogenic activities. As a result, the topic of this paper is the creation of a hybrid methodology for evaluating the aforementioned implications. The "Okyena for a Free Future" project in Manso Abore, in Ghana's Ashanti region, is used as a case study for the methodology. OFF proposes the construction of a school hub that can accompany the entire community towards social and economic development while also taking climate resilience and adaptation measures into consideration. In this environment, perhaps more than in others, the necessity to provide actions that can contribute to community expansion without compromising the development of future generations is clear. The A'WOT model, together with other assessment methods like Stakeholder Analysis and Scenario Building, enables taking multiple factors into account at once to handle the world's increasing complexity. By doing so, it is feasible to highlight the perspectives of the key players and provide decision-makers with a logical foundation for choice dilemmas involving various, frequently at odds objectives. By assessing the viability of implementing NBS solutions, the model aims to facilitate the deployment of alternative techniques.

Keywords: Mixed-methods · A'WOT analysis · Nature-based solutions

1 Introduction

The most recent estimates, the global population might reach approximately 8.5 billion by 2030 and 9.7 billion by 2050. The population will peak at approximately 10,4 billion in 2080 and remain at that level until 2100 [1]. The proportion of world population in

O. Gervasi et al. (Eds.): ICCSA 2023 Workshops, LNCS 14108, pp. 398–414, 2023.
https://doi.org/10.1007/978-3-031-37117-2_27

working age (from 25 to 64 years) is even more increasing. Nowadays, the greatest barrier to equitable growth is inequality, which may be measured using Gini index [2]. Over the past three decades, world inequality has increased as result of liberalist policies of privatization and deregulation [3]. In addition, new potential drivers of inequality, such as digital transformation and climate change, have emerged in recent years and are expected to have a negative impact on inequality if not supported by suitable countermeasures.

In general, Sub-Saharan Africa (SSA) in the last 10 years reported an increasing trendline of the Gini index, as a result of the growing disparity due to the socioeconomic gap between the communities within the SSA Countries. It is estimated that SSA will dominate global population growth until 2050. [2]. The change in age distribution appears to be an opportunity that Sub-Saharan Africa to accelerate economic growth per capita. According to the World Bank, Ghana's Gini index was 43,5 in 2016, indicating significant economic disparity within the nation [3].

Due to a variety of factors such as the increase in population, migration and uncontrolled urbanization, the potential of the African continent for a better quality of life remains untapped.

A commitment supports less developed nations, also through technical and financial aids, in the design and implementation of sustainable and resilient structures using local materials. In Ghana, the achievement of sustainability has stalled, as shown by both overall and average performances by SDG (Fig. 1). Its rank is in part in part due to the lack of special legislation. The target remains one of the major obstacles to ensure a sustainable future for the country's population.

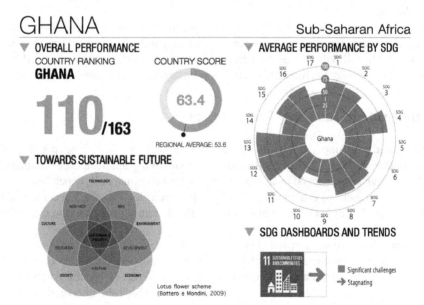

Fig. 1. Sustainable Development Report for Ghana, performance of goal 11 and lotus flower scheme for the problem under investigation.

Although the disparity with the global north countries, SSA countries are significantly moving for climate adaptation and provision of services to communities and with care of the environment. In this sense, SSA have found in Nature-Based Solutions (NBS) an opportunity to achieve sustainable and resilient challenges [2].

Specifically, NBS are defined as "actions to protect, sustainably manage, and restore natural or modified ecosystems, which ad- dress societal challenges in an effective and adaptive manner, while providing benefits for human well-being and biodiversity" [4]. NBS aim to support the achievement of Sustainable Development Goals (SDGs) [5–10], with a particular attention on Goal 11 "Making cities and communities more sustainable and resilient", as well as to protect human well-being by enhancing the resilience of ecosystems, their capacity for renewal, and their service provision. Their deployment is a comprehensive response to the environmental challenges faced by all those impacted by climate change (e.g., flooding, air and water pollution, among others).

The term NBS was first used by the World Bank in 2008 [11], and then adopted by the International Union for Conservation of Nature (IUCN) in 2012 [12, 13].

More recently, the World Resources Institute (WRI) partnered with the World Bank and the African Development Bank to conduct in SSA a regional inventory to collect projects that implemented NBS in the decade 2012–21 [14].

The paper aims to explore the current challenge of NBS implementation in SSA nations, through the development of a multi-methodological proposal to evaluate the feasibility of alternative NBS scenarios. This proposal is composed by a Stakeholders Analysis, a SWOT + STEEP Analysis, and Scenario Building to frame the decision problem, and by the multicriteria ranking technique "A'WOT" for the problem assessment and solution.

The purpose is to provide to public administrations, financiers, and developers a model for the development of a coherent and integrated decision-making process that can facilitate the NBS design, assessment and, implementation in global-south countries to respond effectively to climate resilience uncertainty and socio-economic issues.

2 Integrated Multi-level Methodology

The proposed multi-methodological approach is structured by considering specific evaluation phases that can favor the addressing of sustainability and resilience paradigms. Each phase can be associated to an evaluation tool (or more than one), depending on the complexity to reach the evaluation goal. [8]. In this multi-level method, specific evaluation tools are highly recognized and shared in the literature to support the evaluation process (Table1).

Stakeholder analysis is included in the cognitive analysis phase because it is essential for understanding the engaged players to enhance decision-making process during the design and implementation of an intervention. The SWOT + STEEP Analysis can provide a photograph of the current state of the area in which the intervention should be located. Scenario building can develop narratives to envision alternative futures and thus support the assessment of alternatives.

The A'WOT model aims to analyze the alternatives developed via Scenario Building and to continue with project design through the monitoring phase.

Table 1. Phase of sustainability project and tools (Elab. From [16]).

Evaluation phases	Evaluation tools
1. Cognitive analysis	Stakeholders Analysis
2. Consultation	SWOT + STEEP Analysis
3. Definition of strategic framework	Scenario Building
4. Systemic evaluation	A'WOT Model
5. Monitoring	DPSIR Model

The research focuses on the application of these mixed methodologies to support the selection of the most sustainable design alternative according to the "Lotus flower model" [8].

2.1 Framing of the Problem

After completing the cognitive framework pertaining to the case study and context, it is essential to introduce the Stakeholders Analysis as the first decision-making tool. This analysis identifies the public and private actors capable of influencing the transformation of the urban fabric. In addition to the actors, consideration must also be given to the project's stakeholders, who, despite not necessarily being directly involved in project decisions, can influence the potential success/acceptance of the intervention [15, 16]. It is essential to identify the actors and stakeholders and their level of power/interest, as well as the exchanged relationships between them. A combination of Power Interest Matrix (P/I) and Social Network Analysis (SNA) is therefore proposed.

Power/Interest Matrix
The Power/Interest matrix (P/I) illustrates each stakeholder's power and interest levels in a particular decision-making process [16]. It permits stakeholders to be mapped according to their level of interest and decision-making authority. The identification of stakeholders is accomplished by evaluating the types of actors and cognitive resources possessed by each one. This generates as output a map based on qualitative evaluations converted to a numeric scale to produce a final ranking.

Social Network Analysis
SNA is a methodology that has evolved from sociology and anthropology. Within the decision-making process, the relationships between the various actors and the various types of resources they exchange with one another are taken into account. According to this strategy, it is possible to visualize the size and shape of the network, as well as the coalitions and key DMs. The relationships between stakeholders can affect the over- all performance of the decision-making process [17].

The combination of these two methods enables consideration of all involved parties and their interdependent relationships [18]. Thus, it will be possible to identify competing interests during the ex-ante phase, while minimizing negative externalities during the in itinere and ex-post phases.

SWOT + STEEP Analysis

The SWOT analysis is a decision-making tool that helps to rationalize decision-making processes. It is a well-known technique that was developed in the 1960s [19] to analyze the strengths (S), weaknesses (W), opportunities (O), and threats (T) of a given problem. This appears like a four-quadrant matrix that identifies the context's endogenous (strengths and weaknesses) and exogenous (opportunities and threats) fac- tors. Since the 1980s, its usage was extended to other fields, such as business economics, and founded a fertile arena in public sector to analyze and support policy decisions. This tool well fits when is combined with STEEP analysis, which considers the following factors: (i) Society; (ii) Technology; (iii) Environment; (iv) Economy; (v) Policy. In this contribution, the STEEP analysis has been adapted to fit the rural context, since the specificity of the case study, thus resulting in the following components:

1. Socioeconomic factors to assess sociological components and economic dynamics in the rural area;
2. Urban infrastructure and services to evaluate the availability of services and infrastructure;
3. Ecology and environment to understand the health state of the environment and plan land management;
4. Governance and policy to assess the presence/absence of plans, programs, projects or funds and to understand the hierarchy of the power in the community;
5. Construction and craftsmanship to evaluate the local potential related to traditional techniques.

The SWOT + STEEP analysis generates a four-quadrant diagram in conjunction with the adapted STEEP components to analyze the site-specific characteristics of the case study and its complex dynamics.

Scenario Building

To support policy decisions effectively, scenario building plays an important role in modeling plausible future conditions. A scenario is defined as "a set of hypothetical future events constructed to clarify a possible chain of causal events and their decision points" [20].

Thus, traditional planning has given way to strategic planning, which is founded on a long-term, place-based, multidisciplinary approach. By considering the interests of all parties, this method makes it possible to strengthen political consensus [21, 22]. Scenario planning stimulates strategic thinking, enables the identification of alternative futures, and supports decision-making under conditions of uncertainty [23].

In the relevant literature, a reasonable number of three-five scenarios is generally suggested, including in this range the zero-option (or inertial scenario), which provides the same services and resources without any change over time. Its inclusion in the eval- uation favors more propensity of the DMs in accepting scenarios comparison. Thereby, an operational transition towards sustainable integrated spatial planning is possible.

2.2 Evaluation of the Problem

The systemic evaluation phase allows for the assessment of the optimal design alternative considering the previous analyses. Starting with a SWOT analysis and Scenario Building, the Multicriteria Analysis technique (MCA) is implemented, which is a useful tool for resolving uncertain problems [24]. MCA can be combined within integrated frameworks owing to its qualitative-quantitative methodology [8, 18]. Particularly, it is used as an umbrella term to collect a series of evaluation techniques that attempt to explicitly take into account multiple criteria simultaneously. The goal is to bring out the points of view of the involved actors and provide DMs with a rational basis for choice problems that are increasingly characterized by a multiplicity of often conflicting objectives/criteria [25]. The A'WOT method, which combines SWOT analysis and the AHP technique, is suitable to achieve the sustainability objective [26, 27].

A'WOT

The A'WOT model is a hybrid approach that overcomes certain AHP and SWOT analysis limitations [28–30]. It enables the evaluation of the best alternative in a decision-making process on the basis of the SWOT analysis's highlighted contextual characteristics. The following steps characterize the method:

- Contextual cognitive synthesis;
- Drafting SWOT analysis;
- Cascade structuring according to the AHP decomposition principle;
- Evaluation and weighting of the elements according to the principle of comparative judgements by means of surveys/questions or desk judgements;
- Synthesis of local and global priorities;
- Sensitivity analysis, for instance using the "What-if?" method [31].

The cascade configuration is typical of AHP and is distinguished by [32]:

- Goal: to determine the most sustainable alternative among the generated scenarios;
- Criteria: strengths, weaknesses, opportunities, and threats;
- Sub-criteria: SWOT items subdivided into strengths, weaknesses, opportunities, and threats;
- Alternatives: definition of a finite set of scenarios. They are described in Sect. 3.

The evaluation model can be developed by using dedicated software such as SuperDecisions by CreativeFoundations. Utilizing pairwise comparison and Saaty's scale, the weighting of the elements is determined. Saaty's scale is a nine-score comparison scale that is used by DMs in expressing the intensity of the elements within a hierarchy through pairwise comparison [33]. There are three levels of comparison: (i) At the level of criteria; (ii) At the level of sub- criteria; and (iii) At the level of alternatives.

The following steps must be taken to determine the weight of each alternative:

- Solve the principal eigenvector and normalize the result;
- Weight the eigenvector according to the priority of the element with which it was compared. In this way, a ranking of all the hierarchy priorities is obtained;

- Sum all weighted eigenvectors. This step allows to synthesize the priorities previously obtained in the considered scenarios, thus obtaining the final ranking.

To ensure consistency of judgements, the Consistency Ratio must be always ≤ 10%. A survey can be developed by choosing a participatory or a desktop modality via questionnaires, interviews, workshops, and so on. In the second scenario, picking a key stakeholder is crucial to preventing subjectively affecting the outcomes.

Local priorities and global priorities are elicited at the level of sub-criteria and alternatives, respectively, and are distinguished in the summary of priorities. Thus, it is possible to determine which project strengths, weaknesses, opportunities, and threats will require the most consideration.

Lastly, the sensitivity analysis is helpful to examine the stability of the results and thus of the evaluation model when the weights of the criteria are altered. However, due to the limited space, this was not incorporated into the paper.

3   Application

3.1   Case Study: The Ashanti Region of Ghana

The study area is affected by environmental issues such as Galamsey sites, deforestation, and flooding, which requires the consideration of the role of nature-based solutions (NBS) in the characterization of the scenarios.

"Okyena for a Free Future" (OFF) is a public project developed within the framework of Italian educational institutions, construction holdings and local public authorities, which aims to promote the construction of a vocational school complex in the rural area of Manso Abore, in the Ashanti region of Ghana.

The government-designated intervention area encompasses approximately 19 hectares and is characterized by a vast expanse of virgin forest and a small portion contaminated by illegal mining (Fig. 2). As there are no local, territorial, or government

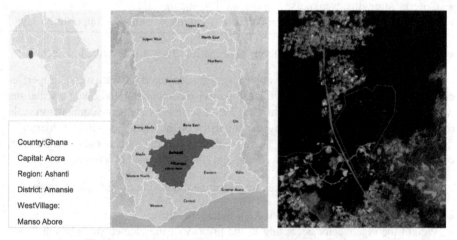

Fig. 2. Map of the intervention plot in Manso Abore, Ghana.

plans with clear indications regarding the area's transformation, these characteristics serve as the starting point for reflection.

Due to the absence of a long-term urban planning forecast, the multi-level methodology is here employed to support the design of a long-term strategy. Particularly, the objective will be to determine the optimal scenario for promoting the region and the community from a social, economic, and environmental standpoint, with a focus on sustainability and climate resilience. The integrated method is then applied to the plot and the surrounding rural territory, beginning with the cognitive analysis and concluding with the scenario selection. Managing the inherent area's complexity and contradictions is the most difficult aspect of the decision-making process.

3.2 Stakeholders Analysis

Once the key stakeholders were identified, they were categorized based on their degree of influence and level of interest using the Power/Interest matrix [17]. According to the SNA model, the above analysis was supplemented by an analysis of the existing and potential relationships between the various stakeholders [18]. The picture below

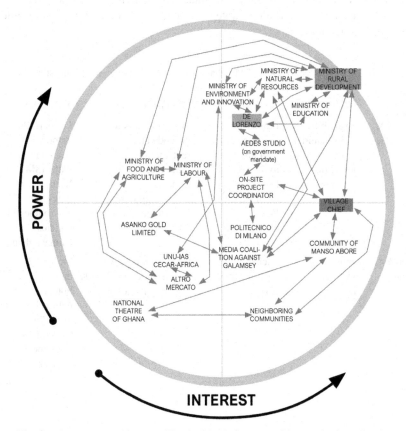

Fig. 3. The output od SNA combined with P/I for the problem under investigation.

depicts the outcomes of the applied mixed method (Fig. 3). The analysis demonstrates that the Ministry of Rural Development is the most influencing public actor. Similarly, a leading Italian company in design, development, and production of technical and vocational training equipment, represents the major private developer as the project's primary funder. The village chief is the central intermediary between the Manso Abore local community, the neighboring communities, and the highest institutional offices.

All other actors and stakeholders must be involved in the decision-making process, more or less actively depending on the quadrant they fall into, to guarantee the highest level of transparency and promote the acceptance of decisions by all parties.

Only by implementing this strategy will it be possible to minimize and mitigate conflicts resulting from divergent opinions and thereby increase the intervention's chances of success.

3.3 SWOT + STEEP Analysis

The SWOT analysis coupled with the STEEP analysis enabled the identification of the intervention area's defining characteristics. According to Table 2, the environmental theme, which is related to the themes of degradation and pollution, plays a crucial role in the region. In addition, education, strategic vision, and the durability of interventions emerged as additional topics.

Table 2. The output of SWOT + STEEP analysis for the problem under investigation.

	STRENGTHS	WEAKNESSES	OPPORTUNITIES	TREATHS
Ecology & Environment	Availability of NBS materials Forest as flood protection element	Floods Environmental degradation due to illegal mining Loss of biodiversity Water contamination	Water projects for groundwater reclamation Land reclamation projects Converting mining areas to new economic horizons	Uncontrolled deforestation Non-compliance with ASM laws Lack of long-term environmental policies Climate change
Governance & Policy	Trust in the village headman	Lack of government control	Cooperation between communities and NGOs Capacity Building	Slow bureaucracy Potential political instability Government investment dependency

(*continued*)

Table 2. (*continued*)

	STRENGTHS	WEAKNESSES	OPPORTUNITIES	TREATHS
Construction & Craft	Widespread vernacular building Government project for building innovation	Unsustainable European construction techniques Products without certifications Use of materials with low durability	Traditional solutions for climate adaptation	Materials with poor resistance to harsh climatic events
Facilities & Services	Health Hub Civic center Primary school Main paved road	Distance between the two village cores Supply difficulties Unplanned construction Lack of infrastructure for public mobility	Government-sponsored rural development Project area as a hub between the two village cores	Absence of urban regulations Lack of long-term strategic vision Great distances without infrastructural development
Society & Economy	Local labour availability Economically active population equal to 77% Availability of mineral and agricultural resources	High illiteracy rate Inequalities in access to education Sanitary conditions Migration Social economic conflicts	Community value Collaboration with fair trade market	Economic policies with negative repercussions on the territory Cyclic poverty network

3.4 Scenario Building

Based on the state of the art as determined by the SWOT + STEEP analysis, alternative future scenario definitions were established. The case study presented the following scenarios:

- Scenario 0 is the inertial scenario, as predicated on maintaining the territory's current technological level. It must be considered to promote a conscious and rational choice that also includes the possibility of non-intervention;
- Scenario 1 is the trend scenario proposed by the Ghanaian government. It entails the construction of a vocational school center and services such as a market, residences, and agricultural areas;

- Scenario 2 envisions the strategic scenario. It proposes the incorporation of NBS solutions, such as the use of local materials, reforestation, reclamation of land degraded by Galamsey, and the implementation of rainwater harvesting strategies.

At this stage, storytelling is a valuable tool for facilitating the communication of the vision. The following comic (Fig. 4) depicts the narrative for Scenario 2.

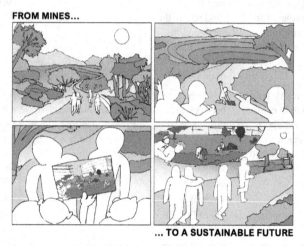

Fig. 4. Storytelling to support Scenario Building for the problem under investigation.

3.5 Development of A'WOT

The A'WOT methodology is implemented while taking into account the limitations im- posed by the geographical distance with respect to the case study. Nowadays, it is currently impossible to administer questionnaires to the involved parties, so the point of view assumed for the application is that of the Ministry of Rural Development, the key stakeholder identified by the Stakeholders Analysis.

The software SuperDecisions was employed for the implementation of the method. After completing the preliminary analysis and drafting the SWOT + STEEP Analysis, the cascade network was generated (Fig. 5).

The principle of decomposition is consistently applied. Criteria and sub-criteria meet the requirements for completeness, redundancy, operability, size, and diachronic impacts. The advantage of this mixed method lies in the ability to evaluate the key aspects that emerged during the state-of-the-art analysis in relation to the project alternatives, thereby proposing a coherent and rational methodology.

We then move on to the Saaty's scale principle of comparative evaluation. Since this evaluation can be conceived as a pre-test to be replicated subsequently with real actors and stakeholders, thanks to the evaluation tools applied before it has been easier to investigate public bodies interests and expectations with respect to rural development issue. The pairwise comparison at the criterion level assigns equal weight to each section

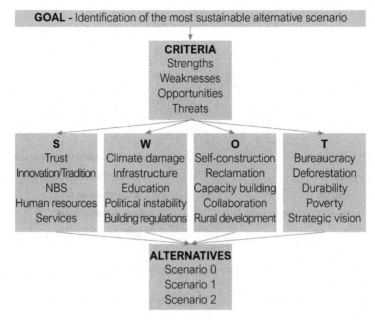

Fig. 5. Structuring of the decision problem through the A'WOT analysis and the AHP method.

of the SWOT analysis. Pairwise comparisons at the level of sub-criteria and alternatives were conducted taking into account the results of previous analyses (Fig. 6).

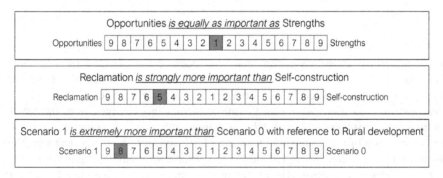

Fig. 6. Examples of pairwise comparison for criteria, sub-criteria and alternatives.

At this stage, it is necessary to ensure that the rate of inconsistency is below 10%.

The software then processes local (Fig. 7) and global priorities (Fig. 8) using the calculation method described previously.

The just-presented findings correspond with the major themes that emerged from the SWOT analysis. At the sub-criteria level, NBS solutions (49%) and the potential offered by the combination of technology and tradition (29%) appear to be the project's greatest strengths. As environmental degradation (37%) and a lack of building regulations (30%)

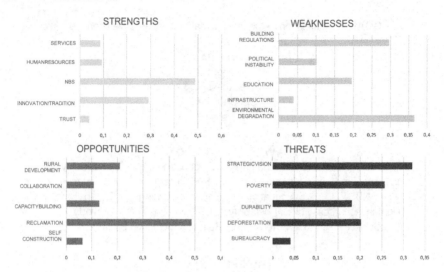

Fig. 7. Sub-criteria priority vectors.

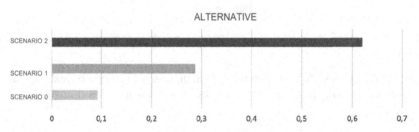

Fig. 8. Alternatives final ranking.

would exacerbate an already critical situation, special consideration must be given to these issues. The issue of land reclamation (49%) and rural development (21%) are highlighted as opportunities. Lastly, the absence of a strategic vision (32%), The just-presented findings correspond with the major themes that emerged from the SWOT analysis. At the sub-criteria level, NBS solutions (49%) and the potential offered by the combination of technology and tradition (29%) appear to be the project's greatest strengths. As environmental degradation (37%) and a lack of building regulations (30%) would exacerbate an already critical situation, special consideration must be given to these issues. The issue of land reclamation (49%) and rural development (21%) are highlighted as opportunities. Lastly, the absence of a strategic vision (32%), poverty (26%), and deforestation (20%) remain exogenous factors that must be man- aged. In terms of global priorities, Scenario 2 (62%) characterized by the implementation of NBS solutions is deemed preferable. Scenario 1 (29%) does not meet the actual needs of the community because it proposes short-term solutions that would not break.

4 Discussion and Conclusions

The proposed process, based on conventional evaluation tools, such as SWOT analysis and Scenario Building, and by mixed methodologies, such as the Stakeholders Analysis P/I and SNA and the A'WOT method, is an effective guideline for a decision- making process aimed at sustainability in its many facets (lotus flower). The article attempts to demonstrate the interconnected nature of the phases of the sustainability project [8], emphasizing their strict relationships.

Specifically, the SWOT analysis generated during the cognitive phase served as the foundation for the systemic assessment phase, establishing a solid chain of relationships between knowledge and decisions.

Promote innovative strategies to enhance decision-making is a process fraught with complexity, as it involves a multitude of variables, including various actors with opposing and frequently competing interests. Sustainability requires a multidimensional and interdisciplinary approach [34], which is why the A'WOT method is especially useful in this field. It enables the simultaneous evaluation of multiple variables, beginning with the state of the art on the territory and culminating in a consensus decision.

In contexts such as SSA, where long-term strategic vision is frequently lacking, the development of an integrated, multi-level methodology is even more crucial to envision potential development scenarios. In fact, the application of a multi-methodological model can support the planning process to be more place-based and to guarantee a multi-level governance as well. This achievement could guarantee safe, inclusive, and sustainable quality of life, while protecting and valorising both cultural and natural heritage.

However, the process should not be considered complete. The implementation of the sensitivity analysis is the first step to ensure the consistency of the results. Secondly, the model is supposed to be replicated with real actors and stakeholders to compare the results. Furthermore, no monitoring tool is addressed in the paper. Specifically, this phase is necessary for both the ex-ante and ongoing evaluations of the project's development, as well as for making any necessary adjustments as the project progresses. The presented case study facilitates the employment of a monitoring tool by using the DPSIR model. The DPSIR can identify determinants, pressures, status, impacts, and societal responses to changes in the environment [35].

The proposed methodology, supplemented by future research on monitoring, is intended to serve as a guideline for the promotion of sustainable projects towards the attainment of the SDGs, with regard to Goal 11 for the resilient and sustainable development of human settlements, with an eye on future generations.

Integration of the A'WOT with the biophysical and economic assessment of the eco- system services that NBS solutions can provide as response to climate shocks and disturbances [36–38], strategic management [39, 40] as well as the investigation of the interdependencies between dependent and independent variables, is an additional area of research. In this sense, various development scenarios are envisioned, including the extension of the multicriteria hierarchical model into a network [33], the application of the Dynamic SWOT [41], and regression analysis [42]. An additional promising step is the combination of the A'WOT with Geographic Information Systems (GIS) and thus allowing to produce suitability maps for the localization of NBS solutions in the territory under investigation [26].

Acknowledgements. The authors wish to thank AEDES srl Architecture Engineering Design for their valuable contribution in providing data and insights about the developed framework. The work was developed within the teaching course "Strumenti per la Valutazione della Sostenibilità Ambientale", Accademic Year 2022–23, of the Master Degree Programme in Architectural Engineering of Politecnico di Milano.

References

1. United Nations: Revision of World Population Prospects (2022). https://population.un.org/wpp/Publications/. Accessed 11 May 2023
2. Gini, C.: Sulla misura della concentrazione e della variabilità dei caratteri. Premiate officine grafiche C. Ferrari (1914)
3. THE WORLD BANK, https://data.worldbank.org. Accessed 11 May 2023
4. World Inequality Lab: World Inequality Report (2022). https://wir2022.wid.world/www-site/uploads/2023/03/D_FINAL_WIL_RIM_RAPPORT_2303.pdf. Accessed 11 May 2023
5. United Nations, https://www.who.int/news-room/fact-sheets/detail/millennium-development-goals-(mdgs). Accessed 11 May 2023
6. United Nations, https://sdgs.un.org, Accessed Jan 1 2023
7. World Commission on Environment and Development: Report of the World Commission on Environment and Development: Our Common Future Towards Sustainable Development, Part II. Common Challenges Population and Human Resources 4. (1987)
8. Mondini, G.: Valutazione e complessità. In Bottero, M., Mondini, G. Valutazioni di sostenibilità, Piani, Programmi, Progetti. Celid, Turin (2009)
9. Bottero, M., Ferretti, V., Mondini, G.: From the environmental debt to the environmental loan: Trends and future challenges for intergenerational discounting. Environ Dev Sustain. **15**, 1623–1644 (2013)
10. Mondini, G.: Valutazioni integrate per la gestione delle nuove sfide sociali, Valori e Valutazioni. DEI Tipografia del Genio civile. **17**, 15–17 (2016)
11. Oliver, E., Marsters, L.: Nature-Based Solutions in Sub-Saharan Africa for Climate and Water Resilience: A Methodology for Evaluating the Regional Status of Investments in Nature-Based Solutions from a Scan of Multilateral Development Bank Portfolios, Technical Note. Washington, DC: World Resources Institute (2022). https://doi.org/10.46830/writn.22.00054
12. IUCN, https://portals.iucn.org/library/node/46486. Accessed Jan 1 2023
13. World Bank: World Development Report 2008: Agriculture for Development. Washington DC (2007). http://hdl.handle.net/10986/5990
14. IUCN-International Union for Conservation of Nature: The IUCN Programme 2013–2016 (2012). https://www.iucn.org/sites/default/files/2022-05/wcc-5th-003.pdf
15. Mendelow, A.: Stakeholder mapping. In: 2nd international conference on information System., Cambridge (1991)
16. Dente, B.: Understanding Policy Decisions. In: Understanding Policy Decisions. SAST, pp. 1–27. Springer, Cham (2014). https://doi.org/10.1007/978-3-319-02520-9_1
17. Yang, R.J.: An investigation of stakeholder analysis in urban development projects: Empirical or rationalistic perspectives. Int. J. Project Manage. **32**, 838–849 (2014)
18. Bottero, M., Assumma, V., Caprioli, C., Dell'Ovo, M.: Decision making in urban development: The application of a hybrid evaluation method for a critical area in the city of Turin (Italy). Sustain Cities Soc. **72**, (2021)
19. Humphrey, A.: SWOT analysis for management consulting, SRI alumni Newsletter. Sri International California (2006)

20. Gharajedaghi, J.: Systems and thinking. Managing chaos and complexity: a Platform for Designing Business Architecture. Elsevier (2006)
21. Kahn, H.: On Escalation. In: Bobbitt Philip and Freedman, L. and T.G.F. (ed.) US Nuclear Strategy: A Reader. pp. 283–336. Palgrave Macmillan UK, London (1989)
22. Godet, M.: The art of scenarios and strategic planning: tools and pitfalls. Technol Forecast Soc Change. **65**, 3–22 (2000)
23. Van de Kerkhof, M.: Making a difference: On the constraints of consensus building and the relevance of deliberation in stakeholder dialogues. Policy Sci. **39**, 279–299 (2006)
24. Figueira, J., Greco, S., Ehrogott, M.: Multiple Criteria Decision Analysis: State of the Art Surveys. Springer, New York, New York (2005)
25. Dell'Anna, F., Dell'Ovo, M.: A stakeholder-based approach managing conflictual values in urban design processes. The case of an open prison in Barcelona. Land use policy. 114, (2022)
26. Bottero, M., D'Alpaos, C., Marello, A.: An application of the a'WOT analysis for the management of cultural heritage assets: The case of the historical farmhouses in the aglie castle (Turin). Sustainability (Switzerland). **12**, (2020)
27. Treves, A., Bottero, M., Caprioli, C., Comino, E.: The reintroduction of Castor fiber in Piedmont (Italy): An integrated SWOT-spatial multicriteria based approach for the analysis of suitability scenarios. Ecol Indic. **118**, 106748 (2020)
28. Kurttila, M., Pesonen, M., Kangas, J., Kajanus, M.: Utilizing the analytic hierarchy process AHP in SWOT analysis a hybrid method and its application to a forest-certification case. Forest Policy and Econom. Elsevier **1**(1), 41–52 (2000)
29. Kangas, J., Pesonen, M., Kurttila, M., Kajanus, M.: A'WOT: INTEGRATING THE AHP WITH SWOT ANALYSIS (2001)
30. Kajanus, M., Kangas, J., Kurttila, M.: The use of value focused thinking and the A'WOT hybrid method in tourism management. Tour Manag. **25**, 499–506 (2004)
31. Saltelli, A., Annoni, P.: How to avoid a perfunctory sensitivity analysis. Environ. Model. Softw. **25**, 1508–1517 (2010)
32. Saaty, T.: The Analytic Hierarchy Process (AHP) for Decision Making (1980)
33. Saaty, T.L.: Analytic Hierarchy Process (2005)
34. Bennett, E.M.: Bright spots: seeds of a good Anthropocene. Front Ecol Environ. **14**, 441–448 (2016)
35. Huang, H.-F., Kuo, J., Lo, S.-L.: Review of PSR framework and development of a DPSIR model to assess greenhouse effect in Taiwan. Environ Monit Assess. **177**, 623–635 (2011)
36. Quagliolo, C., Assumma, V., Comino, E., Mondini, G., Pezzoli, A.: An Integrated Method to Assess Flood Risk and Resilience in the MAB UNESCO Collina Po (Italy). In: Calabrò, F., Della Spina, L., Piñeira Mantiñán, M.J. (eds.) New Metropolitan Perspectives, pp. 2545–2555. Springer International Publishing, Cham (2022)
37. Assumma, V., Quagliolo, C., Comino, E., Mondini, G.: Definition of an Integrated Theoretical Framework to Assess the NBS Suitability in Flood Risk Areas. In: Gervasi, O., Murgante, B., Misra, S., Rocha, A.M.A.C., and Garau, C. (eds.) Computational Science and Its Applications – ICCSA 2022 Workshops. pp. 228–237. Springer International Publishing, Cham (2022). https://doi.org/10.1007/978-3-031-10542-5_16
38. Stanganelli, M., Torrieri, F., Gerundo, C., Rossitti, M.: A Strategic Performance-Based Planning Methodology to Promote the Regeneration of Fragile Territories. In: La Rosa, D., Privitera, R. (eds.) INPUT 2021. LNCE, vol. 146, pp. 149–157. Springer, Cham (2021). https://doi.org/10.1007/978-3-030-68824-0_16
39. Bezzi, C.: La SWOT "dinamica" o "relazionale." (2005)
40. Kangas, J., Kangas, A., Leskinen, P., Pykäläinen, J.: MCDM methods in strategic planning of forestry on state-owned lands in finland: applications and experiences. J. Multi- Criteria Decision Anal. **10**, 257–271 (2001)

41. Kangas, J., Kurttila, M., Kajanus, M., Kangas, A.: Evaluating the management strategies of a forestland estate - The S-O-S approach. J Environ Manage. **69**, 349–358 (2003)
42. Chaikumbung, M.: The effects of institutions and cultures on people's willingness to pay for climate change policies: a meta-regression analysis. Energy Policy **177**, 113513 (2023)

Supporting the Resources Allocation for Inner Areas by the Use of the FITradeoff Method

Marta Dell'Ovo[1]([✉]) [iD], Alessandra Oppio[1] [iD], Eduarda Asfora Frej[2] [iD],
and Adiel Teixeira de Almeida[2] [iD]

[1] Department of Architecture and Urban Studies (DAStU), Politecnico di Milano, Via Bonardi, 3, 20133 Milano, Italy
{marta.dellovo,alessandra.oppio}@polimi.it

[2] CDSID - Center for Decision Systems and Information Development, Universidade Federal de Pernambuco – UFPE, Av. Acadêmico Hélio Ramos, s/n – Cidade Universitária, Recife, PE 50740-530, Brazil
{eafrej,almeida}@cdsid.org.br

Abstract. Slow Tourism is recognized as a driver able to enhance sustainable development in fragile areas characterized by the distance from centers offering essential services, low level of accessibility and affected by depopulation. In this context it is strategic to adopt robust methodologies able to invert this trend and to answer in an effective way to this issue. It is moreover important to identify the peculiarities of each area in order to define specific strategies to be applied. The current research aims to propose and test a methodology to support the Decision Makers (DM) in allocating resources for the valorization of minor real estate heritage for the regeneration of the entire territory by understanding which assets deserve or are more strategic to be renewed. The FITradeoff method (Flexible and Interactive Tradeoff) has been applied to solve the decision problem and support the DM in making a coherent choice in line with the characteristic of the territory.

Keywords: Slow tourism · Multicriteria decision-making (MCDM) · FITradeoff method · Decision Support System (DSS)

1 Introduction

The National Strategy for Inland Areas (SNAI) is an Italian public policy aimed at tackling depopulation in inner areas, which are defined and classified according to their distance from centers offering essential services and their level of accessibility [1]. In this context, SNAI's main objective is to reverse the demographic trend in these territories, to be pursued through two main actions: a) the first focuses on adapting the supply of essential services in order to create the conditions for the development of the territory; b) the second aims at implementing actions in favor of local development, intended to generate labor demand through the reuse and enhancement of territorial capital. Moreover, the Covid-19 pandemic has accelerated the process of both economic and qualitative impoverishment of these places, congesting health services, causing difficulties for certain sectors of work and their training, and making internet access problematic due to weak digital connections [2].

O. Gervasi et al. (Eds.): ICCSA 2023 Workshops, LNCS 14108, pp. 415–428, 2023.
https://doi.org/10.1007/978-3-031-37117-2_28

Slow tourism has been recognized by SNAI as a potential driver of long-run and sustainable developments given the characteristics of the Italian context and the presence of different potential attractions [3, 4]. This new perception of tourism is based on itinerant destinations, through which it is possible to promote the territory and the different proposals present in it. The emergence of slow tourism offers important development scenarios for the Italian inner areas [5, 6], and allows the valorization of that minor real estate heritage no longer in use, such as stations, mills, tollhouses, rural and service buildings, through the implementation of a redevelopment process offering opportunities for new forms of entrepreneurship, work and widespread utility. Given this opportunity, it becomes necessary and strategic to understand how to enhance these strengths, solve current issues and criticalities and allocate potential resources [7].

Within this context the aim of the current contribution is to propose a methodology to support the Decision Makers (DM) in allocating resources for the valorization of minor real estate heritage crossed by slow tourism lines; in detail cycle routs will be considered. The analysis is based on the researches proposed by [8–11] which defined already consistent sets of criteria able to evaluate both the Attractiveness and Vulnerability of inner areas; in addition the FITradeoff method has been applied given its potentials in interacting with the DM and the easy comprehension and visualization of the results. Moreover, considering the slow tourism context and the reuse of abandoned buildings, the presence of multiple values involved and several dimensions to analyze requires the adoption of a multicriteria approach how suggested by [12–15].

The paper is divided into five different sections. After a brief introduction aimed at exploring the decision problem, the methodology applied to rank the buildings selected to be valorized is presented. Section 3 describes the overall approach while the fourth its application and then some conclusions and future perspectives are drawn.

2 FITradeoff Decision Process: Combining Elicitation by Decomposition and Holistic Evaluation

The FITradeoff method (Flexible and Interactive Tradeoff) was developed by [16] to solve multicriteria decision problems with partial information within the scope of the Multiattribute Value Theory (MAVT). This method carries the whole axiomatic structure of the classical tradeoff procedure developed by [17], but improves its applicability for decision makers with easier elicitation questions, since only preference statements are requested from the DMs, instead of declaring indifferent points.

This method is suitable for solving Multicriteria Decision-Model (MCDM) choice problems [16], but also ranking problems [18], sorting problems [19] and portfolio problems [20, 21]. The FITradeoff method works based on partial information obtained by the DM from the declaration of preferences, through an interactive process, and such information is converted into inequalities that act as constraints for linear programming (LP) models that run searching for a recommendation for the DM. Mathematical models change according to the problematic being treated, but the preferences elicitation process is similar for all decision problematics. For the choice problematic, the LP model runs searching for potentially optimal alternatives at each interaction, and the process works based on a progressive reduction of potentially optimal alternatives until a satisfactory solution for the DM is found [16]. In the ranking problematic, dominance relations between alternatives are tested based on LP models that search for the maximum difference between alternatives global values [18], and a ranking of the alternatives is constructed based on these dominance relations found. In the sorting problematic, the minimum and maximum values of each alternative for the current weights space are obtained through LP models, and then decision rules are applied to allocate alternatives into predefined categories based on those values [19]. The portfolio problematic with FITradeoff has two different approaches; the first one works based on the classical combinatorial approach for solving portfolio problems [21] and the second one works based on a heuristic approach thank ranks alternatives based on their benefit-to-cost ration [20]. In this work, the FITradeoff for ranking problematic is applied.

In the FITradeoff method, the two basic paradigms of preference modeling are combined within the decision process [22]: elicitation by decomposition and holistic evaluation. In the elicitation by decomposition, the decision maker compares elements in the consequences space, considering tradeoffs amongst criteria [17]. This is a cartesian process, from which inequalities that involve criteria scaling constants values are obtained. In the holistic evaluation, the decision maker compares elements in the alternatives space, aided by visualization graphics provided by the FITradeoff decision support system (DSS). Based on holistic judgments made by the DM, inequalities comparing global values of two alternatives are obtained. The information obtained by both types of elicitation are joined to form a space of weights, i.e., a set of possible weights vector compatible with the preference structure of the DM. Then, LP models search for a recommendation for the DM considering the current space of weights which define the consistency and robustness of the result.

The FITradeoff method is operated by a flexible and interactive decision support system available for free at www.cdsid.org.br/fitradeoff. This method has been applied in a wide range of practical applications, such as supplier selection problems [23]; location of health units [24]; ordering special operations of Brazilian Federal Police [25]; energy policy related problems [26, 27]; selection of scheduling rules [28]; selection of agricultural technology packages [29]; selection of strategic information systems [30]. Simulation studies performed by [31] show that the FITradeoff method presents a relatively high convergence speed, in a sense that in 90% of the cases simulated, the subset of potentially optimal alternatives is reduced to up to 8 alternatives after the ranking of criteria scaling constants, considering problems with up to 70 alternatives.

3 Methodology

The methodology of this work is summarized in Fig. 1, it consists mainly of seven phases:

1. The first step consists on defining all stakeholders and experts that will be part of the evaluation for this problem and the identification of the Decision Maker (DM), in charge of taking the final decision;

2. Criteria were then defined based on a deep search on the literature, the availability of information and according to the objective to be achieved, in this specific context according to attractiveness and vulnerability aspects;

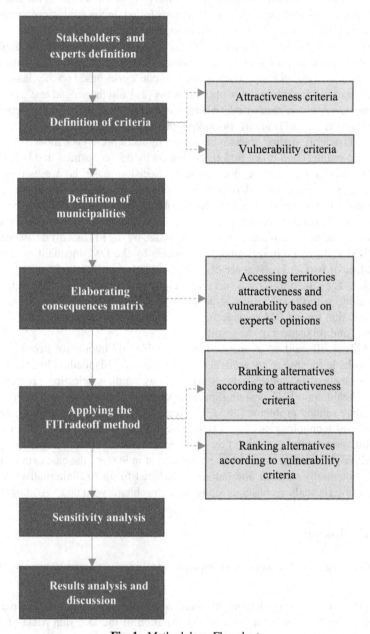

Fig. 1. Methodology Flowchart

3. Then, a set of minor real estate heritage is stablished to be evaluated with respect to the criteria previously identifies;
4. The performance of each alternative in each criterion was then defined based on the consultation of official national website;
5. The FITradeoff method was then applied twice: to rank the buildings according to the attractiveness criteria and according to vulnerability criteria;
6. The sensitivity analysis has been performed to validate the results obtained;
7. Finally, the results were analyzed and discussed in order to draw insightful recommendations and to try to answer to the resource allocation problem.

The approach proposed could be replicated for analyzing other case studies, and phases better specified considering the peculiarities of each context.

4   Application

Given the methodological framework defined, within this context the application will be presented. For what concerns the stakeholders identifications, in order to be consistent and objective within the all evaluation process, groups of experts have been interviewed in the different phases of the methodology. In detail their experience have been requested both in a preliminary phase to understand the decision context and its boundaries and also for the set of criteria validation. Given in fact, the purpose of proceeding by taking a technical decision, as DM in charge of applying the FITradeoff method has been selected an actor belonging to the expert category [32] with experiences in the project appraisal evaluation, cultural heritage valorization and with specific knowledges in the inner areas promotion.

Considering the decision problem consisting in allocating resources with the aim of valorizing minor real estate heritage located in proximity of cycle routs, and starting from the researches developed by [8–11], two different value trees have been identified. Both the attractiveness and the vulnerability of municipalities crossed by the cycle routs VENTO[1] (which connects VENezia to TOrino) have been analyzed. In detail within this context, in order to test the methodologies and investigating homogenous territories, municipalities belonging to the Province of Alessandria and Vercelli (Piedmont Region, Italy) have been selected and more in particular the buildings located in those areas (Fig. 2). The identification of most significant buildings has been guided by a detailed on-site survey and the study of their intrinsic characteristics i.e. the typology, the ownership, the degree of conservation, the dimension and the estimated cost for the recovery. This preliminary analysis allowed to identify a set of eight buildings and their performances have been detected by consulting official geoportal and websites (ISTAT - National Institute of Statistics; Copernicus Atmosphere Monitoring Service; Urban Index – Indicatori per le Politiche Urbane; etc.). Tables 1 and 2 presents respectively the Attractiveness and the Vulnerability performance matrix. A detailed description of the criteria defined has been provided by [8–11].

---

[1] VENTO was founded in 2010 as part of a multidisciplinary research group working at the Department of Architecture and Urban Studies of the Politecnico di Milano with the aim of analysing the issue of bicycle infrastructure with a tourism function in Italy.

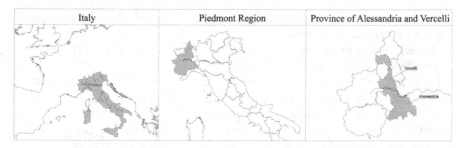

Fig. 2. Location of the case study

Table 1. Attractiveness performance matrix

Objective	Criteria	U.M	Building 1	Building 2	Building 3	Building 4	Building 5	Building 6	Building 7	Building 8
Attractiveness	**Parks and protected areas**	**meter**	0	0	322	34	37	72	170	1460
	Natural areas	**meter**	0	0	322	34	37	310	170	1460
	Cultural heritage	**n° within 5 km**	23	13	100	10	10	24	12	15
	Landscape	**n° within 5 km**	1	0	0	2	2	0	0	0
	Hospitality	**meter**	2200	1700	1600	1800	1200	1100	4800	3500
	High quality wine - yards	**meter**	800	20	0	3000	840	0	0	780
	Connectivity	**meter**	300	70	0	0	0	0	95	1900
	Interchange nodes	**meter**	1800	2600	2400	5400	5200	2100	8800	7800

4.1 DM Interaction and FITradeoff Method Application

Once the consequences have been detected, the elicitation of the DM's preferences can be processed in order to rank the buildings according to the two value trees previously presented. The interview started by presenting the overall purpose of the analysis and the meaning of the different criteria involved. The DM has been selected since confident with the problem to be faced, the methodology to be applied and also with the terminology used to explain the phases. After this introduction, the interaction proceeded by asking to rank the criteria scaling constants by the support of the pairwise comparison.

The elicitation started with the criteria belonging to the Attractiveness dimension and then the judgment between two potential consequences as required by the methodology. The first elicitation process resulted in the following preference: 1. Interchange nodes; 2. Connectivity; 3. Hospitality; 4. Cultural Heritage; 5. High quality wine – yards; 6. Parks and protected areas; 7. Natural areas; 8. Landscape, and it has been justified by the high degree of importance of a place to be accessible in order to be attractive. After this interaction already a ranking of the eight building has been found divided

Table 2. Vulnerability performance matrix

Objective	Criteria	U.M	Building 1	Building 2	Building 3	Building 4	Building 5	Building 6	Building 7	Building 8
Vulnerability	Per capita income	€/freq	18317,2	18921	21179,6	19855,3	16990,4	19981,6	19015	0
	Unemployment rate	%	7,3	9,22	10,71	8,98	11,97	11,51	11,41	2,91
	Local units of the manufacturing sector	%	4	5	257	7	4	752	23	0
	Industrial concentration in the manufacturing sector	%	0,14	0,18	0,2	0,33	0,18	0,58	0,27	0,06
	Percentage of Utilized Agricultural Area (UAA) out of the total	%	92,8	90,5	89	73,6	88,2	77,2	72,5	92,4
	Digital divides from fixed and mobile networks	%	0	14,6	10,8	45,1	95,3	2,7	3,3	90,5
	1st Grade school failure rate	%	10,67	12,57	6,92	8,94	8,73	7,58	9,74	12,16
	Old age index	% Ratio	231,5	261,3	225,8	208,5	280,4	220,8	196,4	190,2
	Population density	inhab/km2	51,76	85,34	403,8	49,75	85,81	405,63	60,67	53,05
	Foreign population	%	54	2854	17	66	102	34	4	25
	Average ten-year rate of resident population's change	%	0,6	-1,5	-5,4	3,9	-4,3	-4,1	1	7,6
	Accessibility index to urban centers (road)	(1–5)	2	3	3	2	2	2	1	2
	Average annual PM10 concentration	$\mu g/m^3$	25,1	24,6	24,9	25,1	25,2	25	24,8	24,5
	Drinking water per capita, fed into the municipal network	m3/inhab/yr	71,7	65,7	91,3	47,5	43,4	75,7	52,8	54,6
	Estimated building density	m3/km2	21077,9	26903,7	97130,1	17146,2	37073,6	91121,6	23156,7	0

(*continued*)

Table 2. (*continued*)

Objective	Criteria	U.M	Building 1	Building 2	Building 3	Building 4	Building 5	Building 6	Building 7	Building 8
	Non-use rate of buildings	%	12,3	1,5	4,9	1,1	6,2	5	6,7	0
	Per capita waste production	kg	246,5	324,8	495,6	287,8	324,5	257,8	257,8	257,8
	Soil consumed per capita	m2/inhab	1501	1289,5	397,2	1084,6	695	291,4	762,6	1453,2
	Seismic hazard	Ag	0,037	0,037	0,039	0,041	0,044	0,051	0,058	0,066

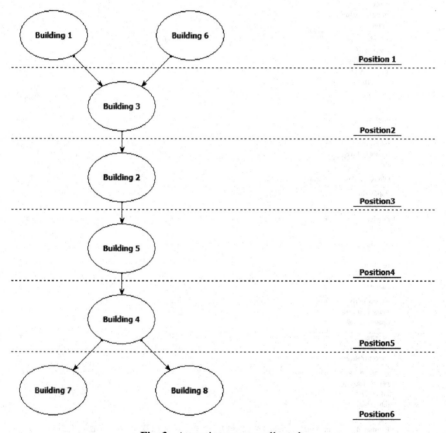

Fig. 3. Attractiveness overall result

in three levels, but the DM was not satisfied with the results and decided to proceed continuing the elicitation by decomposition which allows to compare and decide among two consequences. After fifteen questions the DM decided to stop the interaction and to visualize the results, in fact, for the final ranking six levels have been obtained and Building 1 and 6 were tied for first place (Fig. 3). Considering the overall results and the partial ones visualized according to the performances got for the different criteria (Fig. 4) and provided by the holistic evaluations, the DM decided that Building 6 as an average was the most attractive by considering the set of criteria defined.

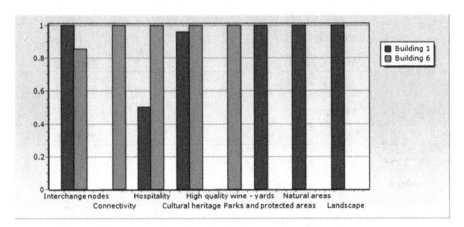

Fig. 4. Attractiveness partial results

After the elicitation developed for the attractiveness, the same process has been carried out for the vulnerability dimension resulting in: 1. Seismic hazard; 2. 1st Grade school failure rate; 3. Digital divides from fixed and mobile networks; 4. Accessibility index to urban centers (road); 5. Percentage of Utilized Agricultural Area (UAA) out of the total; 6. Drinking water per capita, fed into the municipal network; 7. Soil consumed per capita; 8. Average ten-year rate of resident population's change; 9. Population density; 10. Old age index; 11. Local units of the manufacturing sector; 12. Unemployment rate; 13. Per capita income; 14. Foreign population; 15. Non-use rate of buildings; 16. Industrial concentration in the manufacturing sector; 17. Average annual PM10 concentration; 18. Per capita waste production; 19. Estimated building density, and it has been justified by the presence of features that cannot be modified or improved. Only one level has been found after the first interaction and the DM decided to go on with the elicitation by decomposition. After twenty-one answers the DM decided to stop the interview given the high effort and the time required; five levels have been obtained and Building 1, 2 and 3 were tied for first place (Fig. 5). Also in this case the DM decided to proceed by visualizing the partial results according to the holistic evaluation and considering the different graphs which the method presents (Fig. 6), Building 3 has been judged as the asset located in the least vulnerable areas.

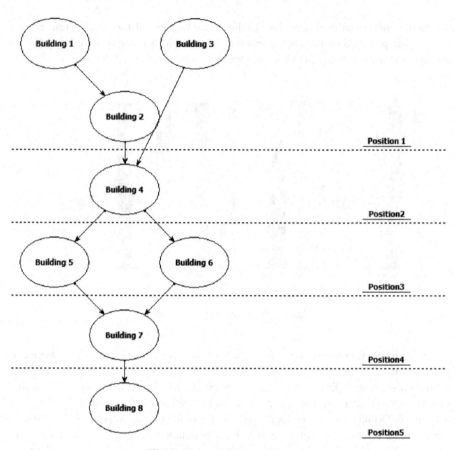

Fig. 5. Vulnerability overall result

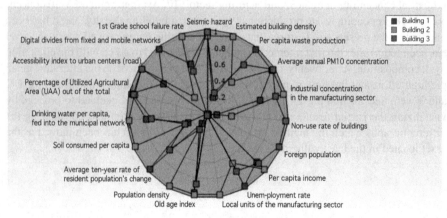

Fig. 6. Vulnerability partial result

4.2 Discussion of the Results

Given the differences in the results obtained, the DM decided to visualize for both the dimensions the sensitivity analysis by considering 10% of variation to the criteria involved to understand the stability of the decision and validate it. Figures 7 and 8 presents respectively the sensitivity analysis performed for the Attractiveness and for the Vulnerability.

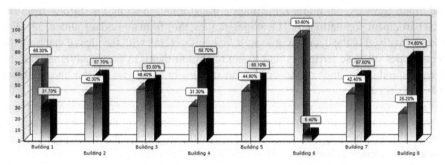

Fig. 7. Attractiveness sensitivity analysis

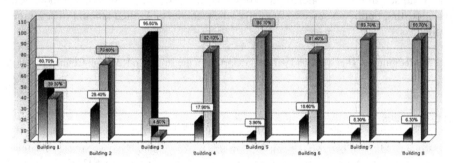

Fig. 8. Vulnerability sensitivity analysis

Both the figures show how the results obtained are not stable and only by varying the consequences space for the criteria involved of 10% the changes are quite sensitive.

In fact, after this visualization the DM was not very confident in taking a final decision but analyzing better together Figs. 7 and 8, found out how the most stable alternative, which keeps a satisfying overall performance with and without the 10% of variation and ranked in both the graph in the first positions is Building 1. In fact, while a high performance obtained for the Attractiveness correspond to the location of the building in an area very attractive, for the vulnerability the result has to be read in reverse, a high performance corresponds to a territory that is not very vulnerable and therefore very resilient. This further explanation allows to better understand how Building 1 classifies in the top ranks of both Attractiveness and Vulnerability.

5   Conclusions

The research proposed aims at supporting the DM in taking more conscious decision about the allocation of resources for the valorization of minor real estate heritage and promoting the slow tourism in inner areas. Marginal territories, in constant depopulation, call for policies and new methodologies capable of implementing authentic tourism oriented towards sustainable development for territories and local communities. This does not mean replicating the economies that have worked in the most attractive territories and urban contexts, but rather reflecting on transformation scenarios starting from the least participant populations and local specificities, thus from unused resources [33]. The criteria involved in the decision process have been selected with the idea of catching the peculiarities of those territories and trying to exploit them. In fact, analyzing both the strengths and criticalities of the same context helps in having awareness and in taking coherent decisions.

The extra effort charged by the DM in answering to the second interview consisting in the Vulnerability dimension has been strongly affected by the number of criteria involved. This criticality could be overcome by reducing the number and trying to check if double counting are present.

The study could be further implemented and validated by the involvement of different categories of stakeholders [34], in particular political and bureaucratic in order to have a real impact on public policies and strengthen the necessity of robust methodologies for allocating public resources, especially where there is a limited amount of resources available.

Acknowledgment. This work had partial support from the Brazilian Research Council (CNPq).

References

1. Rossitti, M., Dell'ovo, M., Oppio, A., Torrieri, F.: The Italian National Strategy for Inner Areas (SNAI): A critical analysis of the indicator grid. Sustainability **13**, 6927 (2021). https://doi.org/10.3390/SU13126927
2. Balducci, A.: I territori fragili di fronte al Covid I Scienze del Territorio. Scienze del Territorio. Special issue, 169–176 (2020)
3. Andreoli, A., Silvestri, F.: Tourism as a driver of development in the inner areas. Italian J. Plan. Pract. **7**, 80–99 (2017)
4. Pileri, P., Moscarelli, R. (eds.): Cycling & Walking for Regional Development. RD, Springer, Cham (2021). https://doi.org/10.1007/978-3-030-44003-9
5. Stanganelli, M., Torrieri, F., Gerundo, C., Rossitti, M.: A strategic performance-based planning methodology to promote the regeneration of fragile territories. In: La Rosa, D., Privitera, R. (eds.) INPUT 2021. LNCE, vol. 146, pp. 149–157. Springer, Cham (2021). https://doi.org/10.1007/978-3-030-68824-0_16
6. Dezio, C.: Restart from resources. Rural heritage as Antifragile Territorial Capital. Valori Valutazioni. **24**, 209–217 (2020)
7. Colucci, E., et al.: Documenting cultural heritage in an INSPIRE-based 3D GIS for risk and vulnerability analysis. https://doi.org/10.1108/JCHMSD-04-2021-0068

8. Dell'Ovo, M., Dezio, C., Mottadelli, M., Oppio, A.: How to support cultural heritage-led development in Italian inner areas: A multi-methodological evaluation approach (2022). https://doi.org/10.1080/09654313.2022.2135367

9. Dell'Ovo, M., Dezio, C., Oppio, A.: Bringing values at the center of policies for inner areas regeneration in the Covid-19 age. Territorio - Sezione Open Access. 43–51 (2021). https://doi.org/10.3280/TR2021-097-SUPPLEMENTOOA12926

10. Dezio, C., Dell'Ovo, M., Oppio, A.: The antifragile potential of line tourism: Towards a multimethodological evaluation model for Italian inner areas cultural heritage. Smart Innovation, Systems and Technologies. 178 SIST, 1819–1829 (2021). https://doi.org/10.1007/978-3-030-48279-4_172/COVER

11. Oppio, A., Dell'Ovo, M.: Cultural heritage preservation and territorial attractiveness: A spatial multidimensional evaluation approach. Res. Developm. 105–125 (2021). https://doi.org/10.1007/978-3-030-44003-9_9/COVER

12. Uyan, M., Sert, E., Osmanli, N., Gulmez, K.: Determination of winter tourism potential areas in Türkiye using a GIS-based multi-criteria analysis. J. Geograph. Inst. Jovan Cvijic SASA **73**, 79–92 (2023). https://doi.org/10.2298/IJGI2301079U

13. Bottero, M.C., Dell'Anna, F., Gobbo, G.L.: A PROMETHEE-based approach for designing the reuse of an abandoned railway in the Monferrato Region, Italy. Int. J. Multicriteria Decis. Mak. **8**, 60–63 (2019). https://doi.org/10.1504/IJMCDM.2019.098027

14. Lupi, C., Giaccio, V., Mastronardi, L., Giannelli, A., Scardera, A.: Exploring the features of agritourism and its contribution to rural development in Italy. Land Use Policy **64**, 383–390 (2017). https://doi.org/10.1016/J.LANDUSEPOL.2017.03.002

15. Diti, I., Torreggiani, D., Tassinari, P.: Rural landscape and cultural routes: A multicriteria spatial classification method tested on an Italian case study. J. Agricult. Eng. **46**, 23–29 (2015). https://doi.org/10.4081/JAE.2015.451

16. De Almeida, A.T., De Almeida, J.A., Costa, A.P.C.S., De Almeida-Filho, A.T.: A new method for elicitation of criteria weights in additive models: Flexible and interactive tradeoff. Eur. J. Oper. Res. **250**, 179–191 (2016). https://doi.org/10.1016/J.EJOR.2015.08.058

17. Keeney, R.L., Raiffa, H.: Decision analysis with multiple conflicting objectives (1976)

18. Frej, E.A., de Almeida, A.T., Costa, A.P.C.S.: Using data visualization for ranking alternatives with partial information and interactive tradeoff elicitation. Oper. Res. Int. J. **19**(4), 909–931 (2019). https://doi.org/10.1007/s12351-018-00444-2

19. Kang, T.H.A., Frej, E.A., de Almeida, A.T.: Flexible and interactive tradeoff elicitation for multicriteria sorting problems. **37** (2020). https://doi.org/10.1142/S0217595920500207

20. Frej, E.A., Ekel, P., de Almeida, A.T.: A benefit-to-cost ratio based approach for portfolio selection under multiple criteria with incomplete preference information. Inf. Sci. (N. Y.) **545**, 487–498 (2021). https://doi.org/10.1016/J.INS.2020.08.119

21. Marques, A.C., Frej, E.A., de Almeida, A.T.: Multicriteria decision support for project portfolio selection with the FITradeoff method. Omega (United Kingdom). **111** (2022). https://doi.org/10.1016/J.OMEGA.2022.102661

22. de Almeida, A.T., Frej, E.A., Roselli, K. reis P.: Combining holistic and decomposition paradigms in preference modeling with the flexibility of FITradeoff. Cent. Eur. J. Oper. Res. **29**, 7–47 (2021)

23. Asfora, E., Reis, L., Roselli, P., Araújo De Almeida, J., Teixeira De Almeida, A.: A multicriteria decision model for supplier selection in a food industry based on FITradeoff method. (2017). https://doi.org/10.1155/2017/4541914

24. Dell'Ovo, M., Frej, E.A., Oppio, A., Capolongo, S., Morais, D.C., de Almeida, A.T.: Multicriteria decision making for healthcare facilities location with visualization based on FITradeoff method. Lect. Notes Bus. Inf. Process. **282**, 32–44 (2017). https://doi.org/10.1007/978-3-319-57487-5_3/COVER

25. da Cunha, C.P.C.B., de Miranda Mota, C.M., de Almeida, A.T., Frej, E.A., Roselli, L.R.P.: Applying the FITradeoff method for aiding prioritization of special operations of Brazilian Federal Police. Lect. Notes Bus. Inf. Process. **405**, 110–125 (2020). https://doi.org/10.1007/978-3-030-64399-7_8/COVER

26. Abreu Kang, T.H., da Costa Soares Júnior, A.M., de Almeida, A.T.: Evaluating electric power generation technologies: A multicriteria analysis based on the FITradeoff method. Energy **165**, 10–20 (2018). https://doi.org/10.1016/J.ENERGY.2018.09.165

27. Fossile, D.K., Frej, E.A., Gouvea da Costa, S.E., Pinheiro de Lima, E., Teixeira de Almeida, A.: Selecting the most viable renewable energy source for Brazilian ports using the FITradeoff method. J. Clean Prod. **260**, 121107 (2020). https://doi.org/10.1016/J.JCLEPRO.2020.121107

28. Pergher, I., Frej, E.A., Roselli, L.R.P., de Almeida, A.T.: Integrating simulation and FITradeoff method for scheduling rules selection in job-shop production systems. Int. J. Prod. Econ. 227 (2020). https://doi.org/10.1016/J.IJPE.2020.107669

29. Anselmo, P., et al.: Selecting an agricultural technology package based on the flexible and interactive tradeoff method. Ann. Oper. Res. **314**, 377–392 (2022). https://doi.org/10.1007/s10479-018-3020-y

30. Paula, A., De Gusmão, H., Medeiros, C.P.: A Model for Selecting a Strategic Information System Using the FITradeoff. (2016). https://doi.org/10.1155/2016/7850960.

31. Mendes, J.A.J., Frej, E.A., de Almeida, A.T., de Almeida, J.A.: Evaluation of flexible and interactive tradeoff method based on numerical simulation experiments. Pesquisa Operacional **40**, e231191 (2020). https://doi.org/10.1590/0101-7438.2020.040.00231191

32. Dente, B.: Understanding Policy Decisions. Springer, Cham (2014). https://doi.org/10.1007/978-3-319-02520-9

33. De Rossi, A Cura Di A.: Riabitare l'italia - le aree interne tra abbandoni e riconquiste. **594** (2018)

34. Assumma, V., Bottero, M., Ishizaka, A., Tasiou, M.: Group analytic hierarchy process sorting II method: An application to evaluate the economic value of a wine region landscape. Environ. Model. Assess. **26**(3), 355–369 (2021). https://doi.org/10.1007/s10666-020-09744-4

Renewable Energy Sources and Ecosystem Services: Measuring the Impacts of Ground-Mounted Photovoltaic Panels

Caterina Caprioli$^{(\boxtimes)}$ ⓘ, Federico Dell'Anna ⓘ, and Francesco Fiermonte ⓘ

Interuniversity Department of Regional and Urban Studies and Planning (DIST), Politecnico di Torino, Viale Mattioli, 39, 10125 Turin, TO, Italy
{caterina.caprioli,federico.dellanna,
francesco.fiermonte}@polito.it

Abstract. Europe is facing complex challenges related to rising natural gas prices and the need for energy independence due to the energy crisis of 2022. To address these challenges, the European Commission presented the REPowerEU plan, which aims to accelerate the deployment of renewable energy sources (RESs), achieve greater energy autonomy, accelerate the green transition, and facilitate investments in renewable energies by 2027. Among the different RESs, the potential of ground-mounted photovoltaic (GMPV) panels in Europe is demonstrated by the spread of large-scale solar installations. Although promoting renewable energy through GMPV technology is in line with the seventh Sustainable Development Goal, it may conflict with the 15th SDG, which aims to protect terrestrial ecosystems. To identify potential impacts that may be generated by the installation of GMPVs in relation to ecosystem services (ESs), this study explores evaluation methodologies for their integration into decision support frameworks. The research reviews different methods available to quantify and/or monetize different impacts for provisioning, regulating and maintenance, cultural ESs and compares three methodological frameworks that can be used to integrate these results into decision-making: Cost-Benefit Analysis (CBA), Multi-Criteria Decision Analysis (MCDA), and COmpoSIte Modeling Assessment (COSIMA). The outcomes could be useful in supporting public and private decision-makers to structure an evaluation framework useful in defining suitable areas where to install GMPVs according to the costs, co-benefits, and negative externalities generated.

Keywords: Renewable Energy Ecosystem Services (REES) · Habitat services · Solar park

1 Introduction

The energy crisis of 2022 has led Europe to face, on the one hand, very complex challenges related to rising natural gas prices and, on the other, the need to diversify energy supplies to increase the continent's energy independence [1]. In response to the difficulties and upheavals in the global energy market, the European Commission presented the

O. Gervasi et al. (Eds.): ICCSA 2023 Workshops, LNCS 14108, pp. 429–443, 2023.
https://doi.org/10.1007/978-3-031-37117-2_29

REPowerEU plan intending to bring forward to 2027 the targets already set for 2030 by giving a decisive boost to the deployment of renewable energies, achieving greater energy autonomy, accelerating the green transition and facilitating investments in renewable energies [2]. To implement the REPowerEU programme, Member States will not only work on the natural gas sector through joint exploration and trading, construction of storage and transport infrastructure. Indeed, the EU wants to increase the use of solar energy through the EU Solar Strategy, which recognizes the potential of rooftop photovoltaics in contributing to the climate and energy goals of the European Green Deal [3].

While the installation of rooftop photovoltaics requires the involvement of many small private investments to achieve the targets set, the installation of ground-mounted photovoltaic (GMPV) panels could lead to the promotion of larger projects that speed up the energy transition. On the one hand, this is driven by the promotion of renewable energy expansion through incentives from European governments. On the other hand, economies of scale come into play with larger projects becoming an important factor for the profitability of a project. The spread of GMPV in Europe is also demonstrated by data from the European Photovoltaic Industry Association (EPIA), which records how large-scale solar installations have grown significantly in recent years, exceeding the capacity of those installed on rooftops [4]. Indeed, in 2020, the total installed capacity of large-scale solar installations in Europe reached 23 GW, and the GMPV size is expected to continue to grow to 60% by 2025.

Although promoting renewable energy through GMPV is in line with the seventh of the Sustainable Development Goals (SDGs), which aims to ensure affordable, reliable, sustainable, and modern energy access for all, it may conflict with others [5]. In fact, the 15th SDG aims to protect, restore, and promote the sustainable use of terrestrial ecosystems, halt and reverse soil degradation, and halt biodiversity loss that are potentially threatened by the GMPV market. Moreover, the implementation of these infrastructures cannot be separated from the preservation of the landscape as heritage. This entails having to take into consideration the system of values with which the landscape is endowed, their protection and preservation [6]. The land use change (LUC) due to the development of renewable energy resources (RESs), not just photovoltaic (PV), poses both opportunities and risks to ecosystems [7]. As such, given the heightened awareness of the ecological emergency and the exponential growth of renewable energy in response to the increase in global per capita energy consumption, it is necessary to consider the potential risks of implementing RESs at the expense of natural ecosystems. On one hand, many studies show that the development of energy-efficient buildings and industrial processes, as well as electric vehicles, requires fewer energy inputs [8]. On the other hand, it is not possible to overlook the infrastructure needed to meet the remaining demand, also for new RES. Developing the scientific understanding of land consumption and related ecosystem services (ESs) for GMPVs becomes critical as solar energy covers an important role in European energy policies, dominating the entire renewable energy sector both now and in view of future forecasts.

In this study, we identify the potential impacts that can be generated by the installation of GMPVs in relation to ESs and explore evaluation methodologies for their integration into decision support frameworks. In detail, the research reviews the different methods available to quantify and/or monetize different impacts and introduces three methodological frameworks that can be used to integrate these results into decision-making: Cost-Benefit Analysis (CBA), Multi-Criteria Decision Analysis (MCDA), and a composite decision support by combining them, i.e., the COmpoSIte Modeling Assessment (COSIMA). The study could be useful in supporting public and private decision-makers to structure an evaluation framework useful in defining suitable areas where to install GMPVs according to the costs, co-benefits and negative externalities generated.

After the Introduction, the chapter is structured as follows; Sect. 2 describes the different ESs generated by RESs with a focus on GMPVs; Sect. 3 explores the assessment and valuation methods of related ESs; decision-making frameworks and their potentials are presented in Sect. 4; Sect. 5 summarizes conclusions and future perspectives.

2 Ecosystem Services Related to RES

2.1 An Overview of Ecosystem Service Impacts in RES

RES offers a variety of benefits on both the environment quality and human life, spanning the reduction of greenhouse gas emissions from fossil and some types of air pollution, the diversification of energy supply reducing dependence on imported fuels and the creation of economic development and jobs in manufacturing and installation [9].

However, the spread of RES currently involves trade-offs with the environment and biodiversity protection. In order to consider both environmental and social issues in RES development, a comprehensive analysis of the benefits and impacts produced by RES is required from an ecosystem service perspective. The research discussion regarding the ES offered or impacted by RES is still ongoing [10]. From the CICES classification, "renewable abiotic energy" and "renewable biofuels" have been included as services: respectively, for the first group, they consider wind, hydro, solar, tidal, and thermal, while, for the second, plant and animal-based resources [11]. Recently, Schetke et al. (2018) [12] refer to them as Renewable Energy Ecosystem Services (REES).

However, these two interpretations (i.e., by the CICES group and Schetke et al. 2018 [12]) do not imply that the different types of RES (i.e., biomass, geothermal energy, hydropower, photovoltaic systems and wind power) produce various benefits and impacts with respect to the other ecosystem services. RES is also viewed as problematic both in terms of provisioning services, regulating and maintaining, and cultural ones [10, 13, 14].

One of the most critical impacts on provisioning services generated by the development of all RES is land use competition. Additionally, for biomass production, the removal of branches or leaves in wood management may impact soil fertility by removing nutrient-rich residues [10].

Several impacts can be observed on the habitat and, therefore, on regulating and maintenance services: for example, wind power may have destructive and disturbance effects on the air routes of specific birds and bats species [15]; deep and near-surface geothermal systems can modify habitats due to soil temperature changes [8]; hydropower can affect various physical and hydrological alternations resulting in habitat and biotope losses, decrease in ecological integrity and connectivity [16].

Concerning cultural services, RES can have a visual impact on the traditional and pristine landscape due to the construction of technical and artificial elements, particularly for both wind power and GMPV systems [10]. Additionally, hydropower can even destroy the existing natural and cultural landscape [17].

2.2 Ground-Mounted PV and ES

Photovoltaic energy is generally considered to have benign environmental impacts, as it does not generate noise or chemical pollutants during use. It is one of the most viable renewable energy technologies for use in urban and non-urban settings, such as scenic areas and national parks, where the ability to avoid pylons and cables is a great advantage [18]. However, it is also necessary to consider the negative aspects that these infrastructures, especially large ones installed on the ground, can generate [10]. Picking up on what was said in the previous section, here we explore in detail the positive and negative impacts generated by GMPVs in relation to ESs.

Provisioning Services. The resources that natural and semi-natural ecosystems generate, such as the production of food, drinking water, timber and fuel refer to the category of provisioning services. Agriculture, which serves as the foundation to produce the tangible goods required for human nutrition, is included in this typology. When installed in previously farmed areas, medium and large GMPV plants consume land and take up less space that could have been used for cultivation [19]. Therefore, energy production is likely to be considered competitive with food production, as in the case of crops dedicated to the production of renewable energy sources, such as agricultural and forestry biomass [20]. Agrovoltaic (AV) systems are one strategy that is emerging to address this problem and enable the coexistence of GMPV and agricultural production [21]. When preserving productive farmland, ensuring energy security, and environmental protection are equally important, this solution could become significant. In this sense, AVs can entail combining the development of GMPV solar energy with one or more of the agricultural activities listed below, such as crop cultivation (also known as "AV-cropping"), animal husbandry (also known as "AV-animal"), or habitat improvement to enhance ESs ("AV-habitat") [22, 23]. AVs can increase the effectiveness of the use of land, the use of water, and the production of energy while also demonstrating the viability of these dual land uses to mutually benefit different ecosystem goods and services. The cultivation of agricultural species that require semi-shaded environments, on-site habitat improvement measures like the establishment and maintenance of native grasses and forages, and the associated potential ecosystem services of these strategies for agricultural production are all examples of benefits that can be multiple in this sense [24].

Regulating and Maintenance Services. Among the many regulating ecosystem services are those that keep ecosystems healthy and functioning properly, control water, erosion, pollination, and safeguard against hydrogeological disruption brought on by wind and rain. The stabilization of the climate is just one example of the many services in this category that benefit people both now and in the future. The preservation of biodiversity is another crucial component. In terms of GMPV, the impacts associated with ESs are highly dependent on previous land uses. Impacts could be positive if disused areas, such as brownfield areas, industrial sites or former caves, are redeveloped, or if selective agricultural extensification occurs. In this case, the development of a photovoltaic field could provide benefits in terms of regeneration of areas that cannot be dedicated to agricultural use due to location or environmental concerns [10]. Negative effects, on the other hand, are likely to occur in ecologically sensitive areas due to shading effects and microclimatic changes. Another issue is the fragmentation of ecological corridors for certain animal species because of the fencing required around the facilities [25–27]. However, it is worth mentioning that the above-mentioned strategies related to AV systems can provide a combination of solutions to limit impacts on habitats, preserve biodiversity and ensure regulatory services related to carbon sequestration and erosion control. Solar panels can be mounted on pile or screw foundations, such as stakes, rather than heavy foundations, to reduce negative effects on the natural functioning of the soil (filtering and buffering characteristics). To improve the fence, a space can be left between the base of the barrier and the ground. Passages can also be created by modifying the structure of the fence to allow animals to walk freely.

Cultural Services. Natural ecosystems contribute to the maintenance of human health by producing opportunities for spiritual enrichment, cognitive development and recreational experiences [28]. One of the drawbacks of GMPVs is related precisely to their presence in lowland and hillside landscapes often associated with agricultural nature, cultural identification, and space for recreation. Generally, GMPVs are significantly distinguishable from the natural or agricultural environment in which they are often built because of their size, regular geometry, and highly reflective surfaces [29]. In this regard, GMPV infrastructure views have been recognized as a potential source of negative aesthetic impact on national park units, wilderness areas, national historic and scenic highway corridors, residential towns, and other visually sensitive places. In regions with a high value for scenic views, it should be prioritized to examine the visual effects induced by GMPV [11]. In this regard, visual compatibility standards that maximize GMPV context integration can be found [30]. Furthermore, as seen above, it is well recognized in the literature that the installation of GMPV can lead to a change in land use. While the occupation of an agricultural field can lead to the loss of temporary ES, the occupation of public land can lead to the overturning of the recreational and spiritual benefits provided by the area. In this regard, the tangible and intangible components of the landscape must both be considered in order to understand how the PV system influences the perception of the landscape in urban, rural and natural contexts [31].

3 ES Assessment for Ground-Mounted PV

These two decades (and more) of research and applications on ESs have intensively investigated how to express their values and benefits [32]. A first major effort sought to translate these values into economic and monetary scales, since the loss or gain of ESs often involves economic costs to be compensated or avoided [33–35]. A second crucial step coincides with the increasing attention on environmental issues that require the quantification of the amount of ecological and biophysical values produced by a territory [34, 36]. The research in this field has strongly increased also thanks to the development of GIS technologies and a variety of tools able to translate land use changes into quantified physical values for each ES [37, 38], such as INVEST [39]. A third ongoing process has regarded the assessment of cultural and social values produced by a territory or an area. Some tentative works were done to consider these subjective and individually different opinions in evaluation procedures, using qualitative assessments, narrations and constructed scales, deliberative processes, locally defined metrics or guiding principles [40], but also econometric models.

According to these three families of values, this section provides a comprehensive overview of how to assess the loss or gain of ESs due to the development of GMPV. In particular, Table 1 summarizes all the possible indicators, i.e., physical, monetary and qualitative, to be used for the assessment of each benefit or impact generated according to an ES perspective. Moreover, the last two columns of Table 1 respectively suggest the most suitable appraised methods for the assessment of each ES according to the indicator used and some examples of applications in which similar work was done.

From Table 1, it is evident the ability of physical indicators to cover the entire list of benefits and impacts compared to monetary and qualitative scales. Their quantification is often easy to be performed knowing the characteristics of the project developed or using GIS data. However, the variability of units of measurement does not allow to have a comprehensive assessment of GMPV in a specific territory, without the use of specific procedures able to convert them into a unique scale. On the contrary, monetary indicators solve this conversion problem, since each impact is estimated from the beginning through a monetary scale. The use of market valuation, both based on market or cost-based prices, are quite easy to be estimated. This approach, however, is not without drawbacks. Firstly, it has to deal with the difficulty of some estimating procedures, such as revealed and stated preferences, which require the collection of a huge amount of data for high quality and representativeness of the estimation procedure. Secondly, these monetary indicators are not always able to quantify all the impacts. As for the case of GMPV, benefits such as plant community changes or biodiversity increase are hard to be assessed from this economic perspective. Finally, regarding qualitative indicators, they represent a more flexible way to evaluate some benefits and impacts, in particular when physical or monetary indicators are hard to be quantified. However, also these indicators require specific procedures to convert them into a unique scale for obtaining an overall performance of all benefits and impacts produced, as for physical indicators. At the same time, as for monetary indicators, qualitative scales are not always the most suitable way to assess some ESs.

From these considerations, it is clear that specific evaluation methods and, particularly, a combination of them is necessary to assess multiple ecosystem services.

Table 1. Ground-mounted photovoltaic panel (GMPV) impacts on ecosystem services (ESs) and related indicators and appraisal methods.

CICES ES categories	Impacts	Physical indicator (PI)	Monetary indicator (MI)	Qualitative indicator (QI)	Appraisal methods	Sources
Provisioning services	Competition with Food/Fodder/Wood production	sqm or tons year^{-1}	€/tons year^{-1}	Degree of suitability of crop production	PI: GIS-based MI: Market valuation (market prices) QI: GIS-based/Spatial MCA	PI: [41] MI: [42] QI: [43]
	Land-mix for pastures, honey production, as well as cultivation of plants (e.g., aloe vera, lettuce, aquafarming)	sqm or kg (tons)	€/kg year^{-1} or €/ton year^{-1}		MI: Market valuation (market prices)	[44–46]
Regulating and maintaining ser-vices	Plant community changes	sqm or number of species unable to survive		Nominal		[47]
	Biodiversity increases if combined with plants for pollination	sqm				[46, 48]
	Alternation of green corridors in case of fence constructions	sqm	€/sqm		MI: Market valuation (cost-based: compensation costs)	[49]
Cultural services	Visual impact on "pristine" or "traditional" landscapes due to the construction of technical/artificial elements	• Visibility coefficient from settle-ments/panoramic view; • Distance coefficient from settle-ments/panoramic view; • Number of PV; • Number of close inhabitants (or total impact matrix)	€/ab	Level	PI: e.g., Multicriteria analysis for total impact matrix MI: Stated preferences (contingent valuation or choice experiment) QI: survey	PI: [50] MI: [51, 52]

(continued)

Table 1. (*continued*)

CICES ES categories	Impacts	Physical indicator (PI)	Monetary indicator (MI)	Qualitative indicator (QI)	Appraisal methods	Sources
	Occupation of public land use areas	sqm	€/sqm or €/ab (or reduction of dwelling values)		MI: Stated preferences (contingent valuation or choice experiment) or Revealed preferences (hedonic pricing)	PI: [53] MI: [28, 54–56]

4   Integrated Frameworks for the ESs Evaluation of GMPV

When dealing with large-scale energy investment decision problems and wanting to include impacts on ESs, specific evaluation tools are needed to consider not only technical and economic aspects, but also environmental and/or social impacts in the decision-making process [57, 58]. In the scientific literature, the most frequently used approaches to include economic and extra-economic aspects are Cost-Benefit Analysis (CBA) [59] and Multi-Criteria Decision Analysis (MCDA) [60]. However, new hybrid methods are emerging that integrate these two analyses, such as COmpoSIte Modeling Assessment (COSIMA) [61]. In this section, we review these three key methodological frameworks, explaining the methodological background, advantages, and disadvantages in the GMPV investments evaluations (Table 2).

4.1   Cost-Benefit Analysis

According to the European Commission [59], CBA is an analytical tool used in investment decisions to evaluate project alternatives from a social perspective. In theoretical terms, CBA introduces economic analysis into the financial analysis, typical of private investment, allowing the positive and negative externalities generated by the project to be considered in the assessment. A disadvantage of the method is the need to translate all impacts into monetary terms. While the monetization of direct costs is trivial, such as the cost of food lost due to land use change, nonmarket goods are more difficult to quantify, such as recreational or spiritual SEs. In the latter case, specific valuation approaches based on the concept of Willingness To Pay (WTP) and opportunity cost are needed [62]. The CBA method involves calculating performance indicators such as Net Present Value (NPV), Internal Rate of Return (IRR) and Benefit/Cost ratio (B/C) to assess the feasibility of projects, as well as comparing different alternatives. Due to limitations related to impacts monetization, ESs that could be examined are: estimation of food and wood production loss, land-mix use benefits, biodiversity increase trought alternation of green corridors, visual impact and occupation of public land valuation.

Table 2. Methodological frameworks available for decision-making.

	CBA	MCDA	COSIMA
Description	The project benefits and costs are expressed in monetary terms and adjusted for the time value of money	Different project alternatives are compared against predetermined criteria	Different project alternatives are compared considering CBA and MCDA outcomes
Input data	Monetary indicator	Monetary indicator Physical indicator Qualitative indicator	Monetary indicator Physical indicator Qualitative indicator
Output data	NPV, IRR, B/C	Aggregated index	TRR
Pros	Project feasibility Standardized approach Time weight	Stakeholders' engagement Multiple impacts	Project feasibility Stakeholders' engagement Economic and extra-economic impact Time weight
Cons	No stakeholders' engagement	No conventional procedure	No conventional procedure
ESs impacts evaluated	Competition with food Wood production Land-mix use Alternation of green corridors Visual impact Occupation of public land	Competition with food Wood production Land-mix use Plant community changes Biodiversity increases Alternation of green corridors Visual impact Occupation of public land	Competition with food Wood production Land-mix use Plant community changes Biodiversity increases Alternation of green corridors Visual impact Occupation of public land

4.2 Multi-criteria Decision Analysis

MCDA is a family of evaluation methods that allow the consideration of a multiplicity of qualitative and quantitative characteristics of the alternatives that can be considered simultaneously. The basic assumption of this family of techniques is that the object of analysis can be broken down into simple factors (criteria) and analyzed separately [63]. Some techniques result in a standardized aggregate index that allows a comparison of the performance of alternatives according to the selected set of criteria. Furthermore, the MCDA allows the different views of stakeholders to emerge, involving them in the definition of the importance of the criteria. However, it is a less well-known approach in the field of evaluation than other more conventional cost-based methods. In an MCDA framework, the opinion of decision-makers is incorporated into the decision-making process to capture a wide range of perspectives through the criteria weighting phase. In terms of ES related to the installation of GMPVs, having the opportunity to consider multiple impacts expressed with different scales of measurement, the MCDA allows for the inclusion of a greater number of them: competition with food, timber production and the opportunity of mixed land use expressed in physical or monetary terms; the changes in plant communities expressed with quantitative or qualitative scales; the increase in biodiversity through the combination of plants with GMPV or the creation of green corridors; the assessment of visual impact and occupation of public land with specific coefficients or economic evaluation approaches.

4.3 COmpoSIte Modeling Assessment

COSIMA analysis can be briefly explained as an analysis that combines the advantages of CBA and MCDA analysis to provide a feasibility assessment and comparison between alternative projects. In fact, COSIMA measures the performance of each alternative by including both nonmonetary criteria and monetizable benefits and costs through an index that aggregates the results of both CBA and MCDA analyses, namely the Total Rate of Return (TRR) [64]. Therefore, the COSIMA framework is very useful when performance is measured on different rating scales. The COSIMA technique implicates the involvement of stakeholders, incorporating their views into the decision-making process to capture a wide range of perspectives through the criteria weighting stage. Moreover, temporal weighting of impacts, a key feature of CBA, would allow different value judgments on future effects to be taken into account by assigning different weights to short-term and long-term effects [65–67]. In terms of impacts on the ES related to the implementation of GMPV, the method allows the same number of impacts to be included as in the MCDA technique, but also offers the possibility of expressing the evaluation in monetary terms by considering the ES proper in the CBA.

5 Discussion and Conclusions

The paper provided a comprehensive discussion about the losses or gains resulting from the development of GMPVs according to an ES perspective. Specifically, the research collected potential indicators—physical, monetary, and qualitative—that may be used to evaluate each benefit or effect produced by RES. From this analysis, the work suggested different methods available to quantify and/or monetize different impacts for provisioning, regulating and maintenance, and cultural ESs. Three methodological frameworks are proposed in order to integrate all these benefits/impacts into decision-making: i.e., CBA, MCDA, and COSIMA. Although they are all decision-making techniques, there are some significant differences between these approaches that define their advantages and disadvantages. CBA is a quantitative approach to comparing costs and benefits all expressed in monetary terms. Although a well-established technique based on European Commission manuals, CBA has limitations that do not allow its wide use in the energy sector. First and foremost, the monetization of impacts requires specific analyses that transform quantitative parameters, often expressed in physical units, into monetary terms. Instead, in some cases, it is impossible to estimate the monetary value of some impacts leading to their exclusion in the assessment (such as plant community changes or biodiversity increases if combined with plants for pollination). MCDA, on the other hand, considers multiple criteria, including economic, social and environmental factors, to evaluate the performance of a given project. One of the advantages of MCDA is that it involves creating a matrix of different criteria and weighting them according to the importance expressed by the decision-maker. This provides a truthful assessment that allows for the engagement of crucial stakeholders in the decision-making process. In addition, using different measurement scales (qualitative or quantitative) allows the inclusion of more criteria. COSIMA is a hybrid approach that combines the strengths of CBA and MCDA. Indeed, it may include quantitative (monetary and non-monetary) and qualitative data, which can be weighted according to their level of importance. The model also can be used to determine the overall net present value of an option, considering monetary criteria alone, or extend the valuation to include extra-economic criteria of an intangible nature. The flexibility of the COSIMA approach thus allows the inclusion of different valuation criteria, chosen by the decision maker, until an all-inclusive valuation is achieved making the method most suitable for investigating GMPVs projects.

The findings may assist both public and private decision-makers in the identification of appropriate locations to place GMPVs based on the associated costs, co-benefits, and negative externalities.

Future perspectives of the present research will regard the application of one of the methods to a real-world case study where a GMPV need to be developed. This application can highlight its potentialities and limits to include all benefits and impacts of a GMPV installation, as well as to support the decision-making process. Moreover, the application could highlight the possible presence of other gains or losses generated by GMPVs or more useful metrics to assess them.

References

1. Ciot, M.: The impact of the Russian-Ukrainian conflict on Green Deal implementation in central–southeastern Member States of the European Union. Reg. Sci. Policy Pract. **15**(1), 122–143 (2023). https://doi.org/10.1111/rsp3.12591
2. European Commission. REPowerEU: A Plan to Rapidly Reduce Dependence on Russian Fossil Fuels and Fast Forward the Green Transition. https://eur-lex.europa.eu/legal-content/EN/TXT/HTML/?uri=CELEX:52022DC0230
3. European Commission. EU Solar Energy Strategy. https://eur-lex.europa.eu/legal-content/EN/TXT/HTML/?uri=CELEX:52022DC0221
4. European Photovoltaic Industry Association. Connecting the Sun Competing in the Energy Sector - On the Road to Large Scale PV Grid Integration. Brussels (2012)
5. United Nations. Transforming Our World: the 2030 Agenda for Sustainable Development (2015). https://sdgs.un.org/publications/transforming-our-world-2030-agenda-sustainable-development-17981#:~:text=View%20PDF%3A%2021252030%20Agenda%20for%20Sustainable%20Development%20web.pdf
6. Rossitti, M., Torrieri, F.: How to manage conflicting values in minor islands: a mcda methodology towards alternative energy solutions assessment. In: Gervasi, O., et al. (eds.) ICCSA 2021. LNCS, vol. 12955, pp. 582–598. Springer, Cham (2021). https://doi.org/10.1007/978-3-030-87007-2_42

7. Randle-Boggis, R.J..: Realising co-benefits for natural capital and ecosystem services from solar parks: a co-developed, evidence-based approach. Renew. Sustain. Energy Rev. **125**, 109775 (2020). https://doi.org/10.1016/J.RSER.2020.109775
8. van de Ven, D.-J., et al.: The potential land requirements and related land use change emissions of solar energy. Sci. Rep. **11**(1), 2907 (2021). https://doi.org/10.1038/s41598-021-82042-5
9. United Nations (UN): Climate Action Summit. (2019). https://www.un.org/en/climatechange/2019-climate-action-summit
10. Hastik, R., et al.: Renewable energies and ecosystem service impacts. Renew. Sustain. Energy Rev. **48**, 608–623 (2015). https://doi.org/10.1016/j.rser.2015.04.004
11. Picchi, P., van Lierop, M., Geneletti, D., Stremke, S.: Advancing the relationship between renewable energy and ecosystem services for landscape planning and design: a literature review. Ecosyst. Serv. **35**, 241–259 (2019). https://doi.org/10.1016/j.ecoser.2018.12.010
12. Schetke, S., Lee, H., Graf, W., Lautenbach, S.: Application of the ecosystem service concept for climate protection in Germany. Ecosyst. Serv. **29**, 294–305 (2018). https://doi.org/10.1016/j.ecoser.2016.12.017
13. Jackson, A.L.R.: Renewable energy vs. biodiversity: Policy conflicts and the future of nature conservation. Glob. Environ. Chang. **21**(4), 1195–1208 (2011). https://doi.org/10.1016/j.gloenvcha.2011.07.001
14. van der Horst, D.: NIMBY or not? Exploring the relevance of location and the politics of voiced opinions in renewable energy siting controversies. Energy Policy **35**(5), 2705–2714 (2007). https://doi.org/10.1016/j.enpol.2006.12.012
15. Directorate-General for Environment (European Commission). Wind energy developments and Natura 2000 (2013). https://op.europa.eu/en/publication-detail/-/publication/65364c77-b5b8-4ab6-919d-8f4e3c6eb5c2
16. Bratrich, C., et al.: Green hydropower: a new assessment procedure for river management. River Res. Appl. **20**(7), 865–882 (2004). https://doi.org/10.1002/rra.788
17. Renöfält, B., Jansson, R., Nilsson, C.: Effects of hydropower generation and opportunities for environmental flow management in Swedish riverine ecosystems. Freshw. Biol. **55**(1), 49–67 (2010). https://doi.org/10.1111/j.1365-2427.2009.02241.x
18. Tsoutsos, T., Frantzeskaki, N., Gekas, V.: Environmental impacts from the solar energy technologies. Energy Policy **33**(3), 289–296 (2005). https://doi.org/10.1016/S0301-4215(03)00241-6
19. Chiabrando, R., Fabrizio, E., Garnero, G.: The territorial and landscape impacts of photovoltaic systems: definition of impacts and assessment of the glare risk. Renew. Sustain. Energy Rev. **13**(9), 2441–2451 (2009). https://doi.org/10.1016/j.rser.2009.06.008
20. Srinivasan, S.: The food v. fuel debate: A nuanced view of incentive structures. Renew. Energy **34**(4), 950–954 (2009). https://doi.org/10.1016/j.renene.2008.08.015
21. Semeraro, T., Scarano, A., Santino, A., Emmanuel, R., Lenucci, M.: An innovative approach to combine solar photovoltaic gardens with agricultural production and ecosystem services. Ecosyst. Serv. **56**, 101450 (2022). https://doi.org/10.1016/J.ECOSER.2022.101450
22. Huang, L., et al.: Effects of grassland restoration programs on ecosystems in arid and semiarid China. J. Environ. Manage. **117**, 268–275 (2013). https://doi.org/10.1016/J.JENVMAN.2012.12.040
23. Walston, L.J., et al.: Opportunities for agrivoltaic systems to achieve synergistic food-energy-environmental needs and address sustainability goals. Front. Sustain. Food Syst. **6**, 374 (2022). https://doi.org/10.3389/FSUFS.2022.932018/BIBTEX
24. Barron-Gafford, G.A., et al.: Agrivoltaics provide mutual benefits across the food–energy–water nexus in drylands. Nat. Sustain. **2**(9), 848–855 (2019). https://doi.org/10.1038/S41893-019-0364-5
25. Hernandez, R.R., et al.: Environmental impacts of utility-scale solar energy. Renew. Sustain. Energy Rev. **29**, 766–779 (2014). https://doi.org/10.1016/J.RSER.2013.08.041

26. McCombie, C., Jefferson, M.: Renewable and nuclear electricity: Comparison of environmental impacts. Energy Policy **96**, 758–769 (2016). https://doi.org/10.1016/J.ENPOL.2016.03.022

27. Kim, J.Y., Koide, D., Ishihama, F., Kadoya, T., Nishihiro, J.: Current site planning of medium to large solar power systems accelerates the loss of the remaining semi-natural and agricultural habitats. Sci. Total Environ. **779**, 146475 (2021). https://doi.org/10.1016/j.scitotenv.2021.146475

28. Bravi, M., Bottero, M., Dell'Anna, F.: An application of the life satisfaction approach (LSA) to value the land consumption and ecosystem services. J. Knowl. Econ. (2023). https://doi.org/10.1007/s13132-023-01150-x

29. Chiabrando, R., Fabrizio, E., Garnero, G.: On the applicability of the visual impact assessment OAI SPP tool to photovoltaic plants. Renew. Sustain. Energy Rev. **15**(1), 845–850 (2011). https://doi.org/10.1016/j.rser.2010.09.030

30. Zorzano-Alba, E., et al.: Visibility assessment of new photovoltaic power plants in areas with special landscape value. Appl. Sci. **12**(2), 703 (2022). https://doi.org/10.3390/app12020703

31. Grodsky, S.M., Hernandez, R.R.: Reduced ecosystem services of desert plants from ground-mounted solar energy development. Nat. Sustain. **3**(12), 1036–1043 (2020). https://doi.org/10.1038/s41893-020-0574-x

32. Caprioli, C., Bottero, M., Zanetta, E., Mondini, G.: Ecosystem services in land-use planning: an application for assessing transformation scenarios at the local scale. In: Bevilacqua, C., Calabrò, F., Della Spina, L. (eds.) NMP 2020. SIST, vol. 178, pp. 1332–1341. Springer, Cham (2021). https://doi.org/10.1007/978-3-030-48279-4_124

33. European Environment Agency. Green infrastructure and territorial cohesion (2011). https://doi.org/10.2800/88266

34. TEEB (The Economics of Ecosystems & Biodiversity). Mainstreaming the economics of nature: A synsthesis of the approach, conclusions and recommendations of TEEB (2010). https://teebweb.org/publications/teeb-for/synthesis/

35. Bottero, M., Bravi, M., Giaimo, C., Barbieri, C.A.: Ecosystem services: from bio-physical to economic values. In: Mondini, G., Oppio, A., Stanghellini, S., Bottero, M., Abastante, F. (eds.) Values and Functions for Future Cities. GET, pp. 37–50. Springer, Cham (2020). https://doi.org/10.1007/978-3-030-23786-8_3

36. Caprioli, C., Oppio, A., Baldassarre, R., Grassi, R., Dell'Ovo, M.: A multidimensional assessment of ecosystem services: from grey to green infrastructure. In: Gervasi, O., et al. (eds.) ICCSA 2021. LNCS, vol. 12955, pp. 569–581. Springer, Cham (2021). https://doi.org/10.1007/978-3-030-87007-2_41

37. Oppio, A., Dell'Ovo, M., Caprioli, C., Bottero, M.: A proposal to assess the benefits of urban ecosystem services. In: Calabrò, F., Della Spina, L., Piñeira Mantiñán, M.J. (eds.) New Metropolitan Perspectives: Post COVID Dynamics: Green and Digital Transition, between Metropolitan and Return to Villages Perspectives, pp. 1947–1955. Springer International Publishing, Cham (2022). https://doi.org/10.1007/978-3-031-06825-6_187

38. Assumma, V., Bottero, M., Caprioli, C., Datola, G., Mondini, G.: Evaluation of ecosystem services in mining basins: an application in the piedmont region (Italy). Sustainability **14**(2), 872 (2022). https://doi.org/10.3390/su14020872

39. Sharp, R., et al.: InVEST User's Guide (2018). https://doi.org/10.13140/RG.2.2.32693.78567

40. Gómez-Baggethun, E., de Groot, R., Lomas, P.L., Montes, C.: The history of ecosystem services in economic theory and practice: from early notions to markets and payment schemes. Ecol. Econ. (2010). https://doi.org/10.1016/j.ecolecon.2009.11.007

41. Nonhebel, S.: Renewable energy and food supply: will there be enough land? Renew. Sustain. Energy Rev. **9**(2), 191–201 (2005). https://doi.org/10.1016/j.rser.2004.02.003

42. Sacchelli, S., et al.: Trade-off between photovoltaic systems installation and agricultural practices on arable lands: an environmental and socio-economic impact analysis for Italy. Land Use Policy **56**, 90–99 (2016). https://doi.org/10.1016/j.landusepol.2016.04.024

43. Sliz-Szkliniarz, B.: Energy Planning in Selected European Regions: Methods for Evaluating the Potential of Renewable Energy Sources. KIT Scientific Publishing (2013)

44. Lytle, W., et al.: Conceptual design and rationale for a new agrivoltaics concept: pasture-raised rabbits and solar farming. J. Clean. Prod. **282**, 124476 (2021). https://doi.org/10.1016/j.jclepro.2020.124476

45. Dinesh, H., Pearce, J.M.: The potential of agrivoltaic systems. Renew. Sustain. Energy Rev. **54**, 299–308 (2016). https://doi.org/10.1016/j.rser.2015.10.024

46. Semeraro, T., Pomes, A., Del Giudice, C., Negro, D., Aretano, R.: Planning ground based utility scale solar energy as green infrastructure to enhance ecosystem services. Energy Policy **117**, 218–227 (2018). https://doi.org/10.1016/j.enpol.2018.01.050

47. Armstrong, A., Waldron, S., Whitaker, J., Ostle, N.J.: Wind farm and solar park effects on plant-soil carbon cycling: uncertain impacts of changes in ground-level microclimate. Glob. Chang. Biol. **20**(6), 1699–1706 (2014). https://doi.org/10.1111/gcb.12437

48. Peschel, T.: Solar parks – Opportunities for Biodiversity: A report on biodiversity in and around ground-mounted photovoltaic plants, Berlin (2010)

49. Sijtsma, F.J., et al.: Ecological impact and cost-effectiveness of wildlife crossings in a highly fragmented landscape: a multi-method approach. Landscape Ecol. **35**(7), 1701–1720 (2020). https://doi.org/10.1007/s10980-020-01047-z

50. Hurtado, J.: Spanish method of visual impact evaluation in wind farms. Renew. Sustain. Energy Rev. **8**(5), 483–491 (2004). https://doi.org/10.1016/j.rser.2003.12.009

51. Botelho, A., Pinto, L., Sousa, P., Sousa, S.: Using contingent valuation to measure welfare losses to local communities due to the impacts of photovoltaic farms. In: Conference: VIth GECAMB, Leiria (2014)

52. Botelho, A., Lourenço-Gomes, L., Pinto, L., Sousa, S., Valente, M.: Using stated preference methods to assess environmental impacts of forest biomass power plants in Portugal. Environ. Dev. Sustain. **18**(5), 1323–1337 (2016). https://doi.org/10.1007/s10668-016-9795-6

53. Gill, S.E., Handley, J.F., Ennos, A.R., Pauleit, S., Theuray, N., Lindley, S.J.: Characterising the urban environment of UK cities and towns: a template for landscape planning. Landsc. Urban Plan. **87**(3), 210–222 (2008). https://doi.org/10.1016/j.landurbplan.2008.06.008

54. Bottero, M., Caprioli, C., Foth, M., Mitchell, P., Rittenbruch, M., Santangelo, M.: Urban parks, value uplift and green gentrification: an application of the spatial hedonic model in the city of Brisbane. Urban For. Urban Green. **74**, 127618 (2022). https://doi.org/10.1016/j.ufug.2022.127618

55. García, J.H., Cherry, T.L., Kallbekken, S., Torvanger, A.: Willingness to accept local wind energy development: does the compensation mechanism matter? Energy Policy **99**, 165–173 (2016). https://doi.org/10.1016/j.enpol.2016.09.046

56. Tyrväinen, L., Miettinen, A.: Property prices and urban forest amenities. J. Environ. Econ. Manage. **39**(2), 205–223 (2000). https://doi.org/10.1006/jeem.1999.1097

57. Bottero, M., Dell'Anna, F., Morgese, V.: Evaluating the transition towards post-carbon cities: a literature review. Sustainability **13**(2), 567 (2021). https://doi.org/10.3390/su13020567

58. Strantzali, E., Aravossis, K.: Decision making in renewable energy investments: a review. Renew. Sustain. Energy Rev. **55**, 885–898 (2016). https://doi.org/10.1016/j.rser.2015.11.021

59. European Commission. Guide to Cost-benefit Analysis of Investment Projects: Economic appraisal tool for Cohesion Policy 2014–2020 (2014) https://doi.org/10.2776/97516

60. Wang, J.-J., Jing, Y.-Y., Zhang, C.-F., Zhao, J.-H.: Review on multi-criteria decision analysis aid in sustainable energy decision-making. Renew. Sustain. Energy Rev. **13**(9), 2263–2278 (2009). https://doi.org/10.1016/j.rser.2009.06.021

61. Barfod, M.B., Salling, K.B., Leleur, S.: Composite decision support by combining cost-benefit and multi-criteria decision analysis. Decis. Support Syst. **51**(1), 167–175 (2011). https://doi.org/10.1016/j.dss.2010.12.005

62. Dell'Anna, F., Bravi, M., Bottero, M.: Urban green infrastructures: how much did they affect property prices in Singapore? Urban For. Urban Green. **68**, 127475 (2022). https://doi.org/10.1016/j.ufug.2022.127475

63. Figueira, J., Greco, S., Ehrgott, M.: Multiple Criteria Decision Analysis: State of the Art Surveys. Springer New York, New York, NY (2005)

64. Barfod, M.B., Jensen, A.V., Leleur, S.: Examination of decision support systems for composite CBA and MCDA assessments of transport infrastructure projects. Lect. Notes Econ. Math. Syst. **648**, 167–176 (2011). https://doi.org/10.1007/978-3-642-19695-9_14

65. Dell'Anna, F., Pederiva, G., Vergerio, G., Becchio, C., Bottero, M.: Supporting sustainability projects at neighbourhood scale: Green visions for the San Salvario district in Turin guided by a combined assessment framework. J. Clean. Prod. **384**, 135460 (2023). https://doi.org/10.1016/j.jclepro.2022.135460

66. Salling, K.B., Leleur, S., Jensen, A.V.: Modelling decision support and uncertainty for large transport infrastructure projects: The CLG-DSS model of the Øresund Fixed Link. Decis. Support Syst. **43**(4), 1539–1547 (2007). https://doi.org/10.1016/j.dss.2006.06.009

67. Barfod, M.B., Salling, K.B.: A new composite decision support framework for strategic and sustainable transport appraisals. Transp. Res. Part A Policy Pract. **72**, 1–15 (2015). https://doi.org/10.1016/j.tra.2014.12.001

NBS Design and Implementation in Urban Systems: Dimensions, Challenges and Issues to Construct a Comprehensive Evaluation Framework

Giulia Datola$^{(\boxtimes)}$ ⓘ and Alessandra Oppio ⓘ

Department of Architecture and Urban Studies (DAStU), Politecnico di Milano, 20133 Milano, Italy
{giulia.datola,alessandra.oppio}@polimi.it

Abstract. The paper explores the recent challenge of implementing Nature-Based Solutions (NBS) in urban systems, as they represent an opportunity to address social, economic, and environmental issues.

Furthermore, the design and implementation of NBS in the urban context are also supported by international and national policies, such as the European Green Deal, the Sustainable Development Goals (SDGs) and the Italian Recovery and Resilience Plan (PNRR). However, despite the growing attention on this topic, there are some critical aspects still unexplored. The European Commission discuss in-depth about these aspects, declaring them as the key points to set future research. Specifically, it has been pointed out that one of the main critical issues to be investigated concerns the development and test of Decision Support Systems (DSS), evaluation tools and models to comprehensively assess NBS interventions to support their design and implementation in urban systems. According to this scenario, this paper is inserted into this research topic. More in detail, the present dissertation is a position paper that underlines the main criticalities concerning the NBS evaluation and identifies a methodological framework and some evaluation techniques that could be used to structure an evaluation framework to overcome the highlighted gaps to answer real operative requirements.

Keywords: Nature-Based Solutions (NBS) · evaluation framework · multidimensional scales and impacts · monetary and non-monetary evaluation · PNRR

1 Introduction

Societies are dealing with a wide range of issues and stresses, related to both local and global phenomena including climate change and natural catastrophes [1]. These pressures imply threats to human health and well-being, the depletion of natural resources, and the security of food, water, and energy [1–3].

According to this scenario, Nature-Based Solutions (NBS) have been suggested as a possible policy strategy to address and solve several urban challenges due to their

O. Gervasi et al. (Eds.): ICCSA 2023 Workshops, LNCS 14108, pp. 444–454, 2023.
https://doi.org/10.1007/978-3-031-37117-2_30

potential to provide multidimensional impacts and advantages and promote the wellness of people and communities [1].

In fact, the European Union (EU) is approaching these multifaceted societal issues through the new and innovative perspective represented by NBS design and implementation in urban systems [3, 4]. The objective is trying to maximize the interactions among nature, society, and the economy [1, 4–7]. Scholars and practitioners discuss the fact that the suitability of NBS design and implementation to achieve multidimensional benefits has never been more relevant, important or urgently needed than now to address the multifaceted stresses and pressures of societies and urban systems [8].

Among various NBS definitions and descriptions, the most commonly adopted is the one provided by the European Commission (EC) [7] which describes NBS as "*solutions that are inspired and supported by nature, which are cost-effective, simultaneously provide environmental, social and economic benefits and help build resilience. Such solutions bring more, and more diverse, nature and natural features and processes into cities, landscapes and seascapes through locally adapted, resource-efficient and systemic interventions*" [9]. This description provides a broad framework that includes several interpretations and practical applications [3, 10].

In this sense, NBS have emerged as both a challenge and an opportunity to assist urban communities in the transition to greater sustainability and adaptation to climate change [11]. According to this scenario, NBS have been proposed as a sustainable approach to supporting the transition of sustainable and resilient development in cities [12]. According to this scenario, exponential attention has been observed in implementing NBS in urban systems. In fact, from the research on the Scopus platform, considering the keywords "Nature-Based Solutions" AND "cities" it has been possible to see an

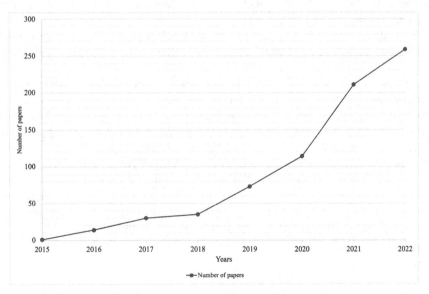

Fig. 1. Development of the literature about NBS and cities

exponential increase in production paper since 2018, as Fig. 1 represents. From the year 2015 with only one paper, moved to 2022 with 259 papers.

In this sense, it is possible to stress the fact that NBS within their design and implementation in urban systems have recently emerged as one of the main policy drivers for transitioning cities [1]. Therefore, NBS can be considered a great opportunity for innovation [1, 5–7].

According to the observed great attention on NBS design and implementation in urban systems, this paper addresses the NBS alignment with the international frameworks to underline their significance in supporting the transition of cities to sustainable and resilient development. Moreover, this paper aims at exploring the criticalities observed in the field of the evaluation of NBS intervention, to stress the necessity of the development and testing of Decision Support Systems (DSS), evaluation tools and models that can conduct a comprehensive assessment to consider all the multifaceted aspects concerning NBS. More in detail, the present research is configured as a position paper to identify some evaluation techniques that could be used to structure an evaluation framework to overcome the highlighted gaps and answer real operative requirements.

2 NBS Alignment with International Frameworks

The regeneration, requalification and transformation of urban areas and territories is the current challenge, which must consider environmental quality and social justice [14]. As stated in the previous part, transforming cities and regions into sustainable and resilient living places has become a key global priority and the NBS implementation can contribute to this global challenge [6]. According to this scenario, it is necessary and useful to point out the alignment of NBS implementation with some of the most important international frameworks [1, 13, 14].

From different works proposed by several scholars [1, 13, 14], it is possible to address that NBS design and implementation in urban systems is aligned with several international frameworks.

First of all, the New Urban Agenda specifically refers to NBS for urban and territorial planning [15]. Article 157 says *"we will support science, research and innovation, including a focus on social, technological, digital and nature-based innovation, robust science-policy interfaces in urban and territorial planning and policy formulation and institutionalized mechanisms for sharing and exchanging information, knowledge and expertise, including the collection, analysis, standardization and dissemination of geographically based, community-collected, high-quality, timely and reliable data disaggregated by income, sex, age, race, ethnicity, migration status, disability, geographic location and other characteristics relevant in national, subnational and local contexts."*[1]

As well as, the NBS design and implementation are aligned with:

– The EU adaptation strategy [16];
– Paris agreement [17];

---

[1] United Nations, 2016, p. 39.

– Sendai Framework [18]

Moreover, it can be stated that NBS can enhance and contribute to a number of Sustainable Development Goals (SDGs) [1]. More specifically, NBS address not only SDGs concerning nature and natural processes such as SDGs 14 and 15. In fact, researchers highlighted that NBS should improve in a general manner the access to recreational/green areas [1]. As well as, the improvement of green areas and green infrastructure networks should engage the SDGS 10 (reducing inequalities) and SGD 3 (improving well-being) [1]. Moreover, NBS should contribute considerably to SDG 11 related to "making cities and human settlements inclusive, safe, resilient and sustainable". In fact, NBS implementation can achieve target 11.3, or rather "inclusive and sustainable urbanization", as well as target 11.4 "protect the world's cultural and natural heritage", target 11. 5 "reduce the adverse effects of natural disasters", target 11.6 "reduce the environmental impact of cities", target 11.7 "provide access to safe and inclusive green and public space". In the same way, NBS can support the reaching of some SDG 13 targets, such as 13.1 "strengthen resilience and adaptive capacity to climate related disasters" and 13.2 "integrate climate change measures into policies and planning",

Moreover, NBS are also engaged in the European Recovery and Resilience Plans (RRPs), and in the Italian National Plan of Recovery and Resilience (PNRR) [19]. The RRPs are focused on the mitigation of the economic and social impacts due to the coronavirus pandemic and on the enhancement of sustainable and resilient development to face both digital and climatic and transitions challenges [19]. The EU defines the six pillars that have to be investigated by RRPs, or rather: (1) green transition, (2) digital transformation, (3) economic cohesion, productivity and competitiveness, (4) social and territorial cohesion, (5) health, economic, social, and institutional resilience, and (6) policies for the next generation [19]. Therefore, the RRP is a plan based on the enhancement of economic growth and increasing job opportunities. The Italian PNRR is organized into 16 Components, that are grouped into six missions: (1) digitalization, (2) ecological transition, (3) sustainable mobility, (4) research and education, (5) social cohesion and inclusion, and (6) health. More in detail, the ecological transition takes the highest percentage of the total funding program with respect to the other missions [19]. Therefore, the design and implementation of NBS intervention is engaged in the mission of PNRR.

3   Problem Statement

As declared in previous sections, NBS have been proposed as a promising approach.

To address several multidimensional urban problems due to the potential, they have to deliver multiple benefits and foster well-being for individuals and communities [1, 12]. However, there are some gaps that need to be explored in the context of NBS design intervention. The EC analyses these lacks and states that one of the main critical issues to be investigated concerns the development and the test of DSS, evaluation tools and models to comprehensively assess NBS interventions to support their implementation in urban systems, as well as the monitoring and assessment of their impacts are needed to guide urban policy-making. In fact, the analysis of the existing and proposed evaluation frameworks highlights several issues and empirical gaps that have to be addressed to define a robust evaluation framework to support and inform policy decisions in European urban projects [12].

In general, the debate is focuses on the necessity of understanding and evaluating the economic, social, political and cultural dimensions of the design and implementation of NBS [4].

Therefore, this section lists the most discussed criticalities concerning the evaluation of NBS design and implementation. More in detail, these gaps have been collected from the combination and the comparison of research papers [1, 3, 10–12, 20] and the report by the EU focused on the NBS state-of-the-art [4].

These main issues can be listed as follows:

– *NBS is an umbrella term that engages a wide range of concepts and practices* [4].

In the literature, NBS is an umbrella term in which different interventions can be classified and engaged. There are several solutions that can use nature ranging from small scales such as green rooftops or green walls in cities to broad-scale for climate change mitigation and adaptation such as forestation [10]. This condition influences in a negative way the organization and structuring of an effective evaluation framework, according to the wide range of possible solutions to evaluate. Therefore, it is necessary to draw and define the limits of what can be classified as NBS or not.

– *Issue of economic evaluation, quantification and monetization of NBS* [5].

One of the main issues concerning the evaluation of NBS implementation regards the evaluation of economic efficiency. In fact, NBS have the potential to be cost-efficient and resource-efficient [1]. Moreover, it is necessary to quantify and monetize NBS benefits to support the decision process.

Whiteoak in the EU report on the state of the art of NBS intervention in the European context stresses that the rigorous use of economic analyses may reveal more NBS options than would otherwise be identified [4].

– *Issue of the consideration in the evaluation framework of the time scale.*

The topic of how different impacts can affect over time urban systems is not an issue in the context of urban sustainability and transformation. Therefore, also the theme of NBS implementation is engaged in this trouble. In fact, interventions should be investigated according to their short-, medium-, and long-term effects [12].

From the literature review, it has been observed that the short-term effects are the most investigated [12]. Moreover, the analysis of the short-term effects is appropriate for specific environmental impacts, but not suitable for other aspects, such as climate change which requires a long-term approach, as well as social impacts [6, 12, 13].

Therefore, in the literature, it is unclear and less explored which approaches would be more suitable in the long-term evaluation and which would be more effective immediately after implementation [21].

In fact, it is necessary to point out that regarding the different solution types, the achievement of benefits required can vary in time scale, or rather different co-benefits can be produced at different time steps [22]. Therefore, NBS implementation effectiveness should be assessed according to different time thresholds in order to evaluate short-time effects (1–5 years), medium-time effects (5–10 years) and long-time effects (over 10 years) [4].

– *Criticalities in considering spatial scale in the evaluation, supporting the definition of the adequate spatial scale of intervention.*

As discussed before, there are different types of NBS implementation interventions, that can embrace the different level scale of interventions [5]. In fact, NBS can be related to the micro-level of a single building (e.g., green walls), the meso-level of a whole city (e.g., constructed wetlands) and the macro-level of an entire country [20]. Moreover, it is important to underline that the scale of a solution affects effectiveness in terms of the provision of services and the level of tackling challenges.

– *The challenge of social impacts valuation and the differentiation of impacts for different socio-economic group.*

In the literature, it is discussed that NBS can have different impacts concerning different social groups [23]. In fact, it has been observed that certain social groups are sometimes excluded from engaging with NBS, or others implying the effect of the green gentrification [23]. To be effective, the evaluation framework should include methodologies to assess the magnitude of these social impacts, as well as their different nature and implication according to different social groups.

– *Issue of considering the interactions between different impacts.*

As underlined by the literature, NBS affect social, environmental, and economic spheres, which are interrelated due to the fact cities are conceptualized as ecosystems [24]. Therefore, it should be recognized also in the evaluation phase the interaction between these dimensions, as well as impacts. Evaluation frameworks should identify potential interactions and interrelations (cause-effects relations) among different types of impacts [3].

4   Proposing Method

As stated in the previous section, NBS address social, economic, and environmental dimensions. According to the analysis of the observed lacks in the field of NBS evaluation, the authors also move their reflection about some aspects that should be addressed in the assessment of NBS design and implementation.

These aspects mainly concern (1) the changing value of the real estate market, that is also strictly related to the gentrification phenomenon [25], and (2) the issue of budget evaluation [4].

Thus, above these reflections and the issues discussed in the previous section, it is possible to underline that when dealing with NBS design and implementation it is necessary to support the definition of the strategy by addressing: the cost of intervention and the economic revenues, the real estate market and the real estate value, the social and environmental impacts, and the spatial and temporal scales.

Therefore, this section aims at proposing some methodologies that should be applied to investigate these aspects.

First of all, a taxonomy of NBS intervention to support the evaluation process is required. In detail, the authors aim at proposing a taxonomy that collects different types of NBS intervention, according to their nature and scale of intervention to clarify their design and better support the selection of the most suitable evaluation framework, as well as to support the evaluation of the intervention cost. In this sense, this proposal aims at making the several NBS interventions more accessible to different stakeholders and improving the coherence in research and policy dialogue [1].

Concerning the issue of the spatial scale of the intervention, the method of alternative design should be selected to explore this topic [26, 27]. More in detail, the alternative design method should be used to investigate and compare micro-scale and large-scale intervention in an urban context to identify the better alternative and scale of intervention according to the objective and purposes.

Moreover, also the application of the Geographic Information System (GIS) is suggested to map the intervention and evaluate its effectiveness [28].

For what concerns about the cost of the investment is important to address the available budget and how to invest it. Therefore, it should be useful and interesting to explore the method of the Portfolio Decision Analysis also in the context of the NBS evaluation [29], in order to purpose to include urban NBS into institutional investment portfolios through regulatory and supervisory action and certification schemes [4].

On the other hand, for the evaluation of the changing in the value of the real estate market, one of the possible methods to use is the Hedonic Price Method (HPM), as it is widely used in the literature to evaluate how urban green infrastructure should affect the market value of housing [30].

Moreover, according to both the multifaceted effects of NBS and to the fact that urban systems are ecosystems [24], it is necessary to address the combination and the relationships among these effects. In this sense, Cognitive Maps and/or System Dynamics Model (SDM) should be an efficient method to design the causal relationships that occur among different dimensions and effects [31–34]. As well, SDM should be also used to evaluate the effects of NBS intervention on temporal scale, thanks to its ability to describe the evolution of complex systems over time and support the definition of development strategies by considering their effects in the temporal scale [2], addressing also the long-term effects. Moreover, in the context of the temporal scale, monitoring evaluation methods can be proposed, such as co-axial matrix [35] by using indicators that are able to address peculiarities of the context, as well as SDGs targets.

Table 1 summarizes the discussed issues of NBS evaluation with the proposed method to overcome these criticalities.

Table 1. List of evaluation issues within the proposed methods to overcome them

Evaluation issue	Proposed method or combined methods
Economic evaluation	Portfolio Decision Analysis; Hedonic Price
Time scale of intervention	System Dynamics Model (SDM) for scenario evaluation over time and impacts assessment; Co-axial matrix for monitoring the intervention
Determination of the properly spatial scale of the intervention	Alternatives Design and GIS
Social impacts of different socio-demographic group	System Dynamics Model (SDM) as a participative process
Interaction between multidimensional impacts	Cognitive Maps and System Dynamics Model (SDM)

5 Discussion and Conclusion

This paper briefly explores the current interest in NBS implementation as an opportunity and challenge to face social, economic, and environmental issues. According to this scenario, the present research highlights how NBS implementation is aligned and can contribute to the different national, and international frameworks (Sect. 2).

Moreover, this paper analyses which are the main lack of NBS evaluation addressed in the literature [4]. According to this statement and some critical reflections, the authors propose and list some methodologies that should be used, among others, to address some of the discussed issues.

As an example, the method of the alternatives design and the GIS should be integrated to support the definition of the properly scale of intervention. As well as, these methodologies should be used to create a multimethodological framework with SDM which can be used to evaluate the designed alternative according to its multidimensional impacts over time.

Therefore, above this discussion, it is possible to state and underline that the evaluation of NBS interventions is a crucial step in implementation design. In fact, NBS evaluation is related to the governance in supporting, defining and designing the most suitable intervention [4, 12, 13]. In fact, what clearly emerged is that it is required an evaluation framework able to support the project selection, according to the assessment of its multidimensional aspects and impacts (economic, social and environmental) in both spatial and temporal scales.

Therefore, according to the discussed statement, future research in NBS evaluation should address the integration of quantitative and qualitative evaluation approaches to understanding the multifaceted issues, as well as their interaction and distribution over time [4, 8–10, 12, 13, 20, 36, 37]. Moreover, the proposed evaluation framework should also be a repeatable and context-sensitive approach at the same time. This condition should be achieved by using indicators able to be used in different contexts and addressing the peculiarities of the evaluation [8].

According to the complexity of these challenges, an accurate NBS implementation requires the contribution of experts and stakeholders across different disciplines and sectors to be implicated in the design, financing, and decision-making processes [4, 8–10, 12, 13, 20, 36, 37].

In conclusion, it can be addressed that this paper explores the current attention of NBS design and implementation in urban systems to support cities in sustainable and resilient development. At the same time, it underlines how NBS can address the tasks of different international and national frameworks, highlighting which are the main operative needs and proposing a reflection on some points and suggestions for other researchers engaged in this field with a specific focus on the PNRR challenges.

Acknowledgement. This study was carried out within the Agritech National Research Center and received funding from the European Union Next-GenerationEU (PIANO NAZIONALE DI RIPRESA E RESILIENZA (PNRR) – MISSIONE 4 COMPONENTE 2, INVESTIMENTO 1.4 – D.D. 1032 17/06/2022, CN00000022). This manuscript reflects only the authors' views and opinions, neither the European Union nor the European Commission can be considered responsible for them.

Furthermore, the authors wish to thank Professor Alexis Tsoukias for his support in reflecting on which methodologies should be examined in addressing NBS design and implementation.

References

1. Faivre, N., Fritz, M., Freitas, T., de Boissezon, B., Vandewoestijne, S.: Nature-based solutions in the EU: innovating with nature to address social, economic and environmental challenges. Environ. Res. **159**, 509–518 (2017). https://doi.org/10.1016/j.envres.2017.08.032
2. Gómez Martín, E., Máñez Costa, M., Egerer, S., Schneider, U.A.: Assessing the long-term effectiveness of nature-based Solutions under different climate change scenarios. Sci. Total Environ. **794**, 148515 (2021). https://doi.org/10.1016/j.scitotenv.2021.148515
3. Davies, C., Chen, W.Y., Sanesi, G., Lafortezza, R.: The European Union roadmap for implementing nature-based solutions: a review. Environ. Sci. Policy **121**, 49–67 (2021). https://doi.org/10.1016/j.envsci.2021.03.018
4. Calfapietra, C., Whiteoak, K., Innovation, Bulkeley, H., Naumann, S., Vojinovic, Z., Wild, T.: Nature-based solutions : state of the art in EU-funded projects. (T. Freitas, S. Vandewoestijne, & T. Wild, Eds.). Publications Office of the European Union (2020). https://doi.org/10.2777/236007
5. Sowińska-Świerkosz, B., García, J.: A new evaluation framework for nature-based solutions (NBS) projects based on the application of performance questions and indicators approach. Sci. Total Environ. **787**, 147615 (2021). https://doi.org/10.1016/j.scitotenv.2021.147615
6. Dumitru, A., Wendling, L., Eiter, S., Pilla, F.: Evaluating the Impact of Nature-based Solutions: A Handbook for Practitioners (2021). https://doi.org/10.13140/RG.2.2.10757.47843
7. Hanson, H.I., Wickenberg, B., Alkan Olsson, J.: Working on the boundaries—How do science use and interpret the nature-based solution concept? Land Use Policy, **90**, 104302 (2020). https://doi.org/10.1016/j.landusepol.2019.104302
8. Cohen-Shacham, E., Walters, G., Maginnis, S., Janzen, C.: Nature-based solutions to address global societal challenges. (E. Cohen-Shacham, G. Walters, C. Janzen, & S. Maginnis, Eds.).

IUCN International Union for Conservation of Nature (2016). https://doi.org/10.2305/IUCN. CH.2016.13.en

9. Bauduceau, N., Berry, P., Cecchi, C., Elmqvist, T., Fernandez, M., Hartig, T.: Noring, L. (2015). Towards an EU research and innovation policy agenda for nature-based solutions & re-naturing cities: Final report of the horizon 2020 expert group on'nature-based solutions and re-naturing cities'

10. Nesshöver, C., et al.: The science, policy and practice of nature-based solutions: an interdisciplinary perspective. Sci. Total Environ. **579**, 1215–1227 (2017). https://doi.org/10.1016/j. scitotenv.2016.11.106

11. Frantzeskaki, N., et al.: Examining the policy needs for implementing nature-based solutions in cities: Findings from city-wide transdisciplinary experiences in Glasgow (UK), Genk (Belgium) and Poznań (Poland). Land Use Policy **96**, 104688 (2020). https://doi.org/10.1016/j. landusepol.2020.104688

12. Dumitru, A., Frantzeskaki, N., Collier, M.: Identifying principles for the design of robust impact evaluation frameworks for nature-based solutions in cities. Environ. Sci. Policy **112**, 107–116 (2020). https://doi.org/10.1016/j.envsci.2020.05.024

13. Raymond, C.M., et al.: A framework for assessing and implementing the co-benefits of nature-based solutions in urban areas. Environ. Sci. Policy **77**, 15–24 (2017). https://doi.org/10.1016/j.envsci.2017.07.008

14. European Environment Agency. Nature-based solutions in Europe: Policy, knowledge and practice for climate change adaptation and disaster risk reduction. EEA Report (2021). https://www.eea.europa.eu/publications/nature-based-solutions-in-europe

15. United Nations. New Urban Agenda Habitat III: Summary. Habitat III Secretariat (2016). 978-92-1-132731-1

16. European commission. Communication from the commission to the european parliament, the council, the european economic and social committee and the committee of the regions an eu strategy on adaptation to climate change (2013). Brussel

17. Delbeke, J., Runge-Metzger, A., Slingenberg, Y., Werksman, J.: The Paris Agreement. In: Towards a Climate-Neutral Europe, pp. 24–45. London: Routledge (2019). https://doi.org/10.4324/9789276082569-2

18. UNISDR. Sendai Framework for Disaster Risk Reduction. UN World Conference (2015)

19. Di Pirro, E., et al.: The embeddedness of nature-based solutions in the recovery and resilience plans as multifunctional approaches to foster the climate transition: the cases of Italy and Portugal. Land **11**(8), 1254 (2022). https://doi.org/10.3390/land11081254

20. Raymond, C., et al.: An impact evaluation framework to support planning and evaluation of nature-based solutions projects. Report prepared by the EKLIPSE Expert Working Group on Nature-based Solutions to Promote Climate Resilience in Urban Areas. Centre for Ecology and Hydrology (2017)

21. Kabisch, N., Korn, H., Stadler, J., Bonn, A. (eds.): Nature-Based Solutions to Climate Change Adaptation in Urban Areas: Linkages between Science, Policy and Practice. Springer International Publishing, Cham (2017)

22. Giordano, R., Pluchinotta, I., Pagano, A., Scrieciu, A., Nanu, F.: Enhancing nature-based solutions acceptance through stakeholders' engagement in co-benefits identification and trade-offs analysis. Sci. Total Environ. **713**, 136552 (2020). https://doi.org/10.1016/j.scitotenv.2020. 136552

23. Sowińska-Świerkosz, B., García, J.: What are Nature-based solutions (NBS)? Setting core ideas for concept clarification. Nature-Based Solutions **2**, 100009 (2022). https://doi.org/10. 1016/j.nbsj.2022.100009

24. Douglas, I., Goode, D., Houck, M.C., Maddox, D.: The Routledge Handbook of Urban Ecology. Taylor \& Francis (2010). https://books.google.it/books?id=5J%5C_HBQAAQBAJ

25. Sax, D.L., Nesbitt, L., Quinton, J.: Improvement, not displacement: A framework for urban green gentrification research and practice. Environ. Sci. Policy **137**, 373–383 (2022). https://doi.org/10.1016/j.envsci.2022.09.013

26. Pluchinotta, I., Kazakçi, A.O., Giordano, R., Tsoukiàs, A.: Design theory for generating alternatives in public decision making processes. Group Decis. Negot. **28**(2), 341–375 (2019). https://doi.org/10.1007/s10726-018-09610-5

27. Colorni, A., Tsoukiàs, A.: Designing alternatives in decision problems. J. Multi-Criteria Decis. Anal. **27**(3–4), 150–158 (2020). https://doi.org/10.1002/mcda.1709

28. Mahmood, R., Zhang, L., Li, G.: Assessing effectiveness of nature-based solution with big earth data: 60 years mangrove plantation program in Bangladesh coast. Ecol. Process. **12**(1), 11 (2023). https://doi.org/10.1186/s13717-023-00419-y

29. Salo, A., Keisler, J., Morton, A. (eds.): Portfolio Decision Analysis: Improved Methods for Resource Allocation. Springer New York, New York, NY (2011)

30. Dell'Anna, F., Bravi, M., Bottero, M.: Urban Green infrastructures: how much did they affect property prices in Singapore? Urban For. Urban Greening **68**, 127475 (2022). https://doi.org/10.1016/j.ufug.2022.127475

31. Axelrod, R.: Structure of decision: The cognitive maps of political elites. Structure of Decision: The Cognitive Maps of Political Elites (2015). https://www.scopus.com/inward/record.uri?eid=2-s2.0-85016362307&partnerID=40&md5=fc296bd0c6fcbb681e0ac7c5545189a5

32. Bottero, M., Datola, G., Monaco, R.: The use of fuzzy cognitive maps for evaluating the reuse project of military barracks in Northern Italy. In: Calabrò, F., Della Spina, L., Bevilacqua, C. (eds.) ISHT 2018. SIST, vol. 100, pp. 691–699. Springer, Cham (2019). https://doi.org/10.1007/978-3-319-92099-3_77

33. Forrester, J.W.: Lessons from system dynamics modeling. Syst. Dyn. Rev. **3**, 136–149 (1987)

34. Bala, B.K., Arshad, F.M., Noh, K.M.: Systems thinking: system dynamics. In: System Dynamics. STBE, pp. 15–35. Springer, Singapore (2017). https://doi.org/10.1007/978-981-10-2045-2_2

35. Assumma, V., Datola, G., Mondini, G.: New Cohesion policy 2021–2027: the role of indicators in the assessment of the SDGs targets performance. In: Gervasi, O., et al. (eds.) ICCSA 2021. LNCS, vol. 12955, pp. 614–625. Springer, Cham (2021). https://doi.org/10.1007/978-3-030-87007-2_44

36. Nika, C.E., Gusmaroli, L., Ghafourian, M., Atanasova, N., Buttiglieri, G., Katsou, E.: Nature-based solutions as enablers of circularity in water systems: a review on assessment methodologies, tools and indicators. Water Res. **183**, 115988 (2020). https://doi.org/10.1016/j.watres.2020.115988

37. Sandin, L., et al.: Working with nature-based solutions. Nordisk Ministerråd (2023). https://doi.org/10.6027/temanord2022-562

How to Address Marginalization in Small Towns: An MCDA Approach to Evaluating Different Strategies in Campania Region

Marco Rossitti[1]([✉]) [iD], Fabiana Forte[2] [iD], and Francesca Torrieri[3] [iD]

[1] Politecnico di Milano, Via E. Bonardi 3, 20133 Milano, Italy
marco.rossitti@polimi.it

[2] DADI, Università Degli Studi della Campania Luigi Vanvitelli, Via San Lorenzo, 81031 Aversa, Italy

[3] DII, Università Degli Studi di Napoli Federico II, Piazzale V. Tecchio 80, 80125 Napoli, Italy

Abstract. In recent years, the struggle against territorial marginalization in small towns has been central to national and international policy agendas. In Italy, several structural incentives and policies have been set to deal with this issue, but only some villages could capture the opportunities provided. In addition, some small towns have stood out for innovative and spontaneous strategies to tackle marginalization. In this context, the research compares different de-marginalizing strategies and tools recently implemented by some small villages in Campania Region (Italy). More in detail, it focuses on three municipalities: Mirabella Eclano (Av), where, as part of the de-marginalization strategy, is adopted the legal instrument "administrative barter"; Guardia Sanframondi (BN), where the shrinking dynamics are tackled by attracting new residents; and Preturo Irpino (AV), where the implemented strategy rests on migrants reception and integration. Since marginalization is universally acknowledged as a multi-dimensional phenomenon, the comparison is performed through an MCDA approach based on social, economic, and spatial criteria relevant to interpreting and counteracting it. On the one hand, the results from this comparison can guide the replicability and adaptation of the considered strategies to other realities. On the other hand, it allows reflecting on the selected strategies' capacity to address the different 'marginalization' dimensions included in the analysis.

Keywords: Marginalization · Small villages · Strategies · MCDA · Comparison

1 Introduction

The struggle against territorial marginalization has been central to national and international policy agendas in recent years. The 20th-century leading urbanization model's crisis, indeed, has triggered reflections about the role of marginal areas in promoting sustainable and balanced territorial development [1]. Considering marginalization as "an involuntary position and condition of an individual or group at the margin of social, political, economic, ecological, and biophysical systems, that prevent them from access

O. Gervasi et al. (Eds.): ICCSA 2023 Workshops, LNCS 14108, pp. 455–467, 2023.
https://doi.org/10.1007/978-3-031-37117-2_31

to resources, assets, services, restraining freedom of choice, preventing the development of capabilities, and eventually causing extreme poverty" [2], well returns the complexity related to dealing with this phenomenon at the territorial level. Indeed, marginalization cannot be reduced to a mere accessibility issue but must be intended as a multidimensional phenomenon, thus raising the necessity for tailored and integrated strategies to be addressed [3].

In Italy, the consequent marginality-tackling challenge has found a privileged implementation territorial context in the small-town dimension. Small towns are defined as municipalities with less than 5000 inhabitants, but the small town categorization also includes 600 municipalities with more than 5000 inhabitants due to adverse economic or demographic conditions [4, 5]. Indeed, most of them are characterized by a severe socio-economic marginality, made evident by the ongoing negative demographic trend with the consequent depletion of their human capital [6].

In any case, small towns are relevant nationally since they account for 69% of Italian municipalities, cover 70% of the national territorial surface, and host almost 17% of the Italian resident population. The relevance of the ongoing marginalization phenomenon in this territorial reality can be immediately grasped from a demographic perspective. Indeed, small towns are experiencing a steady depopulation process: their average drop in resident population stands at 3% between 2012 and 2017 [4].

The increasing attention on the marginality, with specific reference to the inner areas and the small towns, characterized by and extraordinary "territorial capital" [7, 8], has led the Italian Government to develop several structural incentives and policies to tackle this marginalization dynamics. The most relevant ones can be identified in:

- The National Strategy for Inner Areas (SNAI). It was launched in 2014 as the national declination of the European Strategy toward territorial cohesion [9]. It aims to tackle the negative demographic trends affecting some marginal areas, defined as "inner areas", by promoting local development initiatives and rebalancing essential services (education, healthcare, and mobility) [10]. The funding for the SNAI implementation's first cycle (2014–2020), drawing both on national and European resources, accounts for around 2, 1 billion euros [11];
- The Budget Law 2021 – Funding for Marginal Municipalities. The law provides 180 million euros of funding to promote the recovery of existing buildings belonging to the municipality's real estate assets, to support new business activities starting, and to incentivize residence transfer in small towns [12];
- The PNRR 2021 – National Plan Borghi. It allocates 760 million euros to support the recovery of built heritage assets and economic development based on local vocations and specificities [13].

Besides these structural incentives and policies, some small towns implemented marginalization-tackling strategies based on specific juridical tools, fiscal incentives, and innovative actions. Among them, for instance, it is possible to consider the initiative "Case a 1 euro" (Houses for one euro) through which public administrations create conditions for an easy access to housing, while promoting the recovery and maintenance of the municipal built heritage assets.

These strategies stand as a local declination of a broader national policy effort. For this reason, understanding their implementation opportunities and effectiveness, according to the reference territorial context's specificities, can be a valuable tool for better orienting planning decisions toward tackling marginalization in small towns.

Based on these premises, the paper deals with this understanding attempt by providing a methodological approach to compare different marginalization-tackling strategies implemented in small towns and drawing out some preliminary reflections on their effectiveness and implementation opportunities. This approach is tested on a case study: different marginalization-tackling strategies implemented in three small towns from Campania Region. In this sense, Sect. 2 introduces the case study by describing the three selected reference territorial contexts and the peculiarities of the implemented strategies. Section 3 describes the adopted approach that acknowledges the marginalization phenomenon's multi-dimensional nature and finds an appropriate methodological reference in Multi-Criteria Decision Analysis. Section 4 describes the methodological approach implementation to the different strategies comparison, whose results are discussed in Sect. 5. Finally, Sect. 6 considers the proposed approach's opportunities as an operative tool for small towns-focused planning, its replicability, and room for improvement.

2 Strategies to Address Marginalization in Small Towns: Evidence from Campania Region

The marginalization phenomenon, a common trait of small-town realities in the whole national territory, is even exacerbated in the Southern Regions, which suffer from an overall socioeconomic underdevelopment condition [14]. Among them, the small-town reality is particularly relevant in Campania Region since it accounts for 61% of municipalities and covers 58% of the regional territorial surface [4]. For this reason, it can be worth searching for marginalization-tackling strategies to be taken as study elements for the comparison within this territorial context. More in detail, the paper focuses on three different strategies related to different small towns in Campania Region, and implemented in recent years:

- "Attracting new residents" in Guardia Sanframondi (BN). Guardia Sanframondi is a small town in Benevento Province with a resident population of 4611 units in 2022 (Fig. 1). The implemented marginalization-tackling strategy, dating back to 2016, aimed at tackling the ongoing steady demographic shrinking by attracting new residents. This strategy, promoted by the municipality's mayor, was inspired by an unexpected and unofficial event: a Scottish journalist and writer, Clare Galloway, fell in love with the municipality and decided to devote to it an episode of the American TV show 'How Hunters International'. Such a media promotion created an international interest in Guardia Sanframondi that the major decided to leverage by joining different international fairs and organizing several international events in the municipality;

- "Administrative barter" in Mirabella Eclano (AV). Mirabello Eclano is a small town in the north of Avellino Province with a resident population of 6808 units in 2022. In this territorial context, indeed, the declining birth rate is flanked by an increase in the number of young people leaving due to the lack of job opportunities. The implemented marginalization-tackling strategy leverages the "administrative barter".

Fig. 1. Guardia Sanframondi's historical center (photo by M. Rossitti, 2022)

It is a juridical tool introduced by the "Decreto Sblocca Italia" in 2014 [15] and integrated by the Italian Public Contract Code, D. Lgs. n. 50/2016 [16], as modified by the D. Lgs. n. 57/2017, art. 190. The administrative barter is a contract between a public administration and a private citizen: it consists of an exemption or reduction of local taxes in return for community services (i.e., cleaning and maintenance works for public spaces, recovery of abandoned buildings and open spaces) [17]. The Mirabella Eclano municipality deliberated the application of the "administrative barter" juridical tool in 2017 [6].

- "Migrants reception" in Petruro Irpino (AV). Petruro Irpino is a small town in Avellino Province with a resident population of 293 units in 2022. The implemented marginalization-tackling strategy, focusing on migrants' reception and integration, finds similar applications in several small towns spread over the national territory [18]. The Preturo Irpino municipality launched a SPRAR project to host asylum seekers from different countries. Indeed, the SPRAR (System for the Protection of Asylum-Seekers and Refugees) is a legal institute introduced by the Law n. 189/2002, regulating the collaboration among local administrations and third-sector entities to promote the effective reception and integration of migrants voluntarily [19]. Concerning Petruro Irpino, the municipality set several reception and integration activities based on the direct engagement of the existing local community (education and training programs) [20].

3   An MCDA Approach to Comparing Marginalization-Tackling Strategies in Campania Region

The willingness to understand the effectiveness and implementation opportunities of various strategies, dealing with marginalization in different ways, calls for the definition of a robust methodological approach toward their assessment and comparison. In this perspective, recognizing the multi-dimensional nature of the marginalization issue, which affects multiple dimensions of territorial development (demographic, economic, socio-cultural), hints at adopting Multi-Criteria Decision Analysis (MCDA) as methodological ground. Indeed, MCDA methodologies allow for comparing alternatives based on a heterogenous set of qualitative or quantitative indicators, thus dealing with evaluation issues involving multiple dimensions [21–23]. Their application can be traced to two macro-phases, which can be identified as:

- The Problem Structuring phase. It involves the alternatives definition and the decision issue's modeling into a decision tree, which displays: the overall objective for the evaluation task; the related specific objectives in the form of criteria; the sub-criteria to detail specific objectives, and the indicators to measure alternatives' performance according to each sub-criteria [24];
- The Method Implementation phase. It focuses on the different alternatives' performance measurements and the data processing or aggregation, thus providing the analysis results [25].

Scientific literature in the MCDA field shows the existence of about 100 different methodologies [25]. Thus, choosing the appropriate multicriteria method to support the addressed evaluation task stands as a challenging and fundamental research point toward the methodological approach robustness.

3.1 MCDA to Comparing Marginalization-Tackling Strategies: Which Methodology?

The willingness to identify the appropriate methodology for comparing the different marginalization-tackling strategies calls for a comparative assessment of the suitability of the MCDA methods according to the evaluation task's specificities.

Given the impossibility of considering all the 100 available MCDA methodologies, this comparison requires a field choice. It can consist in focusing on the most frequently applied methodologies [26], which are:

- Analytic Hierarchy Process (AHP);
- Analytic Network Process (ANP);
- Elimination Et Choix Traduisant la Réalité (ELECTRE);
- Multi-attribute utility theory (MAUT);
- Measuring Attractiveness by a Categorical Based Evaluation (MACBETH);
- Preference Ranking Organization Method for Enrichment Evaluation (PROMETHEE);
- Technique for Order of Preference by Similarity to Ideal Solution (TOPSIS).

The selected MCDA methodologies' comparison can be performed using an evaluation framework including exogenous and endogenous criteria [27]. More in detail, exogenous criteria deal with the reference context for the method's application, while endogenous criteria consider the different methodologies' specific features. According to the evaluation task's specificities, relevant exogenous criteria for the methods' comparison can be identified in:

- The "number of evaluation elements". It focuses on the number of alternatives and sub-criteria to be taken as a reference for the evaluation.
- The "typology of indicators". It considers the reference variables for measuring alternatives' performances according to the selected sub-criteria.

Regarding endogenous criteria, instead, they can be identified in:

- The "solution approach". It expresses the approach to solving evaluation problems;
- The "type of solutions". It considers the kind of solution achievable through a specific method's application and can be interpreted in light of the specificities of the addressed evaluation task.

Once this minimum reference criteria set is defined, it is possible to perform the MCDA methodologies' comparison by building a descriptive matrix of their features (Table 1). Such a matrix, indeed, can be used as an information frame for the MCDA methods' choice according to its suitability for the specific task under consideration.

In this perspective, the comparison among different marginalization-tackling strategies can be configured as an evaluation issue with a small number of sub-criteria and alternatives potentially involving both qualitative and quantitative indicators. According to it, an acceptable and even more interesting solution can be represented by alternatives with the same score but different solutions, thus admitting an outranking solution approach. Thus, entering the MCDA methodologies' descriptive matrix with this evaluation task's specification returns the Elimination Et Choix Traduisant la Réalité (ELECTRE) as the appropriate MCDA tool to support the comparison among different strategies in small towns.

Table 1. MCDA methodologies' comparison based on exogenous and endogenous criteria

MCDA methodologies	Exogenous criteria		Endogenous criteria	
	Number of evaluation elements	*Typology of indicators*	*Solution approach*	*Type of solutions*
AHP	Large number of sub-criteria and small number of alternatives	Mixed	Full aggregation approach	The alternative with the highest global score
ANP	Large number of sub-criteria and small number of alternatives	Mixed	Full aggregation approach	The alternative with the highest global score
ELECTRE	Small number of sub-criteria and alternatives	Mixed	Outranking approach	Alternatives with the same score but different behaviors / The alternative with the highest global score
MAUT	Small number of sub-criteria and large number of alternatives	Quantitative	Full aggregation approach	The alternative with the highest global score
MACBETH	Large number of sub-criteria and alternatives	Qualitative	Full aggregation approach	The alternative with the highest global score
PROMETHEE	Large number of sub-criteria and alternatives	Mixed	Outranking approach	Alternatives with the same score but different behaviors / The alternative with the highest global score
TOPSIS	Large number of sub-criteria and alternatives	Mixed	Goal, aspiration, or reference-level approach	Medium

The ELECTRE is an MCDA method based on processing a system of pairwise comparisons among the alternatives to be assessed [28]. Indeed, its grounding idea is to measure the degree to which scores and associated weights confirm or contradict the dominant pairwise relationship among options [29]. The steps for performing a multicriteria evaluation based on the ELECTRE method can be identified in:

1. The Decision tree framing. This step belongs to all the multicriteria methodologies and requires identifying the relevant criteria for the assessment, the related sub-criteria and, for each sub-criteria, the related indicator;
2. The Impact matrix definition. It requires the measurement of the alternatives to be assessed according to the defined sub-criteria and indicators;
3. The Impact matrix standardization. It requires adopting a standardization procedure to turn the measured performances into dimensionless values ranging from 0 to 1;
4. The Pairwise comparison of alternatives. It derives a dominance relationship for each pair of alternatives using a net concordance index, an expression of how much an alternative is better than the others, and a net discordance index, expressing to what degree an alternative is worse than the others;
5. The Alternatives' final ranking definition. It requires combing each alternative's net concordance and net discordance index.

4 The ELECTRE Method Implementation to Compare Marginalization-Tackling Strategies in Small Towns

Once the ELECTRE method is identified as the appropriate reference methodology for the addressed evaluation task, it is possible to compare the selected marginalization strategies in Campania Regions' small towns. In this sense, the pre-mentioned steps for the ELECTRE implementation are declined to the case study's specificities by resorting to the software Definite 3.0 (Fig. 2).

Starting from the Decision tree framing, the overall objective is identified in understanding which strategy can be more effective in tackling marginalization in small towns. The criteria are defined according to the different main dimensions of the marginalization phenomenon at the territorial scale: demographic, economic, and socio-cultural. Sub-criteria and indicators are then selected through a literature review referring to the SNAI's Indicators Grid 2014–2020 [30] and the Rete Rurale Nazionale's Context Indicators 2014–2020 [31] (Table 2).

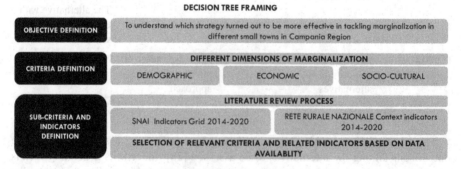

Fig. 2. Decision tree framing

The Decision tree framing, thus, provides all the necessary evaluation elements to build up the Impact matrix (Table 2) by measuring the different marginalization-tackling strategies' performances according to the selected sub-criteria and indicators (Table 3).

Table 2. Definition of criteria, indicators, scale, and units of measurement

Criteria	Sub-criteria	Indicator	Scale	U.M	min/max
Demographic	Population dynamics	Percentage variation in the resident population between 2014 and 2022	*Ratio*	%	max
	Population structure	Variation in the aging index between 2014 and 2022	*Ratio*	%	max
Economic	Real estate market dynamics	Percentage variation in the real estate market value between 2014 and 2022	*Ratio*	%	max
	Wealth market dynamics	Per Capita Income variation between 2014 and 2020	*Ratio*	%	max
	Labor market dynamics	Variation in the employment rate between 2014 and 2020	*Ratio*	%	max
Socio-cultural	Tourism attractiveness	Percentage variation in the number of bed-places in tourist accommodations between 2014 and 2019	*Ratio*	%	max
	Local community vitality	Variation of third-sector entities between 2014 and 2022	*Ratio*	n	max

The measured performances are standardized by applying the standardization procedure by maximum row score and are taken as the basis for the pairwise comparison of the considered strategies. Finally, the anti-marginalization strategies ranking stems from adopting an indifferent system of weights, thus assuming that all the sub-criteria have the same importance in evaluating the strategies' effectiveness.

5 Results

Applying the Electre method, based on the defined decision tree and considering an indifferent system of weights, returns the "Migrant reception and integration" strategy, implemented in Petruro Irpino, as the favorable one for tackling marginalization in small towns (Fig. 3).

Table 3. Impact matrix

Sub-criteria	U.m	Guardia Sanframondi	Mirabella Eclano	Petruro Irpino
Percentage variation in the resident population between 2014 and 2022	%	−9,78%	−11,90%	−5,79%
Variation in the aging index between 2014 and 2022	%	72,45%	11,97%	−141,76%
Percentage variation in the real estate market value between 2014 and 2022	%	−20,71%	−13,41%	0,00%
Per Capita Income variation between 2014 and 2020	%	14,81%	8,03%	2,67%
Variation in the employment rate between 2014 and 2020	%	5,18%	2,92%	4,79%
Percentage variation in the number of bed places in touristic accommodations between 2014 and 2019	%	67%	373%	0%
Variation of third-sector entities between 2014 and 2022	n	1	0	1

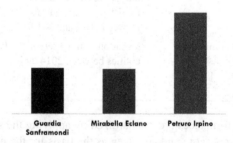

Fig. 3. Marginalization-tackling strategies' ranking

However, some interesting observations can be drawn out by analyzing the partial results from the comparison (Fig. 4).

Indeed, if the "Migrants reception and integration" stands out as the most effective strategy in tackling marginalization from a demographic perspective, focusing on the economic and socio-cultural dimensions provides slightly different results. More in detail, considering the economic dimension, "Migrants reception and integration" emerge as effective as the "Attracting new residents" one in tackling marginalization.

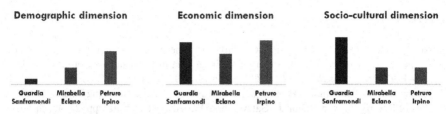

Fig. 4. Partial results from the marginalization-tackling strategies' comparison

Instead, considering marginalization from a socio-cultural perspective, "Attracting new residents" stands out as the favorable strategy to be implemented.

6   Final Considerations and Future Perspectives

The paper proposes a methodological approach toward comparing different marginalization-tackling strategies, resting on different tools and actions, implemented in some of Campania Region's small towns. It moves from recognizing the complexity of marginalization and addresses it as a multi-dimensional phenomenon. In this sense, it attempts to capture the strategies' effectiveness and implementation opportunities by considering the different relevant dimensions for its declination at the territorial scale. Its, even partial, results hint at a higher effectiveness of strategies resting on attracting new forms of residents rather than giving incentives to the local community's staying. Of course, this preliminary finding must be confirmed by extending the analysis to other territorial realities and a broader range of strategies.

Indeed, the paper is an initial research step towards comprehensively assessing marginalization-tackling strategies in Campania Region and at the national level. At this stage, it limits the comparison to three strategies. Its further development, thus, will be firstly devoted to drawing out a complete census of all the implemented strategies against marginalization in small towns in the Campania Region.

The results from the comparison, based on applying the ELECTRE method, are obtained by adopting an indifferent system of weights. In this sense, further research efforts should be devoted to defining the weights of the different marginalization dimensions through interaction with relevant stakeholders. Together with it, the set of sub-criteria, currently limited due to the data availability, will be enriched by considering further sub-criteria able to capture other aspects of the investigated phenomena. Finally, once a complete picture of marginalization-tackling strategies is built, the proposed approach can be refined by clustering small towns based on their features (i.e., resident population). Such a clustering operation, indeed, can lead to deepening and better catering the investigation of the different strategies' effectiveness toward making them a useful information level to orient further possible operational strategies for the valorization of the territorial capital and the human capital – especially young people – of this territorial context. In any case it must be emphasized that any perspectives of development for this areas, characterized by competitive factors "non-relocatable", are possible only through a shared approach, in line with cohesion policy.

References

1. Rossitti, M., Torrieri, F.: The THEMA tool to support heritage-based development strategies for marginal areas: evidence from an Italian inner area in Campania Region. Region **9**(2), 109–129 (2022). https://doi.org/10.18335/reion.v9i2.394
2. Gatzweiler, F.W., Baumüller, H.: Marginality—A Framework for Analyzing Causal Complexities of Poverty. In: von Braun, J., Gatzweiler, F.W. (eds.) Marginality, pp. 27–40. Springer Netherlands, Dordrecht (2014). https://doi.org/10.1007/978-94-007-7061-4_2
3. Moretto, V., Elia, G., Ghiani, G.: Leveraging knowledge discovery and knowledge visualization to define the "inner areas": an application to an Italian province. J. Knowl. Manag. **26**(10), 2743–2771 (2022). https://doi.org/10.1108/JKM-10-2021-0773
4. ANCI: Atlante dei Piccoli Comuni (2019). https://www.anci.it/atlante-dei-piccoli-comuni/
5. Lupatelli, G.: L'economia dei piccoli comuni. In: INU, Rapporto del Territorio 2016. INU-Istituto Nazionale di Urbanistica, Roma (2016)
6. Forte, F., Maffei, L., De Paola, P.: Which future for small towns? Interaction of socio-economic factors and real estate market in Irpinia. Valori e Valutazioni **25**, 45–52 (2020). https://siev.org/7-25-2020/
7. Camagni, R.: Per un concetto di capitale territoriale. In: Borri D., Ferlaino F., Crescita e sviluppo regionale: strumenti sistemi e azioni. Franco Angeli, Milano (2009)
8. Dell'Ovo, M., Dezio, C., Mottadelli, M., Oppio, A.: How to support cultural heritage-led development in Italian inner areas: a multi-methodological evaluation approach. Eur. Plan. Stud. (2022). https://doi.org/10.1080/09654313.2022.2135367
9. Barca, F., Casavola, P., Lucatelli, S.: Strategia nazionale per le aree interne: definizione, obiettivi, strumenti e governance. Materiali Uval 31 (2014). https://www.miur.gov.it/documents/20182/890263/strategia_nazionale_aree_interne.pdf/d10fc111-65c0-4acd-b253-63efae626b19
10. Lucatelli, S.: La strategia nazionale, il riconoscimento delle aree interne. Territorio **74**, 80–86 (2015). https://doi.org/10.3280/TR2015-074014
11. Agenzia per la Coesione Territoriale: Fonti di finanziamento, Risorse assegnate e Avanzamenti di spesa (2020). https://www.agenziacoesione.gov.it/strategia-nazionale-aree-interne/fonti-di-finanziamento-e-risorse-assegnate/
12. Agenzia per la Coesione Territoriale: Fondo di sostegno ai comuni marginali 2021–2023 (2021). https://www.agenziacoesione.gov.it/news_istituzionali/fondo-di-sostegno-ai-comuni-marginali-2021–2023/?print-posts=pdf#:~:text=Il%20fondo%20%C3%A8%20dotato%20complessivamente,alla%20media%20e%20con%20un
13. Ministero della Cultura: PNRR Borghi. Avviso pubblico per la selezione dei progetti (2022). https://media.beniculturali.it/mibac/fles/boards/be78e33bc8ca0c99bff70aa174035096/Card/Borghi20212021/BorghiRecovery.pdf
14. Musolino, D.: The North-South Divide in Italy: Reality or Perception? Eur. Spat. Res. Policy **25**(1), 29–53 (2018). https://doi.org/10.18778/1231-1952.25.1.03
15. Decreto-legge 12 settembre 2014, n. 1333 Misure urgenti per l'apertura dei cantieri, la realizzazione delle opere pubbliche, la digitalizzazione del Paese, la semplificazione burocratica, l'emergenza del dissesto idrogeologico e per la ripresa delle attività produttive (2014). https://www.gazzettaufficiale.it/eli/id/2014/09/12/14G00149/sg
16. Decreto Legislativo 18 aprile 2016, n.50 Codice dei Contratti pubblici. https://www.codicecontrattipubblici.com/
17. Crepaldi, G.: Il baratto amministrativo: sussidiarietà, collaborazione ed esigenze di risparmio. Responsabilità civile e previdenza **83**(1), 17–51 (2018)

18. Morgante, F.C., Oppio, A., Torrieri, F., Rossitti, M.: Real estate market and migrants' flows to small towns: empirical evidence from sales and rent prices analysis. In: Napoli, G., Mondini, G., Oppio, A., Rosato, P., Barbaro, S. (eds.) Values, Cities and Migrations: Real Estate Market and Social System in a Multi-cultural City, pp. 187–198. Springer International Publishing, Cham (2023). https://doi.org/10.1007/978-3-031-16926-7_14

19. Legge 30 luglio 2022, n. 189 Modifica alla normativa in materia di immigrazione e di asilo. https://presidenza.governo.it/USRI/confessioni/norme/legge_189_2002.pdf

20. Sale della terra: SAI – Comune di Petruro Irpino. https://consorziosaledellaterra.it/project/sprar-petruro-irpino/

21. Mavrotas, G.: Effective implementation of the ε-constraint method in multi-objective mathematical programming. Appl. Math. Comput. **213**(2), 455–465 (2009). https://doi.org/10.1016/j.amc.2009.03.037

22. Assumma, V., Bottero, M., Ishizaka, A., Tasiou, M.: Group Analytic hierarchy process sorting ii method: an application to evaluate the economic value of a wine region landscape. Environ. Model. Assess. **26**(3), 355–369 (2021). https://doi.org/10.1007/s10666-020-09744-4

23. Bottero, M., Caprioli, C., Datola, G., Oppio, A., Torrieri, F.: Regeneration of Rogoredo railway: a combined approach using multi-criteria and financial analysis. Valori e Valutazioni **31**, 89–102 (2022). https://doi.org/10.48264/VVSIEV-20223107

24. Cegan, J.C., Filion, A.M., Keisler, J.M., Linkov, I.: Trends and applications of multi-criteria decision analysis in environmental sciences: literature review. Environ. Syst. Decisions **37**(2), 123–133 (2017). https://doi.org/10.1007/s10669-017-9642-9

25. Saaty, T.L.: The modern science of multicriteria decision making and its practical applications: the AHP/ANP approach. Oper. Res. **61**(5), 1101–1118 (2013). https://doi.org/10.1287/opre.2013.1197

26. Guitoni, A., Martel, J.M., Vincke, P., North, P.B.: A Framework to Choose a Discrete Multicriterion Aggregation Procedure. Defence Research Establishment Valcatier (DREV), Ottawa (1998). https://pdfs.semanticscholar.org/27d5/9c846657268bc840c4df8df98e85de66c562.pdf

27. Guarini, M.R., Battisti, F., Chiovitti, A.: Public initiatives of settlement transformation: a theoretical-methodological approach to selecting tools of multicriteria decision analysis. Buildings **8**(1), 1 (2018). https://doi.org/10.3390/buildings8010001

28. Vincke, P.: Multiple Criteria Decision-Aid. John Wiley & Sons, New York (1992)

29. Figueira, J.R., Greco, S., Roy, B., Slowinski, R.: An overview of ELECTRE methods and their recent extensions. J. Multi-Criteria Decision Anal. **20**(1–2), 61–85 (2013). https://doi.org/10.1002/mcda.1482

30. Agenzia per la Coesione Territoriale: Indicatori per la "Diagnosi aperta" delle aree-progetto: indicatori utilizzati durante l'istruttoria (2017). https://www.agenziacoesione.gov.it/strategia-nazionale-aree-interne/la-selezione-delle-aree/

31. Rete Rurale Nazionale: La Banca Dati degli Indicatori di Contesto 2014–2020 (2020). https://www.reterurale.it/indicatoricontesto

Learning Urban Sustainability by Playing

Isabella M. Lami⬥, Francesca Abastante⬥, Marika Gaballo⬥, Beatrice Mecca(✉)⬥,
and Elena Todella⬥

Department of Regional and Urban Studies and Planning (DIST), Politecnico di Torino,
Viale Mattioli 39, 10125 Turin, Italy
`beatrice.mecca@polito.it`

Abstract. Sustainability and the concept of sustainable development are currently
adopted as a founding paradigm of global, national and regional development
strategies. As such, they necessarily permeate new visions of urban development
as well, leading to reflections of economic, environmental and social sustainability
in urban planning and design practices. In this context, the paper aims to reflect
on the capability and usefulness of Serious Games in conveying knowledge with
respect to the development of sustainable cities to students, as future planners
and architects in urban areas. Such games are part of the several participatory
approaches and models of urban innovation and planning and have an explicitly educational purpose with respect to tackling complex problems. Given their
increasing application in the field of sustainability, but their limited use in the
context of sustainable cities, this paper explores two serious games (Urbax and
urbEN), developed in urban and territorial settings within two different European
projects, to reflect on their potential capability to convey specific ways of action
and knowledge with respect to the issues considered in Sustainable Development
Goal 11 (SDG11) of Agenda 2030. The analysis allows observing that although
the two games were not initially designed to align with specific SDG11 targets or
convey information on sustainable cities, both demonstrate the potential capability
in spreading specific knowledge for urban sustainability.

Keywords: Serious Game · urban sustainability · Sustainable Development
Goal 11

1 Introduction

Urban transformation can be considered a wicked problem [1, 2], namely a complex
problem for which there is no simple method of solution. Indeed, they do not foresee a
single right strategy for resolution, due to the fact that every attempt can affect different
stakeholders, and there are no clear stopping rules. All urban transformations see the
interfacing of different actors, who have different interests – economic, environmental
and social – which often prove to be misaligned and unrelated. In this sense, each of
them stands up for their own interests following peculiar strategies thus often leading to
conflicting situations with implications on the transformation. Nowadays, this situation
is more complexified by the sustainability issues that closely affect our cities. Indeed,

O. Gervasi et al. (Eds.): ICCSA 2023 Workshops, LNCS 14108, pp. 468–482, 2023.
https://doi.org/10.1007/978-3-031-37117-2_32

sustainability and the 2030 Agenda have become the founding paradigm of global, national, and regional development strategies [3–6] and of urban interventions.

Traditionally, real estate development processes see as their main driver the creation of economic value [7] and consequently, as a main yardstick for observing their feasibility, their economic sustainability is verified. However, in the current context, the sustainable development approach applied to urban planning and design brings with it implications of broadening reasoning on how to operate on cities and on which values are to be created in addition to the economic value.

In this context, conveying information, knowledge and possible ways of action turns out to be fundamental in undergraduate courses in architecture and territorial planning, whose students will be the future architects and planners of our cities and therefore may represent the end users of these games. In this regard, Serious Games prove to be a useful tool for conveying the complexity of urban transformations to future planners and architects by involving them in a process of "learning by playing" [8]. Serious Games represent one of the emerging participatory models of urban innovation and planning [9] and their application appears to be growing considering the sustainability context [10]. As reported by [10] Serious Games can support making players aware of the challenges associated with sustainability, provide knowledge and understanding of sustainability, and encourage players to implement environmentally, economically, and socially balanced solutions. Indeed, in simulating urban transformation processes, the play in the role of specific stakeholders, the outline of possible transformation strategies and the interaction with other actors enable students to understand real urban problems. However, their use in the field of urban planning and sustainable city development still appears to be limited. Thus, this paper intends to fit into this gap and aims to address the following research question: *can Serious Games developed in urban settings be a useful tool to convey specific knowledge with respect to the development of sustainable cities?*

To answer this question, a comparison of two Serious Games developed in urban and territorial settings is provided, to observe in which way they can support in spreading knowledge with respect to the Sustainable Development Goal 11 (SDG11). The 2030 Agenda represents an internationally recognized framework of goals that provides strategic guidance on sustainable development [3]; within this framework, SDG11 constitutes the goal of urban relevance "to make cities and human settlements inclusive, safe, resilient and sustainable". The intent, therefore, is to cross-reference the reading of the two games with the different SDG11 Targets, to observe on which specific points they may be useful. It is worth noticing that the two Serious Games are not specifically originated from the SDG11 of the urban Agenda 2030, however the comparison provided allows us to observe how these models can differently convey specific knowledge or ways of action regarding urban sustainability, and more in detail with respect to some SDG11 Targets. The two Serious Games considered in this paper, in whose development the first author has been, respectively, the scientific coordinator of the whole project and the scientific coordinator for Politecnico di Torino, and the second authors of this paper were actively involved in the most recent project, are the following:

i. URBAX2 (Urban Planning System in Europe), developed as part of the European Leonardo da Vinci project, a European Union action program for the improvement and development of vocational training in Europe;

ii. urbEN (Urban Energy Management Game), developed within the framework of the Erasmus + project "Locally Organized Transition of Urban Sustainable Spaces" (LOTUS) that involves a consortium of partners from different European countries, including universities, research centres, and community organizations.

The paper is organized as follows: Sect. 2 briefly defines Serious Games and outlines the two pedagogical tools URBAX2 and urbEN. Section 3 provides the design of the research and Sect. 4 identifies the sustainability lessons that can be learned by playing. Lastly, Sect. 5 summarizes the conclusion.

2 Serious Games as a Learning Tool in Urban Complex Decision-Making

Serious Games are part of the participatory approaches and models of urban innovation and planning and are games with explicitly educational purpose. These are carefully designed to be played "seriously" to highlight complex problems [11]. Serious Games were developed in the military field in 1948 [9] and then implemented in various disciplines to support learning, knowledge transfer, and management of research and practice problems [12, 13]. Indeed, the scientific community recognizes such games as motivating and supportive of distributed learning [8, 10, 12, 13].

Serious Games prove to be useful from a learning perspective since [14]: i) tell stories of real-world contexts; ii) offer new ways of communication; iii) stimulate interaction between players/actors; iv) set specific goals and help the achievement of these through the definition of reasoned strategies; v) stimulate problem-solving and allow for effective support of decision-making processes.

Starting from the recent literature review conducted by [15], which proposes a classification of existing Serious Games with respect to their links with the SDGs, some elements can be highlighted concerning their potential with respect to the context of urban sustainability and the parallel limitedness of application in this context. The analysis [15] reviews 67 currently functioning Serious Games related to the SDGs context and notes that some of them are developed as board games, thus according to traditional methods, and some are developed online according to more innovative methods. These are used by allowing interaction between the different players involved, encouraging playful public participation aimed at teaching on the one hand and entertaining those involved in the game on the other. In this sense, the use of such games in the urban context to improve virtuous behaviour turns out to be feasible. In parallel, the literature review in [15] notes that most of the games were designed primarily with respect to the themes of sustainable environmental actions, climate change, water management, and sustainable urban development. Concerning the latter, it can be observed that 27 of the analyzed games refer to SDG11, thus 40 percent of the sample, however, only 13, thus 19 percent, deal with the topic of sustainable urban development; in the other cases SDG11 is crossed but the topic dealt with is more specific than other SDGs. In this sense, it can be seen that the field of application of Serious Games to the context of SDG11 still appears to be currently limited.

2.1 URBAX2 (Urban Planning System in Europe 2)

URBAX2 is a pedagogical tool that aims to represent the relationships between urban markets and public policies in the field of urban planning, with a focus on the definition of land uses and supported by a software [16]. This was created as an evolution of the previous URBAX pedagogical tool, developed and used within the French system, in order to adapt its use to other European systems (Italy, UK, Germany, Sweden and Spain). The broader context in which the development of URBAX is set considers the incessant restructuring and planning transformations dictated by contingent situations, which cities have undergone in recent decades [16]: actors define and manage urban space, so to diminish developments that are not fully foreseen, there is a need for tools that support the understanding of how planning activities work within the urban market framework.

Accordingly, professional training in the field of urban planning and development should clarify not only the technical-administrative mechanisms characteristic of planning interventions, but also the dynamics that develop between the different actors involved [16].

From this perspective, URBAX2 is designed to enhance students' understanding of the effects of private actors' actions and public policies on the market and private land ownership. What characterizes URBAX2 is its ability to provide support by representing in a sufficiently realistic way the dynamics of the urban context and the derived effects at the socio-economic level of the actions implemented by local actors.

The educational objective of this serious game is threefold [17]: i) to foster an understanding of the strategies of urban actors; ii) to convey knowledge of the urban planning system in order to propose comprehensive urban planning strategies; and iii) to disseminate the ability to use planning tools and methods related to a historic district, new neighbourhoods and areas of economic activity.

Accordingly, URBAX2 considers the following four roles corresponding to the four main functions typical of local urban planning scenarios: the city government, the organization building low-income housing projects, economic operators (industrial investors) and real estate operators (construction companies). The simulation considers a theoretical city of 8,000 inhabitants in a declining situation: the city's buildings are in poor condition, there are brown areas in the surroundings, economic activities are declining, and the population is decreasing. In this context, game players are required to develop the city with few resources through acquisitions, transactions, building permits and construction, while the socioeconomic effects of their actions are automatically simulated by the software [18].

Through the game, players learn about social interactions, which is one of the key elements of local planning [19]: negotiations and agreements are one of the ways in which relationships develop between subjects and between subjects and plan. Also, during the game, actions of buying and selling land and buildings, applying for building permits, construction work by developers, investment by industrial operators, and management of the master plan by municipal administrators come into play.

The URBAX and URBAX2 serious games have been used in European educational settings proving to be a valuable tool for training students in the urban planning system.

2.2   UrbEN (Urban Energy Management Game)

UrbEN is an educational simulation tool in the form of a role-playing game on urban energy management aiming to educate and engage users on the complex issues surrounding sustainable urban energy management [20]. The broader context in which urbEN development is set considers the increasing need to support municipal citizens, and companies in their transition toward a zero-carbon future, due to the challenges posed by climate change [21]. Achieving sustainable urban energy systems requires the involvement of diverse actors from both public and private sectors [22, 23], who operate within a complex web of interactions at regional, national, and European levels. Therefore, educators in the field of urban planning and development must incorporate the dynamic integration of new energy concepts into their curriculum to equip future urban planners with the necessary skills and knowledge to navigate the challenges and opportunities presented by the transition toward sustainable urban energy systems [24].

In this perspective, urbEN is designed to enhance the innovative and creative capacities of students in the field of urban energy management, enabling them to effectively address the challenges associated with urban energy transition. This gamified approach enables students to evaluate different interests and integrate them into a holistic and comprehensive perspective.

Hence, in order to put forward a local energy autonomy planning strategy the serious game's educational objective is twofold, aiming at understanding: i) the local actors' energy strategies; ii) the interactions between elements of the local system. Accordingly, the following seven roles corresponding to actors investing in the production and storage of renewable energy and in energy sobriety are included within urbEN: the Local Authority (LA), a Non-Governmental Organization (NGO) representing civil society, two energy operators (local and national), an entrepreneur, a property developer, and a farmer. The simulation involves a virtual city in which the player assumes the role of one of the seven urban energy actors responsible for making decisions about energy use, production, and distribution.

Through a series of challenges and scenarios during the serious game, the players learn about energy efficiency, renewable energy, smart grids, and other key concepts in sustainable urban energy management. Moreover, the serious game also features educational resources and tools that provide additional information and support for players.

It is worth noting that although a serious game may be based on a scientific model, it is not in itself one. Indeed, urbEN aim is to have players understand basic notions within a short time frame and in a playful way [25]. Therefore, the serious game is focused solely on the energy issue, despite the awareness that climate change is not solely an energy-related issue [26, 27].

The urbEN serious game has so far been used in educational settings succeeding in providing an engaging and interactive way to learn about urban energy management and raise awareness of the critical issue of sustainable energy in cities.

3 Research Design

Based on the simulation of urban dynamics through the two serious games described, this paper aims to observe whether and how they convey learning of knowledge and ways of action for sustainable development and more specifically for which SDG11 Targets. With this in mind, the research was organized according to two phases (Fig. 1).

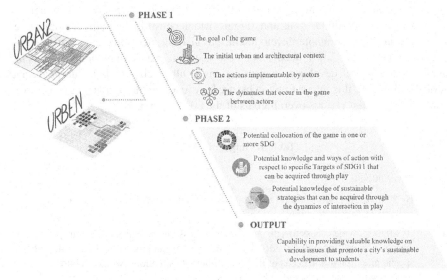

Fig. 1. Overall design of the research

A first phase explores three aspects of the selected games: i) the initial urban and architectural goal and context; ii) the real estate, energy, social, and environmental investment actions that can be implemented in the game by the different actors, with a view to achieving individual private and collective public goals; iii) the dynamics established in the game among the different actors, derived from the needs of each actor to achieve his or her personal goals. The first two aspects were detected and analysed in the materials relating to the rules and instructions of games and those relating to the pedagogical elements of the game. The last aspect was instead detected and observed following the applications of the two Serious Games in first person by all the authors of this paper in the case of the game urbEN and by the first author in the case of URBAX, in different occasions of tests and training activities, and with students of the courses of planning and architecture at the Politecnico di Torino and with students of Economics courses at the University of North Eastern Piedmont.

A second phase consists in the observation of three implications directly derived from the three aspects of the game just listed above: i) considering the goal and the context, it is observed in which potential SDGs of the 2030 Agenda the game can be placed; ii) on the basis of the actions that can be implemented in the game, those that can be directly attributed to the specific Targets of the urban goal, thus SDG11, are highlighted; iii) considering the dynamics among the actors, it is outlined what indirect understandings of sustainable strategies can be derived from the active game.

3.1 The Goals of the 2030 Agenda and the SDG11 Targets

The 2030 Agenda and SDGs were approved in 2015 and entered into force in January 2016 in order to guide international action with respect to sustainable development and thus with the aim of guiding development efforts between 2015–2030. This agenda defines a set of international goals and Targets, which constitute not only the objectives to be achieved for sustainable development, but also the benchmarks for sustainability assessments [7, 28–30]. Indeed, since now sustainable development constitutes the founding paradigm of development new visions at all levels - global, European, and national - [3–6, 31], it is interesting to observe how learning through games can convey knowledge about the various overall goals of the 2030 Agenda.

Table 1. Target of SDG11

Target	Description
11.1	By 2030, ensure access for all to adequate, safe and affordable housing and basic services and upgrade slums
11.2	By 2030, provide access to safe, affordable, accessible and sustainable transport systems for all, improving road safety, notably by expanding public transport, with special attention to the needs of those in vulnerable situations, women, children, persons with disabilities and older persons
11.3	By 2030, enhance inclusive and sustainable urbanization and capacity for participatory, integrated and sustainable human settlement planning and management in all countries
11.4	Strengthen efforts to protect and safeguard the world's cultural and natural heritage
11.5	By 2030, significantly reduce the number of deaths and the number of people affected and substantially decrease the direct economic losses relative to global gross domestic product caused by disasters, including water-related disasters, with a focus on protecting the poor and people in vulnerable situations
11.6	By 2030, reduce the adverse per capita environmental impact of cities, including by paying special attention to air quality and municipal and other waste management
11.7	By 2030, provide universal access to safe, inclusive and accessible, green and public spaces, in particular for women and children, older persons and persons with disabilities
11.a	Support positive economic, social and environmental links between urban, peri-urban and rural areas by strengthening national and regional development planning
11.b	By 2020, substantially increase the number of cities and human settlements adopting and implementing integrated policies and plans towards inclusion, resource efficiency, mitigation and adaptation to climate change, resilience to disasters, and develop and implement, in line with the Sendai Framework for Disaster Risk Reduction 2015–2030, holistic disaster risk management at all levels

In the specific urban context covered within this paper, the goal of urban relevance is SDG 11, which considers 9 Targets that are monitored globally with 15 indicators [30]. Table 1 provides an overview of the 9 urban Targets.

4 Sustainability Lessons Learned by Playing

This section aims to show the cross-analysis of the two Serious Games – URBAX2 and urbEN – considering the elements outlined in the two phases of the research design. In this sense, Table 2 outlines the context and overall goal of each game, followed by the potential SDGs of placement. Accordingly, the recalled SDGs would constitute the sustainable context of the games, thus the scientific reference against which the game can contribute to providing sustainable development knowledge.

Table 2. Placement of the two serious games under analysis in relation to the SDGs of Agenda 2030

Serious Game	Urban and architectural context of the game	Main goal of the game	Potential SDGs
URBAX2	Theoretical city of about 8,000 citizens in a declining situation: the city's buildings are in poor condition, there are brown areas in the surrounding area, economic activities are declining, and the population is decreasing.	The players in the game are called upon to develop a declining city, reactivating its markets by acting at the urban and architectural levels with attention to land uses.	11 SUSTAINABLE CITIES AND COMMUNITIES
urbEN	Theoretical city comprising built-up areas (center, medium- and low-density neighborhoods), uncultivated urban areas, and a public housing district. At some distance from the center there are two villages, which can potentially be expanded. The remaining space is rural.	Game players are called upon to develop the city and neighboring villages in terms of energy management. So they are responsible for making decisions about the use, production and distribution of energy.	11 SUSTAINABLE CITIES AND COMMUNITIES / 7 AFFORDABLE AND CLEAN ENERGY

As Table 1 highlights, URBAX2 seems to align with SDG11 as it focuses on interventions in buildings and urban context to improve the economic, environmental, and social conditions of a declining city. UrbEN is based on an economically and socially functioning urban and architectural context, and the development of the city through the game focuses on energy issues, thus on the use and production of energy within the city. Although energy monitoring is not a primary focus of SDG11, the implications of energy actions and other SDG-related issues like climate change, education quality, industries, and infrastructure are interconnected with the city. Moreover, the game refers also to issues related to housing affordability, or land use control, that are essentials for SDG11. Therefore, SDG11 constitutes the main reference goal as the main context, together with SDG7 related to energy.

Continuing with the exploration of the two games and thus of the actions that can be implemented by the different actors, it is possible to observe how both ensure the acquisition of knowledge on different SDG11 targets. Table 3 reports for each game the actions that can be traced back to the urban goal Targets considering the actors to whom implementation is granted (for more information on the set of actions and actors in the game see [18, 32]).

As can be observed from Table 3 the URBAX game can convey knowledge to students relative to five targets. Indeed:

- *Target 11.1, affordable housing.* In the role of constructors, students are asked to think about the development of housing that must meet the market demand and social status of the district. Thus, housing with affordable or higher prices depends on the target population. In addition, in the role of local government, they may decide to act with subsidies, and tax benefits for the renovation of properties if the socioeconomic characteristics of the district's population do not allow for spontaneous renovation. In this sense, the opportunity to act on the properties is given to everyone in order to favour their improvement from the point of view of adequacy and safety.
- *Target 11.2, transport system.* In the role of local government, students are called upon to improve the blocks of the district in which they operate in order to increase its attractiveness. Besides creating public facilities, it's important to consider and act upon public transportation connections and services. If the current cultural background is rooted in sustainable paradigms, students can learn about them in various academic courses and apply them while reflecting and directing their actions within the game. In this regard, they will consider sustainable, safe, and accessible transportation services while taking into account the occupants' social status and socio-economic categories in the district.
- *Target 11.3, land use.* The game in general, as noted in Table 1, fits into this target as it considers urban and architectural development with a focus on land use. Specifically, in the role of local government, students are asked to manage land use, thus observing building permits and projects submitted and received from other actors and reflecting on their implementation in relation to the amount of land consumed in the district. They are also the ones who regulate land use in the district and in this sense delineate buildable land, thus reflecting on edge density [33] and the amount of buildable land. In addition, they may decide to act with subsidies, tax benefits for property rehabilitation, which may limit new construction interventions with direct implications on land use.
- *Target 11.6, air pollution and waste management.* The action of building renovation by direct builders and indirect local government touches on the possibility of reflection with respect to the decrease in air pollution due to improved energy performance of buildings.

Table 3. Implementable actions in the two serious games under analysis that can be traced back to the SDG11 Targets

Actor	Action	Target SDG11
URBAX2		
Local Government	Improving the attractiveness of the district: creation of public services, public open spaces	11.2;11.7
	Regulating land use: providing building permits	11.3
	District intervention with subsidies, tax benefits for property renovation	11.1; 11.3; 11.6
Constructor	Construction of housing in line with the social status of the district: affordable housing	11.1
urbEN		
Local Authority	Electric public transportation: link between town centre and peripheral villages	11.2; 11.6
	Cycling path: cycling path linking villages to the town centre	11.2
	Thermal renovation of public buildings: Increasing energy efficiency of public facilities such as schools, theatres, municipal rooms, administrative premises, sport and leisure centres, community centres	11.6
National energy network company and Local energy network company	Solar panels on farm buildings and on farming land and on hypermarket roof space	11.6
	Geothermal energy	11.6
Property Developer	Green affordable housing: High energy efficiency mix of affordable and social housing for lower middle class	11.1
	Ordinary affordable housing: Medium energy efficiency mix of affordable and social housing for lower middle class	11.1
	Green single family homes operation: green low-density housing	11.1
	Ordinary single family homes operation: ordinary low-density housing	11.1
Private Company	Renovation scheme for social housing: thermal renovation of DEV's social housing properties	11.6
	Electric public transportation: link between town centre and peripheral villages	11.2; 11.6
Farmer	Solar panels on farm buildings: photovoltaic panels on farm buildings roofs	11.6

- *Target 11.7, safe, inclusive and accessible green and public spaces.* In the role of local government, students reflect on and consider the creation of public open spaces, which should be safe and accessible spaces.

As for urbEN, it can convey knowledge on three specific SDG11 targets with different specific actions. In detail:

- *Target 11.1, affordable housing.* Reflections and knowledge with respect to this issue are mainly acquired through the direct role of the property developer, who builds, and in the indirect role of the local authority, which requires, encourages and accepts the development of certain actions. Students, indeed, take note of and reflect on: the development of green and/or ordinary affordable housing for the middle class, with medium to high energy efficiency; the construction of low-density family housing; the renewal of the thermal performance of the social housing they own.
- *Target 11.2, transport system.* In the role of the local authority, students reflect and disseminate to other stakeholders, possibly seeking funders such as the private developer, on actions to improve transportation services, particularly acting on the implementation of electric public transportation and new bicycle routes.
- *Target 11.6, air pollution and waste management.* In the role of the local authority, local and national energy companies, property developer, farmer, and private companies, students learn theoretical aspects and ways of action to reduce air emissions, implementing actions in the game such as: placing solar panels on buildings, developing geothermal energy systems, renewing energy efficiency of public and private buildings, and developing electric public transport services.

As far as the dynamics of the game are concerned, one main stimulus for reasoning – applicable to both games under analysis – considering sustainable strategies at the urban level can be observed, namely that of enacting trade-offs. Indeed, each actor is free to favour or hinder public policy according to its own interests, and in this sense the local authority can, especially in the case of hostile actors, enact compromise strategies. This means interacting and negotiating with actors to find meeting points, suggesting the implementation of more sustainable actions on certain dimensions of sustainability such as environmental and social to compensate actions that are profitable economically but not very sustainable with respect to the other dimensions. These mechanisms may entail an indirect understanding of sustainability, of its different dimensions, and of sustainable practices to be implemented strategically for the common good. Moreover, these dynamics can lead to a greater awareness and understanding of urban dynamics, its actors, with related interests and needs in relation to sustainable issues, potentially leading to a positive change in attitude and in the structuring of intervention strategies for sustainable development.

Above all, the game allows for an understanding that for sustainable urban development all actors are crucial and to be considered within the strategies, whether they are public or private actors and hostile or sympathetic to cooperation: sustainable urban transition cannot take place without the interaction and intervention of all actors.

5 Discussion and Conclusion

This paper explores two serious games to answer the question: can Serious Games developed in an urban context be a useful tool to convey specific knowledge with respect to the development of sustainable cities?

The analysis allows observing that although the two games were not initially designed to align with specific SDG11 targets or convey information on sustainable cities, both demonstrate the potential to provide knowledge and ways of action related to different SDG11 goals. On the one hand, URBAX2 was developed prior to the approval of the 2030 Agenda and aimed at fostering an understanding of urban actors' strategies and conveying knowledge of the urban system to propose comprehensive urban planning strategies. On the other hand, the urbEN game was developed considering the concept of sustainability but mainly focused on the energy transition of cities, thus just one of the many issues that involve the urban context and that need to be considered for the development of sustainable, safe, resilient and inclusive cities. Accordingly, it seems to us that Serious Games have considerable potential with respect to the transmission of knowledge regarding specific targets of the SDG11. Indeed, both the serious games in analysis allow for reasoning about how to operate in cities following economic, environmental, and social sustainability logics.

In this perspective, the results of the analysis make it possible to observe that the conceptualization of sustainability in the urban and architectural context can be seen as a lens that enables attention to certain aspects of urban transformations, which if conducted according to good practices would positively promote the development in terms of the three pillars of sustainability. Thus, even serious games that do not explicitly prioritize sustainability, such as URBAX, can provide valuable knowledge on various issues that promote a city's sustainable development. Reflections on urban district development will thus likely take into account sustainable, safe, and inclusive actions. For example, the URBAX game, which considers as a goal the reactivation of a declining city through action at the urban and architectural levels with attention to land uses, would imply that: a) regulating and managing land use leads to reflections with respect to strategies aimed at minimizing the consumption of virgin land; b) reactivating the markets of a city in decline determines the creation of services and consequent housing for the population, the realization of which must take into account different socioeconomic situations and thus consider affordable housing; c) the presence of housing in poor condition may lead to reflections in terms of benefits derived from its renovation both in social terms, with respect to the health of users, and in environmental terms, with respect to the reduction of air pollution and land consumption. In a different way, the urbEN game considers within the design of the game inputs traceable to SDG11 targets as actions necessary to achieve an energy transition goal, such as the construction of affordable housing for the middle class with a high level of energy performance.

The use of such games in conveying knowledge about urban sustainability to future architects and planners could potentially have implications related to policymaking. Indeed, the games allow students to experiment and implement strategies as private and public actors by learning shared skills in urban planning, market and strategic logic needed by PA workers. The municipality is the "place" where urban planning is carried out and the PA is the entity that can intervene directly on the planning of urban space through provisions of use, funding, incentives and direct interventions, therefore knowing certain dynamics can be an element in favor of a careful policymaking. In line with this, it could be considered that the application of the game with real PA subjects and other stakeholders could highlight the importance of implementing certain actions or limiting others with a view to shared and conscious sustainable development. For example, it is very difficult that in reality a private actor put aside his/her own economic interests in favour of benefits for society or for the environment, so observing how his/her personal action can actually have positive spillover effects on the welfare of the city could potentially lead him to think according to different strategic patterns.

Among the recognizable limitations in the application of these games is undoubtedly the need to decomplexify reality. This element leads to making some mechanisms oversimplified or establishing game elements governed by dominant dynamics imposed *a priori*. Another limitation observed in applications may be that whereby all or most students assume the goal proposed by the local authority (in the game) as their own, sometimes sacrificing even the primary goals of the actors they are impersonating. This certainly leads to a successful sustainable outcome of the game, however, it may be an overly positive view of reality, which, instead, clashes with multiple issues, interests and priorities.

Although this paper only examines two serious games, it recognizes that there is a vast array of other serious games that exist and can potentially convey specific knowledge on sustainable cities [15]. This paper emphasizes the potential of serious games as tools to transfer this knowledge and highlights the need for future analysis of other serious games developed in urban settings. Furthermore, it suggests that designing a new game that focuses specifically on transferring knowledge about all the issues considered in SDG11 could be a promising avenue for future research and development. The potential for using these tools to promote sustainable urban development can be maximized by exploring more serious games and creating new ones.

References

1. Rittel, H.W.J., Webber, M.M.: Dilemmas in a general theory of planning. Policy Sci. **4**, 155 (1973)
2. Lami, I.M.: The context of urban renewals as a 'Super-Wicked' problem. In: Calabrò, F., Della Spina, L., Bevilacqua, C. (eds.) ISHT 2018. SIST, vol. 100, pp. 249–255. Springer, Cham (2019). https://doi.org/10.1007/978-3-319-92099-3_29
3. United Nations General Assembly: Resolution adopted by the General Assembly on 25 September 2015, 2015. https://www.un.org/en/development/desa/population/migration/gen eralassembly/docs/globalcompact/A_RES_70_1_E.pdf. Accessed 16 Mar 2023
4. European Commission: Communication from the Commission to the European Parliament, the European Council, the Council, the European Economic and Social Committee and the Committee of the regions. The European Green Deal. (2019). https://ec.europa.eu/info/sites/default/files/european-green-deal-communication_en.pdf. Accessed 23 Mar 2023
5. MATTM: Strategia Nazionale per lo Sviluppo Sostenibile, Ministero dell'Ambiente e della Tutela del Territorio e del Mare, 2017. https://www.regione.piemonte.it/web/sites/default/files/media/documenti/2020-6/ssweb_snsvs_ottobre2017.pdf. Accessed 20 Mar 2023
6. PNRR: Piano Nazionale di Ripresa e Resilienza (2021). https://www.governo.it/sites/governo.it/files/PNRR.pdf. Accessed 20 Mar 2023

7. Lami I.M., Abastante F., Gaballo M., Mecca B., Todella E.: An updated picture of target 11.1 and 11.3: Pathways of implementation in the light of Covid-19. AIP Conference Proceedings, 2574, 120004, (2022) https://doi.org/10.1063/5.0105557

8. Cravero, S., Strada, F., Lami, I.M., Bottino, A.: Learning sustainability by making games. the experience of a challenge as a novel approach for Education for Sustainable Development. International Conference on Higher Education Advances Open Access Pages 651 - 6592021 7th International Conference on Higher Education Advances, HEAd (2021) Virtual, Online22 June 2021through 23 June 2021Code 178646

9. Wilkinson, P.: A brief history of serious games. In: Dörner, R., Göbel, S., Kickmeier-Rust, M., Masuch, M., Zweig, K. (eds.) Entertainment Computing and Serious Games. LNCS, vol. 9970, pp. 17–41. Springer, Cham (2016). https://doi.org/10.1007/978-3-319-46152-6_2

10. Ouariachi, T., Olvera-Lobo, M.D., Gutiérrez-Pérez, J.: Serious Games and Sustainability. In: Filho, W.L. (ed.) Encyclopedia of Sustainability in Higher Education, pp. 1450–1458. Springer International Publishing, Cham (2019). https://doi.org/10.1007/978-3-030-11352-0_326

11. ABT, C. C.: Serious Game, The Viking Press, New York, (1970)

12. Gee, J.: What video games have to teach us about learning and literacy. Comput. Entertainment (CIE) 1(1), 20 (2003)

13. Gentile, D.A.: The multiple dimensions of video game effects. Child Dev. Perspectives 5, 75–81 (2011)

14. Mouahebh, H., Fahli, A., Moussetadm, M., Eljamali, S.: The serious game: what educational benefits?. Procedia Soc. Behavioral Sci. 46, 5502–5508 (2012)

15. Cravero, V.: Methods, strategies and tools to improve citizens' engagement in the smart cities' context: a serious Games classification. Valori e Valutazioni 24, 45–60 (2020)

16. Lami, I.M. (ed.): An Overview on Planning Systems and Urban Markets in Europe. Aracne (2006)

17. Viitanen, K., Mierzejewska, M.: Playing the Urbax Game with students – Finnish Experiences. In: Lami, I.M. (ed.): An Overview on Planning Systems and Urban Markets in Europe. Aracne (2006)

18. Urbax21. http://www.urbax.eu/en/home/. Accessed 24 Mar 2023

19. Fubini, A.: Urbax: a planning practice teaching tool. In: Lami, I.M. (ed.): An Overview on Planning Systems and Urban Markets in Europe. Aracne (2006)

20. Lotus - Locally Organized Transitions for Urban Sustainable Spaces. https://lotus-transitio n.eu/. Accessed 04 Apr 2023

21. International Energy Agency (IEA): Energy Technology Perspectives 2020. (2020). https://www.iea.org/reports/energy-technology-perspectives-2020. Accessed 24 Mar 2023

22. Kern, F., Bulkeley, H.: Cities, europeanization and multi-level governance: governing climate change through transnational municipal networks. J. Common Market Stud. 47(2), 309–332 (2009)

23. Bulkeley, H., Castán Broto, V.: Government by experiment? Global cities and the governing of climate change. Trans. Inst. Br. Geogr. 38(3), 361–375 (2013)

24. Schmid, S., Knapp, S., Droege, P.: Urban energy transitions: Places, processes and politics of socio-technical change. Routledge (2018)

25. Lami, I.M., Todella, E.: Locally organized transitions for urban sustainable spaces. In: Locally Organized Transitions for Urban Sustainable Spaces. vol. 1, pp. 262 (2022)https://doi.org/10.5281/zenodo.7500720

26. Bulkeley, H.: Cities and the governing of climate change. Annu. Rev. Environ. Resour. 35, 229–253 (2010)

27. Kates, R.W., Travis, W.R., Wilbanks, T.J.: Transformational adaptation when incremental adaptations to climate change are insufficient. Proc. Natl. Acad. Sci. 109(19), 7156–7161 (2012)

28. United Nations General Assembly: Global indicator framework for the Sustainable Development Goals and targets of the 2030 Agenda for Sustainable Development. United Nation, New York (2017)

29. Abastante, F., Lami, I.M., Mecca, B.: How Covid-19 influences the 2030 agenda: do the practices of achieving the sustainable development goal 11 need rethinking and adjustment? Valori e Valu/tazioni **26**, 11–23 (2020). https://doi.org/10.48264/VVSIEV-20202603

30. United Nations: Global indicator framework for the Sustainable Development Goals and targets of the 2030 Agenda for Sustainable Development (2022). https://unstats.un.org/sdgs/indicators/Global%20Indicator%20Framework%20after%202022%20refinement_Eng.pdf. Accessed 20 Mar 2023

31. Mecca, B., Gaballo, M., Todella, E.: Measuring and evaluating Urban sustainability. Valori e Valutazioni **32**, 17–29 (2023)

32. Print&Play Urban Energy Serious Game urbEN. https://zenodo.org/record/7411604#.ZB2zOXbMJPa. Accessed 24 Mar 2023

33. Lami, I.M., Abastante, F., Gaballo, M., Mecca, B., Todella, E.: Fostering sustainable cities through additional SDG11-related indicators. Valori e Valutazioni **32**, 45–61 (2023)

The Canvas Model to Support the Circular Urban Regeneration Projects

Mariarosaria Angrisano[✉] [ID]

Pegaso Telematic University, Naples, Italy
Mariarosaria.angrisano@unipegaso.it

Abstract. In contemporary cities, abandoned industrial areas represent a significant problem. They are considered true "urban voids" characterized by underutilized land and buildings that have a negative impact on the urban environment, the local economy and resident's quality of life. However, underutilized heritage can serve as a valuable resource that enhances productivity across multiple dimensions, generating economic, social, and environmental value.

In this perspective, circular economy offers a co-evolutive perspective in conservation/management of the disused heritage.

Circular economy applied to urban regeneration aims to create socially inclusive and equitable cities through strategies that improve the quality of life for all residents, promote social cohesion, and enhance access to essential services and amenities.

Business Models are recognized as very useful support tools in urban regeneration processes. Through the analysis of community needs, available resources, and market trends, Business Models allow for the identification of sustainable and economically advantageous development perspectives.

This paper aims to provide an overview of how specific business models can support sustainable brownfield regeneration projects from a circular economy perspective. Specifically, the Smart City Model Canvas was applied to assess the feasibility of a reuse project for the disused buildings in the former Siri industrial area in Terni, Italy.

Keywords: Dismissed area · Cultural heritage · Urban regeneration · Circular economy · Smart city model canvas

1 Introduction

The problem of dismissed areas in cities refers to the existence of abandoned or neglected urban spaces, often found on former industrial or commercial sites.

These areas have undergone various transformations over time, leading to their complete abandonment and creating what are known as "urban voids" [3–5]. The causes of abandonment can be attributed to the crisis of some traditional economic sectors of industrial production. The decline of the european industrial system began around the 1960s, coinciding with the energy crisis and the transition from large to small and medium enterprises. From a redevelopment perspective, brownfields can represent an important opportunity to redefine the future layout of the city [6].

This has left many cities with large areas that are obsolete and show clear signs of environmental degradation and even poverty. Such brownfields have increasingly become a source of political concern and have spurred the emergence of various land-use regeneration initiatives. Different cities in Europe, such as Amsterdam, Rotterdam, London, Antwerp, Hamburg, Marseille, Lisbon, Porto, etc. are addressing the issue of reuse of these abandoned areas by implementing new policy mechanisms based on the general principles of sustainable urban planning able to improve their socio-economic and ecological resilience [7–9].

In this regard, the circular economy is seen as a model for addressing urban problems. It is an economy that considers metabolic processes and analyzes the waste stream, as well as the issue of energy and its central role [7, 8]. It focuses on the use of high-quality energy sources that are obtained from the surrounding environment [10–12].

Innovative circular business and financial models play a crucial role in support-ing urban regeneration efforts by providing frameworks and strategies for sustainable development [13].

The aim of this paper is to provide an overview about business models can sup-port sustainable brownfield regeneration projects, according to the circular economy perspective.

Specifically, the attention is fosuced onf "Smart City Model Canvas", a strategic tool that uses visual language to break down complex projects and simplify them. It is an operational approach that stimulates creativity and challenges established mecha-nisms and habits, focusing on potential users and reversing perspectives by starting from customers' needs [14–16].

This business model was applied to assess the feasibility of a regeneration project of the former Siri industrial area in Terni, Italy.

2 The Circular Economy as a Development Model for the Regeneration of Dismissed Urban Areas

As anticipated in the previous paragraph, there are a lot of european cities characterize by urban areas in a state of complete abandonment, correspond to former industrial zones.

Sometimes these urban spaces are the places where environmental degradation, social fragmentation and marginalization manifest themselves as frequent phenomena [17].

For several years, industrial areas suffered a loss of productive function until they were decommissioned. They were identified as extraneous to the urban fabric, ruins without identity, losing their architectural and social value.

Industrial areas, once decommissioned, create "urban voids" that are problematic due to safety issues, social and environmental degradation. But, investing in their rede-velopment means turning a problem into a strength, returning new valuable spaces to the area [18].

In particular, the "open wound of urban cities" is represented by neighborhoods that have abandoned historic buildings [19]. There are numerous examples of urban regeneration as Bilbao, La Ruhr, Glasgow, Lipsia, Rotterdam, Amsterdam, Liverpool, Barcelona, London, Hamburg, Barcelona, Turin, Lyon, etc. [19].

For example, in London the projects of King's Cross Central and Battersea Power Station redevelopment have transformed former industrial sites into vibrant mixed-use neighborhoods [20]. In Rotterdam, the M4H District and the Merwe-Vierhavens area are examples of successful brownfield regeneration projects, creating innovative spaces for creative industries, startups, and sustainable development [21].

The 22@Barcelona project has revitalized the Poblenou district, converting it into a knowledge and innovation hub, attracting technology companies and research institutions [22]. In Lyon, the Confluence district, located at the confluence of the Rhône and Saône rivers, has undergone a major transformation, creating a sustainable urban neighborhood with residential, commercial and recreational spaces [23].

The winning strategies of these best practices is tied to the ex industrial buildings reuse, according to the circular economy principles.

Infact, the perspective of circular economy linked to the circular adaptive reuse of cultural heritage is the possible way to define the projects for the regeneration of dismissed urban areas.

The circular economy model has been defined by Ellen Macarthur Foundation as an economic model which is "regenerative by design", with the aim to retain as much value as possible of products, parts, and materials [24], focusing on the life-cycle of materials to "close-the-loop" by recovering all wastes as a resource for new productive cycles [24].

Ellen Macarthur Foundation define the "cradle-to-cradle" strategy as a process in which all materials and products are collected and renewed at the end of their useful lives [24].

Instead, circular adaptive reuse refers to the process of recovering and redeveloping old industrial sites to transform them into a new use, different from the one for which they were conceived and built. The strategy of circular adaptive reuse is the only possible approach for the preservation of historic industrial monuments that are generally unsuitable and too obsolete to host new production sites [25].

Adaptive reuse is also the most sustainable solution for the rehabilitation of these urban areas: demolishing buildings, disposing of residual materials and having to construct new buildings using new materials and machinery implies the expenditure of more energy (in terms of resources and consumption) than is required for an asset redevelopment process.

According to Fusco Girard, the "ideal" project of reuse is to transform a dead (in general) site into a living system, to be managed as a complex adaptive system, i.e. an organism capable of continuous learning and adaptation capacity to a changing/dynamic context, through re-organization, repair, regulation, and therefore capable of evolution and resilience [11].

The site object of the re-functionalization process should be transformed into an ecosystem that can also contribute to the vitality of the local context, in a symbiotic relationship (for example, giving and receiving renewable energies etc.), involving other topics and activities especially in management, potentially resulting in the creation of other ecosystems [11, 26, 27].

In the context of the circular economy, functional reuse suggests that there are differences between it and the linear model in terms of design, implementation, and particularly management.

2.1 Smart City Model Canvas

Business Model Canvas (BMC) is a tool originally developed by Alexander Osterwalder and Yves Pigneur (2010) to visually represent the logic of a company and how it organises its operations to create and deliver value. The BMC consists of a model coposed of nine blocks, each of which deals with a specific aspect of the business model. This structure allows companies to develop innovative business models by reorganising or re-engineering the content of any of the nine blocks to reveal a new market and business opportunity [28].

Business models can help the different stakeholders involved in urban planning to organise future design choices on the basis of community needs. In particular, the Canvas business model can be interpreted as a "participatory process" capable of rapidly building design strategies to improve the quality of urban spaces [29, 30].

Canvas model is a visual prototyping tool that helps operators and stakeholders during the conception and development phases of an urban planning or real estate project [31, 32]. It is a prototip that providing users with a visual overview and a quick perspective of an urban project.

This tool is particularly useful during meetings and workshops to highlight validated facts, unvalidated assumptions, project risks and opportunities, skills and information gaps and even identify dangerous blind spots in the project team [32].

In other words, the Canvas model is an easy-to-use tool to research, prototype and gradually develop an urban project without getting lost in the process or neglecting its important elements.

In this research, a particular attention was given to Smart City Model Canvas, a model experimented within a European research "Replicare Project-Horizon 2020" - REnaissance of PLaces with Innovative Citizenship and Technology [32].

Smart City Model Canvas is as the integration of two business canvas models già esistenti:

1. The first is an adaptation of the traditional BMC, better suited to companies whose primary goal is not profit maximization but the achievement of a particular mission [14–15].
2. The second is the adaptation of the BMC, which is based on the triple-layered business model canvas [15] i.e., a model that considers the three levels of sustainability that a company must pursue: economic, social, and environmental.

The Smart City Model Canvas is thus an adaptation of these two models, but reoganized to identify the objectives that municipality (or company) should pursue in implementing an urban regeneration project. While the traditional BMC is one consisting of nine elements, the CMC is composed of fourteen blocks (see Fig. 1).

The first block refers to the identification of the "value proposition" considered comeaning the central element of the City Model Canvas. It indicates what benefits are generated/expected from the project. The "value proposition" should address specific

6. Key partnerships	7. Key activities	2. Value proposition	4. Buy-in & support	
Who can help the city deliver the proposed value to the beneficiaries? Who can access key resources that the city council does not have?	What must the city council do to create and deliver the proposed value?	What specific problems does the proposed service solve or alleviate?	Whose buy-in is needed in order to deploy the service (legal, policy, procurement, etc.)?	3. Beneficiaries
	8. Key infrastructure & key resources		5. Deployment	Who will directly benefit from the proposed services?
	What key resources does the city council have to create and deliver the value?		How will the city solve the problems of the Value proposition specifically?	

9. Budget costs	10. Revenue streams
What costs will the creation and delivery of the proposed services entail?	What sources of revenue for the city do the proposed services provide? What other sources of revenue does the city have?

11. Environmental cost	12. Environmental benefits
What negative environmental impacts can the proposed services cause?	What environmental benefits will the proposed services deliver?

13. Social costs	14. Social benefits
What are some of the potential social risks that the proposed service entails? Who is most vulnerable as a result?	What social benefits will the proposed services bring about? For whom will these benefits materialise?

Fig. 1. Smart City Model Canvas [15]

needs identified by the population and provide a clear picture of how those needs will be addressed by the business model. Generally, there should be at least one value proposition for each type of benefit identified [15].

The second block concerns the identification of the direct and indirect "beneficiates" of the project actions, i.e., the recipients for whom the strategy proposes to solve specific needs or problems ("pain points") [15].

The third block relates to "buy-in & support". This element refers to the stakeholders involved in the project (groups or entities, companies, government organizations, etc.) whose approval is necessary for its successful implementation.

The fourth block "deployment & delivery" indicates how the value proposition will be delivered to the client or beneficiary, i.e., it explains to the different stakeholders how the different project actions will be developed [15].

The fifth block addresses the "key partner(ship)s", i.e. the various partnerships that will be activated for the implementation and operation of the project.

The sixth block refers to "key activities", or the activities that should be undertaken for the business model (the project actions) to be effective [15].

The seventh block is on "key resources and key infrastructure". For a company, key resources are the main assets it needs to create a value proposition and provide a product or service to customers. Depending on the company's goal, the most important resource may be human capital, money, patents, trademarks ecc. In the case of the city, the key resources are not only the financial and physical assets it can use, but also the political and strategic resources it can deploy in support of certain policies [15].

The eighth block refers to "economic costs", i.e. the costs that the city will incur to implement regeneration project services. These costs will range from the initial project investment to the "soft" incentives that will be offered to users.

The ninth block is "revenue/income streams". This refers to all sources of revenue that the municipality and stakeholders involved will get from the project. Cities have a number of revenue streams to evaluate, including taxation, smart service fees, and external subsidies.

The tenth step refers to "environmental costs". These include impacts on land use, water and fuel requirements, greenhouse gas emissions along the production chain, etc. Environmental costs can be monitored through indicators, when data are available.

The eleventh step refers to "environmental benefits" tracked by specific indicators where data are available [15]. In the absence of data, this can be a useful exercise to determine existing data needs and information gaps. The exercise of assessing the environmental impacts and benefits of urban regeneration strategies in each sector will help the city get a clearer picture of where to focus its attention and resources.

The twelfth block refers to "social impacts" or the social sustainability of projects. The element of social impacts refers to the negative costs that the strategy may have on the city's residents and communities. The challenge for the city is to define what social impacts to consider and how to measure them.

The thirteenth block refers to "social benefits". It focuses on the positive social value creation aspects of the urban regeneration strategy. These are elements that arise specifically from interventions on the city, but can include indirect benefits [15]. As with social impacts, social benefits should be measured with specific indicators that allow the city to assess over time whether its interventions are having a positive or negative impact on the social well-being of society.

3   The Case Studie: The Regeneration Project of Siri Ex Industrial Area in Terni (Italy)

Terni is an Italian city of 106.285 inhabitants, its historical vocation coincides with its industrial nature from the mid-19th century onwards, only to undergo a slow and unstoppable decline after the second post-war period [28].

The city of Terni, already in Roman times, was configured as a city of water due to the presence of multiple springs and their high potential. Terni in Latin is a translation of "Interamna Nahars", a city between two rivers (Nera and Serra). Water was used for agriculture through channelization. The Nera was a navigable river and allowed river connections to Rome and the Marmore Falls (165 m, the highest in Europe) also built by the Romans.

Over time, the water resource has increasingly become the potential source of hydro-electric energy to serve industry and urban settlements, so much so that the city of Florence (Italian city), too, finds much of its energy resources in this area.

It was after the Italy Unification that the city experienced a turning point in its development. Local administrators took steps to establish an arms factory in Terni and, along with it, an iron and steel industry was also set up, which would later considerably influence the economic and social development of the city.

In 1884, Italy's first iron and steel industry, the Alti Forni society, Fonderie and Acciaierie of Terni, was founded. Terni's industry grew so massively and quickly that the city went from 14.000 inhabitants in 1871 to 31.400 in just twenty years [33].

The definitive development of the city came in the early 1900s thanks to the strong growth of the chemical industry.

Among these important industries, SIRI (Italian Industrial Research Society) was established in 1925 and occupied the complex of the former Ferriera Pontificia, built in 1794 [15]. The industrial complex produced synthetic ammonia, used for explosives and nitrogenous fertilisers. The industry occupied a flat area of over 40.000 square metres between the Nera river and the slopes of the Obito hill (see Fig. 2).

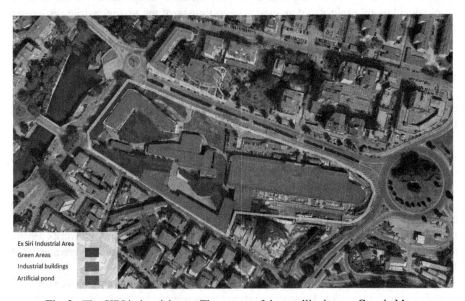

Fig. 2. The SIRI industrial area. The source of the satellite image: Google Maps.

Subsequently, when progressive difficulties in industrial activity emerged due to changing market and technological conditions, the plant closed in 1985 [33].

The growth of the factory took place unequally, with new buildings leaning against the pre-existing ones, leaving a large free area in the middle, where the pond that was fed by the waters of the Nera River still stands.

The industrial complex had important architectural, environmental and industrial archaeological values.

After its closure, in 1985, the SIRI industrial site went through a phase of progressive decline and abandonment.

In 1998, the Municipality of Terni lauched a project to regenerate the entire area, with the aim of recovering and enhancing the industrial archaeology buildings and the surrounding park.

Specifically, the renovation work covered an area of 44.210 square metres, involving the recovery of four buildings, called CAOS site, that were converted into new functions:

modern art museum, palaeontological museum, civic museum archaeological section, refreshment areas, theatre-auditorium and new residences [34].

The entire area (in which the buildings are located) was reclaimed through the creation of an urban park with bicycle and pedestrian paths. The project cost 6.248.612 € of which 3.111.136,36 € was financed by the Region, 1.045.825,02 € by the municipality, and 2.091.650,44 € by private individuals. The project was completed in 2009 [34].

The regeneration of this large urban area was made possible by a series of complex urban planning instruments and acts (Urban Redevelopment Programme, the Complex Urban Programme).

The conditions on which the entire recovery project was based by the awareness that the industrial buildings, although not characterised by a significant formal value or typological layout, represented an evocative testimony of the first industrial settlement in the city of Terni.

With the recovery project, the intention was to testimony of an important historical phase of the city, adopting a correct restoration criterion that would make it compatible with the new planned functions.

The redevelopment of this area is part of a larger urban planning project, aimed at creating new urban spaces to be integrated with the nearby historic centre, characterised by the preservation of the industrial memory.

The recovered buildings were in an advanced state of decay, having been abandoned for many years. Atmospheric agents, seismic events and vegetation growth to a lack of maintenance had severely damaged them, causing part of the roofs to collapse and considerable cracks in the load-bearing walls.

Specifically, thanks to this project, all the building facades were recovered. Some exterior spaces have retained their original layout, such as the driveway. The original housing system and some infrastructural elements, including water intake works for the power plants, were extended and restored. All of the pre-existing buildings are now used for cultural services.

The building, which today is destined for the Museum of Contemporary Art (optical cone 5, in Fig. 3) (see Fig. 3), was renovated by preserving and replacing the degraded structural parts, maintaining the formal and material characteristics while respecting the overall integrity of the public complex.

The external volume has not been changed, only the plasterwork and the reconstruction of the collapsed parapets and the excessively degraded masonry parts were redone.

The areas that were used as chemical laboratories and warehouses saw an adaptation of the roofs, floors and masonry where damaged.

The warehouses used as former experimental laboratories (optical cone 4, 9, 1, in Fig. 3) are the ones with the greatest height and formal value, presents significant aesthetic elements. In fact, the "decò" style decorative bands (present under the roofing imposte), the "Palladian" cut window frames framed by the face brick arches of the façade and the wooden trusses with metal tie-rods have been recovered.

The former electrolysis halls were in a very poor state of preservation, especially the masonry and roofing.

In order to meet the need to continuously obtain electricity through water, a reservoir was recovered that is fed by conduits from the Nera River.

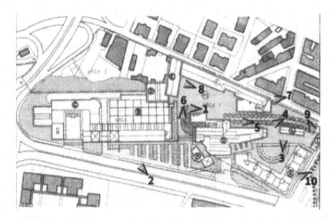

Fig. 3. The buildings that were redeveloped in the municipality's project for the conversion of the ex Siri industrial area

After several years since the opening of all these new activities, the municipality made an overall assessment of the economic, social and environmental impacts generayed by the project, which showed clear imbalances.

It emerged that the residential, commercial and tertiary functions, located in the two towers (optical cone 10 in Fig. 3) and in the hypermarket (optical cone 2 in Fig. 3) are characterised by autonomous productivity. The cultural, social and museum functions are in a fragile condition, i.e. they are characterised by a deficit between income and expenditure. This requires support actions by local institutions, both public and private, either alternatively or in synergy.

The museum system was managed for eight years at a cost of €1.859.620,04 plus VAT. The municipality of Terni also pays the concessionaire € 230.000/year as a subsidy for the use of certain areas [34]. An analysis of the 2019 budget revealed a lack of attractiveness of the museum system [34]. The costs of tickets and the rental of rooms to third parties do not cover all the costs incurred by the operators on an annual basis [34].

The real attractor is therefore the hypermarket, which, however, does not determine any external effect on the site and appears as an autonomous entity in relation to the other functions.

After analyzing the impacts generated by the area redevelopment project, the question was raised on what indications, what proposals can be made to improve this status quo? What solutions to reduce the contradictions between the private functions (that are self-sustainable economically and financially) and public functions?

To answer these questions, a design solution for the regeneration of this industrial site is proposed with the aim to improve the attractiveness of the site. The design proposal consists in the industrial building's energy renovation, which have already been redeveloped in the project carried out by the municipality, in coherence with the European Green Deal (2019) [35].

Infact, one of the critical points is the energy issue related to the operation of the rehabilitated historical buildings, a large amount of energy is spent, with negative repercussions in terms of both environmental and economic impacts.

One of the main project objectives was to transform the buildings (used for cultural activities) into zero-impact architectural fabrications, through the installation of an integrated system for the energy production: photovoltaic panels and a hydrogen system that produces energy through the process of electrolysis.

In particular, the project envisages the installation of 3 kWh of photovoltaic panels for every 200 square metres of surface area (contemporary art museum, archaeological museum, Secci theatre) and storage batteries, to the extent of 6.5 kWh for every 9 kWh of panels for the production of electrical energy, which would be partly used during operating hours, partly stored for the times when it is not possible to produce from solar radiation, and partly for the production of hydrogen through electrolysis, restoring the pipes and reservoirs that brought water to the site directly from the Nera river.

The energy that will be produced by the panels is divided between that used directly, that stored in the battery, and that used for the production of hydrogen through the electrolytic process. The hydrogen produced will then be used for domestic water heaing and space heating in winter [36–38].

This project was developed in collaboration with Giacomo Palombi, a student of Pegaso Telematic University, resident in the Terni city. For this reason, it was possible to organize a workshop within the municipality to evaluate the feasibility of the project using the Smart City Canvas business model.

4   The Smart City Model Canvas Applied to the Regeneration Project of the Former SIRI Industrial Area

The Smart City Model Canvas was used as a business evaluation tool during the workshop organised with different Terni local stakeholders (students, members of associations, members of the municipality, small entrepreneurs and citizens) with the aim to discuss and understand what concrete actions are necessary to realize the buildings energy efficiency project.

It was possible to organise this event thanks to the participation of student Giacomo Palombi, a resident of Terni, who was developing his thesis work.

The workshop was based on an adaptation of the World Café method [39]. The World Café is a participative method that focuses on the expertise and experiences of its members to investigate a problem.

This approach has the benefit of allowing participants to form relationships and learn from one another while looking into a problem [40, 41].

The workshop was characterized by an opening session for participants to share expertise, group discussions, and a closing session for discussing the results of such conversations.

Before starting the activities, the workshop participants discussed about the impacts of the previous recovery project fir the regeneration of Siri ex industrial area, implemented by the Municipality of Terni. No significant social, economic and environmental impacts were identified, as it was found that the real attractor is the hypermarket and not the cultural sites, which, however, does not determine any external effect on the site, and appears as an autonomous entity in relation to the other functions.

The energy issue was identified as the unresolved critical node of the previous project, also because the massive presence of industries means that the city is one of the most polluted in the country, particularly with high numbers of annual PM10 particle exceedances and presence of heavy metals in the air.

Having clarified these issues, the designers explained the new energy efficiency project for the industrial archaeology buildings within the site. The project, as explained in Sect. 3, involves the use of renewable energy sources and the use of hydrogen as an energy carrier for the operation of the buildings.

After this step, stakeholders began to discuss of the project, following the steps suggested by the Canvas model (see Table 1).

Table 1. Smart City Model Canvas for the renovation project ex Siri industrial area

Topics	Actions
Key partnerships	- plant service providers; - public administration; - contractor cooperatives; - residents; - business owners
Key activities	- monitoring activities of the entire project implementation; - relationship management with project beneficiaries; - awareness campaigns with different stakeholders involved in the project, especially with citizens
Value proposition	- energy efficiency strategies for historic buildings; - create business opportunities in the energy efficiency and renewable energy sector
Buy-in & support	- involvement of managers of historic buildings in the building energy efficiency project
Beneficiares	- residents of new housing; - business owners; - managers of cultural activities; - businesses that install photovoltaic panels; - start-ups and local businesses
Deployment	- building retrofitting; - installation of photovoltaic system

(*continued*)

Table 1. (*continued*)

Topics	Actions
Key infrastructure & key resources	- new energy networks; - abandoned historic buildings
Budget costs	- costs for the photovoltaic panel's installation; - costs for testing facilities; - costs of retrofitting for buildings
Revenue streams	- saving energy purchase; - selling surplus energy
Social costs	- possible increase in housing prices due to project
Environmental costs	- environmental impact of new construction
Environmental benefits	- reduced energy waste due to photovoltaic system; - reduced emissions due to better energy production and lower consumption; - general awareness of energy use by users
Social benefits	- improved living conditions through more efficient heating system, better access to clean energy

4.1 Results

The results of the Smart City Canvas model applied for the Terni case study have clarified the strategies to be deployed for transforming the industrial buildings into con-structions with almost zero energy impact.

During the workshop, there were some points of the business model that were most taken into consideration, such as the identification of "Key partnerships" to determine partners who can actively contribute to the implementation of interventions.

Also, the identification of "value propositions" was a topic considered very interesting by stakeholders, because they have identified the benefits for future users of the site.

When they discuss about the "budget costs", a reflection was made on the possible sources of funding for the project.

All workshop participants unanimously agreed that economic investments should focus on reducing CO_2 emissions while promoting new economic development, new employment opportunities, improved welfare, and the protection of ecosystem services.

Regarding the "Environmental costs, environmental benefits, social costs, and social benefits" it was recognized that the technological solution adopted for enhancing the energy efficiency of the industrial buildings would result in several positive impacts both environmentally and socially, with significant benefits particularly in terms of emissions reduction.

5 Conclusion

Reusing industrial cultural heritage within the circular economy framework can drive a new development model that promotes the circulation of processes, leveraging synergies in the financial, economic, social, cultural, and institutional sectors through innovative partnerships involving the public and private sectors for the management of common goods [42].

Economically, investments in adaptive reuse create jobs, income, attract new capital, creative start-ups, and contribute to tourism and local businesses.

Socially, adaptive reuse preserves the character of neighborhoods, enhances community identity and involvement, improves services, and enhances safety perception.

From an environmental perspective, adaptive reuse aims to reduce traditional energy consumption, increase the use of renewable energy, and reduce carbon emissions in alignment with the goals of the European Green Deal.

Adaptive reuse strategies for the regeneration of industrial buildings they can be evaluated through specific business models.

Business models are crucial for driving the transition and governance of a "smart economy" and "smart society", leveraging ICT to promote growth, environmental sustainability, and social inclusion [43].

The smart city business model serves as an initial step in identifying or creating new models that can be utilized by specific companies, research organizations, or private citizens.

The results of the Smart City Urban Canvas model implemented in Terni have shown that participants feel actively involved in the preservation of cultural heritage perceived as "common good". The team involved has identified potential opportunities for innovation, revenue generation, and sustainable growth. Togheter, they have identified the possible risks of the project. The most interesting outcome was the discussion held together on the actions to propose for further improving the project. Some participants put forward intriguing solutions for project funding, including the idea of launching a crowdfunding campaign.

In conclusion, the application of the business model canvas provides a structured approach to analyze, develop, and communicate the regeneration project's business model.

The future aim of this research is to understand if it is possible to combine multicriteria evaluation tools with the Smart City Model Canvas with the purpose of developing an evaluation framework capable of assessing the economic, social, and environmental impacts of an urban regeneration project.

References

1. Bulkeley, H., Broto, V.C.: Government by experiment? Global cities and the governing of climate change. Trans. Inst. British Geograph. **38**(3), 361–375 (2013)
2. https://www.Un.Org/Sustainabledevelopment/Cities/ (Accessed 15 July 2022)
3. Fusco Girard, L., Nocca, F.: Climate change and health impacts in urban areas: towards hybrid evaluation tools for new governance. Atmosphere **11**, 1344 (2020)

4. Di Giovanni, A.: Urban voids as a resource for the design of contemporary public spaces. Planum. The Journal of Urbanism no. 37 vol II. Magazine Section (2018).
5. Assumma, V., Bottero, M., Datola, G., Pezzoli, A., Quagliolo, C.: Climate Change and Urban Resilience. Preliminary Insights from an Integrated Evaluation Framework in Bevilacqua, C., Calabrò, F., Della Spina, L. (eds.) New Metropolitan Perspectives. NMP 2020. Smart Innovation, Systems and Technologies, vol. 178, Springer, Cham, pp. 676–685, ISSN: 2190–3026, https://doi.org/10.1007/978-3-030-48279-4_63, incluso nel database ISI Web of Knowledge e Scopus (2021)
6. Newman, P., Jennings, I.: Cities as sustainable ecosystems: Principles and practices. Island Press) (2008)
7. Gravagnuolo, A., Angrisano, M., Fusco Girard, L.: Circular economy strategies in eight historic port cities: criteria and indicators towards a circular city assessment framework. Sustainability 11(13), 3512 (2019) https://doi.org/10.3390/su11133512
8. Roegen, G., The entropy law and the economic process, Harvard University Press: Cambridge, Massachusetts, United States (1971)
9. Haase, D., Nuissl, H., Wiest, K.: The urban-to-rural gradient of land use change and its implications for multifunctional landscapes. Landsc. Urban Plan. 125, 234–240 (2014)
10. Steffen, W., Jäger, J., Carson, D.J., Bradsha W.: Challenges of a Changing Earth. In: Proceedings of the Global Change Open Science Conference, Amsterdam, the Netherlands,10–13 July (2001)
11. Fusco, G.L.: The circular economy in transforming a died heritage site into a living ecosystem, to be managed as a complex adaptive organism. Aestimum 77, (2020). https://doi.org/10.13128/aestim-9788
12. Foster, G.: Circular economy strategies for adaptive reuse of cultural heritage buildings to reduce environmental impacts. Resour. Conserv., Recycl., n. 152, 104507 (2020)
13. Imrie, R., Lees, L., Raco, M.: Regenerating London: Governance, sustainability and community in a global city. Routledge (2009)
14. Osterwalder, A., Pigneur, Y.: Business Model Generation: A Handbook for Visionaries, Game Changers, and Challengers. John Wiley & Sons (2010)
15. Blank, S.: The Mission Model Canvas – An Adapted Business Model Canvas for Mission-Driven Organizations. Retrieved May 11, 2017, from https://steveblank.com/2016/02/23/the-mission-model-canvas-an-adaptedbusiness-model-canvas-for-mission-driven-organizations/
16. Joyce, A., Paquin, R.L.: The triple layered business model canvas: a tool to design more sustainable business models. J. Clean. Prod. 135, 1474–1486 (2016). https://doi.org/10.1016/j.jclepro.2016.06.067
17. Fusco, G.L.: Multidimensional evaluation processes to manage creative, resilient and sustainable city. AESTIMUM 59. Dicembre 2011, 123–139 (2011)
18. Bottero, M., Caprioli C., Datola G., Oppio A., Torrieri F.: Regeneration of Rogoredo railways scali: a combined approach using multi-criteria and financial analysis, Valori e Valutazioni, 31, 89–102 (2022). https://doi.org/10.48264/VVSIEV-20223107
19. Angrisano, M., Fusco Girard, L., Bianchi, A.: A literature review about Life Cycle Assessment as a tool to support circular economy innovation in the built environment sector. BDC Unina, vol. 19, n. 1. ISSN 2284–4732 (2019)
20. LWARB.: London's Circular Economy Route Map—Circular London; LWARB: London, UK (2017)
21. Gemeente Rotterdam. Roadmap Circular Economy Rotterdam; Gemeente Rotterdam: Rotterdam, The Netherlands (2016)
22. https://use.metropolis.org/case-studies/22-barcelona
23. https://www.lyon-confluence.fr/en/reconquering-strategic-territory
24. Heesen, B.: Case Studies. In: Effective Strategy Execution. MP, pp. 137–211. Springer, Heidelberg (2016). https://doi.org/10.1007/978-3-662-47923-0_6

25. Cerreta, M., Poli, G., Somma, M.: Assessing Infrastructures Alternatives: The Implementation of a Fuzzy Analytic Hierarchy Process (F-AHP). In: Gervasi, O., et al. (eds.) ICCSA 2021. LNCS, vol. 12955, pp. 504–516. Springer, Cham (2021). https://doi.org/10.1007/978-3-030-87007-2_36

26. Cerreta, M., Muccio, E., Poli, G., Regalbuto, S., Romano, F.: A multidimensional evaluation for regenerative strategies: towards a circular city-port model implementation. In: Bevilacqua, C., Calabrò, F., Della Spina, L. (eds.) NMP 2020. SIST, vol. 178, pp. 1067–1077. Springer, Cham (2021). https://doi.org/10.1007/978-3-030-48279-4_100

27. Cerreta, M., Muccio, E., Poli, G., Regalbuto, S., Romano, F.: City-Port Circular Model: Towards a Methodological Framework for Indicators Selection. In: Gervasi, O., et al. (eds.) ICCSA 2020. LNCS, vol. 12251, pp. 855–868. Springer, Cham (2020). https://doi.org/10.1007/978-3-030-58808-3_61

28. https://it.wikipedia.org/wiki/Terni. Consulted on 10 October (2022)

29. Datola G., Bottero M., De Angelis E.: Addressing Social Inclusion Within Urban Resilience: A System Dynamics Approach in Bevilacqua, C., Calabrò, F., Della Spina, L. (eds.) New Metropolitan Perspectives. NMP 2020. Smart Innovation, Systems and Technologies, vol. 178, Springer, Cham, pp. 510–519, ISSN: 2190–3026 (2021). https://doi.org/10.1007/978-3-030-48279-4_48, incluso nel database ISI Web of Knowledge e Scopus

30. Bottero, M., Caprioli, C., Datola, G., Caruso, N.: Assessing the impacts of a social housing project through the Community Impact Evaluation (CIE) methodology in Gervasi O. et al. (eds.): ICCSA 2022 Workshops, LNCS 13380, pp. 183–194 (2022). https://doi.org/10.1007/978-3-031-10542-5_13

31. European Commission, 2017. Deliverable 2.2. Report on the Business Models of the Lighthouse cities

32. https://www.beople.it/business-model-canvas

33. http://cms.provincia.terni.it/on. Consulted on 1 september, 2022

34. https://www.caos.museum/

35. European Commission. The European Green Deal; European Commission: Bruxelles, Belgium, 2019

36. www.planete-energies.com/en/media/article/japan-and-its-advanced-hydrogen-research

37. Wei, H., Wang, C., Yang, S., Yin, B, Liu, X.: Integrated design of hydrogen production and thermal energy storage functions of Al-Bi-Cu composite powders. Int. J. Hydrogen Energy **48**(40), 14931–14940. https://doi.org/10.1016/j.ijhydene.2023.01.006

38. https://www.nims.go.jp/eng/

39. Brown, J., Isaacs, D.: The World Cafe: Shaping our futures ´through conversations that matter. Berrett-Koehler Publishers (2005)

40. Bergold, J., Thomas, S: Participatory research methods: a methodological approach in motion. Historical Social Res. **37**(4), 191–222, GESIS (2012)

41. European Commission. Faro Convention (2005). https://www.coe.int/en/web/culture-and-her itage/faro-convention

42. Datola, G., Assumma, V., Bottero, M.: Assessing the economic value of the unmovable cultural assets for improving their resilience: the case study of the Church of Santa Maria dei Miracoli in Calabrò, F., Della Spina, L., José Piñeira Mantiñán, M. (eds.) New Metropolitan Perspectives NMP 2022. Lecture Notes in Networks and Systems, vol. 482. Springer, Cham. (2022) https://doi.org/10.1007/978-3-031-06825-6_245

43. Norberg Schulz, C.: Genius Loci. Paesaggio Ambiente Architettura. Electa (1979)

Supporting the Management Plan of a World Heritage Site Nomination Through a Multi-step Evaluation Approach

Sebastiano Barbieri(✉) ⓘ, Marta Bottero ⓘ, Caterina Caprioli ⓘ,
and Giulio Mondini ⓘ

Dipartimento Interateneo di Scienze, Progetto e Politiche del Territorio, Politecnico di Torino,
Viale Mattioli, 39, 10125 Torino, TO, Italy
{sebastiano.barbieri,marta.bottero,caterina.caprioli}@polito.it,
giulio.mondini@formerfaculty.polito.it

Abstract. The nomination of a site to the World Heritage List must be supported by a nomination document and a management plan. The management plan emphasizes the Outstanding Universal Value of the site, as well as it defines protection objectives and how to pursue them. However, neither UNESCO documents nor research applications provide a shared framework for the tools or methodologies that can support the different phases of the management plan. Within this context, the present paper started with an analysis of both management plans already implemented for UNESCO-listed sites and contributions provided by research applications. The result of this in-depth analysis suggests the proposal of a multi-step approach able to guide the entire decision-making process and to support the development of the management plan of a World Heritage Site nomination required by the World Heritage Convention. This approach could represent a guiding tool for researchers, practitioners, and decision-makers in the case of real-world site nomination and management for the World Heritage List. The mixed-method approach proposed starts with framing and structuring goals, objectives and values, as well as actors and stakeholders involved, and ends with the design, evaluation and monitoring of the project strategies. In particular, the proposed methodology for developing the management plan of a World Heritage-nominated site is constituted by four main working phases: (1) the problem framing and structuring, (2) the analysis of risks and resources, (3) the design of the strategies, and (4) the evaluation and monitoring phase. Each of these phases is supported by specific assessment methods and tools, both qualitative and quantitative.

Keywords: UNESCO site management plan · Cultural heritage · Sustainable assessment

1 Introduction

In 1946, United Nations (UN) founded UNESCO, a specialized agency based in Paris, with many goals for the promotion of culture, science, education, and collaboration between nations. Specifically, one goal is the intercultural understanding of heritages that have exceptional value and require specific protection and safeguarding. The concept of "exceptional value" was first introduced in 1972 during the general UNESCO conference "Concerning the Protection of the World Cultural and Natural Heritage". The introductory article of the convention clarifies the meaning of "cultural heritage", classifying it into monuments, groups of buildings, and sites, and the meaning of "natural heritage" as natural features, geological and physiographical formations and, natural sites and natural areas. In 1992, additionally to these classifications, the "cultural landscape" was included, that represents joint creations of man and nature [1]. Moreover, this article specifies the criteria for being considered an Outstanding Universal Value (OUV). In particular, the world cultural, natural and landscape heritage must have a value from an historical point of view (i.e., commemorative value), from an artistic point of view (i.e., aesthetic value), from a scientific point of view, from an aesthetic point of view, from an ethnological point of view or for its anthropological value [2]. They could be valuables as an expression of a specific culture, but then, they are "outstanding" because they represent examples, or the most representative example, of a particular type of cultural heritage [3]. The site proposed to be in World Heritage List (WHL) must face at least one of the 10 criteria established by UNESCO (i. "to represent a masterpiece of human creative genius"; ii. "to exhibit an important interchange of human values [...]"; iii. "to bear a unique or at least exceptional testimony to a cultural tradition [...]"; iv. "to be an outstanding example of a type of building, architectural or technological ensemble or landscape [...]"; v. "to be an outstanding example of a traditional human settlement [...]"; vi. "to be directly or tangibly associated with events or living traditions [...]"; vii. "to contain superlative natural phenomena or areas of exceptional natural beauty and aesthetic importance"; viii. "to be outstanding examples representing major stages of earth's history [...]"; ix. "to be outstanding examples representing significant on-going ecological and biological processes in the evolution and development of [...] ecosystems [...]"; x. "to contain the most important and significant natural habitats for in-situ conservation of biological diversity [...]"). Furthermore, a site must respond to the requirements of integrity and authenticity and distinguish itself from other listed territories based on an in-depth comparative analysis [4].

Sites nominated to be included in the list need to be managed and protected to maintain the OUV. In particular, the purpose of a management system is to keep the asset's value unaltered for present and future generations [2]. The greater complexity of our world requires a suitable management approach able to consider the various factors that can affect cultural properties, such as natural disasters, political and financial constraints, human conflicts, as well as the diverse values in play (e.g., intangible and ecological) [5]. In the European context, the protection of OUV is demanded by each state which follows the directives issued by the European Union and then, according to their governance structure, to the competent authorities. Additionally, the Budapest Declaration [6] stipulated that states should strengthen the protection of world heritage. The guidelines drawn up in 1972 required that each site, in the nomination procedure, produces its own Management Plan (MP). This plan should address the combination of heritage protection and sustainable territorial development. This is because sustainable development can be understood as support for the environmental/cultural resources to be protected, but most importantly as a means by which heritage contributes to improving the environmental, social and economic dimensions [5]. However, there is no unique way to develop the MP, and UNESCO documents provide limited help in tools or methodologies that can support the different phases of MP implementation of World Heritage Site (WHS).

Within this context, the paper proposes an overview of the main practices in the development of MPs for WHSs nomination, with particular reference to the assessment methods and evaluation approaches used to frame, plan and managing them. The paper analyzes both MPs already implemented for UNESCO-listed sites and contributions provided by research applications. This overview allows us to propose a multi-step evaluation approach that supports all the phases required by the MP. In particular, starting from the proposal of an integrated approach for a spatially explicit framing of the WHS, a combination of other qualitative and quantitative assessment methods is presented to guide the planning and managing phases.

After this Introduction, the paper will focus on the Italian legal framework for protecting and managing WHSs. This special attention will be given to the Italian case, both for the largest number of sites included in the WHL (i.e., 58 until now) [7] and for the specific methodology defined for the development of MPs [5]. In Sect. 3, the overview of recent MPs and contributions in literature is presented and analyzed. Section 4 will propose a multi-step evaluation approach able to produce an integrated and comprehensive understanding of the state, challenges, opportunities, and threats that guide the decision-making process and the development of a strategic MP. Moreover, the main evaluation methods able to support the development of MP plan for the nomination of WHS are described in order to highlight their main role and abilities. Finally, the Conclusions will summarize the main contents of the paper, highlighting future perspectives of the research.

2 Italian Legal Framework

According to the Convention concerning the Protection of the World Cultural and Natural Heritage, "each State Party to this Convention recognizes that the duty of ensuring the identification, protection, conservation, presentation and transmission to future generations of the cultural and natural heritage [...] belongs primarily to that State. It will do all it can to this end, to the utmost of its own resources" [1].

In Italy, the normative framework can be divided into these main levels [8]:

- European/National level, where *ad hoc* directives for the protection of culture and landscape are included in the Constitution.
- Regional level, which provides guidelines for the protection of its elements, qualifying the landscape through conservation planning tools, such as landscape and territorial regional plans, i.e., Piano Paesaggistico Regionale (PPR) or Piano Territoriale Regionale (PTR). The first is an instrument of protection and promotion of the landscape, aimed at regulating its transformations and supporting its strategic role in the sustainable development of the territory. The second defines the strategies and objectives of the regional level, entrusting the implementation to the entities operating at provincial and local levels. In some cases, these two plans are integrated into a single regional plan.

- Provincial level, which identifies the most sensitive areas through the Piano Territoriale di Coordinamento Provinciale (PTCP) or, in the case of Metropolitan Cities, the metropolitan plans (e.g., PTGM, PTM).
- Local level, which defines the rules for the protection of sites included in the WHL through local plans. Each municipality where it is located a site included in the WHL has to modify its local plan to adapt its regulations, according to the guidelines approved by the region [8].

Concerning the MP, Italy regulates it in Law no. 77 of 20th February 2006, which imposes the development of MPs, not only for new sites but also for those already existing. A MP is a tool to evaluate and manage the anthropogenic dynamics that can lead the protected site to be damaged, or significantly change its qualities. On the one hand, the MP must define the protection guidelines for the site. On the other hand, it supports the process of adoption of the plans at the local level, which are those who actively build concrete actions for the protection of the site. The concrete implementation of MPs must be guaranteed by the proposers, providing for this purpose all the tools for effective protection of the area, and regularly publishing reports on the status of protection and implementation of the safeguard for individual areas. MP defines a management system that analyzes the values to be included and considered for the WHL and identifies strengths and weaknesses, goals, and strategies to achieve the expected results through specific actions. This plan is carried out through agreements between all those responsible for the site's protection, enhancement, and promotion.

3 Literature Review

To have an overview of the most useful evaluation methods to support the development of MPs, the analysis examined three kinds of documents:

- The guidelines at UE and Italian levels for the development of MPs;
- Scientific papers regarding evaluation methodologies employed in the development of MPs;
- Existing MPs developed for nomination to WHL.

Concerning the guidelines, two documents were in-depth analysed, the 2013 UNESCO manual "Managing Cultural World Heritage" [5] was analysed, and "the Italian model", developed by the Ministry of Cultural Heritage in 2004. The first document structures the process through 3 main steps. (1) The planning phase consists of a collection of data and information about the stakeholders involved in the process, the characteristics of the site (as strengths and weaknesses), as well as all the available resources and timing. Moreover, this phase states the actions that should be taken to achieve the goals. (2) The implementation phase articulates and details the strategies identified before, verifying that the planned actions produce the results expected and achieve the goals set. (3) The last phase, i.e., the monitoring phase, is devoted to verifying that the management system is feasible and eventually defining corrective actions [5]. The Italian guidelines for the MP implementation, instead, divides the process into four phases. (1) The first identifies the motivations and values of why the site is nominated. (2) The second phase collects all the data useful to understand the peculiarities of the site in terms of strengths and weaknesses, but also threats and opportunities. It also develops a Stakeholder Analysis to determine who influences the decision-making process. For the development of these phases, the document suggests the use of spatial tools, such as Geographic Information System (GIS), which make it possible to organize, elaborate and map all useful information. (3) The third phase regards the protection and conservation of the site. In this phase, the conservation status of the artifacts, the damage and the risk factors are analysed and evaluated, as well as the available resources (i.e., economic, technical and human) are verified for the protection of the heritage site. (4) The final stage is the formulation of the projects, detailed in objectives, strategies, tactics and actions that are necessary to intervene in the preservation of the protected heritage. The projects are designed over at least 5 years and then specified for each year. The annual structure allows general control of the suitability of the plan [9].

Besides the analysis of the national and international documents, a literature search was conducted, aimed to collect evaluation methods and approaches used to conduct the development of MPs. This literature review led to the knowledge of several assessment methods by showing the stages in which they were used. Initial searches within the literature, using the Scopus database, identified some papers dealing with topics related to UNESCO nominations, without specifying the stage at which they were used or without explaining which method was best suited. In some of these cases, it was possible to identify the assessment method able to develop a specific part of the MP. Appiotti et al. (2020) [10], for example, use different methods such as questionnaires, SWOT analysis, Stakeholder Analysis, and Multi-Criteria Analysis (MCA) to develop the proposed strategy, corresponding to the implementation phase for the European document or the third phase for the Italian model. Ferretti (2021) [11] uses the same methods for both the implementation phase and the planning phase, supporting the entire process with the GIS tool. Santoro et al. (2021) [12] only use public participation as a tool to enhance the Ligurian case of the Cinque Terre, while Bottazzi et al. (2006) [13] evaluate the tourism demand of the same site through a set of indicators and Choice Models. Appiotti et al., (2020) [10], instead, identify methods useful for the implementation and risk assessment phase. Specifically, they use tools such as sets of indicators for MCA, supplemented by questionnaires, SWOT, and Stakeholder Analysis, and as always by the GIS tool.

A third analysis investigates existing MPs developed for sites that have recently joined the WHL. The Plans analysed are summarized in Table 1, which reports the assessment methods identified in the documents under investigation, indicating at which stage they are found (referring to the two guideline documents of the European Commission and the Italian Ministry). In particular, each phase of the European document process is assigned to a colour: light blue for the planning phase, yellow for the implementation phase, green for the monitoring phase, and orange if the method is used in every step of the process. Similarly, each phase of the Italian document is assigned to a number: "1" for the application and universal meaning of the site phase, "2" for the knowledge project, "3" for the protection project, "4" for the strategic project of the local cultural system and, finally, the symbol "*" refers to the entire process. From Table 1, it is clear that the most used methods are SWOT and Stakeholder Analysis for the planning stages, while indicator systems are the most used for monitoring, sometimes supported by matrices. In all MPs, the GIS tool is used to support the entire process, from planning

Table 1. Assessment methods used at different stages of MPs

MANAGEMENT PLANS	FOCUS GROUP	SWOT ANALYSIS	STAKEHOLDERS ANALYSIS	INDICATOR SYSTEM	MDCA	CHOICE MODELS	MATRIX	GIS
Venice and its Lagoon (Italy)	*	2	2	5				*
The Porticoes of Bologna (Italy)			2	5			5	2
Le colline del Prosecco di Conegliano e Valdobbiadene (Italy)		2	1, 2, 4	5				*
Ivrea, industrial city of the 20th century (Italy)				5				1, 2
Padua's fourteenth-century fresco cycles (Italy)	4	1, 2	2	5				1, 2
Venetian Works of Defence between the 16th and 17th Centuries (Italy, Croatia, Montenegro)		2	2	5			2	
Chaîne des Puys - Limagne fault tectonic arena (France)		2		5				1, 2
Amburgo Cathedral (Germany)			2					1, 2
Kojate Greenland: Norse and Inuit Farming at the Edge of the Ice Cap			2	5			5	
Mathildenhöhe Darmstadt (Germany)								*

EU - Planning phase = blue, Implementing phase = yellow, Monitoring phase = green, during all process = orange;
Italy - Application and universal meaning of the site = 1, Knowledge project = 2, Protection project = 3, Strategic project of the local cultural system = 4, during all process = *

to monitoring. For example, Padua's plan [14], the plan for the porticos of Bologna [15], the Prosecco Hills [16], and the plan for Venice and its lagoon [17] are the most complete regarding the use of evaluation methods, at all stages of the process. Bologna's plan uses participation tools throughout the process, organizing moments of information exchange and sharing. In particular, they used focus groups, in which the population and associations interacted and discussed the implementation of the plan. The phase in which evaluation methods are least used is the implementation phase: only Padua's plan conducted some focus groups and Prosecco Hills' plan used Stakeholder Analysis. It is also evident that quantitative or quali-quantitative methodologies, such as the MCA, are less used compared to qualitative approaches. In particular, MCA and choice models do not seem to be applied, at least for the analysed plans, at any stage of the process in contrast to the research applications. These methods are, in fact, found in some of the analysed papers, specifically Bottazzi et al. (2006) [13] for the use of choice models and Ferretti (2021) [11] or Appiotti et al. (2020) [10] for MCAs.

The entire analysis of documents allows for some considerations about the methods and models used. In general, existing MPs adopt methods and tools described into guidelines and directives without much experimentation. They mainly used qualitative methods (e.g., SWOT Analysis and Stakeholder Analysis) and sets of indicators for monitoring. Conversely, from the analysis of the documents in the literature, some authors tried to experiment with more sophisticated models and methodologies such as Choice Models, questionnaires, MCA, and Spatial Multi-Criteria Analysis (S-MCA).

4   A Multi-step Approach

The analysis of previous examples and applications in literature (Sect. 3) have highlighted different ways to tackle the development of the MP of WHSs during its nomination. Each of them has shed a light on the role of qualitative and quantitative evaluation approaches to support the decision-making process for the nomination of UNESCO sites and, specifically, for the development of MPs. However, neither the manual on how to manage Cultural World Heritage produced by UNESCO [5], nor the guidelines for the development of a MP by the Italian National Commission for UNESCO Sites and Local Tourist Systems [9], nor the research applications provide a shared framework on the tools or methodologies that can comprehensively support the different phases that compose the MP.

In this paper, we propose a multi-phase approach as a guiding tool for managing the entire process for the nomination of UNESCO sites. The multi-phase approach is one of the ways of designing and combining methods in decision-making theory [18]. This approach supports the development of a step-by-step process, where qualitative analyses are conducted in the first stages to highlight goals, objectives and values, as well as actors and stakeholders involved; then, quantitative analyses help to design, evaluate and monitor the project strategies [19]. In particular, the proposed methodology for the development of a MP is constituted by four main working phases: (1) the problem framing and structuring, (2) the analysis of risks and resources, (3) the design of the strategies, and (4) the evaluation and monitoring phase. In particular, Fig. 1 shows this multi-step approach, highlighting the connections among the different phases, as well as the most suitable approach (quantitative or qualitative) to be used. In Sects. 4.1, 4.2, 4.3 and 4.4, these four steps are in-depth described, presenting the most suitable methods to be used.

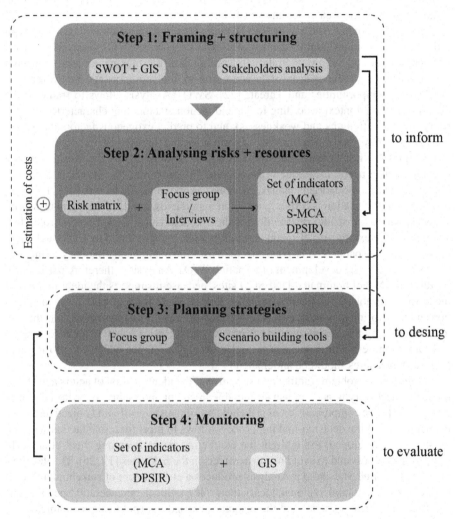

Fig. 1. Multi-step approach for managing WHSs in MPs

4.1 Framing and Structuring the Decision Context

Adequate problem framing and structuring are pivotal for a high-quality decision-making process [20]. This frame should be clear about the issue or opportunity being studied as well as what has to be accomplished (i.e., the decision objectives). Problem framing and structuring in territorial planning and regeneration processes are generally developed through SWOT analysis, Strategic Choice Approach, cognitive mapping [11]. Additionally, the explicit consideration of the spatial dimension, using geographical maps, can significantly contribute to the territorial planning and management processes due to their inherent spatial nature, which is illustrated by the heterogeneous distribution of the characteristics of the area under analysis [21].

Within this context, the use of SWOT Analysis in combination with GIS data can provide adequate knowledge of the decision-making process. SWOT Analysis is a decision support tool that allows the rationalization of decision-making processes, through the organization of the relevant data according to four components, i.e., Strengths, Weaknesses, Opportunities and Threats [22]. SWOT Analysis allows to frame of the decision-making context according to the endogenous factors that characterize the territory (through strengths and weaknesses), and to predict exogenous factors that externally may or may not happen (through opportunities and threats) [19, 23]. In the context of managing UNESCO sites, the SWOT Analysis is suggested by the World Heritage Committee as a useful technique to be adopted [5]. However, the SWOT is generally implemented as a 4-quadrants matrix, by simply pinpointing the factors [24]. This way of collecting information is certainly useful in many fields, but it is limiting in territorial analysis, where the spatial distribution of the characteristics plays a crucial role [11]. Within this context, the use of spatial data, elaborated and processed by a GIS and, then, organized into a spatial SWOT Analysis, increases the quality and efficiency of the outcomes obtained. The development of a spatial SWOT Analysis is therefore particularly useful in the MP of nominated UNESCO sites, because it supports the identification of the most vulnerable areas within the region (Weaknesses) that require defense intervention and monitoring measures, as well as the environmental and physical aspects that are most affected by human intervention (Threats) and the most valuable areas (Strengths and Opportunities) within the region under investigation, for which monitoring and protection measures should be anticipated [11].

Moreover, in problem framing and structuring, the identification of actors and stakeholders is necessary to accomplish sustainable, resilient and inclusive territorial strategies [11, 25]. The comprehension of stakeholders' interests, needs, and objectives, since the beginning of the decision-making process allows to meet their satisfaction with the project to be developed, to highlight the conflicting interests among them at an early stage of the process and to avoid negative effects in the next ones [19, 26]. The development of structured Stakeholder Analysis produces a clear picture of stakeholders' level of intervention (national, regional, local), their role (political, bureaucratic, special interest, general interest, experts) and the resources carried out (political, economic, legal, cognitive) [27]. Additionally, by using specific tools, such as Power-Interest Matrix, Stakeholder Circle or Social Network Analysis is possible to map stakeholders' power, interest, urgency and proximity in a specific decision-making process, and their possible relationships [28–31]. In the context of managing nominated UNESCO sites, an analysis of the stakeholders is suggested by the World Heritage Committee [5]. However, most of the MPs simply list the stakeholders, without collecting the information and knowledge from using Stakeholder Analysis tools.

4.2 Analyzing Risks and Resources

The development of an assessment model of risks is fundamental for the conservation and management of heritage sites. The increasing risks that we have to face, both caused by natural events and man-made actions, require a systematic organization and collection of information and data [10]. Without them, it becomes hard to define adequate measures for the conservation of protected sites both in the short and long term.

In particular, for the nomination of a WHS, the analysis of the risks has to consider the analysis of actual and potential damages to the building, as well as to the environment [9]. Since the main focus in this step is on the heritage site, the analysis should start with the development of a risk matrix. The risk matrix is used in risk assessment to identify the level of risk according to the probability and severity of the event. In the matrix, it is, therefore, possible to locate the risks from the most certain to the rare probability of occurrence and from the minor to the most catastrophic severity. This allows to classify from very high risks to rare. Ni et al. (2010) [32] review a widely applied semi-quantitative tool for risk assessment, namely the risk matrix approach (RMA) as well as its typical variations. Besides the simplicity of the risk matrix, it represents a useful and easy-to-understand tool for enhancing risk visibility and supporting management decision-making. Its potential can be increased by involving experts and local stakeholders in the identification of the risks, through focus groups or interviews.

Once the matrix is filled, a set of indicators can be defined to monitor the most critical and certain risks over time. According to the specificity of the site under investigation, other methods and tools can support the analysis of the risks, such as using a DPSIR framework [33], S-MCA or spatial risk analysis tool [34], such as the Severity Risk Index (SRI) [35], which considers the spatial and temporal evolution of the extreme events.

In parallel to this phase, it can be useful, as suggested by the Italian National Commission for UNESCO Sites and Local Tourist Systems, to identify and estimate the financial resources available and acquired from the different governmental levels (i.e., local, regional or national).

4.3 Planning Strategies

A crucial step in the MP is the definition of the projects to be developed after the inclusion in the WHL. Each project has to be detailed according to the goals to be achieved, the strategies, tactics and actions, as well as in the prediction of the expected results [9]. This phase represents the creative moment in the MP, in which the characteristics of the local system, social and economic aspects and valorization have to be put together to form the development model. The development model has to identify intervention priorities and the articulation of the actions according to different time spans, in order to guarantee the real applicability of the proposed actions.

In the context of project definition in times of uncertainty and complexity, as for heritage sites, scenario building (also called scenario planning) has assumed increasing emphasis [36]. According to Kahn (1967) [37], one of the fathers of scenario planning theory, a scenario is intended as "a set of hypothetical events set in the future constructed to clarify a possible chain of causal events as well as their decision points". Scenario planning is in fact able to deal with uncertainty and complexity in the entire decision-making process, increasing the consideration of a variety of potential future alternatives in a holistic, coherent, systematic and comprehensive manner [36, 38–40]. A variety of approaches and techniques can be used for scenario building, ranging from simple to complex, and qualitative to quantitative. Among the others, we can list STEEP or PESTEL analysis, interviews with stakeholders and comprehensive structural analysis using sophisticated computer tools (e.g., Micmac, SMIC and Mactor analysis), Wilson Matrix, Fuzzy Cognitive Map (FCM) based scenarios, trend impact and cross-impact analysis, double uncertainty 2x2 matrix or morphological analysis. For a comprehensive overview of all approaches and techniques for scenario planning, it is possible to see Amer et al. (2013) [36].

In the context of MPs of WHSs, scenario building techniques can therefore support the definition of projects through a strategic planning. Theoretical and operational examples of scenario building and scenario planning approaches in UNESCO sites can also be examined in Amer et al. (2013) [36], Assumma et al. (2022) [41], and Godet (2000) [42]. Due to its interdisciplinary approach and the long-term placed-based vision, strategic planning can play a bigger part in planning processes. Since MPs provide guidance for strategies and actions but not defined projects to be developed, this phase could start with interviews or focus groups with experts and stakeholders, then structuring the information gathered through scenario building tools, such as the Wilson Matrix.

4.4 Evaluating and Monitoring

The MP of a tentative site for WHL ends with the definition of indicators that progressively measure the goals achieved or not [9]. To support this phase, a coherent set of indicators must be defined, to take a picture of the state of the system and make eventually corrections to them, through specific actions or policies [43]. The list of indicators must reflect the objectives contained in the MPs, as well as the place-based characteristics of the territory under analysis [44]. In most cases, this list will cover the multidimensionality involved in a complex decision-making process, i.e., social, environmental, economic and cultural aspects [45]. In particular, there are several procedures to organize them, such as the DPSIR framework or MCA. Eventually, MCA can be used to produce a synthetic index, which combines all the information obtained from the multiple indicators representing the state of the system from an overall perspective.

Additionally, it could be useful in this phase to develop coaxial matrices. They allow to understand the interrelations among the strategies proposed, the possible impacts, the environmental components and the different assets involved. In this way, the plan is able to guide the definition of mitigation or monitoring actions [46].

The collection of all the data and their monitoring requires a close relationship with local municipalities and stakeholders [9]. Within this context, the use of an open GIS allows to produce a constantly connected network of shared information.

5   Conclusions

The present paper investigated the evaluation methods and tools that can support the nomination for the WHL and, in particular, the development of the MP. The study started by analysing recent papers and MPs to understand which methodologies were the most useful and used. This analysis showed that the SWOT and the Stakeholder Analysis are primarily adopted in the planning phase, while sets of indicators are selected for the monitoring phase. The implementation phase, instead, is the less investigated one. However, the cases of Padua and Bologna showed that surveys and focus groups can be useful tools in this phase for collecting information and data. In addition, the various phases can be deeply supported by the GIS tool and the use of matrices.

This in-depth analysis results in the proposal of a multi-step and mixed-method approach able to guide the entire process of MP development for WHS, according to the main contents required by the MP. This approach can be seen as a guiding tool for real-world sites nominated for the WHL, which starts from framing and structuring goals, objectives and values, as well as actors and stakeholders involved, and ends with the design, evaluation and monitoring of the project strategies. Deciding what strategies and how to develop them requires a set of strategic decisions, each characterized by multiple objectives and stakeholders, conflicting aspects, intangible elements and high levels of uncertainty (e.g. [47–49]). The adoption of a framework, constituted by existing tools and methods, can facilitate the decision-making process. It can guide decision-makers, researchers, and practitioners in all the fundamental steps of the MP for a WHS.

Future developments of the present work will apply the proposed multi-phase approach to a site nominated to the UNESCO list. Its application to a real-world case study can highlight its potentialities and limits, with particular reference to the specific context under investigation, the scale, and the actors involved.

References

1. UNESCO: Convention Concerning the Protection of the World Cultural and Natural Heritage
2. Cameron, C., Jokilehto, J., ICOMOS: The World Heritage List what is OUV? ; defining the outstanding universal value of cultural world heritage properties (2008)
3. Jokilehto, J.: World Heritage: Defining the Outstanding Universal Value (2006)
4. UNESCO: Operational Guidelines for the Implementation of the World Heritage Convention (2021)
5. Wijesuriya, G., Thompson, J., Young, C.: Managing Cultural World Heritage. UNESCO World Heritage Centre (2013)
6. UNESCO: The Budapest Declaration on World Heritage - Convention concerning the protection of the World Cultural and Natural Heritage (2002)
7. UNESCO: Patrimonio Mondiale. https://www.unesco.it/it/italienellunesco/detail/188#:~:text=In%20base%20alla%20Convenzione%20l,%E2%80%99umanit%C3%A0.%3A%2058%20siti. Accessed 30 Mar 2023
8. Pontiglione, I.: Valutazione Economica Spazializzata del Paesaggio del Roero (2018)
9. Ministero per i Beni e le Attività Culturali: Il modello del Piano di Gestione dei Beni Culturali iscritti alla lista del Patrimonio dell'Umanità - Linee Guida (2004)
10. Appiotti, F., et al.: Definition of a risk assessment model within a European interoperable database platform (EID) for cultural heritage. J. Cult. Herit. **46**, 268–277 (2020). https://doi.org/10.1016/j.culher.2020.08.001

11. Ferretti, V.: Framing territorial regeneration decisions: purpose, perspective and scope. Land Use Policy **102** (2021). https://doi.org/10.1016/j.landusepol.2021.105279

12. Santoro, A., Venturi, M., Agnoletti, M.: Landscape perception and public participation for the conservation and valorization of cultural landscapes: the case of the cinque terre and porto venere unesco site. Land (Basel). **10**, 1–24 (2021). https://doi.org/10.3390/land10020093

13. Bottazzi, C., Bottero, M., Mondini, G., Raineri, D.: Evaluation of the tourist demand in Management Plans for UNESCO sites: the case of the Cinque Terre Park (Italy). In: 2006 First International Symposium on Environment Identities and Mediterranean Area, pp. 367–372. IEEE (2006). https://doi.org/10.1109/ISEIMA.2006.345006

14. Comune di Padova: Giotto's Scrovegni Chapel and Padua's fourteenth-century fresco cycles Management Plan (2021)

15. Comune di Bologna: The Porticoes of Bologna - Management plan (2020)

16. Ministry of Cultural Heritage and Tourism, I.: Le colline del Prosecco di Conegliano e Valdobbiadene - Management Plan (2019)

17. Comune di Venezia: Venezia e la sua Laguna Patrimonio Mondiale UNESCO - Piano di Gestione 2012–2018 (2012)

18. Meissner, H.I., Creswell, J.W., Klassen, A.C., Clark, V.L.P., Smith, K.C.: Best practices for mixed methods research in the health sciences (2011)

19. Bottero, M., Assumma, V., Caprioli, C., Dell'Ovo, M.: Decision making in urban development: the application of a hybrid evaluation method for a critical area in the city of Turin (Italy). Sustain Cities Soc. **72**, 103028 (2021). https://doi.org/10.1016/j.scs.2021.103028

20. Spetzler, C., Winter, H., Meyer, J.: Decision quality: value creation from better business decisions (2016)

21. Ferretti, V., Montibeller, G.: Key challenges and meta-choices in designing and applying multi-criteria spatial decision support systems. Decis. Supp. Syst. **84**, 41–52 (2016). https://doi.org/10.1016/j.dss.2016.01.005

22. Humphrey, A.: SWOT analysis for management consulting. SRI Alumni Newsl. **1**, 7–8 (2005)

23. Treves, A., Bottero, M., Caprioli, C., Comino, E.: The reintroduction of Castor fiber in Piedmont (Italy): an integrated SWOT-spatial multicriteria based approach for the analysis of suitability scenarios. Ecol Indic. **118**, 106748 (2020). https://doi.org/10.1016/j.ecolind.2020.106748

24. Geneletti, D., Bagli, S., Napolitano, P., Pistocchi, A.: Spatial decision support for strategic environmental assessment of land use plans: a case study in Southern Italy. Environ. Impact Assess. Rev. **27**, 408–423 (2007). https://doi.org/10.1016/j.eiar.2007.02.005

25. Dell'Anna, F., Dell'Ovo, M.: A stakeholder-based approach managing conflictual values in urban design processes: the case of an open prison in Barcelona. Land Use Policy **114**, 105934 (2022). https://doi.org/10.1016/j.landusepol.2021.105934

26. Gill, L., Lange, E., Morgan, E., Romano, D.: An Analysis of usage of different types of visualisation media within a collaborative planning workshop environment. Environ. Plan. B Plan. Des. **40**, 742–754 (2013). https://doi.org/10.1068/b38049

27. Dente, B.: Understanding Policy Decisions, pp. 1–27. Springer, Heidelberg (2014)

28. Mendelow, A.L.: Environmental scanning--the impact of the stakeholder concept. In: ICIS 1981 Proceedings, vol. 20 (1981)

29. Bourne, L., Walker, D.H.T.: Visualising and mapping stakeholder influence. Manag. Decis. **43**, 649–660 (2005). https://doi.org/10.1108/00251740510597680

30. Guilarte, M., Marin, B., Mayntz, R.: Policy networks: empirical evidence and theoretical considerations. Contemp Sociol. **23**, 425 (1994). https://doi.org/10.2307/2075363

31. Rhodes, R.A.W., Peters, B.G.: Understanding govenance: policy networks, governance, reflexivity and accountability. Public Adm. **76**, 408–409 (1998). https://doi.org/10.1111/1467-9299.00107

32. Ni, H., Chen, A., Chen, N.: Some extensions on risk matrix approach. Saf. Sci. **48**, 1269–1278 (2010). https://doi.org/10.1016/j.ssci.2010.04.005

33. de Bisthoven, L.J., et al.: Social-ecological assessment of Lake Manyara basin, Tanzania: a mixed method approach. J. Environ. Manag. **267**, 11059 (2020). https://doi.org/10.1016/j.jen vman.2020.110594

34. Ferretti, V., Bottero, M., Mondini, G.: Decision making and cultural heritage: an application of the multi-attribute value theory for the reuse of historical buildings. J. Cult. Herit. **15**, 644–655 (2014). https://doi.org/10.1016/j.culher.2013.12.007

35. Trakas, D.N., Panteli, M., Hatziargyriou, N.D., Mancarella, P.: Spatial risk analysis of power systems resilience during extreme events. Risk Anal. **39**, 195–211 (2019). https://doi.org/10.1111/risa.13220

36. Amer, M., Daim, T.U., Jetter, A.: A review of scenario planning. Futures **46**, 23–40 (2013). https://doi.org/10.1016/j.futures.2012.10.003

37. Kahn, H., Wiener, A.J.: The next thirty-three years: a framework for speculation. Daedalus **96**, 705–732 (1967)

38. Coates, J.F.: Scenario planning. Technol. Forecast. Soc. Change **65**, 115–123 (2000). https://doi.org/10.1016/S0040-1625(99)00084-0

39. Jetter, A.J.M.: Educating the guess: strategies, concepts and tools for the fuzzy front end of product development. In: PICMET 2003: Portland International Conference on Management of Engineering and Technology Technology Management for Reshaping the World, pp. 261–273. Portland State University (2003). https://doi.org/10.1109/PICMET.2003.1222803

40. Burt, G., van der Heijden, K.: First steps: towards purposeful activities in scenario thinking and future studies. Futures **35**, 1011–1026 (2003). https://doi.org/10.1016/S0016-3287(03)000 65-X

41. Assumma, V., Bottero, M., De Angelis, E., Lourenço, J.M., Monaco, R., Soares, A.J.: Scenario building model to support the resilience planning of winemaking regions: the case of the Douro territory (Portugal). Sci. Total Environ. **838**, 155889 (2022). https://doi.org/10.1016/j.scitot env.2022.155889

42. Godet, M.: The art of scenarios and strategic planning. Technol. Forecast. Soc. Change **65**, 3–22 (2000). https://doi.org/10.1016/S0040-1625(99)00120-1

43. Berisha, E., Caprioli, C., Cotella, G.: Unpacking SDG target 11.a: what is it about and how to measure its progress? City Environ. Interact. **14**, 100080 (2022). https://doi.org/10.1016/j.cacint.2022.100080

44. Cassatella, C., Bagliani, F.: The management and upkeep of landscape. Considerations from the management plans for the UNESCO World Heritage Sites (2014)

45. Peano, A., Bottero, M., Cassatella, C.: Proposal for a set of indicators. In: Landscape Indicators, pp. 193–215. Springer, Dordrecht (2011). https://doi.org/10.1007/978-94-007-036 6-7_9

46. Picuno, P., Tortora, A., Capobianco, R.L.: Analysis of plasticulture landscapes in Southern Italy through remote sensing and solid modelling techniques. Landsc. Urban Plan **100**, 45–56 (2011). https://doi.org/10.1016/j.landurbplan.2010.11.008

47. Leccis, F.: Regeneration programmes: enforcing the right to housing or fostering gentrification? the example of bankside in London. Land Use Policy **89**, 104217 (2019). https://doi.org/10.1016/j.landusepol.2019.104217

48. Omidipoor, M., Jelokhani-Niaraki, M., Moeinmehr, A., Sadeghi-Niaraki, A., Choi, S.-M.: A GIS-based decision support system for facilitating participatory urban renewal process. Land Use Policy **88**, 104150 (2019). https://doi.org/10.1016/j.landusepol.2019.104150

49. Ferretti, V., Grosso, R.: Designing successful urban regeneration strategies through a behavioral decision aiding approach. Cities **95**, 102386 (2019). https://doi.org/10.1016/j.cities.2019.06.017

Evaluating Nature-Based Solutions Impacts: A Preliminary Framing of Assessment Methods

Vanessa Assumma[1](✉) ⓘ, Giulia Datola[2] ⓘ, Carlotta Quagliolo[3] ⓘ,
and Alessandra Oppio[2] ⓘ

[1] Department of Architecture, Università di Bologna, 40136 Bologna, Italy
vanessa.assumma@unibo.it
[2] Department of Architecture and Urban Studies, Politecnico di Milano, 20133 Milan, Italy
{giulia.datola,alessandra.oppio}@polimi.it
[3] Interuniversity Department of Regional and Urban Studies and Planning, Politecnico di Torino, 10125 Torino, Italy
carlotta.quagliolo@polito.it

Abstract. Nature-based Solutions (NBS) are increasingly promoted to support resilient urban planning. However, integrating NBS into traditional urban planning requires knowledge about the NBS impacts within the environmental, economic, and social spheres. The objective of this paper is to contribute to this knowledge, by systematically identifying assessment methods 'both qualitative and quantitative' for NBS impacts evaluation. This literature review is not fully comprehensive, whereas this study represents a first attempt and aims at guiding future research in this field. The literature review is developed according to a threefold approach that represents the sustainability paradigm, i.e., environmental compatibility, economic development, and social equality. From the literature review imbalances are detected between the environmental, economic, and social spheres.

This contribution is addressed to public and private bodies dealing with NBS, regarding urban practitioners addressing a comprehensive NBS impacts assessment within urban and territorial transformations.

The results of this literature review underline criticalities in dealing with NBS issues comprehensively.

Keywords: Nature-Based Solutions (NBS) · Multiple impact evaluation · Monetary and non-monetary evaluation · Quanti-Qualitative assessment

1 Introduction

As cities are rapidly growing and densifying, urban green spaces play an increasingly vital role in the sustainability challenges associated with urbanization [1]. In Europe, over the latest years, funds such as the Next Generation Europe to the European Regional Development Fund are soliciting country members' governments at all levels with huge amounts of economic financing to invest in nature and secure the future for generations. Planning and evaluation of urban and territorial transformations are given great consideration to reach high and ambitious targets like climate neutrality and net zero emissions by 2050. In this exceptional time, it must be recognized that several of these efforts are remaining on charter. This becomes evident in some realities when these economic financings reach a local level (i.e. municipal, neighbourhood, or building). Good intentions clash with political, technical, and financial barriers. For example, the reporting of well-known and emerging best practices on budgeting the nature neutrality (e.g. Colombian, English, French, or Italian experiences [2–4]) seems to be still observed by local bodies through a "lanternosophy" approach; or it can happen that when public and private sectors are willing to cooperate, there is a high probability to unbalancing the project dimensions, sometimes due to policy agendas ticking and economic revenues. With an exception for strategic and pilot experiences, a foresight vision capable to orient the implementation of the project for a "Good Anthropocene" is still missing operatively (Bennet et al., 2016). On the one hand, new constructions look mainly at costs and revenues and risk investments to support and secure finance, even if private subjects often must agree on (environmental) mitigation and compensation actions with public bodies. Environmental quality, community safety, and well-being took a backseat too frequently and then excluded from the process cause of the lack of economic resources. The effects of these choices are quite evident showing their implication today. On the other hand, reconstruction and regeneration processes deal with (and should make that here and after) externalities to produce socio-economic benefits. Particularly, the need for a reform of public expenditure with regard to green finance should be evident to all the parties more than ever. The concept of Nature-based solutions (NBS) comes as an alternative that can act at several levels, being more than just an aesthetical improvement.

NBS appears as an attempt to face this issue. NBS is a term introduced by the European Commission (EC) in 2015. EU defines NBS as *"Solutions that aim to help societies address a variety of environmental, social, and economic challenges in sustainable ways. They are actions inspired by, supported by or copied from nature, both using and enhancing existing solutions to challenges as well as exploring more novel solutions. Nature-based solutions use the features and complex system processes of nature, such as its ability to store carbon and regulate water flows, in order to achieve desired outcomes, such as reduced disaster risk and an environment that improves human well-being and socially inclusive green growth"* [5].

NBS are transversal to hot research topics such as ecosystem adaptation, green, blue, and grey infrastructures, Natural Climate Solutions (NCS), ecological engineering, Disaster Risk Reduction (DRR) and Disaster Risk Management (DRM) [6].

In light of this evidence, the authors identified the following research questions: i) *"What are the tools that can support an integrated assessment and design of an NBS project?"*, and ii) *"How to support a NBS implementation across the environmental quality, the social inclusion and safety, and the economic feasibility?"*.

NBS is considered the new planning tool to overcome the boundaries of traditional approaches 'predict and prevent', while playing a crucial role in addressing societal challenges and providing benefits through the supply of Ecosystem Services (ES). By connecting people with nature, NBS have a proven positive impact on citizens' well-being such as on public health, physical and social resilience, equity, inclusiveness, and social equity [7]. At the same time, they can reduce the carbon footprint of cities, if wisely designed, constructed, and managed [8]. Their effects referred to ES depend on the way the NBS are aligned with the physical, social, economic, and environmental driving forces in an urban district [9] or more in general in a territory.

The increasing attention to NBS impacts by proving their effectiveness influence positively the willingness to include these solutions in spatial transformations. Determining NBS costs distributed over time (within climate scenarios) helps to better integrate such solutions into urban and territorial planning and project design as well [10]. However, designing and evaluating long-term adaptation strategies is still a challenge [11]. They depend on complex and uncertain factors that cannot be all foresighted, but it is possible to envision impacting strategies, thanks to the support of scenario-based tools [12, 13]. The various methodologies that can assess a wide range of NBS impacts within the environmental, economic, and social challenges, demonstrate the NBS impacts assessment framework as complex and interdisciplinary. Therefore, the current demand is providing a comprehensive evaluation framework that embraces all the NBS implementation aspects [14].

The objective of this study is to review the NBS impacts assessment methods by collecting and analyzing the existing quanti-qualitative methodologies within the environmental, economic, and social spheres. These spheres were selected because they represent the pillars of sustainable development, which NBS implementation strives to implement and achieve in its multidimensionality. Hence, this contribution represents a first attempt to collect such methodologies in an integrated way to support climate change adaptation planning.

This study is addressed to both public and private bodies, with attention on urban practitioners in addressing a more comprehensive NBS impacts assessment while helping to integrate such solutions in spatial planning strategies and project interventions.

2 Methodology

This study proposes a preliminary insight to collect qualitative, quantitative, monetary, and non-monetary evaluation frameworks to address NBS impacts in urban and territorial transformations, according to the social, economic, and environmental dimensions. Three different preliminary literature reviews are developed according to the threefold force of the sustainability paradigm (Fig. 1).

The first review concerns the identification of the most applied evaluation methods in the environmental field. The second review is of economic type, that collects the main valuation techniques to estimate NBS feasibility in both the economic-financial and the socio-economic terms, along the project cycle and alternative solutions. The third review is a preliminary insight to collect several assessment frameworks applied in the social sphere to address the social impacts of NBS implementation.

This methodological research aims to deliver an overview of the most applied evaluation methods of the environmental, economic, and social spheres, that are retained and suitable for NBS design, construction, and implementation while examining both shortcomings and challenges. The three literature reviews go beyond the single-based risk approach to focus on the multiple risks assessment (e.g., floods, landslides, heatwaves, or climate change, among others).

The three reviews have been developed parallelly and have been carried out using the same methodological framework (Fig. 1). The expected output is to integrate the results of each review into an overall discussion to support the final users actively involved in the NBS project and assessment phases.

AN INTEGRATED ASSESSMENT FOR NATURE-BASED SOLUTIONS

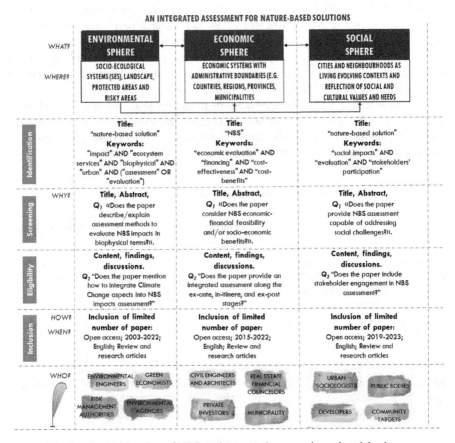

Fig. 1. Threefold review of NBS environmental, economic, and social spheres.

3 Analysis of the Evaluation Methodologies

In this paper, the attention is devoted only to publications of relevant literature, with the purpose to deepen this analysis and including policy documents and reports in a next study of the authors. The research was performed using the Scopus platform, according to the environmental, economic, and social lens.

3.1 Environmental Sphere

For the systematic literature review, the search of peer-reviewed articles was limited to the last 20 years, from 2003 to 2022. The concept of NBS is very recent, thus making it unnecessary to account for a longer time span. The articles were retrieved from Scopus in April 2023 using a search string by including various terms (see Fig. 1).

The screening phase (see criteria in Fig. 1) was performed to analyse papers describing quantitative or qualitative environmental assessment methods in urban contexts. As results of the search phase, 36 articles (review and research peer reviewed papers) of which only 19 are open access. Results from the abstract screening gave a number of three articles (see Table 1). Those papers excluded are focused on the concept of urban resilience, or ecosystem services mapping as well as the stakeholders risk perception to promote NBS, or specific on agricultural field (for example [15–17]).

Raymond et al. (2017) presented a set of principles to ensure holistic co-benefit assessments. The need to consider how to monitor and evaluate the effectiveness of NBS interventions into any NBS policy is crucial as well as considering how such assessments are embedded within a holistic process of option selection.

Table 1. Contributions found on NBS environmental sphere.

Authors and year	Description	Risk typology	Spatial dimension	Climate change aspect
Raymond et al. (2017) [20]	Holistic assessment framework for NBS co-benefits (and costs): socio-cultural and socio-economic systems, biodiversity, ecosystems, and climate	Multi-risk	Not mentioned	Not mentioned
Kumar et al. (2021) [19]	Review on methods, including ground-based measurements (e.g., gauging stations, wireless sensor network) and remote sensing observations used to monitor the performance of NBS	Hydro-meteorological risk (floods, droughts, heatwaves, landslides, storm surges and coastal erosion)	Not mentioned	Not mentioned
Ommer et al. (2022) [18]	Development of a comprehensive guidance on quantitative pre-assessment of potential co-benefits and disbenefits of NBS tackling Disaster Risk Reduction (DRR)	Multi-risk	Not mentioned	General overview

Later, another attempt to review existing NBS co-benefit assessment frameworks and quantification methods has been done [1]. Ommer et al. (2022) reviews methodologies that can be adopted for the pre-assessment of NBS co-benefits and disbenefits. This analysis summarizes frameworks and tools introduced into NBS assessment by presenting their focus, assessment type, and approached indicators [18].

More in detail, Kumar et al. (2021) presents various NBS performance indicators for the ecological/environmental sphere focused on the hydro-meteorological risk [19].

3.2 Economic Sphere

Before providing a literature review on the economic sphere, some preliminary remarks are needed. In the latest years, NBS have been (re)discovered by investors as capable of expressing a "good value for money"[21]. This is a high opportunity to get in this historical time. On the one hand, the global economy uncertainty and carrying at the same time secure and predictable revenues. On the other hand, the attention on losses, damages, and effects unequally distributed at spatial and social levels [22]. This can facilitate to rethink the design and planning of territory under Climate Change, thus looking for a zeroing of land and biodiversity degradation. The United Nations Environmental Programme (UNEP) published a financial gap equal to about USD 403 billion/year, where USD 133 billion/year are invested in NBS, whereas USD 536 billion/year are financing that need of NBS [23]. Yet finance flows to NBS are currently only USD 154 billion/year, which is less than half of the USD 384 billion/year investment in NBS needed by 2025 and only one-third of the investment needed by 2030 (USD 484 billion/year) [24]. Public-private partnerships play a crucial role to enable the environment's quality as capitalization of private capital. Even if this scenario is very appealing, its implementation in the next future will depend on governance, such as green public reforms in countries with different systems of governments, new forms of investment, or the estimation of NBS benefits as loan from the future.

The support of both traditional and novel economic tools can make the change happen. The location area, the project intentionality, and the *desiderata* by economic subjects (i.e. public bodies, developers, banks, real estate and financial advisors) can lead to the building of an economic framework by choosing specific evaluation tools and not others. Additional factors are the NBS level (e.g. building blocks, transformation areas, or water bodies) and the expected transformation. For example, a NBS project should strategically be supported by localisation studies to identify the most suitable site in terms of environmental compatibility, social well-being, and economic income [25].

NBS financial sustainability and intentionality are crucial requirements for feasibility investment, thus making even more central the common saying "no budget, no party". The project feasibility must satisfy both costs and revenues by considering profitability indicators to well support socio-economic benefits estimation. The NBS catalogue for urban resilience by World Bank provides costs grouped in costs of land, construction and implementation, and maintenance [26]. They can vary according to country, location, projects factors, and to general market rules that may influence on land, labor, and material prices.

In the light of this context, a set of queries have been submitted in the Scopus database by considering the combination of the following keywords:

- Q1 "NBS" AND "economic evaluation" = 18 results They are all ranged between 2015 and 2022. Most of the results belong to subject areas out of the topic of this paper (e.g. "Medicine", or "Immunology and Microbiology"). They are filtered and only three studies are considered ("Environment Science", "Agricultural and Biological Science", and "Social Science");
- Q2: "NBS" AND "economic evaluation" AND "financing" = One result. The addition of "financing" keyword has drastically reduced the results [6];
- Q3: "NBS" AND "monetary" AND "decision making"= One result. The study [27] surveys both contextual and attitudinal domains of NBS to identify barriers and drivers related to flood risk;
- Q4: "NBS" AND "cost-effectiveness" AND "co-benefits"= Six results. To complete the literature review with the investigation of NBS and socio-economic, a last query was submitted to Scopus, by changing the query. They are centered on subject areas "Environmental science" and "Social Science", "Earth and Planetary Science", and "Energy".

Despite the high interest in the field, the literature search has highlighted that economic part is not sufficiently explored yet than the environmental and social spheres. In fact, despite the changing and/or addition of keywords of the queries, few meaningful results are found and retained suitable for the aim of the paper (Table 2):

Table 2. Contributions found on NBS economic sphere.

Author and Year	Description	Project phases		
		Project idea	Definition project	Executive project
Wild et al. (2017) [28]	Comparison of benefits of urban greening development scenarios	✓	✓	
Hagedoon et al. (2021) [6]	NBS economic evaluation through stated preference methods, focusing on time than monetary contributions	✓		
Quagliolo et al. (2022) [10]	Cost and benefits for NBS implementation and costs of operation and maintenance	✓	✓	✓
Raymond et al. (2017) [20]	Seven-stage process for co-benefit assessment within policy and project implementation	✓	✓	

(*continued*)

Table 2. (*continued*)

Author and Year	Description	Project phases		
		Project idea	Definition project	Executive project
Debele et al. (2019) [29]	NBS costs, benefits, and effectiveness for hard engineering structures for the management of HMR impact	✓	✓	
Kumar et al. (2021) [19]	Assessments of NBS performance in different risky contexts, according to a co-construction approach in the experimentation and modelling	✓	✓	✓
Menon (2021) [30]	NBS cost-effectiveness as a remedy and generation of co-benefits for health and biodiversity	✓	✓	
Vail Castro (2022) [31]	Optimization tools to support NBS in hydrological, environmental, and social co-benefits (SWMM, Gini index)	✓	✓	✓

Even if these keywords stressed a hole in this NBS arena, it is possible to detect a slight increase in publications. The selected studies look for monetization of NBS benefits and the produced ES as a revenue stream. Most of the contributions concentrate on the estimation of NBS benefits, damage cost, avoided costs, and the difficulty of standardizing procedures to monetize the value (i.e. use and non-use).

There is also a certain short-sightedness on the financing issue in terms of lack of suitable financial instruments, high transaction costs for small project sizes, and the lack of tracked financial performance increase thus the perception of risk to invest in NBS. In addition, governments priorities agendas and the financial coping capacity of the world countries could influence the budget availability, amplifying in some cases the scissors between developed and developing countries [6].

Hence, the authors make a parallelism to state that economic techniques traditionally employed in the fields of building engineering, architecture, and spatial planning, can be adapted to estimate the NBS economic value. Indeed, awareness has only recently been raised to include construction and implementation costs in an integrated vision (and thus together environmental and social features). Moreover, technical project and economic evaluations are strictly related for their parallel and simultaneous development.

The following techniques can support the several phases of an NBS project, from the idea, passing from the design, until to the project as-built (Table 3). These are listed according to the approach, the project phases, and the contribution that each one can provide to NBS. Some of them can be replicated in more phases for a refinement of the project evaluation, such as the Life Cycle Costing Analysis (LCCA) or the Multi-Criteria Analysis (MCA).

Table 3. Overview of economic techniques according to the NBS project cycle phases

Project phases	Economic approach	Techniques	Contribution
Phase 1 – Project idea	Synthetic	Parametric estimating	Span evaluation of the project based on parameter(s) to identify the scale of project costs
Phase 2 – Definitive Project	Mixed	Multi-Criteria Analysis (MCA)	Identification of the most suitable project between alternatives. Project actions ranking
		Single and Multiple Regression Analysis (MRA)	Estimation of benefit or damage to obtain a variation in well-being. Willingness to Pay (WTP) / Willingness to Accept (WTA) for an NBS and/or damages that can be prevented/mitigated by the project
		Discount-Cash Flow Analysis (DFCA)	Provision of the future cash-flows, including timing, entity and investment risk
		Cost-Benefit Analysis (CBA)	It complements feasibility study of the project through the estimation of the effects of a public investment and including alternative locations of resources
		Life Cycle Cost Analysis (LCCA)	Obtaining of the lowest whole project cost, in terms of construction, implementation, management and dismission. Possible refinement for a lowering of costs

(*continued*)

Table 3. (*continued*)

Project phases	Economic approach	Techniques	Contribution
		Life Cycle Cost-Effectiveness (LCCE)	Estimation of project costs and selection of the best investment program
		Sales Comparison Approach (SCA) or General Appraisal System (GAS)	Estimation of the NBS value market through a comparison with similar comparable
Phase 3 – Executive Project	Analytic	Estimate Metric Calculation (EMC)	Measurement of project elements and cost estimation on related prices
Phase 4 – Project as Built	Mixed	Direct costing or Full costing or Activity Based Costing (ABC)	Management control of the costs based on the project activities
		Monitoring indicators	Key Performance Indicators (KPI) indicators for the achievement of objectives, the project performance during the construction and after the implementation

3.3 Social Sphere

As for the other analysed spheres, before discussing the specific literature review, it is useful to underline some preliminary remarks. The NBS is actually proposed in urban systems to address and face the current challenge and support cities in the transition to sustainable development. Moreover, the interest in this type of intervention is increasing according to their ability to address social challenges [32] and mitigate the exposure of the population to environmental hazards and other risks related to climate change [14].

According to this statement declared by the literature, a preliminary literature review about the evaluation of NBS impacts in the social sphere was made using the Scopus database. A set of research questions have been asked in the Scopus platform considering the combination of the following keywords, to select only papers in journals:

- "Nature-based solutions" AND "social impacts" = 13 results. These papers are inserted in the time between 2021 and 2023. This fact strongly underlines the novelty of this research topic. They are mainly related to the topic of environmental science and policy and one of the listed papers discusses the problem of green gentrification. However, no none of the listed papers proposes an evaluation framework to be used to evaluate social impacts, or they are not strictly focused on the NBS.

- "Nature-based solutions" AND "social impacts" = 0 result.
- "Nature-based solutions" AND "social impacts" = 0 result.
- "Nature-based solutions" AND "evaluation" AND "social impacts" = Two results. These two papers belong to 2022 and they do not provide a method to assess social impacts, but they address the topic of social impacts evaluation through a methodological framework.

According to these results, other questions have been queried, enlarging the perspective of the research domain. In fact, it addressed the dimension of social participation. Therefore, the question asked is the following:

- "Nature-based solutions" AND "stakeholders' participation" = 21 results. In this case, the time reference is from 2019 to 2023.

Therefore, discussing and providing some critical reflections about the developed literature review is possible.

First of all, the exploration of this topic is very recent, as underlined by the time scales of the results and the small number of papers.

Secondly, most of the considerable papers propose a qualitative evaluation framework constructed by interviews and questionnaires, such as the case study of Barcelona [33, 34].

Thirdly, the stakeholders engagement is the most discusses topic dealing with NBS and the social sphere, due to the fact that the participation of stakeholders is crucial for the effective implementation and management of NBS [14, 35]. In fact, a solution should be ideal from an environmental point of view but it may not be accepted by society [35].

Moreover, it is also necessary to underline that most of the social issues of NBS are evaluated through the ES approach [20].

4 Conclusion and Future Perspectives

This paper has explored the most relevant evaluation approaches suitable to assess NBS impact in the social, economic, and environmental spheres, according to the fact that NBS implementation aims to achieve sustainable development in its multidimensionality [1, 4, 36]. Existing research supported the state of the art of the fact NBS and have the potential to simultaneously provide multiple benefits [14, 37].

NBS can play a very important role within strategic guidelines and recommendations being defined such as for superordinated spatial planning (e.g. metropolitan level, or basin level), to be adopted as technical references within the revision of regulatory planning and in the design of the vision of new municipal plans. This can help public authorities to define the most performing solution in terms of environmental, social, and economic sustainability [38].

The review on the environmental sphere has highlighted that pre-assessment of ecological indicators is more commonly practiced than of socio-economic indicators as the mirror of the global challenges of socio-economic data collection and availability. At the same time, certain direct environmental impacts of NBS have been more researched and documented (e.g. flood protection, habitat conservation) and often focused on their effectiveness to mitigate climate change effects on urban areas. However, frameworks on how to integrate climate change scenarios into NBS impacts assessment in terms of bio-physical effects are missing and the research on this topic is still scarce and fragmented [14].

The main findings of the performed reviews concern the evidence of major gaps in the field of NBS evaluation, especially in the economic and social spheres. On the other hand, the most examined topic concern the assessment of the environmental impacts.

As a future perspective to follow the extended research of the authors, the next steps will use the same approach for the three spheres, thus looking for potentially different results.

The study proposed by Dimitru and colleagues (for reference please see the paper [14]) states that environmental impacts are specifically addressed in 60% of the reviewed articles, while only about 30% address social and health-related impacts, and about 10% economic impacts [14].

Therefore, from this preliminary insight, it is possible to state that the evaluation of the potential impacts of NBS on social, and economic outcomes are understudied and not systematically evaluated today.

A fruitful exploration of the economic frontiers emerges: revenue streams, fiscal interventions (e.g. Tax Increment Financing [39]) flood risk insurance [40], carbon cred-its [41], Biodiversity-Net Gain (BNG), and nutrient neutrality; public-private partnership to decrease the risk of investment, integrating NBS within traditional projects to influence the size of the investment.

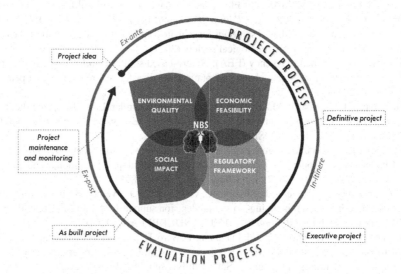

Fig. 2. NBS integrated assessment within real project and evaluation processes.

The multi-directional effects of NBS underline the importance of a holistic approach to their design, construction, and implementation in spatial context by considering both synergies and potential trade-offs [20, 42–45] (Fig. 2).

Co-participation, co-evaluation, and co-design are three fundamental pillars for a winning NBS [46]. In this sense, frameworks like Geo-design can help the communication and the integration of NBS intervention in a territory according to landscape and urban characteristics. Geodesign can promote merging economic, social, and environmental interests into shared solutions [47].

Acknowledgement. Giulia Datola carried out this research within the Agritech National Research Center and received funding from the European Union Next-GenerationEU (PIANO NAZIONALE DI RIPRESA E RESILIENZA (PNRR) – MISSIONE 4 COMPONENTE 2, INVESTIMENTO 1.4 – D.D. 1032 17/06/2022, CN00000022).

References

1. Davis, M., Naumann, S.: Making the case for sustainable urban drainage systems as a nature-based solution to urban flooding. In: Kabisch, N., Korn, H., Stadler, J., Bonn, A. (eds.) Nature-based Solutions to Climate Change Adaptation in Urban Areas. TPUST, pp. 123–137. Springer, Cham (2017). https://doi.org/10.1007/978-3-319-56091-5_8
2. Landholm, D., et al.: Unlocking nature-based solutions in Colombia: Technical Report Unlocking nature-based solutions in Colombia TECHNICAL REPORT Unlocking nature-based solutions in Colombia: Technical Report (2022)
3. Serra-Llobet, A., et al.: Restoring Rivers and Floodplains for Habitat and Flood Risk Reduction: Experiences in Multi-Benefit Floodplain Management From California and Germany. Frontiers Media S.A. (2022). https://doi.org/10.3389/FENVS.2021.778568/BIBTEX
4. Stafford, R., et al.: Nature-based solutions for climate change in the UK: a report by the British ecological society the British ecological society (2021)
5. European Environmental Agency (EEA): Nature-based solutions in Europe: Policy, knowledge and practice for climate change adaptation and disaster risk reduction. , Copenhagen, Denmark (2021)
6. Hagedoorn, L.C., Koetse, M.J., van Beukering, P.J.H., Brander, L.M.: Reducing the finance gap for nature-based solutions with time contributions. Ecosyst. Serv. **52**, 101371 (2021). https://doi.org/10.1016/J.ECOSER.2021.101371
7. European Environmental Agency (EEA): Urban adaptation to climate change in Europe - Challenges and opportunities for cities together with supportive national and European policies. , Luxembourg (2012). https://doi.org/10.2800/41895
8. Grêt-Regamey, A., Altwegg, J., Sirén, E.A., van Strien, M.J., Weibel, B.: Integrating ecosystem services into spatial planning—a spatial decision support tool. Landsc. Urban Plan. **165**, 206–219 (2017). https://doi.org/10.1016/J.LANDURBPLAN.2016.05.003
9. Langemeyer, J., Wedgwood, D., McPhearson, T., Baró, F., Madsen, A.L., Barton, D.N.: Creating urban green infrastructure where it is needed – a spatial ecosystem service-based decision analysis of green roofs in Barcelona. Sci. Total Environ. **707**, 135487 (2020). https://doi.org/10.1016/j.scitotenv.2019.135487
10. Quagliolo, C., Roebeling, P., Mendonça, R., Pezzoli, A., Comino, E.: Integrating biophysical and economic assessment : review of nature-based adaptation to urban flood extremes. Urban Sci. **6**, 1–23 (2022)
11. Aerts, J.C.J.H.: A review of cost estimates for flood adaptation. Water (Switzerland) **10**, 1646 (2018). https://doi.org/10.3390/w10111646
12. Godet, M.: The art of scenarios and strategic planning: tools and pitfalls. Technol. Forecast. Soc. Change. **65**, 3–22 (2000). https://doi.org/10.1016/S0040-1625(99)00120-1

13. Amer, M., Daim, T.U., Jetter, A.: A review of scenario planning. Futures **46**, 23–40 (2013). https://doi.org/10.1016/J.FUTURES.2012.10.003

14. Dumitru, A., Frantzeskaki, N., Collier, M.: Identifying principles for the design of robust impact evaluation frameworks for nature-based solutions in cities. Environ. Sci. Policy. **112**, 107–116 (2020). https://doi.org/10.1016/j.envsci.2020.05.024

15. Sarabi, S., Han, Q., de Vries, B., Romme, A.G.L.: The nature-based solutions planning support system: a playground for site and solution prioritization. Sustain. Cities Soc. **78**, 103608 (2022). https://doi.org/10.1016/j.scs.2021.103608

16. Kumar, B.M., Kunhamu, T.K.: Nature-Based Solutions Nature-based solutions in agriculture : a review of the coconut (Cocos nucifera L .) -based farming systems in Kerala, the Land of Coconut Trees. Nature-Based Solut. **2**, 100012 (2022). https://doi.org/10.1016/j.nbsj.2022. 100012

17. Santoro, S., Pluchinotta, I., Pagano, A., Pengal, P., Cokan, B., Giordano, R.: Assessing stakeholders' risk perception to promote Nature Based Solutions as flood protection strategies: the case of the Glinščica river (Slovenia). Sci. Total Environ. **655**, 188–201 (2019). https://doi. org/10.1016/j.scitotenv.2018.11.116

18. Ommer, J., et al.: Quantifying co-benefits and disbenefits of nature-based solutions targeting disaster risk reduction. Int. J. Disast. Risk Reduct. **75**, 102966 (2022). https://doi.org/10.1016/ j.ijdrr.2022.102966

19. Kumar, P., et al.: Nature-based solutions efficiency evaluation against natural hazards: modelling methods, advantages and limitations. Sci. Total Environ. **784**, 147058 (2021). https:// doi.org/10.1016/j.scitotenv.2021.147058

20. Raymond, C.M., et al.: A framework for assessing and implementing the co-benefits of nature-based solutions in urban areas. Environ. Sci. Policy. **77**, 15–24 (2017). https://doi.org/10.1016/ j.envsci.2017.07.008

21. Hall, C.: Nature-based Solutions "Good Value for Money" – UN – ESG Investor, https://www. esginvestor.net/nature-based-solutions-good-value-for-money-un/. Accessed 05 Apr 2023

22. Kosolapova, E., Rosen, T., Templeton, J., Wagner, L.: State of Global Environmental Governance. International Institute for Sustainable Development Earth Negotiations Bulletin (2022)

23. United Nations: UN Environment Programme Annual Report. https://wedocs.unep.org/bitstr eam/handle/20.500.11822/37946/UNEP_AR2021.pdf. Accessed 31 Mar 2023

24. Wild, T., Bulkeley, H., Naumann, S., Vojinovic, Z., Calfapietra, C., Whiteoak, K.: Nature-based solutions: State of the art in EU-funded projects (2020). https://doi.org/10.2777/236007

25. Bottero, M., Mondini, G.: Valutazione e sostenibilità. Piani, programmi, progetti. CELID (2009)

26. World Bank: A Catalogue of Nature-Based Solutions for Urban Resilience. , Washington D.C. (2021)

27. Han, S., Kuhlicke, C.: Barriers and drivers for mainstreaming nature-based solutions for flood risks: the case of South Korea. Int. J. Disast. Risk Sci. **12**(5), 661–672 (2021). https://doi.org/ 10.1007/s13753-021-00372-4

28. Wild, T.C., Henneberry, J., Gill, L.: Comprehending the multiple 'values' of green infrastructure – valuing nature-based solutions for urban water management from multiple perspectives. Environ. Res. **158**, 179–187 (2017). https://doi.org/10.1016/J.ENVRES.2017.05.043

29. Debele, S.E., et al.: Nature-based solutions for hydro-meteorological hazards: revised concepts, classification schemes and databases. Environ. Res. **179**, 108799 (2019). https://doi. org/10.1016/J.ENVRES.2019.108799

30. Menon, J.S., Sharma, R.: Nature-based solutions for co-mitigation of air pollution and urban heat in Indian cities. Front. Sustain. Cities. **3** (2021). https://doi.org/10.3389/FRSC.2021. 705185

31. Vail Castro, C.: Optimizing nature-based solutions by combining social equity, hydro-environmental performance, and economic costs through a novel Gini coefficient. J. Hydrol. X. **16** (2022). https://doi.org/10.1016/J.HYDROA.2022.100127

32. Pauleit, S., Zölch, T., Hansen, R., Randrup, T.B., Konijnendijk van den Bosch, C.: Nature-based solutions and climate change – four shades of green. In: Kabisch, N., Korn, H., Stadler, J., Bonn, A. (eds.) Nature-based Solutions to Climate Change Adaptation in Urban Areas. TPUST, pp. 29–49. Springer, Cham (2017). https://doi.org/10.1007/978-3-319-56091-5_3

33. Ramírez-Agudelo, N.A., Badia, M., Villares, M., Roca, E.: Assessing the benefits of nature-based solutions in the Barcelona metropolitan area based on citizen perceptions. Nature-Based Solut. **2**, 100021 (2022). https://doi.org/10.1016/j.nbsj.2022.100021

34. Giordano, R., Pluchinotta, I., Pagano, A., Scrieciu, A., Nanu, F.: Enhancing nature-based solutions acceptance through stakeholders' engagement in co-benefits identification and trade-offs analysis. Sci. Total Environ. **713**, 136552 (2020). https://doi.org/10.1016/j.scitotenv.2020.136552

35. Sowińska-Świerkosz, B., García, J.: A new evaluation framework for nature-based solutions (NBS) projects based on the application of performance questions and indicators approach. Sci. Total Environ. **787**, 147615 (2021). https://doi.org/10.1016/j.scitotenv.2021.147615

36. Commission, E., et al.: Nature-based solutions : state of the art in EU-funded projects. Publications Office of the European Union (2020). https://doi.org/10.2777/236007

37. Haase, D., et al.: A quantitative review of urban ecosystem service assessments: concepts, models, and implementation. Ambio **43**(4), 413–433 (2014). https://doi.org/10.1007/s13280-014-0504-0

38. Stanganelli, M., Torrieri, F., Gerundo, C., Rossitti, M.: A strategic performance-based planning methodology to promote the regeneration of fragile territories. In: La Rosa, D., Privitera, R. (eds.) INPUT 2021. LNCE, vol. 146, pp. 149–157. Springer, Cham (2021). https://doi.org/10.1007/978-3-030-68824-0_16

39. Toxopeus, H., Polzin, F.: Reviewing financing barriers and strategies for urban nature-based solutions. J. Environ. Manag. **289**, 112371 (2021). https://doi.org/10.1016/J.JENVMAN.2021.112371

40. Vannucci, E., Pagano, A.J., Romagnoli, F.: Climate change management: a resilience strategy for flood risk using Blockchain tools. Decis. Econ. Financ. **44**, 177–190 (2021). https://doi.org/10.1007/S10203-020-00315-6/TABLES/4

41. Uzsoki, D., Casier, L., Wuennenberg, L.: Financial instruments to create and maintain NBS. In: Croci, E., Lucchitta, B. (eds.) Nature-Based Solutions for More Sustainable Cities – A Framework Approach for Planning and Evaluation, pp. 255–266. Emerald Publishing Limited (2021). https://doi.org/10.1108/978-1-80043-636-720211021

42. Bravi, M., Bottero, M., Dell'Anna, F.: An application of the life satisfaction approach (LSA) to value the land consumption and ecosystem services. J. Knowl. Econ. (2023). https://doi.org/10.1007/S13132-023-01150-X

43. Dell'ovo, M., Bassani, S., Stefanina, G., Oppio, A.: Memories at risk: How to support decisions about abandoned industrial heritage regeneration. Valori e Valutazioni. **2020**, 107–115 (2020)

44. Caprioli, C., Bottero, M., De Angelis, E.: Combining an agent-based model, hedonic pricing and multicriteria analysis to model green gentrification dynamics. Comput. Environ. Urban Syst. **102**, 101955 (2023). https://doi.org/10.1016/J.COMPENVURBSYS.2023.101955

45. Colucci, E., et al.: Documenting cultural heritage in an INSPIRE-based 3D GIS for risk and vulnerability analysis. https://doi.org/10.1108/JCHMSD-04-2021-0068

46. Kumar, P., et al.: Towards an operationalisation of nature-based solutions for natural hazards. Sci. Total Environ. **731**, 138855 (2020). https://doi.org/10.1016/J.SCITOTENV.2020.138855

47. Somma, M., Campagna, M., Canfield, T., Cerreta, M., Poli, G., Steinitz, C.: Collaborative and sustainable strategies through geodesign: the case study of bacoli. In: Gervasi, O., Murgante, B., Misra, S., Rocha, A.M.A.C., Garau, C. (eds) Computational Science and Its Applications – ICCSA 2022 Workshops. ICCSA 2022. Lecture Notes in Computer Science, vol. 13379, pp. 210–224. Springer, Cham (2022). https://doi.org/10.1007/978-3-031-10545-6_15

An Evaluation Model to Support Strategic Urban Planning in Italy: The Application of Community Impact Evaluation

Giulio Cavana[✉] [ORCID] and Federico Dell'Anna[ORCID]

Interuniversity Department of Regional and Urban Studies and Planning (DIST), Politecnico di Torino, Viale Mattioli, 39, 10125 Turin, TO, Italy
{giulio.cavana,federico.dellanna}@polito.it

Abstract. Cities and their transformation have increasingly been placed at the center of the debate on how to reach a more sustainable and inclusive society. Indeed, urban planning is not seen any more as a technocratic top-down practice, but rather as a process able to summarize different perspectives on the development of cities. In this sense, public participation has been progressively seen as a fundamental practice in the attempt to democratize the process of defining the directions that such development should take, and to prioritize actions to be taken in the transformation of the territory. Such cooperative attempt would benefit from the use of formalized tools, in order to enhance the transparency of the process and to identify potential conflictual interests and priorities, and, thus promoting negotiation, also including those social groups usually excluded from the decision-making process. The present chapter proposes a methodological framework based on the integration of SWOT, and Stakeholder Analysis into a Community Impact Evaluation (CIE), in order to support Decision-Makers in the preliminary phases of the revision process of land use plans. Such methodology would allow to base the consultation process on a solid and shared informative framework, and to identify the different stakeholder potentially impacted by the outcomes of the implementation of the plan. Finally, the formalization of impacts and goals into matrices would allow to evaluate the potential outcomes that might affect the different stakeholders, and to monitor the effects that the induced transformations would have on them and on the public interests.

Keywords: SWOT analysis · Stakeholder analysis · Participatory planning · Strategic Environmental Assessment (SEA)

1 Introduction

In recent decades, a large number of initiatives has focused on cities in an attempt to foster the achievement of a more sustainable society [1, 2]. Among these, the 2030 Agenda for Sustainable Development [3], specifically addresses cities with its 11th Sustainable Development Goal (SDG), aiming at making "cities and human settlements inclusive, safe, resilient and sustainable". In this sense, the urban environment is conceived as

O. Gervasi et al. (Eds.): ICCSA 2023 Workshops, LNCS 14108, pp. 528–542, 2023.
https://doi.org/10.1007/978-3-031-37117-2_36

a possible source of solutions rather than a cause of potential harmful challenges [4], representing an opportunity to rethink the design of future cities with greater attention to environmental and social inclusion aspects [3]. Furthermore, the application of several new interpretative frameworks to the city, such as the resilience paradigm [5–7], and the circular economy one [8, 9] have implied the management and planning of cities as complex and adaptive systems [10], and the proliferation of evaluation tool in supporting the decision-making process towards its transformation [11].

Indeed, the complex nature of the urban environment in terms of its environmental, economic and social dimensions, is further complicated by the presence of a variety of actors and stakeholders pursuing different goals (both individual and shared) in the production of the city [12, 13].

In the context of increasing pressure on urban space [14], land use planning is still a prominent tool capable to pool together stakeholders' interests [15], allowing the exploitation of resources preserving the balance between public and private interests [16, 17].

Indeed, land use planning tools could be seen as a product of the mediation between general and specific interests in the definition of the overall vision of the development of a territory or a city, with the possibility to favor some at the expenses of others, while determining the territorial and environmental requirements that are considered non-negotiable [18].

At the European level, a common sectoral approach has been observed, in which land-use planning is referred to as the practice to regulate land uses and physical urban form, by exercising authority on use of properties and the rights to transform land; while also a broader scope considering other features of territorial development (i.e. guiding of investments, accessibility to jobs and services, etc.) is envisioned [19].

The COMPASS project has identified 251 different planning instruments across EU Member States, spanning over three main administrative level: national, sub-national and local. Especially at the local scale, these planning instrument have been recognized as mostly regulatory in nature, with a trend to move toward a more strategic/framework-setting nature, especially in large municipalities. Such regulatory nature, in particular, has been often criticized, while a more strategic approach, able to coordinate different actors and interests (both private and public) have been encouraged, especially during the early stage of the policy cycle [19].

A similar pattern is observable in the Italian context, where the planning system has been recognized as limited in showing adaptability to economic and socio-political changes [20]. This limitation has led to a paradigm shift in urban planning, in which the traditional deterministic approach has been superseded by a more programmatic one, in which the flexibility and adaptation to the objective of the community are the value of the social contract constituted by the plan [18] (see Sect. 2).

In general, at the EU level, land use planning is witnessing a modification path in which competences are being rescaled and procedures simplified in order to create instruments able to better adapt to modification of circumstances of contemporaneity issues, assuring the integration of different sectoral policies, while enhancing transparency and citizens engagement [19]. This evolution, together with a trend toward a more strategic approach to land-use planning claim for a more collaborative process in the governance of the urban environment [21]. This strategic approach to municipal planning, in which participation is seen as a re-appropriation of the transformation of the city by citizens, needs new formalized methods to guide the discussion with the local community in order to include their voices in the definition of the shared vision of the city [16, 18].

With reference to the Italian context, a number of municipalities have recognized the importance of active participation and involvement of citizenship in city policy-making. The leader of this new agreement is the municipality of Bologna, which has established the "Patto per l'Amministrazione condivisa dei beni comuni" thanks to the work carried out by Labsus, the laboratory for subsidiarity [22]. It is a programmatic document that summarizes the strategic agreement between the administration and the city's civic organizations that proposes shared administration and planning, two innovative ways of collaborating with the public administration that aim to expand the number and type of actors involved in shared administration and policy-making in the city. In addition, shared planning is a process that does not end at the stage of defining projects and interventions to be implemented, but also continues in the implementation stage through active cooperation among all stakeholders and evaluation on the progress of ongoing activities to agree on any corrective and/or supplementary interventions. In this context, evaluation tools that systematize the created relationships, the resources exchanged in these arrangements, and assess the impacts of choices at various stages of implementation of the actions taken, become increasingly important.

In order to support the citizens' consultation and participation during the drafting phase of municipal plans, as well as to provide the stakeholders involved in the process with a common framework to assess both the existing conditions of the urban status and the strategic vision that is the common base of the urban planning practice, this contribution proposes a methodological framework based on the integration of a set of methods to evaluate the interaction between current conditions of the urban configuration, the stakeholders' interest and participation, and the impact that the foreseen strategic vision will have on those two aspects. In particular, the research proposes the combination of SWOT [23] and Stakeholder analysis [24], and the integration of them into a Community Impact Evaluation (CIE) with an attempt to facilitate communication between the various stakeholders involved in the city's planning process by considering their different interests [25]. The rest of the contribution is structured as follows: in Sect. 2 a brief overview of the urban management debate resulting in the current strategic approach to urban planning is presented, together with an argumentation in favor of the introduction of formalized methodologies to support participatory processes. In Sect. 3 an integrated methodology is proposed. In Sect. 4 the resulting tool to support the participatory process is introduced, while Sect. 5 outlines the conclusions and future perspectives.

2 Regulatory Plans in Italy: Limits and Constraints

2.1 From a Deterministic Approach

City planning in Italy is regulated at the national level by Law No. 1150/1942 (National urban planning law) which provides for a three-level planning system: a coordinated territorial plan scale (Piani Territoriali di Coordinamento, PTC), the urban general plan at the city scale (Piano Regolatore Generale, PRG), and detailed implementation plans

(Piani Particolareggiati di Esecuzione, PPE), entrusting these two last levels to municipalities. With the progressive reduction of the hierarchical institution enforced by the
national law promulgated in 1942 [26], and the absence of updates to it, each regional
authority has tried to bridge the gap resulting in a proliferation of plans that differs greatly
from one another due to the compliance to the different geographical, political, social
and economic contexts in which they were generated [18]. This delay of the centralized
level in revising the national law, and the consequent necessity of the regional level to
respond to the changed socio-economic conditions of the context in which the latter was
operating, have led to a series of experimentation characterized by a high innovative
content in the governance of the territory for which some authors have coined the term
"asymmetric city planning federalism" [27].

This differentiation is also highlighted by the wide variety of names that indicate the
same territorial level of the laws enforced by each municipality in different regions: being
them PRG, Municipal Structural Plan (Piano Strutturale Comunale, PSC), Municipal
City Planning Plan (Piano Urbanistico Comunale, PUC) Territorial Asset Plan (Piano di
Assetto del Territorio, PAT).

A part from the struggle of municipalities to make the planning obligation to be
respected, another issue is represented by the low capability of the same municipalities
to update their planning instrument [16, 27]. A recent study by ISPRA (Istituto Superiore
per la Protezione e la Ricerca Ambientale) focusing on the status of the urban planning
tools in Italy has highlighted that out of 85 cities analyzed, only 23 of them have a plan
adopted after 2010, while 40 of them dates back between 2000 and 2010. The remaining
cities count on urban plans adopted in the last century: 7 from 1990 to 1999, 15 before
1990, and 2 in the 60s [26].

Traditional urban planning tools have been characterized by a deterministic nature,
based on zoning and regulatory impositions in order to define the future structure of the
city [16, 18]. This approach has determined the governing of the territory in terms of
admitted land uses, their private or public regime of property, and the extension of their
possible exploitation (surfaces and cubic footage), with no correlation to the economic
development nor the quality of the city [26, 27].

The logic of imposition of binding measures by the central administration has shown
its limit [16] with the emergence of new strategic approaches more attentive to environmental and quality features, as well as to a more inclusion of stakeholders interests and
consensus [26]. Even though these attempts have been considered capable of supersed-
ing these limitations, they could nonetheless have a negative impact on the concerted
government of the urban environment [16].

2.2 Toward a Strategic Approach

The revision of the more traditional regulatory structure, amid the Italian Planning Association (Istituto Nazionale di Urbanistica, INU), resulted in a new approach aiming at
overcoming some of the issues related to the old generation of plans [20]. This perspective aims at identifying programmatic solutions open to the initiatives of private operators
preserving a certain degree of flexibility. This new approach does not reject the values of
the urban planning, but rather incorporates the possibility of changing the rules in place
in order to respond to possible changes in the community that has established them [18].

This attempt has been translated in a definition of the urban plan as consisting of different "components", characterized by different "velocities" [27], intended as the differentiated capacity of the components of the plan to respond in a more coherent way to the different changing trends of the territory and its dynamics. In particular, a more strategic and programmatic component has the goal of defining the invariant characteristics of the territory layout and has the duty to interpret the common perspective and vision of the community that has produced it, while a more operative component aims at defining the transformations that are predicted in the short-medium term, with also the duty to translate the strategic-programmatic component in the peculiarity of the territory. Finally, a third component is added with the specific duty of managing of the existing city with prescriptive validity. As stated before, due to the "asymmetric city planning federalism" of the regional level, the constitution of urban plans differs depending on the region to which the municipality is subordinated, this holds true also in this aspect, for which, in different regions, these components are formalized in two or three different urban management tools [16]. Furthermore, this nuanced definition of the urban planning is also reflected in the normative validity of the content of the plans, in which binding regulations are combined with more flexible rules and indications, in the attempt to adapt its regulatory function to the mutability of the socio-economic conditions that determine their introduction [27].

One of the facets that the new strategic approach to urban planning tries to embrace is that of quality, intended not only as the compliance to a set of rules and norms, but also as the morphological quality of the city and its spaces devoted to an enhancement of the population living conditions.

Central to this new conception of the urban planning (and result of the early experimentation conducted to overcome the original rigidity of urban plans in the 80s and 90s) is the common strategic vision of the future of the city, conceived as the shared ground on which the urban transformation and development has to base its moves [4, 27, 28]. This further evolution, formalized in new tools mainly devoted to stress this strategic vocation such as the Strategic Plans adopted at several territorial levels, is based on two primary characteristics: the network and the visionary ones. The former emphasizes the fact that the common strategic vision must seek to achieve the widest level of consensus among the various stakeholders and actors who are members of the network, while the latter is due to its objective of providing a vision for the city's future on which these members agree [27].

2.3 Monitor, Communicate, Participate

The emphasis placed on the need to achieve a common vision in the governance of the city and its transformation could also be seen in the methods used to support the drafting of the plan (both in its embryonic and operative phases) as well as in the form of communication used to define its characteristics.

Regarding these aspects, the introduction of the knowledge frameworks (Quadri Conoscitivi) goes in this direction: this preliminary documentation has the specific purpose of defining a common basis for the evaluation of the initial configuration of the matter on which the subsequent phases of the urban planning exercise will focus, and their production is directly linked to the willingness of the public administration to make the evaluation and knowledge system explicit.

Among the tools early introduced to both evaluate the impact of the planning decisions and to guarantee the transparency of the process, the Strategic Environmental Assessment (SEA) plays a pivotal role in the recognition of the environmental issue in the territorial governance [16, 29]. Introduced for the first time by Directive 2001/42/CE and adopted in the Italian context by Legislative decree 152/2006, SEA constitutes a specific administrative assessment tool aiming at fostering the integration of environmental considerations from development of plans and programs, and throughout their entire life-cycle. The purposes of using SEA are to support the collaboration among experts in highlighting the possible environmental impacts that the implementation of the plan could generate, and to guarantee the transparency of the decision-making process in the consultation with competent authorities and stakeholders [30, 31]. Despite the necessity for this tool in the evaluation of the sustainability of the plan in its generation and operational phase [27], a study highlighted that the minority of the urban plans produced at municipal level (37% out of 85 considered cities) have introduced the SEA in the definition of their plans or variants of them, in fact, most of the plans actually in force in several municipalities date back before the introduction of SEA by Legislative decree 152/2006 [26].

The aim to enhance communication and participation in the genealogy of urban plans, further expanded with the focus on the transparency of the evaluation of their impacts and implications, resulted also in the evolution of the documents that constitute an urban plan. Several examples have introduced different forms of graphical representation in order to foster the participatory process in order to rapidly communicate the objectives as well as the possible evolution scenarios implied by the decisions taken in the process. Urban design has entered the formation of the plan in this sense [28]. Exemplary case could be seen in the plan of the city of Bologna, in which the "seven cities" individuated by the plan [27] are conceptually designed in order to define their idea rather than their formal materialization [32]. The representation of the "seven cities", in fact, moves apart from the canonical bi-dimensional representation, adopting an axonometric infographic representation, in order to better communicate the reasoning behind their conceptualization rather than strictly defining their spatial characteristics [33]. The latter has also allowed the support of the participatory process by providing an easy to understand communication of the objectives and strategies of the plan during its drafting phase, engaging also with a non-expert audience [34].

Another aspect that deconstructs the idea of planning viewed as a set of impositions in a top-down direction is the co-planning one. This collaborative attempt to achieve the agreement upon decisions at different levels of the ruling hierarchy, and the multiplication of actors in the constitution of the common vision of the city, highlight the necessity to establish a framework of communication and participation based on evaluation methods and formalized protocols that would allow the different stakeholders and actors to negotiate on the same informational framework being able to speak the same language.

3 An Integrated Methodology for Urban Plan Evaluation

3.1 What is Needed

The contemporary strategic governance of the cities faces several dimensions of complexity such as the interaction of several actors and elements in it [35], the dissolution of commonly used methods, the disentanglement of the financial city from the physical one [28], the dissolution of space-time boundaries, and the necessity to intercept the private capital [20]. On top of that, the fast mutation of boundary conditions, and the uncertainty of the interpretability of reality [36] led to the necessity to consider at the same time the long-time perspective (strategy) and the short/medium-term one (tactic) in the co-creation of the urban environment [28].

This paradigm shift has to root its arguments in the common vision of the city produced by who inhabit and construct it [28] representing a moment of collective political engagement [27].

The formation of such vision has to be the result of an iterative process in which the strategic features, as well as the potentiality of development and transformations, are individuated, discussed and negotiated, and the voices and expectation of the vast pool of stakeholders are considered and formalized in the attempt to achieve an expression of direct democracy [4, 27].

Aim of the present chapter is to contribute to the formalization of this process by extending a methodology proposed for the evaluation of urban regeneration projects [37–39]. The methodology proposed combine different methods in the attempt to evaluate the different characteristics and potentialities of the existing urban environment through a SWOT analysis, and to highlight the different stakeholders and actors that participate in the process of formation of the strategic vision by means of a Stakeholder analysis. Finally, these two methods (SWOT and Stakeholders analysis) are integrated in a CIE matrix (Fig. 1).

3.2 SWOT Analysis

SWOT analysis is a tool used in support to decision-making processes with the aim to rationalize the set of information known regarding a specific context [40, 41]. In the acronym of its name is contained the system used in such formalization, for which the pieces of information are clustered in the categories of Strengths (S), Weaknesses (W), Opportunities (O), and Threats (T).

The first two (S and W) are intended as internal features, while the second pair (O and T) are the external ones. Strengths and Opportunities are those characteristics supporting the possible success of the project (considering it in the broader sense also of the production of a plan). On the other hand, Weaknesses and Threats might constitute obstacles (existing or potential) to the completion of the latter.

Among the various formalizations of SWOT components, the STEEP framework groups them into five categories, namely, Social (SO), Technological (TE), Environmental (EN), Economic (EC), and Political (PO). The outcome of the SWOT analysis is then to support the identification of the strategies more likely to maximize the internal Strengths and the external Opportunities and to reduce the endogenous Weaknesses and

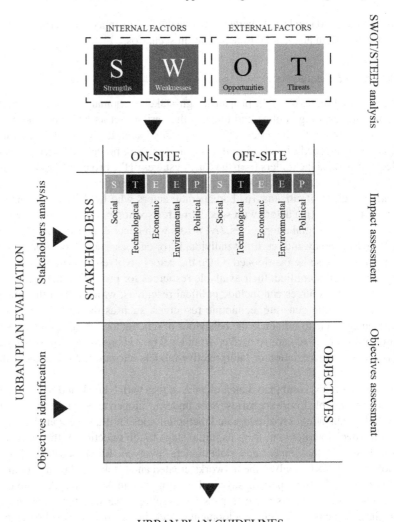

Fig. 1. Methodological framework.

the exogenous Threats, with the optimal integration of projects and context as ultimate goal.

Pratibha et al. [42] used SWOT analysis for the city of Mohol (India) to explore the changing needs and demands of the population for the preparation of an integrated development plan with modified planning standards. Sang and Lin [43] presented a brownfield-related design project in a post-industrial area in Beijing, China. The design phase includes the application of SWOT analysis to analyse the strengths, weaknesses, opportunities, and threats of the site to discuss the goals and strategies of this project for its future redevelopment. SWOT analysis thus seems to be a newer tool, generally employed in decision making to better visualize the factors that characterize the context, and future the urban and spatial transformation scenarios.

3.3 Stakeholder Analysis

During the initial stages of public project design, stakeholder analysis might be employed to examine the existing context and identify the various actors who hold the power to either promote or hinder the process [24]. To ensure that all the needs of the parties who are directly or indirectly involved in the decision-making process are met, it is recommended to involve stakeholders from the earliest stages of the project [44]. In stakeholder analysis, the actors can be divided into five categories, including (i) political actors who advocate on behalf of citizens, (ii) bureaucratic actors who hold legal responsibilities in moving requests, (iii) actors with special interests who are directly impacted by the choice between potential alternatives, (iv) actors with general interests who lack political or legal legitimacy and represent individuals (or entities, such as environmentalists) who might otherwise be overlooked. Once the actors involved in the decision-making process have been identified, their available resources for promoting their interests are analysed. These resources can include political resources, which reflect the amount of support an actor can generate, economic resources, such as the capacity to mobilize funds or other assets to influence the behaviour of other actors, legal resources, such as power or positions of advantage derived from legal provisions, and cognitive resources, such as access to information or interpretative models relevant to the decision-making process.

Bottero et al. [45] combined Stakeholder Analysis with STEEP and SWOT analyses to support sustainable future scenarios for an underdeveloped area in north-western Italy (Turin, Italy). The adoption of integrated methodologies facilitated the analysis of each stage of the decision problem, from its initial stage to the selection of the most suitable scenario based on the context and stakeholders involved. Rădulescu et al. [46] used stakeholder analysis to analyse the networks created and established by actors involved in brownfield projects as part of sustainable strategies in Romania. As studies have shown, stakeholder analysis makes it possible to set up a participatory approach in the design phase that can lead to the development of stakeholder-oriented evaluation models and consider the multiplicity of interests and resources brought into play by the various actors involved in the decision-making process.

3.4 Community Impact Evaluation

CIE methodology is a qualitative evaluation tool that could be used both during the preliminary design phases of a project to assess its impacts [47], and during its life-cycle to monitor the correspondence between initial assumption and ongoing effects [48]. The steps involved to perform the methodology can be summarized as follows [49]. In the first one, the project to be evaluated and the context in which it will generate an impact are described. In the second step, the actors involved in the project are mapped based on their spatial location (on-site and off-site) and over time (short and medium-long term), and classified into two macro-groups: operators/producers, who are active actors responsible for developing the territory, and the consumers, passive subjects who use goods and services. The third step identifies the objectives of the project and the involved actors, which is a crucial phase to evaluate the project's ability to meet the interests of the actors involved. The assessment considers three macro-categories of impacts according to Lichfield's studies: monetary, non-monetary, and mixed [50]. Monetary impacts include financial (F) and tax (FIS) impacts, while non-monetary impacts take into account the social impacts (SOC) for both public and private actors, cultural impacts (CUL) that affect the cultural and knowledge sphere, and environmental impacts (ENV). Mixed impacts refer to economic impacts (ECO) that can be both monetary and non-monetary.

Finally, the information gathered with the two previous methods are systematized in a co-axial matrix in which the impacts of the component of the common vision are verified and assessed against the components of the SWOT and the identified stakeholders, on a qualitative scale.

Due to its versatility, CIE has been applied in many areas, including urban planning and transformation. Torre et al. [51] experimented with CIE to evaluate the interaction between different transformation objectives and scenarios for a historic building located in Peschici (southern Italy), emphasizing the possibility of carping the potential for the different stakeholders involved. Bottero et al. [48] investigated the different implementation phases of an urban regeneration project in Barcelona (Spain) highlighting the communicative capacity of the method's results and the flexibility of its application in different time steps.

4 Results and Discussion

The combined methodology allows to map the strategic vision of a potential project (the urban plan in this case) with its impacts on the different stakeholders involved, clustered into the structure of the STEEP. In particular, by listing the different stakeholders in the rows of the matrix and the impacts in the column, it is possible to evaluate how these stakeholders are impacted by the current situation in which the city find itself (time 0, representing the actual situation). Integrating the goals that the strategic vision of the plan forecasts (Fig. 2), it is possible to highlight the negative or positive transformations that such objectives will induce and, thus, the changes in impacts that the stakeholders will benefit or suffer from the implementation of the vision (time 1, representing the implementation of the strategic vision).

This process aims to enhance transparency and to identify the different positive and negative impacts that a strategic vision for the future of a city could have on different types of actors and stakeholders, thus reducing the risk of delivering over-simplified or conformed visions of a city, without considering its intrinsic complexity [52].

Several are the advantages that could be named for the application of the combined methodology in the formation of the strategic vision of the plan. A first one is that the matrix helps to establish the complexity of impacts on stakeholders (political, bureaucratic, general interest, special interest, experts) according to different dimensions (social, technological, economic, environmental, political).

The application of the methodology makes it possible to spatialize the effects of the strategic vision both within (on-site) and outside (off-site) formal boundaries, thus,

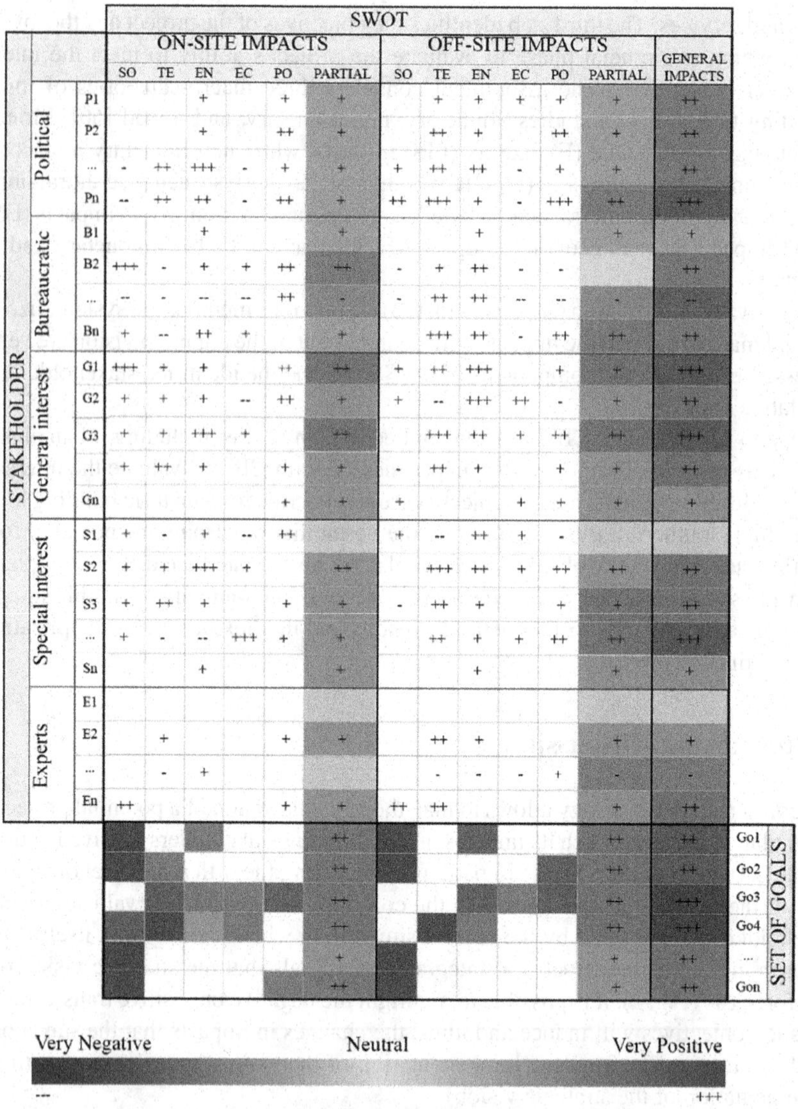

			SWOT												
			ON-SITE IMPACTS						OFF-SITE IMPACTS						GENERAL IMPACTS
STAKEHOLDER			SO	TE	EN	EC	PO	PARTIAL	SO	TE	EN	EC	PO	PARTIAL	
Political		P1			+		+	+		+	+	+	+	+	++
		P2			+		++	+		++	+		++	+	++
		...	-	++	+++	-	+	+	+	++	++	-	+	+	++
		Pn	--	++	++	-	++	+	++	+++	+	-	+++	++	+++
Bureaucratic		B1			+			+			+			+	+
		B2	+++	-	+	+	++	++	-	+	++	-	-		++
		...	--	-	--	--	++	-	-	++	++	--	--	-	--
		Bn	+	--	++	+		+		+++	++	-	++	++	++
General interest		G1	+++	+	+		++	++	+	++	+++		+	+	+++
		G2	+	+	+	--	++	+	+	--	+++	++	-	+	++
		G3	+	+	+++	+		++	+++	++	+	++		++	+++
		...		+	++	+	+	+	-	++	+		+	+	++
		Gn					+	+	+		+		+	+	+
Special interest		S1	+	-	+	--	++		+	--	++	+	-		
		S2	+	+	+++	+		++		+++	++	+	++	++	++
		S3	+	++	+		+	+	-	++	+		+	+	++
		...	+	-	--	+++	+	+		++	+	+	++	++	+++
		Sn			+			+			+			+	+
Experts		E1													
		E2		+			+	+		++	+			+	+
		...		-	+					-	-	-	+	-	-
		En	++				+	+	++	++				+	++
SET OF GOALS		Go1						++						++	++
		Go2						++						++	++
		Go3						++						++	+++
		Go4						++						++	++
		...						+						+	++
		Gon						++						+	++

Very Negative   Neutral   Very Positive

--   +++

Fig. 2. Illustrative example of a co-axial matrix integrating CIE, SWOT and Stakeholder Analysis (source: Authors elaboration, color image available in the online version).

understanding also the relationships that could be established on a broader scale. Furthermore, the use of the matrix would help DMs and stakeholders to prioritize the impacts and the objectives in order to neutralize possible negative consequences that would arise from the formalization of the strategic vision, keeping its flexible discursive and not specialist dimension in the communication and negotiation among the different experts, actors, and private citizens that would convene to the participatory table. Finally, the holistic view, that will be produced by the matrix on the different components that structure the city, will have the advantage to prevent possible risks or negative outcomes that might generate in time either on clusters of stakeholders, or on different dimensions of the context (with a particular reference to the categories of the STEEP analysis).

It is worth underlying that such formalization of the decision process has the advantage of making the negotiation of the strategic vision for the city visible and will help the communication of the different needs and desires within the stakeholders that will participate in the public definition of the matrix itself (that could be viewed as a moment of public discussion and participatory planning). The mapping of the objectives of the strategy against the impact on the stakeholders will inform the non-negotiable features of the plan, ultimately making them explicit.

5 Conclusions and Future Perspectives

In recent decades, the role that the development of cities would have on society has been largely highlighted. In this direction, the negotiation and the communication of the strategic vision that the urban community agree upon is attracting more and more attention. This latter trend could be seen also in the Italian urban planning community, in which the traditional tools used in the management of the city are progressively incorporating the strategic aspect in order to both overcome several limitations generated by the National Law adopted more than 80 years ago.

To support the discussion among stakeholders in the definition and negotiation of such strategic vision, this contribution has proposed an integrated methodology aiming at enhancing the transparency of the process by adopting a formalized scheme that would allow to integrate the different points of view of the individuals and groups involved (stakeholder analysis), with a clear communication (and shared interpretation) of the analysis of the context (SWOT), and to map the possible consequences that the goals of the negotiated vision would have on these two.

The methodology proposed in this contribution might be used by municipalities in the early phase of the revision of urban plans such as the constitution of the Preliminary Project Technical Proposal (SEA) to clarify the expected impacts on the different segments of society, and align the proposed plan to the three bottom line approach to sustainability. Furthermore, by making these impacts evident, the public Decision-Maker could focus the attention on the more conflictual features of the proposed plan, increasing the amount of information required in decision-making process and creating dedicated negotiation focus groups. Finally, using matrices to connect the current and expected configuration of the territory, with the stakeholders involved and the plan goals, it could be possible to monitor the ongoing results of the plan, thus evaluating possible corrective measures in its implementation.

The final aim of such methodology is not to provide a standardized solution to the issues (and potentialities) of cities, but to accompany the broader community and entities that surround and live the urban environment in the formation of the idea of its future asset. In doing so, the risk to provide a homologated vision of the future of the city could be prevented, or, at least, the effects of such attempt would be clear to the broader public, and the possible alternative voices of different groups could be better considered and mediated.

The present contribution is methodological in its nature, the application of the proposed framework to a real case study would allow to test it, and also to integrate and improve several aspects that have not been considered yet, such as the participatory methods that could be used in constructing the three "entries" of the methodology (namely the SWOT components, the stakeholder analysis, and the definition of the set of goals).

Finally, in the long run, it would be interesting to test the methodology in its capability to monitor the development of the goals of the strategic vision, as well as the possible modification that might occur in time regarding the socio-economic context, in order to allow DMs to correct or redefine their initial statements according to the changed conditions.

References

1. United Nations: How to make cities more resilient: a handbook for local government leaders (2012)
2. United Nations: How to make cities more resilient: a handbook for local government leaders (2017)
3. United Nations: Transforming our world: the 2030 Agenda for Sustainable Development. (2015)
4. U.N. Habitat: "Inclusive and sustainable urban planning: a guide for municipalities." Nairobi: UN Habitat (2007)
5. Meerow, S., Newell, J.P., Stults, M.: Defining urban resilience: a review. Landsc. Urban Plan. **147**, 38–49 (2016)
6. Masnavi, M.R., Gharai, F., Hajibandeh, M.: Exploring urban resilience thinking for its application in urban planning: a review of literature. Int. J. Environ. Sci. Technol. **16**(1), 567–582 (2018). https://doi.org/10.1007/s13762-018-1860-2
7. Sharifi, A., Yamagata, Y.: Resilience-Oriented Urban Planning. In: Yamagata, Y., Sharifi, A. (eds.) Resilience-Oriented Urban Planning. LNE, vol. 65, pp. 3–27. Springer, Cham (2018). https://doi.org/10.1007/978-3-319-75798-8_1
8. Girard, L.F., Nocca, F., Gravagnuolo, A.: Matera: City of nature, city of culture, city of regeneration. Towards a landscape-based and culture-based urban circular economy. Aestimum 74, 5–42. (2019)
9. Williams, J.: Circular cities: what are the benefits of circular development? Sustainability (Switzerland) **13**(10), 5725 (2021)
10. Desouza, K.C., Flanery, T.H.: Designing, planning, and managing resilient cities: a conceptual framework. Cities **35**, 89–99 (2013)
11. Suppa, A.R., Cavana, G., Binda, T.: Supporting the EU Mission "100 Climate-Neutral Cities by 2030": A Review of Tools to Support Decision-Making for the Built Environment at District or City Scale. In: Gervasi, O., Murgante, B., Misra, S., Rocha A.M.A.C., Garau, C. (eds.) Computational Science and Its Applications – ICCSA 2022 Workshops. ICCSA 2022. Lecture Notes in Computer Science, vol 13380, pp. 151–168. Springer, Cham (2022). https://doi.org/10.1007/978-3-031-10542-5_11
12. Harvey, D.: The Condition of Postmodernity: An Enquiry into the Origins of Cultural Change. Blackwell, Oxford (1989)
13. Harvey, D.: Flexible accumulation through urbanization reflections on "post-modernism" in the american city. Perspecta, pp. 251–272 (1990)
14. Kędra, A., Maleszyk, P., Visvizi, A.: Engaging citizens in land use policy in the smart city context. Land Use Policy **129**, 106649 (2023)

15. Usai, N.: Grandi strutture per il tempo libero. Trasformazione urbana e governance territoriale. Franco Angeli, Milano (2011)
16. Colavitti, A.M., Usai, N., Bonfiglioli, S.: Urban planning in Italy: the future of urban general plan and governance. Eur. Plan. Stud. **21**, 167–186 (2013)
17. Giaimo, C.: Nuovi Piani per la città sostenibile. Urbanistica Informazioni **236**, 7–8 (2011)
18. Bedini, M.A., Bronzini, F., Imbesi, P.N.: Italian urban plans: diversified approaches and methods for assessing their quality. Plan. Pract. Res. **34**, 346–364 (2019)
19. Nadin, V., et al.: COMPASS–Comparative Analysis of Territorial Governance and Spatial Planning Systems in Europe: Applied Research, pp. 2016–2018 (2018)
20. Caldarice, O., Cozzolino, S.: Institutional contradictions and attempts at innovation. Evidence from the Italian urban facility planning. Europ. Plann. Stud. **27**(1), 68–85 (2019)
21. Thomson, C.S., Karrbom Gustavsson, T., Karvonen, A.: Grand challenges facing our cities: where construction management research meets the urban field. Constr. Manag. Econ. **39**, 874–878 (2021)
22. Arena, G.: A Bologna, nove anni dopo, l'amministrazione condivisa è diventata strutturale, https://www.labsus.org/2023/01/bologna-nove-anni-dopo-lamministrazione-condivisa-e-diventata-strutturale/ Accessed 1 Apr 2023
23. Humphrey, A.: SWOT analysis for management consulting. SRI alumni Newsletter **1**, 7–8 (2005)
24. Dente, B.: Understanding Policy Decisions. SAST. Springer, Cham (2014). https://doi.org/10.1007/978-3-319-02520-9
25. Lichfield, N.: Community impact evaluation. Plan. Theory **6**(12), 55–79 (1994)
26. ISPRA: Qualità dell'ambiente urbano - XI Rapporto. Edizione 2015 (2015)
27. Benevolo, L., Piroddi, E. (eds.): Il nuovo manuale di urbanistica: Fonti e componenti della disciplina-Pratica dell'urbanistica-Lo stato della pianificazione urbana in Italia-venti città a confronto. Mancuso, Roma (2009)
28. Gabellini, P.: Le mutazioni dell'urbanistica. Principi, tecniche, competenze. 1st edn, Carrocci editore, Roma (2018)
29. Fidanza, A.: La Vas: raccordo tra sviluppo e ambiente. Urbanistica Informazioni **236**, 24–26 (2011)
30. Sugoni, G., Assumma, V., Bottero, M.C., Mondini, G.: Development of a decision-making model to support the strategic environmental assessment for the revision of the municipal plan of Turin (Italy). Land **12**, 609 (2023)
31. Roscelli, R. (ed.): Manuale di estimo: valutazioni economiche ed esercizio della professione. De Agostini - UTET Università, Novara (2014)
32. Gabellini, P.: Il disegno urbanistico. La Nuova Italia Scientifica, Roma (1996)
33. http://www.comune.bologna.it/psc/documenti/850, Accessed 1 Apr 2023
34. http://informa.comune.bologna.it/iperbole/media/files/flyer_sette_citta_english_low.pdf, Accessed 1 Apr 2023
35. Amin, A., Thrift, N.: Cities: Reimagining the Urban. Polity Press, Cambridge (2002)
36. Mondini, G.: Editorial Valori & Valutazioni **24**, 1–3 (2020)
37. Dell'Anna, F., Dell'Ovo, M.: A stakeholder-based approach managing conflictual values in urban design processes. The case of an open prison in Barcelona. Land Use Policy **114**, 105934 (2022)
38. Bottero, M., Caprioli, C., Datola, G., Caruso, N.: Assessing the Impacts of a Social Housing Project Through the Community Impact Evaluation (CIE) Methodology. In: Gervasi, O., Murgante, B., Misra, S., Rocha, A.M.A.C., Garau, C. (eds.) Computational Science and Its Applications – ICCSA 2022 Workshops. ICCSA 2022. Lecture Notes in Computer Science, vol 13380. Springer, Cham (2022). https://doi.org/10.1007/978-3-031-10542-5_13

39. Lami, I.M., Beccuti, B.: Evaluation of a project for the radical transformation of the Port of Genoa-Italy: according to community impact evaluation (CIE). Manag. Environ. Qual. **21**(1), 58–77 (2010)
40. Abed, A., Yaklef, M.: Exploring a sustainable strategy for brownfield regeneration. The case of Halawah Farm, Amman City, Jordan. J. Settlements Spatial Plann. **6**, 87–96 (2020)
41. Halla, F.: A SWOT analysis of strategic urban development planning: the case of Dar es Salaam city in Tanzania. Habitat Int. **31**(1), 130–142 (2007)
42. Pratibha, B., Rakesh, J., Radhika, M., Shivaji, P.: A proposed integrated development plan using modified planning standards for a small Urban town: a case study of Mohol town, Dist. Solapur, India. Civil Eng. Architect. **11**, 586–601 (2023)
43. Sang, K., Lin, G.: A landscape design strategy for the regeneration of brownfield: the case of shougang industrial park in China. In: Krüger, E.L., Karunathilake, H.P., Alam, T. (eds.) Resilient and Responsible Smart Cities: The Path to Future Resiliency, pp. 115–125. Springer International Publishing, Cham (2023). https://doi.org/10.1007/978-3-031-20182-0_9
44. Caprioli, C., Bottero, M.: Addressing complex challenges in transformations and planning: a fuzzy spatial multicriteria analysis for identifying suitable locations for urban infrastructures. Land Use Policy **102**, 105147 (2021)
45. Bottero, M., Assumma, V., Caprioli, C., Dell'Ovo, M.: Decision making in urban development: The application of a hybrid evaluation method for a critical area in the city of Turin (Italy). Sustain. Cities Society **72**, 103028 (2021)
46. Rădulescu, C.M., Ştefan, O., Rădulescu, G.M.T., Rădulescu, A.T.G.M., Rădulescu, M.V.G.M.: Management of stakeholders in urban regeneration projects. Case study: Baia-Mare, Transylvania. Sustainability (Switzerland) **8**(3), 238 (2016)
47. Brennan, N., Van Rensburg, T.M., Morris, C.: Public acceptance of large-scale wind energy generation for export from Ireland to the UK: evidence from Ireland. J. Environ. Plann Manage. **60**(11), 1967–1992 (2017)
48. Bottero, M., Bragaglia, F., Caruso, N., Datola, G., Dell'Anna, F.: Experimenting community impact evaluation (CIE) for assessing urban regeneration programmes: The case study of the area 22@ Barcelona. Cities **99**, 102464 (2020)
49. Coscia, C., De Filippi, F.: The use of collaborative digital platforms in the perspective of shared administration. The MiraMap project in Turin (2016)
50. Lichfield, D.: Integrated planning and environmental assessment. Eval. Plann. GeoJ. L. **47**, 151–175 (1998)
51. Torre, C.M., Morano, P., Tajani, F.: Experimenting CIE and CBA in Urban Restoration. In: Gervasi, O., et al. (eds.) ICCSA 2017. LNCS, vol. 10406, pp. 639–650. Springer, Cham (2017). https://doi.org/10.1007/978-3-319-62398-6_45
52. Crippa, J., Silva, M.G., Ribeiro, N.D., Ruschel, R.: Urban branding and circular economy: a bibliometric analysis. Environ. Dev. Sustain. **25**, 2173–2200 (2023)

Mathematical Methods for Image Processing and Understanding (MMIPU 2023)

Mathematical Models and Neural Networks for the Description and the Correction of Typical Distortions of Historical Manuscripts

Pasquale Savino and Anna Tonazzini[✉]

Istituto di Scienza e Tecnologie dell'Informazione, Consiglio Nazionale delle Ricerche,
Via G. Moruzzi 1, 56124 Pisa, Italy
{pasquale.savino,anna.tonazzini}@isti.cnr.it

Abstract. Historical manuscripts are very often degraded by the seeping or transparency of the ink from the page opposite side. Suppressing the interfering text can be of great aid to philologists and paleographers who aim at interpreting the primary text, and nowadays also for the automatic analysis of the text. We formerly proposed a data model, which approximately describes this damage, to generate an artificial training set able to teach a shallow neural network how to classify pixels in clean or corrupted. This NN has proved to be effective in classifying manuscripts where the degradation can be also widely variable. In this paper, we modify the architecture of the NN to better account for ink saturation in text overlay areas, by including a specific class for these pixels. From the experiments, the improvement of the classification and then the restoration is significant.

Keywords: Ancient manuscript virtual restoration · Degraded document binarization · Shallow multilayer neural networks

1 Introduction

Historical and archival manuscripts are usually damaged by a whole series of factors, primarily due to the natural degradation of the materials over time and conditions. The basic requirement for the fruition of these manuscripts is the removal of the degradations in order to make the main text fully understandable. However, this may not be sufficient for a comprehensive fruition, since these manuscripts can contain other elements, such as annotations, miniatures, watermarks, drawings, etc., that should be preserved due to their historical and informative value. Therefore, a right balance is needed between the removal of useless and harmful elements and the conservation (or enhancement) of elements which, although unrelated to the primary text, are very important for the history of the manuscript.

Degraded document binarization can be efficient in separating the main text from other patterns, which can be considered as a complex background to be removed in total [2–5, 20]. However, binarization alone cannot solve cases of very strong degradation, as we will show later. Furthermore, it produces a two-class image, in black and white, which inevitably has lost interesting details of the manuscript Thus, virtual restoration assumes the important role of preserving and highlighting the useful elements, while removing the useless ones that can disturb or even make impossible the scholar study [22].

The bleed-through degradation is the most frequent and impairing degradation in ancient manuscripts. This occurs when both sides of the paper are written. Methods specifically designed for bleed-through reduction are distinguished into blind methods, which exploit the information of the front side alone [6, 7, 16], and non-blind methods, where the often available two sides of the manuscript page are jointly exploited [8–10, 17, 28]. The non-blind methods can provide a very fine virtual restoration, with the counterpart that they require a perfect alignment of the two images [12–14].

In [29] we proposed a simple multilayer shallow neural networks with back-propagation training [23], to solve the non-blind case. We implemented the NN in such a way that it auto-adapts to the manuscript to be restored, i.e. it does not require a preliminary learning from many other manuscripts already classified. This can be realized, for example, when an existing data model can be used for generating simulated training samples. In our case, we experimented with a previously proposed data model, approximately describing the degradation affecting recto-verso manuscripts [11]. A training set was built starting from ground-truths drawn from the clean zones of the manuscript at hand, and then mixed accordingly to the model. The experimental results presented in [29] on heavily damaged manuscripts seemed encouraging in terms of degradation cancellation. We accounted for variable degradation, also very strong. This makes our NN, built on the basis of a single exemplar manuscript, to be potentially effective on other manuscripts of the same corpus but with degradation of different entity, or different pages of a same book.

The difficulty with very strong levels of bleed-through is to succeed in distinguish them from the situations in which the primary text and the opposite text overlap (we call the occlusions). In particular, a NN trained to recognize bleed-through of levels very similar to that of the main text could produce random responses in those cases. In this paper we focus on modifications to the network architecture and learning with the aim to try to get rid of this great difficulty. With respect to the network architecture, we introduce an extra output class to classify the text overlapping pixels as occlusions rather than as mere foreground text pixels. As regards the construction of the training set, we assume a data model that explicitly includes the conditions for the occlusions to occur.

The paper is organized as follows. In Sect. 2 we describe the method adopted for the construction of the adaptive training set, using a specific data model. Section 3 provides some operative details about the shallow NN architecture and the learning and recall phases. Section 4 analyzes from a qualitative point of view some preliminary results, both synthetic and real, in comparison to state-of-the-art binarization methods for degraded historical manuscripts. Finally, Sect. 5 concludes the paper.

2   Construction of the Training Set

The first step of the virtual restoration process for historical recto-verso manuscripts described in this paper is to classify the pixels of each side into four different classes that we call *foreground, background, bleed-through,* and *occlusion,* respectively. These classes represent the main text, the clean paper texture with, eventually, other marks, the seeping ink and the areas where the two sides are both written and the two texts overlap. In the previous work [29] we considered three classes only, by merging the occlusion pixels with the text pixels. This reflects the appearance of only one side of the paper, as occlusions do are text and, without knowledge of the opposite side, cannot be identified with certainty. However, as we will see in the experimental results, using three classes only resulted in an overestimation of the bleed-through class.

As a classifier, we use a neural network (NN) that needs a training set with ground truths to learn how to discriminate the pixels. As mentioned, we do not use an external dataset based on similar manuscripts already classified, but our NN is trained using the same manuscript we want to classify.

Thus, to build the training set, we select N pairs of patches from the manuscript containing clean text, and then symmetrically mix them using a data model for seeping ink that describes the observed optical density of each side as the weighted sum of the ideal densities of the two sides. Defining the optical density as $D_s(t) = -log\left(\frac{s(t)}{p}\right)$, at pixel t, with $s(t)$ being the intensity, and p the mean value of the paper support, the model is expressed in the following way:

$$D_x^{obs}(t) = \begin{cases} D_x(t), & \text{if } t \text{ is text in both sides} \\ D_x(t) + q_y(t)D_{h_y \otimes s_y}(t), & \text{elsewhere} \end{cases} \tag{1}$$

where x and y indicate the two sides, which must be perfectly aligned after reflection of one of the two. Equation (1) holds for the opposite side by exchanging the role of x and y. In Eq. (1), D^{obs} and D are the observed and the ideal optical density, respectively, and $\otimes$ indicates convolution between the ideal intensity s and a Point Spread Functions (PSF), h, describing the smearing of ink penetrating the paper. Finally, the space-variant quantities q_x and q_y, whose maximum allowed range is $[0, 1]$, have the physical meaning of ink penetration percentages from one side to the other. The first condition of the model Eq. (1) means that we assume that the density of the foreground text does not increase due to ink seepage, just as it happens in the majority of the cases.

In previous works [11,14,15], we neglected the ink saturation effect, and proposed to invert the equation in the second condition of the model for virtually restoring the recto-verso pair. To make the inversion possible, we assumed that the hyperparameters q and h are known in advance. Based on the observed densities of the two sides, we first inverted the model by assuming an identically zero ideal density in the opposite side, thus obtaining estimates of the ink penetration percentages at each pixel. The system can then be solved with respect to the ideal density maps, from which the virtually restored manuscript sides are obtained. To manage the text superposition areas (whose ideal density is not zero), the obtained images were corrected using some technicalities.

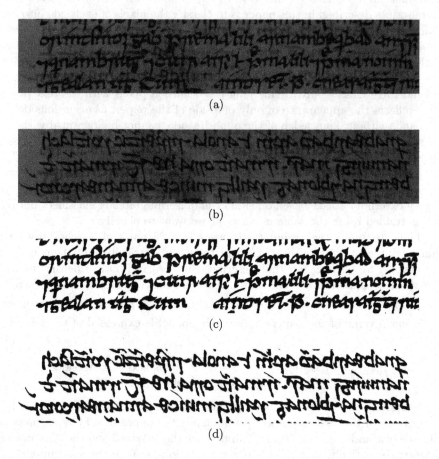

Fig. 1. The manuscripts used for the experiments: (a) and (b) real recto and reflected verso of the 15-th pair of manuscripts in the database [27]; (c) and (d) their corresponding manually generated binary ground-truths.

Here we propose to solve the direct problem of Eq. (1) for generating the data necessary for the training set, rather than solving the inverse problem for estimating the ideal densities, which are known in this case. Operatively, each patch out of the selected N pairs containing clean text is first binarized by the Sauvola algorithm, in order to extract the map of the clean text and the map of the background. Comparing the binary map of both members of the pair allows for locate the four classes in each side, including the occlusions. Then, as said, the original, non-binary pairs of patches are fed to the system in Eq. (1) in a forward manner, with different values of the ink seepage percentage, so that we synthetically generate samples of recto-verso text with bleed-through. The first condition in Eq. (1) permits to simulate the saturation of the ink, that is, when a pixel is foreground text in both sides, the value of the density is set to that of the recto pixel (verso pixel, respectively). For the generation of a single pair of patches the model is taken as stationary, i.e. with fixed ink seeping percentage. However, the construction of several pairs with different percentage values means that, as a whole, samples of non-stationary degradation will be presented to the network.

3   Neural Network: Architecture, Learning and Recall

We adopted a simple feedforward network with the architecture of a multilayer shallow neural networks with one hidden layer and ten neurons, and a backpropagation training [23]. In the specific, we used the function `patternnet` of the Matlab Deep Learning Toolbox. This net is a pattern recognition NN that can be trained to classify inputs according to target classes.

The network processes the two sides of the manuscript simultaneously, on a pixel-by-pixel basis. For each pixel, we consider as features the two density values in the two sides. As already mentioned, as target classes we consider the four different classes of background, foreground, bleed-through and occlusion.

By construction, for the pair of patches used for building the training set we exactly know the classification of each pixel of each side. Thus, the target classes of the generated samples are directly available. The data set is then randomly subdivided into training set (the 70% of pairs) and validation set (the remaining 30%). As mentioned, we use the Matlab `patternnet` net with a single hidden layer constituted of 10 nodes. As minimization algorithm (`training function`) we chose the scaled conjugate gradient, and the cross entropy for measuring the net performance (`performance function`) during training. Tests performed with a higher number of neurons did not provide significant improvement in the quality of the results.

In the experiments, the number of patches N used for constructing the data set was varying between 2 and 10, the size of the patches was chosen between 50×50 and 400×400, and the number of different values of ink seepage percentage was from 10 to 20. The architectural simplicity of the network guarantees very short learning times. Typical learning times are of the order of a few seconds if the indicated parameters are used.

From the output of the NN, which consists in the classification of each pixel as one of the four classes, it is immediate to obtain the binarized version of the manuscript, by merging the pixels classified as text and occlusion in a same class, and, similarly, bleed-through noise and background in another single class. When the goal is instead that of obtaining a virtually restored version of the manuscript, which preserves as much as possible its original appearance and informative features, the foreground text pixels, the occlusion pixels and the background pixels are given their original value, whereas the noisy pixels are replaced with samples drawn from the closest safe background region. For this latter task, in [21] we tested various state-of-the art still image inpainting techniques, and selected as the best and simplest one for our purposes the exemplar-based image inpainting technique described in [19].

4   Experimental Results

We evaluate the results of our virtual restoration method from a qualitative point of view, and comparing the NN classification result with the binarization produced by the algorithm that was the winner of the H-DIBCO-2018 competition [1]. This algorithm implements a segmentation method based on a Laplacian energy, and is described in [24,25].

Both for the learning and classification phases, the manuscripts are converted to grayscale, as the color information is unessential here for the purpose of classification. For virtual restoration, the restored versions of the color manuscripts can be straightforwardly recovered from the classification of the grayscale versions, since the three RGB channels share the same classes.

A first experiment was totally synthetic, in the sense that the recto-verso images to restore were numerically built based on the ground-truths available for one of the recto-verso pairs contained in the database [26,27], i.e. the 15-th pair out of a total of 25 pairs. In a second experiment, we restored the same recto-verso pair used for the synthetic case, this time as it appears in the database, i.e. with its real degradation. We processed the couple of RGB images with the NN trained on them. Since the recto-verso pair was already registered, we did not include the block alignment mechanism necessary in the case of misaligned recto-verso pairs, and described in [14,29].

Figures 1 (a) and (b) show the recto and the reflected verso of the chosen pair, with the real degradation that affect them. Figures 1 (c) and (d) show the binary ground-truths, manually built, that accompany that recto-verso pair in the database. This ground-truths represent the correct foreground texts of the two manuscript sides, and serve as comparison to evaluate the performance of algorithms of binarization of degraded historically manuscripts, as well as, indirectly, of algorithms of virtual restoration.

In the synthetic experiments we built an artificial clean recto-verso pair by placing the clean foreground texts on a textured background obtained by inpainting. The foreground texts were obtained by picking up the RGB values of the real degraded images of Figs. 1 (a) and (b), at the positions of the black pixels in the corresponding binary ground-truth maps (Figs. 1 (c) and (d)). Figure 2 (a) and (b) show this clean, ideal manuscript pair. An artificially degraded pair has then be obtained by mixing the ideal one through the data model of Eq. 1, where the percentage of penetrating ink has been increased from 0.1 to 0.9 (left to right) (Figs. 2 (c) and (d)).

In Fig. 3 the results of applying the NN (training and recall) on those images are shown. The training set was constructed by selecting pairs of clean patches from the degraded images themselves, and were mixed with percentages of ink penetration spanning from 0.1 to 0.9, in such a way to cover all the range of different amounts of degradation in the data. We built two different networks, one having as output only three classes (foreground, background and bleed-through), and the other characterized by the fourth class of the occlusions.

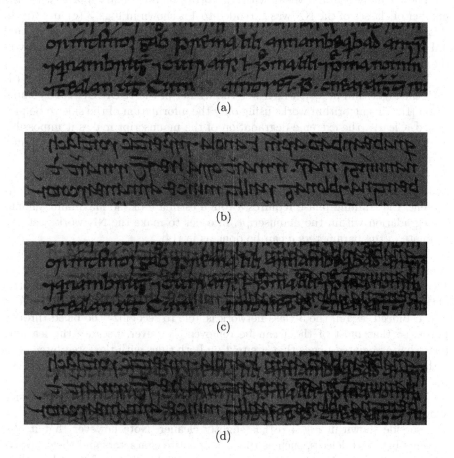

Fig. 2. Generation of a synthetic manuscript pair: (a) and (b) clean, ideal recto and verso created by the images in Fig. 1; (c) and (d) degraded recto and verso numerically constructed by feeding the images (a) and (b) to the data model of Eq. (1).

The virtually restored verso, with the corresponding binary image, when the number of classes of the NN was set to 3 is shown in Figs. 3 (a) and (b). Note how the reconstructed text sometimes appears corroded, fragmentary, with missing strokes. As already mentioned in the introduction, the fact that here the degradation is very strong, reaching up to $q = 0.9$, the lack of a specific class for the occlusions causes text pixels on both sides to be attributed to the bleed-through class and then deleted.

The virtually restored verso, with the corresponding binary image, when the number of classes of the NN was extended to 4 is shown in Figs. 3 (c) and (d). In this case the text is reconstructed much better, the characters are complete and full. Conversely, the bleed-through cleanup is slightly less effective, especially in the more severely degraded right-hand side of the manuscript.

Finally, Fig. 3 (e) shows the binarization of the degraded verso of Fig. 2 (d) with the algorithm in [24], which was the winner of the H-DIBCO-2018 competition [1]. This algorithm works using only the information of the side to be processed. Clearly, the extreme degradation of the manuscript makes it impossible to discriminate noise from the text of interest without information contributed by the opposite side of the page.

In the real experiment, we compared the performance of the 3-class NN and the 4-class NN on the degraded real images of Figs. 1 (a) and 1 (b). At present, the training phase requires a rough estimate of the maximum amount of degradation within the manuscript, in order to make the NN work best. An estimate of the parameters q can be done as in [14].

Thus, in this cases the training set was constructed by limiting the maximum value of the ink penetration percentage to 0.5, as the degradation is not as extreme as in the synthetic case. Our results still demonstrate clear superiority of the 4-classes NN with respect to the 3-classes NN, as shown for the verso side in Fig. 4. Indeed, again, the 3-class network is able to recognize the bleed-through pixels, so that most of them can be removed. However, because the learning phase has associated pixels that are text on both sides with the foreground class rather than with the specific occlusion class, some ambiguity remains between the foreground class and the bleed-through class.

With respect to the binary version of the restored manuscript (verso side shown in Fig. 4 (d)), this time the one obtained through the algorithm in [24] ((verso side shown in Fig. 4 (e)) is slightly cleaner. Note however that it also presents big local defects, such as the lack of entire characters and the excessive thickness of others, for example in the area highlighted with the red box. This area is shown enlarged in Fig. 5 for both methods, in comparison with the binary ground-truth provided in the public database.

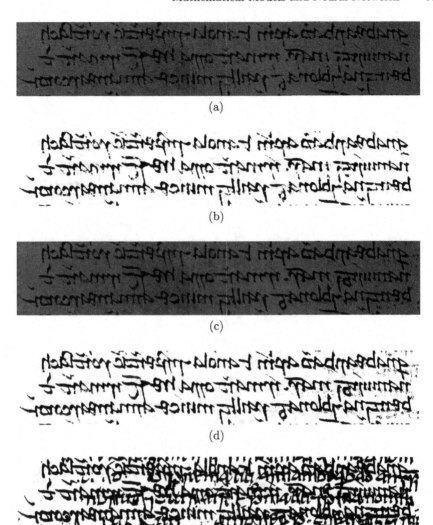

Fig. 3. Virtual restoration of the synthetic pair shown in Figs. 2 (c) and 2 (d): (a) and (b) verso restored with the 3-classes NN and the corresponding binary version; (c) and (d) verso restored with the 4-classes NN and the corresponding binary version; (e) degraded verso of Fig. 2 (d) binarized with the algorithm in [24].

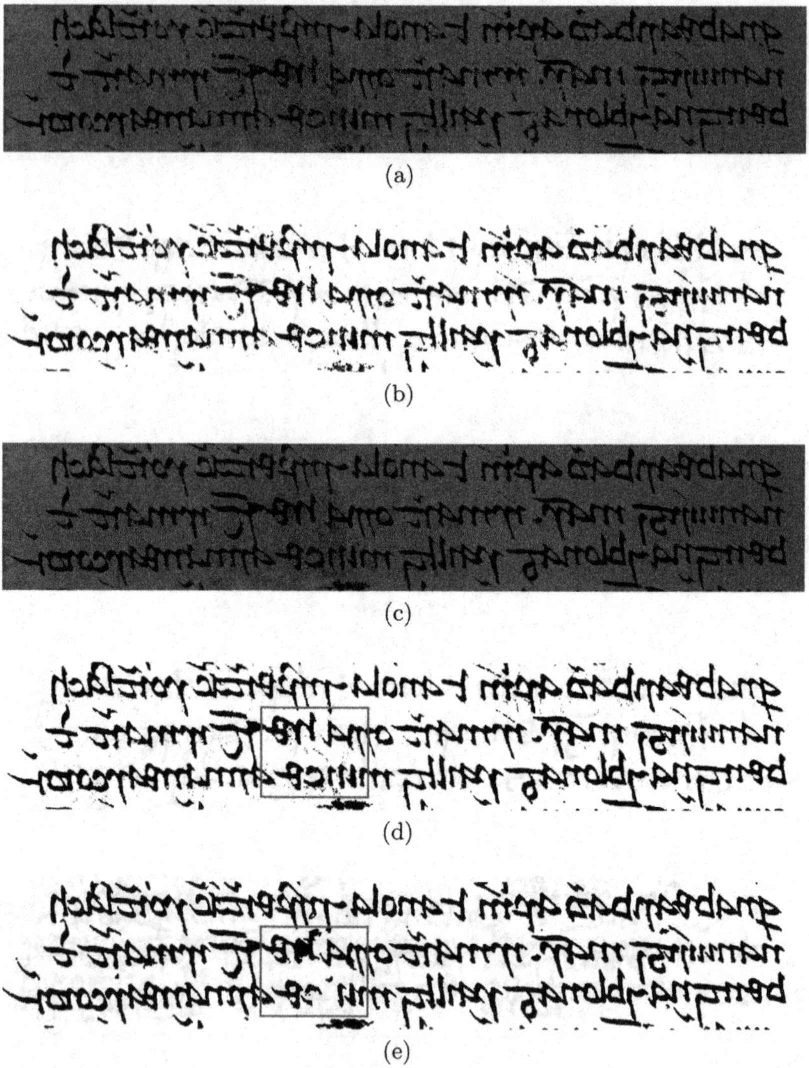

(a)

(b)

(c)

(d)

(e)

Fig. 4. Virtual restoration of the real pair shown in Figs. 1 (a) and 1 (b): (a) and (b) verso restored with the 3-classes NN and the corresponding binary version; (c) and (d) verso restored with the 4-classes NN and the corresponding binary version; (e) binarization of the verso of Fig. 1 (b) with the algorithm in [24].

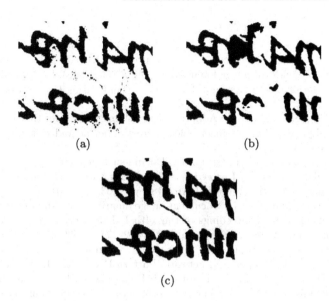

(a)   (b)

(c)

Fig. 5. Enlarged detail of the binary maps highlighted in red in Fig. 4: (a) our result; (b) the H-DIBCO-18 result [24]; (c) the binary ground-truth provided in the public database [27] (Color figure online).

5   Conclusions

We have shown that, exploiting the information contained on both the recto and verso of an ancient manuscript affected by ink penetration, it is possible to train a very simple shallow NN to correctly classify pixels in primary text, paper background, bleed-through noise and overlaid texts, without the need for an external training set. The example-target class pairs are generated from the data images themselves with the help of a data model that describes the degradation. After classification, the output of the NN can be used to produce a binarization of the foreground text or a virtual restoration version of the manuscript that maintains both the fullness of information content and the aesthetics of the original. The method improves on our previous proposals regarding the correct classification of the pixels corresponding to the occlusions between the two texts. In terms of binarization, we compare our results with those provided by the winning algorithm of the H-DIBCO-2018 [1] competition. The superiority of our method is evident in a synthetic case constructed in such a way as to cover the extent of degradation from almost zero to the maximum allowed. For moderate, rather uniform, real degradation, the binarization method performs slightly better, albeit with large local errors. Since the data model used is independent of the neural network paradigm, we intend to test our approach with other more sophisticated neural networks. We will also try to resolve the residual ambiguity between the two classes bleed-through and occlusion by using more descriptors.

References

1. Pratikakis, I., Zagori, K., Kaddas, P., Gatos, B.: ICFHR 2018 competition on handwritten document image binarization (H-DIBCO 2018). In Proceedings of the 16th International Conference on Frontiers in Handwriting Recognition (ICFHR), pp. 489–493 (2018)
2. Pai, Y., Chang, Y., Ruan, S.: Adaptive thresholding algorithm: Efficient computation technique based on intelligent block detection for degraded document images. Pattern Recognit. **43**, 3177–3187 (2010)
3. Westphal, F., Lavesson, N., Grahn, H.: Document image binarization using recurrent neural networks. In: Proceedings of the 13th IAPR International Workshop on Document Analysis Systems (DAS2018), pp. 263–268 (2018)
4. Tensmeyer, R., Martinez, T.: Document image binarization with fully convolutional neural networks. In: Proceedings of the 14th IAPR International Conference on Document Analysis and Recognition (ICDAR 2017), pp. 99–104 (2017)
5. Vo, Q., Kim, S., Yang, H., Lee, G.: Binarization of degraded document images based on hierarchical deep supervised network. Pattern Recognit. **74**, 568–586 (2018)
6. Fadoua, D., Le Bourgeois, F., Emptoz, H: Restoring ink bleed-through degraded document images using a recursive unsupervised classification technique. In: Bunke, H., Spitz, A.L. (eds.) DAS 2006. LNCS, vol. 3872, pp. 38–49. Springer, Heidelberg (2006). https://doi.org/10.1007/11669487_4
7. Sun, B., Li, S., Zhang, X.P., Sun, J.: Blind bleed-through removal for scanned historical document image with conditional random fields. IEEE Trans. Image Process. 5702–5712 (2016)
8. Rowley-Brooke, R., Pitié, F., Kokaram, A.: A non-parametric framework for document bleed-through removal. In: Proceedings of the IEEE Conference on Computer Vision and Pattern Recognition, pp. 2954–2960 (2013)
9. Huang, Y., Brown, M.S., Xu, D.: User assisted ink-bleed reduction. IEEE Trans. Image Process. **19**(10), 2646–2658 (2010)
10. Hanif, M., Tonazzini, A., Savino, P., Salerno, E.: Non-local sparse image in paintig for document bleed-through removal. J. Imaging **4**, 68 (2018)
11. Tonazzini, A., Savino, P., Salerno, E.: A non-stationary density model to separate overlapped texts in degraded documents. Signal Image Video Process. **9**, 155–164 (2015)
12. Rowley-Brooke, R., Pitié, F., Kokaram, A.C.: Non-rigid recto-verso registration using page outline structure and content preserving warps. In: Proceedings of the 2nd International Workshop on Historical Document Imaging and Processing, pp. 8–13 (2013)
13. Wang, J., Tan, C.L.: Non-rigid registration and restoration of double-sided historical manuscripts. In: Proceedings of the International Conference on Document Analysis and Recognition (ICDAR), pp. 1374–1378 (2011)
14. Savino, P., Tonazzini, A.: Digital restoration of ancient color manuscripts from geometrically misaligned recto-verso pairs. J. Cultural Heritage **19**, 511–521 (2016)
15. Savino, P., Tonazzini, A., Bedini, L.: Bleed-through cancellation in non-rigidly misaligned recto-verso archival manuscripts based on local registration. Int. J. Doc. Anal. Recognit. **22**, 163–176 (2019)
16. Tonazzini, A., Bedini, L., Salerno, E.: Independent component analysis for document restoration. Int. J. Doc. Anal. Recognit. **7**, 17–27 (2004)
17. Tonazzini, A., Bedini, L.: Restoration of recto-verso colour documents using correlated component analysis. EURASIP J. Adv. Signal Process. **58**, 2013 (2013)

18. Tonazzini, A., Salerno, E., Bedini, L.: Fast correction of bleed-through distortion in grayscale documents by a blind source separation technique. Int. J. Doc. Anal. Recogn. **10**, 17–25 (2007)
19. Criminisi, A., Pérez, P., Toyama, K.: Region filling and object removal by exemplar-based image inpainting. IEEE Trans. Image Process. **13**, 1200–1212 (2004)
20. He, S., Schomaker, L.: DeepOtsu: Document enhancement and binarization using iterative dep learning. Pattern Recogn. **9**, 379–390 (2019)
21. Savino, P., Tonazzini, A.: A Procedure for the routinary correction of back-to-front degradations in archival manuscripts. In: Nguyen, N.T., et al. (eds.) ICCCI 2020. LNCS (LNAI), vol. 12496, pp. 838–849. Springer, Cham (2020). https://doi.org/10.1007/978-3-030-63007-2_66
22. Tonazzini, A., Savino, P., Salerno, E., Hanif, M., Debole, F.: Virtual restoration and content analysis of ancient degraded manuscripts. Int. J. Inf. Sci. Technol. **3**, 16–25 (2019)
23. Hagan, M.T., Demuth, H.B., Beale, M.H.: Neural Network Design. PWS Publishing, Boston (1996)
24. Xiong, W., Jia, X., Xu, J., Xiong, Z., Liu, M., Wang, J.: Historical document image binarization using background estimation and energy minimization. In: Proceedings of the 24th International Conference on Pattern Recognition (ICPR 2018), pp. 3716–3721 (2018)
25. Xiong, W., Zhou, L., Yue, L., Li, L., Wang, S.: An enhanced binarization framework for degraded historical document images. EURASIP J. Image Video Process. (2021)
26. Rowley-Brooke, R., Pitié, F., Kokaram, A.: A ground truth bleed-through document image database. In: Zaphiris, P., Buchanan, G., Rasmussen, E., Loizides, F. (eds.) TPDL 2012. LNCS, vol. 7489, pp. 185–196. Springer, Heidelberg (2012). https://doi.org/10.1007/978-3-642-33290-6_21
27. Irish Script On Screen Project (2012). www.isos.dias.ie
28. Hanif, M., et al.: Blind bleed-through removal in color ancient manuscripts. Multim. Tools Appl. (2022). https://doi.org/10.1007/s11042-022-13755-6
29. Savino, P., Tonazzini, A.: A shallow neural net with model-based learning for the virtual restoration of recto-verso manuscripts. 1st International Virtual Conference on Visual Pattern Extraction and Recognition for Cultural Heritage Understanding VIPERC 2022 (2022). https://ceur-ws.org/Vol-3266/paper3.pdf

A Mathematical Model for the Analysis of Eye Fundus Images in Healthy and Diabetic Patients

Arianna Travaglini[1,2] and Gianluca Vinti[1(✉)]

[1] Department of Mathematics and Computer Science, University of Perugia,
1, Via Vanvitelli, 06123 Perugia, Italy
arianna.travaglini@unifi.it, gianluca.vinti@unipg.it
[2] Department of Mathematics and Computer Science "U.Dini" - DIMAI,
University of Florence, 67/a, Viale Giovanni Battista Morgagni, 50134 Firenze, Italy

Abstract. In this paper, we provide a study on eye fundus images of healthy and diabetic patients. Taking benefits from its reconstruction and enhancing properties, the sampling Kantorovich algorithm is used to process the considered images, after registration and averaging processes. Moreover, a hybrid segmentation procedure applied on superficial capillary plexus images (SCP) and one using the local Phansalkar method on choriocapillary images (CC) are exploited in order to asses a cluster counting process which is based on finding connected regions according to the 8–*adjacency* criterion. The results achieved on the healthy and diabetic patients show that the novel strategy allows to obtain accurate data from both a mathematical and a clinical point of view.

Keywords: SK algorithm · approximation results · digital image processing · registration · segmentation · cluster counting · diabetic patients

1 Introduction

The optical coherence tomography angiography (OCTA) is a relatively new technique used in ocular medical imaging in order to obtain visual representation of the ocular fundus [1]. Even if fluorangiography is considered the best imaging technique to represent the deep eye tissue, it requires the injection of a contrast agent. Instead, OCTA is a non invasive technique, since provides the visualization of the retinal perfusion without injection of any contrast agent. However,

A. Travaglini and G. Vinti have been partially supported within the 2022 GNAMPA-INdAM Project "Enhancement e segmentazione di immagini mediante operatori di tipo campionamento e metodi variazionali per lo studio di applicazioni biomediche" and G. Vinti within the projects Ricerca di Base 2019 dell'Università degli Studi di Perugia— "Integrazione, Approssimazione, Analisi Nonlineare e loro Applicazioni" and "Innovation, digitalisation and sustainability for the diffused economy in Central Italy - VITALITY (proposal identification code n. ECS_00000041)".

it has some limitations such as artifacts, which may be due to the OCT image acquisition itself or eye motion. For this reasons, many studies on image quality enhancement and noise reduction have been carried out (see, e.g., [2,3]) and more are still going on. In [4] a study on SCP (superficial capillary plexus) and CC (choriocapillary plexus) of healthy patients has been carried out using mainly the above techniques.

In this paper we want to extend the research on diabetic patients, who are potentially characterized by diseased eyes. Indeed, diabetes can cause diabetic macular edema, which is a swelling of the macula [5]. This condition has the potential to gradually obliterate the sharp vision in this area of the eye, resulting in partial vision loss or blindness.

The main purpose of this study is to improve the quality of OCTA eye images (both SCP and CC) coming from 20 healthy and 16 diabetic subjects, by applying a series of digital image processing techniques. For each healthy patient eye, six SCP images and six CC images were acquired by the OCTA scan; while for diabetic subjects we have at disposal five SCP and five CC images. At first, image registration techniques are performed in order to overlap each SCP image with the target one, chosen as the less noisy. The same coordinates are used to register are the CC images, since it is possible to assume that the choriocapillary tissue is rigidly connected to the superficial capillary plexus. Then, the resulting images are averaged and, resized and filtered by the SK algorithm, which consists in the implementation of the reconstruction (convergence) result of a given signal/image by means of the sampling Kantorovich operators (see, e.g., [6,7]).

For these operators, approximation results in the general setting of Orlicz spaces and, in particular, in L^p−spaces, as well as in the space of continuous and uniformly continuous functions, were provided in previous studies (see, e.g., [6–13]).

The SK algorithm, which behaves simultaneously as a low-pass filter and as a rescaling method for the increasing of the information content of images, plays a crucial role in the entire process exploited in this work. Indeed, it has been proved to be a powerful mathematical tool for the reconstruction and improvement of images. In this sense, several interesting outcomes have been attained as a result of this implementation, both in the engineering and biomedical fields [4,14–20]. Additionally, we note that the SK algorithm's efficiency in image rescaling has been assessed in relation with some interpolation and quasi-interpolation techniques, in terms of PSNR and CPU time [21].

In order to deduce quantitative assessments which could allow a comparison between healthy and diabetic patients, a *cluster counting* process has been adopted. This method is based on the fact that the eye vessels' network tends to be fully connected, i.e. it is ideally possible to go through all the capillaries with a single path, (arguments in favor of this assumption can be found in [22]). In order to do this, a segmentation process, which exploits a hybrid thresholding technique presented in [4], has been used on SCP images, starting from the well–known Otsu [23] and Phansalkar [24] local methods; the latter, which is particularly suitable when dealing with images characterized by a nonuniform staining, has been instead used on CC images (see, e.g., [25,26]). As mentioned above, since the vascularization of the retina is assumed to be fully connected, the selected criterion for the cluster counting analysis is that of the 8–adjacency.

Finally, the cluster counting assessment results important also for estabilishing a comparison between the only averaged image and that reconstructed with the SK algorithm after the averaging process, both for healthy and diabetic patients.

The paper is organized as follows: in Sect. 2 we report the fundamental approximation results for the family of sampling Kantorovich operators as well as some examples of kernels, whose choice plays a fundamental role in the application of the SK algorithm. In Sect. 3, the main methods for the processing of the considered images are described, i.e. the SK algorithm and the others digital image processing (DIP) techniques that are helpful for the whole procedure. The segmentation methods for the cluster counting analysis are described in Sect. 4. The experimental data are provided in Sect. 5, while in Sect. 6 we present the numerical achievements of the current study. Finally, Sect. 7 summarizes some remarks for the conclusions of the paper.

2   Approximation Properties of Sampling Kantorovich Operators

In the last years the family of sampling Kantorovich operators have been widely studied for their applications to signal and digital image processing (see, e.g., [4,14–20]).

The multidimensional version of the above operators [7] are defined by

$$(K_w^\chi f)(\underline{x}) = \sum_{\underline{k} \in \mathbb{Z}^n} \chi(w\underline{x} - t_{\underline{k}}) \left[\frac{w^n}{A_{\underline{k}}} \int_{R_{\underline{k}}^w} f(\underline{u}) d\underline{u} \right] \quad (\underline{x} \in \mathbb{R}^n), \tag{1}$$

where $f : \mathbb{R}^n \to \mathbb{R}$ is a locally integrable function such that the above series is convergent for each $\underline{x} \in \mathbb{R}^n$, $\chi : \mathbb{R}^n \to \mathbb{R}$ represents the so called *kernel*, i.e. a function which satisfies the following assumptions (see, e.g., [6,27]):

(χ_1) $\chi \in L^1(\mathbb{R}^n)$ and it is locally bounded on the origin;
(χ_2) $\sum_{\underline{k} \in \mathbb{Z}^n} \chi(\underline{u} - t_{\underline{k}}) = 1$, for every $\underline{u} \in \mathbb{R}^n$;
(χ_3) for some $\beta > 0$, the discrete absolute moment of order β of χ is finite, i.e.,

$$m_{\beta,\Pi^n}(\chi) = \sup_{\underline{u} \in \mathbb{R}^n} \sum_{\underline{k} \in \mathbb{Z}^n} |\chi(\underline{u} - t_{\underline{k}})| \, \|\underline{u} - t_{\underline{k}}\|_2^\beta < +\infty,$$

where $\| \cdot \|_2$ is the Euclidean norm, $\Delta_{k_i} := t_{k+i} - t_k > 0$, for every $i = 1, \dots, n$ and $\underline{k} = (k_1, \dots, k_n) \in \mathbb{Z}^n$, where $\Pi^n := (t_{\underline{k}})_{\underline{k} \in \mathbb{Z}^n}$ a strictly monotone increasing sequence of real numbers with δ, Δ such that $\delta \leq t_{k+1} - t_k \leq \Delta$,

$$R_{\underline{k}}^w := \left[\frac{t_{k_1}}{w}, \frac{t_{k_1+1}}{w} \right] \times \left[\frac{t_{k_2}}{w}, \frac{t_{k_2+1}}{w} \right] \times \cdots \times \left[\frac{t_{k_n}}{w}, \frac{t_{k_n+1}}{w} \right] \quad (w > 0),$$

and $A_{\underline{k}} := \Delta_{k_1} \cdot \Delta_{k_2} \cdot \dots \cdot \Delta_{k_n}$.

The family (1) has been firstly introduced, in its one-dimensional version, in [6] with the aim to provide an extension, to the general setting of Orlicz spaces [8,12,13], of the generalized sampling operators, introduced by P.L. Butzer in [28].

The following approximation results for the family of sampling Kantorovich operators need to be recalled in order to deal with the application to digital images and their reconstruction.

In particular, when one deals with continuous signals, the following convergence theorem holds.

Theorem 1 ([7]). *Let the kernel χ satisfy $(\chi_i), i = 1, 2, 3$ and let $f : \mathbb{R}^n \to \mathbb{R}$ be a continuous and bounded function. Then, for every $\underline{x} \in \mathbb{R}^n$,*

$$\lim_{w \to +\infty} (K_w^\chi f)(\underline{x}) = f(\underline{x}).$$

Further, if the function f is uniformly continuous and bounded, then

$$\lim_{w \to +\infty} \|K_w^\chi f - f\|_\infty = 0,$$

where $\| \cdot \|_\infty$ denotes the uniform norm.

Moreover, the following L^p−convergence theorem, which can be obtained as a particular case of a modular convergence theorem in Orlicz spaces, allows to reconstruct not necessarily continuous signals and hence will be useful for the application to digital images.

Theorem 2 ([7]). *Let the kernel χ satisfy $(\chi_i), i = 1, 2, 3$; then for every $f \in L^p(\mathbb{R}^n)$, $1 \le p < +\infty$, we have*

$$\lim_{w \to +\infty} \|K_w^\chi f - f\|_p = 0,$$

and the following estimate holds

$$\|K_w^\chi f\|_p \le \delta^{-n/p} (m_{0,\Pi^n}(\chi))^{(p-1)/p} \|\chi\|_1^{1/p} \|f\|_p,$$

where $\| \cdot \|_p$ denotes the usual L^p−norm.

Other than the above results, the family of sampling Kantorovich operators (1) have been extensively studied under various theoretical aspects. Indeed, the saturation order in $L^p(\mathbb{R})$-spaces and a characterization of the Favard classes for the family (1) based upon bandlimited kernels have been established in [10,11]. Furthermore, the behaviour of the first derivative of the sampling Kantorovich operators, when both differentiable and not differentiable signals are taken into account, has been studied in [9]. Finally, the family (1) has been implemented in MATLAB© and the resulting algorithm, later called SK algorithm, has been analyzed in terms of CPU time and compared with other reconstruction algorithms known in the literature in [21]. The pseudo-code of its implementation can be found in [17].

A fundamental role, in the theory of sampling Kantorovich operators, is played by the kernel function, i.e. the function which satisfies the assumptions $(\chi_1)-(\chi_3)$. In literature there are several examples of such functions, among them we can mention the one-dimensional central B-spline of order r (see, e.g., [6,27]):

$$M_r(x) := \frac{1}{(r-1)!} \sum_{i=0}^{r} (-1)^r \binom{r}{i} \left(\frac{r}{2} + x - i\right)_+^{r-1},$$

where the function $(x)_+ = \max\{x, 0\}$ denotes the positive part of $x \in \mathbb{R}$.

Its multidimensional version can be constructed from the one-dimensional one, according to the procedure provided in [29], as the following tensor product,

$$M_r^n(\underline{x}) := \prod_{i=1}^{n} M_r(x_i), \quad \underline{x} = (x_1, \dots, x_n) \in \mathbb{R}^n.$$

Another useful class of product type kernels, which has been chosen for the reconstruction of both SCP and CC images (see Sect. 3), is given by the so called Jackson-type kernels:

$$J_k^n(\underline{x}) := \prod_{i=1}^{n} J_k(x_i), \quad \underline{x} \in \mathbb{R}^n, \tag{2}$$

where the one-dimensional Jackson-type kernels are defined by:

$$J_k(x) = c_k sinc^{2k}\left(\frac{x}{2k\pi\alpha}\right),$$

with $x \in \mathbb{R}$, $k \in \mathbb{N}$, $\alpha \geq 1$, and where c_k is a non-zero normalization coefficient given by

$$c_k := \left[\int_{\mathbb{R}} sinc^{2k}\left(\frac{u}{2k\pi\alpha}\right) du\right]^{-1},$$

see e.g., [27]. Other than the tensor product kernels, another kind of kernels are the radial kernels. Examples of them are given by the so called Wendland kernels, which are compactly supported radial basis functions [30,31]. They are defined by considering the function

$$\phi_{m,0}(r) := (1-r)_+^m := \begin{cases} (1-r)^m, & \text{if } r \leq 1 \\ 0, & \text{if } r > 1 \end{cases}, \quad r = \|\underline{x}\|_2 \quad (\underline{x} \in \mathbb{R}^n),$$

then the Wendland kernels are defined by the following recursive formula

$$\phi_{m,k+1}(r) := \int_r^{+\infty} t\phi_{m,k}(t)dt, \quad k = 0, 1, \dots,$$

with $r = \|\underline{x}\|_2$, $\underline{x} \in \mathbb{R}^n$ (see, e.g., [32]).

For other useful examples of kernels, see also [6,29,33,34].

Now, before applying the bidimensional sampling Kantorovich operators to image reconstruction, it is necessary to recall that a bidimensional grayscale image can be represented as:

$$I(x,y) := \sum_{i=1}^{m} \sum_{j=1}^{m} a_{ij} \cdot \mathbf{1}_{ij}(x,y) \quad (x,y) \in \mathbb{R}^2,$$

where a_{ij} are the elements of the matrix A which represents the image,

$$\mathbf{1}_{ij}(x,y) := \begin{cases} 1, & (x,y) \in (i-1,i] \times (j-1,j], \\ 0, & \text{otherwise,} \end{cases}$$

are the characteristics functions of the sets $(i-1,i] \times (j-1,j]$, $i,j = 1,2,\ldots,m$, and I is a step function, e.g. belonging to $L^p(\mathbb{R}^2)$, $1 \le p < +\infty$, with compact support. Therefore, the family of bidimensional sampling Kantorovich operators can then be applied to the function I, considering one of the above mentioned family of kernels.

Furthermore, since it acts as a rescaling algorithm, the above implementation allows to obtain an image with an increasing information content with respect to the original one. Moreover, we remark that the SK algorithm's ability to reconstruct a given image I with any specified sampling rate is one of its key benefits: by increasing the sampling rate, it is possible to obtain an improved version of the rescaled image I.

3   Methodology

As already said, the OCTA is an innovative and clinically promising imaging technique for acquiring images of the retinal and sub-retinal vasculature. OCTA requires repeated scans at the same location to detect motion: it identifies blood vessels by detecting the blood flow-induced change in the OCT reflectance signal [1]. However, variations in flow speed and patient movements can introduce noise and artifacts into OCTA data. In order to overcome this problem, multiple en face OCTA pictures may be averaged together to attenuate noise, enhance vascular continuity, and considerably improve both qualitative and quantitative assessments [35, 36]. However if we average the images without doing any other registration first, the result will be a blurred image, with a lower quality than the initial ones (see Fig. 1).

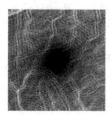

Fig. 1. Example of images averaged without a registration process: on the left an SCP (superficial capillary plexus) image; on the right a CC (choriocapillary tissue) image.

This is due to the time interval between each scan, which causes the eye to make small movements and results in image misalignment. Therefore, the first step is to register the images according to a rigid transformation (affine): the *Turboreg* plugin of *Fiji* (see, e.g., [37]), a commonly used algorithm to do motion correction, is exploited to implement the registration. It tries to align two images by minimizing their *Mean Square Error (MSE)*, while translating and rotating one of them. The Mean Square Error is a similarity index which is defined by

$$MSE = \sum_{i=1}^{M} \sum_{j=1}^{N} \frac{|I_A(i,j) - I_B(i,j)|^2}{MN},$$

where $I_A(i,j)$ and $I_B(i,j)$ are two $M \times N$ images.

However, since the eye is made up of organic tissues and fluids that are constantly deformed, a mere affine registration is not sufficient. Indeed, the resulting averaged image is still too blurred. Therefore, a supplementary type of registration is needed: a landmark based one, using the plugin *bUnwarpJ* [38], deforms elastically the image in order to align salient points previously extracted. The elastic deformations are represented by B–splines functions and the result of these operations can be seen in Fig. 2.

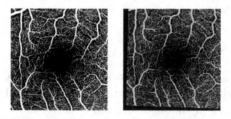

Fig. 2. Original SCP image (left) and its corresponding after both registration processes (right).

As we can see in Fig. 2, the empty space left when the registered image is dislocated, is filled with black pixels. This causes a darkening effect in the areas near the edge on the post–average image.

To detect salient points, the feature extraction plugin *Extract Mops Correspondences* has been exploited. It uses the *Difference of gaussian detector* to detect interest points according to a local feature descriptor, the *Multi-Scale Oriented Patches*, or *MOPS* [39].

At this point, every SCP image is registered on the target one, which is chosen as the less noisy. The average image obtained (Fig. 3) is now less blurred than that one in Fig. 1 and, as a result, the noise is reduced, allowing to better distinguish the vessels from the background.

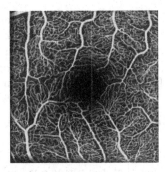

Fig. 3. Example of a SCP image after the registration and averaging process.

Despite CC images pattern's makes it difficult to automatically detect fiducial points, it is possible to assume that the choriocapillary tissue is rigidly connected to the superficial capillary plexus, being them parts of the same body. For this reason, the coordinates of the transformation made on each SCP image have been saved and then applied to each corresponding CC. Therefore the final transformation on SCP and CC images is exactly the same (Fig. 4).

Fig. 4. Example of a CC image after the registration and averaging process.

The reconstruction process on both the SCP and CC images ends with the application of the sampling Kantorovich operator. All the images have been processed using the SK algorithm with the bidimensional Jackson type kernel (see Sect. 2) with $k = 12$ and the scaling factor $R = 2$. Note that in [4], the validity of the SK algorithm for the reconstruction of SCP images has been confirmed, in terms of the PSNR index, by the comparison with the fluorangiography reference images. Similar outcome for the CC images processed with the SK algorithm: their matching with the gold standard image, represented by a histological image, has been confirmed by a texture analysis. These results motivate the choice of the SK algorithm for the processing of the images of healthy and diabetic subjects of the present study.

The sampling Kantorovich operator offers different advantages. Indeed, it operates an integral average which acts as a *low–pass filter*, so that high frequencies are eliminated and consequently the noise is reduced. Moreover, thanks to its zooming factor, it rescales the image, increasing its information content and allowing a better analysis of the eye images, from a clinical point of view.

4 Segmentation Techniques for Cluster Counting Analysis

Starting from the assumption that the retina's vascularization ideally consists, from the anatomical point of view, of a single cluster constituted by a fully connected network [22], a segmentation procedure is needed in order to carry out a cluster counting process. For this scope, the hybrid segmentation method introduced in [4] has been exploited on SCP images, in order to overcome, from one side, the retinal vessel over–segmentation issues caused by the Phansalkar method [24], and, from the other side, the problems related to the white artifacts in the macula, caused by the local Otsu method [23], as can be seen in Fig. 5. The result of the hybrid segmentation can be seen in Fig. 6.

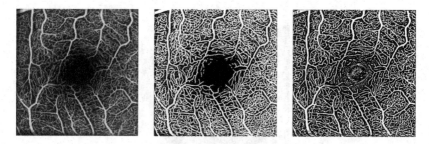

Fig. 5. An example of application of local Phansalkar thresholding (center), local Otsu thresholding (right) on the original SCP (Superficial Capillary Plexus) image (left).

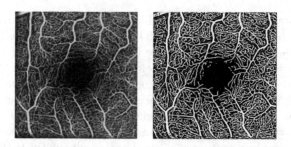

Fig. 6. Example of the application of the hybrid thresholding method (right) on a SCP image (the left).

Instead, the local Phansalkar method has been chosen for the segmentation of CC images, since it results particularly suitable when dealing with low-contrast images, characterized by a nonuniform staining (see, e.g., [25,26]), as can be seen in Fig. 7.

Fig. 7. Example of the application of the local Phansalkar thresholding method (right) on a CC image (left)

All these local thresholding methods have been applied with a radius of 7 pixels on the only averaged images and with a radius of 15 pixels on the images reconstructed by the SK algorithm.

5 Experimental Data

We have evaluated the above procedure on the images of thirtysix eyes from eighteen different patients. Twenty of them are clinically healthy, without any known eye disease, while the other sixteen suffer from diabetes. Even though the latter patients do not have any known eye disease, people suffering from diabetes have a high probability of developing eye pathologies, such as diabetic macular edema or diabetic retinopathy [5]. For each healthy patient eye, six SCP images and six CC images were acquired by the OCTA scan with short intervals of time between one and the other; while for diabetic subjects we have at disposal five SCP and five CC images (see Figs. 8 and 9).

The SPECTRALIS HRA+OCT2 (Heidelberg Engineering, Heidelberg, Germany) was used to capture OCTA images. This device is capable of capturing 85,000 A-scans per second with a 3.9-μm axial and 6-μm lateral resolution. It makes use of an algorithm for probabilistic amplitude decorrelation and an 870nm light source with a 50nm bandwidth. To minimize motion artifacts, TruTrack®Active Eye Tracking Technology was employed. The acquisitions were carried out using the high-resolution pre-set, with a $10° \times 10°$ (3.1 mm × 3.1 mm)-15° angle volume scan (512 B-scans with 6 m space between consecutive B-scans using an averaging technique of 5 frames/scan) centred in the foveal region. C-scan (also known as "en-face") angiograms were evaluated using the viewer software (Heyex Software, version 1.9.201.0, Heidelberg Engineering, Heidelberg, Germany). These grayscale images have been converted in 8-bit images in order to apply our processing techniques.

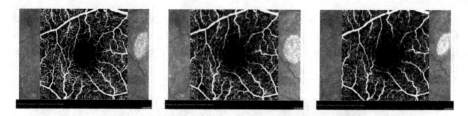

Fig. 8. Examples of three original SCP images from a diabetic patient eye.

Fig. 9. Examples of three original CC images scanned at the same time of the corresponding SCP images in Fig. 8.

6   Numerical Results

In order to numerically evaluate the results obtained, we have calculated the number of connected components (clusters) of the images. The medical literature suggests that the vessels of the healthy eyes are very interconnected, and this results in a low number of clusters (ideally only one cluster). Therefore, a decrease in the cluster's number means that the results are good. Due to the above mentioned interconnection, the 8–*adjacency* criterion has been applied on the thresholded images, in order to operate a cluster counting process. In particular, we have applied the hybrid thresholding technique described in [4] on the SCP images, while the local Phansalkar method on the CC images (see, e.g., [25,26]). The cluster counting process has been done on two types of images so that comparisons can be made:

- on the averaged images where the SK algorithm has not been applied (AVG);
- on the images where the SK algorithm has been applied after the averaging process (AVG+SK).

Results are shown in the following tables.

In particular, Table 1 refers to the *SCP* images of healthy patients. The results show that the images where the SK algorithm has been applied have a lower number of clusters than the only averaged images. This represents an improvement of the image quality, as the vessels' network proves to be more connected. The same positive trend is confirmed in Table 2, showing that our image processing techniques works well also on diabetic patients' images. Indeed, the number of clusters decreases after the reconstruction, while the areas of the clusters increase.

Table 1. From the left to the right: the number describing the progressive number of healthy patients (SCP Healty Eye Nr.); the method (Method) used to process the image (AVG=averaging only, AVG+SK=SK algorithm applied after averaging); the number of clusters of the vessels' network (Nr. cluster); the mean of the area of all the previous clusters (Mean Area, in pixels) and the corresponding standard deviation (Std. Dev. Area, in pixels); the number of pixels of the whole image (Img. Pixels). The values representing areas (Mean Area and Std. Dev. Area) have been scaled according to the image dimension in order to compare the results.

SCP Healthy Eye Nr.	Method	Nr. Clusters	Mean Area	St. Dev. Area	Img. Pixels
1	AVG	1223	296.3	8819.3	902500
2	AVG	746	493.2	12571.7	902500
3	AVG	1601	234.8	7642.2	902500
4	AVG	1691	226.5	7880.0	902500
5	AVG	1536	224.7	7901.2	902500
6	AVG	1471	244.3	8763.0	902500
7	AVG	1321	289.1	9732.8	902500
8	AVG	1310	289.1	9534.8	902500
9	AVG	1526	222.0	7395.0	902500
10	AVG	1885	180.7	6634.1	902500
11	AVG	3655	69.1	1124.0	902500
12	AVG	3448	83.7	1752.3	902500
13	AVG	1315	258.3	8519.4	902500
14	AVG	1873	181.1	6485.0	902500
15	AVG	1735	214.1	6977.8	902500
16	AVG	1461	265.0	8736.2	902500
17	AVG	1508	235.7	7474.1	902500
18	AVG	1216	297.1	9124.4	902500
19	AVG	1140	326.0	10116.0	902500
20	AVG	1070	341.1	10429.0	902500
Mean		1637	248.6	7880.6	
1	AVG+SK	963	384.3	9855.9	3610000
2	AVG+SK	562	667.7	14887.6	3610000
3	AVG+SK	1241	305.6	8885.5	3610000
4	AVG+SK	1312	294.2	9032.9	3610000
5	AVG+SK	1172	298.7	9240.8	3610000
6	AVG+SK	1154	315.6	10080.8	3610000
7	AVG+SK	941	411.6	11873.5	3610000
8	AVG+SK	972	394.2	11206.4	3610000
9	AVG+SK	1226	283.3	8435.3	3610000
10	AVG+SK	1499	232.4	7543.5	3610000
11	AVG+SK	2928	94.4	1200.6	3610000
12	AVG+SK	2709	114.1	2178.3	3610000
13	AVG+SK	992	346.5	9997.7	3610000
14	AVG+SK	1281	266.3	6251.3	3610000
15	AVG+SK	1336	282.1	8152.7	3610000
16	AVG+SK	1104	356.3	10201.0	3610000
17	AVG+SK	1191	305.1	8638.4	3610000
18	AVG+SK	969	378.7	10326.5	3610000
19	AVG+SK	870	433.4	11814.9	3610000
20	AVG+SK	870	425.9	11825.6	3610000
Mean		1265	329.5	9081.5	

Table 2. From the left to the right: the number describing the progressive number of diabetic patients (SCP Diabetic Eye Nr.); the method (Method) used to process the image (AVG = averaging only, AVG+SK=SK algorithm applied after averaging); the number of clusters of the vessels' network (Nr. cluster); the mean of the area of all the previous clusters (Mean Area, in pixels) and the corresponding standard deviation (Std. Dev. Area, in pixels); the number of pixels of the whole image (Img. Pixels). The values representing areas (Mean Area and Std. Dev. Area) have been scaled according to the image dimension in order to compare the results.

SCP Diabetic Eye Nr.	Method	Nr. Clusters	Mean Area	St. Dev. Area	Img. Pixels
1	AVG	2748	110.4	1401.6	960400
2	AVG	1859	175.2	4100.2	960400
3	AVG	1860	181.0	2548.0	960400
4	AVG	3868	56.2	447.5	960400
5	AVG	2480	96.7	975.5	960400
6	AVG	2236	110.2	133.2	960400
7	AVG	2147	131.8	3440.7	960400
8	AVG	1795	185.6	4218.0	960400
9	AVG	2213	145.3	2138.7	960400
10	AVG	3619	89.8	871.6	960400
11	AVG	2444	131.4	1620.4	1010000
12	AVG	2559	135.8	3877.2	1010000
13	AVG	2334	96.5	2333.7	1010000
14	AVG	2402	97.3	1939.6	1010000
15	AVG	3630	67.9	609.0	1010000
16	AVG	2279	131.9	3131.4	1010000
Mean		2529	121.4	2174.1	
1	AVG+SK	2239	143.6	1455.7	3841600
2	AVG+SK	1504	222.0	3613.1	3841600
3	AVG+SK	1569	221.9	2710.8	3841600
4	AVG+SK	3473	72.3	486.8	3841600
5	AVG+SK	2035	121.5	1292.4	3841600
6	AVG+SK	1830	141.8	1442.2	3841600
7	AVG+SK	1868	159.2	2703.6	3841600
8	AVG+SK	1474	233.4	4884.0	3841600
9	AVG+SK	1780	188.7	2476.3	3841600
10	AVG+SK	3121	107.2	767.1	3841600
11	AVG+SK	2082	159.4	2762.3	4040000
12	AVG+SK	2179	162.2	4235.2	4040000
13	AVG+SK	1998	115.8	2620.4	4040000
14	AVG+SK	2022	119.34	2186.1	4040000
15	AVG+SK	3062	90.2	728.0	4040000
16	AVG+SK	1852	168.5	3576.4	4040000
Mean		2131	151.7	2371.3	

Table 3. From the left to the right: the number describing the progressive number of diabetic patients (CC Healthy Eye Nr.); the method (Method) used to process the image (AVG = averaging only, AVG+SK=SK algorithm applied after averaging); the number of clusters of the vessels' network (Nr. cluster); the mean of the area of all the previous clusters (Mean Area, in pixels) and the corresponding standard deviation (Std. Dev. Area, in pixels); the number of pixels of the whole image (Img. Pixels). The values representing areas (Mean Area and Std. Dev. Area) have been scaled according to the image dimension in order to compare the results.

CC Healthy Eye Nr.	Method	Nr. Clusters	Mean Area	St. Dev. Area	Img. Pixels
1	AVG	282	2998.1	50251.7	902500
2	AVG	278	2979.9	49412.1	902500
3	AVG	88	8963.6	84030.8	902500
4	AVG	468	1638.8	35250.4	902500
5	AVG	355	2090.0	39146.4	902500
6	AVG	305	2450.4	42103.7	902500
7	AVG	556	1418.4	33229.3	902500
8	AVG	548	1462.2	33741.6	902500
9	AVG	752	868.3	23457.0	902500
10	AVG	509	1311.6	29395.8	902500
11	AVG	2087	275.2	11832.7	902500
12	AVG	1067	638.8	20538.7	902500
13	AVG	265	2818.7	45731.4	902500
14	AVG	173	4340.9	57013.0	902500
15	AVG	1234	498.8	16991.8	902500
16	AVG	441	1693.6	35407.8	902500
17	AVG	473	1447.3	31289.3	902500
18	AVG	565	1157.2	27330.4	902500
19	AVG	453	1653.6	34929.9	902500
20	AVG	492	1474.7	32459.3	902500
Mean		570	2109.0	36677.2	
1	AVG+SK	214	4044.7	59051.4	3610000
2	AVG+SK	206	4107.6	58658.3	3610000
3	AVG+SK	38	21475.8	132354.2	3610000
4	AVG+SK	363	2171.9	41158.6	3610000
5	AVG+SK	199	9310.1	54955.0	3610000
6	AVG+SK	201	3921.3	54699.7	3610000
7	AVG+SK	429	1911.3	39353.9	3610000
8	AVG+SK	318	2622.3	46446.9	3610000
9	AVG+SK	510	1375.3	30856.4	3610000
10	AVG+SK	263	2747.8	44436.0	3610000
11	AVG+SK	1462	425.3	15581.6	3610000
12	AVG+SK	704	1033.9	27181.3	3610000
13	AVG+SK	111	7080.2	74523.0	3610000
14	AVG+SK	129	5957.4	67586.0	3610000
15	AVG+SK	563	1230.3	28927.9	3610000
16	AVG+SK	282	2794.7	46819.6	3610000
17	AVG+SK	236	3146.8	48211.2	3610000
18	AVG+SK	301	2383.3	41241.6	3610000
19	AVG+SK	353	2183.2	40767.3	3610000
20	AVG+SK	408	1854.0	37155.0	3610000
Mean		365	3788.9	49496.7	

Table 4. From the left to the right: the number describing the progressive number of diabetic patients (CC Diabetic Eye Nr.); the method (Method) used to process the image (AVG = averaging only, AVG+SK=SK algorithm applied after averaging); the number of clusters of the vessels' network (Nr. cluster); the mean of the area of all the previous clusters (Mean Area, in pixels) and the corresponding standard deviation (Std. Dev. Area, in pixels); the number of pixels of the whole image (Img. Pixels). The values representing areas (Mean Area and Std. Dev. Area) have been scaled according to the image dimension in order to compare the results.

CC Diabetic Eye Nr.	Method	Nr. Clusters	Mean Area	St. Dev. Area	Img. Pixels
1	AVG	2782	209.8	10154.7	960400
2	AVG	4928	77.5	1213.6	960400
3	AVG	1414	450.0	16129.1	960400
4	AVG	2685	207.3	9860.5	960400
5	AVG	4098	107.8	4754.2	960400
6	AVG	3242	140.1	5216.3	960400
7	AVG	794	943.6	26180.5	960400
8	AVG	410	1891.4	38066.7	960400
9	AVG	1925	306.4	12690.1	960400
10	AVG	3734	122.1	4472.3	960400
11	AVG	159	5555.9	69979.1	1010000
12	AVG	843	842.9	23518.3	1010000
13	AVG	1224	584.9	19892.0	1010000
14	AVG	938	766.2	23139.4	1010000
15	AVG	3864	131.8	5528.1	1010000
16	AVG	4664	86.3	1136.1	1010000
Mean		2357	776.5	16995.7	
1	AVG+SK	1967	322.1	13398.3	3841600
2	AVG+SK	3910	104.0	2461.4	3841600
3	AVG+SK	749	956.9	25729.2	3841600
4	AVG+SK	1780	351.2	14057.1	3841600
5	AVG+SK	3106	155.5	6371.8	3841600
6	AVG+SK	2298	220.0	8929.5	3841600
7	AVG+SK	580	1364.9	32578.7	3841600
8	AVG+SK	217	3830.1	56265.5	3841600
9	AVG+SK	1047	638.2	20070.6	3841600
10	AVG+SK	2603	197.6	7808.6	3841600
11	AVG+SK	96	9568.7	93701.4	4040000
12	AVG+SK	567	1323.4	30844.0	4040000
13	AVG+SK	767	1010.3	27368.8	4040000
14	AVG+SK	568	1386.5	32845.2	4040000
15	AVG+SK	2508	232.9	10592.7	4040000
16	AVG+SK	3441	130.0	3094.4	4040000
Mean		1638	1362.0	24132.3	

The results shown in Tables 3 and 4 indicate that the process works well for CC images, too. When the SK algorithm is applied, increases the links between vessels also in case of CC images.

The above cluster counting analysis shows a stronger vessel's connection, both for SCP and CC images, whenever the SK algorithm is applied. Moreover, we point out that the variation in size of the images taken into account does not affect the analysis performed. Indeed, the comparisons have been made between one AVG image and its corresponding AVG+SK image, having the foresight to scale the values representing areas. Instead, for what concerns the number of clusters, it has been tested that a larger sized image results in a greater number of clusters. Indeed, by duplicating (without interpolation) the size of the only averaged images, the number of clusters increases. As a consequence, the results achieved on the images reconstructed by the SK algorithm are not only the most reliable, since the number of clusters decreases, but also the most conservatives, since we obtain a lower number of connected regions on a double sized image with respect to the only averaged one.

Finally, we note that diabetic patients' images have a number of clusters on average higher than healthy patients, confirming the clinical incidence of the disease on retinal pathologies.

7 Conclusions

For the processing and improvement of digital images, the reconstruction capabilities of sampling Kantorovich operators have proved to be highly beneficial. Indeed, in [4] it has been already shown that the SK algorithm improves both the quality of SCP and CC images of healthy subjects. In the present study, we extend the analysis also on diabetic subjects: after registration and averaging processes, the SK algorithm is applied in order to rescale and enhance the eye images of the healthy and diabetic patients considered. By exploiting the hybrid thresholding technique presented in [4], the SCP images are binarized, avoiding the retinal vessel over-segmentation and the white artifacts in the macula, caused respectively by local Phansalkar's and Otsu's thresholding methods. A novel approach of this study consists in the application of the local Phansalkar thresholding technique on the CC images, as it results particularly suitable on low-contrast images, characterized by nonuniform staining (see, e.g., [25,26]).

Finally, a cluster counting analysis has been conducted by finding the connected regions in the thresholded images, according to the 8–adjacency criterion. This choice is motivated by the fact that retina vessels' network is assumed to be ideally fully connected. The cluster counting process proved that the images reconstructed by the SK algorithm (after the averaging process) have a lower number of clusters than the only averaged images. Indeed, it improves the representation of vessels' network, as it acts as a resizing algorithm and as a low-pass filter, eliminating the noise contained in high frequencies, also on diabetic patients, who are prone to eye diseases. The variation of the number of clusters between healthy and diabetic patients can be used to analyze the differences between the retinal trees of the two categories, which results to be a clinical indication of the disease.

In conclusion, the outcome of our study shows an effective improvement on the image quality, and, consequently, a more accurate medical diagnosis of eye diseases that can be observed both from a visual and a numerical point of view.

Acknowledgements. The authors wish to thank prof. C. Cagini and prof. M. Lupidi of the Ophthalmology Section of the Department of Medicine and Surgery of the University of Perugia for having kindly provided the images used in this work.

Moreover, A. Travaglini and G. Vinti are members of the Gruppo Nazionale per l'Analisi Matematica, la Probabilitá e le loro Applicazioni (GNAMPA) of the Istituto Nazionale di Alta Matematica (INdAM), of the network RITA (Research ITalian network on Approximation) and of the UMI group "Teoria dell'Approssimazione e Applicazioni."

References

1. Hagag, A.M., Gao, S.S., Jia, Y., Huang, D.: Optical coherence tomography angiography: technical principles and clinical applications in ophthalmology. Taiwan J. Ophthalmol. **7**(3), 115–129 (2017)
2. Sakamoto, A., Hangai, M., Yoshimura, N.: Spectral-domain optical coherence tomography with multiple B-scan averaging for enhanced imaging of retinal diseases. Ophthalmology **115**(6), 1071–1078 e7 (2008)
3. Sander, B., Larsen, M., Thrane, L., Hougaard, J.L., Jorgensen, T.M.: Enhanced optical coherence tomography imaging by multiple scan averaging. Br. J. Ophthalmol. **89**(2), 207–212 (2005)
4. Cagini, C., et al.: Improvement of retinal OCT angiograms by Sampling Kantorovich algorithm in the assessment of retinal and choroidal perfusion. Appl. Math. Comput. **427**(4), 127152 (2022)
5. Skarbez, K., Priestley, Y., Hoepf, M., Koevary, S.B.: Comprehensive review of the effects of diabetes on ocular health. Expert Rev. Ophthalmol. **5**(4), 557–577 (2010)
6. Bardaro, C., Butzer, P.L., Stens, R.L., Vinti, G.: Kantorovich-type generalized sampling series in the setting of Orlicz spaces. Sampling Theory Signal Image Process. **6**(1), 29–52 (2007)
7. Costarelli, D., Vinti, G.: Approximation by multivariate generalized sampling Kantorovich operators in the setting of Orlicz spaces. Bollettino dell'Unione Matematica Italiana **4**(3), 445–468 (2011)
8. Bardaro, C., Musielak, J., Vinti, G.: Nonlinear Integral Operators and Applications. De Gruyter Series in Nonlinear Analysis and Applications, New York, Berlin (2003)
9. Cantarini, M., Costarelli, D., Vinti, G.: Approximation of differentiable and not differentiable signals by the first derivative of sampling Kantorovich operators. J. Math. Anal. Appl. **509**(1), Art. Number 125913 (2021)
10. Costarelli, D., Vinti, G.: Saturation by the Fourier transform method for the sampling Kantorovich series based on bandlimited Kernels. Anal. Math. Phys. **9**(4), 2263–2280 (2019). https://doi.org/10.1007/s13324-019-00334-6
11. Costarelli, D., Vinti, G.: Approximation properties of the sampling Kantorovich operators: regularization, saturation, inverse results and Favard classes in L^p-spaces. J. Fourier Anal. Appl. **28**, 1–42 (2022)

12. Musielak, J.: Orlicz Spaces and Modular Spaces, 1st edn. LNM. Springer, Berlin (1983). https://doi.org/10.1007/BFb0072210
13. Rao, M.M., Ren, Z.D.: Theory of Orlicz Spaces. Dekker Inc., New York-Basel-Hong Kong (1991)
14. Asdrubali, F., et al.: Mathematical models for the improvement of detection techniques of industrial noise sources from acoustic images. Math. Methods Appl. Sci. **44**(13), 10448–10459 (2021)
15. Cluni, F., Gusella, V., Vinti, G.: Masonry elastic characteristics assessment by thermographic images. Meccanica **54**(9), 1339–1349 (2019)
16. Costarelli, D., Pozzilli, P., Seracini, M., Vinti, G.: Enhancement of cone-beam computed tomography dental-maxillofacial images by sampling Kantorovich algorithm. Symmetry **13**(8), Art. number 1450 (2021)
17. Costarelli, D., Seracini, M., Travaglini, A., Vinti, G.: Alzheimer biomarkers esteem by sampling Kantorovich algorithm. Math. Methods Appl. Sci. 1–15 (2023). https://doi.org/10.1002/mma.9268
18. Costarelli, D., Seracini, M., Vinti, G.: A segmentation procedure of the pervious area of the aorta artery from CT images without contrast medium. Math. Methods Appl. Sci. **43**(1), 114–133 (2020)
19. Osowska-Kurczab, A., et al.: Improvement of renal image recognition through resolution enhancement. Expert Syst. Appl. **213**(4), 118836 (2023)
20. Travaglini, A., Vinti, G., Scalera, G.B., Scialpi, M.: A large scale analysis for testing a mathematical model for the study of vascular pathologies. Mathematics **11**(8), Art. Number 1831 (2023)
21. Costarelli, D., Seracini, M., Vinti, G.: A comparison between the sampling Kantorovich algorithm for digital image processing with some interpolation and quasi-interpolation methods. Appl. Math. Comput. **374**(2) (2020)
22. Provis, J.M.: Development of the primate retinal vasculature. Prog. Retin. Eye Res. **20**(6), 799–821 (2001)
23. Otsu, N.: A threshold selection method from Gray-level histograms. IEEE Trans. Syst. Man Cybern. Syst. **9**(1), 62–66 (1979)
24. Phansalkar, N., More, S., Sabale, A., Joshi, M.: Adaptive local thresholding for detection of nuclei in diversity stained cytology images. In: International Conference on Communications and Signal Processing, pp. 218–220 (2011)
25. Laiginhas, R., Cabral, D., Falcão, M.: Evaluation of the different thresholding strategies for quantifying choriocapillaris using optical coherence tomography angiography. Quant. Imaging Med. Surg. **10**(10), 1994–2005 (2020)
26. Spaide, R.F.: Choriocapillaris flow features follow a power law distribution: implications for characterization and mechanisms of disease progression. Am. J. Ophthalmol. **170**, 58–67 (2016)
27. Butzer, P.L., Nessel, R.J.: Fourier Analysis and Approximation, 1st edn. Academic Press, New York-London (1971)
28. Butzer, P.L.: A survey of the Whittaker-Shannon sampling theorem and some of its extensions. J. Math. Res. Exposition **3**, 185–212 (1983)
29. Butzer, P.L., Fischer, A., Stens, R.L.: Generalized sampling approximation of multivariate signals; theory and some applications. Note di Matematica **10**(1), 173–191 (1990)
30. Wendland, H.: Piecewise polynomial, positive definite and compactly supported radial functions of minimal degree. Adv. Comput. Math. **4**, 389–396 (1995)
31. Wendland, H.: Scattered Data Approximation, Cambridge Monographs on Applied and Computational Mathematics, vol. 17. Cambridge University Press, Cambridge (2005)

32. Costarelli, D., Piconi, M., Vinti, G.: The multivariate Durrmeyer-sampling type operators in functional spaces. Dolomites Res. Notes Approx. **15**, 128–144 (2023)
33. Kivinukk, A., Tamberg, G.: On approximation properties of sampling operators by dilated Kernels. In: 8th International Conference on Sampling Theory and Applications, SampTA 2009, Marseille, 18–22 May 2009
34. Orlova, O., Tamberg, G.: On approximation properties of generalized Kantorovich-type sampling operators. J. Approx. Theory **201**, 73–86 (2016)
35. Uji, A., Balasubramanian, S., Lei, J., Baghdasaryan, E., Al-Sheikh, M., Sadda, S.R.: Impact of multiple En Face image averaging on quantitative assessment from optical coherence tomography angiography images. Ophthalmology **124**(7), 944–952 (2017)
36. Uji, A., et al.: Multiple enface image averaging for enhanced optical coherence tomography angiography imaging. Acta Ophthalmol. **96**(7), 820–827 (2018)
37. Thévenaz, P., Ruttimann, U.E., Unser, M.A.: A pyramid approach to subpixel registration based on intensity. IEEE Trans. Image Process. **7**(1), 27–41 (1998). A Publication of the IEEE Signal Processing Society
38. Arganda-Carreras, I., Sorzano, C.O., Kybic, J., Ortíz-de-Solórzano, C.: bUnwarpJ : consistent and elastic registration in ImageJ. In: Methods and Applications (2008)
39. Brown, M., Szeliski, R., Winder, S.: Multi-image matching using multi-scale oriented patches. In: Proceedings of the 2005 IEEE Computer Society Conference on Computer Vision and Pattern Recognition, vol. 1, pp. 510–517 (2005)

Mapped Variably Scaled Kernels: Applications to Solar Imaging

Francesco Marchetti[1]([✉])[iD], Emma Perracchione[2][iD], Anna Volpara[3][iD], Anna Maria Massone[3][iD], Stefano De Marchi[1][iD], and Michele Piana[3][iD]

[1] University of Padova, Padua, Italy
{francesco.marchetti,stefano.demarchi}@unipd.it
[2] Polytechnic of Torino, Turin, Italy
emma.perracchione@polito.it
[3] University of Genova, Genoa, Italy
{volpara,massone,piana}@dima.unige.it

Abstract. Variably scaled kernels and mapped bases constructed via the so-called fake nodes approach are two different strategies to provide adaptive bases for function interpolation. In this paper, we focus on kernel-based interpolation and we present what we call mapped variably scaled kernels, which take advantage of both strategies. We present some theoretical analysis and then we show their efficacy via numerical experiments. Moreover, we test such a new basis for image reconstruction tasks in the framework of hard X-ray astronomical imaging.

Keywords: Variably scaled kernels · Mapped bases interpolation · Hard X-ray imaging

1 Introduction

Kernel-based interpolation is an effective approach to deal with the scattered data interpolation problem, where data sites do not necessarily belong to some particular structure or grid [17,30]. Therefore, because of its flexibility and the achievable accuracy, it finds application in many different contexts [20], including image reconstruction and the numerical solution of partial differential equations. The effectiveness of radial kernel-based interpolation, which is also known as Radial Basis Function (RBF) interpolation, very often relies on a good choice of the so-called *shape parameter*, which rules the shape of basis functions. However, in many situations, a fine tuning of this shape parameter is not sufficient to construct basis functions that are tailored with respect to both the data distribution and the target function to be recovered.

Therefore, in order to gain more adaptivity in the interpolation process, Variably Scaled Kernels (VSKs) have been introduced in [6], and further analyzed in [8] in the more general framework of kernel-based regression networks, and in [16] in the context of persistent homology. The VSK setting has also been employed in the reconstruction of functions presenting jumps, leading to the

O. Gervasi et al. (Eds.): ICCSA 2023 Workshops, LNCS 14108, pp. 577–592, 2023.
https://doi.org/10.1007/978-3-031-37117-2_39

definition of Variably Scaled Discontinuous Kernels (VSDKs) [13], which turned out to be effective in medical image reconstruction tasks in the field of Magnetic Particle Imaging (MPI) [12].

An alternative approach for constructing data-dependent or target-dependent basis functions, the so-called Fake Nodes Approach (FNA), has been introduced in [14] in the framework of univariate polynomial interpolation, and then extended to rational barycentric approximation [4] and general multivariate interpolation, including the RBF framework [15]. In particular, in latter paper the authors showed that the VSDK setting and the FNA can lead to very similar results when facing the Gibbs phenomenon in the reconstruction of discontinuous functions. Moreover, in [11] an effective scheme for dealing with both Gibbs and Runge's phenomena has been proposed.

In this paper, our purpose is to design a unified kernel-based approach for function interpolation by taking advantage of both the VSK setting and the FNA, which are recalled in Sect. 2 and 3, respectively. The resulting kernels that we call Mapped VSKs (MVSKs) are defined in Sect. 4 and provided with an original theoretical contribution, which includes a focus on the discontinuous case tested in Sect. 5. In Sect. 6 we present the application of the proposed method to the inverse problems of solar hard X-ray imaging and, specifically, we consider data from the on the ESA *Spectrometer/Telescope for Imaging X-rays (STIX)* telescope, on board of Solar Orbiter mission. Finally, in Sect. 7 we draw some conclusions.

2   Variably Scaled Kernel-Based Approximation

We refer to [17, 30] for the following introduction.

Let $\Omega \subseteq \mathbb{R}^d$, $d \in \mathbb{N}$, and $X = X_N = \{\boldsymbol{x}_i, \ i = 1, \ldots, N\} \subset \Omega$ be a set of possible scattered distinct nodes, $N \in \mathbb{N}$. Suppose that we wish to reconstruct an unknown function $f : \Omega \longrightarrow \mathbb{R}$ from its values at X_N, i.e. from the vector $\boldsymbol{f} = (f(\boldsymbol{x}_1), \ldots, f(\boldsymbol{x}_N))^\mathsf{T} = (f_1, \ldots, f_N)^\mathsf{T}$. In kernel-based interpolation, this is obtained by considering an approximating function of the form

$$R_{f,X}(\boldsymbol{x}) = \sum_{i=1}^{N} c_i \kappa_\varepsilon(\boldsymbol{x}, \boldsymbol{x}_i), \quad \boldsymbol{x} \in \Omega,$$

where $\boldsymbol{c} = (c_1, \ldots, c_N)^\mathsf{T} \in \mathbb{R}^N$ and $\kappa_\varepsilon : \Omega \times \Omega \longrightarrow \mathbb{R}$ is a strictly positive definite kernel, which depends on a *shape parameter* $\varepsilon > 0$. In the following, we may use the shortened notation $\kappa = \kappa_\varepsilon$. The interpolation conditions are imposed by employing $\boldsymbol{c}$ so that

$$\mathsf{K}\boldsymbol{c} = \boldsymbol{f}, \tag{1}$$

where $\mathsf{K} = (\mathsf{K}_{i,j}) = \kappa(\boldsymbol{x}_i, \boldsymbol{x}_j)$, $i, j = 1, \ldots, N$, is the so-called interpolation (or collocation or simply kernel) matrix. The vector $\boldsymbol{c}$ that satisfies (1) is unique as long as κ is strictly positive definite. Moreover, we assume κ_ε to be *radial*, i.e. there exists a univariate function $\varphi_\varepsilon : \mathbb{R}_{\geq 0} \longrightarrow \mathbb{R}$ such that $\kappa_\varepsilon(\boldsymbol{x}, \boldsymbol{y}) = \varphi_\varepsilon(r)$, with $r := \|\boldsymbol{x} - \boldsymbol{y}\|_2$.

The interpolant $R_{f,X}$ belongs to the dot-product space

$$\mathcal{H}_\kappa = \text{span}\left\{\kappa(\cdot,\boldsymbol{x}),\ \boldsymbol{x} \in \Omega\right\},$$

whose completion with respect to the norm $\|\cdot\|_{\mathcal{H}_\kappa} = \sqrt{(\cdot,\cdot)_{\mathcal{H}_\kappa}}$ induced by the bilinear form $(\cdot,\cdot)_{\mathcal{H}_\kappa}$ is the *native space* $\mathcal{N}_\kappa$ associated to κ. The well-known pointwise error bound [17, Theorem 14.2, p. 117]

$$|f(\boldsymbol{x}) - R_{f,X}(\boldsymbol{x})| \le P_{\kappa,X}(\boldsymbol{x})\|f\|_{\mathcal{N}_\kappa}, \quad f \in \mathcal{N}_\kappa, \quad \boldsymbol{x} \in \Omega, \tag{2}$$

involves the *power function* $P_{\kappa,X} = \|\kappa(\cdot,x) - \boldsymbol{\kappa}(\cdot)^\mathsf{T}\mathsf{K}^{-1}\boldsymbol{\kappa}(\boldsymbol{x})\|_{\mathcal{H}_\kappa}$, where $\boldsymbol{\kappa}(\boldsymbol{x}) := (\kappa(\boldsymbol{x},\boldsymbol{x}_1),\dots,\kappa(\boldsymbol{x},\boldsymbol{x}_N))^\mathsf{T}$. In the estimate (2), a noteworthy property is that the error is split into a first term that only depends on the nodes and on the kernel, and a second term that relies on the underlying function f.

A different perspective is provided by the following error bound, which takes into account the so-called *fill distance*

$$h_{X,\Omega} := \sup_{x \in \Omega} \min_{\boldsymbol{x}_k \in X} \|\boldsymbol{x} - \boldsymbol{x}_k\|_2.$$

Assuming Ω to be bounded and satisfying an interior cone condition, and $\kappa \in C^{2k}(\Omega \times \Omega)$, there exists $C_\kappa(\boldsymbol{x})$ such that

$$|f(\boldsymbol{x}) - R_{f,X}(\boldsymbol{x})| \le C_\kappa(\boldsymbol{x}) h_{X,\Omega}^k \|f\|_{\mathcal{N}_\kappa(\Omega)}. \tag{3}$$

The factor $C_\kappa(\boldsymbol{x})$ depends on the maximum of kernel derivatives of degree $2k$ in a neighborhood of $\boldsymbol{x} \in \Omega$, and $h_{X,\Omega}^k$ needs to be *small enough*; we refer to [17, Section 14.5] for a detailed presentation of this result.

While the theoretically achievable convergence rate is influenced by the fill distance and the smoothness of the kernel, two terms play an important role in affecting the conditioning of the interpolation process:

- The *separation distance* $q_X := \dfrac{1}{2}\min_{i \ne j}\|\boldsymbol{x}_i - \boldsymbol{x}_j\|_2$.
- The value of the shape parameter ε of the kernel κ_ε.

Precisely, the interpolation process gets more ill-conditioned as the separation distance becomes smaller, which is what usually happens in practice when increasing the number of interpolation nodes, thus reducing the value of the fill-distance (this is often denoted as a *trade-off* principle in RBF literature). As far as the shape parameter is concerned, a large value produces very localized basis functions that lead to a well-conditioned but likely inaccurate approximation scheme, while by lowering such value we may obtain a more accurate reconstruction at the price of an ill-conditioned setting. As a consequence, the tuning of the shape parameter is a non trivial problem in kernel-based interpolation.

In order to partially overcome such instability issues, in [6] the authors introduced Variably Scaled Kernels (VSKs), which are defined as follows. Letting $\psi : \Omega \longrightarrow \mathbb{R}$ be a scaling or shape function and $\kappa : (\Omega \times \mathbb{R}) \times (\Omega \times \mathbb{R}) \longrightarrow \mathbb{R}$ a kernel, a VSK $\kappa_\psi : \Omega \times \Omega \longrightarrow \mathbb{R}$ is defined as

$$\kappa_\psi(\boldsymbol{x},\boldsymbol{y}) := \kappa((\boldsymbol{x},\psi(\boldsymbol{x})),(\boldsymbol{y},\psi(\boldsymbol{y})),$$

for $x, y \in \Omega$. Note that we can consider the related native space $\mathcal{N}_{\kappa_\psi}$ spanned by the functions $\kappa_\psi(\cdot, x)$, $x \in \Omega$. Among the properties of VSKs, we recall that:

A1. The theoretical analysis of the VSK setting reduces to the analysis of the classical framework in the augmented space $\Omega \times \mathbb{R}$.
A2. The spaces $\mathcal{N}_\kappa$ and $\mathcal{N}_{\kappa_\psi}$ are isometrically isomorphic.

Although we may consider different values of ε, as done e.g. in the context of moving least squares [21], in the VSK framework the shape parameter is often set to $\varepsilon = 1$. Therefore, the role played by the shape function is duplex. On the one hand, the tuning of the shape parameter is substituted with the choice of the shape function. On the other hand, ψ can lead to an improvement in the conditioning of the approximation process by increasing the value of the separation distance in the augmented domain $\Omega \times \mathbb{R}$. Note that κ_ψ is (strictly) positive definite if so is κ.

3   Interpolation via Mapped Bases

In this section, we present the so called Fake Nodes Approach (FNA) for the kernel-based approximation framework; for a more general and comprehensive treatment we refer to [15].

Let $S : \Omega \longrightarrow \mathbb{R}^d$ be an injective map. Our purpose is to construct an interpolant $R^S_{f,X}$ of the function f in the space

$$\mathcal{H}_{\kappa^S} = \mathrm{span}\left\{\kappa^S(\cdot, x), \; x \in \Omega\right\},$$

where $\kappa^S(x, y) := \kappa(S(x), S(y))$. We have

$$R^S_{f,X}(x) = \sum_{i=1}^{N} c_i^S \kappa^S(x, x_i) = \sum_{i=1}^{N} c_i^S \kappa(S(x), S(x_i)) = R_{g,X}(S(x)), \quad x \in \Omega,$$

where $g_{|S(X)} = f_{|X}$. In other words, the construction of the interpolant $R^S_{f,X} \in \mathcal{H}_{\kappa^S}$ is equivalent to the construction of a classical interpolant $R_{g,S(X)} \in \mathcal{H}_\kappa$ at the *fake* nodes $S(X)$. Similarly to the VSK setting, the FNA is provided with the following properties (cf. A1 and A2):

B1. The theoretical analysis of the FNA interpolant reduces to the analysis of the interpolant in the classical framework. This was proved in [15, Proposition 3.4] and it is linked to the inheritance property of the *Lebesgue constant* [7].
B2. The spaces $\mathcal{N}_\kappa$ and $\mathcal{N}_{\kappa^S}$ are isometrically isomorphic (a direct consequence of Theorem 1 and Proposition 1 stated below).

In previous works, the FNA has been mainly employed for two main purposes. The first is using S to obtain an interpolation design $S(X)$ that leads to a more stable interpolation process with respect to the original set of nodes. For example, this can be achieved in a polynomial-based framework by mapping onto the set of (tensor-product) Chebyshev-Lobatto nodes in the (multi) one-dimensional case. In addition, as we will discuss in Subsect. 4.2, S can be constructed in a target-dependent fashion to emulate the possible discontinuities of the underlying function and thus recover accuracy near jump points.

4 Mapped VSKs

4.1 The General Framework

In Sects. 2 and 3, we outlined two different approaches, which however present some similarities and are employed for analogous purposes. In the following, we discuss how the VSK setting and the FNA can be merged in a unified framework. We start by giving the following definition.

Definition 1. *Let $S : \Omega \longrightarrow \mathbb{R}^d$ be an injective map, $\psi : \Omega \longrightarrow \mathbb{R}$ be a shape function and let $\kappa : (S(\Omega) \times \mathbb{R}) \times (S(\Omega) \times \mathbb{R}) \longrightarrow \mathbb{R}$ be a kernel. Then, a Mapped VSK (MVSK) $\kappa_\psi^S : \Omega \times \Omega \longrightarrow \mathbb{R}$ is defined as*

$$\kappa_\psi^S(\boldsymbol{x}, \boldsymbol{y}) := \kappa((S(\boldsymbol{x}), \psi(\boldsymbol{x})), (S(\boldsymbol{y}), \psi(\boldsymbol{y})),$$

for $\boldsymbol{x}, \boldsymbol{y} \in \Omega$.

We remark that κ_ψ^S might be defined in different possible equivalent manners. However, the advantage of Definition 1 lies in the separation between the actions of S and ψ: The function S works in the original dimension $\mathbb{R}^d$, while ψ rules the coordinate of the input in the augmented dimension. Under certain assumptions, a MVSK reduces to a mapped or VSK.

Proposition 1. *Let κ_ψ^S be a MVSK on $\Omega \times \Omega$ built upon a radial kernel κ. Then:*

1. *If $\psi(\boldsymbol{x}) \equiv \alpha \in \mathbb{R}$, then $\kappa_\psi^S = \kappa^S$.*
2. *If $S(\boldsymbol{x}) - S(\boldsymbol{y}) = \boldsymbol{x} - \boldsymbol{y}$, (e.g., S is the identity map), then $\kappa_\psi^S = \kappa_\psi$.*

Proof. By hypothesis, there exists $\varphi : [0, +\infty) \longrightarrow \mathbb{R}$ such that $\kappa(\boldsymbol{x}, \boldsymbol{y}) = \varphi(\|\boldsymbol{x} - \boldsymbol{y}\|_2)$. Therefore, we can write

$$\kappa_\psi^S(\boldsymbol{x}, \boldsymbol{y}) = \varphi(\|(S(\boldsymbol{x}), \psi(\boldsymbol{x})) - (S(\boldsymbol{y}), \psi(\boldsymbol{y}))\|_2)$$
$$= \varphi(\sqrt{(S(\boldsymbol{x}) - S(\boldsymbol{y}))^2 + (\psi(\boldsymbol{x}) - \psi(\boldsymbol{y}))^2}),$$

from which the two theses follow.

We also prove the following.

Theorem 1. *The spaces $\mathcal{H}_\kappa$ and $\mathcal{H}_{\kappa_\psi^S}$ are isometric.*

Proof. By defining the map $\Lambda_\psi^S(\boldsymbol{x}) := (S(\boldsymbol{x}), \psi(\boldsymbol{x}))$ we can see κ_ψ^S as the pullback of κ in the sense provided in [29, Equation 2.52]. Then, the proof follows from [29, Theorem 2.9]. Indeed, since S is injective then so is Λ_ψ^S, which implies

$$\bigcap_{\boldsymbol{x}\in\Omega} \ker\left(\delta_{\Lambda_\psi^S(\boldsymbol{x})}\right) = \{\boldsymbol{0}\},$$

where we consider the evaluation functional $\delta_{\Lambda_\psi^S(\boldsymbol{x})}(f) = f(\Lambda_\psi^S(\boldsymbol{x})), f \in \mathcal{H}_\kappa$.

As a consequence of Theorem 1, the native spaces $\mathcal{N}_\kappa$ and $\mathcal{N}_{\kappa_\psi^S}$ are isometrically isomorphic (cf. [6, Section 3]).

Independently of the target function to be recovered, we recall that the conditioning of the interpolation problem is related to the ℓ_2-conditioning of the kernel matrix $\mathrm{cond}(\mathsf{K}) = \lambda_{\max}/\lambda_{\min}$, being $\lambda_{\max}, \lambda_{\min}$ the maximum and minimum eigenvalue, respectively. It is known that $\lambda_{\min}$ decays according to the separation distance q_X, in a way that is influenced by the regularity of the kernel (see [17, Chapter 16]). In this direction, MVSKs can be employed in order to increase the separation distance and thus improve the conditioning of the interpolation scheme, e.g., by separating clustered nodes. On the other hand, diminishing the fill distance may improve the accuracy of the method (see (3)). We will experiment on this in Sect. 5.

4.2   Working with Mapped Discontinuous Kernels

In the following, we focus on the case of discontinuous functions. First, we briefly review in which manners VSKs and the FNA were used in the discontinuous setting.

Variably Scaled Discontinuous Kernels (VSDKs). The idea proposed in [13] and further investigated in [12] was to define the scaling function ψ to be discontinuous at the jumps of the target function $f : \Omega \longrightarrow \mathbb{R}$. In order to do so, we assume $\Omega \subset \mathbb{R}^d$ to be a bounded set such that:

- Ω is the union of m pairwise disjoint sets Ω_k, $k \in \{1, \ldots, m\}$.
- Each subset Ω_k, $k = 1, \ldots, m$, has a Lipschitz boundary.
- The discontinuity points of f are contained in the union of the boundaries of the subsets Ω_k, $k = 1, \ldots, m$.

Then, letting $\boldsymbol{\alpha} = (\alpha_1, \ldots, \alpha_m)$, $\alpha_i \in \mathbb{R}$, the scaling function ψ is such that:

- ψ is piecewise constant, such that $\psi(\boldsymbol{x})|_{\Omega_k} = \alpha_k$.
- $\alpha_i \neq \alpha_j$ if Ω_i and Ω_j are neighboring sets.

The theoretical analysis carried out in the referring papers then focused on radial kernels whose related univariate function φ has the following Fourier decay

$$(\mathrm{F}\varphi)(\boldsymbol{\omega}) \sim (1 + \|\boldsymbol{\omega}\|^2)^{-s-\frac{1}{2}}, \quad s > \frac{d-1}{2}. \tag{4}$$

The native space of the kernels that satisfy (4), e.g. Matérn and Wendland kernels, is a Sobolev space [30, Chapter 10]. In order to present an error bound in terms of Sobolev spaces norm for the VSDK setting, we introduce two necessary ingredients:

1. The *regional* fill-distance

$$h_k := h_{X,\Omega_k} = \sup_{x \in \Omega_k} \min_{x_k \in X \cap \Omega_k} \|x - x_k\|_2$$

and the *global* fill distance

$$h := \max_{k \in \{1,\dots,m\}} h_k.$$

2. Letting $s \geq 0$ and $1 \leq p \leq \infty$, we define the space

$$\mathcal{WP}_p^s(\Omega) := \left\{ f : \Omega \longrightarrow \mathbb{R} \mid f|_{\Omega_k} \in \mathcal{W}_p^s(\Omega_k), \ k \in \{1,\dots,m\} \right\},$$

which contains the piecewise smooth functions f on Ω whose restriction to any subregion Ω_k, $k = 1,\dots,m$, is contained in the standard Sobolev space $\mathcal{W}_p^s(\Omega_k)$. The space $\mathcal{WP}_p^s(\Omega)$ is endowed with the norm

$$\|f\|_{\mathcal{WP}_p^s(\Omega)}^p = \sum_{k=1}^{m} \|f|_{\Omega_k}\|_{\mathcal{W}_p^s(\Omega_k)}^p.$$

In the outlined assumptions and letting $R_{f,X}^{\psi}$ be the kernel-based interpolant of f at X built upon the VSDK κ_ψ, in [12, Theorem 3.4] the authors proved the following. Let $s > 0$, $1 \leq q \leq \infty$ and $t \in \mathbb{N}_0$ such that $\lfloor s \rfloor > t + \frac{d}{2}$. Then, for $f \in \mathcal{WP}_2^s(\Omega)$ and *sufficiently* small h we have that

$$\|f - R_{f,X}^{\psi}\|_{\mathcal{WP}_q^t(\Omega)} \leq Ch^{s-t-d(1/2-1/q)_+} \|f\|_{\mathcal{WP}_2^s(\Omega)}, \tag{5}$$

where the constant $C > 0$ is independent of h.

The S-Gibbs Map in the FNA. In the mapped bases approach, similarly to the VSDK framework, the intuition is to map the nodes in order to create some *gaps* in presence of discontinuities. To do so, considering the collection of subsets $\Omega_1,\dots,\Omega_m$ employed to construct VSDKs, the so-called *S-Gibbs map* is designed as

$$S(x) = x + \sum_{k=1}^{m} \beta_k \chi_{\Omega_k}(x),$$

where $\beta_k = (k\beta,\dots,k\beta) \in \mathbb{R}^d$, $\beta \in \mathbb{R}$, and χ_{Ω_k} is the characteristic function corresponding to Ω_k. In [15, Section 4.2], the authors discussed the analogies between a VSDK κ_ψ and a mapped kernels κ^S constructed via the S-Gibbs map. It turned out that these two approaches can lead to *similar* results for certain values of the vectors of parameters α and β_k. This is due to the fact that the interpolation matrices are *close* being the kernel radial.

Mapped VSDKs (MVSDKs). In the mixed approach with the mapped VSK kernel κ_ψ^S, we deal with the jumps of the underlying function as follows.

– We define ψ as in the VSDKs framework. Therefore, the role of the shape function is to mimic the jumps of the target function and thus to prevent the appearance of the Gibbs phenomenon.
– Since the discontinuities are already addressed by ψ, we employ S to map the set of nodes X to obtain improved distributions locally on each Ω_k, meaning that we aim at diminishing the global fill distance and increasing the global separation distance defined as

$$q := \min_{k \in \{1,\dots,m\}} q_k,$$

being $q_k := q_{X_k} = \dfrac{1}{2} \min_{i \neq j} \|\boldsymbol{x}_i - \boldsymbol{x}_j\|_2, \ \boldsymbol{x}_i, \boldsymbol{x}_j \in \Omega_k$.

Recalling the error estimate in (5), this proposed construction for MVSDKs may lead to better results, being h smaller. Moreover, by increasing the separation distance, an improvement in the conditioning of the scheme with respect to classical VSDKs is likely to be obtained. We test these aspects in some numerical examples in the next section.

5   Numerical Tests with MVSDKs

The purpose of this section is to provide a numerical example to show the benefits of the MVSDK framework in comparison to VSDKs and classical RBF interpolation. To do so, we set $\Omega = [-1,1]^2$ and letting $\boldsymbol{x} = (x_1, x_2)$ we consider the target function

$$f : \Omega \longrightarrow \mathbb{R}, \quad f(\boldsymbol{x}) = \begin{cases} x_1 + x_2, & x_1 < -0.3, \\ \sin(x_1 - 2x_2), & 0 \leq x_1 < 0.5, \\ 0, & \text{otherwise.} \end{cases}$$

To deal with the jumps of f, we define the shape function

$$\psi : \Omega \longrightarrow \mathbb{R}, \quad \psi(\boldsymbol{x}) = \begin{cases} 0, & x_1 < -0.3, \\ 1, & -0.3 \leq x_1 < 0, \\ 2, & 0 \leq x_1 < 0.5, \\ 3, & x_1 \geq 0.5. \end{cases}$$

As far as the nodes are concerned, we let G_N be a set of N nodes that are sampled from a bivariate normal distribution with mean $\boldsymbol{\mu} = (0,0)$ and covariance matrix $\Sigma = 0.1 \cdot \mathsf{I}$, being I the 2×2 identity matrix. We can then consider the following mapping function $S : \Omega \longrightarrow \Omega$ defined as

$$S(x_1, x_2) = \left(1 + \text{erf}\left(\frac{x_1}{\sqrt{0.2}}\right), 1 + \text{erf}\left(\frac{x_2}{\sqrt{0.2}}\right) \right) - 1,$$

where erf is the well-known *error function*. To clarify the idea behind the construction of S, it is known from classical probability theory that if $z_1, \ldots, z_n$ are sampled according to a normal distribution of mean μ and standard deviation σ, then $0.5(1 + \text{erf}((z_i - \mu)/(\sqrt{2}\sigma)))$, $i = 1, \ldots, n$, are distributed uniformly in $[0, 1]$. Therefore, our set of nodes G_N is mapped to a uniform distribution in the square $[-1, 1]^2$, as displayed in Fig. 1. We point out that possible nodes in G_N that are not in Ω are removed from the set.

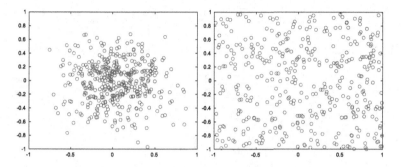

Fig. 1. $N = 400$. Left: G_N. Right: $S(G_N)$.

Consequently, the mapped set $S(G_N)$ is very likely to present smaller fill distance and larger separation distance than G_N. The interpolation results are evaluated on a finer $M \times M$ equispaced grid Ξ_{M^2} in Ω. Precisely, we compute the Root Mean Square Error (RMSE)

$$\text{RMSE} = \sqrt{\frac{1}{M^2} \sum_{k=1}^{M^2} \big(f(\boldsymbol{\xi}_k) - \iota(\boldsymbol{\xi}_k)\big)^2}, \tag{6}$$

where $\boldsymbol{\xi}_k \in \Xi_{M^2}$ and $\iota = R_{f,G_N}$, R_{f,G_N}^{ψ}, $R_{f,G_N}^{\psi,S}$ are the interpolants constructed via the classical, the VSDK and the MVSDK. The shape parameter ε is chosen between 200 equispaced values in the interval $[0.01, 50]$ via Leave-One-Out Cross Validation (LOOCV) [23]. Finally, we let N vary between 10 and 500 and we test two radial kernels:

$$\varphi_W(r) = (1 - \varepsilon r)_+^2 \quad \text{Wendland } C^0,$$
$$\varphi_M(r) = e^{-\varepsilon r}(15 + 15\varepsilon r + 6(\varepsilon r)^2 + (\varepsilon r)^3) \quad \text{Matérn } C^6 .$$

In Fig. 2, we show the behavior of the separation and fill distances, while in Fig. 3 we show the RMSEs achieved with both φ_W and φ_M.

The plots in Fig. 2 display the benefits in employing S in the MVSDK in terms of diminished fill distance and increased separation distance. In Fig. 3, we observe that MVSDKs are more effective in the case of the chosen Matérn kernel. This is due to the fact that this kernel is more regular than the chosen Wendland

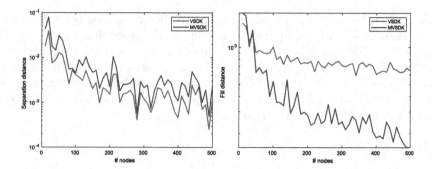

Fig. 2. The separation distance (left) and the fill distance (right) varying N.

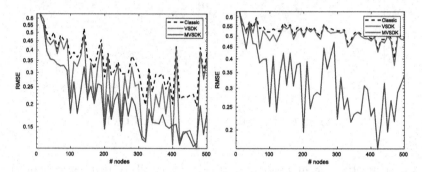

Fig. 3. The RMSE obtained using φ_W (left) and φ_M (right) varying N.

kernel, therefore it is more prone to provide an ill-conditioned interpolation process. Furthermore, we remark that the sets of nodes G_N, $N = 10, \ldots, 500$ are not nested, and they are clustered around the origin. Therefore, we can not expect an accurate recovering of the function f, nor convergence increasing N.

6   Applications to the STIX Imaging Framework

In order to test the proposed MVSKs in real applied sciences, we focus on solar hard X-ray imaging and, specifically, on the ESA STIX telescope [28], on board of Solar Orbiter mission (see Fig. 4). Hard X-ray telescopes provide experimental measurements, named visibilities, of the Fourier transform of the incoming photon flux at specific points of the spatial frequency plane. In the case of STIX, 30 subcollimators relying on the Moiré pattern technology provide $N = 60$ visibilities on 10 circles of the frequency plane with increasing radii from about 2.79×10^{-3} arcsec^{-1} to 7.02×10^{-2} arcsec^{-1} (see Fig. 4). We observe that the visibilities lying in the lower half plane are obtained by reflecting the visibilities in the upper half with respect to the origin.

Fig. 4. The Spectrometer/Telescope for Imaging X-rays (STIX).

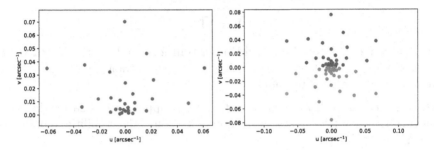

Fig. 5. STIX visibilities: reflecting with respect to the origin leads to a total number of 60 visibilities.

We denote by **f** the vector whose components are the discretized values of the incoming flux, by **F** the discretized Fourier transform sampled at the set of points $\{\mathbf{u}_i = (u_i, v_i)\}_{i=1}^{N}$ in the (u, v)-plane and with **V** the vector whose n components are the observed visibilities. Then, the image formation model in this framework can be approximated by

$$\mathbf{V} = \mathbf{F}\mathbf{f} \ . \tag{7}$$

6.1 The Imaging Process

Many inversion methods have been formulated to express the STIX observations as images, see e.g. [2,3,5,9,18,24,25]. The approach that we propose consists of two steps: interpolation of the visibilities so that we obtain the visibility surfaces and the inversion of the so generated surfaces with rather standard techniques. This idea was already used for the dismissed NASA telescope Reuven Ramaty High Energy Solar Spectroscopic Imager (RHESSI) [22], and its IDL implementation called uv_smooth [25], can be find in the NASA Solar SoftWare (SSW) tree.

The uv_smooth code addresses Eq. (7) by means of an interpolation and extrapolation procedure in which the interpolation step is carried out via an algorithm based on spline functions and the extrapolation step is realized by means of a soft-thresholding scheme [1,10]. As far as the second step is concerned, we will rely on the well-established projected Landweber iterative method [27]. The first step instead will be carried out with our MVSKs.

6.2   MVSKs for STIX

To employ MVSKs, we need to define a scaling function ψ and a mapping S.

The choice of ψ. In order to define the scaling function, we take advantage of a first approximation of the inverse problem obtained via a standard back-projection algorithm [26] that computes the discretized inverse Fourier transform of the visibilities by means of the IDL source code `vis_bpmap` available in the NASA SSW tree. The so-constructed image is then forward Fourier transformed to obtain ψ. Once the interpolated visibility surface $\overline{\mathbf{V}}$ has been computed, the image reconstruction problem reads as follows

$$\overline{\mathbf{V}} = \overline{\mathbf{F}}\mathbf{f} \ , \tag{8}$$

where $\overline{\mathbf{F}}$ is the $N^2 \times N^2$ discretized Fourier transform and $\overline{\mathbf{f}}$ is the $N^2 \times 1$ vector to reconstruct. In the following we will point out the advantages of interpolating the visibilities with our technique.

The Choice of S. To present in details the mapping S chosen for the STIX imaging framework, let us first deepen the definition of the visibilities represented in Fig. 5 (left). We have

$$u_i = (L_1 + L_2)\frac{\cos(\alpha_i^f)}{\rho_i^f} - L_2\frac{\cos(\alpha_i^r)}{\rho_i^r}, \ v_i = (L_1 + L_2)\frac{\sin(\alpha_i^f)}{\rho_i^f} - L_2\frac{\sin(\alpha_i^r)}{\rho_i^r},$$

where $L_1 = 550$, $L_2 = 47$ and $\alpha_i^f, \rho_i^f, \alpha_i^r, \rho_i^r$ are discussed in [19]. We define the map

$$S(u,v) = C\log(\|(u,v)\|_2)(\cos(\arctan(v/u)), \sin(\arctan(v/u))),$$

where C is a normalizing factor used to retain the order of magnitude of the original visibilities after the mapping. In Fig. 6, we can observe that the mapped visibilities are distributed in a circular crown with no clustering around the origin.

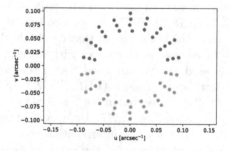

Fig. 6. Mapped STIX visibilities.

6.3 Numerical Results

On Jul 2022 STIX recorded a flare during the during the time interval 23:41:15–23:41:41 UT. The energy range of the event is 15–25 keV. In Fig. 7 we reported the reconstruction carried out with the interpolation/extrapolation algorithm where we respectively interpolate with: classical radial kernels, VSKs and MVSKs. Moreover, as a further comparison we also consider mem_ge [24] which is a well established implementation of the maximum entropy approach and it is used by the solar physics community. We note that all methods present artifacts but the shape of the source reconstructed by interpolating with MVSKs is more similar to the one computed with mem_ge. To have a quantitative feedback on the accuracy, we show in Fig. 8 the visibility fits obtained with the four different approaches. We further observe that the chi squares values of mem_ge and uv_smooth + MVSKs are similar and are the lowest.

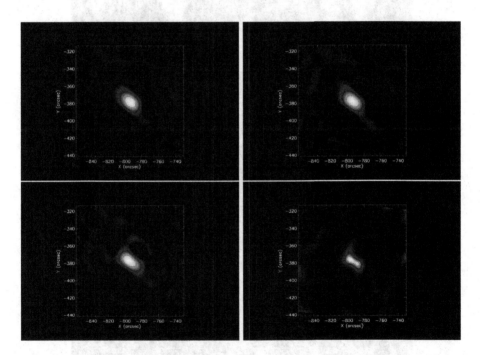

Fig. 7. Left to right, top to bottom: reconstruction of the flaring source with: uv_smooth + classical radial kernels, uv_smooth + VSKs, uv_smooth + MVSKs and mem_ge.

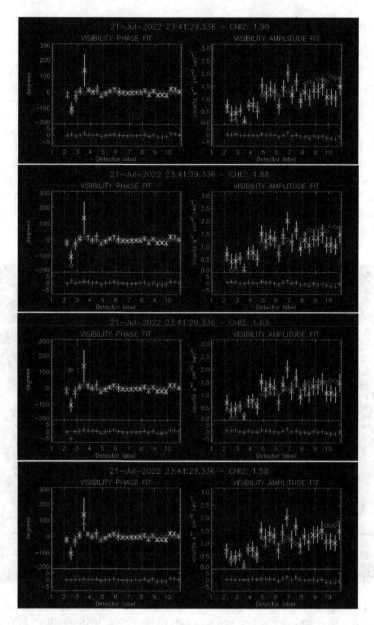

Fig. 8. Top to bottom: visibility fits of the flaring source with: uv_smooth + classical radial kernels, uv_smooth + VSKs, uv_smooth + MVSKs and mem_ge.

7 Conclusions

In this work, we defined MVSKs by mixing VSKs with the FNA. After providing some theoretical details, we performed some numerical simulations that showed the advantages of using MVSDKs with respect to classical RBF kernels and VSDKs. Then, we applied our method in the framework of hard X-ray astronomical imaging. The obtained results encourage further investigations on this research line.

Acknowledgments. EP and AM are supported by the project: "Physics-based AI for predicting extreme weather and spaceweather events (AIxtreme)", Founded by Fondazione Compagnia di San Paolo. FM acknowledges the financial support of the Programma Operativo Nazionale (PON) "Ricerca e Innovazione" 2014–2020. The authors kindly acknowledge the financial contribution from the AI-FLARES ASI-INAF n.2018-16-HH.0 agreement. This research has been accomplished within GNCS-INδAM.

References

1. Allavena, S., Piana, M., Benvenuto, F., Massone, A.M.: An interpolation/extrapolation approach to X-ray imaging of solar flares. Inverse Probl. Imag. **6**, 147 (2012)
2. Aschwanden, M.J., Schmal, E.: The RHESSI team: reconstruction of RHESSI solar flare images with a forward-fitting method. Sol. Phys. **210**, 193–211 (2002)
3. Benvenuto, F., Schwartz, R., Piana, M., Massone, A.M.: Expectation maximization for hard X-ray count modulation profiles. Astron. Astrophys. **555**, A61 (2013)
4. Berrut, J.P., De Marchi, S., Elefante, G., Marchetti, F.: Treating the Gibbs phenomenon in barycentric rational interpolation and approximation via the *S*-Gibbs algorithm. Appl. Math. Lett. **103**, 106196, 7 (2020)
5. Bonettini, S., Anastasia, C., Prato, M.: A new semiblind deconvolution approach for Fourier-based image restoration: an application in astronomy. SIAM J. Imaging Sci. **6**, 1736–1757 (2013)
6. Bozzini, M., Lenarduzzi, L., Rossini, M., Schaback, R.: Interpolation with variably scaled kernels. IMA J. Numer. Anal. **35**(1), 199–219 (2015)
7. Brutman, L.: Lebesgue functions for polynomial interpolation - a survey. Ann. Numer. Math. **4**(1/4), 111–128 (1996)
8. Campi, C., Marchetti, F., Perracchione, E.: Learning via variably scaled kernels. Adv. Comput. Math. **47**(4), 23 (2021). Paper No. 51. https://doi.org/10.1007/s10444-021-09875-6
9. Cornwell, T., Evans, K.F.: A simple maximum entropy deconvolution algorithm. Astron. Astrophys. **143**(1), 77–83 (1985)
10. Daubechies, I., Defrise, M., De Mol, C.: An iterative thresholding algorithm for linear inverse problems with a sparsity constraint. Commun. Pure Appl. Math. **57**(11), 1413–1457 (2004)
11. De Marchi, S., Elefante, G., Marchetti, F.: Stable discontinuous mapped bases: the Gibbs-Runge-avoiding stable polynomial approximation (GRASPA) method. Comput. Appl. Math. **40**(8), 17 (2021). Paper No. 299
12. De Marchi, S., Erb, W., Marchetti, F., Perracchione, E., Rossini, M.: Shape-driven interpolation with discontinuous kernels: error analysis, edge extraction, and applications in magnetic particle imaging. SIAM J. Sci. Comput. **42**(2), B472–B491 (2020)
13. De Marchi, S., Marchetti, F., Perracchione, E.: Jumping with variably scaled discontinuous kernels (VSDKs). BIT Numer. Math. **60**, 441–463 (2020)

14. De Marchi, S., Marchetti, F., Perracchione, E., Poggiali, D.: Polynomial interpolation via mapped bases without resampling. J. Comput. Appl. Math. **364**, 112347, 12 (2020)
15. De Marchi, S., Marchetti, F., Perracchione, E., Poggiali, D.: Multivariate approximation at fake nodes. Appl. Math. Comput. **391**, 17 (2021). Paper No. 125628
16. De Marchi, S., Lot, F., Marchetti, F., Poggiali, D.: Variably scaled persistence kernels (VSPKs) for persistent homology applications. J. Comput. Math. Data Sci. **4**, 100050 (2022)
17. Fasshauer, G.E.: Meshfree Approximation Methods with MATLAB. World Scientific (2007)
18. Felix, S., Bolzern, R., Battaglia, M.: A compressed sensing-based image reconstruction algorithm for solar flare x-ray observations. Astrophys. J. **849**(1), 10 (2017)
19. Giordano, S., Pinamonti, N., Piana, M., Massone, A.M.: The process of data formation for the Spectrometer/Telescope for Imaging X-rays (STIX) in Solar Orbiter. SIAM J. Imaging Sci. **8**(2), 1315–1331 (2015)
20. Guastavino, S., Benvenuto, F.: Convergence rates of spectral regularization methods: a comparison between ILL-posed inverse problems and statistical kernel learning. SIAM J. Numer. Anal. **58**(6), 3504–3529 (2020)
21. Karimnejad Esfahani, M., De Marchi, S., Marchetti, F.: Moving least squares approximation using variably scaled discontinuous weight function. Constr. Math. Anal. **6**(1), 38–54 (2023)
22. Lin, R.P., et al.: The Reuven Ramaty High-Energy Solar Spectroscopic Imager (RHESSI). Sol. Phy. **210**(1–2), 3–32 (2002)
23. Ling, L., Marchetti, F.: A stochastic extended Rippa's algorithm for LpOCV. Appl. Math. Lett. **129**, 107955 (2022)
24. Massa, P., et al.: MEM_GE: a new maximum entropy method for image reconstruction from solar X-ray visibilities. Astrophys. J. **894**(1), 46 (2020)
25. Massone, A.M., Emslie, A.G., Hurford, G.J., Prato, M., Kontar, E.P., Piana, M.: Hard X-ray imaging of solar flares using interpolated visibilities. Astrophys. J. **703**, 2004–2016 (2009)
26. Mersereau, R., Oppenheim, A.: Digital reconstruction of multidimensional signals from their projections. Proc. IEEE **62**(10) (1974)
27. Piana, M., Bertero, M.: Projected Landweber method and preconditioning. Inverse Probl. **13**(2), 441–463 (1997)
28. Krucker, S., et al.: The Spectrometer/Telescope for Imaging X-rays (STIX). Astron. Astrophys. **642**, A15 (2020)
29. Saitoh, S., Sawano, Y.: Theory of Reproducing Kernels and Applications, Developments in Mathematics, vol. 44. Springer, Singapore (2016). https://doi.org/10.1007/978-981-10-0530-5
30. Wendland, H.: Scattered Data Approximation, Cambridge Monographs on Applied and Computational Mathematics, vol. 17. Cambridge University Press, Cambridge (2005)

Fruit Fly Detection and Classification in IoT Setup

Syed M. Fasih, Asad Ali, Talha Mabood$^{(\boxtimes)}$, Atif Ullah, Muhammad Hanif,
and Waqar Ahmad

Faculty of Computer Science and Engineering, Ghulam Ishaq Khan Institute
of Engineering Sciences and Technology, Topi, Swabi, Pakistan
talhamabood400@gmail.com

Abstract. In the 21st century, advancements in hardware and processing speeds have enabled the deployment of machine learning algorithms
such as YOLOv5 on Internet of Things (IoT) devices. These AI-based
IoT devices are powerful computers suitable for embedded applications,
AI IoT, and edge computing, delivering the performance of a modern
AI module at a reduced cost. This conference paper presents a modified
version of YOLOv5 called YOLOv5-FlyEye, optimized for embedded systems such as the Nvidia Jetson Nano. The proposed modification achieves
high performance in detecting and classifying fruit flies by reducing the
computational complexity of the YOLOv5 algorithm. The study aims to
demonstrate the potential of AI-based IoT devices in the field of agriculture, particularly in pest detection and monitoring, and contributes to
the development of optimized algorithms for efficient and cost-effective
embedded systems.

Keywords: Deep Learning · YOLOv5 · Embedded Systems · Edge
Computing

1 Introduction

The conventional methods for identifying pests in orchards mostly rely on human
experience and visual inspection, which can be highly subjective and inconsistent
across different individuals. Moreover, orchards are typically vast in size, which
makes it time-consuming and labor-intensive to inspect them solely through
human eyes. To address the issues of poor objectivity and low efficiency associated with these traditional methods, there is an urgent need for a new pest identification technology for orchards. In recent years, deep learning-based computer
vision has emerged as a powerful tool with various applications in fields such as
facial recognition and autonomous driving. While GPU computing power limitations previously hindered the development of this technology, advancements in
computing power have gradually overcome this limitation. Consequently, more
and more researchers have started to apply computer vision techniques to solve
problems related to image recognition and detection in agriculture. Edge computing and embedded systems are transforming the technological landscape for

O. Gervasi et al. (Eds.): ICCSA 2023 Workshops, LNCS 14108, pp. 593–607, 2023.
https://doi.org/10.1007/978-3-031-37117-2_40

future innovations. Edge computing and embedded systems are developing for hardware specific applications such as machine learning. Embedded machine learning represents a hot topic in both academic research and industry. Emerging innovations such as TinyML is contributing to the field of embedded machine learning to make this world a better place for coming generations. Earlier, machine learning algorithms were not as efficient and computer hardware's were not good enough to support machine learning deployment on embedded scale. But with recent advancements in algorithms such as, Yolov5, MobileNet SSD and TensorFlow lite which are lighter and perform the task with lower number of floating-point operations. Moreover, with improved hardware, we can deploy machine learning algorithms for edge computing. In this paper, we are using Nvidia Jetson Nano development kit for deploying machine learning algorithms to demonstrate the ability of SBC's. Nvidia Jetson nano is equipped with NVIDIA Maxwell GPU, Quad-Core ARM Cortex-A57 processor and 4GB LPDDR4 memory. It uses Nvidia's provided Jetpack-Os which runs a Linux operating system. Figure 1 shows an image of Nvidia Jetson Nano.

2   Literature Review

Various automatic systems have been created to detect and monitor insect pests, with the aim of enhancing integrated pest management in precision agriculture. There are now many automatic detection traps available for significant pests, and these technologies hold great potential for the timely identification and monitoring of dangerous and quarantined pests. Outlined below is a brief overview of several methods employed for the detection of pests, including infrared sensors, audio sensors, and classification based on images.

2.1   Automatic Monitoring of Lepidoptera Pest Species

Worldwide, insects like moths and butterflies can significantly reduce crop yields and have the capacity to lay a large number of eggs, which can result in significant losses when populations are well established [1,2]. Currently, delta traps with pheromone lures are the standard surveillance technique for these insects. However, the development of automatic detection and identification models is quite difficult due to the variety of poses that these insects can adopt when attached to sticky traps [3].

To automatically identify various kinds of moths and butterflies using machine learning techniques, several researchers have created tools and models. The nymphalid butterfly Bicyclus anynana has eyespot patterns that can be automatically recognised by Silveira and Monteiro using a machine learning system with features based on circularity and symmetry. Other butterfly species' patterns could also be recognised by the software with success [4].

Other researchers created a pyramidal stacked de-noising auto-encoder (IpS-DAE) that can produce a deep neural network for moth identification regardless of the pose of insects using a mix of form, colour, texture, and numerical features retrieved for moth description. This model was able to identify 98.13% of moth genera without categorising the species [3,5].

2.2 Automatic Monitoring of Sucking Insects

Growers in greenhouses are particularly concerned about sucking bugs since they can result in considerable crop losses. Among the pests that cause the most trouble in congested greenhouse environments are thrips, aphids, and whiteflies. Sticky traps are frequently set up in greenhouses to keep an eye on the populations of these pests. However, given the small size and intricate morphology of these pests, in addition to the low effectiveness of weary or inexperienced human observers, this can be a challenging task for non-specialized professionals [6].

To monitor and identify pests, useful integrated pest management (IPM) strategies have been developed in addition to image processing techniques. A model for estimating silver leaf whitefly Bemisia tabaci density was put out by Qiao et al. and is based on an image processing system that makes use of yellow sticky traps from greenhouses. In order to score and identify Bemisia tabaci and the western flower thrips Franklinella occidentalis on sticky traps, Sun et al. applied a unique smart vision method using two-dimensional Fourier transformed spectra, achieving good correlation with human vision accuracy [6].

For the highly accurate identification and monitoring of Franklinella occidentalis and Bemisia tabaci, Espinoza et al. integrated artificial neural networks with image processing (segmentation, morphological and colour property estimates). To analyse both whiteflies and thrips with an accuracy of 85% to 95%, Lu et al. presented a convolutional network (CNN) classifier model in conjunction with a generative adversarial network (GAN) picture augmentation. A model-fitting embedded system for the inexpensive detection of aphids, whiteflies, and thrips was proposed by Xia et al. [6,7].

2.3 Automatic Identification and Monitoring of Fruit Flies

One of the major obstacles to the cultivation of horticulture and fruit in the Mediterranean, tropical, and subtropical regions of the world is the presence of frugivorous fruit flies (Diptera: Tephritidae) [8]. Each year, these pests result in crop losses reaching billions of dollars worldwide, with Brazil alone experiencing losses of USD 242 million [9]. Fruit fly damage can result in crop losses of up to 80% to 100% depending on the crop and the lack of control measures. The fruit fly is a member of the Dacini tribe and includes 932 recognised species, 10% of which are currently considered to be pests of commercial fruit and vegetable production, leading to quarantine problems and trade embargos [8].

A limited number of highly polyphagous and invasive pest species that, if they enter and establish in a place, competitively dominate the native fauna are aggravating the problem of fruit flies worldwide [10–12]. Sprays of pesticides, mass trapping with pheromone lures, and the release of sterile males can all be used to control these pests. The timing of treatment determines the effectiveness of the control approach, which is more effective when the pest is discovered early. An automatic detection system will be helpful to avoid and monitor the infestation of these quarantine pests in a quicker manner due to the low threshold of control of these pests [12].

3   Machine Learning Algorithms

Machine learning algorithms are a type of artificial intelligence that enable computers to learn from data and make predictions or decisions without being explicitly programmed. These algorithms use statistical models and optimization techniques to identify patterns and relationships in data, and can be used for a wide range of tasks, from image and speech recognition to natural language processing and predictive analytics.

The goal of machine learning is to create models that can make accurate predictions or decisions on new, unseen data. This involves a process of training the algorithm on a large dataset, tuning its parameters, and testing its performance on a separate validation dataset. With the increasing availability of large datasets and powerful computing resources, machine learning algorithms are rapidly advancing and being applied to an ever-growing number of domains and industries. For the detection and classification purpose, YOLO algorithm is used.

3.1   YOLOv5

YOLO (You Only Look Once) is an object detection algorithm that uses deep convolutional neural networks to detect objects in images and videos. YOLOv5 is the version of the algorithm, released in 2020, and is an improvement over previous versions in terms of accuracy and speed.

YOLOv5 is an object detection algorithm that uses a single-stage architecture with a focus on speed and accuracy. It is built on top of the EfficientDet-D7 backbone, which is a high-performance convolutional neural network (CNN) designed for object detection. YOLOv5 also incorporates several key features that improve its performance, such as anchor-based predictions, focal loss, and class-balanced sampling. The YOLOv5 algorithm uses a single neural network to detect objects in an image. The input image is divided into a grid of cells, and each cell is responsible for predicting a set of bounding boxes and object classes. The predicted bounding boxes are then refined and filtered based on their confidence scores and non-maximum suppression is used to eliminate redundant detections.

The YOLOv5 algorithm is based on a deep neural network architecture called CSP (Cross-Stage Partial Network). This architecture consists of a series of convolutional layers that extract features from the input image, followed by a set of detection layers that make predictions based on the extracted features. As it involves CSP (Cross-Stage Partial Network) into Darknet, creating CSPDarknet as its backbone. CSPNet addresses the problem of repeated gradients information in largescale backbones. It also integrates gradient changes into feature maps of the convolved images, thereby decreasing the parameters and number of Floating-Point Operations (FLOPs). A decrease in FLOPs is considered a crucial element in embedded deep learning because a lower value of FLOPs ensures inference speed and accuracy while reducing the model size.

Deep learning models that are smaller, faster, and more efficient, such as YOLOv5 yield great performance on jetson Nano's GPU. The YOLOv5 uses a path aggregation network (PANet) as its neck to boost information flow. PANet involves a feature pyramid network (FPN) structure with an improved bottom-up path, this results in better propagation of low-level features. At the same time, adaptive feature pooling, which links the feature grid and all feature levels, is used to make useful information in each feature level propagate directly to the following subnetwork. PANet improves the utilization of accurate localization signals in lower layers, which can enhance the location accuracy of the object. Further, YOLOv5 also address the problem of multi-scale detection. Such detections involve variations in the size of objects, for example, when detecting crops using a UAV, the footage is subjected to certain scaling, perspective distortion and other factors. There are some variants of YOLOv5. These are as follows:

YOLOv5s. YOLOv5s is a variant of the YOLOv5 algorithm that is designed to be small and fast while still maintaining high accuracy. The "s" in YOLOv5s stands for "small," and it is intended for use cases where computational resources and memory are limited, but real-time object detection is still required.

Compared to the larger YOLOv5 models (YOLOv5m and YOLOv5l), YOLOv5s has fewer layers and parameters, which allows it to be deployed on low-power edge devices with limited resources. Specifically, YOLOv5s has 12 convolutional layers and a total of 7.5 million parameters, which is significantly fewer than the 44 layers and 88 million parameters of YOLOv5m.

One of the key features of YOLOv5s is its use of a CSP (Cross Stage Partial) architecture, which allows for faster and more efficient computation. This architecture is based on the idea of splitting the input data into two streams, which are then processed in parallel by two separate convolutional blocks. The outputs of these blocks are then concatenated and passed through another set of convolutional layers to produce the final predictions. Another important feature of YOLOv5s is its use of a dynamic anchor assignment strategy. This strategy involves adjusting the anchor boxes during training based on the statistics of the training data, which helps to improve the model's accuracy on objects of different sizes and aspect ratios.

YOLOv5n. Edge computing has become an increasingly important trend in computer vision, as more and more applications require real-time object detection on low-power devices. YOLOv5n is an optimized version of the popular YOLOv5 object detection model, designed specifically for edge devices with limited computing resources. In order to achieve high performance and efficiency on these devices, several technical considerations must be taken into account when optimizing the model architecture and training process.

- Precision and accuracy: One of the key trade-offs when optimizing YOLOv5 for edge devices is achieving a balance between precision and accuracy. Since YOLOv5n is designed for low-power devices, it may use lower precision arithmetic to reduce the computational and memory requirements of the model.

However, lower precision can also reduce the accuracy of the model, so it is important to carefully evaluate the impact of different precision levels on the model's performance.

- Compression techniques: In addition to quantization and pruning, there are several other compression techniques that can be used to reduce the size of the YOLOv5n model. For example, weight sharing, which involves using the same weights for multiple layers of the network, can significantly reduce the number of parameters in the model without sacrificing performance.
- Data augmentation: Data augmentation is a technique used to artificially increase the size of the training dataset by applying random transformations to the input images. This can help to improve the robustness of the YOLOv5n model and reduce the risk of overfitting, which can be a concern when working with limited training data.
- Quantization-aware training: Quantization-aware training is a technique that involves training the YOLOv5n model with quantization in mind, rather than quantizing the model after training. By taking into account the impact of quantization on the model during training, it is possible to achieve better performance and accuracy on low-power devices.

4   Methodology

4.1   Deep Learning Approach

Introducing an efficient approach to address the problem of low inference speed on IoT devices (e.g. NVIDIA Jetson Nano) running YOLOv5 while maintaining sufficient accuracy. We propose modifications to an existing YOLOv5 architecture to achieve superior results while reducing the floating point operations (FLOPs) significantly.

In this paper we discarded the use of standard convolution operation and used Ghosted convolution. Ghosted convolution is a technique used in convolutional neural networks (CNNs) that was introduced in the GhostNet architecture. In traditional CNNs, convolutions are performed on the entire input tensor, resulting in a large number of parameters and computations. Ghosted convolution, on the other hand, are a type of convolution that involves splitting the input feature maps into two parts, the primary feature map and the ghost feature map. The ghost feature map is generated by convolving the primary feature map with a set of lower-dimensional convolution filters. The output of this convolution is then upsampled and added back to the primary feature map to produce the final output [13].

The use of ghosted convolutions in GhostNet allows for more efficient feature extraction while reducing the computational complexity and memory requirements of the network. This is because the ghost feature maps are generated using lower-dimensional convolution filters, which reduces the number of parameters needed to learn and the computational cost of the convolution operation.

Overall, the use of intrinsic feature maps and ghosted convolutions in Ghost-Net allows for a more efficient and effective deep neural network architecture.

The key idea behind GhostNet is the use of a Ghost module, which is a modified version of a standard convolutional layer. The Ghost module splits the input into two parts, with one part being passed through a cheap operation (e.g. depth-wise convolution), while the other part is passed through a regular convolutional layer. The cheap operation is then used to refine the output of the regular convolution, resulting in a more accurate output while using fewer computational resources.

The Ghost module is defined as follows, where $F(x)$ represents a regular convolution, $G(x)$ represents a cheap operation, and W represents the learnable parameters of the layer:

$$H(x) = F(x) + GW(x)$$

To illustrate this with an example, let's consider an image classification task. Suppose we have an input image x and we want to apply the Ghost module to extract features from it. Regular Convolution (F(x)), we first pass the input image x through a regular convolution operation, which applies a set of learnable filters to extract spatial features. This operation captures complex patterns and details in the image. Cheaper Operation (G(x)), alongside the regular convolution, we perform a cheaper operation that requires fewer computational resources. This operation might involve simpler operations like downsampling, pooling, or applying a small number of filters. The purpose of this operation is to capture more general features or global information from the image. Combining the Results, after obtaining the outputs from both the regular convolution and the cheaper operation, we apply the Ghost module. We multiply the output of the cheaper operation, GW(x), by the learnable parameters W. This multiplication scales the cheaper operation's output based on the learned weights. Finally, we add this scaled output to the output of the regular convolution, F(x), resulting in the final output H(x) of the Ghost module. By combining both the expensive and cheaper operations, the Ghost module aims to strike a balance between computational efficiency and capturing detailed and global features. The learnable parameters W allow the module to adaptively control the influence of the cheaper operation, enabling it to learn the most effective combination of features for a given task.

In the GhostNet architecture, ghosted convolution can be used in conjunction with other techniques such as squeeze-and-excitation (SE) blocks and mobile inverted bottleneck (MBConv) blocks to create a lightweight and efficient CNN. The resulting network has fewer parameters and computations compared to traditional CNNs, while still achieving high accuracy on a variety of computer vision tasks.

In summary, ghosted convolution is a technique that can be used in CNNs to reduce the number of parameters and computations while maintaining accuracy. It achieves this by splitting the input tensor into smaller tensors, which are then convolved separately. The GhostNet architecture uses ghosted convolution in combination with other techniques to create a lightweight and efficient CNN [13,14].

Proposed YOLOv5 Architecture. The customized YOLOv5 architecture namely Yolov5-FlyEye has two main parts, the backbone and the head. The backbone consists of a series of convolutional layers that are used to extract features from the input image. The backbone starts with a 6-layer Convolutional Neural Network (CNN) with 32 output channels, a kernel size of 6, a stride of 2, and padding of 2. This layer is followed by a Ghost convolutional layer with 64 output channels, a kernel size of 3, and a stride of 2, which downsamples the feature maps by a factor of 2.

The backbone then consists of a series of C3Ghost modules arranged in specific manner to form the Yolov5-FlyEye.

In a YOLOv5 model, the "head" refers to the top part of the architecture that takes in features from the backbone and outputs predictions for object detection. The head of the YOLOv5 model is responsible for predicting the bounding boxes and class probabilities for the objects in the input image.

The head consists of a series of layers, including GhostConv (a type of convolutional layer that uses less computation), Upsample (to increase the size of the feature maps), Concat (to concatenate feature maps from different layers), and C3Ghost (a type of GhostConv layer with three parallel branches).

At the prediction level we have removed the P5/32-large and P6/64-xlarge layer from the architecture because out dataset includes the detection of objects that may vary between small and medium sizes. Therefore we used the P3/8-small and P4/16-medium layers at the prediction level.

In the YOLOv5 head, the small prediction level is represented by feature maps from the P3 layer of the backbone network that have been downsampled by a factor of 8. These feature maps have a resolution of 80×80 pixels and are processed by three convolutional layers with ghost convolution filters to generate object detection predictions.

The medium prediction level is represented by feature maps from the P4 layer of the backbone network that have been downsampled by a factor of 16. These feature maps have a resolution of 40×40 pixels and are processed by three convolutional layers with ghost convolution filters to generate object detection predictions.

The object detection predictions for the small and medium prediction levels are then combined using a "Detect" operation that applies anchor-based object detection to the concatenated feature maps. These predictions are used to generate the final bounding box and class predictions for the YOLOv5 model.

Overall, the head architecture is designed to combine information from multiple resolution levels and perform detection on objects of varying sizes, while minimizing computational cost.

5   Dataset

In any model, dataset plays vital role in performance irrespective of algorithm. In our case we are having two species of fruit flies. On which our data is trained. If any other specie of fly is detected then it would be classified as foreign fly. This custom dataset has been collected from Bactrocera zonata and Bactrocera dorsalis. Bactrocera zonata, also known as the peach fruit fly, is known to attack a variety of fruits, including peaches, plums, pomegranates, and citrus fruits. It has also been reported to attack some vegetables, such as eggplant and tomato. Bactrocera dorsalis, also known as the Oriental fruit fly, is known to infest over 250 different types of fruit, including citrus, mangoes, bananas, guava, and papaya. It can also attack some vegetables, such as peppers and tomatoes. The dataset was taken from [15].

We also used a dataset from [16], which consists of 200 images of yellow fruit flies in the trap are consolidated into two parts, namely training dataset and test dataset, with the proportion of 75% and 25%, respectively.

Overall, both Bactrocera zonata and Bactrocera dorsalis are highly destructive pests that can cause significant damage to fruit and vegetable crops. Effective control measures, such as the use of insecticides, biological control agents, and quarantine measures, are essential for preventing the spread of these pests and minimizing their impact on agricultural production.

In order to classify rest of the flies from fruit flies, we also collected data of butterflies from [17]. That will be considered as foreign fly. We aquired all the above mentioned dataset from three sources and merged them to create a single dataset.

After the dataset is created, we implemented the algorithm. The dataset details are given below having testing set and validation set as follows (Table 1).

Table 1. Table showing dataset split ratio

Data split	Image Count	Image Percentage
Training Set	2500	84%
Validation Set	399	13%
Testing Set	85	3%

It is necessary to preprocess the data. The goal of preprocessing is to enhance the quality of the data and to optimize its use for a specific machine learning algorithm. By applying preprocessing techniques, machine learning models can be trained more accurately and efficiently, leading to better predictions and insights.

Preprocessing techniques may include removing irrelevant or duplicated data, handling missing values, scaling or normalizing data, reducing noise, and transforming data into a different format or representation (Table 2).

After preprocessing is done, augmentation is performed on the dataset. In augmentation, blur of 0.75px and three outputs per training example are produced (Table 3).

Table 2. Table with augmentation and detail columns.

Type of Preprocessing	Detail
Auto-Orient	Applied
Resize	Stretch to 640×640

Table 3. Table with augmentation and detail.

Augmentation	Detail
Blur	Applied up to 0.75px

Annotation group is also a vital component in any models. So the table below contain the annotation group as well as details about the dataset (Table 4).

Table 4. Table showing dataset version detail.

Attribute	Detail
Version ID	3
Annotation Group	Flies

The dataset was labeled using Roboflow, which is an online platform for managing, annotating, and augmenting computer vision datasets. The following image shows a collage of the labeled dataset.

6   Results

To ensure how well our customized version of Yolov5 namely Yolov5-FlyEye performs against the two Yolov5n and Yolov5s variants. We found out that Yolov5-FlyEye outperforms both Yolov5s and Yolov5n by slight margin when subjected to same training hyperparameter values. The following shows the comparison of mean average precision at iou 0.5–0.95 against the Floating point operations (GFLOPs) (Fig. 2).

The Fig. 3 shows how the Yolov5-FlyEye performs against the Yolov5n and Yolov5s for precision vs epoch metric.

The hyper-parameters for the training of the three yolov5 variants were the same. The Table 5 highlights the hyper-parameters used for the training.

Since we are deploying the Yolov5-FlyEye on embedded device namely Nvidia Jetson Nano, we aim to lower the computational complexity of the model. We aimed to lower the floating point operations (FLOPs) which determine the computational complexity of the model while achieving superior performance than other variants used for comparison. The Table 6 shows the GFLOPs, the GPU used for training and the sizes of the weight files produced from the three Yolov5

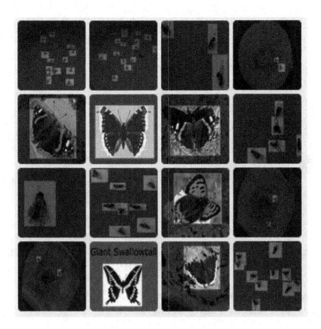

Fig. 1. Labeled Dataset

Table 5. Hyper-parameters

Hyper-parameter	YOLOv5 FlyEye	YOLOv5n	YOLOv5s
Input resolution	640 × 640	640 × 640	640 × 640
Number of layers	271	157	157
Training batch size	16	16	16
Epochs	177	191	192
Patience	30	30	30
Optimizer	Adam	Adam	Adam
Learning rate	0.001	0.001	0.001
Momentum	0.937	0.937	0.937
Weight decay	0.0005	0.0005	0.0005
IoU threshold	0.55	0.55	0.55

variants. The comparison shows that our proposed Yolov5 architecture namely Yolov5-FlyEye outperforms the Yolov5n and Yolov5s. The following table shows the comparison. If we look at the Table 6, we can see that our proposed Yolov5 architecture has 23% lower computational complexity with respect to Yolov5n and 78% lower computational complexity than the Yolov5s.

After training we performed inference to check how well object detection works on the test images. The Fig. 4 shows the detection results.

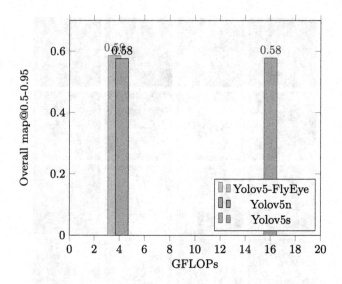

Fig. 2. Bar chart showing the performance of Yolov5-FlyEye, Yolov5n, and Yolov5s models on a detection task as a function of GFLOPs.

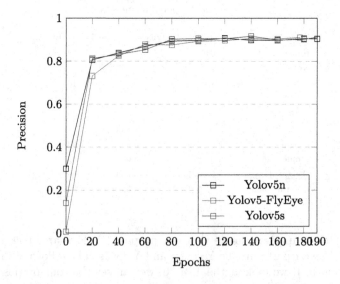

Fig. 3. Graph showing the precision of Yolov5-FlyEye, Yolov5n, and Yolov5s models on a detection task as function of epochs

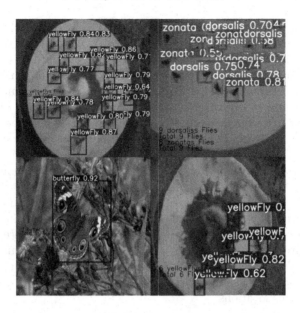

Fig. 4. Inference on test images

Table 6. Yolov5 Training Details

Model	GPU	Weight file size	GFLOPs
Yolov5-FlyEye	NVIDIA RTX A2000-12GB	3.2 MB	3.5
Yolov5n	NVIDIA RTX A2000-12GB	4.2 MB	4.6
Yolov5s	NVIDIA RTX A2000-12GB	14.7 MB	15.8

7   Conclusion

In conclusion, this conference paper highlights the potential of AI-based Internet of Things (IoT) devices in the field of agriculture by presenting the modified version of YOLOv5 called YOLOv5-FlyEye. The results demonstrate that the proposed modification achieves high performance in detecting and classifying fruit flies on embedded systems such as the Nvidia Jetson Nano. The optimized algorithm reduces the computational complexity of YOLOv5, making it suitable for efficient and cost-effective embedded systems. These findings contribute to the development of AI-based IoT devices for pest detection and monitoring in agriculture, showcasing the power of modern AI modules in edge computing applications. The advancements in hardware and processing speeds have enabled the deployment of machine learning algorithms such as YOLOv5 on IoT devices, paving the way for a new era of embedded AI computing. Moving forward, future work can explore the application of the YOLOv5-FlyEye algorithm on a wider range of embedded systems and devices to evaluate its performance in diverse environments. Further optimization of the algorithm can be carried out to improve its accuracy and speed, making it even more efficient for real-time pest detection and monitoring. There are a number of things that should be done better for IoT's future work. Real-time monitoring could be one potential avenue for advancement. The Flytrap application now depends on data kept on the Think talk server, which may cause delays in getting crucial information. By sending data from the Jetson board to the mobile application directly, the system can be improved to enable real-time monitoring. Users would be able to get alerts and notifications in real-time as a result, getting more timely and useful information. The creation of a centralised board that can link to numerous cameras dispersed throughout an orchard or farming area represents another potential future avenue for IoT in the context of Flytrap. This would make it possible to develop a monitoring system that is more thorough, can gather information from many sources, and can give a more thorough account of pest activity in various locations.

Acknowledgment. We would like to express my sincere gratitude to my supervisor Dr Muhammad Hanif and co-supervisor Dr Waqar Ahmed for their invaluable support and guidance throughout the process of writing this conference paper. Their expertise and insights were instrumental in shaping the direction of our research and in refining our ideas. Their feedback and constructive criticism were immensely helpful in improving the quality of our manuscript. We are deeply grateful for the time and effort they have dedicated to mentoring us and helping us grow. Without their guidance, this paper would not have been possible.

References

1. Bradshaw, C.J., et al.: Massive yet grossly underestimated global costs of invasive insects. Nat. Commun. **7**, 12986 (2016)
2. Gautam, M.P., Singh, H., Kumar, S., Kumar, V., Singh, G., Singh, S.N.: Diamondback moth, Plutella xylostella (Linnaeus) (Insecta: Lepidoptera: Plutellidae) a major insect of cabbage in India: a review. J. Entomol. Zool. Stud. **6**, 1394–1399 (2018)
3. Wen, C., Wu, D., Hu, H., Pan, W.: Pose estimation-dependent identification method for field moth images using deep learning architecture. Biosyst. Eng. **136**, 117–128 (2015)
4. Silveira, M., Monteiro, A.: Automatic recognition and measurement of butterfly eyespot patterns. Biosystems **95**, 130–136 (2009)
5. Guarnieri, A., Maini, S., Molari, G., Rondelli, V.: Automatic trap for moth detection in integrated pest management. Bull. Insectol. **64**, 247–251 (2011)
6. Wang, J., Lin, C., Ji, L., Liang, A.: A new automatic identification system of insect images at the order level. Knowl. Based Syst. **33**, 102–110 (2012)
7. Thenmozhi, K., Reddy, U.S.: Crop pest classification based on deep convolutional neural network and transfer learning. Comput. Electron. Agric. **164**, 104906 (2019)

8. Hendrichs, J., Vera, M.T., De Meyer, M., Clarke, A.R.: Resolving cryptic species complexes of major tephritid pests. Zookeys **540**, 5–39 (2015)
9. Oliveira, C.M., Auad, A.M., Mendes, S.M., Frizzas, M.R.: Economic impact of insect pests in Brazilian agriculture. J. Appl. Entomol. **137**, 1–15 (2012)
10. Duyck, P., David, P., Quilici, S.: A review of relationships between interspecific competition and invasions of fruit flies (Diptera: Tephritidae). Ecol. Enthomol. **29**, 511–520 (2004)
11. Duyck, P., David, P., Junod, G., Brunel, C., Dupont, R., Quilici, S.: Importance of competition mechanisms in successive invasions by polyphagous tephritis in La Reunion. Ecology **87**, 1770–1780 (2006)
12. Potamitis, I., Rigakis, I., Tatlas, N.: Automated surveillance of fruit flies. Sensors **17**, 110 (2017)
13. Han, K., Wang, Y., Tian, Q., Guo, J., Xu, C., Xu, C.: GhostNet: more features from cheap operations, pp. 1577–1586 (2020)
14. Zhang, Y., Cai, W., Fan, S., Song, R., Jin, J.: Object detection based on YOLOv5 and GhostNet for orchard pests. Information **13**, 548 (2022)
15. Tariq, S., Hakim, A., Siddiqi, A.A., Owais, M.: An image dataset of fruit fly species. Mendeley Data **V1** (2022). https://doi.org/10.17632/hgz2n5jxhp.1
16. Le, A.D., Pham, D.A., Pham, D.T., Vo, H.B.: AlertTrap: a study on object detection in remote insect trap monitoring system using on-the-edge deep learning platform (2022)
17. Wang, J., Markert, K., Everingham, M.: Learning models for object recognition from natural language descriptions. In: Proceedings of the 20th British Machine Vision Conference (BMVC2009), September 2009

A Finite Differences-Based Metric for Magnetic Resonance Image Inpainting

Marco Seracini[1]([envelope])[ID], Claudia Testa[2,3][ID], and Stephen R. Brown[4,5][ID]

[1] Department of Biomedical and Neruomotorial Sciences, University of Bologna,
via Massarenti 9, 40138 Bologna, Italy
marco.seracini2@unibo.it

[2] IRCCS, Istituto delle Scienze Neurologiche di Bologna, via Altura 3, 40139 Bologna, Italy
claudia.testa@unibo.it

[3] Department of Physics and Astronomy "Augusto Righi", University of Bologna,
viale Berti Pichat 6/2, 40127 Bologna, Italy

[4] Massachusetts Institute of Technology, 77 Massachusetts Ave, Cambridge, MA 02139, USA
srbrown@mit.edu

[5] Aprovechar Lab L3C, Montpelier, VT, USA
srbrown@aprovechar.org

Abstract. In this article, using a patch-based approach, we inpaint two different T_1 and T_2 sets of Magnetic Resonance images of phantoms by the application of a new metric formulated with the introduction of finite differences. We show that the new approach allows us to exactly reconstruct the missing part of the image, when the unknown patch is present in the search domain. Moreover, we show that higher finite difference order terms are needed when the contrast of the area to inpaint is reduced.

Keywords: Texture Synthesis · Inpainting by Patch · Image Processing

1 Introduction

In the literature, the so called *inpainting problem* consists in filling zones of missing information in an image, digitally represented by a two-dimensional discrete set [18].

To fill those areas of missing information, different approaches and solutions have been proposed and described in the literature ([2, 7–9, 11, 14, 22, 26, 29]). Among those, an interesting promising one was introduced by [8, 29]: for each missing point in the to-be-inpainted area a suitable neighborhood of the point is scrolled all over the known image data (in what follows also referred to as search domain) and the correct value is chosen maximizing a similarity measure between the neighborhood and the given signal. The described method, despite its conceptual simplicity, provides very good results in a relatively affordable execution time [13, 20, 28].

Subsequently, in [7], a mathematical formalization of the algorithm has been provided through a functional, named *Inpainting Energy* (E_I). E_I quantifies the difference between a neighborhood of the missing points and the known part of the signal itself.

© The Author(s), under exclusive license to Springer Nature Switzerland AG 2023
O. Gervasi et al. (Eds.): ICCSA 2023 Workshops, LNCS 14108, pp. 608–622, 2023.
https://doi.org/10.1007/978-3-031-37117-2_41

Despite the goodness of the achieved results, these methods mask a conceptual weakness because they neglect the *under-the-surface* structural information hidden in the known part of the signal, i.e., in the structure of the surface of the image function (see Fig. 1). In fact, to evaluate the similarity between two functions (or signals) it is possible to take into account, together with their pointwise difference, also the similarity between their derivatives (or their finite differences). This structural information is therefore connected with the concept of the derivatives or, in this specific discrete case, of the finite differences [17,19,23].

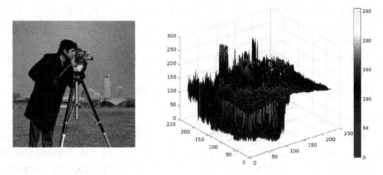

Fig. 1. Cameraman picture (on the left) and its three-dimensional representation as a surface with a two dimensional support (on the right).

For this reason, introducing a methodology that cares about these structural aspects gives support to:

– a better understanding of the logic behind the inpainting process;
– a faster convergence to a stable solution;
– better results.

Finite differences have been used in image and signal reconstruction mainly with regularization purposes [3,25,31]: this approach is based on the assumptions, sometimes arbitrary, about certain regularity properties of the signal to reconstruct. Differently, with our method we stay true to the inpainting-by-patch logic.

Moreover, the inclusion of the finite differences assures a faster convergence to the solution, supported by the evolution of the inpainting error at each iteration.

Finally, the quality of the results is improved. On one hand, in case of aesthetic needs (computer graphics, arts or photography, only to name some) to consider satisfactory the achieved results, the inpainted area has to be not *eye-distinguishable*, by a human observer, from the known part of it. This way to evaluate the quality of the reconstruction is user-dependant and completely detached from the ground truth. This approach is evidently not suitable in case of medical images that are going to be used for diagnostic purposes.

In medical cases, we require the achieved reconstructions to be representative of the effective nature of the investigated biological tissue (i.e., healthy or not). The missing of a reference in the most of the real medical investigations, e.g., because it is not possible to perform the extraction of the suspicious tissue from the patient body, allows to test the procedure only on *ad hoc* built objects, referred to as phantoms. In particular, we:

- take the images of a set of phantoms;
- delete some zones from them;
- perform the search of the missing parts in the pristine images, such that we expect the reconstruction to be without errors of any kind;
- check the similarity between the achieved reconstructions and the pristine images.

A meaningful example of medical images is represented by the ones coming from Magnetic Resonance (MR) Imaging systems, which are widely used, e.g., for structural and functional brain investigations [12, 24].

The reasons for the partial loss and degradation of the signal in MR images are artifacts due to local magnetic field inhomogeneities, due to motion, to eddy currents, to low signal to noise ratio. In particular susceptibilities variations and eddy currents can produce loss of signal in regions of the image.

To face these problems in the post processing stage, given the practical difficulties and the economic expense to repeat the MR exams on individuals, the attempts to reconstruct the missing areas have widely employed, in the recent years, various structures of Neural Networks (NN) and Deep Learning (DL) techniques [1, 16, 21]. The main drawback of NN-based approaches is that a complete mathematical model is missing, such that their results can not be stated to be a priori valid in general, even if they are usually visually impressive.

The goal of our work is to study how the introduction of a finite differences term in the formulation of E_I improves the quality and reliability of the reconstructions, as with general images, and in the specific MRI case.

In particular, we want to prove that the minimization of the inpainting energy, as defined in [7], is not enough to achieve back the pristine images, even if the missing parts are effectively present in the search domain. Moreover, due to the limited available number of images, our analysis is focused on *deterministic* methods only, given the impossibility to adequately train NN and DL.

The main novelties introduced in this work concern the use of the finite differences of any order (also higher than one) for the inpainting process and the experimental test of this procedure on real medical Magnetic Resonance images.

The article is structured as follows: in Sect. 2 the formalization of the algorithm is provided. The more applied part of the work is exposed in Sect. 3, and Sect. 4 where the MR dataset, the numerical implementation and the numerical results are respectively described. A final paragraph in Sect. 5 summarizes the achieved results.

2   Algorithm Formalization

Working with an n-bits coded image function I, of size $M \times N$, containing the area Ω to be inpainted (see Fig. 2), we consider a function χ of the point to inpaint. In [28, 29] the mean square error (MSE) is calculated between χ and whatever plausible patch in the given image. We denote it by MSE_χ.

From the minimization of MSE_χ the value of each missing point comes (e.g., [7]). In Fig. 2 a graphical example of this procedure is provided. Anyway, this process can bring to multiple different values, such that an unique solution can not always exist. We can group these equivalent values as belonging to the same class of equivalence. To reduce the number of the values belonging to the same class, we introduce, in the computation of the value for the inpainting, a new term, taking into account of the finite differences of any order.

Then the inpainting-by-patch task can be conceptually outlined in two main subproblems:

1. individuate the *content-driven* solutions depending on E_{C_T};
2. individuate the *structure-driven* solutions depending on E_{S_T}.

E_{C_T} is the mean square error of the signal respect with a given patch of support χ in the image; E_{S_T} is the mean square error of the signal finite differences respect with a given patch of support χ. The *content-driven* solutions are those values that minimize the MSE_χ while the *structure-driven* solutions are those ones that minimize the mean square error calculated on the finite differences. The final inpainted results come from the best possible match of both of these conditions, opportunely combined together. We denote this combination with E_T.

Moreover, to make the contribution of E_{C_T} and E_{S_T} comparable, also in the physical dimensionality sense, normalization coefficients $w_{S_k} = \frac{1}{2^k}$, where k is the order of the finite differences, are needed. Note that, in this case $\sum_{k=1}^{\infty} w_{S_k} = 1$, such that, to the limit, the contribution of the finite differences equals the contribution of the content term.

In Algorithm 1 we show the pseudo-code we have used for the calculation of the E_{C_T} and E_{S_T} contributions.

3   MR Dataset

MR images have been acquired by a 3T scanner (Siemens, Skyra) at the IRCCS Institute of Neurological Sciences, Bellaria Hospital (Italy), using a 64 channels head/neck

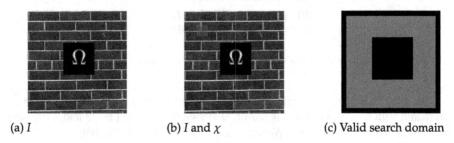

(a) I (b) I and χ (c) Valid search domain

Fig. 2. From left to right: (a) image I contianing the to-be-inpainted area Ω; (b) in blue, bordered in orange, the support of the neighborhood function χ, centered in a point of the valid search domain; (c) the green area represents the set for which the inpainting energy is well defined. The black border is half the size of χ. (Color figure online)

Algorithm 1 Pseudo-code of the algorithm used for the inpainting procedure. The value of maxint represents the maximum possible value available in the calculation system. Ts denotes the given part of the image from which the values of the missing points are deduced.

procedure INPAINT(I=Image,Ω=To-Be-Inpainted area,Ts=Training Set)

    for each point of coordinates (i, j) in Ω **do**
        $E_{T_{min}} = maxint$
$loop:$
        for each point of coordinates (h, k) in Ts **do**
            calculate E_{C_T}
            calculate E_{S_T}
            $E_T = E_{C_T} + E_{S_T}$
            if $E_T < E_{T_{min}}$ **then**
                $I(i, j) \leftarrow Ts(h, k)$
            else
                $goto\ loop:$

coil. To evaluate hardware performance and quantitative parameters (such as geometry distortion, slice thickness accuracy, intensity uniformity, ghosting artifact, and high contrast spatial resolution) of the images an ACR phantom (American College of Radiology [30]) was used. T_1 and T_2 sequences were acquired.

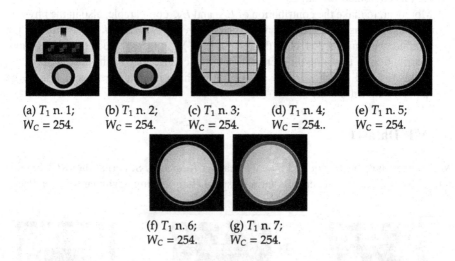

(a) T_1 n. 1; $W_C = 254.$

(b) T_1 n. 2; $W_C = 254.$

(c) T_1 n. 3; $W_C = 254.$

(d) T_1 n. 4; $W_C = 254..$

(e) T_1 n. 5; $W_C = 254.$

(f) T_1 n. 6; $W_C = 254.$

(g) T_1 n. 7; $W_C = 254.$

Fig. 3. Set of MR acquisitions of seven different phantoms wth their W_C, T_1 sequence.

The MR T_1 sequence provides a set of better contrast images in ACR phantom, if compared with the T_2 one. For this reason, under each image in Figs. 3 and 4 we show the corresponding value of their Weber contrast, defined as follows [10]:

$$W_C := \frac{I_{max} - I_{min}}{I_{min}}.$$

Moreover, to quantify the quality of the reconstructions the Peak Signal to Noise Ratio (PSNR) has been used [27].

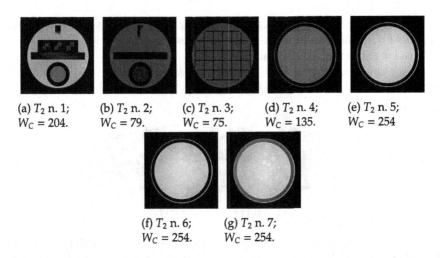

(a) T_2 n. 1; (b) T_2 n. 2; (c) T_2 n. 3; (d) T_2 n. 4; (e) T_2 n. 5;
$W_C = 204$. $W_C = 79$. $W_C = 75$. $W_C = 135$. $W_C = 254$

(f) T_2 n. 6; (g) T_2 n. 7;
$W_C = 254$. $W_C = 254$.

Fig. 4. Set of MR acquisitions of seven different phantoms with their W_C, T_2 sequence.

Moreover, to make the contribution of E_{C_T} and E_{S_T} comparable, also in the physical dimensionality sense, we put $w_{S_k} = \frac{1}{2^k}$, that is also a theoretical set of appropriate values. Note that, in this case $\sum_{k=1}^{\infty} w_{S_k} = 1$, such that, to the limit, the contribution of the finite differences equals the contribution of the content term.

4   Numerical Results

In this section we show some meaningful numerical results achieved with and without the introduction of the finite differences. We use a square neighborhood χ of side $2L+1$.

The first example is represented by a quasi periodic texture (de Bonet's sample number 161 [6]), Ω has the size of 12×14 pixels (the black rectangle in Fig. 5).

In the same Fig. 5 the results of inpainting Ω for different values of L are shown, by only using the content-driven term (i.e., $E_T = E_{C_T}$).

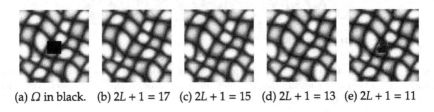

(a) Ω in black. (b) $2L + 1 = 17$ (c) $2L + 1 = 15$ (d) $2L + 1 = 13$ (e) $2L + 1 = 11$

Fig. 5. Inpainting of Ω by mean of $E_T = E_{C_T}$, for different values of $2L + 1$. In (a) the image to inpaint with Ω in black. Then, (b) to (e), the results after the inpainting with $2L+1 = 17, 15, 13, 11$ respectively. The minimum value that visually guarantees a suitable final result is $2L+1 = 13$. We stress that all the reconstructions achieved for different values of $2L+1$ are numerically different, even if to the naked eye they look visually identical.

From the same figure we can see that increasing the support of the neighborhood χ until $2L+1 = 13$, the reconstruction quality improves. On the other hand, for $2L+1 > 13$ the final images appear visually equivalent.

On the contrary, by using $E_T = E_{C_T} + E_{S_T}$, even the case $2L + 1 = 11$ results in a correct reconstruction, as shown in Fig. 6.

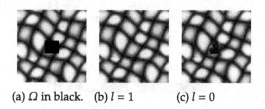

(a) Ω in black.   (b) $l = 1$ (c) $l = 0$

Fig. 6. From left to right: (a) image to be inpainted with Ω of size 12×14 pixels; (b) inpainting result using $E_T = E_{C_T} + E_{S_T}(l = 1)$; (c) inpainting result using $E_T = E_{C_T}$ only. Both the reconstructions have been performed with $2L+1 = 11$. The better performance deriving from the contribution of E_{S_T} is visually evident.

In [7] they formulated the expression of the inpainting energy and showed that it has a decreasing trend. To evaluate the behavior of the minimization of the functional when introducing the finite differences we recorded the values of $E_T = E_{C_T} + E_{S_T}$ at each iteration. Its trend is converging faster to a lower minimum than the case not using the finite differences; the trend exhibits also less oscillations and a higher rate of regularity of the convergence process (see Figs. 8 and 11).

The same tests, performed increasing the size of Ω to 41×41 pixels, result in what shown in Fig. 7. The associated energy trends are in Fig. 8.

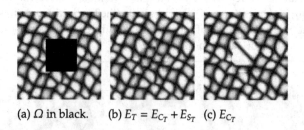

(a) Ω in black.   (b) $E_T = E_{C_T} + E_{S_T}$ (c) E_{C_T}

Fig. 7. (a) Initial Ω, size 41×41 pixels; (b) inpainting result using $E_T = E_{C_T} + E_{S_T}$ (first order finite differences); (c) inpainting result using E_{C_T} only. Both the reconstructions have been performed with $2L+1 = 11$. The better performance deriving from the introduction of E_{S_T} is, again, visually evident.

Further examples of reconstruction of images, taken from the Brodatz database [4], are available in Fig. 9 and 10, together with their energy trends (see Fig. 11 again).

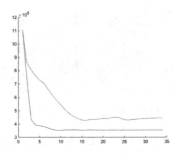

Fig. 8. The figure shows two E_T trends when varying L: in red $E_T = E_{C_T}$, in blue $E_T = E_{C_T} + E_{S_T}$. The contribution of the finite differences brings to a faster and more regular convergence to the minimum value.

(a) Pristine I.   (b) Ω in black.   (c) $E_T = E_{C_T}$.   (d) $E_T = E_{C_T} + E_{S_T}$.

Fig. 9. Inpainting of texture D1 taken from Brodatz database with $2L + 1 = 23$. From left to right: (a) pristine image; (b) image to be inpainted (Ω in black, size 16×16); (c) inpainting by mean of $E_T = E_{C_T}$ and (d) $E_T = E_{C_T} + E_{S_T}$. The result achieved using the first order finite difference are visually closer to the pristine image with respect to the case when the finite differences have not been used. (Color figure online)

In Fig. 9 the result achieved introducing the structural term appears free from shadowing artifacts: in this case the pristine image has not been used as search domain, such that a perfect (i.e.,with zero error) reconstruction is not generally possible.

In Fig. 10 the result achieved introducing the finite differences appears more compliant with the geometrical structure of the texture, if compared with the images obtained using content-driven only.

From the previous considerations we can infer that the introduction of E_{S_T} allows us to carry more structural information in the final reconstruction.

After these general examples we have tested the effects of introducing the finite differences in MR phantom images and we have compared the achieved results with the ones coming from the Matlab function *inpaintExamplar*, based on [5, 15] and generally taken as reference in the inpainting-by-patch-approach. In the follwing examples the pristine image has been used as search domain for the determination of the best value to inpaint. Only in those cases, when the missing part in Ω is contained in the image itself (or in the used search domain), a zero-error reconstruction is possible (e.g., in a

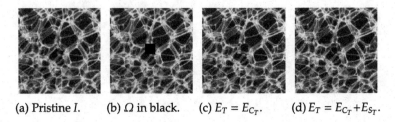

(a) Pristine I.   (b) Ω in black.   (c) $E_T = E_{C_T}$.   (d) $E_T = E_{C_T} + E_{S_T}$.

Fig. 10. Inpainting of texture D111 taken from Brodatz database with $2L + 1 = 27$. From left to right: (a) pristine image; (b) image to be inpainted (Ω in black, size 16×16); (c) inpainting by mean of $E_T = E_{C_T}$ and (d) $E_T = E_{C_T} + E_{S_T}$. The result achieved using the first order finite difference are visually closer to the pristine image with respect to the case when the finite differences have not been used. (Color figure online)

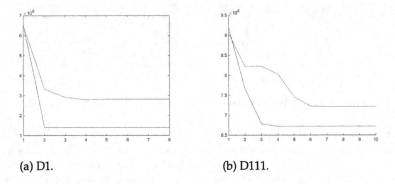

(a) D1.   (b) D111.

Fig. 11. The figure shows the E_T trends: in red $E_T = E_{C_T}$, in blue $E_T = E_{C_T} + E_{S_T}$ $l = 1$. From left to right: (a) image D1 from Brodatz database; (b) image D111 from Brodatz database. Including finite differences determines a faster and more regular convergence to a lower minimum value. (Color figure online)

periodic pattern). This property is strongly auspicable because such a kind of behavior guarantees that, if the zero minimum exists for the functional, the algorithm is capable to converge to it. Viceversa, if the algorithm is not capable to reach the absolute minimum, in those case when it exists, we have, a priori, less control on the quality of the final reconstruction.

In Fig. 12 we show the reconstructions of the T_1 sequence dataset of phantoms. The inpainting performed introducing the finite differences contributions allows us to reconstruct the pristine image without errors of any kind, given a suitable order of the finite difference l. On the other hand, in the case of [5, 15] the reconstructions appear sometimes to be visually not correct (see the first column M_{Dt} image), other times not identical to the pristine image. To quantify the quality of the reconstruction the values of the PSNR are shown in Table 1. For this set of images, all having the same maximum contrast $W_C = 254$, the finite differences of the first order are enough to perfectly reconstruct the original image.

Table 1. Values of the PSNR for the reconstructions of the T_1 dataset. In the T_1# columns the number of the phantom (from 1 to 7); in the Method columns the used method to inpaint, e.g., without the contribution of the finite differences [5, 15] and with their contributions $E_T = E_{C_T} + E_{S_T}$; in the W_C columns the Weber contrast for the area to be inpainted, calculated in the pristine image; in the l columns the finite differences order used to inpaint; in the last columns the PSNR. In this case, where all the images have maximum contrast $W_C = 254$, $l = 1$ is enough to perfectly reconstruct the pristine image.

T_1#	Method	W_C	l	PSNR	T_1#	Method	W_C	l	PSNR
1	[5, 15]	254	0	9.286	5	[5, 15]	254	0	20.882
1	$E_T = E_{C_T} + E_{S_T}$		1	$+\infty$	5	$E_T = E_{C_T} + E_{S_T}$		1	$+\infty$
2	[5, 15]	254	0	15.943	6	[5, 15]	254	0	37.759
2	$E_T = E_{C_T} + E_{S_T}$		1	$+\infty$	6	$E_T = E_{C_T} + E_{S_T}$		1	$+\infty$
3	[5, 15]	254	0	29.932	7	[5, 15]	254	0	32.060
3	$E_T = E_{C_T} + E_{S_T}$		1	$+\infty$	7	$E_T = E_{C_T} + E_{S_T}$		1	$+\infty$
4	[5, 15]	254	0	36.752					
4	$E_T = E_{C_T} + E_{S_T}$		1	$+\infty$					

In Fig. 13 the reconstructions of the T_2 dataset of phantoms are shown. Also in this case, the inpainting performed introducing the finite differences contributions allows to reconstruct the pristine image without errors of any kind, given a suitable order of the finite difference l. Differently from the T_1 sequence, for this set of images the value of W_C is lower, according to the properties of the T_2 sequence, such that it is necessary to introduce a higher order of finite differences, to guarantee a zero error reconstruction of the pristine image.

The values of the PSNR for the achieved reconstructions are shown in Table 2. Given the lower contrast with respect to the analogous T_1 acquisitions, a higher order of finite differences l is needed to correctly reconstruct the pristine image. The most demanding case is the phantom number 3, having the lower contrast $W_C = 75$ in the whole dataset.

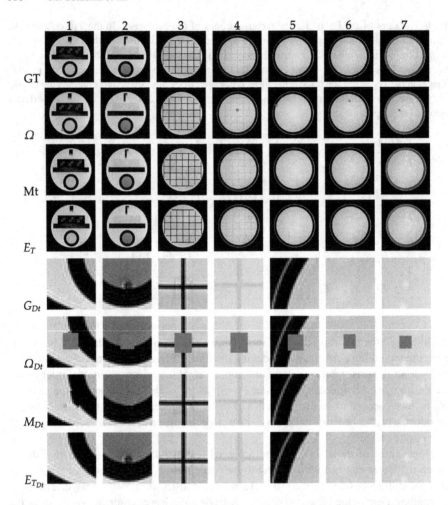

Fig. 12. Reconstructions of the set of MR acquisitions of seven different phantoms, T_1 sequence. From the first row: ground truth (GT); the area to be inpainted in green (Ω); inpainted result by [5,15] (Mt), i.e., with no contribution of the finite differences; inpainted result by the introduction of E_{S_T} in E_T (E_T); magnification of GT (G_{Dt}); magnification of Ω (Ω_{Dt}); magnification of Mt (M_{Dt}); magnification of E_T ($E_{T_{Dt}}$). For every image we used $l = 1$.

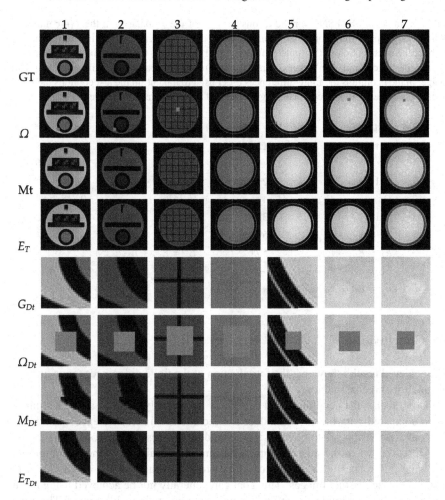

Fig. 13. Reconstructions of the set of MR acquisitions of seven different phantoms, T_2 sequence. From the first row: ground truth (GT); the area to be inpainted in green (Ω); inpainted result by [5, 15] (Mt), i.e., with no contribution of the finite differences; inpainted result by the introduction of E_{S_T} in E_T (E_T); magnification of GT (G_{Dt}); magnification of Ω (Ω_{Dt}); magnification of Mt (M_{Dt}); magnification of E_T ($E_{T_{Dt}}$). The value chosen for l varies according to W_C: lower the contrast, higher l. The values of l are available in Table 2.

Table 2. Values of the PSNR for the reconstructions of the T_2 dataset. In the T_1# columns the number of the phantom (from 1 to 7); in the Method columns the used method to inpaint, e.g., without the contribution of the finite differences [5,15] and with their contributions $E_T = E_{C_T} + E_{S_T}$; in the W_C columns the Weber contrast for the area to be inpainted, calculated in the pristine image; in the l columns the finite differences order used to inpaint; in the last columns the PSNR. In case of images with low contrast a higher order of finite differences l is needed.

T_2#	Method	W_C	l	PSNR	T_2#	Method	W_C	l	PSNR
1	[5,15]	204	0	12.009	4	[5,15]		0	45.821
1	$E_T = E_{C_T} + E_{S_T}$		1	+∞	4	$E_T = E_{C_T} + E_{S_T}$	135	1	61.0568
2	[5,15]	79	0	21.229	4	$E_T = E_{C_T} + E_{S_T}$	254	2	+∞
2	$E_T = E_{C_T} + E_{S_T}$		1	+∞	5	[5,15]		0	18.368
3	[5,15]	75	0	38.858	5	$E_T = E_{C_T} + E_{S_T}$		1	+∞
3	$E_T = E_{C_T} + E_{S_T}$		1	59.1454	6	[5,15]		0	35.364
3	$E_T = E_{C_T} + E_{S_T}$		2	59.6284	6	$E_T = E_{C_T} + E_{S_T}$	254	1	+∞
3	$E_T = E_{C_T} + E_{S_T}$		3	+∞	7	[5,15]		0	33.181
3	$E_T = E_{C_T} + E_{S_T}$		3	+∞	7	$E_T = E_{C_T} + E_{S_T}$	254	1	+∞

5   Conclusions

The achieved results show that the introduction of the finite differences terms improves the quality of reconstruction.

In particular, the new functional converges numerically faster to a lower minimum when compared with the case that does not include the finite differences. In addition, the convergence appears to be more regular and to have less oscillations.

Moreover, when the missing part of the image is available in the search domain, the finite differences term allows to achieve results without errors of any kind, i.e., identical to the pristine images. This goal can generally not be achieved using current inpainting-by-patch implementation that does not employ finite differences. This aspect is particular important to guarantee the algorithm to reach the absolute minimum, when it is available in the search domain. This importance increases considerably in case of medical diagnostic images.

In addition, our results show that lower is the contrast of the image to reconstruct, higher is the order of the finite differences needed to achieve back the pristine image. To the best of our knowledge it is the first time that finite differences are used to inpaint using an inpainting-by-patch approach. Even if in some cases the reconstruction not using the finite differences provides visually acceptable results, what achieved is not congruent with the ground truth, point that is crucial for medical images.

This behavior depends on the fact that the number of the candidate, i.e., of the metrically equivalent patches to inpaint, increase as the contrast decreases. The contribution of higher finite differences is needed to add constraints and prune the number of equivalent candidates, consequently reducing the probability to generate errors.

References

1. K. Armanious, Y. Mecky, S. Gatidis, B. Yang, Adversarial inpainting of medical image modalities, in ICASSP 2019–2019 IEEE International Conference on Acoustics, Speech and Signal Processing (ICASSP), pp. 3267–3271 (2019)
2. Ashikhmin, M.: Synthesizing natural textures. In: The proceedings of 2001 ACM Symposium on Interactive 3D Graphics, pp. 217–226 (2001)
3. Brezis, Haim: Functional Analysis, Sobolev Spaces and Partial Differential Equations. Springer, New York (2011). https://doi.org/10.1007/978-0-387-70914-7
4. Brodatz, P.: Textures: A Photographic Album for Artists and Designers. Dover, New York (1996)
5. Crimisi, A., Perez, P., Toyama, K.: Region filling and object removal by exemplar-based image inpainting. IEEE Trans. Image Process. **13**(9), 1200–1212 (2004)
6. De Bonet, J.S.: Multiresolution sampling procedure for analysis and synthesis of texture images. In: SIGGRAPH 1997 Conference Proceedings, pp, 361–368 (1997)
7. Demanet, L., Song, B., Chan, T.: Image Inpainting by Correspondence Maps: a Deterministic Approach, Applied and Computational Mathematics, 1100 (2003)
8. Efros, A., Freeman, W.T.: Image quilting for texture synthesis and transfer. In: Proceedings of SIGGRAPH 2001, pp. 341–346 (2001)
9. Efros, A.A., Leung, T.K.: Texture synthesis by non-parametric sampling. In: Proceedings of the International Conference on Computer Vision, vol. 2, pp. 1033–1038 (1999)
10. Fechner, G.T.: Elemente der Psychophysik [Elements of psychophysics], vol. 2 (1860)
11. Gatys, L., Ecker, A.S., Bethge, M.: Image texture synthesis using convolutional neural networks. In: Advances in Neural Information Processing Systems 28 NIPS 2015 (2015)
12. Evangelisti, S., et al.: Brain functional MRI responses to blue light stimulation in Leber's hereditary optic neuropathy. Biochem. Pharmacol. **191**(114488) (2021)
13. Gersho, A., Gray, R.M.: Vector Quantization and Signal Compression. Kluwer Academic Publishers (1992)
14. Hertzmann, A., Jacobs, C.E., Oliver, N., Curless, B., Salesin, D.H.: Image analogies, SIGGRAPH 2001 Proceedings of the 28th Annual Conference On Computer Graphics And Interactive Techniques, pp. 327–340 (2001)
15. Le Meur, O., Ebdelli, M., Guillemot, C.: Hierarchical super-resolution-based-inpainting. IEEE Trans. Image Process. **22**(10), 3779–3790 (2013)
16. Manjón, J.V., et al.: Blind MRI brain lesion inpainting using deep learning. In: Burgos, N., Svoboda, D., Wolterink, J.M., Zhao, C. (eds.) Simulation and Synthesis in Medical Imaging. SASHIMI 2020. LNCS. vol. 12417. Springer, Cham (2020). https://doi.org/10.1007/978-3-030-59520-3_5
17. Marr, D., Hildreth, E.: Theory of edge detection. Proc. Royal Soc. London **B-207**, 187–217 (1980)
18. Masnou, S., Morel, J.: Level lines based disocclusion. In: Proceedings 1998 International Conference on Image Processing, ICIP 1998, vol. 3, pp. 259–263 (1998)
19. Mumford, D., Shah, J.: Optimal approximations by piecewise smooth functions and associated variational problems. Comm. Pure Applied. Math. **42**, 577–685 (1989)
20. Nene, S., Nayar, S.: A simple algorithm for nearest neighbor search in high dimensions. IEEE Trans. Pattern Anal. Mach. Intell. **19**, 989–1003 (1998)
21. Nguyen, B., et al.: Unsupervised region-based Anomaly detection in brain MRI with With Adversarial Image Inpainting. In: 2021 IEEE 18th International Symposium on Biomedical Imaging (ISBI), Nice, France, pp. 1127–1131 (2021)
22. Portilla, J., Simoncelli, E.: Texture characterization via joint statistics of wavelet coefficient magnitudes. In: Fifth International Conference on Image Processing, vol. 1, pp. 62–66 (1998)

23. Rudin, L., Osher, S., Fatemi, E.: Nonlinear total variation based noise removal algorithms. Phys. D **60**, 259–268 (1992)
24. Testa, C., et al.: Stridor-related gray matter alterations in multiple system atrophy: A pilot study. Parkinsonism Relat. Disord. **62**, 226–230 (2019)
25. Tikhonov, A.N., Arsenin, V.Y.: Solutions of Ill-Posed Problems. Wiley, New York (1977)
26. Vese, L.A.: Modeling textures with total variation minimization and oscillating patterns in image processing. J. Sci. Comput. **19**(1–3), 553–572 (2003)
27. Wang, Z., Bovik, A.C.: Mean squared error: Love it or leave it? A new look at signal fidelity measures. IEEE Signal Process. Mag. **26**(1), 98–117 (2009)
28. Wei, L.: Deterministic texture analysis and synthesis using tree structure vector quantization. In: XII Brazilian Symposium on Computer Graphics and Image Processing, pp. 299–308 (1999)
29. Wei, L.Y., Levoy, M.: Fast texture synthesis using tree-structured vector quantization. In: Proceedings of SIGGRAPH 2000, pp. 479–488 (2000)
30. Weinreb, J., Wilcox, P.A., Hayden, J., Lewis, R., Froelich, J.: ACR MRI accreditation: yesterday, today, and tomorrow. J. Am. Coll. Radiol. **2**(6), 494–503 (2005)
31. Wilson, D.L., Baddeley, A.J., Owens, R.A.: A new metric for grey-scale image comparison. Int. J. Comput. Vision **24**(1), 5–17 (1997)

Improving Color Image Binary Segmentation Using Nonnegative Matrix Factorization

Ciro Castiello[1,3], Nicoletta Del Buono[2,3(✉)], and Flavia Esposito[2,3]

[1] Department of Computer Science, Bologna, Italy
ciro.castiello@uniba.it
[2] Department of Mathematics, University of Bari Aldo Moro, Bari, Italy
{nicoletta.delbuono,flavia.esposito}@uniba.it
[3] Members of INDAM-GNCS Research Group, Bari, Italy

Abstract. Image segmentation is the process of dividing a digital image into multiple segments or regions, each of which represents a different object or part of the image or shares certain visual characteristics. The goal of image segmentation is to simplify the representation of an image into something that is more meaningful and easier to analyze. Typically, segmentation creates histograms indicating edges and boundaries that use local information such as color. The color space used determines the segmentation results: while RGB is the most fundamental and widely used color space, other color spaces can also be adopted for segmentation to emphasize different aspects of an image. No single color space, however, is capable of producing satisfactory results for all types of color image segmentation tasks.

Nonnegative Matrix Factorization (NMF) is a powerful data reduction and exploration tool efficiently used to extract features that provide part-based representation for a wide range of data types. In this paper, we propose an NMF-based method for integrating different color space information from an image and then extracting from it an "optimal color space representation" which is used to improve the results of a threshold segmentation algorithm. The proposed approach uses NMF on histograms of different color spaces to generate a meta-histogram representation of the given image, which is then binary segmented. Experimental results showed that the features extracted from the proposed NMF-based approach are able to improve segmentation outcomes obtained by conventional segmentation algorithms like Otsu method.

Keywords: Image segmentation · Nonnegative Matrix Factorization · Data Integration · Color Spaces · Feature extraction

1 Introduction

In image analysis and pattern recognition, segmentation is a crucial stage. Image segmentation seeks to identify homogeneous areas, surfaces, and boundaries (such as lines or curves) in a picture that correlates to significant areas of the observed image. Moreover, segmentation is the process of categorizing each individual pixel in a picture, where identified common pixels share characteristics like gray level, color, texture, and gradients.

Formally, let I denote an image and $\mathcal{H}$ define a certain homogeneity property of it. The segmentation of I is a partition $\mathcal{P}$ of I into a set of N disjointed regions $\mathcal{R}_k$ for $k = 1, \ldots, N$ such that: (i) $\mathcal{P}$ covers the whole image I, i.e., $I = \cup_{k=1}^{N} \mathcal{R}_k$ with $\mathcal{R}_k \cap \mathcal{R}_j = \varnothing$ for $k \neq j$; (ii) each region is homogeneous with respect to a property $\mathcal{H}$, i.e., $\mathcal{H}(\mathcal{R}_k) = true$; (iii) two adjacent regions cannot be merged into a single region satisfying the property $\mathcal{H}$, i.e., $\mathcal{H}(\mathcal{R}_k \cup \mathcal{R}_j) \neq true$ for any adjacent $\mathcal{R}_k$ and $\mathcal{R}_j$ [3,12]. Image segmentation is performed on some features of the image I (such as color information or texture); segmentation mechanisms are thus designed to exploit only some of the image information's characteristics. There are many types of segmentation algorithms, each with its own strengths and limitations, depending on the nature of the image and the desired outcome; however, a fully efficient image segmentation algorithm is still a long way off. Color images contain more information than grayscale images. Several color image segmentation approaches are based on pixel color features; they assume that the distribution of pixel colors (homogeneous colors) corresponds to meaningful objects either in the image plane or in the color space in which the image is represented. A point in the RGB color space is determined by the color component levels of the associated pixel in the image, namely the red (R), green (G), and blue (B). RGB color space is commonly used for color image segmentation and, often, its linear or nonlinear transformations are used to define other color spaces. Different color spaces can be used to individuate other images' pixel color characteristics, however, the outcomes of image segmentation depend on the space that is used. Many studies attempted to identify the best color representation for a specific segmentation method or investigated the ability of color space to improve segmentation outcomes [3,8,10,13,15]. The performance of an image segmentation technique depends on the specific color space image representation, and it should be emphasized that no single color space can provide good results for the segmentation of all types of images.

In this work, we aim to segment color images discriminating principally from background to foreground. Information related to various color spaces is used by integrating the histograms associated to different color channels and we propose to use Nonnegative Matrix Factorization (NMF) to derive an "optimal color space" features hidden within a set of classical color spaces. NMF, in particular, represents an efficient method for extracting and processing image information represented in different 3D color spaces, which can then be used to improve the segmentation performance of a well-known thresholding region-based segmentation method, namely the Otsu algorithm.

In the following section, we review some basic concepts needed to introduce the proposal. In particular, we revise color spaces commonly used to describe a color image and generate useful image histograms, as well as some fundamental concepts of thresholding image segmentation techniques (such as the Otsu algorithm). Then the NMF learning method is introduced and applied to integrate different color space representations of a given image I. NMF is able to extract features (also known as factors) able to integrate and describe the optimal color space information hidden in a given image. These new features will provide a meta-histogram representation of I that can be then used to segment the image. In Sect. 4, the proposed NMF-based approach demonstrated its ability to improve segmentation outcomes when compared to the conventional Otsu segmentation algorithm on different types of color images. We conclude the paper by outlining some observations and potential future research.

2   Color Spaces and Thresholding Segmentation

A color space is a three-dimensional geometric representation of colors that uses three numerical values to characterize each specific color. There are a variety of color spaces that enable the special definition of certain attributes of color image pixels. The RGB color space is the most widely utilized, since it captures color as it is seen by humans -a combination of the tristimuli R (red), G (green), and B (blue), often known as primary colors. The RGB space can be transformed linearly or nonlinearly to create other color spaces. According to a rough classification [3,14], the four most common color spaces are: (i) the primary spaces (based on the trichromatic theory and representing any color by combining the right amounts of the three primary colors), (ii) the luminance–chrominance spaces (in which one component represents the luminance and the two others the chrominance), (iii) the perceptual spaces (that quantify the color perception using the intensity, the hue, and the saturation), and (iv) the independent axis spaces (which provide as less correlated components as possible in some statistical sense).

Some of these color spaces are adopted in this paper to represent the color image I to segment. Each color channel in the different color image representations will then integrate into a new structured data matrix. This enlarged representation of the image I allows extracting from it the hidden properties of the image I which can be used as basis information for a threshold-based segmentation algorithm.

Primary spaces. The primary spaces are based on trichromatic theory and can be used to match any color by combining appropriate amounts of three primary colors. They are divided into two types: real primary spaces, in which the primary colors are physically realizable (as in RGB), and imaginary primary spaces, in which the primaries do not exist physically (in the sense that they cannot be generated with any light spectrum).

Any primary space can be converted into RGB space using matrix linear transformations on color space components (particularly, additive or subtractive color models are used). In terms of the imaginary primary space XYZ, it defines the coordinate Y as luminance, while the coordinates X and Z carry information about all possible chromaticities at that luminance (that is how the cones in the human eye respond to light waves of varying frequencies). As previously stated, not every set of XYZ tristimulus values corresponds to a color visible to human eyes.

Luminance-Crominance spaces. Other characteristics of color include luminance and chrominance information, which are used to define the luminance-chrominance spaces $LChr_1Chr_2$. The luminance component L, in particular, can represent the lightness, brightness, luminous intensity, or luma of a color image pixel, whereas the two components Chr_1, Chr_2 represent color chrominance, typically represented as two color-difference components. Luminance-chrominance space can be created using either linear or nonlinear transformations from RGB color space. An example is the YC_bC_r luminance-chrominance space, in which one dimension (the Y color component) is the luminance (specifying the perceived brightness) and the chrominance components C_b and C_r represent the difference between the blue (B) and red (R) channels and a reference value, respectively [3]. The $L^*a^*b^*$ space, instead is derived from a nonlinear transformation of the RGB space. Its first coordinate L^* represents the color lightness of the image from black to white on a scale of zero to 100, while the a^* and the b^* components represent chromaticity with no specific numeric limits (i.e., the position of the color between magenta and green and the position of the color between yellow and blue, respectively). This color space describes all colors visible to the human eye and serves as a device-independent reference model.

Perceptual spaces. Perceptual spaces attempt to quantify subjective human color perception using: (i) brightness/intensity which characterizes the luminous level of a color stimulus (how dark or luminous an area appears), (ii) hue which measures how an area appears to be similar to one of the main primary colors (red, green, blue, and yellow), (iii) saturation which allows one to estimate an area's colorfulness in relation to its brightness (it represents the purity of a perceived color). Complex transformation functions from and to RGB space can be used to obtain perceptual spaces. The HSV is a perceptual color space that can be obtained by cylindrical-coordinate transformation of RGB; it represents a color pixel by a given hue (the chromatic content), saturation (the ratio of chromatic and achromatic contents), and brightness.

Independent spaces. Using methods such as Principal Component or Independent Component analysis, the classical space RGB can be transformed into a new color space. The color space $I_1I_2I_3$ can be obtained using principal components, where the first and most discriminant coordinate represents a luminance component, and the other two color components represent the blue-red and magenta-green color oppositions, respectively.

2.1 Segmentation by Histograms

The methods based on pixel property analysis in a color space make use of the characterization of each pixel by its color representation. The basic assumption is that homogeneous image plane regions correspond to a class of pixels with similar color properties. Color histograms can be used to identify these classes and segment the original image. The majority of gray-level image segmentation techniques are applicable to color images: they can be applied to each component of a color space and the results can then be combined to obtain a final segmentation of a color image. Histogram thresholding is a popular technique for gray-level image segmentation. The histogram of a single component color image can be divided into a number of peaks, each corresponding to a region of pixels with similar properties. A histogram method assumes that there is a threshold value corresponding to the valley between two adjacent peaks that can distinguish two different adjacent regions. However, because color information is represented by a three-dimensional color space, representing a color image's histogram and then selecting a proper threshold in this histogram reveals to be a difficult task [4].

Otsu Algorithm. The simplest type of segmentation is thresholding, in which each image pixel is divided into foreground and background points using a preset intensity value k (threshold), separating the picture objects and backdrop into distinct sets. Otsu method is a thresholding technique that works by finding an optimal threshold value that maximizes the separation between the two regions. The basic idea behind this method is to minimize the intra-class variance defined as the weighted sum of the variances of the foreground and background regions. It is computed as

$$\sigma(k) = \frac{(m_G P_1 - m(k))^2}{P_1(1 - P_1)},$$

where m_G is the mean of the image intensity, $m(k)$ is the cumulative mean at a level k, and P_1 is the probability that a pixel is assigned to one class. The optimal threshold value is the one minimizing this intra-class variance and can be computed as $\bar{k} = \mathrm{argmax}_{k=0,...,L-1}\, \sigma(k)$, being L the number of the distinct intensity level of the image. The main steps performed by Otsu algorithm are described in Algorithm 1.

Algorithm 1. Otsu algorithm

1: Calculate the pixel frequency distribution histogram of I;
2: Normalize the histogram so that it sums to one, and calculate the cumulative sum;
3: Calculate the cumulative mean and cumulative variance of pixel values;
4: For each threshold value t calculate the intra-class variance;
5: Find $\tilde{k}$ that maximizes the intra-class variance;
6: Use $\tilde{k}$ to binarize I.

---

3 Integrating Image Color Features via Low-Rank Factorization

As previously discussed, the color image I can be represented using different color spaces, each of them highlighting some embedded image property. However, none of these representations have proven to outperform the others in terms

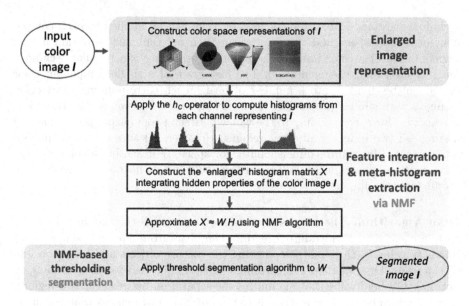

Fig. 1. Flow-chart of NMF-based segmentation algorithm. The sequential phases of the proposed approach are: creation of an enlarged representation of the input color image, feature integration, and meta-histograms extraction, and a final threshold segmentation step. (Color figure online)

of segmentation results for all types of images. As a result, choosing the best color space remains one of the most difficult aspects of color image segmentation. In this paper, rather than looking for the best color space representation, we propose to integrate different color space image properties and derive from them new global features which describe I. Particularly, we propose to integrate histograms derived by different color space representations of I via a low-rank matrix factorization to automatically extract an "integrated representation". The new characterization will allow sharing hidden properties in each single color image histogram representation. This extracted knowledge can then be used as input features of any segmentation method, such as the thresholding Otsu approach described in Algorithm 1. In the following, we formalize the main steps this integration approach is based on, while Fig. 1 sketches its main phases.

3.1 Enlarged Histogram Matrix Representation of Color Images

Images can be represented as three-dimensional nonnegative data, with two of the dimensions (rows and columns) describing the position of each pixel in the image and the third being the pixel intensity value of the gray/color channel used to represent the image. The histogram of a gray-scale image shows the number of image pixels found at each different intensity. Because there are 256 different intensities in an 8-bit gray-scale image, the histogram can be formalized as a vector of 256 numbers displaying the distribution of pixels among those grayscale values. In a color image I, histograms can be computed for each individual channel of the color space used to represent I. For example, if the RGB color space is used, histograms of the red, green, and blue channels can be generated.

Let $I \in \mathbb{R}^{p \times q}$ be a color image with pq pixels and let RGB, YC_bC_r, $L^*a^*b^*$ and HSV be the color spaces chosen to describe I. Formally, let h_C indicate the n-bin histogram operator which computes the distribution of image pixel intensities in the color channel C:

$$h_C : \mathbb{R}^{p \times q} \rightarrow \mathbb{R}^n_+. \tag{1}$$

From each of the previously considered color channels, we apply the operator h_C to the given image I to obtain the "enlarged" histogram matrix representation of I, that is

$$X = [h_R, h_G, h_B, h_Y, h_{C_b}, h_{C_r}, h_{L^*}, h_{a^*}, h_{b^*}, h_H, h_S, h_V]. \tag{2}$$

The matrix $X \in \mathbb{R}^{n \times 12}_+$ is a nonnegative matrix whose columns are histograms of the color channel in the chosen color image representation of I. It represents all the underlying color distributions in I measured in the chosen color components and provides an integrated representation of the hidden properties of the color image I. It represents –in a single structured matrix– different characteristics of the image I. In fact, the HSV color space codifies intensity, hue, and luminosity, which are not covered by the RGB color space. The YCbCr space allows for the comparison of color luminance, as well as blue and red chromaticity, whereas the L*a*b* space extracts luminance, hue, and saturation while separating luminance from chromaticity.

3.2   Feature Integration and Meta-Histograms Extraction

Since the enlarged histogram matrix X is nonnegative and incorporates different color representations of the picture I, we may decompose it using NMF[6,9,11]. This is a low-rank dimensionality reduction technique for feature extraction, data analysis, and signal processing that has found wide use in image processing too. NMF decomposes a nonnegative data matrix $X \in \mathbb{R}^{n \times m}_+$ into a basis matrix $W \in \mathbb{R}^{n \times r}_+$ and an encoding factor $H \in \mathbb{R}^{r \times m}_+$, both having non-negative elements, such that $X \approx WH$; with the rank value r usually chosen so that $(n + m)r < nm$. NMF provides an additive combination of non-negative matrix factors representing realistic building blocks for the original data. When factorizing the enlarged histogram matrix $X \in \mathbb{R}^{n \times 12}_+$, that integrates histograms of some fundamental color channel of the image I, the factor W can be interpreted as the meta-histogram factor since it represents an additive combination of color histograms. The columns of W extract hidden information from the different representations of the picture I and can be considered as an "ideal" color representation of image pixels. The matrix factor W stores the information of the image in the selected 3-D color spaces and can be adopted to segment I.

The segmentation of color images usually presents different issues. Firstly, the choice of the color space: color information is represented by tristimulus R,G, and

B or by their linear/nonlinear transformations. Secondly, when dealing with a thresholding algorithm: selecting the cutoff value in the histogram is not a trivial job, and detecting the clusters of points within this space will be computationally expensive. Using the information embedded in different color spaces, the meta-histogram factor W computed by NMF could produce some improvement in the segmentation process.

3.3   The NMF-Based Segmentation Approach

The approach proposed in this paper is based on the idea of using NMF to integrate different features extracted from a given color image using a histogram of image pixel intensities in the selected color channel. The generated data matrix X, which incorporates several picture features, is then factorized into W and H, where each column of the basis matrix W serves as a meta-histogram for any segmentation technique based on thresholding. Particularly, we apply Otsu method described in Algorithm 1. We refer to this method as NMF+Otsu. As regarding the computation of the NMF of the enlarged matrix X, to obtain $W \in \mathbb{R}^{n \times r}$ and $H \in \mathbb{R}^{r \times 12}$ we used the 2-block coordinate descent method Alternating Nonnegative Least Square (ANLS), based on the alternating solution two convex sub-problems related to the NMF factorization of X, that is:

$$\min_{H \geq 0} \|X - WH\|_F^2, \quad \text{with } W \text{ fixed}$$

and

$$\min_{W \geq 0} \|X^\top - H^\top W^\top\|_F^2, \quad \text{with } H \text{ fixed}.$$

The algorithm adopted to solve the ANLS is based on the following update rules [1]:

$$W_{ia}^{k+1} = W_{ia}^k \frac{(X(H^k)^\top)_{ia}}{(W^k H^k (H^k)^\top)_{ia}}, \quad \forall i, a \tag{3}$$

$$H_{bj}^{k+1} = H_{bj}^k \frac{((W^{k+1})^\top X)_{bj}}{((W^{k+1})^\top W^{k+1} H^k)_{bj}}, \quad \forall b, j \tag{4}$$

being k the iteration step and the final value of k represents the total number of iterations performed by the algorithm before reaching its stopping criterium. The ANLS algorithm has been initialized using random nonnegative factors W_0 [5].

The rank value has been selected as $r = 3$, coherently with the dimension of the color spaces used to describe the meta-histogram information extracted from I. The Otsu algorithm then uses the columns of the factor W as input meta-histograms to adaptively detect r thresholds. A probability mask can be finally produced by averaging the segmentation outcomes for each meta-histogram.

4   Numerical Experiments

To demonstrate the effectiveness of the proposed NMF-based segmentation strategy, namely NMF+Otsu, we reported here some experimental results on some well-known color images. Lacking commonly used metrics, to evaluate the image segmentation results, we selected empirical goodness and discrepancy which simply qualitatively evaluate segmentation results with respect to the original image according to human intuition (as described in [16]).

Moreover, the NMF+Otsu approach has been compared with the standard Otsu segmentation method (namely, Otsu). Accuracy and Precision measures have been used as additional quantitative metrics for images having foreground truth image segmentation results. Particularly, $Precision = \frac{TP}{TP+FP}$ is the proportion of pixels in the segmentation that correspond to boundary pixels in the ground truth; while pixel accuracy is computed as $Accuracy = \frac{TP+TN}{TP+TN+FP+FN}$ where TP indicates the number of pixels classified correctly for a given class c, FP the number of pixels classified incorrectly as class c, TN the number of pixels classified correctly as not c, and FN the number of pixels classified incorrectly as not c.

4.1   Experimental Results

To assess the qualitative validity of the proposed NMF-based methodology, the segmentation results on different color images are presented. Firstly, Fig. 2 illustrates the original color images used as benchmarks: (a) Palm tree on the seafront with a shadowed sky as background; (b) two flower vases with clear background and flower stems inside; (c) some Martini glasses with a gray background and back lighting. Figure 3 illustrates the color channels used to represent the two flower vases image in the selected color spaces. It should be observed that twelve initial feature histograms can be extracted using four color spaces.

Figure 4 illustrates the qualitative comparisons between NMF+Otsu and Otsu algorithm on the three used color images (palm tree on the seafront, flower vase, six Martini glasses) to discriminate principally from background to foreground. As it can be observed, for all three images, Otsu algorithm (applied on the histogram obtained from a single space image representation) is able to identify and extract the main objects in the image with respect to the background on which they are located (palm three, sea and wall in Fig. 4a; the two vases and parts of the flowers in Fig. 4b; the six glasses in Fig. 4c). However, the final segmentation also includes parts of clouds in the sky for the Palm image or parts of the shadows generated by the light on the background on which the vases and the glasses are located in. Instead, the NMF+Otsu proposed approach produced a better segmentation of all the images. For instance, a clear simplification of the numerous segments within the image can be seen for the flower vases image where the shadow areas formed by the vessels are not treated as segments pertaining to the vessels themselves. Moreover, in the Martini glasses image, it can be appreciated a distinct distinction between the glasses and their

(a)   (b)   (c)

Fig. 2. Original color images used to test the empirical goodness of the proposed approach: (a) Palm tree on the seafront with a shadowed sky as background; (b) Flower vases with clear background and some flower stem inside; (c) Six Martini glasses in the gray background and with back lighting.

shadows, and also it exhibits a well-defined separation between the glasses and the background.

To better evaluate the efficiency of our proposed method we also test it on some pictures with ground truth, selected from a dataset adopted for a Kaggle challenge [7]. The three images considered are depicted in Fig. 5 with their corresponding ground truth.

We compare three different approaches to produce a segmented image for each picture by applying: (i) Otsu method on the gray image (used as its standard description, i.e., a thresholding algorithm acting on a single histogram), (ii) Otsu method on each band of the color image (i.e., Otsu on each of the color 12 bands before the application of NMF reduction), and (iii) the proposed NMF+Otsu approach. Results for each selected image can be observed in panel (a) of Figs. 6, 7, and 8, respectively. It is important to note that the NMF+Otsu approach in this paper has also the advantage of supplying a probability mask. This mask will display a probability grayscale that the user or the expert of domain, may interpret and utilize to independently segment the image under consideration. The probabilities mask for each selected images are shown in Figs. 6a, 7b, and 8b, respectively; whereas results for panels (a) are associated with a binarization of the mask values equal to 0.5.

Beside the advantage of the probability mask, the use of this particular dataset, which provides the ground truth as well, gives us the possibility to make also a quantitative comparison between the methods under analysis. Table 1 reports the values of the quantitative metrics for images in Fig. 5. The last column of Table 1 reports the accuracy and precision values for NMF+Otsu, which works on the extracted meta-histogram features. Evaluation has been performed using a binarization threshold. As can be observed, for the more complex pictures (Vessel and running dog) the NMF-based approach overcomes the basic threshold algorithm, providing highly accurate results.

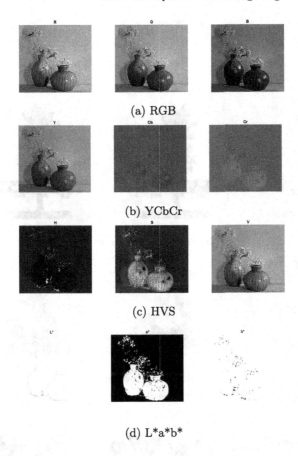

(a) RGB

(b) YCbCr

(c) HVS

(d) L*a*b*

Fig. 3. Color spaces used to describe the flower vase image (nine and twelve initial feature histograms can be extracted using three or four color spaces, respectively).

(a) Palm tree on the seafront

(b) Flower vases

(c) Martini glasses

Fig. 4. Qualitative results obtained using Otsu and NMF+Otsu segmentation process with different color image inputs.

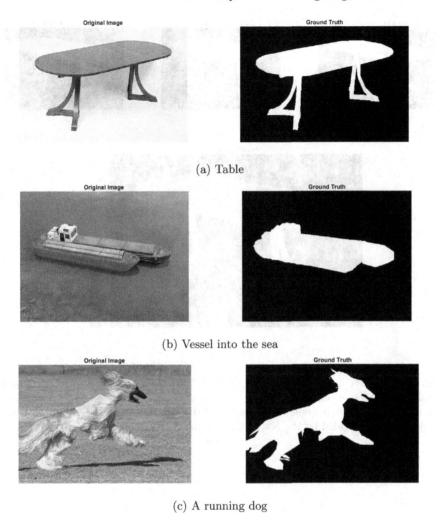

(a) Table

(b) Vessel into the sea

(c) A running dog

Fig. 5. Test color images used with corresponding ground truth. These images are from the image database in [7].

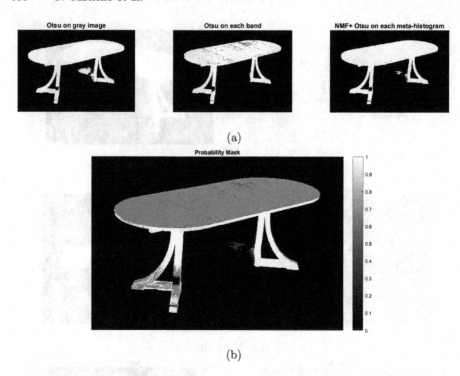

(a)

(b)

Fig. 6. The three panels (a) report (from left to right) the segmentation results obtained from Otsu algorithm applied to the grayscale image, on each color channel, and of NMF+Otsu framework. The panel (b) reports the probability mask which is additionally provided by the NMF+Otsu framework. (Color figure online)

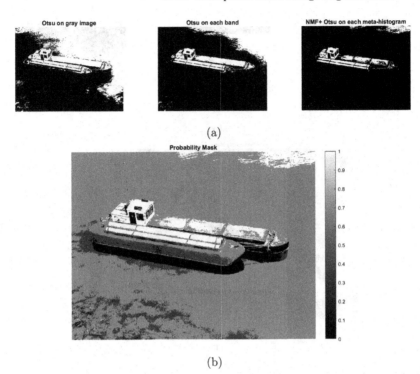

(a)

(b)

Fig. 7. The three panels (a) report (from left to right) the segmentation results obtained from Otsu algorithm applied to the grayscale image, on each color channel, and the segmentation provided by NMF+Otsu framework. The panel (b) reports the probability mask which is additionally provided by the NMF+Otsu framework on the vessel pictured. (Color figure online)

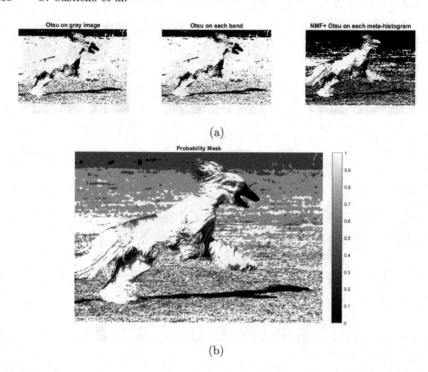

(a)

(b)

Fig. 8. The three panels (a) report (from left to right) the segmentation results obtained from Otsu algorithm applied to the grayscale image, on each color channel, and the segmentation provided by NMF+Otsu. The panel (b) reports the probability mask of the dog picture additionally obtained with the NMF+Otsu approach. (Color figure online)

Table 1. Accuracy and precision of the segmentation results for the test color images with ground truth. Highest values are marked in bold.

	Otsu on gray image	Otsu on each color histogram	NMF+Otsu on meta-histograms
Table image			
Accuracy	98.24	98.78	**98.83**
Precision	93.28	**96.99**	95.88
Vessel image			
Accuracy	56.48	76.47	**85.79**
Precision	20.99	37.07	**76.75**
Dog image			
Accuracy	34.42	34.42	**71.77**
Precision	21.28	21.28	**39.75**

5 Summary and Discussion

In this paper, we addressed the problem of segmenting color images discriminating principally from background to foreground. Information related to various color channels, represented by color spaces, is used by integrating the different associated histograms and extracting hidden knowledge that can be used to improve the segmentation process. Particularly, given a color image I to segment, it is firstly represented using different color channels (four color spaces are used each of them having three color features). This information is then integrated into a new data matrix X embedding features extracted by the histogram operator on each original color feature. This is the enlarged histogram matrix representation of the image I. Hence, the new data matrix X is mined using Nonnegative Matrix Factorization algorithm to extract meta-histograms on which a thresholding algorithm is applied to segment the original image providing a probability mask.

The proposed NMF-based approach is demonstrated to provide better binary segmentation results compared with Otsu algorithm on single color space or on gray image representation. It has the advantage of creating a probability mask that indicates, for each pixel of the color image, an associated probability that pixel is or is not a feature pixel. It can also synthesize the image information expressed through the histogram operator on various color channels. Future developments will include the detection of various objects in color image, rather than just concentrating on the foreground and background.

This probability mask could be also used to feed a supervised learning algorithm for image classification tasks. Future works would concentrate to define different models based on constrained NMF that can improve the extraction of latent properties of the meta-histograms such as sparsity and soft-orthogonality [2].

Acknowledgments. This work was supported in part by the GNCS-INDAM (Gruppo Nazionale per il Calcolo Scientifico of Istituto Nazionale di Alta Matematica) Francesco Severi, P.le Aldo Moro, Roma, Italy. The author F.E. was funded by REFIN Project, grant number 363BB1F4, Reference project idea UNIBA027 "Un modello numerico-matematico basato su metodologie di algebra lineare e multilineare per l'analisi di dati genomici".

References

1. Berry, M., Browne, M., Langville, A., Pauca, P., Plemmons, R.: Algorithms and applications for approximate nonnegative matrix factorization. Comput. Stat. Data Anal. **52**(1), 155–173 (2007)
2. Del Buono, N., Esposito, F., Selicato, L.: Methods for hyperparameters optimization in learning approaches: an overview. In: Nicosia, G., Ojha, V., La Malfa, E., Jansen, G., Sciacca, V., Pardalos, P., Giuffrida, G., Umeton, R. (eds.) LOD 2020. LNCS, vol. 12565, pp. 100–112. Springer, Cham (2020). https://doi.org/10.1007/978-3-030-64583-0_11

3. Busin, L., Shi, J., Vandenbroucke, N., Macaire, L.: Color space selection for color image segmentation by spectral clustering. In: Proceedings of IEEE International Conference on Signal and Image Processing Applications- ICSIPA 2009, pp. 262–267 (2009)
4. Cheng, H.D., Jiang, X.H., Sun, Y., Wang, J.L.: Color image segmentation: Advances and prospects. Patt. Recogn. **34**, 2259–2281 (2001)
5. Esposito, F.: A review on initialization methods for nonnegative matrix factorization: Towards omics data experiments. Mathematics **9**, 1006 (2021)
6. Esposito, F., Buono, N.D., Selicato, L.: Nonnegative matrix factorization models for knowledge extraction from biomedical and other real world data. PAMM **20**(1), e202000032 (2021)
7. Everingham, M., Van Gool, L., Williams, C.K.I., Winn, J., Zisserman, A.: The PASCAL Visual Object Classes Challenge 2012 (VOC 2012) Results. http://www.pascal-network.org/challenges/VOC/voc2012/workshop/index.html
8. Garcia-Lamont, F., Cervantes, J., López, A., Rodriguez, L.: Segmentation of images by color features: A survey. Neurocomputing **292**, 1–27 (2018)
9. Gillis, N.: Nonnegative Matrix Factorization. SIAM (2020)
10. Jurio, A., Pagola, M., Galar, M., Lopez-Molina, C., Paternain, D.: A comparison study of different color spaces in clustering based image segmentation. In: Hüllermeier, E., Kruse, R., Hoffmann, F. (eds.) IPMU 2010. CCIS, vol. 81, pp. 532–541. Springer, Heidelberg (2010). https://doi.org/10.1007/978-3-642-14058-7_55
11. Lee, D.D., Seung, H.S.: Algorithms for non-negative matrix factorization. In Proceedings of Neural Information Processing Systems, vol. 13, pp. 556–562. MIT Press (2000)
12. Lucchese, L., Mitra, S.: Color image segmentation: A state-of-the-art survey. Proc. Indian National Sci. Acad. **2**, 01 (2001)
13. Martinkauppi, B., Hadid, A., Pietikäinen, M.: Skin color in face analysis. In: Li, S., Jain, A., (eds.) Handbook of Face Recognition. Springer-Verlag (2011). https://doi.org/10.1007/978-0-85729-932-1_9
14. Vandenbroucke, N., Macaire, L., Postaire, J.-G.: Color image segmentation by pixel classification in an adapted hybrid color space application to soccer image analysis. Comput. Vis. Image Underst. **90**(2), 190–216 (2003)
15. Yang, J., Liu, C., Zhang, L.: Color space normalization: Enhancing the discriminating power of color spaces for face recognition. Patt. Recog. **43**, 1454–1466 (2010)
16. Zhang, Y.: A survey on evaluation methods for image segmentation. Patt. Recog. **29**(8), 1335–1346 (1996)

Truncated Minimal-Norm Gauss–Newton Method Applied to the Inversion of FDEM Data

Federica Pes[(✉)] [iD]

University of Pisa, 56124 Pisa, Italy
federica.pes@dcci.unipi.it

Abstract. Electromagnetic induction techniques are among the most popular methods for non-invasive investigation of the soil. The collection of data is allowed by frequency domain electromagnetic devices. Starting from these data, the reconstruction of some soil properties is a challenging task, as the inverse problem is ill-posed, meaning that the problem is underdetermined, ill-conditioned, that is, the solution is sensitive to the presence of noise in the data, and nonlinear. Iterative procedures are commonly used to solve nonlinear inverse problems and the Gauss–Newton method is one of the most popular. When the problem is ill-conditioned, the Gauss–Newton method is coupled with regularization techniques, to transform the problem into a well-conditioned one. In this paper, we propose a minimal-norm regularized solution method based on the Gauss–Newton iteration to invert FDEM data. Some numerical examples on synthetic data, regarding the reconstruction of a vertical portion of the soil, show good performances.

Keywords: Inverse problems · Nonlinear least-squares · Gauss–Newton method · Regularization · FDEM

1 Introduction

In many scientific and engineering applications, it is necessary to solve an inverse problem in order to interpret indirect physical measurements. An example of inverse problem, which will be analyzed in numerical experiments of this paper, concerns the study of the subsoil in a non-destructive way, by propagating electromagnetic waves, to obtain information about some properties. This geophysical application is described by a nonlinear model. In the following, we develop the theory for solving nonlinear least-squares problems, that can be adapted to the mentioned geophysical model. Typically, this kind of problems can be solved using iterative algorithms, such as the Gauss–Newton method. Moreover, if the problem is ill-conditioned, then it is necessary to combine the iterative method with regularization techniques to obtain an accurate solution.

The paper is organized as follows. In Sect. 2 we review the Gauss–Newton method and its modified version to compute the minimal-norm solution as well as some basic computational tools. Section 3 is devoted to recalling some well-known

O. Gervasi et al. (Eds.): ICCSA 2023 Workshops, LNCS 14108, pp. 641–658, 2023.
https://doi.org/10.1007/978-3-031-37117-2_43

regularization techniques and to introduce the truncated MNGN2. Section 4 briefly describes a nonlinear model involved in applied geophysics and its discretization. In Sect. 5 we show some numerical examples that test the different regularization techniques to reconstruct a two-dimensional vertical section of the ground and we illustrate some advantages of the TMNGN2 method. Finally, Sect. 6 contains concluding remarks and outlines future research.

2   Mathematical Background

We consider the nonlinear least-squares problem

$$\min_{\mathbf{x}\in\mathbb{R}^n} \|\mathbf{r}(\mathbf{x})\|_2^2, \qquad \mathbf{r}(\mathbf{x}) = F(\mathbf{x}) - \mathbf{b}, \tag{1}$$

where $F : \mathbb{R}^n \to \mathbb{R}^m$ is a nonlinear and at least twice continuously Fréchet differentiable function, $\mathbf{r}(\mathbf{x})$ represents the residual vector function between the model expectation $F(\mathbf{x})$ and the known vector $\mathbf{b} \in \mathbb{R}^m$ of measured data, and $\|\cdot\|_2$ denotes the Euclidean norm, i.e., $\|\mathbf{r}(\mathbf{x})\|_2^2 = \sum_{i=1}^m (r_i(\mathbf{x}))^2$. The problem (1) arises very frequently in data-fitting applications, in particular for parametrized physical, chemical, or financial system in which the minimum sum of squared errors measures the discrepancy between the model and the output of the system at various observation points.

Nonlinear least-squares problems can be solved using optimization approaches, as Newton's method [3,35], but more efficient and less expensive variants are often used instead. Indeed, Newton's method requires the computation of partial second derivatives of $\mathbf{r}(\mathbf{x})$ at each iteration. By ignoring the second-order term [30,37], Newton's method yields the Gauss–Newton method. If the functions $r_i(\mathbf{x})$ are mildly nonlinear in a neighborhood of the solution or if the problem is consistent (i.e., $\mathbf{r}(\mathbf{x}) = \mathbf{0}$), the behavior of the Gauss–Newton method is alike to that of Newton's method.

The *Gauss–Newton method* is based on a sequence of linear approximations of $\mathbf{r}(\mathbf{x})$, so that only first-order differential information on the model is needed. Starting with an initial guess $\mathbf{x}^{(0)}$, if $\mathbf{x}^{(k)}$ denotes the current approximation, then the new approximation is

$$\mathbf{x}^{(k+1)} = \mathbf{x}^{(k)} + \alpha_k \mathbf{s}^{(k)}, \qquad k = 0, 1, 2, \dots, \tag{2}$$

where the step $\mathbf{s}^{(k)}$ is computed as a solution to the linear least-squares problem

$$\min_{\mathbf{s}\in\mathbb{R}^n} \|J(\mathbf{x}^{(k)})\mathbf{s} + \mathbf{r}(\mathbf{x}^{(k)})\|_2^2. \tag{3}$$

Here, $J(\mathbf{x}) \in \mathbb{R}^{m\times n}$ represents the Jacobian matrix of the function $\mathbf{r}(\mathbf{x})$,

$$[J(\mathbf{x})]_{ij} = \frac{\partial r_i(\mathbf{x})}{\partial x_j}, \qquad i = 1,\dots,m, \quad j = 1,\dots,n.$$

To improve convergence, we employ line search with the parameter $\alpha_k > 0$, which can be estimated by any strategy that guarantees a reduction in the norm of the residual. The choice of the step length is a trade-off between giving a substantial reduction in the norm of the residual and, at the same time, not spending too much time finding the solution. If the scalar α_k is chosen too small, convergence is slow. We choose the step length by the *Armijo–Goldstein principle* [1,3,22]: it is determined as the largest number in the sequence $1/2^i$, $i = 0, 1, \ldots$, for which the following inequality holds

$$\|\mathbf{r}_k\|_2^2 - \|\mathbf{r}(\mathbf{x}^{(k)} + \alpha_k \mathbf{s}^{(k)})\|_2^2 \geq \frac{1}{2}\alpha_k\|J_k\mathbf{s}^{(k)}\|_2^2, \tag{4}$$

where $J_k = J(\mathbf{x}^{(k)})$ and $\mathbf{r}_k = \mathbf{r}(\mathbf{x}^{(k)})$. The solution of the least-squares problem (3) is given by

$$\mathbf{s}^{(k)} = -J_k^\dagger \mathbf{r}_k, \tag{5}$$

where $J_k^\dagger$ represents the Moore-Penrose pseudoinverse of J_k. This is a descent direction if J_k has full rank. Under this assumption, if $m \geq n$ the pseudoinverse is defined as $J_k^\dagger = (J_k^T J_k)^{-1} J_k^T$, otherwise, if $m < n$, it is $J_k^\dagger = J_k^T (J_k J_k^T)^{-1}$.

According to the definition given by Hadamard [25], problem (3) can be ill-posed, in particular, the uniqueness of the solution is not always ensured. This occurs when the system is underdetermined ($m < n$), or when the Jacobian matrix J is rank-deficient at the point $\mathbf{x}^{(k)}$.

In case of a non-unique solution, the one computed by Eq. (5) is the so-called minimal-norm solution, that is the one obtained by solving the minimal-norm linear least-squares problem

$$\min_{\mathbf{s}\in\mathbb{R}^n} \|\mathbf{s}\|_2^2, \quad \text{s.t. } \mathbf{s} \in \left\{\arg\min_{\mathbf{s}\in\mathbb{R}^n} \|J_k\mathbf{s} + \mathbf{r}_k\|_2^2\right\}. \tag{6}$$

To select a different solution for the step $\mathbf{s}^{(k)}$ of the new iterate $\mathbf{x}^{(k+1)}$, a matrix $L \in \mathbb{R}^{p\times n}$ ($p \leq n$) can be introduced in the objective function of problem (6), that is,

$$\min_{\mathbf{s}\in\mathbb{R}^n} \|L\mathbf{s}\|_2^2, \quad \text{s.t. } \mathbf{s} \in \left\{\arg\min_{\mathbf{s}\in\mathbb{R}^n} \|J_k\mathbf{s} + \mathbf{r}_k\|_2^2\right\}. \tag{7}$$

The matrix L is typically a diagonal weighting matrix or a $p \times n$ discrete approximation of a derivative operator, in which case L is a banded matrix with full row rank. For example, the matrices

$$D_1 = \begin{bmatrix} -1 & 1 & & \\ & \ddots & \ddots & \\ & & -1 & 1 \end{bmatrix} \quad \text{and} \quad D_2 = \begin{bmatrix} 1 & -2 & 1 & & \\ & \ddots & \ddots & \ddots & \\ & & 1 & -2 & 1 \end{bmatrix}, \tag{8}$$

of size $(n-1) \times n$ and $(n-2) \times n$, respectively, are approximations to the first and second derivative operators.

We remark that both problems (6) and (7) impose a regularity constraint on the update vector $\mathbf{s}$ for the solution $\mathbf{x}^{(k)}$, and not on the solution itself. The consequence of imposing a regularity constraint directly on the solution $\mathbf{x}$ of problem (1)

$$\min_{\mathbf{x}\in\mathbb{R}^n} \|L\mathbf{x}\|_2^2, \quad \text{s.t. } \mathbf{x} \in \left\{\arg\min_{\mathbf{x}\in\mathbb{R}^n} \|F(\mathbf{x}) - \mathbf{b}\|_2^2\right\}$$

has been analyzed in [20, 37, 38]. Considering an iterative method of the type (3), the step $\mathbf{s}^{(k)}$ is the solution of the linearized problem

$$\min_{\mathbf{s} \in \mathbb{R}^n} \|L(\mathbf{x}^{(k)} + \alpha \mathbf{s})\|_2^2, \quad \text{s.t. } \mathbf{s} \in \left\{ \arg \min_{\mathbf{s} \in \mathbb{R}^n} \|J_k \mathbf{s} + \mathbf{r}_k\|_2^2 \right\}. \tag{9}$$

In [37], the authors have shown that the iteration of the minimal-norm Gauss–Newton (MNGN) method is obtained by subtracting a projection term onto the null space of J_k to the iteration (2)

$$\mathbf{x}^{(k+1)} = \mathbf{x}^{(k)} + \alpha_k \mathbf{s}^{(k)} - \mathcal{P}_{\mathcal{N}(J_k)} \mathbf{x}^{(k)}, \qquad k = 0, 1, 2, \ldots,$$

where $\mathcal{P}_{\mathcal{N}(J_k)}$ denotes the orthogonal projector onto the null space of J_k. Then, in [38], in order to avoid some issues in the convergence caused by the projection term, the more efficient implementation (MNGN2) is proposed

$$\mathbf{x}^{(k+1)} = \mathbf{x}^{(k)} + \alpha_k \mathbf{s}^{(k)} - \beta_k \mathcal{P}_{\mathcal{N}(J_k)} \mathbf{x}^{(k)}, \qquad k = 0, 1, 2, \ldots, \tag{10}$$

where the parameter β_k controls that the projection does not cause an increase in the residual. In the same paper, some techniques to estimate it are explained in detail.

In the case of an ill-conditioned problem, it is necessary to regularize it. Classical regularization techniques are the T(G)SVD and the Tikhonov method. In this paper, we introduce the truncated MNGN2 method, that is a regularized version of the MNGN2 method (10). We stress that the MNGN2 method has been introduced in [38] for well-conditioned problems. Herein, we extend it for ill-conditioned problems. Moreover, we apply the truncated MNGN2 algorithm to an applied geophysics problem, with the aim of reconstructing a 2D section of the subsurface.

We end this section by introducing some useful tools. We recall the definition of the singular value decomposition (SVD) of a matrix J as well as that of the generalized singular value decomposition (GSVD) of a matrix pair (J, L) [24].

The SVD is a matrix decomposition of the form

$$J = U \Sigma V^T, \tag{11}$$

where the diagonal matrix $\Sigma \in \mathbb{R}^{m \times n}$ contains the *singular values* ordered such that $\sigma_1 \geq \sigma_2 \geq \cdots \geq \sigma_r > 0$, with $r = \text{rank}(J) \leq \min(m, n)$, and the matrices $U = [\mathbf{u}_1, \ldots, \mathbf{u}_m] \in \mathbb{R}^{m \times m}$ and $V = [\mathbf{v}_1, \ldots, \mathbf{v}_n] \in \mathbb{R}^{n \times n}$ have orthonormal columns.

Let $J \in \mathbb{R}^{m \times n}$ and $L \in \mathbb{R}^{p \times n}$ be matrices with $\text{rank}(J) = r$ and $\text{rank}(L) = p$. Suppose that $m + p \geq n$ and

$$\text{rank}\left(\begin{bmatrix} J \\ L \end{bmatrix}\right) = n,$$

or, equivalently, that $\mathcal{N}(J) \cap \mathcal{N}(L) = \{0\}$. The GSVD of the matrix pair (J, L) is defined by the factorizations

$$J = U \Sigma_J W^{-1}, \qquad L = V \Sigma_L W^{-1}, \tag{12}$$

where $U \in \mathbb{R}^{m \times m}$ and $V \in \mathbb{R}^{p \times p}$ are matrices with orthonormal columns $\mathbf{u}_i$ and $\mathbf{v}_i$, respectively, and $W \in \mathbb{R}^{n \times n}$ is nonsingular. If $m \geq n \geq r$, the structure of the matrices $\Sigma_J \in \mathbb{R}^{m \times n}$ and $\Sigma_L \in \mathbb{R}^{p \times n}$ is

$$\Sigma_J = \begin{bmatrix} O_{n-r} & & \\ & C & \\ \hline & & I_d \\ \hline O_{(m-n) \times n} \end{bmatrix}, \qquad \Sigma_L = \begin{bmatrix} I_{p-r+d} & & \\ & S & \Big| O_{p \times d} \end{bmatrix},$$

where $d = n - p$, and the blocks C and S are nonnegative diagonal matrices such that

$$C = \mathrm{diag}(c_1, \ldots, c_{r-d}), \qquad 0 < c_1 \leq c_2 \leq \cdots \leq c_{r-d} < 1,$$
$$S = \mathrm{diag}(s_1, \ldots, s_{r-d}), \qquad 1 > s_1 \geq s_2 \geq \cdots \geq s_{r-d} > 0,$$

with $c_i^2 + s_i^2 = 1$, for $i = 1, \ldots, r - d$. The identity matrix of size k is denoted by I_k, while O_k and $O_{k \times \ell}$ are zero matrices of size k and $k \times \ell$, respectively; if one of the dimensions of the identity or zero submatrices vanishes, the block has to be omitted. The *generalized singular values* are the scalars $\gamma_i = c_i / s_i$, and they appear in nondecreasing order. If $r \leq m < n$, the matrix $\Sigma_J \in \mathbb{R}^{m \times n}$ has the form

$$\Sigma_J = \begin{bmatrix} O_{m \times (n-m)} & \Big| O_{m-r} & \\ & C & \\ & I_d \end{bmatrix},$$

where the blocks are defined as above, and the structure of $\Sigma_L \in \mathbb{R}^{p \times n}$ is the same as the previous one.

3   TGSVD, TMNGN2, and Tikhonov Regularization

In applications, typically, the measured data vector $\mathbf{b}$ is prone to noise caused by measurement errors. This results in a perturbed data vector

$$\mathbf{b} = \widehat{\mathbf{b}} + \mathbf{e}, \qquad \mathbf{e} \in \mathbb{R}^m,$$

where $\widehat{\mathbf{b}} \in \mathbb{R}^m$ is the exact data vector and $\mathbf{e} \in \mathbb{R}^m$ represents the noise vector. Due to error propagation, the computed solution may deviate significantly from the exact solution, especially in ill-conditioned problems. It is well-known that the concept of inverse problem is closely related to that of ill-conditioning. A nonlinear operator $F(\mathbf{x})$ is considered ill-conditioned in a domain $\Omega \subset \mathbb{R}^n$ when the condition number $\kappa(J)$ of the Jacobian $J = J(\mathbf{x})$ is very large for any $\mathbf{x} \in \Omega$. In such cases, a common approach is to apply a regularization procedure at each step of the Gauss–Newton method: the initial least-squares problem is replaced by a nearby better conditioned problem, whose solution is less sensitive to the error $\mathbf{e}$ in the right-hand side $\mathbf{b}$ and to round-off errors introduced during the solution process. For a more detailed discussion regarding regularization of inverse problems, we refer to [19, 27].

One of the most widely used methods to do so is the truncated singular value decomposition applied to the system matrix. The TSVD solves (6) after substituting J_k by its best rank-ℓ approximation. Here, ℓ is the regularization parameter, which has to be wisely estimated. Choosing its value amounts to finding a compromise between fidelity to the original model and numerical stability.

Fixed a value for the truncation parameter $1 \leq \ell \leq r$, the iteration of the truncated Gauss–Newton method becomes

$$\mathbf{x}_\ell^{(k+1)} = \mathbf{x}_\ell^{(k)} - \alpha_k \sum_{i=1}^{\ell} \frac{\mathbf{u}_i^T \mathbf{r}(\mathbf{x}_\ell^{(k)})}{\sigma_i} \mathbf{v}_i, \qquad k = 0, 1, 2, \ldots, \tag{13}$$

where $\mathbf{u}_i$ and $\mathbf{v}_i$ are the left and right singular vectors of J_k, respectively; see Eq. (11). We remark that the singular value decomposition of the matrix J_k changes at each step of the Gauss–Newton method, and that the rank r may change too. In order not to burden the notation we write $\mathbf{u}_i$, $\mathbf{v}_i$, σ_i, and r without specifying the dependence on k.

On the other hand, if the step $\mathbf{s}^{(k)}$ is determined by regularizing problem (7), the iteration is expressed in terms of the GSVD of the matrix pair (J_k, L):

$$\mathbf{x}_\ell^{(k+1)} = \mathbf{x}_\ell^{(k)} - \alpha_k \sum_{i=p-\ell+1}^{p} \frac{\mathbf{u}_{i-N}^T \mathbf{r}(\mathbf{x}_\ell^{(k)})}{c_{i-n+r}} \mathbf{w}_i - \alpha_k \sum_{i=p+1}^{n} (\mathbf{u}_{i-N}^T \mathbf{r}(\mathbf{x}_\ell^{(k)})) \mathbf{w}_i,$$

where the integer $0 \leq \ell \leq p - n + r$ is the regularization parameter, $\mathbf{u}_{i-N}$ and $\mathbf{w}_i$ are the column vectors of the matrices U and W of (12), respectively, and the integer $N = \max(n - m, 0)$ allows us to condense in a single formula both the overdetermined and underdetermined case. As in the previous formulation, the GSVD of (J_k, L) changes at each iteration, therefore the same observation made before on the abuse of notation by not indicating the dependence on k of $\mathbf{u}_{i-N}$, $\mathbf{w}_i$, c_{i-n+r}, and r is valid.

The truncated MNGN2 method solves (9), when $L = I_n$, considering the best rank-ℓ approximation of J_k. As remarked in Section 2, the iteration of the TMNGN2 method differs from that of the truncated Gauss–Newton (13) for the presence of a projection term. Indeed it is of the form

$$\mathbf{x}_\ell^{(k+1)} = \mathbf{x}_\ell^{(k)} - \alpha_k \sum_{i=1}^{\ell} \frac{\mathbf{u}_i^T \mathbf{r}(\mathbf{x}_\ell^{(k)})}{\sigma_i} \mathbf{v}_i - \beta_k \sum_{i=\ell+1}^{n} (\mathbf{v}_i^T \mathbf{x}_\ell^{(k)}) \mathbf{v}_i, \qquad k = 0, 1, 2, \ldots.$$

Similarly, if $L \neq I_n$, the TMNGN2 iteration depends on the GSVD of (J_k, L) and it is given by

$$\mathbf{x}_\ell^{(k+1)} = \mathbf{x}_\ell^{(k)} - \alpha_k \sum_{i=p-\ell+1}^{p} \frac{\mathbf{u}_{i-N}^T \mathbf{r}(\mathbf{x}_\ell^{(k)})}{c_{i-n+r}} \mathbf{w}_i - \alpha_k \sum_{i=p+1}^{n} (\mathbf{u}_{i-N}^T \mathbf{r}(\mathbf{x}_\ell^{(k)})) \mathbf{w}_i$$
$$- \beta_k \sum_{i=1}^{p-\ell} (\widehat{\mathbf{w}}^i \mathbf{x}_\ell^{(k)}) \mathbf{w}_i,$$

where $\widehat{\mathbf{w}}^i$ are the row vectors of the matrix W^{-1}; see Eq. (12). The non-regularized version of the last two formulas has been obtained in [38].

Another approach consists of regularizing the least-squares problem (3) by the Tikhonov method, that is, solving the minimization problem

$$\min_{\mathbf{s}\in\mathbb{R}^n} \left\{ \|J_k\mathbf{s} + \mathbf{r}_k\|_2^2 + \lambda^2\|L\mathbf{s}\|_2^2 \right\},\tag{14}$$

for a fixed value of the parameter $\lambda > 0$ and a chosen regularization matrix $L \in \mathbb{R}^{p\times n}$. The regularization parameter λ controls the balance between the two terms of the functional, i.e., the weights attributed to the residual term and to the regularization term. Equivalently, (14) can be written as

$$\min_{\mathbf{s}\in\mathbb{R}^n} \left\| \begin{bmatrix} J_k \\ \lambda L \end{bmatrix} \mathbf{s} + \begin{bmatrix} \mathbf{r}_k \\ \mathbf{0} \end{bmatrix} \right\|_2^2.$$

The solution of (14) is given by

$$\mathbf{s} = -(J_k^T J_k + \lambda^2 L^T L)^{-1} J_k^T \mathbf{r}_k.$$

Then, if $L = I_n$, after substituting the SVD of J_k, the iteration of the Gauss–Newton method with Tikhonov regularization is

$$\mathbf{x}_\lambda^{(k+1)} = \mathbf{x}_\lambda^{(k)} - \alpha_k \sum_{i=1}^r \frac{\sigma_i(\mathbf{u}_i^T\mathbf{r}(\mathbf{x}_\lambda^{(k)}))}{\sigma_i^2 + \lambda^2}\mathbf{v}_i, \qquad k = 0, 1, 2, \ldots,$$

where $\{\mathbf{u}_i, \mathbf{v}_i, \sigma_i\}$ are the singular triplets of J_k (Eq. (11)). If $L \neq I_n$, considering the GSVD of the matrix pair (J_k, L), the iterative method becomes

$$\mathbf{x}_\lambda^{(k+1)} = \mathbf{x}_\lambda^{(k)} - \alpha_k \sum_{i=n-r+1}^p \frac{c_{i-n+r}(\mathbf{u}_{i-N}^T\mathbf{r}(\mathbf{x}_\lambda^{(k)}))}{c_{i-n+r}^2 + \lambda^2 s_{i-n+r}^2}\mathbf{w}_i - \alpha_k \sum_{i=p+1}^n (\mathbf{u}_{i-N}^T\mathbf{r}(\mathbf{x}_\lambda^{(k)}))\mathbf{w}_i,$$

where $\mathbf{u}_{i-N}$ and $\mathbf{w}_i$ are the column vectors of the matrices U and W of (12), respectively, and $N = \max(n - m, 0)$.

3.1 Regularization Parameter Estimation

The solution vectors obtained through the Gauss–Newton method, regularized by TGSVD/TMNGN2 or by the Tikhonov approach, will be denoted by $\mathbf{x}_\ell$ or $\mathbf{x}_\lambda$ at convergence, respectively, where ℓ and λ are the corresponding regularization parameters. A regularization method should also incorporate a technique for estimating the optimal regularization parameter.

Most of the methods for determining the regularization parameter are based on residual norms and, in the case of the L-curve, also on the (semi)norm of the solution. Assuming the knowledge of the error norm $\|\mathbf{e}\|_2$ or of a good estimate of it, the discrepancy principle introduced by Morozov [34] can be used to determine the parameter. In real situations, when the noise is unknown, heuristic techniques, as the L-curve criterion [26, 28, 29] or the generalized cross-validation [8, 21, 23], allow to estimate the regularization parameter without information on the noise level. There are many contributions dedicated to developing and analyzing different methods to select the regularization parameter. In this regard, the interested reader can see [7, 27, 32, 36, 39] and references therein.

In the numerical experiments reported in this paper, we determine the regularization parameters by the L-curve criterion. In the upcoming subsection we remind what it consists of.

L-curve. This method is based on a plot of the logarithm of the (semi)norm $\|L\mathbf{s}_{\text{reg}}\|_2$ of the regularized solution versus the logarithm of the corresponding residual norm $\|J_k\mathbf{s}_{\text{reg}} + \mathbf{r}_k\|_2$. With the subscript "reg" we refer in general to both parameters ℓ and λ, depending on the approach adopted to regularize. The L-curve is also a powerful graphical tool for the analysis of discrete ill-posed problems, since it graphically represents the compromise between the minimization of these two quantities, which is the core of any regularization method.

When the regularization parameter is continuous, as in Tikhonov regularization, the L-curve is a continuous curve. In case of regularization methods with a discrete regularization parameter, such as TGSVD/TMNGN2, the L-curve consists of a finite set of points

$$\left(\log \|J_k\mathbf{s}_{\text{reg}} + \mathbf{r}_k\|_2, \ \log \|L\mathbf{s}_{\text{reg}}\|_2 \right), \qquad\qquad \text{in TGSVD},$$

$$\left(\log \|J_k\mathbf{s}_{\text{reg}} + \mathbf{r}_k\|_2, \ \log \|L(\mathbf{x}^{(k)} + \alpha\mathbf{s}_{\text{reg}})\|_2 \right), \qquad \text{in TMNGN2}.$$

This criterion chooses the regularization parameter corresponding to the point of maximum curvature on the log-log plot of the L-curve, which corresponds to the corner of the "L"-shape.

4   A Nonlinear Model for FDEM Data Inversion

In this section, we briefly describe a nonlinear model typical of applied geophysics. It is based on electromagnetic induction techniques that allow to investigate in a non-destructive way some soil properties. Mathematically, it is represented by a system of first kind integral equations.

Before describing the nonlinear model, we recall that, in 1980, a linear model was developed by McNeill [33] to reproduce the readings of one of the first available ground conductivity meters (GCM), the Geonics EM-38. Regarding this model and the possibility of recovering the distribution of the electrical conductivity, in [5], a Tikhonov regularization technique was implemented to reconstruct the conductivity profile from measurements obtained by positioning a GCM at various heights above the ground, while in [9] the Tikhonov approach was optimized by a projected conjugate gradient algorithm.

More recently, in [15], the linear system has been studied under the hypothesis that the values of the unknown function are known at the boundaries. The aforementioned paper led to propose subsequently a numerical method to compute the solution of a system of first kind integral equations in the presence of boundary constraints. The algorithm descends from the Riesz representation theorem and the solution is sought in a reproducing kernel Hilbert space. A first version of the algorithm is introduced in [16], that addresses the idea for a single integral equation. Afterwards, in [17] the theory is generalized for a system of integral equations of the first kind.

In 1982, Wait [40] described a nonlinear forward model for predicting the electromagnetic response of the subsoil. In [31], the technique adopted in [5] was extended and applied to a nonlinear model for the same physical system, previously described in [41]. A regularized inversion algorithm was studied in [12,14] and then it was extended to process complex-valued datasets [13]. The algorithm was coded in Matlab and included in the publicly available software package FDEMtools [10] which includes a graphical user interface (GUI), that has already been employed in real-world applications [4,13,18]. In [6] the authors propose to solve a variational problem to obtain a 2D reconstruction of some properties of a soil vertical section. Recently, the FDEMtools package has been updated by inserting some variants for the computation of the minimal-norm solution regarding the resolution of the inverse problem, as well as a GUI for a forward modelling [11].

In the model, the soil is assumed to have a layered structure with n layers below ground level, starting from $z_1 = 0$. Each subsoil layer, of thickness d_k (meters), ranges from depth z_k to z_{k+1}, $k = 1, \ldots, n-1$, and is characterized by an electrical conductivity σ_k (Siemens/meter) and a magnetic permeability μ_k (Henry/meter), for $k = 1, \ldots, n$. The thickness of the deepest layer d_n, starting at z_n, is considered infinite.

A GCM is an FDEM induction device composed of two coils, namely a transmitter and a receiver, positioned at a fixed distance ρ from each other. The two coils, operating at frequency f in Hertz, are at height h above the ground with their axes oriented either vertically or horizontally with respect to the ground surface. Both the depth z and the height h are measured in meters. The transmitting coil generates a primary electromagnetic (EM) field H_P above the ground, which then propagates into it. H_P induces eddy currents in the conductive parts of the subsurface, generating in succession a secondary EM field H_S, that propagates towards the ground surface. This signal is detected by the receiver. The GCM measures the ratio between the secondary EM field produced by such currents and the primary field. The reader interested on the working principles of the instrument is referred to [11] for a detailed discussion.

Mathematically, the nonlinear model, derived from Maxwell's equations, consists of two integral equations of the first kind. Let $u_k(\lambda) = \sqrt{\lambda^2 + i\sigma_k\mu_k\omega}$, where i is the unit imaginary number and $\omega = 2\pi f$ is the angular frequency of the electromagnetic wave generated by the device. The variable λ is non-negative and it measures the ratio between the depth below the ground surface and the inter-coil distance ρ. If we denote the characteristic admittance in the kth layer by

$$N_k(\lambda) = \frac{u_k(\lambda)}{\mathrm{i}\mu_k\omega}, \quad k = 1, \ldots, n,$$

then the surface admittance $Y_k(\lambda)$ at the top of the same layer verifies the recursion

$$\begin{cases} Y_n(\lambda) = N_n(\lambda), \\ Y_k(\lambda) = N_k(\lambda)\dfrac{Y_{k+1}(\lambda) + N_k(\lambda)\tanh(d_k u_k(\lambda))}{N_k(\lambda) + Y_{k+1}(\lambda)\tanh(d_k u_k(\lambda))}, \quad k = n-1, \ldots, 1. \end{cases} \tag{15}$$

as shown in [40]. Let us define the reflection factor as

$$R_\omega(\lambda) = \frac{N_0(\lambda) - Y_1(\lambda)}{N_0(\lambda) + Y_1(\lambda)},$$

where $Y_1(\lambda)$ is computed by the recursion formula (15) and $N_0(\lambda) = \lambda/(\mathrm{i}\mu_0\omega)$, with $\mu_0 = 4\pi10^{-7}$H/m the value of the vacuum magnetic permeability, that is the permeability of the free space. The ratio of the secondary field to the primary one is given by the following system of two integral equations of the first kind

$$M_\nu(\boldsymbol{\sigma}, \boldsymbol{\mu}; h, \omega, \rho) = -\rho^{3-\nu} \int_0^\infty \lambda^{2-\nu} e^{-2h\lambda} R_\omega(\lambda) J_\nu(\rho\lambda)\, d\lambda, \quad \nu = 0, 1,$$

by setting $\nu = 0$ and $\nu = 1$ for the vertical and horizontal orientation of the coils, respectively. In the above equation, $\boldsymbol{\sigma} = [\sigma_1, \ldots, \sigma_n]^T$, $\boldsymbol{\mu} = [\mu_1, \ldots, \mu_n]^T$, and J_ν denotes the first kind Bessel function of order ν.

As is usual in many applications, we let the magnetic permeability take the constant value μ_0 in all layers. It is reasonable to make this assumption if the ground does not contain ferromagnetic materials. Recent FDEM devices can record multiple measurements with different operating frequencies $\omega_1, \ldots, \omega_{m_\omega}$ or different inter-coil distances $\rho_1, \ldots, \rho_{m_\rho}$ at different heights $h_1, \ldots, h_{m_h}$ above the ground. Considering also both orientations of the coils, we have $m = 2m_\rho m_\omega m_h$ measurements. We denote them by $\mathbf{b} = [b_1, \ldots, b_m]^T$, and the model prediction by $M(\boldsymbol{\sigma})$, where

$$M(\boldsymbol{\sigma}) = \begin{bmatrix} M_0(\boldsymbol{\sigma}) \\ M_1(\boldsymbol{\sigma}) \end{bmatrix}.$$

Then, the problem of data inversion consists of computing the conductivity vector $\boldsymbol{\sigma}$ which determines the best fit to the data vector $\mathbf{b}$, that is, the one which solves the problem

$$\min_{\boldsymbol{\sigma} \in \mathbb{R}^n} \|\mathbf{r}(\boldsymbol{\sigma})\|_2^2, \quad \text{with } \mathbf{r}(\boldsymbol{\sigma}) = M(\boldsymbol{\sigma}) - \mathbf{b}.$$

This is the one-dimensional discretization of the problem, i.e., considering the measurements collected by the instrument at a fixed point above the ground.

We now consider a 2D discretization of the problem. In practice, by moving the device along a straight path above the ground, it is possible to collect data at several points. We depict the two-dimensional vertical section of the ground as the rectangle $[0, a] \times [0, b]$, where $[0, a]$ represents the horizontal path along which the instrument is moved, and $[0, b]$ is the depth under the ground; see Fig. 1. Our intention is to reconstruct the electrical conductivity as an image.

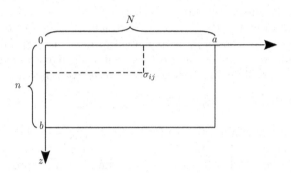

Fig. 1. 2D scheme of a vertical portion of the subsoil. The electrical conductivity of the ith layer in the jth dataset is denoted by σ_{ij}.

Given the two-dimensional section of the ground and assuming to have N equispaced measurement sets, let σ_{ij} be the electrical conductivity of the ith layer in the jth dataset, and $\boldsymbol{\sigma}_j = [\sigma_{1j}, \dots, \sigma_{nj}]^T$, $j = 1, \dots, N$. Let the corresponding dataset be $\mathbf{b}_j = [b_{1j}, \dots, b_{mj}]^T$. We group them in the matrices

$$\mathbf{S} = (\sigma_{ij}) = [\boldsymbol{\sigma}_1, \dots, \boldsymbol{\sigma}_N] \in \mathbb{R}^{n \times N}, \qquad \mathbf{B} = (b_{pj}) = [\mathbf{b}_1, \dots, \mathbf{b}_N] \in \mathbb{C}^{m \times N}.$$

We want to solve the nonlinear least-squares problem

$$\min_{\mathbf{S}} \|\mathbf{M}(\mathbf{S}) - \mathbf{B}\|_F^2 = \sum_{j=1}^{N} \min_{\boldsymbol{\sigma}_j} \|M(\boldsymbol{\sigma}_j) - \mathbf{b}_j\|_2^2, \tag{16}$$

where $\| \cdot \|_F$ denotes the Frobenius norm and $\mathbf{M}(\mathbf{S}) = [M(\boldsymbol{\sigma}_1), \dots, M(\boldsymbol{\sigma}_N)]$ contains the readings predicted by the model. In (16) the two-dimensional problem is brought to N independent one-dimensional problems. Therefore, each one-dimensional problem is solved independently from each others and the obtained solutions are placed side by side to obtain the two-dimensional reconstruction. Each nonlinear least-squares problem for a single column is solved by the Gauss–Newton method regularized by the TGSVD or by the Tikhonov approach, as well as by the TMNGN2 method, as explained in Sect. 3. For each $j = 1, \dots, N$, we initialize the starting point $\boldsymbol{\sigma}_j^{(0)}$ with a vector whose components are randomly and uniformly distributed within the intervals $(0.48, 0.52)$, $(1.48, 1.52)$, and $(1.49, 1.51)$. We observe that this differs from the initial point chosen in previous papers, e.g., in [13,14], where the authors adopted a vector with all equal entries (e.g., $[0.5,\ldots,0.5]^T$ or $[1.5,\ldots,1.5]^T$). Our choice emphasizes, in the numerical experiments, that the TMNGN2 method is not affected by a random starting point, as it happens instead in the classical regularization method if we do not use a vector with equal components.

For all iterative methods, the damping parameter α_k is determined by coupling the Armijo–Goldstein principle (4) to the positivity constraint $\sigma_j^{(k)} \geq 0$. Moreover, for the TMNGN2 method, the second relaxation parameter β_k is determined by an automatic procedure based on the comparison between the residue obtained from TMNGN2 and the residual of Gauss–Newton at the same step; the algorithm to choose β_k is explained in detail in [38]. For all iterative methods, we adopt the following stopping criterion: fixed a tolerance $\tau > 0$, we iterate until the difference between two successive approximations is small enough

$$\|\sigma_j^{(k)} - \sigma_j^{(k-1)}\|_2 < \tau \|\sigma_j^{(k)}\|_2,$$

or until a chosen maximum number of iterations $K_{\max}$ is reached. In our numerical tests, we set $\tau = 10^{-8}$ and $K_{\max} = 100$. An additional stopping rule is considered, in order to detect the unboundedness of the approximate solution for a particular value of the regularization parameter. The iteration is interrupted if the ratio between the norms of the kth approximate solution and the starting point $\sigma_j^{(0)}$ is larger than a certain threshold, which in the numerical experiments of this paper is set to 10^8. This indicates that the solution is growing without bound and is therefore unlikely to converge to a meaningful result. This stopping rule is useful in the case where the regularization parameter is not well chosen and the computed solution is unbounded. By interrupting the iteration, the user can investigate the cause of the unboundedness and adjust the regularization parameter accordingly. Without this stopping rule, the iteration may continue indefinitely, leading to an overflow or to misleading results.

5 Numerical Experiments

This section is devoted to analyzing the behavior of different regularized solution methods for the inversion problem. In particular, we compare the results obtained by applying the TGSVD with the minimization of the Tikhonov functional and with the TMNGN2 method.

All the computations were carried out in Matlab version 9.10 (R2021a) on an Intel(R) Xeon(R) Gold 6136 server with 128 GB of RAM memory and 32 cores, running the Ubuntu/Linux operating system.

We consider synthetic data by generating two test models for the electrical conductivity. They are illustrated in the first picture of Fig. 2 and Fig. 4. To generate the synthetic data, we choose a particular configuration of the Geophex GEM-2 device, with both orientations of the coils, with inter-coil distance $\rho = 1.66$ m, six different operating frequencies $f = 775, 1175, 3925, 9825, 21725, 47025$ Hz, and two measuring heights $h = 0.8, 1.6$ m above the ground. Therefore, we have $m = 24$ data for each position $j = 1,\ldots,N$. Chosen $N = 50$ soundings along a 10 m path, the forward model generates the matrix $\widehat{\mathbf{B}}$ of dimension $m \times N$ of the exact synthetic measurements. To simulate experimental errors, we add a noise vector to each column of $\widehat{\mathbf{B}}$

$$\mathbf{e}_j = \frac{\varepsilon \|\widehat{\mathbf{b}}_j\|_2}{\sqrt{m}} \mathbf{w}, \qquad j = 1, \ldots, N,$$

where $\mathbf{w}$ is a normally distributed random vector with zero mean and unitary variance and ε stands for the noise level. In our experiments, we set $\varepsilon = 10^{-3}$. We discretize the soil by $n = 60$ layers up to the depth of 3.5 m, each of which is of equal thickness. As a regularization matrix L we tested D_1 and D_2; see Eq. (8).

In Table 1 we report the relative restoration error (RRE) for each computed solution, defined by

$$\text{RRE}(\mathbf{S}) = \frac{\|\mathbf{S} - \mathbf{S}_{\text{exact}}\|_F}{\|\mathbf{S}_{\text{exact}}\|_F},$$

where $\mathbf{S}_{\text{exact}}$ is the exact solution.

Table 1. RRE obtained with different regularization techniques: the TGSVD, Tikhonov, and TMNGN2 methods. The algorithms are tested with different regularization matrices D_1 and D_2 and different starting points (random components uniformly distributed in the interval $(0.48, 0.52)$ and $(1.48, 1.52)$ for Example 1 and $(0.48, 0.52)$ and $(1.49, 1.51)$ for Example 2).

	Example 1				Example 2			
	(0.48, 0.52)		(1.48, 1.52)		(0.48, 0.52)		(1.49, 1.51)	
	D_1	D_2	D_1	D_2	D_1	D_2	D_1	D_2
TGSVD	0.1569	0.2303	0.1549	0.2304	0.1701	0.1851	0.1690	0.1799
Tikhonov	0.1576	0.2276	0.1578	0.2295	0.1653	0.1758	0.1661	0.1782
TMNGN2	0.1730	0.2152	0.1730	0.2152	0.1708	0.1782	0.1789	0.1780

From the errors shown in Table 1, it can be observed that for almost all algorithms, the errors obtained by regularizing the problem with the matrix D_1 are smaller, compared to the regularization matrix D_2.

Taking into consideration the matrix D_1 as a regularization matrix, we can observe that the RRE of the solutions obtained with the TGSVD and Tikhonov are smaller than the one obtained with the TMNGN2 method. In any case, however, in the right panel of Fig. 2 we can see some horizontal irregularities.

These are caused by the lack of regularity of the solutions obtained with the TGSVD and the Tikhonov regularization. This lack of regularity can be shown by a graph of the electrical conductivity corresponding to only one column of $\mathbf{S}$. Figure 3 depicts $\mathbf{S}(:, 33)$ on the left pane and $\mathbf{S}(:, 48)$ on the right for all iterative methods compared to the exact electrical conductivity in the same column. These irregularities do not occur in the solution computed with the TMNGN2 method.

By examining the RRE in Table 1, when $L = D_2$, the TMNGN2 recovers a better solution compared to the others, except in Example 2 and starting point in $(1.49, 1.51)$. Figure 4 displays this case.

In both Fig. 2 and Fig. 4, we can notice some vertical artifacts or irregularities caused by the fact that we are solving N inverse problems independently of each other and we are chunking together their solutions. To avoid these irregular lines, one could think of reconstructing the 2D-solution as if it were an image. In this case, regularizers typically used in image restoration could be involved, which also induce horizontal regularization.

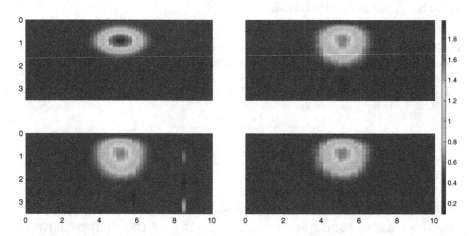

Fig. 2. Example 1. The exact solution (top-left) is compared to the solutions computed by TGSVD (top-right), by TMNGN2 (bottom-left), and by Tikhonov (bottom-right). The problem is regularized with matrix D_1. The initial point has random components uniformly distributed in the interval $(0.48, 0.52)$.

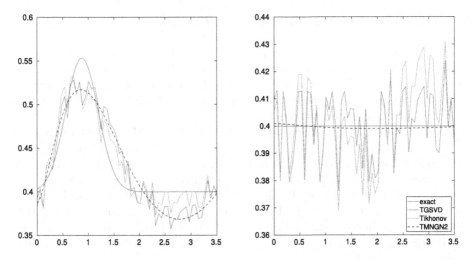

Fig. 3. Example 1. Electrical conductivity obtained from the 33rd (left) and 48th (right) dataset. The exact conductivity is compared to the solutions computed by TGSVD, by TMNGN2, and by Tikhonov. The problem is regularized with matrix D_1. The initial point has random components uniformly distributed in the interval $(0.48, 0.52)$.

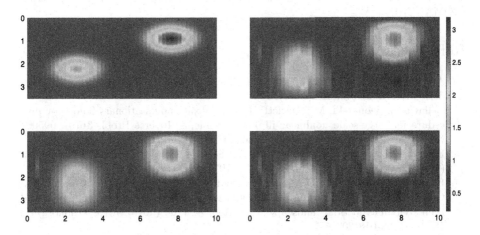

Fig. 4. Example 2. The exact solution (top-left) is compared to the solutions computed by TGSVD (top-right), by TMNGN2 (bottom-left), and by Tikhonov (bottom-right). The problem is regularized with matrix D_2. The initial point has random components uniformly distributed in the interval $(1.49, 1.51)$.

6   Conclusions and Future Developments

In this paper, we have tested the TMNGN2 method and we have compared it with TGSVD and Tikhonov regularization on an applied geophysics problem with the aim of reconstructing a 2D portion of the subsurface. We noticed that, compared to classical regularization methods, TMNGN2 does not suffer from an initial point with random entries.

The 2D reconstruction of a portion of the subsoil considered as an image and not arranging the 1D reconstructions side by side, will be a subject of study and research in the near future. This should allow to introduce "horizontal" regularization, by considering other regularization matrices that are usually used in image restoration, which would improve the reconstruction and avoid vertical irregularities, caused by a "side by side" reconstruction. Moreover, the applicability to 2D reconstructions is limited by the computational complexity of the SVD. As done for instance in [2], the SVD could be replaced by Krylov subspace regularization methods.

Acknowledgements. The author would like to thank Giuseppe Rodriguez for many precious discussions on the subject. The author is member of the GNCS group of INdAM and this research was partially funded by the INdAM-GNCS 2022 project "Metodi e modelli di regolarizzazione per problemi malposti di grandi dimensioni", by the INdAM-GNCS 2023 project "Tecniche numeriche per lo studio dei problemi inversi e l'analisi delle reti complesse", and by Fondazione di Sardegna, Progetto biennale bando 2021, "Computational Methods and Networks in Civil Engineering (COMANCHE)".

References

1. Armijo, L.: Minimization of functions having Lipschitz continuous first partial derivatives. Pac. J. Math. **16**(1), 1–3 (1966)
2. Bellavia, S., Donatelli, M., Riccietti, E.: An inexact non stationary Tikhonov procedure for large-scale nonlinear ill-posed problems. Inverse Probl. **36**(9), 095007 (2020). https://doi.org/10.1088/1361-6420/ab8f84
3. Björck, Å.: Numerical Methods for Least Squares Problems. SIAM, Philadelphia (1996). https://doi.org/10.1137/1.9781611971484
4. Boaga, J., Ghinassi, M., D'Alpaos, A., Deidda, G.P., Rodriguez, G., Cassiani, G.: Geophysical investigations unravel the vestiges of ancient meandering channels and their dynamics in tidal landscapes. Sci. Rep. **8**, 1708 (2018). https://doi.org/10.1038/s41598-018-20061-5
5. Borchers, B., Uram, T., Hendrickx, J.M.H.: Tikhonov regularization of electrical conductivity depth profiles in field soils. Soil Sci. Soc. Am. J. **61**(4), 1004–1009 (1997)
6. Buccini, A., Díaz de Alba, P.: A variational non-linear constrained model for the inversion of FDEM data. Inverse Probl. **38**(1), 014001 (2022). https://doi.org/10.1088/1361-6420/ac3c54
7. Buccini, A., Park, Y., Reichel, L.: Comparison of A-posteriori parameter choice rules for linear discrete ill-posed problems. J. Comput. Appl. Math. **373**, 112138 (2020). https://doi.org/10.1016/j.cam.2019.02.005

8. Buccini, A., Reichel, L.: Generalized cross validation for ℓ_p-ℓ_q minimization. Numer. Algorithms **88**, 1595–1616 (2021). https://doi.org/10.1007/s11075-021-01087-9

9. Deidda, G.P., Bonomi, E., Manzi, C.: Inversion of electrical conductivity data with Tikhonov regularization approach: some considerations. Ann. Geophys. **46**(3), 549–558 (2003). https://doi.org/10.4401/ag-3427

10. Deidda, G.P., Díaz de Alba, P., Fenu, C., Lovicu, G., Rodriguez, G.: FDEMtools: a MATLAB package for FDEM data inversion. Numer. Algorithms **84**, 1313–1327 (2020). https://doi.org/10.1007/s11075-019-00843-2

11. Deidda, G.P., Díaz de Alba, P., Pes, F., Rodriguez, G.: Forward electromagnetic induction modelling in a multilayered half-space: an open-source software tool. Remote Sens. **15**(7), 1772 (2023). https://doi.org/10.3390/rs15071772

12. Deidda, G.P., Díaz de Alba, P., Rodriguez, G.: Identifying the magnetic permeability in multi-frequency EM data inversion. Electron. Trans. Numer. Anal. **47**, 1–17 (2017)

13. Deidda, G.P., Díaz de Alba, P., Rodriguez, G., Vignoli, G.: Inversion of multi-configuration complex EMI data with minimum gradient support regularization: a case study. Math. Geosci. **52**(7), 945–970 (2020). https://doi.org/10.1007/s11004-020-09855-4

14. Deidda, G.P., Fenu, C., Rodriguez, G.: Regularized solution of a nonlinear problem in electromagnetic sounding. Inverse Probl. **30**(12), 125014 (2014). https://doi.org/10.1088/0266-5611/30/12/125014

15. Díaz de Alba, P., Fermo, L., van der Mee, C., Rodriguez, G.: Recovering the electrical conductivity of the soil via a linear integral model. J. Comput. Appl. Math. **352**, 132–145 (2019). https://doi.org/10.1016/j.cam.2018.11.034

16. Díaz de Alba, P., Fermo, L., Pes, F., Rodriguez, G.: Minimal-norm RKHS solution of an integral model in geo-electromagnetism. In: 2021 21st International Conference on Computational Science and Its Applications (ICCSA), Cagliari, Italy, pp. 21–28, September 2021. https://doi.org/10.1109/ICCSA54496.2021.00014

17. Díaz de Alba, P., Fermo, L., Pes, F., Rodriguez, G.: Regularized minimal-norm solution of an overdetermined system of first kind integral equations. Numer. Algorithms **92**, 471–502 (2023). https://doi.org/10.1007/s11075-022-01282-2

18. Dragonetti, G., et al.: Calibrating electromagnetic induction conductivities with time-domain reflectometry measurements. Hydrol. Earth Syst. Sci. **22**, 1509–1523 (2018). https://doi.org/10.5194/hess-22-1509-2018

19. Engl, H.W., Hanke, M., Neubauer, A.: Regularization of Inverse Problems. Kluwer, Dordrecht (1996)

20. Eriksson, J., Wedin, P.A., Gulliksson, M.E., Söderkvist, I.: Regularization methods for uniformly rank-deficient nonlinear least-squares problems. J. Optim. Theor. Appl. **127**, 1–26 (2005). https://doi.org/10.1007/s10957-005-6389-0

21. Fenu, C., Reichel, L., Rodriguez, G., Sadok, H.: GCV for Tikhonov regularization by partial SVD. BIT Numer. Math. **57**, 1019–1039 (2017). https://doi.org/10.1007/s10543-017-0662-0

22. Goldstein, A.A.: Constructive Real Analysis. Harper and Row (1967)

23. Golub, G.H., Heath, M., Wahba, G.: Generalized cross-validation as a method for choosing a good ridge parameter. Technometrics **21**(2), 215–223 (1979). https://doi.org/10.2307/1268518

24. Golub, G.H., Van Loan, C.F.: Matrix Computations, 3rd edn. The John Hopkins University Press, Baltimore (1996)

25. Hadamard, J.: Lectures on Cauchy's Problem in Linear Partial Differential Equations. Yale University Press, New Haven (1923)

26. Hansen, P.C.: Analysis of discrete ill-posed problems by means of the L-curve. SIAM Rev. **34**(4), 561–580 (1992). https://doi.org/10.1137/1034115
27. Hansen, P.C.: Rank-Deficient and Discrete Ill-Posed Problems. SIAM, Philadelphia (1998). https://doi.org/10.1137/1.9780898719697
28. Hansen, P.C., Jensen, T.K., Rodriguez, G.: An adaptive pruning algorithm for the discrete L-curve criterion. J. Comput. Appl. Math. **198**(2), 483–492 (2007). https://doi.org/10.1016/j.cam.2005.09.026
29. Hansen, P.C., O'Leary, D.P.: The use of the L-curve in the regularization of discrete ill-posed problems. SIAM J. Sci. Comput. **14**(6), 1487–1503 (1993). https://doi.org/10.1137/0914086
30. Hansen, P.C., Pereyra, V., Scherer, G.: Least Squares Data Fitting with Applications. Johns Hopkins University Press, Baltimore (2012)
31. Hendrickx, J.M.H., Borchers, B., Corwin, D.L., Lesch, S.M., Hilgendorf, A.C., Schlue, J.: Inversion of soil conductivity profiles from electromagnetic induction measurements: theory and experimental verification. Soil Sci. Soc. Am. J. **66**(3), 673–685 (2002). https://doi.org/10.2136/sssaj2002.6730
32. Hochstenbach, M.E., Reichel, L., Rodriguez, G.: Regularization parameter determination for discrete ill-posed problems. J. Comput. Appl. Math. **273**, 132–149 (2015). https://doi.org/10.1016/j.cam.2014.06.004
33. McNeill, J.D.: Electromagnetic terrain conductivity measurement at low induction numbers. Technical Note TN-6 Geonics Limited (1980)
34. Morozov, V.A.: The choice of parameter when solving functional equations by regularization. Dokl. Akad. Nauk SSSR **175**(6), 1225–1228 (1962)
35. Ortega, J.M., Rheinboldt, W.C.: Iterative Solution of Nonlinear Equations in Several Variables. Academic Press, New York (1970). https://doi.org/10.1137/1.9780898719468
36. Park, Y., Reichel, L., Rodriguez, G., Yu, X.: Parameter determination for Tikhonov regularization problems in general form. J. Comput. Appl. Math. **343**, 12–25 (2018). https://doi.org/10.1016/j.cam.2018.04.049
37. Pes, F., Rodriguez, G.: The minimal-norm Gauss-Newton method and some of its regularized variants. Electron. Trans. Numer. Anal. **53**, 459–480 (2020). https://doi.org/10.1553/etna_vol53s459
38. Pes, F., Rodriguez, G.: A doubly relaxed minimal-norm Gauss-Newton method for underdetermined nonlinear least-squares problems. Appl. Numer. Math. **171**, 233–248 (2022). https://doi.org/10.1016/j.apnum.2021.09.002
39. Reichel, L., Rodriguez, G.: Old and new parameter choice rules for discrete ill-posed problems. Numer. Algorithms **63**, 65–87 (2013). https://doi.org/10.1007/s11075-012-9612-8
40. Wait, J.R.: Geo-Electromagnetism. Academic Press, New York (1982)
41. Ward, S.H., Hohmann, G.W.: Electromagnetic theory for geophysical applications. In: Electromagnetic Methods in Applied Geophysics: Volume 1, Theory, pp. 130–311. Society of Exploration Geophysicists (1988). https://doi.org/10.1190/1.9781560802631.ch4

Blind Source Separation of Color Noisy Blurred Images

Giulio Biondi⬤, Antonio Boccuto⬤, and Ivan Gerace(✉)⬤

Department of Mathematics and Computer Science, University of Perugia,
Perugia, Italy
{giulio.biondi,antonio.boccuto,ivan.gerace}@unipg.it

Abstract. Blind Source Separation (BSS) is a relevant problem in the signal processing research area, with a broad application sphere. In this work, we consider a BSS problem with recto–verso images subject to show–through and bleed–through effects; in particular, we suppose that the observed image is obtained using a two-step linear process: the recto and verso images are separately blurred using a blur operator with known coefficients and then mixed. Our algorithm, Blind Estimation Technique Imposing Smoothness and Non–Overlapping (BETIS–NO), built on top of previous work, computes the entries of the mixture matrix, which regulates the intensity of recto–verso mixing for the document reconstruction; the introduction of second–order discontinuities and additional constraints on source images, i.e., minimum entropy, non–Gaussianity, and correct overlapping, leads to improved quality of the reconstruction.

Keywords: Blind Source Separation · Regularization · Indirect Maximum A Priori estimation · Graduate Non–Convex algorithm

1 Introduction

This paper deals with the Blind Source Separation (BSS) problem, a popular topic within the broader research area of signal processing. The BSS problem consists of separating source signals from a group of mixed signals without knowing the mixing coefficients and is relevant to several research fields, e.g., separating individual speech signals from mixed audio signals in the cocktail party problem [2], classifying images, detecting changes in images, identifying the structure of buildings in thermographic images for seismic engineering [9], and estimating the Cosmic Microwave Background (CMB) from galactic and extragalactic emissions (see, e.g., [12,20]).

In this work, we focus on digitally restoring degraded written documents, which can suffer damage from various sources such as weathering, ink seepage, humidity, powder, mold, and light transmission. Over time, these factors can cause paper and ink to deteriorate, leading to the degradation and decay of written records. In particular, we address two types of effects in degraded written documents: show–through and bleed–through. Show–through is caused by the transparency of the paper, resulting in the text from one side appearing on the other due to the light used in the scanning process. Conversely, bleed–through is caused by ink seeping through the paper, producing a similar effect to show–through. The physical model for show-through distortion is complex, considering factors such as paper features, transmittance parameters, the reflectance of the verso, and how light spreads through the paper.

Removing the bleed–through (or the show–through) patterns from a digital document scan is generally challenging, especially in ancient documents, where the interferences are often significant. Indeed, dealing with heavy bleed-through using a simple threshold technique is practically ineffective since the intensities of the unwanted ink filtered from the back can be similar to those of the main text. For instance, in [21], several threshold techniques are compared for separating text in degraded historical documents; in general, both global and local thresholds do not provide satisfactory results.

In this work, we assume that the decayed image is formed through a two-step linear process: the recto and verso images are separately blurred using a blur operator with known coefficients and then mixed [8,13,28]. The mixture matrix defines the mixing intensity and will be subject to estimation during the document reconstruction phase. The problem is said to be non–blind when the mixture matrix is known; both the blind and the non–blind problems are ill–posed (see also [16]). Regularization techniques can convert an ill–posed non–blind BSS problem into a well–posed one by addressing the instability problem. Such techniques require solving a nearby well–posed problem with specific known properties, which has a unique stable solution. Piecewise smoothness is often assumed for the estimated sources, and the solution to the inverse problem is determined by minimizing an appropriate energy function.

To solve the blind BSS problem of estimating the mixture matrix, we use a target function. We start by considering a mixture matrix and computing the related sources by minimizing the energy function. Then, we evaluate the properties of the result using the target function, defined as a combination of various terms that represent constraints based on our prior knowledge about the solution. Using this function, we can determine the effectiveness of the estimated solution in meeting our restrictions and producing the desired results. This technique is called *Indirect Maximum A Priori* (IMAP) estimation (see, e.g., [8,10,12,13,15]).

In particular, in this article, differing from how it was done in [8], where the *Blind Estimation Technique Imposing Smoothness* (BETIS) technique was proposed, we impose that the ideal sources are piecewise linear, do not present adjacent parallel discontinuities (see also [3,5,6]), and are non–Gaussian (see also [18,19]). Additionally, we impose that the values of the front and back are partially overlapping, classifying our method as a *Correlated Component Analysis* (CCA) technique [1,4]. Furthermore, we introduce a new measure of the system entropy and use it in the target function.

A stochastic algorithm such as *Simulated Annealing* (SA) minimizes the target function. During the target function minimization, it is necessary tominimize the energy function, which is generally non-convex; for this purpose, we apply a *Graduate Non-Convexity* (GNC)-algorithm (see, e.g., [3,6,7,11,17,22–25,27,29]). We refer to our technique as *Blind Estimation Technique Imposing Smoothness and Non–Overlapping* (BETIS–NO).

The paper is structured as follows. In Sect. 2, we describe the background mathematical model; in Sect. 3, we first deal with the non–blind reconstruction, using regularization techniques; in Sect. 4, we deal with the blind problem using an IMAP approach; in Sect. 5, we show the effectiveness of our algorithm using the presented experimental results.

2   Mathematical Model

We begin with defining the *source recto-verso document* as a vector $\mathbf{s} \in \mathbb{R}^{6MN}$, where M and N are the dimensions of the recto and the verso of the analyzed document, structured as follows:

$$\mathbf{s} = \left((\mathbf{s}_f^{(r)})^T \ (\mathbf{s}_f^{(g)})^T \ (\mathbf{s}_f^{(b)})^T \ (\mathbf{s}_v^{(r)})^T \ (\mathbf{s}_v^{(g)})^T \ (\mathbf{s}_v^{(b)})^T \right)^T, \tag{1}$$

where each block of the vector $\mathbf{s}$ in (Eq. 1) is an $M \times N$-dimensional vector, taken in the lexicographic order. Hereafter, the index f (resp., v) corresponds to the front (resp., verso), while the symbols (r), (g), (b) are associated with the colors red, green, and blue, respectively.

We assume that the blur operator acting on the visible (resp., hidden) side of the image is given by

$$H_k = \begin{pmatrix} H_k^{(r,r)} & H_k^{(r,g)} & H_k^{(r,b)} \\ H_k^{(g,r)} & H_k^{(g,g)} & H_k^{(g,b)} \\ H_k^{(b,r)} & H_k^{(b,g)} & H_k^{(b,b)} \end{pmatrix},$$

where $k = 1$ (resp., $k = 2$). The $H_k^{(u,v)}$'s, $u, v \in \{r, g, b\}$, $k = 1, 2$, can be easily derived from a given blur mask $M_k^{(u,v)} \in \mathbb{R}^{(2\rho+1) \times (2\rho+1)}$, whose radius is denoted by ρ (see, e.g., [6,14]). We assume that the observed document is obtained using the following model:

$$\mathbf{m} = \begin{pmatrix} \mathbf{m}_f^{(r)} \\ \mathbf{m}_f^{(g)} \\ \mathbf{m}_f^{(b)} \\ \mathbf{m}_v^{(r)} \\ \mathbf{m}_v^{(g)} \\ \mathbf{m}_v^{(b)} \end{pmatrix} = \begin{pmatrix} a_{1,1}H_1 & a_{1,2}H_2 \\ a_{2,1}H_1 & a_{2,2}H_2 \end{pmatrix} \begin{pmatrix} \mathbf{s}_f^{(r)} \\ \mathbf{s}_f^{(g)} \\ \mathbf{s}_f^{(b)} \\ \mathbf{s}_v^{(r)} \\ \mathbf{s}_v^{(g)} \\ \mathbf{s}_v^{(b)} \end{pmatrix} + \mathbf{n} = \mathcal{H}(A)\mathbf{s} + \mathbf{n}, \tag{2}$$

where

$$A = \begin{pmatrix} a_{1,1} & a_{1,2} \\ a_{2,1} & a_{2,2} \end{pmatrix}$$

is the mixture matrix, which describes how the observed images are obtained from the ideal source images, and the vector $\mathbf{n}$, of dimension MN, is the additive noise, which we assume to be white, Gaussian, with zero mean and a known variance σ^2.

The linear *Blind Source Separation* (BSS) problem consists in reconstructing the original source $\mathbf{s}$ and to evaluate the matrix A, starting from the mixture vector $\mathbf{m}$. Here we assume that the linear operators $H_k^{(u,v)}$, $u, v \in \{r, g, b\}$, $k = 1, 2$, and the variance of the noise are known.

3   Non-blind Reconstruction

Let us consider first the non–blind problem, in which the mixture matrix A is known. This problem is ill–posed in the sense of Hadamard (see, e.g., [16]). To regularize the problem, we now introduce the second–order finite difference operators. Note that it has been proved experimentally that the use of such operators yields better results than that of operators of first or third order (see, e.g., [7]). A *clique* c of order 2 is a subset of points of a square grid on which the second–order finite difference is defined. We denote by the symbol C_2 the set of all cliques of order 2, namely $C_2 = \{c = \{(i, j), (h, l), (r, q)\} : i = h = r, j = l + 1 = q + 2$ or $i = h + 1 = r + 2, j = l = q\}$. Every element of C_2 is uniquely associated with a discontinuity of order 2, which is labeled with a hidden line element.

We denote the second order finite difference operator of the vector $\mathbf{s}_k^{(e)}$, $e \in \{r, g, b\}$, $k = 1, 2$, associated with the clique c, by $D_c^2 \mathbf{s}_k^{(e)}$, that is, if $c = \{(i, j), (h, l), (r, q)\} \in C_2$, then $D_c^2 \mathbf{s}_k^{(e)} = s_k^{(e)}(i, j) - 2s_k^{(e)}(h, l) + s_k^{(e)}(r, q)$. Let us introduce the concept of *adjacent clique of order 2*, used to define the non-parallelism constraint, whose importance is apparent in Fig. 1. The original image in (a) is blurred to obtain (b); (c) is reconstructed from (b) without imposing the non-parallelism constraint, while the image in (d) is obtained by enforcing it. The reconstructions of Figure Fig. 1(c) and (d) present significant differences in terms of artifacts, which are also evident in the corresponding line process plots (e) and (f). Note that this example is given in the simplified case where only the reconstruction of a blurred image is required.

Given a vertical clique $c = \{(i, j), (i + 1, j), (i + 2, j)\}$, $i = 3, \ldots, M - 2$, $j = 1, \ldots, N$, we define its preceding clique $c - 1$ as follows:

$$c - 1 = \{(i - 2, j), (i - 1, j), (i, j)\}.$$

If c is a horizontal clique, $c = \{(i, j), (i, j + 1), (i, j + 2)\}$, $i = 1, \ldots, M$, $j = 3, \ldots, N - 2$, then its preceding clique $c - 1$ is defined by setting

$$c - 1 = \{(i, j - 2), (i, j - 1), (i, j)\}.$$

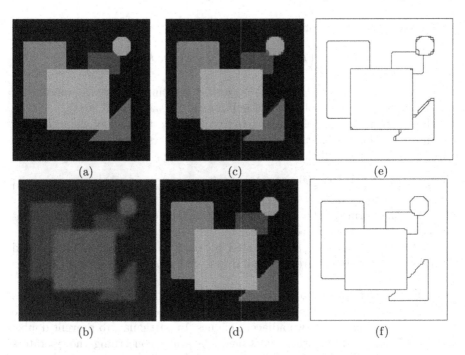

Fig. 1. The original (resp., blurred) image is in (a) (resp., (b)); the image reconstructed without (resp., with) non-parallelism constraint is given in (c) (resp., (d)), with line elements drawn in (e) (resp., (f)).

Given a mixture matrix A, We define a *regularized solution* $\widetilde{\mathbf{s}}$ as an argument of the minimum of the energy function defined by

$$E_A(\mathbf{s}) = \|\mathbf{m} - \mathcal{H}(A)\mathbf{s}\|_2^2 + \sum_{k=1}^{2} \sum_{c \in C_2} \varphi(N_c^2 \mathbf{s}_k, N_{c-1}^2 \mathbf{s}_k) \tag{3}$$

$$+ \sum_{k=1}^{2} \sum_{c \in C_2} \varphi(V_c^2 \mathbf{s}_k, V_{c-1}^k \mathbf{s}_k),$$

where $\|\cdot\|_2$ is the Euclidean norm, and the first term of the right hand of (Eq. 3) indicated a data faithfulness constraint. The second term in the right hand of (Eq. 3) expresses the intra–channel smoothness of the images. The third term indicates a correlation between the different channels, i.e., an inter–channel smoothness. Intra–channel and inter–channel smoothness are measured using the operators N_c^2 and V_c^2, respectively, and φ is a stabilizer associated with the requested degree of smoothness and which relaxes it when one expects a discontinuity (see, e.g., [5,6]).

We begin with defining the operator N_c^2, i.e. the norm of the vector of the finite differences of the intensities of the red, green, and blue channels evaluated on the clique c of second order, as follows:

$$N_c^2 \mathbf{s}_k = \left\| \left(D_c^2 \mathbf{s}_k^{(r)}, D_c^2 \mathbf{s}_k^{(g)}, D_c^2 \mathbf{s}_k^{(b)} \right) \right\|_2, \quad k = 1, 2, \tag{4}$$

where $\mathbf{s}_k = ((\mathbf{s}_k^{(r)})^T, (\mathbf{s}_k^{(g)})^T, (\mathbf{s}_k^{(b)})^T)^T$, and D_c^2 is a finite difference operator of order 2 applied to a suitable set c of adjacent pixels, as defined above.

The inter-channel correlation is strictly related to the clue of the objects in the image; for this reason, the finite difference operators should enforce the same coherent behavior for all the channels. Thus we define the following operators:

$$V_c^2 \mathbf{s}_k = \left\| \left(D_c^2 \mathbf{s}_k^{(r)} - D_c^2 \mathbf{s}_k^{(g)}, D_c^2 \mathbf{s}_k^{(r)} - D_c^2 \mathbf{s}_k^{(b)}, D_c^2 \mathbf{s}_k^{(g)} - D_c^2 \mathbf{s}_k^{(b)} \right) \right\|_2, \quad k = 1, 2, \tag{5}$$

which are the norms of the vector of the inter-channel differences of the intra-channel derivatives of the second order.

In (Eq. 3), N_c^2 and V_c^2 are weighted by suitable stabilizers, which should regulate the requested degree of smoothness and relax it when discontinuities are expected.

To have a more precise reconstruction, it is fundamental that discontinuities are not thick; that is, the object contours are not blurred. So, it is advisable to avoid discontinuities at two adjacent cliques. In particular, to prevent double discontinuities, we deal with a function φ, bivariate concerning the operators defined in (Eq. 4) and (Eq. 5) in the cliques c and $c-1$, respectively. When $c-1$ is not defined, we assume directly that the adjacent discontinuity is null.

Thus, we use a two-variable function $\varphi : \mathbb{R} \times \mathbb{R} \to \mathbb{R}$ (see also [6]), defined by

$$\varphi(t_1, t_2) = \begin{cases} g_1(t_1), & \text{if } |t_2| \leq s, \\[2mm] \left(1 - \frac{2(|t_2|-s)^2}{(\zeta-s)^2} \right) g_1(t_1) + \frac{2(|t_2|-s)^2}{(\zeta-s)^2} g_2(t_1), & \text{if } s < |t_2| \leq \frac{\zeta+s}{2}, \\[2mm] \frac{2(|t_2|-\zeta)^2}{(\zeta-s)^2} g_1(t_1) + \left(1 - \frac{2(|t_2|-\zeta)^2}{(\zeta-s)^2} \right) g_2(t_1), & \text{if } \frac{\zeta+s}{2} < |t_2| < \zeta, \\[2mm] g_2(t_1), & \text{if } |t_2| \geq \zeta, \end{cases} \tag{6}$$

where

$$s = \frac{\sqrt{\alpha}}{\lambda},$$

and ζ is such that $\zeta - s$ is a positive and sufficiently small quantity, and for $i = 1, 2$ we have

$$g_i(t_1) = \begin{cases} \lambda^2 t_1^2, & \text{if } |t_1| < q_i, \\[2mm] \alpha_i - \frac{\tau}{2}(|t_1| - r_i)^2, & \text{if } q_i \leq |t_1| \leq r_i, \\[2mm] \alpha_i, & \text{if } |t_1| > r_i, \end{cases}$$

$$\alpha_i = \begin{cases} \alpha, & \text{if } i = 1, \\ \alpha + \varepsilon, & \text{if } i = 2, \end{cases} \qquad q_i = \frac{\sqrt{\alpha_i}}{\lambda^2} \left(\frac{2}{\tau} + \frac{1}{\lambda^2} \right)^{-1/2},$$

τ is a large enough real constant, and

$$r_i = \frac{\alpha_i}{\lambda^2 q_i}, \quad i = 1, 2.$$

The graph of the function in (Eq. 6) for some values of the parameters is pictured in Fig. 2(a).

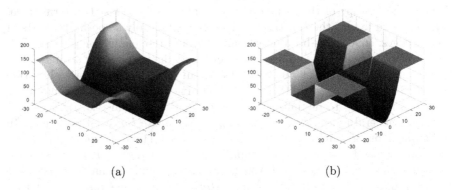

(a)   (b)

Fig. 2. Used stabilizers with $\lambda = 1$, $\alpha = \varepsilon = 80$.

Observe that, when $\zeta - s = 0$ and τ tends to $+\infty$, we get an ideal model with Boolean line variables (see Fig. 2(b)), where λ^2 is a regularization parameter, which regulates the smoothness of the solution, α is the cost to introduce a discontinuity on the image. Such a cost is incremented by ε if there is a parallel discontinuity. In [5] a duality-type theorem was proved, which states that the use of a suitable bivariate function, as the one defined in (Eq. 6), preserves the edges in the reconstructed images and prevents parallel edges from appearing. Additionally, in (Eq. 6) the underlying line elements assume a continuous range of values.

4   IMAP Estimation

Now we deal with the blind problem. In this context, both the sources and the mixture matrix are unknown. The estimate of the mixture matrix is defined as

$$\widetilde{A} = \arg \min_A F(A, \mathbf{s}(A)),$$

where F is the *target function*, that is constructed in order to find the solution which best fits the a priori knowledge, and

$$\mathbf{s}(A) = \arg\min_{\mathbf{s}} E_A(\mathbf{s}).$$

The solution to the blind problem is given by $(\tilde{\mathbf{s}} = \mathbf{s}(\tilde{A}), \tilde{A})$. Such a technique is called *Indirect Maximum A Priori* (IMAP) (see, e.g., [8,10,12,13,15]). In this paper, we propose the following target function:

$$F(\mathbf{s}(A)) = \omega_1 \, NG(\mathbf{s}(A)) + \omega_2 \, OV(\mathbf{s}(A)) + \omega_3 \, EN(\mathbf{s}(A)) \tag{7}$$

$$+ \sum_{k=1}^{2} \sum_{c \in C_2} \varphi(N_c^2 \mathbf{s}_k, N_{c-1}^2 \mathbf{s}_k) + \sum_{k=1}^{2} \sum_{c \in C_2} \varphi(V_c^2 \mathbf{s}_k, V_{c-1}^k \mathbf{s}_k),$$

where $NG(\mathbf{s}(A))$ measures the non–Gaussianity of the estimated source $\mathbf{s}(A)$, $OV(\mathbf{s}(A))$ expresses the overlapping degree of $\mathbf{s}_1(A)$ over $\mathbf{s}_2(A)$, $EN(\mathbf{s}(A))$ denotes the entropy of the estimated source $\mathbf{s}(A)$ and the last two terms measure to which extent the constructed sources are suitably smooth and without double edges, concerning both inter-channel and intra-channel components. The parameters ω_i, $i = 1, 2, 3$, express the strength of the imposed constraints.

To minimize the target function $F(\mathbf{s}(A))$ in (Eq. 7), a stochastic algorithm such as *Simulated Annealing* (SA) is used. During the target function minimization, it is necessary to minimize the energy function $E(\mathbf{s})$ in (Eq. 3). Note that $E(\mathbf{s})$ is in general non-convex. So, we apply a *Graduate Non-Convexity* (GNC)-technique in order to minimize $E(\mathbf{s})$ (see, e.g., [3,6,7,11,17,22–25,27,29]). Hereafter, we refer to the proposed technique as BETIS–NO (*Blind Estimation Technique Imposing Smoothness and Non-Overlapping*), while we name its previous version proposed in [8] as BETIS (*Blind Estimation Technique Imposing Smoothness*).

4.1   The Non–Gaussianity Constraint

To measure the Gaussianity of a grayscale image $\mathbf{y} \in \mathbb{R}^{NM}$, we first find the histogram of $\mathbf{y}$, by defining the following function:

$$d_{\mathbf{y}}(\eta) = \#(\{y_{i,j} : y_{i,j} = \eta, \, i = 1, \ldots, M, \, j = 1, \ldots, N\}), \quad \eta = 0, 1, \ldots, 255,$$

where $\#(\cdot)$ denotes the cardinality of a generic set; in the color case, three histograms can be computed, one for each color component. Now, we denote by $\Phi_{\mu,\sigma}$ the Gaussian function with mean μ and standard deviation σ, and define the distance of a histogram of an image $\mathbf{y}$ from a Gaussian curve of mean μ and variance σ by setting

$$G(\mathbf{y}, \mu, \sigma) = \sum_{\eta=0}^{255} (d_{\mathbf{y}}(\eta) - \Phi_{\mu,\sigma}(\eta))^2. \tag{8}$$

Given a fixed image $\mathbf{y}$, we deal with finding that values of μ and σ which minimize the function G defined in (Eq. 8). This function is not convex in (μ, σ). So, we estimate a suitable componentwise minimum. Starting with the mean

μ and the standard deviation σ of the histogram $d(\mathbf{y})$, we apply the following heuristic (where h is a suitable small enough step):

```
change=true;
while change
        change=false;
        while G(y, μ, σ) > G(y, μ − h, σ)
                μ = μ − h;
                change=true;
        end while
        while G(y, μ, σ) > G(y, μ + h, σ)
                μ = μ + h;
                change=true;
        end while
        while G(y, μ, σ) > G(y, μ, σ − h)
                σ = σ − h;
                change=true;
        end while
        while G(y, μ, σ) > G(y, μ, σ + h)
                σ = σ + h;
                change=true;
        end while
end while
```

We define as $\mu(\mathbf{y})$ and $\sigma(\mathbf{y})$ those expressions obtained in the above heuristic. Thus, we define the *non–Gaussianity* of the estimated source $\mathbf{s}$ by

$$NG(\mathbf{s}) = \sum_{k=1}^{2} \sum_{e \in \{r,g,b\}} \frac{1}{\mathbf{G}(\mathbf{s}_{\mathbf{k}}^{(\mathbf{e})}, \mu(\mathbf{s}_{\mathbf{k}}^{(\mathbf{e})}), \sigma(\mathbf{s}_{\mathbf{k}}^{(\mathbf{e})}))}.$$

4.2   Overlapping Constraint

In a document, there is an overlapping when a value different from the background of the recto overlaps with an analogous element of the verso. To correctly separate two images, it is advisable to estimate the overlapping level present in the ideal sources. A technique to determine such a level was given in [4] in the case of non–blurred and non–noisy images, and a related quick algorithm was presented. Thus, to reduce computational costs, we use such an estimate by calling it $RO(\mathbf{s})$. We define our error concerning a correct overlapping level as

$$OV(\mathbf{s}) = \left(RO(\mathbf{s}) - \sum_{e \in \{r,g,b\}} \sum_{i=1}^{N} \sum_{j=1}^{M} \left((\overline{m}_1^{(e)} - s_1^{(e)}(i,j))(\overline{m}_2^{(e)} - s_1^{(e)}(i,j)) \right)^2 \right)^2$$

where $\overline{m}_k^{(e)}$, $k = 1, 2$, is the median of the image $s_k^{(e)}$. We assume that such medians correspond with the background of the involved images.

4.3   Entropy Constraint

To measure the entropy, it is necessary to compute the number of states ι of the studied system; in our case ι expresses the gray levels present in an image $\mathbf{y}$, i.e.

$$\iota(\mathbf{y}) = \#(\{\eta \in \{0, \ldots, 255\} : d_{\mathbf{y}}(\eta) \neq 0\}).$$

In Fig. 3(a) and (c), the two possible ideal sources are shown, while in (e) mixture of the ideal images after separately blurring them and adding noise. Please note that the blurring level is generally different between the front and the verso; moreover, the cardinality of the set of states is directly correlated to the sharpness of an image: sharper images have fewer states, as visible in Fig. 3(b), (d), and (e).

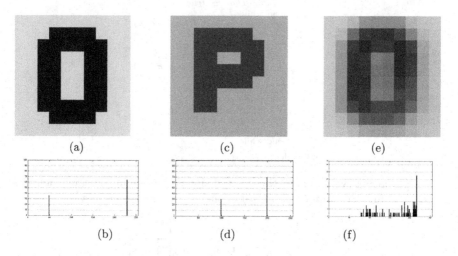

(a)   (c)   (e)

(b)   (d)   (f)

Fig. 3. In (a) and (c), there are the front and the verso of the ideal document, respectively; a mixture of such sources is given in (e). In (b), (d), and (f), there are the corresponding histograms.

Thus, we define the *entropy level* of the estimated source **s** as

$$EN(\mathbf{s}) = k_B \, \ln \left(\sum_{k=1}^{2} \sum_{e \in \{r,g,b\}} \iota(\mathbf{s}_k^{(e)}) \right),$$

where k_B is the Boltzmann constant.

5   Experimental Results

The presented experimental results are divided into two parts. In the former, we show a quantitative comparison between BETIS presented in [8] and the here proposed BETIS–NO. For this purpose, synthetic data are generated through the linear model given in (Eq. 2) and then reconstructed; the quality of reconstructions is measured by the MSE (mean square error) between the real and the reconstructed sources. Note that other algorithms in the literature are not directly comparable because of the difference in the data generation model. We also chose to replicate the same experimental results given in [8] to evaluate the BETIS algorithm to provide a better comparison with it. Later, we evaluate qualitatively our algorithm in the reconstruction of real data mixtures.

The following blur masks are used to generate synthetic data from ideal images:

$$M_1^{(u,u)} = \begin{pmatrix} 0 & 1 & 2 & 1 & 0 \\ 1 & 2 & 4 & 2 & 1 \\ 2 & 4 & 9 & 4 & 2 \\ 1 & 2 & 4 & 2 & 1 \\ 0 & 1 & 2 & 1 & 0 \end{pmatrix}, \quad M_2^{(u,u)} = \begin{pmatrix} 0 & 1 & 2 & 1 & 0 \\ 1 & 2 & 2 & 2 & 1 \\ 2 & 2 & 6 & 2 & 2 \\ 1 & 2 & 2 & 2 & 1 \\ 0 & 1 & 2 & 1 & 0 \end{pmatrix},$$

for $u \in \{r,g,b\}$, while $M_k^{(u,v)} = \frac{1}{3}M_k^{(u,u)}$ for $u,v \in \{r,g,b\}$, $u \neq v$, $k = 1,2$. A Gaussian noise is added, with the characteristics in Sect. 2, and standard deviation $\sigma = 5$. The parameters used in the reconstruction are always $\lambda = 0.5$, $\alpha = 10$, $\epsilon = 10$, $\omega_1 = 5 \cdot 10^5$, $\omega_2 = 0.5$, and $\omega_3 = 1 \cdot 10^4$.

Here we assume that the sum of all the rows of the mixture matrix is equal to one, since we expect the background color of the source to be the same as that of the data (see [4]).

In Fig. 4, in (a) and (b) the front and retro ideal images are shown; in (c) and (d) the generated mixtures are present; in (e) and (f) we see the sources estimated by BETIS, while in (g) and (h) there are those estimated by BETIS–NO.

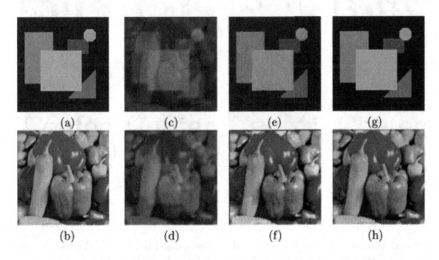

Fig. 4. (a) and (b): ideal images; (c) and (d): generated mixtures; (e) and (f): sources estimated by BETIS; (g) and (h): sources estimated by BETIS–NO.

In Fig. 5 and Fig. 6 we show, in the same order as in Fig. 4, the respective documents and the related reconstructions.

In Table 1 the mixture matrices used to generate the synthetic data and those obtained in BETIS and BETIS–NO are shown. In Table 2 we present the mean square errors between the ideal sources and those estimated by BETIS and BETIS–NO. It is apparent that the reconstruction computed by BETIS–NO is significantly closer to the original than that of BETIS, due to the introduction of the new proposed constraints.

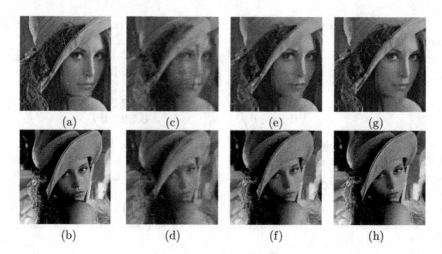

Fig. 5. (a) and (b): ideal images; (c) and (d): generated mixtures; (e) and (f): sources estimated by BETIS; (g) and (h): sources estimated by BETIS–NO.

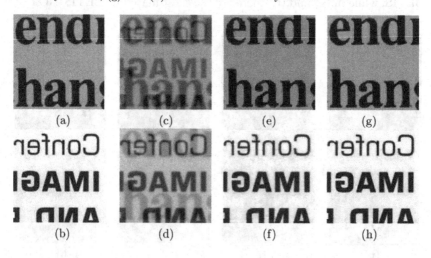

Fig. 6. (a) and (b): ideal images; (c) and (d): generated mixtures; (e) and (f): sources estimated by BETIS; (g) and (h): sources estimated by BETIS–NO.

Table 1. Original and estimated mixture matrices

Experiment	Real mixture matrix	Mixture matrix obtained by BETIS	Mixture matrix obtained by BETIS–NO
1	$\begin{pmatrix} 0.7124 & 0.2876 \\ 0.4281 & 0.5719 \end{pmatrix}$	$\begin{pmatrix} 0.7489 & 0.2511 \\ 0.4784 & 0.5216 \end{pmatrix}$	$\begin{pmatrix} 0.7165 & 0.2835 \\ 0.4305 & 0.5695 \end{pmatrix}$
2	$\begin{pmatrix} 0.7023 & 0.2977 \\ 0.3812 & 0.6188 \end{pmatrix}$	$\begin{pmatrix} 0.7367 & 0.2633 \\ 0.3925 & 0.6075 \end{pmatrix}$	$\begin{pmatrix} 0.7038 & 0.2962 \\ 0.3841 & 0.6159 \end{pmatrix}$
3	$\begin{pmatrix} 0.7103 & 0.2897 \\ 0.3086 & 0.6914 \end{pmatrix}$	$\begin{pmatrix} 0.7023 & 0.2977 \\ 0.3112 & 0.6888 \end{pmatrix}$	$\begin{pmatrix} 0.7105 & 0.2895 \\ 0.3074 & 0.6926 \end{pmatrix}$

Table 2. MSE of the algorithms BETIS and BETIS–NO

Experiment	BETIS		BETIS–NO	
	MSE recto	MSE verso	MSE recto	MSE verso
1	430.8025	604.8162	6.6897	11.4097
2	357.5233	192.1110	54.9735	26.0081
3	574.7180	186.4750	87.3849	22.8117

Now we present some results obtained starting from the real mixtures. In Fig. 7, we show the reconstructions using BETIS and BETIS–NO of a document affected by the show–through effect. No blur operator was considered in this case. It is visibly evident that the result obtained by BETIS–NO improves that given by BETIS.

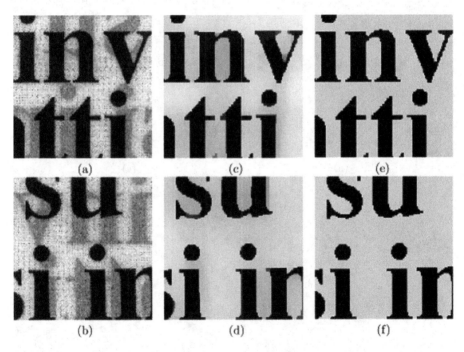

Fig. 7. (a) and (b): real mixtures; (c) and (d): sources estimated by BETIS; (e) and (f): sources estimated by BETIS–NO.

The data document in Fig. 8 (a) and (b) is taken from the database created as part of the *Irish Script on Screen* (ISOS) project of the School of Celtic Studies of the Dublin Institute for Advanced Studies, in conjunction with the SIGMEDIA group of the Department of Electrical and Electronic Engineering at Trinity College Dublin (see [26]). This database contains ancient documents affected by bleed–through. Here, we empirically assumed that the blur masks are as follows.

$$M_1^{(u,u)} = \begin{pmatrix} 0 & 0 & 0 \\ 0 & 1 & 0 \\ 0 & 0 & 0 \end{pmatrix}, \quad M_2^{(u,u)} = \begin{pmatrix} 0 & 1 & 0 \\ 1 & 4 & 1 \\ 0 & 1 & 0 \end{pmatrix},$$

for $u \in \{r, g, b\}$, while $M_k^{(u,v)} = \frac{1}{6} M_k^{(u,u)}$ for $u, v \in \{r, g, b\}$, $u \neq v$, $k = 1, 2$. In Fig. 8(c) and (d) the reconstruction obtained by BETIS–NO is presented.

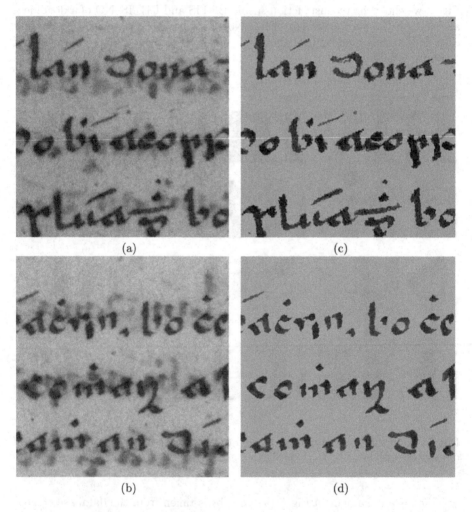

Fig. 8. (a) and (b): real mixtures; (c) and (d): sources estimated by BETIS–NO.

Conclusions

In this work, we dealt with a BSS problem in which we assumed that the decayed image is formed through a two-step linear process: the recto and verso images are separately blurred using a blur operator with known coefficients and then mixed. Our algorithm estimates the entries of the mixture matrix, which controls the intensity of recto-verso mixing for the document reconstruction. Our IMAP-type approach, BETIS–NO, is built on top of previous work [8] and enhanced by introducing second–order discontinuities and additional constraints on source images, i.e., minimum entropy, non–Gaussianity, and correct overlapping. The experimental results show the promising capability of the algorithm in reconstructing original documents, measured for synthetic data through MSE, and analyzed through visual inspection for real data. We could further extend the proposed technique by incorporating the blur mask's estimation into the mixture matrix's estimation; however, by increasing the degrees of freedom in our field of research, a significant increase in computational cost must be expected.

References

1. Barros, A.K.: The independence assumption: dependent component analysis. In: Girolami, M. (eds.) Advances in Independent Component Analysis. Perspectives in Neural Computing. Springer, London (2000). https://doi.org/10.1007/978-1-4471-0443-8_4

2. Benlin, X., Fangfang, L., Xingliang, M., Huazhong, J.: Study on independent component analysis application in classification and change detection of multispectral images. In: The International Archives of the Photogrammetry, Remote Sensing, and Spatial Information Sciences, vol. 37, pp. 871–876 (2008)

3. Boccuto, A., Gerace, I.: Image reconstruction with a non-parallelism constraint. In: Proceedings of the International Workshop on Computational Intelligence for Multimedia Understanding, Reggio Calabria, Italy, 27–28 October 2016, pp. 1–5. IEEE Conference Publications (2016)

4. Boccuto, A., Gerace, I., Giorgetti, V.: A blind source separation technique for document restoration. SIAM J. Imaging Sci. $12(2)$, 1135–1162 (2019)

5. Boccuto, A., Gerace, I., Martinelli, F.: Half-quadratic image restoration with a non-parallelism constraint. J. Math. Imaging Vis. $59(2)$, 270–295 (2017)

6. Boccuto, A., Gerace, I., Pucci, P.: Convex approximation technique for interacting line elements deblurring: a new approach. J. Math. Imaging Vis. $44(2)$, 168–184 (2012)

7. Cricco, F., De Santi, G., Gerace, I.: A deterministic algorithm for deblurring considering higher order smoothness constraints. In: Proceedings of the 2003 International Workshop on Spectral Methods and Multirate Signal Processing SMMSP2004, Vienna, Austria, 11/12 September 2004, pp. 325–332 (2004)

8. Cricco, F., Gerace, I.: An IMAP estimation for the joint separation and restoration of mixed degraded color images. In: Proceedings of the 7th Conference on Applied and Industrial Mathematics in Italy, Venice (Italy), 20–24 September 2004, pp. 260–269 (2004)

9. Cluni, F., Costarelli, D., Minotti, A.M., Vinti, G.: Applications of sampling Kantorovich operators to thermographic images for seismic engineering. J. Comput. Anal. Appl. $19(4)$, 602–617 (2015)

10. Discepoli, M., Gerace, I., Pandolfi, R.: Blind image restoration from multiple views by IMAP estimation. In: Modern Information Processing From Theory to Applications, pp. 441–452 (2006)
11. Evangelopoulos, X., Brockmeier, A. J., Mu, T., Goulermas, J. Y.: A graduated nonconvexity relaxation for large-scale seriation. In: Proceedings of the 2017 SIAM International Conference on Data Mining, Houston, Texas (USA), pp. 462–470 (2017)
12. Fedeli, L., Gerace, I., Martinelli, F.: Unsupervised blind separation and deblurring of mixtures of sources. In: Proceedings of Knowledge-Based Intelligent Information and Engineering Systems. LNCS, Vietri sul Mare, Italy, vol. 4694, pp. 25–32 (2007)
13. Gerace, I., Cricco, F., Tonazzini, A.: An extended maximum likelihood approach for the robust blind separation of autocorrelated images from noisy mixtures. In: Puntonet, C.G., Prieto, A. (eds.) ICA 2004. LNCS, vol. 3195, pp. 954–961. Springer, Heidelberg (2004). https://doi.org/10.1007/978-3-540-30110-3_120
14. Gerace, I., Pandolfi, R.: A color image restoration with adjacent parallel lines inhibition. In: Proceedings of the 12th International Conference on Image Analysis and Processing, 17–19 September 2003, Mantova, Italy, 6 p. (2003)
15. Gerace, I., Pandolfi, R., Pucci, P.: A new estimation of blur in the blind restoration problem. In: Proceedings of the 2003 International Conference on Image Processing, Barcelona, Spain, 14–17 September 2003, pp. 261–264 (2003)
16. Gillis, N.: Sparse and unique nonnegative matrix factorization through data preprocessing. J. Mach. Learn. Res. **13**, 3349–3386 (2012)
17. Hazan, E., Levy, K.Y., Shalev-Shwartz, S.: On graduated optimization for stochastic non-convex problems. In: Proceedings of the 33rd International Conference on Machine Learning, New York, NY, USA, vol. 48, pp. 1–9, 2016. JMLR: W& CP (2016)
18. Hyvärinen, A.: Fast and robust fixed-point algorithms for independent component analysis. IEEE Trans. Neural Netw. **10**, 626–634 (1999)
19. Hyvärinen, A.: Gaussian moments for noisy independent component analysis. IEEE Sig. Proc. Lett. **6**, 145–147 (1999)
20. Kuruoglu, E., Bedini, L., Paratore, M.T., Salerno, E., Tonazzini, A.: Source separation in astrophysical maps using independent factor analysis. Neural Netw. **16**(3–4), 479–491 (2003)
21. Leedham, G., Varma, S., Patankar, A., Govindaraju, V.: Separating text and background in degraded document images - a comparison of global thresholding techniques for multi-stage thresholding. In: Proceedings of the 8th International Workshop on Frontiers in Handwriting Recognition, Niagara on the Lake, Canada, pp. 244–249 (2002)
22. Liu, Z.-Y., Qiao, H.: GNCCP-graduated nonconvexity and concavity procedure. IEEE Trans. Pattern Anal. Mach. Intell. **36**(6), 1258–1267 (2014)
23. Liu, Z.-Y., Qiao, H., Su, J.-H.: MAP inference with MRF by graduated nonconvexity and concavity procedure. In: Loo, C.K., Yap, K.S., Wong, K.W., Teoh, A., Huang, K. (eds.) ICONIP 2014. LNCS, vol. 8835, pp. 404–412. Springer, Cham (2014). https://doi.org/10.1007/978-3-319-12640-1_49
24. Nikolova, M., Ng, M.K., Tam, C.-P.: On ℓ_1 data fitting and concave regularization for image recovery. SIAM J. Sci. Comput. **35**(1), A397–A430 (2013)
25. Nikolova, M., Ng, M.K., Zhang, S., Ching, W.-K.: Efficient reconstruction of piecewise constant images using nonsmooth nonconvex minimization. SIAM J. Imaging Sci. **1**(1), 2–25 (2008)

26. Rowley-Brooke, R., Pitié, F., Kokaram, A.: A ground truth bleed-through document image database. In: Zaphiris, P., Buchanan, G., Rasmussen, E., Loizides, F. (eds.) TPDL 2012. LNCS, vol. 7489, pp. 185–196. Springer, Heidelberg (2012). https://doi.org/10.1007/978-3-642-33290-6_21

27. Smith, T., Egeland, O.: Dynamical pose estimation with graduated non-convexity for outlier robustness. Model. Identif. Control (MIC) J. **43**(2), 79–89 (2022)

28. Tonazzini, A., Gerace, I., Martinelli, F.: Document image restoration and analysis as separation of mixtures of patterns: from linear to nonlinear models. In: Gunturk, B.K., Li, X. (eds.) Image Restoration - Fundamentals and Advances, pp. 285–310. CRC Press, Taylor & Francis, Boca Raton (2013)

29. Yang, H., Antonante, P., Tzoumas, V., Carlone, L.: Graduated non-convexity for robust spatial perception: from non-minimal solvers to global outlier rejection. IEEE Robot. Autom. Lett. **5**(2), 1127–1134 (2020)

Quadratically Transformed Luminance Chrominance Spaces

Giulio Biondi[(✉)] [ID], Antonio Boccuto [ID], and Ivan Gerace [ID]

Department of Mathematics and Computer Science, University of Perugia, Perugia, Italy
{giulio.biondi,antonio.boccuto,ivan.gerace}@unipg.it

Abstract. Several color spaces defined in the literature are obtained from the RGB space through non-linear transforms, potentially limiting their applicability in a regularization context. Therefore, in this paper, we introduce three new color spaces, QTLC-r_*^2, QTLC-g_*^2, and QTLC-r_*g_*, and the corresponding quadratic mappings from the RGB space. To test their uniformity, we use them to consider the image defading problem through a novel two-step technique: first, we define a fast heuristic to restore the natural color saturation; then, we propose a regularization technique to deblur the image. We experimentally observe that presumably thanks to its higher uniformity, the QTLC-r_*g_* space produces natural-looking images in the reconstruction and should be preferred to the QTLC-r_*^2 and QTLC-g_*^2 spaces.

Keywords: uniform color space · defading problem · deblurring · regularization technique

1 Introduction

A color space is said to be *uniform* if the adjacent colors in it are similar to the human eye [9,11]. The classical color spaces, as RGB (*Red-Green-Blue*) and CMYK (*Cyan-Magenta-Yellow-Black*), are not uniform. The uniform color spaces, in general, are defined as employing luminance and chrominance components, since these two components have different properties. The most known classical space constructed in this way is the CIE $L^*a^*b^*$ space. Unfortunately, in general, the transform from RGB to CIE $L^*a^*b^*$ is not polynomial and not easily manageable. The aim of this article is to study some new color spaces which are defined using luminance and chrominance, using a quadratic transform to compute the coordinates of color from the RGB space to them. In particular we define three different color spaces, which we call QTLC-r_*^2 (*Quadratically Transformed Luminance Chrominance-r_*^2*), QTLC-g_*^2, and QTLC-r_*g_*. The choice of quadratic transforms and rational numerical coefficients for the proposed mappings aims to define simple models yet deliver performance comparable to existing state-of-the-art methods, to enhance their applicability to downstream tasks, e.g., image demosaicing (see, e.g., [3,13]) and optical flow (see, e.g., [12,16]). In

O. Gervasi et al. (Eds.): ICCSA 2023 Workshops, LNCS 14108, pp. 676–693, 2023.
https://doi.org/10.1007/978-3-031-37117-2_45

this work, to test such spaces, we deal with the defading image problem [1]. The problem of faded images refers to the loss of quality and detail in an image over time due to environmental factors such as light exposure, temperature, and humidity. This results in the colors becoming less vibrant, the contrast is reduced, and the details becoming less sharp. Faded images can also be caused by the deterioration of the physical materials used to store the image, such as film or paper. This can be a significant issue for individuals, archives, and museums that aim to preserve historical images and visual artifacts. To address this problem, several methods are available for restoring faded images, including digital restoration techniques (see, e.g., [1, 15, 19, 21]) and chemical treatments for physical media. However, there are several reasons why digital restoration may be preferred over physical restoration for faded images.

- Speed and convenience: Digital restoration can be performed quickly and easily using specialized software and hardware. On the other hand, physical restoration can be time-consuming and labor-intensive.
- Non-invasivity: Digital restoration requires no physical intervention with the original image. On the other hand, physical restoration can sometimes further damage the image.
- Flexibility: Digital restoration allows for easy adjustments and changes to the image during restoration. Physical restoration, once completed, cannot be easily altered.
- Reproduction: Digital restoration allows for the creation of multiple copies of the restored image, which can be distributed and shared more easily than physical copies.
- Preservation: Digital restoration enables the preservation of the restored image in a digital format, which can be easily backed up and protected against future degradation. Physical restoration is subject to ongoing degradation and requires ongoing preservation efforts.
- Accessibility: Digital restoration makes the restored image more widely accessible to a larger audience, including people with disabilities and those in remote locations. Physical restoration is typically limited to those who can physically access the location where the image is housed.

The *defading image problem* consists in estimating the ideal source image, given a faded image. To solve this problem, we proceed in two phases. In the former, we define a simple heuristic to recover the correct color saturation of the image. However, some unsupervised techniques are described in the literature (see, e.g., [6, 20]). Concerning the latter, we propose a novel two-step approach. In the first we reconstruct the luminance component and use a regularization technique, through which the solution is defined as the minimizer of a suitable energy function. In such a function, some constraints are included, which impose that the second–order finite differences of luminance are small enough, and allow the existence of discontinuities of the values of luminance. Indeed, we can assume that luminance is a piecewise linear function [7]; moreover, to further increase the quality of the reconstruction, we inhibit the existence of parallel adjacent discontinuities (see, e.g., [2, 4, 5]). To minimize the energy function, we use a GNC

(*Graduate Non-Convexity*) technique (see, e.g., [2,5,7,10,14,17,18,22,23]). In the second step, we assume that chrominance is a piecewise constant function and that the discontinuities present in such a function correspond to those estimated for the luminance. So, the regularized solution is defined as a minimizer of a different energy function. Since such a function is convex, the minimization can be performed by a SOR (*Successive Over Relaxation*) algorithm. The experimental results show how the QTLC-r_*g_* space gives the most natural results in reconstructing faded images.

The article is structured as follows. In Sect. 2 we introduce three new color spaces, in Sect. 3 we deal with the defading problem, and in Sect. 4 we present our experimental results.

2   New Luminance-Chrominance Spaces

In this section, we introduce some new spaces defined using luminance and chrominance, obtained by a transform from the RGB space. In particular, we consider Adobe RGB, where each color is encoded as a triple $(r, g, b) \in [0, 1]^3$. Let us first consider the following coordinate change

$$
\begin{cases}
l = \dfrac{1}{4} r + \dfrac{1}{2} g + \dfrac{1}{4} b, \\[2mm]
r_* = \dfrac{r - l}{l}, \\[2mm]
g_* = \dfrac{g - l}{l}.
\end{cases}
$$

We determine the value of the luminance coordinate l as a linear combination of the terms r, g, b, so that the sum of the involved coefficients is equal to 1 and, to describe a realistic model, the coefficient corresponding to the green color is the largest one since the human eye perceives green better than the other colors. The pair of coordinates (r_*, g_*) represents the chrominance of the color; note that, in this color space, every gray corresponds to the origin $(0, 0)$.

Now we find three quadratic transforms that map the subspace (r_*, g_*) into the subspace (α, β); in particular, we focus on mapping the Aqua Green, Magenta, Gray, and Blue colors into $(\alpha, \beta) = (-1, 0)$, $(\alpha, \beta) = (1, 0)$, $(\alpha, \beta) = (0, 0)$, and $(\alpha, \beta) = (0, -1)$, respectively (see Table 1), so that complementary colors are symmetrical with respect to the origin. In Fig. 1 the desired color mapping is illustrated.

We consider the following transforms:

$$
\begin{cases}
\alpha = \dfrac{19}{40} r_* - \dfrac{5}{8} g_* - \dfrac{3}{20} r_*^2 \\[3mm]
\beta = \dfrac{3}{8} r_* + \dfrac{5}{8} g_*,
\end{cases}
\tag{1}
$$

Table 1. Color coordinates in the spaces (r,g,b), $(l,\bar{r},\bar{g})$, (l,r_*,g_*), (l,α,β).

	r	g	b	l	r_*	g_*	α	β
Gray	k	k	k	k	0	0	0	0
Magenta	1	0	1/2	3/8	5/3	−1	1	0
Aqua Green	0	1	1/2	5/8	−1	3/5	−1	0
Blue	0	0	1	1/4	−1	−1	0	−1

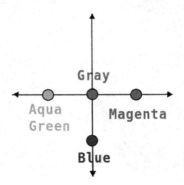

Fig. 1. Colors mapping in the proposed spaces

$$
\begin{cases}
\alpha = \dfrac{3}{8}r_* - \dfrac{19}{24}g_* - \dfrac{5}{12}g_*^2 \\[2mm]
\beta = \dfrac{3}{8}r_* + \dfrac{5}{8}g_*,
\end{cases}
\tag{2}
$$

$$
\begin{cases}
\alpha = \dfrac{5}{8}r_* - \dfrac{3}{8}g_* + \dfrac{1}{4}r_* g_* \\[2mm]
\beta = \dfrac{3}{8}r_* + \dfrac{5}{8}g_*,
\end{cases}
\tag{3}
$$

Note that β reduces to a linear function of r_* and g_*; furthermore, a quadratic term is necessary for the transforms to be well-defined.

The spaces obtained by the transform in (Eq. 1), (Eq. 2), and (Eq. 3) are called *Quadratically Transformed Luminance Chrominance* r_*^2 (QTLC-r_*^2), *Quadratically Transformed Luminance Chrominance* g_*^2 (QTLC-g_*^2), and *Quadratically Transformed Luminance Chrominance* $r_* g_*$ (QTLC-$r_* g_*$), respectively. In Fig. 2, in (a), (b), and (c), the sections of the QTLC-r_*^2, QTLC-g_*^2, and QTLC-$r_* g_*$ spaces are represented for $l = 180$, respectively. Figure 2 (d) shows the section of the CIE $L^*a^*b^*$ space for $l = 100$; in the CIE $L^*a^*b^*$ space $l \in [0, 100]$ and, for the chrominance components, $a^* \in [-500, 500]$, and $b^* \in [-200, 200]$. In (a), in correspondence with the orange color, a sharp gradient can be observed; in (b), in the lower right section, there is a compenetration

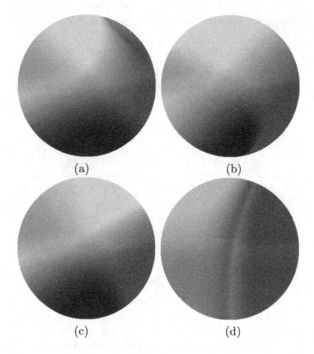

(a)   (b)

(c)   (d)

Fig. 2. Sections of the spaces QTLC-r_*^2 (a), QTLC-g_*^2 (b), QTLC-$r_* g_*$ (c) for $l = 180$, and in the CIE $L^*a^*b^*$ space for $l = 100$ (d).

between the blue and the magenta clues; the plot of (c), instead, shows a closer behavior to that of a uniform space. From visual inspections on various values of l, the behavior appears to be consistent. In Fig. 3 the luminance component in the QTLC-r_*^2, QTLC-g_*^2, and QTLC-$r_* g_*$ spaces (b) and in the CIE $L^*a^*b^*$ space (c) are shown next to the source image (a); the chrominance components, instead, are visualized in Fig. 4. Each row shows, from left to right, the α, β, and total chrominance (α, β) for, respectively, the QTLC-r_*^2, QTLC-g_*^2, and QTLC-$r_* g_*$ spaces; in the final row, the a^*, b^* and (a^*, b^*) components in the CIE $L^*a^*b^*$ space. For all the QTLC spaces, the representations do not show appreciable differences. Moreover, regardless of the space, luminance is associated with image details, while chrominance is used for color distribution. Note that these two properties can be modeled as functions whose behavior is close to be piecewise linear and piecewise constant, respectively.

3   The Defading Image Problem

We now show how the spaces introduced in the previous section can be used to solve the defading image problem. Old images can be faded because of light damage, air exposure, mold and fungi, improper storage, or water damage. Due

(a)   (b)   (c)

Fig. 3. (a) The source image; (b) the luminance component in the QTLC-r_*^2, QTLC-g_*^2, and QTLC-$r_* g_*$ spaces; (c) the luminance component in the CIE $L^*a^*b^*$ space.

to these effects, we get both a variation of saturation of the involved colors and a blur on the image.

Our proposed method is divided into two phases. The former emphasizes the involved colors by intensifying the contrasts and is necessary to get the correct saturation in the estimated ideal image. In the latter, the analyzed image is deblurred.

3.1 Analysis of the Contrast

For testing, we employ a simple heuristic to intensify the contrast of a faded image. First, we analyze the luminance value. A faded image of size $n \times m$ can be expressed as $f = (\mathbf{l}, \boldsymbol{\alpha}, \boldsymbol{\beta}) \in \mathbb{R}^{n \times m \times 3}$, where $(\mathbf{l}, \boldsymbol{\alpha}, \boldsymbol{\beta})$ are, respectively, the vectors in lexicographic form of the luminance, α-chrominance and β-chrominance. It is necessary to determine empirically a value l_0 of the luminance, which we want to be constant. So, the luminance value at every pixel $(i,j) \in \{1,\ldots,n\}^2$ is modified according to the following algorithmic law:

$$l(i,j) := (c_l(l(i,j) - l_0) + l_0)^{(+)},$$

where $c_l > 0$ is the contrast parameter, which expresses the sharpness of the contrast, and $\tau^{(+)} = \max\{\tau, 0\}$. The choice of c_l is made empirically, according to the characteristics of the image.

Concerning the value of chrominance, we proceed analogously. In particular, we consider the positive and the negative values of α and β separately. Namely, we fix four different saturation values, which we want to be constant, which we call α_0^+, α_0^-, β_0^+, β_0^-, which correspond to the values of Magenta, Aqua Green, Yellow and Blue, respectively. Note that α_0^+ and β_0^+ are positive, while α_0^- and β_0^- are negative. Moreover, we fix the contrast parameter for the four involved colors, which we call c_α^+, c_α^-, c_β^+, c_β^-. For every $(i,j) \in \{1,\ldots,n\} \times \{1,\ldots,m\}$

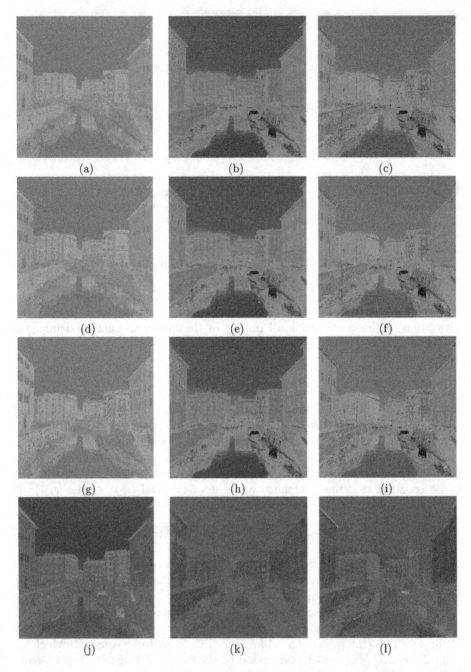

Fig. 4. The α (a), β (b) and total (c) chrominance associated with the QTLC-r_*^2 space; the α (d), β (e) and total (α, β) (f) chrominance related to the QTLC-g_*^2 space; the α (g), β (h) and total (i) chrominance corresponding to the QTLC-$r_*\,g_*$ space; the a^* (j), b^* (k) and (a^*, b^*) (l) components in the CIE $L^*a^*b^*$ space. (Color figure online)

we apply

$$\alpha(i,j) = \begin{cases} (c_\alpha^+(\alpha(i,j) - l_\alpha^+) + l_\alpha^+)^{(+)} \text{ if } \alpha(i,j) \geq 0, \\ \\ (c_\alpha^-(\alpha(i,j) - l_\alpha^-) + l_\alpha^-)^{(-)} \text{ if } \alpha(i,j) < 0, \end{cases}$$

$$\beta(i,j) = \begin{cases} (c_\beta^+(\beta(i,j) - l_\beta^+) + l_\beta^+)^{(+)} \text{ if } \beta(i,j) \geq 0, \\ \\ (c_\beta^-(\beta(i,j) - l_\beta^-) + l_\beta^-)^{(-)} \text{ if } \beta(i,j) < 0, \end{cases}$$

where $\tau^{(-)} = \min\{\tau, 0\}$.

3.2   The Deblurring Technique

In our approach, luminance and chrominance are deblurred separately. Indeed, as we can see in Fig. 4 (b), luminance corresponds to the analyzed color image transformed into a grayscale image, while chrominance corresponds to an image with almost constant color stains. Such a difference requires the two components to be treated separately; for this reason, we model luminance using a piecewise linear function, and chrominance of a piecewise constant function.

Luminance Deblurring. The problem of luminance deblurring is similar to that of reconstructing the original grayscale image from a grayscale image blurred and/or corrupted by noise. The direct problem is stated as follows:

$$\mathbf{l} = A\widetilde{\mathbf{l}} + \mathbf{n_l},$$

where the vectors $\mathbf{l}, \widetilde{\mathbf{l}}$, of dimension $n\,m$, are the observed luminance and the ideal one in the lexicographic order, respectively. The vector $\mathbf{n_l}$, of dimension $n\,m$, is the additive noise on the luminance, which we assume to be white, Gaussian, with zero mean and a known variance σ^2. The $(n\,m) \times (n\,m)$-matrix A is a linear operator, which represents the blur acting on the luminance. Each pixel of the blur luminance is assumed to be obtained by a weighted average of its neighbors. Given a positive matrix $M \in \mathbb{R}^{(2h+1)\times(2h+1)}$, called *blur mask*, the entries of matrix A can be defined by:

$$a_{(i,j),(i+w,j+v)} = \begin{cases} \dfrac{m_{h+1+w,h+1+v}}{\nu_{i,j}}, \text{ if } |w|, |v| \leq h, \\ \\ 0, \qquad\qquad\quad \text{otherwise}, \end{cases}$$

where $\nu_{i,j} = \sum_{i=\xi_1}^{\xi_2} \sum_{j=\xi_3}^{\xi_4} m_{i,j}$, $\xi_1 = \max\{1, 2 + h - i\}$, $\xi_2 = \min\{2h + 1, n - i + h + 1\}$, $\xi_3 = \max\{1, 2 + h - j\}$, and $\xi_4 = \min\{2h + 1, n - j + h + 1\}$.

In this work, we reduce the problem to a luminance restoration problem, which consists in finding an estimation $\widetilde{\mathbf{l}}$ of the unknown original luminance, given the blurred luminance l, the matrix A and the variance of the noise σ^2; for the sake of simplicity, A is determined empirically. This is an ill-posed inverse problem in the sense of Hadamard (see, e.g., [8]).

To solve ill-posed problems, a *regularization technique* is used in order to find a unique solution, stable concerning the noise. To improve the quality of the results, some binary elements called *line variables*, can be considered (see, e.g., [5]). These elements consider the discontinuities present in the luminance $\widetilde{\mathbf{l}}$ the ideal luminances have discontinuities in correspondence with the edges of different objects. A *clique c* of order 1 (resp., 2) is a subset of points of a square grid on which the first (resp., second) order finite difference is defined. We denote by the symbol C_1 (resp., C_2) the set of all cliques of order 1 (resp., 2), namely $C_1 = \{c = \{(i,j),(h,l)\} : i = h, j = l + 1 \text{ or } i = h + 1, j = l\}$ (resp., $C_2 = \{c = \{(i,j),(h,l),(r,q)\} : i = h = r, j = l + 1 = q + 2 \text{ or } i = h + 1 = r + 2, j = l = q\}$). We denote the first (resp., second) order finite difference operator of the vector $\widetilde{\mathbf{l}}$ associated with the clique c by $D_c^k \widetilde{\mathbf{l}}$, $k = 1, 2$, that is, if $c = \{(i,j),(h,l)\} \in C_1$, then $D_c^1 \mathbf{x} = x_{i,j} - x_{h,l}$, (resp., if $c = \{(i,j),(h,l),(r,q)\} \in C_2$, then $D_c^2 \mathbf{x} = x_{i,j} - 2x_{h,l} + x_{r,q}$). Note that the second–order differences are used for the luminance restoration problem, while the first order differences will be considered in the next paragraph for the chrominance deblurring.

Now, let us introduce the auxiliary variables associated with the discontinuities of the luminance $\widetilde{\mathbf{l}}$. A good estimation of the discontinuities is crucial to restoring luminance quality. Such variables have the role of eliminating the regularity constraint, where discontinuities should appear. To every clique c we associate a weight $w_c \in \{0, 1\}$, called *line variable*; in particular, a value of 1 corresponds to a discontinuity in luminance in c. The vector $\mathbf{w}$ is the set of all line variables w_c. Thus, the original luminance is considered as a pair $(\widetilde{\mathbf{l}}, \mathbf{w})$, where $\widetilde{\mathbf{l}}$ is the matrix of the luminance levels of pixels, and $\mathbf{w}$ is the vector of the set of all components w_c, $c \in C_2$. Let us introduce the concept of *adjacent clique of order* 2, which is used to define the non-parallelism constraint. Given a vertical clique $c = \{(i,j),(i+1,j),(i+2,j)\}$, $i = 3, \ldots, M - 2$, $j = 1, \ldots, N$, we define its preceding clique $c - 1$ as follows:

$$c - 1 = \{(i - 2, j), (i - 1, j), \ldots, (i, j)\}.$$

If c is a horizontal clique, $c = \{(i,j),(i,j+1),(i,j+2)\}$, $i = 1, \ldots, M$, $j = 3, \ldots, N - 2$, then its preceding clique $c - 1$ is defined by setting

$$c - 1 = \{(i, j - 2), (i, j - 1), (i, j)\}.$$

We use the convention that if $c - 1$ does not exist, then $w_{c-1} = 0$.

A regularized solution to the restoration problem is achieved as the minimum of the *primal energy function*, given by

$$E(\widetilde{\mathbf{l}}, \mathbf{w}) = \|A\widetilde{\mathbf{l}} - \mathbf{l}\|^2 + \sum_{c \in C_2} \left[\lambda^2 (D_c^2 \widetilde{\mathbf{l}})^2 (1 - w_c) + \theta w_c \right] + \sum_{c \in C_2} \varepsilon \, w_c \, w_{c-1}. \quad (4)$$

The first term of (Eq. 4) measures the faithfulness of the solution to the data. The second one is a regularization term related to a smoothness condition on $\tilde{\mathbf{l}}$. The *regularization parameter* λ^2 allows us to establish an appropriate degree of smoothness in the solution. The positive parameter θ is used to avoid having too many discontinuities in the restored luminance. The last term, $\varepsilon \geq 0$, is added to the energy function to make parallel close discontinuities in the restored luminance unlikely to appear. The importance of ε is apparent in Fig. 5; the image in (b) is reconstructed from the blurred image in (a) by setting $\varepsilon = 0$, i.e., not using it, while the image in (d) by setting ε to an appropriate strictly positive value. Although the reconstructions of Fig. 5 (b) and (d) appear similar to the human eye, the underlying quality for the latter is higher, as visible in the corresponding line process plots (c) and (e).

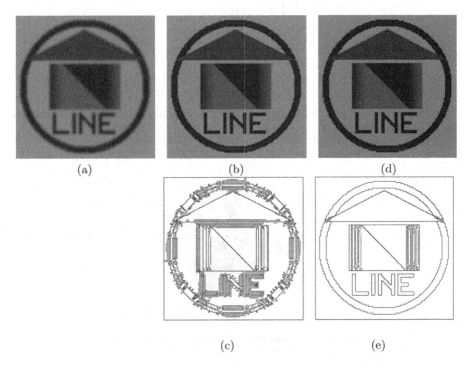

| (a) | (b) | (d) |

| (c) | (e) |

Fig. 5. In (a) the original blurred image; in (b) and (c) a reconstruction with $\varepsilon = 0$ and the corresponding line process plot; in (d) and (e), a reconstruction with $\varepsilon > 0$ and the corresponding line process plot.

To reduce the computational cost of the minimization of (Eq. 4), the *dual energy function* through the minimization of the primal energy function concerning the line process $\mathbf{w}$ is used. Namely, we get (see, e.g., [4,5])

$$E_d(\tilde{\mathbf{l}}) = \inf_{\mathbf{w}} E(\tilde{\mathbf{l}}, \mathbf{w}).$$

In general, the direct calculation of the dual energy function is difficult, so we consider the following good approximation of the dual energy function (see, e.g., [5]):

$$E_d(\tilde{\mathbf{l}}) = \|A\tilde{\mathbf{l}} - \mathbf{1}\|^2 + \sum_{c \in C_2} \psi(D_c^2 \tilde{\mathbf{l}}, D_{c-1}^2 \tilde{\mathbf{l}}),$$

where

$$\psi(t_1, t_2) = \begin{cases} \begin{cases} \lambda^2 t_1^2, & \text{if } |t_1| < s, \\ \theta, & \text{if } |t_1| \geq s, \end{cases} & \text{if } |t_2| < s, \\ \begin{cases} \lambda^2 t_1^2, & \text{if } |t_1| < \bar{s}, \\ \theta + \varepsilon, & \text{if } |t_1| \geq \bar{s}, \end{cases} & \text{if } |t_2| \geq s. \end{cases} \tag{5}$$

The quantity

$$s = \sqrt{\theta}/\lambda \tag{6}$$

is a *threshold* for creating a discontinuity, while $\bar{s} = \sqrt{\theta + \varepsilon}/\lambda$ is a *superthreshold* for creating a close parallel discontinuity. The function ψ in (Eq. 5) is plotted for particular values of λ, θ and $\varepsilon > 0$.

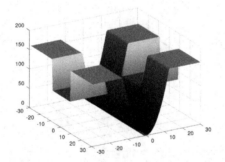

Fig. 6. Used stabilizers with $\lambda = 1$, $\theta = \varepsilon = 80$

The dual energy function E_d is not convex, and thus requires appropriate optimization strategies. A classical deterministic technique for minimizing the dual energy function is the GNC (*Graduated Non-Convexity*) algorithm (see, e.g., [2,5,7,10,14,17,18,22,23]). Algorithms for minimizing a non-convex function depend on the choice of the starting point; to perform a suitable choice of this point, the The GNC technique finds a finite family of approximating functions $\{E_d^{(p)}\}_p$, such that the first one is convex, and the last one is the original dual energy function. The GNC algorithm is defined as follows:

initialize $\tilde{\mathbf{l}}$;

while $E_d^{(p)} \neq E_d$ do

- find the minimum of the function $E_d^{(p)}$ starting from the initial point $\tilde{\mathbf{l}}$;
- $\tilde{\mathbf{l}} = \arg\min E_d^{(p)}(\tilde{\mathbf{l}})$;
- update the parameter p.

Chrominance Deblurring. Now we deal with reconstructing the chrominance component. The direct problem is formulated as follows:

$$\boldsymbol{\alpha} = A\,\tilde{\boldsymbol{\alpha}} + \mathbf{n}_\alpha, \quad \boldsymbol{\beta} = A\,\tilde{\boldsymbol{\beta}} + \mathbf{n}_\beta,$$

where the vectors $\boldsymbol{a}$, $\tilde{\boldsymbol{\alpha}}$, $(\boldsymbol{\beta}, \tilde{\boldsymbol{\beta}})$, of dimension $n\,m$, are the observed chrominance α-component (β-component) and the ideal one in the lexicographic order, respectively. Note that we assume that the A matrix is the same as in the luminance step; experiments show that such a choice delivers satisfying reconstructions. The $n\,m$-dimensional vector $\mathbf{n}_\alpha$ (resp. $\mathbf{n}_\beta$) is the additive noise on the chrominance α-component (β-component), which is supposed to be white, Gaussian, with zero mean and a known variance σ^2.

We define the estimate of the solution as a minimizer of the following energy function:

$$E(\tilde{\boldsymbol{\alpha}}, \boldsymbol{\beta}) = \|A\tilde{\boldsymbol{\alpha}} - \boldsymbol{\alpha}\|^2 + \|A\tilde{\boldsymbol{\beta}} - \boldsymbol{\beta}\|^2 + \sum_{c \in C_1} \lambda^2 (D_c^1 \tilde{\boldsymbol{\alpha}})^2 + (D_c^1 \tilde{\boldsymbol{\beta}})^2)(1 - \tilde{w}_c). \quad (7)$$

where the first two terms of the right hand of (Eq. 7) are the faithfulness with data of the α- and the β-component of the chrominance, respectively, and the third addend is a smoothness term, in which λ^2 is the regularization parameter, which we assume to be the same as that used to reconstruct the luminance. Note that we use a finite difference operator of the first order, since we assume that chrominance is represented by a piecewise constant function. Moreover the line variables $\tilde{w}_c$, with $c \in C_1$, are fixed by means of the estimated luminance $\tilde{l}$, as follows:

$$\tilde{w}_c = \begin{cases} 1 \text{ if } D_c^1 \tilde{\mathbf{l}} \geq s, \\ 0 \text{ otherwise,} \end{cases}$$

where s is as in (Eq. 6). Note that the energy function defined in (Eq. 7) is convex, and hence the minimization can be performed using a SOR-type algorithm.

4   Experimental Results

We present the application of the proposed algorithm to a set of faded images, to demonstrate the reconstruction capability and visually compare the results when different color spaces are used.

In Fig. 7 and Fig. 8 the observed and the corresponding reconstructed images are shown, using respectively the spaces QTLC-r_*^2 and QTLC-g_*^2. The parameters used in the defading phase in both cases are $l_0 = 100$, $c_l = 1.2$, $l_\alpha^+ = 0.4$, $c_\alpha^+ = 1.2$, $l_\alpha^- = 0.01$, $c_\alpha^- = 1.4$, $l_\beta^+ = 0.03$, $c_\beta^+ = 1.3$, $l_\beta^- = 0.01$, and $c_\beta^- = 1.5$; while the parameters used in the deblurring phase are $\lambda = 1$, $\theta = 10$, and $\epsilon = 10$. Moreover, we assume that the following blur mask blurs the observed data:

$$M = \begin{pmatrix} 5 & 10 & 5 \\ 10 & 20 & 10 \\ 5 & 10 & 5 \end{pmatrix}$$

(a)   (b)

Fig. 7. (a): the observed image of dimension $n = 1160$; (b): the image reconstructed using the space QTLC-r_*^2.

Regarding the QTLC-r_*g_* space, we experimentally observed a higher degree of freedom in the choice of the parameter values for the defading process. Such behavior could be attributed to a superior uniformity of the space if compared to the previous two; for this reason, QTLC-r_*g_* should be the space of choice due to its more consistent capability of preserving color naturalness. In Fig. 9, (b) is reconstructed from (a), using the following defading parameters: $l_0 = 100$, $c_l = 1.1$, $l_\alpha^+ = 0.32$, $c_\alpha^+ = 1.6$, $l_\alpha^- = 0.005$, $c_\alpha^- = 3.8$, $l_\beta^+ = 0.08$, $c_\beta^+ = 1.5$, $l_\beta^- = 0.01$, and $c_\beta^- = 2$. The restoration capabilities of the three QTLC spaces and the LAB space are visually compared with the source image in Fig. 10. (b), (c), and (d) are obtained from (a) using respectively, the QTLC-r_*^2 (b), QTLC-g_*^2 (c), QTLC-$r_* g_*$ with the following common parameter values: $l_0 = 100$, $c_l = 1.1$, $l_\alpha^+ = 0.99$, $c_\alpha^+ = 1.1$, $l_\alpha^- = 0.005$, $c_\alpha^- = 2.8$, $l_\beta^+ = 0.08$, $c_\beta^+ = 1.5$, $l_\beta^- = 0.01$, $c_\beta^- = 1.5$; in (e) the CIE $L^*a^*b^*$ is employed, with $l_0 = 70$, $c_l = 1.1$, $l_{a*}^+ = 50$, $c_{a*}^+ = 1.3$, $l_{a*}^- = -15$, $c_{a*}^- = 1.3$, $l_{b*}^+ = 10$, $c_{b*}^+ = 1.3$, $l_{b*}^- = -15$, $c_{b*}^- = 1.3$. In both cases, the parameters taken to obtain Fig. 7 and Fig. 8 are used in the deblurring phase.

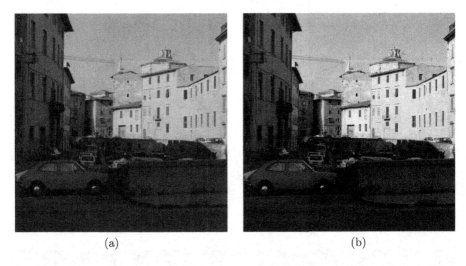

Fig. 8. (a): the observed image of dimension $n = 1166$; (b): the image reconstructed using the space QTLC-g_*^2.

Fig. 9. (a): the observed image of dimension $n = 1180$; (b): the image reconstructed using the space QTLC-$r_* g_*$.

In Fig. 11, details of the reconstructions obtained from the source in Fig. 10 are shown to highlight the differences between the QTLC spaces. (a) and (b) show a section of the bridge for the QTLC-r_*^2 and QTLC-$r_* g_*$ spaces; in the former, the colors tend to be over-saturated, while in the latter, they are more realistic. (c) and (d), instead, present a detail of the water in the canal for the QTLC-g_*^2 and QTLC-$r_* g_*$ spaces; in the first, the colors tend to be metallic, while in the QTLC-$r_* g_*$ reconstruction, the water hue is more natural.

Fig. 10. (a): the observed image of dimension $n = 1077$; the image reconstructed using the QTLC-r_*^2 (b), QTLC-g_*^2 (c), QTLC-$r_* g_*$ (d), and CIE $L^* a^* b^*$ (e) spaces.

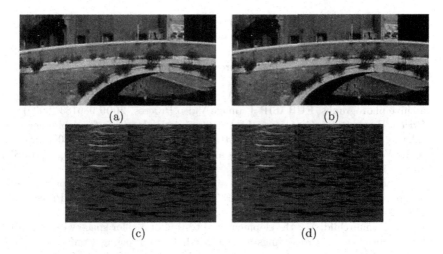

Fig. 11. A close-up of the bridge in Fig. 10, from the image reconstructed with QTLC-r_*^2 (a) and QTLC-$r_* g_*$(b); A close-up of the water section in Fig. 10, from the image reconstructed with QTLC-g_*^2 (c) and QTLC-$r_* g_*$(d)

Conclusions

In this work, we defined three new color spaces obtained by means of a quadratic transform from the RGB space. To test the uniformity of such spaces, we employed them to deal with the image defading problem, using a novel two-step technique: first, we defined a fast heuristic to restore the correct color saturation; then, we proposed a regularization technique to deblur the analyzed image. We experimentally observed that presumably thanks to its higher uniformity, the QTLC-$r_* g_*$ space widens the range of parameter values that produce natural-looking images in the reconstruction and should thus be preferred to the QTLC-r_*^2 and QTLC-g_*^2 spaces.

References

1. Ahmed, A.M.T.: Color restoration techniques for faded colors of old photos, printings, and paintings. In: Proceedings of 2009 IEEE International Conference on Electro/Information Technology, pp. 151–156 (2009)
2. Boccuto, A., Gerace, I.: Image reconstruction with a non-parallelism constraint. In: Proceedings of the International Workshop on Computational Intelligence for Multimedia Understanding, Reggio Calabria, Italy, 27–28 October 2016, pp. 1–5. IEEE Conference Publications (2016)
3. Boccuto, A., Gerace, I., Giorgetti, V., Rinaldi, M.: A fast algorithm for the demosaicing problem concerning the Bayer pattern. Open Signal Process. J. **6**, 1–14 (2019)

4. Boccuto, A., Gerace, I., Martinelli, F.: Half-quadratic image restoration with a non-parallelism constraint. J. Math. Imaging Vision **59**(2), 270–295 (2017)

5. Boccuto, A., Gerace, I., Pucci, P.: Convex approximation technique for interacting line elements deblurring: A new approach. J. Math. Imag. Vis. **44**(2), 168–184 (2012)

6. Bruni, V., Ramponi, G., Restrepo, A., Vitulano, D.: Context-based defading of archive photographs. EURASIP J. Image Video Process. **2009** 986183 (2009)

7. Cricco, F., De Santi, G., Gerace, I.: A deterministic algorithm for deblurring considering higher order smoothness constraints. In: Proceedings of the 2003 International Workshop on Spectral Methods and Multirate Signal Processing (SMMSP) 2004, Vienna, pp. 325–332 (2004)

8. Demoment, G.: Image reconstruction and restoration: Overview of common estimation structures and problems. IEEE Trans. Acoust. Speech Signal Process. **37**, 2024–2036 (1989)

9. Ebner, F., Fairchild, M.: Development and testing of a color space with improved hue uniformity. In: Proceedings of The Sixth Color Imaging Conference: Color Science, Systems, and Applications, Scottsdale, Arizona, USA, pp. 8–13 (1998)

10. Evangelopoulos, X., Brockmeier, A.J., Mu, T., Goulermas, J.Y.: A graduated non-convexity relaxation for large-scale seriation. In: Proceedings of the 2017 SIAM International Conference on Data Mining, Houston, Texas, pp. 462–470 (2017)

11. Fairchild, M.D.: Color and Image Appearance Models. Color Appearance Models. John Wiley and Sons (2005)

12. Gerace, I., Martinelli, F., Pucci, P.: A deterministic algorithm for optical flow estimation. Commun. Appl. Indust. Math. **1**(2), 249–268 (2010)

13. Gunturk, B.K., Altunbasak, Y., Mersereau, R.M.: Color plane interpolation using alternating projections. IEEE Trans. Image Process. **11**(9), 997–1013 (2002)

14. Hazan, E., Levy, K.Y., Shalev-Shwartz, S.: On graduated optimization for stochastic non-convex problems. In: Proceedings of the 33rd International Conference on Machine Learning, New York, 2016. JMLR: W& CP, vol. 48, pp. 1–9 (2016)

15. Kyung, W.J., Kim, K.M., Kim, D.C., Ha, Y.H.: Color correction for a faded image using classification in LCybCrg color space. In: 2011 IEEE International Conference on Consumer Electronics-Berlin (ICCE-Berlin), pp. 189–193 (2011)

16. Liu, W., Ribeiro, E.: A survey on image-based continuum-body motion estimation. Image Vis. Comput. **29**(8), 509–523 (2011)

17. Liu, Z.-Y., Qiao, H.: GNCCP-graduated nonconvexity and concavity procedure. IEEE Trans. Pattern Anal. Mach. Intell. **36**(6), 1258–1267 (2014)

18. Liu, Z.-Y., Qiao, H., Su, J.-H.: MAP inference with MRF by graduated non-convexity and concavity procedure. In: Loo, C.K., Yap, K.S., Wong, K.W., Teoh, A., Huang, K. (eds.) ICONIP 2014. LNCS, vol. 8835, pp. 404–412. Springer, Cham (2014). https://doi.org/10.1007/978-3-319-12640-1_49

19. Nikitenko, D., Wirth, M., Trudel, K.: Applicability of white-balancing algorithms to restoring faded colour slides: An empirical evaluation. J. Multim. **3**(5), 9–18 (2008)

20. Restrepo, A., Ramponi, G.: Filtering and luminance correction for aged photographs. In: Image Processing: Algorithms and Systems VI, Proceedings of SPIE, San Jose, Calif, vol. 6812, pp. 26–31 (2008)

21. Panetta, K.A., Wharton, E.J., Agaian, S.S.: Human visual system-based image enhancement and logarithmic contrast measure. IEEE Trans. Syst. Man Cybernet. **38**(1), 174–188 (2008)
22. Smith, T., Egeland, O.: Dynamical pose estimation with graduated non-convexity for outlier robustness. Model. Identificat. Control **43**(2), 79–89 (2022)
23. Yang, H., Antonante, P., Tzoumas, V., Carlone, L.: Graduated non-convexity for robust spatial perception: From non-minimal solvers to global outlier rejection. IEEE Robot. Automat. Lett. **5**(2), 1127–1134 (2020)

Author Index

A

Abastante, Francesca 468
Ahmad, Waqar 593
Aktas, Mehmet S. 16
Ali, Asad 593
Alifieris, Charalambos 133
Angrisano, Mariarosaria 359, 483
Aquino, José Miguel Sánchez 110
Assumma, Vanessa 398, 512

B

Barbieri, Sebastiano 498
Bayas, Marcia 32
Bekmanova, Gulmira 191
Bianchi, Irene 226
Biondi, Giulio 179, 659, 676
Boccuto, Antonio 659, 676
Bosone, Martina 259
Bottero, Marta 498
Brown, Stephen R. 608
Bustos, Samuel 123

C

Campuzano, Maria 32
Cannatella, Daniele 328
Caprioli, Caterina 429, 498
Cardone, Barbara 345
Casprini, Danny 379
Castiello, Ciro 623
Cavana, Giulio 528
Cerreta, Maria 239, 277, 295
Chamaidi, Theodora 133
Corti, Martina 398

D

D'Agostino, Angela 311
Daldanise, Gaia 295
Datola, Giulia 444, 512
de Almeida, Adiel Teixeira 415
De Marchi, Stefano 577
Del Buono, Nicoletta 623

Dell'Anna, Federico 429, 528
Dell'Ovo, Marta 415
Di Martino, Ferdinando 239, 345
Duque, Vilma 3

E

Esposito, Flavia 623

F

Fasih, Syed M. 593
Fernandes, A. J. G. 70, 166
Fernandes, António J. G. 97
Fernandes, António 123
Fiermonte, Francesco 429
Forte, Fabiana 455
Franzoni, Valentina 179
Frej, Eduarda Asfora 415

G

Gaballo, Marika 468
Gaibor, Samuel Baldomero Bustos 110
Gerace, Ivan 659, 676
González, Carlos Mendoza 44
González, José Catuto 44
Guarda, T. 70
Guarda, Teresa 97, 123
Guin, Washington Daniel Torres 110
Gultekin, Emrullah 16

H

Hanif, Muhammad 593

I

Imbriaco, Alessandro 209

J

Jiménez, Luis Enrique Chuquimarca 110

K

Kato, Takumi 58
Katsikis, Nikos 328

O. Gervasi et al. (Eds.): ICCSA 2023 Workshops, LNCS 14108, pp. 695–696, 2023.
https://doi.org/10.1007/978-3-031-37117-2

L
La Rocca, Ludovica   209
Lami, Isabella M.   468
Linzan, Soraya   150
Lopes, Isabel M.   97
Lopes, Isabel   70, 123, 166

M
Mabood, Talha   593
Malisova, Katerina   133
Mamalis, Dimitrios   133
Marchetti, Francesco   577
Massone, Anna Maria   577
Mazón, Luis   3
Mazzarella, Chiara   209
Mecca, Beatrice   468
Milani, Alfredo   179
Miraglia, Vittorio   345
Mondini, Giulio   498
Mukanova, Assel   191

N
Nocca, Francesca   359
Nomikos, Evangelos   133

O
Omarbekova, Assel   191
Ongarbayev, Yerkyn   191
Oppio, Alessandra   379, 415, 444, 512

P
Padrão, Pascoal   166
Pérez, Maritza   150
Perracchione, Emma   577
Pes, Federica   641
Pham-Quoc, Cuong   82
Piana, Michele   577
Pirelli, Barbara   259
Pittau, Francesco   398
Poli, Giuliano   311

Q
Quagliolo, Carlotta   512

R
Raiola, Maria Lucia   295
Regalbuto, Stefania   209
Ribeiro, Isabel   123
Ribeiro, Maria I. B.   97
Ribeiro, Maria Isabel   70
Rigakis, Chrysostomos   133
Rossitti, Marco   455
Rovira, Ronald   32

S
Sacco, Sabrina   239
Savino, Pasquale   545
Seracini, Marco   608
Somma, Maria   209
Song, Jinlai   328
Stavrakis, Modestos   133
Suárez, Marjorie Alexandra Coronel   110

T
Testa, Claudia   608
Todella, Elena   468
Tonazzini, Anna   545
Torrieri, Francesca   379, 455
Tosoni, Ilaria   226
Travaglini, Arianna   558
Tumbaco, Mónica   150

U
Ukenova, Aru   191
Ullah, Atif   593

V
Vannelli, Giovangiuseppe   311
Ventre, Sveva   277
Vera, Andrade   44
Vera, Gonzalo   3
Villao, Datzania   3, 150
Vinti, Gianluca   558
Vito, Domenico   259
Vlachogiannis, Evangelos   133
Volpara, Anna   577

Y
Yergesh, Banu   191

Z
Zizzania, Piero   311

Printed in the United States
by Baker & Taylor Publisher Services